Stephen Walther

ASP.NET 2.0

UNLEASHED

SAMS | 800 East 96th Street, Indianapolis, Indiana 46240

ASP.NET 2.0 Unleashed

International Standard Book Number: 0-672-32823-2

Library of Congress Catalog Card Number: 2006901233

Printed in the United States of America

First Printing: June 2006

06   4   3   2   1

Trademarks

Warning and Disclaimer

Bulk Sales

Sams Publishing offers excellent discounts on this book when ordered in quantity for bulk purchases or special sales. For more information, please contact

> **U.S. Corporate and Government Sales**
> **1-800-382-3419**
> corpsales@pearsontechgroup.com

For sales outside of the U.S., please contact:

> **International Sales**
> international@pearsoned.com

Editor-in-Chief
Karen Gettman

Acquisitions Editor
Neil Rowe

Development Editor
Mark Renfrow

Managing Editor
Gina Kanouse

Project Editor
George Nedeff

Copy Editors
Margo Catts

Indexer
Erika Millen

Proofreader
Suzanne Thomas

Publishing Coordinator
Cindy Teeters

Book Designer
Gary Adair

Technical Editor
Alex Lowe

Page Layout
Nonie Ratcliff

Contents at a Glance

Table of Contents

Part II   Designing ASP.NET Websites

About the Author

Stephen Walther is a Microsoft Software Legend, a Microsoft ASP.NET MVP, and a member of the INETA Speaker's Bureau. He has spoken at a number of major conferences including Microsoft TechEd, Microsoft DevDays, and ASP.NET Connections.

He wrote several ASP.NET best-practice applications for Microsoft. He was the lead developer of the ASP.NET Community Starter Kit and the Issue Tracker Starter Kit.

His company, Superexpert ASP.NET Training (www.AspWorkshops.com), has provided ASP.NET training to companies and organizations across the United States including NASA, the National Science Foundation, the U.S. House of Representatives, Boeing, Lockheed Martin, Verizon, and Microsoft.

Dedication

This book is dedicated to my wife, Ruth Walther, who is my favorite person in the world.

Acknowledgments

I want to thank a number of people at Microsoft for taking the time to answer my questions about ASP.NET: Scott Guthrie, Susan Chory, Bradley Millington, Mike Harder, Andres Sanabria, Nikhil Kothari, Matthew Gibbs, Rob Howard, and Stefan Schackow.

I also want to thank Alex Lowe for taking on the huge project of being the technical editor for this book. His patience and feedback were very much appreciated. Charles Carroll also provided many valuable suggestions for improving this book.

Also, I want to thank Nathan Wiger and Corey Gray, the world-renowned experts on all excellent forms of beer, for giving me permission to use their beer label images for the ASP.NET Beer Store described in the final chapter of this book.

Finally, I want to thank Neil Rowe for all the support and encouragement that he gave me while I was writing this book.

We Want to Hear from You!

As the reader of this book, *you* are our most important critic and commentator. We value your opinion and want to know what we're doing right, what we could do better, what areas you'd like to see us publish in, and any other words of wisdom you're willing to pass our way.

As an associate publisher for Sams Publishing, I welcome your comments. You can email or write me directly to let me know what you did or didn't like about this book—as well as what we can do to make our books better.

Please note that I cannot help you with technical problems related to the topic of this book. We do have a User Services group, however, where I will forward specific technical questions related to the book.

When you write, please be sure to include this book's title and author as well as your name, email address, and phone number. I will carefully review your comments and share them with the author and editors who worked on the book.

Email: feedback@samspublishing.com

Mail: Paul Boger
           Associate Publisher
           Sams Publishing
           800 East 96th Street
           Indianapolis, IN 46240 USA

For more information about this book or another Sams Publishing title, visit our website at www.samspublishing.com. Type the ISBN (excluding hyphens) or the title of a book in the Search field to find the page you're looking for.

Introduction

ASP.NET is Microsoft's flagship technology for building highly interactive, highly scalable websites. Some of the largest websites hosted on the Internet were built with the ASP.NET Framework, including the Dell website (www.Dell.com), parts of the Martha Stewart website (www.MarthaStewart.com), parts of the eBay website (www.eBay.com), the XBOX website (www.xbox.com), the MySpace website (www.MySpace.com), and the Microsoft website itself (www.Microsoft.com). If you need to build a highly interactive website that can scale to handle thousands of simultaneous users, then ASP.NET is the technology to use.

The ASP.NET 2.0 Framework is the latest version of the Microsoft ASP.NET Framework. The ASP.NET 2.0 Framework introduces more than 50 new controls. However, simply counting the number of new controls does not provide you with an accurate picture of the extent of the new features included in the ASP.NET 2.0 Framework. Many of the most important changes are framework-level changes.

Following are just a few of the significant new features of ASP.NET 2.0:

- **A new declarative data access model**—By taking advantage of the new data access controls, you can display and edit a set of database records without writing a single line of code.

- **Master Pages and Themes**—By taking advantage of Master Pages and Themes, you can easily create a common style and layout for all the pages in your website.

- **Membership API**—By taking advantage of the Membership API, you can build an entire user registration system that stores user information in a Microsoft SQL Server database table or Active Directory without writing any code.

- **Web Parts**—By taking advantage of Web Parts, you can build portal applications that can be customized by users or administrators at runtime.

- **SQL Cache Invalidation**—By taking advantage of SQL Cache Invalidation, you can cache database records in memory and reload the records automatically when the data in the underlying database changes.

- **AJAX**—By taking advantage of AJAX, you can update a web page without posting the page back to the web server.

Who Should Read This Book?

ASP.NET 2.0 Unleashed is intended for professional programmers who need to create a website. This book is a comprehensive reference for building websites with ASP.NET 2.0. The CD that accompanies this book contains hundreds of code samples that you can start using immediately while building your website.

If you are new to building websites with ASP.NET, you can use this book to teach yourself everything you need to know to build one with the ASP.NET Framework. If you are an experienced ASP.NET developer, you can use this book to learn about the new features of ASP.NET 2.0.

The final part of this book contains a complete sample application: an online store. The complete code for this application is included on the CD that accompanies this book.

What Do You Need to Know Before You Read This Book?

This book assumes that you know either the Visual Basic .NET or C# programming language. If you are completely new to the .NET Framework, then I recommend that you read an introductory book on either Visual Basic .NET or C# before reading this book.

In the body of the book, all the code samples are presented in Visual Basic .NET. However, this was not intended as any kind of insult to C# programmers. The CD that accompanies this book includes every code sample translated into the C# programming language.

To get the most from the database chapters, you should have some experience working with a database such as Microsoft SQL Server, Oracle, or Microsoft Access. You should know how to perform basic database operations with SQL.

Changes to This Book

This book has been completely rewritten from the first edition. I dumped the first edition of the book from my laptop's hard drive and started from scratch.

The first edition of this book, *ASP.NET Unleashed*, was written five years ago when the first version of the ASP.NET Framework was released. Like most developers, I've undergone a number of changes over the last five years.

First, you'll notice that this edition of this book emphasizes web standards much more than the first edition. When I wrote the first edition of this book, I didn't care about web standards. At that time, I assumed that Internet Explorer had won the browser wars and the only thing that mattered was getting pages to work in Internet Explorer.

I was young, stupid, and naive. After the first edition of this book was published, a new browser named Firefox appeared. Everyone, once again, is starting to be concerned with creating cross-browser–compatible websites. The best way to create cross-browser–compatible websites is to follow web standards.

All the code samples in this book were written to conform to both XHTML and accessibility standards. You'll notice that almost all the page layout and formatting is performed with Cascading Style Sheets. Furthermore, the book includes notes on how to use different technologies included with the ASP.NET Framework in a manner that is compatible with web standards.

You'll also notice that the screenshots in this book do not all display Internet Explorer. To emphasize the fact that you can build standards-compliant web pages with ASP.NET, I rotated the screenshots among Internet Explorer, Firefox, and Opera.

Second, like many developers, I've become obsessed with the topic of AJAX (Asynchronous JavaScript and XML). AJAX enables you to build web applications that more closely resemble desktop applications. By taking advantage of AJAX, you can update content in a web page without posting the page back to the web server.

I was very happy to learn that Microsoft included the basic infrastructure that you need to build AJAX applications as part of the ASP.NET 2.0 Framework. AJAX samples are scattered throughout this book. In Chapter 7, for example, you learn how to display different quotations randomly in a page by using AJAX. In Chapter 33 you learn how to insert, edit, and display database records by using AJAX.

How This Book Is Organized

Although I encourage you to read this book from start to finish, reading chapter by chapter, I realize that not everyone has time to do so. If necessary, you can use this book solely as a reference and jump to a chapter only when the need arises. It may be helpful, therefore, to have an idea of the overall organization of this book.

- **Part I: Building ASP.NET Pages**—The chapters in this part provide you with an overview of the basic controls included in the ASP.NET Framework. You learn how to build interactive Web Forms with the form controls. You also learn how to validate form data with the validation controls. Finally, you learn how to upload files and display interactive calendars and wizards with the rich controls.

- **Part II: Designing ASP.NET Websites**—The chapters in this part discuss how you can create a common layout and style for the pages in your website. You learn how to use Master Pages to share content across multiple pages. You also learn how to use Themes to create a consistent page style.

- **Part III: Performing Data Access**—The chapters in this part focus on data access. You learn how to use the new GridView control to display, page, sort, and edit a set of database records. You learn how to use the new DetailsView and FormView controls to display and edit a single database record at a time.

- **Part IV: Building Components**—The chapters in this part focus on building custom components. You learn how to design and create multi-tiered applications. You also learn how to build data access components by taking advantage of the new features of ADO.NET 2.0. For example, you learn how to build a Stored Procedures with the .NET Framework.

- **Part V: Site Navigation**—The chapters in this part discuss the new navigation controls such as the TreeView and Menu controls. You learn how to use these controls with a Site Map to allow users to navigate a website easily. You also learn how to use the `VirtualPathProvider` class to abstract a website from the file system. For example, you learn how to store the pages in a website in a Microsoft SQL Server database.

- **Part VI: Security**—The chapters in this part focus on the new Login controls and Membership API. You learn how to create a user registration and authentication system. You learn how to store Membership information in either a SQL Server database or Active Directory.

- **Part VII: Building ASP.NET Applications**—The chapters discuss a variety of topics related to building ASP.NET applications. For example, you learn how to improve the performance of your ASP.NET applications by taking advantage of caching. You also learn how to localize your ASP.NET applications so that they can be translated easily and presented in multiple human languages.

- **Part VIII: Building Applications with Web Parts**—The chapters in this part are devoted to Web Parts. By taking advantage of Web Parts, you can build portal applications that can be customized by users or administrators at runtime.

- **Part IX: Custom Control Building**—The chapters in this part concentrate on extending the ASP.NET Framework with custom controls. For example, you learn how to create a `WebWindow` control that enables you to create virtual windows in a web page.

- **Part X: Sample Application**—The last part of this book contains a single chapter that describes a sample application. There you learn how to build an e-commerce website with the ASP.NET Framework: the ASP.NET Beer Store.

Viewing the Code Samples

All the code samples for this book are included on the CD that accompanies this book. If you want to view the code samples for a particular chapter, copy the corresponding folder from the CD onto your local hard drive and open the folder in Microsoft Visual Web Developer.

The code samples are also posted at the Superexpert website (www.superexpert.com). You can view "live" versions of any of the code samples by visiting this website. Please visit the Superexpert website to view the latest errata and content updates for this book, as well.

PART I

Building ASP.NET Pages

IN THIS PART

Overview of the ASP.NET Framework

Let's start by building a simple ASP.NET page.

> **NOTE**
>
> For information on installing ASP.NET, see the last section of this chapter.

If you are using Visual Web Developer or Visual Studio .NET, you first need to create a new website. Start Visual Web Developer and select the menu option File, New Web Site. The New Web Site dialog box appears (see Figure 1.1). Enter the folder where you want your new website to be created in the Location field and click the OK button.

After you create a new website, you can add an ASP.NET page to it. Select the menu option Website, Add New Item. Select Web Form and enter the value **FirstPage.aspx** in the Name field. Make sure that both the `Place Code in Separate File` and `Select Master Page` check boxes are unchecked, and click the Add button to create the new ASP.NET page (see Figure 1.2).

The code for the first ASP.NET page is contained in Listing 1.1.

LISTING 1.1 FirstPage.aspx

```
<%@ Page Language="VB" %>
<!DOCTYPE html PUBLIC "-//W3C//DTD XHTML 1.0
Transitional//EN"
    "http://www.w3.org/TR/xhtml1/DTD/
xhtml1-transitional.dtd">
<script runat="server">
```

LISTING 1.1   Continued

```
    Sub Page_Load()
        lblServerTime.Text = DateTime.Now.ToString()
    End Sub

</script>
<html xmlns="http://www.w3.org/1999/xhtml" >
<head>
    <title>First Page</title>
</head>
<body>
    <form id="form1" runat="server">
    <div>

    Welcome to ASP.NET 2.0! The current date and time is:

    <asp:Label
        id="lblServerTime"
        Runat="server" />

    </div>
    </form>
</body>
</html>
```

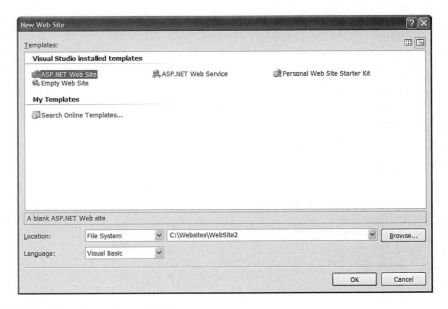

FIGURE 1.1   Creating a new website.

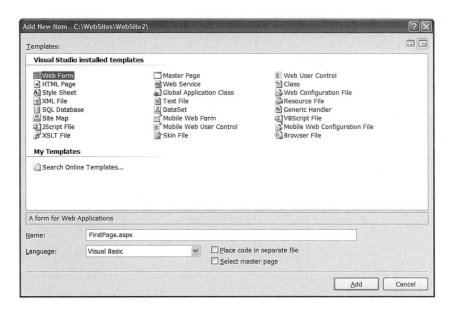

FiGURE 1.2   Adding a new ASP.NET page.

NOTE

The CD that accompanies this book contains C# versions of all the Visual Basic .NET code samples.

The ASP.NET page in Listing 1.1 displays a brief message and the server's current date and time. You can view the page in Listing 1.1 in a browser by right-clicking the page and selecting View in Browser (see Figure 1.3).

The page in Listing 1.1 is an extremely simple page. However, it does illustrate the most common elements of an ASP.NET page. The page contains a directive, a code declaration block, and a page render block.

The first line, in Listing 1.1, contains a directive. It looks like this:

```
<%@ Page Language="VB" %>
```

A directive always begins with the special characters <%@ and ends with the characters %>. Directives are used primarily to provide the compiler with the information it needs to compile the page.

For example, the directive in Listing 1.1 indicates that the code contained in the page is Visual Basic .NET (VB .NET) code. The page is compiled by the Visual Basic .NET compiler and not another compiler such as the C# compiler.

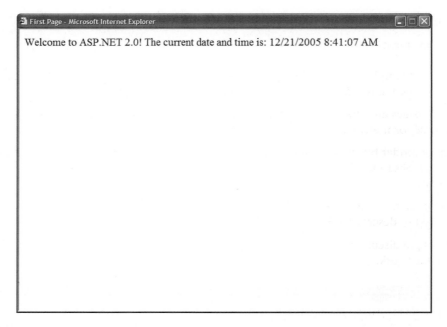

FIGURE 1.3   Viewing `FirstPage.aspx` in a browser.

The next part of the page begins with the opening `<script runat="server">` tag and ends with the closing `</script>` tag. The `<script>` tag contains something called the *code declaration block*.

The code declaration block contains all the methods used in the page. It contains all the page's functions and subroutines. The code declaration block in Listing 1.1 includes a single subroutine named `Page_Load()`, which looks like this:

```
Sub Page_Load()
  lblServerTime.Text = DateTime.Now.ToString()
End Sub
```

This subroutine assigns the current date and time to the `Text` property of a `Label` control contained in the body of the page named `lblServerTime`.

The `Page_Load()` subroutine is an example of an event handler. This subroutine handles the `Page Load` event. Each and every time the page loads, the subroutine automatically executes and assigns the current date and time to the `Label` control.

The final part of the page is called the *page render block*. The page render block contains everything that is rendered to the browser. In Listing 1.1, the render block includes everything between the opening and closing `<html>` tags.

The majority of the page render block consists of everyday HTML. For example, the page contains the standard HTML `<head>` and `<body>` tags. In Listing 1.1, there are two special things contained in the page render block.

First, notice that the page contains a `<form>` tag that looks like this:

```
<form id="form1" runat="server">
```

This is an example of an ASP.NET control. Because the tag includes a `runat="server"` attribute, the tag represents an ASP.NET control that executes on the server.

ASP.NET pages are often called *web form* pages because they almost always contain a server-side form element.

The page render block also contains a Label control. The Label control is declared with the `<asp:Label>` tag. In Listing 1.1, the Label control is used to display the current date and time.

Controls are the heart of the ASP.NET framework. Most of the ink contained in this book is devoted to describing the properties and features of the ASP.NET controls.

Controls are discussed in more detail shortly. However, first you need to understand the .NET Framework.

> **NOTE**
>
> By default, ASP.NET pages are compatible with the XHTML 1.0 Transitional standard. You'll notice that the page in Listing 1.1 includes an XHTML 1.0 Transitional DOCTYPE. For details on how the ASP.NET framework complies with both XHTML and accessibility standards, see my article at the Microsoft MSDN website (msdn.Microsoft.com), entitled "Building ASP.NET 2.0 Web Sites Using Web Standards."

ASP.NET and the .NET Framework

ASP.NET is part of the Microsoft .NET Framework. To build ASP.NET pages, you need to take advantage of the features of the .NET Framework. The .NET Framework consists of two parts: the Framework Class Library and the Common Language Runtime.

Understanding the Framework Class Library

The .NET Framework contains thousands of classes that you can use when building an application. The Framework Class Library was designed to make it easier to perform the most common programming tasks. Here are just a few examples of the classes in the framework:

- `File` **class**—Enables you to represent a file on your hard drive. You can use the `File` class to check whether a file exists, create a new file, delete a file, and perform many other file related tasks.

- `Graphics` **class**—Enables you to work with different types of images such as GIF, PNG, BMP, and JPEG images. You can use the `Graphics` class to draw rectangles, arcs, ellipsis, and other elements on an image.

- `Random` **class**—Enables you to generate a random number.

- `SmtpClient` **class**—Enables you to send email. You can use the `SmtpClient` class to send emails that contain attachments and HTML content.

These are only four examples of classes in the Framework. The .NET Framework contains almost 13,000 classes you can use when building applications.

You can view all the classes contained in the Framework by opening the Microsoft .NET Framework SDK documentation and expanding the Class Library node (see Figure 1.4). If you don't have the SDK documentation installed on your computer, then see the last section of this chapter.

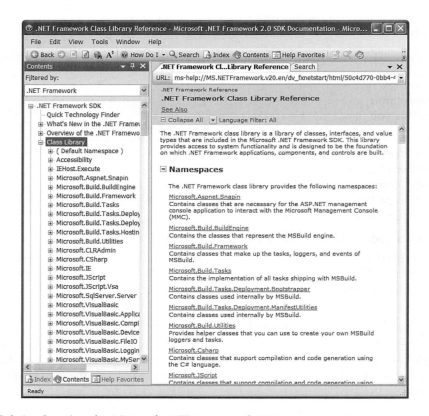

FIGURE 1.4   Opening the Microsoft .NET Framework SDK Documentation.

> **NOTE**
>
> The Microsoft .NET Framework 2.0 includes 18,619 types; 12,909 classes; 401,759 public methods; 93,105 public properties; and 30,546 public events.

Each class in the Framework can include properties, methods, and events. The properties, methods, and events exposed by a class are the members of a class. For example, here is a partial list of the members of the SmtpClient class:

- Properties
    - Host—The name or IP address of your email server
    - Port—The number of the port to use when sending an email message
- Methods
    - Send—Enables you to send an email message synchronously
    - SendAsync—Enables you to send an email message asynchronously
- Events
    - SendCompleted—Raised when an asynchronous send operation completes

If you know the members of a class, then you know everything that you can do with a class. For example, the SmtpClient class includes two properties named Host and Port, which enable you to specify the email server and port to use when sending an email message.

The SmtpClient class also includes two methods you can use to send an email: Send() and SendAsync(). The Send method blocks further program execution until the send operation is completed. The SendAsync() method, on the other hand, sends the email asynchronously. Unlike the Send() method, the SendAsync() method does not wait to check whether the send operation was successful.

Finally, the SmtpClient class includes an event named SendCompleted, which is raised when an asynchronous send operation completes. You can create an event handler for the SendCompleted event that displays a message when the email has been successfully sent.

The page in Listing 1.2 sends an email by using the SmtpClient class and calling its Send() method.

LISTING 1.2   SendMail.aspx

```
<%@ Page Language="VB" %>
<%@ Import Namespace="System.Net.Mail" %>
<!DOCTYPE html PUBLIC "-//W3C//DTD XHTML 1.0 Transitional//EN"
  "http://www.w3.org/TR/xhtml1/DTD/xhtml1-transitional.dtd">
<script runat="server">

    Sub Page_Load()
        Dim client As New SmtpClient()
        client.Host = "localhost"
        client.Port = 25
```

LISTING 1.2   Continued

```
        client.Send("steve@somewhere", "bob@somewhere.com", _
            "Let's eat lunch!", "Lunch at the Steak House?")
    End Sub

</script>
<html xmlns="http://www.w3.org/1999/xhtml" >
<head id="Head1" runat="server">
    <title>Send Mail</title>
</head>
<body>
    <form id="form1" runat="server">
    <div>

    Email sent!

    </div>
    </form>
</body>
</html>
```

The page in Listing 1.2 calls the `SmtpClient Send()` method to send the email. The first parameter is the from: address; the second parameter is the to: address; the third parameter is the subject; and the final parameter is the body of the email.

> **WARNING**
>
> The page in Listing 1.2 sends the email by using the local SMTP Server. If your SMTP Server is not enabled, then you'll receive the error `An existing connection was forcibly closed by the remote host`. You can enable your local SMTP Server by opening Internet Information Services, right-clicking Default SMTP Virtual Server, and selecting Start.

Understanding Namespaces

There are almost 13,000 classes in the .NET Framework. This is an overwhelming number. If Microsoft simply jumbled all the classes together, then you would never find anything. Fortunately, Microsoft divided the classes in the Framework into separate namespaces.

A *namespace* is simply a category. For example, all the classes related to working with the file system are located in the `System.IO` namespace. All the classes for working a Microsoft SQL Server database are located in the `System.Data.SqlClient` namespace.

Before you can use a class in a page, you must indicate the namespace associated with the class. There are multiple ways of doing this.

First, you can fully qualify a class name with its namespace. For example, because the File class is contained in the System.IO namespace, you can use the following statement to check whether a file exists:

```
System.IO.File.Exists("SomeFile.txt")
```

Specifying a namespace each and every time you use a class can quickly become tedious (it involves a lot of typing). A second option is to import a namespace.

You can add an <%@ Import %> directive to a page to import a particular namespace. In Listing 1.2, we imported the System.Net.Mail namespace because the SmtpClient is part of this namespace. The page in Listing 1.2 includes the following directive near the very top of the page:

```
<%@ Import Namespace="System.Net.Mail" %>
```

After you import a particular namespace, you can use all the classes in that namespace without qualifying the class names.

Finally, if you discover that you are using a namespace in multiple pages in your application, then you can configure all the pages in your application to recognize the namespace.

> **NOTE**
>
> A web configuration file is a special type of file that you can add to your application to configure your application. Be aware that the file is an XML file and, therefore, all the tags contained in the file are case sensitive. You can add a web configuration file to your application by selecting Website, Add New Item and selecting Web Configuration File. Chapter 26, "Configuring Applications," discusses web configuration files in detail.

If you add the web configuration file in Listing 1.3 to your application, then you do not need to import the System.Net.Mail namespace in a page to use the classes from this namespace. For example, if you include the Web.config file in your project, you can remove the <%@ Import %> directive from the page in Listing 1.2.

LISTING 1.3   Web.Config

```xml
<?xml version="1.0"?>
<configuration>
    <system.web>
      <pages>
        <namespaces>
          <add namespace="System.Net.Mail"/>
        </namespaces>
      </pages>
    </system.web>
</configuration>
```

You don't have to import every namespace. The ASP.NET Framework gives you the most commonly used namespaces for free. These namespaces are

- `System`
- `System.Collections`
- `System.Collections.Specialized`
- `System.Configuration`
- `System.Text`
- `System.Text.RegularExpressions`
- `System.Web`
- `System.Web.Caching`
- `System.Web.SessionState`
- `System.Web.Security`
- `System.Web.Profile`
- `System.Web.UI`
- `System.Web.UI.WebControls`
- `System.Web.UI.WebControls.WebParts`
- `System.Web.UI.HTMLControls`

The default namespaces are listed inside the `pages` element in the root web configuration file located at the following path:

`\WINDOWS\Microsoft.NET\Framework\[version]\CONFIG\Web.Config`

Understanding Assemblies

An assembly is the actual `.dll` file on your hard drive where the classes in the .NET Framework are stored. For example, all the classes contained in the ASP.NET Framework are located in an assembly named `System.Web.dll`.

More accurately, an assembly is the primary unit of deployment, security, and version control in the .NET Framework. Because an assembly can span multiple files, an assembly is often referred to as a "logical" dll.

> **NOTE**
>
> The .NET Framework (version 2.0) includes 51 assemblies.

There are two types of assemblies: private and shared. A private assembly can be used by only a single application. A shared assembly, on the other hand, can be used by all applications located on the same server.

Shared assemblies are located in the Global Assembly Cache (GAC). For example, the System.Web.dll assembly and all the other assemblies included with the .NET Framework are located in the Global Assembly Cache.

> **NOTE**
>
> The Global Assembly Cache is located physically in your computer's \WINDOWS\Assembly folder. There is a separate copy of every assembly in your \WINDOWS\Microsoft.NET\ Framework\v2.0.50727 folder. The first set of assemblies is used at runtime and the second set is used at compile time.

Before you can use a class contained in an assembly in your application, you must add a reference to the assembly. By default, an ASP.NET application references the most common assemblies contained in the Global Assembly Cache:

- mscorlib.dll
- System.dll
- System.Configuration.dll
- System.Web.dll
- System.Data.dll
- System.Web.Services.dll
- System.Xml.dll
- System.Drawing.dll
- System.EnterpriseServices.dll
- System.Web.Mobile.dll

To use any particular class in the .NET Framework, you must do two things. First, your application must reference the assembly that contains the class. Second, your application must import the namespace associated with the class.

In most cases, you won't worry about referencing the necessary assembly because the most common assemblies are referenced automatically. However, if you need to use a specialized assembly, you need to add a reference explicitly to the assembly. For example, if you need to interact with Active Directory by using the classes in the System. DirectoryServices namespace then you will need to add a reference to the System. DirectoryServices.dll assembly to your application.

Each class entry in the .NET Framework SDK documentation lists the assembly and name-space associated with the class. For example, if you look up the MessageQueue class in the documentation, you'll discover that this class is located in the System.Messaging name-space located in the System.Messaging.dll assembly.

If you are using Visual Web Developer, you can add a reference to an assembly explicitly by selecting the menu option Website, Add Reference, and selecting the name of the assembly that you need to reference. For example, adding a reference to the System. Messaging.dll assembly results in the web configuration file in Listing 1.4 being added to your application.

LISTING 1.4   Web.Config

```
<?xml version="1.0"?>
<configuration>
<system.web>
  <compilation>
  <assemblies>
  <add
    assembly="System.Messaging, Version=2.0.0.0,
    Culture=neutral, PublicKeyToken=B03F5F7F11D50A3A"/>
  </assemblies>
  </compilation>
</system.web>
</configuration>
```

If you prefer not to use Visual Web Developer, then you can add the reference to the System.Messaging.dll assembly by creating the file in Listing 1.4 by hand.

Understanding the Common Language Runtime

The second part of the .NET Framework is the Common Language Runtime (CLR). The Common Language Runtime is responsible for executing your application code.

When you write an application for the .NET Framework with a language such as Visual Basic .NET or C#, your source code is never compiled directly into machine code. Instead, the Visual Basic or C# compiler converts your code into a special language named MSIL (Microsoft Intermediate Language).

MSIL looks very much like an object-oriented assembly language. However, unlike a typical assembly language, it is not CPU specific. MSIL is a low-level and platform-independent language.

When your application actually executes, the MSIL code is "just-in-time" compiled into machine code by the JITTER (the Just-In-Time compiler). Normally, your entire application is not compiled from MSIL into machine code. Instead, only the methods that are actually called during execution are compiled.

In reality, the .NET Framework understands only one language: MSIL. However, you can write applications using languages such as Visual Basic .NET and C# for the .NET Framework because the .NET Framework includes compilers for these languages that enable you to compile your code into MSIL.

You can write code for the .NET Framework using any one of dozens of different languages, including

- Ada

- Apl

- Caml

- COBOL

- Eiffel

- Forth

- Fortran

- JavaScript

- Oberon

- PERL

- Pascal

- PHP

- Python

- RPG

- Scheme

- Small Talk

The vast majority of developers building ASP.NET applications write the applications in either Visual Basic .NET or C#. Many of the other .NET languages in the preceding list are academic experiments.

Once upon a time, if you wanted to become a developer, you concentrated on becoming proficient at a particular language. For example, you became a C++ programmer, a COBOL programmer, or a Visual Basic Programmer.

When it comes to the .NET Framework, however, knowing a particular language is not particularly important. The choice of which language to use when building a .NET application is largely a preference choice. If you like case-sensitivity and curly braces, then you should use the C# programming language. If you want to be lazy about casing and you don't like semicolons, then write your code with Visual Basic .NET.

All the real action in the .NET Framework happens in the Framework Class Library. If you want to become a good programmer using Microsoft technologies, you need to learn how to use the methods, properties, and events of the 13,000 classes included in the Framework. From the point of view of the .NET Framework, it doesn't matter whether you are using these classes from a Visual Basic .NET or C# application.

Understanding ASP.NET Controls

ASP.NET controls are the heart of the ASP.NET Framework. An ASP.NET control is a .NET class that executes on the server and renders certain content to the browser.

For example, in the first ASP.NET page created at the beginning of this chapter, a Label control was used to display the current date and time. The ASP.NET framework includes over 70 controls, which enable you to do everything from displaying a list of database records to displaying a randomly rotating banner advertisement.

In this section, you are provided with an overview of the controls included in the ASP.NET Framework. You also learn how to handle events that are raised by controls and how to take advantage of View State.

Overview of ASP.NET Controls

The ASP.NET Framework (version 2.0) contains over 70 controls. These controls can be divided into eight groups:

- **Standard Controls**—The standard controls enable you to render standard form elements such as buttons, input fields, and labels. We examine these controls in detail in the following chapter, "Using the Standard Controls."

- **Validation Controls**—The validation controls enable you to validate form data before you submit the data to the server. For example, you can use a RequiredFieldValidator control to check whether a user entered a value for a required input field. These controls are discussed in Chapter 3, "Using the Validation Controls."

- **Rich Controls**—The rich controls enable you to render things such as calendars, file upload buttons, rotating banner advertisements, and multi-step wizards. These controls are discussed in Chapter 4, "Using the Rich Controls."

- **Data Controls**—The data controls enable you to work with data such as database data. For example, you can use these controls to submit new records to a database table or display a list of database records. These controls are discussed in detail in Part III of this book, "Performing Data Access."

- **Navigation Controls**—The navigation controls enable you to display standard navigation elements such as menus, tree views, and bread crumb trails. These controls are discussed in Chapter 17, "Using the Navigation Controls."

- **Login Controls**—The login controls enable you to display login, change password, and registration forms. These controls are discussed in Chapter 20, "Using the Login Controls."

- **Web Part Controls**—The Web Part controls enable you to build personalizable portal applications. These controls are discussed in Part VIII, "Building Applications with Web Parts."

- **HTML Controls**—The HTML controls enable you to convert any HTML tag into a server-side control. We discuss this group of controls in the next section of this chapter.

With the exception of the HTML controls, you declare and use all the ASP.NET controls in a page in exactly the same way. For example, if you want to display a text input field in a page, then you can declare a `TextBox` control like this:

```
<asp:TextBox id="TextBox1" runat="Server" />
```

This control declaration looks like the declaration for an HTML tag. Remember, however, unlike an HTML tag, a control is a .NET class that executes on the server and not in the web browser.

When the TextBox control is rendered to the browser, it renders the following content:

```
<input name="TextBox1" type="text" id="TextBox1" />
```

The first part of the control declaration, the `asp:` prefix, indicates the namespace for the control. All the standard ASP.NET controls are contained in the `System.Web.UI.WebControls` namespace. The prefix `asp:` represents this namespace.

Next, the declaration contains the name of the control being declared. In this case, a `TextBox` control is being declared.

This declaration also includes an ID attribute. You use the ID to refer to the control in the page within your code. Every control must have a unique ID.

> **NOTE**
>
> You should always assign an ID attribute to every control even when you don't need to program against it. If you don't provide an ID attribute, then certain features of the ASP.NET Framework (such as two-way databinding) won't work.

The declaration also includes a `runat="Server"` attribute. This attribute marks the tag as representing a server-side control. If you neglect to include this attribute, then the `TextBox` tag would be passed, without being executed, to the browser. The browser would simply ignore the tag.

Finally, notice that the tag ends with a forward slash. The forward slash is shorthand for creating a closing `</asp:TextBox>` tag. You can, if you prefer, declare the `TextBox` control like this:

```
<input name="TextBox1" type="text" id="TextBox1"></asp:TextBox>
```

In this case, the opening tag does not contain a forward slash and an explicit closing tag is included.

Understanding HTML Controls

You declare HTML controls in a different way than you declare standard ASP.NET controls. The ASP.NET Framework enables you to take any HTML tag (real or imaginary) and add a `runat="server"` attribute to the tag. The `runat="server"` attribute converts the HTML tag into a server-side ASP.NET control.

For example, the page in Listing 1.5 contains a <span> tag, which has been converted into an ASP.NET control.

LISTING 1.5   HtmlControls.aspx

```
<%@ Page Language="VB" %>
<!DOCTYPE html PUBLIC "-//W3C//DTD XHTML 1.0 Transitional//EN"
  "http://www.w3.org/TR/xhtml1/DTD/xhtml1-transitional.dtd">
<script runat="server">

    Sub Page_Load()
        spanNow.InnerText = DateTime.Now.ToString("T")
    End Sub

</script>
<html xmlns="http://www.w3.org/1999/xhtml" >
<head id="Head1" runat="server">
    <title>HTML Controls</title>
</head>
<body>
    <form id="form1" runat="server">
    <div>

    At the tone, the time will be:
    <span id="spanNow" runat="server" />

    </div>
    </form>
</body>
</html>
```

Notice that the <span> tag in Listing 1.5 looks just like a normal HTML <span> tag except for the addition of the `runat="server"` attribute.

Because the <span> tag in Listing 1.5 is a server-side HTML control, you can program against it. In Listing 1.5, the current date and time are assigned to the <span> tag in the `Page_Load()` method.

The HTML controls are included in the ASP.NET Framework to make it easier to convert existing HTML pages to use the ASP.NET Framework. I rarely use the HTML controls in this book because, in general, the standard ASP.NET controls provide all the same functionality and more.

Understanding and Handling Control Events

The majority of the ASP.NET controls support one or more events. For example, the ASP.NET Button control supports the Click event. The Click event is raised on the server after you click the button rendered by the Button control in the browser.

The page in Listing 1.6 illustrates how you can write code that executes when a user clicks the button rendered by the Button control (in other words, it illustrates how you can create a Click event handler):

LISTING 1.6   ShowButtonClick.aspx

```
<%@ Page Language="VB" %>
<!DOCTYPE html PUBLIC "-//W3C//DTD XHTML 1.0 Transitional//EN"
  "http://www.w3.org/TR/xhtml1/DTD/xhtml1-transitional.dtd">
<script runat="server">

    Sub btnSubmit_Click(ByVal sender As Object, ByVal e As EventArgs)
        Label1.Text = "Thanks!"
    End Sub
</script>
<html xmlns="http://www.w3.org/1999/xhtml" >
<head id="Head1" runat="server">
    <title>Show Button Click</title>
</head>
<body>
    <form id="form1" runat="server">
    <div>

    <asp:Button
        id="btnSubmit"
        Text="Click Here"
        OnClick="btnSubmit_Click"
        Runat="server" />

    <br /><br />

    <asp:Label
        id="Label1"
        Runat="server" />
```

LISTING 1.6   Continued

```
      </div>
    </form>
  </body>
</html>
```

Notice that the Button control in Listing 1.6 includes an OnClick attribute. This attribute points to a subroutine named btnSubmit_Click(). The btnSubmit_Click() subroutine is the handler for the Button Click event. This subroutine executes whenever you click the button (see Figure 1.5).

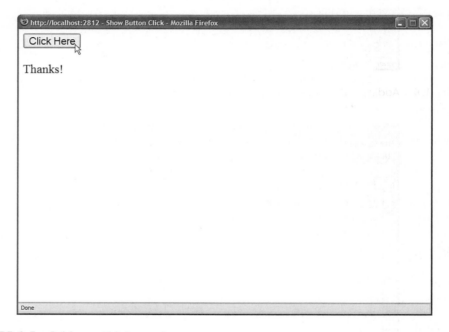

FIGURE 1.5   Raising a Click event.

You can add an event handler automatically to a control in multiple ways when using Visual Web Developer. In Source view, add a handler by selecting a control from the top-left drop-down list and selecting an event from the top-right drop-down list. The event handler code is added to the page automatically (see Figure 1.6).

In Design view, you can double-click a control to add a handler for the control's default event. Double-clicking a control switches you to Source view and adds the event handler.

Finally, from Design view, after selecting a control on the designer surface you can add an event handler from the Properties window by clicking the Events button (the lightning bolt) and double-clicking next to the name of any of the events (see Figure 1.7).

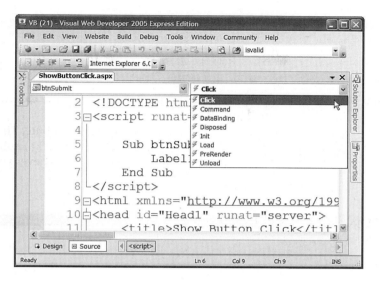

FIGURE 1.6 Adding an event handler from Source view.

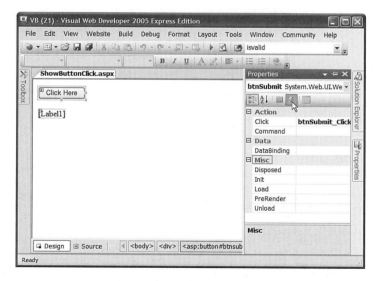

FIGURE 1.7 Adding an event handler from the Properties window.

It is important to understand that all ASP.NET control events happen on the server. For example, the Click event is not raised when you actually click a button. The Click event is not raised until the page containing the Button control is posted back to the server.

The ASP.NET Framework is a server-side web application framework. The .NET Framework code that you write executes on the server and not within the web browser. From the perspective of ASP.NET, nothing happens until the page is posted back to the server and can execute within the context of the .NET Framework.

Notice that two parameters are passed to the `btnSubmit_Click()` handler in Listing 1.6. All event handlers for ASP.NET controls have the same general signature.

The first parameter, the object parameter named `sender`, represents the control that raised the event. In other words, it represents the `Button` control which you clicked.

You can wire multiple controls in a page to the same event handler and use this first parameter to determine the particular control that raised the event. For example, the page in Listing 1.7 includes two `Button` controls. When you click either `Button` control, the text displayed by the `Button` control is updated (see Figure 1.8).

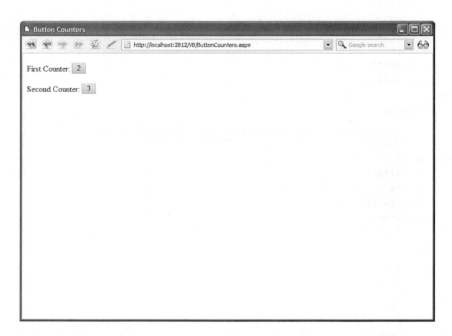

FIGURE 1.8   Handling two `Button` controls with one event handler.

LISTING 1.7   `ButtonCounters.aspx`

```
<%@ Page Language="VB" %>
<!DOCTYPE html PUBLIC "-//W3C//DTD XHTML 1.0 Transitional//EN"
 "http://www.w3.org/TR/xhtml1/DTD/xhtml1-transitional.dtd">
<script runat="server">

    Sub Button_Click(ByVal sender As Object, ByVal e As EventArgs)
        Dim btn As Button = CType(sender, Button)
        btn.Text = (Int32.Parse(btn.Text) + 1).ToString()
```

LISTING 1.8   Continued

```
    End Sub
</script>
<html xmlns="http://www.w3.org/1999/xhtml" >
<head id="Head1" runat="server">
    <title>Button Counters</title>
</head>
<body>
    <form id="form1" runat="server">
    <div>

    First Counter:
    <asp:Button
        id="Button1"
        Text="0"
        OnClick="Button_Click"
        Runat="server" />

    <br /><br />

    Second Counter:
    <asp:Button
        id="Button2"
        Text="0"
        OnClick="Button_Click"
        Runat="server" />

    </div>
    </form>
</body>
</html>
```

The second parameter passed to the `Click` event handler, the `EventArgs` parameter named e, represents any additional event information associated with the event. No additional event information is associated with clicking a button, so this second parameter does not represent anything useful in either Listing 1.6 or Listing 1.7.

When you click an `ImageButton` control instead of a `Button` control, on the other hand, additional event information is passed to the event handler. When you click an `ImageButton` control, the X and Y coordinates of where you clicked are passed to the handler.

The page in Listing 1.8 contains an `ImageButton` control that displays a picture. When you click the picture, the X and Y coordinates of the spot you clicked are displayed in a Label control (see Figure 1.9).

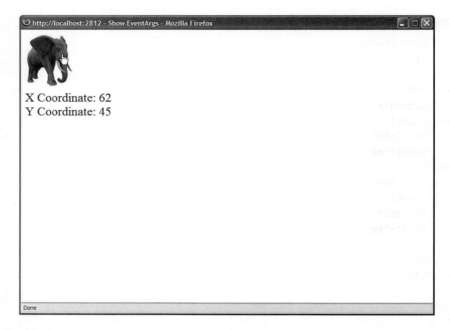

FIGURE 1.9   Clicking an `ImageButton`.

LISTING 1.9   `ShowEventArgs.aspx`

```
<%@ Page Language="VB" %>
<!DOCTYPE html PUBLIC "-//W3C//DTD XHTML 1.0 Transitional//EN"
    "http://www.w3.org/TR/xhtml1/DTD/xhtml1-transitional.dtd">
<script runat="server">

    Sub btnElephant_Click(ByVal sender As Object, ByVal e As ImageClickEventArgs)
        lblX.Text = e.X.ToString()
        lblY.Text = e.Y.ToString()
    End Sub
</script>
<html xmlns="http://www.w3.org/1999/xhtml" >
<head id="Head1" runat="server">
    <title>Show EventArgs</title>
</head>
<body>
    <form id="form1" runat="server">
    <div>

    <asp:ImageButton
        id="btnElephant"
        ImageUrl="Elephant.jpg"
```

LISTING 1.9   Continued

```
        OnClick="btnElephant_Click"
        Runat="server" />

    <br />
    X Coordinate:
    <asp:Label
        id="lblX"
        Runat="server" />
    <br />
    Y Coordinate:
    <asp:Label
        id="lblY"
        Runat="server" />

    </div>
    </form>
</body>
</html>
```

Notice that the second parameter passed to the btnElephant_Click() method is an ImageClickEventArgs parameter. Whenever the second parameter is not the default EventArgs parameter, you know that additional event information is being passed to the handler.

Understanding View State

The HTTP protocol, the fundamental protocol of the World Wide Web, is a stateless protocol. Each time you request a web page from a website, from the website's perspective, you are a completely new person.

The ASP.NET Framework, however, manages to transcend this limitation of the HTTP protocol. For example, if you assign a value to a Label control's Text property, the Label control retains this value across multiple page requests.

Consider the page in Listing 1.9. This page contains a Button control and a Label control. Each time you click the Button control, the value displayed by the Label control is incremented by 1 (see Figure 1.10). How does the Label control preserve its value across postbacks to the web server?

LISTING 1.9   ShowViewState.aspx

```
<%@ Page Language="VB" %>
<!DOCTYPE html PUBLIC "-//W3C//DTD XHTML 1.0 Transitional//EN"
    "http://www.w3.org/TR/xhtml1/DTD/xhtml1-transitional.dtd">
<script runat="server">
```

LISTING 1.9   Continued

```
    Sub btnAdd_Click(ByVal sender As Object, ByVal e As EventArgs)
        lblCounter.Text = (Int32.Parse(lblCounter.Text) + 1).ToString()
    End Sub
</script>
<html xmlns="http://www.w3.org/1999/xhtml" >
<head id="Head1" runat="server">
    <title>Show View State</title>
</head>
<body>
    <form id="form1" runat="server">
    <div>

    <asp:Button
        id="btnAdd"
        Text="Add"
        OnClick="btnAdd_Click"
        Runat="server" />

    <asp:Label
        id="lblCounter"
        Text="0"
        Runat="server" />

    </div>
    </form>
</body>
</html>
```

The ASP.NET Framework uses a trick called View State. If you open the page in Listing 1.9 in your browser and select View Source, you'll notice that the page includes a hidden form field named __VIEWSTATE that looks like this:

```
<input type="hidden" name="__VIEWSTATE" id="__
  VIEWSTATE" value="/wEPDwUKLTc2ODE1OTYxNw9kFgICBA9kFgIC
  Aw8PFgIeBFRleHQFATFkZGT3tMnThg9KZpGak55p367vfInj1w==" />
```

This hidden form field contains the value of the Label control's Text property (and the values of any other control properties that are stored in View State). When the page is posted back to the server, the ASP.NET Framework rips apart this string and re-creates the values of all the properties stored in View State. In this way, the ASP.NET Framework preserves the state of control properties across postbacks to the web server.

By default, View State is enabled for every control in the ASP.NET Framework. If you change the background color of a Calendar control, the new background color is remembered across postbacks. If you change the selected item in a DropDownList, the selected item is remembered across postbacks. The values of these properties are automatically stored in View State.

FIGURE 1.10   Preserving state between postbacks.

View State is a good thing, but sometimes it can be too much of a good thing. The __VIEWSTATE hidden form field can become very large. Stuffing too much data into View State can slow down the rendering of a page because the contents of the hidden field must be pushed back and forth between the web server and web browser.

You can determine how much View State each control contained in a page is consuming by enabling tracing for a page (see Figure 1.11). The page in Listing 1.10 includes a Trace="true" attribute in its <%@ Page %> directive, which enables tracing.

LISTING 1.10   ShowTrace.aspx

```
<%@ Page Language="VB" Trace="true" %>
<!DOCTYPE html PUBLIC "-//W3C//DTD XHTML 1.0 Transitional//EN"
    "http://www.w3.org/TR/xhtml1/DTD/xhtml1-transitional.dtd">
<script runat="server">

    Sub Page_Load()
        Label1.Text = "Hello World!"
        Calendar1.TodaysDate = DateTime.Now
    End Sub
```

LISTING 1.10   Continued

```
</script>
<html xmlns="http://www.w3.org/1999/xhtml" >
<head id="Head1" runat="server">
    <title>Show Trace</title>
</head>
<body>
    <form id="form1" runat="server">
    <div>

    <asp:Label
        id="Label1"
        Runat="server" />
    <asp:Calendar
        id="Calendar1"
        TodayDayStyle-BackColor="Yellow"
        Runat="server" />

    </div>
    </form>
</body>
</html>
```

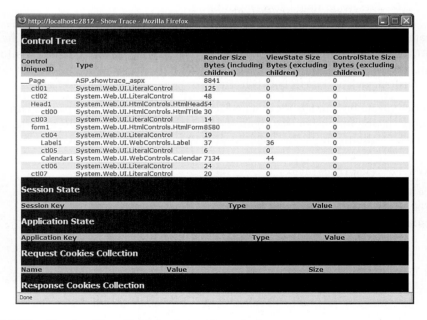

FIGURE 1.11   Viewing View State size for each control.

When you open the page in Listing 1.10, additional information about the page is appended to the bottom of the page. The Control Tree section displays the amount of View State used by each ASP.NET control contained in the page.

Every ASP.NET control includes a property named `EnableViewState`. If you set this property to the value `False`, then View State is disabled for the control. In that case, the values of the control properties are not remembered across postbacks to the server.

For example, the page in Listing 1.11 contains two Label controls and a Button control. The first Label has View State disabled and the second Label has View State enabled. When you click the button, only the value of the second Label control is incremented past 1.

LISTING 1.11   DisableViewState.aspx

```
<%@ Page Language="VB" %>
<!DOCTYPE html PUBLIC "-//W3C//DTD XHTML 1.0 Transitional//EN"
    "http://www.w3.org/TR/xhtml1/DTD/xhtml1-transitional.dtd">
<script runat="server">

    Sub btnAdd_Click(ByVal sender As Object, ByVal e As EventArgs)
        Label1.Text = (Int32.Parse(Label1.Text) + 1).ToString()
        Label2.Text = (Int32.Parse(Label2.Text) + 1).ToString()
    End Sub
</script>
<html xmlns="http://www.w3.org/1999/xhtml" >
<head id="Head1" runat="server">
    <title>Disable View State</title>
</head>
<body>
    <form id="form1" runat="server">
    <div>

    Label 1:
    <asp:Label
        id="Label1"
        EnableViewState="false"
        Text="0"
        Runat="server" />

    <br />

    Label 2:
    <asp:Label
        id="Label2"
        Text="0"
        Runat="server" />
```

LISTING 1.11   Continued

```
    <br /><br />

    <asp:Button
        id="btnAdd"
        Text="Add"
        OnClick="btnAdd_Click"
        Runat="server" />

    </div>
    </form>
</body>
</html>
```

Sometimes, you might want to disable View State even when you aren't concerned with the size of the __VIEWSTATE hidden form field. For example, if you are using a Label control to display a form validation error message, you might want to start from scratch each time the page is submitted. In that case, simply disable View State for the Label control.

> **NOTE**
>
> The ASP.NET Framework version 2.0 includes a new feature called Control State. Control State is similar to View State except that it is used to preserve only critical state information. For example, the GridView control uses Control State to store the selected row. Even if you disable View State, the GridView control remembers which row is selected.

Understanding ASP.NET Pages

This section examines ASP.NET pages in more detail. You learn about dynamic compilation and code-behind files. We also discuss the events supported by the Page class.

Understanding Dynamic Compilation

Strangely enough, when you create an ASP.NET page, you are actually creating the source code for a .NET class. You are creating a new instance of the System.Web.UI.Page class. The entire contents of an ASP.NET page, including all script and HTML content, are compiled into a .NET class.

When you request an ASP.NET page, the ASP.NET Framework checks for a .NET class that corresponds to the page. If a corresponding class does not exist, the Framework automatically compiles the page into a new class and stores the compiled class (the assembly) in the Temporary ASP.NET Files folder located at the following path:

```
\WINDOWS\Microsoft.NET\Framework\[version]\Temporary ASP.NET Files
```

The next time anyone requests the same page in the future, the page is not compiled again. The previously compiled class is executed and the results are returned to the browser.

Even if you unplug your web server, move to Borneo for 3 years, and start up your web server again, the next time someone requests the same page, the page does not need to be re-compiled. The compiled class is preserved in the Temporary ASP.NET Files folder until the source code for your application is modified.

When the class is added to the Temporary ASP.NET Files folder, a file dependency is created between the class and the original ASP.NET page. If the ASP.NET page is modified in any way, the corresponding .NET class is automatically deleted. The next time someone requests the page, the Framework automatically compiles the modified page source into a new .NET class.

This process is called *dynamic compilation*. Dynamic compilation enables ASP.NET applications to support thousands of simultaneous users. Unlike an ASP Classic page, for example, an ASP.NET page does not need to be parsed and compiled each and every time it is requested. An ASP.NET page is compiled only when an application is modified.

> **NOTE**
>
> You can precompile an entire ASP.NET application by using the `aspnet_compiler.exe` command-line tool. If you precompile an application, users don't experience the compilation delay resulting from the first page request.

> **NOTE**
>
> You can disable dynamic compilation for a single page, the pages in a folder, or an entire website with the `CompilationMode` attribute. When the `CompilationMode` attribute is used with the `<%@ Page %>` directive, it enables you to disable dynamic compilation for a single page. When the `compilationMode` attribute is used with the `pages` element in a web configuration file, it enables you to disable dynamic compilation for an entire folder or application.
>
> Disabling compilation is useful when you have thousands of pages in a website and you don't want to load an assembly into memory for every page. When the `CompilationMode` attribute is set to the value `Never`, the page is never compiled and an assembly is never generated for the page. The page is interpreted at runtime.
>
> You cannot disable compilation for pages that include server-side code. In particular, a no compile page cannot include a server-side `<script>...</script>` block. On the other hand, a no compile page can contain ASP.NET controls and databinding expressions.

In case you are curious, I've included the source code for the class that corresponds to the `FirstPage.aspx` page in Listing 1.12 (I've cleaned up the code slightly to make it shorter). I copied this file from the Temporary ASP.NET Files folder after enabling debugging for the application.

LISTING 1.12 FirstPage.aspx Source

```
Option Strict Off
Option Explicit On

Imports Microsoft.VisualBasic
Imports System
Imports System.Collections
Imports System.Collections.Specialized
Imports System.Configuration
Imports System.Text
Imports System.Text.RegularExpressions
Imports System.Web
Imports System.Web.Caching
Imports System.Web.Profile
Imports System.Web.Security
Imports System.Web.SessionState
Imports System.Web.UI
Imports System.Web.UI.HtmlControls
Imports System.Web.UI.WebControls
Imports System.Web.UI.WebControls.WebParts

Namespace ASP

    <System.Runtime.CompilerServices.CompilerGlobalScopeAttribute()> _
    Public Class firstpage_aspx
        Inherits Global.System.Web.UI.Page
        Implements System.Web.SessionState.IRequiresSessionState, System.Web.
IHttpHandler

        Protected WithEvents lblServerTime As Global.System.Web.UI.WebControls.
Label
        Protected WithEvents form1 As Global.System.Web.UI.HtmlControls.HtmlForm
        Private Shared __initialized As Boolean
        Private Shared __fileDependencies As Object

    Sub Page_Load()
            lblServerTime.Text = DateTime.Now.ToString()
        End Sub

        Public Sub New()
            MyBase.New
            Dim dependencies() As String
            CType(Me,System.Web.UI.Page).AppRelativeVirtualPath = "~/FirstPage.
aspx"
```

LISTING 1.12   Continued

```
        If (Global.ASP.firstpage_aspx.__initialized = false) Then
            dependencies = New String(0) {}
            dependencies(0) = "~/FirstPage.aspx"
            Global.ASP.firstpage_aspx.__fileDependencies =
Me.GetWrappedFileDependencies(dependencies)
            Global.ASP.firstpage_aspx.__initialized = true
        End If
        Me.Server.ScriptTimeout = 30000000
    End Sub


    Protected ReadOnly Property Profile() As System.Web.Profile.DefaultProfile
        Get
            Return CType(Me.Context.Profile,System.Web.Profile.DefaultProfile)
        End Get
    End Property


    Protected ReadOnly Property ApplicationInstance() As System.Web.
HttpApplication
        Get
            Return CType(Me.Context.ApplicationInstance,System.
Web.HttpApplication)
        End Get
    End Property


    Private Function __BuildControllblServerTime() As Global.System.Web.UI.
WebControls.Label
        Dim __ctrl As Global.System.Web.UI.WebControls.Label
        __ctrl = New Global.System.Web.UI.WebControls.Label
        Me.lblServerTime = __ctrl
        __ctrl.ApplyStyleSheetSkin(Me)
        __ctrl.ID = "lblServerTime"
        Return __ctrl
    End Function


    Private Function __BuildControlform1() As
Global.System.Web.UI.HtmlControls.HtmlForm
        Dim __ctrl As Global.System.Web.UI.HtmlControls.HtmlForm
        __ctrl = New Global.System.Web.UI.HtmlControls.HtmlForm
        Me.form1 = __ctrl
        __ctrl.ID = "form1"
        Dim __parser As System.Web.UI.IParserAccessor =
CType(__ctrl,System.Web.UI.IParserAccessor)
        __parser.AddParsedSubObject(New System.Web.UI.LiteralControl(""&
```

LISTING 1.12   Continued

```
Global.Microsoft.VisualBasic.ChrW(13)&Global.Microsoft.VisualBasic.ChrW(10)
&"    <div>"&Global.Microsoft.VisualBasic.ChrW(13)&Global.Microsoft.
VisualBasic.ChrW(10)&"    "&Global.Microsoft.VisualBasic.ChrW(13)&Global.
Microsoft.VisualBasic.ChrW(10)&"    Welcome to ASP.NET 2.0! The current date
and time is:"&Global.Microsoft.VisualBasic.ChrW(13)&Global.Microsoft.
VisualBasic.ChrW(10)&"    "& _
                        " "&Global.Microsoft.VisualBasic.ChrW(13)&
Global.Microsoft.VisualBasic.ChrW(10)&"    "))
            Dim __ctrl1 As Global.System.Web.UI.WebControls.Label
            __ctrl1 = Me.__BuildControllblServerTime
            __parser.AddParsedSubObject(__ctrl1)
            __parser.AddParsedSubObject(New System.Web.UI.LiteralControl(""
&Global.Microsoft.VisualBasic.ChrW(13)&Global.Microsoft.VisualBasic.ChrW(10)&
"    "&Global.Microsoft.VisualBasic.ChrW(13)&Global.Microsoft.VisualBasic.ChrW(10)&
"    </div>"&Global.Microsoft.VisualBasic.ChrW(13)&Global.Microsoft.VisualBasic.
ChrW(10)&"    "))
            Return __ctrl
        End Function


        Private Sub __BuildControlTree(ByVal __ctrl As firstpage_aspx)
            Me.InitializeCulture
            Dim __parser As System.Web.UI.IParserAccessor = CType(__ctrl,
System.Web.UI.IParserAccessor)
            __parser.AddParsedSubObject(New System.Web.UI.LiteralControl(""&
Global.Microsoft.VisualBasic.ChrW(13)&Global.Microsoft.VisualBasic.
ChrW(10)&"<!DOCTYPE html PUBLIC ""-//W3C//DTD XHTML 1.0 Transitional//EN""
""http://www.w3.o"& _
                        "rg/TR/xhtml1/DTD/xhtml1-
transitional.dtd"">"&Global.Microsoft.VisualBasic.ChrW(13)&Global.Microsoft.
VisualBasic.ChrW(10)))
            __parser.AddParsedSubObject(New
System.Web.UI.LiteralControl(""&Global.Microsoft.VisualBasic.
ChrW(13)&Global.Microsoft.VisualBasic.ChrW(10)&"<html xmlns=
""http://www.w3.org/1999/xhtml""
 >"&Global.Microsoft.VisualBasic.ChrW(13)&
Global.Microsoft.VisualBasic.ChrW(10)&"<head>"&Global.Microsoft.VisualBasic.
ChrW(13)&Global.Microsoft.VisualBasic.ChrW(10)&"    <title>First Page</ti"& _
                        "tle>"&Global.Microsoft.VisualBasic.ChrW(13)&
Global.Microsoft.VisualBasic.ChrW(10)&"</head>"&
Global.Microsoft.VisualBasic.ChrW(13)&Global.Microsoft.VisualBasic.
ChrW(10)&"<body>"&Global.Microsoft.VisualBasic.ChrW(13)&Global.
Microsoft.VisualBasic.ChrW(10)&"    "))
            Dim __ctrl1 As Global.System.Web.UI.HtmlControls.HtmlForm
```

LISTING 1.12   Continued

```
                __ctrl1 = Me.__BuildControlform1
                __parser.AddParsedSubObject(__ctrl1)
                __parser.AddParsedSubObject(New System.Web.UI.LiteralControl(""&
Global.Microsoft.VisualBasic.ChrW(13)&Global.Microsoft.
VisualBasic.ChrW(10)&"</body>"&Global.Microsoft.VisualBasic.
ChrW(13)&Global.Microsoft.VisualBasic.ChrW(10)&
"</html>"&Global.Microsoft.VisualBasic.ChrW(13)&
Global.Microsoft.VisualBasic.ChrW(10)))
        End Sub


        Protected Overrides Sub FrameworkInitialize()
            MyBase.FrameworkInitialize
            Me.__BuildControlTree(Me)
            Me.AddWrappedFileDependencies(Global.ASP.firstpage_aspx._
_fileDependencies)
            Me.Request.ValidateInput
        End Sub


        Public Overrides Function GetTypeHashCode() As Integer
            Return 579569163
        End Function


      Public Overrides Sub ProcessRequest(ByVal context As System.Web.HttpContext)
            MyBase.ProcessRequest(context)
        End Sub
    End Class
End Namespace
```

The class in Listing 1.12 inherits from the System.Web.UI.Page class. The ProcessRequest() method is called by the ASP.NET Framework when the page is displayed. This method builds the page's control tree, which is the subject of the next section.

Understanding Control Trees

In the previous section, you learned that an ASP.NET page is really the source code for a .NET class. Alternatively, you can think of an ASP.NET page as a bag of controls. More accurately, because some controls might contain child controls, you can think of an ASP.NET page as a control tree.

For example, the page in Listing 1.13 contains a DropDownList control and a Button control. Furthermore, because the <%@ Page %> directive has the Trace="true" attribute, tracing is enabled for the page.

LISTING 1.13   ShowControlTree.aspx

```
<%@ Page Language="VB" Trace="true" %>
<!DOCTYPE html PUBLIC "-//W3C//DTD XHTML 1.0 Transitional//EN"
 "http://www.w3.org/TR/xhtml1/DTD/xhtml1-transitional.dtd">
<html xmlns="http://www.w3.org/1999/xhtml" >
<head id="Head1" runat="server">
    <title>Show Control Tree</title>
</head>
<body>
    <form id="form1" runat="server">
    <div>

    <asp:DropDownList
        id="DropDownList1"
        Runat="server">
        <asp:ListItem Text="Oranges" />
        <asp:ListItem Text="Apples" />
    </asp:DropDownList>

    <asp:Button
        id="Button1"
        Text="Submit"
        Runat="server" />

    </div>
    </form>
</body>
</html>
```

When you open the page in Listing 1.12 in your browser, you can see the control tree for the page appended to the bottom of the page. It looks like this:

```
__Page ASP.showcontroltree_aspx
    ctl02 System.Web.UI.LiteralControl
    ctl00 System.Web.UI.HtmlControls.HtmlHead
        ctl01 System.Web.UI.HtmlControls.HtmlTitle
    ctl03 System.Web.UI.LiteralControl
    form1 System.Web.UI.HtmlControls.HtmlForm
        ctl04 System.Web.UI.LiteralControl
        DropDownList1 System.Web.UI.WebControls.DropDownList
        ctl05 System.Web.UI.LiteralControl
        Button1 System.Web.UI.WebControls.Button
        ctl06 System.Web.UI.LiteralControl
    ctl07
```

The root node in the control tree is the page itself. The page has an ID of __Page. The page class contains all the other controls in its child controls collection.

The control tree also contains an instance of the HtmlForm class named form1. This control is the server-side form tag contained in the page. It contains all the other form controls—the DropDownList and Button controls—as child controls.

Notice that there are several LiteralControl controls interspersed between the other controls in the control tree. What are these controls?

Remember that everything in an ASP.NET page is converted into a .NET class, including any HTML or plain text content in a page. The LiteralControl class represents the HTML content in the page (including any carriage returns between tags).

> **NOTE**
>
> Normally, you refer to a control in a page by its ID. However, there are situations in which this is not possible. In those cases, you can use the FindControl() method of the Control class to retrieve a control with a particular ID. The FindControl() method is similar to the JavaScript getElementById() method.

Using Code-Behind Pages

The ASP.NET Framework (and Visual Web Developer) enables you to create two different types of ASP.NET pages. You can create both single-file and two-file ASP.NET pages.

All the code samples in this book are written as single-file ASP.NET pages. In a single-file ASP.NET page, a single file contains both the page code and page controls. The page code is contained in a <script runat="server"> tag.

As an alternative to a single-file ASP.NET page, you can create a two-file ASP.NET page. A two-file ASP.NET page is normally referred to as a *code-behind* page. In a code-behind page, the page code is contained in a separate file.

> **NOTE**
>
> Code-behind pages work in a different way in the ASP.NET 2.0 Framework than they did in the ASP.NET 1.x Framework. In ASP.NET 1.x, the two halves of a code-behind page were related by inheritance. In the ASP.NET 2.0 Framework, the two halves of a code-behind page are related by a combination of partial classes and inheritance.

For example, Listing 1.14 and Listing 1.15 contain the two halves of a code-behind page.

> **VISUAL WEB DEVELOPER NOTE**
>
> When using Visual Web Developer, you create a code-behind page by selecting Website, Add New Item, selecting the Web Form Item, and checking the Place Code in Separate File check box before adding the page.

LISTING 1.14   FirstPageCodeBehind.aspx

```
<%@ Page Language="VB" AutoEventWireup="false"
CodeFile="FirstPageCodeBehind.aspx.vb" Inherits="FirstPageCodeBehind" %>
<!DOCTYPE html PUBLIC "-//W3C//DTD XHTML 1.0 Transitional//EN"
"http://www.w3.org/TR/xhtml1/DTD/xhtml1-transitional.dtd">
<html xmlns="http://www.w3.org/1999/xhtml" >
<head id="Head1" runat="server">
    <title>First Page Code-Behind</title>
</head>
<body>
    <form id="form1" runat="server">
    <div>

    <asp:Button
        id="Button1"
        Text="Click Here"
        Runat="server" />

    <br /><br />

    <asp:Label
        id="Label1"
        Runat="server" />

    </div>
    </form>
</body>
</html>
```

LISTING 1.15   FirstPageCodeBehind.aspx.vb

```
Partial Class FirstPageCodeBehind
    Inherits System.Web.UI.Page


    Protected Sub Page_Load(ByVal sender As Object, ByVal e As System.EventArgs)
    Handles Me.Load
        Label1.Text = "Click the Button"
    End Sub


    Protected Sub Button1_Click(ByVal sender As Object, ByVal e
        As System.EventArgs) Handles Button1.Click
```

LISTING 1.15   Continued

```
        Label1.Text = "Thanks!"
    End Sub

End Class
```

The page in Listing 1.14 is called the *presentation page*. It contains a Button control and a Label control. However, the page does not contain any code. All the code is contained in the code-behind file.

> **VISUAL WEB DEVELOPER NOTE**
>
> You can flip to the code-behind file for a page by right-clicking a page and selecting View Code.

The code-behind file in Listing 1.15 contains the `Page_Load()` and `Button1_Click()` handlers. The code-behind file in Listing 1.15 does not contain any controls.

Notice that the page in Listing 1.14 includes both a `CodeFile` and `Inherits` attribute in its `<%@ Page %>` directive. These attributes link the page to its code-behind file.

How Code-Behind Works: The Ugly Details

In the previous version of the ASP.NET Framework (ASP.NET 1.x), two classes were generated by a code-behind page. One class corresponded to the presentation page and one class corresponded to the code-behind file. These classes were related to one another through class inheritance. The presentation page class inherited from the code-behind file class.

The problem with this method of associating presentation pages with their code-behind files was that it was very brittle. Inheritance is a one-way relationship. Anything that is true of the mother is true of the daughter, but not the other way around. Any control that you declared in the presentation page was required to be declared in the code-behind file. Furthermore, the control had to be declared with exactly the same ID. Otherwise, the inheritance relationship would be broken and events raised by a control could not be handled in the code-behind file.

In the beta version of ASP.NET 2.0, a completely different method of associating presentation pages with their code-behind files was used. This new method was far less brittle. The two halves of a code-behind page were no longer related through inheritance, but through a new technology supported by the .NET 2.0 Framework called *partial classes*.

> **NOTE**
>
> Partial classes are discussed in Chapter 14, "Building Components."

Partial classes enable you to declare a class in more than one physical file. When the class gets compiled, one class is generated from all the partial classes. Any members of one partial class—including any private fields, methods, and properties—are accessible to any other partial classes of the same class. This makes sense because partial classes are combined eventually to create one final class.

The advantage of using partial classes is that you don't need to worry about declaring a control in both the presentation page and code-behind file. Anything that you declare in the presentation page is available automatically in the code-behind file, and anything you declare in the code-behind file is available automatically in the presentation page.

The beta version of the ASP.NET 2.0 Framework used partial classes to relate a presentation page with its code-behind file. However, certain advanced features of the ASP.NET 1.x Framework were not compatible with using partial classes. To support these advanced features, a more complex method of associating presentation pages with code-behind files is used in the final release of the ASP.NET 2.0 Framework.

> **NOTE**
>
> The ASP.NET 1.x Framework enabled you to create a custom base Page class and inherit every ASP.NET page in an application from the custom Page class. Relating pages and code-behind files with partial classes conflicted with inheriting from a custom base Page class. In the final release of the ASP.NET 2.0 Framework, you can once again create custom base Page classes. For a sample of a custom base Page class, see the final section of Chapter 5, "Designing Websites with Master Pages."

The final release of the ASP.NET 2.0 Framework uses a combination of inheritance and partial classes to relate presentation pages and code-behind files. The ASP.NET 2.0 Framework generates three classes whenever you create a code-behind page.

The first two classes correspond to the presentation page. For example, when you create the `FirstPageCodeBehind.aspx` page, the following two classes are generated automatically in the Temporary ASP.NET Files folder:

```
Partial Public Class FirstPageCodeBehind

  Protected WithEvents Button1 As Global.System.Web.UI.WebControls.Button
  Protected WithEvents Label1 As Global.System.Web.UI.WebControls.Label
  ... additional class code ...

End Class

Public Class firstpagecodebehind_aspx
  Inherits FirstPageCodeBehind

  ... additional class code ...

End Class
```

A third class is generated that corresponds to the code-behind file. Corresponding to the `FirstPageCodeBehind.aspx.vb` file, the following class is generated:

```
Partial Class FirstPageCodeBehind
  Inherits System.Web.UI.Page

  Protected Sub Button1_Click(ByVal sender As Object, ByVal e As System.EventArgs) _
      Handles Button1.Click
    Label1.Text = "Thanks!"
  End Sub

End Class
```

The `firstpagecodebehind_aspx` class is executed when the `FirstPageCodeBehind.aspx` page is requested from a browser. This class inherits from the `FirstPageCodeBehind` class. The `FirstPageCodeBehind` class is a partial class. It gets generated twice: once by the presentation page and once by the code-behind file.

The final release of the ASP.NET 2.0 Framework uses a combination of partial classes and inheritance to relate presentation pages and code-behind files. Because the page and code-behind classes are partial classes, unlike the previous version of ASP.NET, you no longer need to declare controls in both the presentation and code-behind page. Any control declared in the presentation page is accessible in the code-behind file automatically. Because the page class inherits from the code-behind class, the ASP.NET 2.0 Framework continues to support advanced features of the ASP.NET 1.x Framework such as custom base Page classes.

Deciding Between Single-File and Code-Behind Pages

So, when should you use single-file ASP.NET pages and when should you use code-behind pages? This decision is a preference choice. There are intense arguments over this topic contained in blogs spread across the Internet.

I've heard it argued that code-behind pages are superior to single-file pages because code-behind pages enable you to more cleanly separate your user interface from your application logic. The problem with this argument is that the normal justification for separating your user interface from your application logic is code reuse. Building code-behind pages really doesn't promote code reuse. A better way to reuse application logic across multiple pages is to build separate component libraries. (Part IV of this book explores this topic.)

My personal preference is to build ASP.NET applications using single-file ASP.NET pages because this approach requires managing fewer files. However, I've built many applications using the code-behind model (such as some of the ASP.NET Starter Kits) without suffering dire consequences.

> **NOTE**
>
> The previous version of Visual Studio .NET did not support building single-file ASP.NET pages. If you wanted to create single-file ASP.NET pages in the previous version of ASP.NET, you had to use an alternate development environment such as Web Matrix or Notepad.

Handling Page Events

Whenever you request an ASP.NET page, a particular set of events is raised in a particular sequence. This sequence of events is called the *page execution lifecycle*.

For example, we have already used the Page Load event in previous code samples in this chapter. You normally use the Page Load event to initialize the properties of controls contained in a page. However, the Page Load event is only one event supported by the Page class.

Here is the sequence of events that are raised whenever you request a page:

1. PreInit

2. Init

3. InitComplete

4. PreLoad

5. Load

6. LoadComplete

7. PreRender

8. PreRenderComplete

9. SaveStateComplete

10. Unload

Why so many events? Different things happen and different information is available at different stages in the page execution lifecycle.

For example, View State is not loaded until after the InitComplete event. Data posted to the server from a form control, such as a TextBox control, is also not available until after this event.

Ninety-nine percent of the time, you won't handle any of these events except for the Load and the PreRender events. The difference between these two events is that the Load event happens before any control events and the PreRender event happens after any control events.

The page in Listing 1.16 illustrates the difference between the Load and PreRender events. The page contains three event handlers: one for the Load event, one for the Button Click event, and one for the PreRender event. Each handler adds a message to a Label control (Figure 1.12).

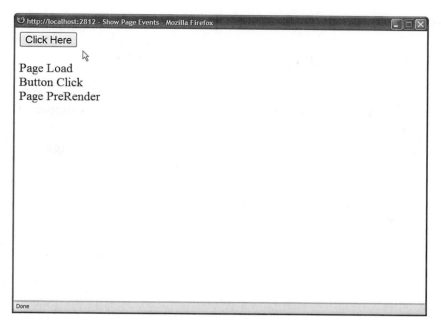

FIGURE 1.12   Viewing the sequence of page events.

LISTING 1.16   ShowPageEvents.aspx

```
<%@ Page Language="VB" %>
<!DOCTYPE html PUBLIC "-//W3C//DTD XHTML 1.0 Transitional//EN"
    "http://www.w3.org/TR/xhtml1/DTD/xhtml1-transitional.dtd">
<script runat="server">

    Sub Page_Load()
        Label1.Text = "Page Load"
    End Sub

    Sub Button1_Click(ByVal sender As Object, ByVal e As EventArgs)
        Label1.Text &= "<br />Button Click"
    End Sub

    Sub Page_PreRender()
        Label1.Text &= "<br />Page PreRender"
    End Sub
</script>
<html xmlns="http://www.w3.org/1999/xhtml" >
<head id="Head1" runat="server">
    <title>Show Page Events</title>
```

LISTING 1.16   Continued

```
</head>
<body>
    <form id="form1" runat="server">
    <div>

    <asp:Button
        id="Button1"
        Text="Click Here"
        OnClick="Button1_Click"
        Runat="server" />

    <br /><br />

    <asp:Label
        id="Label1"
        Runat="server" />

    </div>
    </form>
</body>
</html>
```

When you click the Button control, the Click event does not happen on the server until after the Load event and before the PreRender event.

The other thing you should notice about the page in Listing 1.16 is the way the event handlers are wired to the Page events. ASP.NET pages support a feature named AutoEventWireUp, which is enabled by default. If you name a subroutine Page_Load(), the subroutine automatically handles the Page Load event; if you name a subroutine Page_ PreRender(), the subroutine automatically handles the Page PreRender event, and so on.

> **WARNING**
>
> AutoEventWireUp does not work for every page event. For example, it does not work for the Page_InitComplete() event.

Using the Page.IsPostBack Property

The Page class includes a property called the IsPostBack property, which you can use to detect whether the page has already been posted back to the server.

Because of View State, when you initialize a control property, you do not want to initialize the property every time a page loads. Because View State saves the state of control properties across page posts, you typically initialize a control property only once, when the page first loads.

In fact, many controls don't work correctly if you re-initialize the properties of the control with each page load. In these cases, you must use the `IsPostBack` property to detect whether or not the page has been posted.

The page in Listing 1.17 illustrates how you can use the `Page.IsPostBack` property when adding items to a `DropDownList` control.

LISTING 1.17   `ShowIsPostBack.aspx`

```
<%@ Page Language="VB" %>
<!DOCTYPE html PUBLIC "-//W3C//DTD XHTML 1.0 Transitional//EN"
    "http://www.w3.org/TR/xhtml1/DTD/xhtml1-transitional.dtd">
<script runat="server">

    Sub Page_Load()
        if Not Page.IsPostBack Then
            ' Create collection of items
            Dim items As New ArrayList()
            items.Add("Apples")
            items.Add("Oranges")

            ' Bind to DropDownList
            DropDownList1.DataSource = items
            DropDownList1.DataBind()
        End If
    End Sub

    Sub Button1_Click(ByVal sender As Object, ByVal e As EventArgs)
        Label1.Text = DropDownList1.SelectedItem.Text
    End Sub
</script>
<html xmlns="http://www.w3.org/1999/xhtml" >
<head id="Head1" runat="server">
    <title>Show IsPostBack</title>
</head>
<body>
    <form id="form1" runat="server">
    <div>

    <asp:DropDownList
        id="DropDownList1"
        Runat="server" />

    <asp:Button
        id="Button1"
        Text="Select"
```

LISTING 1.17   Continued

```
        OnClick="Button1_Click"
        Runat="server" />

    <br /><br />

    You selected:
    <asp:Label
        id="Label1"
        Runat="server" />

    </div>
    </form>
</body>
</html>
```

In Listing 1.17, the code in the Page_Load() event handler executes only once when the page first loads. When you post the page again, the IsPostBack property returns True and the code contained in the Page_Load() handler is skipped.

If you remove the IsPostBack check from the Page_Load() method, then you get a strange result. The DropDownList always displays its first item as the selected item. Binding the DropDownList to a collection of items re-initializes the DropDownList control. Therefore, you want to bind the DropDownList control only once, when the page first loads.

Debugging and Tracing ASP.NET Pages

The sad fact of life is that you spend the majority of your development time when building applications debugging the application.

In this section, you learn how to get detailed error messages when developing ASP.NET pages. You also learn how you can display custom trace messages that you can use when debugging a page.

Debugging ASP.NET Pages

If you need to view detailed error messages when you execute a page, you need to enable debugging for either the page or your entire application. You can enable debugging for a page by adding a Debug="true" attribute to the <%@ Page %> directive. For example, the page in Listing 1.18 has debugging enabled.

LISTING 1.18   ShowError.aspx

```
<%@ Page Language="VB" Debug="true" %>
<!DOCTYPE html PUBLIC "-//W3C//DTD XHTML 1.0 Transitional//EN"
 "http://www.w3.org/TR/xhtml1/DTD/xhtml1-transitional.dtd">
<script runat="server">
```

LISTING 1.18   Continued

```
    Sub Page_Load()
        Dim Blow
        Label1.Text = Blow.Up()
    End Sub

</script>
<html xmlns="http://www.w3.org/1999/xhtml" >
<head id="Head1" runat="server">
    <title>Show Error</title>
</head>
<body>
    <form id="form1" runat="server">
    <div>

    <asp:Label
        id="Label1"
        Runat="server" />

    </div>
    </form>
</body>
</html>
```

When you open the page in Listing 1.18 in your web browser, a detailed error message is displayed (see Figure 1.13).

> **WARNING**
>
> Make sure that you disable debugging before placing your application into production. When an application is compiled in debug mode, the compiler can't make certain performance optimizations.

Rather than enable debugging for a single page, you can enable debugging for an entire application by adding the web configuration file in Listing 1.19 to your application.

LISTING 1.19   Web.Config

```
<?xml version="1.0"?>
<configuration>
<system.web>
  <compilation debug="true" />
</system.web>
</configuration>
```

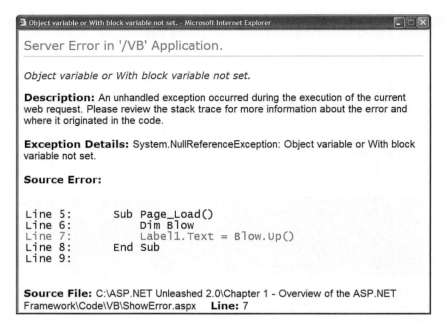

FIGURE 1.13   Viewing a detailed error message.

When debugging an ASP.NET application located on a remote web server, you need to disable custom errors. For security reasons, by default, the ASP.NET Framework doesn't display error messages when you request a page from a remote machine. When custom errors are enabled you don't see errors on a remote machine. The modified web configuration file in Listing 1.20 disables custom errors.

LISTING 1.20   Web.Config

```
<?xml version="1.0"?>
<configuration>
<system.web>
  <compilation debug="true" />
  <customErrors mode="Off" />
</system.web>
</configuration>
```

Debugging Pages with Visual Web Developer

If you are using Visual Web Developer, then you can display compilation error messages by performing a build on a page or an entire website. Select the menu option Build, Build Page or the menu option Build, Build Web Site. A list of compilation error messages and warnings appears in the Error List window (see Figure 1.14). You can double-click any of the errors to navigate directly to the code that caused the error.

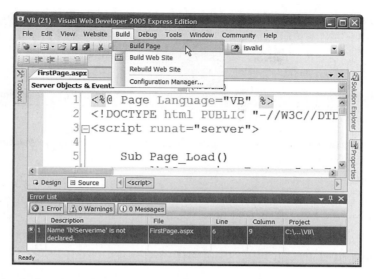

FIGURE 1.14   Performing a build in Visual Web Developer.

If you need to perform more advanced debugging, you can use the Visual Web Developer's debugger. The debugger enables you to set breakpoints and step line by line through your code.

You set a breakpoint by double-clicking the left-most column in Source view. When you add a breakpoint, a red circle appears (see Figure 1.15).

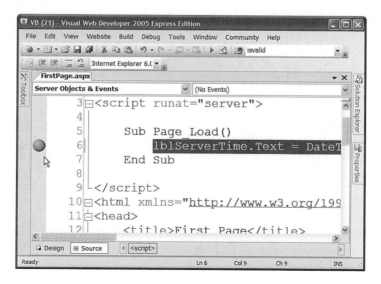

FIGURE 1.15   Setting a breakpoint.

After you set a breakpoint, run your application by selecting the menu option Debug, Start Debugging. Execution stops when the breakpoint is hit. At that point, you can hover your mouse over any variable or control property to view the current value of the variable or control property.

> **NOTE**
>
> You can designate one of the pages in your application as the Start Page. That way, whenever you run your application, the Start Page is executed regardless of the page that you have open. Set the Start Page by right-clicking a page in the Solution Explorer window and selecting the menu option Set As Start Page.

After you hit a breakpoint, you can continue execution by selecting Step Into, Step Over, or Step Out from the Debug menu or the toolbar. Here's an explanation of each of these options:

- **Step Into**—Executes the next line of code.

- **Step Over**—Executes the next line of code without leaving the current method.

- **Step Out**—Executes the next line of code and returns to the method that called the current method.

When you are finished debugging a page, you can continue, stop, or restart your application by selecting a particular option from the Debug menu or the toolbar.

Tracing Page Execution

If you want to output trace messages while a page executes, then you can enable tracing for a particular page or an entire application. The ASP.NET Framework supports both page-level tracing and application-level tracing.

The page in Listing 1.21 illustrates how you can take advantage of page-level tracing.

LISTING 1.21   PageTrace.aspx

```
<%@ Page Language="VB" Trace="true" %>
<!DOCTYPE html PUBLIC "-//W3C//DTD XHTML 1.0 Transitional//EN"
    "http://www.w3.org/TR/xhtml1/DTD/xhtml1-transitional.dtd">
<script runat="server">

    Sub Page_Load()
        For counter As Integer = 0 To 9
            ListBox1.Items.Add("item " & counter.ToString())
            Trace.Warn("counter=" & counter.ToString())
        Next
    End Sub
```

LISTING 1.21   Continued

```
</script>
<html xmlns="http://www.w3.org/1999/xhtml" >
<head id="Head1" runat="server">
    <title>Page Trace</title>
</head>
<body>
    <form id="form1" runat="server">
    <div>

    <asp:ListBox
        id="ListBox1"
        Runat="server" />

    </div>
    </form>
</body>
</html>
```

Notice that the <%@ Page %> directive in Listing 1.21 includes a trace="true" attribute. This attribute enables tracing and causes a Trace Information section to be appended to the bottom of the page (see Figure 1.16).

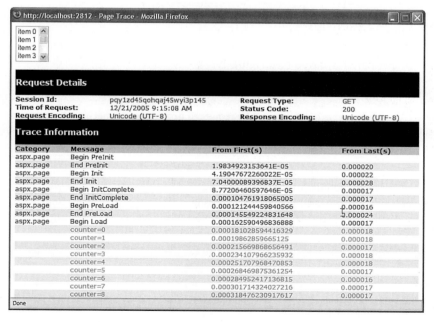

FIGURE 1.16   Viewing page trace information.

Notice, furthermore, that the `Page_Load()` handler uses the `Trace.Warn()` method to write messages to the Trace Information section. You can output any string to the Trace Information section that you please. In Listing 1.21, the current value of a variable named counter is displayed.

You'll want to take advantage of page tracing when you need to determine exactly what is happening when a page executes. You can call the `Trace.Warn()` method wherever you need in your code. Because the Trace Information section appears even when there is an error in your page, you can use tracing to diagnose the causes of any page errors.

One disadvantage of page tracing is that everyone in the world gets to see your trace information. You can get around this problem by taking advantage of application-level tracing. When application-level tracing is enabled, trace information appears only when you request a special page named `Trace.axd`.

To enable application-level tracing, you need to add the web configuration file in Listing 1.22 to your application.

LISTING 1.22   Web.Config

```
<?xml version="1.0"?>
<configuration>
<system.web>
    <trace enabled="true" />
</system.web>
</configuration>
```

After you add the `Web.Config` file in Listing 1.22 to your application, you can request the `Trace.axd` page in your browser. The last 10 page requests made after application-level tracing is enabled are displayed (see Figure 1.17).

> **WARNING**
>
> By default, the `Trace.axd` page cannot be requested from a remote machine. If you need to access the `Trace.axd` page remotely, you need to add a `localOnly="false"` attribute to the trace element in the web configuration file.

If you click the View Details link next to any of the listed page requests, you can view all the trace messages outputted by the page. Messages written with the `Trace.Warn()` method are displayed by the `Trace.axd` page even when page-level tracing is disabled.

> **NOTE**
>
> You can use the new `writeToDiagnosticsTrace` attribute of the trace element to write all trace messages to the Output window of Visual Web Developer when you run an application. You can use the new `mostRecent` attribute to display the last 10 page requests rather than the 10 page requests after tracing was enabled.

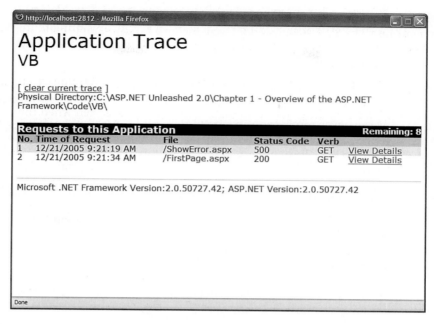

FIGURE 1.17   Viewing application trace information.

Installing the ASP.NET Framework

The easiest way to install the ASP.NET Framework is to install Visual Web Developer Express. Visual Web Developer Express is included on the CD that accompanies this book. (You also can download the latest version from www.ASP.net, which is the official Microsoft ASP.NET website.)

Installing Visual Web Developer Express also installs the following components:

- Microsoft .NET Framework version 2.0
- SQL Server Express

Visual Web Developer Express is compatible with the following operating systems:

- Windows 2000 Service Pack 4
- Windows XP Service Pack 2
- Windows Server 2003 Service Pack 1
- Windows x64 editions
- Windows Vista

I strongly recommend that you also download the .NET Framework SDK (Software Development Kit). The SDK includes additional documentation, sample code, and tools for building ASP.NET applications. You can download the SDK from the Microsoft MSDN website located at msdn.microsoft.com.

You can install Visual Web Developer Express on a computer that already has Visual Studio .NET 2003 installed. The two development environments can co-exist peacefully.

Furthermore, the same web server can serve both ASP.NET 1.1 pages and ASP.NET 2.0 pages. Each version of the .NET Framework is installed in the following folder:

```
C:\WINDOWS\Microsoft.NET\Framework
```

For example, on my computer, I have the following three versions of the .NET Framework installed (version 1.0, version 1.1, and version 2.0):

```
C:\WINDOWS\Microsoft.NET\Framework\v1.0.3705
C:\WINDOWS\Microsoft.NET\Framework\v1.1.4322
C:\WINDOWS\Microsoft.NET\Framework\v2.0.50727
```

Each folder includes a command-line tool named aspnet_regiis.exe. You can use this tool to associate a particular virtual directory on your machine with a particular version of the .NET Framework.

For example, executing the following command from a command prompt enables a particular version of ASP.NET for a virtual directory named MyApplication:

```
aspnet_regiis -s W3SVC/1/ROOT/MyApplication
```

By executing the aspnet_regiis.exe tool located in the different .NET Framework version folders, you can map a particular virtual directory to any version of the ASP.NET Framework.

Summary

In this chapter, you were introduced to the ASP.NET 2.0 Framework. First, we built a simple ASP.NET page. You learned about the three main elements of an ASP.NET page: directives, code declaration blocks, and page render blocks.

Next, we discussed the .NET Framework. You learned about the 13,000 classes contained in the Framework Class Library and you learned about the features of the Common Language Runtime.

You also were provided with an overview of ASP.NET controls. You learned about the different groups of controls included in the .NET Framework. You also learned how to handle control events and take advantage of View State.

We also discussed ASP.NET pages. You learned how ASP.NET pages are dynamically compiled when they are first requested. We also examined how you can divide a single-file ASP.NET page into a code-behind page. You learned how to debug and trace the execution of an ASP.NET page.

At the end of the chapter we covered installation issues in getting the ASP.NET Framework up and running. You learned how to map different Virtual Directories to different versions of the ASP.NET Framework.

CHAPTER **2**

Using the Standard Controls

In this chapter, you learn how to use the core controls contained in the ASP.NET 2.0 Framework. These are controls that you'll use in just about any ASP.NET application that you build.

You learn how to display information to users by using the Label and Literal controls. You learn how to accept user input with the TextBox, CheckBox, and RadioButton controls. You also learn how to submit forms with the button controls.

At the end of this chapter, you learn how to group form fields with the Panel control. Finally, you learn how to link from one page to another with the HyperLink control.

Displaying Information

The ASP.NET Framework includes two controls you can use to display text in a page: the Label control and the Literal control. Whereas the Literal control simply displays text, the Label control supports several additional formatting properties.

Using the Label Control

Whenever you need to modify the text displayed in a page dynamically, you can use the Label control. For example, the page in Listing 2.1 dynamically modifies the value of a Label control's Text property to display the current time (see Figure 2.1).

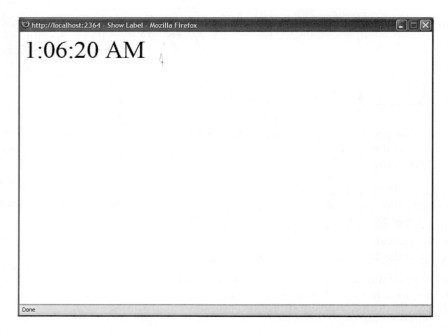

FIGURE 2.1   Displaying the time with a `Label` control.

LISTING 2.1   ShowLabel.aspx

```
<%@ Page Language="VB" %>
<!DOCTYPE html PUBLIC "-//W3C//DTD XHTML 1.0 Transitional//EN"
➥"http://www.w3.org/TR/xhtml1/DTD/xhtml1-transitional.dtd">
<script runat="server">

    Sub Page_Load()
        lblTime.Text = DateTime.Now.ToString("T")
    End Sub
</script>
<html xmlns="http://www.w3.org/1999/xhtml" >
<head id="Head1" runat="server">
    <title>Show Label</title>
</head>
<body>
    <form id="form1" runat="server">
    <div>

    <asp:Label
        id="lblTime"
        Runat="server" />
```

LISTING 2.1   Continued

```
    </div>
    </form>
</body>
</html>
```

Any string that you assign to the Label control's Text property is displayed by the Label when the control is rendered. You can assign simple text to the Text property or you can assign HTML content.

As an alternative to assigning text to the Text property, you can place the text between the Label control's opening and closing tags. Any text that you place before the opening and closing tags gets assigned to the Text property.

By default, a Label control renders its contents in an HTML <span> tag. Whatever value you assign to the Text property is rendered to the browser enclosed in a <span> tag.

The Label control supports several properties you can use to format the text displayed by the Label (this is not a complete list):

- BackColor—Enables you to change the background color of the label.

- BorderColor—Enables you to set the color of a border rendered around the label.

- BorderStyle—Enables you to display a border around the label. Possible values are NotSet, None, Dotted, Dashed, Solid, Double, Groove, Ridge, Inset, and Outset.

- BorderWidth—Enables you to set the size of a border rendered around the label.

- CssClass—Enables you to associate a Cascading Style Sheet class with the label.

- Font—Enables you to set the label's font properties.

- ForeColor—Enables you to set the color of the content rendered by the label.

- Style—Enables you to assign style attributes to the label.

- ToolTip—Enables you to set a label's title attribute. (In Microsoft Internet Explorer, the title attribute is displayed as a floating tooltip.)

In general, I recommend that you avoid using the formatting properties and take advantage of Cascading Style Sheets to format the rendered output of the Label control. The page in Listing 2.2 contains two Label controls: The first is formatted with properties and the second is formatted with a Cascading Style Sheet (see Figure 2.2).

LISTING 2.2   FormatLabel.aspx

```
<%@ Page Language="VB" %>
<!DOCTYPE html PUBLIC "-//W3C//DTD XHTML 1.0 Transitional//EN"
➥"http://www.w3.org/TR/xhtml1/DTD/xhtml1-transitional.dtd">
<html xmlns="http://www.w3.org/1999/xhtml" >
```

LISTING 2.2   Continued

```
<head id="Head1" runat="server">
    <style type="text/css">
        div
        {
            padding:10px;
        }
        .labelStyle
        {
            color:red;
            background-color:yellow;
            border:Solid 2px Red;
        }
    </style>
    <title>Format Label</title>
</head>
<body>
    <form id="form1" runat="server">
    <div>

    <asp:Label
        id="lblFirst"
        Text="First Label"
        ForeColor="Red"
        BackColor="Yellow"
        BorderStyle="Solid"
        BorderWidth="2"
        BorderColor="red"
        Runat="server" />

    <br /><br />

    <asp:Label
        id="lblSecond"
        Text="Second Label"
        CssClass="labelStyle"
        Runat="server" />

    </div>
    </form>
</body>
</html>
```

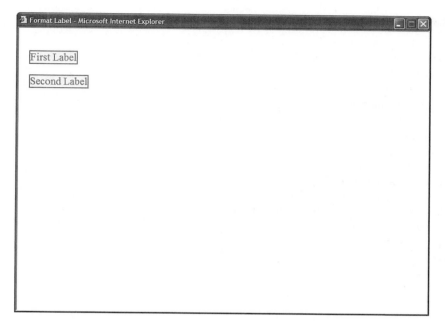

FIGURE 2.2   Formatting a label.

You should use a Label control when labeling the fields in an HTML form. The Label control includes a property named the AssociatedControlID property. You can set this property to point at an ASP.NET control that represents a form field.

For example, the page in Listing 2.3 contains a simple form that contains fields for entering a first and last name. Label controls are used to label the two TextBox controls.

LISTING 2.3   LabelForm.aspx

```
<%@ Page Language="VB" %>
<!DOCTYPE html PUBLIC "-//W3C//DTD XHTML 1.0 Transitional//EN"
➥"http://www.w3.org/TR/xhtml1/DTD/xhtml1-transitional.dtd">
<html xmlns="http://www.w3.org/1999/xhtml" >
<head id="Head1" runat="server">
    <title>Label Form</title>
</head>
<body>
    <form id="form1" runat="server">
    <div>

    <asp:Label
        id="lblFirstName"
        Text="First Name:"
        AssociatedControlID="txtFirstName"
```

LISTING 2.3   Continued

```
         Runat="server" />
    <br />
    <asp:TextBox
         id="txtFirstName"
         Runat="server" />

    <br /><br />

    <asp:Label
         id="lblLastName"
         Text="Last Name:"
         AssociatedControlID="txtLastName"
         Runat="server" />
    <br />
    <asp:TextBox
         id="txtLastName"
         Runat="server" />

    </div>
    </form>
</body>
</html>
```

When you provide a Label control with an AssociatedControlID property, the Label control is rendered as an HTML <label> tag instead of an HTML <span> tag. For example, if you select View Source on your web browser, you'll see that the first Label in Listing 2.3 renders the following content to the browser:

```
<label for="txtFirstName" id="lblFirstName">First Name:</label>
```

Always use a Label control with an AssociatedControlID property when labeling form fields. This is important when you need to make your website accessible to persons with disabilities. If someone is using an assistive device, such as a screen reader, to interact with your website, the AssociatedControlID property enables the assistive device to associate the correct label with the correct form field.

A side benefit of using the AssociatedControlID property is that clicking a label when this property is set automatically changes the form focus to the associated form input field.

WEB STANDARDS NOTE

Both the WCAG 1.0 and Section 508 accessibility guidelines require you to use the <label for> tag when labeling form fields. For more information, see http://www.w3.org/wai and http://www.Section508.gov.

Using the Literal Control

The Literal control is similar to the Label control. You can use the Literal control to display text or HTML content in a browser. However, unlike the Label control, the Literal control does not render its content inside of a <span> tag.

For example, the page in Listing 2.4 uses a Literal control in the page's <head> tag to dynamically modify the title displayed in the browser title bar. The current date is displayed in the Literal control (see Figure 2.3).

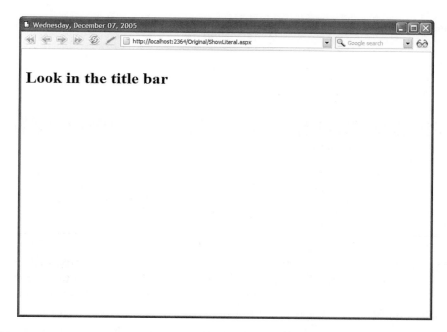

FIGURE 2.3   Modifying the browser title with a Literal control.

LISTING 2.4   ShowLiteral.aspx

```
<%@ Page Language="VB" %>
<!DOCTYPE html PUBLIC "-//W3C//DTD XHTML 1.0 Transitional//EN"
➥"http://www.w3.org/TR/xhtml1/DTD/xhtml1-transitional.dtd">
<script runat="server">
    Sub Page_Load()
        ltlTitle.Text = DateTime.Now.ToString("D")
    End Sub
</script>
<html xmlns="http://www.w3.org/1999/xhtml" >
<head>
    <title><asp:Literal id="ltlTitle" Runat="Server" /></title>
</head>
```

LISTING 2.4   Continued

```
<body>
    <form id="form1" runat="server">
    <div>

    <h1>Look in the title bar</h1>

    </div>
    </form>
</body>
</html>
```

If you used a Label control in Listing 2.4 instead of a Literal control, the uninterpreted <span> tags would appear in the browser title bar.

> **NOTE**
>
> The page in Listing 2.4 uses a format specifier to format the date before assigning the date to the Label control. The D format specifier causes the date to be formatted in a long format. You can use several standard format specifiers with the ToString() method to format dates, times, currency amounts, and numbers. For a list of these format specifiers, look up the Format Specifiers topic in the index of the Microsoft .NET Framework 2.0 SDK Documentation.

Because the contents of a Literal control are not contained in a <span> tag, the Literal control does not support any of the formatting properties supported by the <span> tag. For example, the Literal control does not support either the CssClass or BackColor properties.

The Literal control does support one property that is not supported by the Label control: the Mode property. The Mode property enables you to encode HTML content. The Mode property accepts any of the following three values:

- PassThrough—Displays the contents of the control without encoding.

- Encode—Displays the contents of the control after HTML encoding the content.

- Transform—Displays the contents of the control after stripping markup that is not supported by the requesting device.

For example, the page in Listing 2.5 contains three Literal controls that are set to the three possible values of the Mode property (see Figure 2.4).

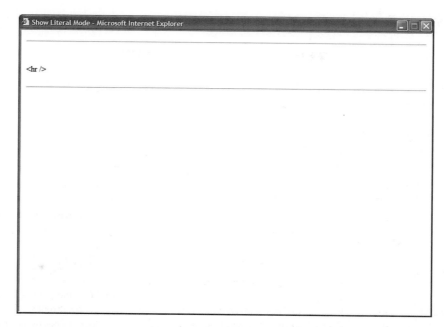

FIGURE 2.4   Three values of the `Literal` control's `Mode` property.

LISTING 2.5   ShowLiteralMode.aspx

```
<%@ Page Language="VB" %>
<!DOCTYPE html PUBLIC "-//W3C//DTD XHTML 1.0 Transitional//EN"
➥"http://www.w3.org/TR/xhtml1/DTD/xhtml1-transitional.dtd">
<html xmlns="http://www.w3.org/1999/xhtml" >
<head id="Head1" runat="server">
    <title>Show Literal Mode</title>
</head>
<body>
    <form id="form1" runat="server">
    <div>

    <asp:Literal
        id="ltlFirst"
        Mode="PassThrough"
        Text="<hr />"
        Runat="server" />

    <br /><br />

    <asp:Literal
        id="ltlSecond"
```

LISTING 2.5   Continued

```
            Mode="Encode"
            Text="<hr />"
            Runat="server" />

    <br /><br />

    <asp:Literal
            id="ltlThird"
            Mode="Transform"
            Text="<hr />"
            Runat="server" />

    </div>
    </form>
</body>
</html>
```

When you request the page in Listing 2.5 with a web browser, the first Literal control displays a horizontal rule, the second Literal control displays the uninterpreted <hr /> tag, and the final Literal control displays another horizontal rule. If you requested the page from a device (such as a WML cell phone) that does not support the <hr> tag, the third <hr /> tag would be stripped.

Accepting User Input

The ASP.NET Framework includes several controls that you can use to gather user input. In this section, you learn how to use the TextBox, CheckBox, and RadioButton controls. These controls correspond to the standard types of HTML input tags.

Using the TextBox Control

The TextBox control can be used to display three different types of input fields depending on the value of its TextMode property. The TextMode property accepts the following three values:

- SingleLine—Displays a single-line input field.

- MultiLine—Displays a multi-line input field.

- Password—Displays a single-line input field in which the text is hidden.

The page in Listing 2.6 contains three TextBox controls that illustrate all three of the TextMode values (see Figure 2.5).

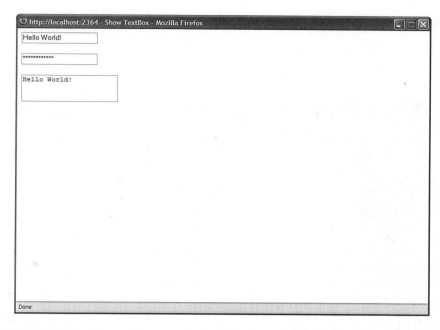

FIGURE 2.5   Displaying `TextBox` controls with different values for `TextMode`.

LISTING 2.6   `ShowTextBox.aspx`

```
<%@ Page Language="VB" %>
<!DOCTYPE html PUBLIC "-//W3C//DTD XHTML 1.0 Transitional//EN"
➥"http://www.w3.org/TR/xhtml1/DTD/xhtml1-transitional.dtd">
<html xmlns="http://www.w3.org/1999/xhtml" >
<head id="Head1" runat="server">
    <title>Show TextBox</title>
</head>
<body>
    <form id="form1" runat="server">
    <div>

    <asp:TextBox
        id="txtUserName"
        TextMode="SingleLine"
        Runat="server" />

    <br /><br />

    <asp:TextBox
        id="txtPassword"
        TextMode="Password"
```

LISTING 2.6   Continued

```
        Runat="server" />

    <br /><br />

    <asp:TextBox
        id="txtComments"
        TextMode="MultiLine"
        Runat="server" />

    </div>
    </form>
</body>
</html>
```

You can use the following properties to control the rendering characteristics of the TextBox control (this is not a complete list):

- AccessKey—Enables you to specify a key that navigates to the TextBox control.

- AutoCompleteType—Enables you to associate an AutoComplete class with the TextBox control.

- AutoPostBack—Enables you to post the form containing the TextBox back to the server automatically when the contents of the TextBox is changed.

- Columns—Enables you to specify the number of columns to display.

- Enabled—Enables you to disable the text box.

- MaxLength—Enables you to specify the maximum length of data that a user can enter in a text box (does not work when TextMode is set to Multiline).

- ReadOnly—Enables you to prevent users from changing the text in a text box.

- Rows—Enables you to specify the number of rows to display.

- TabIndex—Enables you to specify the tab order of the text box.

- Wrap—Enables you to specify whether text word-wraps when the TextMode is set to Multiline.

The TextBox control also supports the following method:

- Focus—Enables you to set the initial form focus to the text box.

And, the TextBox control supports the following event:

- TextChanged—Raised on the server when the contents of the text box are changed.

When the `AutoPostBack` property has the value `True`, the form containing the `TextBox` is automatically posted back to the server when the contents of the `TextBox` changes. For example, the page in Listing 2.7 contains a simple search form. If you modify the contents of the text box and tab out of the `TextBox` control, the form is automatically posted back to the server and the contents of the `TextBox` are displayed (see Figure 2.6).

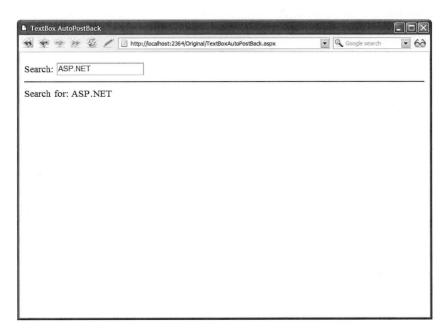

FIGURE 2.6   Reloading a form automatically when the contents of a form field change.

LISTING 2.7   `TextBoxAutoPostBack.aspx`

```
<%@ Page Language="VB" %>
<!DOCTYPE html PUBLIC "-//W3C//DTD XHTML 1.0 Transitional//EN"
➥"http://www.w3.org/TR/xhtml1/DTD/xhtml1-transitional.dtd">
<script runat="server">

    Sub txtSearch_TextChanged(ByVal sender As Object, ByVal e As EventArgs)
        lblSearchResults.Text = "Search for: " & txtSearch.Text
    End Sub
</script>
<html xmlns="http://www.w3.org/1999/xhtml" >
<head id="Head1" runat="server">
    <title>TextBox AutoPostBack</title>
</head>
```

LISTING 2.7 Continued

```
<body>
    <form id="form1" runat="server">
    <div>

    <asp:Label
        id="lblSearch"
        Text="Search:"
        Runat="server" />
    <asp:TextBox
        id="txtSearch"
        AutoPostBack="true"
        OnTextChanged="txtSearch_TextChanged"
        Runat="server" />

    <hr />

    <asp:Label
        id="lblSearchResults"
        Runat="server" />

    </div>
    </form>
</body>
</html>
```

In Listing 2.7, the `TextBox` control's `TextChanged` event is handled. This event is raised on the server when the contents of the `TextBox` have been changed. You can handle this event even when you don't use the `AutoPostBack` property.

> **WEB STANDARDS NOTE**
>
> You should avoid using the `AutoPostBack` property for accessibility reasons. Creating a page that automatically reposts to the server can be very confusing to someone using an assistive device such as a screen reader. If you insist on using the `AutoPostBack` property, you should include a value for the `ToolTip` property that warns the user that the page will be reloaded.

Notice that the `TextBox` control also includes a property that enables you to associate the `TextBox` with a particular `AutoComplete` class. When `AutoComplete` is enabled, the user does not need to re-enter common information—such as a first name, last name, or phone number—in a form field. If the user has not disabled `AutoComplete` on his browser, then his browser prompts him to enter the same value that he entered previously for the form field (even if the user entered the value for a form field at a different website).

For example, the page in Listing 2.8 asks for your first name, last name, and phone number. Each TextBox control is associated with a particular AutoComplete class. The AutoComplete class specifies the type of information associated with the form field. After you complete the form once, if you return to the same form in the future, you are prompted to enter the same responses (see Figure 2.7).

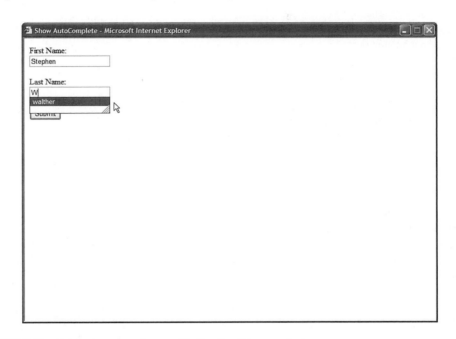

FIGURE 2.7   Using AutoComplete with the TextBox control.

LISTING 2.8   ShowAutoComplete.aspx

```
<%@ Page Language="VB" %>
<!DOCTYPE html PUBLIC "-//W3C//DTD XHTML 1.0 Transitional//EN"
➥"http://www.w3.org/TR/xhtml1/DTD/xhtml1-transitional.dtd">
<html xmlns="http://www.w3.org/1999/xhtml" >
<head id="Head1" runat="server">
    <title>Show AutoComplete</title>
</head>
<body>
    <form id="form1" runat="server">
    <div>

    <asp:Label
        id="lblFirstName"
        Text="First Name:"
```

LISTING 2.8   Continued

```
            AssociatedControlID="txtFirstName"
            Runat="server" />
    <br />
    <asp:TextBox
        id="txtFirstName"
        AutoCompleteType="FirstName"
        Runat="server" />
    <br /><br />
    <asp:Label
        id="lblLastname"
        Text="Last Name:"
        AssociatedControlID="txtLastName"
        Runat="server" />
    <br />
    <asp:TextBox
        id="txtLastName"
        AutoCompleteType="LastName"
        Runat="server" />
    <br /><br />
    <asp:Button
        id="btnSubmit"
        Text="Submit"
        Runat="server" />

    </div>
    </form>
</body>
</html>
```

NOTE

When using Internet Explorer, you can configure AutoComplete by selecting Tools, Internet Options, Content, and clicking the AutoComplete button. The ASP.NET Framework does not support AutoComplete for other browsers such as FireFox or Opera.

Finally, the TextBox control supports the Focus() method. You can use the Focus() method to shift the initial form focus to a particular TextBox control. By default, no form field has focus when a page first opens. If you want to make it easier for users to complete a form, you can set the focus automatically to a particular TextBox control contained in a form.

For example, the page in Listing 2.9 sets the focus to the first of two form fields.

LISTING 2.9   TextBoxFocus.aspx

```
<%@ Page Language="VB" %>
<!DOCTYPE html PUBLIC "-//W3C//DTD XHTML 1.0 Transitional//EN"
➥"http://www.w3.org/TR/xhtml1/DTD/xhtml1-transitional.dtd">
<script runat="server">

    Sub Page_Load()
        txtFirstName.Focus()
    End Sub

</script>
<html xmlns="http://www.w3.org/1999/xhtml" >
<head id="Head1" runat="server">
    <title>TextBox Focus</title>
</head>
<body>
    <form id="form1" runat="server">
    <div>

    <asp:Label
        id="lblFirstName"
        Text="First Name:"
        AssociatedControlID="txtFirstName"
        Runat="server" />
    <br />
    <asp:TextBox
        id="txtFirstName"
        AutoCompleteType="FirstName"
        Runat="server" />
    <br /><br />
    <asp:Label
        id="lblLastname"
        Text="Last Name:"
        AssociatedControlID="txtLastName"
        Runat="server" />
    <br />
    <asp:TextBox
        id="txtLastName"
        AutoCompleteType="LastName"
        Runat="server" />
    <br /><br />
    <asp:Button
        id="btnSubmit"
```

LISTING 2.9   Continued

```
        Text="Submit"
        Runat="server" />

    </div>
    </form>
</body>
</html>
```

In Listing 2.9, the `Page_Load()` event handler sets the form focus to the `txtFirstName`
TextBox control.

> **NOTE**
>
> You can also set the form focus by setting either the `Page.SetFocus()` method or the server-side
> `HtmlForm` control's `DefaultFocus` property.

Using the `CheckBox` Control

The `CheckBox` control enables you to display, well, a check box. The page in Listing 2.10
illustrates how you can use the `CheckBox` control in a newsletter signup form (see
Figure 2.8).

FIGURE 2.8   Displaying a `CheckBox` control.

LISTING 2.10   ShowCheckBox.aspx

```
<%@ Page Language="VB" %>
<!DOCTYPE html PUBLIC "-//W3C//DTD XHTML 1.0 Transitional//EN"
➥"http://www.w3.org/TR/xhtml1/DTD/xhtml1-transitional.dtd">
<script runat="server">

    Sub btnSubmit_Click(ByVal sender As Object, ByVal e As EventArgs)
        lblResult.Text = chkNewsletter.Checked.ToString()
    End Sub
</script>
<html xmlns="http://www.w3.org/1999/xhtml" >
<head id="Head1" runat="server">
    <title>Show CheckBox</title>
</head>
<body>
    <form id="form1" runat="server">
    <div>

    <asp:CheckBox
        id="chkNewsletter"
        Text="Receive Newsletter?"
        Runat="server" />
    <br />
    <asp:Button
        id="btnSubmit"
        Text="Submit"
        OnClick="btnSubmit_Click"
        Runat="server" />
    <hr />

    <asp:Label
        id="lblResult"
        Runat="server" />

    </div>
    </form>
</body>
</html>
```

In Listing 2.10, the `Checked` property is used to determine whether the user has checked the check box.

Notice that the `CheckBox` includes a `Text` property that is used to label the `CheckBox`. If you use this property, then the proper (accessibility standards–compliant) HTML `<label>` tag is generated for the `TextBox`.

The CheckBox control supports the following properties (this is not a complete list):

- AccessKey—Enables you to specify a key that navigates to the TextBox control.
- AutoPostBack—Enables you to post the form containing the CheckBox back to the server automatically when the CheckBox is checked or unchecked.
- Checked—Enables you to get or set whether the CheckBox is checked.
- Enabled—Enables you to disable the TextBox.
- TabIndex—Enables you to specify the tab order of the check box.
- Text—Enables you to provide a label for the check box.
- TextAlign—Enables you to align the label for the check box. Possible values are Left and Right.

The CheckBox control also supports the following method:

- Focus—Enables you to set the initial form focus to the check box.

And, the CheckBox control supports the following event:

- CheckedChanged—Raised on the server when the check box is checked or unchecked.

Notice that the CheckBox control, like the TextBox control, supports the AutoPostBack property. The page in Listing 2.11 illustrates how you can use the AutoPostBack property to post the form containing the check box back to the server automatically when the check box is checked or unchecked.

LISTING 2.11   CheckBoxAutoPostBack.aspx

```
<%@ Page Language="VB" %>
<!DOCTYPE html PUBLIC "-//W3C//DTD XHTML 1.0 Transitional//EN"
➥"http://www.w3.org/TR/xhtml1/DTD/xhtml1-transitional.dtd">
<script runat="server">

    Sub chkNewsletter_CheckedChanged(ByVal sender As Object, ByVal e As EventArgs)
        lblResult.Text = chkNewsletter.Checked.ToString()
    End Sub
</script>

<html xmlns="http://www.w3.org/1999/xhtml" >
<head id="Head1" runat="server">
    <title>CheckBox AutoPostBack</title>
</head>
<body>
    <form id="form1" runat="server">
```

LISTING 2.11 Continued

```
    <div>

    <asp:CheckBox
        id="chkNewsletter"
        Text="Receive Newsletter?"
        AutoPostBack="true"
        OnCheckedChanged="chkNewsletter_CheckedChanged"
        Runat="server" />
    <hr />

    <asp:Label
        id="lblResult"
        Runat="server" />

    </div>
    </form>
</body>
</html>
```

> **NOTE**
>
> The ASP.NET Framework also includes the `CheckBoxList` control that enables you to display a list of check boxes automatically. This control is discussed in detail in Chapter 10, "Using List Controls."

Using the `RadioButton` Control

You always use the `RadioButton` control in a group. Only one radio button in a group of `RadioButton` controls can be checked at a time.

For example, the page in Listing 2.12 contains three RadioButton controls (see Figure 2.9).

LISTING 2.12 ShowRadioButton.aspx

```
<%@ Page Language="VB" %>
<!DOCTYPE html PUBLIC "-//W3C//DTD XHTML 1.0 Transitional//EN"
➥"http://www.w3.org/TR/xhtml1/DTD/xhtml1-transitional.dtd">
<script runat="server">

    Sub btnSubmit_Click(ByVal sender As Object, ByVal e As EventArgs)
        If rdlMagazine.Checked Then
            lblResult.Text = rdlMagazine.Text
        End If
        If rdlTelevision.Checked Then
```

LISTING 2.12   Continued

```
                lblResult.Text = rdlTelevision.Text
        End If
        If rdlOther.Checked Then
                lblResult.Text = rdlOther.Text
        End If
    End Sub
</script>
<html xmlns="http://www.w3.org/1999/xhtml" >
<head id="Head1" runat="server">
    <title>Show RadioButton</title>
</head>
<body>
    <form id="form1" runat="server">
    <div>

    How did you hear about our Website?

    <ul>
        <li>
        <asp:RadioButton
            id="rdlMagazine"
            Text="Magazine Article"
            GroupName="Source"
            Runat="server" />
        </li>
        <li>
        <asp:RadioButton
            id="rdlTelevision"
            Text="Television Program"
            GroupName="Source"
            Runat="server" />
        </li>
        <li>
        <asp:RadioButton
            id="rdlOther"
            Text="Other Source"
            GroupName="Source"
            Runat="server" />
        </li>
    </ul>

    <asp:Button
        id="btnSubmit"
        Text="Submit"
```

LISTING 2.12   Continued

```
        Runat="server" OnClick="btnSubmit_Click" />

    <hr />

    <asp:Label
        id="lblResult"
        Runat="server" />

    </div>
    </form>
</body>
</html>
```

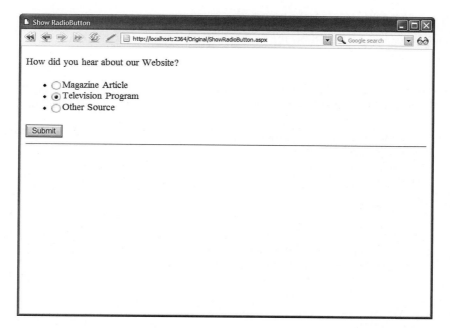

FIGURE 2.9   Displaying RadioButton.

The RadioButton controls in Listing 2.12 are grouped together with the RadioButton control's GroupName property. Only one of the three RadioButton controls can be checked at a time.

The RadioButton control supports the following properties (this is not a complete list):

- AccessKey—Enables you to specify a key that navigates to the RadioButton control.

- AutoPostBack—Enables you to post the form containing the RadioButton back to the server automatically when the radio button is checked or unchecked.

- Checked—Enables you to get or set whether the RadioButton control is checked.

- Enabled—Enables you to disable the RadioButton.

- GroupName—Enables you to group RadioButton controls.

- TabIndex—Enables you to specify the tab order of the RadioButton control.

- Text—Enables you to label the RadioButton control.

- TextAlign—Enables you to align the RadioButton label. Possible values are Left and Right.

The RadioButton control supports the following method:

- Focus—Enables you to set the initial form focus to the RadionButton control.

Finally, the RadioButton control supports the following event:

- CheckedChanged—Raised on the server when the RadioButton is checked or unchecked.

The page in Listing 2.13 demonstrates how you can use the AutoPostBack property with a group of RadioButton controls and detect which RadioButton control is selected.

LISTING 2.13   RadioButtonAutoPostBack.aspx

```
<%@ Page Language="VB" %>
<!DOCTYPE html PUBLIC "-//W3C//DTD XHTML 1.0 Transitional//EN"
➥"http://www.w3.org/TR/xhtml1/DTD/xhtml1-transitional.dtd">
<script runat="server">

    Sub RadioButton_CheckedChanged(ByVal sender As Object, ByVal e As EventArgs)
        Dim selectedRadioButton As RadioButton = CType(sender, RadioButton)
        lblResult.Text = selectedRadioButton.Text
    End Sub
</script>
<html xmlns="http://www.w3.org/1999/xhtml" >
<head id="Head1" runat="server">
    <title>RadioButton AutoPostBack</title>
</head>
<body>
    <form id="form1" runat="server">
    <div>

    How did you hear about our Website?

    <ul>
```

LISTING 2.13 Continued

```
            <li>
            <asp:RadioButton
                id="rdlMagazine"
                Text="Magazine Article"
                GroupName="Source"
                AutoPostBack="true"
                OnCheckedChanged="RadioButton_CheckedChanged"
                Runat="server" />
            </li>
            <li>
            <asp:RadioButton
                id="rdlTelevision"
                Text="Television Program"
                GroupName="Source"
                AutoPostBack="true"
                OnCheckedChanged="RadioButton_CheckedChanged"
                Runat="server" />
            </li>
            <li>
            <asp:RadioButton
                id="rdlOther"
                Text="Other Source"
                GroupName="Source"
                AutoPostBack="true"
                OnCheckedChanged="RadioButton_CheckedChanged"
                Runat="server" />
            </li>
        </ul>

        <hr />

        <asp:Label
            id="lblResult"
            Runat="server" />

        </div>
        </form>
    </body>
    </html>
```

In Listing 2.13, when you select a RadioButton control, the page is automatically posted back to the server, and the value of the Text property of the selected RadioButton control is displayed. Notice that all three of the RadioButton controls are associated with the same `CheckedChanged` event handler. The first parameter passed to the handler represents the particular `RadioButton` that was changed.

> **NOTE**
>
> The ASP.NET Framework also includes the `RadioButtonList` control, which enables you to display a list of radio buttons automatically. This control is discussed in detail in Chapter 10, "Using List Controls."

Submitting Form Data

The ASP.NET Framework includes three controls you can use to submit a form to the server: the `Button`, `LinkButton`, and `ImageButton` controls. These controls have the same function, but each control has a distinct appearance.

In this section, you learn how to use each of these three types of buttons in a page. Next, you learn how to associate client-side scripts with server-side `Button` controls. You also learn how to use a button control to post a form to a page other than the current page. Finally, you learn how to handle a button control's Command event.

Using the `Button` Control

The `Button` control renders a push button that you can use to submit a form to the server. For example, the page in Listing 2.14 contains a `Button` control. When you click the Button control, the time displayed by a `Label` control is updated (see Figure 2.10).

LISTING 2.14   ShowButton.aspx

```
<%@ Page Language="VB" %>
<!DOCTYPE html PUBLIC "-//W3C//DTD XHTML 1.0 Transitional//EN"
➥"http://www.w3.org/TR/xhtml1/DTD/xhtml1-transitional.dtd">
<script runat="server">

    Sub btnSubmit_Click(ByVal sender As Object, ByVal e As EventArgs)
        lblTime.Text = DateTime.Now.ToString("T")
    End Sub
</script>
<html xmlns="http://www.w3.org/1999/xhtml" >
<head id="Head1" runat="server">
    <title>Show Button</title>
</head>
<body>
    <form id="form1" runat="server">
    <div>

    <asp:Button
```

LISTING 2.14 Continued

```
        id="btnSubmit"
        Text="Submit"
        OnClick="btnSubmit_Click"
        Runat="server" />

    <br /><br />

    <asp:Label
        id="lblTime"
        Runat="server" />

    </div>
    </form>
</body>
</html>
```

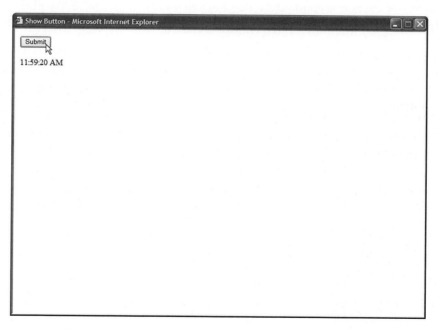

FIGURE 2.10 Displaying a Button control.

The Button control supports the following properties (this is not a complete list):

- AccessKey—Enables you to specify a key that navigates to the Button control.

- CommandArgument—Enables you to specify a command argument that is passed to the Command event.

- CommandName—Enables you to specify a command name that is passed to the Command event.

- Enabled—Enables you to disable the Button control.

- OnClientClick—Enables you to specify a client-side script that executes when the button is clicked.

- PostBackUrl—Enables you to post a form to a particular page.

- TabIndex—Enables you to specify the tab order of the Button control.

- Text—Enables you to label the Button control.

- UseSubmitBehavior—Enables you to use JavaScript to post a form.

The Button control also supports the following method:

- Focus—Enables you to set the initial form focus to the Button control.

The Button control also supports the following two events:

- Click—Raised when the Button control is clicked.

- Command—Raised when the Button control is clicked. The CommandName and CommandArgument are passed to this event.

Using the LinkButton **Control**

The LinkButton control, like the Button control, enables you to post a form to the server. Unlike a Button control, however, the LinkButton control renders a link instead of a push button.

The page in Listing 2.15 contains a simple form. The form includes a LinkButton control that enables you to submit the form to the server and display the contents of the form fields (see Figure 2.11).

LISTING 2.15   ShowLinkButton.aspx

```
<%@ Page Language="VB" %>
<!DOCTYPE html PUBLIC "-//W3C//DTD XHTML 1.0 Transitional//EN"
➥"http://www.w3.org/TR/xhtml1/DTD/xhtml1-transitional.dtd">
<script runat="server">

    Sub lnkSubmit_Click(ByVal sender As Object, ByVal e As EventArgs)
        lblResults.Text = "First Name: " & txtFirstName.Text
        lblResults.Text &= "<br />Last Name: " & txtLastName.Text
    End Sub
</script>
<html xmlns="http://www.w3.org/1999/xhtml" >
```

LISTING 2.15   Continued

```
<head id="Head1" runat="server">
    <title>Show LinkButton</title>
</head>
<body>
    <form id="form1" runat="server">
    <div>

    <asp:Label
        id="lblFirstName"
        Text="First Name:"
        AssociatedControlID="txtFirstName"
        Runat="server" />
    <br />
    <asp:TextBox
        id="txtFirstName"
        Runat="server" />
    <br /><br />
    <asp:Label
        id="lblLastName"
        Text="Last Name:"
        AssociatedControlID="txtLastName"
        Runat="server" />
    <br />
    <asp:TextBox
        id="txtLastName"
        Runat="server" />
    <br /><br />
    <asp:LinkButton
        id="lnkSubmit"
        Text="Submit"
        OnClick="lnkSubmit_Click"
        Runat="server" />

    <br /><br />

    <asp:Label
        id="lblResults"
        Runat="server" />

    </div>
    </form>
</body>
</html>
```

FIGURE 2.11   Displaying a `LinkButton` control.

Behind the scenes, the `LinkButton` control uses JavaScript to post the form back to the server. The hyperlink rendered by the `LinkButton` control looks like this:

```
<a id="lnkSubmit" href="javascript:__doPostBack('lnkSubmit','')">Submit</a>
```

Clicking the `LinkButton` invokes the `JavaScript __doPostBack()` method, which posts the form to the server. When the form is posted, the values of all the other form fields in the page are also posted to the server.

The `LinkButton` control supports the following properties (this is not a complete list):

- `AccessKey`—Enables you to specify a key that navigates to the `Button` control.

- `CommandArgument`—Enables you to specify a command argument that is passed to the `Command` event.

- `CommandName`—Enables you to specify a command name that is passed to the `Command` event.

- `Enabled`—Enables you to disable the `LinkButton` control.

- `OnClientClick`—Enables you to specify a client-side script that executes when the `LinkButton` is clicked.

- `PostBackUrl`—Enables you to post a form to a particular page.

- `TabIndex`—Enables you to specify the tab order of the `LinkButton` control.

- `Text`—Enables you to label the `LinkButton` control.

The LinkButton control also supports the following method:

- Focus—Enables you to set the initial form focus to the LinkButton control.

The LinkButton control also supports the following two events:

- Click—Raised when the LinkButton control is clicked.

- Command—Raised when the LinkButton control is clicked. The CommandName and CommandArgument are passed to this event.

Using the ImageButton Control

The ImageButton control, like the Button and LinkButton controls, enables you to post a form to the server. However, the ImageButton control always displays an image.

The page in Listing 2.16 contains an ImageButton control that posts a simple form back to the server (see Figure 2.12).

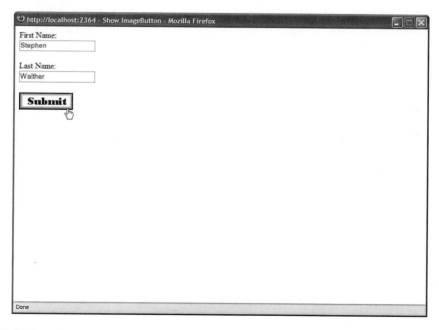

FIGURE 2.12 Displaying an ImageButton control.

LISTING 2.16 ShowImageButton.aspx

```
<%@ Page Language="VB" %>
<!DOCTYPE html PUBLIC "-//W3C//DTD XHTML 1.0 Transitional//EN"
➥"http://www.w3.org/TR/xhtml1/DTD/xhtml1-transitional.dtd">
```

LISTING 2.16   Continued

```
<script runat="server">

    Sub btnSubmit_Click(ByVal sender As Object, ByVal e As ImageClickEventArgs)
        lblResults.Text = "First Name: " & txtFirstName.Text
        lblResults.Text &= "<br />Last Name: " & txtLastName.Text
    End Sub
</script>
<html xmlns="http://www.w3.org/1999/xhtml" >
<head id="Head1" runat="server">
    <title>Show ImageButton</title>
</head>
<body>
    <form id="form1" runat="server">
    <div>

    <asp:Label
        id="lblFirstName"
        Text="First Name:"
        AssociatedControlID="txtFirstName"
        Runat="server" />
    <br />
    <asp:TextBox
        id="txtFirstName"
        Runat="server" />
    <br /><br />
    <asp:Label
        id="lblLastName"
        Text="Last Name:"
        AssociatedControlID="txtLastName"
        Runat="server" />
    <br />
    <asp:TextBox
        id="txtLastName"
        Runat="server" />
    <br /><br />
    <asp:ImageButton
        id="btnSubmit"
        ImageUrl="Submit.gif"
        AlternateText="Submit Form"
        Runat="server" OnClick="btnSubmit_Click" />

    <br /><br />
    <asp:Label
        id="lblResults"
```

LISTING 2.16   Continued

```
        Runat="server" />

    </div>
    </form>
</body>
</html>
```

The `ImageButton` in Listing 2.16 includes both an `ImageUrl` and `AlternateText` property. The `ImageUrl` contains the path to the image that the `ImageButton` displays. The `AlternateText` property is used to provide alternate text for the image used by screen readers and text-only browsers.

> **WEB STANDARDS NOTE**
>
> Always include alternate text for any image. The accessibility guidelines require it. Furthermore, remember that some people turn off images in their browsers for a faster surfing experience.

Notice that the event handler for an `Image` control's `Click` event is different than that for the other button controls. The second parameter passed to the event handler is an instance of the `ImageClickEventArgs` class. This class has the following properties:

- X—The x coordinate relative to the image the user clicked.

- Y—The y coordinate relative to the image the user clicked.

You can use the `ImageButton` control to create a simple image map. For example, the page in Listing 2.17 contains an `ImageButton` that displays an image of a target. If you click the center of the target, then a success message is displayed (see Figure 2.13).

LISTING 2.17   ImageButtonTarget.aspx

```
<%@ Page Language="VB" %>
<!DOCTYPE html PUBLIC "-//W3C//DTD XHTML 1.0 Transitional//EN"
➥"http://www.w3.org/TR/xhtml1/DTD/xhtml1-transitional.dtd">
<script runat="server">

    Sub btnTarget_Click(ByVal sender As Object, ByVal e As ImageClickEventArgs)
        If (e.X > 90 And e.X < 110) And (e.Y > 90 And e.Y < 110) Then
            lblResult.Text = "You hit the target!"
        Else
            lblResult.Text = "You missed!"
        End If
    End Sub
</script>
<html xmlns="http://www.w3.org/1999/xhtml" >
```

LISTING 2.17 Continued

```
<head id="Head1" runat="server">
    <title>ImageButton Target</title>
</head>
<body>
    <form id="form1" runat="server">
    <div>

    <asp:ImageButton
        id="btnTarget"
        ImageUrl="Target.gif"
        Runat="server" OnClick="btnTarget_Click" />

    <br /><br />

    <asp:Label
        id="lblResult"
        Runat="server" />

    </div>
    </form>
</body>
</html>
```

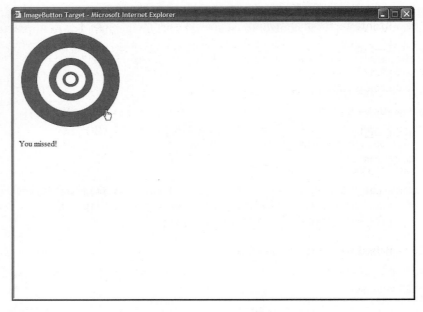

FIGURE 2.13 Retrieving X and Y coordinates from an ImageButton.

> **WEB STANDARDS NOTE**
>
> The ImageButton can be used to create a server-side image map. Server-side image maps are not accessible to persons with disabilities. A better method for creating an ImageMap is to use the ImageMap control, which enables you to create a client-side image map. The ImageMap control is discussed in the next section of this chapter.

The ImageButton control supports the following properties (this is not a complete list):

- AccessKey—Enables you to specify a key that navigates to the ImageButton control.

- AlternateText—Enables you to provide alternate text for the image (required for accessibility).

- DescriptionUrl—Enables you to provide a link to a page that contains a detailed description of the image (required to make a complex image accessible).

- CommandArgument—Enables you to specify a command argument that is passed to the Command event.

- CommandName—Enables you to specify a command name that is passed to the Command event.

- Enabled—Enables you to disable the ImageButton control.

- GenerateEmptyAlternateText—Enables you to set the AlternateText property to an empty string.

- ImageAlign—Enables you to align the image relative to other HTML elements in the page. Possible values are AbsBottom, AbsMiddle, Baseline, Bottom, Left, Middle, NotSet, Right, TextTop, and Top.

- ImageUrl—Enables you to specify the URL to the image.

- OnClientClick—Enables you to specify a client-side script that executes when the ImageButton is clicked.

- PostBackUrl—Enables you to post a form to a particular page.

- TabIndex—Enables you to specify the tab order of the ImageButton control.

The ImageButton control also supports the following method:

- Focus—Enables you to set the initial form focus to the ImageButton control.

The ImageButton control also supports the following two events:

- Click—Raised when the ImageButton control is clicked.

- Command—Raised when the ImageButton control is clicked. The CommandName and CommandArgument are passed to this event.

Using Client Scripts with Button Controls

All three Button controls support an OnClientClick property. You can use this property to execute any client-side code that you need when a button is clicked. The page in Listing 2.18 illustrates how you can use the OnClientClick property to display a confirmation dialog box (see Figure 2.14).

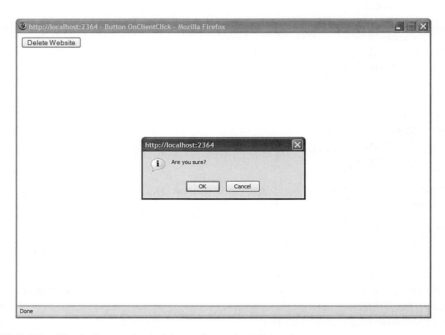

FIGURE 2.14   Displaying a client-side confirmation dialog box.

LISTING 2.18   ButtonOnClientClick.aspx

```
<%@ Page Language="VB" %>
<!DOCTYPE html PUBLIC "-//W3C//DTD XHTML 1.0 Transitional//EN"
➡"http://www.w3.org/TR/xhtml1/DTD/xhtml1-transitional.dtd">
<script runat="server">

    Sub btnDelete_Click(sender AS Object, e As EventArgs)
        lblResult.Text = "All pages deleted!"
    End Sub
</script>
<html xmlns="http://www.w3.org/1999/xhtml" >
<head id="Head1" runat="server">
    <title>Button OnClientClick</title>
</head>
<body>
```

LISTING 2.18 Continued

```
      <form id="form1" runat="server">
      <div>

      <asp:Button
          id="btnDelete"
          Text="Delete Website"
          OnClick="btnDelete_Click"
          OnClientClick="return confirm('Are you sure?');"
          Runat="server" />

      <br /><br />

      <asp:Label
          id="lblResult"
          Runat="server" />

      </div>
      </form>
  </body>
  </html>
```

In Listing 2.18, the Button control includes an OnClientClick property, which executes a JavaScript script when you click the button on the client. The script displays a confirmation dialog box. If the confirmation box returns False, then the button click is canceled and the form containing the button is not posted to the server.

Because the button controls, like most ASP.NET controls, support expando attributes, you can handle other client-side events simply by adding an arbitrary attribute to the control. If the ASP.NET Framework does not recognize an attribute declared on a button control, the framework simply passes the attribute to the browser.

For example, the page in Listing 2.19 contains a button control that includes onmouseover and onmouseout attributes. When you hover your mouse over the button, the text displayed in the button is changed.

LISTING 2.19 ButtonExpando.aspx

```
<%@ Page Language="VB" %>
<!DOCTYPE html PUBLIC "-//W3C//DTD XHTML 1.0 Transitional//EN"
➥"http://www.w3.org/TR/xhtml1/DTD/xhtml1-transitional.dtd">
<html xmlns="http://www.w3.org/1999/xhtml" >
<head id="Head1" runat="server">
    <title>Button Expando</title>
</head>
<body>
```

LISTING 2.19   Continued

```
<form id="form1" runat="server">
<div>

<asp:Button
    id="btnSubmit"
    Text="Submit"
    onmouseover="this.value='Click Here!'"
    onmouseout="this.value='Submit'"
    Runat="server" />

</div>
</form>
</body>
</html>
```

> **NOTE**
>
> You'll get green squiggly warnings under expando attributes in Visual Web Developer—but these warnings can be safely ignored.

Performing Cross-Page Posts

By default, if you click a button control, the page containing the control is posted back to itself and the same page is reloaded. However, you can use the `PostBackUrl` property to post form data to another page.

For example, the page in Listing 2.20 includes a search form. The `Button` control in the page posts the form to another page named `ButtonSearchResults.aspx`. The `ButtonSearchResults.aspx` page is contained in Listing 2.21.

LISTING 2.20   `ButtonSearch.aspx`

```
<%@ Page Language="VB" %>
<!DOCTYPE html PUBLIC "-//W3C//DTD XHTML 1.0 Transitional//EN"
➥"http://www.w3.org/TR/xhtml1/DTD/xhtml1-transitional.dtd">
<html xmlns="http://www.w3.org/1999/xhtml" >
<head id="Head1" runat="server">
    <title>Button Search</title>
</head>
<body>
    <form id="form1" runat="server">
    <div>

    <asp:Label
```

LISTING 2.20 Continued

```
            id="lblSearch"
            Text="Search:"
            Runat="server" />
    <asp:TextBox
        id="txtSearch"
        Runat="server" />
    <asp:Button
        id="btnSearch"
        Text="Go!"
        PostBackUrl="ButtonSearchResults.aspx"
        Runat="server" />
    </div>
    </form>
</body>
</html>
```

LISTING 2.21 ButtonSearchResults.aspx

```
<%@ Page Language="VB" %>
<!DOCTYPE html PUBLIC "-//W3C//DTD XHTML 1.0 Transitional//EN"
➥"http://www.w3.org/TR/xhtml1/DTD/xhtml1-transitional.dtd">
<script runat="server">

    Sub Page_Load()
        If Not IsNothing(PreviousPage) Then
            Dim txtSearch As TextBox =
➥CType(PreviousPage.FindControl("txtSearch"), TextBox)
            lblSearch.Text = String.Format("Search For: {0}", txtSearch.Text)
        End If
    End Sub

</script>
<html xmlns="http://www.w3.org/1999/xhtml" >
<head id="Head1" runat="server">
    <title>Button Search Results</title>
</head>
<body>
    <form id="form1" runat="server">
    <div>

    <asp:Label
        id="lblSearch"
        Runat="server" />
```

LISTING 2.21 Continued

```
    </div>
    </form>
</body>
</html>
```

In the Page_Load event handler in Listing 2.21, the PreviousPage property is used to get a reference to the previous page (the ButtonSearch.aspx page in Listing 2.20). Next, the FindControl() method is used to retrieve the txtSearch TextBox control from the previous page. Finally, the value entered into the TextBox is displayed in a label on the page.

As an alternative to using the FindControl() method to retrieve a particular control from the previous page, you can expose the control through a page property. The page in Listing 2.22 exposes the txtSearch TextBox through a property named SearchString. The page posts the form data to a page named ButtonSearchResultsTyped.aspx, contained in Listing 2.23.

LISTING 2.22 ButtonSearchTyped.aspx

```
<%@ Page Language="VB" %>
<!DOCTYPE html PUBLIC "-//W3C//DTD XHTML 1.0 Transitional//EN"
➥"http://www.w3.org/TR/xhtml1/DTD/xhtml1-transitional.dtd">
<script runat="server">

    Public ReadOnly Property SearchString() As String
        Get
            Return txtSearch.Text
        End Get
    End Property

</script>
<html xmlns="http://www.w3.org/1999/xhtml" >
<head id="Head1" runat="server">
    <title>Button Search Typed</title>
</head>
<body>
    <form id="form1" runat="server">
    <div>

    <asp:Label
        id="lblSearch"
        Text="Search:"
        Runat="server" />
    <asp:TextBox
        id="txtSearch"
        Runat="server" />
```

LISTING 2.22   Continued

```
    <asp:Button
        id="btnSearch"
        Text="Go!"
        PostBackUrl="ButtonSearchResultsTyped.aspx"
        Runat="server" />
    </div>
    </form>
</body>
</html>
```

LISTING 2.23   ButtonSearchResultsTyped.aspx

```
<%@ Page Language="VB" %>
<%@ PreviousPageType VirtualPath="~/ButtonSearchTyped.aspx" %>
<!DOCTYPE html PUBLIC "-//W3C//DTD XHTML 1.0 Transitional//EN"
➥"http://www.w3.org/TR/xhtml1/DTD/xhtml1-transitional.dtd">
<script runat="server">

    Sub Page_Load()
        If Not IsNothing(Page.PreviousPage) Then
            lblSearch.Text = String.Format("Search For: {0}",
➥PreviousPage.SearchString)
        End If
    End Sub

</script>
<html xmlns="http://www.w3.org/1999/xhtml" >
<head id="Head1" runat="server">
    <title>Button Search Results Typed</title>
</head>
<body>
    <form id="form1" runat="server">
    <div>

    <asp:Label
        id="lblSearch"
        Runat="server" />

    </div>
    </form>
</body>
</html>
```

2

Notice that the page in Listing 2.23 includes a `<%@ PreviousPageType %>` directive. This directive casts the value returned by the `PreviousPage` property as an instance of the `ButtonSearchTyped` class. Without this directive, the `PreviousPage` property would return the previous page as an instance of the generic `Page` class.

You can use either method when performing cross-page posts. The first method provides you with an untyped method of retrieving values from the previous page, and the second method provides you with a typed method.

Specifying a Default Button

You can specify a default button for a form by using the `DefaultButton` property of the server-side `Form` control. If you specify a default button, then pressing the keyboard Enter key invokes the button.

For example, the page in Listing 2.24 contains a simple search form. The `<form>` tag sets the `btnSearch` Button control as the default button on the page.

LISTING 2.24 ButtonDefaultButton.aspx

```
<%@ Page Language="VB" %>
<!DOCTYPE html PUBLIC "-//W3C//DTD XHTML 1.0 Transitional//EN"
➡"http://www.w3.org/TR/xhtml1/DTD/xhtml1-transitional.dtd">
<script runat="server">

    Sub btnSearch_Click(ByVal sender As Object, ByVal e As EventArgs)
        lblResult.Text = "Search for: " & txtSearch.Text
    End Sub
</script>
<html xmlns="http://www.w3.org/1999/xhtml" >
<head id="Head1" runat="server">
    <title>Button Default Button</title>
</head>
<body>
    <form id="form1" defaultbutton="btnSearch" runat="server">
    <div>

    <asp:Label
        id="lblSearch"
        Text="Search:"
        AssociatedControlID="txtSearch"
        Runat="server" />
    <asp:TextBox
        id="txtSearch"
        Runat="server" />
```

LISTING 2.24 Continued

```
<asp:Button
    id="btnSearch"
    Text="Search"
    OnClick="btnSearch_Click"
    Runat="server" />
<asp:Button
    id="btnCancel"
    Text="Cancel"
    Runat="server" />

<hr />

<asp:Label
    id="lblResult"
    Runat="server" />

</div>
</form>
</body>
</html>
```

If you open the page in Listing 2.24, type a search phrase, and hit the keyboard Enter key, the form is submitted to the server. Pressing the Enter key causes the btnSearch_Click event handler to execute because the btnSearch button is the default button on the page.

> **NOTE**
>
> You can also specify a DefaultButton with a Panel control. The Panel control is discussed later in this chapter.

Handling the Command Event

All three Button controls support both the Click event and the Command event. The difference between these events is that you can pass a command name and command argument to a Command event handler but not to a Click event handler.

For example, the page in Listing 2.25 contains two Button controls and a BulletedList control. When you click the first button, the items displayed by the BulletedList control are sorted in ascending order, and when you click the second button, the items displayed by the BulletedList control are sorted in descending order (see Figure 2.15).

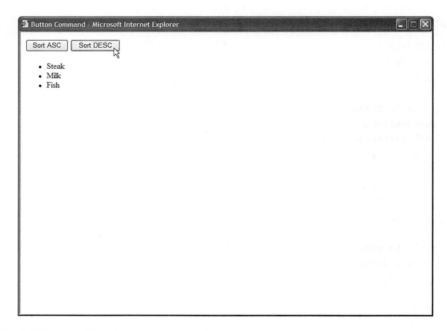

FIGURE 2.15   Handling the Command even\t.

LISTING 2.25   ButtonCommand.aspx

```
<%@ Page Language="VB" %>
<%@ Import Namespace="System.Collections.Generic" %>
<!DOCTYPE html PUBLIC "-//W3C//DTD XHTML 1.0 Transitional//EN"
➡"http://www.w3.org/TR/xhtml1/DTD/xhtml1-transitional.dtd">
<script runat="server">

    Private groceries As New List(Of String)()

    Sub Page_Load()
        groceries.Add("Milk")
        groceries.Add("Steak")
        groceries.Add("Fish")
    End Sub

    Sub Sort_Command(ByVal sender As Object, ByVal e As CommandEventArgs)
        If e.CommandName = "Sort" Then
            Select Case e.CommandArgument.ToString()
                Case "ASC"
                    groceries.Sort(AddressOf SortASC)
                Case "DESC"
                    groceries.Sort(AddressOf SortDESC)
```

LISTING 2.25   Continued

```
            End Select
        End If
    End Sub

    Sub Page_PreRender()
        bltGroceries.DataSource = groceries
        bltGroceries.DataBind()
    End Sub

    Function SortASC(ByVal x As String, ByVal y As String) As Integer
        Return String.Compare(x, y)
    End Function

    Function SortDESC(ByVal x As String, ByVal y As String) As Integer
        Return String.Compare(x, y) * -1
    End Function

</script>
<html xmlns="http://www.w3.org/1999/xhtml" >
<head id="Head1" runat="server">
    <title>Button Command</title>
</head>
<body>
    <form id="form1" runat="server">
    <div>

    <asp:Button
        id="btnSortAsc"
        Text="Sort ASC"
        CommandName="Sort"
        CommandArgument="ASC"
        OnCommand="Sort_Command"
        Runat="server" />

    <asp:Button
        id="btnSortDESC"
        Text="Sort DESC"
        CommandName="Sort"
        CommandArgument="DESC"
        OnCommand="Sort_Command"
        Runat="server" />

    <br /><br />
```

LISTING 2.25   Continued

```
    <asp:BulletedList
        id="bltGroceries"
        Runat="server" />

    </div>
    </form>
</body>
</html>
```

Both Button controls include CommandName and CommandArgument properties. Furthermore, both Button controls are wired to the same Sort_Command() event handler. This event handler checks the CommandName and CommandArgument properties when determining how the elements in the BulletedList should be sorted.

Displaying Images

The ASP.NET framework includes two controls for displaying images: the Image and ImageMap controls. The Image control simply displays an image. The ImageMap control enables you to create a client-side, clickable, image map.

Using the Image Control

The page in Listing 2.26 randomly displays one of three images. The image is displayed by setting the ImageUrl property of the Image control contained in the body of the page.

LISTING 2.26   ShowImage.aspx

```
<%@ Page Language="VB" %>
<!DOCTYPE html PUBLIC "-//W3C//DTD XHTML 1.0 Transitional//EN"
➥"http://www.w3.org/TR/xhtml1/DTD/xhtml1-transitional.dtd">
<script runat="server">

    Sub Page_Load()
        Dim rnd As New Random()
        Select Case rnd.Next(3)
            Case 0
                imgRandom.ImageUrl = "Picture1.gif"
                imgRandom.AlternateText = "Picture 1"
            Case 1
                imgRandom.ImageUrl = "Picture2.gif"
                imgRandom.AlternateText = "Picture 2"
            Case 2
                imgRandom.ImageUrl = "Picture3.gif"
                imgRandom.AlternateText = "Picture 3"
        End Select
    End Sub
```

LISTING 2.26   Continued

```
</script>
<html xmlns="http://www.w3.org/1999/xhtml" >
<head id="Head1" runat="server">
    <title>Show Image</title>
</head>
<body>
    <form id="form1" runat="server">
    <div>

    <asp:Image
        id="imgRandom"
        Runat="server" />

    </div>
    </form>
</body>
</html>
```

The Image control supports the following properties (this is not a complete list):

- AlternateText—Enables you to provide alternate text for the image (required for accessibility).

- DescriptionUrl—Enables you to provide a link to a page that contains a detailed description of the image (required to make a complex image accessible).

- GenerateEmptyAlternateText—Enables you to set the AlternateText property to an empty string.

- ImageAlign—Enables you to align the image relative to other HTML elements in the page. Possible values are AbsBottom, AbsMiddle, Baseline, Bottom, Left, Middle, NotSet, Right, TextTop, and Top.

- ImageUrl—Enables you to specify the URL to the image.

The Image control supports three methods for supplying alternate text. If an image represents page content, then you should supply a value for the AlternateText property. For example, if you have an image for your company's logo, then you should assign the text "My Company Logo" to the AlternateText property.

If an Image control represents something really complex—such as a bar chart, pie graph, or company organizational chart—then you should supply a value for the DescriptionUrl property. The DescriptionUrl property links to a page that contains a long textual description of the image.

Finally, if the image is used purely for decoration (it expresses no content), then you should set the GenerateEmptyAlternateText property to the value True. When this property has the value `True`, then an `alt=""` attribute is included in the rendered `<img>` tag. Screen readers know to ignore images with empty `alt` attributes.

Using the `ImageMap` Control

The `ImageMap` control enables you to create a client-side image map. An image map displays an image. When you click different areas of the image, things happen.

For example, you can use an image map as a fancy navigation bar. In that case, clicking different areas of the image map navigates to different pages in your website.

You also can use an image map as an input mechanism. For example, you can click different product images to add a particular product to a shopping cart.

An `ImageMap` control is composed out of instances of the `HotSpot` class. A `HotSpot` defines the clickable regions in an image map. The ASP.NET framework ships with three `HotSpot` classes:

- `CircleHotSpot`—Enables you to define a circular region in an image map.
- `PolygonHotSpot`—Enables you to define an irregularly shaped region in an image map.
- `RectangleHotSpot`—Enables you to define a rectangular region in an image map.

The page in Listing 2.27 contains a navigation bar created with an `ImageMap` control. The `ImageMap` contains three `RectangleHotSpots` that delimit the three buttons displayed by the navigation bar (see Figure 2.16).

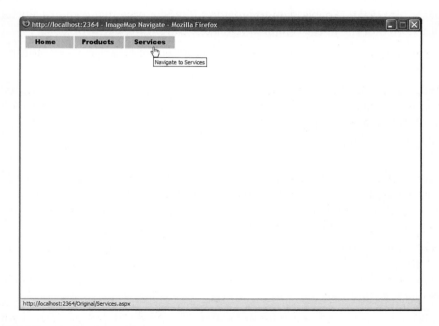

FIGURE 2.16   Navigating with an `ImageMap` control.

LISTING 2.27 ImageMapNavigate.aspx

```
<%@ Page Language="VB" %>
<!DOCTYPE html PUBLIC "-//W3C//DTD XHTML 1.0 Transitional//EN"
➥"http://www.w3.org/TR/xhtml1/DTD/xhtml1-transitional.dtd">
<html xmlns="http://www.w3.org/1999/xhtml" >
<head id="Head1" runat="server">
    <title>ImageMap Navigate</title>
</head>
<body>
    <form id="form1" runat="server">
    <div>

    <asp:ImageMap
        id="mapNavigate"
        ImageUrl="ImageBar.jpg"
        Runat="server">
        <asp:RectangleHotSpot
            NavigateUrl="Home.aspx"
            Left="0"
            Top="0"
            Right="100"
            Bottom="50"
            AlternateText="Navigate to Home" />
        <asp:RectangleHotSpot
            NavigateUrl="Products.aspx"
            Left="100"
            Top="0"
            Right="200"
            Bottom="50"
            AlternateText="Navigate to Products" />
        <asp:RectangleHotSpot
            NavigateUrl="Services.aspx"
            Left="200"
            Top="0"
            Right="300"
            Bottom="50"
            AlternateText="Navigate to Services" />
    </asp:ImageMap>

    </div>
    </form>
</body>
</html>
```

Each RectangleHotSpot includes Left, Top, Right, and Bottom properties that describe the area of the rectangle. Each RectangleHotSpot also includes a NavigateUrl property that contains the URL to which the region of the image map links.

Rather than use an image map to link to different pages, you can use it to post back to the same page. For example, the page in Listing 2.28 uses an ImageMap control to display a menu. When you click different menu items represented by different regions of the image map, the text contained in the TextBox control is changed (see Figure 2.17).

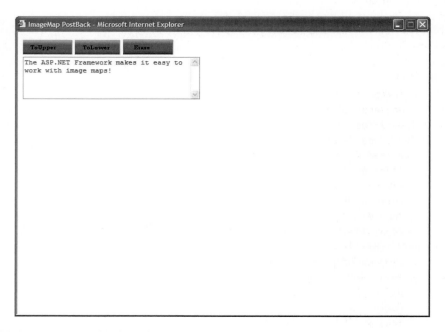

FIGURE 2.17   Posting back to the server with an ImageMap control.

LISTING 2.28   ImageMapPostBack.aspx

```
<%@ Page Language="VB" %>
<!DOCTYPE html PUBLIC "-//W3C//DTD XHTML 1.0 Transitional//EN"
➡"http://www.w3.org/TR/xhtml1/DTD/xhtml1-transitional.dtd">
<script runat="server">

    Sub mapMenu_Click(ByVal sender As Object, ByVal e As ImageMapEventArgs)
        Select Case e.PostBackValue
            Case "ToUpper"
                txtText.Text = txtText.Text.ToUpper()
            Case "ToLower"
                txtText.Text = txtText.Text.ToLower()
            Case "Erase"
```

LISTING 2.28   Continued

```
                txtText.Text = String.Empty
        End Select
    End Sub
</script>
<html xmlns="http://www.w3.org/1999/xhtml" >
<head id="Head1" runat="server">
    <title>ImageMap PostBack</title>
</head>
<body>
    <form id="form1" runat="server">
    <div>

    <asp:ImageMap
        id="mapMenu"
        ImageUrl="MenuBar.gif"
        HotSpotMode="PostBack"
        Runat="server" OnClick="mapMenu_Click">
        <asp:RectangleHotSpot
            PostBackValue="ToUpper"
            Left="0"
            Top="0"
            Right="100"
            Bottom="30"
            AlternateText="To Uppercase" />
        <asp:RectangleHotSpot
            PostBackValue="ToLower"
            Left="100"
            Top="0"
            Right="200"
            Bottom="30"
            AlternateText="To Uppercase" />
        <asp:RectangleHotSpot
            PostBackValue="Erase"
            Left="200"
            Top="0"
            Right="300"
            Bottom="30"
            AlternateText="To Uppercase" />
    </asp:ImageMap>

    <br />

    <asp:TextBox
        id="txtText"
```

LISTING 2.28   Continued

```
            TextMode="MultiLine"
            Columns="40"
            Rows="5"
            Runat="server" />

    </div>
    </form>
</body>
</html>
```

Notice that the ImageMap control has its HotSpotMode property set to the value PostBack.
Also, the ImageMap is wired to a Click event handler named mapMenu_Click.

Each HotSpot contained in the ImageMap control has a PostBackValue property. The
mapMenu_Click handler reads the PostBackValue from the region clicked and modifies the
text displayed by the TextBox control.

The ImageMap control supports the following properties (this is not a complete list):

- AccessKey—Enables you to specify a key that navigates to the ImageMap control.

- AlternateText—Enables you to provide alternate text for the image (required for
  accessibility).

- DescriptionUrl—Enables you to provide a link to a page which contains a detailed
  description of the image (required to make a complex image accessible).

- GenerateEmptyAlternateText—Enables you to set the AlternateText property to an
  empty string.

- HotSpotMode—Enables you to specify the behavior of the image map when you click
  a region. Possible values are Inactive, Navigate, NotSet, and PostBack.

- HotSpots—Enables you to retrieve the collection of HotSpots contained in the
  ImageMap control.

- ImageAlign—Enables you to align the image map with other HTML elements in the
  page. Possible values are AbsBottom, AbsMiddle, Baseline, Bottom, Left, Middle,
  NotSet, Right, TextTop, and Top.

- ImageUrl—Enables you to specify the URL to the image.

- TabIndex—Enables you to specify the tab order of the ImageMap control.

- Target—Enables you to open a page in a new window.

The ImageMap control also supports the following method:

- Focus—Enables you to set the initial form focus to the ImageMap control.

Finally, the ImageMap control supports the following event:

- Click—Raised when you click a region of the ImageMap and the HotSpotMode property is set to the value PostBack.

Using the Panel Control

The Panel control enables you to work with a group of ASP.NET controls.

For example, you can use a Panel control to hide or show a group of ASP.NET controls. The page in Listing 2.29 contains a list of RadioButton controls which can be used to select your favorite programming language. The last RadioButton is labeled Other. If you select the Other radio button, the contents of a Panel control are revealed (see Figure 2.18).

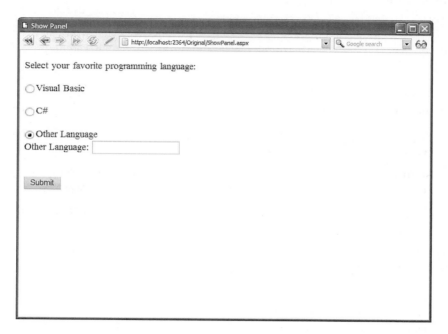

FIGURE 2.18   Hiding and displaying controls with the Panel control.

LISTING 2.29   ShowPanel.aspx

```
<%@ Page Language="VB" %>
<!DOCTYPE html PUBLIC "-//W3C//DTD XHTML 1.0 Transitional//EN"
➥"http://www.w3.org/TR/xhtml1/DTD/xhtml1-transitional.dtd">
<script runat="server">

    Sub btnSubmit_Click(ByVal sender As Object, ByVal e As EventArgs)
        If rdlOther.Checked Then
```

LISTING 2.29   Continued

```
            pnlOther.Visible = True
        Else
            pnlOther.Visible = False
        End If
    End Sub
</script>
<html xmlns="http://www.w3.org/1999/xhtml" >
<head id="Head1" runat="server">
    <title>Show Panel</title>
</head>
<body>
    <form id="form1" runat="server">
    <div>

    Select your favorite programming language:
    <br /><br />
    <asp:RadioButton
        id="rdlVisualBasic"
        GroupName="language"
        Text="Visual Basic"
        Runat="server" />
    <br /><br />
    <asp:RadioButton
        id="rdlCSharp"
        GroupName="language"
        Text="C#"
        Runat="server" />
    <br /><br />
    <asp:RadioButton
        id="rdlOther"
        GroupName="language"
        Text="Other Language"
        Runat="server" />
    <br />
    <asp:Panel
        id="pnlOther"
        Visible="false"
        Runat="server">

        <asp:Label
            id="lblOther"
            Text="Other Language:"
            AssociatedControlID="txtOther"
            Runat="server" />
```

LISTING 2.29   Continued

```
            <asp:TextBox
                id="txtOther"
                Runat="server" />

    </asp:Panel>

    <br /><br />

    <asp:Button
        id="btnSubmit"
        Text="Submit"
        OnClick="btnSubmit_Click"
        Runat="server" />

    </div>
    </form>
</body>
</html>
```

Notice that the Panel control is declared with a Visible property that has the value False. Because the Visible property is set to the value False, the Panel control and any controls contained in the Panel control are not rendered when the page is requested.

If you select the RadioButton control labeled Other, then the Visible property is set to the value True and the contents of the Panel control are displayed.

> **NOTE**
>
> Every control in the ASP.NET framework supports the Visible property. When Visible is set to the value False, the control does not render its contents.

The Panel control supports the following properties (this is not a complete list):

- DefaultButton—Enables you to specify the default button in a Panel. The default button is invoked when you press the Enter button.

- Direction—Enables you to get or set the direction in which controls that display text are rendered. Possible values are NotSet, LeftToRight, and RightToLeft.

- GroupingText—Enables you to render the Panel control as a fieldset with a particular legend.

- HorizontalAlign—Enables you to specify the horizontal alignment of the contents of the Panel. Possible values are Center, Justify, Left, NotSet, and Right.

- ScrollBars—Enables you to display scrollbars around the panel's contents. Possible values are Auto, Both, Horizontal, None, and Vertical.

By default, a Panel control renders a <div> tag around its contents. If you set the GroupingText property, however, the Panel control renders a <fieldset> tag. The value that you assign to the GroupingText property appears in the <fieldset> tag's <legend> tag. Listing 2.30 demonstrates how you can use the GroupingText property (see Figure 2.19).

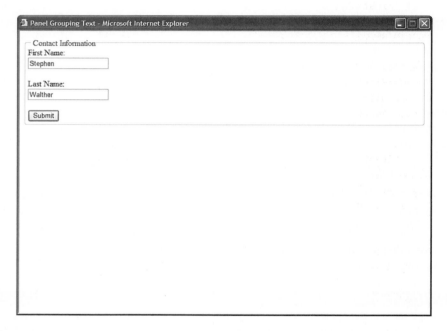

FIGURE 2.19   Setting the GroupingText property.

LISTING 2.30   PanelGroupingText.aspx

```
<%@ Page Language="VB" %>
<!DOCTYPE html PUBLIC "-//W3C//DTD XHTML 1.0 Transitional//EN"
➡"http://www.w3.org/TR/xhtml1/DTD/xhtml1-transitional.dtd">
<html xmlns="http://www.w3.org/1999/xhtml" >
<head id="Head1" runat="server">
    <title>Panel Grouping Text</title>
</head>
<body>
    <form id="form1" runat="server">
    <div>
```

LISTING 2.30   Continued

```
<asp:Panel
    id="pnlContact"
    GroupingText="Contact Information"
    Runat="server">

<asp:Label
    id="lblFirstName"
    Text="First Name:"
    AssociatedControlID="txtFirstName"
    Runat="server" />
<br />
<asp:TextBox
    id="txtFirstName"
    AutoCompleteType="FirstName"
    Runat="server" />
<br /><br />
<asp:Label
    id="lblLastname"
    Text="Last Name:"
    AssociatedControlID="txtLastName"
    Runat="server" />
<br />
<asp:TextBox
    id="txtLastName"
    AutoCompleteType="LastName"
    Runat="server" />
<br /><br />
<asp:Button
    id="btnSubmit"
    Text="Submit"
    Runat="server" />

</asp:Panel>

</div>
</form>
</body>
</html>
```

WEB STANDARDS NOTE

According to the accessibility guidelines, you should use `<fieldset>` tags when grouping related form fields in long forms.

The ScrollBars property enables you to display scrollbars around a panel's contents. For example, the page in Listing 2.31 contains a Panel control that contains a BulletedList control that displays 100 items. The panel is configured to scroll when its contents overflow its width or height (see Figure 2.20).

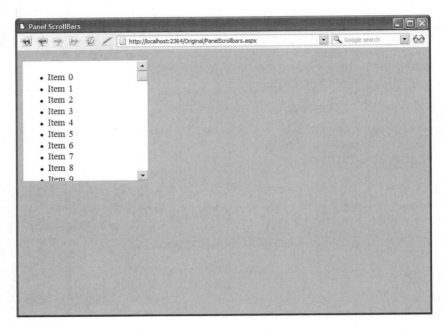

FIGURE 2.20 Displaying scrollbars with a Panel control.

LISTING 2.31 PanelScrollBars.aspx

```
<%@ Page Language="VB" %>
<!DOCTYPE html PUBLIC "-//W3C//DTD XHTML 1.0 Transitional//EN"
➥"http://www.w3.org/TR/xhtml1/DTD/xhtml1-transitional.dtd">
<script runat="server">

    Sub Page_Load()
        For i As Integer = 1 To 100
            bltList.Items.Add("Item " & i.ToString())
        Next
    End Sub

</script>
<html xmlns="http://www.w3.org/1999/xhtml" >
<head id="Head1" runat="server">
    <style type="text/css">
```

LISTING 2.31   Continued

```
    html
    {
        background-color:silver;
    }
    .contents
    {
        background-color:white;
        width:200px;
        height:200px;
    }
    </style>
    <title>Panel ScrollBars</title>
</head>
<body>
    <form id="form1" runat="server">
    <div>

    <asp:Panel
        id="pnlContent"
        ScrollBars="Auto"
        CssClass="contents"
        Runat="server">
        <asp:BulletedList
            id="bltList"
            Runat="server" />
    </asp:Panel>

    </div>
    </form>
</body>
</html>
```

WEB STANDARDS NOTE

Don't use the values Horizontal or Vertical with the ScrollBars property when you want the scrollbars to appear in browsers other than Microsoft Internet Explorer. If you want the scrollbars to appear in FireFox and Opera, use either the value Auto or Both.

When enabling scrollbars with the Panel control, you must specify a particular width and height to display the scrollbars. In Listing 2.31, the width and height are specified in a Cascading Style Sheet class. Alternatively, you can specify the width and height with the Panel control's Width and Height properties.

Using the HyperLink Control

The HyperLink control enables you to create a link to a page. Unlike the LinkButton control, the HyperLink control does not submit a form to a server.

For example, the page in Listing 2.32 displays a hyperlink that randomly links to a page in your application.

LISTING 2.32   ShowHyperLink.aspx

```
<%@ Page Language="VB" %>
<%@ Import Namespace="System.IO" %>
<!DOCTYPE html PUBLIC "-//W3C//DTD XHTML 1.0 Transitional//EN"
➥"http://www.w3.org/TR/xhtml1/DTD/xhtml1-transitional.dtd">
<script runat="server">

    Sub Page_Load()
        lnkRandom.NavigateUrl = GetRandomFile()
    End Sub

    Function GetRandomFile() As String
        Dim files As String() = Directory.GetFiles(
➥MapPath(Request.ApplicationPath), "*.aspx")
        Dim rnd As New Random()
        Dim rndFile As String = files(rnd.Next(files.Length))
        Return Path.GetFileName(rndFile)
    End Function

</script>
<html xmlns="http://www.w3.org/1999/xhtml" >
<head id="Head1" runat="server">
    <title>Show HyperLink</title>
</head>
<body>
    <form id="form1" runat="server">
    <div>

    <asp:HyperLink
        id="lnkRandom"
        Text="Random Link"
        Runat="server" />

    </div>
    </form>
</body>
</html>
```

In the `Page_Load` event handler in Listing 2.32, a random file name from the current application is assigned to the `NavigateUrl` property of the `HyperLink` control.

The `HyperLink` control supports the following properties (this is not a complete list):

- `Enabled`—Enables you to disable the hyperlink.
- `ImageUrl`—Enables you to specify an image for the hyperlink.
- `NavigateUrl`—Enables you to specify the URL represented by the hyperlink.
- `Target`—Enables you to open a new window.
- `Text`—Enables you to label the hyperlink.

Notice that you can specify an image for the `HyperLink` control by setting the `ImageUrl` property. If you set both the `Text` and `ImageUrl` properties, then the `ImageUrl` property takes precedence.

Summary

In this chapter, you were introduced to the core controls of the ASP.NET 2.0 framework. You learned how to display information using the `Label` and `Literal` controls. You also learned how to accept user input using the `TextBox`, `CheckBox`, and `RadioButton` controls.

In the second part of this chapter, you learned how to use the different button controls—the `Button`, `LinkButton`, and `ImageButton` controls—to submit a form. You learned how to post forms between pages. You also learned how to set a default button.

Finally, we discussed the `Panel` and `HyperLink` controls. You learned how to hide and display a group of controls with the `Panel` control. You also learned how to create dynamic links with the `HyperLink` control.

Using the Validation Controls

In this chapter, you learn how to validate form fields when a form is submitted to the web server. You can use the validation controls to prevent users from submitting the wrong type of data into a database table. For example, you can use validation controls to prevent a user from submitting the value "Apple" for a birth date field.

In the first part of this chapter, you are provided with an overview of the standard validation controls included in the ASP.NET 2.0 Framework. You learn how to control how validation errors are displayed, how to highlight validation error messages, and how to use validation groups. You are provided with sample code for using each of the standard validation controls.

Next, we extend the basic validation controls with our own custom validation controls. For example, you learn how to create an AjaxValidator control that enables you to call a server-side validation function from the client.

Overview of the Validation Controls

Six validation controls are included in the ASP.NET 2.0 Framework:

- RequiredFieldValidator—Enables you to require a user to enter a value in a form field.

- RangeValidator—Enables you to check whether a value falls between a certain minimum and maximum value.

- CompareValidator—Enables you to compare a value against another value or perform a data type check.

- RegularExpressionValidator—Enables you to compare a value against a regular expression.

- CustomValidator—Enables you to perform custom validation.

- ValidationSummary—Enables you to display a summary of all validation errors in a page.

You can associate the validation controls with any of the form controls included in the ASP.NET Framework. For example, if you want to require a user to enter a value into a TextBox control, then you can associate a RequiredFieldValidator control with the TextBox control.

> **NOTE**
>
> Technically, you can use the validation controls with any control that is decorated with the ValidationProperty attribute.

The page in Listing 3.1 contains a simple order entry form. It contains three TextBox controls that enable you to enter a product name, product price, and product quantity. Each of the form fields are validated with the validation controls.

LISTING 3.1   OrderForm.aspx

```
<%@ Page Language="VB" %>
<!DOCTYPE html PUBLIC "-//W3C//DTD XHTML 1.0 Transitional//EN"
   "http://www.w3.org/TR/xhtml1/DTD/xhtml1-transitional.dtd">
<script runat="server">

    Protected Sub btnSubmit_Click(ByVal sender As Object, ByVal e
➥As System.EventArgs)
        If Page.IsValid Then
            lblResult.Text = "<br />Product: " & txtProductName.Text
            lblResult.Text &= "<br />Price: " & txtProductPrice.Text
            lblResult.Text &= "<br />Quantity: " & txtProductQuantity.Text
        End If
    End Sub
</script>
<html xmlns="http://www.w3.org/1999/xhtml" >
<head id="Head1" runat="server">
    <title>Order Form</title>
</head>
<body>
    <form id="form1" runat="server">
    <div>

    <fieldset>
```

LISTING 3.1   Continued

```
<legend>Product Order Form</legend>

<asp:Label
    id="lblProductName"
    Text="Product Name:"
    AssociatedControlID="txtProductName"
    Runat="server" />
<br />
<asp:TextBox
    id="txtProductName"
    Runat="server" />
<asp:RequiredFieldValidator
    id="reqProductName"
    ControlToValidate="txtProductName"
    Text="(Required)"
    Runat="server" />

<br /><br />

<asp:Label
    id="lblProductPrice"
    Text="Product Price:"
    AssociatedControlID="txtProductPrice"
    Runat="server" />
<br />
<asp:TextBox
    id="txtProductPrice"
    Columns="5"
    Runat="server" />
<asp:RequiredFieldValidator
    id="reqProductPrice"
    ControlToValidate="txtProductPrice"
    Text="(Required)"
    Display="Dynamic"
    Runat="server" />
<asp:CompareValidator
    id="cmpProductPrice"
    ControlToValidate="txtProductPrice"
    Text="(Invalid Price)"
    Operator="DataTypeCheck"
    Type="Currency"
    Runat="server" />

<br /><br />
```

3

LISTING 3.1   Continued

```
    <asp:Label
        id="lblProductQuantity"
        Text="Product Quantity:"
        AssociatedControlID="txtProductQuantity"
        Runat="server" />
    <br />
    <asp:TextBox
        id="txtProductQuantity"
        Columns="5"
        Runat="server" />
    <asp:RequiredFieldValidator
        id="reqProductQuantity"
        ControlToValidate="txtProductQuantity"
        Text="(Required)"
        Display="Dynamic"
        Runat="server" />
    <asp:CompareValidator
        id="CompareValidator1"
        ControlToValidate="txtProductQuantity"
        Text="(Invalid Quantity)"
        Operator="DataTypeCheck"
        Type="Integer"
        Runat="server" />

    <br /><br />

    <asp:Button
        id="btnSubmit"
        Text="Submit Product Order"
        OnClick="btnSubmit_Click"
        Runat="server" />

    </fieldset>

    <asp:Label
        id="lblResult"
        Runat="server" />

    </div>
    </form>
</body>
</html>
```

A separate RequiredFieldValidator control is associated with each of the three form fields. If you attempt to submit the form in Listing 3.1 without entering a value for a field, then a validation error message is displayed (see Figure 3.1).

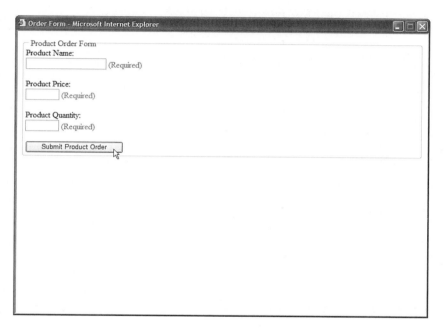

FIGURE 3.1   Displaying a validation error message.

Each RequiredFieldValidator is associated with a particular control through its ControlToValidate property. This property accepts the name of the control to validate on the page.

CompareValidator controls are associated with the txtProductPrice and txtProductQuantity TextBox controls. The first CompareValidator is used to check whether the txtProductPrice text field contains a currency value, and the second CompareValidator is used to check whether the txtProductQuantity text field contains an integer value.

Notice that there is nothing wrong with associating more than one validation control with a form field. If you need to make a form field required and check the data type entered into the form field, then you need to associate both a RequiredFieldValidator and CompareValidator control with the form field.

Finally, notice that the Page.IsValid property is checked in the btnSubmit_Click() handler after the form data is submitted. When using the validation controls, you should always check the Page.IsValid property before doing anything with the data submitted to a page. This property returns the value true when, and only when, there are no validation errors on the page.

Validation Controls and JavaScript

By default, the validation controls perform validation on both the client (the browser) and the server. The validation controls use client-side JavaScript. This is great from a user experience perspective because you get immediate feedback whenever you enter an invalid value into a form field.

> **NOTE**
>
> The `RequiredFieldValidator` will not perform client-side validation until after you attempt to submit a form at least once or you enter and remove data in a form field.

Client-side JavaScript is supported on any uplevel browser. Supported browsers include Internet Explorer, Firefox, and Opera. This is a change from the previous version of ASP.NET, which supported only Internet Explorer as an uplevel browser.

You can use the validation controls with browsers that do not support JavaScript (or do not have JavaScript enabled). If a browser does not support JavaScript, the form must be posted back to the server before a validation error message is displayed.

Even when validation happens on the client, validation is still performed on the server. This is done for security reasons. If someone creates a fake form and submits the form data to your web server, the person still won't be able to submit invalid data.

If you prefer, you can disable client-side validation for any of the validation controls by assigning the value `False` to the validation control's `EnableClientScript` property.

Using `Page.IsValid`

As mentioned earlier, you should always check the `Page.IsValid` property when working with data submitted with a form that contains validation controls. Each of the validation controls includes an `IsValid` property that returns the value `True` when there is not a validation error. The `Page.IsValid` property returns the value `True` when the `IsValid` property for all of the validation controls in a page returns the value `True`.

It is easy to forget to check the `Page.IsValid` property. When you use an uplevel browser that supports JavaScript with the validation controls, you are prevented from submitting a form back to the server when there are validation errors. However, if someone requests a page using a browser that does not support JavaScript, the page is submitted back to the server even when there are validation errors.

For example, if you request the page in Listing 3.1 with a browser that does not support JavaScript and submit the form without entering form data, then the `btnSubmit_Click()` handler executes on the server. The `Page.IsValid` property is used in Listing 3.1 to prevent downlevel browsers from displaying invalid form data.

> **WARNING**
>
> Unfortunately, I've made the mistake of forgetting to include a check of the `Page.IsValid` property several times when building applications. Because you do not normally develop a web application with a downlevel browser, you won't notice the problem described in this section until you start getting invalid data in your database tables.

Setting the Display Property

All the validation controls include a `Display` property that determines how the validation error message is rendered. This property accepts any of the following three possible values:

- Static

- Dynamic

- None

By default, the `Display` property has the value `Static`. When the `Display` property has this value, the validation error message rendered by the validation control looks like this:

```
<span id="reqProductName" style="color:Red;visibility:hidden;">(Required)</span>
```

Notice that the error message is rendered in a `<span>` tag that includes a Cascading Style Sheet style attribute that sets the visibility of the `<span>` tag to `hidden`.

If, on the other hand, you set the `Display` property to the value `Dynamic`, the error message is rendered like this:

```
<span id="reqProductName" style="color:Red;display:none;">(Required)</span>
```

In this case, a Cascading Style Sheet `display` attribute hides the contents of the `<span>` tag.

Both the visibility and display attributes can be used to hide text in a browser. However, text hidden with the `visibility` attribute still occupies screen real estate. Text hidden with the `display` attribute, on the other hand, does not occupy screen real estate.

In general, you should set a validation control's `Display` property to the value `Dynamic`. That way, if other content is displayed next to the validation control, the content is not pushed to the right. All modern browsers (Internet Explorer, Firefox, and Opera) support the Cascading Style Sheet `display` attribute.

The third possible value of the `Display` property is `None`. If you prefer, you can prevent the individual validation controls from displaying an error message and display the error messages with a `ValidationSummary` control. You learn how to use the `ValidationSummary` control later in this chapter.

Highlighting Validation Errors

When a validation control displays a validation error, the control displays the value of its Text property. Normally, you assign a simple text string, such as "(Required)" to the Text property. However, the Text property accepts any HTML string.

For example, the page in Listing 3.2 displays an image when you submit the form without entering a value for the First Name text field (see Figure 3.2).

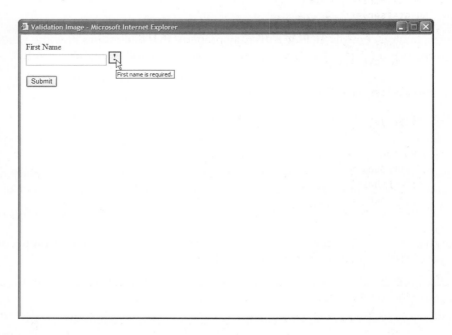

FIGURE 3.2   Displaying an image for a validation error.

LISTING 3.2   ValidationImage.aspx

```
<%@ Page Language="VB" %>
<!DOCTYPE html PUBLIC "-//W3C//DTD XHTML 1.0 Transitional//EN"
  "http://www.w3.org/TR/xhtml1/DTD/xhtml1-transitional.dtd">
<html xmlns="http://www.w3.org/1999/xhtml" >
<head id="Head1" runat="server">
    <title>Validation Image</title>
</head>
<body>
    <form id="form1" runat="server">
    <div>

    <asp:Label
        id="lblFirstName"
```

LISTING 3.2   Continued

```
        Text="First Name"
        AssociatedControlID="txtFirstName"
        Runat="server" />
    <br />
    <asp:TextBox
        id="txtFirstName"
        Runat="server" />
    <asp:RequiredFieldValidator
        id="reqFirstName"
        ControlToValidate="txtFirstName"
        Text="<img src='Error.gif' alt='First name is required.' />"
        Runat="server" />

    <br /><br />

    <asp:Button
        id="btnSubmit"
        Text="Submit"
        Runat="server" />

    </div>
    </form>
</body>
</html>
```

In Listing 3.2, the `Text` property contains an HTML `<img>` tag. When there is a validation error, the image represented by the `<img>` tag is displayed.

Another way that you can emphasize errors is to take advantage of the `SetFocusOnError` property that is supported by all the validation controls. When this property has the value `True`, the form focus is automatically shifted to the control associated with the validation control when there is a validation error.

For example, the page in Listing 3.3 contains two `TextBox` controls that are both validated with `RequiredFieldValidator` controls. Both `RequiredFieldValidator` controls have their `SetFocusOnError` properties enabled. If you provide a value for the first text field and not the second text field and submit the form, the form focus automatically shifts to the second form field.

LISTING 3.3   ShowSetFocusOnError.aspx

```
<%@ Page Language="VB" %>
<!DOCTYPE html PUBLIC "-//W3C//DTD XHTML 1.0 Transitional//EN"
    "http://www.w3.org/TR/xhtml1/DTD/xhtml1-transitional.dtd">
<html xmlns="http://www.w3.org/1999/xhtml" >
```

LISTING 3.3   Continued

```
<head id="Head1" runat="server">
    <title>Show SetFocusOnError</title>
</head>
<body>
    <form id="form1" runat="server">
    <div>

    <asp:Label
        id="lblFirstName"
        Text="First Name"
        AssociatedControlID="txtFirstName"
        Runat="server" />
    <br />
    <asp:TextBox
        id="txtFirstName"
        Runat="server" />
    <asp:RequiredFieldValidator
        id="reqFirstName"
        ControlToValidate="txtFirstName"
        Text="(Required)"
        SetFocusOnError="true"
        Runat="server" />

    <br /><br />

    <asp:Label
        id="lblLastName"
        Text="Last Name"
        AssociatedControlID="txtLastName"
        Runat="server" />
    <br />
    <asp:TextBox
        id="txtLastname"
        Runat="server" />
    <asp:RequiredFieldValidator
        id="reqLastName"
        ControlToValidate="txtLastName"
        Text="(Required)"
        SetFocusOnError="true"
        Runat="server" />

     <br /><br />

     <asp:Button
```

LISTING 3.3   Continued

```
        id="btnSubmit"
        Text="Submit"
        Runat="server" />

    </div>
    </form>
</body>
</html>
```

Finally, if you want to really emphasize the controls associated with a validation error, then you can take advantage of the Page.Validators property. This property exposes the collection of all the validation controls in a page. In Listing 3.4, the Page.Validators property is used to highlight each control that has a validation error (see Figure 3.3).

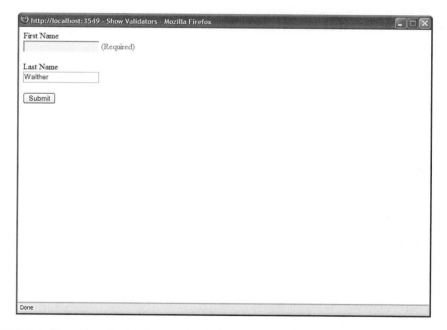

FIGURE 3.3   Changing the background color of form fields.

LISTING 3.4   ShowValidators.aspx

```
<%@ Page Language="VB" %>
<!DOCTYPE html PUBLIC "-//W3C//DTD XHTML 1.0 Transitional//EN"
    "http://www.w3.org/TR/xhtml1/DTD/xhtml1-transitional.dtd">
<script runat="server">
```

LISTING 3.4   Continued

```
    Sub Page_PreRender()
        For Each valControl As BaseValidator In Page.Validators
            Dim assControl As WebControl =
➡Page.FindControl(valControl.ControlToValidate)
            If Not valControl.IsValid Then
                assControl.BackColor = Drawing.Color.Yellow
            Else
                assControl.BackColor = Drawing.Color.White
            End If
        Next
    End Sub
</script>
<html xmlns="http://www.w3.org/1999/xhtml" >
<head id="Head1" runat="server">
    <title>Show Validators</title>
</head>
<body>
    <form id="form1" runat="server">
    <div>

    <asp:Label
        id="lblFirstName"
        Text="First Name"
        AssociatedControlID="txtFirstName"
        Runat="server" />
    <br />
    <asp:TextBox
        id="txtFirstName"
        Runat="server" />
    <asp:RequiredFieldValidator
        id="reqFirstName"
        ControlToValidate="txtFirstName"
        Text="(Required)"
        EnableClientScript="false"
        Runat="server" />

    <br /><br />

    <asp:Label
        id="lblLastName"
        Text="Last Name"
        AssociatedControlID="txtLastName"
        Runat="server" />
    <br />
```

LISTING 3.4 Continued

```
    <asp:TextBox
        id="txtLastname"
        Runat="server" />
    <asp:RequiredFieldValidator
        id="reqLastName"
        ControlToValidate="txtLastName"
        Text="(Required)"
        EnableClientScript="false"
        Runat="server" />

    <br /><br />

    <asp:Button
        id="btnSubmit"
        Text="Submit"
        Runat="server" />

    </div>
    </form>
</body>
</html>
```

The `Page.Validators` property is used in the `Page_PreRender()` handler. The `IsValid` property is checked for each control in the `Page.Validators` collection. If `IsValid` returns `False`, then the control being validated by the validation control is highlighted with a yellow background color.

Using Validation Groups

In the first version of the ASP.NET Framework, there was no easy way to add two forms to the same page. If you added more than one form to a page, and both forms contained validation controls, then the validation controls in both forms were evaluated regardless of which form you submitted.

For example, imagine that you wanted to create a page that contained both a login and registration form. The login form appeared in the left column and the registration form appeared in the right column. If both forms included validation controls, then submitting the login form caused any validation controls contained in the registration form to be evaluated.

In ASP.NET 2.0, you no longer face this limitation. The ASP.NET 2.0 Framework introduces the idea of validation groups. A validation group enables you to group related form fields together.

For example, the page in Listing 3.5 contains both a login and registration form and both forms contain independent sets of validation controls.

LISTING 3.5   ShowValidationGroups.aspx

```
<%@ Page Language="VB" %>
<!DOCTYPE html PUBLIC "-//W3C//DTD XHTML 1.0 Transitional//EN"
    "http://www.w3.org/TR/xhtml1/DTD/xhtml1-transitional.dtd">
<script runat="server">

    Protected Sub btnLogin_Click(ByVal sender As Object, ByVal e As EventArgs)
        If Page.IsValid() Then
            lblLoginResult.Text = "Log in successful!"
        End If
    End Sub

    Protected Sub btnRegister_Click(ByVal sender As Object, ByVal e As EventArgs)
        If Page.IsValid() Then
            lblRegisterResult.Text = "Registration successful!"
        End If
    End Sub
</script>
<html xmlns="http://www.w3.org/1999/xhtml" >
<head id="Head1" runat="server">
    <style type="text/css">
        html
        {
            background-color:silver;
        }
        .column
        {
            float:left;
            width:300px;
            margin-left:10px;
            background-color:white;
            border:solid 1px black;
            padding:10px;
        }
    </style>
    <title>Show Validation Groups</title>
</head>
<body>
    <form id="form1" runat="server">

    <div class="column">
    <fieldset>
```

LISTING 3.5   Continued

```
<legend>Login</legend>
<p>
Please log in to our Website.
</p>
<asp:Label
    id="lblUserName"
    Text="User Name:"
    AssociatedControlID="txtUserName"
    Runat="server" />
<br />
<asp:TextBox
    id="txtUserName"
    Runat="server" />
<asp:RequiredFieldValidator
    id="reqUserName"
    ControlToValidate="txtUserName"
    Text="(Required)"
    ValidationGroup="LoginGroup"
    Runat="server" />
<br /><br />
<asp:Label
    id="lblPassword"
    Text="Password:"
    AssociatedControlID="txtPassword"
    Runat="server" />
<br />
<asp:TextBox
    id="txtPassword"
    TextMode="Password"
    Runat="server" />
<asp:RequiredFieldValidator
    id="reqPassword"
    ControlToValidate="txtPassword"
    Text="(Required)"
    ValidationGroup="LoginGroup"
    Runat="server" />
<br /><br />
<asp:Button
    id="btnLogin"
    Text="Login"
    ValidationGroup="LoginGroup"
    Runat="server" OnClick="btnLogin_Click" />
</fieldset>
```

LISTING 3.5   Continued

```
<asp:Label
    id="lblLoginResult"
    Runat="server" />

</div>

<div class="column">
<fieldset>
<legend>Register</legend>
<p>
If you do not have a User Name, please
register at our Website.
</p>
<asp:Label
    id="lblFirstName"
    Text="First Name:"
    AssociatedControlID="txtFirstName"
    Runat="server" />
<br />
<asp:TextBox
    id="txtFirstName"
    Runat="server" />
<asp:RequiredFieldValidator
    id="reqFirstName"
    ControlToValidate="txtFirstName"
    Text="(Required)"
    ValidationGroup="RegisterGroup"
    Runat="server" />
<br /><br />
<asp:Label
    id="lblLastName"
    Text="Last Name:"
    AssociatedControlID="txtLastName"
    Runat="server" />
<br />
<asp:TextBox
    id="txtLastName"
    Runat="server" />
<asp:RequiredFieldValidator
    id="reqLastName"
    ControlToValidate="txtLastName"
    Text="(Required)"
    ValidationGroup="RegisterGroup"
    Runat="server" />
```

LISTING 3.5   Continued

```
    <br /><br />
    <asp:Button
        id="btnRegister"
        Text="Register"
        ValidationGroup="RegisterGroup"
        Runat="server" OnClick="btnRegister_Click" />
    </fieldset>

    <asp:Label
        id="lblRegisterResult"
        Runat="server" />

    </div>

    </form>
</body>
</html>
```

Notice that the validation controls and the button controls all include `ValidationGroup` properties. The controls associated with the login form all have the value `"LoginGroup"` assigned to their `ValidationGroup` properties. The controls associated with the register form all have the value `"RegisterGroup"` assigned to their `ValidationGroup` properties.

Because the form fields are grouped into different validation groups, you can submit the two forms independently. Submitting the Login form does not trigger the validation controls in the Register form (see Figure 3.4).

You can assign any string to the `ValidationGroup` property. The only purpose of the string is to associate different controls in a form together into different groups.

> **NOTE**
>
> Using validation groups is particularly important when working with Web Parts because multiple Web Parts with different forms might be added to the same page.

Disabling Validation

All the button controls—the `Button`, `LinkButton`, and `ImageButton` control—include a `CausesValidation` property. If you assign the value `False` to this property, then clicking the button bypasses any validation in the page.

Bypassing validation is useful when creating a Cancel button. For example, the page in Listing 3.6 includes a Cancel button that redirects the user back to the `Default.aspx` page.

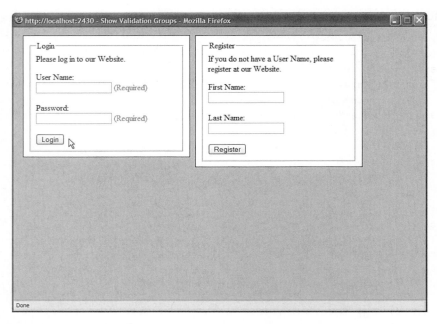

FIGURE 3.4   Using validation groups.

LISTING 3.6   ShowDisableValidation.aspx

```
<%@ Page Language="VB" %>
<!DOCTYPE html PUBLIC "-//W3C//DTD XHTML 1.0 Transitional//EN"
  "http://www.w3.org/TR/xhtml1/DTD/xhtml1-transitional.dtd">
<script runat="server">

    Protected Sub btnCancel_Click(ByVal sender As Object, ByVal e
➥As System.EventArgs)
        Response.Redirect("~/Default.aspx")
    End Sub
</script>
<html xmlns="http://www.w3.org/1999/xhtml" >
<head id="Head1" runat="server">
    <title>Show Disable Validation</title>
</head>
<body>
    <form id="form1" runat="server">
    <div>

    <asp:Label
        id="lblFirstName"
        Text="First Name:"
```

LISTING 3.6   Continued

```
            AssociatedControlID="txtFirstName"
            Runat="server" />
    <asp:TextBox
            id="txtFirstName"
            Runat="server" />
    <asp:RequiredFieldValidator
            id="reqFirstName"
            ControlToValidate="txtFirstName"
            Text="(Required)"
            Runat="server" />
    <br /><br />
    <asp:Button
            id="btnSubmit"
            Text="Submit"
            Runat="server" />
    <asp:Button
            id="btnCancel"
            Text="Cancel"
            OnClick="btnCancel_Click"
            CausesValidation="false"
            Runat="server" />

    </div>
    </form>
</body>
</html>
```

Notice that the Cancel button in Listing 3.6 includes the `CausesValidation` property with the value `False`. If the button did not include this property, then the `RequiredFieldValidator` control would prevent you from submitting the form when you clicked the Cancel button.

Using the `RequiredFieldValidator` Control

The `RequiredFieldValidator` control enables you to require a user to enter a value into a form field before submitting the form. You must set two important properties when using the `RequiredFieldValdiator` control:

- `ControlToValidate`—The ID of the form field being validated.

- `Text`—The error message displayed when validation fails.

The page in Listing 3.1 illustrates how you can use the `RequiredFieldValidator` control to require a user to enter both a first and last name (see Figure 3.5).

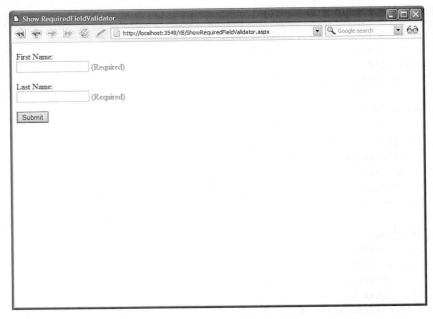

FIGURE 3.5   Requiring a user to enter form field values.

LISTING 3.7   ShowRequiredFieldValidator.aspx

```
<%@ Page Language="VB" %>
<!DOCTYPE html PUBLIC "-//W3C//DTD XHTML 1.0 Transitional//EN"
  "http://www.w3.org/TR/xhtml1/DTD/xhtml1-transitional.dtd">
<html xmlns="http://www.w3.org/1999/xhtml" >
<head id="Head1" runat="server">
    <title>Show RequiredFieldValidator</title>
</head>
<body>
    <form id="form1" runat="server">
    <div>

    <asp:Label
        id="lblFirstName"
        Text="First Name:"
        AssociatedControlID="txtFirstName"
        Runat="server" />
    <br />
    <asp:TextBox
        id="txtFirstName"
        Runat="server" />
    <asp:RequiredFieldValidator
```

LISTING 3.7 Continued

```
        id="reqFirstName"
        ControlToValidate="txtFirstName"
        Text="(Required)"
        Runat="server" />

    <br /><br />

    <asp:Label
        id="lblLastName"
        Text="Last Name:"
        AssociatedControlID="txtLastName"
        Runat="server" />
    <br />
    <asp:TextBox
        id="txtLastName"
        Runat="server" />
    <asp:RequiredFieldValidator
        id="reqLastName"
        ControlToValidate="txtLastName"
        Text="(Required)"
        Runat="server" />

    <br /><br />

    <asp:Button
        id="btnSubmit"
        Text="Submit"
        Runat="server" />

    </div>
    </form>
</body>
</html>
```

By default, the `RequiredFieldValidator` checks for a nonempty string (spaces don't count). If you enter anything into the form field associated with the `RequiredFieldValidator`, then the `RequiredFieldValidator` does not display its validation error message.

You can use the `RequiredFieldValidator` control's `InitialValue` property to specify a default value other than an empty string. For example, the page in Listing 3.8 uses a `RequiredFieldValidator` to validate a `DropDownList` control (see Figure 3.6).

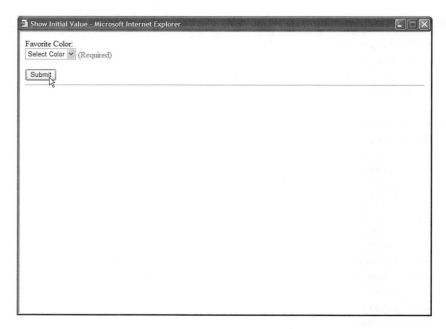

FIGURE 3.6   Using a `RequiredFieldValidator` with a `DropDownList` control.

LISTING 3.8   ShowInitialValue.aspx

```
<%@ Page Language="VB" %>
<!DOCTYPE html PUBLIC "-//W3C//DTD XHTML 1.0 Transitional//EN"
    "http://www.w3.org/TR/xhtml1/DTD/xhtml1-transitional.dtd">
<script runat="server">

    Protected Sub btnSubmit_Click(ByVal sender As Object, ByVal e
➡As System.EventArgs)
        If Page.IsValid Then
            lblResult.Text = dropFavoriteColor.SelectedValue
        End If
    End Sub
</script>
<html xmlns="http://www.w3.org/1999/xhtml" >
<head id="Head1" runat="server">
    <title>Show Initial Value</title>
</head>
<body>
    <form id="form1" runat="server">
    <div>

    <asp:Label
```

LISTING 3.8   Continued

```
        id="lblFavoriteColor"
        Text="Favorite Color:"
        AssociatedControlID="dropFavoriteColor"
        Runat="server" />
    <br />
    <asp:DropDownList
        id="dropFavoriteColor"
        Runat="server">
        <asp:ListItem Text="Select Color" Value="none" />
        <asp:ListItem Text="Red" Value="Red" />
        <asp:ListItem Text="Blue" Value="Blue" />
        <asp:ListItem Text="Green" Value="Green" />
    </asp:DropDownList>
    <asp:RequiredFieldValidator
        id="reqFavoriteColor"
        Text="(Required)"
        InitialValue="none"
        ControlToValidate="dropFavoriteColor"
        Runat="server" />

    <br /><br />

    <asp:Button
        id="btnSubmit"
        Text="Submit"
        Runat="server" OnClick="btnSubmit_Click" />

    <hr />

    <asp:Label
        id="lblResult"
        Runat="server" />

    </div>
    </form>
</body>
</html>
```

The first list item displayed by the `DropDownList` control displays the text "`Select Color`". If you submit the form without selecting a color from the `DropDownList` control, then a validation error message is displayed.

Notice that the `RequiredFieldValidator` control includes an `InitialValue` property. The value of the first list from the `DropDownList` control is assigned to this property.

Using the RangeValidator **Control**

The RangeValidator control enables you to check whether the value of a form field falls between a certain minimum and maximum value. You must set five properties when using this control:

- ControlToValidate—The ID of the form field being validated.
- Text—The error message displayed when validation fails.
- MinimumValue—The minimum value of the validation range.
- MaximumValue—The maximum value of the validation range.
- Type—The type of comparison to perform. Possible values are String, Integer, Double, Date, and Currency.

For example, the page in Listing 3.9 includes a RangeValidator that validates an age form field. If you do not enter an age between 5 and 100, then a validation error is displayed (see Figure 3.7).

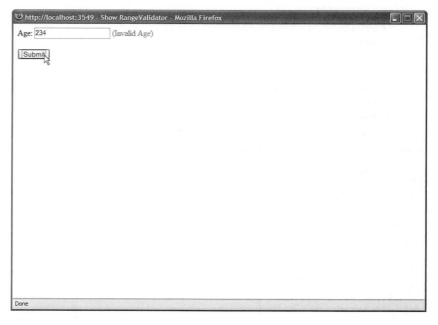

FIGURE 3.7 Validating a form field against a range of values.

LISTING 3.9 ShowRangeValidator.aspx

```
<%@ Page Language="VB" %>
<!DOCTYPE html PUBLIC "-//W3C//DTD XHTML 1.0 Transitional//EN"
 "http://www.w3.org/TR/xhtml1/DTD/xhtml1-transitional.dtd">
```

LISTING 3.9   Continued

```
<html xmlns="http://www.w3.org/1999/xhtml" >
<head id="Head1" runat="server">
    <title>Show RangeValidator</title>
</head>
<body>
    <form id="form1" runat="server">
    <div>

    <asp:Label
        id="lblAge"
        Text="Age:"
        AssociatedControlID="txtAge"
        Runat="server" />
    <asp:TextBox
        id="txtAge"
        Runat="server" />
    <asp:RangeValidator
        id="reqAge"
        ControlToValidate="txtAge"
        Text="(Invalid Age)"
        MinimumValue="5"
        MaximumValue="100"
        Type="Integer"
        Runat="server" />

    <br /><br />

    <asp:Button
        id="btnSubmit"
        Text="Submit"
        Runat="server" />

    </div>
    </form>
</body>
</html>
```

If you submit the form in Listing 3.9 with an age less than 5 or greater than 100, then the validation error message is displayed. The validation message is also displayed if you enter a value that is not a number. If the value entered into the form field cannot be converted into the data type represented by the RangeValidator control's Type property, then the error message is displayed.

If you don't enter any value into the age field and submit the form, no error message is displayed. If you want to require a user to enter a value, you must associate a RequiredFieldValidator with the form field.

Don't forget to set the Type property when using the RangeValidator control. By default, the Type property has the value String, and the RangeValidator performs a string comparison to determine whether a values falls between the minimum and maximum value.

Using the CompareValidator **Control**

The CompareValidator control enables you to perform three different types of validation tasks. You can use the CompareValidator to perform a data type check. In other words, you can use the control to determine whether a user has entered the proper type of value into a form field, such as a date in a birth date field.

You also can use the CompareValidator to compare the value entered into a form field against a fixed value. For example, if you are building an auction website, you can use the CompareValidator to check whether a new minimum bid is greater than the previous minimum bid.

Finally, you can use the CompareValidator to compare the value of one form field against another. For example, you use the CompareValidator to check whether the value entered into the meeting start date is less than the value entered into the meeting end date.

The CompareValidator has six important properties:

- ControlToValidate—The ID of the form field being validated.

- Text—The error message displayed when validation fails.

- Type—The type of value being compared. Possible values are String, Integer, Double, Date, and Currency.

- Operator—The type of comparison to perform. Possible values are DataTypeCheck, Equal, GreaterThan, GreaterThanEqual, LessThan, LessThanEqual, and NotEqual.

- ValueToCompare—The fixed value against which to compare.

- ControlToCompare—The ID of a control against which to compare.

The page in Listing 3.10 illustrates how you can use the CompareValidator to perform a data type check. The page contains a birth date field. If you enter a value that is not a date, then the validation error message is displayed (see Figure 3.8).

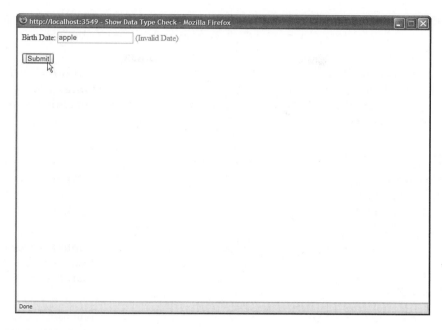

FIGURE 3.8   Performing a data type check.

LISTING 3.10   ShowDataTypeCheck.aspx

```
<%@ Page Language="VB" %>
<!DOCTYPE html PUBLIC "-//W3C//DTD XHTML 1.0 Transitional//EN"
    "http://www.w3.org/TR/xhtml1/DTD/xhtml1-transitional.dtd">
<html xmlns="http://www.w3.org/1999/xhtml" >
<head id="Head1" runat="server">
    <title>Show Data Type Check</title>
</head>
<body>
    <form id="form1" runat="server">
    <div>

    <asp:Label
        id="lblBirthDate"
        Text="Birth Date:"
        AssociatedControlID="txtBirthDate"
        Runat="server" />
    <asp:TextBox
        id="txtBirthDate"
        Runat="server" />
    <asp:CompareValidator
```

LISTING 3.10   Continued

```
        id="cmpBirthDate"
        Text="(Invalid Date)"
        ControlToValidate="txtBirthDate"
        Type="Date"
        Operator="DataTypeCheck"
        Runat="server" />

    <br /><br />

    <asp:Button
        id="btnSubmit"
        Text="Submit"
        Runat="server" />

    </div>
    </form>
</body>
</html>
```

Notice that the page in Listing 3.10 contains a CompareValidator control. Its Type property has the value Date, and its Operator property has the value DataTypeCheck. If you enter a value other than a date into the birth date field, the validation error message is displayed.

> **WARNING**
>
> An important limitation of the CompareValidator concerns how it performs a data type check. You cannot enter a long date into the form in Listing 3.10 (for example, December 25, 1966). You must enter a short date (for example, 12/25/1966). When validating currency amounts, you cannot enter the currency symbol. If these limitations concern you, you can use either the RegularExpression or CustomValidator controls to perform a more flexible data type check.

You can also use the CompareValidator to perform a comparison against a fixed value. For example, the page in Listing 3.11 uses a CompareValidator to check whether a date entered into a form field is greater than the current date (see Figure 3.9).

LISTING 3.11   ShowFixedValue.aspx

```
<%@ Page Language="VB" %>
<!DOCTYPE html PUBLIC "-//W3C//DTD XHTML 1.0 Transitional//EN"
    "http://www.w3.org/TR/xhtml1/DTD/xhtml1-transitional.dtd">
<script runat="server">

    Sub Page_Load()
```

LISTING 3.11   Continued

```
            cmpDate.ValueToCompare = DateTime.Now.ToString("d")
    End Sub
</script>
<html xmlns="http://www.w3.org/1999/xhtml" >
<head id="Head1" runat="server">
    <title>Show Fixed Value</title>
</head>
<body>
    <form id="form1" runat="server">
    <div>

    <asp:Label
        id="lblDate"
        Text="Date:"
        AssociatedControlID="txtDate"
        Runat="server" />
    <asp:TextBox
        id="txtDate"
        Runat="server" />
    <asp:CompareValidator
        id="cmpDate"
        Text="(Date must be greater than now)"
        ControlToValidate="txtDate"
        Type="Date"
        Operator="GreaterThan"
        Runat="server" />

    <br /><br />

    <asp:Button
        id="btnSubmit"
        Text="Submit"
        Runat="server" />

    </div>
    </form>
</body>
</html>
```

Finally, you can use a CompareValidator to compare the value of one form field against another form field. The page in Listing 3.12 contains a meeting start date and meeting end date field. If you enter a value into the first field that is greater than the second field, a validation error is displayed (see Figure 3.10).

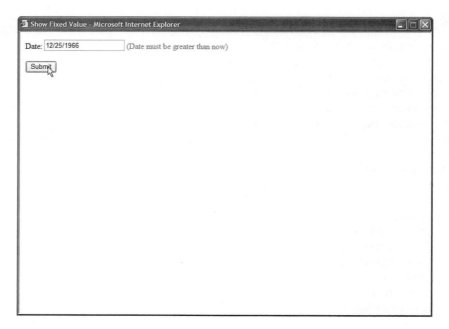

FIGURE 3.9   Comparing a form field against a fixed value.

FIGURE 3.10   Comparing two form fields.

LISTING 3.12   ShowCompareValues.aspx

```
<%@ Page Language="VB" %>
<!DOCTYPE html PUBLIC "-//W3C//DTD XHTML 1.0 Transitional//EN"
    "http://www.w3.org/TR/xhtml1/DTD/xhtml1-transitional.dtd">
<html xmlns="http://www.w3.org/1999/xhtml" >
<head id="Head1" runat="server">
    <title>Show Compare Values</title>
</head>
<body>
    <form id="form1" runat="server">
    <div>

    <asp:Label
        id="lblStartDate"
        Text="Start Date:"
        Runat="server" />
    <asp:TextBox
        id="txtStartDate"
        Runat="server" />

    <br /><br />

    <asp:Label
        id="lblEndDate"
        Text="End Date:"
        Runat="server" />
    <asp:TextBox
        id="txtEndDate"
        Runat="server" />
    <asp:CompareValidator
        id="cmpDate"
        Text="(End date must be greater than start date)"
        ControlToValidate="txtEndDate"
        ControlToCompare="txtStartDate"
        Type="Date"
        Operator="GreaterThan"
        Runat="server" />

    <br /><br />

    <asp:Button
        id="btnSubmit"
        Text="Submit"
        Runat="server" />
```

3

LISTING 3.12   Continued

```
      </div>
      </form>
</body>
</html>
```

Just like the `RangeValidator`, the `CompareValidator` does not display an error if you don't enter a value into the form field being validated. If you want to require that a user enter a value, then you must associate a `RequiredFieldValidator` control with the field.

Using the `RegularExpressionValidator` Control

The `RegularExpressionValidator` control enables you to compare the value of a form field against a regular expression. You can use a regular expression to represent string patterns such as email addresses, Social Security numbers, phone numbers, dates, currency amounts, and product codes.

For example, the page in Listing 3.13 enables you to validate an email address (see Figure 3.11).

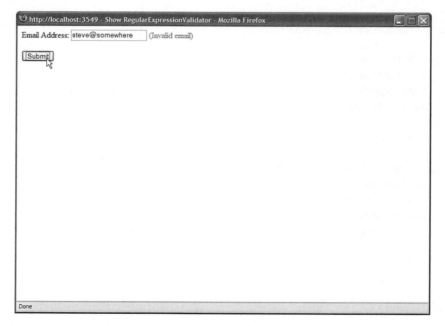

FIGURE 3.11   Validating an email address.

LISTING 3.13   ShowRegularExpressionValidator.aspx

```
<%@ Page Language="VB" %>
<!DOCTYPE html PUBLIC "-//W3C//DTD XHTML 1.0 Transitional//EN"
    "http://www.w3.org/TR/xhtml1/DTD/xhtml1-transitional.dtd">
<html xmlns="http://www.w3.org/1999/xhtml" >
<head id="Head1" runat="server">
    <title>Show RegularExpressionValidator</title>
</head>
<body>
    <form id="form1" runat="server">
    <div>

    <asp:Label
        id="lblEmail"
        Text="Email Address:"
        AssociatedControlID="txtEmail"
        Runat="server" />
    <asp:TextBox
        id="txtEmail"
        Runat="server" />
    <asp:RegularExpressionValidator
        id="regEmail"
        ControlToValidate="txtEmail"
        Text="(Invalid email)"
        ValidationExpression="\w+([-+.']\w+)*@\w+([-.]\w+)*\.\w+([-.]\w+)*"
        Runat="server" />

    <br /><br />

    <asp:Button
        id="btnSubmit"
        Text="Submit"
        Runat="server" />

    </div>
    </form>
</body>
</html>
```

The regular expression is assigned to the `RegularExpressionValidator` control's `ValidationExpression` property. It looks like this:

```
\w+([-+.']\w+)*@\w+([-.]\w+)*\.\w+([-.]\w+)*
```

Regular expressions are not fun to read. This pattern matches a simple email address. The \w expression represents any non-whitespace character. Therefore, roughly, this regular expression matches an email address that contains non-whitespace characters, followed by an @ sign, followed by non-whitespace characters, followed by a period, followed by more non-whitespace characters.

> **NOTE**
>
> There are huge collections of regular expression patterns living on the Internet. The easiest way to find a good regular expression for a pattern is to simply Google it.

Just like the other validation controls, the RegularExpressionValidator doesn't validate a form field unless the form field contains a value. To make a form field required, you must associate a RequiredFieldValidator control with the form field.

> **VISUAL WEB DEVELOPER NOTE**
>
> If you open the property sheet for a RegularExpressionValidator control in Design view and select the ValidationExpression property, you can view a number of canned regular expressions. Visual Web Developer includes regular expressions for patterns such as email addresses, phone numbers, and Social Security numbers.

Using the CustomValidator **Control**

If none of the other validation controls perform the type of validation that you need, you can always use the CustomValidator control. You can associate a custom validation function with the CustomValidator control.

The CustomValidator control has three important properties:

- ControlToValidate—The ID of the form field being validated.
- Text—The error message displayed when validation fails.
- ClientValidationFunction—The name of a client-side function used to perform client-side validation.

The CustomValidator also supports one event:

- ServerValidate—This event is raised when the CustomValidator performs validation.

You associate your custom validation function with the CustomValidator control by handling the ServerValidate event.

For example, imagine that you want to validate the length of a string entered into a form field. You want to ensure that a user does not enter more than 10 characters into a multi-line TextBox control. The page in Listing 3.14 contains an event handler for a CustomValidator control's ServerValidate event, which checks the string's length.

LISTING 3.14   ShowCustomValidator.aspx

```
<%@ Page Language="VB" %>
<!DOCTYPE html PUBLIC "-//W3C//DTD XHTML 1.0 Transitional//EN"
    "http://www.w3.org/TR/xhtml1/DTD/xhtml1-transitional.dtd">
<script runat="server">

    Protected Sub valComments_ServerValidate(ByVal source As Object, ByVal args
➥As System.Web.UI.WebControls.ServerValidateEventArgs)
        If args.Value.Length > 10 Then
            args.IsValid = False
        Else
            args.IsValid = True
        End If
    End Sub
</script>
<html xmlns="http://www.w3.org/1999/xhtml" >
<head id="Head1" runat="server">
    <title>Show CustomValidator</title>
</head>
<body>
    <form id="form1" runat="server">
    <div>

    <asp:Label
        id="lblComments"
        Text="Comments:"
        AssociatedControlID="txtComments"
        Runat="server" />
    <br />
    <asp:TextBox
        id="txtComments"
        TextMode="MultiLine"
        Columns="30"
        Rows="5"
        Runat="server" />
    <asp:CustomValidator
        id="valComments"
        ControlToValidate="txtComments"
        Text="(Comments must be less than 10 characters)"
        OnServerValidate="valComments_ServerValidate"
        Runat="server" />
```

LISTING 3.14   Continued

```
    <br /><br />

    <asp:Button
        id="btnSubmit"
        Text="Submit"
        Runat="server" />

    </div>
    </form>
</body>
</html>
```

The second parameter passed to the ServerValidate event handler is an instance of the ServerValidateEventArgs class. This class has two properties:

- Value—Represents the value of the form field being validated.

- IsValid—Represents whether validation fails or succeeds.

- ValidateEmptyText—Represents whether validation is performed when the form field being validated does not contain a value.

In Listing 3.14, if the string represented by the Value property is longer than 10 characters, then the value False is assigned to the IsValid property and validation fails. Otherwise, the value True is assigned to the IsValid property and the input field passes the validation check (see Figure 3.12).

The ServerValidate event handler in Listing 3.14 is a server-side function. Therefore, validation does not occur until the page is posted back to the web server. If you want to perform validation on both the client (browser) and server, then you need to supply a client-side validation function.

> **WARNING**
>
> If you don't associate a client validation function with a CustomValidator control, then the CustomValidator doesn't render an error message until you post the page back to the server. Because the other validation controls prevent a page from being posted if the page contains any validation errors, you won't see the error message rendered by the CustomValidator control until you pass every other validation check in a page.

The page in Listing 3.15 illustrates how you can associate a client-side validation function with the CustomValidator control. This page also checks the length of the string entered into a TextBox control. However, it checks the length on both the browser and server.

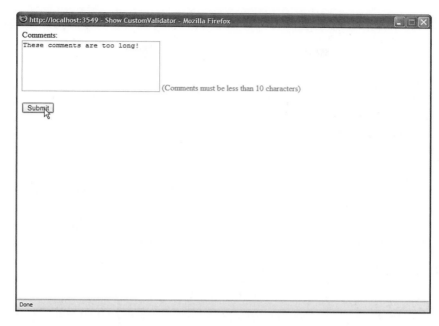

FIGURE 3.12   Validating field length with the CustomValidator control.

LISTING 3.15   ShowCustomValidatorJS.aspx

```
<%@ Page Language="VB" %>
<!DOCTYPE html PUBLIC "-//W3C//DTD XHTML 1.0 Transitional//EN"
    "http://www.w3.org/TR/xhtml1/DTD/xhtml1-transitional.dtd">
<script runat="server">

    Protected Sub valComments_ServerValidate(ByVal source As Object,
➥ByVal args As ServerValidateEventArgs)
        If args.Value.Length > 10 Then
            args.IsValid = False
        Else
            args.IsValid = True
        End If
    End Sub
</script>
<html xmlns="http://www.w3.org/1999/xhtml" >
<head id="Head1" runat="server">
    <script type="text/javascript">

    function valComments_ClientValidate(source, args)
    {
        if (args.Value.length > 10)
```

LISTING 3.15 Continued

```
                args.IsValid = false;
        else
                args.IsValid = true;
    }

    </script>
    <title>Show CustomValidator with JavaScript</title>
</head>
<body>
    <form id="form1" runat="server">
    <div>

    <asp:Label
        id="lblComments"
        Text="Comments:"
        AssociatedControlID="txtComments"
        Runat="server" />
    <br />
    <asp:TextBox
        id="txtComments"
        TextMode="MultiLine"
        Columns="30"
        Rows="5"
        Runat="server" />
    <asp:CustomValidator
        id="valComments"
        ControlToValidate="txtComments"
        Text="(Comments must be less than 10 characters)"
        OnServerValidate="valComments_ServerValidate"
        ClientValidationFunction="valComments_ClientValidate"
        Runat="server" />

    <br /><br />

    <asp:Button
        id="btnSubmit"
        Text="Submit"
        Runat="server" />

    </div>
    </form>
</body>
</html>
```

Notice that the `CustomValidator` control in Listing 3.15 includes a `ClientValidationFunction` property. This property contains the name of a JavaScript function defined in the page's <head> tag.

The JavaScript validation function accepts the same two parameters as the server-side validation function. The first parameter represents the `CustomValidator` control, and the second parameter represents an object that includes both a `Value` and an `IsValid` property. The client-side function is nearly identical to the server-side function (with the important difference that it is written in JavaScript).

Unlike the `RangeValidator`, `CompareValidator`, and `RegularExpressionValidator` controls, you can validate a form field with the `CustomValidator` control even when the form field is left blank. The `CustomValidator` control includes a property named `ValidateEmptyText` property. You can use this property to cause the `CustomValidator` control to validate a form field even when the user hasn't entered a value into the form field. For example, the page in Listing 3.16 contains a `TextBox` that requires a product code that contains exactly four characters.

LISTING 3.16   ShowValidateEmptyText.aspx

```
<%@ Page Language="VB" %>
<!DOCTYPE html PUBLIC "-//W3C//DTD XHTML 1.0 Transitional//EN"
 "http://www.w3.org/TR/xhtml1/DTD/xhtml1-transitional.dtd">
<script runat="server">

    Sub valProductCode_ServerValidate(ByVal source As Object,
➥ByVal args As ServerValidateEventArgs)
        If args.Value.Length = 4 Then
            args.IsValid = True
        Else
            args.IsValid = False
        End If
    End Sub
</script>
<html xmlns="http://www.w3.org/1999/xhtml" >
<head id="Head1" runat="server">
    <title>Show Validate Empty Text</title>
</head>
<body>
    <form id="form1" runat="server">
    <div>

    <asp:Label
        id="lblProductCode"
        Text="Product Code:"
```

LISTING 3.16   Continued

```
              AssociatedControlID="txtProductCode"
              Runat="server" />
      <br />
      <asp:TextBox
              id="txtProductCode"
              Runat="server" />
      <asp:CustomValidator
              id="valProductCode"
              ControlToValidate="txtProductCode"
              Text="(Invalid product code)"
              ValidateEmptyText="true"
              OnServerValidate="valProductCode_ServerValidate"
              Runat="server" />

      <br /><br />

      <asp:Button
              id="btnSubmit"
              Text="Submit"
              Runat="server" />

      </div>
      </form>
</body>
</html>
```

Notice that the CustomValidator control in Listing 3.16 includes a ValidateEmptyText property which has the value True. If the ValidateEmptyText property was not included, and you submitted the form without entering any data, then no validation error would be displayed.

Finally, unlike the other validation controls, you are not required to associate the CustomValidator control with any form field. In other words, you don't need to include a ControlToValidate property.

For example, the page in Listing 3.17 contains a timed test. If you don't answer the question within five seconds, then the CustomValidator control displays a validation error message (see Figure 3.13).

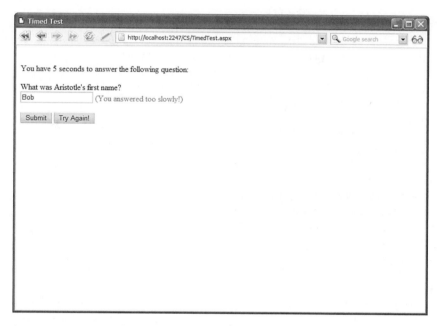

FIGURE 3.13   Performing validation against no particular field.

LISTING 3.17   TimedTest.aspx

```
<%@ Page Language="VB" %>
<!DOCTYPE html PUBLIC "-//W3C//DTD XHTML 1.0 Transitional//EN"
 "http://www.w3.org/TR/xhtml1/DTD/xhtml1-transitional.dtd">
<script runat="server">

    Sub Page_Load()
        If Not Page.IsPostBack Then
            ResetStartTime()
        End If
    End Sub


    Protected Sub btnAgain_Click(ByVal sender As Object, ByVal e
➥As System.EventArgs)
        ResetStartTime()
    End Sub


    Sub ResetStartTime()
        Session("StartTime") = DateTime.Now
    End Sub
```

LISTING 3.17   Continued

```
    Protected Sub valAnswer_ServerValidate(ByVal source As Object, ByVal args
➥As System.Web.UI.WebControls.ServerValidateEventArgs)
        Dim startTime As DateTime = CType(Session("StartTime"), DateTime)
        If startTime.AddSeconds(5) > DateTime.Now Then
            args.IsValid = True
        Else
            args.IsValid = False
        End If
    End Sub
</script>
<html xmlns="http://www.w3.org/1999/xhtml" >
<head id="Head1" runat="server">
    <title>Timed Test</title>
</head>
<body>
    <form id="form1" runat="server">
    <div>

    <p>
    You have 5 seconds to answer the following question:
    </p>

    <asp:Label
        id="lblQuestion"
        Text="What was Aristotle's first name?"
        AssociatedControlID="txtAnswer"
        Runat="server" />
    <br />
    <asp:TextBox
        id="txtAnswer"
        Runat="server" />
    <asp:CustomValidator
        id="valAnswer"
        Text="(You answered too slowly!)"
        OnServerValidate="valAnswer_ServerValidate"
        Runat="server"  />

    <br /><br />

    <asp:Button
        id="btnSubmit"
        Text="Submit"
        Runat="server" />
```

LISTING 3.17   Continued

```
<asp:Button
    id="btnAgain"
    Text="Try Again!"
    CausesValidation="false"
    OnClick="btnAgain_Click"
    Runat="server" />

</div>
</form>
</body>
</html>
```

Using the ValidationSummary **Control**

The ValidationSummary control enables you to display a list of all the validation errors in a page in one location. This control is particularly useful when working with large forms. If a user enters the wrong value for a form field located toward the end of the page, then the user might never see the error message. If you use the ValidationSummary control, however, you can always display a list of errors at the top of the form.

You might have noticed that each of the validation controls includes an ErrorMessage property. We have not been using the ErrorMessage property to represent the validation error message. Instead, we have used the Text property.

The distinction between the ErrorMessage and Text property is that any message that you assign to the ErrorMessage property appears in the ValidationSummary control, and any message that you assign to the Text property appears in the body of the page. Normally, you want to keep the error message for the Text property short (for example, "Required!"). The message assigned to the ErrorMessage property, on the other hand, should identify the form field that has the error (for example, "First name is required!").

> **NOTE**
>
> If you don't assign a value to the Text property, then the value of the ErrorMessage property is displayed in both the ValidationSummary control and the body of the page.

The page in Listing 3.18 illustrates how you can use the ValidationSummary control to display a summary of error messages (see Figure 3.14).

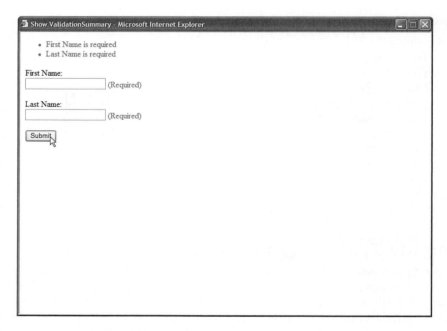

FIGURE 3.14   Displaying a validation summary.

LISTING 3.18   ShowValidationSummary.aspx

```
<%@ Page Language="VB" %>
<!DOCTYPE html PUBLIC "-//W3C//DTD XHTML 1.0 Transitional//EN"
    "http://www.w3.org/TR/xhtml1/DTD/xhtml1-transitional.dtd">
<html xmlns="http://www.w3.org/1999/xhtml" >
<head id="Head1" runat="server">
    <title>Show ValidationSummary</title>
</head>
<body>
    <form id="form1" runat="server">
    <div>

    <asp:ValidationSummary
        id="ValidationSummary1"
        Runat="server" />

    <asp:Label
        id="lblFirstName"
        Text="First Name:"
        AssociatedControlID="txtFirstName"
        Runat="server" />
    <br />
```

LISTING 3.18   Continued

```
<asp:TextBox
    id="txtFirstName"
    Runat="server" />
<asp:RequiredFieldValidator
    id="reqFirstName"
    Text="(Required)"
    ErrorMessage="First Name is required"
    ControlToValidate="txtFirstName"
    Runat="server" />

<br /><br />

<asp:Label
    id="lblLastName"
    Text="Last Name:"
    AssociatedControlID="txtLastName"
    Runat="server" />
<br />
<asp:TextBox
    id="txtLastName"
    Runat="server" />
<asp:RequiredFieldValidator
    id="reqLastName"
    Text="(Required)"
    ErrorMessage="Last Name is required"
    ControlToValidate="txtLastName"
    Runat="server" />

<br /><br />

<asp:Button
    id="btnSubmit"
    Text="Submit"
    Runat="server" />

</div>
</form>
</body>
</html>
```

If you submit the form in Listing 3.18 without entering a value for the first and last name, then validation error messages appear in both the body of the page and in the ValidationSummary control.

The ValidationSummary control supports the following properties:

- DisplayMode—Enables you to specify how the error messages are formatted. Possible values are BulletList, List, and SingleParagraph.

- HeaderText—Enables you to display header text above the validation summary.

- ShowMessageBox—Enables you to display a popup alert box.

- ShowSummary—Enables you to hide the validation summary in the page.

If you set the ShowMessageBox property to the value True and the ShowSummary property to the value False, then you can display the validation summary only within a popup alert box. For example, the page in Listing 3.19 displays a validation summary in an alert box (see Figure 3.15).

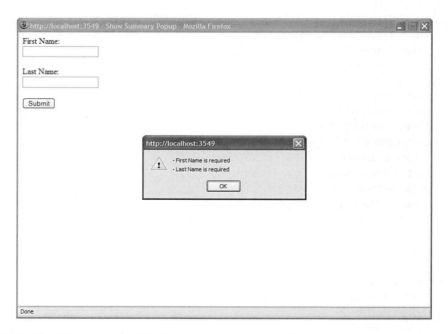

FIGURE 3.15   Displaying a validation summary in an alert box.

LISTING 3.19   ShowSummaryPopup.aspx

```
<%@ Page Language="VB" %>
<!DOCTYPE html PUBLIC "-//W3C//DTD XHTML 1.0 Transitional//EN"
    "http://www.w3.org/TR/xhtml1/DTD/xhtml1-transitional.dtd">
<html xmlns="http://www.w3.org/1999/xhtml" >
<head id="Head1" runat="server">
    <title>Show Summary Popup</title>
```

LISTING 3.19   Continued

```
</head>
<body>
    <form id="form1" runat="server">
    <div>

    <asp:ValidationSummary
        id="ValidationSummary1"
        ShowMessageBox="true"
        ShowSummary="false"
        Runat="server" />

    <asp:Label
        id="lblFirstName"
        Text="First Name:"
        AssociatedControlID="txtFirstName"
        Runat="server" />
    <br />
    <asp:TextBox
        id="txtFirstName"
        Runat="server" />
    <asp:RequiredFieldValidator
        id="reqFirstName"
        ErrorMessage="First Name is required"
        ControlToValidate="txtFirstName"
        Display="None"
        Runat="server" />

    <br /><br />

    <asp:Label
        id="lblLastName"
        Text="Last Name:"
        AssociatedControlID="txtLastName"
        Runat="server" />
    <br />
    <asp:TextBox
        id="txtLastName"
        Runat="server" />
    <asp:RequiredFieldValidator
        id="reqLastName"
        ErrorMessage="Last Name is required"
        ControlToValidate="txtLastName"
        Display="None"
```

LISTING 3.19   Continued

```
            Runat="server" />

    <br /><br />

    <asp:Button
        id="btnSubmit"
        Text="Submit"
        Runat="server" />

    </div>
    </form>
</body>
</html>
```

Notice that both of the RequiredFieldValidator controls have their Display properties set to the value None. The validation error messages appear only in the alert box.

Creating Custom Validation Controls

In this final section, you learn how to create custom validation controls. We create two custom controls. First we create a LengthValidator control that enables you to validate the length of an entry in a form field. Next, we create an AjaxValidator control. The AjaxValidator control performs validation on the client by passing information back to a custom function defined on the server.

You create a new validation control by deriving a new control from the BaseValidator class. As its name implies, the BaseValidator class is the base class for all the validation controls, including the RequiredFieldValidator and RegularExpressionValidator controls.

The BaseValidator class is a MustInherit (abstract) class, which requires you to implement a single method:

- EvaluateIsValid—Returns true when the form field being validated is valid.

The BaseValidator class also includes several other methods that you can override or otherwise use. The most useful of these methods is the following:

- GetControlValidationValue—Enables you to retrieve the value of the control being validated.

When you create a custom validation control, you override the EvaluateIsValid() method and, within the EvaluateIsValid() method, you call GetControlValidationValue to get the value of the form field being validated.

Creating a `LengthValidator` Control

To illustrate the general technique for creating a custom validation control, in this section we will create an extremely simple one. It's a `LengthValidator` control, which enables you to validate the length of a form field.

The code for the `LengthValidator` control is contained in Listing 3.20.

LISTING 3.20   `LengthValidator.vb`

```
Imports System
Imports System.Web.UI
Imports System.Web.UI.WebControls

Namespace myControls

    ''' <summary>
    ''' Validates the length of an input field
    ''' </summary>
    Public Class LengthValidator
        Inherits BaseValidator

        Dim _maximumLength As Integer = 0

        Public Property MaximumLength() As Integer
            Get
                Return _maximumLength
            End Get
            Set(ByVal Value As Integer)
                _maximumLength = value
            End Set
        End Property

        Protected Overrides Function EvaluateIsValid() As Boolean
            Dim value As String =
➥Me.GetControlValidationValue(Me.ControlToValidate)
            If value.Length > _maximumLength Then
                Return False
            Else
                Return True
            End If
        End Function
    End Class
End Namespace
```

Listing 3.20 contains a class that inherits from the `BaseValidator` class. The new class overrides the `EvaluateIsValid` method. The value from the control being validated is retrieved with the help of the `GetControlValidationValue()` method, and the length of the value is compared against the `MaximumLength` property.

> **NOTE**
>
> To use the class in Listing 3.20, you need to add the class to your application's `App_Code` folder. Any class added to this special folder is automatically compiled by the ASP.NET Framework.

The page in Listing 3.21 uses the `LengthValidator` control to validate the length of a comment input field (see Figure 3.16).

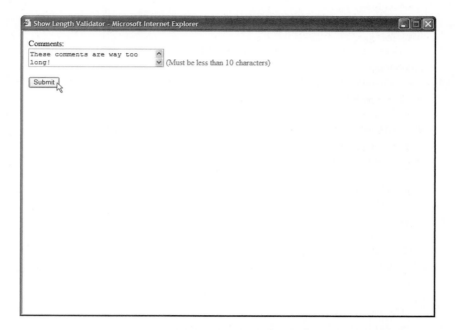

FIGURE 3.16   Validating the length of a field with the `LengthValidator` control.

LISTING 3.21   ShowLengthValidator.aspx

```
<%@ Page Language="VB" %>
<%@ Register TagPrefix="custom" Namespace="myControls" %>
<!DOCTYPE html PUBLIC "-//W3C//DTD XHTML 1.0 Transitional//EN"
    "http://www.w3.org/TR/xhtml1/DTD/xhtml1-transitional.dtd">
<html xmlns="http://www.w3.org/1999/xhtml" >
<head id="Head1" runat="server">
    <title>Show Length Validator</title>
</head>
```

LISTING 3.21   Continued

```
<body>
    <form id="form1" runat="server">
    <div>

    <asp:Label
        id="lblComments"
        Text="Comments:"
        AssociatedControlID="txtComments"
        Runat="server" />
    <br />
    <asp:TextBox
        id="txtComments"
        TextMode="MultiLine"
        Columns="30"
        Rows="2"
        Runat="server" />
    <custom:LengthValidator
        id="valComments"
        ControlToValidate="txtComments"
        Text="(Must be less than 10 characters)"
        MaximumLength="10"
        Runat="server" />

    <br /><br />

    <asp:Button
        id="btnSubmit"
        Text="Submit"
        Runat="server" />

    </div>
    </form>
</body>
</html>
```

Notice that the LengthValidator is registered at the top of the page with the
<%@ Register %> directive. If you need to use the control in multiple pages in your
application, then you can alternatively register the control in the <pages> section of your
application's web configuration file.

Creating an AjaxValidator Control

In this section, we are going to create an extremely useful control named the
AjaxValidator control. Like the CustomValidator control, the AjaxValidator control

enables you to create a custom server-side validation function. Unlike the CustomValidator control, however, the AjaxValidator control enables you to call the custom validation function from the browser.

The AjaxValidator control uses AJAX (Asynchronous JavaScript and XML) to call the server-side validation function from the client. The advantage of using AJAX is that no postback to the server is apparent to the user.

For example, imagine that you are creating a website registration form and you need to validate a User Name field. You want to make sure that the User Name entered does not already exist in the database. The AjaxValidator enables you to call a server-side valida-tion function from the client to check whether the User Name is unique in the database.

The code for the AjaxValidator control is contained in Listing 3.22.

LISTING 3.22   AjaxValidator.vb

```
Imports System
Imports System.Web
Imports System.Web.UI
Imports System.Web.UI.WebControls


Namespace myControls

    ''' <summary>
    ''' Enables you to perform custom validation on both the client and server
    ''' </summary>
    Public Class AjaxValidator
        Inherits BaseValidator
        Implements ICallbackEventHandler

        Public Event ServerValidate As ServerValidateEventHandler

        Dim _controlToValidateValue As String

        Protected Overrides Sub OnPreRender(ByVal e As EventArgs)
            Dim eventRef As String = Page.ClientScript.GetCallbackEventReference(
➥Me, "", "", "")

            ' Register include file
            Dim includeScript As String =
➥Page.ResolveClientUrl("~/ClientScripts/AjaxValidator.js")
            Page.ClientScript.RegisterClientScriptInclude("AjaxValidator",
➥includeScript)

            ' Register startup script
```

LISTING 3.22   Continued

```
            Dim startupScript As String =
➥String.Format("document.getElementById('{0}').evaluationfunction =
➥'AjaxValidatorEvaluateIsValid';", Me.ClientID)
            Page.ClientScript.RegisterStartupScript(Me.GetType(),
➥"AjaxValidator", startupScript, True)

            MyBase.OnPreRender(e)
        End Sub

        ''' <summary>
        ''' Only do the AJAX call on browsers that support it
        ''' </summary>
        Protected Overrides Function DetermineRenderUplevel() As Boolean
            Return Context.Request.Browser.SupportsCallback
        End Function

        ''' <summary>
        ''' Server method called by client AJAX call
        ''' </summary>
        Public Function GetCallbackResult() As String
➥Implements ICallbackEventHandler.GetCallbackResult
            Return ExecuteValidationFunction(_controlToValidateValue).ToString()
        End Function

        ''' <summary>
        ''' Return callback result to client
        ''' </summary>
        Public Sub RaiseCallbackEvent(ByVal eventArgument As String)
➥Implements ICallbackEventHandler.RaiseCallbackEvent
            _controlToValidateValue = eventArgument
        End Sub

        ''' <summary>
        ''' Server-side method for validation
        ''' </summary>
        Protected Overrides Function EvaluateIsValid() As Boolean
            Dim controlToValidateValue As String =
➥Me.GetControlValidationValue(Me.ControlToValidate)
            Return ExecuteValidationFunction(controlToValidateValue)
        End Function

        ''' <summary>
        ''' Performs the validation for both server and client
        ''' </summary>
```

LISTING 3.22   Continued

```
        Private Function ExecuteValidationFunction(ByVal controlToValidateValue
➡As String) As Boolean
            Dim args As New ServerValidateEventArgs(controlToValidateValue,
➡Me.IsValid)
            RaiseEvent ServerValidate(Me, args)
            Return args.IsValid
        End Function

    End Class

End Namespace
```

The control in Listing 3.22 inherits from the `BaseValidator` class. It also implements the `ICallbackEventHandler` interface. The `ICallbackEventHandler` interface defines two methods that are called on the server when an AJAX request is made from the client.

In the `OnPreRender()` method, a JavaScript include file and startup script are registered. The JavaScript include file contains the client-side functions that are called when the `AjaxValidator` validates a form field on the client. The startup script associates the client-side `AjaxValidatorEvaluateIsValid()` function with the `AjaxValidator` control. The client-side validation framework automatically calls this JavaScript function when performing validation.

The JavaScript functions used by the `AjaxValidator` control are contained in Listing 3.23.

LISTING 3.23   `AjaxValidator.js`

```javascript
// Performs AJAX call back to server
function AjaxValidatorEvaluateIsValid(val)
{
    var value = ValidatorGetValue(val.controltovalidate);
    WebForm_DoCallback(val.id, value, AjaxValidatorResult, val,
AjaxValidatorError, true);
    return true;
}


// Called when result is returned from server
function AjaxValidatorResult(returnValue, context)
{
    if (returnValue == 'True')
        context.isvalid = true;
    else
        context.isvalid = false;
    ValidatorUpdateDisplay(context);
}
```

LISTING 3.23   Continued

```
// If there is an error, show it
function AjaxValidatorError(message)
{
    alert('Error: ' + message);
}
```

The `AjaxValidatorEvaluateIsValid()` JavaScript method initiates an AJAX call by calling the `WebForm_DoCallback()` method. This method calls the server-side validation function associated with the `AjaxValidator` control. When the AJAX call completes, the `AjaxValidatorResult()` method is called. This method updates the display of the validation control on the client.

The page in Listing 3.24 illustrates how you can use the `AjaxValidator` control. This page handles the `AjaxValidator` control's `ServerValidate` event to associate a custom validation function with the control.

The page in Listing 3.24 contains a form that includes fields for entering a username and favorite color. When you submit the form, the values of these fields are inserted into a database table named Users.

In Listing 3.24, the validation function checks whether a username already exists in the database. If you enter a username that already exists, a validation error message is displayed. The message is displayed in the browser before you submit the form back to the server (see Figure 3.17).

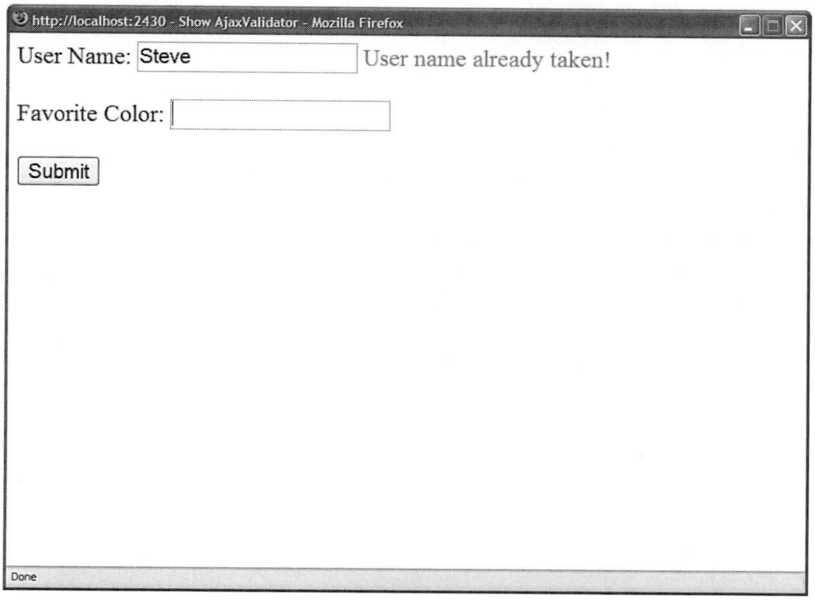

FIGURE 3.17   Using the `AjaxValidator` to check whether a username is unique.

It is important to realize that you can associate any server-side validation function with the AjaxValidator. You can perform a database lookup, call a web service, or perform a complex mathematical function. Whatever function you define on the server is automatically called on the client.

LISTING 3.24   ShowAjaxValidator.aspx

```
<%@ Page Language="VB" %>
<%@ Register TagPrefix="custom" Namespace="myControls" %>
<%@ Import Namespace="System.Data.SqlClient" %>
<%@ Import Namespace="System.Web.Configuration" %>
<!DOCTYPE html PUBLIC "-//W3C//DTD XHTML 1.0 Transitional//EN"
 "http://www.w3.org/TR/xhtml1/DTD/xhtml1-transitional.dtd">
<script runat="server">

    ''' <summary>
    ''' Validation function that is called on both the client and server
    ''' </summary>
    Protected Sub AjaxValidator1_ServerValidate(ByVal source As Object,
➥ByVal args As ServerValidateEventArgs)
        If UserNameExists(args.Value) Then
            args.IsValid = False
        Else
            args.IsValid = True
        End If
    End Sub


    ''' <summary>
    ''' Returns true when user name already exists
    ''' in Users database table
    ''' </summary>
    Private Function UserNameExists(ByVal userName As String) As Boolean
        Dim conString As String =
➥WebConfigurationManager.ConnectionStrings("UsersDB").ConnectionString
        Dim con As New SqlConnection(conString)
        Dim cmd As New SqlCommand("SELECT COUNT(*) FROM Users
➥WHERE UserName=@UserName", con)
        cmd.Parameters.AddWithValue("@UserName", userName)
        Dim result As Boolean = False
        Using con
            con.Open()
            Dim count As Integer = CType(cmd.ExecuteScalar(), Integer)
            If count > 0 Then
                result = True
            End If
        End Using
```

LISTING 3.24   Continued

```
            Return result
        End Function


        ''' <summary>
        ''' Insert new user name to Users database table
        ''' </summary>
        Protected Sub btnSubmit_Click(ByVal sender As Object, ByVal e As EventArgs)
            Dim conString As String =
➡WebConfigurationManager.ConnectionStrings("UsersDB").ConnectionString
            Dim con As New SqlConnection(conString)
            Dim cmd As New SqlCommand("INSERT Users (UserName,FavoriteColor)
➡VALUES (@UserName,@FavoriteColor)", con)
            cmd.Parameters.AddWithValue("@UserName", txtUserName.Text)
            cmd.Parameters.AddWithValue("@FavoriteColor", txtFavoriteColor.Text)
            Using con
                con.Open()
                cmd.ExecuteNonQuery()
            End Using
            txtUserName.Text = String.Empty
            txtFavoriteColor.Text = String.Empty
        End Sub
    </script>
    <html xmlns="http://www.w3.org/1999/xhtml" >
    <head id="Head1" runat="server">
        <title>Show AjaxValidator</title>
    </head>
    <body>
        <form id="form1" runat="server">
        <div>

        <asp:Label
            id="lblUserName"
            Text="User Name:"
            AssociatedControlID="txtUserName"
            Runat="server" />
        <asp:TextBox
            id="txtUserName"
            Runat="server" />
        <custom:AjaxValidator
            id="AjaxValidator1"
            ControlToValidate="txtUserName"
            Text="User name already taken!"
            OnServerValidate="AjaxValidator1_ServerValidate"
```

LISTING 3.24   Continued

```
        Runat="server" />

    <br /><br />
    <asp:Label
        id="lblFavoriteColor"
        Text="Favorite Color:"
        AssociatedControlID="txtFavoriteColor"
        Runat="server" />
    <asp:TextBox
        id="txtFavoriteColor"
        Runat="server" />

    <br /><br />
    <asp:Button
        id="btnSubmit"
        Text="Submit"
        Runat="server" OnClick="btnSubmit_Click" />

    </div>
    </form>
</body>
</html>
```

Summary

In this chapter, you learned how to perform form validation with the ASP.NET 2.0 Framework. First, you were provided with an overview of all the standard validation controls. You learned how to highlight validation error messages and how to take advantage of validation groups to simulate multiple forms in a single page.

In the final section of this chapter, you learned how to create custom validation controls by deriving new controls from the BaseValidator control. We created both a custom LengthValidator and AjaxValidator control.

CHAPTER 4

Using the Rich Controls

In previous chapters we examined the ASP.NET controls that you will use in just about any application. In this chapter we examine a more specialized set of controls known collectively as the *rich controls*.

In the first section, you learn how to accept file uploads at your website. For example, you learn how to enable users to upload images, Microsoft Word documents, or Microsoft Excel spreadsheets.

Next, you learn how to work with the Calendar control. You can use the Calendar control as a date picker. You can also use the Calendar control to display upcoming events (such as a meeting schedule).

In this chapter, we also discuss the AdRotator control. This control enables you to display banner advertisements randomly on your website. The control enables you to store a list of advertisements in an XML file or a database table.

Next, you will learn about the MultiView control. This control enables you to hide and display areas of content on a page. You learn how to use this control to divide a page into different tabs.

Finally, you will learn about the Wizard control, which enables you to display multi-step forms. This control is useful when you need to divide a long form into multiple sub-forms.

Accepting File Uploads

The FileUpload control enables users to upload files to your web application. After the file is uploaded, you can store the file anywhere you please. Normally, you store the file either on the file system or in a database. This section explores both options.

The FileUpload control supports the following properties (this is not a complete list):

- Enabled—Enables you to disable the FileUpload control.
- FileBytes—Enables you to get the uploaded file contents as a byte array.
- FileContent—Enables you to get the uploaded file contents as a stream.
- FileName—Enables you to get the name of the file uploaded.
- HasFile—Returns True when a file has been uploaded.
- PostedFile—Enables you to get the uploaded file wrapped in the HttpPostedFile object.

The FileUpload control also supports the following methods:

- Focus—Enables you to shift the form focus to the FileUpload control.
- SaveAs—Enables you to save the uploaded file to the file system.

The FileUpload control's PostedFile property enables you to retrieve the uploaded file wrapped in an HttpPostedFile object. This object exposes additional information about the uploaded file.

The HttpPostedFile class has the following properties (this is not a complete list):

- ContentLength—Enables you to get the size of the uploaded file in bytes.
- ContentType—Enables you to get the MIME type of the uploaded file.
- FileName—Enables you to get the name of the uploaded file.
- InputStream—Enables you to retrieve the uploaded file as a stream.

The HttpPostedFile class also supports the following method:

- SaveAs—Enables you to save the uploaded file to the file system.

Notice that there is some redundancy here. For example, you can get the name of the uploaded file by using either the FileUpload.FileName property or the HttpPostedFile.FileName property. You can save a file by using either the FileUpload.SaveAs() method or the HttpPostedFile.SaveAs() method.

> **NOTE**
>
> Adding a FileUpload control to a page automatically adds a enctype="multipart/form-data" attribute to the server-side <form> tag.

Saving Files to the File System

The page in Listing 4.1 illustrates how you can upload images to an application by using the FileUpload control.

LISTING 4.1   FileUploadFile.aspx

```
<%@ Page Language="VB" %>
<%@ Import Namespace="System.IO" %>
<!DOCTYPE html PUBLIC "-//W3C//DTD XHTML 1.0 Transitional//EN"
➥"http://www.w3.org/TR/xhtml1/DTD/xhtml1-transitional.dtd">
<script runat="server">

    Sub btnAdd_Click(ByVal sender As Object, ByVal e As EventArgs)
        If (upImage.HasFile) Then
            If (CheckFileType(upImage.FileName)) Then
                Dim filePath As String = "~/UploadImages/" & upImage.FileName
                upImage.SaveAs(MapPath(filePath))
            End If
        End If
    End Sub


    Function CheckFileType(ByVal fileName As String) As Boolean
        Dim ext As String = Path.GetExtension(fileName)
        Select Case ext.ToLower()
            Case ".gif"
                Return True
            Case ".png"
                Return True
            Case ".jpg"
                Return True
            Case ".jpeg"
                Return True
            Case Else
                Return False
        End Select
    End Function

    Sub Page_PreRender()
        Dim upFolder As String = MapPath("~/UploadImages/")
        Dim dir As New DirectoryInfo(upFolder)
        dlstImages.DataSource = dir.GetFiles()
        dlstImages.DataBind()
    End Sub
</script>
<html xmlns="http://www.w3.org/1999/xhtml" >
<head id="Head1" runat="server">
```

4

LISTING 4.1   Continued

```
    <title>FileUpload File</title>
</head>
<body>
    <form id="form1" runat="server">
    <div>

    <asp:Label
        id="lblImageFile"
        Text="Image File:"
        AssociatedControlID="upImage"
        Runat="server" />

    <asp:FileUpload
        id="upImage"
        Runat="server" />

    <br /><br />

    <asp:Button
        id="btnAdd"
        Text="Add Image"
        OnClick="btnAdd_Click"
        Runat="server" />

    <hr />

    <asp:DataList
        id="dlstImages"
        RepeatColumns="3"
        runat="server">
        <ItemTemplate>
        <asp:Image ID="Image1"
            ImageUrl='<%# Eval("Name", "~/UploadImages/{0}") %>'
            style="width:200px"
            Runat="server" />
        <br />
        <%# Eval("Name") %>
        </ItemTemplate>
    </asp:DataList>

    </div>
    </form>
</body>
</html>
```

Listing 4.1 includes both a `FileUpload` control and a `DataList` control. When you upload a file, the file is saved to a folder named `ImageUploads`. The `DataList` control automatically displays the contents of the `ImageUploads` folder. The result is an image gallery (see Figure 4.1).

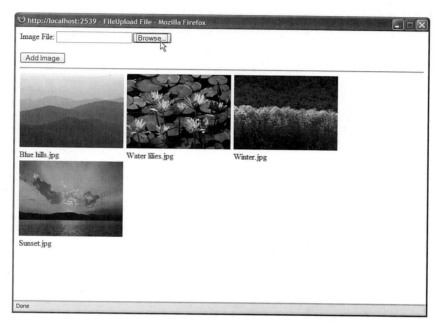

FIGURE 4.1   Displaying a photo gallery.

Notice that the page includes a method named `CheckFileType()`, which prevents users from uploading a file that does not have the `.gif`, `.jpeg`, `.jpg`, or `.png` extension. The method restricts the type of file that can be uploaded based on the file extension.

> **NOTE**
>
> The HTML 4.01 specifications define an `accept` attribute that you should be able to use to filter the files that can be uploaded. Unfortunately, no browser supports the `accept` attribute, so you must perform filtering on the server (or use some JavaScript to check the filename extension on the client).

To save a file to the file system, the Windows account associated with the ASP.NET page must have sufficient permissions to save the file. For Windows 2003 Servers, an ASP.NET page executes in the security context of the NETWORK SERVICE account. In the case of every other operating system, an ASP.NET page executes in the security context of the ASPNET account.

To enable the ASP.NET framework to save an uploaded file to a particular folder, you need to right-click the folder within Windows Explorer, select the Security tab, and provide either the NETWORK SERVICE or ASPNET account Write permissions for the folder (see Figure 4.2).

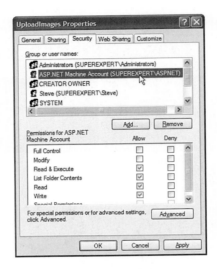

FIGURE 4.2   Adding Write permissions for the ASPNET account.

Saving Files to a Database

You also can use the FileUpload control to save files to a database table. Saving and retrieving files from a database can place more stress on your server. However, it does have certain advantages. First, you can avoid file system permissions issues. Second, saving files to a database enables you to more easily back up your information.

The page in Listing 4.2 enables you to save Microsoft Word documents to a database table (see Figure 4.3).

LISTING 4.2   FileUploadDatabase.aspx

```
<%@ Page Language="VB" %>
<%@ Import Namespace="System.IO" %>
<!DOCTYPE html PUBLIC "-//W3C//DTD XHTML 1.0 Transitional//EN"
➥"http://www.w3.org/TR/xhtml1/DTD/xhtml1-transitional.dtd">
<script runat="server">

    Sub btnAdd_Click(ByVal sender As Object, ByVal e As EventArgs)
        If upFile.HasFile Then
            If CheckFileType(upFile.FileName) Then
                srcFiles.Insert()
```

LISTING 4.2   Continued

```
                End If
            End If
        End Sub

        Function CheckFileType(ByVal fileName As String) As Boolean
            Return Path.GetExtension(fileName).ToLower() = ".doc"
        End Function

    </script>
    <html xmlns="http://www.w3.org/1999/xhtml" >
    <head id="Head1" runat="server">
        <style type="text/css">
            .fileList li
            {
                margin-bottom:5px;
            }
        </style>
        <title>FileUpload Database</title>
    </head>
    <body>
        <form id="form1" runat="server">
        <div>

        <asp:Label
            id="lblFile"
            Text="Word Document:"
            AssociatedControlID="upFile"
            Runat="server" />

        <asp:FileUpload
            id="upFile"
            Runat="server" />

        <asp:Button
            id="btnAdd"
            Text="Add Document"
            OnClick="btnAdd_Click"
            Runat="server" />

        <hr />

        <asp:Repeater
            id="rptFiles"
```

LISTING 4.2   Continued

```
        DataSourceID="srcFiles"
        Runat="server">
        <HeaderTemplate>
        <ul class="fileList">
        </HeaderTemplate>
        <ItemTemplate>
        <li>
        <asp:HyperLink
            id="lnkFile"
            Text='<%#Eval("FileName")%>'
            NavigateUrl='<%#Eval("Id", "~/FileHandler.ashx?id={0}")%>'
            Runat="server" />
        </li>
        </ItemTemplate>
        <FooterTemplate>
        </ul>
        </FooterTemplate>
    </asp:Repeater>

    <asp:SqlDataSource
        id="srcFiles"
        ConnectionString="Server=.\SQLExpress;Integrated Security=True;
            AttachDbFileName=¦DataDirectory¦FilesDB.mdf;User Instance=True"
        SelectCommand="SELECT Id,FileName FROM Files"
        InsertCommand="INSERT Files (FileName,FileBytes) VALUES
(@FileName,@FileBytes)"
        Runat="server">
        <InsertParameters>
            <asp:ControlParameter Name="FileName"
ControlID="upFile" PropertyName="FileName" />
            <asp:ControlParameter Name="FileBytes"
ControlID="upFile" PropertyName="FileBytes" />
        </InsertParameters>
    </asp:SqlDataSource>

    </div>
    </form>
</body>
</html>
```

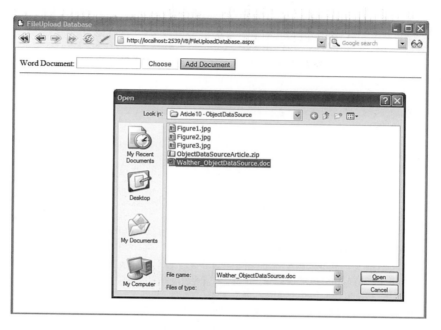

FIGURE 4.3 Uploading Microsoft Word documents.

When you submit the form in Listing 4.2, the `btnAdd_Click()` method executes. This method checks the file extension to verify that the file is a Microsoft Word document. Next, the `SqlDataSource` control's `Insert()` method is called to insert the values of the `FileUpload` control's `FileName` and `FileBytes` properties into a local SQL Express database table. The SQL Express database table, named Files, looks like this:

Column Name	Data Type
Id	Int (IDENTITY)
FileName	NVarchar(50)
FileBytes	Varbinary(max)

The page also displays a list of the current Microsoft Word documents in the database. You can click any file and view the contents of the file. Exactly what happens when you click a file is browser (and browser settings) dependent. With Microsoft Internet Explorer, for example, the document opens directly in the browser.

Clicking the name of a document links you to a page named `FileHandler.ashx`. The `FileHandler.ashx` file is a generic HTTP Handler file. Chapter 25 discusses HTTP Handlers in detail. An HTTP Handler enables you to execute code when someone makes a request for a file with a certain path.

The `FileHandler.ashx` file is contained in Listing 4.3.

LISTING 4.3   FileHandler.ashx

```vb
<%@ WebHandler Language="VB" Class="FileHandler" %>

Imports System
Imports System.Web
Imports System.Data
Imports System.Data.SqlClient

Public Class FileHandler
    Implements IHttpHandler

    Const conString As String = "Server=.\SQLExpress;Integrated Security=True;
➥AttachDbFileName=¦DataDirectory¦FilesDB.mdf;User Instance=True"

    Public Sub ProcessRequest(ByVal context As HttpContext)
➥Implements IHttpHandler.ProcessRequest
        context.Response.ContentType = "application/msword"

        Dim con As SqlConnection = New SqlConnection(conString)
        Dim cmd As SqlCommand = New SqlCommand("SELECT FileBytes
➥FROM Files WHERE Id=@Id", con)
        cmd.Parameters.AddWithValue("@Id", context.Request("Id"))
        Using con
            con.Open()
            Dim file() As Byte = CType(cmd.ExecuteScalar(), Byte())
            context.Response.BinaryWrite(file)
        End Using
    End Sub

    Public ReadOnly Property IsReusable() As Boolean
➥Implements IHttpHandler.IsReusable
        Get
            Return False
        End Get
    End Property

End Class
```

When the `FileHandler.aspx` page is requested, the `ProcessRequest()` method executes. This method grabs a query string item named `Id` and retrieves the matching record from the Files database table. The record contains the contents of a Microsoft Word document as a byte array. The byte array is sent to the browser with the `Response.BinaryWrite()` method.

Uploading Large Files

You must do extra work when uploading large files. You don't want to consume all your server's memory by placing the entire file in memory. When working with a large file, you need to work with the file in more manageable chunks.

First, you need to configure your application to handle large files. Two configuration settings have an effect on posting large files to the server: the httpRuntime maxRequestLength and httpRuntime requestLengthDiskThreshold settings.

The maxRequestLength setting places a limit on the largest form post that the server will accept. By default, you cannot post a form that contains more than 4MB of data—if you try, you'll get an exception. If you need to upload a file that contains more than four megabytes of data, then you need to change this setting.

The requestLengthDiskThreshold setting determines how a form post is buffered to the file system. In the previous version of ASP.NET (ASP.NET 1.1), uploading a large file could do horrible things to your server. The entire file was uploaded into the server memory. While a 10-megabyte video file was uploaded, for example, 10 megabytes of server memory was consumed.

The ASP.NET 2.0 Framework enables you to buffer large files onto the file system. When the size of the file passes the requestLengthDiskThreshold setting, the remainder of the file is buffered to the file system (in the Temporary ASP.NET Files folder).

By default, the ASP.NET framework is configured to buffer any post larger than 80KB to a file buffer. If you are not happy with this setting, then you can modify the requestLengthDiskThreshold to configure a new threshold. (The requestLengthDiskThreshold setting must be less than the maxRequestLength setting.)

The web configuration file in Listing 4.4 enables files up to 10MB to be posted. It also changes the buffering threshold to 100KB.

LISTING 4.4   Web.Config

```
<?xml version="1.0"?>
<configuration>
<system.web>
  <httpRuntime
      maxRequestLength="10240"
      requestLengthDiskThreshold="100" />
</system.web>
</configuration>
```

When working with large files, you must be careful about the way that you handle the file when storing or retrieving the file from a data store. For example, when saving or retrieving a file from a database table, you should never load the entire file into memory.

The page in Listing 4.5 demonstrates how you can save a large file to a database table efficiently.

LISTING 4.5   FileUploadLarge.aspx

```vb
<%@ Page Language="VB" %>
<%@ Import Namespace="System.IO" %>
<%@ Import Namespace="System.Data" %>
<%@ Import Namespace="System.Data.SqlClient" %>
<!DOCTYPE html PUBLIC "-//W3C//DTD XHTML 1.0 Transitional//EN"
➥"http://www.w3.org/TR/xhtml1/DTD/xhtml1-transitional.dtd">
<script runat="server">

    Const conString As String = "Server=.\SQLExpress;Integrated Security=True;
➥AttachDbFileName=¦DataDirectory¦FilesDB.mdf;User Instance=True"

    Sub btnAdd_Click(ByVal s As Object, ByVal e As EventArgs)
        If upFile.HasFile Then
            If CheckFileType(upFile.FileName) Then
                AddFile(upFile.FileName, upFile.FileContent)
                rptFiles.DataBind()
            End If
        End If
    End Sub

    Function CheckFileType(ByVal fileName As String) As Boolean
        Return Path.GetExtension(fileName).ToLower() = ".doc"
    End Function

    Sub AddFile(ByVal fileName As String, ByVal upload As Stream)
        Dim con As New SqlConnection(conString)

        Dim cmd As New SqlCommand("INSERT Files (FileName) Values (@FileName);
➥SELECT @Identity = SCOPE_IDENTITY()", con)

        cmd.Parameters.AddWithValue("@FileName", fileName)
        Dim idParm As SqlParameter = cmd.Parameters.Add("@Identity", SqlDbType.Int)
        idParm.Direction = ParameterDirection.Output

        Using con
            con.Open()
            cmd.ExecuteNonQuery()
            Dim newFileId As Integer = CType(idParm.Value, Integer)
            StoreFile(newFileId, upload, con)
        End Using
    End Sub

    Sub StoreFile(ByVal fileId As Integer, ByVal upload As Stream,
➥ByVal connection As SqlConnection)
```

LISTING 4.5   Continued

```
        Dim bufferLen As Integer = 8040
        Dim br As New BinaryReader(upload)
        Dim chunk As Byte() = br.ReadBytes(bufferLen)

        Dim cmd As New SqlCommand("UPDATE Files SET FileBytes=@Buffer
➥WHERE Id=@FileId", connection)
        cmd.Parameters.AddWithValue("@FileId", fileId)
        cmd.Parameters.Add("@Buffer", SqlDbType.VarBinary, bufferLen).Value = chunk
        cmd.ExecuteNonQuery()


        Dim cmdAppend As New SqlCommand("UPDATE Files
➥SET FileBytes .WRITE(@Buffer, NULL, 0) WHERE Id=@FileId", connection)
        cmdAppend.Parameters.AddWithValue("@FileId", fileId)
        cmdAppend.Parameters.Add("@Buffer", SqlDbType.VarBinary, bufferLen)
        chunk = br.ReadBytes(bufferLen)

        While chunk.Length > 0
            cmdAppend.Parameters("@Buffer").Value = chunk
            cmdAppend.ExecuteNonQuery()
            chunk = br.ReadBytes(bufferLen)
        End While

        br.Close()
    End Sub

</script>
<html xmlns="http://www.w3.org/1999/xhtml" >
<head id="Head1" runat="server">
    <title>FileUpload Large</title>
</head>
<body>
    <form id="form1" runat="server">
    <div>

    <asp:Label
        id="lblFile"
        Text="Word Document:"
        AssociatedControlID="upFile"
        Runat="server" />

    <asp:FileUpload
        id="upFile"
        Runat="server" />
```

4

LISTING 4.5   Continued

```
<asp:Button
    id="btnAdd"
    Text="Add Document"
    OnClick="btnAdd_Click"
    Runat="server" />

<hr />

<asp:Repeater
    id="rptFiles"
    DataSourceID="srcFiles"
    Runat="server">
    <HeaderTemplate>
    <ul class="fileList">
    </HeaderTemplate>
    <ItemTemplate>
    <li>
    <asp:HyperLink
        id="lnkFile"
        Text='<%#Eval("FileName")%>'
        NavigateUrl='<%#Eval("Id", "~/FileHandlerLarge.ashx?id={0}")%>'
        Runat="server" />
    </li>
    </ItemTemplate>
    <FooterTemplate>
    </ul>
    </FooterTemplate>
</asp:Repeater>

<asp:SqlDataSource
    id="srcFiles"
    ConnectionString="Server=.\SQLExpress;Integrated Security=True;
        AttachDbFileName=¦DataDirectory¦FilesDB.mdf;User Instance=True"
    SelectCommand="SELECT Id,FileName FROM Files"
    Runat="server" />

</div>
</form>
</body>
</html>
```

In Listing 4.5, the `AddFile()` method is called. This method adds a new row to the Files database table that contains the filename. Next, the `StoreFile()` method is called. This method adds the actual bytes of the uploaded file to the database. The file contents are divided into 8040-byte chunks. Notice that the SQL UPDATE statement includes a .WRITE clause that is used when the FileBytes database column is updated.

> **NOTE**
>
> Microsoft recommends that you set the buffer size to multiples of 8040 when using the .WRITE clause to update database data.

The page in Listing 4.5 never represents the entire uploaded file in memory. The file is yanked into memory from the file system in 8040-byte chunks and fed to SQL Server in chunks.

When you click a filename, the FileHandlerLarge.ashx HTTP Handler executes. This handler retrieves the selected file from the database and sends it to the browser. The handler is contained in Listing 4.6.

LISTING 4.6   FileHandlerLarge.ashx

```
<%@ WebHandler Language="VB" Class="FileHandlerLarge" %>

Imports System
Imports System.Web
Imports System.Data
imports System.Data.SqlClient

Public Class FileHandlerLarge
    Implements IHttpHandler

    Const conString As String = "Server=.\SQLExpress;Integrated Security=True;
➡AttachDbFileName=¦DataDirectory¦FilesDB.mdf;User Instance=True"

    Sub ProcessRequest(ByVal context As HttpContext)
➡Implements IHttpHandler.ProcessRequest
        context.Response.Buffer = False
        context.Response.ContentType = "application/msword"

        Dim con As New SqlConnection(conString)
        Dim cmd As New SqlCommand("SELECT FileBytes FROM Files WHERE Id=@Id", con)
        cmd.Parameters.AddWithValue("@Id", context.Request("Id"))
        Using con
            con.Open()
            Dim reader As SqlDataReader =
➡cmd.ExecuteReader(CommandBehavior.SequentialAccess)
            If reader.Read() Then
                Dim bufferSize As Integer = 8040
                Dim chunk(bufferSize - 1) As Byte
```

LISTING 4.6   Continued

```
            Dim retCount As Long
            Dim startIndex As Long = 0

            retCount = reader.GetBytes(0, startIndex, chunk, 0, bufferSize)

            While retCount = bufferSize
                context.Response.BinaryWrite(chunk)

                startIndex += bufferSize
                retCount = reader.GetBytes(0, startIndex, chunk, 0, bufferSize)
            End While

            Dim actualChunk(retCount - 1) As Byte
            Buffer.BlockCopy(chunk, 0, actualChunk, 0, retCount - 1)
            context.Response.BinaryWrite(actualChunk)

        End If
      End Using
    End Sub

    Public ReadOnly Property IsReusable() As Boolean
➥Implements IHttpHandler.IsReusable
        Get
            Return False
        End Get
    End Property

End Class
```

The HTTP Handler in Listing 4.6 uses a `SqlDataReader` to retrieve a file from the database. Notice that the `SqlDataReader` is retrieved with a `CommandBehavior.SequentialAccess` parameter. This parameter enables the `SqlDataReader` to load data as a stream. The contents of the database column are pulled into memory in 8040-byte chunks. The chunks are written to the browser with the `Response.BinaryWrite()` method.

Notice that response buffering is disabled for the handler. The `Response.Buffer` property is set to the value `False`. Because buffering is disabled, the output of the handler is not buffered in server memory before being transmitted to the browser.

> **WARNING**
>
> The method of working with large files described in this section works only with SQL Server 2005. When using earlier versions of SQL Server, you need to use the `TEXTPTR()` function instead of the `.WRITE` clause.

Displaying a Calendar

The Calendar control enables you to display a calendar. You can use the calendar as a date picker or you can use the calendar to display a list of upcoming events.

The page in Listing 4.7 displays a simple calendar with the Calendar control (see Figure 4.4).

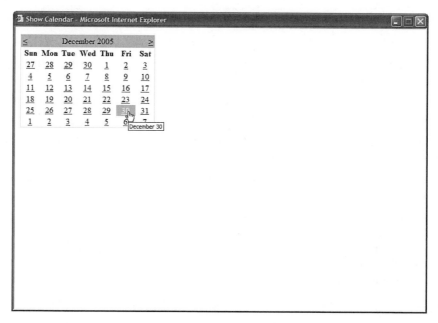

FIGURE 4.4   Displaying a calendar with the Calendar control.

LISTING 4.7   ShowCalendar.aspx

```
<%@ Page Language="VB" %>
<!DOCTYPE html PUBLIC "-//W3C//DTD XHTML 1.0 Transitional//EN"
➥"http://www.w3.org/TR/xhtml1/DTD/xhtml1-transitional.dtd">
<html xmlns="http://www.w3.org/1999/xhtml" >
<head id="Head1" runat="server">
    <title>Show Calendar</title>
</head>
<body>
    <form id="form1" runat="server">
    <div>

    <asp:Calendar
        id="Calendar1"
```

LISTING 4.7   Continued

```
        Runat="server" />

    </div>
    </form>
</body>
</html>
```

The `Calendar` control supports the following properties (this is not a complete list):

- `DayNameFormat`—Enables you to specify the appearance of the days of the week. Possible values are `FirstLetter`, `FirstTwoLetters`, `Full`, `Short`, and `Shortest`.

- `NextMonthText`—Enables you to specify the text that appears for the next month link.

- `NextPrevFormat`—Enables you to specify the format of the next month and previous month link. Possible values are `CustomText`, `FullMonth`, and `ShortMonth`.

- `PrevMonthText`—Enables you to specify the text that appears for the previous month link.

- `SelectedDate`—Enables you to get or set the selected date.

- `SelectedDates`—Enables you to get or set a collection of selected dates.

- `SelectionMode`—Enables you to specify how dates are selected. Possible values are Day, DayWeek, DayWeekMonth, and None.

- `SelectMonthText`—Enables you to specify the text that appears for selecting a month.

- `SelectWeekText`—Enables you to specify the text that appears for selecting a week.

- `ShowDayHeader`—Enables you to hide or display the day names at the top of the `Calendar` control.

- `ShowNextPrevMonth`—Enables you to hide or display the links for the next and previous months.

- `ShowTitle`—Enables you to hide or display the title bar displayed at the top of the calendar.

- `TitleFormat`—Enables you to format the title bar. Possible values are Month and MonthYear.

- `TodaysDate`—Enables you to specify the current date. This property defaults to the current date on the server.

- `VisibleDate`—Enables you to specify the month displayed by the `Calendar` control. This property defaults to displaying the month that contains the date specified by TodaysDate.

The Calendar control also supports the following events:

- DayRender—Raised as each day is rendered.

- SelectionChanged—Raised when a new day, week, or month is selected.

- VisibleMonthChanged—Raised when the next or previous month link is clicked.

Notice that the SelectionMode property enables you to change the behavior of the calendar so that you can not only select days, but also select weeks or months. The page in Listing 4.8 illustrates how you can use the SelectionMode property in conjunction with the SelectedDates property to select multiple dates (see Figure 4.5).

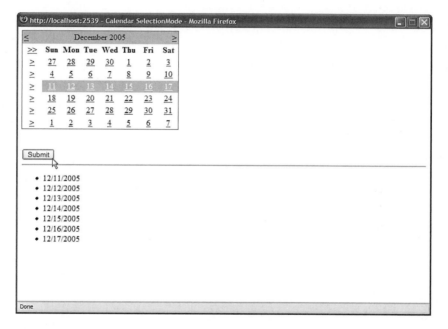

FIGURE 4.5   Selecting weeks and months with a Calendar control.

LISTING 4.8   CalendarSelectionMode.aspx

```
<%@ Page Language="VB" %>
<!DOCTYPE html PUBLIC "-//W3C//DTD XHTML 1.0 Transitional//EN"
➥"http://www.w3.org/TR/xhtml1/DTD/xhtml1-transitional.dtd">
<script runat="server">

    Sub btnSubmit_Click(sender As Object, e As EventArgs)
        bltResults.DataSource = Calendar1.SelectedDates
        bltResults.DataBind()
    End Sub
```

LISTING 4.8   Continued

```
</script>
<html xmlns="http://www.w3.org/1999/xhtml" >
<head id="Head1" runat="server">
    <title>Calendar SelectionMode</title>
</head>
<body>
    <form id="form1" runat="server">
    <div>

    <asp:Calendar
        id="Calendar1"
        SelectionMode="DayWeekMonth"
        runat="server" />

    <br /><br />

    <asp:Button
        id="btnSubmit"
        Text="Submit"
        OnClick="btnSubmit_Click"
        Runat="server" />

    <hr />

    <asp:BulletedList
        id="bltResults"
        DataTextFormatString="{0:d}"
        Runat="server" />

    </div>
    </form>
</body>
</html>
```

When you select a date, or group of dates, from the Calendar control in Listing 4.8, the set of selected dates are displayed in a BulletedList control.

Creating a Pop-up Date Picker

You can use a Calendar control to create a fancy pop-up date picker if you are willing to add a little JavaScript and some Cascading Style Sheet rules to a page. The page in Listing 4.9 contains a TextBox and Calendar control (see Figure 4.6).

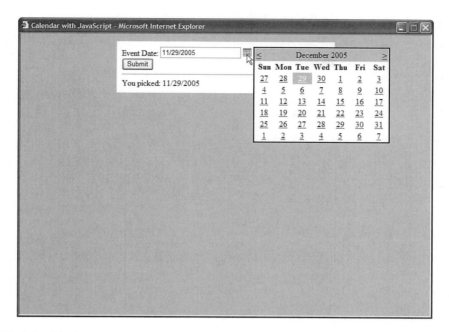

FIGURE 4.6   Displaying a pop-up calendar.

The Calendar control is hidden until you click the calendar image. The #datePicker style sheet rules sets the display property to none. When you click the image of the calendar, the JavaScript displayCalendar() function executes and sets the CSS display property to the value block.

When you select a date from the calendar, the page is posted back to the server and the SelectionChanged server-side event is raised. The SelectionChanged event handler updates the TextBox control with the selected date.

LISTING 4.9   CalendarJS.aspx

```
<%@ Page Language="VB" %>
<!DOCTYPE html PUBLIC "-//W3C//DTD XHTML 1.0 Transitional//EN"
➡"http://www.w3.org/TR/xhtml1/DTD/xhtml1-transitional.dtd">
<script runat="server">

    Sub calEventDate_SelectionChanged(ByVal sender As Object, ByVal e As EventArgs)
        txtEventDate.Text = calEventDate.SelectedDate.ToString("d")
    End Sub


    Sub btnSubmit_Click(ByVal sender As Object, ByVal e As EventArgs)
        lblResult.Text = "You picked: " & txtEventDate.Text
    End Sub
</script>
```

LISTING 4.9   Continued

```
<html xmlns="http://www.w3.org/1999/xhtml" >
<head id="Head1" runat="server">
    <script type="text/javascript">

        function displayCalendar()
        {
            var datePicker = document.getElementById('datePicker');
            datePicker.style.display = 'block';
        }

    </script>
    <style type="text/css">
        #datePicker
        {
            display:none;
            position:absolute;
            border:solid 2px black;
            background-color:white;
        }
        .content
        {
            width:400px;
            background-color:white;
            margin:auto;
            padding:10px;
        }
        html
        {
            background-color:silver;
        }
    </style>
    <title>Calendar with JavaScript</title>
</head>
<body>
    <form id="form1" runat="server">
    <div class="content">

    <asp:Label
        id="lblEventDate"
```

LISTING 4.9   Continued

```
            Text="Event Date:"
            AssociatedControlID="txtEventDate"
            Runat="server" />
    <asp:TextBox
        id="txtEventDate"
        Runat="server" />
    <img src="Calendar.gif" onclick="displayCalendar()" />

    <div id="datePicker">
    <asp:Calendar
        id="calEventDate"
        OnSelectionChanged="calEventDate_SelectionChanged"
        Runat="server" />
    </div>

    <br />
    <asp:Button
        id="btnSubmit"
        Text="Submit"
        Runat="server" OnClick="btnSubmit_Click" />

    <hr />

    <asp:Label
        id="lblResult"
        Runat="server" />

    </div>
    </form>
</body>
</html>
```

Rendering a Calendar from a Database Table

You also can use the Calendar control to display events in a calendar. In this section, we build a simple schedule application that enables you to insert, update, and delete calendar entries. Each schedule entry is highlighted in a Calendar control (see Figure 4.7).

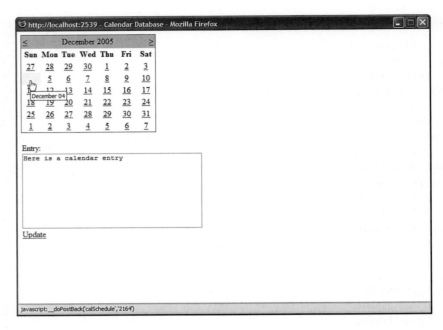

FIGURE 4.7   Displaying a calendar from a database.

The code for the schedule application is contained in Listing 4.10.

LISTING 4.10   CalendarDatabase.aspx

```
<%@ Page Language="VB" ValidateRequest="false" %>
<%@ Import Namespace="System.Data" %>
<!DOCTYPE html PUBLIC "-//W3C//DTD XHTML 1.0 Transitional//EN"
➥"http://www.w3.org/TR/xhtml1/DTD/xhtml1-transitional.dtd">
<script runat="server">

    Private schedule As New DataView()

    Sub Page_Load()
        If calSchedule.SelectedDate = DateTime.MinValue Then
            calSchedule.SelectedDate = calSchedule.TodaysDate
        End If
    End Sub

    Sub Page_PreRender()
        schedule = CType(srcCalendar.Select(DataSourceSelectArguments.Empty),
➥DataView)
        schedule.Sort = "EntryDate"
    End Sub
```

LISTING 4.10   Continued

```
    Sub calSchedule_DayRender(ByVal sender As Object, ByVal e
➥As DayRenderEventArgs)
        If schedule.FindRows(e.Day.Date).Length > 0 Then
            e.Cell.BackColor = System.Drawing.Color.Yellow
        End If
    End Sub
</script>
<html xmlns="http://www.w3.org/1999/xhtml" >
<head id="Head1" runat="server">
    <title>Calendar Database</title>
</head>
<body>
    <form id="form1" runat="server">
    <div>

    <asp:Calendar
        id="calSchedule"
        OnDayRender="calSchedule_DayRender"
        Runat="server" />

    <br />

    <asp:FormView
        id="frmSchedule"
        AllowPaging="True"
        DataKeyNames="EntryDate"
        DataSourceID="srcSchedule"
        Runat="server">
        <EmptyDataTemplate>
        <asp:LinkButton
            id="btnNew"
            Text="Add Entry"
            CommandName="New"
            Runat="server" />
        </EmptyDataTemplate>
        <ItemTemplate>
        <h1><%# Eval("EntryDate", "{0:D}") %></h1>
        <%# Eval("Entry") %>
        <br /><br />
        <asp:LinkButton
            Id="btnEdit"
            Text="Edit Entry"
            CommandName="Edit"
            Runat="server" />
```

LISTING 4.10   Continued

```
<asp:LinkButton
    Id="lnkDelete"
    Text="Delete Entry"
    CommandName="Delete"
    OnClientClick="return confirm('Delete entry?');"
    Runat="server" />
</ItemTemplate>
<EditItemTemplate>
<asp:Label
    id="lblEntry"
    Text="Entry:"
    AssociatedControlID="txtEntry"
    Runat="server" />
<br />
<asp:TextBox
    id="txtEntry"
    Text='<%#Bind("Entry") %>'
    TextMode="MultiLine"
    Columns="40"
    Rows="8"
    Runat="server" />
<br />
<asp:LinkButton
    id="btnUpdate"
    Text="Update"
    CommandName="Update"
    Runat="server" />
</EditItemTemplate>
<InsertItemTemplate>
<asp:Label
    id="lblEntry"
    Text="Entry:"
    AssociatedControlID="txtEntry"
    Runat="server" />
<br />
<asp:TextBox
    id="txtEntry"
    Text='<%#Bind("Entry") %>'
    TextMode="MultiLine"
    Columns="40"
    Rows="8"
    Runat="server" />
<br />
<asp:Button
```

LISTING 4.10   Continued

```
            id="btnInsert"
            Text="Insert"
            CommandName="Insert"
            Runat="server" />
        </InsertItemTemplate>
    </asp:FormView>

    <asp:SqlDataSource
        id="srcSchedule"
        ConnectionString="Server=.\SQLExpress;Integrated Security=True;
            AttachDbFileName=¦DataDirectory¦ScheduleDB.mdf;User Instance=True"
        SelectCommand="SELECT EntryDate,Entry FROM Schedule
➥WHERE EntryDate=@EntryDate"
        InsertCommand="INSERT Schedule (EntryDate,Entry)
➥VALUES (@EntryDate,@Entry)"
        UpdateCommand="UPDATE Schedule SET Entry=@Entry WHERE EntryDate=@EntryDate"
        DELETECommand="DELETE Schedule WHERE EntryDate=@EntryDate"
        Runat="server">
        <SelectParameters>
        <asp:ControlParameter
            Name="EntryDate"
            ControlID="calSchedule"
            PropertyName="SelectedDate" />
        </SelectParameters>
        <InsertParameters>
        <asp:ControlParameter
            Name="EntryDate"
            ControlID="calSchedule"
            PropertyName="SelectedDate" />
        </InsertParameters>
    </asp:SqlDataSource>

    <asp:SqlDataSource
        id="srcCalendar"
        ConnectionString="Server=.\SQLExpress;Integrated Security=True;
            AttachDbFileName=¦DataDirectory¦ScheduleDB.mdf;User Instance=True"
        SelectCommand="SELECT EntryDate FROM Schedule"
        Runat="server">
    </asp:SqlDataSource>

    </div>
    </form>
</body>
</html>
```

The page in Listing 4.10 saves and loads entries from a SQL Express database named ScheduleDB. The contents of the schedule are contained in a table named Schedule which has the following schema:

Column Name	Data Type
EntryDate	DateTime
Entry	Nvarchar(max)

The tricky part in Listing 4.10 is the code for highlighting the current entries in the calendar. In the Page_PreRender event handler, a list of all the current entries is retrieved from the database. The list is represented by a DataView object.

The DayRender event is raised when the Calendar renders each day (table cell). In the DayRender event handler in Listing 4.10, if there is an entry in the database that corresponds to the day being rendered, then the day is highlighted with a yellow background color.

Displaying Advertisements

The AdRotator control enables you to randomly display different advertisements in a page. You can store the list of advertisements in either an XML file or in a database table.

The AdRotator control supports the following properties (this is not a complete list):

- AdvertisementFile—Enables you to specify the path to an XML file that contains a list of banner advertisements.

- AlternateTextField—Enables you to specify the name of the field for displaying alternate text for the banner advertisement image. The default value is AlternateText.

- DataMember—Enables you to bind to a particular data member in the data source.

- DataSource—Enables you to specify a data source programmatically for the list of banner advertisements.

- DataSourceID—Enables you to bind to a data source declaratively.

- ImageUrlField—Enables you to specify the name of the field for the image URL for the banner advertisement. The default value for this field is ImageUrl.

- KeywordFilter—Enables you to filter advertisements by a single keyword.

- NavigateUrlField—Enables you to specify the name of the field for the advertisement link. The default value for this field is NavigateUrl.

- Target—Enables you to open a new window when a user clicks the banner advertisement.

The `AdRotator` control also supports the following event:

- `AdCreated`—Raised after the `AdRotator` control selects an advertisement but before the `AdRotator` control renders the advertisement.

Notice that the `AdRotator` control includes a `KeywordFilter` property. You can provide each banner advertisement with a keyword and then filter the advertisements displayed by the `AdRotator` control by using the value of the `KeywordFilter` property.

This property can be used in multiple ways. For example, if you are displaying more than one advertisement in the same page, then you can filter the advertisements by page regions. You can use the KeywordFilter to show the big banner advertisement on the top of the page and box ads on the side of the page.

You can also use the `KeywordFilter` property to filter advertisements by website section. For example, you might want to show different advertisements on your website's home page than on your website's search page.

> **NOTE**
>
> If you cache a page that contains an AdRotator control, then the AdRotator control is excluded from the cache. In other words, even if you cache a page, randomly selected banner advertisements are still displayed. The `AdRotator` control takes advantage of a new feature of the ASP.NET 2.0 Framework called post-cache substitution. You learn more about this feature in Chapter 23, "Caching Application Pages and Data."

Storing Advertisements in an XML File

You can store the list of advertisements that the AdRotator displays in an XML file by setting the `AdRotator` control's `AdvertisementFile` property. For example, the page in Listing 4.11 contains three `AdRotator` controls that retrieve banner advertisements from an XML file named `AdList.xml` (see Figure 4.8).

LISTING 4.11 `AdRotatorXML.aspx`

```
<%@ Page Language="VB" %>
<!DOCTYPE html PUBLIC "-//W3C//DTD XHTML 1.0 Transitional//EN"
➥"http://www.w3.org/TR/xhtml1/DTD/xhtml1-transitional.dtd">
<html xmlns="http://www.w3.org/1999/xhtml" >
<head id="Head1" runat="server">
    <style type="text/css">
        html
        {
            background-color:silver;
        }
        .content
        {
```

LISTING 4.11   Continued

```
                background-color:white;
                padding:10px;
                border:solid 1px black;
                margin:auto;
                width:400px;
                text-align:center;
            }
            .box
            {
                float:right;
                padding:10px;
                border-left:solid 1px black;
            }
            .clear
            {
                clear:both;
            }
        </style>
        <title>AdRotator XML</title>
</head>
<body>
    <form id="form1" runat="server">
    <div class="content">

    <asp:AdRotator
        id="AdRotator1"
        AdvertisementFile="~/App_Data/AdList.xml"
        KeywordFilter="banner"
        CssClass="banner"
        Runat="server" />

    <br />

    <div class="box">
        <asp:AdRotator
            id="AdRotator2"
            AdvertisementFile="~/App_Data/AdList.xml"
            KeywordFilter="box"
            Runat="server" />
        <br /><br />
        <asp:AdRotator
            id="AdRotator3"
            AdvertisementFile="~/App_Data/AdList.xml"
            KeywordFilter="box"
```

LISTING 4.11   Continued

```
            Runat="server" />
    </div>


    <br />Here is the body text in the page.
    <br />Here is the body text in the page.
    <br />Here is the body text in the page.
    <br />Here is the body text in the page.

    <br class="clear" />
    </div>
    </form>
</body>
</html>
```

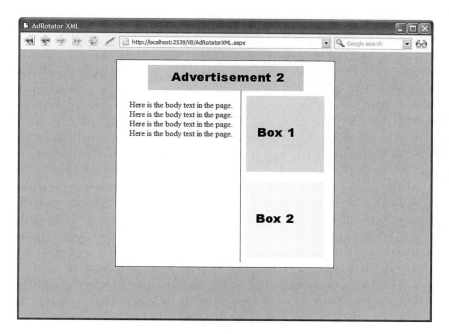

FIGURE 4.8   Displaying advertisements from an XML file.

The page in Listing 4.11 contains an AdRotator control that displays a banner advertisement at the top of the page. The page also contains two AdRotator controls that display box advertisements on the right of the page.

Notice that the first AdRotator has a KeyworldFilter property that has the value banner, and the remaining two AdRotator controls have KeywordFilter properties with the value box. The first `AdRotator` displays only banner advertisements, and the remaining two `AdRotator` controls display only box advertisements.

All three `AdRotator` controls get their list of banner advertisements from a file named `AdList.xml`. This file is located in the `App_Data` folder for security reasons. The files in the `App_Data` folder cannot be opened in a web browser.

> **NOTE**
>
> There is nothing wrong with assigning different XML files to different `AdRotator` controls. For example, you could create distinct `BannerAd.xml` and `BoxAd.xml` files and then you would not have to worry about the `KeywordFilter` property.

The file in Listing 4.12 contains the contents of the `AdList.xml` file.

LISTING 4.12   AdList.xml

```xml
<?xml version="1.0" encoding="utf-8" ?>
<Advertisements>
  <!-- Banner Advertisements -->
  <Ad>
    <ImageUrl>~/Ads/BannerAd1.gif</ImageUrl>
    <Width>300</Width>
    <Height>50</Height>
    <NavigateUrl>http://www.AspWorkshops.com</NavigateUrl>
    <AlternateText>Banner Advertisement 1</AlternateText>
    <Impressions>50</Impressions>
    <Keyword>banner</Keyword>
  </Ad>
  <Ad>
    <ImageUrl>~/Ads/BannerAd2.gif</ImageUrl>
    <Width>300</Width>
    <Height>50</Height>
    <NavigateUrl>http://www.AspWorkshops.com</NavigateUrl>
    <AlternateText>Banner Advertisement 2</AlternateText>
    <Impressions>25</Impressions>
    <Keyword>banner</Keyword>
  </Ad>
  <Ad>
    <ImageUrl>~/Ads/BannerAd3.gif</ImageUrl>
    <Width>300</Width>
    <Height>50</Height>
    <NavigateUrl>http://www.AspWorkshops.com</NavigateUrl>
    <AlternateText>Banner Advertisement 3</AlternateText>
    <Impressions>25</Impressions>
    <Keyword>banner</Keyword>
```

LISTING 4.12   Continued

```
  </Ad>
  <!-- Box Advertisements -->
  <Ad>
    <ImageUrl>~/Ads/BoxAd1.gif</ImageUrl>
    <Width>150</Width>
    <Height>150</Height>
    <NavigateUrl>http://www.AspWorkshops.com</NavigateUrl>
    <AlternateText>Box Advertisement 1</AlternateText>
    <Impressions>50</Impressions>
    <Keyword>box</Keyword>
  </Ad>
  <Ad>
    <ImageUrl>~/Ads/BoxAd2.gif</ImageUrl>
    <Width>150</Width>
    <Height>150</Height>
    <NavigateUrl>http://www.AspWorkshops.com</NavigateUrl>
    <AlternateText>Box Advertisement 2</AlternateText>
    <Impressions>50</Impressions>
    <Keyword>box</Keyword>
  </Ad>
</Advertisements>
```

The `Impressions` attribute in the file in Listing 4.12 determines how often each banner advertisement is displayed. For example, the first banner advertisement is displayed 50% of the time, and the remaining two banner advertisements are displayed 25% of the time.

Storing Advertisements in a Database Table

Rather than store the list of advertisements in an XML file, you can store the list in a database table. For example, the `AdRotator` control contained in Listing 4.13 is bound to a `SqlDataSource` control. The `SqlDataSource` control represents the contents of a database table named `AdList`, which is located in a SQL Express database named `AdListDB`.

LISTING 4.13   AdRotatorDatabase.aspx

```
<%@ Page Language="VB" %>
<!DOCTYPE html PUBLIC "-//W3C//DTD XHTML 1.0 Transitional//EN"
➥"http://www.w3.org/TR/xhtml1/DTD/xhtml1-transitional.dtd">
<html xmlns="http://www.w3.org/1999/xhtml" >
<head id="Head1" runat="server">
    <title>AdRotator Database</title>
</head>
<body>
    <form id="form1" runat="server">
```

LISTING 4.13   Continued

```
    <div>

    <asp:AdRotator
        id="AdRotator1"
        DataSourceID="srcAds"
        Runat="server" />

    <asp:SqlDataSource
        id="srcAds"
        ConnectionString="Server=.\SQLExpress;Integrated Security=True;
            AttachDbFileName=¦DataDirectory¦AdListDB.mdf;User Instance=True"
        SelectCommand="SELECT ImageUrl, Width, Height, NavigateUrl,
➥ AlternateText, Keyword, Impressions
            FROM AdList"
        Runat="server" />

    </div>
    </form>
</body>
</html>
```

To use the page in Listing 4.13, you need to create the AdList database table. This table has the following schema:

Column Name	Data Type
Id	Int (IDENTITY)
ImageUrl	Varchar(250)
Width	Int
Height	Int
NavigateUrl	Varchar(250)
AlternateText	NVarchar(100)
Keyword	NVarchar(50)
Impressions	Int

Notice that the columns in the AdList database table correspond to the attributes in the AdList.xml file discussed in the previous section.

Tracking Impressions and Transfers

Normally, when you are displaying advertisements, you are doing it to make money. Your advertisers will want statistics on how often their advertisements were displayed (the number of impressions) and how often their advertisements were clicked (the number of transfers).

To track the number of times that an advertisement is displayed, you need to handle the AdRotator control's AdCreated event. To track the number of times that an advertisement is clicked, you need to create a redirect handler.

> **WARNING**
>
> If you create an event handler for the AdCreated event and you cache the page, the content rendered by the AdRotator control will also be cached. When handling the AdCreated event, use partial page caching to cache only part of a page and not the AdRotator control itself.

The page in Listing 4.14 displays a banner advertisement with the AdRotator control. The page includes an event handler for the AdRotator control's AdCreated event.

LISTING 4.14   AdRotatorTrack.aspx

```
<%@ Page Language="VB" %>
<!DOCTYPE html PUBLIC "-//W3C//DTD XHTML 1.0 Transitional//EN"
➥"http://www.w3.org/TR/xhtml1/DTD/xhtml1-transitional.dtd">
<script runat="server">

    Sub AdRotator1_AdCreated(ByVal sender As Object, ByVal e As AdCreatedEventArgs)
        ' Update Impressions
        srcAds.InsertParameters("AdId").DefaultValue =
➥e.AdProperties("Id").ToString()
        srcAds.Insert()


        ' Change NavigateUrl to redirect page
        e.NavigateUrl = "~/AdHandler.ashx?id=" & e.AdProperties("Id").ToString()
    End Sub
</script>
<html xmlns="http://www.w3.org/1999/xhtml" >
<head id="Head1" runat="server">
    <title>AdRotator Track</title>
</head>
<body>
    <form id="form1" runat="server">
    <div>

    <asp:AdRotator
        id="AdRotator1"
        DataSourceID="srcAds"
        OnAdCreated="AdRotator1_AdCreated"
        Runat="server" />

    <asp:SqlDataSource
        id="srcAds"
```

4

LISTING 4.14   Continued

```
        ConnectionString="Server=.\SQLExpress;Integrated Security=True;
            AttachDbFileName=¦DataDirectory¦AdListDB.mdf;User Instance=True"
        SelectCommand="SELECT Id, ImageUrl, Width, Height,
➥ NavigateUrl, AlternateText, Keyword, Impressions
            FROM AdList"
        InsertCommand="INSERT AdStats (AdId, EntryDate, Type)
➥ VALUES (@AdId, GetDate(), 0)"
        Runat="server">
        <InsertParameters>
        <asp:Parameter Name="AdId" Type="int32" />
        </InsertParameters>
      </asp:SqlDataSource>

    </div>
    </form>
</body>
</html>
```

The AdCreated event handler does two things. First, it inserts a new record into a database table named AdStats, which records an advertisement impression. Second, the handler modifies the NavigateUrl so that the user is redirected to a handler named AdHandler.ashx.

The AdStats database table looks like this:

Column Name	Data Type
Id	Int (IDENTITY)
AdId	Int
EntryDate	DateTime
Type	Int

The Type column is used to record the type of entry. The value 0 represents an advertisement impression, and the value 1 represents an advertisement transfer.

When you click an advertisement, you link to a file named AdHandler.ashx. This file is contained in Listing 4.15.

LISTING 4.15   AdHandler.ashx

```
<%@ WebHandler Language="VB" Class="AdHandler" %>

Imports System
Imports System.Web
Imports System.Data
imports System.Data.SqlClient
```

LISTING 4.15   Continued

```
Public Class AdHandler
    Implements IHttpHandler

    Const conString As String = "Server=.\SQLExpress;Integrated Security=True;
➡AttachDbFileName=¦DataDirectory¦AdListDB.mdf;User Instance=True"

    Sub ProcessRequest(ByVal context As HttpContext)
➡Implements IHttpHandler.ProcessRequest
        Dim AdId As Integer = Int32.Parse(context.Request("Id"))

        Dim con As New SqlConnection(conString)
        Dim navigateUrl As String = String.Empty
        Using con
            con.Open()
            UpdateTransferStats(AdId, con)
            navigateUrl = GetNavigateUrl(AdId, con)
        End Using

        If Not String.IsNullOrEmpty(navigateUrl) Then
            context.Response.Redirect(navigateUrl)
        End If
    End Sub

    Sub UpdateTransferStats(ByVal advertisementId As Integer, ByVal con
➡As SqlConnection)
        Dim cmdText As String = "INSERT AdStats
➡ (AdId, EntryDate, Type) VALUES "& _
            "(@AdId, GetDate(), 1)"
        Dim cmd As New SqlCommand(cmdText, con)
        cmd.Parameters.AddWithValue("@AdId", advertisementId)
        cmd.ExecuteNonQuery()
    End Sub

    Function GetNavigateUrl(ByVal advertisementId As Integer, ByVal con
➡As SqlConnection) As String
        Dim cmdText As String = "SELECT NavigateUrl FROM AdList WHERE Id=@AdId"
        Dim cmd As New SqlCommand(cmdText, con)
        cmd.Parameters.AddWithValue("@AdId", advertisementId)
        Return cmd.ExecuteScalar().ToString()
    End Function


    Public ReadOnly Property IsReusable() As Boolean
➡Implements IHttpHandler.IsReusable
```

LISTING 4.15   Continued

```
        Get
            Return False
        End Get
    End Property


End Class
```

The handler in Listing 4.15 performs two tasks. First, it inserts a new record into the AdStats database table, recording the fact that a transfer is taking place. Next, it grabs the NavigateUrl from the AdList database table and sends the user to the advertiser's website.

The final page displays advertiser statistics from the AdStats database table (see Figure 4.9). This page is contained in Listing 4.16.

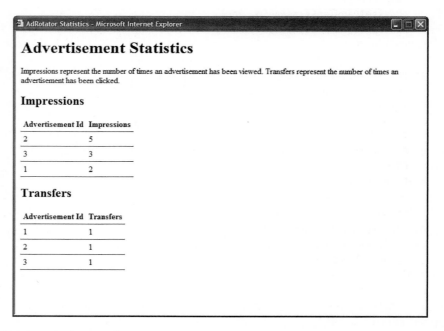

FIGURE 4.9   Displaying advertiser statistics.

LISTING 4.16   AdRotatorStats.aspx

```
<%@ Page Language="VB" %>
<!DOCTYPE html PUBLIC "-//W3C//DTD XHTML 1.0 Transitional//EN"
➥"http://www.w3.org/TR/xhtml1/DTD/xhtml1-transitional.dtd">
<html xmlns="http://www.w3.org/1999/xhtml" >
```

LISTING 4.16 Continued

```
<head id="Head1" runat="server">
    <style type="text/css">
        .grid td,.grid th
        {
            border-bottom:solid 1px black;
            padding:5px;
        }
    </style>
    <title>AdRotator Statistics</title>
</head>
<body>
    <form id="form1" runat="server">
    <div>

    <h1>Advertisement Statistics</h1>
    Impressions represent the number of times an advertisement has been viewed.
    Transfers represent the number of times an advertisement has been clicked.

    <h2>Impressions</h2>

    <asp:GridView
        id="grdImpressions"
        DataSourceID="srcImpressions"
        AutoGenerateColumns="false"
        GridLines="None"
        CssClass="grid"
        Runat="server">
        <Columns>
        <asp:BoundField
            DataField="AdId"
            HeaderText="Advertisement Id" />
        <asp:BoundField
            DataField="Impressions"
            HeaderText="Impressions" />
        </Columns>
    </asp:GridView>

    <asp:SqlDataSource
        id="srcImpressions"
        ConnectionString="Server=.\SQLExpress;Integrated Security=True;
            AttachDbFileName=|DataDirectory|AdListDB.mdf;User Instance=True"
        SelectCommand="SELECT AdId,Count(*) As Impressions
            FROM AdStats
```

LISTING 4.16   Continued

```
                WHERE Type=0
                GROUP BY AdId
                ORDER BY Impressions DESC"
        Runat="server" />

    <h2>Transfers</h2>

    <asp:GridView
        id="grdTransfers"
        DataSourceID="srcTransfers"
        AutoGenerateColumns="false"
        GridLines="None"
        CssClass="grid"
        Runat="server">
        <Columns>
        <asp:BoundField
            DataField="AdId"
            HeaderText="Advertisement Id" />
        <asp:BoundField
            DataField="Transfers"
            HeaderText="Transfers" />
        </Columns>
    </asp:GridView>

    <asp:SqlDataSource
        id="srcTransfers"
        ConnectionString="Server=.\SQLExpress;Integrated Security=True;
            AttachDbFileName=¦DataDirectory¦AdListDB.mdf;User Instance=True"
        SelectCommand="SELECT AdId,Count(*) As Transfers
            FROM AdStats
            WHERE Type=1
            GROUP BY AdId
            ORDER BY Transfers DESC"
        Runat="server" />

    </div>
    </form>
</body>
</html>
```

The page in Listing 4.16 contains two `GridView` controls bound to two `SqlDataSource` controls. The first `GridView` displays statistics on impressions, and the second `GridView` displays statistics on transfers.

Displaying Different Page Views

The `MultiView` control enables you to hide and display different areas of a page. This control is useful when you need to create a tabbed page. It is also useful when you need to divide a long form into multiple forms.

The `MultiView` control contains one or more `View` controls. You use the `MultiView` control to select a particular `View` control to render. (The selected `View` control is the `Active View`.) The contents of the remaining `View` controls are hidden. You can render only one `View` control at a time.

The `MultiView` control supports the following properties (this is not a complete list):

- `ActiveViewIndex`—Enables you to select the `View` control to render by index.

- `Views`—Enables you to retrieve the collection of `View` controls contained in the `MultiView` control.

The `MultiView` control also supports the following methods:

- `GetActiveView`—Enables you to retrieve the selected `View` control.

- `SetActiveView`—Enables you to select the active view.

Finally, the `MultiView` control supports the following event:

- `ActiveViewChanged`—Raised when a new `View` control is selected.

The `View` control does not support any special properties or methods. Its primary purpose is to act as a container for other controls. However, the `View` control does support the following two events:

- `Activate`—Raised when the view becomes the selected view in the `MultiView` control.

- `Deactivate`—Raised when another view becomes the selected view in the `MultiView` control.

Displaying a Tabbed Page View

When you use the `MultiView` control in conjunction with the `Menu` control, you can create a tabbed page view. (To make it look pretty, you need to use some CSS.)

For example, the page in Listing 4.17 contains a `MultiView` control with three `View` controls. The `Menu` control is used to switch between the `View` controls (see Figure 4.10).

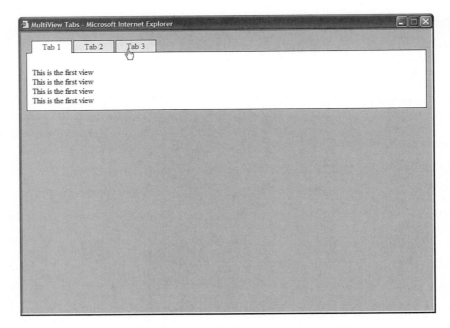

FIGURE 4.10   Displaying a tabbed page with the `MultiView` control.

LISTING 4.17   `MultiViewTabs.aspx`

```
<%@ Page Language="VB" %>
<!DOCTYPE html PUBLIC "-//W3C//DTD XHTML 1.0 Transitional//EN"
➥"http://www.w3.org/TR/xhtml1/DTD/xhtml1-transitional.dtd">
<script runat="server">

    Sub Menu1_MenuItemClick(ByVal sender As Object, ByVal e As MenuEventArgs)
        Dim index As Integer = Int32.Parse(e.Item.Value)
        MultiView1.ActiveViewIndex = index
    End Sub
</script>
<html xmlns="http://www.w3.org/1999/xhtml" >
<head id="Head1" runat="server">
    <style type="text/css">
        html
        {
            background-color:silver;
        }
        .tabs
        {
            position:relative;
            top:1px;
```

LISTING 4.17   Continued

```
                left:10px;
        }
        .tab
        {
            border:solid 1px black;
            background-color:#eeeeee;
            padding:2px 10px;
        }
        .selectedTab
        {
            background-color:white;
            border-bottom:solid 1px white;
        }
        .tabContents
        {
            border:solid 1px black;
            padding:10px;
            background-color:white;
        }
    </style>
    <title>MultiView Tabs</title>
</head>
<body>
    <form id="form1" runat="server">
    <div>

    <asp:Menu
        id="Menu1"
        Orientation="Horizontal"
        StaticMenuItemStyle-CssClass="tab"
        StaticSelectedStyle-CssClass="selectedTab"
        CssClass="tabs"
        OnMenuItemClick="Menu1_MenuItemClick"
        Runat="server">
        <Items>
        <asp:MenuItem Text="Tab 1" Value="0" Selected="true" />
        <asp:MenuItem Text="Tab 2" Value="1" />
        <asp:MenuItem Text="Tab 3" Value="2" />
        </Items>
    </asp:Menu>

    <div class="tabContents">
    <asp:MultiView
        id="MultiView1"
```

4

LISTING 4.17   Continued

```
            ActiveViewIndex="0"
            Runat="server">
            <asp:View ID="View1" runat="server">
                <br />This is the first view
                <br />This is the first view
                <br />This is the first view
                <br />This is the first view
            </asp:View>
            <asp:View ID="View2" runat="server">
                <br />This is the second view
                <br />This is the second view
                <br />This is the second view
                <br />This is the second view
            </asp:View>
            <asp:View ID="View3" runat="server">
                <br />This is the third view
                <br />This is the third view
                <br />This is the third view
                <br />This is the third view
            </asp:View>
        </asp:MultiView>
        </div>

        </div>
        </form>
</body>
</html>
```

In Listing 4.17, the Menu control is associated with a CSS class named tabs. This class relatively positions the Menu control down one pixel to merge the bottom border of the Menu control with the top border of the <div> tag that contains the MultiView. Because the selected tab has a white bottom border, the border between the selected tab and the tab contents disappears.

Displaying a Multi-Part Form

You can use the MultiView control to divide a large form into several sub-forms. You can associate particular commands with button controls contained in a MultiView. When the button is clicked, the MultiView changes the active view.

The MultiView control recognizes the following commands:

- NextView—Causes the MultiView to activate the next View control.

- PrevView—Causes the MultiView to activate the previous View control.

- SwitchViewByID—Causes the MultiView to activate the view specified by the button control's CommandArgument.

- SwitchViewByIndex—Causes the MultiView to activate the view specified by the button control's CommandArgument.

You can use these commands with any of the button controls—Button, LinkButton, and ImageButton—by setting the button control's CommandName property and, in the case of the SwitchViewByID and SwitchViewByIndex, by setting the CommandArgument property.

The page in Listing 4.18 illustrates how you can use the NextView command to create a multiple-part form.

LISTING 4.18   MultiViewForm.aspx

```
<%@ Page Language="VB" %>
<!DOCTYPE html PUBLIC "-//W3C//DTD XHTML 1.0 Transitional//EN"
➥"http://www.w3.org/TR/xhtml1/DTD/xhtml1-transitional.dtd">
<script runat="server">

    Sub View3_Activate(ByVal sender As Object, ByVal e As EventArgs)
        lblFirstNameResult.Text = txtFirstName.Text
        lblColorResult.Text = txtColor.Text
    End Sub
</script>
<html xmlns="http://www.w3.org/1999/xhtml" >
<head id="Head1" runat="server">
    <title>MultiView Form</title>
</head>
<body>
    <form id="form1" runat="server">
    <div>

    <asp:MultiView
        id="MultiView1"
        ActiveViewIndex="0"
        Runat="server">
        <asp:View ID="View1" runat="server">
        <h1>Step 1</h1>
        <asp:Label
            id="lblFirstName"
            Text="Enter Your First Name:"
            AssociatedControlID="txtFirstName"
            Runat="server" />
        <br />
        <asp:TextBox
            id="txtFirstName"
```

4

LISTING 4.18   Continued

```
        Runat="server" />

    <br /><br />

    <asp:Button
        id="btnNext"
        Text="Next"
        CommandName="NextView"
        Runat="server" />

    </asp:View>
    <asp:View ID="View2" runat="server">
    <h1>Step 2</h1>
    <asp:Label
        id="Label1"
        Text="Enter Your Favorite Color:"
        AssociatedControlID="txtColor"
        Runat="server" />
    <br />
    <asp:TextBox
        id="txtColor"
        Runat="server" />

    <br /><br />

    <asp:Button
        id="Button1"
        Text="Next"
        CommandName="NextView"
        Runat="server" />

    </asp:View>
    <asp:View ID="View3" runat="server" OnActivate="View3_Activate">
    <h1>Summary</h1>
    Your First Name:
    <asp:Label
        id="lblFirstNameResult"
        Runat="server" />
    <br /><br />
    Your Favorite Color:
    <asp:Label
        id="lblColorResult"
        Runat="server" />
    </asp:View>
```

LISTING 4.18   Continued

```
    </asp:MultiView>

    </div>
    </form>
</body>
</html>
```

The first two `View` controls in Listing 4.18 contain a `Button` control. These `Button` controls both have a `CommandName` property set to the value `NextView`.

Displaying a Wizard

The `Wizard` control, like the `MultiView` control, can be used to divide a large form into multiple sub-forms. The `Wizard` control, however, supports many advanced features that are not supported by the `MultiView` control.

The `Wizard` control contains one or more `WizardStep` child controls. Only one `WizardStep` is displayed at a time.

The `Wizard` control supports the following properties (this is not a complete list):

- `ActiveStep`—Enables you to retrieve the active `WizardStep` control.

- `ActiveStepIndex`—Enables you to set or get the index of the active `WizardStep` control.

- `CancelDestinationPageUrl`—Enables you to specify the URL where the user is sent when the Cancel button is clicked.

- `DisplayCancelButton`—Enables you to hide or display the Cancel button.

- `DisplaySideBar`—Enables you to hide or display the `Wizard` control's side bar. The side bar displays a list of all the wizard steps.

- `FinishDestinationPageUrl`—Enables you to specify the URL where the user is sent when the Finish button is clicked.

- `HeaderText`—Enables you to specify the header text that appears at the top of the `Wizard` control.

- `WizardSteps`—Enables you to retrieve the `WizardStep` controls contained in the `Wizard` control.

The `Wizard` control also supports the following templates:

- `FinishNavigationTemplate`—Enables you to control the appearance of the navigation area of the finish step.

- `HeaderTemplate`—Enables you control the appearance of the header area of the `Wizard` control.

- `SideBarTemplate`—Enables you to control the appearance of the side bar area of the `Wizard` control.

- `StartNavigationTemplate`—Enables you to control the appearance of the navigation area of the start step.

- `StepNavigationTemplate`—Enables you to control the appearance of the navigation area of steps that are not start, finish, or complete steps.

The `Wizard` control also supports the following methods:

- `GetHistory()`—Enables you to retrieve the collection of `WizardStep` controls that have been accessed.

- `GetStepType()`—Enables you to return the type of `WizardStep` at a particular index. Possible values are `Auto`, `Complete`, `Finish`, `Start`, and `Step`.

- `MoveTo()`—Enables you to move to a particular `WizardStep`.

The `Wizard` control also supports the following events:

- `ActiveStepChanged`—Raised when a new `WizardStep` becomes the active step.

- `CancelButtonClick`—Raised when the Cancel button is clicked.

- `FinishButtonClick`—Raised when the Finish button is clicked.

- `NextButtonClick`—Raised when the Next button is clicked.

- `PreviousButtonClick`—Raised when the Previous button is clicked.

- `SideBarButtonClick`—Raised when a side bar button is clicked.

A `Wizard` control contains one or more `WizardStep` controls that represent steps in the wizard. The `WizardStep` control supports the following properties:

- `AllowReturn`—Enables you to prevent or allow a user to return to this step from a future step.

- `Name`—Enables you to return the name of the `WizardStep` control.

- `StepType`—Enables you to get or set the type of wizard step. Possible values are `Auto`, `Complete`, `Finish`, `Start` and `Step`.

- `Title`—Enables you to get or set the title of the `WizardStep`. The title is displayed in the wizard side bar.

- `Wizard`—Enables you to retrieve the `Wizard` control containing the `WizardStep`.

The WizardStep also supports the following two events:

- Activate—Raised when a WizardStep becomes active.

- Deactivate—Raised when another WizardStep becomes active.

The StepType property is the most important property. This property determines how a WizardStep is rendered. The default value of StepType is Auto. When StepType is set to the value Auto, the position of the WizardStep in the WizardSteps collection determines how the WizardStep is rendered.

You can explicitly set the StepType property to a particular value. If you set StepType to the value Start, then a Previous button is not rendered. If you set the StepType to Step, then both Previous and Next buttons are rendered. If you set StepType to the value Finish, then Previous and Finish buttons are rendered. Finally, when StepType is set to the value Complete, no buttons are rendered.

The page in Listing 4.19 illustrates how you can use a Wizard control to display a multiple part form (see Figure 4.11).

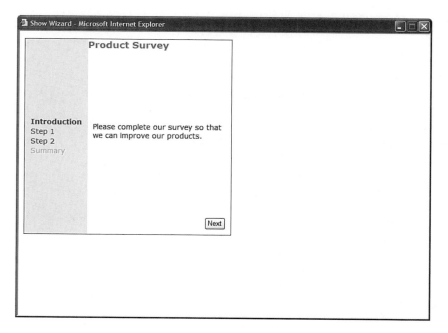

FIGURE 4.11   Displaying a wizard with the Wizard control.

LISTING 4.19   ShowWizard.aspx

```
<%@ Page Language="VB" %>
<!DOCTYPE html PUBLIC "-//W3C//DTD XHTML 1.0 Transitional//EN"
➥"http://www.w3.org/TR/xhtml1/DTD/xhtml1-transitional.dtd">
```

LISTING 4.19   Continued

```
<script runat="server">

    Sub Wizard1_FinishButtonClick(ByVal sender As Object, ByVal e
➥As WizardNavigationEventArgs)
        lblSSNResult.Text = txtSSN.Text
        lblPhoneResult.Text = txtPhone.Text
    End Sub
</script>
<html xmlns="http://www.w3.org/1999/xhtml" >
<head id="Head1" runat="server">
    <style type="text/css">
        .wizard
        {
            border:solid 1px black;
            font:14px Verdana,Sans-Serif;
            width:400px;
            height:300px;
        }
        .header
        {
            color:gray;
            font:bold 18px Verdana,Sans-Serif;
        }
        .sideBar
        {
            background-color:#eeeeee;
            padding:10px;
            width:100px;
        }
        .sideBar a
        {
            text-decoration:none;
        }
        .step
        {
            padding:10px;
        }
    </style>
    <title>Show Wizard</title>
</head>
<body>
    <form id="form1" runat="server">
    <div>
```

LISTING 4.19   Continued

```
<asp:Wizard
    id="Wizard1"
    HeaderText="Product Survey"
    OnFinishButtonClick="Wizard1_FinishButtonClick"
    CssClass="wizard"
    HeaderStyle-CssClass="header"
    SideBarStyle-CssClass="sideBar"
    StepStyle-CssClass="step"
    Runat="server">
    <WizardSteps>
    <asp:WizardStep ID="WizardStep1" Title="Introduction">
    Please complete our survey so that we can improve our
    products.
    </asp:WizardStep>
    <asp:WizardStep ID="WizardStep2" Title="Step 1">
    <asp:Label
        id="lblSSN"
        Text="Social Security Number:"
        AssociatedControlID="txtSSN"
        Runat="server" />
    <br />
    <asp:TextBox
        id="txtSSN"
        Runat="server" />
    </asp:WizardStep>
    <asp:WizardStep ID="WizardStep3" Title="Step 2" StepType="Finish">
    <asp:Label
        id="lblPhone"
        Text="Phone Number:"
        AssociatedControlID="txtPhone"
        Runat="server" />
    <br />
    <asp:TextBox
        id="txtPhone"
        Runat="server" />
    </asp:WizardStep>
    <asp:WizardStep ID="WizardStep4" Title="Summary" StepType="Complete">
    <h1>Summary</h1>
    Social Security Number:
    <asp:Label
        id="lblSSNResult"
        Runat="server" />
    <br /><br />
    Phone Number:
```

LISTING 4.19   Continued

```
        <asp:Label
            id="lblPhoneResult"
            Runat="server" />
        </asp:WizardStep>
        </WizardSteps>
    </asp:Wizard>

    </div>
    </form>
</body>
</html>
```

The `Wizard` control in Listing 4.19 contains four `WizardStep` controls. Notice that the `StepType` property is explicitly set for the last two `WizardStep` controls. When the `Finish` `WizardStep` is rendered, a Finish button is rendered. When the `Complete` `WizardStep` is rendered, no buttons are rendered.

The `Wizard` control's `FinishButtonClick` event is handled with a method named `Wizard1_FinishButtonClick()`. This method updates the final `WizardStep` with a summary of the answers entered in the previous `WizardStep` controls.

Summary

This chapter tackled the rich controls. You learned how to perform file uploads with the `FileUpload` control. You also saw how to accept and display large file uploads by dividing the file into smaller chunks.

You also learned how to use the `Calendar` control to display a date picker and render a schedule of events. Using a tiny bit of JavaScript, you learned how to create a fancy pop-up date picker.

This chapter also discussed the `AdRotator` control. You learned how to store a list of advertisements in both an XML file and a database table. You also learned how to track advertisement impressions and transfers and build a statistics page.

You also learned how to use the `MultiView` control to display different views of a page. You learned how to create a tabbed page by using the `MultiView` control with the `Menu` control. You also learned how to use the `MultiView` to divide a large form into multiple sub-forms.

Finally, we discussed the `Wizard` control. You learned how to use the `Wizard` control to render navigation elements automatically for completing a multiple-step task.

PART II

Designing ASP.NET Websites

IN THIS PART

CHAPTER **5**

Designing Websites with Master Pages

A Master Page enables you to share the same content among multiple content pages in a website. You can use a Master Page to create a common page layout. For example, if you want all the pages in your website to share a three-column layout, you can create the layout once in a Master Page and apply the layout to multiple content pages.

You also can use Master Pages to display common content in multiple pages. For example, if you want to display a standard header and footer in each page in your website, then you can create the standard header and footer in a Master Page.

By taking advantage of Master Pages, you can make your website easier to maintain, extend, and modify. If you need to add a new page to your website that looks just like the other pages in your website, then you simply need to apply the same Master Page to the new content page. If you decide to completely modify the design of your website, you do not need to change every content page. You can modify just a single Master Page to dramatically change the appearance of all the pages in your application.

In this chapter, you learn how to create Master Pages and apply Master Pages to content pages. It describes how you can apply a Master Page to an entire application by registering the Master Page in the web configuration file.

It also explores different methods of modifying content in a Master Page from individual content pages. For example, you learn how to change the title displayed by a Master Page for each content page.

Finally, you learn how to load Master Pages dynamically. Loading Master Pages dynamically is useful when you need to co-brand one website with another website, or when you want to enable individual website users to customize the appearance of your website.

Creating Master Pages

You create a Master Page by creating a file that ends with the `.master` extension. You can locate a Master Page file any place within an application. Furthermore, you can add multiple Master Pages to the same application.

For example, Listing 5.1 contains a simple Master Page.

LISTING 5.1   SimpleMaster.master

```
<%@ Master Language="VB" %>
<!DOCTYPE html PUBLIC "-//W3C//DTD XHTML 1.1//EN"
"http://www.w3.org/TR/xhtml11/DTD/xhtml11.dtd">
<html xmlns="http://www.w3.org/1999/xhtml" >
<head id="Head1" runat="server">
    <style type="text/css">
        html
        {
            background-color:silver;
            font:14px Arial,Sans-Serif;
        }
        .content
        {
            margin:auto;
            width:700px;
            background-color:white;
            border:Solid 1px black;
        }
        .leftColumn
        {
            float:left;
            padding:5px;
            width:200px;
            border-right:Solid 1px black;
            height:700px;

        }
        .rightColumn
        {
            float:left;
            padding:5px;
        }
```

LISTING 5.1   Continued

```
            .clear
            {
                clear:both;
            }
        </style>
        <title>Simple Master</title>
</head>
<body>
    <form id="form1" runat="server">
    <div class="content">
        <div class="leftColumn">

            <asp:contentplaceholder
                id="ContentPlaceHolder1"
                runat="server"/>

        </div>
        <div class="rightColumn">

            <asp:contentplaceholder
                id="ContentPlaceHolder2"
                runat="server"/>

        </div>
        <br class="clear" />
    </div>
    </form>
</body>
</html>
```

Notice that the Master Page in Listing 5.1 looks very much like a normal ASP.NET page. In fact, you can place almost all the same elements in a Master Page that you could place in an ASP.NET page, including HTML, server-side scripts, and ASP.NET controls.

VISUAL WEB DEVELOPER NOTE

You create a Master Page in Visual Web Developer by selecting the Website menu option, Add New Item, and selecting the Master Page item.

There are two special things about the Master Page in Listing 5.1. First, notice that the file contains a `<%@ Master %>` directive instead of the normal `<%@ Page %>` directive. Second, notice that the Master Page includes two ContentPlaceHolder controls.

When the Master Page is merged with a particular content page, the content from the content page appears in the areas marked by `ContentPlaceHolder` controls. You can add as many `ContentPlaceHolders` to a Master Page as you need.

WARNING

There are some things that you can't do in a Master Page that you can do in a content page. For example, you cannot cache a Master Page with the `OutputCache` directive. You also cannot apply a theme to a Master Page.

The Master Page in Listing 5.1 creates a two-column page layout. Each `ContentPlaceHolder` control is contained in a separate `<div>` tag. Cascading Style Sheet rules are used to position the two `<div>` tags into a two-column page layout (see Figure 5.1).

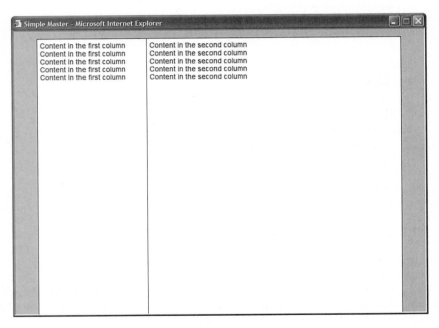

FIGURE 5.1   Creating a two-column Master Page.

WEB STANDARDS NOTE

The Master Page uses Cascading Style Sheets to create the page layout. You should strive to avoid using HTML tables for layout. HTML tables should be used only to display tabular information.

The content page in Listing 5.2 uses the Master Page that was just created.

LISTING 5.2 SimpleContent.aspx

```
<%@ Page Language="VB" MasterPageFile="~/SimpleMaster.master" %>

<asp:Content
    ID="Content1"
    ContentPlaceHolderID="ContentPlaceHolder1"
    Runat="Server">
    Content in the first column
    <br />Content in the first column
    <br />Content in the first column
    <br />Content in the first column
    <br />Content in the first column
</asp:Content>

<asp:Content
    ID="Content2"
    ContentPlaceHolderID="ContentPlaceHolder2"
    Runat="Server">
    Content in the second column
    <br />Content in the second column
    <br />Content in the second column
    <br />Content in the second column
    <br />Content in the second column
</asp:Content>
```

When you open the page in Listing 5.2 in a web browser, the contents of the page are merged with the Master Page.

> **VISUAL WEB DEVELOPER NOTE**
>
> In Visual Web Developer, you create an ASP.NET page that is associated with a particular Master Page by selecting Website, Add New Item, and selecting Web Form. Next, check the check box labeled Select Master Page. When you click Add, a dialog box appears that enables you to select a Master Page.

The Master Page is associated with the content page through the `MasterPageFile` attribute included in the `<%@ Page %>` directive. This attribute contains the virtual path to a Master Page.

Notice that the content page does not contain any of the standard opening and closing XHTML tags. All these tags are contained in the Master Page. All the content contained in the content page must be added with Content controls.

You must place all the content contained in a content page within the Content controls. If you attempt to place any content outside these controls, you get an exception.

The Content control includes a `ContentPlaceHolderID` property. This property points to the ID of a `ContentPlaceHolder` control contained in the Master Page.

Within a Content control, you can place anything that you would normally add to an ASP.NET page, including XHTML tags and ASP.NET controls.

Creating Default Content

You don't have to associate a Content control with every `ContentPlaceHolder` control contained in a Master Page. You can provide default content in a `ContentPlaceHolder` control, and the default content will appear unless it is overridden in a particular content page.

For example, the Master Page in Listing 5.3 includes an additional column, which displays a banner advertisement (see Figure 5.2). The banner advertisement is contained in a `ContentPlaceHolder` control named `contentAd`.

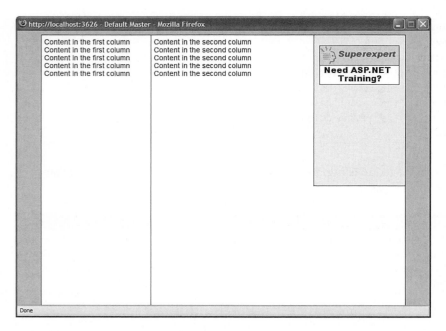

FIGURE 5.2   Displaying default content in a Master Page.

LISTING 5.3   DefaultMaster.master

```
<%@ Master Language="VB" %>
<!DOCTYPE html PUBLIC "-//W3C//DTD XHTML 1.1//EN"
"http://www.w3.org/TR/xhtml11/DTD/xhtml11.dtd">
```

LISTING 5.3   Continued

```
<html xmlns="http://www.w3.org/1999/xhtml" >
<head id="Head1" runat="server">
    <style type="text/css">
        html
        {
            background-color:silver;
            font:14px Arial,Sans-Serif;
        }
        .content
        {
            margin:auto;
            width:700px;
            background-color:white;
            border:Solid 1px black;
        }
        .leftColumn
        {
            float:left;
            padding:5px;
            width:200px;
            border-right:Solid 1px black;
            height:700px;

        }
        .middleColumn
        {
            float:left;
            padding:5px;
        }
        .rightColumn
        {
            float:right;
            width:175px;
            height:300px;
            border-left:solid 1px black;
            border-bottom:solid 1px black;
            background-color:#eeeeee;
            text-align:center;
        }
        .ad
        {
            margin-top:20px;
        }
        .clear
```

LISTING 5.3   Continued

```
        {
            clear:both;
        }
    </style>
    <title>Default Master</title>
</head>
<body>
    <form id="form1" runat="server">
    <div class="content">
        <div class="leftColumn">

            <asp:contentplaceholder
                id="ContentPlaceHolder1"
                runat="server"/>

        </div>
        <div class="middleColumn">

            <asp:ContentPlaceholder
                id="ContentPlaceHolder2"
                runat="server" />

        </div>
        <div class="rightColumn">

            <asp:ContentPlaceHolder
                id="contentAd"
                Runat="server">
                <asp:Image
                    id="imgAd"
                    ImageUrl="~/BannerAd.gif"
                    CssClass="ad"
                    AlternateText="Advertisement for Superexpert ASP Workshops"
                    Runat="server" />
            </asp:ContentPlaceHolder>

        </div>
        <br class="clear" />
    </div>
    </form>
</body>
</html>
```

The content page in Listing 5.4 uses the Master Page in Listing 5.3. It does not include a Content control that corresponds to the contentAd control in the Master Page. When you open the page in a browser, the default banner advertisement is displayed.

LISTING 5.4 DefaultContent.aspx

```
<%@ Page Language="VB" MasterPageFile="~/DefaultMaster.master" %>

<asp:Content
    ID="Content1"
    ContentPlaceHolderID="ContentPlaceHolder1"
    Runat="Server">
    Content in the first column
    <br />Content in the first column
    <br />Content in the first column
    <br />Content in the first column
    <br />Content in the first column
</asp:Content>

<asp:Content
    ID="Content2"
    ContentPlaceHolderID="ContentPlaceHolder2"
    Runat="Server">
    Content in the second column
    <br />Content in the second column
    <br />Content in the second column
    <br />Content in the second column
    <br />Content in the second column
</asp:Content>
```

Of course, you do have the option of adding a Content control that overrides the default content contained in the contentAd control in the Master Page. For example, you might want to display different banner advertisements in different sections of your website.

> **NOTE**
>
> You can nest ContentPlaceHolder controls in a Master Page. If you do this, then you have the option of overriding greater or smaller areas of content in the Master Page.

Nesting Master Pages

When building a large website, you might need to create multiple levels of Master Pages. For example, you might want to create a single site-wide Master Page that applies to all the content pages in your website. In addition, you might need to create multiple section-wide Master Pages that apply to only the pages contained in a particular section.

> **WARNING**
>
> You cannot work with nested Master Pages in Visual Web Developer while in Design view. If you need to nest Master Pages, then you need to stick to Source view.

You can nest Master Pages as many levels as you need. For example, Listing 5.5 contains a Master Page named `Site.master`, which displays a logo image and contains a single content area. It also contains site-wide navigation links.

LISTING 5.5   `Site.master`

```
<%@ Master Language="VB" %>
<!DOCTYPE html PUBLIC "-//W3C//DTD XHTML 1.1//EN"
"http://www.w3.org/TR/xhtml11/DTD/xhtml11.dtd">
<html xmlns="http://www.w3.org/1999/xhtml" >
<head id="Head1" runat="server">
    <style type="text/css">
        html
        {
            background-color:DarkGreen;
            font:14px Georgia,Serif;
        }
        .content
        {
            width:700px;
            margin:auto;
            border-style:solid;
            background-color:white;
            padding:10px;
        }
        .tabstrip
        {
            padding:3px;
            border-top:solid 1px black;
            border-bottom:solid 1px black;
        }
        .tabstrip a
        {
            font:14px Arial;
            color:DarkGreen;
            text-decoration:none;
        }
        .column
        {
            float:left;
            padding:10px;
```

LISTING 5.5   Continued

```
                  border-right:solid 1px black;
          }
          .rightColumn
          {
              float:left;
              padding:10px;
          }
          .clear
          {
              clear:both;
          }
      </style>
      <title>Site Master</title>
</head>
<body>
    <form id="form1" runat="server">

    <div class="content">
        <asp:Image
            id="imgLogo"
            ImageUrl="~/Images/SiteLogo.gif"
            AlternateText="Website Logo"
            Runat="server" />

        <div class="tabstrip">
        <asp:HyperLink
            id="lnkProducts"
            Text="Products"
            NavigateUrl="~/Products.aspx"
            Runat="server" />
         
        <asp:HyperLink
            id="lnkServices"
            Text="Services"
            NavigateUrl="~/Services.aspx"
            Runat="server" />
        </div>
        <asp:contentplaceholder id="ContentPlaceHolder1" runat="server">
        </asp:contentplaceholder>
        <br class="clear" />
        copyright &copy; 2007 by the Company
    </div>
    </form>
</body>
</html>
```

The Master Pages in Listing 5.6 and Listing 5.7 are nested Master Pages. Notice that both Master Pages include a `MasterPageFile` attribute that points to the `Site.master` Master Page.

LISTING 5.6   `SectionProducts.master`

```
<%@ Master Language="VB" MasterPageFile="~/Site.master" %>


<asp:Content
    id="Content1"
    ContentPlaceHolderID="ContentPlaceHolder1"
    Runat="server">
    <div class="column">
        <asp:ContentPlaceHolder
            id="ContentPlaceHolder1"
            Runat="server" />
    </div>
    <div class="column">
        <asp:ContentPlaceHolder
            id="ContentPlaceHolder2"
            Runat="server" />
    </div>
    <div class="rightColumn">
        <asp:ContentPlaceHolder
            id="ContentPlaceHolder3"
            Runat="server" />
    </div>
</asp:Content>
```

LISTING 5.7   `SectionServices.master`

```
<%@ Master Language="VB" MasterPageFile="~/Site.master" %>


<asp:Content
    id="Content1"
    ContentPlaceHolderID="ContentPlaceHolder1"
    Runat="server">
    <div class="column">
        <asp:ContentPlaceHolder
            id="ContentPlaceHolder1"
            Runat="server" />
    </div>
    <div class="rightColumn">
        <asp:ContentPlaceHolder
```

LISTING 5.7   Continued

```
            id="ContentPlaceHolder2"
            Runat="server" />
    </div>
</asp:Content>
```

The Master Page in Listing 5.6 creates a three-column page layout, and the Master Page in Listing 5.7 creates a two-column page layout.

The Products.aspx page in Listing 5.8 uses the SectionProducts.master Master Page. When you request the Products.aspx page, the contents of Site.master, SectionProducts.master, and Products.aspx are combined to generate the rendered output (see Figure 5.3).

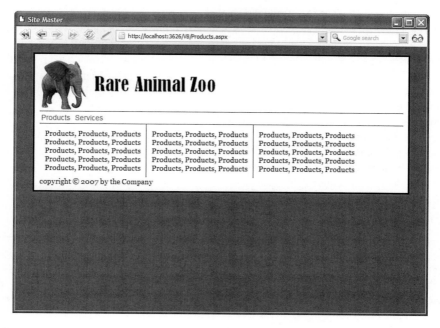

FIGURE 5.3   Nesting Master Pages to display the Products.aspx page.

LISTING 5.8   Products.aspx

```
<%@ Page Language="VB" MasterPageFile="~/SectionProducts.master" %>

<asp:Content
    ID="Content1"
    ContentPlaceHolderID="ContentPlaceHolder1"
    Runat="Server">
```

LISTING 5.8   Continued

```
    Products, Products, Products
    <br />Products, Products, Products
    <br />Products, Products, Products
    <br />Products, Products, Products
    <br />Products, Products, Products
</asp:Content>

<asp:Content
    ID="Content2"
    ContentPlaceHolderID="ContentPlaceHolder2"
    Runat="Server">
    Products, Products, Products
    <br />Products, Products, Products
    <br />Products, Products, Products
    <br />Products, Products, Products
    <br />Products, Products, Products
</asp:Content>

<asp:Content
    ID="Content3"
    ContentPlaceHolderID="ContentPlaceHolder3"
    Runat="Server">
    Products, Products, Products
    <br />Products, Products, Products
    <br />Products, Products, Products
    <br />Products, Products, Products
    <br />Products, Products, Products
</asp:Content>
```

The Services.aspx page in Listing 5.9 uses the SectionService.master Master Page. When this page is opened in a browser, the contents of Site.master, SectionServices.master, and Services.aspx are combined to generate the rendered output (see Figure 5.4).

LISTING 5.9   Services.aspx

```
<%@ Page Language="VB" MasterPageFile="~/SectionServices.master"
    Title="Untitled Page" %>

<asp:Content
    ID="Content1"
    ContentPlaceHolderID="ContentPlaceHolder1"
    Runat="Server">
    Services, Services, Services
```

LISTING 5.9   Continued

```
    <br />Services, Services, Services
    <br />Services, Services, Services
    <br />Services, Services, Services
    <br />Services, Services, Services
</asp:Content>
<asp:Content
    ID="Content2"
    ContentPlaceHolderID="ContentPlaceHolder2"
    Runat="Server">
    Services, Services, Services, Services, Services
    <br />Services, Services, Services, Services, Services
    <br />Services, Services, Services, Services, Services
    <br />Services, Services, Services, Services, Services
    <br />Services, Services, Services, Services, Services
</asp:Content>
```

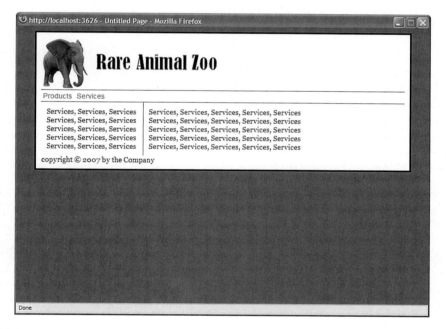

FIGURE 5.4   Nesting Master Pages to display the `Services.aspx` pages.

Using Images and Hyperlinks in Master Pages

You must be careful when using relative URLs in a Master Page. For example, you must be careful when adding images and links to a Master Page. Relative URLs are interpreted in different ways, depending on whether they are used with HTML tags or ASP.NET controls.

If you use a relative URL with an ASP.NET control, then the URL is interpreted relative to the Master Page. For example, suppose that you add the following ASP.NET Image control to a Master Page:

```
<asp:Image ImageUrl="Picture.gif" Runat="Server" />
```

The `ImageUrl` property contains a relative URL. If the Master Page is located in a folder named `MasterPages`, then the URL is interpreted like this:

```
/MasterPages/Picture.gif
```

Even if a content page is located in a completely different folder, the `ImageUrl` is interpreted relative to the folder that contains the Master Page and not relative to the content page.

The situation is completely different in the case of HTML elements. If an HTML element such as an `<img>` or `<a>` tag includes a relative URL, the relative URL is interpreted relative to the content page. For example, suppose you add the following `<img>` tag to a Master Page:

```
<img src="Picture.gif" />
```

The `src` attribute contains a relative URL. This URL is interpreted relative to a particular content page. For example, if you request a content page located in a folder named `ContentPages`, the relative URL is interpreted like this:

```
/ContentPages/Picture.gif
```

Using relative URLs with HTML elements is especially tricky because the URL keeps changing with each content page. If you request content pages from different folders, the relative URL changes. There are three ways that you can solve this problem.

First, you can replace all the HTML elements that use relative URLs with ASP.NET controls. An ASP.NET control automatically reinterprets a relative URL as relative to the Master Page.

> **NOTE**
>
> Relative URLs used by ASP.NET controls in a Master Page are automatically reinterpreted relative to the Master Page. This process of reinterpretation is called *rebasing*. Only ASP.NET control properties decorated with the `UrlProperty` attribute are rebased.

Second, you can avoid relative URLs and use absolute URLs. For example, if your application is named MyApp, then you can use the following `<img>` tag to display an image file located in the `MasterPages` folder:

```
<img src="/MyApp/MasterPages/Picture.gif" />
```

The disadvantage of using absolute URLs is that they make it difficult to change the location of a web application. If the name of your application changes, then the absolute URLs will no longer work and you'll end up with a bunch of broken images and links.

Another option is to use a method to reinterpret relative URLs in a Master Page. For example, the Master Page in Listing 5.10 includes a method named MasterUrl(). This method is used with the <img> tag in the body of the Master Page, which displays the website logo.

LISTING 5.10   MasterPages\ImageMaster.master

```
<%@ Master Language="VB" %>
<!DOCTYPE html PUBLIC "-//W3C//DTD XHTML 1.1//EN"
"http://www.w3.org/TR/xhtml11/DTD/xhtml11.dtd">
<script runat="server">

    Public Function MasterUrl(ByVal url As String) As String
        Return String.Format("{0}/{1}", Me.TemplateSourceDirectory, url)
    End Function
</script>
<html xmlns="http://www.w3.org/1999/xhtml" >
<head id="Head1" runat="server">
    <title>Image Master</title>
</head>
<body>
    <form id="form1" runat="server">
    <div>

    <img src='<%=MasterUrl("Logo.gif") %>' alt="Website Logo" />

    <asp:contentplaceholder id="ContentPlaceHolder1" runat="server" />

    </div>
    </form>
</body>
</html>
```

The Master Page in Listing 5.10 is located in a folder named MasterPages. This folder also includes an image named Logo.gif. This image is displayed with the following HTML tag:

```
<img src='<%=MasterUrl("Logo.gif") %>' alt="Website Logo" />
```

The MasterUrl() method appends the image's filename to the value of the Master Page's TemplateSourceDirectory property. The TemplateSourceDirectory property represents the folder that contains the Master Page.

The content page in Listing 5.11 uses the Master Page and correctly displays the website logo (see Figure 5.5):

FIGURE 5.5   Displaying a Master Page relative image.

LISTING 5.11   `ImageContent.aspx`

```
<%@ Page Language="VB" MasterPageFile="~/MasterPages/ImageMaster.master" %>

<asp:Content
    ID="Content1"
    ContentPlaceHolderID="ContentPlaceHolder1"
    Runat="Server">

    <h1>Content</h1>

</asp:Content>
```

Registering Master Pages in Web Configuration

You can apply a Master Page to every content page in a particular folder or every content page in an entire application. Rather than add a `MasterPageFile` attribute to individual content pages, you can add a configuration option to the web configuration file.

For example, the web configuration file in Listing 5.12 applies the `SimpleMaster.master` Master Page to every page contained in the same folder (or subfolder) as the web configuration file.

LISTING 5.12 `FolderA\Web.Config`

```xml
<?xml version="1.0"?>
<configuration>
<system.web>
  <pages masterPageFile="~/SimpleMaster.master" />
</system.web>
</configuration>
```

The Master Page is applied only to content pages. If a page does not contain any `Content` controls—it is a normal ASP.NET page—then the Master Page is ignored.

You can override the Master Page configured in the web configuration file in the case of a particular content page. In other words, a `MasterPageFile` attribute in a content page takes precedence over a Master Page specified in the web configuration file.

Modifying Master Page Content

Master Pages enable you to display the same content in multiple content pages. You'll quickly discover that you need to override the content displayed by a Master Page in the case of particular content pages.

For example, normally the Master Page contains the opening and closing HTML tags, including the `<title>` tag. This means that every content page will display the same title. Normally, you want each page to display a unique title.

In this section, you learn multiple techniques of modifying Master Page content from a content page.

Using the `Title` Attribute

If you only need to modify the title displayed in each content page, then you can take advantage of the `<%@ Page %>` directive's `Title` attribute. This attribute accepts any string value.

For example, the page in Listing 5.13 includes a `Title` attribute, which sets the title of the current content page to the value `Content Page Title`.

LISTING 5.13 `TitleContent.aspx`

```aspx
<%@ Page Language="VB" MasterPageFile="~/SimpleMaster.master"
    Title="Content Page Title" %>

<asp:Content
    ID="Content1"
```

LISTING 5.13 Continued

```
        ContentPlaceHolderID="ContentPlaceHolder1"
        Runat="Server">
        Content in the first column
        <br />Content in the first column
        <br />Content in the first column
        <br />Content in the first column
        <br />Content in the first column
</asp:Content>

<asp:Content
        ID="Content2"
        ContentPlaceHolderID="ContentPlaceHolder2"
        Runat="Server">
        Content in the second column
        <br />Content in the second column
        <br />Content in the second column
        <br />Content in the second column
        <br />Content in the second column
</asp:Content>
```

There is one requirement for the Title attribute to work. The HTML <head> tag in the Master Page must be a server-side Head tag. In other words, the <head> tag must include the runat="server" attribute. When you create a new Web Form or Master Page in Visual Web Developer, a server-side <head> tag is automatically created.

Using the Page Header Property

If you need to programmatically change the Title or Cascading Style Sheet rules included in a Master Page, then you can use the Page.Header property. This property returns an object that implements the IPageHeader interface. This interface has the following two properties:

- StyleSheet
- Title

For example, the content page in Listing 5.14 uses the SimpleMaster.master Master Page. It changes the Title and background color of the Master Page.

LISTING 5.14 HeaderContent.aspx

```
<%@ Page Language="VB" MasterPageFile="~/SimpleMaster.master" %>
<script runat="server">

    Private Sub Page_Load()
```

LISTING 5.14   Continued

```
        ' Change the title
        Page.Header.Title = String.Format("Header Content ({0})", DateTime.Now)

        ' Change the background color
        Dim myStyle As New Style()
        myStyle.BackColor = System.Drawing.Color.Red
        Page.Header.StyleSheet.CreateStyleRule(myStyle, Nothing, "html")
    End Sub
</script>
<asp:Content
    ID="Content1"
    ContentPlaceHolderID="ContentPlaceHolder1"
    Runat="Server">
    Content in the first column
    <br />Content in the first column
    <br />Content in the first column
    <br />Content in the first column
    <br />Content in the first column
</asp:Content>

<asp:Content
    ID="Content2"
    ContentPlaceHolderID="ContentPlaceHolder2"
    Runat="Server">
    Content in the second column
    <br />Content in the second column
    <br />Content in the second column
    <br />Content in the second column
    <br />Content in the second column
</asp:Content>
```

The Page.Header property returns the server-side <head> tag contained in the Master Page. You can cast the object returned by this property to an HTMLHead control. For example, the page in Listing 5.15 modifies the Master Page <meta> tags (the tags used by search engines when indexing a page).

LISTING 5.15   MetaContent.aspx

```
<%@ Page Language="VB" MasterPageFile="~/SimpleMaster.master" %>
<script runat="server">

    Private Sub Page_Load()
        ' Create Meta Description
```

LISTING 5.15   Continued

```
        Dim metaDesc As New HtmlMeta()
        metaDesc.Name = "DESCRIPTION"
        metaDesc.Content = "A sample of using HtmlMeta controls"

        ' Create Meta Keywords
        Dim metaKeywords As New HtmlMeta()
        metaKeywords.Name = "KEYWORDS"
        metaKeywords.Content = "HtmlMeta,Page.Header,ASP.NET"

        ' Add Meta controls to HtmlHead
        Dim head As HtmlHead = CType(Page.Header, HtmlHead)
        head.Controls.Add(metaDesc)
        head.Controls.Add(metaKeywords)
    End Sub
</script>
<asp:Content
    ID="Content1"
    ContentPlaceHolderID="ContentPlaceHolder1"
    Runat="Server">
    Content in the first column
    <br />Content in the first column
    <br />Content in the first column
    <br />Content in the first column
    <br />Content in the first column
</asp:Content>

<asp:Content
    ID="Content2"
    ContentPlaceHolderID="ContentPlaceHolder2"
    Runat="Server">
    Content in the second column
    <br />Content in the second column
    <br />Content in the second column
    <br />Content in the second column
    <br />Content in the second column
</asp:Content>
```

Notice that the Page_Load() method in Listing 5.15 creates two HtmlMeta controls. The first control represents a Meta Description tag and the second control represents a Meta Keywords tag. Both HtmlMeta controls are added to the HtmlHead control's Controls collection.

When the page is rendered, the following tags are added to the <head> tag:

```
<meta name="DESCRIPTION" content="A sample of using HtmlMeta controls" />
<meta name="KEYWORDS" content="HtmlMeta,Page.Header,ASP.NET" />
```

> **WARNING**
>
> You receive a NullReference exception if you use the Page.Header property when the Master Page does not contain a server-side <head> tag.

Exposing Master Page Properties

You can expose properties and methods from a Master Page and modify the properties and methods from a particular content page. For example, the Master Page in Listing 5.16 includes a public property named BodyTitle.

LISTING 5.16   PropertyMaster.master

```
<%@ Master Language="VB" %>
<!DOCTYPE html PUBLIC "-//W3C//DTD XHTML 1.1//EN"
"http://www.w3.org/TR/xhtml11/DTD/xhtml11.dtd">
<script runat="server">

    Public Property BodyTitle() As String
        Get
            Return ltlBodyTitle.Text
        End Get
        Set(ByVal Value As String)
            ltlBodyTitle.Text = value
        End Set
    End Property
</script>
<html xmlns="http://www.w3.org/1999/xhtml" >
<head id="Head1" runat="server">
    <style type="text/css">
        html
        {
            background-color:silver;
        }
        .content
        {
            margin:auto;
            width:700px;
            background-color:white;
            padding:10px;
        }
```

LISTING 5.16   Continued

```
        h1
        {
            border-bottom:solid 1px blue;
        }
    </style>
    <title>Property Master</title>
</head>
<body>
    <form id="form1" runat="server">
    <div class="content">
    <h1><asp:Literal ID="ltlBodyTitle" runat="server" /></h1>
    <asp:contentplaceholder
        id="ContentPlaceHolder1"
        runat="server" />
    </div>
    </form>
</body>
</html>
```

The `BodyTitle` property enables you to assign a title that is rendered in a header tag in the body of the page (see Figure 5.6).

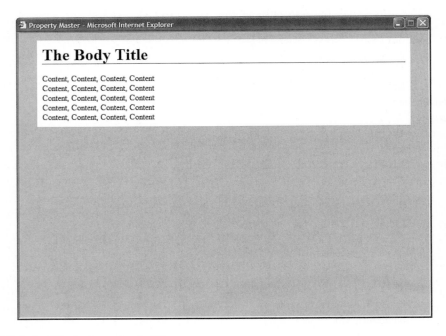

FIGURE 5.6   Displaying a body title.

Because the BodyTitle property is exposed as a public property, you can modify it from a particular content page. The page in Listing 5.17 assigns the value "The Body Title" to the BodyTitle property.

LISTING 5.17   PropertyContent.aspx

```
<%@ Page Language="VB" MasterPageFile="~/PropertyMaster.master" %>
<%@ MasterType VirtualPath="~/PropertyMaster.master" %>
<script runat="server">

    Private  Sub Page_Load()
        If Not Page.IsPostBack Then
            Master.BodyTitle = "The Body Title"
        End If
    End Sub
</script>
<asp:Content
    ID="Content1"
    ContentPlaceHolderID="ContentPlaceHolder1"
    Runat="Server">
    Content, Content, Content, Content
    <br />Content, Content, Content, Content
    <br />Content, Content, Content, Content
    <br />Content, Content, Content, Content
    <br />Content, Content, Content, Content
</asp:Content>
```

You should notice several things about the page in Listing 5.17. First, notice that you can refer to the Master Page by using the Master property. In the Page_Load() method in Listing 5.17, the BodyTitle property of the Master Page is assigned a value with the following line of code:

```
Master.BodyTitle = "The Body Title";
```

You should also notice that the page in Listing 5.17 includes a <%@ MasterType %> directive. This directive automatically casts the value of the Master property to the type of the Master Page. In other words, it casts the Master Page to the PropertyMaster type instead of the generic MasterPage type.

If you want to be able to refer to a custom property in a Master Page, such as the BodyTitle property, then the value of the Master property must be cast to the right type. The BodyTitle property is not a property of the generic MasterPage class, but it is a property of the PropertyMaster class.

Using FindControl with Master Pages

In the previous section, you learned how to modify a property of a control located in a Master Page from a content page by exposing a property from the Master Page. You have an alternative here. If you need to modify a control in a Master Page, you can use the FindControl() method in a content page.

For example, the Master Page in Listing 5.18 includes a Literal control named BodyTitle. This Master Page does not include any custom properties.

LISTING 5.18   FindMaster.master

```
<%@ Master Language="VB" %>
<!DOCTYPE html PUBLIC "-//W3C//DTD XHTML 1.1//EN"
"http://www.w3.org/TR/xhtml11/DTD/xhtml11.dtd">
<html xmlns="http://www.w3.org/1999/xhtml" >
<head id="Head1" runat="server">
    <style type="text/css">
        html
        {
            background-color:silver;
        }
        .content
        {
            margin:auto;
            width:700px;
            background-color:white;
            padding:10px;
        }
        h1
        {
            border-bottom:solid 1px blue;
        }

    </style>
    <title>Find Master</title>
</head>
<body>
    <form id="form1" runat="server">
    <div class="content">
    <h1><asp:Literal ID="ltlBodyTitle" runat="server" /></h1>
    <asp:contentplaceholder
        id="ContentPlaceHolder1"
        runat="server" />
    </div>
    </form>
</body>
</html>
```

The content page in Listing 5.19 modifies the Text property of the Literal control located in the Master Page. The content page uses the FindControl() method to retrieve the Literal control from the Master Page.

LISTING 5.19   FindContent.aspx

```
<%@ Page Language="VB" MasterPageFile="~/FindMaster.master" %>
<script runat="server">

    Private Sub Page_Load()
        If Not Page.IsPostBack Then
            Dim ltlBodyTitle As Literal =
➥CType(Master.FindControl("ltlBodyTitle"), Literal)
            ltlBodyTitle.Text = "The Body Title"
        End If
    End Sub
</script>
<asp:Content
    ID="Content1"
    ContentPlaceHolderID="ContentPlaceHolder1"
    Runat="Server">
    Content, Content, Content, Content
    <br />Content, Content, Content, Content
    <br />Content, Content, Content, Content
    <br />Content, Content, Content, Content
    <br />Content, Content, Content, Content
</asp:Content>
```

The FindControl() method enables you to search a naming container for a control with a particular ID. The method returns a reference to the control.

Loading Master Pages Dynamically

You can associate different Master Pages dynamically with a content page. This is useful in two situations.

First, you can enable the users of your website to customize the appearance of the website by loading different Master Pages. You can display a menu of Master Pages, and allow your users to pick their favorite layout.

Another situation in which loading Master Pages dynamically is useful concerns co-branding. Imagine that your company needs to make its website look like a partner website. When users link to your website from the partner website, you don't want users to know that they are traveling to a new website. You can maintain this illusion by dynamically loading different Master Pages based on a query string passed from a partner website.

A Master Page is merged with a content page very early in the page execution life-cycle. This means that you cannot dynamically load a Master Page during the Page Load event. The only event during which you can load a Master Page is during the Page PreInit event. This is the first event that is raised during the page execution life cycle.

For example, the content page in Listing 5.20 dynamically loads one of two Master Pages named Dynamic1.master and Dynamic2.master.

LISTING 5.20   DynamicContent.aspx

```
<%@ Page Language="VB" MasterPageFile="~/Dynamic1.master" %>
<script runat="server">

    Protected  Sub Page_PreInit(ByVal sender As Object, ByVal e As EventArgs)
        If Not Request("master") Is Nothing Then
            Select Case Request("master")
                Case "Dynamic1"
                    Profile.MasterPageFile = "Dynamic1.master"
                Case "Dynamic2"
                    Profile.MasterPageFile = "Dynamic2.master"
            End Select
        End If

        MasterPageFile = Profile.MasterPageFile
    End Sub
</script>


<asp:Content
    ID="Content1"
    ContentPlaceHolderID="ContentPlaceHolder1"
    Runat="Server">

    Select a Master Page:
    <ul class="selectMaster">
        <li>
        <a href="DynamicContent.aspx?master=Dynamic1">Dynamic Master 1</a>
        </li>
        <li>
        <a href="DynamicContent.aspx?master=Dynamic2">Dynamic Master 2</a>
        </li>
    </ul>

</asp:Content>
```

The page in Listing 5.20 contains two links. Both links include a query string parameter named master, which represents the name of a Master Page. When you click the first link, the `Dynamic1.master` Master Page is loaded (see Figure 5.7) and when you click the second link, the `Dynamic2.master` Master Page is loaded (see Figure 5.8).

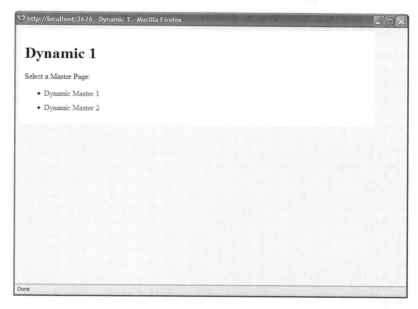

FIGURE 5.7   Displaying the Dynamic1 Master Page.

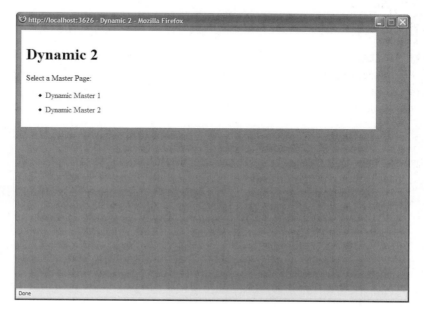

FIGURE 5.8   Displaying the Dynamic2 Master Page.

Notice that the page in Listing 5.20 includes a `Page_PreInit()` event handler. This handler grabs the value of the master query string parameter and assigns the value of this parameter to a `Profile` property. Next, the value of the `Profile` property is assigned to the page's `MasterPageFile` property. Assigning a value to the `MasterPageFile` property causes a Master Page to be dynamically loaded.

Because the name of the Master Page is assigned to a `Profile` property, the selected Master Page loads for a user even if the user returns to the website many years in the future. The `Profile` object automatically persists the values of its properties for a user across multiple visits to a website. The `Profile` is defined in the web configuration file contained in Listing 5.21.

LISTING 5.21   `Web.Config`

```
<?xml version="1.0"?>
<configuration>
  <system.web>
    <profile>
      <properties>
        <add
          name="MasterPageFile"
          defaultValue="Dynamic1.master" />
      </properties>
    </profile>
  </system.web>
</configuration>
```

Loading Master Pages Dynamically for Multiple Content Pages

In the previous section, you learned how to load a Master Page dynamically for a single page in a website. However, what if you need to load a Master Page dynamically for every content page in a website?

The easiest way to apply the same logic to multiple content pages is to create a new base Page class. The file in Listing 5.22 contains a new base `Page` class named `DynamicMasterPage`.

> **NOTE**
>
> Add the file in Listing 5.22 to your application's App_Code folder.

LISTING 5.22   `DynamicMasterPage.vb`

```
Imports Microsoft.VisualBasic

Public Class DynamicMasterPage
```

LISTING 5.22   Continued

```
Inherits Page

Protected Overrides Sub OnPreInit(ByVal e As EventArgs)
    Me.MasterPageFile = CType(Context.Profile("MasterPageFile"), String)
    MyBase.OnPreInit(e)
End Sub

End Class
```

The class in Listing 5.22 inherits from the `Page` class. However, it overrides the base `Page` class's `OnPreInit()` method and adds the logic for loading a Master Page dynamically.

After you create a new base `Page` class, you need to register it in the web configuration file. The web configuration file in Listing 5.23 contains the necessary settings.

LISTING 5.23   Web.config

```
<?xml version="1.0"?>
<configuration>
  <system.web>

    <pages pageBaseType="DynamicMasterPage" />

    <profile>
      <properties>
        <add
          name="MasterPageFile"
          defaultValue="Dynamic1.master" />
      </properties>
    </profile>
  </system.web>
</configuration>
```

After you register the `DynamicMasterPage` class as the base `Page` class, every page in your application automatically inherits from the new base class. Every page inherits the new `OnPreInit()` method and every page loads a Master Page dynamically.

Summary

In this chapter, you learned how to share the same content among multiple pages in an application by taking advantage of Master Pages. In the first section, you learned how to create a Master Page and apply it to multiple content pages. You also learned how to nest Master Pages and how to register a Master Page in the web configuration file.

The next section explored various techniques of modifying a Master Page from a particular content page. You learned how to use the `Title` attribute, how to use the `Page.Header` property, how to expose properties in a Master Page, and how to use the `FindControl()` method.

Finally, you learned how you can dynamically load different Master Pages and associate a particular Master Page with a particular content page at runtime. You learned how you can save a user's Master Page preference by using the `Profile` object.

CHAPTER 6

Designing Websites with Themes

An ASP.NET Theme enables you to apply a consistent style to the pages in your website. You can use a Theme to control the appearance of both the HTML elements and ASP.NET controls that appear in a page.

Themes are different than Master Pages. A Master Page enables you to share content across multiple pages in a website. A Theme, on the other hand, enables you to control the appearance of the content.

In this chapter, you learn how to create and apply ASP.NET Themes. First, you learn how to create Skins. A Skin enables you to modify the properties of an ASP.NET control that have an effect on its appearance. You learn how to create both Default and Named Skins.

Next, you learn how to format both HTML elements and ASP.NET controls by adding Cascading Style Sheets to a Theme. Cascading Style Sheets enable you to control the appearance and layout of pages in a website in a standards-compliant manner.

You also learn how you can create Global Themes, which can be used by multiple applications located on the same server. You learn how to use Global Themes with both File System and HTTP-based websites.

Finally, you learn how to load Themes and Skins dynamically at runtime. You build a page that each user of a website can customize by skinning.

Creating Themes

You create a Theme by adding a new folder to a special folder in your application named App_Themes. Each folder that you add to the App_Themes folder represents a different Theme.

If the App_Themes folder doesn't exist in your application, then you can create it. It must be located in the root of your application.

> **VISUAL WEB DEVELOPER NOTE**
>
> When using Visual Web Developer, you can create a new Theme folder by right-clicking the name of your project in the Solution Explorer window and selecting Add ASP.NET Folder, Theme.

A Theme folder can contain a variety of different types of files, including images and text files. You also can organize the contents of a Theme folder by adding multiple subfolders to a Theme folder.

The most important types of files in a Theme folder are the following:

- Skin Files
- Cascading Style Sheet Files

In the following sections, you learn how to add both Skin files and Cascading Style Sheet files to a Theme.

> **WARNING**
>
> Be careful about how you name your Theme (the folder name). The contents of a Theme folder are automatically compiled in the background into a new class. So you want to be careful not to name a Theme with a class name that conflicts with an existing class name in your project.

Adding Skins to Themes

A Theme can contain one or more Skin files. A Skin enables you to modify any of the properties of an ASP.NET control that have an effect on its appearance.

For example, imagine that you decide that you want every TextBox control in your web application to appear with a yellow background color and a dotted border. If you add the file in Listing 6.1 to the Simple Theme (the App_Themes\Simple folder), then you can modify the appearance of all TextBox controls in all pages that use the Simple Theme.

LISTING 6.1   Simple\TextBox.skin

```
<asp:TextBox
    BackColor="Yellow"
    BorderStyle="Dotted"
    Runat="Server" />
```

Notice that the Skin file in Listing 6.1 is named `TextBox.skin`. You can name a Skin file anything you want. I recommend following a naming convention in which you name the Skin file after the name of the control that the Skin modifies.

A Theme folder can contain a single Skin file that contains Skins for hundreds of controls. Alternatively, a Theme can contain hundreds of Skin files, each of which contains a single Skin. It doesn't matter how you organize your Skins into files because everything in a Theme folder eventually gets compiled into one Theme class.

The Skin file in Listing 6.1 contains a declaration of a `TextBox` control. Notice that the `TextBox` control includes a `BackColor` property that is set to the value Yellow and a `BorderStyle` property that is set to the value Dotted.

You should notice that the `TextBox` control includes a `Runat="Server"` attribute, but it does not include an `ID` attribute. You must always include a `Runat` attribute, but you can never include the `ID` attribute when declaring a control in a Skin.

> **NOTE**
>
> You can't create a Skin that applies to the properties of a User Control. However, you can Skin the controls contained inside a User Control.

The Skin is applied to every page to which the Simple Theme is applied. For example, the page in Listing 6.2 uses the Simple Theme.

LISTING 6.2   `ShowSkin.aspx`

```
<%@ Page Language="VB" Theme="Simple" %>
<!DOCTYPE html PUBLIC "-//W3C//DTD XHTML 1.1//EN"
"http://www.w3.org/TR/xhtml11/DTD/xhtml11.dtd">
<html xmlns="http://www.w3.org/1999/xhtml" >
<head id="Head1" runat="server">
    <title>Show Skin</title>
</head>
<body>
    <form id="form1" runat="server">
    <div>

    <asp:TextBox ID="TextBox1"
        Runat="server" />

    </div>
    </form>
</body>
</html>
```

Notice that the page in Listing 6.2 includes a Theme attribute in its <%@ Page %> directive. This attribute causes the Simple Theme to be applied to the page.

When you open the page in Listing 6.2, the Label control appears with a yellow background color and dotted border. This is the background color and border specified by the Theme (see Figure 6.1).

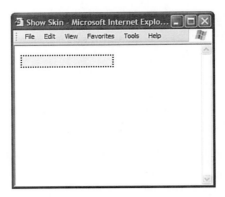

FIGURE 6.1   Using a TextBox Skin.

Only certain control properties are "themeable." In other words, you can create a Skin file that modifies only certain properties of a control. In general, you can use a Skin to modify properties that have an effect on a control's appearance but not its behavior. For example, you can modify the BackColor property of a TextBox control but not its AutoPostBack property.

> **NOTE**
>
> By default, all control properties are themeable (can be modified in a Skin file). However, certain control properties are decorated with the Themeable(False) attribute, which disables theming.

Creating Named Skins

In the previous section, we created something called a Default Skin. A Default Skin is applied to every instance of a control of a certain type. For example, a Default Skin is applied to every instance of a TextBox control.

You also have the option of creating a Named Skin. When you create a Named Skin, you can decide when you want to apply the Skin. For example, you might want required fields in a form to appear with a red border. In that case, you can create a Named Skin and apply the Skin to only particular TextBox controls.

The Skin in Listing 6.3 contains both a Default Skin and a Named Skin for a TextBox control.

LISTING 6.3   `Simple2\TextBox.skin`

```
<asp:TextBox
    SkinID="DashedTextBox"
    BorderStyle="Dashed"
    BorderWidth="5px"
    Runat="Server" />

<asp:TextBox
    BorderStyle="Double"
    BorderWidth="5px"
    Runat="Server" />
```

The first `TextBox` in Listing 6.3 is an example of a Named Skin. Notice that it includes a `SkinID` property. The `SkinID` property represents the name of the Named Skin. You use the value of this property when applying the Skin in a page.

The file in Listing 6.3 also includes a Default Skin for a `TextBox` control. The Default Skin does not include a `SkinID` property. If a `TextBox` control in a page is not associated with a Named Skin, then the Default Skin is applied to the `TextBox`.

A Theme can contain only one Default Skin for each type of control. However, a Theme can contain as many Named Skins as you please. Each Named Skin must have a unique name.

The page in Listing 6.4 contains two `TextBox` controls. The first `TextBox` control includes a `SkinID` attribute. This attribute causes the Named Skin to be applied to the control. The second `TextBox`, on the other hand, does not include a `SkinID` property. The Default Skin is applied to the second `TextBox` control.

LISTING 6.4   `ShowNamedSkin.aspx`

```
<%@ Page Language="VB" Theme="Simple2" %>
<!DOCTYPE html PUBLIC "-//W3C//DTD XHTML 1.1//EN"
"http://www.w3.org/TR/xhtml11/DTD/xhtml11.dtd">
<html xmlns="http://www.w3.org/1999/xhtml" >
<head id="Head1" runat="server">
    <title>Show Named Skin</title>
</head>
<body>
    <form id="form1" runat="server">
    <div>

    <asp:TextBox
        id="txtFirstName"
        SkinID="DashedTextBox"
        Runat="server" />
```

LISTING 6.4   Continued

```
    <br /><br />

    <asp:TextBox
        id="txtLastName"
        Runat="server" />

    </div>
    </form>
</body>
</html>
```

When you open the page in Listing 6.4, the first TextBox appears with a dashed border and the second TextBox appears with a double border (see Figure 6.2).

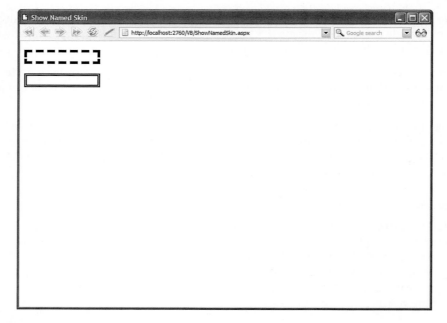

FIGURE 6.2   Using Named Skins.

Themes **versus** StyleSheetThemes

When you apply a Theme to a page, the Skins in the Theme override any existing properties of the controls in the page. In other words, properties in a Skin override properties in a page.

For example, imagine that you create the Skin in Listing 6.5.

LISTING 6.5   `Simple3\Label.skin`

```
<asp:Label
    BackColor="Orange"
    Runat="Server" />
```

The Skin in Listing 6.5 sets the background color of all Label controls to the color Orange.

Now, imagine that you apply the Skin in Listing 6.5 to the ASP.NET page in Listing 6.6.

LISTING 6.6   `ShowSkinTheme.aspx`

```
<%@ Page Language="VB" Theme="Simple3" %>
<!DOCTYPE html PUBLIC "-//W3C//DTD XHTML 1.1//EN"
"http://www.w3.org/TR/xhtml11/DTD/xhtml11.dtd">
<html xmlns="http://www.w3.org/1999/xhtml" >
<head id="Head1" runat="server">
    <title>Show Skin Theme</title>
</head>
<body>
    <form id="form1" runat="server">
    <div>

    <asp:Label
        id="Label1"
        Text="What color background do I have?"
        BackColor="red"
        Runat="server" />

    </div>
    </form>
</body>
</html>
```

The page in Listing 6.6 includes a Label that has a BackColor property which is set to the value Red. However, when you open the page, the BackColor declared in the Skin overrides the BackColor declared in the page and the Label is displayed with an orange background.

The default behavior of Themes makes it very easy to modify the design of an existing website. You can override any existing control properties that have an effect on the appearance of the control.

However, there are situations in which you might want to override Skin properties. For example, you might want to display every Label in your website with an orange background color except for one Label. In that case, it would be nice if there was a way to override the Skin property.

You can override Skin properties by applying a Theme to a page with the StyleSheetTheme attribute instead of the Theme attribute. For example, the page in Listing 6.7 uses the StyleSheetTheme attribute to apply the Simple3 Theme to the page.

LISTING 6.7   ShowSkinStyleSheetTheme.aspx

```
<%@ Page Language="VB" StyleSheetTheme="Simple3" %>
<!DOCTYPE html PUBLIC "-//W3C//DTD XHTML 1.1//EN"
"http://www.w3.org/TR/xhtml11/DTD/xhtml11.dtd">
<html xmlns="http://www.w3.org/1999/xhtml" >
<head id="Head1" runat="server">
    <title>Show Skin Style Sheet Theme</title>
</head>
<body>
    <form id="form1" runat="server">
    <div>

    <asp:Label
        id="Label1"
        Text="What color background do I have?"
        BackColor="red"
        Runat="server" />

    </div>
    </form>
</body>
</html>
```

Notice that the <%@ Page %> directive in Listing 6.7 includes a StyleSheetTheme attribute. When you open the page in Listing 6.7 in a web browser, the Label is displayed with a red background color instead of the orange background color specified by the Theme.

Disabling Themes

Every ASP.NET control includes an EnableTheming property. You can use the EnableTheming property to prevent a Skin from being applied to a particular control in a page.

For example, the page in Listing 6.8 contains two Calendar controls. The second Calendar control has its EnableTheming property set to the value False (see Figure 6.3).

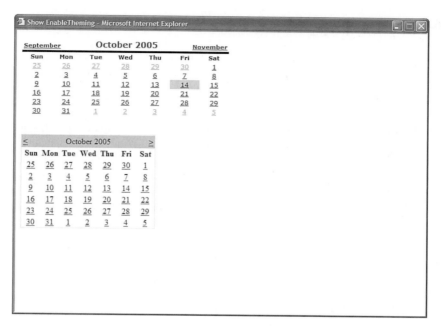

FIGURE 6.3   Disabling a Theme.

LISTING 6.8   ShowEnableTheming.aspx

```
<%@ Page Language="VB" Theme="Simple4" %>
<html xmlns="http://www.w3.org/1999/xhtml" >
<head id="Head1" runat="server">
    <title>Show EnableTheming</title>
</head>
<body>
    <form id="form1" runat="server">
    <div>

    <asp:Calendar
        id="Calendar1"
        Runat="server" />

    <br /><br />

    <asp:Calendar
        id="Calendar2"
        EnableTheming="false"
        Runat="server" />
```

LISTING 6.8   Continued

```
    </div>
    </form>
</body>
</html>
```

The page in Listing 6.8 includes a Theme attribute that applies the Simple Theme to the page. The Simple Theme includes the Skin in Listing 6.9.

LISTING 6.9   Simple4\Calendar.skin

```
<asp:Calendar
    BackColor="White"
    BorderColor="White"
    BorderWidth="1px"
    Font-Names="Verdana"
    Font-Size="9pt"
    ForeColor="Black"
    NextPrevFormat="FullMonth"
    Width="400px"
    Runat="Server">
    <SelectedDayStyle
        BackColor="#333399"
        ForeColor="White" />
    <OtherMonthDayStyle
        ForeColor="#999999" />
    <TodayDayStyle
        BackColor="#CCCCCC" />
    <NextPrevStyle
        Font-Bold="True"
        Font-Size="8pt"
        ForeColor="#333333"
        VerticalAlign="Bottom" />
    <DayHeaderStyle
        Font-Bold="True"
        Font-Size="8pt" />
    <TitleStyle
        BackColor="White"
        BorderColor="Black"
        BorderWidth="4px"
        Font-Bold="True"
        Font-Size="12pt"
        ForeColor="#333399" />
</asp:Calendar>
```

When you open the page in Listing 6.9 in a web browser, the Skin is applied to the first Calendar control but not the second Calendar control.

Registering Themes in the Web Configuration File

Rather than add the Theme or StyleSheetTheme attribute to each and every page to which you want to apply a Theme, you can register a Theme for all pages in your application in the web configuration file.

The Web.Config file in Listing 6.10 applies the Site Theme to every page in an application.

LISTING 6.10   Web.Config

```
<?xml version="1.0"?>
<configuration xmlns="http://schemas.microsoft.com/.NetConfiguration/v2.0">
<system.web>

  <pages theme="Site" />

</system.web>
</configuration>
```

Rather than use the theme attribute, you can use the styleSheetTheme attribute to apply a Theme to the pages in an application. If you use the styleSheetTheme attribute, you can override particular Skin properties in a page.

The web configuration file in Listing 6.11 includes the styleSheetTheme attribute.

LISTING 6.11   Web.Config

```
<?xml version="1.0"?>
<configuration xmlns="http://schemas.microsoft.com/.NetConfiguration/v2.0">
<system.web>

  <pages styleSheetTheme="Site" />

</system.web>
</configuration>
```

After you enable a Theme for an application, you can disable the Theme for a particular page by using the EnableTheming attribute with the <%@ Page %> directive. For example, the page in Listing 6.12 disables any Themes configured in the web configuration file.

LISTING 6.12 `DisablePageTheme.aspx`

```
<%@ Page Language="VB" EnableTheming="false" %>
<!DOCTYPE html PUBLIC "-//W3C//DTD XHTML 1.1//EN"
"http://www.w3.org/TR/xhtml11/DTD/xhtml11.dtd">
<html xmlns="http://www.w3.org/1999/xhtml" >
<head id="Head1" runat="server">
    <title>Disable Page Theme</title>
</head>
<body>
    <form id="form1" runat="server">
    <div>

    <asp:Label
        id="Label1"
        Text="Don't Theme Me!"
        Runat="server" />

    </div>
    </form>
</body>
</html>
```

Adding Cascading Style Sheets to Themes

As an alternative to Skins, you can use a Cascading Style Sheet file to control the appearance of both the HTML elements and ASP.NET controls contained in a page. If you add a Cascading Style Sheet file to a Theme folder, then the Cascading Style Sheet is automatically applied to every page to which the Theme is applied.

For example, the Cascading Style Sheet in Listing 6.13 contains style rules that are applied to several different HTML elements in a page.

LISTING 6.13 `App_Themes\StyleTheme\SimpleStyle.css`

```
html
{
    background-color:gray;
    font:14px Georgia,Serif;
}

.content
{
    margin:auto;
    width:600px;
    border:solid 1px black;
```

LISTING 6.13 Continued

```
    background-color:White;
    padding:10px;
}

h1
{
    color:Gray;
    font-size:18px;
    border-bottom:solid 1px orange;
}

label
{
    font-weight:bold;
}

input
{
    background-color:Yellow;
    border:double 3px orange;
}

.button
{
    background-color:#eeeeee;
}
```

If you add the `SimpleStyle.css` file to a Theme named `StyleTheme` (a folder named `StyleTheme` in the `App_Themes` folder), then the Cascading Style Sheet is applied automatically to the page in Listing 6.14.

LISTING 6.14 ShowSimpleCSS.aspx

```
<%@ Page Language="VB" Theme="StyleTheme" %>
<!DOCTYPE html PUBLIC "-//W3C//DTD XHTML 1.1//EN"
"http://www.w3.org/TR/xhtml11/DTD/xhtml11.dtd">
<html xmlns="http://www.w3.org/1999/xhtml" >
<head id="Head1" runat="server">
    <title>Show Simple CSS</title>
</head>
<body>
    <form id="form1" runat="server">
    <div class="content">
```

LISTING 6.14   Continued

```
<h1>Registration Form</h1>

<asp:Label
    id="lblFirstName"
    Text="First Name:"
    AssociatedControlID="txtFirstName"
    Runat="server" />
<br />
<asp:TextBox
    id="txtFirstName"
    Runat="server" />

<br /><br />

<asp:Label
    id="lblLastName"
    Text="Last Name:"
    AssociatedControlID="txtLastName"
    Runat="server" />
<br />
<asp:TextBox
    id="txtLastName"
    Runat="server" />

<br /><br />

<asp:Button
    id="btnSubmit"
    Text="Submit Form"
    CssClass="button"
    Runat="server" />

    </div>
    </form>
</body>
</html>
```

The Cascading Style Sheet is used to style several HTML elements in Listing 6.14 (see Figure 6.4). For example, the Style Sheet sets the background color of the page to the value Gray. It also centers the `<div>` tag containing the page content.

Because an ASP.NET control renders HTML, the Style Sheet also styles the HTML rendered by the ASP.NET Label, TextBox, and Button controls. An ASP.NET Label control renders an HTML `<label>` tag and the Style Sheet formats all `<label>` tags in bold. Both a TextBox control and a `Button` control render HTML `<input>` tags. The Style Sheet modifies the border and background color of the `<input>` tag.

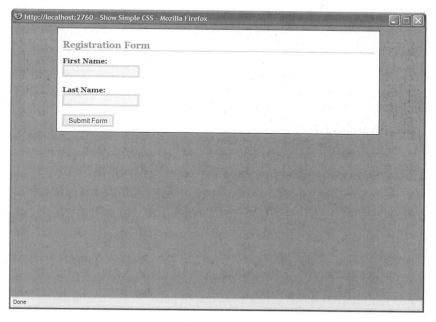

FIGURE 6.4   Styling with Cascading Style Sheets.

Notice that the `Button` control includes a `CssClass` attribute. By providing a control with a `CssClass` attribute, you can target a particular control (or set of controls) in a Cascading Style Sheet. In this case, the background color of the `<input>` tag rendered by the Button control is set to the value `#eeeeee` (light gray).

I recommend that you do all your web page design by using the method discussed in this section. You should place all your page design in an external Cascading Style Sheet located in a Theme folder. In particular, you should not modify the appearance of a control by modifying its properties. Furthermore, you should avoid using Skin files.

The advantage of using Cascading Style Sheets is that they result in leaner and faster loading pages. The more content that you can place in an external Style Sheet, the less content must be loaded each time you make a page request. The contents of an external Style Sheet can be loaded and cached by a browser and applied to all pages in a web application.

If, on the other hand, you modify the appearance of a control by modifying its properties, then additional content must be rendered to the browser each time you make a page request. For example, if you modify a `Label` control's `BackColor` property, then an additional `Style` attribute is rendered when the `Label` control is rendered.

Using Skins is no different than setting control properties. Skins also result in bloated pages. For example, if you create a Skin for a Label control, then the properties of the Label Skin must be merged with each Label control on each page before the Label is rendered.

NOTE

In this book, you will notice that I try to avoid formatting controls by using control properties. Instead, I perform all the formatting in a Style Sheet embedded in the page (using the `<style>` tag). I would prefer to place all the control formatting in an external Style Sheet, but that would require creating a separate file for each code sample, which would make this book much longer than it already threatens to be.

Adding Multiple Cascading Style Sheets to a Theme

You can add as many Cascading Style Sheet files to a Theme folder as you need. When you add multiple Cascading Style Sheets to a Theme, all the Cascading Style Sheets are applied to a page when the Theme is applied to a page.

The order in which an external Style Sheet is linked to a page can be important. For example, style sheet rules in one Style Sheet can override style sheet rules in another Style Sheet.

When you add multiple Style Sheets to a Theme, the style sheets are linked to a page in alphabetical order (in the order of the Style Sheet file name). For example, if the Theme contains three Style Sheet files named ThemeA.css, ThemeB.css, and ThemeC.css, then the following three links are added to a page:

```
<link href="App_Themes/Simple/ThemeA.css" type="text/css" rel="stylesheet" />
<link href="App_Themes/Simple/ThemeB.css" type="text/css" rel="stylesheet" />
<link href="App_Themes/Simple/ThemeC.css" type="text/css" rel="stylesheet" />
```

If you want to control the order in which Style Sheets are applied to a page, then you need to follow a naming convention.

Changing Page Layouts with Cascading Style Sheets

Because you can use a Cascading Style Sheet to change the layout of a page, you can use a Theme to control page layout.

For example, the page in Listing 6.15 contains three `<div>` tags. By default, if you open the page, the contents of the `<div>` tags are stacked one on top of another (see Figure 6.5).

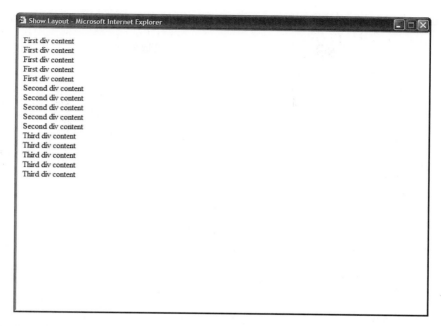

FIGURE 6.5   Page without Cascading Style Sheet.

LISTING 6.15   ShowLayout.aspx

```
<%@ Page Language="VB" %>
<!DOCTYPE html PUBLIC "-//W3C//DTD XHTML 1.1//EN"
"http://www.w3.org/TR/xhtml11/DTD/xhtml11.dtd">
<html xmlns="http://www.w3.org/1999/xhtml" >
<head id="Head1" runat="server">
    <title>Show Layout</title>
</head>
<body>
    <form id="form1" runat="server">

    <div id="div1">
        First div content
        <br />First div content
        <br />First div content
        <br />First div content
        <br />First div content
    </div>

    <div id="div2">
        Second div content
```

LISTING 6.15   Continued

```
        <br />Second div content
        <br />Second div content
        <br />Second div content
        <br />Second div content
    </div>

    <div id="div3">
        Third div content
        <br />Third div content
        <br />Third div content
        <br />Third div content
        <br />Third div content
    </div>

    </form>
</body>
</html>
```

If you add the Cascading Style Sheet in Listing 6.16, you can modify the layout of the <div> tags (see Figure 6.6). The Style Sheet in Listing 6.16 displays the <div> tags in three columns. (The Stylesheet floats each of the <div> tags.)

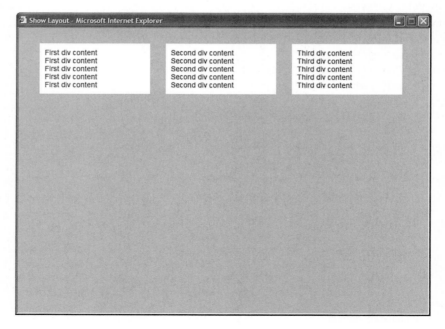

FIGURE 6.6   Using a floating layout.

LISTING 6.16   `Float.css`

```
html
{
    background-color:Silver;
    font:14px Arial,Sans-Serif;
}

#div1
{
    float:left;
    width:25%;
    margin:15px;
    padding:10px;
    background-color:White;
}

#div2
{
    float:left;
    width:25%;
    margin:15px;
    padding:10px;
    background-color:White;
}

#div3
{
    float:left;
    width:25%;
    margin:15px;
    padding:10px;
    background-color:White;
}
```

Alternatively, you can position the <div> tags absolutely by using the left and top style properties. The Style Sheet in Listing 6.17 reverses the order in which the three <div> tags are displayed (see Figure 6.7).

> **NOTE**
>
> The Cascading Style Sheets in this section work equally well with Internet Explorer 6, Firefox 1, and Opera 8.

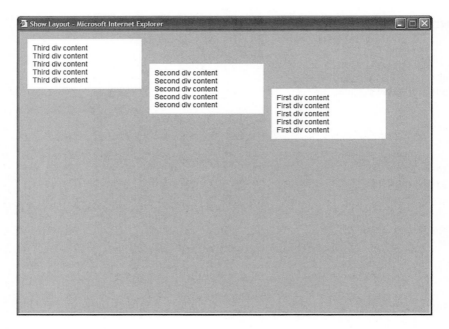

FIGURE 6.7   Using an absolute layout.

LISTING 6.17   Absolute.css

```
html
{
    background-color:Silver;
    font:14px Arial,Sans-Serif;
}

#div3
{
    position:absolute;
    left:15px;
    top:15px;
    width:200px;
    padding:10px;
    background-color:White;
}

#div2
{
    position:absolute;
    left:250px;
```

LISTING 6.17   Continued

```
    top:65px;
    width:200px;
    padding:10px;
    background-color:White;
}

#div1
{
    position:absolute;
    left:485px;
    top:115px;
    width:200px;
    padding:10px;
    background-color:White;
}
```

The point of this section is to demonstrate that Cascading Style Sheets are very powerful. You can create elaborate website designs simply by creating the right Style Sheet. If you want to see some samples of some amazing website designs performed with Cascading Style Sheets, visit the CSS Zen Garden located at http://www.CSSZenGarden.com.

Creating Global Themes

You can share the same Theme among multiple web applications running on the same web server. A Global Theme can contain both Skin files and Cascading Style Sheet files. Creating a Global Theme is useful when you want to create one company-wide website design and apply it to all your company's applications.

You create a Global Theme by adding the Theme to the Themes folder located at the following path:

```
WINDOWS\Microsoft.NET\Framework\[version]\ASP.NETClientFiles\Themes
```

After you add a Theme folder to this path, you can immediately start using the Theme in any file system–based website.

If you want to use the Theme in an HTTP-based website, you need to perform an additional step. You must add the Theme folder to the following path:

```
Inetpub\wwwroot\aspnet_client\system_web\[version]\Themes
```

You can copy the Theme to this folder manually or you can use the aspnet_regiis tool to copy the Theme folder. Execute the aspnet_regiis tool from the command line like this:

```
aspnet_regiis -c
```

The aspnet_regiis tool is located in the Windows\Microsoft.NET\Framework\[version] folder. You can open a command prompt and navigate to this folder to execute the tool. Alternatively, if you have installed the Microsoft .NET Framework SDK 2.0, then you can execute the tool by opening the SDK Command Prompt from the Microsoft .NET Framework SDK v2.0 program group.

Applying Themes Dynamically

You might want to enable each user of your website to customize the appearance of your website by selecting different Themes. Some website users might prefer a green Theme and other website users might prefer a pink Theme.

You can dynamically apply a Theme to a page by handling the Page PreInit event. This event is the first event that is raised when you request a page. You cannot apply a Theme dynamically in a later event such as the Page Load or PreRender events.

For example, the page in Listing 6.15 applies either the green Theme or the pink Theme to the page depending on which link you click in the page body (see Figure 6.8).

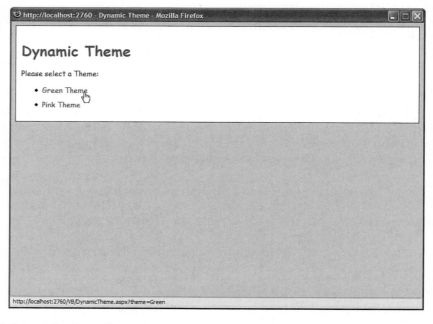

FIGURE 6.8   Selecting a Theme programmatically.

LISTING 6.15   `DynamicTheme.aspx`

```
<%@ Page Language="VB" %>
<!DOCTYPE html PUBLIC "-//W3C//DTD XHTML 1.1//EN"
"http://www.w3.org/TR/xhtml11/DTD/xhtml11.dtd">
<script runat="server">

    Sub Page_PreInit(ByVal s As Object, ByVal e As EventArgs)
        If Not IsNothing(Request("theme")) Then
            Select Case (Request("theme"))
                Case "Green"
                    Profile.UserTheme = "GreenTheme"
                Case "Pink"
                    Profile.UserTheme = "PinkTheme"
            End Select
        End If
        Theme = Profile.UserTheme
    End Sub
</script>

<html xmlns="http://www.w3.org/1999/xhtml" >
<head id="Head1" runat="server">
    <title>Dynamic Theme</title>
</head>
<body>
    <form id="form1" runat="server">
    <div class="content">

    <h1>Dynamic Theme</h1>

    Please select a Theme:
    <ul>
    <li>
        <a href="DynamicTheme.aspx?theme=Green">Green Theme</a>
    </li>
    <li>
        <a href="DynamicTheme.aspx?theme=Pink">Pink Theme</a>
    </li>
    </ul>

    </div>
    </form>
</body>
</html>
```

A particular Theme is applied to the page with the help of the Theme property. You can assign the name of any Theme (Theme folder) to this property in the Page PreInit event, and the Theme will be applied to the page.

Notice that the selected Theme is stored in the Profile object. When you store information in the Profile object, the information is preserved across multiple visits to the website. So, if a user selects a favorite Theme once, the Theme is applied every time the user returns to the website in the future.

The Profile is defined in the web configuration file in Listing 6.16.

LISTING 6.16   Web.Config

```
<?xml version="1.0"?>
<configuration xmlns="http://schemas.microsoft.com/.NetConfiguration/v2.0">
  <system.web>
    <profile>
      <properties>
        <add name="UserTheme" />
      </properties>
    </profile>
  </system.web>
</configuration>
```

Because the control tree has not been created when the PreInit event is raised, you can't refer to any controls in a page. Notice that hyperlinks are used in Listing 6.15 to select a Theme. You could not use a DropDownList control because the DropDownList control would not have been created.

> **NOTE**
>
> If you need to load a Theme dynamically for multiple pages in an application, then you can override the OnPreInit() method of the base Page class. This technique is discussed in the "Loading Master Pages Dynamically for Multiple Content Pages" section of Chapter 5.

Applying Skins Dynamically

You can apply skins dynamically to particular controls in a page. In the Page PreInit event, you can modify a control's SkinID property programmatically.

For example, the page in Listing 6.17 enables a user to select a favorite skin for a GridView control. The GridView control displays a list of movies (see Figure 6.9).

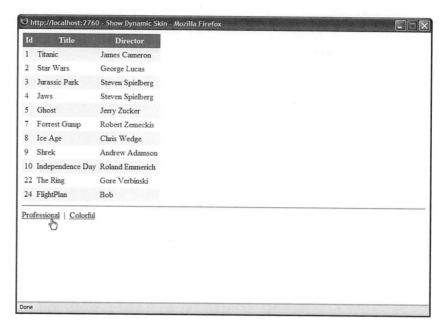

FIGURE 6.9   Applying a Skin programmatically.

LISTING 6.17   ShowDynamicSkin.aspx

```
<%@ Page Language="VB" Theme="DynamicSkin" %>
<!DOCTYPE html PUBLIC "-//W3C//DTD XHTML 1.1//EN"
"http://www.w3.org/TR/xhtml11/DTD/xhtml11.dtd">
<script runat="server">

    Sub Page_PreInit(ByVal s As Object, ByVal e As EventArgs)
        If Not IsNothing(Request("skin")) Then
            Select Case Request("skin")
                Case "professional"
                    grdMovies.SkinID = "Professional"
                Case "colorful"
                    grdMovies.SkinID = "Colorful"
            End Select
        End If
    End Sub
</script>
<html xmlns="http://www.w3.org/1999/xhtml" >
<head id="Head1" runat="server">
    <title>Show Dynamic Skin</title>
</head>
```

LISTING 6.17   Continued

```
<body>
    <form id="form1" runat="server">
    <div>

    <asp:GridView
        id="grdMovies"
        DataSourceID="srcMovies"
        Runat="server" />

     <asp:SqlDataSource
        id="srcMovies"
        ConnectionString="<%$ ConnectionStrings:Movies %>"
        SelectCommand="SELECT Id,Title,Director FROM Movies"
        Runat="server" />

    <hr />

    <a href="showdynamicskin.aspx?skin=professional">Professional</a>
     | 
    <a href="showdynamicskin.aspx?skin=colorful">Colorful</a>

    </div>
    </form>
</body>
</html>
```

A hyperlink is used to select a particular Skin. The Skin is applied to the GridView in the PreInit event when a particular value is assigned to the GridView control's SkinID property.

Of course, I don't recommend doing this. It makes more sense to use a Cascading Style Sheet and modify a control's CssClass property. This alternate approach is demonstrated by the page in Listing 6.18.

LISTING 6.18   ShowDynamicCSS.aspx

```
<%@ Page Language="VB" Theme="DynamicSkin" %>
<!DOCTYPE html PUBLIC "-//W3C//DTD XHTML 1.1//EN"
"http://www.w3.org/TR/xhtml11/DTD/xhtml11.dtd">
<script runat="server">

    Sub btnSubmit_Click(ByVal s As Object, ByVal e As EventArgs)
        grdMovies.CssClass = ddlCssClass.SelectedItem.Text
    End Sub
</script>
```

LISTING 6.18   Continued

```
<html xmlns="http://www.w3.org/1999/xhtml" >
<head id="Head1" runat="server">
    <title>Show Dynamic CSS</title>
</head>
<body>
    <form id="form1" runat="server">
    <div>

    <asp:GridView
        id="grdMovies"
        DataSourceID="srcMovies"
        HeaderStyle-CssClass="Header"
        AlternatingRowStyle-CssClass="Alternating"
        GridLines="none"
        Runat="server" />

     <asp:SqlDataSource
        id="srcMovies"
        ConnectionString="<%$ ConnectionStrings:Movies %>"
        SelectCommand="SELECT Id,Title,Director FROM Movies"
        Runat="server" />

    <hr />

    <asp:Label
        id="lblCssClass"
        Text="Select Style:"
        AssociatedControlID="ddlCssClass"
        Runat="server" />
    <asp:DropDownList
        id="ddlCssClass"
        Runat="server">
        <asp:ListItem Text="Professional" />
        <asp:ListItem Text="Colorful" />
    </asp:DropDownList>
    <asp:Button
        id="btnSubmit"
        Text="Select"
        Runat="server" OnClick="btnSubmit_Click" />

    </div>
    </form>
</body>
</html>
```

Note that in this code sample, unlike the previous one, you can use a `DropDownList` and `Button` control to change the appearance of the `GridView` control when modifying the `CssClass` property. Because you can modify the `CssClass` property during any event before the page is rendered, you can handle the `Button Click` event to modify the value of the `CssClass` property.

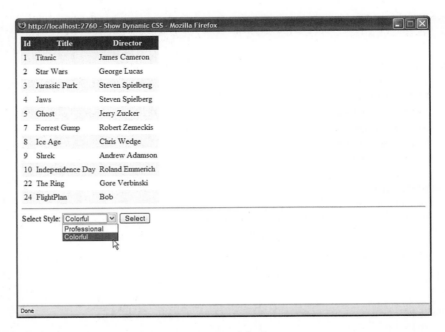

FIGURE 6.10   Modifying a `CssClass` programmatically.

Summary

In this chapter, you learned how to create a consistent look for your website by taking advantage of ASP.NET Themes. In the first section, you learned how to modify the appearance of controls in a page with Skins. You learned how to create both Default and Named Skins. You also learned how to apply a Theme by using the `Theme` attribute and `StyleSheetTheme` attribute.

Next, you learned how to add Cascading Style Sheets to Themes. I recommended that you take advantage of Cascading Style Sheets and avoid Skins whenever possible.

We also discussed how you can create Global Themes. You learned how to create a Theme that you can apply to every application executing on a web server.

Finally, you learned how to dynamically apply Themes. You learned how to use the `PreInit` event to dynamically apply either an entire Theme or a particular Skin at runtime.

CHAPTER 7

Creating Custom Controls with User Controls

A Web User control enables you to build a new control from existing controls. By taking advantage of User controls, you can easily extend the ASP.NET Framework with your own custom controls.

Imagine, for example, that you need to display the same address form in multiple pages in a web application. The address form consists of several TextBox and Validation controls for entering address information. If you want to avoid declaring all the TextBox and Validation controls in multiple pages, you can wrap these controls inside a Web User control.

Anytime that you discover that you need to display the same user interface elements in multiple pages, you should consider wrapping the elements inside a User control. By taking advantage of User controls, you make your website easier to maintain and extend.

In this chapter, you learn how to build custom controls with User controls. It starts with the basics. You learn how to create a simple User control and expose properties and events from the User control.

You then examine how you can use AJAX with a User control. You learn how to modify the content displayed by a User control without posting the page that contains the User control back to the web server.

Finally, you learn how you can load User controls dynamically. You learn how to load a User control at runtime and inject the User control into a page. In the final section of this chapter, dynamically loaded User controls are used to build a multi-page wizard.

Creating User Controls

Let's start by building a simple User control that randomly displays one image from a folder of images (see Figure 7.1). The code for the User control is contained in Listing 7.1.

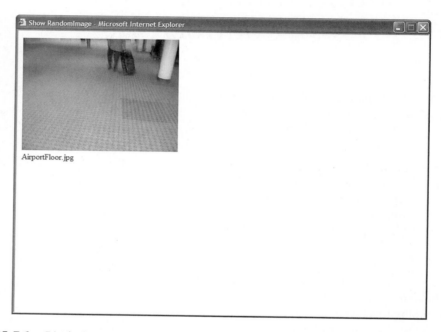

FIGURE 7.1 Displaying an image with the `RandomImage` User control.

LISTING 7.1 `RandomImage.ascx`

```
<%@ Control Language="VB" ClassName="RandomImage" %>
<%@ Import Namespace="System.IO" %>

<script runat="server">

    Private Sub Page_Load()
        Dim imageToDisplay As String = GetRandomImage()
        imgRandom.ImageUrl = Path.Combine("~/Images", imageToDisplay)
        lblRandom.Text = imageToDisplay
    End Sub

    Private Function GetRandomImage() As String
        Dim rnd As New Random()
```

LISTING 7.1   Continued

```
        Dim images() As String = Directory.GetFiles(MapPath("~/Images"), "*.jpg")
        Dim imageToDisplay As String = images(rnd.Next(images.Length))
        Return Path.GetFileName(imageToDisplay)
    End Function
</script>

<asp:Image
    id="imgRandom"
    Width="300px"
    Runat="server" />
<br />
<asp:Label
    id="lblRandom"
    Runat="server" />
```

VISUAL WEB DEVELOPER NOTE

You create a new User control in Visual Web Developer by selecting Website, Add New Item, and selecting the Web User control item.

The file in Listing 7.1 closely resembles a standard ASP.NET page. Like a standard ASP.NET page, the User control contains a Page_Load() event handler. Also, the User control contains standard controls such as the ASP.NET Image and Label controls.

User controls are closely related to ASP.NET pages. Both the UserControl class and the Page class derive from the base TemplateControl class. Because they derive from the same base class, they share many of the same methods, properties, and events.

The important difference between an ASP.NET page and a User control is that a User control is something you can declare in an ASP.NET page. When you build a User control, you are building a custom control.

Notice that the file in Listing 7.1 ends with the .ascx extension. You cannot request this file directly from a web browser. To use the RandomImage User control, you must declare the control in an ASP.NET page.

The page in Listing 7.2 contains the RandomImage User control. When you open the page, a random image is displayed.

LISTING 7.2   ShowRandomImage.aspx

```
<%@ Page Language="VB" %>
<%@ Register TagPrefix="user" TagName="RandomImage"
    Src="~/UserControls/RandomImage.ascx" %>
<!DOCTYPE html PUBLIC "-//W3C//DTD XHTML 1.1//EN"
```

LISTING 7.2   Continued

```
    "http://www.w3.org/TR/xhtml11/DTD/xhtml11.dtd">
<html xmlns="http://www.w3.org/1999/xhtml" >
<head id="Head1" runat="server">
    <title>Show RandomImage</title>
</head>
<body>
    <form id="form1" runat="server">
    <div>

    <user:RandomImage
        ID="RandomImage1"
        Runat="server" />

    </div>
    </form>
</body>
</html>
```

Before you can use a web User control in a page, you must register it. The page in Listing 7.2 includes a `<%@ Register %>` directive that contains the following three attributes:

- `TagPrefix`—Indicates the namespace that you want to associate with the User control for the current page. You can use any string that you want.

- `TagName`—Indicates the name that you want to associate with the User control for the current page. You can use any string that you want.

- `Src`—Indicates the virtual path to the User control (the path to the .ascx file)

The `RandomImage` User control is declared in the body of the page. It looks like this:

```
<user:RandomImage ID="RandomImage1" Runat="Server" />
```

Notice that the declaration of the User control uses the `TagPrefix` and `TagName` specified in the `<%@ Register %>` directive. Furthermore, notice that you provide a User control with both an `ID` and a `Runat` attribute, just as you would for any standard ASP.NET control.

VISUAL WEB DEVELOPER NOTE

You can add a User control to a page in Visual Web Developer simply by dragging the User control from the Solution Explorer window onto the Design surface. The `<%@ Register %>` directive is automatically added to the source of the page.

Registering User Controls in the Web Configuration File

As an alternative to registering a User control in each page in which you need to use it by using the `<%@ Register %>` directive, you can register a User control once for an entire application. You can register a User control in an application's web configuration file.

For example, the web configuration file in Listing 7.3 registers the `RandomImage` control for the application.

LISTING 7.3 `Web.Config`

```
<?xml version="1.0"?>
<configuration>
<system.web>
  <pages>
    <controls>
      <add
        tagPrefix="user"
        tagName="RandomImage"
        src="~/UserControls/RandomImage.ascx"/>
    </controls>
  </pages>
</system.web>
</configuration>
```

After you register a User control in the web configuration file, you can simply declare the User control in any page. For example, the page in Listing 7.4 contains an instance of the `RandomImage` User control, but it does not include the `<%@ Register %>` directive.

LISTING 7.4 `ShowAppRegister.aspx`

```
<%@ Page Language="VB" %>
<!DOCTYPE html PUBLIC "-//W3C//DTD XHTML 1.1//EN"
  "http://www.w3.org/TR/xhtml11/DTD/xhtml11.dtd">
<html xmlns="http://www.w3.org/1999/xhtml" >
<head id="Head1" runat="server">
    <title>Show Application Register</title>
</head>
<body>
    <form id="form1" runat="server">
    <div>

    <user:RandomImage
        ID="RandomImage1"
        Runat="Server" />
```

LISTING 7.4   Continued

```
    </div>
    </form>
</body>
</html>
```

You need to be aware of one important limitation when registering a User control in the web configuration file. A User control cannot be located in the same folder as a page that uses it. For that reason, you should create all your User controls in a subfolder (I typically create a UserControls subfolder for each of my applications).

Exposing Properties from a User Control

The RandomImage User control always displays an image from the Images folder. It would be nice if you could specify the name of the folder that contains the images so that you could use different folder paths in different applications. You can do this by exposing a property from the RandomImage User control.

The modified RandomImage control in Listing 7.5, named PropertyRandomImage, exposes a property named ImageFolderPath.

LISTING 7.5   PropertyRandomImage.ascx

```
<%@ Control Language="VB" ClassName="PropertyRandomImage" %>
<%@ Import Namespace="System.IO" %>
<script runat="server">

    Private _imageFolderPath As String = "~/Images"

    Public Property ImageFolderPath() As String
        Get
            Return _imageFolderPath
        End Get
        Set(ByVal Value As String)
            _imageFolderPath = value
        End Set
    End Property

    Private Sub Page_Load()
        Dim imageToDisplay As String = GetRandomImage()
        imgRandom.ImageUrl = Path.Combine(_imageFolderPath, imageToDisplay)
        lblRandom.Text = imageToDisplay
    End Sub

    Private Function GetRandomImage() As String
        Dim rnd As New Random()
```

LISTING 7.5   Continued

```
        Dim images() As String = Directory.GetFiles(MapPath("~/Images"), "*.jpg")
        Dim imageToDisplay As String = images(rnd.Next(images.Length))
        Return Path.GetFileName(imageToDisplay)
    End Function
</script>

<asp:Image
    id="imgRandom"
    Width="300px"
    Runat="server" />
<br />
<asp:Label
    id="lblRandom"
    Runat="server" />
```

After you expose a property in a User control, you can set the property either declaratively or programmatically. The page in Listing 7.6 sets the `ImageFolderPath` property declaratively.

LISTING 7.6   ShowDeclarative.aspx

```
<%@ Page Language="VB" %>
<%@ Register TagPrefix="user" TagName="PropertyRandomImage"
 Src="~/PropertyRandomImage.ascx" %>
<!DOCTYPE html PUBLIC "-//W3C//DTD XHTML 1.1//EN"
  "http://www.w3.org/TR/xhtml11/DTD/xhtml11.dtd">
<html xmlns="http://www.w3.org/1999/xhtml" >
<head id="Head1" runat="server">
    <title>Show Declarative</title>
</head>
<body>
    <form id="form1" runat="server">
    <div>

    <user:PropertyRandomImage
        ID="PropertyRandomImage1"
        ImageFolderPath="~/Images2"
        Runat="server" />

    </div>
    </form>
</body>
</html>
```

Notice that the `PropertyRandomImage` User control in Listing 7.6 includes an `ImageFolderPath` property. When you request the page, the random images are retrieved from the Images2 folder.

> **VISUAL WEB DEVELOPER NOTE**
>
> Any properties that you add to a User control appear in both Intellisense and the Property window.

The page in Listing 7.7 demonstrates how you can set the `ImageFolderPath` programmatically.

LISTING 7.7   `ShowProgrammatic.aspx`

```
<%@ Page Language="VB" %>
<%@ Register TagPrefix="user" TagName="PropertyRandomImage"
    Src="~/PropertyRandomImage.ascx" %>
<!DOCTYPE html PUBLIC "-//W3C//DTD XHTML 1.1//EN"
  "http://www.w3.org/TR/xhtml11/DTD/xhtml11.dtd">
<script runat="server">

    Protected  Sub Page_Load(ByVal sender As Object, ByVal e As EventArgs)
        PropertyRandomImage1.ImageFolderPath = "~/Images2"
    End Sub

</script>
<html xmlns="http://www.w3.org/1999/xhtml" >
<head id="Head1" runat="server">
    <title>Show Programmatic</title>
</head>
<body>
    <form id="form1" runat="server">
    <div>

    <user:PropertyRandomImage
        ID="PropertyRandomImage1"
        Runat="server" />

    </div>
    </form>
</body>
</html>
```

The page in Listing 7.7 includes a `Page_Load()` event handler. This handler programmatically sets the `ImageFolderPath` to the value Images2.

Exposing Events from a User Control

You can expose custom events from a User control. After you expose the event, you can handle the event in the page that contains the User control.

Exposing events is useful when you need to pass information up to the containing page. Imagine, for example, that you want to create a custom tab strip with a User control. When a user clicks a tab, you want to change the content displayed in the page (see Figure 7.2).

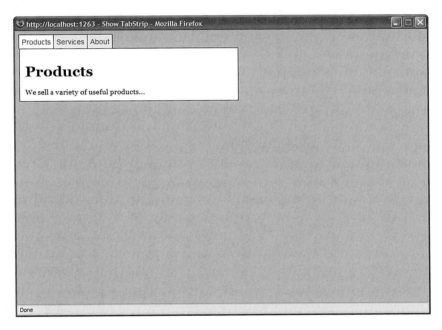

FIGURE 7.2   Displaying a tab strip with a User control.

The User control in Listing 7.8 contains the code for a simple tab strip.

LISTING 7.8   TabStrip.ascx

```
<%@ Control Language="VB" ClassName="TabStrip" %>
<%@ Import Namespace="System.Collections.Generic" %>
<script runat="server">

    Public Event TabClick As EventHandler

    ''' <summary>
    ''' The index of the selected tab
    ''' </summary>
    Public ReadOnly Property SelectedIndex() As Integer
```

LISTING 7.8   Continued

```
        Get
            Return dlstTabStrip.SelectedIndex
        End Get
    End Property

    ''' <summary>
    ''' Create the tabs
    ''' </summary>
    Private Sub Page_Load()
        If Not Page.IsPostBack Then
            ' Create the tabs
            Dim tabs As New List(Of String)()
            tabs.Add("Products")
            tabs.Add("Services")
            tabs.Add("About")

            ' Bind tabs to the DataList
            dlstTabStrip.DataSource = tabs
            dlstTabStrip.DataBind()

            ' Select first tab
            dlstTabStrip.SelectedIndex = 0
        End If
    End Sub

    ''' <summary>
    ''' This method executes when a user clicks a tab
    ''' </summary>
    Protected Sub dlstTabStrip_SelectedIndexChanged(ByVal sender As Object,
➥ByVal e As EventArgs)
        RaiseEvent TabClick(Me, EventArgs.Empty)
    End Sub

</script>

<asp:DataList
    id="dlstTabStrip"
    RepeatDirection="Horizontal"
    OnSelectedIndexChanged="dlstTabStrip_SelectedIndexChanged"
    CssClass="tabs"
    ItemStyle-CssClass="tab"
    SelectedItemStyle-CssClass="selectedTab"
```

LISTING 7.8 Continued

```
    Runat="server">
    <ItemTemplate>
    <asp:LinkButton
        id="lnkTab"
        Text='<%# Container.DataItem %>'
        CommandName="Select"
        Runat="server" />
    </ItemTemplate>
</asp:DataList>
```

The tab strip is created with the help of a DataList control. The DataList control displays links for each of the items created in the Page_Load() event handler.

Notice that the TabStrip control exposes an event named TabClick. This event is raised in the dlstTabStrip_SelectedIndexChanged() event handler when a user clicks a tab.

The page in Listing 7.9 uses the TabStrip control to display different content depending on the tab selected.

LISTING 7.9 ShowTabStrip.aspx

```
<%@ Page Language="VB" %>
<%@ Register TagPrefix="user" TagName="TabStrip" Src="~/TabStrip.ascx" %>
<!DOCTYPE html PUBLIC "-//W3C//DTD XHTML 1.1//EN"
    "http://www.w3.org/TR/xhtml11/DTD/xhtml11.dtd">
<script runat="server">

    Protected Sub TabStrip1_TabClick(ByVal sender As Object,
➥ByVal e As EventArgs)
        MultiView1.ActiveViewIndex = TabStrip1.SelectedIndex
    End Sub
</script>
<html xmlns="http://www.w3.org/1999/xhtml" >
<head id="Head1" runat="server">
    <style type="text/css">
        html
        {
            background-color:silver;
            font:14px Georgia,Serif;
        }
        .tabs a
        {
            color:blue;
```

LISTING 7.9   Continued

```
            text-decoration:none;
            font:14px Arial,Sans-Serif;
        }
        .tab
        {
            background-color:#eeeeee;
            padding:5px;
            border:Solid 1px black;
            border-bottom:none;
        }
        .selectedTab
        {
            background-color:white;
            padding:5px;
            border:Solid 1px black;
            border-bottom:none;
        }
        .views
        {
            background-color:white;
            width:400px;
            border:Solid 1px black;
            padding:10px;
        }
    </style>
    <title>Show TabStrip</title>
</head>
<body>
    <form id="form1" runat="server">
    <div>

    <user:TabStrip
        ID="TabStrip1"
        OnTabClick="TabStrip1_TabClick"
        Runat="Server" />

    <div class="views">
    <asp:MultiView
        id="MultiView1"
        ActiveViewIndex="0"
        Runat="server">
```

LISTING 7.9   Continued

```
        <asp:View ID="Products" runat="server">
            <h1>Products</h1>
            We sell a variety of useful products...
        </asp:View>
        <asp:View ID="Services" runat="server">
            <h1>Services</h1>
            We offer a number of services...
        </asp:View>
        <asp:View ID="About" runat="server">
            <h1>About</h1>
            We were the first company to offer products and services...
        </asp:View>
    </asp:MultiView>
    </div>

    </div>
    </form>
</body>
</html>
```

The page in Listing 7.9 includes an event handler for the `TabStrip` control's `TabClick` event. When you click a tab, the index of the selected tab is retrieved from the tab strip, and the `View` control with the matching index is displayed.

VISUAL WEB DEVELOPER NOTE

You can add a `TabClick` event handler to the `TabStrip` control by selecting the `TabStrip` control from the top-left drop-down list and selecting the `TabClick` event from the top-right drop-down list.

NOTE

The ASP.NET Framework includes a Menu control that you can use to create both tabstrips and pop-up menus. This control is discussed in Chapter 4, "Using the Rich Controls," and Chapter 17, "Using the Navigation Controls."

Creating an `AddressForm` Control

Let's end this section by creating a generally useful Web User control. We'll build an AddressForm User control that you can reuse in multiple pages or reuse multiple times in a single page (see Figure 7.3).

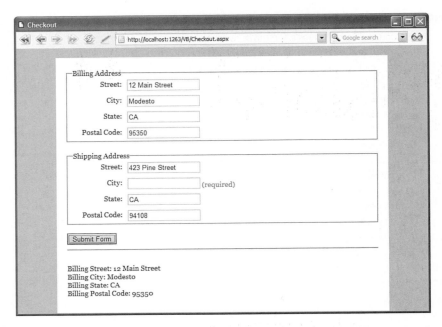

FIGURE 7.3   Displaying multiple address forms with the `AddressForm` User control.

The `AddressForm` User control is contained in Listing 7.10.

LISTING 7.10   `AddressForm.ascx`

```vb
<%@ Control Language="VB" ClassName="AddressForm" %>
<script runat="server">

    Public Property Title() As String
        Get
                Return ltlTitle.Text
        End Get
        Set (ByVal Value As String)
                ltlTitle.Text = value
        End Set
    End Property


    Public Property Street() As String
        Get
                Return txtStreet.Text
        End Get
        Set (ByVal Value As String)
                txtStreet.Text = value
        End Set
    End Property
```

LISTING 7.10 Continued

```
    Public Property City() As String
        Get
                Return txtCity.Text
        End Get
        Set (ByVal Value As String)
                txtCity.Text = value
        End Set
    End Property

    Public Property State() As String
        Get
                Return txtState.Text
        End Get
        Set (ByVal Value As String)
                txtState.Text = value
        End Set
    End Property

    Public Property PostalCode() As String
        Get
                Return txtPostalCode.Text
        End Get
        Set (ByVal Value As String)
                txtPostalCode.Text = value
        End Set
    End Property

</script>

<fieldset>
<legend>
    <asp:Literal
        ID="ltlTitle"
        Text="Address Form"
        runat="server" />
</legend>

<div class="addressLabel">
<asp:Label
    ID="lblStreet"
    Text="Street:"
    AssociatedControlID="txtStreet"
    Runat="server" />
</div>
```

LISTING 7.10   Continued

```
<div class="addressField">
<asp:TextBox
    ID="txtStreet"
    Runat="server" />
<asp:RequiredFieldValidator
    ID="reqStreet"
    Text="(required)"
    ControlToValidate="txtStreet"
    Runat="server" />
</div>

<br class="clear" />

<div class="addressLabel">
<asp:Label
    ID="lblCity"
    Text="City:"
    AssociatedControlID="txtCity"
    Runat="server" />
</div>
<div class="addressField">
<asp:TextBox
    ID="txtCity"
    Runat="server" />
<asp:RequiredFieldValidator
    ID="reqCity"
    Text="(required)"
    ControlToValidate="txtCity"
    Runat="server" />
</div>

<br class="clear" />

<div class="addressLabel">
<asp:Label
    ID="lblState"
    Text="State:"
    AssociatedControlID="txtState"
    Runat="server" />
</div>
<div class="addressField">
<asp:TextBox
    ID="txtState"
    Runat="server" />
```

LISTING 7.10   Continued

```
<asp:RequiredFieldValidator
    ID="reqState"
    Text="(required)"
    ControlToValidate="txtState"
    Runat="server" />
</div>

<br class="clear" />

<div class="addressLabel">
<asp:Label
    ID="lblPostalCode"
    Text="Postal Code:"
    AssociatedControlID="txtPostalCode"
    Runat="server" />
</div>
<div class="addressField">
<asp:TextBox
    ID="txtPostalCode"
    Runat="server" />
<asp:RequiredFieldValidator
    ID="RequiredFieldValidator1"
    Text="(required)"
    ControlToValidate="txtPostalCode"
    Runat="server" />
</div>

<br class="clear" />

</fieldset>
```

The AddressForm control contains form controls for entering your street, city, state, and postal code. Each of these fields is validated by a RequiredFieldValidator control. Finally, the AddressForm includes a Label that can be used to provide a title for the control.

The AddressForm exposes all of its form fields with properties. The control includes public Street, City, State, and PostalCode property, which you can read from the containing page.

The page in Listing 7.11 illustrates how you can use the AddressForm control in a page.

LISTING 7.11   Checkout.aspx

```
<%@ Page Language="VB" %>
<%@ Register TagPrefix="user" TagName="AddressForm" Src="~/AddressForm.ascx" %>
<!DOCTYPE html PUBLIC "-//W3C//DTD XHTML 1.1//EN"
    "http://www.w3.org/TR/xhtml11/DTD/xhtml11.dtd">
<script runat="server">

    Protected Sub btnSubmit_Click(ByVal sender As Object, ByVal e As EventArgs)
        ' Show Billing Address Form Results
        ltlResults.Text = "<br />Billing Street: " + AddressForm1.Street
        ltlResults.Text += "<br />Billing City: " + AddressForm1.City
        ltlResults.Text += "<br />Billing State: " + AddressForm1.State
        ltlResults.Text += "<br />Billing Postal Code: " + AddressForm1.PostalCode

        ltlResults.Text += "<br /><br />"

        ' Show Shipping Address Form Results
        ltlResults.Text += "<br />Shipping Street: " + AddressForm2.Street
        ltlResults.Text += "<br />Shipping City: " + AddressForm2.City
        ltlResults.Text += "<br />Shipping State: " + AddressForm2.State
        ltlResults.Text += "<br />Shipping Postal Code: " + AddressForm2.PostalCode
    End Sub
</script>
<html xmlns="http://www.w3.org/1999/xhtml" >
<head id="Head1" runat="server">
    <style type="text/css">
        html
        {
            background-color:silver;
            font:14px Georgia,Serif;
        }
        .content
        {
            background-color:white;
            width:600px;
            margin:auto;
            padding:20px;
        }
        .addressLabel
        {
            float:left;
            width:100px;
            padding:5px;
            text-align:right;
        }
```

LISTING 7.11   Continued

```
        .addressField
        {
            float:left;
            padding:5px;
        }
        .clear
        {
            clear:both;
        }

    </style>
    <title>Checkout</title>
</head>
<body>
    <form id="form1" runat="server">
    <div class="content">

    <user:AddressForm
        id="AddressForm1"
        Title="Billing Address"
        Runat="server" />

    <br />

    <user:AddressForm
        id="AddressForm2"
        Title="Shipping Address"
        Runat="server" />

    <br />

    <asp:Button
        ID="btnSubmit"
        Text="Submit Form"
        OnClick="btnSubmit_Click"
        Runat="server" />

    <hr />

    <asp:Literal
        id="ltlResults"
        Runat="server" />
```

LISTING 7.11   Continued

```
    </div>
    </form>
</body>
</html>
```

The page in Listing 7.11 contains two instances of the `AddressForm` control: a Billing Address and Shipping Address. When you click the Button control, the address information is retrieved from the `AddressForm` controls and displayed in a Literal control. (In a real application, you would grab the data and store it in a database.)

> **WEB STANDARDS NOTE**
>
> The `AddressForm` User control does not use an HTML table to layout its controls. You should strive to avoid using tables except when displaying tabular information. Instead, Cascading Style Sheet rules are used to position the form elements. The page looks almost identical in Internet Explorer 6, Firefox 1.0, and Opera 8.0.

AJAX and User Controls

AJAX (Asynchronous JavaScript and XML) enables you to update content in a page without posting the page back to the server. Behind the scenes, AJAX uses the XMLHttp ActiveX component (in the case of Microsoft Internet Explorer) or the XMLHttpRequest intrinsic browser object (in the case of other browsers such as FireFox).

In the ASP.NET Framework, AJAX is referred to as *client callbacks*. To add AJAX support to a User control, you must implement the `ICallBackEventHandler` interface and add the necessary JavaScript scripts to process the results of the AJAX call.

Here are the steps for implementing AJAX:

1. Create a client script for invoking the AJAX call. You can get this script with the `Page.ClientScript.GetCallbackEventReference()` method.

2. Create server methods named `RaiseCallbackEvent()` and `GetCallbackResult()`, which returns a string value from the server.

3. Create a client method that receives the value from the server `RaiseCallbackEvent()` method and does something with the value.

For example, the User control in Listing 7.12 randomly displays one of three quotations. The quotation is updated automatically every 10 seconds (see Figure 7.4).

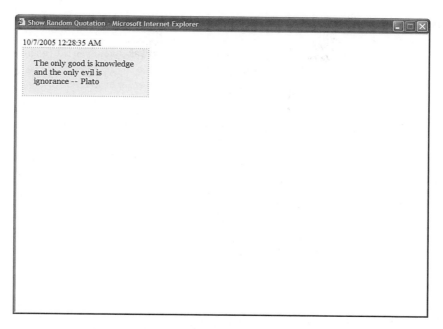

10/7/2005 12:28:35 AM

The only good is knowledge
and the only evil is
ignorance -- Plato

FIGURE 7.4   Using AJAX to display a random quotation.

LISTING 7.12   RandomQuotation.ascx

```
<%@ Control Language="VB" ClassName="RandomQuotation" %>
<%@ Implements Interface="System.Web.UI.ICallbackEventHandler" %>
<%@ Import Namespace="System.Collections.Generic" %>
<script runat="server">

    Public Sub RaiseCallbackEvent(ByVal result As String) Implements ICallbackEven-
tHandler.RaiseCallbackEvent
    End Sub

    Public Function GetCallbackResult() As String Implements ICallbackEven-
tHandler.GetCallbackResult
        Dim quotes As New List(Of String)()
        quotes.Add("All paid jobs absorb and degrade the mind -- Aristotle")
        quotes.Add("No evil can happen to a good man, either in life or after death
-- Plato")
        quotes.Add("The only good is knowledge and the only evil is ignorance --
➥Plato")
        Dim rnd As Random = New Random()
        Return quotes(rnd.Next(quotes.Count))
    End Function
```

LISTING 7.12   Continued

```
    Private Sub Page_Load()
        Dim callback As String = Page.ClientScript.GetCallbackEventReference(Me,
➥Nothing, "UpdateQuote", Nothing, "CallbackError", True)
        Dim startupScript As String = String.Format("setInterval( ""{0}"", 5000 )"
➥, callback)
        Page.ClientScript.RegisterStartupScript(Me.GetType(), "RandomQuotation",
➥ startupScript, True)
    End Sub

</script>

<div id="divQuote" class="quote">
Random Quotation
</div>

<script type="text/javascript">

    function UpdateQuote(result)
    {
        var divQuote = document.getElementById('divQuote');
        divQuote.innerText = result;
    }

    function CallbackError(result)
    {
        alert( result );
    }

</script>
```

The Page_Load() method in Listing 7.12 generates the client script for invoking the AJAX call. A reference to the script that makes the AJAX call is retrieved from the Page.ClientScript.GetCallbackEventReference() method. The JavaScript setInterval() method is used to execute this script every five seconds.

The User control implements the ICallbackEventHandler interface. This interface has two methods that you must implement: RaiseCallbackEvent() and GetCallbackResult(). These two methods are called on the server in order. In Listing 7.12, the RaiseCallbackEvent() does nothing and the GetCallbackResult() method returns the random quotation to the client.

Finally, notice that the User control contains a client script block that contains two JavaScript functions. The first function, named UpdateQuote(), displays the random quotation returned by the RaiseCallbackEvent() in an HTML <div> tag. The second method, named CallbackError(), shows an alert dialog box when an error occurs during performance of the AJAX call.

The page in Listing 7.13 illustrates how you can use the RandomQuotation User control. It contains the User control and it also displays the current time.

LISTING 7.13   ShowRandomQuotation.aspx

```
<%@ Page Language="VB" %>
<%@ Register TagPrefix="user" TagName="RandomQuotation"
    Src="~/RandomQuotation.ascx" %>
<!DOCTYPE html PUBLIC "-//W3C//DTD XHTML 1.1//EN"
    "http://www.w3.org/TR/xhtml11/DTD/xhtml11.dtd">
<html xmlns="http://www.w3.org/1999/xhtml" >
<head id="Head1" runat="server">
    <style type="text/css">
        .quote
        {
            width:200px;
            padding:20px;
            border:Dotted 2px orange;
            background-color:#eeeeee;
            font:16px Georgia,Serif;
        }
    </style>
    <title>Show Random Quotation</title>
</head>
<body>
    <form id="form1" runat="server">
    <div>

    <%= DateTime.Now %>
    <br />

    <user:RandomQuotation
        id="RandomQuotation1"
        Runat="server" />

    </div>
    </form>
</body>
</html>
```

Notice that the random quotation is updated, but that the time on the page does not change. Only the area of the page that contains the random quotation is updated.

Dynamically Loading User Controls

You can dynamically load a User control at runtime and display it in a page. Imagine, for example, that you want to display different featured products randomly on the home page of your website. However, you want to display each featured product with a completely different layout. In that case, you can create a separate User control for each product and load one of the User controls randomly at runtime.

You load a User control with the `Page.LoadControl()` method. This method returns an instance of the `Control` class that you can add to a page. Typically, you add the User control to a `PlaceHolder` control that you have declared on the page.

> **NOTE**
>
> The `PlaceHolder` control was designed to do absolutely nothing. It simply acts as a placeholder on the page where you can add other controls.

For example, the page in Listing 7.14 randomly loads one of the controls from the FeaturedProducts folder and adds the control to the page.

LISTING 7.14   ShowFeaturedProduct.aspx

```
<%@ Page Language="VB" %>
<%@ Import Namespace="System.IO" %>
<!DOCTYPE html PUBLIC "-//W3C//DTD XHTML 1.1//EN"
    "http://www.w3.org/TR/xhtml11/DTD/xhtml11.dtd">
<script runat="server">

    Const randomFolder As String = "~/FeaturedProducts"

    Sub Page_Load(ByVal sender As Object, ByVal e As EventArgs)
        Dim featuredProductPath As String = GetRandomProductPath()
        Dim featuredProduct As Control = Page.LoadControl(featuredProductPath)
        PlaceHolder1.Controls.Add(featuredProduct)
    End Sub

    Private Function GetRandomProductPath() As String
        Dim rnd As New Random()
        Dim files() As String =
➥Directory.GetFiles(MapPath(randomFolder),"*.ascx")
        Dim featuredProductPath As String =
➥    Path.GetFileName(files(rnd.Next(files.Length)))
```

LISTING 7.14   Continued

```
        Return Path.Combine(randomFolder,featuredProductPath)
    End Function

</script>
<html xmlns="http://www.w3.org/1999/xhtml" >
<head id="Head1" runat="server">
    <title>Show Featured Products</title>
</head>
<body>
    <form id="form1" runat="server">
    <div>

    <asp:PlaceHolder
        id="PlaceHolder1"
        Runat="server" />

    </div>
    </form>
</body>
</html>
```

Using the Reference Directive

When you load a User control with the `Page.LoadControl()` method, the User control is returned as an instance of the `System.Web.UI.Control` class. This means that if the User control includes any custom properties, the properties aren't available when you dynamically load the User control.

If you dynamically load a User control, then you need to cast the control to the correct type before you can access any of the control's custom properties. To get a reference to a User control's type, you must use the `<%@ Reference %>` directive.

For example, imagine that you need to create a form that displays different questions depending on the answers that a user provides for previous questions. In that case, you can dynamically load different User controls that contain the different sets of questions.

For example, the page in Listing 7.15 contains a survey form. The first question asks you whether you are currently using ASP Classic or ASP.NET. Depending on your answer, the remainder of the form displays different questions (see Figure 7.5).

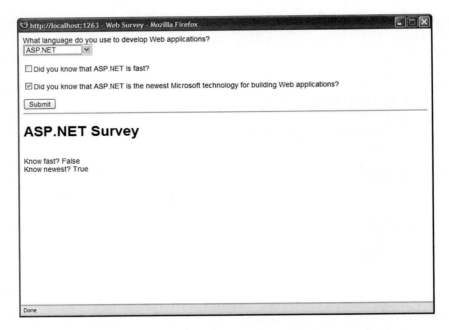

FIGURE 7.5   Displaying a survey form with dynamically loaded questions.

LISTING 7.15   WebSurvey.aspx

```
<%@ Page Language="VB" %>
<%@ Reference Control="~/ASPSurvey.ascx" %>
<%@ Reference Control="~/ASPNetSurvey.ascx" %>
<!DOCTYPE html PUBLIC "-//W3C//DTD XHTML 1.1//EN"
  "http://www.w3.org/TR/xhtml11/DTD/xhtml11.dtd">
<script runat="server">

    Private _survey As Control = Nothing

    Private Sub Page_Load()
        Select Case ddlLanguage.SelectedIndex
            Case 1
                _survey = Page.LoadControl("ASPSurvey.ascx")
            Case 2
                _survey = Page.LoadControl("ASPNetSurvey.ascx")
        End Select

        If Not IsNothing(_survey) Then
            PlaceHolder1.Controls.Add(_survey)
```

LISTING 7.15   Continued

```
            End If
        End Sub


    Protected Sub btnSubmit_Click(ByVal sender As Object, ByVal e As EventArgs)
        Select Case ddlLanguage.SelectedIndex
            Case 1
                Dim aspResults As ASPSurvey = CType(_survey, ASPSurvey)
                ltlResults.Text = "<h1>ASP Survey</h1>"
                ltlResults.Text += "<br />Know slow? "
➥+ aspResults.KnowSlow.ToString()
                ltlResults.Text += "<br />Know outdated? "
➥+ aspResults.KnowOutdated.ToString()
            Case 2
                Dim aspNetResults As ASPNetSurvey = CType(_survey, ASPNetSurvey)
                ltlResults.Text = "<h1>ASP.NET Survey</h1>"
                ltlResults.Text += "<br />Know fast? "
➥+ aspNetResults.KnowFast.ToString()
                ltlResults.Text += "<br />Know newest? "
➥+ aspNetResults.KnowNewest.ToString()
        End Select
    End Sub

</script>
<html xmlns="http://www.w3.org/1999/xhtml" >
<head id="Head1" runat="server">
    <style type="text/css">
        html
        {
            font:14px Arial,Sans-Serif;
        }
    </style>
    <title>Web Survey</title>
</head>
<body>
    <form id="form1" runat="server">
    <div>

    <asp:Label
        id="lblLanguage"
        Text="What language do you use to develop Web applications?"
        Runat="server" />
    <br />
    <asp:DropDownList
        id="ddlLanguage"
```

LISTING 7.15   Continued

```
        ToolTip="Web application language (reloads form)"
        AutoPostBack="true"
        Runat="server">
        <asp:ListItem Text="Select Language" />
        <asp:ListItem Text="ASP Classic"  />
        <asp:ListItem Text="ASP.NET" />
    </asp:DropDownList>

    <br /><br />

    <asp:PlaceHolder
        id="PlaceHolder1"
        Runat="server" />

    <asp:Button
        id="btnSubmit"
        Text="Submit"
        OnClick="btnSubmit_Click"
        Runat="server" />

    <hr />

    <asp:Literal
        id="ltlResults"
        Runat="server" />

    </div>
    </form>
</body>
</html>
```

> **WEB STANDARDS NOTE**
>
> The DropDownList control in Listing 7.15 reloads the page automatically when you select a new option. You should never reload a page without warning the user because this can be very confusing for someone who is using an assistive device such as a screen reader. In Listing 7.15, a warning is added to the ToolTip property of the DropDownList control.

Depending on the user's selection from the DropDownList control, one of two User controls is loaded in the Page_Load() event handler: the ASPSurvey.ascx or the ASPNetSurvey.ascx User control. These controls are contained in Listing 7.16 and Listing 7.17.

When you submit the survey form, the btnSubmit_Click() method executes. This method casts the User control loaded in the form to the correct type. It casts the User control to either the ASPSurvey or the ASPNetSurvey type.

Notice that the page in Listing 7.15 includes two <%@ Reference %> directives. These reference directives enable you to cast the User control to the correct type so that you can access custom properties of the control such as the KnowSlow and KnowOutdated properties.

LISTING 7.16   ASPSurvey.ascx

```
<%@ Control Language="VB" ClassName="ASPSurvey" %>
<script runat="server">

    Public ReadOnly Property KnowSlow() As Boolean
        Get
            Return chkSlow.Checked
        End Get
    End Property

    Public ReadOnly Property KnowOutdated() As Boolean
        Get
            Return chkOutdated.Checked
        End Get
    End Property
</script>

<asp:CheckBox
    id="chkSlow"
    Text="Did you know that ASP Classic is slow?"
    Runat="server" />

<br /><br />

<asp:CheckBox
    id="chkOutdated"
    Text="Did you know that ASP Classic is outdated?"
    Runat="server" />
<br /><br />
```

LISTING 7.17   ASPNetSurvey.ascx

```
<%@ Control Language="VB" ClassName="ASPNetSurvey" %>
<script runat="server">
```

LISTING 7.17   Continued

```
    Public ReadOnly Property KnowFast() As Boolean
        Get
            Return chkFast.Checked
        End Get
    End Property

    Public ReadOnly Property KnowNewest() As Boolean
        Get
            Return chkNewest.Checked
        End Get
    End Property
</script>
<asp:CheckBox
    id="chkFast"
    Text="Did you know that ASP.NET is fast?"
    Runat="server" />

<br /><br />

<asp:CheckBox
    id="chkNewest"
    Text="Did you know that ASP.NET is the newest Microsoft
        technology for building Web applications?"
    Runat="server" />
<br /><br />
```

Creating a Multi-Page Wizard

This final section discusses how you can create a multi-page wizard by dynamically loading different user controls into the same page. This is going to be a complicated sample, but it is a realistic sample of situations when you would want to load User controls dynamically (see Figure 7.6).

Imagine that you must create a form with 200 questions in it. Displaying all 200 questions to a user in a single form would be overwhelming. Instead, it makes more sense to break the form into multiple pages. Each page of questions can be represented with a User control.

First, you need to define an interface, named the IWizardStep interface, which all the User controls will implement. An interface enables you to know, in advance, that a User control supports a particular set of properties or methods.

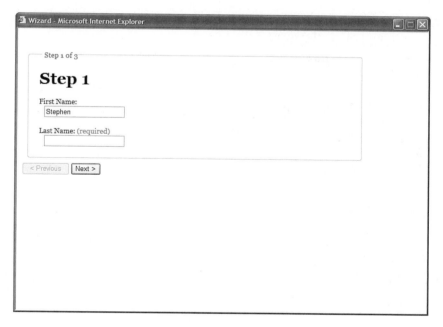

FIGURE 7.6   Displaying a wizard with a series of User controls.

> **NOTE**
>
> You need to add the interface in Listing 7.18 to your application's App_Code folder. In Visual Web Developer, create the interface by selecting Website, Add New Item, and select Class. Visual Web Developer prompts you to create the App_Code folder.

The IWizardStep interface is contained in Listing 7.18.

LISTING 7.18   IWizardStep.vb

```
Public Interface IWizardStep
    Sub LoadStep()
    Function NextStep() As Boolean
End Interface
```

The interface in Listing 7.18 contains two methods: LoadStep() and NextStep(). The LoadStep() method is called when a User control is first loaded. The NextStep() method is called when the Next button is clicked in the wizard.

Notice that the NextStep() method returns a Boolean value. If the NextStep() method returns the value False, then the user doesn't advance to the next wizard step.

This wizard will consist of the three wizard steps contained in Listing 7.19, Listing 7.20, and Listing 7.21.

LISTING 7.19   WizardSteps\Step1.ascx

```
<%@ Control Language="VB" ClassName="Step1" %>
<%@ Implements Interface="IWizardStep" %>
<script runat="server">

    Public Sub LoadStep() Implements IWizardStep.LoadStep
        If Not IsNothing(Session("FirstName")) Then
            txtFirstName.Text = CStr(Session("FirstName"))
        End If
        If Not IsNothing(Session("LastName")) Then
            txtLastName.Text = CStr(Session("LastName"))
        End If
    End Sub

    Public Function NextStep() As Boolean Implements IWizardStep.NextStep
        If Page.IsValid Then
            Session("FirstName") = txtFirstName.Text
            Session("LastName") = txtLastName.Text
            Return True
        End If
        Return False
    End Function
</script>
<h1>Step 1</h1>

<asp:Label
    id="lblFirstName"
    Text="First Name:"
    AssociatedControlID="txtFirstName"
    Runat="server" />
<asp:RequiredFieldValidator
    id="reqFirstName"
    Text="(required)"
    ControlToValidate="txtFirstName"
    Runat="server" />
<br />
<asp:TextBox
    id="txtFirstName"
    Runat="server" />

<br /><br />

<asp:Label
    id="lblLastName"
    Text="Last Name:"
```

LISTING 7.19   Continued

```
    AssociatedControlID="txtLastName"
    Runat="server" />
<asp:RequiredFieldValidator
    id="reqLastName"
    Text="(required)"
    ControlToValidate="txtLastName"
    Runat="server" />
<br />
<asp:TextBox
    id="txtLastName"
    Runat="server" />
```

The wizard step in Listing 7.19 contains a simple form that contains Textbox controls for the user's first and last name. Both TextBox controls are validated with RequiredFieldValidator controls.

Notice that the User control in Listing 7.19 implements the IWizardStep interface. It contains an <%@ Implements %> directive at the top of the control.

The LoadStep() method assigns values to the txtFirstName and txtLastName TextBox controls from Session state. The NextStep() method grabs the values from the txtFirstName and txtLastName TextBox controls and assigns the values to Session state.

The second step of the Wizard is contained in Listing 7.20.

LISTING 7.20   WizardSteps\Step2.ascx

```
<%@ Control Language="VB" ClassName="Step2" %>
<%@ Implements Interface="IWizardStep" %>
<script runat="server">

    Public Sub LoadStep() Implements IWizardStep.LoadStep
        If Not IsNothing(Session("FavoriteColor")) Then
            txtFavoriteColor.Text = CStr(Session("FavoriteColor"))
        End If
    End Sub


    Public Function NextStep() As Boolean Implements IWizardStep.NextStep
        If Page.IsValid Then
            Session("FavoriteColor") = txtFavoriteColor.Text
            Return True
        End If
        Return False
    End Function
</script>
```

LISTING 7.20 Continued

```
<h1>Step 2</h1>

<asp:Label
    id="lblFavoriteColor"
    Text="Favorite Color:"
    AssociatedControlID="txtFavoriteColor"
    Runat="server" />
<asp:RequiredFieldValidator
    id="reqFavoriteColor"
    Text="(required)"
    ControlToValidate="txtFavoriteColor"
    Runat="server" />
<br />
<asp:TextBox
    id="txtFavoriteColor"
    Runat="server" />
```

The User control in Listing 7.20 also implements the IWizardStep interface. In this step, the user enters a favorite color.

The final wizard step is contained in Listing 7.21.

LISTING 7.21 WizardSteps\Step3.ascx

```
<%@ Control Language="VB" ClassName="Step3" %>
<%@ Implements Interface="IWizardStep" %>
<script runat="server">

    Public Sub LoadStep() Implements IWizardStep.LoadStep
        lblFirstName.Text = CStr(Session("FirstName"))
        lblLastName.Text = CStr(Session("LastName"))
        lblFavoriteColor.Text = CStr(Session("FavoriteColor"))
    End Sub

    Public Function NextStep() As Boolean Implements IWizardStep.NextStep
        Return False
    End Function
</script>

<h1>Step 3</h1>

First Name:
<asp:Label
    id="lblFirstName"
    Runat="server" />
```

LISTING 7.21   Continued

```
<br />
Last Name:
<asp:Label
    id="lblLastName"
    Runat="server" />
<br />
Favorite Color:
<asp:Label
    id="lblFavoriteColor"
    Runat="server" />
```

The wizard step in Listing 7.21 displays a summary of answers that the user has provided in the first two wizard steps (see Figure 7.7). Notice that it also implements the IWizardStep interface. Because this is the final wizard step, the NextStep() method always returns the value False.

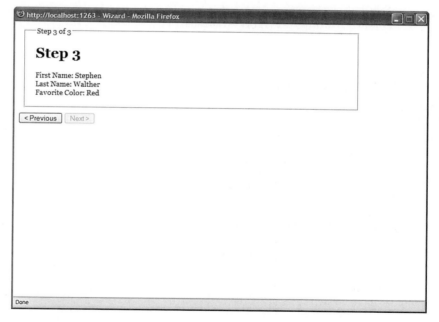

FIGURE 7.7   Displaying the wizard summary step.

The page in Listing 7.22 contains the actual wizard. This page loads each of the wizard steps.

LISTING 7.22   Wizard.aspx

```vb
<%@ Page Language="VB" %>
<%@ Import Namespace="System.Collections.Generic" %>
<!DOCTYPE html PUBLIC "-//W3C//DTD XHTML 1.1//EN"
    "http://www.w3.org/TR/xhtml11/DTD/xhtml11.dtd">
<script runat="server">

    Private _wizardSteps As New List(Of String)()
    Private _currentStep As Control

    ''' <summary>
    ''' The current step in the Wizard
    ''' </summary>
    Public Property StepIndex() As Integer
        Get
            If (IsNothing(ViewState("StepIndex"))) Then
                Return 0
            else
                Return CInt(ViewState("StepIndex"))
            End If
        End Get
        Set (ByVal Value As Integer)
            ViewState("StepIndex") = value
        End Set
    End Property

    ''' <summary>
    ''' Load the list of wizard steps and load
    ''' current step
    ''' </summary>
    Sub Page_Load()
        _wizardSteps.Add("~/WizardSteps/Step1.ascx")
        _wizardSteps.Add("~/WizardSteps/Step2.ascx")
        _wizardSteps.Add("~/WizardSteps/Step3.ascx")

        LoadWizardStep()
    End Sub

    ''' <summary>
    ''' Load the current wizard step
    ''' </summary>
    Private Sub LoadWizardStep()
        _currentStep = Page.LoadControl(_wizardSteps(StepIndex))
        _currentStep.ID = "ctlWizardStep"
        plhWizardStep.Controls.Clear()
```

LISTING 7.22   Continued

```
        plhWizardStep.Controls.Add(_currentStep)
        CType(_currentStep, IWizardStep).LoadStep()
        ltlStep.Text = String.Format("Step {0} of {1}", StepIndex + 1, _wizard-
Steps.Count)
    End Sub


    ''' <summary>
    ''' Disable the Previous and Next
    ''' buttons when appropriate
    ''' </summary>
    Sub Page_PreRender()
        btnPrevious.Enabled = StepIndex > 0
        btnNext.Enabled = StepIndex < _wizardSteps.Count - 1
    End Sub


    ''' <summary>
    ''' Execute the step's NextStep() method
    ''' and move to the next step
    ''' </summary>
    Sub btnNext_Click(ByVal sender As Object, ByVal s As EventArgs)
        Dim success As Boolean = CType(_currentStep, IWizardStep).NextStep()
        If success Then
            If (StepIndex < _wizardSteps.Count - 1) Then
                StepIndex = StepIndex + 1
                LoadWizardStep()
            End If
        End If
    End Sub


    ''' <summary>
    ''' Move to the previous step
    ''' </summary>
    Sub btnPrevious_Click(ByVal sender As Object, ByVal e As EventArgs)
        If StepIndex > 0 Then
            StepIndex = StepIndex - 1
            LoadWizardStep()
        End If
    End Sub


</script>
<html xmlns="http://www.w3.org/1999/xhtml" >
<head id="Head1" runat="server">
    <style type="text/css">
        html
        {
```

LISTING 7.22   Continued

```
                font:14px Georgia,Serif;
        }
        fieldset
        {
            display:block;
            width:600px;
            padding:20px;
            margin:10px;
        }
    </style>
    <title>Wizard</title>
</head>
<body>
    <form id="form1" runat="server">
    <div>

    <asp:Label
        id="lblStepNumber"
        Runat="server" />

    <fieldset>
    <legend><asp:Literal ID="ltlStep" runat="server" /></legend>
        <asp:PlaceHolder
            id="plhWizardStep"
            Runat="server" />
    </fieldset>

    <asp:Button
        id="btnPrevious"
        Text="&lt; Previous"
        CausesValidation="false"
        OnClick="btnPrevious_Click"
        Runat="server" />

    <asp:Button
        id="btnNext"
        Text="Next &gt;"
        OnClick="btnNext_Click"
        Runat="server" />

    </div>
    </form>
</body>
</html>
```

The list of wizard steps is created in the `Page_Load()` method. The path to each wizard step User control is added to a collection of wizard steps.

The `StepIndex` property represents the index of the wizard step to display. Notice that the value of this property is stored in `ViewState` so that the value is available across multiple page requests.

The current wizard step is loaded by the `LoadWizardStep()` method. This method uses the StepIndex to grab the path to the current wizard step. Next, it uses the `Page.LoadControl()` method to actually load the wizard step User control.

After the `LoadWizardStep()` method loads the current wizard step, it calls the control's `LoadStep()` method and initializes the control.

The page also contains a Previous and Next button. When you click the Previous button, the `btnPrevious_Click()` method is called and the `StepIndex` is reduced by one. When you click the Next button, the `btnNext_Click()` method is called.

The `btnNext_Click()` method first calls the current wizard step's `NextStep()` method. If this method returns the value `True`, then one is added to the `StepIndex` property and the next wizard step is loaded. Otherwise, if the `NextStep()` method returns `false`, the next wizard step is not loaded.

Summary

In this chapter, you learned how to build custom controls by creating User controls. The first section covered the basics of User controls. You learned how to create a User control and register it both in a page and in a Web configuration file. You learned how to add custom properties and events to a User control.

You also explored the topic of AJAX and User controls. You learned how to update content in a User control without posting the page that contains the User control back to the web server.

Finally, you learned how to add User controls dynamically to a page. You learned how to use the `<%@ Reference %>` directive to cast a User control to a particular type. You also learned how to create a multi-page wizard by dynamically loading a series of User controls.

PART III

Performing Data Access

IN THIS PART

Overview of Data Access

Any web application worth writing involves data access. In this chapter, you learn how to take advantage of the rich set of controls included in the ASP.NET 2.0 Framework for working with data.

You learn how to take advantage of the DataBound controls to display data in your ASP.NET pages. You also learn how to take advantage of the DataSource controls to represent different sources of data such as databases, XML files, and business objects.

Next, you are provided with an overview of Microsoft SQL Server 2005 Express, which is the royalty-free database included with Visual Web Developer. You learn how to connect to this database and use it for all of your data access needs.

Finally, at the end of this chapter, we build a database-driven application, which illustrates how you can use many of the data controls discussed in this chapter. We build an Employee Directory application.

Using DataBound Controls

You use DataBound controls to generate your application's user interface for working with data. The DataBound controls can be used to display and edit database data, XML data, or just about any other type of data you can imagine.

There are three main types of DataBound controls: list controls, tabular DataBound controls, and hierarchical DataBound controls.

Working with List Controls

List controls are used to display simple option lists. The ASP.NET 2.0 Framework includes the following five list controls:

- `BulletedList`— Displays a bulleted list of items. Each item can be displayed as text, a link button, or a hyperlink.

- `CheckBoxList`—Displays a list of check boxes. Multiple check boxes in the list can be selected.

- `DropDownList`—Displays a drop-down list. Only one item in the drop-down list can be selected.

- `ListBox`—Displays a list box. You can configure this control so that only one item in the list can be selected or multiple items can be selected.

- `RadioButtonList`—Displays a list of radio buttons. Only one radio button can be selected.

All five controls inherit from the same base `ListControl` class. This means that all these controls share a core set of properties and methods. In Chapter 10, "Working with List Controls," you can find detailed instructions on how to use each of the list controls.

The page in Listing 8.1 illustrates how to use all five list controls to display the same set of database records (see Figure 8.1).

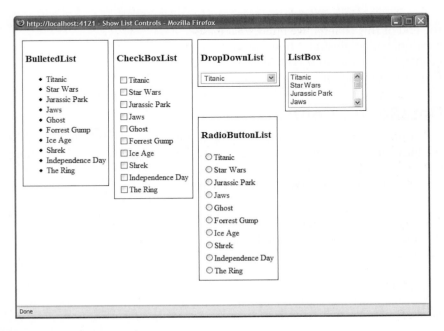

FIGURE 8.1   Using list controls.

LISTING 8.1   ShowListControls.aspx

```
<%@ Page Language="VB" %>
<!DOCTYPE html PUBLIC "-//W3C//DTD XHTML 1.1//EN"
    "http://www.w3.org/TR/xhtml11/DTD/xhtml11.dtd">
<html xmlns="http://www.w3.org/1999/xhtml" >
<head id="Head1" runat="server">
    <style type="text/css">
        .floater
        {
            float:left;
            border:solid 1px black;
            padding:5px;
            margin:5px;
        }
    </style>
    <title>Show List Controls</title>
</head>
<body>
    <form id="form1" runat="server">

    <div class="floater">
    <h3>BulletedList</h3>
    <asp:BulletedList
        id="BulletedList1"
        DataSourceId="srcMovies"
        DataTextField="Title"
        Runat="server" />
    </div>

    <div class="floater">
    <h3>CheckBoxList</h3>
    <asp:CheckBoxList
        id="CheckBoxList1"
        DataSourceId="srcMovies"
        DataTextField="Title"
        Runat="server" />
    </div>

    <div class="floater">
    <h3>DropDownList</h3>
    <asp:DropDownList
        id="DropDownList1"
        DataSourceId="srcMovies"
        DataTextField="Title"
        Runat="server" />
    </div>
```

LISTING 8.1   Continued

```
<div class="floater">
<h3>ListBox</h3>
<asp:ListBox
    id="ListBox1"
    DataSourceId="srcMovies"
    DataTextField="Title"
    Runat="server" />
</div>

<div class="floater">
<h3>RadioButtonList</h3>
<asp:RadioButtonList
    id="RadioButtonList1"
    DataSourceId="srcMovies"
    DataTextField="Title"
    Runat="server" />
</div>

<asp:SqlDataSource
    id="srcMovies"
    ConnectionString="Data Source=.\SQLExpress;
        AttachDbFilename=|DataDirectory|MyDatabase.mdf;
        Integrated Security=True;User Instance=True"
    SelectCommand="SELECT Title FROM Movies"
    Runat="server" />

</form>
</body>
</html>
```

In Listing 8.1, each list control is bound to a `SqlDataSource` control which represents the contents of the Movies database table. For example, the `BulletedList` control is bound to the `DataSource` control like this:

```
<asp:BulletedList
    id="BulletedList1"
    DataSourceID="srcMovies"
    DataTextField="Title"
    Runat="server" />

<asp:SqlDataSource
    id="srcMovies"
    ConnectionString="Data Source=.\SQLExpress;
        AttachDbFilename=|DataDirectory|MyDatabase.mdf;
        Integrated Security=True;User Instance=True"
```

```
SelectCommand="SELECT Title FROM Movies"
Runat="server" />
```

Notice that the `BulletedList` control includes a `DataSourceID` attribute, which points to the ID of the `SqlDataSource` control. The `DataSourceID` attribute associates a `DataBound` control with a `DataSource` control.

Working with Tabular DataBound Controls

The tabular DataBound controls are the main set of controls that you use when working with database data. These controls enable you to display and, in some cases, modify data retrieved from a database or other type of data source.

There are five tabular DataBound controls. These controls can be divided into two types: those that display multiple data items at a time and those that display a single data item at a time.

First, you can use any of the following controls to display a set of data items:

- `GridView`—Displays a set of data items in an HTML table. For example, you can use the `GridView` control to display all the records contained in the Movies database table. This control enables you to display, sort, page, select, and edit data.

- `DataList`—Displays a set of data items in an HTML table. Unlike the `GridView` control, more than one data item can be displayed in a single row.

- `Repeater`—Displays a set of data items using a template. Unlike the `GridView` and `DataList` controls, a `Repeater` control does not automatically render an HTML table.

You can use either of the following two controls to display a single data item at a time:

- `DetailsView`—Displays a single data item in an HTML table. For example, you can use the `DetailsView` control to display a single record from the Movies database table. This control enables you to display, page, edit, and add data.

- `FormView`—Uses a template to display a single data item. Unlike the `DetailsView`, a `FormView` enables you to use to layout a form by using templates .

NOTE

What happened to the DataGrid? The DataGrid was included in the ASP.NET 1.x Framework, but it no longer appears in the Toolbox in Visual Web Developer. The DataGrid is officially deprecated. You should use the `GridView` control instead because the `GridView` is more powerful. For backwards compatibility reasons, the DataGrid is included in the ASP.NET 2.0 Framework so that you can still use it in your pages.

The page in Listing 8.2 illustrates how you can use each of the tabular DataBound controls (see Figure 8.2).

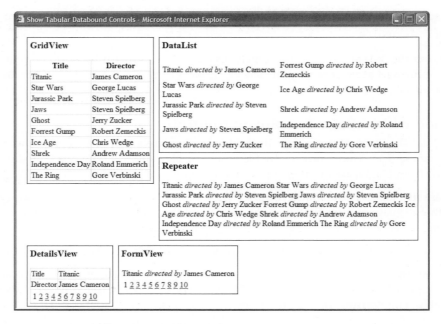

FIGURE 8.2   Using tabular DataBound controls.

LISTING 8.2   ShowTabularDataBound.aspx

```
<%@ Page Language="VB" %>
<!DOCTYPE html PUBLIC "-//W3C//DTD XHTML 1.1//EN"
  "http://www.w3.org/TR/xhtml11/DTD/xhtml11.dtd">
<html xmlns="http://www.w3.org/1999/xhtml" >
<head id="Head1" runat="server">
    <style type="text/css">
        .floater
        {
            float:left;
            border:solid 1px black;
            padding:5px;
            margin:5px;
        }
    </style>
    <title>Show Tabular Databound Controls</title>
</head>
<body>
    <form id="form1" runat="server">

    <div class="floater">
    <h3>GridView</h3>
```

LISTING 8.2   Continued

```
<asp:GridView
    id="GridView1"
    DataSourceId="srcMovies"
    Runat="server" />
</div>

<div class="floater">
<h3>DataList</h3>
<asp:DataList
    id="DataList1"
    DataSourceId="srcMovies"
    RepeatColumns="2"
    Runat="server">
    <ItemTemplate>
    <%#Eval("Title")%>
    <i>directed by</i>
    <%#Eval("Director")%>
    </ItemTemplate>
</asp:DataList>
</div>

<div class="floater">
<h3>Repeater</h3>
<asp:Repeater
    id="Repeater1"
    DataSourceId="srcMovies"
    Runat="server">
    <ItemTemplate>
    <%#Eval("Title")%>
    <i>directed by</i>
    <%#Eval("Director")%>
    </ItemTemplate>
</asp:Repeater>
</div>

<div class="floater">
<h3>DetailsView</h3>
<asp:DetailsView
    id="DetailsView1"
    DataSourceId="srcMovies"
    AllowPaging="true"
    Runat="server" />
</div>
```

LISTING 8.2   Continued

```
<div class="floater">
<h3>FormView</h3>
<asp:FormView
    id="FormView1"
    DataSourceId="srcMovies"
    AllowPaging="true"
    Runat="server">
    <ItemTemplate>
    <%#Eval("Title")%>
    <i>directed by</i>
    <%#Eval("Director")%>
    </ItemTemplate>
</asp:FormView>
</div>

<asp:SqlDataSource
    id="srcMovies"
    ConnectionString="Data Source=.\SQLExpress;
        AttachDbFilename=|DataDirectory|MyDatabase.mdf;
        Integrated Security=True;User Instance=True"
    SelectCommand="SELECT Title,Director FROM Movies"
    Runat="server" />

</form>
</body>
</html>
```

For the moment, don't worry too much about formatting the controls. Each of the tabular DataBound controls supports an abundance of properties that modify the control's behavior and appearance. The GridView control gets a detailed examination in Chapter 11, "Using the GridView Control." The DetailsView and FormView controls are covered in Chapter 12, "Using the DetailsView and FormView Controls." The Repeater and DataList controls are discussed in Chapter 13, "Using the Repeater and DataList controls."

Working with Hierarchical DataBound Controls

A hierarchical DataBound control can be used to display nested data items. For example, you can use hierarchical DataBound controls to display the folder and page structure of your website, the contents of an XML file, or a set of master/detail database records.

The ASP.NET 2.0 Framework includes two hierarchical DataBound controls:

- Menu—Displays data items in a static or dynamic menu.

- TreeView—Displays data items in a tree.

The page in Listing 8.3 illustrates how you can use both the `Menu` and `TreeView` controls. Both controls are bound to an `XmlDataSource` control, which represents the XML file in Listing 8.4 (see Figure 8.3).

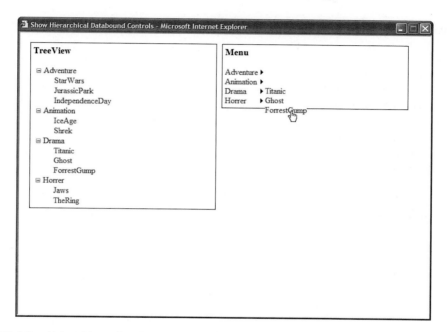

FIGURE 8.3   Using hierarchical DataBound controls.

LISTING 8.3   ShowHierarchicalDataBound.aspx

```
<%@ Page Language="VB" %>
<!DOCTYPE html PUBLIC "-//W3C//DTD XHTML 1.1//EN"
  "http://www.w3.org/TR/xhtml11/DTD/xhtml11.dtd">
<html xmlns="http://www.w3.org/1999/xhtml" >
<head id="Head1" runat="server">
    <style type="text/css">
        .floater
        {
            float:left;
            width:45%;
            border:solid 1px black;
            padding:5px;
            margin:5px;
        }
    </style>
    <title>Show Hierarchical Databound Controls</title>
</head>
```

LISTING 8.3   Continued

```
<body>
    <form id="form1" runat="server">

    <div class="floater">
    <h3>TreeView</h3>
    <asp:TreeView
        id="CheckBoxList1"
        DataSourceId="srcMovies"
        Runat="server" />
    </div>

    <div class="floater">
    <h3>Menu</h3>
    <asp:Menu
        id="BulletedList1"
        DataSourceId="srcMovies"
        Runat="server" />
    </div>

    <asp:XmlDataSource
        id="srcMovies"
        DataFile="~/Movies.xml"
        XPath="/movies/*"
        Runat="server" />

    </form>
</body>
</html>
```

LISTING 8.4   Movies.xml

```
<?xml version="1.0" encoding="utf-8" ?>
<movies>
  <Adventure>
    <StarWars />
    <JurassicPark />
    <IndependenceDay />
  </Adventure>
  <Animation>
    <IceAge />
    <Shrek />
  </Animation>
  <Drama>
    <Titanic />
```

LISTING 8.4   Continued

```
      <Ghost />
      <ForrestGump />
    </Drama>
    <Horrer>
      <Jaws />
      <TheRing />
    </Horrer>
</movies>
```

Again, don't worry about the appearance of the `Menu` and `TreeView` controls in the page rendered by Listing 8.3. Both controls support a rich set of options for modifying the control's appearance. We examine the properties of both of these hierarchical controls in detail in Chapter 17, "Using the Navigation Controls."

Working with Other Controls

You can bind any control in the ASP.NET Framework to the data items represented by a data source. Imagine, for example, that you want to display a photo gallery. In that case, you might want to bind a set of Image controls to a data source.

You can bind any ASP.NET control to a data item by adding the control to a template. For example, the page in Listing 8.5 automatically displays all the pictures in a folder named Photos (see Figure 8.4).

FIGURE 8.4   Binding images to a data source.

LISTING 8.5   ShowPhotos.aspx

```
<%@ Page Language="VB" %>
<%@ Import Namespace="System.IO" %>
<%@ Import Namespace="System.Collections.Generic" %>
<!DOCTYPE html PUBLIC "-//W3C//DTD XHTML 1.1//EN"
  "http://www.w3.org/TR/xhtml11/DTD/xhtml11.dtd">
<script runat="server">

    ''' <summary>
    ''' Bind photos to Repeater
    ''' </summary>
    Sub Page_Load()
        If Not Page.IsPostBack Then
            Repeater1.DataSource = GetPhotos()
            Repeater1.DataBind()
        End If
    End Sub

    ''' <summary>
    ''' Get list of photos from Photo folder
    ''' </summary>
    Public Function GetPhotos() As List(Of String)
        Dim photos As New List(Of String)()
        Dim photoPath As String = MapPath("~/Photos")
        Dim files As String() = Directory.GetFiles(photoPath)
        For Each photo As String In files
            photos.Add("~/Photos/" + Path.GetFileName(photo))
        Next
        Return photos
    End Function

</script>
<html xmlns="http://www.w3.org/1999/xhtml" >
<head id="Head1" runat="server">
    <title>Show Photos</title>
</head>
<body>
    <form id="form1" runat="server">
    <div>

    <asp:Repeater
        id="Repeater1"
        runat="server">
        <ItemTemplate>
```

LISTING 8.5   Continued

```
            <asp:Image
                id="Image1"
                Width="200px"
                ImageUrl='<%# Container.DataItem %>'
                Runat="server" />
        </ItemTemplate>
    </asp:Repeater>

    </div>
    </form>
</body>
</html>
```

Notice that the Repeater control contains an ItemTemplate, and the ItemTemplate contains an ASP.NET Image control. The Image control displays each of the photographs from the Photos folder.

Using DataSource Controls

You bind a DataBound control to a DataSource control. A DataSource control is used to represent a particular type of data.

The ASP.NET 2.0 Framework includes the following five DataSource controls:

- SqlDataSource—Represents data retrieved from a SQL relational database, including Microsoft SQL Server, Oracle, or DB2.

- AccessDataSource—Represents data retrieved from a Microsoft Access database.

- ObjectDataSource—Represents data retrieved from a business object.

- XmlDataSource—Represents data retrieved from an XML document.

- SiteMapDataSource—Represents data retrieved from a Site Map Provider. A Site Map Provider represents the page and folder structure of a website.

The ASP.NET Framework contains two basic types of DataSource controls. The SqlDataSource, AccessDataSource, and ObjectDataSource controls all derive from the base DataSourceControl class. These controls can be used to represent tabular data. The XmlDataSource and SiteMapDataSource controls, on the other hand, derive from the base HierarchicalDataSourceControl control. These two controls can be used to represent both tabular and hierarchical data.

A DataBound control is associated with a particular data source control through its DataSourceID property. For example, the page in Listing 8.6 contains a GridView control bound to a SqlDataSource control (see Figure 8.5).

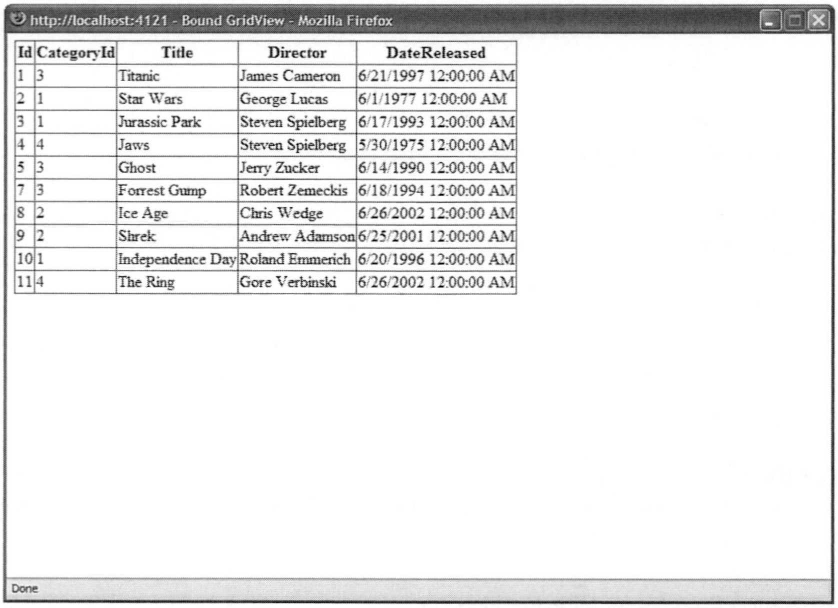

Id	CategoryId	Title	Director	DateReleased
1	3	Titanic	James Cameron	6/21/1997 12:00:00 AM
2	1	Star Wars	George Lucas	6/1/1977 12:00:00 AM
3	1	Jurassic Park	Steven Spielberg	6/17/1993 12:00:00 AM
4	4	Jaws	Steven Spielberg	5/30/1975 12:00:00 AM
5	3	Ghost	Jerry Zucker	6/14/1990 12:00:00 AM
7	3	Forrest Gump	Robert Zemeckis	6/18/1994 12:00:00 AM
8	2	Ice Age	Chris Wedge	6/26/2002 12:00:00 AM
9	2	Shrek	Andrew Adamson	6/25/2001 12:00:00 AM
10	1	Independence Day	Roland Emmerich	6/20/1996 12:00:00 AM
11	4	The Ring	Gore Verbinski	6/26/2002 12:00:00 AM

FIGURE 8.5 Using the `SqlDataSource` control.

LISTING 8.6 `BoundGridView.aspx`

```
<%@ Page Language="VB" %>
<!DOCTYPE html PUBLIC "-//W3C//DTD XHTML 1.1//EN"
  "http://www.w3.org/TR/xhtml11/DTD/xhtml11.dtd">
<html xmlns="http://www.w3.org/1999/xhtml" >
<head id="Head1" runat="server">
    <title>Bound GridView</title>
</head>
<body>
    <form id="form1" runat="server">
    <div>

    <asp:GridView
        id="GridView1"
        DataSourceId="srcMovies"
        Runat="server" />

    <asp:SqlDataSource
        id="srcMovies"
```

LISTING 8.6   Continued

```
            ConnectionString="Data Source=.\SQLExpress;
                AttachDbFilename=¦DataDirectory¦MyDatabase.mdf;
                Integrated Security=True;User Instance=True"
            SelectCommand="SELECT * FROM Movies"
            Runat="server" />

    </div>
    </form>
</body>
</html>
```

Using ASP.NET Parameters with DataSource Controls

Many of the DataSource controls support ASP.NET parameters. You use ASP.NET parameters to modify the commands that a DataSource control executes.

Different types of DataSource controls use ASP.NET parameters to represent different types of things. When you use ASP.NET parameters with a SqlDataSource control, the ASP.NET parameters represent ADO.NET parameters. In other words, they represent parameters used with SQL statements.

When you use parameters with the ObjectDataSource control, the ASP.NET parameters represent method parameters. They represent parameters passed to a particular method of a business object.

The SqlDataSource, AccessDataSource, and ObjectDataSource controls all support the following types of Parameter objects:

- Parameter—Represents an arbitrary static value.

- ControlParameter—Represents the value of a control or page property.

- CookieParameter—Represents the value of a browser cookie.

- FormParameter—Represents the value of an HTML form field.

- ProfileParameter—Represents the value of a Profile property.

- QueryStringParameter—Represents the value of a query string field.

- SessionParameter—Represents the value of an item stored in Session state.

For example, the page in Listing 8.7 contains a DropDownList, GridView, and SqlDataSource control. The DropDownList displays a list of movie categories. When you select a new category, the GridView displays matching movies (see Figure 8.6).

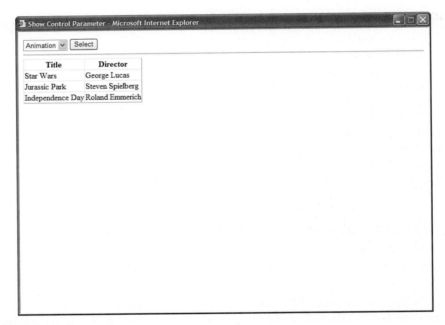

FIGURE 8.6　Using the `ControlParameter` object.

LISTING 8.7　ShowControlParameter.aspx

```
<%@ Page Language="VB" %>
<!DOCTYPE html PUBLIC "-//W3C//DTD XHTML 1.1//EN"
  "http://www.w3.org/TR/xhtml11/DTD/xhtml11.dtd">
<html xmlns="http://www.w3.org/1999/xhtml" >
<head id="Head1" runat="server">
    <title>Show Control Parameter</title>
</head>
<body>
    <form id="form1" runat="server">
    <div>

    <asp:DropDownList
        id="ddlMovieCategory"
        DataSourceID="srcMovieCategories"
        DataTextField="Name"
        DataValueField="Id"
        Runat="server" />

    <asp:Button
        id="btnSelect"
        Text="Select"
```

LISTING 8.7   Continued

```
            ToolTip="Select Movie"
            Runat="server" />

    <hr />

    <asp:GridView
        id="grdMovies"
        DataSourceID="srcMovies"
        Runat="server" />

    <asp:SqlDataSource
        id="srcMovieCategories"
        ConnectionString="Data Source=.\SQLExpress;
            AttachDbFilename=¦DataDirectory¦MyDatabase.mdf;
            Integrated Security=True;User Instance=True"
        SelectCommand="SELECT Id,Name FROM MovieCategories"
        Runat="server" />

    <asp:SqlDataSource
        id="srcMovies"
        ConnectionString="Data Source=.\SQLExpress;
            AttachDbFilename=¦DataDirectory¦MyDatabase.mdf;
            Integrated Security=True;User Instance=True"
        SelectCommand="SELECT Title,Director FROM Movies
            WHERE CategoryId=@Id"
        Runat="server">
        <SelectParameters>
            <asp:ControlParameter
                Name="Id"
                Type="int32"
                ControlID="ddlMovieCategory" />
        </SelectParameters>
    </asp:SqlDataSource>

    </div>
    </form>
</body>
</html>
```

Notice that the SqlDataSource control includes a ControlParameter object. The ControlParameter represents the selected item in the DropDownList control. The value of the ControlParameter is used in the SqlDataSource control's SelectCommand to select movies that match the category selected in the DropDownList control.

Using Programmatic DataBinding

When you bind a DataBound control to a DataSource control, you are taking advantage of *declarative databinding*. When you use declarative databinding, the ASP.NET Framework handles all the messy details of deciding when to retrieve the data items represented by a DataSource control.

In certain situations, you'll want to handle these messy details yourself. For example, you might want to force a GridView control to refresh the data it displays after you add a new record to a database table. Or, you might want to bind a DataBound control to a data source that can't be easily represented by one of the existing DataSource controls. In these situations, you'll want to use *programmatic databinding*.

> **NOTE**
>
> The ASP.NET 1.x Framework supported only programmatic databinding. The first version of the Framework did not include any of the DataSource controls.

Every DataBound control has a `DataSource` property and a `DataBind()` method. By using this property and method, you can programmatically associate a DataBound control with a data source.

For example, the page in Listing 8.8 displays a list of all the fonts installed on your computer (see Figure 8.7).

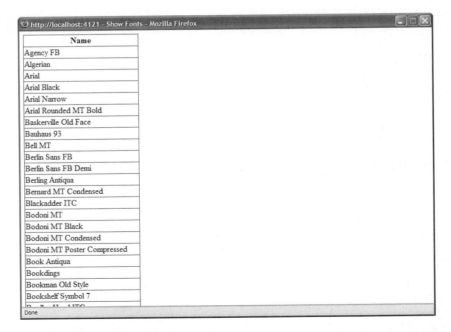

FIGURE 8.7 Programmatic databinding.

LISTING 8.8 ShowFonts.aspx

```
<%@ Page Language="VB" %>
<%@ Import Namespace="System.Drawing.Text" %>
<!DOCTYPE html PUBLIC "-//W3C//DTD XHTML 1.1//EN"
  "http://www.w3.org/TR/xhtml11/DTD/xhtml11.dtd">
<script runat="server">

    Private Sub Page_Load()
        If Not Page.IsPostBack Then
            Dim fonts As New InstalledFontCollection()
            GridView1.DataSource = fonts.Families
            GridView1.DataBind()
        End If
    End Sub

</script>
<html xmlns="http://www.w3.org/1999/xhtml" >
<head id="Head1" runat="server">
    <title>Show Fonts</title>
</head>
<body>
    <form id="form1" runat="server">
    <div>

    <asp:GridView
        id="GridView1"
        Runat="server" />

    </div>
    </form>
</body>
</html>
```

> **NOTE**
>
> The programmatic databinding in Listing 8.8 could have been avoided by taking advantage of the ObjectDataSource control. This DataSource control is discussed in detail in Chapter 15, "Using the ObjectDataSource Control."

The list of fonts is displayed by a GridView control. The actual list of fonts is retrieved from the InstalledFontCollection class (which inhabits the System.Drawing.Text namespace). The list of fonts is assigned to the GridView control's DataSource property, and the DataBind() method is called.

In Listing 8.8, a collection of fonts has been assigned to the DataSource property. In general, you can assign any object that implements the IEnumerable interface to the

`DataSource` property. For example, you can assign collections, arrays, DataSets, DataReaders, DataViews, and enumerations to the `DataSource` property.

> **NOTE**
>
> Particular DataBound controls support different data sources. For example, you can assign any object that implements the `IEnumerable`, `IListSource` or `IDataSource` interface to the `DataSource` property of a GridView control.

When you call the `DataBind()` method, the GridView control actually retrieves its data from the data source. The control iterates through all of the items represented by the data source and displays each item. If you neglect to call the `DataBind()` method, the control will never display anything.

Notice that the GridView is bound to its data source only when the page is requested for the first time. The `Page.IsPostBack` property is used to determine whether or not the page has been posted back to the server. You don't need to rebind the GridView to its data source every time the page is requested because the GridView uses View State to remember the data items that it displays.

You can't mix declarative and programmatic databinding. If you attempt to use both the DataSource and DataSourceID properties, then you will get an exception.

On the other hand, you can call the `DataBind()` method even when you have declaratively bound a control to a DataSource control. When you explicitly call `DataBind()`, the DataBound control grabs the data items from its DataSource control again. Explicitly calling `DataBind()` is useful when you want to refresh the data displayed by a DataBound control.

Understanding Templates and DataBinding Expressions

Almost all the DataBound controls support templates. You can use a template to format the layout and appearance of each of the data items that a DataBound control displays. Within a template, you can use a DataBinding expression to display the value of a data item.

In this section, you learn about the different kinds of templates and DataBinding expressions that you can use with the DataBound controls.

Using Templates

Every DataBound control included in the ASP.NET 2.0 Framework supports templates with the sole exception of the `TreeView` control. The Repeater, DataList, and FormView controls all require you to use templates. If you don't supply a template, then these controls display nothing. The GridView, DetailsView, and Menu controls also support templates, but they do not require a template.

For example, when you use the Repeater control you must supply an ItemTemplate. The Repeater control uses the ItemTemplate to format each of the records that it displays.

Listing 8.9 contains a Repeater control that formats each of the records from the Movies database table (see Figure 8.8).

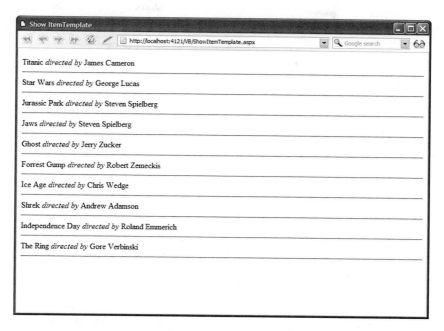

FIGURE 8.8   Using an ItemTemplate.

LISTING 8.9   ShowItemTemplate.aspx

```
<%@ Page Language="VB" %>
<!DOCTYPE html PUBLIC "-//W3C//DTD XHTML 1.1//EN"
    "http://www.w3.org/TR/xhtml11/DTD/xhtml11.dtd">
<html xmlns="http://www.w3.org/1999/xhtml" >
<head id="Head1" runat="server">
    <title>Show ItemTemplate</title>
</head>
<body>
    <form id="form1" runat="server">
    <div>

    <asp:Repeater
        id="Repeater1"
        DataSourceId="srcMovies"
        Runat="server">
        <ItemTemplate>
        <%#Eval("Title")%>
        <i>directed by</i>
        <%#Eval("Director")%>
        <hr />
```

LISTING 8.9   Continued

```
            </ItemTemplate>
        </asp:Repeater>

        <asp:SqlDataSource
            id="srcMovies"
            ConnectionString="Data Source=.\SQLExpress;
                AttachDbFilename=|DataDirectory|MyDatabase.mdf;
                Integrated Security=True;User Instance=True"
            SelectCommand="SELECT Title,Director FROM Movies"
            Runat="server" />

        </div>
        </form>
</body>
</html>
```

A template can contain HTML, DataBinding expressions, and other controls. In Listing 8.9, the template includes the following two DataBinding expressions:

```
<%# Eval("Title") %>
<%# Eval("Director") %>
```

The first DataBinding expression displays the value of the Title column and the second DataBinding expression displays the value of the Director column.

A template can contain other controls—even other DataBound controls. For example, the page in Listing 8.10 displays a list of hyperlinks (see Figure 8.9).

LISTING 8.10   ShowLinks.aspx

```
<%@ Page Language="VB" %>
<!DOCTYPE html PUBLIC "-//W3C//DTD XHTML 1.1//EN"
  "http://www.w3.org/TR/xhtml11/DTD/xhtml11.dtd">
<html xmlns="http://www.w3.org/1999/xhtml" >
<head id="Head1" runat="server">
    <title>Show Links</title>
</head>
<body>
    <form id="form1" runat="server">
    <div>

    <asp:Repeater
        id="Repeater1"
        DataSourceId="srcMovies"
        Runat="server">
        <ItemTemplate>
```

LISTING 8.10   Continued

```
        <asp:HyperLink
            id="HyperLink1"
            Text='<%# Eval("Title") %>'
            NavigateUrl='<%# Eval("Id", "Details.aspx?id={0}") %>'
            runat="server" />
        <br />

        </ItemTemplate>
    </asp:Repeater>


    <asp:SqlDataSource
        id="srcMovies"
        ConnectionString="Data Source=.\SQLExpress;
            AttachDbFilename=¦DataDirectory¦MyDatabase.mdf;
            Integrated Security=True;User Instance=True"
        SelectCommand="SELECT Id, Title FROM Movies"
        Runat="server" />

    </div>
    </form>
</body>
</html>
```

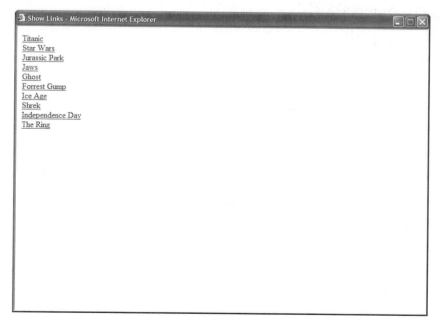

FIGURE 8.9   Displaying a list of hyperlinks.

In Listing 8.10, a HyperLink control is displayed for each item from the data source. The HyperLink control displays the movie title and links to a details page for the movie.

Using DataBinding Expressions

A DataBinding expression is a special type of expression that is not evaluated until runtime. You mark a databinding expression in a page by wrapping the expression in opening <%# and closing %> brackets.

A DataBinding expression isn't evaluated until a control's DataBinding event is raised. When you bind a DataBound control to a DataSource control declaratively, this event is raised automatically. When you bind a DataSource control to a data source programmatically, the DataBinding event is raised when you call the DataBind() method.

For example, the page in Listing 8.11 contains a DataList control that contains a template that includes two DataBinding expressions.

LISTING 8.11   ShowDataList.aspx

```
<%@ Page Language="VB" %>
<!DOCTYPE html PUBLIC "-//W3C//DTD XHTML 1.1//EN"
  "http://www.w3.org/TR/xhtml11/DTD/xhtml11.dtd">
<html xmlns="http://www.w3.org/1999/xhtml" >
<head id="Head1" runat="server">
    <title>Show DataList</title>
</head>
<body>
    <form id="form1" runat="server">
    <div>

    <asp:DataList
        id="DataList1"
        DataSourceId="srcMovies"
        Runat="server">
        <ItemTemplate>
        <b>Movie Title:</b>
        <%#Eval("Title")%>
        <br />
        <b>Date Released:</b>
        <%#Eval("DateReleased", "{0:D}") %>
        <hr />
        </ItemTemplate>
    </asp:DataList>

    <asp:SqlDataSource
        id="srcMovies"
        ConnectionString="Data Source=.\SQLExpress;
            AttachDbFilename=|DataDirectory|MyDatabase.mdf;
            Integrated Security=True;User Instance=True"
```

LISTING 8.11   Continued

```
            SelectCommand="SELECT Title,Director,DateReleased FROM Movies"
            Runat="server" />

        </div>
        </form>
    </body>
</html>
```

The first DataBinding expression displays the title of the movie and the second DataBinding expression displays the date the movie was released (see Figure 8.10).

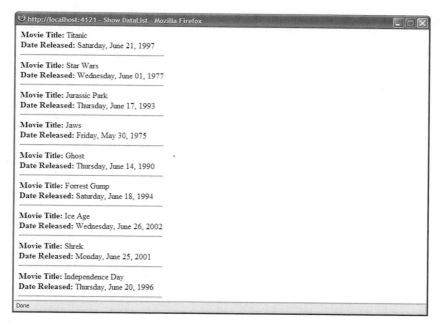

FIGURE 8.10   Using databinding expressions.

Both DataBinding expressions call the Eval() method. The Eval() method is a protected method of the Page class. Behind the scenes, the Page.Eval() method calls the shared (static) DataBinder.Eval() method. If you want to be verbose, instead of using the Eval() method, you could use the following two expressions:

```
<%# DataBinder.Eval(Container.DataItem, "Title") %>
<%# DataBinder.Eval(Container.DataItem, "DateReleased", "{0:D}" ) %>
```

In ASP.NET version 1.x, you had to use DataBinder.Eval() when displaying data items in a template. However, Microsoft took pity on programmers in ASP.NET 2.0 and provided us with the shorter syntax.

> **NOTE**
>
> Technically, the `Eval()` method uses reflection when evaluating the data item to find a property with a certain name. You do pay a performance penalty when you use reflection.
>
> As an alternative, you can improve the performance of your DataBinding expressions by casting the data items to a particular type like this:
>
> `<%# CType(Container.DataItem, System.Data.DataRowView)("Title")%>`

Notice that the second DataBinding expression in Listing 8.11 includes a second parameter. The `Eval()` method, optionally, accepts a format string. You can use the format string to format values such as dates and currency amounts. In Listing 8.11, the format string is used to format the DateReleased column as a long date.

> **NOTE**
>
> Format strings use *format specifiers* such as the D format specifier when formatting strings. You can find a list of format specifiers by looking up Formatting Types in the index of the Microsoft .NET Framework SDK 2.0 documentation.

You can call other methods than the `Eval()` method in a DataBinding expression. For example, the DataBinding expression in Listing 8.12 calls a method named `FormatTitle()` to format the movie titles.

LISTING 8.12   FormatMovieTitles.aspx

```
<%@ Page Language="VB" %>
<!DOCTYPE html PUBLIC "-//W3C//DTD XHTML 1.1//EN"
  "http://www.w3.org/TR/xhtml11/DTD/xhtml11.dtd">
<script runat="server">

    Public Function FormatTitle(ByVal title As Object) As String
        Return "<b>" + title.ToString().ToUpper() + "</b>"
    End Function

</script>
<html xmlns="http://www.w3.org/1999/xhtml" >
<head id="Head1" runat="server">
    <title>Format Movie Titles</title>
</head>
<body>
    <form id="form1" runat="server">
    <div>

    <asp:Repeater
        id="Repeater1"
        DataSourceId="srcMovies"
        Runat="server">
        <ItemTemplate>
```

LISTING 8.12   Continued

```
            <%# FormatTitle(Eval("Title")) %>
            <hr />
            </ItemTemplate>
        </asp:Repeater>


        <asp:SqlDataSource
            id="srcMovies"
            ConnectionString="Data Source=.\SQLExpress;
                AttachDbFilename=¦DataDirectory¦MyDatabase.mdf;
                Integrated Security=True;User Instance=True"
            SelectCommand="SELECT Title FROM Movies"
            Runat="server" />

    </div>
    </form>
</body>
</html>
```

The FormatTitle() method is defined in the page in Listing 8.12. This method formats each of the titles displayed by the Repeater control by making each title bold and upper-case (see Figure 8.11).

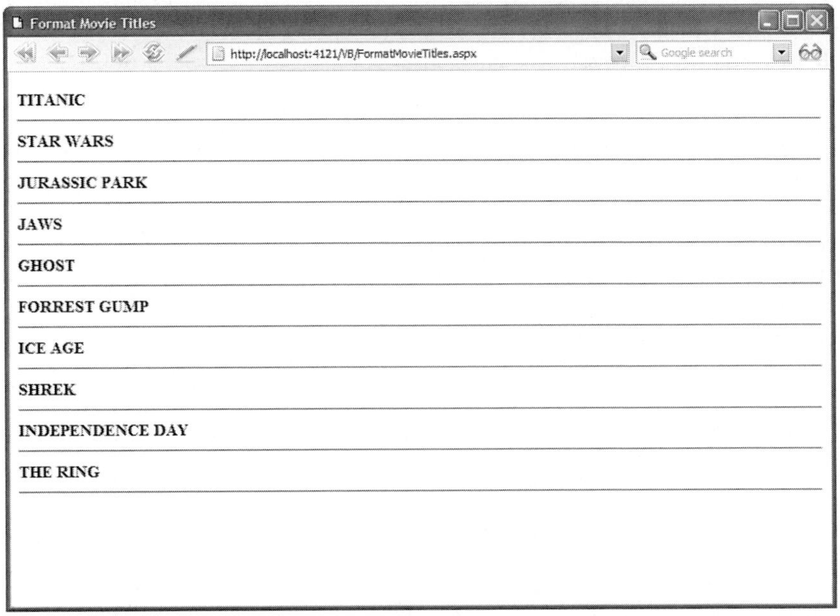

FIGURE 8.11   Formatting movie titles.

Using Two-Way DataBinding Expressions

The ASP.NET 2.0 Framework actually supports two types of templates and two types of DataBinding expressions. The ASP.NET Framework supports both one-way DataBinding expressions and two-way DataBinding expressions.

Up to this point, we have used one-way DataBinding expressions exclusively. In a one-way DataBinding expression, you use the DataBinding expression to display the value of a data item. You use the Eval() method to display the value of a one-way DataBinding expression.

In a two-way DataBinding expression, you not only can display the value of a data item, you also can modify the value of a data item. You use the Bind() method when working with a two-way DataBinding expression.

For example, the page in Listing 8.13 contains a FormView control that includes a template for editing a movie record in the Movies database table (see Figure 8.12).

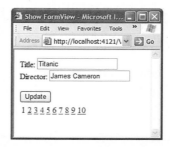

FIGURE 8.12   Editing a movie.

LISTING 8.13   ShowFormView.aspx

```
<%@ Page Language="VB" %>
<!DOCTYPE html PUBLIC "-//W3C//DTD XHTML 1.1//EN"
  "http://www.w3.org/TR/xhtml11/DTD/xhtml11.dtd">
<html xmlns="http://www.w3.org/1999/xhtml" >
<head id="Head1" runat="server">
    <title>Show FormView</title>
</head>
<body>
    <form id="form1" runat="server">
    <div>

    <asp:FormView
        id="FormView1"
        DataKeyNames="Id"
        DataSourceId="srcMovies"
        DefaultMode="Edit"
```

LISTING 8.13 Continued

```
        AllowPaging="true"
        Runat="server">
        <EditItemTemplate>
        <asp:Label
            id="lblTitle"
            Text="Title:"
            AssociatedControlID="txtTitle"
            Runat="server" />
        <asp:TextBox
            id="txtTitle"
            Text='<%#Bind("Title")%>'
            Runat="server" />
        <br />
        <asp:Label
            id="lblDirector"
            Text="Director:"
            AssociatedControlID="txtDirector"
            Runat="server" />
        <asp:TextBox
            id="txtDirector"
            Text='<%#Bind("Director")%>'
            Runat="server" />
        <br />
        <asp:Button
            id="btnUpdate"
            Text="Update"
            CommandName="Update"
            Runat="server" />
        </EditItemTemplate>
    </asp:FormView>

    <asp:SqlDataSource
        id="srcMovies"
        ConnectionString="Data Source=.\SQLExpress;
            AttachDbFilename=¦DataDirectory¦MyDatabase.mdf;
            Integrated Security=True;User Instance=True"
        SelectCommand="SELECT Id, Title,Director,DateReleased FROM Movies"
        UpdateCommand="UPDATE Movies SET Title=@Title,
            Director=@Director WHERE Id=@Id"
        Runat="server" />

    </div>
    </form>
</body>
</html>
```

Notice that the FormView contains an EditItemTemplate. The EditItemTemplate contains three TextBox controls. Each TextBox control has a two-way DataBinding expression assigned to its Text property.

The DataBinding expressions associate the TextBox control properties with the properties of the data item being edited. When you click the Update button, any changes you make to the Text properties are updated in the Movies database table.

> **NOTE**
>
> Templates that support one-way databinding implement the ITemplate interface, and templates that support two-way databinding implement the IBindableTemplate interface.

Overview of SQL Server 2005 Express

Microsoft SQL Server 2005 Express is the version of SQL Server bundled with Visual Web Developer. You can also download this database engine from the Microsoft website (http://msdn.microsoft.com/sql/2005). SQL Server Express is used for almost all the database examples in this book.

In this section, you are provided with a brief overview of the features of this database. You also learn how to connect to SQL Server Express.

Features of SQL Server Express

One of the most important features of SQL Server 2005 Express is that it is a royalty-free database engine. You can download it and use it for free in your applications. You also can distribute the database in commercial applications that you produce for others without paying royalties to Microsoft (registration at the Microsoft site is required to do this).

> **NOTE**
>
> Microsoft SQL Server 2005 Express replaces the Microsoft Desktop Engine version of SQL Server. There won't be an MSDE version of SQL Server 2005.

SQL Server 2005 Express works with the Windows XP, Windows 2000, and the Windows 2003 operating systems. It requires the .NET Framework 2.0 to be installed on its host computer.

Microsoft SQL Server 2005 Express uses the same database engine as the full retail version of SQL Server 2005. However, because it is a free product, Microsoft has limited some of its features to encourage you to upgrade to the full version of SQL Server 2005.

First, unlike the full version of SQL Server 2005, a SQL Server Express database can be no larger than 4 gigabytes. Furthermore, SQL Server Express is limited to using 1 gigabyte of RAM. Also, SQL Server Express uses only a single processor even when used on a multi-processor server.

SQL Server Express also does not support several of the advanced features of the full version of SQL Server 2005. For example, it doesn't support Full-Text Search, Reporting Services, Analysis Services, Notification Services, English Query, Data Transformation Services, or OLAP.

However, unlike Microsoft SQL Server 2000 MSDE, SQL Server Express does not have a Workload Governor. The performance of a SQL Server Express database is never throttled. This means that you can use SQL Server Express for small websites without worrying about performance limitations.

Finally, like the full version of SQL Server 2005, SQL Server Express supports the Common Language Runtime. In other words, you can use Visual Basic .NET or C# to create stored procedures, triggers, user-defined functions and user-defined types. You can learn how to create stored procedures and user-defined types written with VisualBasic.NET in Chapter 16, "Building Data Access Components."

SQL Server 2005 Express Management Tools

You can use three tools to create new database objects when using SQL Server 2005 Express. You can use the Database Explorer in Visual Web Developer, you can use the Microsoft SQL Server Management Studio Express, and you can use the SQLCMD utility.

The Database Explorer included in Visual Web Developer provides you with a user-friendly interface for working with database objects (see Figure 8.13). I assume that you are using the Database Explorer in the case of the database samples in this book.

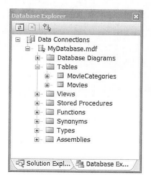

FIGURE 8.13   The Database Explorer window in Visual Web Developer.

Alternatively, you can use the Microsoft SQL Server Management Studio Express (its groovy name is XM). You can download Management Studio from the Microsoft site at http://msdn.microsoft.com/sql/2005. This tool enables you to browse database objects and execute SQL queries (see Figure 8.14).

Finally, SQL Server 2005 Express includes a command-line tool named SQLCMD. You can use the SQLCMD tool to fire off SQL queries from the Command Prompt (see Figure 8.15). This alternative is the most painful, but it works.

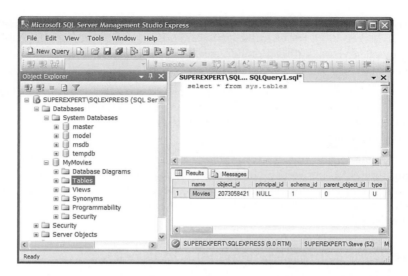

FIGURE 8.14   Using the Microsoft SQL Server Management Studio Express.

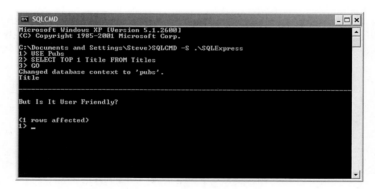

FIGURE 8.15   Executing a SQL query with SQLCMD.

You use SQLCMD by opening a command prompt and connecting to your database with the following command:

```
SQLCMD -S .\SQLExpress
```

Next, you can enter SQL statements at the command prompt. The statements are not executed until you type **GO**. You can get help using SQLCMD by typing **:HELP** after starting the tool. When you are finished using the tool, type **EXIT** to quit.

Server Databases versus Local Databases

You can create two different types of databases with SQL Server Express: Server databases and Local databases.

By default, when you install SQL Server 2005 Express, a named instance of the server is created with the name SQLExpress. You can create a new Server database by connecting to the named instance and adding a new database.

> **NOTE**
>
> To connect to SQL Server 2005 Express from a page served from Internet Information Server, you must add either the ASPNET account (in the case of Windows XP or Windows 2000) or the Network Service account (in the case of Windows 2003) to SQL Server Express. These accounts are created for you automatically when you install the QuickStart Tutorials included with the .NET Framework SDK 2.0 Documentation.

If you own Visual Studio .NET 2005, then you can create a new Server database directly from the Server Explorer window. Simply right-click the Data Connections node in the Server Explorer window and select the menu option Create New SQL Server Database.

Unfortunately, you can't use Visual Web Developer to create a new Server database. This option is grayed out. If you need to create a new Server database, and you don't have Visual Studio .NET 2005, then you need to use Microsoft SQL Server Management Studio Express as discussed in the previous section (see Figure 8.16).

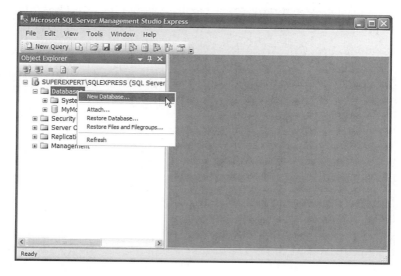

FIGURE 8.16   Creating a new Server database.

When you create a Server database, the database is attached and available to any application running on the server. You can connect to the database easily from any ASP.NET application.

For example, the following connection string enables you to connect to a Server database named MyData:

```
Data Source=.\SQLExpress;Initial Catalog=MyData;Integrated Security=True
```

> **NOTE**
>
> There are many different ways to write a connection string that does the same thing. For example, instead of the Data Source parameter, you can use the Server parameter, and instead of the Initial Catalog parameter, you can use the Database parameter. For a list of all the keywords supported when connecting to a Microsoft SQL Server database, see the SqlConnection.ConnectionString entry in the Microsoft .NET Framework SDK 2.0 documentation.

The other option is to create a Local database instead of a Server database. When you create a Local database, you create the database in your project. The database file is added to the App_Data folder in your website.

Here are the steps for creating a Local database in Visual Web Developer:

1. Open the Add New Item dialog box by selecting the menu option Website, Add New Item (see Figure 8.17).

2. Select Sql Database and provide the database with a name (for example, MyLocalData.mdf).

3. Click Add.

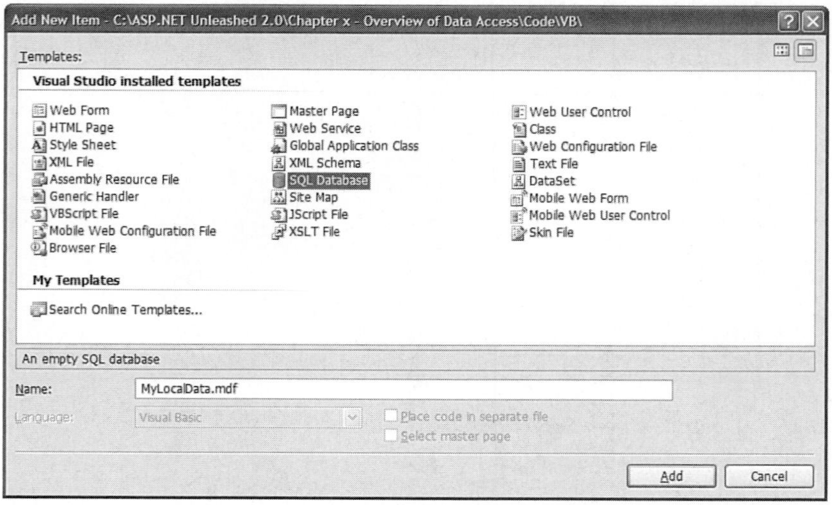

FIGURE 8.17   Creating a new Local database.

When you click Add, Visual Web Developer warns you that it needs to create the App_Data folder (if the folder doesn't already exist). The `MyLocalData.mdf` file will be added to this folder. Click OK to create the new folder.

You can connect to a Local database named `MyLocalData.mdf` by using the following connection string:

```
Data Source=.\SQLEXPRESS;AttachDbFilename=¦DataDirectory¦MyLocalData.mdf;
Integrated Security=True;User Instance=True
```

When you connect to the `MyLocalData.mdf` file, the database is attached automatically to Microsoft SQL Server Express.

The connection string includes an `AttachDbFilename` parameter. This parameter represents the physical path to a database file (`.mdf` file). Notice that the keyword `¦DataDirectory¦` is used in the path. The `¦DataDirectory¦` keyword represents a website's App_Data folder.

Instead of using the `¦DataDirectory¦` keyword, you could supply the entire physical path to a database file. The advantage of using the `¦DataDirectory¦` keyword is that you can move your web application easily to a new location without needing to change the connection string.

Notice that the connection string also includes a `User Instance` parameter. Creating a `User Instance` connection enables you to connect to a Local database without using an Administrator account. Because the ASPNET account is not an Administrator account, you need to add this parameter to use Local databases from ASP.NET pages.

Including the `User Instance` parameter in a connection string causes a separate user instance of SQL Server to execute with the security context of the user. The first time a user creates a User Instance connection, copies of the system databases are copied to a user's application data folder located at the following path:

```
C:\Documents and Settings\[Username]\Local Settings\Application Data\
Microsoft\Microsoft SQL Server Data\SQLEXPRESS
```

A separate set of system databases is created for each user.

> **NOTE**
>
> By default, when a page is served from Internet Information Server, the page executes in the security context of either the ASPNET or Network Service account. When a page is served from the web server included in Visual Web Developer, the page executes in the security context of the current user.

One of the primary advantages of using a Local database rather than a Server database is that a Local database can be moved easily to a new location. If you email a Local database file (the `.mdf` file stored in the App_Data folder) to a friend, your friend can start using the database immediately. The only requirement is that your friend have SQL Server 2005 Express installed on a computer.

I use Local databases for all the code samples in this book. You can simply copy the database files (the .mdf files) from the CD onto your local hard drive to use the sample databases.

Sample Database-Driven Web Application

The chapters that follow get into all the gritty details of the data controls. Before you get lost in the details, however, I want to provide you with a sample of a data-driven web application. I want to provide you with a "real world" application that illustrates what can be built with the data controls.

In this section, a complete Employee Directory application is built, which supports displaying, adding, editing, and deleting employee information. The sample application includes all the necessary form field validation.

One of the amazing things about the ASP.NET 2.0 Framework is how much the new Framework simplifies data access. The sample application consists of a single page that contains very little code. Writing the same application with the ASP.NET 1.x Framework would require pages of code (I won't even mention how much code it would require to write the same application in ASP Classic).

Because the Employee Directory application includes all the required validation code, the page is a little too long to include in the pages of this book. However, it is included on the CD that accompanies this book. Open the page named EmployeeDirectory.aspx.

After you open the EmployeeDirectory.aspx page in your browser, you see a list of employees. This list is rendered by a GridView control (see Figure 8.18).

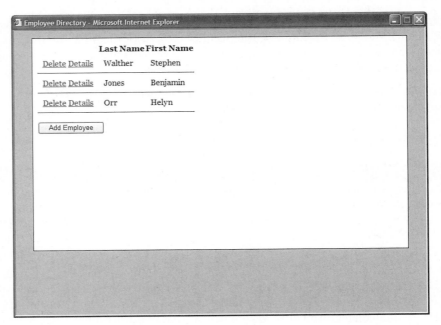

FIGURE 8.18   Displaying a list of employees with the GridView control.

Next to each employee, there is a Delete link and a Details link. If you click Delete, the selected employee is deleted from the database. Notice that a client-side confirmation dialog box appears when you click the Delete link (see Figure 8.19). This dialog box is added to each of the Delete links in the grdEmployees_RowCreated() method. This method is called automatically by the GridView control as the GridView creates each row.

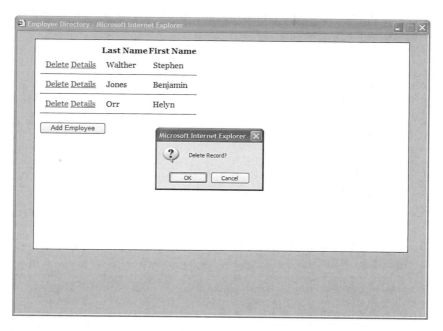

FIGURE 8.19   Deleting employee information.

If you click the Details link, a window appears that displays detailed information for the Employee (see Figure 8.20). The detailed information is rendered by a FormView control. The window that appears is created with an absolutely positioned <div> tag.

If you click Edit when viewing a employee's details, you can edit the employee record. The edit form is contained in the FormView control's EditItemTemplate. Each of the form fields is associated with a RequiredFieldValidator control.

Finally, you can add new employees to the directory by clicking the Add Employee button. The form that appears is also rendered by a FormView control (see Figure 8.21).

WEB STANDARDS NOTE

The Employee Directory application works great in Internet Explorer 6, FireFox 1.0, and Opera 8.0. The only feature of the application that breaks Web standards is the use of the Drop Shadow filter around the pop-up window. The Drop Shadow effect works only in Internet Explorer.

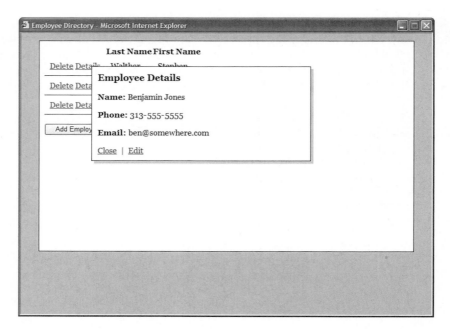

FIGURE 8.20   Displaying employee details.

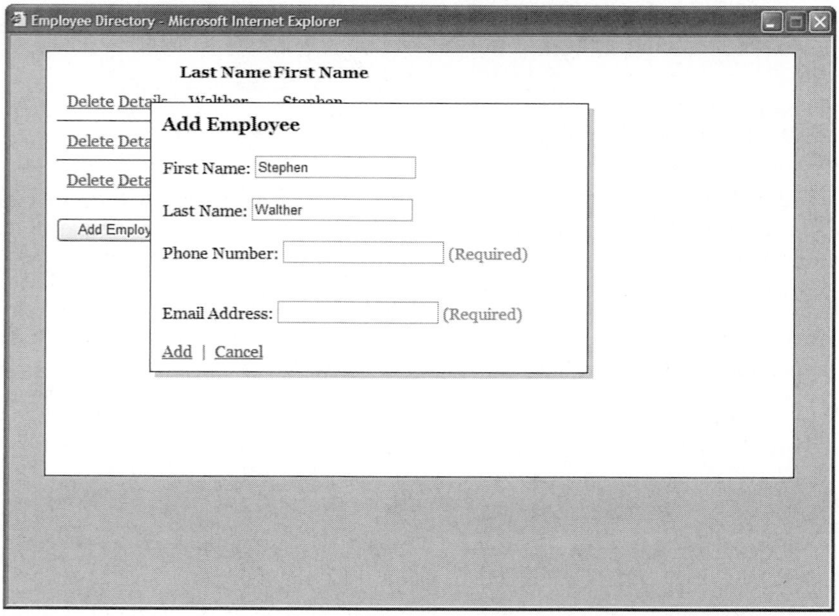

FIGURE 8.21   Adding a new employee.

Summary

In this chapter, you were provided with an overview of the data controls included in the ASP.NET 2.0 Framework. You learned how to use the DataBound controls to render the user interface for working with data. You also were provided with an introduction to the DataSource controls, which can be used to represent different types of data such as database data and XML data.

You also learned about two important features of the DataBound controls. You learned how to use Templates and databinding expressions. You also learned about the difference between one-way databinding and two-way databinding expressions.

Next, you were provided with an overview of SQL Server 2005 Express. You learned how to create a SQL Server Express database. You also learned how to create both Server and Local databases.

Finally, the data controls were used to build a sample application: the Employee Directory application. You learned how to use the controls to build an application that enables you to list, edit, insert, and delete database records.

CHAPTER **9**

Using the SqlDataSource Control

The SqlDataSource control enables you to quickly and easily represent a SQL database in a web page. In many cases, you can take advantage of the SqlDataSource control to write a database-driven web page without writing a single line of code.

You use the SqlDataSource control to represent a connection and set of commands that can be executed against a SQL database. You can use the SqlDataSource control when working with Microsoft SQL Server, Microsoft SQL Server Express, Microsoft Access, Oracle, DB2, MySQL, or just about any other SQL relational database ever created by man.

> **NOTE**
>
> Although you can use the SqlDataSource control when working with Microsoft Access, the ASP.NET Framework does include the AccessDataSource control, which was designed specifically for Microsoft Access. Because using Microsoft Access for a website is not recommended, this book doesn't discuss the AccessDataSource control.

The SqlDataSource control is built on top of ADO.NET. Under the covers, the SqlDataSource uses ADO.NET objects such as the DataSet, DataReader, and Command objects. Because the SqlDataSource control is a control, it enables you to use these ADO.NET objects declaratively rather than programmatically.

The SqlDataSource control is a non-visual control—it doesn't render anything. You use the SqlDataSource control with other controls, such as the GridView or

FormView controls, to display and edit database data. The SqlDataSource control can also be used to issue SQL commands against a database programmatically.

> **NOTE**
>
> The SqlDataSource control is not an appropriate control to use when building more complicated multi-tier applications. The SqlDataSource control forces you to mix your data access layer with your user interface layer. If you want to build a more cleanly architected multi-tier application, then you should use the ObjectDataSource control to represent your database data.
>
> The ObjectDataSource is discussed in detail in Chapter 15, "Using the ObjectDataSource Control."

In this chapter, you learn how to represent connections and commands with the SqlDataSource control. You also learn how to use different types of parameters when executing commands. Finally, you learn how to improve the performance of your database-driven applications by taking advantage of the SqlDataSource control's support for caching database data.

Creating Database Connections

You can use the SqlDataSource control to connect to just about any SQL relational database server. In this section, you learn how to connect to Microsoft SQL Server and other databases such as Oracle. You also learn how you can store the database connection string used by the SqlDataSource securely in your web configuration files.

Connecting to Microsoft SQL Server

By default, the SqlDataSource control is configured to connect to Microsoft SQL Server version 7.0 or higher. The default provider used by the SqlDataSource control is the ADO.NET provider for Microsoft SQL Server.

You represent a database connection string with the SqlDataSource control's ConnectionString property. For example, the page in Listing 9.1 includes a SqlDataSource control that connects to a local SQL Server 2005 database (see Figure 9.1).

LISTING 9.1   ShowLocalConnection.aspx

```
<%@ Page Language="VB" %>
<!DOCTYPE html PUBLIC "-//W3C//DTD XHTML 1.1//EN"
 "http://www.w3.org/TR/xhtml11/DTD/xhtml11.dtd">
<html xmlns="http://www.w3.org/1999/xhtml" >
<head id="Head1" runat="server">
    <title>Show Local Connection</title>
</head>
<body>
    <form id="form1" runat="server">
    <div>
```

LISTING 9.1   Continued

```
<asp:GridView
    id="grdMovies"
    DataSourceID="srcMovies"
    Runat="server" />

<asp:SqlDataSource
    id="srcMovies"
    SelectCommand="SELECT * FROM Movies"
    ConnectionString="Data Source=.\SQLEXPRESS;
        AttachDbFilename=|DataDirectory|MyDatabase.mdf;
        Integrated Security=True;User Instance=True"
    Runat="server" />

    </div>
    </form>
</body>
</html>
```

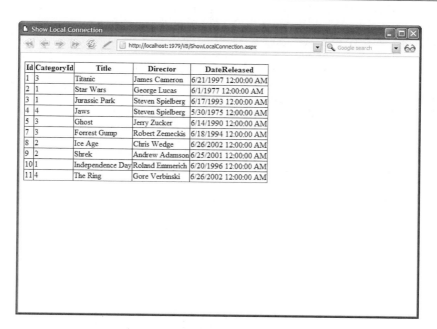

FIGURE 9.1   Displaying the Movies database table.

In Listing 9.1, the SqlDataSource control uses the following connection string:

```
Data Source=.\SQLEXPRESS;
AttachDbFilename=|DataDirectory|MyDatabase.mdf;
Integrated Security=True;User Instance=True
```

This connection string connects to an instance of SQL Server Express located on the local machine and a database file named MyDatabase.mdf. The connection string uses Integrated Security (a Trusted Connection) to connect to the local database.

You can use the following connection string to connect to a database located on a remote server.

```
Data Source=DataServer;Initial Catalog=Northwind;
User ID=webuser;Password=secret
```

This database connection string connects to a SQL Server database located on a remote machine named DataServer. The connection string connects to a database named Northwind.

This second connection string uses SQL Standard Security instead of Integrated Security. It contains a user ID and password that are associated with a SQL Server login.

> **WARNING**
>
> For security reasons, you should never include a connection string that contains security credentials in an ASP.NET page. Theoretically, no one should able to see the source of an ASP.NET page. However, Microsoft does not have a perfect track record. Later in this section, you learn how to store connection strings in the web configuration file.

The .NET Framework includes a utility class, named the SqlConnectionBuilder class, that you can use when working with SQL connection strings. This class automatically converts any connection string into a canonical representation. It also exposes properties for extracting and modifying individual connection string parameters such as the Password parameters.

For example, the page in Listing 9.2 automatically converts any connection string into its canonical representation (see Figure 9.2).

LISTING 9.2   SqlConnectionStringBuilder.aspx

```
<%@ Page Language="VB" %>
<%@ Import Namespace="System.Data.SqlClient" %>
<!DOCTYPE html PUBLIC "-//W3C//DTD XHTML 1.1//EN"
 "http://www.w3.org/TR/xhtml11/DTD/xhtml11.dtd">
<script runat="server">

    Protected Sub btnConvert_Click(ByVal sender As Object, ByVal e As EventArgs)
        Dim builder As New SqlConnectionStringBuilder(txtConnectionString.Text)
        lblResult.Text = builder.ConnectionString
    End Sub

</script>
<html xmlns="http://www.w3.org/1999/xhtml" >
```

LISTING 9.2   Continued

```
<head id="Head1" runat="server">
    <title>SQL Connection String Builder</title>
</head>
<body>
    <form id="form1" runat="server">
    <div>

    <asp:TextBox
        id="txtConnectionString"
        Columns="60"
        Runat="Server" />
    <asp:Button
        id="btnConvert"
        Text="Convert"
        OnClick="btnConvert_Click"
        Runat="Server" />

    <hr />

    <asp:Label
        id="lblResult"
        Runat="server" />

    </div>
    </form>
</body>
</html>
```

After opening the page in Listing 9.2, if you enter a connection string that looks like this:

```
Server=localhost;UID=webuser;pwd=secret;database=Northwind
```

the page converts the connection string to look like this:

```
Data Source=localhost;Initial Catalog=Northwind;User ID=webuser;Password=secret
```

Connecting to Other Databases

If you need to connect to any database server other than Microsoft SQL Server, then you need to modify the SqlDataSource control's ProviderName property.

The .NET Framework includes the following providers:

- System.Data.OracleClient—Use the ADO.NET provider for Oracle when connecting to an Oracle database.

- `System.Data.OleDb`—Use the OLE DB provider when connecting to a data source that supports an OLE DB provider.

- `System.Data.Odbc`—Use the ODBC provider when connecting to a data source with an ODBC driver.

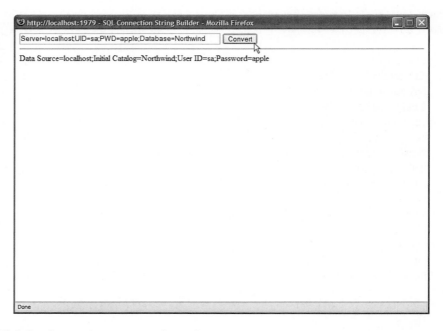

FIGURE 9.2 Converting a connection string.

> **NOTE**
>
> You can configure additional providers that you can use with the SqlDataSource control by adding new entries to the <DbProviderFactories> section of the Machine.config file.

For performance reasons, you should always use the native ADO.NET provider for a database. However, if your database does not have an ADO.NET provider then you need to use either OLE DB or ODBC to connect to the database. Almost every database under the sun has either an OLE DB provider or an ODBC driver.

For example, the page in Listing 9.3 uses the ADO.NET Oracle provider to connect to an Oracle database.

LISTING 9.3 ConnectOracle.aspx

```
<%@ Page Language="VB" %>
<!DOCTYPE html PUBLIC "-//W3C//DTD XHTML 1.1//EN"
 "http://www.w3.org/TR/xhtml11/DTD/xhtml11.dtd">
```

LISTING 9.3   Continued

```
<html xmlns="http://www.w3.org/1999/xhtml" >
<head id="Head1" runat="server">
    <title>Connect Oracle</title>
</head>
<body>
    <form id="form1" runat="server">
    <div>

    <asp:GridView
        id="grdOrders"
        DataSourceID="srcOrders"
        Runat="server" />

    <asp:SqlDataSource
        id="srcOrders"
        ProviderName="System.Data.OracleClient"
        SelectCommand="SELECT * FROM Orders"
        ConnectionString="Data Source=OracleDB;Integrated Security=yes"
        Runat="server" />

    </div>
    </form>
</body>
</html>
```

In Listing 9.3, notice that the `ProviderName` property is set to the value `System.Data.`
`OracleClient`. The connection uses the native ADO.NET Oracle provider instead of the
default provider for Microsoft SQL Server.

> **NOTE**
>
> To connect to an Oracle database, you need to install the Oracle client software on your
> web server.

> **NOTE**
>
> Oracle has produced their own native ADO.NET provider. You can download the Oracle provider
> at `http://www.oracle.com/technology/tech/windows/odpnet/index.html`.

Storing Connection Strings in the Web Configuration File

Storing connection strings in your pages is a bad idea for three reasons. First, it is not a
good practice from the perspective of security. In theory, no one should ever be able to

view the source code of your ASP.NET pages. In practice, however, hackers have discovered security flaws in the ASP.NET framework. To sleep better at night, you should store your connection strings in a separate file.

Also, adding a connection string to every page makes it difficult to manage a website. If you ever need to change your password, then you need to change every page that contains it. If, on the other hand, you store the connection string in one file, you can update the password by modifying the single file.

Finally, storing a connection string in a page can, potentially, hurt the performance of your application. The ADO.NET provider for SQL Server automatically uses connection pooling to improve your application's data access performance. Instead of being destroyed when they are closed, the connections are kept alive so that they can be put back into service quickly when the need arises. However, only connections that are created with the same connection strings are pooled together (an exact character-by-character match is made). Adding the same connection string to multiple pages is a recipe for defeating the benefits of connection pooling.

For these reasons, you should always place your connection strings in the web configuration file. The `Web.Config` file in Listing 9.4 includes a `connectionStrings` section.

LISTING 9.4   Web.Config

```
<?xml version="1.0"?>
<configuration>
  <connectionStrings>
    <add name="Movies" connectionString="Data Source=.\SQLEXPRESS;
      AttachDbFilename=|DataDirectory|MyDatabase.mdf;Integrated Security=True;
User Instance=True" />
  </connectionStrings>
</configuration>
```

You can add as many connection strings to the `connectionStrings` section as you want. The page in Listing 9.5 includes a `SqlDataSource` that uses the Movies connection string.

LISTING 9.5   ShowMovies.aspx

```
<%@ Page Language="VB" %>
<!DOCTYPE html PUBLIC "-//W3C//DTD XHTML 1.1//EN"
 "http://www.w3.org/TR/xhtml11/DTD/xhtml11.dtd">
<html xmlns="http://www.w3.org/1999/xhtml" >
<head id="Head1" runat="server">
    <title>Show Movies</title>
</head>
<body>
    <form id="form1" runat="server">
    <div>
```

LISTING 9.5 Continued

```
    <asp:GridView
        id="grdMovies"
        DataSourceID="srcMovies"
        Runat="server" />

    <asp:SqlDataSource
        id="srcMovies"
        SelectCommand="SELECT * FROM Movies"
        ConnectionString="<%$ ConnectionStrings:Movies %>"
        Runat="server" />

    </div>
    </form>
</body>
</html>
```

The expression <%$ ConnectionStrings:Movies %> is used to represent the connection string. This expression is not case sensitive.

Rather than add a connection string to your project's web configuration file, you can add the connection string to a web configuration file higher in the folder hierarchy. For example, you can add the connection string to the root Web.Config file and make it available to all applications running on your server. The root Web.Config file is located at the following path:

```
C:\WINDOWS\Microsoft.NET\Framework\[version]\CONFIG
```

Encrypting Connection Strings

You can encrypt the <connectionStrings> section of a web configuration file. For example, Listing 9.6 contains an encrypted version of the Web.Config file that was created in Listing 9.4.

LISTING 9.6 Web.Config

```
<?xml version="1.0"?>
<configuration>
  <protectedData>
    <protectedDataSections>
      <add name="connectionStrings" provider="RsaProtectedConfigurationProvider"
        inheritedByChildren="false" />
    </protectedDataSections>
  </protectedData>
  <connectionStrings>
    <EncryptedData Type="http://www.w3.org/2001/04/xmlenc#Element"
```

LISTING 9.6   Continued

```
        xmlns="http://www.w3.org/2001/04/xmlenc#">
        <EncryptionMethod Algorithm="http://www.w3.org/2001/04/xmlenc
#tripledes-cbc" />
        <KeyInfo xmlns="http://www.w3.org/2000/09/xmldsig#">
            <EncryptedKey Recipient="" xmlns="http://www.w3.org/2001/04/xmlenc#">
                <EncryptionMethod Algorithm="http://www.w3.org/2001/04/xmlenc#rsa-1_5" />
                <KeyInfo xmlns="http://www.w3.org/2000/09/xmldsig#">
                    <KeyName>Rsa Key</KeyName>
                </KeyInfo>
                <CipherData>

<CipherValue>MPLyXy7PoZ8E5VPk6K/azkGumO5tpeuWRzxx4PfgKeFwFccKx/8Zc7app++0
4c/dX7jA3uvNniFHTW6eKvrkLOsW2m6MxaeeLEfR9ME51Gy5jLa1KIXfTXKuJbXeZdiwrjCRdIqQpEj4fGZ
➥vr
3KkwI5HbGAqgK4Uu7IfBajdTJM=</CipherValue>
                </CipherData>
            </EncryptedKey>
        </KeyInfo>
        <CipherData>
            <CipherValue>CgnD74xMkcr7N4fgaHZNMps+e+if7dnEZ8xFw07kOBexaX+KyJvqtPuZiD2hW
Dpqt5EOw6YMOFs2uI5ocetbb74+d4kfHorC0bEjLEV+zcsJVGi2dZ80ll6sW+Y99osupaxOfrL3ld3mphM
Yrpcf+xafAs05s2x7H77TY01Y1goRaQ77tnkEIrQNQsHk/5eeptcE+A8scZSlaolFRNSSCdyO1TiKjPHF+
MtI/8qzr2T6yjYM5Z+ZQ5TeiVvpg/6VD7K7dArIDmkFMTuQgdQBSJUQ23dZ5V9Ja9HxqMGCea9NomBdhGC
0sabDLxyPdOzGEAqOyxWKxqQM6Y0JyZKtPDg==</CipherValue>
        </CipherData>
    </EncryptedData>
  </connectionStrings>
</configuration>
```

Notice that the contents of the `<connectionStrings>` section are no longer visible. However, an ASP.NET page can continue to read the value of the Movie database connection string by using the `<%$ ConnectionStrings:Movie %>` expression.

The easiest way to encrypt the `<connectionStrings>` section is to use the `aspnet_regiis` command-line tool. This tool is located in the following folder:

`C:\WINDOWS\Microsoft.NET\Framework\[version]\`

Executing the following command encrypts the `<connectionStrings>` section of a `Web.Config` file located in a folder with the path `c:\Websites\MyWebsite`:

`aspnet_regiis -pef connectionStrings "c:\Websites\MyWebsite"`

The `-pef` option (Protect Encrypt Filepath) encrypts a particular configuration section located at a particular path.

You can decrypt a section with the -pdf option like this:

```
aspnet_regiis -pdf connectionStrings "c:\Websites\MyWebsite"
```

> **NOTE**
>
> Web configuration encryption options are discussed in more detail in Chapter 26, "Configuring Applications."

Executing Database Commands

In this section, you learn how to represent and execute SQL commands with the SqlDataSource control. In particular, you learn how to execute both inline SQL statements and external stored procedures. You also learn how to capture and gracefully handle errors that result from executing SQL commands.

Executing Inline SQL Statements

The SqlDataSource control can be used to represent four different types of SQL commands. The control supports the following four properties:

- SelectCommand

- InsertCommand

- UpdateCommand

- DeleteCommand

You can assign any SQL statement to any of these properties. For example, the page in Listing 9.7 uses all four properties to enable selecting, inserting, updating, and deleting records from the Movies database table (see Figure 9.3).

LISTING 9.7   ShowInlineCommands.aspx

```
<%@ Page Language="VB" %>
<!DOCTYPE html PUBLIC "-//W3C//DTD XHTML 1.1//EN"
  "http://www.w3.org/TR/xhtml11/DTD/xhtml11.dtd">
<html xmlns="http://www.w3.org/1999/xhtml" >
<head id="Head1" runat="server">
    <style type="text/css">
        .detailsView
        {
            margin:0px auto;
            border:solid 4px black;
            background-color:white;
        }
```

LISTING 9.7   Continued

```
        .detailsView td
        {
            padding:8px;
        }
        html
        {
            background-color:silver;
            font-family:Georgia, Serif;
        }
        a
        {
            color:blue;
            text-decoration:none;
        }
    </style>
    <title>Show Inline Commands</title>
</head>
<body>
    <form id="form1" runat="server">
    <div>

    <asp:DetailsView
        id="dtlMovies"
        DataSourceID="srcMovies"
        DataKeyNames="Id"
        AllowPaging="true"
        AutoGenerateEditButton="true"
        AutoGenerateInsertButton="true"
        AutoGenerateDeleteButton="true"
        AutoGenerateRows="false"
        CssClass="detailsView"
        PagerSettings-Mode="NumericFirstLast"
        Runat="server">
        <Fields>
        <asp:BoundField DataField="Id"
            HeaderText="Movie Id:" ReadOnly="true" InsertVisible="false" />
        <asp:BoundField DataField="Title" HeaderText="Movie Title:" />
        <asp:BoundField DataField="Director" HeaderText="Movie Director:" />
        </Fields>
    </asp:DetailsView>

    <asp:SqlDataSource
```

LISTING 9.7   Continued

```
        id="srcMovies"
        SelectCommand="SELECT Id,Title,Director FROM Movies"
        InsertCommand="INSERT Movies (Title,Director,CategoryId,DateReleased)
            VALUES (@Title, @Director,0,'12/15/1966')"
        UpdateCommand="UPDATE Movies SET Title=@Title,
            Director=@Director WHERE Id=@Id"
        DeleteCommand="DELETE Movies WHERE Id=@Id"
        ConnectionString="<%$ ConnectionStrings:Movies %>"
        Runat="server" />

    </div>
    </form>
</body>
</html>
```

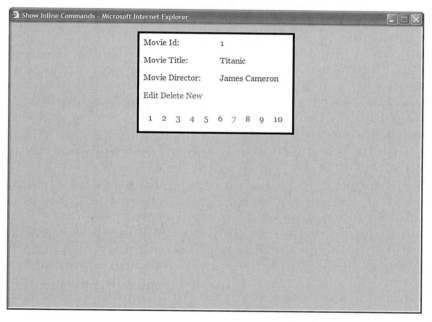

FIGURE 9.3   Executing inline SQL commands.

The page in Listing 9.7 contains a DetailsView control bound to a SqlDataSource control. You can click the Edit link to update an existing record, the New link to insert a new record, or the Delete link to delete an existing record. The DataBound control takes advantage of all four SQL commands supported by the SqlDataSource control.

Executing Stored Procedures

The SqlDataSource control can represent SQL stored procedures just as easily as it can represent inline SQL commands. You can indicate that a command represents a stored procedure by assigning the value StoredProcedure to any of the following properties:

- SelectCommandType

- InsertCommandType

- UpdateCommandType

- DeleteCommandType

You can create a new stored procedure in Visual Web Developer by opening the Database Explorer window, expanding a Data Connection, right-clicking Stored Procedures, and clicking Add New Stored Procedure (see Figure 9.4).

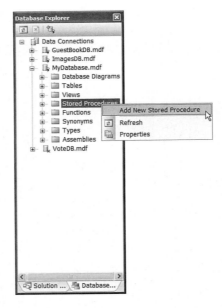

FIGURE 9.4   Creating a new stored procedure in Visual Web Developer.

The stored procedure in Listing 9.8 returns a count of the number of movies in each movie category.

LISTING 9.8   CountMoviesInCategory

```
CREATE PROCEDURE CountMoviesInCategory
AS
SELECT Name As Category, Count(*) As Count
FROM Movies
```

LISTING 9.8   Continued

```
INNER JOIN MovieCategories
ON CategoryId = MovieCategories.Id
GROUP BY Name
```

The page in Listing 9.9 uses the `CountMoviesInCategory` stored procedure to display a report with a GridView control (see Figure 9.5).

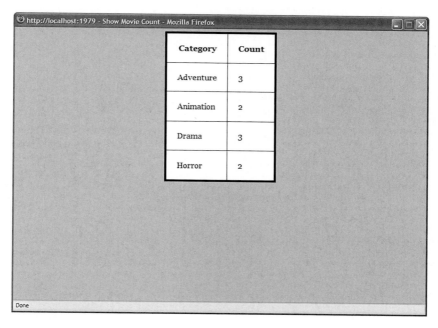

FIGURE 9.5   Showing count of movies in category.

LISTING 9.9   ShowMovieCount.aspx

```
<%@ Page Language="VB" %>
<!DOCTYPE html PUBLIC "-//W3C//DTD XHTML 1.1//EN"
 "http://www.w3.org/TR/xhtml11/DTD/xhtml11.dtd">
<html xmlns="http://www.w3.org/1999/xhtml" >
<head id="Head1" runat="server">
    <style type="text/css">
        .gridView
        {
            margin:0px auto;
            border:solid 4px black;
            background-color:white;
        }
```

LISTING 9.9   Continued

```
        .gridView td, .gridView th
        {
            padding:20px;
        }
        html
        {
            background-color:silver;
            font-family:Georgia, Serif;
        }
    </style>
    <title>Show Movie Count</title>
</head>
<body>
    <form id="form1" runat="server">
    <div>

    <asp:GridView
        id="grdMovies"
        DataSourceID="srcMovies"
        CssClass="gridView"
        Runat="server" />

    <asp:SqlDataSource
        id="srcMovies"
        SelectCommand="CountMoviesInCategory"
        SelectCommandType="StoredProcedure"
        ConnectionString="<%$ ConnectionStrings:Movies %>"
        Runat="server" />

    </div>
    </form>
</body>
</html>
```

Filtering Database Rows

The `SqlDataSource` control includes a `FilterExpression` property that enables you to filter the rows returned by the control. You can define complex Boolean filters that include parameters with this property.

For example, the page in Listing 9.10 retrieves all movies that have titles that match the string entered into the `TextBox` control (see Figure 9.6).

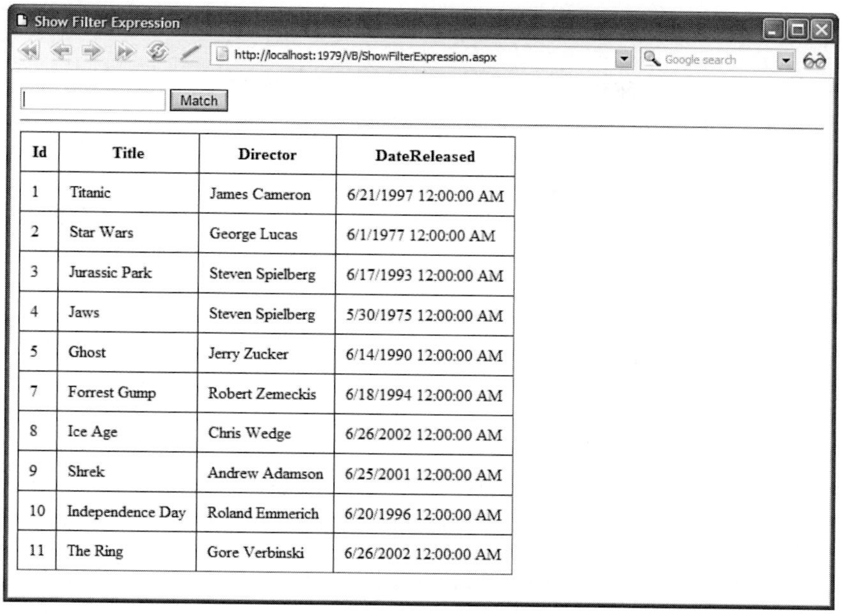

FIGURE 9.6   Show matching movies.

LISTING 9.10   `ShowFilterExpression.aspx`

```
<%@ Page Language="VB" %>
<!DOCTYPE html PUBLIC "-//W3C//DTD XHTML 1.1//EN"
 "http://www.w3.org/TR/xhtml11/DTD/xhtml11.dtd">
<html xmlns="http://www.w3.org/1999/xhtml" >
<head id="Head1" runat="server">
    <style type="text/css">
        td, th
        {
            padding:10px;
        }

    </style>
    <title>Show Filter Expression</title>
</head>
<body>
    <form id="form1" runat="server">
    <div>

    <asp:TextBox
        id="txtTitle"
```

LISTING 9.10   Continued

```
        Runat="server" />
    <asp:Button
        id="btnMatch"
        Text="Match"
        Runat="server" />
    <hr />

    <asp:GridView
        id="grdMovies"
        DataSourceId="srcMovies"
        Runat="server" />

    <asp:SqlDataSource
        id="srcMovies"
        SelectCommand="SELECT Id,Title,Director,DateReleased
            FROM Movies"
        FilterExpression="Title LIKE '{0}%'"
        ConnectionString="<%$ ConnectionStrings:Movies %>"
        Runat="server">
        <FilterParameters>
            <asp:ControlParameter Name="Title" ControlID="txtTitle" />
        </FilterParameters>
    </asp:SqlDataSource>

    </div>
    </form>
</body>
</html>
```

In Listing 9.10, the `FilterExpression` includes the `LIKE` operator and the ? wildcard character. The `LIKE` operator is used to perform partial matches on the movie titles.

Notice that the filter expression includes a `{0}` placeholder. The value of the `txtTitle` TextBox is plugged into this placeholder. You can use multiple parameters and multiple placeholders with the `FilterExpression` property.

> **NOTE**
>
> Behind the scenes, the `SqlDataSource` control uses the `DataView.RowFilter` property to filter database rows. You can find detailed documentation on proper filter syntax by looking up the `DataColumn.Expression` property in the .NET Framework SDK 2.0 Documentation.

Using the `FilterExpression` property is especially useful when caching the data represented by a `SqlDataSource`. For example, you can cache the entire contents of the movies database table in memory and use the `FilterExpression` property to filter the movies displayed on a page. You can display different sets of movies depending on a user's selection from a drop-down list of movie categories.

Changing the Data Source Mode

The `SqlDataSource` control can represent the data that it retrieves in two different ways. It can represent the data using either an ADO.NET DataSet or an ADO.NET DataReader.

By default, the `SqlDataSource` represents records using the ADO.NET DataSet object. The DataSet object provides a static, memory-resident representation of data.

> **NOTE**
>
> Technically, the `SqlDataSource` control returns a `DataView` and not a `DataSet`. Because, by default, the `SqlDataSourceMode` enumeration is set to the value `DataSet`, I'll continue to refer to DataSets instead of `DataViews`.

Several features of the `DataBound` controls work only when the controls are bound to a `DataSet`. For example, the `GridView` control supports paging and sorting data only when the control is bound to a `DataSet`. Furthermore, you can take advantage of the `SqlDataSource` control's support for caching and filtering records only when using a `DataSet`.

The other option is to represent the data that a `SqlDataSource` control returns with a `DataReader` object. The advantage of using a `DataReader` is that it offers significantly better performance than the `DataSet` object. The `DataReader` represents a fast, forward-only representation of data. If you want to grab some database records and display the records in the fastest possible way, use the `DataReader` object.

For example, the page in Listing 9.11 retrieves the records from the Movies database by using a `DataReader`.

LISTING 9.11   ShowDataSourceMode.aspx

```
<%@ Page Language="VB" %>
<!DOCTYPE html PUBLIC "-//W3C//DTD XHTML 1.1//EN"
 "http://www.w3.org/TR/xhtml11/DTD/xhtml11.dtd">
<html xmlns="http://www.w3.org/1999/xhtml" >
<head id="Head1" runat="server">
    <title>Show Data Source Mode</title>
</head>
<body>
    <form id="form1" runat="server">
    <div>

    <asp:GridView
        id="grdMovies"
        DataSourceID="srcMovies"
```

6

LISTING 9.11   Continued

```
        Runat="server" />

    <asp:SqlDataSource
        id="srcMovies"
        DataSourceMode="DataReader"
        SelectCommand="SELECT * FROM Movies"
        ConnectionString="<%$ ConnectionStrings:Movies %>"
        Runat="server" />

    </div>
    </form>
</body>
</html>
```

Notice that the SqlDataSource control's DataSourceMode property is set to the value DataReader.

Handling SQL Command Execution Errors

Whenever you build a software application you need to plan for failure. Databases go down, users enter unexpected values in form fields, networks get clogged. It is miraculous that the Internet works at all.

You can handle errors thrown by the SqlDataSource control by handling any or all of the following four events:

- Deleted—Happens immediately after the SqlDataSource executes its delete command.

- Inserted—Happens immediately after the SqlDataSource executes its insert command.

- Selected—Happens immediately after the SqlDataSource executes its select command.

- Updated—Happens immediately after the SqlDataSource executes its delete command.

Each of these events is passed an EventArgs parameter that includes any exceptions raised when the command was executed. For example, in the SELECT command in Listing 9.12, movies are retrieved from the DontExist database table instead of the Movies database table.

LISTING 9.12   `HandleError.aspx`

```vbnet
<%@ Page Language="VB" %>
<!DOCTYPE html PUBLIC "-//W3C//DTD XHTML 1.1//EN"
  "http://www.w3.org/TR/xhtml11/DTD/xhtml11.dtd">

<script runat="server">

    Protected Sub srcMovies_Selected(ByVal sender As Object,
➥ByVal e As SqlDataSourceStatusEventArgs)
        If Not e.Exception Is Nothing Then
            lblError.Text = e.Exception.Message
            e.ExceptionHandled = True
        End If
    End Sub

</script>

<html xmlns="http://www.w3.org/1999/xhtml" >
<head id="Head1" runat="server">
    <style type="text/css">
        .error
        {
            display:block;
            color:red;
            font:bold 16px Arial;
            margin:10px;
        }
    </style>
    <title>Handle Error</title>
</head>
<body>
    <form id="form1" runat="server">
    <div>

    <asp:Label
        id="lblError"
        EnableViewState="false"
        CssClass="error"
        Runat="server" />

    <asp:GridView
        id="grdMovies"
        DataSourceID="srcMovies"
        Runat="server" />
```

LISTING 9.12   Continued

```
<asp:SqlDataSource
    id="srcMovies"
    SelectCommand="SELECT * FROM DontExist"
    ConnectionString="<%$ ConnectionStrings:Movies %>"
    OnSelected="srcMovies_Selected"
    Runat="server" />

    </div>
    </form>
</body>
</html>
```

If the page in Listing 9.12 is opened in a web browser, an exception is raised when the SqlDataSource control attempts to retrieve the rows from the DontExist database table (because it doesn't exist). In the `srcMovies_Selected()` method, the exception is detected and displayed in a Label control.

Notice that the ExceptionHandled property is used to suppress the exception. If you do not set ExceptionHandled to true, then the page will explode (see Figure 9.7).

FIGURE 9.7   An unhandled exception.

As an alternative to handling exceptions at the level of the `SqlDataSource` control, you can handle the exception at the level of a DataBound control. The `GridView`, `DetailsView`, and `FormView` controls all include events that expose the `Exception` and `ExceptionHandled` properties.

For example, the page in Listing 9.13 includes a `GridView` that handles the exception raised when you attempt to edit the contents of the DontExist database table.

LISTING 9.13   GridViewHandleError.aspx

```
<%@ Page Language="VB" %>
<!DOCTYPE html PUBLIC "-//W3C//DTD XHTML 1.1//EN"
 "http://www.w3.org/TR/xhtml11/DTD/xhtml11.dtd">
<script runat="server">

    Protected Sub grdMovies_RowUpdated(ByVal sender As Object,
➥ByVal e As GridViewUpdatedEventArgs)
        If Not e.Exception Is Nothing Then
            lblError.Text = e.Exception.Message
            e.ExceptionHandled = True
        End If
    End Sub

</script>

<html xmlns="http://www.w3.org/1999/xhtml" >
<head id="Head1" runat="server">
    <style type="text/css">
        .error
        {
            display:block;
            color:red;
            font:bold 16px Arial;
            margin:10px;
        }
    </style>
    <title>GridView Handle Error</title>
</head>
<body>
    <form id="form1" runat="server">
    <div>

    <asp:Label
        id="lblError"
        EnableViewState="false"
        CssClass="error"
```

LISTING 9.13   Continued

```
        Runat="server" />

    <asp:GridView
        id="grdMovies"
        DataKeyNames="Id"
        AutoGenerateEditButton="true"
        DataSourceID="srcMovies"
        OnRowUpdated="grdMovies_RowUpdated"
        Runat="server"  />

    <asp:SqlDataSource
        id="srcMovies"
        SelectCommand="SELECT Id,Title FROM Movies"
        UpdateCommand="UPDATE DontExist SET Title=@Title
            WHERE Id=@ID"
        ConnectionString="<%$ ConnectionStrings:Movies %>"
        Runat="server" />

    </div>
    </form>
</body>
</html>
```

After you open the page in Listing 9.13, you can click the Edit link next to any record to edit the record. If you click the Update link, an exception is raised because the update command attempts to update the DontExist database table. The exception is handled by the GridView control's RowUpdated event handler.

You can handle an exception at both the level of the SqlDataSource control and the level of a DataBound control. The SqlDataSource control's events are raised before the corresponding events are raised for the DataBound control. If you handle an exception by using the ExceptionHandled property in the SqlDataSource control's event handler, then the exception is not promoted to the DataSource control's event handler.

Canceling Command Execution

You can cancel SqlDataSource commands when some criterion is not met. For example, you might want to validate the parameters that you are using with the command before executing the command.

You can cancel a command by handling any of the following events exposed by the SqlDataSource control:

- Deleting—Happens immediately before the SqlDataSource executes its delete command.

- Filtering—Happens immediately before the SqlDataSource filters its data.

- Inserting—Happens immediately before the SqlDataSource executes its insert command.

- Selecting—Happens immediately before the SqlDataSource executes its select command.

- Updating—Happens immediately before the SqlDataSource executes its delete command.

For example, the page in Listing 9.14 contains a DetailsView control bound to a SqlDataSource control that represents the contents of the Movies database table. The DetailsView control enables you to update a particular movie record. However, if you leave one of the fields blank, then the update command is canceled (see Figure 9.8).

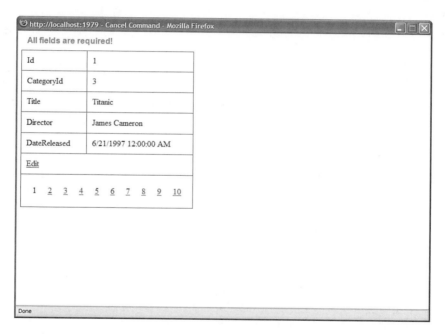

FIGURE 9.8   Canceling a command when a field is blank.

LISTING 9.14   CancelCommand.aspx

```
<%@ Page Language="VB" %>
<%@ Import Namespace="System.Data.SqlClient" %>
<!DOCTYPE html PUBLIC "-//W3C//DTD XHTML 1.1//EN"
   "http://www.w3.org/TR/xhtml11/DTD/xhtml11.dtd">
<script runat="server">
```

LISTING 9.14   Continued

```
''' <summary>
''' Iterate through all parameters and check for Nothing
''' </summary>
Protected Sub srcMovies_Updating(ByVal sender As Object,
➥ByVal e As SqlDataSourceCommandEventArgs)
    Dim param As SqlParameter
    For Each param In e.Command.Parameters
        If param.Value Is Nothing Then
            e.Cancel = True
            lblError.Text = "All fields are required!"
        End If
    Next
End Sub
</script>

<html xmlns="http://www.w3.org/1999/xhtml" >
<head id="Head1" runat="server">
    <style type="text/css">
        .error
        {
            display:block;
            color:red;
            font:bold 16px Arial;
            margin:10px;
        }
        td,th
        {
            padding:10px;
        }
    </style>
    <title>Cancel Command</title>
</head>
<body>
    <form id="form1" runat="server">
    <div>

    <asp:Label
        id="lblError"
        EnableViewState="false"
        CssClass="error"
        Runat="server" />

    <asp:DetailsView
```

LISTING 9.14 Continued

```
            id="dtlMovie"
            DataSourceID="srcMovies"
            DataKeyNames="Id"
            AllowPaging="true"
            AutoGenerateEditButton="true"
            Runat="server" />

    <asp:SqlDataSource
        id="srcMovies"
        SelectCommand="SELECT * FROM Movies"
        UpdateCommand="UPDATE Movies SET Title=@Title,
            Director=@Director,DateReleased=@DateReleased
            WHERE Id=@id"
        ConnectionString="<%$ ConnectionStrings:Movies %>"
        OnUpdating="srcMovies_Updating"
        Runat="server" />

    </div>
    </form>
</body>
</html>
```

The page in Listing 9.14 includes a srcMovies_Updating() method. In this method, each parameter associated with the update command is compared against the value Nothing (null). If one of the parameters is null, an error message is displayed in a Label control.

Using ASP.NET Parameters with the SqlDataSource Control

You can use any of the following ASP.NET Parameter objects with the SqlDataSource control:

- Parameter—Represents an arbitrary static value.

- ControlParameter—Represents the value of a control or page property.

- CookieParameter—Represents the value of a browser cookie.

- FormParameter—Represents the value of an HTML form field.

- ProfileParameter—Represents the value of a Profile property.

- QueryStringParameter—Represents the value of a query string field.

- SessionParameter—Represents the value of an item stored in Session state.

The SqlDataSource control includes five collections of ASP.NET parameters: SelectParameters, InsertParameters, DeleteParameters, UpdateParameters, and FilterParameters. You can use these parameter collections to associate a particular ASP.NET parameter with a particular SqlDataSource command or filter.

In the following sections, you learn how to use each of these different types of parameter objects.

Using the ASP.NET Parameter Object

The ASP.NET parameter object has the following properties:

- ConvertEmptyStringToNull—When true, if a parameter represents an empty string then the empty string is converted to the value Nothing (null) before the associated command is executed.

- DefaultValue—When a parameter has the value Nothing (null), the DefaultValue is used for the value of the parameter.

- Direction—Indicates the direction of the parameter. Possible values are Input, InputOutput, Output, and ReturnValue.

- Name—Indicates the name of the parameter. Do not use the @ character when indicating the name of an ASP.NET parameter.

- Size—Indicates the data size of the parameter.

- Type—Indicates the .NET Framework type of the parameter. You can assign any value from the TypeCode enumeration to this property.

You can use the ASP.NET parameter object to indicate several parameter properties explicitly, such as a parameter's type, size, and default value.

For example, the page in Listing 9.15 contains a DetailsView control bound to a SqlDataSource control. You can use the page to update records in the Movies database table (see Figure 9.9).

LISTING 9.15   ShowDetailsView.aspx

```
<%@ Page Language="VB" %>
<!DOCTYPE html PUBLIC "-//W3C//DTD XHTML 1.1//EN"
    "http://www.w3.org/TR/xhtml11/DTD/xhtml11.dtd">
<html xmlns="http://www.w3.org/1999/xhtml" >
<head id="Head1" runat="server">
    <title>Show DetailsView</title>
</head>
<body>
    <form id="form1" runat="server">
    <div>
```

LISTING 9.15   Continued

```
<asp:DetailsView
    id="dtlMovie"
    DataKeyNames="Id"
    DataSourceID="srcMovies"
    AutoGenerateEditButton="true"
    DefaultMode="Edit"
    AllowPaging="true"
    runat="server" />

<asp:SqlDataSource
    id="srcMovies"
    ConnectionString="<%$ ConnectionStrings:Movies %>"
    SelectCommand="Select * FROM Movies"
    UpdateCommand="UPDATE Movies SET Title=@Title,Director=@Director,
        DateReleased=@DateReleased WHERE Id=@id"
    Runat="server" />

</div>
</form>
</body>
</html>
```

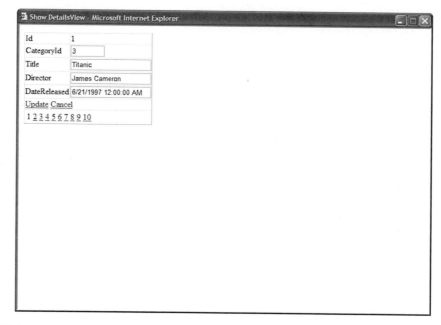

FIGURE 9.9   Updating movie records.

In Listing 9.15, no ASP.NET parameter objects are declared explicitly. The `DetailsView` control automatically creates and adds ADO.NET parameters to the `SqlDataSource` control's update command before the command is executed.

If you want to be explicit about the data types and sizes of the parameters used by a `SqlDataSource` control, then you can declare the parameters. The page in Listing 9.16 declares each of the parameters used when executing the update command.

LISTING 9.16   ShowDetailsViewExplicit.aspx

```
<%@ Page Language="VB" %>
<!DOCTYPE html PUBLIC "-//W3C//DTD XHTML 1.1//EN"
  "http://www.w3.org/TR/xhtml11/DTD/xhtml11.dtd">
<html xmlns="http://www.w3.org/1999/xhtml" >
<head id="Head1" runat="server">
    <title>Show DetailsView Explicit</title>
</head>
<body>
    <form id="form1" runat="server">
    <div>

    <asp:DetailsView
        id="dtlMovie"
        DataKeyNames="Id"
        DataSourceID="srcMovies"
        AutoGenerateEditButton="true"
        DefaultMode="Edit"
        AllowPaging="true"
        runat="server" />

    <asp:SqlDataSource
        id="srcMovies"
        ConnectionString="<%$ ConnectionStrings:Movies %>"
        SelectCommand="Select * FROM Movies"
        UpdateCommand="UPDATE Movies SET Title=@Title,Director=@Director,
            DateReleased=@DateReleased WHERE Id=@id"
        Runat="server">
        <UpdateParameters>
          <asp:Parameter Name="Title"
            Type="String" Size="100" DefaultValue="Untitled" />
          <asp:Parameter Name="Director"
            Type="String" Size="100" DefaultValue="Alan Smithee" />
          <asp:Parameter Name="DateReleased" Type="DateTime" />
          <asp:Parameter Name="id" Type="int32" />
        </UpdateParameters>
    </asp:SqlDataSource>
```

LISTING 9.16   Continued

```
      </div>
      </form>
</body>
</html>
```

In Listing 9.16, each of the parameters used by the update command are provided with an explicit data type. For example, the `DateReleased` parameter is declared to be a `DateTime` parameter (if you didn't assign an explicit type to this parameter, it would default to a string).

Furthermore, the `Title` and `Director` parameters are provided with default values. If you edit a movie record and do not supply a title or director, the default values are used.

> **NOTE**
>
> Another situation in which explicitly declaring `Parameter` objects is useful is when you need to explicitly order the parameters. For example, the order of parameters is important when you use the OLE DB provider with Microsoft Access.

Using the ASP.NET `ControlParameter` Object

You use the `ControlParameter` object to represent the value of a control property. You can use it to represent the value of any control contained in the same page as the `SqlDataSource` control.

The `ControlParameter` object includes all the properties of the `Parameter` object and these additional properties:

- `ControlID`—The ID of the control that the parameter represents.

- `PropertyName`—The name of the property that the parameter represents.

For example, the page in Listing 9.17 includes a `DropDownList` control and a `DetailsView` control. When you select a movie from the `DropDownList`, details for the movie are displayed in the `DetailsView` control (see Figure 9.10).

LISTING 9.17   ShowControlParameter.aspx

```
<%@ Page Language="VB" %>
<!DOCTYPE html PUBLIC "-//W3C//DTD XHTML 1.1//EN"
  "http://www.w3.org/TR/xhtml11/DTD/xhtml11.dtd">
<html xmlns="http://www.w3.org/1999/xhtml" >
<head id="Head1" runat="server">
    <title>Show Control Parameter</title>
</head>
<body>
```

LISTING 9.17   Continued

```
<form id="form1" runat="server">
<div>

<asp:DropDownList
    id="ddlMovies"
    DataSourceID="srcMovies"
    DataTextField="Title"
    DataValueField="Id"
    Runat="server" />
<asp:Button
    id="btnSelect"
    Text="Select"
    Runat="server" />

<hr />

<asp:DetailsView
    id="dtlMovie"
    DataSourceID="srcMovieDetails"
    Runat="server" />

<asp:SqlDataSource
    id="srcMovies"
    SelectCommand="SELECT Id,Title FROM Movies"
    ConnectionString="<%$ ConnectionStrings:Movies %>"
    Runat="server" />

<asp:SqlDataSource
    id="srcMovieDetails"
    SelectCommand="SELECT * FROM Movies
        WHERE Id=@Id"
    ConnectionString="<%$ ConnectionStrings:Movies %>"
    Runat="server">
    <SelectParameters>
        <asp:ControlParameter Name="Id" ControlID="ddlMovies"
            PropertyName="SelectedValue" />
    </SelectParameters>
</asp:SqlDataSource>

</div>
</form>
</body>
</html>
```

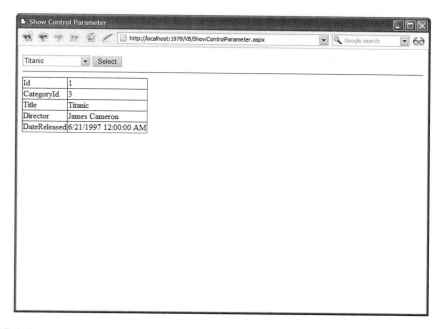

FIGURE 9.10   Show matching movies for each movie category.

Notice that the second `SqlDataSource` control in Listing 9.17 includes a
`ControlParameter` object. The `ControlParameter` represents the ID of the selected movie
in the `DropDownList` control.

When using a `ControlParameter`, you must always set the value of the `ControlID` property to point to a control on the page. On the other hand, you are not always required to
set the `PropertyName` property. If you do not set `PropertyName`, the `ControlParameter`
object automatically looks for a property that is decorated with the
`ControlValueProperty` attribute. Because the `SelectedValue` property of the
`DropDownList` control is decorated with this attribute, you do not really need to set this
property in Listing 9.17.

Because the `Page` class derives from the `control` class, you can use the `ControlParameter`
object to represent the value of a `Page` property.

For example, the page in Listing 9.18 contains a simple guestbook. When a user adds a
new entry to the guestbook, the user's remote IP address is saved automatically with the
guestbook entry (see Figure 9.11).

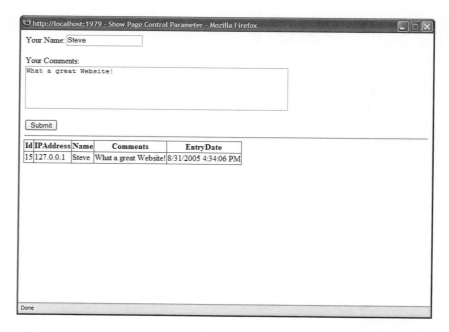

FIGURE 9.11   Saving an IP address in guest book entries.

LISTING 9.18   `ShowPageControlParameter.aspx`

```
<%@ Page Language="VB" %>
<!DOCTYPE html PUBLIC "-//W3C//DTD XHTML 1.1//EN"
  "http://www.w3.org/TR/xhtml11/DTD/xhtml11.dtd">
<script runat="server">

    Public ReadOnly Property IPAddress() As String
        Get
            Return Request.UserHostAddress
        End Get
    End Property

</script>
<html xmlns="http://www.w3.org/1999/xhtml" >
<head id="Head1" runat="server">
    <title>Show Page Control Parameter</title>
</head>
<body>
    <form id="form1" runat="server">
    <div>
```

LISTING 9.18   Continued

```
<asp:FormView
    id="frmGuestBook"
    DataSourceID="srcGuestBook"
    DefaultMode="Insert"
    runat="server">
    <InsertItemTemplate>
    <asp:Label
        id="lblName"
        Text="Your Name:"
        AssociatedControlID="txtName"
        Runat="server" />
    <asp:TextBox
        id="txtName"
        Text='<%# Bind("Name") %>'
        Runat="server" />
    <br /><br />
    <asp:Label
        id="Label1"
        Text="Your Comments:"
        AssociatedControlID="txtComments"
        Runat="server" />
    <br />
    <asp:TextBox
        id="txtComments"
        Text='<%# Bind("Comments") %>'
        TextMode="MultiLine"
        Columns="60"
        Rows="4"
        Runat="server" />
    <br /><br />
    <asp:Button
        id="btnSubmit"
        Text="Submit"
        CommandName="Insert"
        Runat="server" />
    </InsertItemTemplate>
</asp:FormView>

<hr />

<asp:GridView
    id="grdGuestBook"
    DataSourceID="srcGuestBook"
    Runat="server" />
```

LISTING 9.18   Continued

```
            <asp:SqlDataSource
                id="srcGuestBook"
                SelectCommand="SELECT * FROM GuestBook ORDER BY Id DESC"
                InsertCommand="INSERT GuestBook (IPAddress,Name,Comments)
                    VALUES (@IPAddress,@Name,@Comments)"
                ConnectionString="<%$ ConnectionStrings:GuestBook %>"
                Runat="server">
                <InsertParameters>
                    <asp:ControlParameter Name="IPAddress" ControlID="__page"
                        PropertyName="IPAddress" />
                </InsertParameters>
            </asp:SqlDataSource>

        </div>
        </form>
</body>
</html>
```

Notice that the ControlID property is set to the value __page. This value is the automatically generated ID for the Page class. The PropertyName property has the value IPAddress. This property is defined in the page.

Using the ASP.NET CookieParameter **Object**

The CookieParameter object represents a browser-side cookie. The CookieParameter includes all the properties of the base Parameter class and the following additional property:

- CookieName—The name of the browser cookie.

The page in Listing 9.19 illustrates how you can use the CookieParameter object. The page contains a voting form that you can use to vote for your favorite color. A cookie is added to the user's browser to identify the user and prevent someone from cheating by voting more than once (see Figure 9.12).

LISTING 9.19   Vote.aspx

```
<%@ Page Language="VB" %>
<!DOCTYPE html PUBLIC "-//W3C//DTD XHTML 1.1//EN"
  "http://www.w3.org/TR/xhtml11/DTD/xhtml11.dtd">
<script runat="server">

    Private Sub Page_Load()
        If Request.Cookies("VoterId") Is Nothing Then
            Dim identifier As String = Guid.NewGuid().ToString()
            Dim voteCookie As HttpCookie = New HttpCookie("VoterId",identifier)
```

LISTING 9.19   Continued

```
                voteCookie.Expires = DateTime.MaxValue
                Response.AppendCookie(voteCookie)
            End If
        End Sub

    </script>
    <html xmlns="http://www.w3.org/1999/xhtml" >
    <head id="Head1" runat="server">
        <title>Vote</title>
    </head>
    <body>
        <form id="form1" runat="server">
        <div>

        <asp:FormView
            id="frmVote"
            DataSourceID="srcVote"
            DefaultMode="Insert"
            Runat="server">
            <InsertItemTemplate>
            <asp:Label
                id="lblFavoriteColor"
                AssociatedControlID="rdlFavoriteColor"
                Runat="server" />
            <asp:RadioButtonList
                id="rdlFavoriteColor"
                SelectedValue='<%#Bind("Color")%>'
                Runat="server">
                <asp:ListItem Value="Red" Text="Red" Selected="True" />
                <asp:ListItem Value="Blue" Text="Blue" />
                <asp:ListItem Value="Green" Text="Green" />
            </asp:RadioButtonList>
            <br />
            <asp:Button
                id="btnSubmit"
                Text="Submit"
                CommandName="Insert"
                Runat="server" />
            </InsertItemTemplate>
        </asp:FormView>

        <hr />

        <asp:GridView
            id="grdVote"
```

LISTING 9.19   Continued

```
        DataSourceID="srcVote"
        Runat="server" />

    <asp:SqlDataSource
        id="srcVote"
        SelectCommand="SELECT * FROM Vote
            ORDER BY Id DESC"
        InsertCommand="INSERT Vote (VoterId,Color)
            VALUES (@VoterId,@Color)"
        ConnectionString="<%$ ConnectionStrings:Vote %>"
        Runat="server">
        <InsertParameters>
            <asp:CookieParameter Name="VoterId"
                CookieName="VoterId" />
        </InsertParameters>
    </asp:SqlDataSource>

    </div>
    </form>
</body>
</html>
```

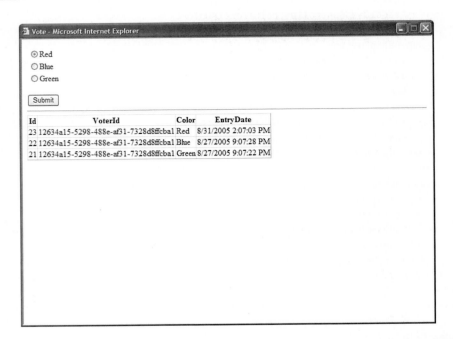

FIGURE 9.12   Vote on your favorite color.

The cookie is added in the Page_Load() method. A unique identifier (GUID) is generated to identify the user uniquely.

Using the ASP.NET FormParameter Object

The FormParameter object represents a form field submitted to the server. Typically, you never work directly with browser form fields because their functionality is encapsulated in the ASP.NET form controls.

The page in Listing 9.20 contains a client-side HTML form that enables you to enter a movie title and director. When the form is submitted to the server, the values of the form fields are saved to the Movies database table (see Figure 9.13).

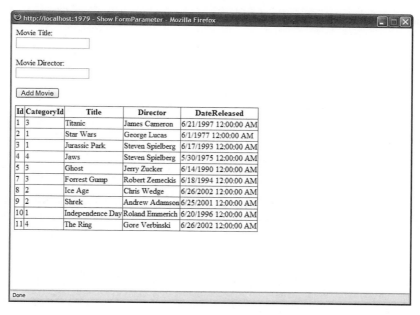

FIGURE 9.13 Using a client-side HTML form.

LISTING 9.20 ShowFormParameter.aspx

```
<%@ Page Language="VB" %>
<!DOCTYPE html PUBLIC "-//W3C//DTD XHTML 1.1//EN"
  "http://www.w3.org/TR/xhtml11/DTD/xhtml11.dtd">
<script runat="server">

    Private  Sub Page_Load()
        If Not Request.Form("AddMovie") Is Nothing Then
            srcMovies.Insert()
        End If
    End Sub
```

LISTING 9.20   Continued

```
</script>
<html xmlns="http://www.w3.org/1999/xhtml" >
<head id="Head1" runat="server">
    <title>Show FormParameter</title>
</head>
<body>
    <form action="ShowFormParameter.aspx" method="post">

    <label for="txtTitle">Movie Title:</label>
    <br />
    <input name="txtTitle" />

    <br /><br />

    <label for="txtDirector">Movie Director:</label>
    <br />
    <input name="txtDirector" />

    <br /><br />
    <input name="AddMovie" type="submit" value="Add Movie" />

    </form>

    <form id="form1" runat="server">
    <div>

    <asp:GridView
        id="grdMovies"
        DataSourceID="srcMovies"
        Runat="server" />

    <asp:SqlDataSource
        id="srcMovies"
        SelectCommand="SELECT * FROM Movies"
        InsertCommand="INSERT Movies (Title,Director,CategoryId,DateReleased)
            VALUES (@Title,@Director,0,'12/25/1966')"
        ConnectionString="<%$ ConnectionStrings:Movies %>"
        Runat="server">
        <InsertParameters>
            <asp:FormParameter Name="Title"
                FormField="txtTitle" DefaultValue="Untitled" />
            <asp:FormParameter Name="Director"
                FormField="txtDirector" DefaultValue="Allen Smithee" />
        </InsertParameters>
```

LISTING 9.20   Continued

```
        </asp:SqlDataSource>

        </div>
        </form>
</body>
</html>
```

Notice that you check whether a form field named AddMovie exists in the `Page_Load()` method. This is the name of the submit button. If this field exists, then you know that the client-side form was submitted and the `SqlDataSource` control's `Insert()` method can be called to add the form fields to the database.

Using the ASP.NET `ProfileParameter` **Object**

The `ProfileParameter` object enables you to represent any of the properties of the `Profile` object. The `ProfileParameter` includes all the properties of the `Parameter` class and the following property:

- `PropertyName`—Indicates the name of the `Profile` property associated with this `ProfileParameter`.

For example, imagine that you are building a Guest Book application and you want to allow users to enter their display names when adding entries to a guest book. You can add a `DisplayName` property to the `Profile` object with the web configuration file in Listing 9.21.

LISTING 9.21   `Web.config`

```
<?xml version="1.0"?>
<configuration>
  <connectionStrings>
    <add name="GuestBook" connectionString="Data Source=.\SQLEXPRESS;
      AttachDbFilename=¦DataDirectory¦GuestBookDB.mdf;
Integrated Security=True;User Instance=True" />
  </connectionStrings>

  <system.web>
    <profile enabled="true">
      <properties>
        <add name="DisplayName" defaultValue="Anonymous" />
      </properties>
    </profile>
  </system.web>

</configuration>
```

NOTE

The Profile object automatically stores user specific information across visits to a website. The Profile object is discussed in detail in Chapter 22, "Maintaining Application State."

The web configuration file in Listing 9.21 includes the definition of a Profile property named DisplayName. Notice that the default value of this property is Anonymous.

The page in Listing 9.22 uses the ProfileParameter object to read the value of the DisplayName property automatically when new entries are added to a Guest Book.

LISTING 9.22   ShowProfileParameter.aspx

```
<%@ Page Language="VB" %>
<!DOCTYPE html PUBLIC "-//W3C//DTD XHTML 1.1//EN"
  "http://www.w3.org/TR/xhtml11/DTD/xhtml11.dtd">
<html xmlns="http://www.w3.org/1999/xhtml" >
<head id="Head1" runat="server">
    <title>Show ProfileParameter</title>
</head>
<body>
    <form id="form1" runat="server">
    <div>

    <asp:FormView
        id="frmGuestBook"
        DataSourceID="srcGuestBook"
        DefaultMode="Insert"
        Runat="server">
        <InsertItemTemplate>
        <asp:Label
            id="lblComments"
            Text="Enter Your Comments:"
            Runat="server" />
        <br />
        <asp:TextBox
            id="txtComments"
            Text='<%# Bind("Comments") %>'
            TextMode="MultiLine"
            Columns="50"
            Rows="4"
            Runat="server" />
        <br />
        <asp:Button
            id="btnInsert"
            Text="Add Comments"
```

LISTING 9.21   Continued

```
            CommandName="Insert"
            Runat="server" />
        </InsertItemTemplate>
    </asp:FormView>

    <hr />

    <asp:GridView
        id="grdGuestBook"
        DataSourceID="srcGuestBook"
        Runat="server" />

    <asp:SqlDataSource
        id="srcGuestBook"
        SelectCommand="SELECT Name,Comments,EntryDate
            FROM GuestBook ORDER BY Id DESC"
        InsertCommand="INSERT GuestBook (Name,Comments)
            VALUES (@Name,@Comments)"
        ConnectionString="<%$ ConnectionStrings:GuestBook %>"
        Runat="server">
        <InsertParameters>
            <asp:ProfileParameter Name="Name" PropertyName="DisplayName" />
        </InsertParameters>
    </asp:SqlDataSource>

    </div>
    </form>
</body>
</html>
```

Notice that the SqlDataSource control in Listing 9.22 includes a ProfileParameter object. This object represents the DisplayName profile property.

Using the QueryStringParameter **Object**

The QueryStringParameter object can represent any query string passed to a page. The QueryStringParameter class includes all the properties of the base Parameter class with the addition of the following property:

- QueryStringField—The name of the query string that the QueryStringParameter represents.

This type of parameter is particularly useful when you build Master/Detail pages. For example, the page in Listing 9.23 displays a list of movie titles. Each movie title links to a page that contains detailed information for the movie.

LISTING 9.23   ShowQueryStringParameterMaster.aspx

```
<%@ Page Language="VB" %>
<!DOCTYPE html PUBLIC "-//W3C//DTD XHTML 1.1//EN"
 "http://www.w3.org/TR/xhtml11/DTD/xhtml11.dtd">
<html xmlns="http://www.w3.org/1999/xhtml" >
<head id="Head1" runat="server">
    <title>Show QueryStringParameter Master</title>
</head>
<body>
    <form id="form1" runat="server">
    <div>

    <asp:GridView
        id="grdMovies"
        DataSourceId="srcMovies"
        AutoGenerateColumns="false"
        ShowHeader="false"
        Runat="server">
        <Columns>
        <asp:HyperLinkField
            DataTextField="Title"
            DataNavigateUrlFields="Id"
            DataNavigateUrlFormatString=
➡"ShowQueryStringParameterDetails.aspx?id={0}" />
        </Columns>
    </asp:GridView>

    <asp:SqlDataSource
        id="srcMovies"
        SelectCommand="SELECT * FROM Movies"
        ConnectionString="<%$ ConnectionStrings:Movies %>"
        Runat="server" />

    </div>
    </form>
</body>
</html>
```

Notice that the ID of the movie is passed to the ShowQueryStringParameterDetails.aspx
page. The movie ID is passed in a query string field named id.

The page in Listing 9.24 displays detailed information for a particular movie.

LISTING 9.24   ShowQueryStringParamterDetails.aspx

```
<%@ Page Language="VB" %>
<!DOCTYPE html PUBLIC "-//W3C//DTD XHTML 1.1//EN"
  "http://www.w3.org/TR/xhtml11/DTD/xhtml11.dtd">
<html xmlns="http://www.w3.org/1999/xhtml" >
<head id="Head1" runat="server">
    <title>Show QueryStringParameter Details</title>
</head>
<body>
    <form id="form1" runat="server">
    <div>

    <asp:DetailsView
        id="dtlMovie"
        DataSourceID="srcMovie"
        Runat="server" />

    <asp:SqlDataSource
        id="srcMovie"
        SelectCommand="SELECT * FROM Movies
            WHERE Id=@Id"
        ConnectionString="<%$ ConnectionStrings:Movies %>"
        Runat="server">
        <SelectParameters>
            <asp:QueryStringParameter
                Name="Id"
                QueryStringField="Id" />
        </SelectParameters>
    </asp:SqlDataSource>

    </div>
    </form>
</body>
</html>
```

Notice that the SqlDataSource control in Listing 9.24 includes a QueryStringParameter. The QueryStringParameter is used to supply the movie ID in the SqlDataSource control's SelectCommand.

Using the SessionParameter Object

The SessionParameter object enables you to represent any item stored in Session state. The SessionParameter object includes all the properties of the base Parameter class and the following property:

- `SessionField`—The name of the item stored in `Session` state that the `SessionParameter` represents.

The page in Listing 9.25 contains a `GridView` that displays a list of movies matching a movie category. The movie category is stored in Session state.

LISTING 9.25   ShowSessionParameter.aspx

```
<%@ Page Language="VB" %>
<!DOCTYPE html PUBLIC "-//W3C//DTD XHTML 1.1//EN"
  "http://www.w3.org/TR/xhtml11/DTD/xhtml11.dtd">
<script runat="server">

    Private Sub Page_Load()
        Session("MovieCategoryName") = "Animation"
    End Sub

</script>
<html xmlns="http://www.w3.org/1999/xhtml" >
<head id="Head1" runat="server">
    <title>Show SessionParameter</title>
</head>
<body>
    <form id="form1" runat="server">
    <div>

    <asp:GridView
        id="grdMovies"
        DataSourceID="srcMovies"
        Runat="server" />

    <asp:SqlDataSource
        id="srcMovies"
        SelectCommand="SELECT Name As Category,Title,Director
            FROM Movies
            INNER JOIN MovieCategories
            ON CategoryId = MovieCategories.id
            WHERE Name=@Name"
        ConnectionString="<%$ ConnectionStrings:Movies %>"
        Runat="server">
        <SelectParameters>
```

LISTING 9.25   Continued

```
        <asp:SessionParameter
            Name="Name"
            SessionField="MovieCategoryName" />
        </SelectParameters>
    </asp:SqlDataSource>

    </div>
    </form>
</body>
</html>
```

Notice that the current movie category is added to the Session object in the Page_Load() method. The SqlDataSource reads the MovieCategoryName item from Session state when it retrieves the list of movies that the GridView displays.

Programmatically Executing SqlDataSource Commands

You aren't required to use the SqlDataSource control only when working with DataBound controls. You can create parameters and execute the commands represented by a SqlDataSource control by working directly with the properties and methods of the SqlDataSource control in your code.

In this section, you learn how to add parameters programmatically to a SqlDataSource control. You also learn how to execute select, insert, update, and delete commands when using the SqlDataSource control.

Adding ADO.NET Parameters

Under the covers, the SqlDataSource control uses ADO.NET objects such as the ADO.NET DataSet, DataReader, Parameter, and Command objects to interact with a database. In particular, any ASP.NET Parameter objects that you declare when working with the SqlDataSource control get converted into ADO.NET Parameter objects.

In some cases, you will want to work directly with these ADO.NET Parameter objects when using the SqlDataSource control. For example, you might want to add additional ADO.NET parameters programmatically before executing a command.

The page in Listing 9.26 automatically adds an ADO.NET parameter that represents the current user's username to the command that the SqlDataSource executes.

LISTING 9.26   AddParameter.aspx

```
<%@ Page Language="VB" %>
<%@ Import Namespace="System.Data.SqlClient" %>
<!DOCTYPE html PUBLIC "-//W3C//DTD XHTML 1.1//EN"
  "http://www.w3.org/TR/xhtml11/DTD/xhtml11.dtd">
```

LISTING 9.26 Continued

```
<script runat="server">

    Protected Sub srcGuestBook_Inserting(ByVal sender As Object,
➡ByVal e As SqlDataSourceCommandEventArgs)
        e.Command.Parameters.Add(New SqlParameter("@Name", User.Identity.Name))
    End Sub

</script>

<html xmlns="http://www.w3.org/1999/xhtml" >
<head id="Head1" runat="server">
    <title>Show ProfileParameter</title>
</head>
<body>
    <form id="form1" runat="server">
    <div>

    <asp:FormView
        id="frmGuestBook"
        DataSourceID="srcGuestBook"
        DefaultMode="Insert"
        Runat="server">
        <InsertItemTemplate>
        <asp:Label
            id="lblComments"
            Text="Enter Your Comments:"
            Runat="server" />
        <br />
        <asp:TextBox
            id="txtComments"
            Text='<%# Bind("Comments") %>'
            TextMode="MultiLine"
            Columns="50"
            Rows="4"
            Runat="server" />
        <br />
        <asp:Button
            id="btnInsert"
            Text="Add Comments"
            CommandName="Insert"
            Runat="server" />
        </InsertItemTemplate>
    </asp:FormView>
```

LISTING 9.26   Continued

```
    <hr />

    <asp:GridView
        id="grdGuestBook"
        DataSourceID="srcGuestBook"
        Runat="server" />

    <asp:SqlDataSource
        id="srcGuestBook"
        SelectCommand="SELECT Name,Comments,EntryDate
            FROM GuestBook ORDER BY Id DESC"
        InsertCommand="INSERT GuestBook (Name,Comments)
            VALUES (@Name,@Comments)"
        ConnectionString="<%$ ConnectionStrings:GuestBook %>"
        Runat="server" OnInserting="srcGuestBook_Inserting" />

    </div>
    </form>
</body>
</html>
```

Notice that the page in Listing 9.26 includes a `srcGuestBook_Inserting()` event handler. This event handler executes immediately before the `SqlDataSource` control executes its insert command. In the event handler, a new ADO.NET `Parameter` is added to the insert command, which represents the current user's username.

> **NOTE**
>
> The names of ADO.NET parameters, unlike ASP.NET parameters, always start with the character @.

Executing Insert, Update, and Delete Commands

The `SqlDataSource` control has methods that correspond to each of the different types of commands that it represents:

- `Delete`—Enables you to execute a SQL delete command.
- `Insert`—Enables you to execute a SQL insert command.
- `Select`—Enables you to execute a SQL select command.
- `Update`—Enables you to execute a SQL update command.

9

For example, the page in Listing 9.27 contains a form for adding new entries to the GuestBook database table. This form is not contained in a `DataBound` control such as the `FormView` or `DetailsView` controls. The form is contained in the body of the page. When you click the Add Entry button, the `SqlDataSource` control's `Insert()` method is executed.

LISTING 9.27   `ExecuteInsert.aspx`

```
<%@ Page Language="VB" %>
<!DOCTYPE html PUBLIC "-//W3C//DTD XHTML 1.1//EN"
  "http://www.w3.org/TR/xhtml11/DTD/xhtml11.dtd">
<script runat="server">

    ''' <summary>
    ''' When button clicked, execute Insert command
    ''' </summary>
    Protected Sub btnAddEnTry_Click(ByVal sender As Object, ByVal e As EventArgs)
        srcGuestBook.InsertParameters("Name").DefaultValue = txtName.Text
        srcGuestBook.InsertParameters("Comments").DefaultValue = txtComments.Text
        srcGuestBook.Insert()
    End Sub

</script>

<html xmlns="http://www.w3.org/1999/xhtml" >
<head id="Head1" runat="server">
    <title>Execute Insert</title>
</head>
<body>
    <form id="form1" runat="server">
    <div>

    <asp:Label
        id="lblName"
        Text="Name:"
        AssociatedControlId="txtName"
        Runat="server" />
    <br />
    <asp:TextBox
        id="txtName"
        Runat="server" />

    <br /><br />

    <asp:Label
        id="lblComments"
```

LISTING 9.27   Continued

```
            Text="Comments:"
            AssociatedControlId="txtComments"
            Runat="server" />
        <br />
        <asp:TextBox
            id="txtComments"
            TextMode="MultiLine"
            Columns="50"
            Rows="2"
            Runat="server" />

        <br /><br />

        <asp:Button
            id="btnAddEntry"
            Text="Add Entry"
            Runat="server" OnClick="btnAddEntry_Click" />

        <hr />

        <asp:GridView
            id="grdGuestBook"
            DataSourceId="srcGuestBook"
            Runat="server" />

        <asp:SqlDataSource
            id="srcGuestBook"
            ConnectionString="<%$ ConnectionStrings:GuestBook %>"
            SelectCommand="SELECT Name,Comments FROM GuestBook
                ORDER BY Id DESC"
            InsertCommand="INSERT GuestBook (Name,Comments)
                VALUES (@Name,@Comments)"
            Runat="server">
            <InsertParameters>
                <asp:Parameter Name="Name" />
                <asp:Parameter Name="Comments" />
            </InsertParameters>
        </asp:SqlDataSource>

    </div>
    </form>
</body>
</html>
```

Executing Select Commands

The procedure for executing a select command is different from executing insert, update, and delete commands because a select command returns data. This section discusses how you can execute the SqlDataSource control's Select() method programmatically and represent the data that the method returns.

Remember that a SqlDataSource control can return either a DataView or DataReader depending on the value of its DataSourceMode property. The SqlDataSource control's Select() method returns an object of type IEnumerable. Both DataViews and DataReaders implement the IEnumerable interface.

To understand how you can call the Select() method programmatically, look at the following simple photo gallery application. This application enables you to upload images to a database table and display them in a page (see Figure 9.14).

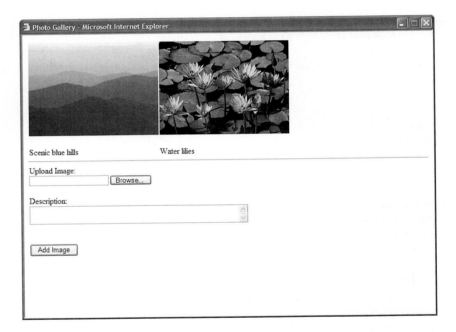

FIGURE 9.14   A photo gallery application.

First, you need to create the page that displays the images and contains the form for adding new images. The PhotoGallery.aspx page is contained in Listing 9.28.

LISTING 9.28   PhotoGallery.aspx

```
<%@ Page Language="VB" %>
<!DOCTYPE html PUBLIC "-//W3C//DTD XHTML 1.1//EN"
   "http://www.w3.org/TR/xhtml11/DTD/xhtml11.dtd">
```

LISTING 9.28   Continued

```
<html xmlns="http://www.w3.org/1999/xhtml" >
<head id="Head1" runat="server">
    <title>Photo Gallery</title>
</head>
<body>
    <form id="form1" runat="server">
    <div>

    <asp:DataList
        id="dlstImages"
        DataSourceID="srcImages"
        RepeatColumns="3"
        Runat="server">
        <ItemTemplate>
        <asp:Image ID="Image1"
            ImageUrl='<%# String.Format("DynamicImage.ashx?id={0}", Eval("Id")) %>'
            Width="250"
            Runat="server" />
        <br />
        <%# Eval("Description") %>
    </ItemTemplate>
    </asp:DataList>

    <hr />

    <asp:FormView
        id="frmImage"
        DataSourceID="srcImages"
        DefaultMode="Insert"
        Runat="server">
        <InsertItemTemplate>
        <asp:Label
            id="lblImage"
            Text="Upload Image:"
            AssociatedControlId="upImage"
            Runat="server" />
        <br />
        <asp:FileUpload
            id="upImage"
            FileBytes='<%# Bind("Image") %>'
            Runat="server" />

        <br /><br />
```

LISTING 9.28   Continued

```
            <asp:Label
                id="lblDescription"
                Text="Description:"
                AssociatedControlID="txtDescription"
                Runat="server" />
            <br />
            <asp:TextBox
                id="txtDescription"
                Text='<%# Bind("Description") %>'
                TextMode="MultiLine"
                Columns="50"
                Rows="2"
                Runat="server" />

            <br /><br />

            <asp:Button
                id="btnInsert"
                Text="Add Image"
                CommandName="Insert"
                Runat="server" />
            </InsertItemTemplate>
    </asp:FormView>

    <asp:SqlDataSource
        id="srcImages"
        SelectCommand="SELECT ID,Description FROM Images"
        InsertCommand="INSERT Images (Image,Description)
            VALUES (@Image,@Description)"
        ConnectionString="<%$ ConnectionStrings:Images %>"
        Runat="server" />

    </div>
    </form>
</body>
</html>
```

The page in Listing 9.28 has a FormView control that contains a FileUpload control. You can use the FileUpload control to upload images from your local hard drive to the application's database table.

Also, the page contains a DataList control that is used to display the image. Notice that the Image control contained in the DataList control's ItemTemplate points to a file named `DynamicImage.ashx`. The `DynamicImage.ashx` file represents an HTTP Handler that renders a particular image. The `DynamicImage.ashx` handler is contained in Listing 9.29.

> **NOTE**
>
> HTTP handlers are discussed in detail in Chapter 25, "Working with the HTTP Runtime."

LISTING 9.29   `DynamicImage.ashx`

```vb
<%@ WebHandler Language="VB" Class="DynamicImage" %>

Imports System.Data
Imports System.Web
Imports System.Web.Configuration
Imports System.Web.UI
Imports System.Web.UI.WebControls

''' <summary>
''' Displays an image corresponding to the Id passed
''' in a query string field
''' </summary>
Public Class DynamicImage
        Implements IHttpHandler

    Public Sub ProcessRequest(ByVal context As HttpContext)
➥Implements IHttpHandler.ProcessRequest
        ' Get the Id of the image to display
        Dim imageId As String = context.Request.QueryString("Id")

        ' Use SqlDataSource to grab image bytes
        Dim src As SqlDataSource = New SqlDataSource()
        src.ConnectionString =
➥ WebConfigurationManager.ConnectionStrings("Images").ConnectionString
        src.SelectCommand = "SELECT Image FROM Images WHERE Id=" + imageId

        ' Return a DataView
        Dim view As DataView =
➥CType(src.Select(DataSourceSelectArguments.Empty), DataView)
        context.Response.BinaryWrite(CType(view(0)("Image"), Byte()))

        ' Return a DataReader
        'src.DataSourceMode = SqlDataSourceMode.DataReader
        'Dim reader As IDataReader =
➥CType(src.Select(DataSourceSelectArguments.Empty), IDataReader)
        'reader.Read()
```

9

LISTING 9.29   Continued

```
'context.Response.BinaryWrite(CType(reader("Image"), Byte()))
'reader.Close()

End Sub

Public ReadOnly Property IsReusable() As Boolean
➥Implements IHttpHandler.IsReusable
    Get
        Return False
    End Get
End Property

End Class
```

In the `ProcessRequest()` method, an instance of the `SqlDataSource` control is created. The `SqlDataSource` control's `ConnectionString` and `SelectCommand` properties are initialized. Finally, the `SqlDataSource` control's `Select()` command is executed and the results are rendered with the `Response.BinaryWrite()` method.

Notice that the return value from the `Select()` method is cast explicitly to a `DataView` object. You need to cast the return value to either a `DataView` or `IDataReader` for it to work with the results of the `Select()` method.

In Listing 9.29, the image bytes are returned in a `DataView`. To illustrate how you can use the `Select()` method to return a DataReader, I've also included the code for returning the image with a `DataReader`, but I've added comments to the code so that it won't execute.

Caching Database Data with the `SqlDataSource` Control

The easiest way to dramatically improve the performance of a database-driven website is through caching. Retrieving data from a database is one of the slowest operations that you can perform in a web page. Retrieving data from memory, on the other hand, is lightning fast. The `SqlDataSource` control makes it easy to cache data in your server's memory.

Caching is discussed in detail in Chapter 23, "Caching Application Pages and Data." In that chapter, you learn about all the different caching options supported by the `SqlDataSource` control. However, because it is so easy to cache data with the `SqlDataSource` control and caching has such a dramatic impact on performance, I wanted to provide you with a quick sample of how you can use the `SqlDataSource` control to cache data in this chapter.

The page in Listing 9.30 displays a list of movies that are cached in memory.

LISTING 9.30   CacheSqlDataSource.aspx

```
<%@ Page Language="VB" %>
<!DOCTYPE html PUBLIC "-//W3C//DTD XHTML 1.1//EN"
  "http://www.w3.org/TR/xhtml11/DTD/xhtml11.dtd">
<script runat="server">

    Protected Sub srcMovies_Selecting(ByVal sender As Object,
➥ByVal e As System.Web.UI.WebControls.SqlDataSourceSelectingEventArgs)
        lblMessage.Text = "Selecting data from database"
    End Sub
</script>
<html xmlns="http://www.w3.org/1999/xhtml" >
<head id="Head1" runat="server">
    <title>Cache SqlDataSource</title>
</head>
<body>
    <form id="form1" runat="server">
    <div>

    <asp:Label
        id="lblMessage"
        EnableViewState="false"
        Runat="server" />
    <br /><br />

    <asp:GridView
        id="grdMovies"
        DataSourceID="srcMovies"
        Runat="server" />

    <asp:SqlDataSource
        id="srcMovies"
        EnableCaching="True"
        CacheDuration="3600"
        SelectCommand="SELECT * FROM Movies"
        ConnectionString="<%$ ConnectionStrings:Movies %>"
        OnSelecting="srcMovies_Selecting"
        Runat="server" />

    </div>
    </form>
</body>
</html>
```

9

In Listing 9.30, two properties of the `SqlDataSource` control related to caching are set. First, the `EnableCaching` property is set to the value `True`. Next, the `CacheDuration` property is set to a value that represents `3,600` seconds (one hour). The movies are cached in memory for a maximum of one hour. If you don't supply a value for the `CacheDuration` property, the default value is `Infinite`.

WARNING

It is important to understand that there is no guarantee that the `SqlDataSource` control will cache data for the amount of time specified by its `CacheDuration` property. Behind the scenes, the `SqlDataSource` control uses the `Cache` object for caching. This object supports scavenging. When memory resources become low, the `Cache` object automatically removes items from the cache.

Notice that the page in Listing 9.30 includes a `srcMovies_Selecting()` event handler. This handler is called only when the movies are retrieved from the database rather than from memory. In other words, you can use this event handler to detect when the movies are dropped from the cache (see Figure 9.15).

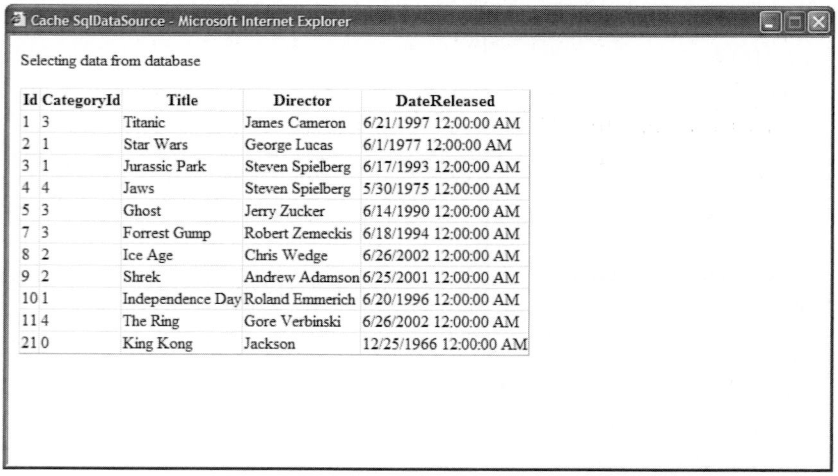

Selecting data from database

Id	CategoryId	Title	Director	DateReleased
1	3	Titanic	James Cameron	6/21/1997 12:00:00 AM
2	1	Star Wars	George Lucas	6/1/1977 12:00:00 AM
3	1	Jurassic Park	Steven Spielberg	6/17/1993 12:00:00 AM
4	4	Jaws	Steven Spielberg	5/30/1975 12:00:00 AM
5	3	Ghost	Jerry Zucker	6/14/1990 12:00:00 AM
7	3	Forrest Gump	Robert Zemeckis	6/18/1994 12:00:00 AM
8	2	Ice Age	Chris Wedge	6/26/2002 12:00:00 AM
9	2	Shrek	Andrew Adamson	6/25/2001 12:00:00 AM
10	1	Independence Day	Roland Emmerich	6/20/1996 12:00:00 AM
11	4	The Ring	Gore Verbinski	6/26/2002 12:00:00 AM
21	0	King Kong	Jackson	12/25/1966 12:00:00 AM

FIGURE 9.15   Caching the data represented by a `SqlDataSource` control.

The page in Listing 9.30 illustrates only one type of caching that you can use with the `SqlDataSource` control. In Chapter 23, you learn about all the advanced caching options supported by the `SqlDataSource` control. For example, by taking advantage of SQL cache dependencies, you can reload the cached data represented by a `SqlDataSource` control automatically when data in a database is changed. For more information, see the final section of Chapter 23, "Caching Application Pages and Data."

Summary

In this chapter, you learned how to use the `SqlDataSource` control to connect and execute commands against a SQL relational database. In the first section, you learned how to represent database connection strings with the `SqlDataSource` control. You learned how to store connection strings in the web configuration file and encrypt the connection strings.

Next, you learned how to execute both inline SQL commands and stored procedures. You also learned how to cancel commands and handle errors gracefully.

This chapter also discussed the different types of ASP.NET parameters that you can use with the `SqlDataSource` control. You learned how to use the `Parameter`, `ControlParameter`, `CookieParameter`, `FormParameter`, `ProfileParameter`, `SessionParameter`, and `QueryStringParameter` objects.

Finally, you learned how to improve the performance of your database-driven applications through caching. You learned how you can cache the data represented by a `SqlDataSource` control in server memory and avoid accessing the database with each page request.

CHAPTER 10

Using List Controls

The List controls enable you to display simple lists of options. For example, you can use the RadioButtonList control to display a group of radio buttons, or the BulletedList control to display a list of links.

In this chapter, you learn how to use each of the List controls included in the ASP.NET Framework. In particular, it discusses the DropDownList, RadioButtonList, ListBox, CheckBoxList, and BulletedList controls. You learn how to bind the different types of List controls to a data source such as a database table. You also learn how to work directly with the list items contained by a List control.

Finally, at the end of this chapter, you learn how to build a custom List control. We create a client-side multi-select List control, which enables you to select multiple list items at a time.\

Overview of the List Controls

All five of the List controls inherit from the base ListControl class. This means that all the List controls share a common set of properties and methods. In this section, you are provided with an overview of the common features of the List controls.

Declaring List Items

The List controls render a list of options. Each option is represented by an instance of the ListItem class. For example, you can use the page in Listing 10.1 to render a set of options for selecting your favorite movie (see Figure 10.1).

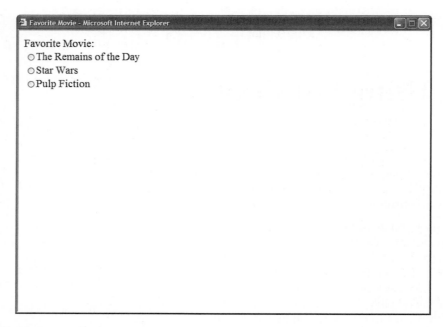

FIGURE 10.1 Displaying a list of movies.

LISTING 10.1 FavoriteMovie.aspx

```
<%@ Page Language="VB" %>
<!DOCTYPE html PUBLIC "-//W3C//DTD XHTML 1.1//EN"
"http://www.w3.org/TR/xhtml11/DTD/xhtml11.dtd">
<html xmlns="http://www.w3.org/1999/xhtml" >
<head id="Head1" runat="server">
    <title>Favorite Movie</title>
</head>
<body>
    <form id="form1" runat="server">
    <div>

    <asp:Label
        id="lblMovies"
        Text="Favorite Movie:"
        AssociatedControlID="rblMovies"
        Runat="server" />

    <asp:RadioButtonList
        id="rblMovies"
        Runat="server">
```

LISTING 10.1   Continued

```
        <asp:ListItem
            Text="The Remains of the Day"
            Value="movie1" />
        <asp:ListItem
            Text="Star Wars"
            Value="movie2" />
        <asp:ListItem
            Text="Pulp Fiction"
            Value="movie3" />
    </asp:RadioButtonList>

    </div>
    </form>
</body>
</html>
```

The page in Listing 10.1 contains a `RadioButtonList` control. This control contains three `ListItem` controls which correspond to the three radio buttons. All the List controls use the `ListItem` control to represent individual list items.

The `ListItem` control supports the following five properties:

- `Attributes`   Enables you to add HTML attributes to a list item.
- `Enabled`   Enables you to disable a list item.
- `Selected`   Enables you to mark a list item as selected.
- `Text`   Enables you to specify the text displayed by the List Item.
- `Value`   Enables you to specify a hidden value associated with the List Item.

You use the `Text` property to indicate the text that you want the option to display, and the `Value` property to indicate a hidden value associated with the option. For example, the hidden value might represent the value of a primary key column in a database table.

The `Selected` property enables you to show a list item as selected. Selected radio buttons and check boxes appear checked. The selected option in a `DropDownList` is the default option displayed. Selected options in a `ListBox` appear highlighted. And, in the case of a `BulletedList` control, the `selected` property has no effect whatsoever.

The `Enabled` property has different effects when used with different List controls. When you set a `ListItem` control's `Enabled` property to the value `False` when using the `DropDownList` or `ListBox` controls, the list item is not rendered to the browser. When you use this property with a `CheckBoxList`, `RadioButtonList`, or `BulletedList` control, then the list item is ghosted and non-functional.

Binding to a Data Source

You can bind any of the List controls to a data source. The List controls support both declarative databinding and programmatic databinding.

For example, the page in Listing 10.2 contains a `DropDownList` control that is bound to the Movies database table with declarative databinding (see Figure 10.2).

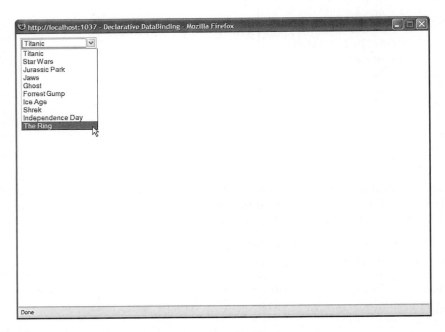

FIGURE 10.2   Displaying list items with declarative databinding.

LISTING 10.2   DeclarativeDataBinding.aspx

```
<%@ Page Language="VB" %>
<!DOCTYPE html PUBLIC "-//W3C//DTD XHTML 1.1//EN"
"http://www.w3.org/TR/xhtml11/DTD/xhtml11.dtd">
<html xmlns="http://www.w3.org/1999/xhtml" >
<head id="Head1" runat="server">
    <title>Declarative DataBinding</title>
</head>
<body>
    <form id="form1" runat="server">
    <div>

    <asp:DropDownList
        id="ddlMovies"
        DataSourceID="srcMovies"
```

LISTING 10.2   Continued

```
            DataTextField="Title"
            DataValueField="Id"
            Runat="server" />

        <asp:SqlDataSource
            id="srcMovies"
            SelectCommand="SELECT Id, Title FROM Movies"
            ConnectionString="<%$ ConnectionStrings:Movies %>"
            Runat="server" />

    </div>
    </form>
</body>
</html>
```

Notice that the DropDownList control's DataSourceID property points to the ID of the SqlDataSource control. When you open the page in Listing 10.2, the SqlDataSource control retrieves the records from the Movies database table. The DropDownList control grabs these records from the SqlDataSource control and creates a ListItem control for each data item.

You also should notice that the DropDownList control has both its DataTextField and DataValueField properties set. When the DropDownList control creates each of its list items, it uses the values of the DataTextField and DataValueField properties to set the Text and Value properties of each list item.

As an alternative to declarative databinding, you can programmatically bind any of the List controls to a data source. For example, the page in Listing 10.3 binds a ListBox control to a collection which represents a shopping cart (see Figure 10.3).

LISTING 10.3   ProgrammaticDataBinding.aspx

```
<%@ Page Language="VB" %>
<%@ Import Namespace="System.Collections.Generic" %>
<!DOCTYPE html PUBLIC "-//W3C//DTD XHTML 1.1//EN"
"http://www.w3.org/TR/xhtml11/DTD/xhtml11.dtd">
<script runat="server">

    ''' <summary>
    ''' Represents an item in the
    ''' shopping cart
    ''' </summary>
    Public Class CartItem
        Private _id As Integer
        Public _description As String
```

LISTING 10.3   Continued

```vb
        Public ReadOnly Property Id() As Integer
            Get
                Return _id
            End Get
        End Property


        Public ReadOnly Property Description() As String
            Get
                Return _description
            End Get
        End Property


        Public Sub New(ByVal id As Integer, ByVal description As String)
            _id = id
            _description = description
        End Sub
    End Class


    Private Sub Page_Load()
        If Not IsPostBack Then
            ' Create shopping cart
            Dim shoppingCart As New List(Of CartItem)()
            shoppingCart.Add(New CartItem(1, "Notebook Computer"))
            shoppingCart.Add(New CartItem(2, "HD Plasma Television"))
            shoppingCart.Add(New CartItem(3, "Lava Lamp"))


            ' Bind ListBox to shopping cart
            lstShoppingCart.DataSource = shoppingCart
            lstShoppingCart.DataBind()
        End If
    End Sub
</script>
<html xmlns="http://www.w3.org/1999/xhtml" >
<head id="Head1" runat="server">
    <title>Programmatic DataBinding</title>
</head>
<body>
    <form id="form1" runat="server">
    <div>


    <asp:ListBox
        id="lstShoppingCart"
        DataTextField="Description"
        DataValueField="Id"
```

LISTING 10.3   Continued

```
        Runat="server" />

    </div>
    </form>
</body>
</html>
```

In Listing 10.3, the ListBox is bound to the collection in the Page_Load() method. Notice that the DataTextField and DataValueField properties of the ListBox control represent properties of the CartItem class.

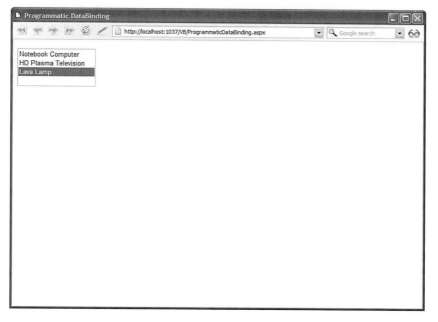

FIGURE 10.3   Show list items with programmatic binding.

> **NOTE**
>
> A List control's DataTextField and DataValueField properties can refer to any public property of a class, but you cannot bind a List control to a public field.

Determining the Selected List Item

Displaying options with the List controls is all very nice, but at some point you need to be able to determine which option a user has selected. The List controls support three properties that you can use to determine the selected list item:

- SelectedIndex   Gets or sets the index of the selected list item.

- SelectedItem   Gets the first selected list item.

- SelectedValue   Gets or sets the value of the first selected list item.

For example, the page in Listing 10.4 enables you to select an item from the DropDownList control and display the value of the selected item's Text property (see Figure 10.4).

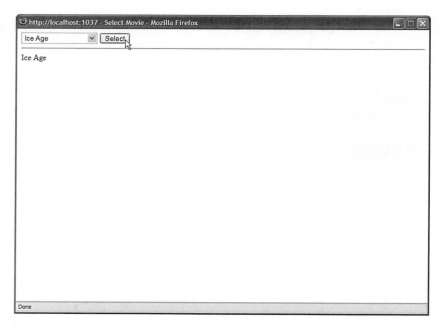

FIGURE 10.4   Selecting an item from a DropDownList control.

LISTING 10.4   SelectMovie.aspx

```
<%@ Page Language="VB" %>
<!DOCTYPE html PUBLIC "-//W3C//DTD XHTML 1.1//EN"
"http://www.w3.org/TR/xhtml11/DTD/xhtml11.dtd">
<script runat="server">

    Protected  Sub btnSelect_Click(ByVal sender As Object, ByVal e As EventArgs)
        lblSelectedMovie.Text = ddlMovies.SelectedItem.Text
    End Sub
</script>
<html xmlns="http://www.w3.org/1999/xhtml" >
<head id="Head1" runat="server">
    <title>Select Movie</title>
```

LISTING 10.4   Continued

```
</head>
<body>
    <form id="form1" runat="server">
    <div>

    <asp:DropDownList
        id="ddlMovies"
        DataSourceID="srcMovies"
        DataTextField="Title"
        DataValueField="Id"
        Runat="server" />

    <asp:Button
        id="btnSelect"
        Text="Select"
        OnClick="btnSelect_Click"
        Runat="server" />

    <hr />

    <asp:Label
        id="lblSelectedMovie"
        Runat="server" />

    <asp:SqlDataSource
        id="srcMovies"
        SelectCommand="SELECT Id, Title FROM Movies"
        ConnectionString="<%$ ConnectionStrings:Movies %>"
        Runat="server" />

    </div>
    </form>
</body>
</html>
```

The SelectedItem property is used to retrieve the selected ListItem control from the DropDownList control. The value of the selected item's Text property is displayed in the Label control.

You can use these properties when you want to associate a List control with another DataBound control. For example, the page in Listing 10.5 contains a DropDownList control that displays a list of movie categories and a GridView control that displays a list of movies that match the selected category (see Figure 10.5).

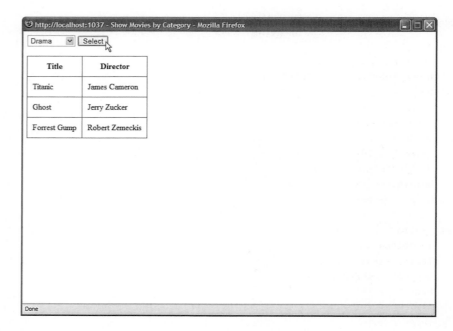

FIGURE 10.5   Master/Details form with a list control.

LISTING 10.5   ShowMoviesByCategory.aspx

```
<%@ Page Language="VB" %>
<!DOCTYPE html PUBLIC "-//W3C//DTD XHTML 1.1//EN"
"http://www.w3.org/TR/xhtml11/DTD/xhtml11.dtd">
<html xmlns="http://www.w3.org/1999/xhtml" >
<head id="Head1" runat="server">
    <style type="text/css">
        .gridView
        {
            margin-top:20px;
        }
        .gridView td, .gridView th
        {
            padding:10px;
        }
    </style>
    <title>Show Movies by Category</title>
</head>
<body>
    <form id="form1" runat="server">
    <div>
```

LISTING 10.5   Continued

```
    <asp:DropDownList
        id="ddlMovieCategory"
        DataSourceID="srcMovieCategories"
        DataTextField="Name"
        DataValueField="Id"
        Runat="server" />

    <asp:Button
        id="btnSelect"
        Text="Select"
        Runat="server" />

    <asp:GridView
        id="grdMovies"
        DataSourceID="srcMovies"
        CssClass="gridView"
        Runat="server" />

    <asp:SqlDataSource
        id="srcMovieCategories"
        SelectCommand="SELECT Id, Name FROM MovieCategories"
        ConnectionString="<%$ ConnectionStrings:Movies %>"
        Runat="server" />

    <asp:SqlDataSource
        id="srcMovies"
        SelectCommand="SELECT Title,Director FROM Movies
            WHERE CategoryId=@Id"
        ConnectionString="<%$ ConnectionStrings:Movies %>"
        Runat="server">
        <SelectParameters>
        <asp:ControlParameter
            Name="Id"
            ControlID="ddlMovieCategory"
            PropertyName="SelectedValue" />
        </SelectParameters>
    </asp:SqlDataSource>

    </div>
    </form>
</body>
</html>
```

The DropDownList control is bound to the srcMovieCategories SqlDataSource control, and the GridView control is bound to the srcMovies SqlDataSource control. The srcMovies SqlDataSource control includes a ControlParameter, which represents the SelectedValue property of the DropDownList control. When you select a movie category from the DropDownList control, the selected value changes and the GridView control displays a list of matching movies.

Appending Data Items

You can mix the list items that you declare in a List control and the list items that are added to the control when it is bound to a data source. This is useful when you want to display a default selection.

For example, imagine that you are creating a form in which you want to require a user to pick an item from a List control. In this situation, you should add a default item to the List Control so you can detect whether a user has actually picked an item.

You can mix declarative list items with databound list items by assigning the value True to the AppendDataBoundItems property. The page in Listing 10.6 illustrates how you can add a default list item to a List control (see Figure 10.6).

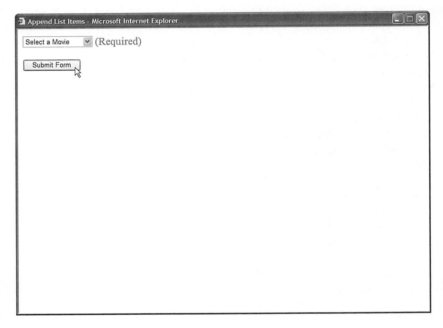

FIGURE 10.6   Displaying a default list item.

LISTING 10.6 AppendListItems.aspx

```
<%@ Page Language="VB" %>
<!DOCTYPE html PUBLIC "-//W3C//DTD XHTML 1.1//EN"
"http://www.w3.org/TR/xhtml11/DTD/xhtml11.dtd">
<html xmlns="http://www.w3.org/1999/xhtml" >
<head id="Head1" runat="server">
    <title>Append List Items</title>
</head>
<body>
    <form id="form1" runat="server">
    <div>

    <asp:DropDownList
        id="ddlMovies"
        DataSourceID="srcMovies"
        DataTextField="Title"
        DataValueField="Id"
        AppendDataBoundItems="True"
        Runat="server">
        <asp:ListItem
            Text="Select a Movie"
            Value="" />
    </asp:DropDownList>

    <asp:RequiredFieldValidator
        id="valMovies"
        Text="(Required)"
        ControlToValidate="ddlMovies"
        Runat="server" />

    <br /><br />

    <asp:Button
        id="btnSubmit"
        Text="Submit Form"
        Runat="server" />

    <asp:SqlDataSource
        id="srcMovies"
        SelectCommand="SELECT Id, Title FROM Movies"
        ConnectionString="<%$ ConnectionStrings:Movies %>"
        Runat="server" />
```

LISTING 10.6   Continued

```
    </div>
    </form>
</body>
</html>
```

The page in Listing 10.6 includes both a DropDownList control and a RequiredFieldValidator control. The DropDownList control includes a list item that displays the text "Select a Movie." The Value property of this list item is set to the empty string. If you attempt to submit the form without selecting a list item other than the default list item, then the RequiredFieldValidator displays an error message.

Notice that the DropDownList control includes an AppendDataBoundItems property which is set to the value True. If you neglect to set this property, then the databound list items overwrite any declarative list items.

Enabling Automatic PostBacks

All the List controls, except for the BulletedList control, support a property named the AutoPostBack property. When this property is assigned the value True, the form containing the List control is automatically posted back to the server whenever a new selection is made.

For example, the page in Listing 10.7 contains a DropDownList control that has its AutoPostBack property enabled. When you select a new item from the DropDownList control, the page is automatically posted back to the server and the Label control displays the selected item.

LISTING 10.7   AutoPostBackListControl.aspx

```
<%@ Page Language="VB" %>
<!DOCTYPE html PUBLIC "-//W3C//DTD XHTML 1.1//EN"
"http://www.w3.org/TR/xhtml11/DTD/xhtml11.dtd">
<script runat="server">

    Protected Sub ddlMovies_SelectedIndexChanged(ByVal sender As Object,
➥ ByVal e As EventArgs)
        lblSelectedMovie.Text = ddlMovies.SelectedItem.Text
    End Sub

</script>
<html xmlns="http://www.w3.org/1999/xhtml" >
<head id="Head1" runat="server">
    <title>AutoPostBack List Control</title>
</head>
<body>
```

LISTING 10.7   Continued

```
<form id="form1" runat="server">
<div>

<asp:DropDownList
    id="ddlMovies"
    DataSourceID="srcMovies"
    DataTextField="Title"
    DataValueField="Id"
    AutoPostBack="true"
    OnSelectedIndexChanged="ddlMovies_SelectedIndexChanged"
    Runat="server" />

<br /><br />

<asp:Label
    id="lblSelectedMovie"
    Runat="server" />

<asp:SqlDataSource
    id="srcMovies"
    SelectCommand="SELECT Id, Title FROM Movies"
    ConnectionString="<%$ ConnectionStrings:Movies %>"
    Runat="server" />

</div>
</form>
</body>
</html>
```

When you enable the `AutoPostBack` property, a JavaScript `onchange()` event handler is added to the List control. The onchange event is supported by all recent browsers including Firefox 1.0 and Opera 8.0.

Notice that the `DropDownList` control has a `SelectedIndexChanged` event handler named `ddlMovies_SelectedIndexChanged()`. The `SelectedIndexChanged` event is raised whenever you make a new selection in the List control (independent of the `AutoPostBack` property). The `ddlMovies_SelectedIndexChanged()` method displays the selected list item in a Label control.

WEB STANDARDS NOTE

You should avoid using the `AutoPostBack` property because it creates accessibility problems for persons with disabilities. If you can't use a mouse, and you are interacting with a website through the keyboard, having a page post back to the server whenever you make a selection change is a very frustrating experience.

Using the Items Collection

All the list items rendered by a List control are contained in the List control's list item collection. This collection is exposed by the Items property.

You can work directly with the list items in this collection. For example, you can add or remove particular list items or you can change the order of the list items.

The page in Listing 10.8 contains two ListBox controls and two button controls. When you click the Add button, a list item is moved from the first ListBox to the second ListBox control. When you click Remove, the list item is moved back to the original List control (see Figure 10.7).

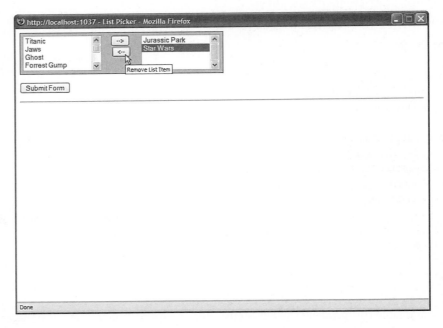

FIGURE 10.7   Using the ListPicker to select list items.

LISTING 10.8   ListPicker.aspx

```
<%@ Page Language="VB" %>
<!DOCTYPE html PUBLIC "-//W3C//DTD XHTML 1.1//EN"
"http://www.w3.org/TR/xhtml11/DTD/xhtml11.dtd">
<script runat="server">

    ''' <summary>
    ''' Move item from All Movies to Favorite Movies
    ''' </summary>
    Protected  Sub btnAdd_Click(ByVal sender As Object, ByVal e As EventArgs)
        Dim item As ListItem =  lstAllMovies.SelectedItem
```

LISTING 10.8   Continued

```
          If Not IsNothing (item) Then
             lstAllMovies.Items.Remove(item)
             lstFavoriteMovies.ClearSelection()
             lstFavoriteMovies.Items.Add(item)
          End If
      End Sub


      ''' <summary>
      ''' Move item from Favorite Movies to All Movies
      ''' </summary>
      Protected  Sub btnRemove_Click(ByVal sender As Object, ByVal e As EventArgs)
          Dim item As ListItem =  lstFavoriteMovies.SelectedItem
          If Not IsNothing (item) Then
             lstFavoriteMovies.Items.Remove(item)
             lstAllMovies.ClearSelection()
             lstAllMovies.Items.Add(item)
          End If
      End Sub


      ''' <summary>
      ''' When the form is submitted,
      ''' show the contents of the
      ''' Favorite Movies ListBox
      ''' </summary>
      Protected  Sub btnSubmit_Click(ByVal sender As Object, ByVal e As EventArgs)
          For Each item As ListItem In lstFavoriteMovies.Items
              lblResults.Text &= "<li>" & item.Text
          Next
      End Sub
</script>
<html xmlns="http://www.w3.org/1999/xhtml" >
<head id="Head1" runat="server">
    <style type="text/css">
        .listPicker
        {
            border:solid 1px black;
            padding:5px;
            width:380px;
            background-color:silver;
        }
        .listPicker select
        {
            width:100%;
        }
    </style>
    <title>List Picker</title>
</head>
```

LISTING 10.8   Continued

```
<body>
    <form id="form1" runat="server">


        <div class="listPicker">
        <div style="float:left;width:40%">
        <asp:ListBox
            id="lstAllMovies"
            DataSourceID="srcMovies"
            DataTextField="Title"
            DataValueField="Id"
            Runat="server" />
        </div>
        <div style="float:left;width:20%;text-align:center">
        <asp:Button
            id="btnAdd"
            Text="--&gt;"
            ToolTip="Add List Item"
            Runat="server" OnClick="btnAdd_Click" />
        <br />
        <asp:Button
            id="btnRemove"
            Text="&lt;--"
            ToolTip="Remove List Item"
            Runat="server" OnClick="btnRemove_Click" />
        </div>
        <div style="float:left;width:40%">
        <asp:ListBox
            id="lstFavoriteMovies"
            Runat="server" />
        </div>
        <br style="clear:both" />
        </div>

        <p>
        <asp:Button
            id="btnSubmit"
            Text="Submit Form"
            Runat="server" OnClick="btnSubmit_Click" />
        </p>

        <hr />
```

LISTING 10.8 Continued

```
<asp:Label
    id="lblResults"
    EnableViewState="false"
    Runat="server" />

<asp:SqlDataSource
    id="srcMovies"
    SelectCommand="SELECT Id, Title FROM Movies"
    ConnectionString="<%$ ConnectionStrings:Movies %>"
    Runat="server" />

</form>
</body>
</html>
```

The first ListBox in Listing 10.8 is bound to the Movies database table. You can use the ListBox controls to pick your favorite movies by moving movie titles from the first ListBox to the second ListBox.

When you click the Add button, the btnAdd_Click() method executes. This method grabs the selected item from the All Movies ListBox and adds it to the Favorite Movies ListBox. The Remove button does exactly the opposite.

Notice that both the btnAdd_Click() and btnRemove_Click() methods call the ClearSelection() method of the ListBox class. This method iterates through all the list items and sets the Selected property for each list item to the value False. If multiple list items are selected, an exception is thrown.

> **NOTE**
>
> One problem with the page discussed in this section is that the page must be posted back to the server each time you move an item from the first ListBox to the second ListBox. At the end of this chapter, you learn how to create a MultiSelectList control, which uses a client-side script to get around this limitation.

Working with the DropDownList Control

The DropDownList control enables you to display a list of options while requiring a minimum of screen real estate. A user can select only one option at a time when using this control.

The page in Listing 10.9 illustrates how you can use the DropDownList control to display all the movie titles from the Movies database table (see Figure 10.8).

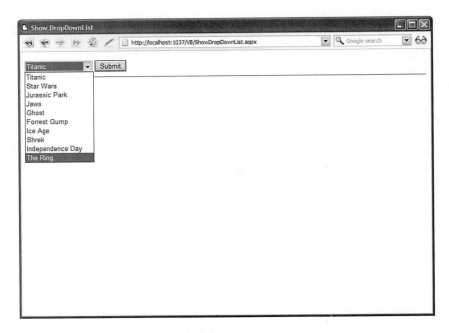

FIGURE 10.8 Displaying list items with the DropDownList control.

LISTING 10.9 ShowDropDownList.aspx

```
<%@ Page Language="VB" %>
<!DOCTYPE html PUBLIC "-//W3C//DTD XHTML 1.1//EN"
"http://www.w3.org/TR/xhtml11/DTD/xhtml11.dtd">
<script runat="server">

    Protected  Sub btnSubmit_Click(ByVal sender As Object, ByVal e As EventArgs)
        lblMovie.Text = ddlMovies.SelectedItem.Text
    End Sub
</script>
<html xmlns="http://www.w3.org/1999/xhtml" >
<head id="Head1" runat="server">
    <title>Show DropDownList</title>
</head>
<body>
    <form id="form1" runat="server">
    <div>

    <asp:DropDownList
        id="ddlMovies"
        DataSourceID="srcMovies"
```

LISTING 10.9 Continued

```
            DataTextField="Title"
            DataValueField="Id"
            Runat="server" />

    <asp:Button
        id="btnSubmit"
        Text="Submit"
        OnClick="btnSubmit_Click"
        Runat="server" />

    <hr />

    <asp:Label
        id="lblMovie"
        Runat="server" />

    <asp:SqlDataSource
        id="srcMovies"
        SelectCommand="SELECT Id, Title FROM Movies"
        ConnectionString="<%$ ConnectionStrings:Movies %>"
        Runat="server" />

    </div>
    </form>
</body>
</html>
```

The `DropDownList` control renders an HTML `<select>` tag. One problem with the HTML `<select>` tag is that it has an infinite z index. In other words, you can't place other objects, such as an absolutely positioned `<div>` tag, in front of a `DropDownList` control in a page.

One way to get around this problem is to use a third-party control such as the `EasyListBox` control (available at http://www.EasyListBox.com). This control works fine when other objects are layered over it. It also supports several advanced features such as multiple columns and images in list items.

Working with the `RadioButtonList` Control

The `RadioButtonList` control, like the `DropDownList` control, enables a user to select only one list item at a time. The `RadioButttonList` control displays a list of radio buttons that can be arranged either horizontally or vertically.

The page in Listing 10.10 illustrates how you can use the `RadioButtonList` control to display a list of movie titles (see Figure 10.9).

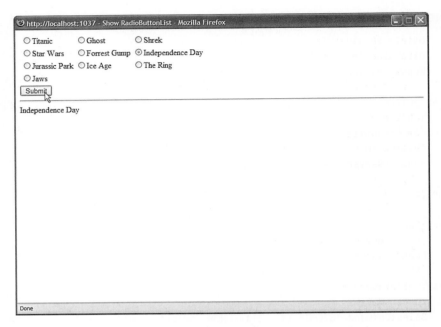

FIGURE 10.9   Displaying list items with the `RadioButtonList` control.

LISTING 10.10   ShowRadioButtonList.aspx

```
<%@ Page Language="VB" %>
<!DOCTYPE html PUBLIC "-//W3C//DTD XHTML 1.1//EN"
"http://www.w3.org/TR/xhtml11/DTD/xhtml11.dtd">
<script runat="server">

    Protected  Sub btnSubmit_Click(ByVal sender As Object, ByVal e As EventArgs)
        lblMovie.Text = rblMovies.SelectedItem.Text
    End Sub
</script>
<html xmlns="http://www.w3.org/1999/xhtml" >
<head id="Head1" runat="server">
    <title>Show RadioButtonList</title>
</head>
<body>
    <form id="form1" runat="server">
    <div>

    <asp:RadioButtonList
        id="rblMovies"
        DataSourceID="srcMovies"
```

LISTING 10.10   Continued

```
            DataTextField="Title"
            DataValueField="Id"
            RepeatColumns="3"
            Runat="server" />

    <asp:Button
        id="btnSubmit"
        Text="Submit"
        Runat="server" OnClick="btnSubmit_Click" />

    <hr />

    <asp:Label
        id="lblMovie"
        Runat="server" />

    <asp:SqlDataSource
        id="srcMovies"
        SelectCommand="SELECT Id, Title FROM Movies"
        ConnectionString="<%$ ConnectionStrings:Movies %>"
        Runat="server" />

    </div>
    </form>
</body>
</html>
```

In Listing 10.10, the radio buttons are rendered in a three-column layout. The `RadioButtonList` control includes three properties that have an effect on its layout:

- `RepeatColumns`   The number of columns of radio buttons to display.

- `RepeatDirection`   The direction that the radio buttons are repeated. Possible values are Horizontal and Vertical.

- `RepeatLayout`   Determines whether the radio buttons are displayed in an HTML table. Possible values are Table and Flow.

By default, the radio buttons rendered by the `RadioButtonList` control are rendered in an HTML table. If you set the `RepeatLayout` property to the value `Flow`, then the radio buttons are not rendered in a table. Even when the `RadioButtonList` renders its items in Flow layout mode, you can specify multiple columns.

Working with the `ListBox` Control

The `ListBox` control is similar to the `DropDownList` control with two important differences. First, the `ListBox` control requires more screen real estate because it always displays a certain number of list items. Furthermore, unlike the `DropDownList` control, the `ListBox` control enables a user to select multiple items.

The page in Listing 10.11 illustrates how you can enable a user to select a single item from a `ListBox` control (see Figure 10.10).

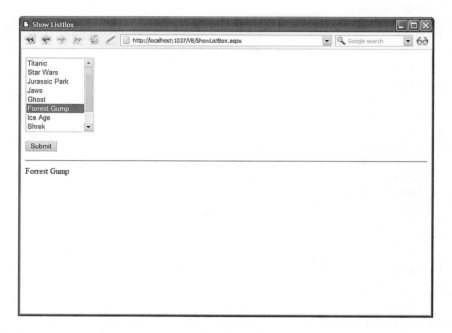

FIGURE 10.10   Displaying list items with the `ListBox` control.

LISTING 10.11   ShowListBox.aspx

```
<%@ Page Language="VB" %>
<!DOCTYPE html PUBLIC "-//W3C//DTD XHTML 1.1//EN"
"http://www.w3.org/TR/xhtml11/DTD/xhtml11.dtd">
<script runat="server">

    Protected  Sub btnSubmit_Click(ByVal sender As Object, ByVal e As EventArgs)
        lblMovie.Text = lstMovies.SelectedItem.Text
    End Sub
</script>
<html xmlns="http://www.w3.org/1999/xhtml" >
<head id="Head1" runat="server">
```

LISTING 10.11   Continued

```
    <title>Show ListBox</title>
</head>
<body>
    <form id="form1" runat="server">
    <div>

    <asp:ListBox
        id="lstMovies"
        DataSourceID="srcMovies"
        DataTextField="Title"
        DataValueField="Id"
        Rows="8"
        Runat="server" />

    <p>
    <asp:Button
        id="btnSubmit"
        Text="Submit"
        OnClick="btnSubmit_Click"
        Runat="server" />
    </p>

    <hr />

    <asp:Label
        id="lblMovie"
        Runat="server" />

    <asp:SqlDataSource
        id="srcMovies"
        SelectCommand="SELECT Id, Title FROM Movies"
        ConnectionString="<%$ ConnectionStrings:Movies %>"
        Runat="server" />

    </div>
    </form>
</body>
</html>
```

Notice that the ListBox control in Listing 10.11 includes a Rows property. The Rows property determines the number of list items that the ListBox displays.

You can also configure the ListBox control to enable a user to select multiple items. This is illustrated in the page in Listing 10.12 (see Figure 10.11).

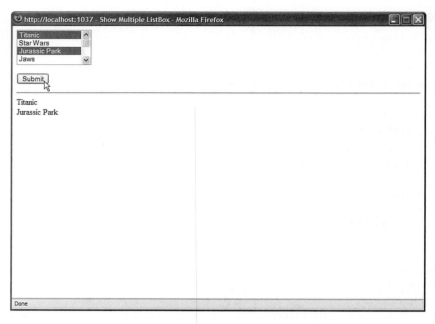

FIGURE 10.11   Selecting multiple list items.

LISTING 10.12   ShowMultipleListBox.aspx

```
<%@ Page Language="VB" %>
<!DOCTYPE html PUBLIC "-//W3C//DTD XHTML 1.1//EN"
"http://www.w3.org/TR/xhtml11/DTD/xhtml11.dtd">
<script runat="server">

    Protected  Sub btnSubmit_Click(ByVal sender As Object, ByVal e As EventArgs)
        For Each item As ListItem In lstMovies.Items
            If item.Selected Then
                lblMovie.Text &= "<li>" & item.Text
            End If
        Next
    End Sub
</script>
<html xmlns="http://www.w3.org/1999/xhtml" >
<head id="Head1" runat="server">
    <title>Show Multiple ListBox</title>
</head>
<body>
    <form id="form1" runat="server">
    <div>
```

LISTING 10.12   Continued

```
    <asp:ListBox
        id="lstMovies"
        DataSourceID="srcMovies"
        DataTextField="Title"
        DataValueField="Id"
        SelectionMode="Multiple"
        Runat="server" />

    <p>
    <asp:Button
        id="btnSubmit"
        Text="Submit"
        OnClick="btnSubmit_Click"
        Runat="server" />
    </p>

    <hr />

    <asp:Label
        id="lblMovie"
        EnableViewState="false"
        Runat="server" />

    <asp:SqlDataSource
        id="srcMovies"
        SelectCommand="SELECT Id, Title FROM Movies"
        ConnectionString="<%$ ConnectionStrings:Movies %>"
        Runat="server" />

    </div>
    </form>
</body>
</html>
```

Notice that the ListBox in Listing 10.12 includes a SelectionMode property that is set to the value Multiple. A user can select multiple items from the ListBox by using the Ctrl or Shift key when clicking more than one list item.

> **WARNING**
>
> Most users don't understand how to select multiple items from a ListBox control. If you want to enable users to pick multiple items, a better approach is to use either the CheckBoxList control (discussed in the next section) or the MultiSelectList control (discussed in the final section of this chapter).

When you click the Submit button in Listing 10.12, all the selected list items are displayed in a Label control. The SelectedItem, SelectedIndex, and SelectedValue properties return only the first list item selected. When multiple items are selected, you need to iterate through the Items collection of the ListBox control to detect the selected items.

Working with the CheckBoxList Control

The CheckBoxList control renders a list of check boxes. The check boxes can be rendered horizontally or vertically. Unlike the other List controls, a user always can select multiple items when using a CheckBoxList control.

For example, the page in Listing 10.13 contains a CheckBoxList control that renders its list items in two columns (see Figure 10.12).

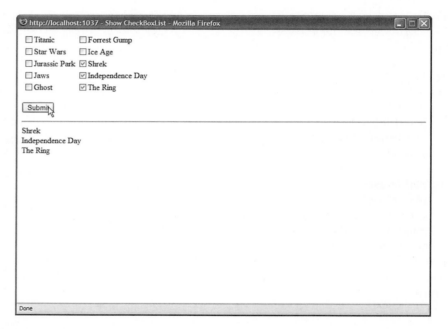

FIGURE 10.12   Displaying list items with the CheckBoxList control.

LISTING 10.13   ShowCheckBoxList.aspx

```
<%@ Page Language="VB" %>
<!DOCTYPE html PUBLIC "-//W3C//DTD XHTML 1.1//EN"
"http://www.w3.org/TR/xhtml11/DTD/xhtml11.dtd">
<script runat="server">

    Protected  Sub btnSubmit_Click(ByVal sender As Object, ByVal e As EventArgs)
        For Each item As ListItem In cblMovies.Items
```

LISTING 10.13 Continued

```
                if (item.Selected)
                    lblMovie.Text &= "<li>" & item.Text
                End If
            Next
        End Sub
    </script>
    <html xmlns="http://www.w3.org/1999/xhtml" >
    <head id="Head1" runat="server">
        <title>Show CheckBoxList</title>
    </head>
    <body>
        <form id="form1" runat="server">
        <div>

        <asp:CheckBoxList
            id="cblMovies"
            DataSourceID="srcMovies"
            DataTextField="Title"
            DataValueField="Id"
            RepeatColumns="2"
            Runat="server" />

        <p>
        <asp:Button
            id="btnSubmit"
            Text="Submit"
            OnClick="btnSubmit_Click"
            Runat="server" />
        </p>

        <hr />

        <asp:Label
            id="lblMovie"
            EnableViewState="false"
            Runat="server" />

        <asp:SqlDataSource
            id="srcMovies"
            SelectCommand="SELECT Id, Title FROM Movies"
            ConnectionString="<%$ ConnectionStrings:Movies %>"
            Runat="server" />
```

LISTING 10.13   Continued

```
        </div>
        </form>
</body>
</html>
```

When you click the Submit button, the values of the Text property of any selected check boxes are displayed in a Label control. The selected check boxes are retrieved from the CheckBoxList control's Items property.

The CheckBoxList control includes three properties that affect its layout:

- RepeatColumns   The number of columns of check boxes to display.

- RepeatDirection   The direction in which the check boxes are rendered. Possible values are Horizontal and Vertical.

- RepeatLayout   Determines whether the check boxes are displayed in an HTML table. Possible values are Table and Flow.

Normally, a CheckBoxList control renders its list items in an HTML table. When the RepeatLayout property is set to the value Flow, the items are not rendered in a table.

Working with the BulletedList Control

The BulletedList control renders either an unordered (bulleted) or ordered (numbered) list. Each list item can be rendered as plain text, a LinkButton control, or a link to another web page.

For example, the page in Listing 10.14 uses the BulletedList control to render an unordered list of movies (see Figure 10.13).

LISTING 10.14   ShowBulletedList.aspx

```
<%@ Page Language="VB" %>
<!DOCTYPE html PUBLIC "-//W3C//DTD XHTML 1.1//EN"
"http://www.w3.org/TR/xhtml11/DTD/xhtml11.dtd">
<html xmlns="http://www.w3.org/1999/xhtml" >
<head id="Head1" runat="server">
    <title>Show BulletedList</title>
</head>
<body>
    <form id="form1" runat="server">
    <div>

    <asp:BulletedList
        id="blMovies"
        DataSourceID="srcMovies"
```

LISTING 10.14   Continued

```
            DataTextField="Title"
            Runat="server" />

    <asp:SqlDataSource
            id="srcMovies"
            SelectCommand="SELECT Title FROM Movies"
            ConnectionString="<%$ ConnectionStrings:Movies %>"
            Runat="server" />

    </div>
    </form>
</body>
</html>
```

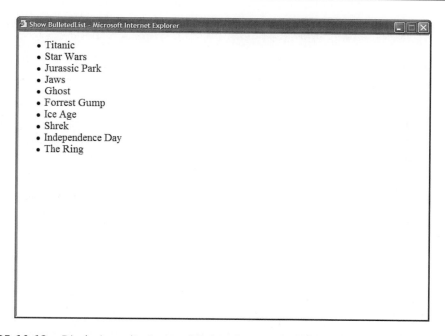

FIGURE 10.13   Displaying a list items with the BulletedList control.

You can control the appearance of the bullets that appear for each list item with the BulletStyle property. This property accepts the following values:

- Circle

- CustomImage

- Disc

- LowerAlpha

- LowerRoman

- NotSet

- Numbered

- Square

- UpperAlpha

- UpperRoman

You can set `BulletStyle` to `Numbered` to display a numbered list. If you set this property to the value `CustomImage` and assign an image path to the `BulletImageUrl` property, then you can associate an image with each list item. For example, the page in Listing 10.15 displays an image named `Bullet.gif` with each list item (see Figure 10.14).

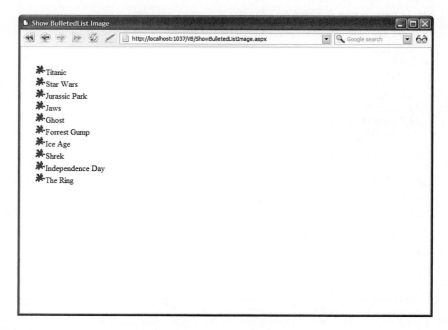

FIGURE 10.14   Displaying image bullets.

LISTING 10.15   ShowBulletedListImage.aspx

```
<%@ Page Language="VB" %>
<!DOCTYPE html PUBLIC "-//W3C//DTD XHTML 1.1//EN"
"http://www.w3.org/TR/xhtml11/DTD/xhtml11.dtd">
<html xmlns="http://www.w3.org/1999/xhtml" >
<head id="Head1" runat="server">
    <title>Show BulletedList Image</title>
</head>
<body>
    <form id="form1" runat="server">
    <div>

    <asp:BulletedList
        id="blMovies"
        DataSourceID="srcMovies"
        DataTextField="Title"
        BulletStyle="CustomImage"
        BulletImageUrl="~/Images/Bullet.gif"
        Runat="server" />

    <asp:SqlDataSource
        id="srcMovies"
        SelectCommand="SELECT Title FROM Movies"
        ConnectionString="<%$ ConnectionStrings:Movies %>"
        Runat="server" />

    </div>
    </form>
</body>
</html>
```

You can modify the appearance of each list item by modifying the value of the DisplayMode property. This property accepts one of the following values from the BulletedListDisplayMode enumeration:

- HyperLink   Each list item is rendered as a link to another page.

- LinkButton   Each list item is rendered by a LinkButton control.

- Text   Each list item is rendered as plain text.

For example, the page in Listing 10.16 displays a list of links to other websites (see Figure 10.15).

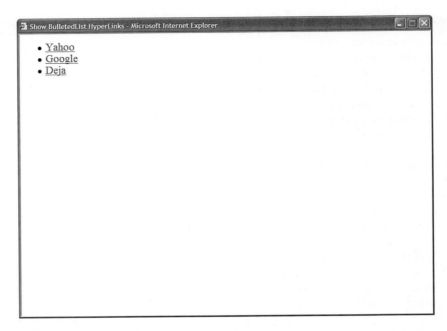

FIGURE 10.15   Displaying list items as hyperlinks.

LISTING 10.16   ShowBulletedListHyperLinks.aspx

```
<%@ Page Language="VB" %>
<!DOCTYPE html PUBLIC "-//W3C//DTD XHTML 1.1//EN"
"http://www.w3.org/TR/xhtml11/DTD/xhtml11.dtd">
<html xmlns="http://www.w3.org/1999/xhtml" >
<head id="Head1" runat="server">
    <title>Show BulletedList HyperLinks</title>
</head>
<body>
    <form id="form1" runat="server">

    <asp:BulletedList
        id="blWebsites"
        DisplayMode="HyperLink"
        Target="_blank"
        Runat="server">
        <asp:ListItem
            Text="Yahoo"
```

LISTING 10.16   Continued

```
              Value="http://www.Yahoo.com" />
          <asp:ListItem
              Text="Google"
              Value="http://www.Google.com" />
          <asp:ListItem
              Text="Deja"
              Value="http://www.Deja.com" />
      </asp:BulletedList>

    </form>
</body>
</html>
```

Each list item has both its Text and Value properties set. The Text property contains the text that is displayed for the list item, and the Value property contains the URL for the other website. Notice that the Target property is set to the value _blank. When you click one of the hyperlinks, the page is opened in a new window.

> **WARNING**
>
> The BulletedList control is different from the other List controls because it does not support the SelectedIndex, SelectedItem, and SelectedValue properties.

Creating a Custom List Control

All the List controls inherit from the base ListControl class. If you are not happy with the existing List controls, there is nothing to prevent you from building your own.

In this section, we create a custom List control named the MultiSelectList control. This control renders two list boxes and an Add and Remove button. You can click the buttons to move items between the two list boxes (see Figure 10.16).

The custom control uses client-side JavaScript to move the items between the two list boxes. Using JavaScript enables you to avoid posting the page back to the server each time a list item is moved. The client-side JavaScript is standards compliant so it will work with Internet Explorer 6.0, FireFox 1.0, and Opera 8.0.

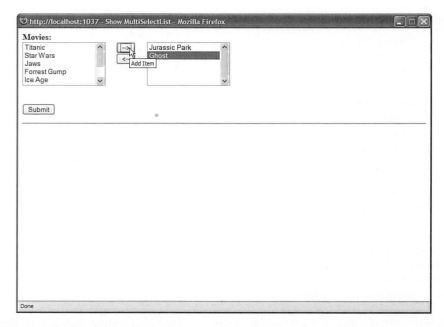

FIGURE 10.16   Using the `MultiSelectList` control.

The code for the custom `MultiSelectList` is contained in Listing 10.17.

LISTING 10.17   MultiSelectList.vb

```vb
Imports System
Imports System.Web
Imports System.Web.UI
Imports System.Web.UI.WebControls
Imports System.Collections.Specialized

Namespace myControls


    ''' <summary>
    ''' Enables you to select mulitple list items
    ''' from two list boxes
    ''' </summary>
    <ValidationProperty("SelectedItem")> _
    Public Class MultiSelectList
        Inherits ListControl
        Implements IPostBackDataHandler
        Private _rows As Integer = 5
```

LISTING 10.17   Continued

```
''' <summary>
''' This control is contained in a div
''' tag
''' </summary>
Protected Overrides ReadOnly Property TagKey() As HtmlTextWriterTag
    Get
        Return HtmlTextWriterTag.Div
    End Get
End Property


''' <summary>
''' The number of rows of list items to display
''' </summary>
Public Property Rows() As Integer
    Get
        Return _rows
    End Get
    Set(ByVal Value As Integer)
        _rows = Value
    End Set
End Property



''' <summary>
''' Name passed to client-side script
''' </summary>
Private ReadOnly Property BaseName() As String
    Get
        Return ClientID & ClientIDSeparator
    End Get
End Property

''' <summary>
''' Name of unselected items list box
''' </summary>
Private ReadOnly Property UnselectedListName() As String
    Get
        Return BaseName & "unselected"
    End Get
End Property

''' <summary>
''' Name of selected items list box
''' </summary>
```

LISTING 10.17   Continued

```vb
        Private ReadOnly Property SelectedListName() As String
            Get
                Return BaseName & "selected"
            End Get
        End Property


        ''' <summary>
        ''' Name of hidden input field
        ''' </summary>
        Private ReadOnly Property HiddenName() As String
            Get
                Return BaseName & "hidden"
            End Get
        End Property


        ''' <summary>
        ''' Register client scripts
        ''' </summary>
        Protected Overrides Sub OnPreRender(ByVal e As EventArgs)
            Page.RegisterRequiresPostBack(Me)

            ' Register hidden field
            Page.ClientScript.RegisterHiddenField(HiddenName, String.Empty)

            ' Register Include File
            If Not Page.ClientScript.IsClientScriptIncludeRegistered("MultiSe-
lectList") Then
                Page.ClientScript.RegisterClientScriptInclude("MultiSelectList",
➥Page.ResolveUrl("~/ClientScripts/MultiSelectList.js"))
            End If

            ' Register submit script
            Dim submitScript As String =
➥String.Format("multiSelectList_submit('{0}')", BaseName)
            Page.ClientScript.RegisterOnSubmitStatement(Me.GetType(), Me.ClientID,
submitScript)

            MyBase.OnPreRender(e)
        End Sub


        ''' <summary>
        ''' Render list boxes and buttons
        ''' </summary>
```

LISTING 10.17   Continued

```vb
    Protected Overrides Sub RenderContents(ByVal writer As HtmlTextWriter)
        ' Render Unselected
        RenderUnselected(writer)

        ' Render Buttons
        RenderButtons(writer)

        ' Render Selected
        RenderSelected(writer)

        ' Render clear break
        writer.AddStyleAttribute("clear", "both")
        writer.RenderBeginTag(HtmlTextWriterTag.Br)
        writer.RenderEndTag()
    End Sub

    ''' <summary>
    ''' Render the buttons
    ''' </summary>
    Private Sub RenderButtons(ByVal writer As HtmlTextWriter)
        writer.AddStyleAttribute("float", "left")
        writer.AddStyleAttribute(HtmlTextWriterStyle.Width, "20%")
        writer.AddStyleAttribute(HtmlTextWriterStyle.TextAlign, "center")
        writer.RenderBeginTag(HtmlTextWriterTag.Div)

        Dim addScript As String = String.Format("return
➥multiSelectList_add('{0}');", BaseName)
        writer.AddAttribute(HtmlTextWriterAttribute.Onclick, addScript)
        writer.AddAttribute(HtmlTextWriterAttribute.Title, "Add Item")
        writer.RenderBeginTag(HtmlTextWriterTag.Button)
        writer.Write("--&gt;")
        writer.RenderEndTag()
        writer.WriteBreak()
        Dim removeScript As String = String.Format("return
➥multiSelectList_remove('{0}');", BaseName)
        writer.AddAttribute(HtmlTextWriterAttribute.Onclick, removeScript)
        writer.AddAttribute(HtmlTextWriterAttribute.Title, "Remove Item")
        writer.RenderBeginTag(HtmlTextWriterTag.Button)
        writer.Write("&lt;--")
        writer.RenderEndTag()

        writer.RenderEndTag()
    End Sub
```

LISTING 10.17   Continued

```
''' <summary>
''' Render unselected list box
''' </summary>
Private Sub RenderUnselected(ByVal writer As HtmlTextWriter)
    writer.AddStyleAttribute("float", "left")
    writer.AddStyleAttribute(HtmlTextWriterStyle.Width, "40%")
    writer.RenderBeginTag(HtmlTextWriterTag.Div)
    writer.AddAttribute(HtmlTextWriterAttribute.Size, _rows.ToString())
    writer.AddStyleAttribute(HtmlTextWriterStyle.Width, "100%")
    writer.AddAttribute(HtmlTextWriterAttribute.Id, UnselectedListName)
    writer.AddAttribute(HtmlTextWriterAttribute.Name, UnselectedListName)
    writer.RenderBeginTag(HtmlTextWriterTag.Select)
    For Each item As ListItem In Items
        If Not item.Selected Then
            RenderListItem(writer, item)
        End If
    Next
    writer.RenderEndTag()
    writer.RenderEndTag()
End Sub

''' <summary>
''' Render selected list items
''' </summary>
Private Sub RenderSelected(ByVal writer As HtmlTextWriter)
    writer.AddStyleAttribute("float", "left")
    writer.AddStyleAttribute(HtmlTextWriterStyle.Width, "40%")
    writer.RenderBeginTag(HtmlTextWriterTag.Div)
    writer.AddAttribute(HtmlTextWriterAttribute.Size, _rows.ToString())
    writer.AddStyleAttribute(HtmlTextWriterStyle.Width, "100%")
    writer.AddAttribute(HtmlTextWriterAttribute.Id, SelectedListName)
    writer.AddAttribute(HtmlTextWriterAttribute.Name, SelectedListName)
    writer.RenderBeginTag(HtmlTextWriterTag.Select)
    For Each item As ListItem In Items
        If item.Selected Then
            RenderListItem(writer, item)
        End If
    Next
    writer.RenderEndTag()
    writer.RenderEndTag()
End Sub

''' <summary>
''' Render a list item
```

LISTING 10.17 Continued

```
    ''' </summary>
        Private Sub RenderListItem(ByVal writer As HtmlTextWriter, ByVal item As
➥ListItem)
            writer.AddAttribute(HtmlTextWriterAttribute.Value, item.Value)
            writer.RenderBeginTag(HtmlTextWriterTag.Option)
            writer.Write(item.Text)
            writer.RenderEndTag()
        End Sub


    ''' <summary>
    ''' Process postback data
    ''' </summary>
        Public Function LoadPostData(ByVal postDataKey As String,
➥ByVal postCollection As NameValueCollection) As Boolean Implements
➥  IPostBackDataHandler.LoadPostData
            EnsureDataBound()
            ClearSelection()

            Dim values As String = postCollection(HiddenName)
            If values <> String.Empty Then
                Dim splitValues() As String = values.Split(","c)
                For Each value As String In splitValues
                    Items.FindByValue(value).Selected = True
                Next
            End If
            Return False
        End Function


    ''' <summary>
    ''' Required by the IPostBackDataHandler interface
    ''' </summary>
        Public Sub RaisePostDataChangedEvent() Implements
IPostBackDataHandler.RaisePostDataChangedEvent
        End Sub


    End Class
End Namespace
```

Notice that the TagKey property of the base ListControl class is overridden. The elements
of the control are contained in an HTML <div> tag.

The MultiSelectList renders its user interface in the RenderContents() method. This
method renders the two list boxes and button controls. Each unselected list item is
rendered in the first list box and each selected item is rendered in the second list box.

Furthermore, the `MultiSelectList` control implements the `IPostBackDataHandler` interface. When a user posts a page that contains the `MultiSelectList` control to the server, each item that the user selected is retrieved and the Items collection of the List control is updated.

The control takes advantage of a client-side JavaScript library contained in a file named `MultiSelectList.js`. This JavaScript library is registered in the control's `OnPreRender()` method. The `MultiSelectList.js` library is contained in Listing 10.18.

LISTING 10.18 `MultiSelectList.js`

```
function multiSelectList_add(baseName)
{
    var unselectedList = document.getElementById(baseName + 'unselected');
    var selectedList = document.getElementById(baseName + 'selected');

    // Copy selected items
    for (var i=0;i < unselectedList.options.length;i++)
    {
        if (unselectedList.options[i].selected)
        {
            var item = unselectedList.removeChild(unselectedList.options[i]);
            selectedList.appendChild(item);
        }
    }

    // Prevent post
    return false;
}


function multiSelectList_remove(baseName)
{
    var unselectedList = document.getElementById(baseName + 'unselected');
    var selectedList = document.getElementById(baseName + 'selected');

    // Copy unselected items
    for (var i=0;i < selectedList.options.length;i++)
    {
        if (selectedList.options[i].selected)
        {
            var item = selectedList.removeChild(selectedList.options[i]);
            unselectedList.appendChild(item);
        }
    }
}
```

LISTING 10.18   Continued

```
    // Prevent post
    return false;
}



// This function executes when the page
// is submitted. It stuffs all the
// selected items into a hidden field
function multiSelectList_submit(baseName)
{

    var hidden = document.getElementById(baseName + 'hidden');

    var selectedList = document.getElementById(baseName + 'selected');

    var values = new Array();
    for (var i=0;i<selectedList.options.length;i++)
        values.push(selectedList.options[i].value);

    hidden.value = values.join(',');

}
```

Listing 10.18 contains three JavaScript functions. The first two functions simply move list items from one list box to the other list box. The `multiSelectList_submit()` function is called immediately before a page containing the `MultiSelectList` control is posted to the server. This control records each of the selected list items (the items in the second list box) to a hidden form field.

The page in Listing 10.19 illustrates how you can use the `MultiSelectList` control.

LISTING 10.19   ShowMultiSelectList.aspx

```
<%@ Page Language="VB" %>
<%@ Register TagPrefix="custom" Namespace="myControls" %>
<!DOCTYPE html PUBLIC "-//W3C//DTD XHTML 1.1//EN"
"http://www.w3.org/TR/xhtml11/DTD/xhtml11.dtd">
<script runat="server">
    Protected  Sub btnSubmit_Click(ByVal sender As Object, ByVal e As EventArgs)
        For Each item As ListItem In MultiSelectList1.Items
            If item.Selected Then
                lblSelected.Text &= String.Format("<li>{0} ({1})",
➥item.Text, item.Value)
```

LISTING 10.18 Continued

```
            End If
        Next
    End Sub

</script>
<html xmlns="http://www.w3.org/1999/xhtml" >
<head id="Head1" runat="server">
    <title>Show MultiSelectList</title>
</head>
<body>
    <form id="form1" runat="server">
    <div>

    <b>Movies:</b>

    <custom:MultiSelectList
        id="MultiSelectList1"
        DataSourceID="srcMovies"
        DataTextField="Title"
        DataValueField="Id"
        Style="width:400px"
        Runat="server" />

    <asp:RequiredFieldValidator
        id="val"
        ControlToValidate="MultiSelectList1"
        Text="Required"
        Runat="server" />

    <asp:SqlDataSource
        id="srcMovies"
        SelectCommand="SELECT Id, Title FROM Movies"
        ConnectionString="<%$ ConnectionStrings:Movies %>"
        Runat="server" />

    <p>
    <asp:Button
        id="btnSubmit"
        Text="Submit"
        Runat="server" OnClick="btnSubmit_Click" />
    </p>

    <hr />
```

LISTING 10.18   Continued

```
    <asp:Label
        id="lblSelected"
        EnableViewState="false"
        Runat="server" />

    </div>
    </form>
</body>
</html>
```

In the page in Listing 10.19, the `MultiSelectList` control is bound to a `SqlDataSource` control, which represents the contents of the Movies database table. You can select movie titles in the `MultiSelectList` control by moving movie titles from one list box to the second list box. When you click the Submit button, the selected movies are displayed in a Label control.

Summary

In this chapter, you learned how to use List controls to display simple option lists. You learned how to work with the `DropDownList`, `RadioButtonList`, `ListBox`, `CheckBoxList`, and `BulletedList` controls.

You also saw the common features of the List controls. You learned how to append data items to a List control and automatically post a form containing a List control back to the server.

Finally, you worked through the creation of a custom List control, which involved deriving a new control from the base `ListControl` class. The custom List control takes advantage of client-side JavaScript to enable users to select multiple list items without requiring a page to be posted back to the server when each item is selected.

CHAPTER 11

Using the GridView Control

The GridView control is the workhorse of the ASP.NET 2.0 Framework. It is one of the most feature-rich and complicated of all the ASP.NET controls. The GridView control enables you to display, select, sort, page, and edit data items such as database records.

> **NOTE**
>
> The GridView control supersedes the DataGrid control included in the ASP.NET 1.x Framework. The DataGrid control is still included in ASP.NET 2.0 for backward compatibility, but you should use the GridView instead because it is a more powerful control.

In this chapter, you learn everything you ever wanted to know about the GridView control. You learn how to use all the basic features of the GridView control. For example, you learn how to use this control to display, select, sort, page, and edit database records. You also learn how to use AJAX with the GridView control when sorting and paging records.

You also get the chance to tackle several advanced topics. For example, you learn how to highlight certain rows in a GridView depending on the data the row represents. You also learn how to display column summaries.

Finally, you learn how to extend the GridView control by building custom GridView fields. At the end of this chapter, we build a LongTextField, a DeleteButtonField, and a ValidatedField.

GridView **Control Fundamentals**

In this section, you learn how to take advantage of all the basic features of the GridView control. In particular, you learn how to display, select, sort, page, and edit database data with a GridView control. We also discuss GridView formatting options.

Displaying Data

The GridView renders its data items in an HTML table. Each data item is rendered in a distinct HTML table row. For example, the page in Listing 11.1 demonstrates how you can use the GridView to display the contents of the Movies database table (see Figure 11.1).

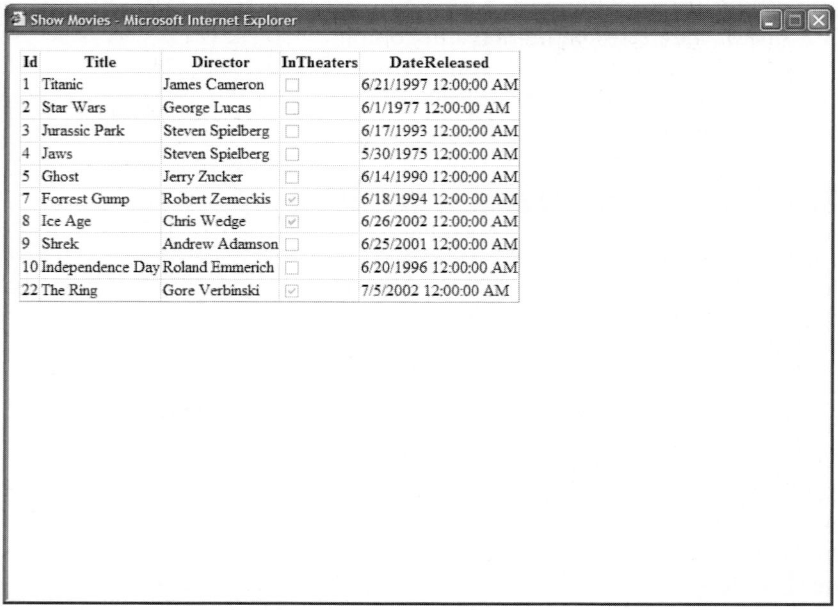

Show Movies - Microsoft Internet Explorer

Id	Title	Director	InTheaters	DateReleased
1	Titanic	James Cameron	☐	6/21/1997 12:00:00 AM
2	Star Wars	George Lucas	☐	6/1/1977 12:00:00 AM
3	Jurassic Park	Steven Spielberg	☐	6/17/1993 12:00:00 AM
4	Jaws	Steven Spielberg	☐	5/30/1975 12:00:00 AM
5	Ghost	Jerry Zucker	☐	6/14/1990 12:00:00 AM
7	Forrest Gump	Robert Zemeckis	☑	6/18/1994 12:00:00 AM
8	Ice Age	Chris Wedge	☑	6/26/2002 12:00:00 AM
9	Shrek	Andrew Adamson	☐	6/25/2001 12:00:00 AM
10	Independence Day	Roland Emmerich	☐	6/20/1996 12:00:00 AM
22	The Ring	Gore Verbinski	☑	7/5/2002 12:00:00 AM

FIGURE 11.1   Displaying data with the GridView control.

LISTING 11.1   ShowMovies.aspx

```
<%@ Page Language="VB" %>
<!DOCTYPE html PUBLIC "-//W3C//DTD XHTML 1.1//EN"
  "http://www.w3.org/TR/xhtml11/DTD/xhtml11.dtd">
<html xmlns="http://www.w3.org/1999/xhtml" >
<head id="Head1" runat="server">
    <title>Show Movies</title>
</head>
<body>
    <form id="form1" runat="server">
```

LISTING 11.1   Continued

```
    <div>

    <asp:GridView
        id="grdMovies"
        DataSourceID="srcMovies"
        Runat="server" />

    <asp:SqlDataSource
        id="srcMovies"
        ConnectionString="<%$ ConnectionStrings:Movies %>"
        SelectCommand="SELECT Id,Title,Director,InTheaters,DateReleased
            FROM Movies"
        Runat="server" />

    </div>
    </form>
</body>
</html>
```

In Listing 11.1, the `GridView` control is bound to a `SqlDataSource` control, which represents the Movies database table. The `GridView` is associated with its data source through its `DataSourceID` property.

Notice that the `GridView` control automatically renders a check box for any Boolean fields. In the case of Listing 11.1, the `GridView` renders a check box for the InTheaters database column. For all other types of fields, the `GridView` simply renders the contents of the field.

> **WEB STANDARDS NOTE**
>
> The `GridView` control was designed to meet XHTML and accessibility guidelines. For example, the control uses the `<th>` tag to render its headers. Furthermore, each header tag includes a `scope="col"` attribute.

> **VISUAL WEB DEVELOPER NOTE**
>
> You can add a `GridView` and `SqlDataSource` control to a page quickly by dragging a database table from the Database Explorer window onto a page in Design view. When you drag a database table onto the page, a `SqlDataSource` is automatically created, which retrieves all the rows and all the columns from a database table.

The `GridView` control also supports programmatic databinding. In Listing 11.2, the `GridView` control is used to display a list of shopping list items represented by a Generic List collection.

LISTING 11.2   ShowShoppingList.aspx

```
<%@ Page Language="VB" %>
<%@ Import Namespace="System.Collections.Generic" %>
<!DOCTYPE html PUBLIC "-//W3C//DTD XHTML 1.1//EN"
   "http://www.w3.org/TR/xhtml11/DTD/xhtml11.dtd">
<script runat="server">

    Sub Page_Load()
        ' Build shopping list
        Dim shoppingList As New List(Of String)()
        shoppingList.Add("Bread")
        shoppingList.Add("Milk")
        shoppingList.Add("Beer")
        shoppingList.Add("Waffles")

        ' Bind to GridView
        grdShoppingList.DataSource = shoppingList
        grdShoppingList.DataBind()
    End Sub

</script>
<html xmlns="http://www.w3.org/1999/xhtml" >
<head id="Head1" runat="server">
    <title>Show Shopping List</title>
</head>
<body>
    <form id="form1" runat="server">
    <div>

    <asp:GridView
        id="grdShoppingList"
        Runat="server" />

    </div>
    </form>
</body>
</html>
```

Notice that the `GridView` is bound to the shopping list in the `Page_Load()` method. Its `DataSource` property points to the List collection, and its `DataBind()` method is called to load the items from the List collection and display them.

Selecting Data

You can enable a user to select a particular row in a GridView control. This is useful when you want to build single-page Master/Details forms. For example, the page in Listing 11.3 contains two GridView controls. The first GridView displays a list of movie categories. When you select a category, the second GridView displays a list of matching movies (see Figure 11.2).

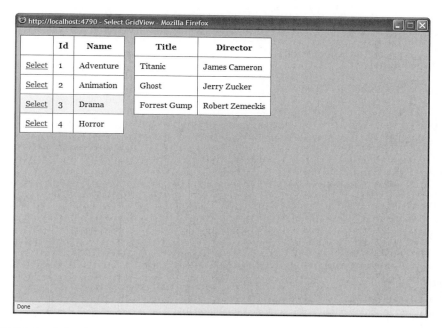

FIGURE 11.2   Selecting a GridView row.

LISTING 11.3   SelectGridView.aspx

```
<%@ Page Language="VB" %>
<!DOCTYPE html PUBLIC "-//W3C//DTD XHTML 1.1//EN"
   "http://www.w3.org/TR/xhtml11/DTD/xhtml11.dtd">
<html xmlns="http://www.w3.org/1999/xhtml" >
<head id="Head1" runat="server">
    <style type="text/css">
        html
        {
            background-color:silver;
            font-family:Georgia, Serif;
        }
        .gridView
```

LISTING 11.3   Continued

```
        {
            float:left;
            margin-right:20px;
            background-color:white;
        }
        .gridView td, .gridView th
        {
            padding:10px;
        }
        .selectedRow
        {
            background-color:yellow;
        }
    </style>
    <title>Select GridView</title>
</head>
<body>
    <form id="form1" runat="server">
    <div>

    <asp:GridView
        id="grdMovieCategories"
        DataKeyNames="Id"
        DataSourceID="srcMovieCategories"
        AutoGenerateSelectButton="true"
        SelectedRowStyle-CssClass="selectedRow"
        CssClass="gridView"
        Runat="server" />

    <asp:GridView
        id="grdMovies"
        DataSourceID="srcMovies"
        CssClass="gridView"
        Runat="server" />

    <asp:SqlDataSource
        id="srcMovieCategories"
        ConnectionString="<%$ ConnectionStrings:Movies %>"
        SelectCommand="SELECT Id, Name FROM MovieCategories"
        Runat="server" />

    <asp:SqlDataSource
        id="srcMovies"
```

LISTING 11.3   Continued

```
        ConnectionString="<%$ ConnectionStrings:Movies %>"
        SelectCommand="SELECT Title,Director FROM Movies
            WHERE CategoryId=@CategoryId"
        Runat="server">
        <SelectParameters>
        <asp:ControlParameter
            Name="CategoryId"
            ControlID="grdMovieCategories"
            PropertyName="SelectedValue" />
        </SelectParameters>
    </asp:SqlDataSource>

    </div>
    </form>
</body>
</html>
```

Notice that the first GridView has its AutoGenerateSelectButton property enabled. When this property has the value True, a Select link is displayed next to each row.

You can determine which row is selected in a GridView control by using any of the following properties:

- SelectedDataKey—Returns the DataKey object associated with the selected row (useful when there are multiple data keys).

- SelectedIndex—Returns the (zero-based) index of the selected row.

- SelectedValue—Returns the data key associated with the selected row.

- SelectedRow—Returns the actual row (GridViewRow object) associated with the selected row.

In most cases, you use the SelectedValue property to determine the value associated with a particular row. The SelectedValue property returns the data key associated with a row. The following section discusses data keys.

> **NOTE**
>
> If you want to customize the appearance of the Select link, then you can use a CommandField control instead of using the AutoGenerateSelectButton property. The CommandField control is discussed later in this chapter in the section entitled "Using Fields with the GridView Control."

Using Data Keys

You associate a value with each row in a GridView by providing a value for the GridView control's DataKeyNames property. You can assign the name of a single database column to this property or you can assign a comma-separated list of column names to this property.

For example, the Employees database table uses two columns—the employee first and last name—as a primary key. The page in Listing 11.4 displays employee details when you select a particular employee (see Figure 11.3).

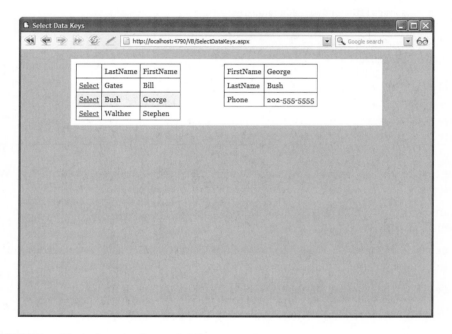

FIGURE 11.3   Displaying employee details.

LISTING 11.4   SelectDataKeys.aspx

```
<%@ Page Language="VB" %>
<!DOCTYPE html PUBLIC "-//W3C//DTD XHTML 1.1//EN"
    "http://www.w3.org/TR/xhtml11/DTD/xhtml11.dtd">
<html xmlns="http://www.w3.org/1999/xhtml" >
<head id="Head1" runat="server">
    <style type="text/css">
        html
        {
            background-color:silver;
        }
        .content
```

LISTING 11.4   Continued

```
        {
            width:600px;
            margin:auto;
            background-color:white;
        }
        .column
        {
            float:left;
            padding:10px;
            width:265px;
        }
        .column td,.column th
        {
            padding:5px;
            font:14px Georgia, Serif
        }
        .selectedRow
        {
            background-color:yellow;
        }
    </style>
    <title>Select Data Keys</title>
</head>
<body>
    <form id="form1" runat="server">
    <div class="content">
    <div class="column">

    <asp:GridView
        id="grdEmployees"
        DataSourceID="srcEmployees"
        DataKeyNames="LastName,FirstName"
        AutoGenerateSelectButton="true"
        SelectedRowStyle-CssClass="selectedRow"
        Runat="server" />

    </div>
    <div class="column">

    <asp:DetailsView
        id="dtlEmployees"
        DataSourceID="srcEmployeeDetails"
        Runat="server" />

    </div>
```

LISTING 11.4   Continued

```
    <br style="clear:both" />
    </div>

    <asp:SqlDataSource
        id="srcEmployees"
        ConnectionString="<%$ ConnectionStrings:Employees %>"
        SelectCommand="SELECT LastName,FirstName
            FROM Employees"
        Runat="server" />

    <asp:SqlDataSource
        id="srcEmployeeDetails"
        ConnectionString="<%$ ConnectionStrings:Employees %>"
        SelectCommand="SELECT * FROM Employees
            WHERE FirstName=@FirstName AND LastName=@LastName"
        Runat="server">
        <SelectParameters>
        <asp:ControlParameter
            Name="FirstName"
            ControlID="grdEmployees"
            PropertyName='SelectedDataKey("FirstName")' />
        <asp:ControlParameter
            Name="LastName"
            ControlID="grdEmployees"
            PropertyName='SelectedDataKey("LastName")' />
        </SelectParameters>
    </asp:SqlDataSource>

    </form>
</body>
</html>
```

In Listing 11.4, notice that the `SelectedDataKey` property is used to retrieve the primary key of the selected employee. The `SelectedDataKey` property is used in both of the `ControlParameters` contained in the second `SqlDataSource` control. If you use `SelectedValue` instead of `SelectedDataKey`, then you can return only the value of the first data key and not both values.

A `GridView` stores data keys in a collection called the `DataKeys` collection. This collection is exposed by the `GridView` control's `DataKeys` property. You can retrieve the data key associated with any row by using a statement that looks like this:

```
DIM key As Object = Gridview1.DataKeys(6).Value
```

This statement returns the value of the data key associated with the seventh row in the GridView (remember that the rows collection is zero based).

If you have assigned multiple data keys to each row, then you can use a statement that looks like this:

```
Dim key As Object = GridView1.DataKeys(6).Values("LastName")
```

This statement retrieves the value of the LastName key for the seventh row in the GridView.

Sorting Data

You can sort the rows rendered by a GridView control by enabling the AllowSorting property. For example, the page in Listing 11.5 illustrates how you can sort the contents of the Movies database table.

LISTING 11.5   SortGrid.aspx

```
<%@ Page Language="VB" %>
<!DOCTYPE html PUBLIC "-//W3C//DTD XHTML 1.1//EN"
    "http://www.w3.org/TR/xhtml11/DTD/xhtml11.dtd">
<html xmlns="http://www.w3.org/1999/xhtml" >
<head id="Head1" runat="server">
    <title>Sort Grid</title>
</head>
<body>
    <form id="form1" runat="server">
    <div>

    <asp:GridView
        id="grdMovies"
        DataSourceID="srcMovies"
        AllowSorting="true"
        Runat="server" />

    <asp:SqlDataSource
        id="srcMovies"
        ConnectionString="<%$ ConnectionStrings:Movies %>"
        SelectCommand="SELECT Id,Title,DateReleased FROM Movies"
        Runat="server" />

    </div>
    </form>
</body>
</html>
```

When AllowSorting has the value True, column headers are rendered as links. When you click a column header, you can sort the rows contained in the GridView in the order of the selected column.

NOTE

When using explicitly specified fields with a GridView, such as BoundFields, you need to specify values for the fields's SortExpression properties. Otherwise, nothing happens when you click a header.

Notice that the GridView supports ascending and descending sorts. In other words, if you click a column header more than once, the rows toggle between being sorted in ascending and descending order.

Sorting with AJAX

By default, whenever you click a column header to sort the rows contained in a GridView, the page containing the GridView is posted back to the server. When sorting records with the GridView control, you can avoid posting the entire page back to the server by taking advantage of AJAX (Asynchronous JavaScript and XML).

You enable AJAX by including the EnableSortingAndPagingCallbacks property when declaring the GridView. The page in Listing 11.6 illustrates how you can take advantage of AJAX when sorting records.

LISTING 11.6   AjaxSorting.aspx

```
<%@ Page Language="VB" %>
<!DOCTYPE html PUBLIC "-//W3C//DTD XHTML 1.1//EN"
    "http://www.w3.org/TR/xhtml11/DTD/xhtml11.dtd">
<html xmlns="http://www.w3.org/1999/xhtml" >
<head id="Head1" runat="server">
    <title>AJAX Sorting</title>
</head>
<body>
    <form id="form1" runat="server">
    <div>
    <%= DateTime.Now.ToString("T") %>

    <asp:GridView
        id="grdMovies"
        DataSourceID="srcMovies"
        AllowSorting="true"
        EnableSortingAndPagingCallbacks="true"
        Runat="server" />

    <asp:SqlDataSource
```

LISTING 11.6   Continued

```
            id="srcMovies"
            ConnectionString="<%$ ConnectionStrings:Movies %>"
            SelectCommand="SELECT Id,Title,DateReleased FROM Movies"
            Runat="server" />

    </div>
    </form>
</body>
</html>
```

The page in Listing 11.6 displays the current time at the top of the page. Notice that the time is not updated when you sort the records in the GridView. The entire page is not posted back to the server; only the content of the GridView control is updated.

> **WARNING**
>
> When using AJAX with the GridView control, you cannot use TemplateFields. Furthermore, you cannot display a Select button when AJAX is enabled.

Customizing the Sorting Interface

You can customize the appearance of the sort links by handling the GridView control's RowDataBound event. This event is raised for each row rendered by the GridView after the GridView is bound to its data source.

For example, the page in Listing 11.7 displays an image that represents whether a column is sorted in ascending or descending order (see Figure 11.4).

LISTING 11.7   ImageSorting.aspx

```
<%@ Page Language="VB" %>
<!DOCTYPE html PUBLIC "-//W3C//DTD XHTML 1.1//EN"
    "http://www.w3.org/TR/xhtml11/DTD/xhtml11.dtd">
<script runat="server">

    Protected Sub grdMovies_RowDataBound(ByVal sender As Object,
➥ByVal e As GridViewRowEventArgs)
        If e.Row.RowType = DataControlRowType.Header Then
            For Each cell As TableCell In e.Row.Cells
                Dim sortLink As LinkButton = CType(cell.Controls(0), LinkButton)
                If sortLink.Text = grdMovies.SortExpression Then
                    If grdMovies.SortDirection = SortDirection.Ascending Then
                        sortLink.Text +=
➥" <img src='asc.gif' title='Sort ascending' />"
                    Else
```

LISTING 11.7   Continued

```
                        sortLink.Text +=
➥" <img src='desc.gif' title='Sort descending' />"
                    End If
                End If
            Next
        End If
    End Sub

</script>
<html xmlns="http://www.w3.org/1999/xhtml" >
<head id="Head1" runat="server">
    <style type="text/css">
        img
        {
            border:0px;
        }
    </style>
    <title>Image Sorting</title>
</head>
<body>
    <form id="form1" runat="server">
    <div>

    <asp:GridView
        id="grdMovies"
        DataSourceID="srcMovies"
        AllowSorting="true"
        Runat="server" OnRowDataBound="grdMovies_RowDataBound" />

    <asp:SqlDataSource
        id="srcMovies"
        ConnectionString="<%$ ConnectionStrings:Movies %>"
        SelectCommand="SELECT Id,Title,Director FROM Movies"
        Runat="server" />

    </div>
    </form>
</body>
</html>
```

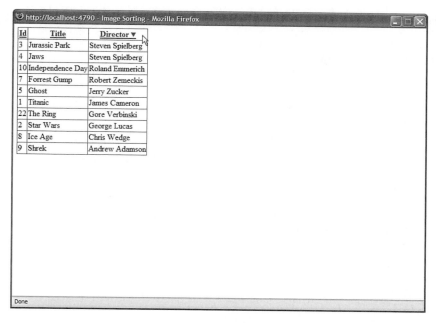

FIGURE 11.4   Displaying an image when sorting.

In Listing 11.7, the image is added to the header row in the `grdMovies_RowDataBound()` method. The current row's `RowType` property is checked to verify that the row is a header row. Next, an HTML `<img>` tag is added to the `LinkButton` that matches the column that is currently selected for sorting.

If you need to completely customize the appearance of the sorting user interface, then you can call the `GridView` control's `Sort()` method programmatically. This approach is illustrated in the page in Listing 11.8 (see Figure 11.5).

LISTING 11.8   `CustomSorting.aspx`

```
<%@ Page Language="VB" %>
<!DOCTYPE html PUBLIC "-//W3C//DTD XHTML 1.1//EN"
  "http://www.w3.org/TR/xhtml11/DTD/xhtml11.dtd">
<script runat="server">

    Sub btnSort_Click(s As object, e As EventArgs)
        grdMovies.Sort(ddlSort.Text, SortDirection.Ascending)
    End Sub
</script>
```

LISTING 11.8   Continued

```
<html xmlns="http://www.w3.org/1999/xhtml" >
<head id="Head1" runat="server">
    <title>Custom Sorting</title>
</head>
<body>
    <form id="form1" runat="server">
    <div>

    <asp:DropDownList
        id="ddlSort"
        Runat="server">
        <asp:ListItem Text="Id" />
        <asp:ListItem Text="Title" />
        <asp:ListItem Text="Director" />
    </asp:DropDownList>
    <asp:Button
        id="btnSort"
        Text="Sort"
        Runat="server" OnClick="btnSort_Click" />

    <asp:GridView
        id="grdMovies"
        DataSourceID="srcMovies"
        Runat="server" />

    <asp:SqlDataSource
        id="srcMovies"
        ConnectionString="<%$ ConnectionStrings:Movies %>"
        SelectCommand="SELECT Id,Title,Director FROM Movies"
        Runat="server" />

    </div>
    </form>
</body>
</html>
```

The page in Listing 11.8 includes a DropDownList control, which you can use to sort the contents of the GridView. When a list item is selected from the DropDownList control and the Sort button is clicked, the btnSort_Click() method executes. This method calls the Sort() method of the GridView control to sort the contents of the GridView.

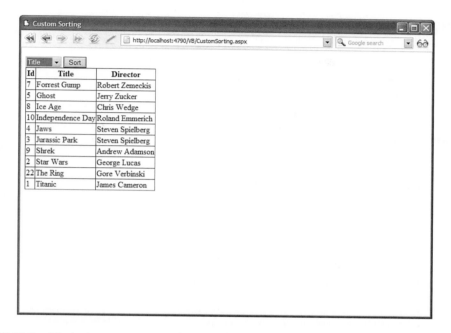

FIGURE 11.5　Displaying a custom sorting interface.

Paging Through Data

When working with a large number of database rows, it is useful to be able to display the rows in different pages. You can enable paging with the GridView control by enabling its AllowPaging property.

For example, the page in Listing 11.9 enables you to page through the records in the Movies database table (see Figure 11.6).

LISTING 11.9　PageGrid.aspx

```
<%@ Page Language="VB" %>
<!DOCTYPE html PUBLIC "-//W3C//DTD XHTML 1.1//EN"
    "http://www.w3.org/TR/xhtml11/DTD/xhtml11.dtd">
<html xmlns="http://www.w3.org/1999/xhtml" >
<head id="Head1" runat="server">
    <title>Page Grid</title>
</head>
<body>
    <form id="form1" runat="server">
    <div>

    <asp:GridView
```

LISTING 11.9   Continued

```
        id="grdMovies"
        DataSourceID="srcMovies"
        AllowPaging="true"
        PageSize="3"
        Runat="server" />

    <asp:SqlDataSource
        id="srcMovies"
        ConnectionString="<%$ ConnectionStrings:Movies %>"
        SelectCommand="SELECT Id,Title,Director FROM Movies"
        Runat="server" />

    </div>
    </form>
</body>
</html>
```

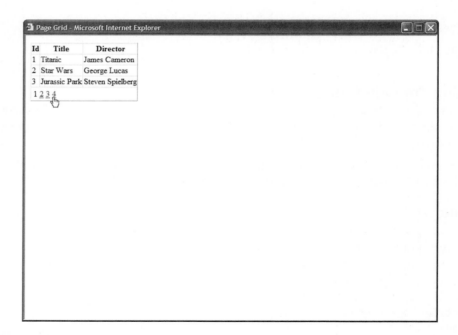

FIGURE 11.6   Paging through records in a GridView control.

The GridView in Listing 11.9 displays three database records per page. You can modify the number of records displayed per page by modifying the GridView control's PageSize property. (If you don't specify a value for PageSize, then the GridView defaults to displaying 10 records per page.)

> **WARNING**
>
> This section describes how you can enable *user interface paging* with the GridView control. When you use user interface paging, all the database records are loaded into memory and divided into separate pages. For example, when paging through a database table that contains three billion database records, all three billion records are loaded into memory even when you display only three records in a single page. You should not use user interface paging when working with large sets of data. Instead, use the ObjectDataSource control's support for *data source paging*. This option is discussed in Chapter 15, "Using the ObjectDataSource Control."

Paging with AJAX

The default behavior of the GridView control is to post back to the server each and every time you navigate to a new page of records. However, there is an alternative. You can take advantage of AJAX (Asynchronous JavaScript and XML) when paging through records with the GridView control.

The page in Listing 11.10 illustrates how you can use AJAX with the GridView control.

LISTING 11.10 AjaxPaging.aspx

```
<%@ Page Language="VB" %>
<!DOCTYPE html PUBLIC "-//W3C//DTD XHTML 1.1//EN"
    "http://www.w3.org/TR/xhtml11/DTD/xhtml11.dtd">
<html xmlns="http://www.w3.org/1999/xhtml" >
<head id="Head1" runat="server">
    <title>AJAX Page</title>
</head>
<body>
    <form id="form1" runat="server">
    <div>
    <%= DateTime.Now.ToString("T") %>
    <asp:GridView
        id="grdMovies"
        DataSourceID="srcMovies"
        AllowPaging="true"
        EnableSortingAndPagingCallbacks="true"
        PageSize="3"
        Runat="server" />

    <asp:SqlDataSource
        id="srcMovies"
        ConnectionString="<%$ ConnectionStrings:Movies %>"
        SelectCommand="SELECT Id,Title,Director FROM Movies"
        Runat="server" />
```

LISTING 11.10   Continued

```
        </div>
        </form>
</body>
</html>
```

Notice that the GridView in Listing 11.10 includes an EnableSortingAndPagingCallbacks property that is assigned the value True. This property enables AJAX.

The page in Listing 11.10 displays the current time at the top of the page. When you page through the records rendered by the GridView control, notice that the time does not change. Only the contents of the GridView control are modified.

> **WARNING**
>
> When using AJAX with the GridView control, you cannot use TemplateFields. Furthermore, you cannot display a Select button when AJAX is enabled.

Customizing the Paging Interface

By default, when paging is enabled, the GridView renders a list of page numbers at the bottom of the grid. You can modify the user interface for paging through records by modifying the GridView control's PagerSettings property. For example, the page in Listing 11.11 contains a GridView that renders First, Previous, Next, and Last links at both the top and bottom of the GridView (see Figure 11.7).

LISTING 11.11   PageGridPreviousNext.aspx

```
<%@ Page Language="VB" %>
<!DOCTYPE html PUBLIC "-//W3C//DTD XHTML 1.1//EN"
    "http://www.w3.org/TR/xhtml11/DTD/xhtml11.dtd">
<html xmlns="http://www.w3.org/1999/xhtml" >
<head id="Head1" runat="server">
    <title>Page Grid Previous Next</title>
</head>
<body>
    <form id="form1" runat="server">
    <div>

    <asp:GridView
        id="grdMovies"
        DataSourceID="srcMovies"
        AllowPaging="true"
        PageSize="3"
        PagerSettings-Mode="NextPreviousFirstLast"
        PagerSettings-Position="TopAndBottom"
```

LISTING 11.11   Continued

```
            PagerStyle-HorizontalAlign="Center"
            Runat="server" />

        <asp:SqlDataSource
            id="srcMovies"
            ConnectionString="<%$ ConnectionStrings:Movies %>"
            SelectCommand="SELECT Id,Title,Director FROM Movies"
            Runat="server" />

    </div>
    </form>
</body>
</html>
```

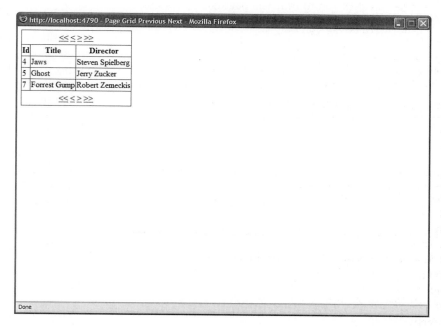

FIGURE 11.7   Modifying pager settings.

The PagerSettings class supports the following properties:

- FirstPageImageUrl—Enables you to display an image for the first page link.

- FirstPageText—Enables you to specify the text for the first page link.

- LastPageImageUrl—Enables you to display an image for the last page link.

- LastPageText—Enables you to specify the text for the last page link.

- Mode—Enables you to select a display mode for the pager user interface. Possible values are NextPrevious, NextPreviousFirstLast, Numeric, and NumericFirstLast.

- NextPageImageUrl—Enables you to display an image for the next page link.

- NextPageText—Enables you to specify the text for the next page link.

- PageButtonCount—Enables you to specify the number of page number links to display.

- Position—Enables you to specify the position of the paging user interface. Possible values are Bottom, Top, TopAndBottom.

- PreviousPageImageUrl—Enables you to display an image for the previous page link.

- PreviousPageText—Enables you to specify the text for the previous page link.

- Visible—Enables you to hide the paging user interface.

The PageButtonCount requires more explanation. Imagine that you are displaying the contents of a database table that contains 3 billion records and you are displaying two records per page. In that case, you would need to render an overwhelming number of page numbers. The PageButtonCount property enables you to limit the number of page numbers displayed at once. When PageButtonCount has a value less than the number of page numbers, the GridView renders ellipsis, which enables a user to move between ranges of page numbers.

The GridView control includes a PagerTemplate, which enables you to completely customize the appearance of the paging user interface. For example, the page in Listing 11.12 uses a Menu control in a PagerTemplate to display a list of page numbers. The PagerTemplate also includes two LinkButton controls, which represent a Previous and Next link (see Figure 11.8).

LISTING 11.12   PageTemplateGrid.aspx

```
<%@ Page Language="VB" %>
<!DOCTYPE html PUBLIC "-//W3C//DTD XHTML 1.1//EN"
    "http://www.w3.org/TR/xhtml11/DTD/xhtml11.dtd">
<script runat="server">

    Protected Sub grdMovies_DataBound(ByVal sender As Object, ByVal e As EventArgs)
        Dim menuPager As Menu =
➥CType(grdMovies.BottomPagerRow.FindControl("menuPager"), Menu)
        For i As Integer = 0 To grdMovies.PageCount - 1
            Dim item As New MenuItem()
            item.Text = String.Format("[{0}]", i + 1)
            item.Value = i.ToString()
            If grdMovies.PageIndex = i Then
```

LISTING 11.12   Continued

```
                    item.Selected = True
                End If
                menuPager.Items.Add(item)
            Next
        End Sub


        Protected  Sub menuPager_MenuItemClick(ByVal sender As Object,
    ➥ByVal e As MenuEventArgs)
            grdMovies.PageIndex = Int32.Parse(e.Item.Value)
        End Sub
    </script>

    <html xmlns="http://www.w3.org/1999/xhtml" >
    <head id="Head1" runat="server">
        <style type="text/css">
            .menu td
            {
                padding:5px 0px;
            }
            .selectedPage a
            {
                font-weight:bold;
                color:red;
            }
        </style>
        <title>Page Template Grid</title>
    </head>
    <body>
        <form id="form1" runat="server">
        <div>

        <asp:GridView
            id="grdMovies"
            DataSourceID="srcMovies"
            AllowPaging="true"
            PageSize="3"
            Runat="server" OnDataBound="grdMovies_DataBound">
            <PagerTemplate>
            <table>
            <tr><td>
            <asp:LinkButton
                id="lnkPrevious"
                Text="&lt; Prev"
                CommandName="Page"
```

LISTING 11.12   Continued

```
                CommandArgument="Prev"
                ToolTip="Previous Page"
                Runat="server" />
            </td><td>
            <asp:Menu
                id="menuPager"
                Orientation="Horizontal"
                OnMenuItemClick="menuPager_MenuItemClick"
                StaticSelectedStyle-CssClass="selectedPage"
                CssClass="menu"
                Runat="server" />
            </td><td>
            <asp:LinkButton
                id="lnkNext"
                Text="Next &gt;"
                CommandName="Page"
                CommandArgument="Next"
                ToolTip="Next Page"
                Runat="server" />
            </td></tr>
            </table>
            </PagerTemplate>
    </asp:GridView>

    <asp:SqlDataSource
        id="srcMovies"
        ConnectionString="<%$ ConnectionStrings:Movies %>"
        SelectCommand="SELECT Id,Title,Director FROM Movies"
        Runat="server" />

    </div>
    </form>
</body>
</html>
```

The GridView in Listing 11.12 includes a PagerTemplate that contains a Menu control. When the GridView is bound to its data source, the grdMovies_DataBound() method executes and creates menu items that correspond to each page in the GridView. When you click a menu item, the page index of the GridView is updated.

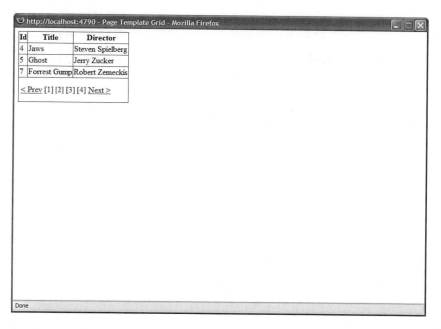

FIGURE 11.8   Using a template for the paging interface.

To customize the PagerTemplate, you can add button controls to the template such as the Button, ImageButton, or LinkButton controls. Set the CommandName property of the button control to the value Page and the CommandArgument property to one of the following values:

- Next—Causes the GridView to display the next page of data items.
- Prev—Causes the GridView to display the previous page of data items.
- First—Causes the GridView to display the first page of data items.
- Last—Causes the GridView to display the last page of data items.
- Integer Value—Causes the GridView to display a particular page of data items.

Editing Data

The GridView control also enables you to edit database data. The amazing thing is that you can use the GridView to edit the contents of a database table row without writing a single line of code.

The page in Listing 11.13 illustrates how you can update and delete records in the Movies database table by using the GridView control (see Figure 11.9).

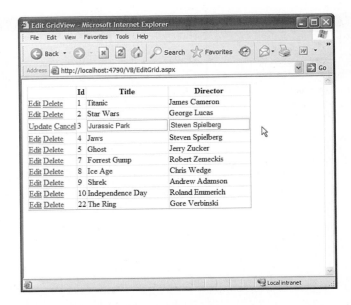

FIGURE 11.9   Editing records with the GridView.

LISTING 11.13   EditGrid.aspx

```
<%@ Page Language="VB" MaintainScrollPositionOnPostback="true" %>
<!DOCTYPE html PUBLIC "-//W3C//DTD XHTML 1.1//EN"
  "http://www.w3.org/TR/xhtml11/DTD/xhtml11.dtd">
<html xmlns="http://www.w3.org/1999/xhtml" >
<head id="Head1" runat="server">
    <title>Edit GridView</title>
</head>
<body>
    <form id="form1" runat="server">
    <div>

    <asp:GridView
        id="grdMovies"
        DataSourceID="srcMovies"
        DataKeyNames="Id"
        AutoGenerateEditButton="true"
        AutoGenerateDeleteButton="true"
        Runat="server" />

    <asp:SqlDataSource
        id="srcMovies"
        ConnectionString="<%$ ConnectionStrings:Movies %>"
```

LISTING 11.13   Continued

```
            SelectCommand="SELECT Id,Title,Director FROM Movies"
            UpdateCommand="UPDATE Movies SET Title=@Title, Director=@Director
                WHERE Id=@Id"
            DeleteCommand="DELETE Movies WHERE Id=@Id"
            Runat="server" />

    </div>
    </form>
</body>
</html>
```

In Listing 11.13, notice that the GridView control has both its AutoGenerateEditButton and AutoGenerateDeleteButton properties enabled. When these properties are enabled, Edit and Delete links are automatically rendered next to each row in the GridView.

> **NOTE**
>
> You can take advantage of the <%@ Page %> directive's MaintainScrollPositionOnPostback attribute to scroll a page back automatically to the same position whenever the page is posted back to the server. For example, if you add this attribute and click an Edit link rendered by a GridView, the page automatically scrolls to the record being edited. This attribute works with Internet Explorer 6+, Firefox 1+, and Opera 8+.

When you click an Edit link, you can edit a particular database row. The GridView automatically renders a check box for any Boolean columns and a text field for any other type of column.

> **NOTE**
>
> The GridView control does not support inserting new records into a database table. If you need to insert new records, use either the DetailsView or FormView control.

Furthermore, notice that the GridView control includes a DataKeyNames property. When editing and deleting rows with the GridView, you need to assign the name of the primary key field from the database table being modified to this property. In Listing 11.13, the Movies ID column is assigned to the DataKeyNames property.

Finally, notice that the SqlDataSource control associated with the GridView control includes a SelectCommand, UpdateCommand, and DeleteCommand property. These properties contain the SQL statements that are executed when you display, insert, and delete records with the GridView control.

The SQL statements contained in both the UpdateCommand and DeleteCommand include parameters. For example, the UpdateCommand looks like this:

```
UPDATE Movies SET Title=@Title, Director=@Director
WHERE Id=@Id
```

The @Title and @Director parameters represent the new values for these columns that a user enters when updating a record with the GridView control. The @Id parameter represents the primary key column from the database table.

Handling Concurrency Issues

The GridView control can track both the original and modified value of each database column. The GridView control tracks the original and updated values of a column so that you can handle concurrency conflicts. Imagine that you are building a massive order entry system. Your company has hundreds of employees modifying orders with a page that contains a GridView control. If two employees open the same customer record at the same time, then one employee might overwrite changes made by the other employee.

You can prevent this type of concurrency conflict by using the page in Listing 11.14.

LISTING 11.14   Concurrency.aspx

```
<%@ Page Language="VB" %>
<!DOCTYPE html PUBLIC "-//W3C//DTD XHTML 1.1//EN"
    "http://www.w3.org/TR/xhtml11/DTD/xhtml11.dtd">
<html xmlns="http://www.w3.org/1999/xhtml" >
<head id="Head1" runat="server">
    <title>Concurrency</title>
</head>
<body>
    <form id="form1" runat="server">
    <div>

    <asp:GridView
        id="grdMovies"
        DataSourceID="srcMovies"
        DataKeyNames="Id"
        AutoGenerateEditButton="true"
        Runat="server" />

    <asp:SqlDataSource
        id="srcMovies"
        ConflictDetection="CompareAllValues"
        OldValuesParameterFormatString="original_{0}"
        ConnectionString="<%$ ConnectionStrings:Movies %>"
        SelectCommand="SELECT Id,Title,Director FROM Movies"
        UpdateCommand="UPDATE Movies SET Title=@Title, Director=@Director
```

LISTING 11.14 Continued

```
                WHERE Id=@original_Id AND Title=@original_Title
                AND Director=@original_Director"
        Runat="server" />

    </div>
    </form>
</body>
</html>
```

In Listing 11.14, the SqlDataSource control includes both a ConflictDetection and OldValuesParameterFormatString property. These two properties cause the SqlDataSource control to track both the original and modified versions of each column.

The ConflictDetection property can have one of the following two values:

- CompareAllValues

- OverwriteChanges

By default, the ConflictDetection property has the value OverwriteChanges, which causes the SqlDataSource control to overwrite the previous value of a column with its new value. When ConflictDetection is set to the value CompareAllValues, the SqlDataSource tracks both the original and modified version of each column.

The OldValuesParameterFormatString property is used to provide a distinguishing name for the original value of a column. For example, the value of the SqlDataSource control's UpdateCommand looks like this:

```
UPDATE Movies SET Title=@Title, Director=@Director
WHERE Id=@original_Id AND Title=@original_Title
AND Director=@original_Director
```

The @original_Id, @original_Title, and @original_Director parameters represent the original values of these columns. If the value of the Title or Director columns has changed in the underlying database, then the record is not updated. In other words, if someone else beats you to the record change, then your modifications are ignored.

Displaying Empty Data

The GridView includes two properties that enable you to display content when no results are returned from the GridView control's data source. You can use either the EmptyDataText property or the EmptyDataTemplate property to handle empty data.

For example, the page in Listing 11.15 contains a movie search form. If you enter a search string that does not match the start of any movie title, then the contents of the EmptyDataText property are displayed (see Figure 11.10).

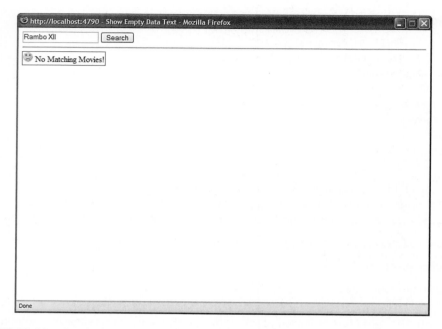

FIGURE 11.10   Displaying a message when no records match.

LISTING 11.15   ShowEmptyDataText.aspx

```
<%@ Page Language="VB" %>
<!DOCTYPE html PUBLIC "-//W3C//DTD XHTML 1.1//EN"
    "http://www.w3.org/TR/xhtml11/DTD/xhtml11.dtd">
<script runat="server">

    Sub btnSubmit_Click(sender As object, e As EventArgs)
        grdMovies.Visible = True
    End Sub
</script>


<html xmlns="http://www.w3.org/1999/xhtml" >
<head id="Head1" runat="server">
    <title>Show Empty Data Text</title>
</head>
<body>
    <form id="form1" runat="server">
    <div>

    <asp:TextBox
        id="txtTitle"
        Runat="server" />
```

LISTING 11.15   Continued

```
    <asp:Button
        id="btnSubmit"
        Text="Search"
        OnClick="btnSubmit_Click"
        Runat="server" />
    <hr />

    <asp:GridView
        id="grdMovies"
        DataSourceID="srcMovies"
        EmptyDataText="<img src='sad.gif'/> No Matching Movies!"
        Visible="false"
        Runat="server" />

    <asp:SqlDataSource
        id="srcMovies"
        ConnectionString="<%$ ConnectionStrings:Movies %>"
        SelectCommand="SELECT Title,Director FROM Movies
            WHERE Title LIKE @Title+'%'"
        Runat="server">
        <SelectParameters>
        <asp:ControlParameter
            Name="Title"
            ControlID="txtTitle"
            PropertyName="Text" />
        </SelectParameters>
    </asp:SqlDataSource>

    </div>
    </form>
</body>
</html>
```

If you use the search form in Listing 11.15 to search for a movie that doesn't exist, then an icon of a frowning face and the text No Matching Movies! is displayed.

Notice that the initial value of the GridView control's Visible property is set to False. The GridView is displayed only after you click the button. If you did not add this additional logic, then the EmptyDataText message would be displayed when the page is first opened.

As an alternative to using the EmptyDataText property, you can use an EmptyDataTemplate to display content when a data source does not return any results. For example, the page in Listing 11.16 prompts you to enter a new movie when no matching movies are found (see Figure 11.11).

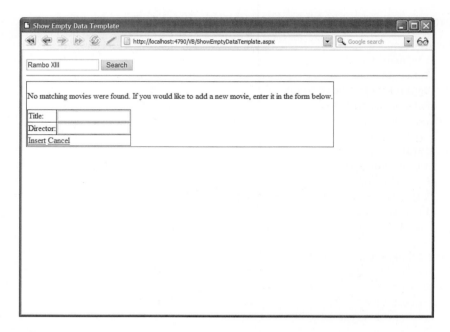

FIGURE 11.11   Displaying a template when no records match.

LISTING 11.16   ShowEmptyDataTemplate.aspx

```
<%@ Page Language="VB" %>
<!DOCTYPE html PUBLIC "-//W3C//DTD XHTML 1.1//EN"
    "http://www.w3.org/TR/xhtml11/DTD/xhtml11.dtd">
<script runat="server">

    Protected Sub btnSubmit_Click(ByVal sender As Object, ByVal e As EventArgs)
        grdMovies.Visible = True
    End Sub


    Protected Sub dtlMovie_ItemInserted(ByVal sender As Object,
➥ ByVal e As DetailsViewInsertedEventArgs)
        txtTitle.Text = CType(e.Values("Title"), String)
        grdMovies.DataBind()
    End Sub
</script>
<html xmlns="http://www.w3.org/1999/xhtml" >
<head id="Head1" runat="server">
    <title>Show Empty Data Template</title>
</head>
<body>
    <form id="form1" runat="server">
```

LISTING 11.16   Continued

```
<div>

<asp:TextBox
    id="txtTitle"
    Runat="server" />
<asp:Button
    id="btnSubmit"
    Text="Search"
    OnClick="btnSubmit_Click"
    Runat="server" />
<hr />

<asp:GridView
    id="grdMovies"
    DataSourceID="srcMovies"
    Visible="false"
    Runat="server">
    <EmptyDataTemplate>
    <p>
    No matching movies were found. If you would like
    to add a new movie, enter it in the form below.
    </p>
    <asp:DetailsView
        id="dtlMovie"
        DataSourceID="srcMovies"
        DefaultMode="Insert"
        AutoGenerateInsertButton="true"
        AutoGenerateRows="false"
        Runat="server" OnItemInserted="dtlMovie_ItemInserted">
        <Fields>
        <asp:BoundField
            HeaderText="Title:"
            DataField="Title" />
        <asp:BoundField
            HeaderText="Director:"
            DataField="Director" />
        </Fields>
    </asp:DetailsView>

    </EmptyDataTemplate>
</asp:GridView>

<asp:SqlDataSource
    id="srcMovies"
```

LISTING 11.16   Continued

```
        ConnectionString="<%$ ConnectionStrings:Movies %>"
        SelectCommand="SELECT Title,Director FROM Movies
            WHERE Title LIKE @Title+'%'"
        InsertCommand="INSERT Movies (Title, Director)
            VALUES (@Title, @Director)"
        Runat="server">
        <SelectParameters>
        <asp:ControlParameter
            Name="Title"
            ControlID="txtTitle"
            PropertyName="Text" />
        </SelectParameters>
    </asp:SqlDataSource>

    </div>
    </form>
</body>
</html>
```

The `EmptyDataTemplate` in Listing 11.16 contains some text and a `DetailsView` control that you can use to insert a new movie into the Movies database table. You can add any HTML content or ASP.NET controls to an `EmptyDataTemplate` that you need.

Formatting the `GridView` Control

The `GridView` control includes a rich set of formatting properties that you can use to modify its appearance. I recommend that you don't use most of these properties because using these properties results in bloated pages. Instead, I recommend that you use Cascading Style Sheets to format the `GridView` control.

The `GridView` control includes a `CssClass` property. The control also exposes several `Style` objects that include the `CssClass` property:

- `AlternatingRowStyle`—Enables you to format every other row.

- `FooterStyle`—Enables you to format the footer row.

- `HeaderStyle`—Enables you to format the header row.

- `PagerStyle`—Enables you to format the pager row.

- `RowStyle`—Enables you to format each row.

- `SelectedRowStyle`—Enables you to format the selected row.

For example, the page in Listing 11.17 contains a `GridView` that is formatted with Cascading Style Sheet rules (see Figure 11.12).

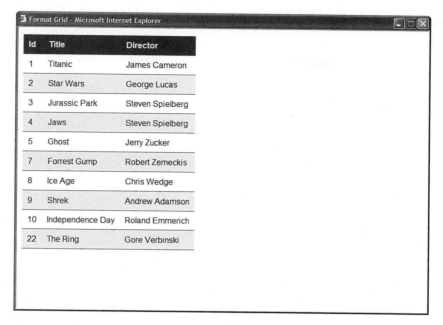

FIGURE 11.12   A GridView control formatted with CSS.

LISTING 11.17   FormatGrid.aspx

```
<%@ Page Language="VB" %>
<!DOCTYPE html PUBLIC "-//W3C//DTD XHTML 1.1//EN"
    "http://www.w3.org/TR/xhtml11/DTD/xhtml11.dtd">
<html xmlns="http://www.w3.org/1999/xhtml" >
<head id="Head1" runat="server">
    <style type="text/css">
        .grid
        {
            font:16px Arial, Sans-Serif;
        }
        .grid td, .grid th
        {
            padding:10px;
        }
        .header
        {
            text-align:left;
            color:white;
            background-color:blue;
        }
```

LISTING 11.17   Continued

```
            .row td
            {
                border-bottom:solid 1px blue;
            }
            .alternating
            {
                background-color:#eeeeee;
            }
            .alternating td
            {
                border-bottom:solid 1px blue;
            }
        </style>
        <title>Format Grid</title>
</head>
<body>
    <form id="form1" runat="server">
    <div>

    <asp:GridView
        id="grdMovies"
        DataSourceID="srcMovies"
        GridLines="None"
        CssClass="grid"
        HeaderStyle-CssClass="header"
        RowStyle-CssClass="row"
        AlternatingRowStyle-CssClass="alternating"
        Runat="server" />

    <asp:SqlDataSource
        id="srcMovies"
        ConnectionString="<%$ ConnectionStrings:Movies %>"
        SelectCommand="SELECT Id,Title,Director FROM Movies"
        Runat="server" />

    </div>
    </form>
</body>
</html>
```

In Listing 11.17, the column header text is left aligned. Also notice that banding is added to the table rendered by the GridView. Alternating rows are rendered with a gray background.

The GridView control has a few formatting properties that you might need to use even when formatting a GridView with Cascading Style Sheets. For example, in Listing 11.17, the GridLines property was assigned the value None to suppress the default rendering of borders around each table cell. Here is a list of these properties.

- GridLines—Renders borders around table cells. Possible values are Both, Vertical, Horizontal, and None.

- ShowFooter—When True, renders a footer row at the bottom of the GridView.

- ShowHeader—When True, renders a header row at the top of the GridView.

Using View State with the GridView Control

By default, the GridView control stores the values of all the columns contained in all the rows that it renders in ViewState. In other words, all the rows that the GridView retrieves from its data source are stuffed in a hidden form field.

The advantage of using ViewState is that the GridView does not need to query the database for the same set of records every time a page containing the GridView is displayed. The records are retrieved from the database only when the page first loads.

The disadvantage of using ViewState is that it means that a lot of information might need to be pushed over the wire to a user's browser. All ViewState information is stored in a hidden form field. When a large number of rows are displayed, this hidden form field can become enormous. When ViewState becomes too large, it can significantly impact a page's performance.

You can disable ViewState by assigning the value False to the GridView control's EnableViewState property. Even if you disable ViewState, you can still display, sort, page, and edit database records with the GridView control (The GridView uses ControlState to track vital state information.) When displaying a large number of records, you should turn ViewState off.

You can view the amount of ViewState that a GridView is using by enabling tracing for the page that contains the GridView. Add the Trace="True" attribute to the Page directive like this:

```
<%@ Page Trace="true" %>
```

When tracing is enabled, a Control Tree section is appended to the end of a page when the page is rendered in a browser. The Control Tree section displays the ViewState size used by each control contained in the page.

Using Fields with the GridView Control

In all the sample code in the previous section, the GridView control was used to automatically render an HTML table that contains a list of data items. However, there is a problem with allowing the GridView to render its columns automatically. The result does not look very professional.

For example, the column headers are simply the names of the underlying database columns. Displaying the column name EntryDate as a column header seems, well, a little cheesy. We really need to be able to specify custom column headers.

Another problem with enabling the GridView to render its columns automatically is that you give up any control over column formatting. For example, the BoxOfficeTotals column is displayed as a decimal amount without any currency formatting. The EntryDate column always displays in short-date and long-time format.

Furthermore, it would be nice to be able to display the values of certain columns as images, drop-down lists, or hyperlinks. If you use the automatically generated columns, then you are stuck with the user interface you are given.

The solution to all these problems is to specify explicitly the fields that a GridView displays. The GridView control supports the following types of fields:

- BoundField—Enables you to display the value of a data item as text.
- CheckBoxField—Enables you to display the value of a data item as a check box.
- CommandField—Enables you to display links for editing, deleting, and selecting rows.
- ButtonField—Enables you to display the value of a data item as a button (image button, link button, or push button).
- HyperLinkField—Enables you to display the value of a data item as a link.
- ImageField—Enables you to display the value of a data item as an image.
- TemplateField—Enables you to customize the appearance of a data item.

The following sections examine how you can take advantage of each of these different types of fields.

> **NOTE**
>
> You can create custom fields that work with the GridView control. This option is explored in the final section of this chapter.

Using BoundFields

A BoundField always displays the value of a data item as text when a row is in normal display mode. When a row is selected for editing, a BoundField displays the value of a data item in a single line text field.

The most important three properties of the BoundField class are the DataField, DataFormatString, and HeaderText properties. The page in Listing 11.18 illustrates how to use these properties when displaying a list of movies (see Figure 11.13).

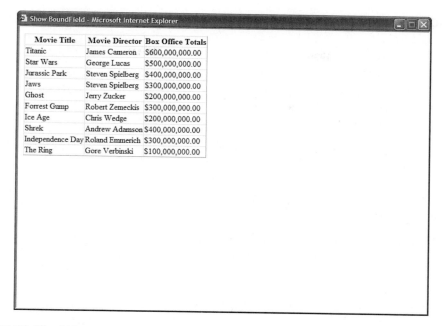

FIGURE 11.13   Using BoundFields with the GridView control.

LISTING 11.18   ShowBoundField.aspx

```
<%@ Page Language="VB" %>
<!DOCTYPE html PUBLIC "-//W3C//DTD XHTML 1.1//EN"
    "http://www.w3.org/TR/xhtml11/DTD/xhtml11.dtd">
<html xmlns="http://www.w3.org/1999/xhtml" >
<head id="Head1" runat="server">
    <title>Show BoundField</title>
</head>
<body>
    <form id="form1" runat="server">
    <div>

    <asp:GridView
        id="grdMovies"
        DataSourceID="srcMovies"
        AutoGenerateColumns="false"
        Runat="server">
        <Columns>
        <asp:BoundField
            DataField="Title"
            HeaderText="Movie Title" />
```

LISTING 11.18   Continued

```
            <asp:BoundField
                DataField="Director"
                HeaderText="Movie Director" />
            <asp:BoundField
                DataField="BoxOfficeTotals"
                DataFormatString="{0:c}"
                HtmlEncode="false"
                HeaderText="Box Office Totals" />
        </Columns>
    </asp:GridView>

    <asp:SqlDataSource
        id="srcMovies"
        ConnectionString="<%$ ConnectionStrings:Movies %>"
        SelectCommand="SELECT * FROM Movies"
        Runat="server" />

    </div>
    </form>
</body>
</html>
```

Notice that the `GridView` control includes an `AutoGenerateColumns` property that is assigned the value `False`. If you don't disable automatically generated columns, then both columns represented by the `BoundFields` and all the columns from the data source are displayed redundantly.

In Listing 11.18, `BoundFields` are used to display the Title, Director, and BoxOfficeTotals columns. The `DataField` property is used to represent the column that a `BoundField` displays. The `HeaderText` property determines the column header.

The `BoundField` used to display the BoxOfficeTotals column includes a `DataFormatString` property. This format string formats the values of the BoxOfficeTotals column as a currency amount. Notice that the `BoundField` also includes an `HtmlEncode` property that is set to the value `False`. When formatting a field, you need to prevent the `GridView` from encoding the field.

> **WARNING**
>
> When using the `DataFormatString` property, always set the `HtmlEncode` property to `False`. Otherwise, the formatting is not applied. This is a change from the previous version of ASP.NET.

> **NOTE**
>
> For more information about string formatting, see the Formatting Types topic in the Microsoft .NET Framework SDK 2.0 documentation.

A BoundField supports several other useful properties:

- AccessibleHeaderText—Enables you to add an HTML abbr attribute to the column header.

- ApplyFormatInEditMode—Enables you to apply the DataFormatString to the field when the row is in edit display mode.

- ConvertEmptyStringToNull—Enables you to convert an empty string "" into the value Nothing (null) when editing a column.

- DataField—Enables you to specify the name of the field that the BoundField displays.

- DataFormatString—Enables you to use a format string to format a data item.

- FooterStyle—Enables you to format the column footer.

- FooterText—Enables you to display text in the column footer.

- HeaderImageUrl—Enables you to display an image in the column header.

- HeaderStyle—Enables you to format the column header.

- HeaderText—Enables you to display text in the column header.

- HtmlEncode—Enables you to HTML-encode the value of a data item, which enables you to avoid script injection attacks.

- InsertVisible—Enables you to not display a column when inserting a new record (does not apply to the GridView control).

- ItemStyle—Enables you to format a data item.

- NullDisplayText—Enables you to specify text that is displayed when a data item has the value Nothing (null).

- ReadOnly—Enables you to prevent the data item from being edited in edit mode.

- ShowHeader—Enables you to display the column header.

- SortExpression—Enables you to associate a sort expression with the column.

- Visible—Enables you to hide a column.

Using CheckBoxFields

A CheckBoxField, as you can probably guess, displays a check box. When a row is not in edit mode, the check box is displayed but it is disabled.

The page in Listing 11.19 illustrates how you can use a `CheckBoxField` (see Figure 11.14).

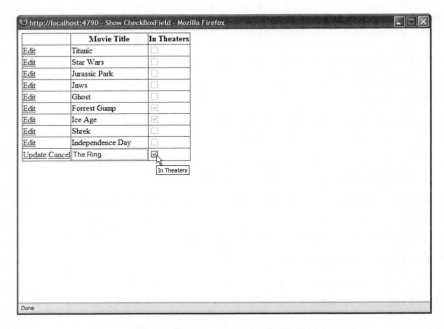

FIGURE 11.14   Using the **CHECKBOXFIELD** with the **GRIDVIEW** control.

LISTING 11.19   ShowCheckBoxField.aspx.

```
<%@ Page Language="VB" %>
<!DOCTYPE html PUBLIC "-//W3C//DTD XHTML 1.1//EN"
    "http://www.w3.org/TR/xhtml11/DTD/xhtml11.dtd">
<html xmlns="http://www.w3.org/1999/xhtml" >
<head id="Head1" runat="server">
    <title>Show CheckBoxField</title>
</head>
<body>
    <form id="form1" runat="server">
    <div>

    <asp:GridView
        id="grdMovies"
        DataSourceID="srcMovies"
        DataKeyNames="Id"
        AutoGenerateColumns="false"
        AutoGenerateEditButton="true"
        Runat="server">
```

LISTING 11.19   Continued

```
        <Columns>
        <asp:BoundField
            DataField="Title"
            HeaderText="Movie Title" />
        <asp:CheckBoxField
            DataField="InTheaters"
            HeaderText="In Theaters" />
        </Columns>
    </asp:GridView>

    <asp:SqlDataSource
        id="srcMovies"
        ConnectionString="<%$ ConnectionStrings:Movies %>"
        SelectCommand="SELECT Id,Title,InTheaters FROM Movies"
        UpdateCommand="UPDATE Movies SET
            Title=@Title, InTheaters=@InTheaters
            WHERE Id=@Id"
        Runat="server" />

    </div>
    </form>
</body>
</html>
```

The CheckBoxField inherits from the BoundField class, so it includes all the properties of the BoundField class. It also supports the following property:

- Text—Displays text next to each check box.

Using CommandFields

You can use a CommandField to customize the appearance of the Edit, Delete, Update, Cancel, and Select buttons displayed by the GridView control. For example, the page in Listing 11.20 uses icons for the standard edit buttons (see Figure 11.15).

LISTING 11.20   ShowCommandField.aspx

```
<%@ Page Language="VB" %>
<!DOCTYPE html PUBLIC "-//W3C//DTD XHTML 1.1//EN"
    "http://www.w3.org/TR/xhtml11/DTD/xhtml11.dtd">
<html xmlns="http://www.w3.org/1999/xhtml" >
<head id="Head1" runat="server">
    <title>Show CommandField</title>
</head>
```

LISTING 11.20 Continued

```
<body>
    <form id="form1" runat="server">
    <div>

    <asp:GridView
        id="grdMovies"
        DataSourceID="srcMovies"
        DataKeyNames="Id"
        AutoGenerateColumns="false"
        Runat="server">
        <Columns>
        <asp:CommandField
            ButtonType="Image"
            ShowEditButton="true"
            EditText="Edit Movie"
            EditImageUrl="Edit.gif"
            UpdateText="Update Movie"
            UpdateImageUrl="Update.gif"
            ShowCancelButton="true"
            CancelText="Cancel Edit"
            CancelImageUrl="Cancel.gif"
            ShowDeleteButton="true"
            DeleteText="Delete Movie"
            DeleteImageUrl="Delete.gif" />
        <asp:BoundField
            DataField="Title"
            HeaderText="Movie Title" />
        <asp:BoundField
            DataField="Director"
            HeaderText="Movie Director" />
        </Columns>
    </asp:GridView>

    <asp:SqlDataSource
        id="srcMovies"
        ConnectionString="<%$ ConnectionStrings:Movies %>"
        SelectCommand="SELECT Id,Title,Director FROM Movies"
        UpdateCommand="UPDATE Movies SET
            Title=@Title, Director=@Director
            WHERE Id=@Id"
        DeleteCommand="DELETE Movies
            WHERE Id=@Id"
        Runat="server" />
```

LISTING 11.20 Continued

```
    </div>
    </form>
</body>
</html>
```

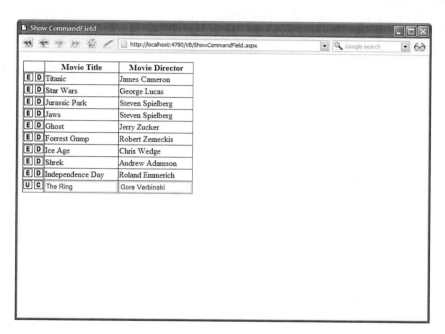

FIGURE 11.15   Using a CommandField with the GridView control.

Notice that you do not enable the AutoGenerateEditButton or AutoGenerateDeleteButton properties when using a CommandField. Instead, you use the CommandField to set up the standard editing buttons explicitly.

The CommandField supports the following properties:

- ButtonType—Enables you to specify the type of button displayed by the CommandField. Possible values are Button, Image, and Link.

- CancelImageUrl—Enables you to specify an image to display for the Cancel button.

- CancelText—Enables you to specify the text to display for the Cancel button.

- CausesValidation—Enables you to disable validation when an edit button is clicked.

- DeleteImageUrl—Enables you to specify an image to display for the Delete button.

- DeleteText—Enables you to specify the text to display for the Delete button.

- `EditImageUrl`—Enables you to specify an image to display for the Edit button.

- `EditText`—Enables you to specify the text to display for the Edit button.

- `InsertImageUrl`—Enables you to specify an image to display for the Insert button.

- `InsertText`—Enables you to specify the text to display for the Insert button.

- `NewImageUrl`—Enables you to specify an image to display for the New button (does not apply to `GridView`).

- `NewText`—Enables you to specify the text to display for the New button.

- `SelectImageUrl`—Enables you to specify the image to display for the Select button.

- `SelectText`—Enables you to specify the text to display for the Select button.

- `ShowCancelButton`—Enables you to display the Cancel button.

- `ShowDeleteButton`—Enables you to display the Delete button.

- `ShowEditButton`—Enables you to display the Edit button.

- `ShowInsertButton`—Enables you to display the Insert button (does not apply to `GridView`).

- `ShowSelectButton`—Enables you to display the Select button.

- `UpdateImageUrl`—Enables you to specify the image to display for the Update button.

- `UpdateText`—Enables you to specify the text to display for the Update button.

- `ValidationGroup`—Enables you to associate the edit buttons with a validation group.

Using Button Fields

You use a `ButtonField` to display a button in a `GridView`. You can use a `ButtonField` to represent a custom command or one of the standard edit commands.

For example, the `GridView` in Listing 11.21 contains two `ButtonFields` that a user can click to change the display order of the movie category records (see Figure 11.16).

LISTING 11.21   ShowButtonField.aspx

```
<%@ Page Language="VB" %>
<!DOCTYPE html PUBLIC "-//W3C//DTD XHTML 1.1//EN"
    "http://www.w3.org/TR/xhtml11/DTD/xhtml11.dtd">
<script runat="server">

    Sub grdMovieCategories_RowCommand(ByVal sender As Object,
➥ByVal e As GridViewCommandEventArgs)
        Dim index As Integer = Int32.Parse(CType(e.CommandArgument, String))
```

LISTING 11.21   Continued

```
        Dim id As Integer =
➥ CType(grdMovieCategories.DataKeys(index).Values("Id"), Integer)
        Dim position As Integer =
➥ CType(grdMovieCategories.DataKeys(index).Values("Position"), Integer)
        Select Case e.CommandName
            Case "Up"
                position = position - 1
            Case "Down"
                position = position + 1
        End Select
        srcMovieCategories.UpdateParameters("Id").DefaultValue = id.ToString()
        srcMovieCategories.UpdateParameters("Position").DefaultValue =
➥ position.ToString()
        srcMovieCategories.Update()
    End Sub
</script>
<html xmlns="http://www.w3.org/1999/xhtml" >
<head id="Head1" runat="server">
    <title>Show ButtonField</title>
</head>
<body>
    <form id="form1" runat="server">
    <div>

    <asp:GridView
        id="grdMovieCategories"
        DataSourceID="srcMovieCategories"
        DataKeyNames="Id,Position"
        AutoGenerateColumns="false"
        OnRowCommand="grdMovieCategories_RowCommand"
        Runat="server">
        <Columns>
        <asp:ButtonField
            Text="Move Up"
            CommandName="Up" />
        <asp:ButtonField
            Text="Move Down"
            CommandName="Down" />
        <asp:BoundField
            DataField="Position"
            HeaderText="Position" />
        <asp:BoundField
            DataField="Name"
            HeaderText="Category Name" />
        </Columns>
    </asp:GridView>
```

LISTING 11.21   Continued

```
<asp:SqlDataSource
    id="srcMovieCategories"
    ConnectionString="<%$ ConnectionStrings:Movies %>"
    SelectCommand="SELECT Id, Name, Position FROM MovieCategories
        ORDER BY Position"
    UpdateCommand="UPDATE MovieCategories SET
        Position=@Position WHERE Id=@Id"
    Runat="server">
    <UpdateParameters>
    <asp:Parameter
        Name="Id" />
    <asp:Parameter
        Name="Position" />
    </UpdateParameters>
</asp:SqlDataSource>

    </div>
    </form>
</body>
</html>
```

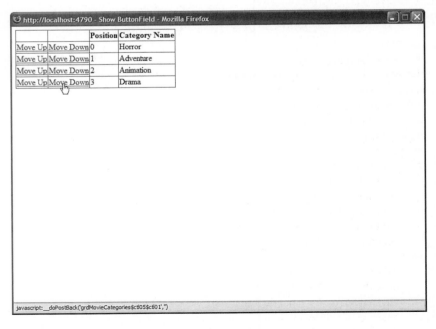

FIGURE 11.16   Using ButtonFields with the GridView control.

When you click either the Move Up or Move Down buttons in the page in Listing 11.21, the GridView control's RowCommand event is raised. This event is handled by the grdMovieCategories_RowCommand() method.

The grdMovieCategories_RowCommand() retrieves the index of the row containing the button that was clicked. The row index is grabbed from the GridViewCommandEventArgs's CommandArgument property passed as the second parameter to the event handler.

The grdMovieCategories_RowCommand() method updates the position of a record by setting the SqlDataSource control's Update parameters and calling the SqlDataSource control's Update() method.

A ButtonField supports the following properties:

- ButtonType—Enables you to specify the type of button displayed by the CommandField. Possible values are Button, Image, and Link.

- CausesValidation—Enables you to disable validation when the button is clicked.

- CommandName—Enables you to associate a standard edit command with the ButtonField. Possible values include Delete, Edit, Update, and Cancel.

- DataTextField—Enables you to use a data column to specify the button text.

- DataTextFormatString—Enables you to format the button text.

- Text—Enables you to specify the button text.

- ValidationGroup—Enables you to associate the button with a validation group.

Notice that you can use CommandName to associate a ButtonField with one of the standard edit commands. For example, you can create a Delete button by assigning the value Delete to the CommandName property.

Using HyperLinkField

You use a HyperLinkField to create a link to another page. A HyperLinkField is particularly useful when you need to build two page Master/Detail forms.

For example, the page in Listing 11.22 displays a list of movie categories, and the page in Listing 11.23 displays a list of movies that match the selected category.

LISTING 11.22   Master.aspx

```
<%@ Page Language="VB" %>
<html xmlns="http://www.w3.org/1999/xhtml" >
<head id="Head1" runat="server">
    <title>Master</title>
</head>
<body>
    <form id="form1" runat="server">
```

LISTING 11.22 Continued

```
    <div>

    <asp:GridView
        id="grdMovieCategories"
        DataSourceID="srcMovieCategories"
        AutoGenerateColumns="false"
        Runat="server">
        <Columns>
        <asp:HyperLinkField
            HeaderText="Movie Categories"
            DataTextField="Name"
            DataNavigateUrlFields="Id"
            DataNavigateUrlFormatString="Details.aspx?id={0}" />
        </Columns>
    </asp:GridView>

    <asp:SqlDataSource
        id="srcMovieCategories"
        ConnectionString="<%$ ConnectionStrings:Movies %>"
        SelectCommand="SELECT Id, Name FROM MovieCategories"
        Runat="server" />

    </div>
    </form>
</body>
</html>
```

LISTING 11.23 Details.aspx

```
<%@ Page Language="VB" %>
<!DOCTYPE html PUBLIC "-//W3C//DTD XHTML 1.1//EN"
  "http://www.w3.org/TR/xhtml11/DTD/xhtml11.dtd">
<html xmlns="http://www.w3.org/1999/xhtml" >
<head id="Head1" runat="server">
    <title>Details</title>
</head>
<body>
    <form id="form1" runat="server">
    <div>

    <asp:GridView
        id="grdMovies"
        DataSourceID="srcMovies"
```

LISTING 11.23 Continued

```
            Runat="server" />

    <asp:SqlDataSource
        id="srcMovies"
        ConnectionString="<%$ ConnectionStrings:Movies %>"
        SelectCommand="SELECT Title,Director FROM Movies
            WHERE CategoryId=@CategoryId"
        Runat="server">
        <SelectParameters>
        <asp:QueryStringParameter
            Name="CategoryId"
            QueryStringField="id" />
        </SelectParameters>
    </asp:SqlDataSource>

    </div>
    </form>
</body>
</html>
```

The page in Listing 11.22 includes a GridView control that contains a HyperLinkField.
The HyperLinkField creates a link to the Details.aspx page and passes the movie category ID as a query string parameter.

The HyperLinkField looks like this:

```
<asp:HyperLinkField
    HeaderText="Movie Categories"
    DataTextField="Name"
    DataNavigateUrlFields="Id"
    DataNavigateUrlFormatString="Details.aspx?id={0}" />
```

The DataNavigateUrlFields property represents the fields used with the
DataNavigateFormatString. The DataNavigateFormatString plugs the value of the
ID column from the DataNavigateUrlFields into the {0} placeholder.

> **NOTE**
>
> The DataNavigateUrlFields property accepts a comma-separated list of column names. You
> can use multiple placeholders in the DataNavigateUrlFormatString.

When you link to the page in Listing 11.23, the list of matching movies is displayed.
Notice that the SqlDataSource control includes a QueryStringParameter that represents
the movie category ID query string parameter.

You also can use HyperLinkFields when working with frames. For example, the page in Listing 11.24 employs a GridView to display a list of movies. The page also includes an iframe (inline frame), which displays details for a particular movie. The iframe displays the page contained in Listing 11.25 (see Figure 11.17).

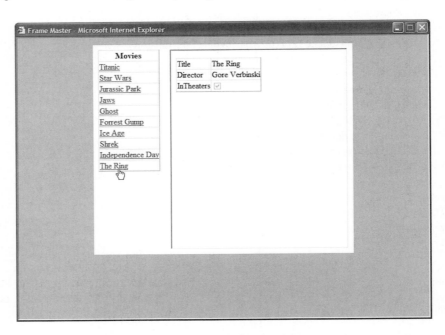

FIGURE 11.17   Displaying a single-page Master/Detail form.

LISTING 11.24   FrameMaster.aspx

```
<%@ Page Language="VB" %>
<!DOCTYPE html PUBLIC "-//W3C//DTD XHTML 1.0 Transitional//EN"
    "http://www.w3.org/TR/xhtml1/DTD/xhtml1-transitional.dtd">
<html xmlns="http://www.w3.org/1999/xhtml" >
<head id="Head1" runat="server">
    <style type="text/css">
        html
        {
            background-color:silver;
        }
        .content
        {
            width:500px;
            margin:auto;
            background-color:white;
        }
```

LISTING 11.24   Continued

```
        .column
        {
            padding:10px;
            float:left;
        }
        #FrameDetails
        {
            width:100%;
            height:400px;
        }
    </style>
    <title>Frame Master</title>
</head>
<body>
    <form id="form1" runat="server">
    <div class="content">

    <div class="column">

    <asp:GridView
        id="grdMovies"
        DataSourceID="srcMovies"
        AutoGenerateColumns="false"
        Runat="server">
        <Columns>
        <asp:HyperLinkField
            HeaderText="Movies"
            DataTextField="Title"
            DataNavigateUrlFields="Id"
            DataNavigateUrlFormatString="FrameDetails.aspx?id={0}"
            Target="FrameDetails" />
        </Columns>
    </asp:GridView>

    <asp:SqlDataSource
        id="srcMovies"
        ConnectionString="<%$ ConnectionStrings:Movies %>"
        SelectCommand="SELECT * FROM Movies"
        Runat="server" />

    </div>
    <div class="column">

    <iframe name="FrameDetails" id="FrameDetails"></iframe>
```

LISTING 11.24   Continued

```
        </div>

        <br style="clear:both" />
        </div>
        </form>
</body>
</html>
```

LISTING 11.25   FrameDetails.aspx

```
<%@ Page Language="VB" %>
<!DOCTYPE html PUBLIC "-//W3C//DTD XHTML 1.0 Transitional//EN"
    "http://www.w3.org/TR/xhtml1/DTD/xhtml1-transitional.dtd">
<html xmlns="http://www.w3.org/1999/xhtml" >
<head id="Head1" runat="server">
    <title>Frame Details</title>
</head>
<body>
    <form id="form1" runat="server">
    <div>

    <asp:DetailsView
        id="dtlMovie"
        DataSourceID="srcMovieDetails"
        Runat="server" />

    <asp:SqlDataSource
        id="srcMovieDetails"
        ConnectionString="<%$ ConnectionStrings:Movies %>"
        SelectCommand="SELECT Title, Director, InTheaters
            FROM Movies WHERE Id=@MovieId"
        Runat="server">
        <SelectParameters>
        <asp:QueryStringParameter
            Name="MovieId"
            QueryStringField="id" />
        </SelectParameters>
    </asp:SqlDataSource>

    </div>
    </form>
</body>
</html>
```

Notice that the HyperLinkField contained in Listing 11.24 includes a Target property. The Target property contains the name of the iframe. When you click a movie link, the FrameDetails.aspx page opens in the named iframe.

The HyperLinkField supports the following properties:

- DataNavigateUrlFields—Represents the field or fields from the data source to use with the DataNavigateUrlFormatString.

- DataNavigateUrlFormatString—Represents a format string that can be used to create the hyperlink.

- DataTextField—Represents a field from the data source to use for the hyperlink label.

- DataTextFormatString—Represents a format string that can be used to format the hyperlink label.

- NavigateUrl—Represents a fixed link to another page.

- Target—Represents the target of a link. Possible values include _blank, _parent, _self, and _top. You can also supply the name of a frame or iframe.

- Text—Represents fixed text to display as the label for the hyperlink.

Using ImageField

You use an ImageField to display an image stored on the server's hard drive. You can't use an ImageField to display images stored in a database table.

The page in Listing 11.26 illustrates how you can use the ImageField when creating a simple photo gallery (see Figure 11.18).

LISTING 11.26   ShowImageField.aspx

```
<%@ Page Language="VB" %>
<!DOCTYPE html PUBLIC "-//W3C//DTD XHTML 1.1//EN"
  "http://www.w3.org/TR/xhtml11/DTD/xhtml11.dtd">
<script runat="server">

    Protected Sub frmPhoto_ItemInserting(ByVal sender As Object,
➥ByVal e As FormViewInsertEventArgs)
        ' Get the FileUpload control
        Dim upPhoto As FileUpload = CType(frmPhoto.FindControl("upPhoto"),
➥FileUpload)
        srcImages.InsertParameters("FileName").DefaultValue = upPhoto.FileName

        ' Save contents to file system
```

LISTING 11.26   Continued

```
        Dim savePath As String = MapPath("~/Photos/" + upPhoto.FileName)
        upPhoto.SaveAs(savePath)
    End Sub

</script>

<html xmlns="http://www.w3.org/1999/xhtml" >
<head id="Head1" runat="server">
    <title>Show ImageField</title>
</head>
<body>
    <form id="form1" runat="server">
    <div>

    <asp:GridView
        id="grdImages"
        DataSourceID="srcImages"
        AutoGenerateColumns="false"
        ShowHeader="false"
        Runat="server">
        <Columns>
        <asp:ImageField
            DataImageUrlField="FileName"
            DataImageUrlFormatString="~/Photos/{0}"
            DataAlternateTextField="AltText"
            ControlStyle-Width="200px" />
        </Columns>
    </asp:GridView>

    <asp:SqlDataSource
        id="srcImages"
        ConnectionString="<%$ ConnectionStrings:Photos %>"
        SelectCommand="SELECT FileName, AltText FROM Photos"
        InsertCommand="INSERT Photos (FileName, AltText)
            VALUES (@FileName, @AltText)"
        Runat="server">
        <InsertParameters>
            <asp:Parameter Name="FileName" />
        </InsertParameters>
    </asp:SqlDataSource>

    <hr />
    <asp:FormView
```

LISTING 11.26 Continued

```
            id="frmPhoto"
            DefaultMode="Insert"
            DataSourceID="srcImages"
            OnItemInserting="frmPhoto_ItemInserting"
            Runat="server">
            <InsertItemTemplate>
            <h1>Add Photo</h1>
            <asp:Label
                id="lblPhoto"
                Text="Photo:"
                AssociatedControlID="upPhoto"
                Runat="server" />
            <br />
            <asp:FileUpload
                id="upPhoto"
                Runat="server" />
            <br />
            <asp:Label
                id="lblAltText"
                Text="Alternate Text:"
                AssociatedControlID="txtAltText"
                Runat="server" />
            <br />
            <asp:TextBox
                id="txtAltText"
                Text='<%# Bind("AltText") %>'
                Columns="50"
                Runat="server" />
            <br />
            <asp:Button
                id="btnInsert"
                Text="Add New Photo"
                CommandName="Insert"
                Runat="server" />
            </InsertItemTemplate>
        </asp:FormView>

    </div>
    </form>
</body>
</html>
```

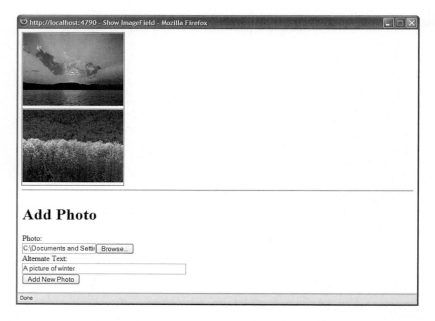

FIGURE 11.18 Using an ImageField with the GridView control.

The GridView in Listing 11.26 contains an ImageField that looks like this:

```
<asp:ImageField
    DataImageUrlField="FileName"
    DataImageUrlFormatString="~/Photos/{0}"
    DataAlternateTextField="AltText"
    ControlStyle-Width="200px" />
```

The DataImageUrlField property contains the name of a field from the data source that represents the path to an image on the server hard drive. The DataImageUrlFormatString enables you to format this path. Finally, the DataAlternateTextField enables you to specify the value of the alt attribute used by the <img> tag.

WEB STANDARDS NOTE

Always supply an alt attribute for your <img> tags so that blind users of your web application can interpret an image's meaning. In the case of purely decorative images, create an empty alt attribute (alt="").

An ImageField supports the following properties:

- AlternateText—Enables you to specify fixed alternate text.

- DataAlternateTextField—Enables you to specify a field that represents the alternate text.

- DataAlternateTextFormatString—Enables you to format the alternate text.

- DataImageUrlField—Enables you to specify a field that represents the image path.

- DataImageUrlFormatString—Enables you to format the image path.

- NullImageUrl—Enables you to specify an alternate image when the DataImageUrlField is Nothing (null).

Using TemplateField

A TemplateField enables you to add any content to a GridView column that you need. A TemplateField can contain HTML, DataBinding expressions, or ASP.NET controls.

TemplateFields are particularly useful when you are using a GridView to edit database records. You can use a TemplateField to customize the user interface and add validation to the fields being edited.

For example, the page in Listing 11.27 contains a GridView that enables you to edit the records contained in the Movies database table. TemplateFields are used to render the user interface for editing the movie title and category columns (see Figure 11.19).

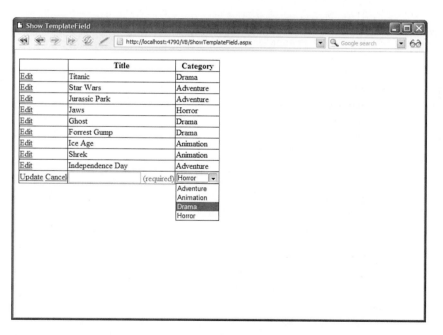

FIGURE 11.19   Using TemplateFields with the GridView control.

LISTING 11.27   ShowTemplateField.aspx

```
<%@ Page Language="VB" %>
<!DOCTYPE html PUBLIC "-//W3C//DTD XHTML 1.1//EN"
  "http://www.w3.org/TR/xhtml11/DTD/xhtml11.dtd">
<html xmlns="http://www.w3.org/1999/xhtml" >
<head id="Head1" runat="server">
    <title>Show TemplateField</title>
</head>
<body>
    <form id="form1" runat="server">
    <div>

    <asp:GridView
        id="grdMovies"
        DataSourceID="srcMovies"
        DataKeyNames="Id"
        AutoGenerateColumns="false"
        AutoGenerateEditButton="true"
        Runat="server">
        <Columns>
        <asp:TemplateField HeaderText="Title">
            <ItemTemplate>
            <%# Eval("Title") %>
            </ItemTemplate>
            <EditItemTemplate>
            <asp:TextBox
                id="txtTitle"
                Text='<%# Bind("Title") %>'
                Runat="server" />
            <asp:RequiredFieldValidator
                id="valTitle"
                ControlToValidate="txtTitle"
                Text="(required)"
                Runat="server" />
            </EditItemTemplate>
        </asp:TemplateField>
        <asp:TemplateField HeaderText="Category">
            <ItemTemplate>
            <%# Eval("Name") %>
            </ItemTemplate>
            <EditItemTemplate>
            <asp:DropDownList
                id="ddlCategory"
                DataSourceID="srcMovieCategories"
                DataTextField="Name"
```

LISTING 11.27   Continued

```
                    DataValueField="Id"
                    SelectedValue='<%# Bind("CategoryId") %>'
                    Runat="server" />
            </EditItemTemplate>
        </asp:TemplateField>
        </Columns>
    </asp:GridView>

    <asp:SqlDataSource
        id="srcMovies"
        ConnectionString='<%$ ConnectionStrings:Movies %>'
        SelectCommand="SELECT Movies.Id, Title, CategoryId, Name
            FROM Movies JOIN MovieCategories
            ON MovieCategories.Id = Movies.CategoryId"
        UpdateCommand="UPDATE Movies SET Title=@Title, CategoryId=@CategoryId
            WHERE Id=@Id"
        Runat="server" />

    <asp:SqlDataSource
        id="srcMovieCategories"
        ConnectionString='<%$ ConnectionStrings:Movies %>'
        SelectCommand="SELECT Id, Name FROM MovieCategories"
        Runat="server" />

    </div>
    </form>
</body>
</html>
```

The GridView in Listing 11.27 contains two TemplateFields. The first TemplateField enables you to display and edit the value of the Title column. The contents of the ItemTemplate are displayed when a row *is not* selected for editing. The contents of the EditItemTemplate are displayed when the row *is* selected for editing.

The EditItemTemplate for the Title column includes a RequiredFieldValidator control. This RequiredFieldValidator control prevents a user from updating a record without entering a value for the Title column.

The second TemplateField displays the value of the movie category column. The EditItemTemplate contains a DropDownList control, which enables you to change the movie category associated with the record being edited.

A TemplateField supports the following six types of templates:

- AlternatingItemTemplate—The contents of this template are displayed for every other row rendered by the GridView.

- `EditItemTemplate`—The contents of this template are displayed when a row is selected for editing.

- `FooterTemplate`—The contents of this template are displayed in the column footer.

- `HeaderTemplate`—The contents of this template are displayed in the column header.

- `InsertItemTemplate`—The contents of this template are displayed when a new data item is inserted (does not apply to the `GridView` control).

- `ItemTemplate`—The contents of this template are displayed for every row rendered by the `GridView`.

Working with `GridView` Control Events

The `GridView` control includes a rich set of events that you can handle to customize the control's behavior and appearance. These events can be divided into three groups.

First, the `GridView` control supports the following set of events that are raised when the control displays its rows:

- `DataBinding`—Raised immediately before the `GridView` is bound to its data source.

- `DataBound`—Raised immediately after a `GridView` is bound to its data source.

- `RowCreated`—Raised when each row in the `GridView` is created.

- `RowDataBound`—Raised when each row in the `GridView` is bound to data.

Second, the `GridView` control includes the following set of events that are raised when you are editing records:

- `RowCommand`—Raised when an event is raised by a control contained in the `GridView`.

- `RowUpdating`—Raised immediately before a `GridView` updates a record.

- `RowUpdated`—Raised immediately after a `GridView` updates a record.

- `RowDeleting`—Raised immediately before a `GridView` deletes a record.

- `RowDeleted`—Raised immediately after a `GridView` deletes a record.

- `RowCancelingEdit`—Raised when you cancel updating a record.

Finally, the `GridView` control supports the following events related to sorting, selecting, and paging:

- `PageIndexChanging`—Raised immediately before the current page is changed.

- `PageIndexChanged`—Raised immediately after the current page is changed.

- `Sorting`—Raised immediately before sorting.

- Sorted—Raised immediately after sorting.

- SelectedIndexChanging—Raised immediately before a row is selected.

- SelectedIndexChanged—Raised immediately after a row is selected.

In this section, you learn how to handle the RowDataBound event (my favorite event included with the GridView control) to create GridView special effects. You learn how to handle the RowDataBound event to highlight particular rows, show column summaries, and create nested Master/Detail forms.

Highlighting GridView Rows

Imagine that you want to highlight particular rows in a GridView. For example, when displaying a table of sales totals, you might want to highlight the rows in which the sales are greater than a certain amount.

You can modify the appearance of individual rows in a GridView control by handling the RowDataBound event. For example, the page in Listing 11.28 displays every movie that has a box office total greater than $300,000.00 with a yellow background color (see Figure 11.20).

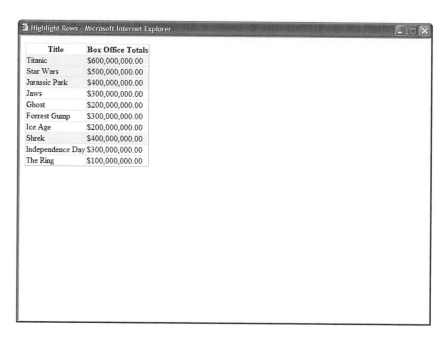

FIGURE 11.20   Highlighting rows in the GridView control.

LISTING 11.28   `HighlightRows.aspx`

```
<%@ Page Language="VB" %>
<!DOCTYPE html PUBLIC "-//W3C//DTD XHTML 1.1//EN"
    "http://www.w3.org/TR/xhtml11/DTD/xhtml11.dtd">
<script runat="server">

    Protected Sub grdMovies_RowDataBound(ByVal sender As Object,
➥ByVal e As GridViewRowEventArgs)
        If e.Row.RowType = DataControlRowType.DataRow Then
            Dim boxOfficeTotals As Decimal =
➥CType(DataBinder.Eval(e.Row.DataItem, "BoxOfficeTotals"), Decimal)
            If boxOfficeTotals > 300000000 Then
                e.Row.BackColor = System.Drawing.Color.Yellow
            End If
        End If
    End Sub
</script>
<html xmlns="http://www.w3.org/1999/xhtml" >
<head id="Head1" runat="server">
    <title>Highlight Rows</title>
</head>
<body>
    <form id="form1" runat="server">
    <div>

    <asp:GridView
        id="grdMovies"
        DataSourceID="srcMovies"
        OnRowDataBound="grdMovies_RowDataBound"
        AutoGenerateColumns="false"
        Runat="server">
        <Columns>
        <asp:BoundField
            DataField="Title"
            HeaderText="Title" />
        <asp:BoundField
            DataField="BoxOfficeTotals"
            DataFormatString="{0:c}"
            HtmlEncode="false"
            HeaderText="Box Office Totals" />
        </Columns>
    </asp:GridView>

    <asp:SqlDataSource
```

LISTING 11.28   Continued

```
        id="srcMovies"
        ConnectionString="<%$ ConnectionStrings:Movies %>"
        SelectCommand="SELECT * FROM Movies"
        Runat="server" />

    </div>
    </form>
</body>
</html>
```

In Listing 11.28, the grdMovies_RowDataBound() method is executed when the GridView renders each of its rows (including its header and footer). The second parameter passed to this event handler is an instance of the GridViewRowEventArgs class. This class exposes a GridViewRow object that represents the row being bound.

The GridViewRow object supports several useful properties (this is not a complete list):

- Cells—Represents the collection of table row cells associated with the row being bound.

- DataItem—Represents the data item associated with the row being bound.

- DataItemIndex—Represents the index of the data item in its DataSet associated with the row being bound.

- RowIndex—Represents the index of the row being bound.

- RowState—Represents the state of the row being bound. Possible values are Alternate, Normal, Selected, Edit. Because these values can be combined (for example, the RowState can be Alternate Edit), use a bitwise comparison with RowState.

- RowType—Represents the type of row being bound. Possible values are DataRow, Footer, Header, NullRow, Pager, Separator.

In Listing 11.28, the RowType property is used to verify that the row is a DataRow (not a header row or some other type of row). The DataItem property is used to retrieve the database record associated with the row. Notice that the DataBinder.Eval() method is used to retrieve the value of the BoxOfficeColumn.

Displaying Column Summaries

Imagine that you want to display a column total at the bottom of a column. In that case, you can handle the GridView RowDataBound event to sum the values in a column and display the summary in the column footer.

For example, the page in Listing 11.29 contains a GridView control that displays a summary column representing the total box office sales of all movies (see Figure 11.21).

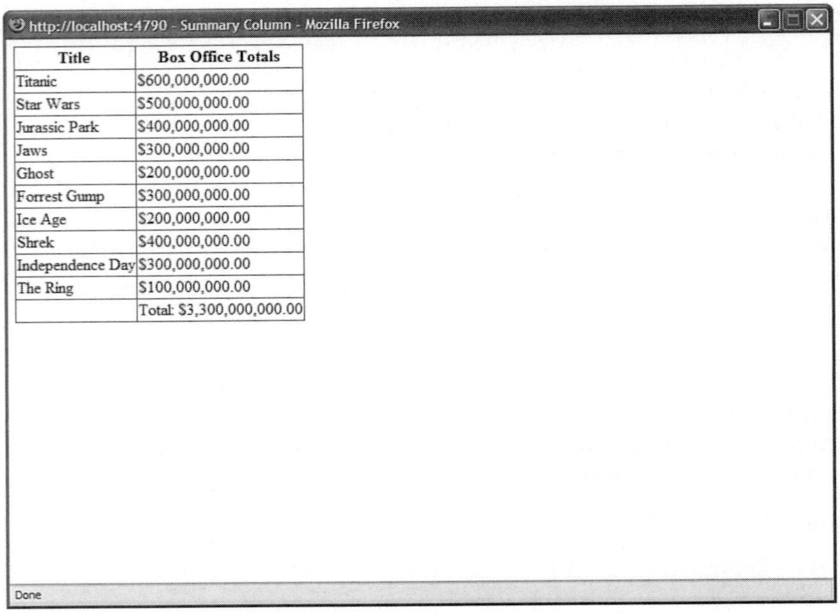

FIGURE 11.21   Displaying a column summary.

LISTING 11.29   SummaryColumn.aspx

```
<%@ Page Language="VB" %>
<!DOCTYPE html PUBLIC "-//W3C//DTD XHTML 1.1//EN"
  "http://www.w3.org/TR/xhtml11/DTD/xhtml11.dtd">
<script runat="server">

    Private _boxOfficeTotalsTotal As Decimal = 0

    Protected Sub grdMovies_RowDataBound(ByVal sender As Object,
➥ByVal e As GridViewRowEventArgs)
        If e.Row.RowType = DataControlRowType.DataRow Then
            Dim boxOfficeTotals As Decimal =
➥CType(DataBinder.Eval(e.Row.DataItem, "BoxOfficeTotals"), Decimal)
            _boxOfficeTotalsTotal += boxOfficeTotals
        End If
        If e.Row.RowType = DataControlRowType.Footer Then
            Dim lblSummary As Label = CType(e.Row.FindControl("lblSummary"), Label)
            lblSummary.Text = String.Format("Total: {0:c}", _boxOfficeTotalsTotal)
        End If
    End Sub
End Sub
```

LISTING 11.29 Continued

```
</script>
<html xmlns="http://www.w3.org/1999/xhtml" >
<head id="Head1" runat="server">
    <title>Summary Column</title>
</head>
<body>
    <form id="form1" runat="server">
    <div>

    <asp:GridView
        id="grdMovies"
        DataSourceID="srcMovies"
        OnRowDataBound="grdMovies_RowDataBound"
        AutoGenerateColumns="false"
        ShowFooter="true"
        Runat="server">
        <Columns>
        <asp:BoundField
            DataField="Title"
            HeaderText="Title" />
        <asp:TemplateField HeaderText="Box Office Totals">
        <ItemTemplate>
            <%# Eval("BoxOfficeTotals", "{0:c}") %>
        </ItemTemplate>
        <FooterTemplate>
            <asp:Label
                id="lblSummary"
                Runat="server" />
        </FooterTemplate>
        </asp:TemplateField>
        </Columns>
    </asp:GridView>

    <asp:SqlDataSource
        id="srcMovies"
        ConnectionString="<%$ ConnectionStrings:Movies %>"
        SelectCommand="SELECT * FROM Movies"
        Runat="server" />

    </div>
    </form>
</body>
</html>
```

Notice that the GridView control uses a TemplateField to represent the BoxOfficeTotals column. The TemplateField includes a <FooterTemplate> that contains a Label control. The grdMovies_RowDataBound() method displays the total of the box office totals in this Label control.

Displaying Nested Master/Details Forms

You also can handle the RowDataBound event to create nested Master/Details forms. The page in Listing 11.30 displays a list of movie categories and displays a list of matching movies under each category (see Figure 11.22).

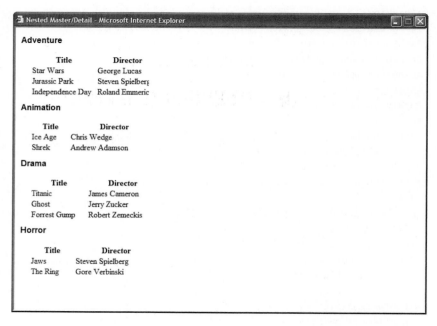

FIGURE 11.22   Displaying a nested Master/Detail form.

LISTING 11.30   NestedMasterDetail.aspx

```
<%@ Page Language="VB" %>
<!DOCTYPE html PUBLIC "-//W3C//DTD XHTML 1.1//EN"
    "http://www.w3.org/TR/xhtml11/DTD/xhtml11.dtd">
<script runat="server">

    Protected Sub grdMovieCategories_RowDataBound(ByVal sender As Object,
➥ByVal e As GridViewRowEventArgs)
        If e.Row.RowType = DataControlRowType.DataRow Then
            Dim categoryId As Integer =
➥CType(DataBinder.Eval(e.Row.DataItem,"Id"), Integer)
```

LISTING 11.30   Continued

```
            Dim srcMovies As SqlDataSource =
➥CType(e.Row.FindControl("srcMovies"), SqlDataSource)
            srcMovies.SelectParameters("CategoryId").DefaultValue =
➥categoryId.ToString()
        End If
    End Sub

</script>
<html xmlns="http://www.w3.org/1999/xhtml" >
<head id="Head1" runat="server">
    <style type="text/css">
        .categories h1
        {
            font:bold 16px Arial, Sans-Serif;
        }
        .movies
        {
            margin-left:20px;
            margin-bottom:10px;
            width:100%;
        }
    </style>
    <title>Nested Master/Detail</title>
</head>
<body>
    <form id="form1" runat="server">
    <div>

    <asp:GridView
        id="grdMovies"
        DataSourceID="srcMovieCategories"
        OnRowDataBound="grdMovieCategories_RowDataBound"
        AutoGenerateColumns="false"
        CssClass="categories"
        ShowHeader="false"
        GridLines="none"
        Runat="server">
        <Columns>
        <asp:TemplateField>
        <ItemTemplate>
            <h1><%# Eval("Name") %></h1>
            <asp:GridView
                id="grdMovies"
                DataSourceId="srcMovies"
```

LISTING 11.30   Continued

```
                CssClass="movies"
                GridLines="none"
                Runat="server" />

        <asp:SqlDataSource
            id="srcMovies"
            ConnectionString="<%$ ConnectionStrings:Movies %>"
            SelectCommand="SELECT Title,Director FROM Movies
                WHERE CategoryId=@CategoryId"
            Runat="server">
            <SelectParameters>
                <asp:Parameter Name="CategoryId" />
            </SelectParameters>
        </asp:SqlDataSource>
    </ItemTemplate>
    </asp:TemplateField>
    </Columns>
</asp:GridView>

<asp:SqlDataSource
    id="srcMovieCategories"
    ConnectionString="<%$ ConnectionStrings:Movies %>"
    SelectCommand="SELECT Id,Name FROM MovieCategories"
    Runat="server" />

</div>
</form>
</body>
</html>
```

The grdMovieCategories_RowDataBound() method handles the RowDataBound event. This event handler grabs the movie category ID from the current row's DataItem property. Next, it retrieves the SqlDataSource control contained in the grdMovieCategories TemplateField. Finally, it assigns the movie category ID to a parameter contained in the SqlDataSource control's SelectParameters collection.

> **NOTE**
>
> Notice that you must use the FindControl() method to get the SqlDataSource control from the TemplateField. The templates in a TemplateField each create their own naming containers to prevent naming collisions. The FindControl() method enables you to search a naming container for a control with a matching ID.

Extending the GridView Control

Like any other control in the ASP.NET framework, if you don't like any aspect of the GridView control, you always have the option of extending the control. In this section, you learn how to extend the GridView control with custom fields.

To create a custom field, you can inherit a new class from any of the existing fields or any of the following base classes:

- DataControlField—The base class for all fields.

- ButtonFieldBase—The base class for all button fields, such as the ButtonField and CommandField.

In this section, you learn how to create a long text field, a delete button field, and a validated field.

Creating a Long Text Field

None of the existing GridView fields do a good job of handling large amounts of text. You can fix this problem by creating a custom field, named the LongTextField, which you can use to display the value of text columns regardless of the length of the text.

In normal display mode, the LongTextField displays the text in a scrolling <div> tag. In edit display mode, the text appears in a multi-line TextBox control (see Figure 11.23).

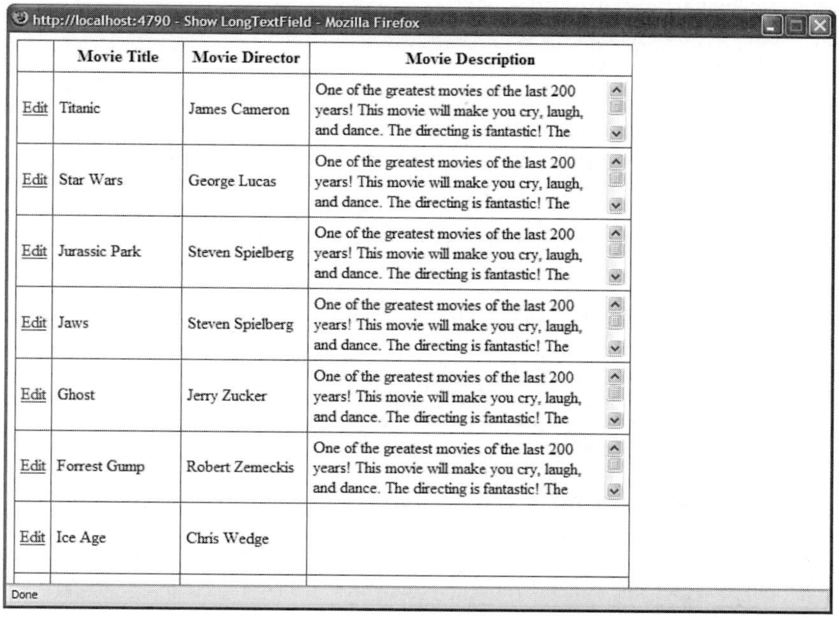

FIGURE 11.23   Displaying a long text field.

To create a custom field, we'll inherit a new class from the base `BoundField` control. The custom `LongTextField` is contained in Listing 11.31.

LISTING 11.31   LongTextField.vb

```vb
Imports System
Imports System.Web.UI
Imports System.Web.UI.WebControls
Imports System.Web.UI.HtmlControls

Namespace myControls
    ''' <summary>
    ''' Enables you to display a long text field
    ''' </summary>
    Public Class LongTextField
        Inherits BoundField

        Private _width As Unit = New Unit("250px")
        Private _height As Unit = New Unit("60px")

        ''' <summary>
        ''' The width of the field
        ''' </summary>
        Public Property Width() As Unit
            Get
                Return _width
            End Get
            Set(ByVal Value As Unit)
                _width = Value
            End Set
        End Property

        ''' <summary>
        ''' The height of the field
        ''' </summary>
        Public Property Height() As Unit
            Get
                Return _height
            End Get
            Set(ByVal Value As Unit)
                _height = Value
            End Set
        End Property

        ''' <summary>
        ''' Builds the contents of the field
```

LISTING 11.31   Continued

```
''' </summary>
Protected Overrides Sub InitializeDataCell(ByVal cell
➡As DataControlFieldCell, ByVal rowState As DataControlRowState)
        ' If not editing, show in scrolling div
        If (rowState And DataControlRowState.Edit) = 0 Then
            Dim div As HtmlGenericControl = New HtmlGenericControl("div")
            div.Attributes("class") = "longTextField"
            div.Style(HtmlTextWriterStyle.Width) = _width.ToString()
            div.Style(HtmlTextWriterStyle.Height) = _height.ToString()
            div.Style(HtmlTextWriterStyle.Overflow) = "auto"

            AddHandler div.DataBinding, AddressOf div_DataBinding

            cell.Controls.Add(div)
        Else
            Dim txtEdit As TextBox = New TextBox()
            txtEdit.TextMode = TextBoxMode.MultiLine
            txtEdit.Width = _width
            txtEdit.Height = _height

            AddHandler txtEdit.DataBinding, AddressOf txtEdit_DataBinding

            cell.Controls.Add(txtEdit)
        End If
    End Sub

    ''' <summary>
    ''' Called when databound in display mode
    ''' </summary>
    Private Sub div_DataBinding(ByVal s As Object, ByVal e As EventArgs)
        Dim div As HtmlGenericControl = CType(s, HtmlGenericControl)

        ' Get the field value
        Dim value As Object = Me.GetValue(div.NamingContainer)

        ' Assign the formatted value
        div.InnerText = Me.FormatDataValue(value, Me.HtmlEncode)
    End Sub

    ''' <summary>
    ''' Called when databound in edit mode
    ''' </summary>
    Private Sub txtEdit_DataBinding(ByVal s As Object, ByVal e As EventArgs)
        Dim txtEdit As TextBox = CType(s, TextBox)
```

LISTING 11.31   Continued

```
            ' Get the field value
            Dim value As Object = Me.GetValue(txtEdit.NamingContainer)

            ' Assign the formatted value
            txtEdit.Text = Me.FormatDataValue(value, Me.HtmlEncode)
        End Sub

    End Class
End Namespace
```

In Listing 11.31, the `InitializeDataCell()` method is overridden. This method is responsible for creating all the controls that the custom field contains.

First, a check is made to determine whether the field is being rendered when the row is selected for editing. Notice that a bitwise comparison must be performed with the `rowState` parameter because the `rowState` parameter can contain combinations of the values `Alternate`, `Normal`, `Selected`, and `Edit` (for example, the `RowState` can be both `Alternate` and `Edit`).

When the row is not in edit mode, a `<div>` tag is created to contain the text. An `HtmlGenericControl` represents the `<div>` tag. When the `GridView` is bound to its data source, the `<div>` tags get the value of its `innerText` property from the `div_DataBinding()` method.

When the row is selected for editing, a multi-line `TextBox` control is created. When the `GridView` is bound to its data source, the `TextBox` control's `Text` property gets its value from the `txtEdit_DataBinding()` method.

You can experiment with the `LongTextField` with the page in Listing 11.32. This page uses the `LongTextField` to display the value of the Movie Description column.

LISTING 11.32   ShowLongTextField.aspx

```
<%@ Page Language="VB" %>
<%@ Register TagPrefix="custom" Namespace="myControls" %>
<!DOCTYPE html PUBLIC "-//W3C//DTD XHTML 1.1//EN"
    "http://www.w3.org/TR/xhtml11/DTD/xhtml11.dtd">
<html xmlns="http://www.w3.org/1999/xhtml" >
<head id="Head1" runat="server">
    <style type="text/css">
        .grid td, .grid th
        {
            padding:5px;
        }
    </style>
```

LISTING 11.32 Continued

```
    <title>Show LongTextField</title>
</head>
<body>
    <form id="form1" runat="server">
    <div>

    <asp:GridView
        id="grdMovies"
        CssClass="grid"
        DataSourceID="srcMovies"
        DataKeyNames="Id"
        AutoGenerateColumns="false"
        AutoGenerateEditButton="true"
        Runat="server">
        <Columns>
        <asp:BoundField
            DataField="Title"
            HeaderText="Movie Title" />
        <asp:BoundField
            DataField="Director"
            HeaderText="Movie Director" />
        <custom:LongTextField
            DataField="Description"
            Width="300px"
            Height="60px"
            HeaderText="Movie Description" />
        </Columns>
    </asp:GridView>

    <asp:SqlDataSource
        id="srcMovies"
        ConnectionString="<%$ ConnectionStrings:Movies %>"
        SelectCommand="SELECT Id, Title, Director, Description
            FROM Movies"
        UpdateCommand="UPDATE Movies SET
            Title=@Title,Director=@Director,Description=@Description
            WHERE Id=@Id"
        Runat="server" />

    </div>
    </form>
</body>
</html>
```

Creating a Delete Button Field

I don't like the Delete button rendered by the GridView control's CommandField. The problem is that it does not provide you with any warning before you delete a record. In this section, we fix this problem by creating a Delete button that displays a client-side confirmation dialog box (see Figure 11.24).

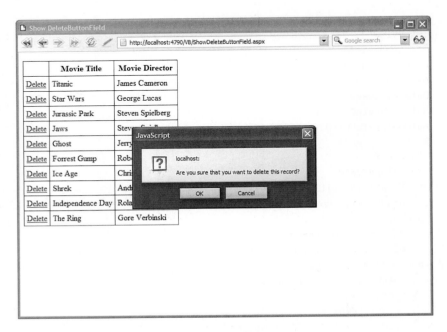

FIGURE 11.24   Displaying a confirmation dialog box.

The DeleteButtonField inherits from the ButtonField class. The code for the custom field is contained in Listing 11.33.

LISTING 11.33   DeleteButtonField.vb

```
Imports System
Imports System.Web.UI.WebControls

Namespace myControls
    ''' <summary>
    ''' Displays a confirmation before deleting a record
    ''' </summary>
    Public Class DeleteButtonField
        Inherits ButtonField

        Private _confirmText As String = "Delete this record?"
```

LISTING 11.33   Continued

```
        Public Property ConfirmText() As String
            Get
                Return _confirmText
            End Get
            Set(ByVal Value As String)
                _confirmText = value
            End Set
        End Property


        Public Sub New()
            Me.CommandName = "Delete"
            Me.Text = "Delete"
        End Sub


        Public Overrides Sub InitializeCell(ByVal cell As DataControlFieldCell,
➡ ByVal cellType As DataControlCellType, ByVal rowState As DataControlRowState,
➡ByVal rowIndex As Integer)
                MyBase.InitializeCell(cell, cellType, rowState, rowIndex)
                If cellType = DataControlCellType.DataCell Then
                    Dim button As WebControl = CType(cell.Controls(0), WebControl)
                    button.Attributes("onclick") = String.Format(
➡"return confirm('{0}');", _confirmText)
                End If
        End Sub


    End Class
End Namespace
```

Most of the work in Listing 11.33 is handled by the base `ButtonField` class. The `InitializeCell()` method is overridden so that the button can be grabbed. The button is added to the cell by the base `ButtonField`'s `InitializeCell()` method.

To create the confirmation dialog box, an `onclick` attribute is added to the button. If the JavaScript confirm statement returns `false`, then the button click is canceled.

You can test the `DeleteButtonField` with the page in Listing 11.34. This page enables you to delete records from the Movies database table.

LISTING 11.34   ShowDeleteButtonField.vb

```
<%@ Page Language="VB" %>
<%@ Register TagPrefix="custom" Namespace="myControls" %>
<!DOCTYPE html PUBLIC "-//W3C//DTD XHTML 1.1//EN"
  "http://www.w3.org/TR/xhtml11/DTD/xhtml11.dtd">
<html xmlns="http://www.w3.org/1999/xhtml" >
```

LISTING 11.34   Continued

```
<head id="Head1" runat="server">
    <style type="text/css">
        .grid td, .grid th
        {
            padding:5px;
        }
    </style>
    <title>Show DeleteButtonField</title>
</head>
<body>
    <form id="form1" runat="server">
    <div>

    <asp:GridView
        id="grdMovies"
        CssClass="grid"
        DataSourceID="srcMovies"
        DataKeyNames="Id"
        AutoGenerateColumns="false"
        Runat="server">
        <Columns>
        <custom:DeleteButtonField
            ConfirmText="Are you sure that you want to delete this record?" />
        <asp:BoundField
            DataField="Title"
            HeaderText="Movie Title" />
        <asp:BoundField
            DataField="Director"
            HeaderText="Movie Director" />
        </Columns>
    </asp:GridView>

    <asp:SqlDataSource
        id="srcMovies"
        ConnectionString="<%$ ConnectionStrings:Movies %>"
        SelectCommand="SELECT Id, Title, Director FROM Movies"
        DeleteCommand="DELETE Movies WHERE Id=@Id"
        Runat="server" />

    </div>
    </form>
</body>
</html>
```

Creating a Validated Field

In this final section, we create a `ValidatedField` custom field. This field automatically validates the data that a user enters into a `GridView` when editing a record. The `ValidatedField` uses a `RequiredFieldValidator` to check whether a user has entered a value, and a `CompareValidator` to check whether the value is the correct data type (see Figure 11.25).

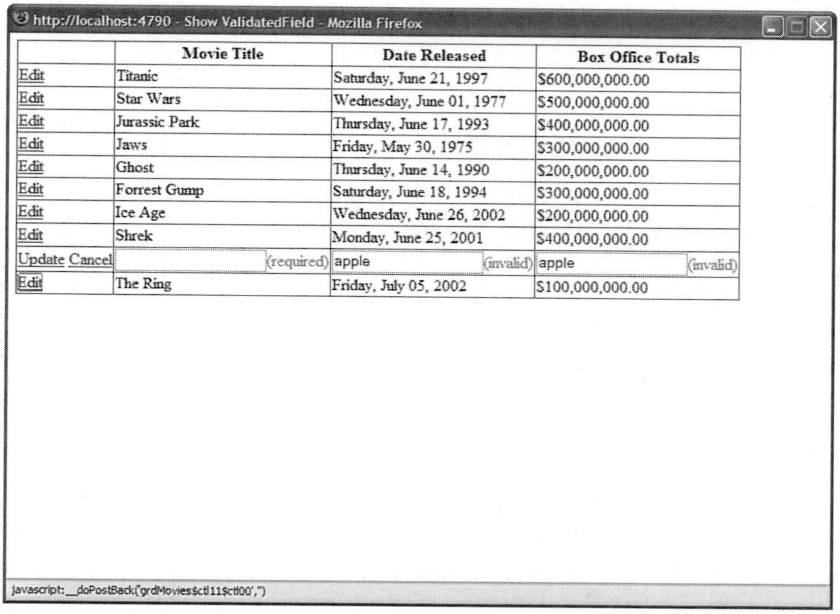

	Movie Title	Date Released	Box Office Totals
Edit	Titanic	Saturday, June 21, 1997	$600,000,000.00
Edit	Star Wars	Wednesday, June 01, 1977	$500,000,000.00
Edit	Jurassic Park	Thursday, June 17, 1993	$400,000,000.00
Edit	Jaws	Friday, May 30, 1975	$300,000,000.00
Edit	Ghost	Thursday, June 14, 1990	$200,000,000.00
Edit	Forrest Gump	Saturday, June 18, 1994	$300,000,000.00
Edit	Ice Age	Wednesday, June 26, 2002	$200,000,000.00
Edit	Shrek	Monday, June 25, 2001	$400,000,000.00
Update Cancel	(required)	apple (invalid)	apple (invalid)
Edit	The Ring	Friday, July 05, 2002	$100,000,000.00

FIGURE 11.25 Using the ValidatedField to edit a record.

The ValidatedField is a composite field. The field contains three child controls—a `TextBox`, `RequiredFieldValidator`, `CompareValidator`—wrapped up in a container control.

The code for the `ValidatedField` is contained in Listing 11.35.

LISTING 11.35 `ValidatedField.vb`

```
Imports System
Imports System.Collections.Specialized
Imports System.Web.UI
Imports System.Web.UI.WebControls

Namespace myControls
    ''' <summary>
    ''' Adds RequiredFieldValidator and CompareValidator
```

LISTING 11.35   Continued

```vb
''' to BoundField
''' </summary>
Public Class ValidatedField
    Inherits BoundField

    Private _validationDataType As ValidationDataType =
ValidationDataType.String

    Public Property ValidationDataType() As ValidationDataType
        Get
            Return _validationDataType
        End Get
        Set(ByVal Value As ValidationDataType)
            _validationDataType = Value
        End Set
    End Property

    ''' <summary>
    ''' Get value from TextBox
    ''' </summary>
    Public Overrides Sub ExtractValuesFromCell(ByVal dictionary As
➥ IOrderedDictionary, ByVal cell As DataControlFieldCell,
➥ByVal rowState As DataControlRowState, ByVal includeReadOnly As Boolean)
        Dim edit As EditContainer = CType(cell.Controls(0), EditContainer)
        If dictionary.Contains(DataField) Then
            dictionary(DataField) = edit.Text
        Else
            dictionary.Add(DataField, edit.Text)
        End If
    End Sub

    ''' <summary>
    ''' Called when field is bound to data source
    ''' </summary>
    Protected Overrides Sub OnDataBindField(ByVal sender As Object,
➥ ByVal e As EventArgs)
        Dim source As Control = CType(sender, Control)

        ' Get the field value
        Dim value As Object = Me.GetValue(source.NamingContainer)

        ' If the control is a table cell, display the text
        If TypeOf source Is DataControlFieldCell Then
```

LISTING 11.35   Continued

```
                Dim formattedValue As String = Me.FormatDataValue(value,
➥Me.HtmlEncode)
            If formattedValue = String.Empty Then
                formattedValue = " "
            End If
            CType(source, DataControlFieldCell).Text = formattedValue
        End If


        ' If the control is an editor, display the editor
        If TypeOf source Is EditContainer Then
            Dim formattedValue As String = String.Empty
            Select Case _validationDataType
                Case ValidationDataType.Date
                    Dim vdate As DateTime = CType(value, DateTime)
                    formattedValue = vdate.ToShortDateString()
                Case ValidationDataType.Currency
                    Dim dec As Decimal = CType(value, Decimal)
                    formattedValue = dec.ToString("F")
                Case Else
                    formattedValue = value.ToString()
            End Select
            CType(source, EditContainer).Text = formattedValue
        End If
    End Sub

    ''' <summary>
    ''' Build the field
    ''' </summary>
    Protected Overrides Sub InitializeDataCell(ByVal cell As
➥DataControlFieldCell, ByVal rowState As DataControlRowState)
        If (rowState And DataControlRowState.Edit) = 0 Then
            AddHandler cell.DataBinding, AddressOf Me.OnDataBindField
        Else
            Dim editor As EditContainer =
➥New EditContainer(DataField, _validationDataType)
            AddHandler editor.DataBinding, AddressOf Me.OnDataBindField
            cell.Controls.Add(editor)
        End If
    End Sub
End Class

''' <summary>
''' This control is added to the field
''' </summary>
```

LISTING 11.35   Continued

```
Public Class EditContainer
    Inherits Control
    Implements INamingContainer

    Private _dataField As String
    Private _validationDataType As ValidationDataType

    Private _txtEdit As TextBox
    Private _valReq As RequiredFieldValidator
    Private _valCompare As CompareValidator

    Public Sub New(ByVal dataField As String,
➡ByVal validationDataType As ValidationDataType)
        _dataField = dataField
        _validationDataType = validationDataType
    End Sub

    ''' <summary>
    ''' Expose the TextBox control's Text property
    ''' </summary>
    Public Property Text() As String
        Get
            EnsureChildControls()
            Return _txtEdit.Text
        End Get
        Set(ByVal Value As String)
            EnsureChildControls()
            _txtEdit.Text = Value
        End Set
    End Property

    ''' <summary>
    ''' Add TextBox, RequiredFieldValidator, and
    ''' CompareValidator
    ''' </summary>
    Protected Overrides Sub CreateChildControls()
        ' Add the textbox
        _txtEdit = New TextBox()
        _txtEdit.ID = "txtEdit"
        Controls.Add(_txtEdit)

        ' Add a RequiredFieldValidator control
        _valReq = New RequiredFieldValidator()
        _valReq.Display = ValidatorDisplay.Dynamic
```

LISTING 11.35   Continued

```
                _valReq.Text = "(required)"
                _valReq.ControlToValidate = _txtEdit.ID
                Controls.Add(_valReq)

                ' Add a CompareValidator control
                _valCompare = New CompareValidator()
                _valCompare.Display = ValidatorDisplay.Dynamic
                _valCompare.Operator = ValidationCompareOperator.DataTypeCheck
                _valCompare.Type = _validationDataType
                _valCompare.Text = "(invalid)"
                _valCompare.ControlToValidate = _txtEdit.ID
                Controls.Add(_valCompare)
        End Sub
    End Class
End Namespace
```

The file in Listing 11.35 contains two classes. It contains the ValidatedField class and the EditContainer class.

The ValidatedField class derives from the BoundField class and overrides the InitializeDataCell() method. When a row is not selected for editing, the field simply displays the value of the data item associated with it. When a row is selected for editing, the field creates a new EditContainer control.

The EditContainer control contains a TextBox, RequiredFieldValidator, and CompareValidator. Notice that the EditContainer implements the INamingContainer interface. Implementing this interface prevents naming collisions when more than one instance of the ValidatedField is used in a GridView row.

The ValidatedField is used in the page in Listing 11.36. This page contains a GridView control that you can use to edit the Movies database table. The GridView control includes three ValidatedFields: one for the Title, DateReleased, and BoxOfficeTotals columns.

If you edit a column, and attempt to submit the column without entering a value, then a validation error is displayed. Furthermore, if you attempt to enter a value that is not a date for the DateReleased column or a value that is not a currency amount for the BoxOfficeTotals column, then a validation error is displayed.

LISTING 11.36   ShowValidatedField.aspx

```
<%@ Page Language="VB" %>
<%@ Register TagPrefix="custom" Namespace="myControls" %>
<!DOCTYPE html PUBLIC "-//W3C//DTD XHTML 1.1//EN"
    "http://www.w3.org/TR/xhtml11/DTD/xhtml11.dtd">
<html xmlns="http://www.w3.org/1999/xhtml" >
<head id="Head1" runat="server">
```

LISTING 11.36   Continued

```
    <title>Show ValidatedField</title>
</head>
<body>
    <form id="form1" runat="server">
    <div>

    <asp:GridView
        id="grdMovies"
        DataKeyNames="Id"
        DataSourceID="srcMovies"
        AutoGenerateEditButton="true"
        AutoGenerateColumns="false"
        Runat="server">
        <Columns>
        <custom:ValidatedField
            DataField="Title"
            HeaderText="Movie Title" />
        <custom:ValidatedField
            DataField="DateReleased"
            DataFormatString="{0:D}"
            HtmlEncode="false"
            ValidationDataType="Date"
            HeaderText="Date Released" />
        <custom:ValidatedField
            DataField="BoxOfficeTotals"
            DataFormatString="{0:c}"
            HtmlEncode="false"
            ValidationDataType="Currency"
            HeaderText="Box Office Totals" />
        </Columns>
    </asp:GridView>

    <asp:SqlDataSource
        id="srcMovies"
        ConnectionString="<%$ ConnectionStrings:Movies %>"
        SelectCommand="SELECT * FROM Movies"
        UpdateCommand="UPDATE Movies SET Title=@Title,
            DateReleased=@DateReleased, BoxOfficeTotals=@BoxOfficeTotals
            WHERE Id=@Id"
        Runat="server" />

    </div>
    </form>
</body>
</html>
```

Summary

In this chapter, you learned how to use the GridView control to display, select, sort, page, and edit database records. You also learn how to customize the appearance of the columns rendered by a column by using different types of fields. In particular, you learned how to use BoundFields, CheckboxFields, CommandFields, ImageFields, TemplateFields, ButtonFields, and HyperLinkFields.

Next, you learned how to handle the RowDataBound event to create GridView special effects. For example, you learned how to add column summaries to a GridView.

Finally, you learned how to extend the GridView control with custom fields. We created custom fields, which enable you to display large text fields, display a confirmation dialog box before a record is deleted, and display validation error messages when editing a record.

CHAPTER **12**

Using the DetailsView and FormView Controls

The DetailsView and FormView controls, the subject of this chapter, enable you to work with a single data item at a time. Both controls enable you to display, edit, insert, and delete data items such as database records. Furthermore, both controls enable you to page forward and backward through a set of data items.

The difference between the two controls concerns the user interface that the controls render. The DetailsView control always renders each field in a separate HTML table row. The FormView control, on the other hand, uses a template that enables you to completely customize the user interface rendered by the control.

Using the DetailsView Control

In this section, you learn how to use the DetailsView control when working with database records. In particular, you learn how to display, page, edit, insert, and delete database records with the DetailsView. You also learn how to format the appearance of the DetailsView control.

Displaying Data with the DetailsView Control

A DetailsView control renders an HTML table that displays the contents of a single database record. The DetailsView supports both declarative and programmatic databinding.

For example, the page in Listing 12.1 displays a record from the Movies database table, using declarative databinding (see Figure 12.1).

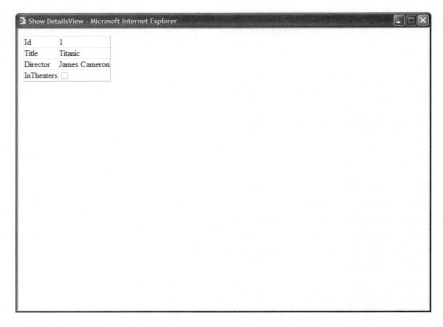

FIGURE 12.1   Displaying a movie record.

LISTING 12.1   `ShowDetailsView.aspx`

```
<%@ Page Language="VB" %>
<!DOCTYPE html PUBLIC "-//W3C//DTD XHTML 1.1//EN"
    "http://www.w3.org/TR/xhtml11/DTD/xhtml11.dtd">
<html xmlns="http://www.w3.org/1999/xhtml" >
<head id="Head1" runat="server">
    <title>Show DetailsView</title>
</head>
<body>
    <form id="form1" runat="server">
    <div>

    <asp:DetailsView
        id="dtlMovies"
        DataSourceID="srcMovies"
        Runat="server" />

    <asp:SqlDataSource
        id="srcMovies"
        ConnectionString="<%$ ConnectionStrings:Movies %>"
        SelectCommand="SELECT Id,Title,Director,InTheaters FROM Movies
```

LISTING 12.1 Continued

```
            WHERE Id=1"
        Runat="server" />

    </div>
    </form>
</body>
</html>
```

In Listing 12.1, the SQL Select statement associated with the `SqlDataSource` control retrieves the first movie from the Movies database table. The `DetailsView` control is bound to the `SqlDataSource` control through its `DataSourceID` property.

You also can bind a `DetailsView` control programmatically to a data source. The page in Listing 12.2 contains a `DetailsView` that is bound to a collection of employees.

LISTING 12.2 ShowEmployee.aspx

```
<%@ Page Language="VB" %>
<%@ Import Namespace="System.Collections.Generic" %>
<!DOCTYPE html PUBLIC "-//W3C//DTD XHTML 1.1//EN"
    "http://www.w3.org/TR/xhtml11/DTD/xhtml11.dtd">
<script runat="server">

    ''' <summary>
    ''' Represents an employee
    ''' </summary>
    Public Class Employee
        Public _firstName As String
        Public _lastName As String
        Public _retired As Boolean

        Public ReadOnly Property FirstName() As String
            Get
                Return _firstName
            End Get
        End Property

        Public ReadOnly Property LastName() As String
            Get
                Return _lastName
            End Get
        End Property

        Public ReadOnly Property Retired() As Boolean
```

LISTING 12.2   Continued

```
            Get
                Return _retired
            End Get
        End Property

        Public Sub New(ByVal firstName As String, ByVal lastName As String,
➥ByVal retired As Boolean)
            _firstName = firstName
            _lastName = lastName
            _retired = retired
        End Sub
    End Class

    ''' <summary>
    ''' Load employees into DetailsView
    ''' </summary>
    Private Sub Page_Load()
        ' Create employees collection with one employee
        Dim NewEmployee As New Employee("Steve", "Walther", False)
        Dim employees As New List(Of Employee)()
        employees.Add(NewEmployee)

        ' Bind employees to DetailsView
        dtlMovies.DataSource = employees
        dtlMovies.DataBind()
    End Sub

</script>
<html xmlns="http://www.w3.org/1999/xhtml" >
<head id="Head1" runat="server">
    <title>Show Employee</title>
</head>
<body>
    <form id="form1" runat="server">
    <div>

    <asp:DetailsView
        id="dtlMovies"
        Runat="server" />

    </div>
    </form>
</body>
</html>
```

In Listing 12.2, an `Employee` class is defined, which contains properties for the employee first name, last name, and retirement status. In the `Page_Load()` method, a new employee is created and added to a generic collection. This collection is bound to the `DetailsView` control.

Using Fields with the `DetailsView` Control

If you need more control over the appearance of the `DetailsView`, including the particular order in which columns are displayed, then you can use fields with the `DetailsView` control. The `DetailsView` control supports exactly the same fields as the `GridView` control:

- `BoundField`—Enables you to display the value of a data item as text.
- `CheckBoxField`—Enables you to display the value of a data item as a check box.
- `CommandField`—Enables you to display links for editing, deleting, and selecting rows.
- `ButtonField`—Enables you to display the value of a data item as a button (image button, link button, or push button).
- `HyperLinkField`—Enables you to display the value of a data item as a link.
- `ImageField`—Enables you to display the value of a data item as an image.
- `TemplateField`—Enables you to customize the appearance of a data item.

> **NOTE**
>
> Another option is to create custom fields for the `DetailsView` control. You can create custom fields that work with the `DetailsView` control in exactly the same way as you create custom fields that work with the `GridView` control. Custom fields for the `GridView` control are discussed in the final section of Chapter 11, "Using the `GridView` Control."

The page in Listing 12.3 contains a `DetailsView` control that contains three `BoundFields`. The `BoundFields` display the values of the Title, Director, and BoxOfficeTotals database columns (see Figure 12.2).

LISTING 12.3   `ShowFields.aspx`

```
<%@ Page Language="VB" %>
<!DOCTYPE html PUBLIC "-//W3C//DTD XHTML 1.1//EN"
    "http://www.w3.org/TR/xhtml11/DTD/xhtml11.dtd">
<html xmlns="http://www.w3.org/1999/xhtml" >
<head id="Head1" runat="server">
    <title>Show Fields</title>
</head>
<body>
    <form id="form1" runat="server">
```

LISTING 12.3   Continued

```
<div>

<asp:DetailsView
    id="dtlMovies"
    DataSourceID="srcMovies"
    AutoGenerateRows="false"
    Runat="server">
    <Fields>
    <asp:BoundField
        DataField="Title"
        HeaderText="Movie Title:" />
    <asp:BoundField
        DataField="Director"
        HeaderText="Movie Director:" />
    <asp:BoundField
        DataField="BoxOfficeTotals"
        DataFormatString="{0:c}"
        HtmlEncode="false"
        HeaderText="Box Office Totals:" />
    </Fields>
</asp:DetailsView>

<asp:SqlDataSource
    id="srcMovies"
    ConnectionString="<%$ ConnectionStrings:Movies %>"
    SelectCommand="SELECT Id,Title,Director,BoxOfficeTotals FROM Movies
        WHERE Id=1"
    Runat="server" />

</div>
</form>
</body>
</html>
```

Notice that the `DetailsView` control has an `AutoGenerateRows` property that has the value
`False`. When you specify fields for a `DetailsView` control, you'll want to include this
property so that the fields do not appear more than once.

Each of the `BoundFields` in Listing 12.3 includes a `HeaderText` attribute that is used to
specify the label for the field. In addition, the `BoundField` associated with the
BoxOfficeTotals column includes a `DataFormatString` property that is used to format the
value of the column as a currency amount.

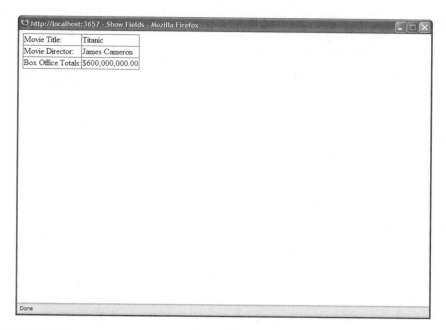

FIGURE 12.2   Using BoundFields with the DetailsView control.

> **WARNING**
>
> Make sure that you disable HTML encoding by setting the HtmlEncode property to the value
> False when you use the DataFormatString property. Otherwise the format string is ignored.

Displaying Empty Data with the DetailsView Control

The DetailsView control includes two properties that you can use to display a message
when no results are returned from its data source. You can use the EmptyDataText property to display an HTML string, or the EmptyDataTemplate property to display more
complicated content.

For example, the SqlDataSource in Listing 12.4 does not return a record because no
record in the Movies database table has an ID of –1.

LISTING 12.4   ShowEmptyDataText.aspx

```
<%@ Page Language="VB" %>
<!DOCTYPE html PUBLIC "-//W3C//DTD XHTML 1.1//EN"
  "http://www.w3.org/TR/xhtml11/DTD/xhtml11.dtd">
<html xmlns="http://www.w3.org/1999/xhtml" >
<head id="Head1" runat="server">
```

LISTING 12.4   Continued

```
    <title>Show Empty Data Text</title>
</head>
<body>
    <form id="form1" runat="server">
    <div>

    <asp:DetailsView
        id="dtlMovies"
        DataSourceID="srcMovies"
        EmptyDataText="<b>No Matching Record!</b>"
        Runat="server" />

    <asp:SqlDataSource
        id="srcMovies"
        ConnectionString="<%$ ConnectionStrings:Movies %>"
        SelectCommand="SELECT Id,Title,Director,InTheaters FROM Movies
            WHERE Id=-1"
        Runat="server" />

    </div>
    </form>
</body>
</html>
```

When you open the page in Listing 12.4, the contents of the `EmptyDataText` property are displayed.

If you need to display more complicated content when no results are returned, such as ASP.NET controls, then you can specify an `EmptyDataTemplate`. The page in Listing 12.5 illustrates how you can use the `EmptyDataTemplate` to display complicated HTML content (see Figure 12.3).

LISTING 12.5   `ShowEmptyDataTemplate.aspx`

```
<%@ Page Language="VB" %>
<!DOCTYPE html PUBLIC "-//W3C//DTD XHTML 1.1//EN"
"http://www.w3.org/TR/xhtml11/DTD/xhtml11.dtd">
<html xmlns="http://www.w3.org/1999/xhtml" >
<head id="Head1" runat="server">
    <style type="text/css">
        .noMatch
        {
            background-color:#ffff66;
```

LISTING 12.5   Continued

```
              padding:10px;
              font-family:Arial,Sans-Serif;
          }
          .noMatch h1
          {
              color:red;
              font-size:16px;
              font-weight:bold;
          }
      </style>
      <title>Show Empty Data Template</title>
</head>
<body>
    <form id="form1" runat="server">
    <div>

    <asp:DetailsView
        id="dtlMovies"
        DataSourceID="srcMovies"
        Runat="server">
        <EmptyDataTemplate>
        <div class="noMatch">
            <h1>No Matching Results!</h1>
            Please select a different record.
        </div>
        </EmptyDataTemplate>
    </asp:DetailsView>

    <asp:SqlDataSource
        id="srcMovies"
        ConnectionString="<%$ ConnectionStrings:Movies %>"
        SelectCommand="SELECT Id,Title,Director,InTheaters FROM Movies
            WHERE Id=-1"
        Runat="server" />

    </div>
    </form>
</body>
</html>
```

12

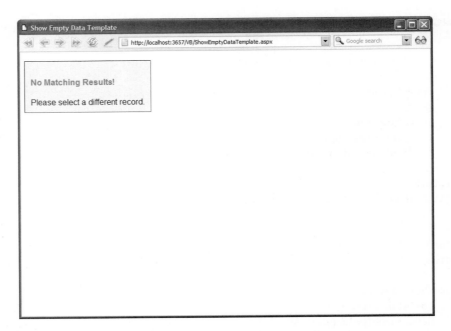

FIGURE 12.3   Displaying content when no results are returned.

Paging through Data with the DetailsView Control

You can use the DetailsView to page through a set of database records by enabling the DetailsView control's AllowPaging property. The page in Listing 12.6 illustrates how you can page through the records in the Movies database table (see Figure 12.4).

LISTING 12.6   ShowPaging.aspx

```
<%@ Page Language="VB" %>
<!DOCTYPE html PUBLIC "-//W3C//DTD XHTML 1.1//EN"
    "http://www.w3.org/TR/xhtml11/DTD/xhtml11.dtd">
<html xmlns="http://www.w3.org/1999/xhtml" >
<head id="Head1" runat="server">
    <title>Show Paging</title>
</head>
<body>
    <form id="form1" runat="server">
    <div>

    <asp:DetailsView
        id="dtlMovies"
        DataSourceID="srcMovies"
        AllowPaging="true"
```

LISTING 12.6   Continued

```
        Runat="server" />

    <asp:SqlDataSource
        id="srcMovies"
        ConnectionString="<%$ ConnectionStrings:Movies %>"
        SelectCommand="SELECT Id,Title,Director,InTheaters FROM Movies"
        Runat="server" />

    </div>
    </form>
</body>
</html>
```

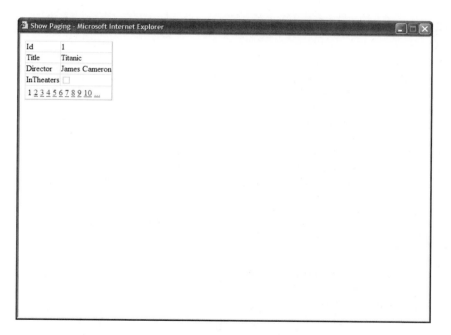

FIGURE 12.4   Paging through records with the DetailsView control.

WARNING

In this section, you learn how to take advantage of user interface paging when paging through records with the DetailsView control. Although user interface paging is convenient, it is not efficient. When working with large sets of records, you should use data source paging. This option is described in Chapter 15, "Using the ObjectDataSource Control."

Paging with AJAX

By default, when you page through records with the DetailsView control, the page is posted back to the server each and every time you click a page number. As an alternative, you can take advantage of AJAX to page through records. When you take advantage of AJAX, only the DetailsView control and not the entire page is updated when you navigate to a new page of records.

> **NOTE**
>
> AJAX (Asynchronous JavaScript and XML) enables you to retrieve content from a web server without reloading the page. AJAX works with all modern browsers including Microsoft Internet Explorer 6.0, Firefox 1.0, and Opera 8.0.

The page in Listing 12.7 illustrates how you can use AJAX with the DetailsView control.

LISTING 12.7   ShowAJAX.aspx

```
<%@ Page Language="VB" %>
<!DOCTYPE html PUBLIC "-//W3C//DTD XHTML 1.1//EN"
    "http://www.w3.org/TR/xhtml11/DTD/xhtml11.dtd">
<html xmlns="http://www.w3.org/1999/xhtml" >
<head id="Head1" runat="server">
    <title>Show Paging</title>
</head>
<body>
    <form id="form1" runat="server">
    <div>

    <%= DateTime.Now %>

    <asp:DetailsView
        id="dtlMovies"
        DataSourceID="srcMovies"
        AllowPaging="true"
        EnablePagingCallbacks="true"
        Runat="server" />

    <asp:SqlDataSource
        id="srcMovies"
        ConnectionString="<%$ ConnectionStrings:Movies %>"
        SelectCommand="SELECT Id,Title,Director,InTheaters FROM Movies"
        Runat="server" />

    </div>
    </form>
</body>
</html>
```

Notice that the DetailsView control in Listing 12.7 includes an EnablePagingCallbacks property which has the value True. This property enables AJAX while paging with the DetailsView.

Furthermore, notice that the page in Listing 12.7 displays the current time. The time is not updated when you navigate to a new page of records. The time is not updated because the entire page is not updated. When you navigate to a new page, only the contents of the DetailsView are updated.

Customizing the Paging Interface

You can customize the appearance of the paging interface by modifying the PagerSettings property. For example, the DetailsView control in Listing 12.8 displays first, previous, next, and last links instead of page numbers (see Figure 12.5).

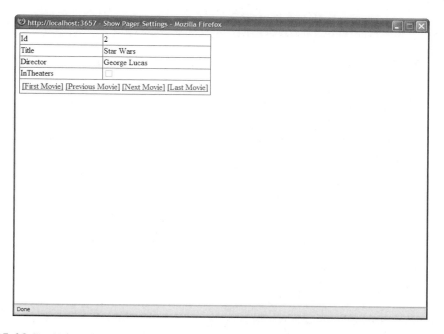

FIGURE 12.5   Using PagerSettings to customize the paging interface.

LISTING 12.8   ShowPagerSettings.aspx

```
<%@ Page Language="VB" %>
<!DOCTYPE html PUBLIC "-//W3C//DTD XHTML 1.1//EN"
   "http://www.w3.org/TR/xhtml11/DTD/xhtml11.dtd">
<html xmlns="http://www.w3.org/1999/xhtml" >
<head id="Head1" runat="server">
    <title>Show Pager Settings</title>
</head>
```

LISTING 12.8   Continued

```
<body>
    <form id="form1" runat="server">
    <div>

    <asp:DetailsView
        id="dtlMovies"
        DataSourceID="srcMovies"
        AllowPaging="true"
        Runat="server">
        <PagerSettings
            Mode="NextPreviousFirstLast"
            FirstPageText="[First Movie]"
            LastPageText="[Last Movie]"
            NextPageText="[Next Movie]"
            PreviousPageText="[Previous Movie]" />
    </asp:DetailsView>

    <asp:SqlDataSource
        id="srcMovies"
        ConnectionString="<%$ ConnectionStrings:Movies %>"
        SelectCommand="SELECT Id,Title,Director,InTheaters FROM Movies"
        Runat="server" />

    </div>
    </form>
</body>
</html>
```

The `PagerSettings` class supports the following properties:

- `FirstPageImageUrl`—Enables you to display an image for the first page link.

- `FirstPageText`—Enables you to specify the text for the first page link.

- `LastPageImageUrl`—Enables you to display an image for the last page link.

- `LastPageText`—Enables you to specify the text for the last page link.

- `Mode`—Enables you to select a display mode for the pager user interface. Possible values are `NextPrevious`, `NextPreviousFirstLast`, `Numeric`, and `NumericFirstLast`.

- `NextPageImageUrl`—Enables you to specify the text for the next page link.

- `NextPageText`—Enables you to specify the text for the next page link.

- `PageButtonCount`—Enables you to specify the number of page number links to display.

- Position—Enables you to specify the position of the paging user interface. Possible values are Bottom, Top, TopAndBottom.

- PreviousPageImageUrl—Enables you to display an image for the previous page link.

- PreviousPageText—Enables you to specify the text for the previous page link.

- Visible—Enables you to hide the paging user interface.

If you need to customize the paging interface completely, then you can use a template. For example, the page in Listing 12.9 displays a list of page numbers in a drop-down list control (see Figure 12.6).

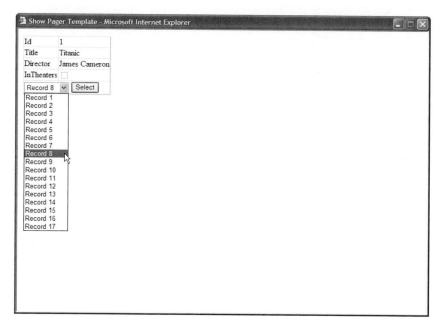

FIGURE 12.6   Using a PagerTemplate to customize the paging interface.

LISTING 12.9   ShowPagerTemplate.aspx

```
<%@ Page Language="VB" %>
<!DOCTYPE html PUBLIC "-//W3C//DTD XHTML 1.1//EN"
 "http://www.w3.org/TR/xhtml11/DTD/xhtml11.dtd">
<script runat="server">

    Protected Sub dtlMovies_DataBound(ByVal sender As Object, ByVal e As EventArgs)
        Dim ddlPager As DropDownList =
➥ CType(dtlMovies.BottomPagerRow.Cells(0).FindControl("ddlPager"), DropDownList)
```

LISTING 12.9   Continued

```
        For i As Integer = 0 To dtlMovies.PageCount - 1
            Dim item As New ListItem(String.Format("Record {0}", i + 1),
➥i.ToString())
            If dtlMovies.PageIndex = i Then
                item.Selected = True
            End If
            ddlPager.Items.Add(item)
        Next
    End Sub


    Protected Sub btnPage_Click(ByVal sender As Object, ByVal e As EventArgs)
        Dim ddlPager As DropDownList =
➥ CType(dtlMovies.BottmPagerRow.Cells(0).FindControl("ddlPager"), DropDownList)
        dtlMovies.PageIndex = Int32.Parse(ddlPager.SelectedValue)
    End Sub
</script>
<html xmlns="http://www.w3.org/1999/xhtml" >
<head id="Head1" runat="server">
    <title>Show Pager Template</title>
</head>
<body>
    <form id="form1" runat="server">
    <div>

    <asp:DetailsView
        id="dtlMovies"
        DataSourceID="srcMovies"
        AllowPaging="true"
        OnDataBound="dtlMovies_DataBound"
        Runat="server">
        <PagerTemplate>
            <asp:DropDownList
                id="ddlPager"
                Runat="server" />
            <asp:Button
                id="btnPage"
                Text="Select"
                Runat="server" OnClick="btnPage_Click" />
        </PagerTemplate>
    </asp:DetailsView>

    <asp:SqlDataSource
        id="srcMovies"
```

LISTING 12.9   Continued

```
        ConnectionString="<%$ ConnectionStrings:Movies %>"
        SelectCommand="SELECT Id,Title,Director,InTheaters FROM Movies"
        Runat="server" />

    </div>
    </form>
</body>
</html>
```

After you open the page in Listing 12.9, you can select a record from the `DropDownList` control and navigate to the record by clicking the `Button` control.

Updating Data with the `DetailsView` Control

You can use the `DetailsView` control to update existing database records. In order to update an existing record, assign the value True to the `DetailsView` control's AutoGenerateEditButton property as illustrated in Listing 12.10 (see Figure 12.7).

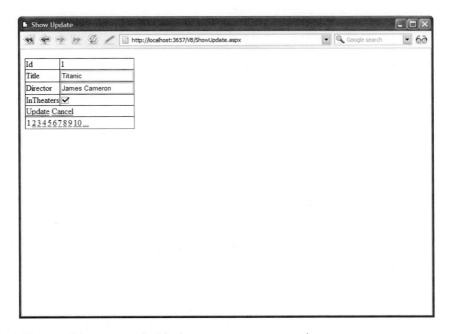

FIGURE 12.7   Editing a record with the `DetailsView` control.

LISTING 12.10   ShowUpdate.aspx

```
<%@ Page Language="VB" %>
<!DOCTYPE html PUBLIC "-//W3C//DTD XHTML 1.1//EN"
    "http://www.w3.org/TR/xhtml11/DTD/xhtml11.dtd">
<html xmlns="http://www.w3.org/1999/xhtml" >
<head id="Head1" runat="server">
    <title>Show Update</title>
</head>
<body>
    <form id="form1" runat="server">
    <div>

    <asp:DetailsView
        id="dtlMovies"
        DataKeyNames="Id"
        AutoGenerateEditButton="true"
        AllowPaging="true"
        DataSourceID="srcMovies"
        Runat="server" />

    <asp:SqlDataSource
        id="srcMovies"
        ConnectionString="<%$ ConnectionStrings:Movies %>"
        SelectCommand="SELECT Id,Title,Director,InTheaters FROM Movies"
        UpdateCommand="UPDATE Movies SET Title=@Title,Director=@Director,
            InTheaters=@InTheaters WHERE Id=@Id"
        Runat="server" />

    </div>
    </form>
</body>
</html>
```

When you open the page in Listing 12.10, the record appears in Read Only mode. You can click the Edit button to switch the DetailsView into Edit mode and update the record.

Notice that the DetailsView control includes a DataKeyNames property and an AutoGenerateEditButton property. The DataKeyNames property contains the name of the primary key column. The AutoGenerateEditButton property automatically generates the user interface for editing the record.

Notice that the SqlDataSource control includes an UpdateCommand. The UpdateCommand updates the Title, Director, and InTheaters database columns.

If you want the `DetailsView` control to initially appear in Edit mode, then you can set the `DetailsView` control's `DefaultMode` property to the value `Edit`. For example, the page in Listing 12.11 contains a Master/Detail form. If you select any of the records in the `GridView`, you can edit the record with the `DetailsView` control (see Figure 12.8).

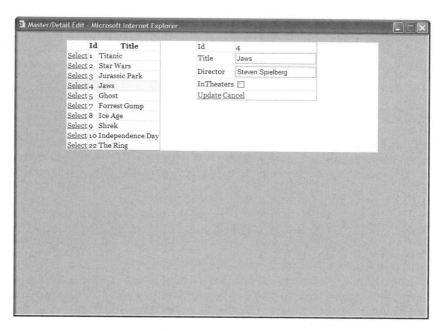

FIGURE 12.8   Displaying a Master/Detail form with the `DetailsView` control.

LISTING 12.11   MasterDetailEdit.aspx

```
<%@ Page Language="VB" %>
<!DOCTYPE html PUBLIC "-//W3C//DTD XHTML 1.1//EN"
  "http://www.w3.org/TR/xhtml11/DTD/xhtml11.dtd">
<script runat="server">

    Private Sub Page_Load()
        If Not Page.IsPostBack Then
            grdMovies.SelectedIndex = 0
        End If
    End Sub


    Protected Sub dtlMovies_ItemUpdated(ByVal sender As Object,
➡ ByVal e As DetailsViewUpdatedEventArgs)
        grdMovies.DataBind()
    End Sub
```

LISTING 12.11   Continued

```
</script>
<html xmlns="http://www.w3.org/1999/xhtml" >
<head id="Head1" runat="server">
    <style type="text/css">
        html
        {
            background-color:silver;
            font:14px Georgia,Serif;
        }
        .content
        {
            margin:auto;
            width:600px;
            background-color:white;
        }
        .column
        {
            float:left;
            width:250px;
        }
        .selectedRow
        {
            background-color:yellow;
        }
    </style>
    <title>Master/Detail Edit</title>
</head>
<body>
    <form id="form1" runat="server">
    <div class="content">

    <div class="column">
    <asp:GridView
        id="grdMovies"
        DataSourceID="srcMovies"
        DataKeyNames="Id"
        AutoGenerateSelectButton="true"
        SelectedRowStyle-CssClass="selectedRow"
        Runat="server" />
    </div>

    <div class="column">
    <asp:DetailsView
```

LISTING 12.11   Continued

```
            id="dtlMovies"
            DefaultMode="Edit"
            AutoGenerateEditButton="true"
            AllowPaging="true"
            DataSourceID="srcMovieDetails"
            DataKeyNames="Id"
            OnItemUpdated="dtlMovies_ItemUpdated"
            Runat="server" />

    <asp:SqlDataSource
        id="srcMovies"
        ConnectionString="<%$ ConnectionStrings:Movies %>"
        SelectCommand="SELECT Id,Title FROM Movies"
        Runat="server" />
    </div>

    <asp:SqlDataSource
        id="srcMovieDetails"
        ConnectionString="<%$ ConnectionStrings:Movies %>"
        SelectCommand="SELECT Id,Title,Director,InTheaters FROM
            Movies WHERE Id=@MovieId"
        UpdateCommand="UPDATE Movies SET Title=@Title,Director=@Director,
            InTheaters=@InTheaters WHERE Id=@Id"
        Runat="server">
        <SelectParameters>
            <asp:ControlParameter Name="MovieId" ControlID="grdMovies" />
        </SelectParameters>
    </asp:SqlDataSource>

    </div>
    </form>
</body>
</html>
```

Notice that the `DetailsView` control includes a `DefaultMode` property that is set to the value `Edit`. When you select a record, the record is displayed by the `DetailsView` in Edit mode by default.

Using Templates when Editing

By default, you don't get any validation when editing records with the `DetailsView` control. In other words, there is nothing to prevent you from attempting to submit a null value to a database column that does not accept null values. If you need to perform validation, then you need to use templates with the `DetailsView` control.

The page in Listing 12.12 uses TemplateFields for the Title and BoxOfficeTotals columns. Both TemplateFields contain a RequiredFieldValidator. The BoxOfficeTotals column also includes a CompareValidator to check whether the value entered is a currency value (see Figure 12.9).

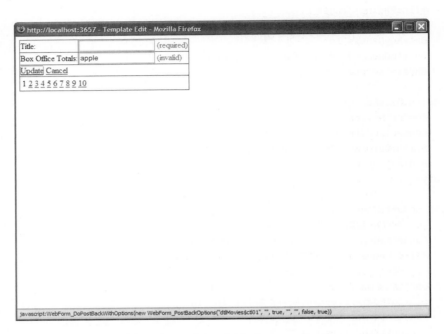

FIGURE 12.9   Using a template when editing with the DetailsView control.

LISTING 12.12   TemplateEdit.aspx

```
<%@ Page Language="VB" %>
<!DOCTYPE html PUBLIC "-//W3C//DTD XHTML 1.1//EN"
  "http://www.w3.org/TR/xhtml11/DTD/xhtml11.dtd">
<html xmlns="http://www.w3.org/1999/xhtml" >
<head id="Head1" runat="server">
    <title>Template Edit</title>
</head>
<body>
    <form id="form1" runat="server">
    <div>

    <asp:DetailsView
        id="dtlMovies"
        AutoGenerateRows="false"
        AutoGenerateEditButton="true"
```

LISTING 12.12   Continued

```
    AllowPaging="true"
    DefaultMode="Edit"
    DataSourceID="srcMovies"
    DataKeyNames="Id"
    Runat="server">
    <Fields>
    <asp:TemplateField HeaderText="Title:">
    <EditItemTemplate>
    <asp:TextBox
        id="txtTitle"
        Text='<%# Bind("Title") %>'
        runat="server" />
    <asp:RequiredFieldValidator
        id="reqTitle"
        ControlToValidate="txtTitle"
        Text="(required)"
        Display="Dynamic"
        Runat="server" />
    </EditItemTemplate>
    </asp:TemplateField>
    <asp:TemplateField HeaderText="Box Office Totals:">
    <EditItemTemplate>
    <asp:TextBox
        id="txtBoxOfficeTotals"
        Text='<%# Bind("BoxOfficeTotals", "{0:f}") %>'
        runat="server" />
    <asp:RequiredFieldValidator
        id="reqBoxOfficeTotals"
        ControlToValidate="txtBoxOfficeTotals"
        Text="(required)"
        Display="Dynamic"
        Runat="server" />
    <asp:CompareValidator
        id="cmpBoxOfficeTotals"
        ControlToValidate="txtBoxOfficeTotals"
        Text="(invalid)"
        Display="Dynamic"
        Operator="DataTypeCheck"
        Type="currency"
        Runat="server" />
    </EditItemTemplate>
    </asp:TemplateField>
    </Fields>
</asp:DetailsView>
```

12

LISTING 12.12 Continued

```
<asp:SqlDataSource
    id="srcMovies"
    ConnectionString="<%$ ConnectionStrings:Movies %>"
    SelectCommand="SELECT Id,Title,BoxOfficeTotals FROM Movies"
    UpdateCommand="UPDATE Movies SET Title=@Title,
        BoxOfficeTotals=@BoxOfficeTotals WHERE Id=@Id"
    Runat="server" />

</div>
</form>
</body>
</html>
```

If you attempt to edit a record, and you do not provide a value for the Title or BoxOfficeTotals columns, then a validation error is displayed. Also, if you enter anything other than a currency amount for the BoxOfficeTotals column, a validation error message is displayed.

Handling Concurrency Issues

What happens when two users edit the same record at the same time? By default, the last user to update the database record wins. In other words, one user can overwrite changes made by another user.

Imagine that Sally opens a page to edit a database record. After opening the page, Sally leaves for her two-week vacation in Las Vegas. While Sally is vacationing, Jim edits the same record and submits his changes. When Sally returns from vacation, she submits her changes. Any modifications that Jim makes are overwritten by Sally's changes.

If you need to prevent this scenario, then you can take advantage of optimistic concurrency. The SqlDataSource control's ConflictDetection property supports the following two values:

- CompareAllValues

- OverwriteChanges

By default, the ConflictDetection property has the value OverwriteChanges. If you set this property to the value CompareAllValues, then the SqlDataSource tracks both the original and modified versions of each column.

For example, the page in Listing 12.13 doesn't allow a user to update a record when the original record has been modified after the user has opened the page.

LISTING 12.13   Concurrency.aspx

```
<%@ Page Language="VB" %>
<!DOCTYPE html PUBLIC "-//W3C//DTD XHTML 1.1//EN"
"http://www.w3.org/TR/xhtml11/DTD/xhtml11.dtd">
<html xmlns="http://www.w3.org/1999/xhtml" >
<head id="Head1" runat="server">
    <title>Concurrency</title>
</head>
<body>
    <form id="form1" runat="server">
    <div>

    <asp:DetailsView
        id="dtlMovies"
        DataKeyNames="Id"
        AutoGenerateEditButton="true"
        AllowPaging="true"
        DataSourceID="srcMovies"
        Runat="server" />

    <asp:SqlDataSource
        id="srcMovies"
        ConnectionString="<%$ ConnectionStrings:Movies %>"
        SelectCommand="SELECT Id,Title,Director,InTheaters FROM Movies"
        UpdateCommand="UPDATE Movies
            SET Title=@Title,Director=@Director,InTheaters=@InTheaters
            WHERE Title=@original_Title
            AND Director=@original_Director
            AND InTheaters=@InTheaters
            AND Id=@original_Id"
        ConflictDetection="CompareAllValues"
        OldValuesParameterFormatString="original_{0}"
        Runat="server" />

    </div>
    </form>
</body>
</html>
```

Notice the contents of the UpdateCommand in Listing 12.13. The current values are
compared against the original values for each database column when updating a record. If
the current and original values don't match, then the record is not updated.

The SqlDataSource has both its ConflictDetection and
OldValuesParameterFormatString properties set. The OldValuesParameterFormatString
specifies the prefix added to the parameters that represent the original field values.

Inserting Data with the `DetailsView` Control

You can use the `DetailsView` control to insert new records into a database table. For example, the page in Listing 12.14 enables you to insert a new record into the Movies database table.

LISTING 12.14   `ShowInsert.aspx`

```
<%@ Page Language="VB" %>
<!DOCTYPE html PUBLIC "-//W3C//DTD XHTML 1.1//EN"
  "http://www.w3.org/TR/xhtml11/DTD/xhtml11.dtd">
<html xmlns="http://www.w3.org/1999/xhtml" >
<head id="Head1" runat="server">
    <title>Show Insert</title>
</head>
<body>
    <form id="form1" runat="server">
    <div>

    <asp:DetailsView
        id="dtlMovies"
        AllowPaging="true"
        DataSourceID="srcMovies"
        AutoGenerateInsertButton="true"
        Runat="server" />

    <asp:SqlDataSource
        id="srcMovies"
        ConnectionString="<%$ ConnectionStrings:Movies %>"
        SelectCommand="SELECT Title,Director,InTheaters FROM Movies"
        InsertCommand="INSERT Movies (Title,Director,InTheaters)
            VALUES (@Title,@Director,@InTheaters)"
        Runat="server" />

    </div>
    </form>
</body>
</html>
```

Notice that the `DetailsView` control in Listing 12.14 includes an `AutoGenerateInsertButton` property that has the value `True`. This property automatically generates the user interface for inserting a new record.

After you open the page in Listing 12.14, you can click the New button to display a form for inserting a new record. When you click the Insert button, the SQL command represented by the `SqlDataSource` control's `InsertCommand` property is executed.

If you want the DetailsView control to display an insert form by default, then you can assign the value Insert to the DetailsView control's DefaultMode property. This approach is illustrated by the page in Listing 12.15 (see Figure 12.10).

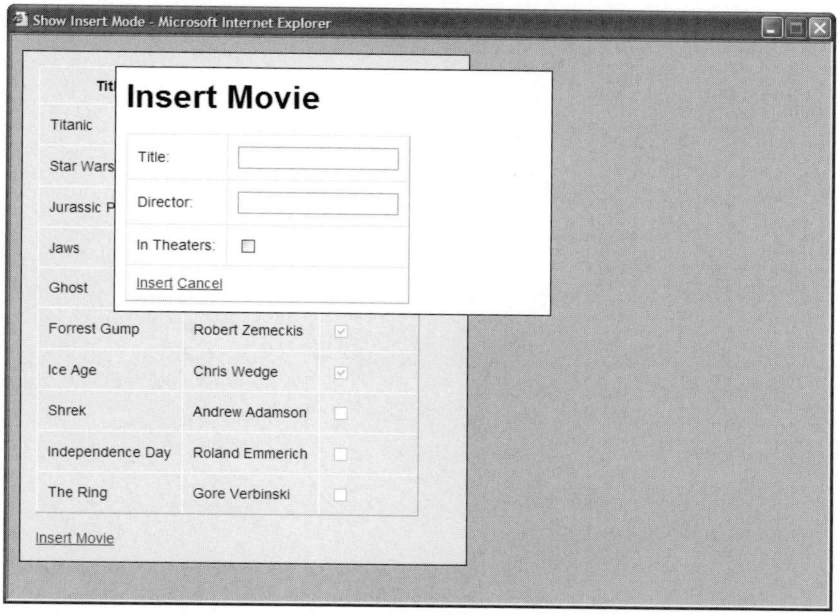

FIGURE 12.10   Inserting a record with the DetailsView control.

LISTING 12.15   ShowInsertMode.aspx

```
<%@ Page Language="VB" %>
<!DOCTYPE html PUBLIC "-//W3C//DTD XHTML 1.1//EN"
  "http://www.w3.org/TR/xhtml11/DTD/xhtml11.dtd">
<html xmlns="http://www.w3.org/1999/xhtml" >
<head id="Head1" runat="server">
    <style type="text/css">
        html
        {
            background-color:silver;
            font:14px Arial,Sans-Serif;
        }
        td,th
        {
            padding:10px;
        }
        #divDisplay
```

LISTING 12.15   Continued

```
        {
            border:solid 1px black;
            width:400px;
            padding:15px;
            background-color:#eeeeee;
        }
        #divInsert
        {
            display:none;
            border:solid 1px black;
            width:400px;
            position:absolute;
            top:30px;
            left:100px;
            padding:10px;
            background-color:white;
        }

    </style>
    <script type="text/javascript">
        function showInsert()
        {
            var divInsert = document.getElementById('divInsert');
            divInsert.style.display = 'block';
        }
    </script>
    <title>Show Insert Mode</title>
</head>
<body>
    <form id="form1" runat="server">
    <div id="divDisplay">
    <asp:GridView
        id="grdMovies"
        DataSourceID="srcMovies"
        Runat="server" />
    <br />
    <a href="JavaScript:showInsert();">Insert Movie</a>
    </div>

    <div id="divInsert">
    <h1>Insert Movie</h1>
    <asp:DetailsView
        id="dtlMovies"
        DataSourceID="srcMovies"
        AutoGenerateInsertButton="true"
```

LISTING 12.15   Continued

```
            AutoGenerateRows="false"
            DefaultMode="Insert"
            Runat="server">
            <Fields>
            <asp:BoundField
                DataField="Title"
                HeaderText="Title:" />
            <asp:BoundField
                DataField="Director"
                HeaderText="Director:" />
            <asp:CheckBoxField
                DataField="InTheaters"
                HeaderText="In Theaters:" />
            </Fields>
    </asp:DetailsView>
    </div>

    <asp:SqlDataSource
        id="srcMovies"
        ConnectionString="<%$ ConnectionStrings:Movies %>"
        SelectCommand="SELECT Title,Director,InTheaters FROM Movies"
        InsertCommand="INSERT Movies (Title,Director,InTheaters)
            VALUES (@Title,@Director,@InTheaters)"
        Runat="server" />

    </form>
</body>
</html>
```

The page in Listing 12.15 contains both a `GridView` and `DetailsView` control. The `DetailsView` control is hidden until you click the Insert Movie link. This link executes a JavaScript function named `ShowInsert()`, which displays the `DetailsView` control.

> **NOTE**
>
> You can hide a column when a `DetailsView` control is in Insert mode with the `BoundField` control's `InsertVisible` property. This property is useful, for example, when you want to prevent users from inserting a value for an identity column.

Deleting Data with the `DetailsView` Control

You can delete records with the `DetailsView` control by enabling its `AutoGenerateDeleteButton` property. The page in Listing 12.16 enables you to both insert and delete records in the Movies database table.

LISTING 12.16   ShowDelete.aspx

```
<%@ Page Language="VB" %>
<!DOCTYPE html PUBLIC "-//W3C//DTD XHTML 1.1//EN"
    "http://www.w3.org/TR/xhtml11/DTD/xhtml11.dtd">
<html xmlns="http://www.w3.org/1999/xhtml" >
<head id="Head1" runat="server">
    <title>Show Delete</title>
</head>
<body>
    <form id="form1" runat="server">
    <div>

    <asp:DetailsView
        id="dtlMovies"
        AllowPaging="true"
        DataSourceID="srcMovies"
        DataKeyNames="Id"
        AutoGenerateInsertButton="true"
        AutoGenerateDeleteButton="true"
        AutoGenerateRows="false"
        Runat="server">
        <Fields>
        <asp:BoundField
            DataField="Id"
            HeaderText="ID:"
            InsertVisible="false" />
        <asp:BoundField
            DataField="Title"
            HeaderText="Title:" />
        <asp:BoundField
            DataField="Director"
            HeaderText="Director:" />
        <asp:CheckBoxField
            DataField="InTheaters"
            HeaderText="In Theaters:" />
        </Fields>
    </asp:DetailsView>

    <asp:SqlDataSource
        id="srcMovies"
        ConnectionString="<%$ ConnectionStrings:Movies %>"
        SelectCommand="SELECT Id,Title,Director,InTheaters FROM Movies"
        InsertCommand="INSERT Movies (Title,Director,InTheaters)
            VALUES (@Title,@Director,@InTheaters)"
```

LISTING 12.16   Continued

```
            DeleteCommand="DELETE Movies WHERE id=@Id"
            Runat="server" />

    </div>
    </form>
</body>
</html>
```

When deleting records, you need to supply a value for the DetailsView control's DataKeyNames property. Notice that a parameter named @Id is used to represent the value of the ID column in the DeleteCommand property.

Working with DetailsView **Control Events**

The DetailsView control supports the following events:

- DataBinding—Raised immediately before the DetailsView control is bound to its data source.

- DataBound—Raised immediately after the DetailsView control is bound to its data source.

- ItemCommand—Raised when any control contained in the DetailsView raises an event (for example, when you click a button rendered by a ButtonField).

- ItemCreated—Raised when a DetailsView renders a data item.

- ItemDeleting—Raised immediately before a data item is deleted.

- ItemDeleted—Raised immediately after a data item is deleted.

- ItemInserting—Raised immediately before a data item is inserted.

- ItemInserted—Raised immediately after a data item is inserted.

- ItemUpdating—Raised immediately before a data item is updated.

- ItemUpdated—Raised immediately after a data item is updated.

- ModeChanging—Raised immediately before the DetailsView control's mode is changed.

- ModeChanged—Raised immediately after the DetailsView control's mode is changed.

- PageIndexChanging—Raised immediately before the current page is changed.

- PageIndexChanged—Raised immediately after the current page is changed.

Notice that several of these events reflect similar events exposed by the DataSource controls. For example, the SqlDataSource control includes Inserting and Inserted events, which mirror the DetailsView control's ItemInserting and ItemInserted events.

The page in Listing 12.17 demonstrates how to use the ItemInserted event to handle any errors which might be raised when inserting a new record into a database table (see Figure 12.11).

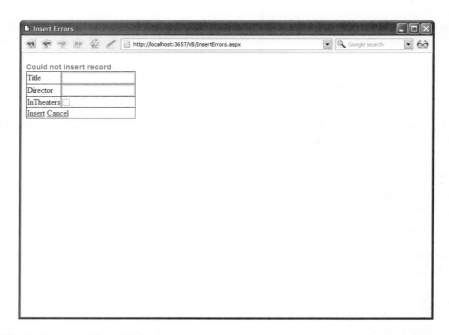

FIGURE 12.11   Handling database insert errors.

LISTING 12.17   InsertErrors.aspx

```
<%@ Page Language="VB" %>
<!DOCTYPE html PUBLIC "-//W3C//DTD XHTML 1.1//EN"
  "http://www.w3.org/TR/xhtml11/DTD/xhtml11.dtd">
<script runat="server">

    Protected Sub dtlMovies_ItemInserted(ByVal sender As Object,
➥ByVal e As DetailsViewInsertedEventArgs)
        If Not IsNothing(e.Exception) Then
            e.ExceptionHandled = True
            e.KeepInInsertMode = True
            lblError.Visible = True
        End If
    End Sub
</script>
<html xmlns="http://www.w3.org/1999/xhtml" >
<head id="Head1" runat="server">
```

LISTING 12.17   Continued

```
    <style type="text/css">
        .error
        {
            color:red;
            font:bold 14px Arial,Sans-Serif;
        }
    </style>
    <title>Insert Errors</title>
</head>
<body>
    <form id="form1" runat="server">
    <div>

    <asp:Label
        id="lblError"
        Text="Could not insert record"
        Visible="false"
        EnableViewState="false"
        CssClass="error"
        Runat="server" />

    <asp:DetailsView
        id="dtlMovies"
        AllowPaging="true"
        DataSourceID="srcMovies"
        AutoGenerateInsertButton="true"
        OnItemInserted="dtlMovies_ItemInserted"
        Runat="server" />

    <asp:SqlDataSource
        id="srcMovies"
        ConnectionString="<%$ ConnectionStrings:Movies %>"
        SelectCommand="SELECT Title,Director,InTheaters FROM Movies"
        InsertCommand="INSERT Movies (Title,Director,InTheaters)
            VALUES (@Title,@Director,@InTheaters)"
        Runat="server" />

    </div>
    </form>
</body>
</html>
```

If you attempt to insert a record without providing values for the Title or Director column, then the error message contained in the Label control is displayed.

When you insert a record, the `DetailsView` control raises the `ItemInserted` event. The second parameter passed to the event handler for this method contains a property that exposes any exceptions raised when inserting the record. In Listing 12.17, if there is an exception, then the exception is suppressed with the `ExceptionHandled` property. Furthermore, the `KeepInInsertMode` property prevents the `DetailsView` from automatically switching out of Insert mode.

Formatting the `DetailsView` Control

The `DetailsView` control includes an abundance of properties for formatting the control. I recommend that you format the `DetailsView` control by taking advantage of Cascading Style Sheets. All the following properties expose a Style object that includes a `CssClass` property:

- `CssClass`—Enables you to associate a style sheet class with the `DetailsView` control.
- `AlternatingRowStyle`—Represents every other row rendered by the `DetailsView` control.
- `CommandRowStyle`—Represents the row that contains the edit buttons.
- `EditRowStyle`—Represents rows when the `DetailsView` control is in Edit mode.
- `EmptyDataRowStyle`—Represents the row displayed when the data source does not return any data items.
- `FieldHeaderStyle`—Represents the cell displayed for the field labels.
- `FooterStyle`—Represents the footer row.
- `HeaderStyle`—Represents the header row.
- `InsertRowStyle`—Represents rows when the `DetailsView` control is in Insert mode.
- `PagerStyle`—Represents the row or rows that display the paging user interface.
- `RowStyle`—Represents the rows displayed by the `DetailsView` control.

Furthermore, you can take advantage of the following properties when formatting a `DetailsView` control:

- `GridLines`—Enables you to specify the appearance of the rules that appear around the cells of the table rendered by a `DetailsView` control. Possible values are None, Horizontal, Vertical, and Both.
- `HeaderText`—Enables you to specify text that appears in the header of the `DetailsView` control.
- `FooterText`—Enables you to specify text that appears in the footer of the `DetailsView` control.

The page in Listing 12.18 uses several of these properties to format a DetailsView control (see Figure 12.12).

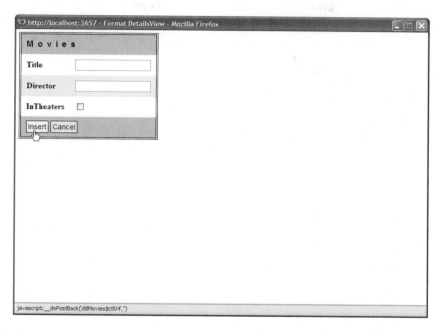

FIGURE 12.12   Formatting a DetailsView control with CSS.

LISTING 12.18   FormatDetailsView.aspx

```
<%@ Page Language="VB" %>
<!DOCTYPE html PUBLIC "-//W3C//DTD XHTML 1.1//EN"
  "http://www.w3.org/TR/xhtml11/DTD/xhtml11.dtd">
<html xmlns="http://www.w3.org/1999/xhtml" >
<head id="Head1" runat="server">
    <style type="text/css">
        .movies td,.movies th
        {
            padding:10px;
        }
        .movies
        {
            border:double 4px black;
        }
        .header
        {
            letter-spacing:8px;
```

LISTING 12.18   Continued

```
                font:bold 16px Arial,Sans-Serif;
                background-color:silver;
            }
            .fieldHeader
            {
                font-weight:bold;
            }
            .alternating
            {
                background-color:#eeeeee;
            }
            .command
            {
                background-color:silver;
            }
            .command a
            {
                color:black;
                background-color:#eeeeee;
                font:14px Arials,Sans-Serif;
                text-decoration:none;
                padding:3px;
                border:solid 1px black;
            }
            .command a:hover
            {
                background-color:yellow;
            }
            .pager td
            {
                padding:2px;
            }
        </style>
        <title>Format DetailsView</title>
    </head>
<body>
    <form id="form1" runat="server">
    <div>

    <asp:DetailsView
        id="dtlMovies"
        DataSourceID="srcMovies"
```

LISTING 12.18   Continued

```
            AutoGenerateInsertButton="true"
            AllowPaging="true"
            GridLines="None"
            HeaderText="Movies"
            CssClass="movies"
            HeaderStyle-CssClass="header"
            FieldHeaderStyle-CssClass="fieldHeader"
            AlternatingRowStyle-CssClass="alternating"
            CommandRowStyle-CssClass="command"
            PagerStyle-CssClass="pager"
            Runat="server" />

    <asp:SqlDataSource
        id="srcMovies"
        ConnectionString="<%$ ConnectionStrings:Movies %>"
        SelectCommand="SELECT Title,Director,InTheaters FROM Movies"
        InsertCommand="INSERT Movies (Title,Director,InTheaters)
            VALUES (@Title,@Director,@InTheaters)"
        Runat="server" />

    </div>
    </form>
</body>
</html>
```

Using the FormView Control

You can use the FormView control to do anything that you can do with the DetailsView control. Just as you can with the DetailsView control, you can use the FormView control to display, page, edit, insert, and delete database records. However, unlike the DetailsView control, the FormView control is entirely template driven.

I end up using the FormView control much more than the DetailsView control. The FormView control provides you with more control over the layout of a form. Furthermore, adding validation controls to a FormView is easier than adding validation controls to a DetailsView control.

> **WEB STANDARDS NOTE**
>
> Unfortunately, from a web standards perspective, the FormView control does, in fact, render an HTML table. It creates an HTML table that contains a single cell.

Displaying Data with the FormView Control

You can display a database record with the FormView control by using an ItemTemplate. For example, the page in Listing 12.19 displays a record from the Movies database table (see Figure 12.13).

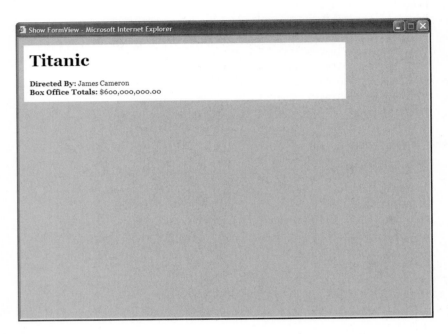

FIGURE 12.13   Displaying a database record with the FormView control.

LISTING 12.19   ShowFormView.aspx

```
<%@ Page Language="VB" %>
<!DOCTYPE html PUBLIC "-//W3C//DTD XHTML 1.1//EN"
  "http://www.w3.org/TR/xhtml11/DTD/xhtml11.dtd">
<html xmlns="http://www.w3.org/1999/xhtml" >
<head id="Head1" runat="server">
    <style type="text/css">
    html
    {
        background-color:silver;
    }
    #content
    {
        margins:auto;
        width:600px;
        padding:10px;
```

LISTING 12.19   Continued

```
            background-color:white;
            font:14px Georgia,Serif;
        }
        </style>
        <title>Show FormView</title>
</head>
<body>
    <form id="form1" runat="server">
    <div id="content">

    <asp:FormView
        id="frmMovies"
        DataSourceID="srcMovies"
        Runat="server">
        <ItemTemplate>
        <h1><%# Eval("Title") %></h1>
        <b>Directed By:</b>
        <%# Eval("Director") %>
        <br />
        <b>Box Office Totals:</b>
        <%#Eval("BoxOfficeTotals", "{0:c}") %>
        </ItemTemplate>
    </asp:FormView>

    <asp:SqlDataSource
        id="srcMovies"
        ConnectionString="<%$ ConnectionStrings:Movies %>"
        SelectCommand="SELECT Id,Title,Director,BoxOfficeTotals FROM Movies
            WHERE Id=1"
        Runat="server" />

    </div>
    </form>
</body>
</html>
```

Notice that the FormView control's DataSourceID property points to the SqlDataSource control. The SqlDataSource control retrieves the first record from the Movies database table.

Notice that the ItemTemplate contains databinding expressions that display the values of the Title, Director, and BoxOfficeTotals columns. The Eval() method retrieves the values of these columns. The databinding expression for the BoxOfficeTotals column formats the value of the column as a currency amount.

Paging Through Data with the FormView Control

You can enable users to navigate through a set of data items by enabling paging. You can allow the FormView control to automatically render the paging interface or you can use a PagerTemplate to customize the paging interface.

The page in Listing 12.20 automatically renders an additional row that contains buttons for navigating between data items.

LISTING 12.20   ShowFormViewPaging.aspx

```
<%@ Page Language="VB" %>
<!DOCTYPE html PUBLIC "-//W3C//DTD XHTML 1.1//EN"
  "http://www.w3.org/TR/xhtml11/DTD/xhtml11.dtd">
<html xmlns="http://www.w3.org/1999/xhtml" >
<head id="Head1" runat="server">
    <style type="text/css">
    html
    {
        background-color:silver;
    }
    #content
    {
        margins:auto;
        width:600px;
        padding:10px;
        background-color:white;
        font:14px Georgia,Serif;
    }
    a
    {
        color:blue;
    }
    </style>
    <title>Show FormView Paging</title>
</head>
<body>
    <form id="form1" runat="server">
    <div id="content">

    <asp:FormView
        id="frmMovies"
        DataSourceID="srcMovies"
        AllowPaging="true"
        Runat="server">
        <ItemTemplate>
        <h1><%# Eval("Title") %></h1>
```

LISTING 12.20   Continued

```
            <b>Directed By:</b>
            <%# Eval("Director") %>
            <br />
            <b>Box Office Totals:</b>
            <%#Eval("BoxOfficeTotals", "{0:c}") %>
            </ItemTemplate>
    </asp:FormView>

    <asp:SqlDataSource
        id="srcMovies"
        ConnectionString="<%$ ConnectionStrings:Movies %>"
        SelectCommand="SELECT Id,Title,Director,BoxOfficeTotals FROM Movies"
        Runat="server" />

    </div>
    </form>
</body>
</html>
```

Notice that the FormView in Listing 12.20 includes an AllowPaging property that is assigned the value True. Adding this property generates the paging interface automatically.

> **NOTE**
>
> Unlike the DetailsView and GridView controls, the FormView control does not support AJAX.

> **WARNING**
>
> This section describes user interface paging. User interface paging is not an efficient method to use when paging through large record sets because all the data must be loaded into memory. In Chapter 15, "Using the ObjectDataSource Control," you learn how to implement data source paging.

You can customize the appearance of the automatically rendered paging interface with the PagerSettings property, which exposes the PagerSettings class. The PagerSettings class supports the following properties:

- FirstPageImageUrl—Enables you to display an image for the first page link.
- FirstPageText—Enables you to specify the text for the first page link.
- LastPageImageUrl—Enables you to display an image for the last page link.
- LastPageText—Enables you to specify the text for the last page link.

- `Mode`—Enables you to select a display mode for the pager user interface. Possible values are `NextPrevious`, `NextPreviousFirstLast`, `Numeric`, and `NumericFirstLast`.

- `NextPageImageUrl`—Enables you to specify the text for the next page link.

- `NextPageText`—Enables you to specify the text for the next page link.

- `PageButtonCount`—Enables you to specify the number of page number links to display.

- `Position`—Enables you to specify the position of the paging user interface. Possible values are `Bottom`, `Top`, `TopAndBottom`.

- `PreviousPageImageUrl`—Enables you to display an image for the previous page link.

- `PreviousPageText`—Enables you to specify the text for the previous page link.

- `Visible`—Enables you to hide the paging user interface.

If you need to customize the appearance of the paging interface completely, then you can create a `PagerTemplate`. The page in Listing 12.21 uses the `PagerTemplate` to create a custom paging interface. The `PagerTemplate` displays the current page number. It also contains buttons for navigating to the previous and next page (see Figure 12.14).

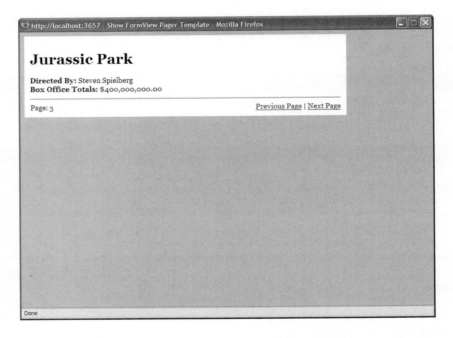

FIGURE 12.14   Using a `PagerTemplate` with the `FormView` control.

LISTING 12.21   ShowFormViewPagerTemplate.aspx

```
<%@ Page Language="VB" %>
<!DOCTYPE html PUBLIC "-//W3C//DTD XHTML 1.1//EN"
    "http://www.w3.org/TR/xhtml11/DTD/xhtml11.dtd">
<html xmlns="http://www.w3.org/1999/xhtml" >
<head id="Head1" runat="server">
    <style type="text/css">
    html
    {
        background-color:silver;
    }
    #content
    {
        margins:auto;
        width:600px;
        padding:10px;
        background-color:white;
        font:14px Georgia,Serif;
    }
    .frmMovies
    {
        width:100%;
    }
    </style>
    <title>Show FormView Pager Template</title>
</head>
<body>
    <form id="form1" runat="server">
    <div id="content">

    <asp:FormView
        id="frmMovies"
        DataSourceID="srcMovies"
        AllowPaging="true"
        CssClass="frmMovies"
        Runat="server">
        <ItemTemplate>
        <h1><%# Eval("Title") %></h1>
        <b>Directed By:</b>
        <%# Eval("Director") %>
        <br />
        <b>Box Office Totals:</b>
        <%#Eval("BoxOfficeTotals", "{0:c}") %>
        </ItemTemplate>
```

LISTING 12.21   Continued

```
<PagerTemplate>
<hr />
<div style="float:left">
Page: <%# frmMovies.PageIndex + 1 %>
</div>

<div style="float:right;white-space:nowrap">
<asp:LinkButton
    id="lnkPrevious"
    Text="Previous Page"
    CommandName="Page"
    CommandArgument="Prev"
    Runat="server" />

<asp:LinkButton
    id="lnkNext"
    Text="Next Page"
    CommandName="Page"
    CommandArgument="Next"
    Runat="server" />
</div>
</PagerTemplate>
</asp:FormView>

<asp:SqlDataSource
    id="srcMovies"
    ConnectionString="<%$ ConnectionStrings:Movies %>"
    SelectCommand="SELECT Id,Title,Director,BoxOfficeTotals FROM Movies"
    Runat="server" />

</div>
</form>
</body>
</html>
```

Notice that each button contained in the `PagerTemplate` has both a `CommandName` and `CommandArgument` property. The `CommandName` is set to the value `Page`. The `CommandArgument` specifies a particular type of paging operation.

You can use the following values for the `CommandArgument` property:

- `First`—Navigates to the first page
- `Last`—Navigates to the last page

- Prev—Navigates to the previous page
- Next—Navigates to the next page
- number—Navigates to a particular page number

Editing Data with the FormView Control

You can edit a database record with the FormView control. For example, you can use the page in Listing 12.22 to edit any of the records in the Movies database table (see Figure 12.15).

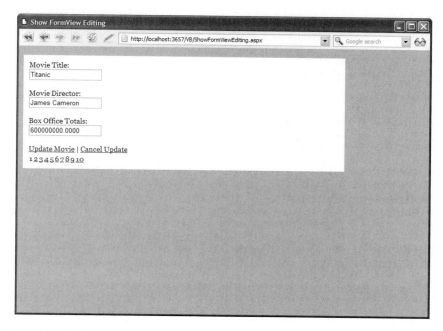

FIGURE 12.15   Editing a record with the FormView control.

LISTING 12.22   ShowFormViewEditing.aspx

```
<%@ Page Language="VB" %>
<!DOCTYPE html PUBLIC "-//W3C//DTD XHTML 1.1//EN"
  "http://www.w3.org/TR/xhtml11/DTD/xhtml11.dtd">
<html xmlns="http://www.w3.org/1999/xhtml" >
<head id="Head1" runat="server">
    <style type="text/css">
    html
    {
        background-color:silver;
    }
```

LISTING 12.22 Continued

```
    #content
    {
        margins:auto;
        width:600px;
        padding:10px;
        background-color:white;
        font:14px Georgia,Serif;
    }
    a
    {
        color:blue;
    }
    </style>
    <title>Show FormView Editing</title>
</head>
<body>
    <form id="form1" runat="server">
    <div id="content">

    <asp:FormView
        id="frmMovies"
        DataSourceID="srcMovies"
        DataKeyNames="Id"
        AllowPaging="true"
        Runat="server">
        <ItemTemplate>
        <h1><%# Eval("Title") %></h1>
        <b>Directed By:</b>
        <%# Eval("Director") %>
        <br />
        <b>Box Office Totals:</b>
        <%#Eval("BoxOfficeTotals", "{0:c}") %>
        <hr />
        <asp:LinkButton
            id="lnkEdit"
            Text="Edit Movie"
            CommandName="Edit"
            Runat="server" />
        </ItemTemplate>
        <EditItemTemplate>
        <asp:Label
            id="lblTitle"
            Text="Movie Title:"
```

LISTING 12.22   Continued

```
                AssociatedControlID="txtTitle"
                Runat="server" />
        <br />
        <asp:TextBox
            id="txtTitle"
            Text='<%# Bind("Title") %>'
            Runat="server" />
        <br /><br />
        <asp:Label
            id="lblDirector"
            Text="Movie Director:"
            AssociatedControlID="txtDirector"
            Runat="server" />
        <br />
        <asp:TextBox
            id="txtDirector"
            Text='<%# Bind("Director") %>'
            Runat="server" />
        <br /><br />
        <asp:Label
            id="lblBoxOfficeTotals"
            Text="Box Office Totals:"
            AssociatedControlID="txtBoxOfficeTotals"
            Runat="server" />
        <br />
        <asp:TextBox
            id="txtBoxOfficeTotals"
            Text='<%# Bind("BoxOfficeTotals") %>'
            Runat="server" />
        <br /><br />
        <asp:LinkButton
            id="lnkUpdate"
            Text="Update Movie"
            CommandName="Update"
            Runat="server" />
        ⋮
        <asp:LinkButton
            id="lnkCancel"
            Text="Cancel Update"
            CommandName="Cancel"
            Runat="server" />
        </EditItemTemplate>
    </asp:FormView>
```

12

LISTING 12.22   Continued

```
    <asp:SqlDataSource
        id="srcMovies"
        ConnectionString="<%$ ConnectionStrings:Movies %>"
        SelectCommand="SELECT Id,Title,Director,BoxOfficeTotals
            FROM Movies"
        UpdateCommand="UPDATE Movies SET Title=@Title,
            Director=@Director,BoxOfficeTotals=@BoxOfficeTotals
            WHERE Id=@Id"
        Runat="server" />

    </div>
    </form>
</body>
</html>
```

You should notice several things about the `FormView` control in Listing 12.22. First, notice that the `FormView` control includes a `DataKeyNames` property that contains the name of the primary key from the data source. You need to specify a primary key when editing records.

Next, notice that the `FormView` control's `ItemTemplate` includes a `LinkButton` that looks like this:

```
<asp:LinkButton
  id="lnkEdit"
  Text="Edit Movie"
  CommandName="Edit"
  Runat="server" />
```

This `LinkButton` includes a `CommandName` property with the value `Edit`. Clicking the link switches the `FormView` control into Edit mode. You could use any other control here that supports the `CommandName` property such as a `Button` or `ImageButton` control.

Next, notice that the `FormView` control includes an `EditItemTemplate`. This template contains the form for editing the record. Each form field uses a two-way databinding expression. For example, the form field for editing the movie title looks like this:

```
<asp:TextBox
  id="txtTitle"
  Text='<%# Bind("Title") %>'
  Runat="server" />
```

The `Bind("Title")` method binds the Title column to the `Text` property of the `TextBox` control.

Finally, notice that the EditItemTemplate includes both a LinkButton for updating the database record and a LinkButton for canceling the update. The LinkButton for updating the record looks like this:

```
<asp:LinkButton
    id="lnkUpdate"
    Text="Update Movie"
    CommandName="Update"
    Runat="server" />
```

This LinkButton includes a CommandName property, which has the value Update. When you click this LinkButton, the SQL statement represented by the SqlDataSource control's UpdateCommand is executed.

> **NOTE**
>
> If you want the FormView control to be in Edit mode by default, then you can assign the value Edit to the FormView control's DefaultMode property.

Inserting Data with the FormView Control

You can use the FormView control to insert new records into a database table. For example, the page in Listing 12.23 enables you to insert a new movie record into the Movies database table.

LISTING 12.23   ShowFormViewInserting.aspx

```
<%@ Page Language="VB" %>
<!DOCTYPE html PUBLIC "-//W3C//DTD XHTML 1.1//EN"
  "http://www.w3.org/TR/xhtml11/DTD/xhtml11.dtd">
<html xmlns="http://www.w3.org/1999/xhtml" >
<head id="Head1" runat="server">
    <style type="text/css">
    html
    {
        background-color:silver;
    }
    #content
    {
        margins:auto;
        width:600px;
        padding:10px;
        background-color:white;
        font:14px Georgia,Serif;
    }
    a
```

LISTING 12.23   Continued

```
    {
        color:blue;
    }
    </style>
    <title>Show FormView Inserting</title>
</head>
<body>
    <form id="form1" runat="server">
    <div id="content">

    <asp:FormView
        id="frmMovies"
        DataSourceID="srcMovies"
        AllowPaging="true"
        Runat="server">
        <ItemTemplate>
        <h1><%# Eval("Title") %></h1>
        <b>Directed By:</b>
        <%# Eval("Director") %>
        <br />
        <b>In Theaters:</b>
        <%#Eval("InTheaters") %>
        <hr />
        <asp:LinkButton
            id="lnkNew"
            Text="New Movie"
            CommandName="New"
            Runat="server" />
        </ItemTemplate>
        <InsertItemTemplate>
        <asp:Label
            id="lblTitle"
            Text="Movie Title:"
            AssociatedControlID="txtTitle"
            Runat="server" />
        <br />
        <asp:TextBox
            id="txtTitle"
            Text='<%# Bind("Title") %>'
            Runat="server" />
        <br /><br />
        <asp:Label
            id="lblDirector"
```

LISTING 12.23   Continued

```
                    Text="Movie Director:"
                    AssociatedControlID="txtDirector"
                    Runat="server" />
            <br />
            <asp:TextBox
                id="txtDirector"
                Text='<%# Bind("Director") %>'
                Runat="server" />
            <br /><br />
            <asp:CheckBox
                id="chkInTheaters"
                Text="In Theaters"
                Checked='<%# Bind("InTheaters") %>'
                Runat="server" />
            <br /><br />
            <asp:LinkButton
                id="lnkInsert"
                Text="Insert Movie"
                CommandName="Insert"
                Runat="server" />
            ¦
            <asp:LinkButton
                id="lnkCancel"
                Text="Cancel Insert"
                CommandName="Cancel"
                Runat="server" />
        </InsertItemTemplate>
    </asp:FormView>

    <asp:SqlDataSource
        id="srcMovies"
        ConnectionString="<%$ ConnectionStrings:Movies %>"
        SelectCommand="SELECT Id,Title,Director,InTheaters
            FROM Movies"
        InsertCommand="INSERT Movies (Title,Director,InTheaters)
            VALUES (@Title,@Director,@InTheaters)"
        Runat="server" />

    </div>
    </form>
</body>
</html>
```

You should notice several things about the page in Listing 12.23. First, notice that the `ItemTemplate` includes a `LinkButton` control that looks like this:

```
<asp:LinkButton
  id="lnkNew"
  Text="New Movie"
  CommandName="New"
  Runat="server" />
```

When you click this `LinkButton` control, the `FormView` switches into Insert mode and displays the contents of the `InsertTemplate`. Notice that the `CommandName` property has the value `New`.

The `FormView` control includes an `InsertItemTemplate` that contains the form for inserting a new movie record. Each form field uses a two-way databinding expression. For example, the `InTheaters CheckBox` looks like this:

```
<asp:CheckBox
  id="chkInTheaters"
  Text="In Theaters"
  Checked='<%# Bind("InTheaters") %>'
  Runat="server" />
```

The `Bind("InTheaters")` method binds the value of the `CheckBox` control's `Checked` property to the `InTheaters` database column.

The `InsertItemTemplate` contains a `LinkButton` for inserting the record and a `LinkButton` for canceling the insert operation. The `LinkButton` for inserting a record looks like this:

```
<asp:LinkButton
  id="lnkInsert"
  Text="Insert Movie"
  CommandName="Insert"
  Runat="server" />
```

Notice that this `LinkButton` control includes a `CommandName` property that has the value `Insert`. When you click the `LinkButton`, the SQL command represented by the `SqlDataSource` control's `InsertCommand` is executed.

> **NOTE**
>
> You can place the `FormView` control into Insert mode by default by assigning the value `Insert` to the control's `DefaultMode` property.

Deleting Data with the `FormView` Control

You can use the `FormView` control to delete database records. For example, the page in Listing 12.24 enables you to delete records from the Movies database table (see Figure 12.16).

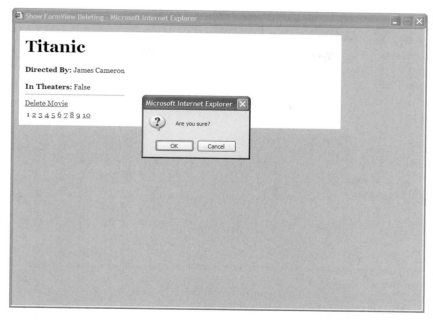

FIGURE 12.16   Deleting a record with the FormView control.

LISTING 12.24   ShowFormViewDeleting.aspx

```
<%@ Page Language="VB" %>
<!DOCTYPE html PUBLIC "-//W3C//DTD XHTML 1.1//EN"
    "http://www.w3.org/TR/xhtml11/DTD/xhtml11.dtd">
<html xmlns="http://www.w3.org/1999/xhtml" >
<head id="Head1" runat="server">
    <style type="text/css">
    html
    {
        background-color:silver;
    }
    #content
    {
        margins:auto;
        width:600px;
        padding:10px;
        background-color:white;
        font:14px Georgia,Serif;
    }
    a
    {
        color:blue;
    }
```

LISTING 12.24   Continued

```
    </style>
    <title>Show FormView Deleting</title>
</head>
<body>
    <form id="form1" runat="server">
    <div id="content">

    <asp:FormView
        id="frmMovies"
        DataSourceID="srcMovies"
        DataKeyNames="Id"
        AllowPaging="true"
        Runat="server">
        <ItemTemplate>
        <h1><%# Eval("Title") %></h1>
        <b>Directed By:</b>
        <%# Eval("Director") %>
        <br />
        <b>In Theaters:</b>
        <%#Eval("InTheaters") %>
        <hr />
        <asp:LinkButton
            id="lnkDelete"
            Text="Delete Movie"
            CommandName="Delete"
            OnClientClick="return confirm('Are you sure?');"
            Runat="server" />
        </ItemTemplate>
    </asp:FormView>

    <asp:SqlDataSource
        id="srcMovies"
        ConnectionString="<%$ ConnectionStrings:Movies %>"
        SelectCommand="SELECT Id,Title,Director,InTheaters
            FROM Movies"
        DeleteCommand="DELETE Movies WHERE Id=@Id"
        Runat="server" />

    </div>
    </form>
</body>
</html>
```

Notice that the `FormView` control includes a `DataKeyNames` property, which contains the name of the primary key column from the data source. When deleting records with the `FormView` control, you need to indicate the primary key column.

Furthermore, notice that the `ItemTemplate` includes a `LinkButton` for deleting a record. The `LinkButton` looks like this:

```
<asp:LinkButton
  id="lnkDelete"
  Text="Delete Movie"
  CommandName="Delete"
  OnClientClick="return confirm('Are you sure?');"
  Runat="server" />
```

This `LinkButton` includes a `CommandName` property that has the value `Delete`. When you click the `LinkButton`, the SQL command represented by the `SqlDataSource` control's `DeleteCommand` property is executed.

Notice, also, that the `LinkButton` includes an `OnClientClick` property that calls the JavaScript `confirm()` method to display a confirmation dialog box. This extra script prevents users from accidentally deleting database records.

Summary

In this chapter, you learned how to work with individual database records by using the `DetailsView` and `FormView` controls. You learned how to use both controls to display, page, edit, insert, and delete database records. You also learned how to format the appearance of both controls.

Using the Repeater and DataList Controls

Both the Repeater and DataList controls—the subjects of this chapter—enable you to display a set of data items at a time. For example, you can use these controls to display all the rows contained in a database table.

The Repeater control is entirely template driven. You can format the rendered output of the control in any way that you please. For example, you can use the Repeater control to display records in a bulleted list, a set of HTML tables, or even in a comma-delimited list.

The DataList control is also template driven. However, unlike the Repeater control, the default behavior of the DataList control is to render its contents into an HTML table. The DataList control renders each record from its data source into a separate HTML table cell.

In this chapter, you learn how to use both of these controls to display database data. You also learn how to use each of the different types of templates that each of the controls supports. Finally, you can see how to handle the different types of events that the controls expose.

Using the Repeater Control

The Repeater control provides you with the maximum amount of flexibility in rendering a set of database records. You can format the output of the Repeater control in any way that you please. In this section, you learn how to display data with the Repeater control and handle Repeater control events.

Displaying Data with the Repeater Control

To display data with the Repeater control, you must create an ItemTemplate. For example, the page in Listing 13.1 displays the contents of the Movies database table (see Figure 13.1).

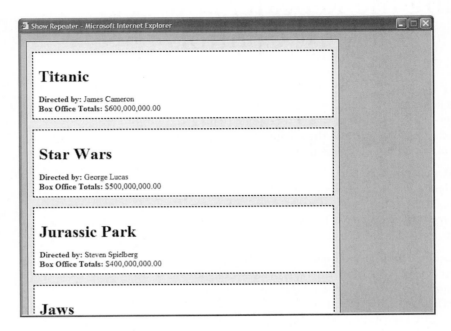

FIGURE 13.1   Displaying data with a Repeater control.

LISTING 13.1   ShowRepeater.aspx

```
<%@ Page Language="VB" %>
<!DOCTYPE html PUBLIC "-//W3C//DTD XHTML 1.1//EN"
  "http://www.w3.org/TR/xhtml11/DTD/xhtml11.dtd">
<html xmlns="http://www.w3.org/1999/xhtml" >
<head id="Head1" runat="server">
    <style type="text/css">
    html
    {
        background-color:silver;
    }
    .content
    {
        width:600px;
        border:solid 1px black;
        background-color:#eeeeee;
```

LISTING 13.1   Continued

```
    }
    .movies
    {
        margin:20px 10px;
        padding:10px;
        border:dashed 2px black;
        background-color:white;
    }
    </style>
    <title>Show Repeater</title>
</head>
<body>
    <form id="form1" runat="server">
    <div class="content">

    <asp:Repeater
        id="rptMovies"
        DataSourceID="srcMovies"
        Runat="server">
        <ItemTemplate>
        <div class="movies">
        <h1><%#Eval("Title") %></h1>
        <b>Directed by:</b> <%# Eval("Director") %>
        <br />
        <b>Box Office Totals:</b> <%# Eval("BoxOfficeTotals","{0:c}") %>
        </div>
        </ItemTemplate>
    </asp:Repeater>

    <asp:SqlDataSource
        id="srcMovies"
        ConnectionString="<%$ ConnectionStrings:Movies %>"
        SelectCommand="SELECT Title,Director,BoxOfficeTotals
            FROM Movies"
        Runat="server" />

    </div>
    </form>
</body>
</html>
```

The Repeater control in Listing 13.1 displays each record in a separate HTML <div> tag. A databinding expression is used to display the value of each column.

In Listing 13.1, declarative databinding is used to bind the Repeater to the `SqlDataSource`. You also can databind a Repeater control programmatically.

For example, the page in Listing 13.2 contains a Repeater control that renders a JavaScript array. The Repeater control is programmatically databound to the list of files in the Photos directory.

LISTING 13.2   ShowRepeaterPhotos.aspx

```
<%@ Page Language="VB" %>
<%@ Import Namespace="System.IO" %>
<!DOCTYPE html PUBLIC "-//W3C//DTD XHTML 1.1//EN"
    "http://www.w3.org/TR/xhtml11/DTD/xhtml11.dtd">
<script runat="server">

    Sub Page_Load()
        If Not Page.IsPostBack Then
            Dim dir As New DirectoryInfo(MapPath("~/Photos"))
            rptPhotos.DataSource = dir.GetFiles("*.jpg")
            rptPhotos.DataBind()
        End If
    End Sub
</script>
<html xmlns="http://www.w3.org/1999/xhtml" >
<head id="Head1" runat="server">
    <style type="text/css">
        .photo
        {
            width:400px;
            background-color:white;
            filter:progid:DXImageTransform.Microsoft.Fade(duration=2);
        }
    </style>
    <script type="text/javascript">
    var photos = new Array();
    window.setInterval(showImage, 5000);

    function showImage()
    {
        if (photos.length > 0)
        {
            var index = Math.floor(Math.random() * photos.length);
            var image = document.getElementById('imgPhoto');
            image.src = photos[index];
```

LISTING 13.2   Continued

```
            if (image.filters)
            {
                image.filters[0].Apply();
                image.filters[0].Play();
            }
        }
    }
    </script>
    <title>Show Repeater Photos</title>
</head>
<body>
    <form id="form1" runat="server">
    <div>


    <img id="imgPhoto" alt="" class="photo" />
    <script type="text/javascript">
    <asp:Repeater
        id="rptPhotos"
        Runat="server">
        <ItemTemplate>
        <%# Eval("Name", "photos.push('Photos/{0}')") %>
        </ItemTemplate>
    </asp:Repeater>
    showImage();
    </script>


    </div>
    </form>
</body>
</html>
```

The page in Listing 13.2 randomly displays a different photo every five seconds. A random image is selected from the JavaScript array and displayed by the JavaScript showImage() function. An Internet Explorer transition filter is used to create a fade-in effect.

WEB STANDARDS NOTE

The transition filter is an Internet Explorer–only extension to Cascading Style Sheets. The page still works with Opera 8 and Firefox 1, but you don't get the fade-in effect.

Using Templates with the Repeater Control

The Repeater control supports five different types of templates:

- ItemTemplate—Formats each item from the data source.

- AlternatingItemTemplate—Formats every other item from the data source.

- SeparatorTemplate—Formats between each item from the data source.

- HeaderTemplate—Formats before all items from the data source.

- FooterTemplate—Formats after all items from the data source.

You are required to use only an ItemTemplate; the other types of templates can be used at your own discretion. The order in which you declare the templates in the Repeater control does not matter.

You can use the AlternatingItemTemplate to create a banding effect (as in old-time computer paper). In other words, you can use the AlternatingItemTemplate to display alternating rows with a different background color. This approach is illustrated by the page in Listing 13.3 (see Figure 13.2).

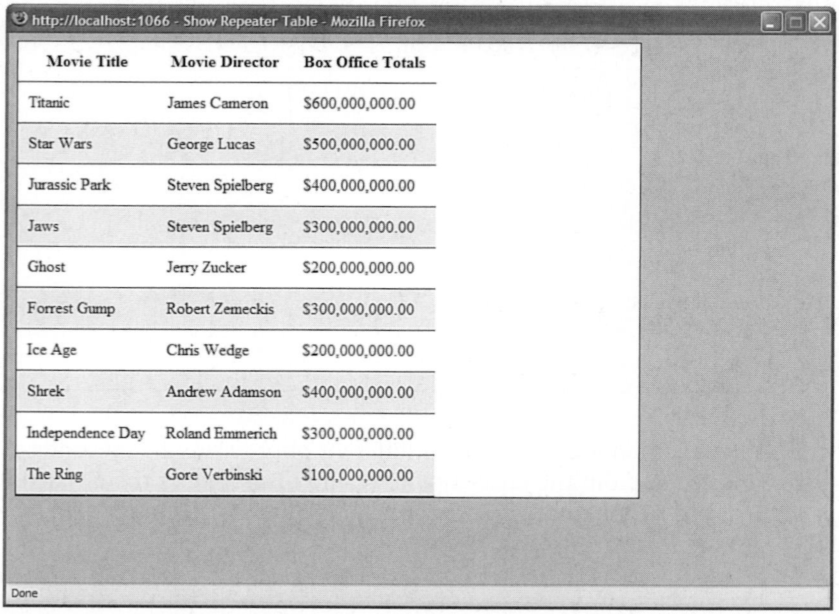

FIGURE 13.2   Displaying an HTML table with the Repeater control.

LISTING 13.3   ShowRepeaterTable.aspx

```
<%@ Page Language="VB" %>
<!DOCTYPE html PUBLIC "-//W3C//DTD XHTML 1.1//EN"
    "http://www.w3.org/TR/xhtml11/DTD/xhtml11.dtd">
<html xmlns="http://www.w3.org/1999/xhtml" >
<head id="Head1" runat="server">
    <style type="text/css">
    html
    {
        background-color:silver;
    }
    .content
    {
        width:600px;
        border:solid 1px black;
        background-color:white;
    }
    .movies
    {
        border-collapse:collapse;
    }
    .movies th,.movies td
    {
        padding:10px;
        border-bottom:1px solid black;
    }
    .alternating
    {
        background-color:#eeeeee;
    }
    </style>
    <title>Show Repeater Table</title>
</head>
<body>
    <form id="form1" runat="server">
    <div class="content">

    <asp:Repeater
        id="rptMovies"
        DataSourceID="srcMovies"
        Runat="server">
        <HeaderTemplate>
        <table class="movies">
        <tr>
            <th>Movie Title</th>
```

13

LISTING 13.3   Continued

```
            <th>Movie Director</th>
            <th>Box Office Totals</th>
        </tr>
        </HeaderTemplate>
        <ItemTemplate>
        <tr>
            <td><%#Eval("Title") %></td>
            <td><%#Eval("Director") %></td>
            <td><%#Eval("BoxOfficeTotals","{0:c}") %></td>
        </tr>
        </ItemTemplate>
        <AlternatingItemTemplate>
        <tr class="alternating">
            <td><%#Eval("Title") %></td>
            <td><%#Eval("Director") %></td>
            <td><%#Eval("BoxOfficeTotals","{0:c}") %></td>
        </tr>
        </AlternatingItemTemplate>
        <FooterTemplate>
        </table>
        </FooterTemplate>
    </asp:Repeater>

    <asp:SqlDataSource
        id="srcMovies"
        ConnectionString="<%$ ConnectionStrings:Movies %>"
        SelectCommand="SELECT Title,Director,BoxOfficeTotals
            FROM Movies"
        Runat="server" />

    </div>
    </form>
</body>
</html>
```

The Repeater control in Listing 13.3 renders an HTML table in which every other row appears with a gray background color. Notice that this Repeater control uses four out of five of the templates supported by the Repeater: the ItemTemplate, AlternatingItemTemplate, HeaderTemplate, and FooterTemplate.

Notice that the AlternatingItemTemplate contains almost exactly the same content as the ItemTemplate. The only difference is that the `<tr>` tag includes a class attribute that changes its background color.

The SeparatorTemplate is used to add content between each data item from the data source. For example, the page in Listing 13.4 uses a SeparatorItemTemplate to create a tab strip with the Repeater control (see Figure 13.3).

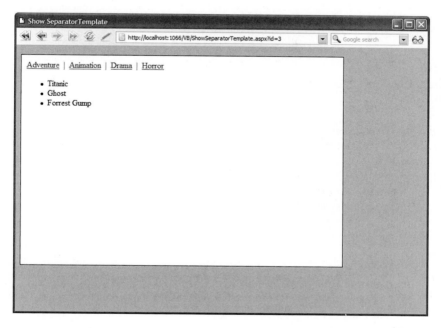

FIGURE 13.3   Displaying a tab strip with the Repeater control.

LISTING 13.4   ShowSeparatorTemplate.aspx

```
<%@ Page Language="VB" %>
<!DOCTYPE html PUBLIC "-//W3C//DTD XHTML 1.1//EN"
    "http://www.w3.org/TR/xhtml11/DTD/xhtml11.dtd">
<html xmlns="http://www.w3.org/1999/xhtml" >
<head id="Head1" runat="server">
    <style type="text/css">
    html
    {
        background-color:silver;
    }
    .content
    {
        width:600px;
        height:400px;
        padding:10px;
        border:solid 1px black;
```

LISTING 13.4   Continued

```
        background-color:white;
    }
    a
    {
        color:blue;
    }
    </style>
    <title>Show SeparatorTemplate</title>
</head>
<body>
    <form id="form1" runat="server">
    <div class="content">

    <asp:Repeater
        id="rptMovieCategories"
        DataSourceID="srcMovieCategories"
        Runat="server">
        <ItemTemplate>
        <asp:HyperLink
            id="lnkMenu"
            Text='<%#Eval("Name")%>'
            NavigateUrl='<%#Eval("Id","ShowSeparatorTemplate.aspx?id={0}")%>'
            Runat="server" />
        </ItemTemplate>
        <SeparatorTemplate>
         | 
        </SeparatorTemplate>
    </asp:Repeater>

    <asp:Repeater
        id="rptMovies"
        DataSourceID="srcMovies"
        Runat="server">
        <HeaderTemplate>
        <ul>
        </HeaderTemplate>
        <ItemTemplate>
        <li><%#Eval("Title")%></li>
        </ItemTemplate>
        <FooterTemplate>
        </ul>
        </FooterTemplate>
    </asp:Repeater>
```

LISTING 13.4   Continued

```
<asp:SqlDataSource
    id="srcMovieCategories"
    ConnectionString="<%$ ConnectionStrings:Movies %>"
    SelectCommand="SELECT Id, Name
        FROM MovieCategories"
    Runat="server" />

<asp:SqlDataSource
    id="srcMovies"
    ConnectionString="<%$ ConnectionStrings:Movies %>"
    SelectCommand="SELECT Title FROM Movies
        WHERE CategoryId=@CategoryId"
    Runat="server">
    <SelectParameters>
    <asp:QueryStringParameter
        Name="CategoryId"
        QueryStringField="Id" />
    </SelectParameters>
</asp:SqlDataSource>

    </div>
    </form>
</body>
</html>
```

The page in Listing 13.4 contains two Repeater controls. The first Repeater control displays a tab strip of movie categories. The second Repeater control displays a bulleted list of matching movies.

Handling Repeater Control Events

The Repeater control supports the following events:

- DataBinding—Raised when the Repeater control is bound to its data source.

- ItemCommand—Raised when a control contained in the Repeater control raises an event.

- ItemCreated—Raised when each Repeater item is created.

- ItemDataBound—Raised when each Repeater item is bound.

The page in Listing 13.5 illustrates how you can use the DataBinding, ItemCommand, and ItemDataBound events. This page uses a Repeater control to update, delete, and insert database records (see Figure 13.4).

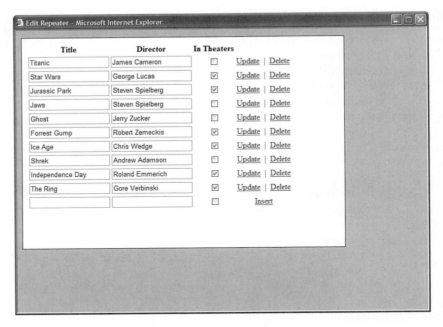

FIGURE 13.4   Editing database records with the Repeater control.

LISTING 13.5   EditRepeater.aspx

```
<%@ Page Language="VB" %>
<!DOCTYPE html PUBLIC "-//W3C//DTD XHTML 1.1//EN"
   "http://www.w3.org/TR/xhtml11/DTD/xhtml11.dtd">
<script runat="server">

    ' The name of the primary key column
    Dim DataKeyName As String = "Id"

    ''' <summary>
    ''' Stores the primary keys in ViewState
    ''' </summary>
    ReadOnly Property Keys() As Hashtable
        Get
            If IsNothing(ViewState("Keys")) Then
                ViewState("Keys") = New Hashtable()
            End If
            Return CType(ViewState("Keys"), Hashtable)
        End Get
    End Property

    ''' <summary>
```

LISTING 13.5   Continued

```
'''  Build the primary key collection
'''  </summary>
Protected Sub rptMovies_ItemDataBound(ByVal sender As Object,
➡ ByVal e As RepeaterItemEventArgs)
    If e.Item.ItemType = ListItemType.Item Or e.Item.ItemType
➡= ListItemType.AlternatingItem Then
        Keys.Add(e.Item.ItemIndex, DataBinder.Eval(e.Item.DataItem, "Id"))
    End If
End Sub


'''  <summary>
'''  Clear the primary keys when Repeater is rebound
'''  to its data source
'''  </summary>
Protected Sub rptMovies_DataBinding(ByVal sender As Object,
➡ByVal e As EventArgs)
    Keys.Clear()
End Sub


'''  <summary>
'''  When you click the Update,Insert, or Delete
'''  button, this method executes
'''  </summary>
Protected Sub rptMovies_ItemCommand(ByVal source As Object,
➡ByVal e As RepeaterCommandEventArgs)
    Select Case e.CommandName
        Case "Update"
            UpdateMovie(e)
            Exit Sub
        Case "Insert"
            InsertMovie(e)
            Exit Sub
        Case "Delete"
            DeleteMovie(e)
            Exit Sub
    End Select
End Sub


'''  <summary>
'''  Update a movie record
'''  </summary>
Private Sub UpdateMovie(ByVal e As RepeaterCommandEventArgs)
    ' Get the form fields
    Dim txtTitle As TextBox = CType(e.Item.FindControl("txtTitle"), TextBox)
```

13

LISTING 13.5   Continued

```
        Dim txtDirector As TextBox = CType(e.Item.FindControl("txtDirector"),
➡ TextBox)
        Dim chkInTheaters As CheckBox = CType(e.Item.FindControl("chkInTheaters"),
CheckBox)

        ' Set the DataSource parameters
        srcMovies.UpdateParameters("Id").DefaultValue =
➡Keys(e.Item.ItemIndex).ToString()
        srcMovies.UpdateParameters("Title").DefaultValue = txtTitle.Text
        srcMovies.UpdateParameters("Director").DefaultValue = txtDirector.Text
        srcMovies.UpdateParameters("InTheaters").DefaultValue =
➡ chkInTheaters.Checked.ToString()

        ' Fire the UpdateCommand
        srcMovies.Update()
    End Sub

    ''' <summary>
    ''' Insert a movie record
    ''' </summary>
    Private Sub InsertMovie(ByVal e As RepeaterCommandEventArgs)
        ' Get the form fields
        Dim txtTitle As TextBox = CType(e.Item.FindControl("txtTitle"), TextBox)
        Dim txtDirector As TextBox =
➡CType(e.Item.FindControl("txtDirector"), TextBox)
        Dim chkInTheaters As CheckBox =
➡CType(e.Item.FindControl("chkInTheaters"), CheckBox)

        ' Set the DataSource parameters
        srcMovies.InsertParameters("Title").DefaultValue = txtTitle.Text
        srcMovies.InsertParameters("Director").DefaultValue = txtDirector.Text
        srcMovies.InsertParameters("InTheaters").DefaultValue =
➡ chkInTheaters.Checked.ToString()

        ' Fire the InsertCommand
        srcMovies.Insert()
    End Sub

    ''' <summary>
    ''' Delete a movie record
    ''' </summary>
    Private Sub DeleteMovie(ByVal e As RepeaterCommandEventArgs)
        ' Set the DataSource parameters
```

LISTING 13.5   Continued

```
            srcMovies.DeleteParameters("Id").DefaultValue =
➥Keys(e.Item.ItemIndex).ToString()

            ' Fire the DeleteCommand
            srcMovies.Delete()
    End Sub
</script>
<html xmlns="http://www.w3.org/1999/xhtml" >
<head id="Head1" runat="server">
    <style type="text/css">
    html
    {
        background-color:silver;
    }
    .content
    {
        width:600px;
        height:400px;
        padding:10px;
        border:solid 1px black;
        background-color:white;
    }
    .movies td
    {
        text-align:center;
    }
    a
    {
        color:blue;
    }
    </style>
    <title>Edit Repeater</title>
</head>
<body>
    <form id="form1" runat="server">
    <div class="content">

    <asp:Repeater
        id="rptMovies"
        DataSourceID="srcMovies"
        OnItemCommand="rptMovies_ItemCommand"
        OnItemDataBound="rptMovies_ItemDataBound"
        OnDataBinding="rptMovies_DataBinding"
        Runat="server">
```

13

LISTING 13.5   Continued

```
<HeaderTemplate>
<table class="movies">
<tr>
    <th>Title</th>
    <th>Director</th>
    <th>In Theaters</th>
</tr>
</HeaderTemplate>
<ItemTemplate>
<tr>
    <td>
    <asp:TextBox
        id="txtTitle"
        Text='<%#Eval("Title")%>'
        Runat="server" />
    </td>
    <td>
    <asp:TextBox
        id="txtDirector"
        Text='<%#Eval("Director")%>'
        Runat="server" />
    </td>
    <td>
    <asp:CheckBox
        id="chkInTheaters"
        Checked='<%#Eval("InTheaters")%>'
        Runat="server" />
    </td>
    <td>
    <asp:LinkButton
        id="lnkUpdate"
        CommandName="Update"
        Text="Update"
        Runat="server" />
     | 
    <asp:LinkButton
        id="lnkDelete"
        CommandName="Delete"
        Text="Delete"
        OnClientClick="return confirm('Are you sure?');"
        Runat="server" />
    </td>
</tr>
</ItemTemplate>
```

LISTING 13.5   Continued

```
        <FooterTemplate>
        <tr>
            <td>
            <asp:TextBox
                id="txtTitle"
                Runat="server" />
            </td>
            <td>
            <asp:TextBox
                id="txtDirector"
                Runat="server" />
            </td>
            <td>
            <asp:CheckBox
                id="chkInTheaters"
                Runat="server" />
            </td>
            <td>
            <asp:LinkButton
                id="lnkInsert"
                CommandName="Insert"
                Text="Insert"
                Runat="server" />
            </td>
        </tr>
        </table>
        </FooterTemplate>
    </asp:Repeater>

    <asp:SqlDataSource
        id="srcMovies"
        ConnectionString="<%$ ConnectionStrings:Movies %>"
        SelectCommand="SELECT Id,Title,Director,InTheaters
            FROM Movies"
        UpdateCommand="UPDATE Movies SET Title=@Title,
            Director=@Director,InTheaters=@InTheaters
            WHERE Id=@Id"
        InsertCommand="INSERT Movies (Title,Director,InTheaters)
            VALUES (@Title,@Director,@InTheaters)"
        DeleteCommand="DELETE Movies WHERE Id=@Id"
        Runat="server">
        <UpdateParameters>
            <asp:Parameter Name="Id" />
            <asp:Parameter Name="Title" />
            <asp:Parameter Name="Director" />
```

13

LISTING 13.5   Continued

```
              <asp:Parameter Name="InTheaters" />
          </UpdateParameters>
          <InsertParameters>
              <asp:Parameter Name="Title" />
              <asp:Parameter Name="Director" />
              <asp:Parameter Name="InTheaters" />
          </InsertParameters>
          <DeleteParameters>
              <asp:Parameter Name="Id" />
          </DeleteParameters>
      </asp:SqlDataSource>

      </div>
      </form>
</body>
</html>
```

In Listing 13.5, the `ItemDataBound` event handler builds a collection of primary keys from the data source. The collection of primary keys is stored in ViewState so that they will be available after a postback to the server.

The `DataBinding` event handler clears the primary key collection when the Repeater is rebound to its data source (after a record is updated or deleted). If you don't clear the collection, then you get duplicates of the primary keys and an exception is raised.

The `ItemCommand` event handler takes care of processing the button click events. When you click an Insert, Update, or Delete button, the event bubbles up and raises the `ItemCommmand` event. The `ItemCommand` event handler grabs the values from the form fields and calls the `Insert()`, `Update()`, or `Delete()` methods of the SqlDataSource control.

Using the DataList Control

The DataList control, like the Repeater control, is template driven. Unlike the Repeater control, by default, the DataList renders an HTML table. Because the DataList uses a particular layout to render its content, you are provided with more formatting options when using the DataList control.

In this section, you learn how to use the DataList control to display data. You also learn how to render database records in both single-column and multi-column HTML tables. We also explore how you can edit data with the DataList control.

Displaying Data with the DataList Control

To display data with the DataList control, you must supply the control with an ItemTemplate. The contents of the ItemTemplate are rendered for each data item from the data source.

For example, the page in Listing 13.6 uses a DataList to display the contents of the Movies database table. The ItemTemplate displays the values of the Title, Director, and BoxOfficeTotals columns (see Figure 13.5).

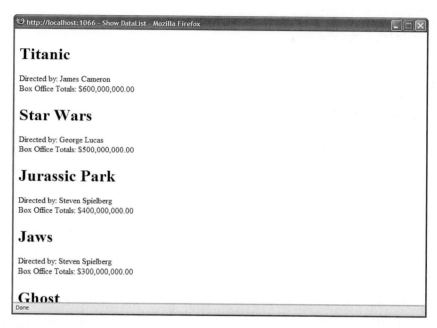

FIGURE 13.5   Displaying database records with the DataList control.

LISTING 13.6   ShowDataList.aspx

```
<%@ Page Language="VB" %>
<!DOCTYPE html PUBLIC "-//W3C//DTD XHTML 1.1//EN"
    "http://www.w3.org/TR/xhtml11/DTD/xhtml11.dtd">
<html xmlns="http://www.w3.org/1999/xhtml" >
<head id="Head1" runat="server">
    <title>Show DataList</title>
</head>
<body>
    <form id="form1" runat="server">
    <div>

    <asp:DataList
        id="dlstMovies"
        DataSourceID="srcMovies"
        Runat="server">
        <ItemTemplate>
```

LISTING 13.6   Continued

```
        <h1><%#Eval("Title")%></h1>
        Directed by:
        <%#Eval("Director") %>
        <br />
        Box Office Totals:
        <%#Eval("BoxOfficeTotals","{0:c}") %>
        </ItemTemplate>
    </asp:DataList>

    <asp:SqlDataSource
        id="srcMovies"
        ConnectionString="<%$ ConnectionStrings:Movies %>"
        SelectCommand="SELECT Title,Director,BoxOfficeTotals
            FROM Movies"
        Runat="server" />

    </div>
    </form>
</body>
</html>
```

The DataList in Listing 13.6 renders an HTML table. Each data item is rendered into a separate table cell (<td> tag). The rendered output of the DataList control in Listing 13.6 looks like this:

```
<table id="dlstMovies" cellspacing="0" border="0"
  style="border-collapse:collapse;">
<tr>
  <td>
  <h1>Titanic</h1>
  Directed by:
  James Cameron
  <br />
  Box Office Totals:
  $600,000,000.00
  </td>
</tr>
<tr>
  <td>
  <h1>Star Wars</h1>
  Directed by:
  George Lucas
  <br />
  Box Office Totals:
```

```
$500,000,000.00
  </td>
</tr>
...
</table>
```

The default behavior of the DataList control is to render an HTML table. However, you can override this default behavior and display the contents of each data item in a separate HTML <span> tag. This approach is illustrated in Listing 13.7.

LISTING 13.7   ShowFlowDataList.aspx

```
<%@ Page Language="VB" %>
<html xmlns="http://www.w3.org/1999/xhtml" >
<head id="Head1" runat="server">
    <title>Show Flow DataList</title>
</head>
<body>
    <form id="form1" runat="server">
    <div>

    <asp:DataList
        id="dlstMovies"
        DataSourceID="srcMovies"
        RepeatLayout="Flow"
        Runat="server">
        <ItemTemplate>
        <%#Eval("Title")%>
        </ItemTemplate>
    </asp:DataList>

    <asp:SqlDataSource
        id="srcMovies"
        ConnectionString="<%$ ConnectionStrings:Movies %>"
        SelectCommand="SELECT Title FROM Movies"
        Runat="server" />

    </div>
    </form>
</body>
</html>
```

Notice that the DataList control in Listing 13.7 includes a `RepeatLayout` property that has the value `Flow`. Each movie title is rendered in a <span> tag followed by a line-break tag (<br>).

The `RepeatLayout` property accepts one of the following two values:

- `Table`—Data Items are rendered in HTML table cells.
- `Flow`—Data Items are rendered in HTML `<span>` tags.

Displaying Data in Multiple Columns

You can render the contents of a `DataList` control into a multi-column table in which each data item occupies a separate table cell. Two properties modify the layout of the HTML table rendered by the DataList control:

- `RepeatColumns`—The number of columns to display.
- `RepeatDirection`—The direction to render the cells. Possible values are `Horizontal` and `Vertical`.

For example, the page in Listing 13.8 displays the contents of the Movies database table in a three-column layout (see Figure 13.6).

FIGURE 13.6   Displaying a multi-column DataList.

LISTING 13.8   MultiColumnDataList.aspx

```
<%@ Page Language="VB" %>
<html xmlns="http://www.w3.org/1999/xhtml" >
<head id="Head1" runat="server">
```

LISTING 13.8   Continued

```
    <title>MultiColumn DataList</title>
</head>
<body>
    <form id="form1" runat="server">
    <div>

    <asp:DataList
        id="dlstMovies"
        DataSourceID="srcMovies"
        RepeatColumns="3"
        GridLines="Both"
        Runat="server">
        <ItemTemplate>
        <h1><%#Eval("Title")%></h1>
        Directed by:
        <%#Eval("Director") %>
        <br />
        Box Office Totals:
        <%#Eval("BoxOfficeTotals","{0:c}") %>
        </ItemTemplate>
    </asp:DataList>

    <asp:SqlDataSource
        id="srcMovies"
        ConnectionString="<%$ ConnectionStrings:Movies %>"
        SelectCommand="SELECT Title,Director,BoxOfficeTotals
            FROM Movies"
        Runat="server" />

    </div>
    </form>
</body>
</html>
```

Notice that the DataList control in Listing 13.8 includes a RepeatColumns property that has the value 3.

If you set the RepeatDirection property to the value Horizontal and do not assign a value to the RepeatColumns property, then the DataList renders its data items horizontally without end.

> **NOTE**
>
> You can display data items in multiple columns when the DataList is in Flow layout mode. In that case, <br> tags are used to create the row breaks.

Using Templates with the DataList Control

The DataList control supports all the same templates as the Repeater control:

- **ItemTemplate**—Formats each item from the data source.
- **AlternatingItemTemplate**—Formats every other item from the data source.
- **SeparatorTemplate**—Formats between each item from the data source.
- **HeaderTemplate**—Formats before all items from the data source.
- **FooterTemplate**—Formats after all items from the data source

In addition, the DataList supports the following templates:

- EditItemTemplate—Displayed when a row is selected for editing.
- SelectedItemTemplate—Displayed when a row is selected.

The DataList control in Listing 13.9 includes both a HeaderTemplate and a FooterTemplate. The HeaderTemplate contains the caption for the table. The FooterTemplate contains a Label control that displays the total for all the preceding rows (see Figure 13.7).

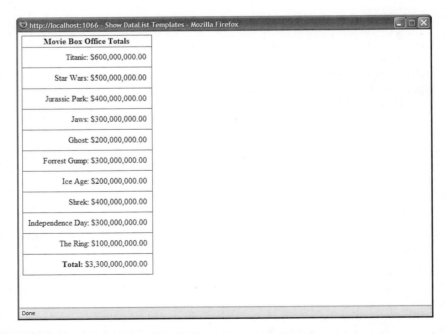

FIGURE 13.7   Displaying a HeaderTemplate and FooterTemplate.

LISTING 13.9   ShowDataListTemplates.aspx

```
<%@ Page Language="VB" %>
<!DOCTYPE html PUBLIC "-//W3C//DTD XHTML 1.1//EN"
   "http://www.w3.org/TR/xhtml11/DTD/xhtml11.dtd">
<script runat="server">

    Dim totals As Decimal

    Protected Sub dlstMovies_ItemDataBound(ByVal sender As Object,
➥ ByVal e As DataListItemEventArgs)
        If Not IsNothing(e.Item.DataItem) Then
            totals += CType(DataBinder.Eval(e.Item.DataItem,
➥"BoxOfficeTotals"), Decimal)
        End If
        If e.Item.ItemType = ListItemType.Footer Then
            Dim lblTotal As Label = CType(e.Item.FindControl("lblTotal"), Label)
            lblTotal.Text = totals.ToString("c")
        End If
    End Sub
</script>
<html xmlns="http://www.w3.org/1999/xhtml" >
<head id="Head1" runat="server">
    <style type="text/css">
    .movies td
    {
        padding:10px;
        text-align:right;
    }
    </style>
    <title>Show DataList Templates</title>
</head>
<body>
    <form id="form1" runat="server">
    <div>

    <asp:DataList
        id="dlstMovies"
        DataSourceID="srcMovies"
        GridLines="Horizontal"
        UseAccessibleHeader="true"
        OnItemDataBound="dlstMovies_ItemDataBound"
        CssClass="movies"
        Runat="server" >
        <HeaderTemplate>
        Movie Box Office Totals
```

13

LISTING 13.9 Continued

```
        </HeaderTemplate>
        <ItemTemplate>
        <%#Eval("Title")%>:
        <%#Eval("BoxOfficeTotals","{0:c}") %>
        </ItemTemplate>
        <FooterTemplate>
        <b>Total:</b>
        <asp:Label
            id="lblTotal"
            Runat="server" />
        </FooterTemplate>
    </asp:DataList>

    <asp:SqlDataSource
        id="srcMovies"
        ConnectionString="<%$ ConnectionStrings:Movies %>"
        SelectCommand="SELECT Title,BoxOfficeTotals
            FROM Movies"
        Runat="server" />

    </div>
    </form>
</body>
</html>
```

The total displayed in the FooterTemplate is calculated by the ItemDataBound event handler. The Label control is extracted by the FindControl() method and the total is assigned to the control's Text property.

Selecting Data with the DataList Control

You can use a DataList control as a menu by taking advantage of the control's SelectedValue property. For example, the page in Listing 13.10 enables you to pick a movie category and display a list of matching movies (see Figure 13.8).

LISTING 13.10 SelectDataList.aspx

```
<%@ Page Language="VB" %>
<!DOCTYPE html PUBLIC "-//W3C//DTD XHTML 1.1//EN"
    "http://www.w3.org/TR/xhtml11/DTD/xhtml11.dtd">
<html xmlns="http://www.w3.org/1999/xhtml" >
<head id="Head1" runat="server">
    <style type="text/css">
    html
```

LISTING 13.10   Continued

```
    {
        background-color:orange;
    }
    .content
    {
        margin:auto;
        width:600px;
        background-color:white;
    }
    .column
    {
        float:left;
        width:250px;
        padding:20px;
    }
    .movies td
    {
        padding:10px;
    }
    a
    {
        padding:10px;
        color:red;
    }
    a:hover
    {
        background-color:Gold;
    }
    </style>
    <title>Select DataList</title>
</head>
<body>
    <form id="form1" runat="server">
    <div class="content">

    <div class="column">
    <asp:DataList
        id="dlstMovieCategories"
        DataSourceID="srcMovieCategories"
        DataKeyField="Id"
        GridLines="Both"
        CssClass="movies"
        Runat="server">
        <ItemTemplate>
```

LISTING 13.10   Continued

```
        <asp:LinkButton
            id="lnkMovie"
            Text='<%#Eval("Name") %>'
            CommandName="Select"
            Runat="server" />
    </ItemTemplate>
</asp:DataList>
</div>

<div class="column">
<asp:DataList
    id="dlstMovieDetails"
    DataSourceID="srcMovieDetails"
    Runat="server">
    <ItemTemplate>
    <h1><%#Eval("Title")%></h1>
    Directed by:
    <%#Eval("Director") %>
    <br />
    Box Office Totals:
    <%#Eval("BoxOfficeTotals","{0:c}") %>
    </ItemTemplate>
</asp:DataList>
</div>
<br style="clear:both" />
</div>

<asp:SqlDataSource
    id="srcMovieCategories"
    ConnectionString="<%$ ConnectionStrings:Movies %>"
    SelectCommand="SELECT Id, Name FROM MovieCategories"
    Runat="server" />

<asp:SqlDataSource
    id="srcMovieDetails"
    ConnectionString="<%$ ConnectionStrings:Movies %>"
    SelectCommand="SELECT Title,Director,BoxOfficeTotals
        FROM Movies WHERE CategoryId=@CategoryId"
    Runat="server">
    <SelectParameters>
    <asp:ControlParameter
        Name="CategoryId"
        ControlID="dlstMovieCategories"
        PropertyName="SelectedValue" />
```

LISTING 13.10   Continued

```
        </SelectParameters>
    </asp:SqlDataSource>
    </form>
</body>
</html>
```

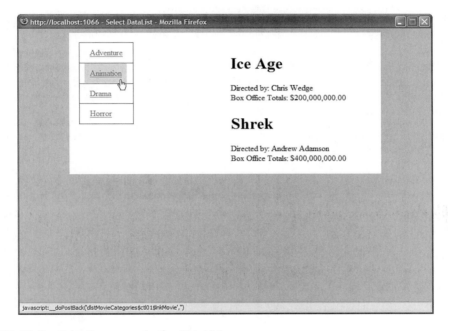

FIGURE 13.8   Selecting a row in the DataList.

The page in Listing 13.10 contains two DataList controls. The first control displays a menu of movie categories and the second DataList control displays a list of matching movies.

Notice that the first DataList in Listing 13.10 includes a `DataKeyField` property. The `DataKeyField` property accepts the name of a primary key column from the data source. When this property is set, the DataList control's DataKeys collection is populated with the primary keys from the data source when the control is bound to its data source.

The first DataList contains a LinkButton inside its ItemTemplate, which looks like this:

```
<asp:LinkButton
  id="lnkMovie"
  Text='<%#Eval("Name") %>'
  CommandName="Select"
  Runat="server" />
```

Because the LinkButton control's `CommandName` property has the value `Select`, clicking the button changes the value of the DataList control's `SelectedValue` property. The DataList control's `SelectedValue` property is used by the second `SqlDataSource` control to return movies that match the selected category.

NOTE

Unlike the `GridView`, `DetailsView`, and `FormView` controls, you cannot assign the names of multiple primary key columns to the DataKeyField property.

Editing Data with the DataList Control

You can use the DataList control to edit database records. However, editing with the DataList control requires more coding than editing with other DataBound controls such as the `GridView`, `FormView`, or `DetailsView` controls.

The page in Listing 13.11 illustrates how you can edit and delete database records with the DataList control (see Figure 13.9).

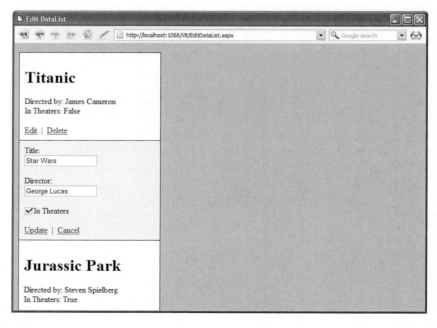

FIGURE 13.9   Editing database records with the DataList control.

LISTING 13.11   EditDataList.aspx

```
<%@ Page Language="VB" MaintainScrollPositionOnPostback="true" %>
<!DOCTYPE html PUBLIC "-//W3C//DTD XHTML 1.1//EN"
    "http://www.w3.org/TR/xhtml11/DTD/xhtml11.dtd">
<script runat="server">

    Protected Sub dlstMovies_EditCommand(ByVal source As Object,
➥ByVal e As DataListCommandEventArgs)
        dlstMovies.EditItemIndex = e.Item.ItemIndex
        dlstMovies.DataBind()
    End Sub

    Protected Sub dlstMovies_UpdateCommand(ByVal source As Object,
➥ByVal e As DataListCommandEventArgs)
        ' Get form fields
        Dim txtTitle As TextBox = CType(e.Item.FindControl("txtTitle"), TextBox)
        Dim txtDirector As TextBox = CType(e.Item.FindControl("txtDirector"),
➥TextBox)
        Dim chkInTheaters As CheckBox = CType(e.Item.FindControl("chkInTheaters"),
CheckBox)

        ' Assign parameters
        srcMovies.UpdateParameters("Id").DefaultValue =
➥dlstMovies.DataKeys(e.Item.ItemIndex).ToString()
        srcMovies.UpdateParameters("Title").DefaultValue = txtTitle.Text
        srcMovies.UpdateParameters("Director").DefaultValue = txtDirector.Text
        srcMovies.UpdateParameters("InTheaters").DefaultValue =
chkInTheaters.Checked.ToString()

        ' Call SqlDataSource Update
        srcMovies.Update()

        ' Take out of Edit mode
        dlstMovies.EditItemIndex = -1
    End Sub

    Protected Sub dlstMovies_DeleteCommand(ByVal source As Object,
➥ByVal e As DataListCommandEventArgs)
        ' Assign parameters
        srcMovies.DeleteParameters("Id").DefaultValue =
➥ dlstMovies.DataKeys(e.Item.ItemIndex).ToString()
```

13

LISTING 13.11   Continued

```
                ' Call SqlDataSource Delete
                srcMovies.Delete()
        End Sub


        Protected Sub dlstMovies_CancelCommand(ByVal source As Object,
➥ByVal e As DataListCommandEventArgs)
                dlstMovies.EditItemIndex = -1
                dlstMovies.DataBind()
        End Sub
</script>
<html xmlns="http://www.w3.org/1999/xhtml">
<head id="Head1" runat="server">
    <style type="text/css">
    html
    {
        background-color:silver;
    }
    .movies
    {
        background-color:white;
    }
    .movies td,.movies th
    {
        padding:10px;
        border:solid 1px black;
    }
    .edit
    {
        background-color:yellow;
    }
    a
    {
        color:blue;
    }
    </style>
    <title>Edit DataList</title>
</head>
<body>
    <form id="form1" runat="server">
    <div>

    <asp:DataList
        id="dlstMovies"
        DataSourceID="srcMovies"
```

LISTING 13.11   Continued

```
DataKeyField="Id"
GridLines="None"
OnEditCommand="dlstMovies_EditCommand"
OnCancelCommand="dlstMovies_CancelCommand"
OnUpdateCommand="dlstMovies_UpdateCommand"
OnDeleteCommand="dlstMovies_DeleteCommand"
CssClass="movies"
EditItemStyle-CssClass="edit"
Runat="server">
<ItemTemplate>
<h1><%#Eval("Title")%></h1>
Directed by:
<%#Eval("Director") %>
<br />
In Theaters:
<%#Eval("InTheaters") %>
<br /><br />
<asp:LinkButton
    id="lnkEdit"
    CommandName="Edit"
    Text="Edit"
    Runat="server" />
 | 
<asp:LinkButton
    id="lnkDelete"
    CommandName="Delete"
    Text="Delete"
    OnClientClick="return confirm('Are you sure?');"
    Runat="server" />
</ItemTemplate>
<EditItemTemplate>
<asp:Label
    id="lblTitle"
    Text="Title:"
    AssociatedControlID="txtTitle"
    Runat="server" />
<br />
<asp:TextBox
    id="txtTitle"
    Text='<%#Eval("Title")%>'
    Runat="server" />
<br /><br />
<asp:Label
    id="lblDirector"
```

13

LISTING 13.11   Continued

```
            Text="Director:"
            AssociatedControlID="txtDirector"
            Runat="server" />
        <br />
        <asp:TextBox
            id="txtDirector"
            Text='<%#Eval("Director")%>'
            Runat="server" />
        <br /><br />
        <asp:CheckBox
            id="chkInTheaters"
            Text="In Theaters"
            Checked='<%#Eval("InTheaters")%>'
            Runat="server" />
        <br /><br />
        <asp:LinkButton
            id="lnkUpdate"
            CommandName="Update"
            Text="Update"
            Runat="server" />
         | 
        <asp:LinkButton
            id="lnkCancel"
            CommandName="Cancel"
            Text="Cancel"
            Runat="server" />
        </EditItemTemplate>
</asp:DataList>

<asp:SqlDataSource
    id="srcMovies"
    ConnectionString="<%$ ConnectionStrings:Movies %>"
    SelectCommand="SELECT Id,Title,Director,InTheaters
        FROM Movies"
    UpdateCommand="UPDATE Movies SET Title=@Title,
        Director=@Director,InTheaters=@InTheaters
        WHERE Id=@Id"
    DeleteCommand="DELETE Movies WHERE Id=@Id"
    Runat="server">
    <UpdateParameters>
        <asp:Parameter Name="Id" />
        <asp:Parameter Name="Title" />
        <asp:Parameter Name="Director" />
        <asp:Parameter Name="InTheaters" />
    </UpdateParameters>
```

LISTING 13.11   Continued

```
        <DeleteParameters>
            <asp:Parameter Name="Id" />
        </DeleteParameters>
    </asp:SqlDataSource>

    </div>
    </form>
</body>
</html>
```

The ItemTemplate contained in the DataList in Listing 13.11 includes an Edit LinkButton and a Delete LinkButton. When you click the Edit LinkButton, the DataList raises its `EditCommand` event and the `dlstMovies_Edit()` method is executed. Clicking the Delete LinkButton raises the `DeleteCommand` event and the `dlstMovies_Delete()` method is executed.

The `dlstMovies_Edit()` method sets the `EditItemIndex` property of the DataList control. The EditItemTemplate is displayed for the item in the DataList that matches the `EditItemIndex`.

The EditItemTemplate includes form fields for editing a movie record and an Update and Cancel LinkButton. These LinkButtons raise the `UpdateCommand` and `CancelCommand` events, and execute the corresponding event handlers.

> **NOTE**
>
> Notice that the `<%@ Page %>` directive includes a `MaintainScrollPositionOnPostback` attribute. This attribute causes a page to scroll to the same position whenever you post the page back to the server. For example, when you click the Edit link next to a row in the DataList, the page scrolls to the Edit link that you clicked. This attribute works with Internet Explorer 6+, FireFox 1+, and Opera 8+.

Formatting the DataList Control

The DataList control includes a rich set of properties that you can use to format the HTML rendered by the control. If you want to associate Cascading Style Sheet rules with different elements of the DataList, then you can take advantage of any of the following properties:

- `CssClass`—Enables you to associate a CSS class with the DataList.

- `AlternatingItemStyle`—Enables you to format every other row of the DataList.

- `EditItemStyle`—Enables you to format the DataList row selected for editing.

- `FooterStyle`—Enables you to format the footer row of the DataList.

- `HeaderStyle`—Enables you to format the header row of the DataList.

- ItemStyle—Enables you to format each row displayed by the DataList.

- SelectedItemStyle—Enables you to format the selected row in the DataList.

- SeparatorStyle—Enables you to format the row separator displayed by the DataList.

When formatting the DataList, you also need to work with the following properties:

- GridLines—Enables you to add rules around the cells in the DataList. Possible values are None, Horizontal, Vertical, and Both.

- ShowFooter—Enables you to show or hide the footer row.

- ShowHeader—Enables you to show or hide the header row.

- UseAccessibleHeader—Enables you to render HTML <th> tags instead of <td> tags for the cells in the header row.

> **WEB STANDARDS NOTE**
>
> To make a page that contains a DataList more accessible to persons with disabilities, you should always include a HeaderTemplate and enable the UserAccessibleHeader property.

The page in Listing 13.12 illustrates how you can take advantage of several of these formatting properties (see Figure 13.10).

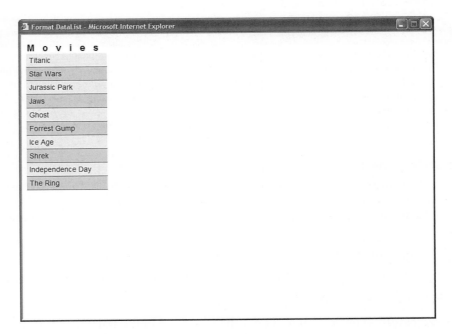

FIGURE 13.10   Formatting a DataList.

LISTING 13.12   FormatDataList.aspx

```
<%@ Page Language="VB" %>
<!DOCTYPE html PUBLIC "-//W3C//DTD XHTML 1.1//EN"
    "http://www.w3.org/TR/xhtml11/DTD/xhtml11.dtd">
<html xmlns="http://www.w3.org/1999/xhtml" >
<head id="Head1" runat="server">
    <style type="text/css">
    html
    {
        background-color:#Silver;
    }
    .movies
    {
        font:14px Arial,Sans-Serif;
    }
    .header
    {
        font-size:18px;
        letter-spacing:15px;
    }
    .item
    {
        padding:5px;
        background-color:#eeeeee;
        border-bottom:Solid 1px blue;
    }
    .alternating
    {
        padding:5px;
        background-color:LightBlue;
        border-bottom:Solid 1px blue;
    }
    </style>
    <title>Format DataList</title>
</head>
<body>
    <form id="form1" runat="server">
    <div>

    <asp:DataList
        id="dlstMovies"
        DataSourceID="srcMovies"
        UseAccessibleHeader="true"
        CssClass="movies"
        HeaderStyle-CssClass="header"
```

LISTING 13.12   Continued

```
            ItemStyle-CssClass="item"
            AlternatingItemStyle-CssClass="alternating"
            Runat="server">
            <HeaderTemplate>
            Movies
            </HeaderTemplate>
            <ItemTemplate>
            <%#Eval("Title")%>
            </ItemTemplate>
        </asp:DataList>

        <asp:SqlDataSource
            id="srcMovies"
            ConnectionString="<%$ ConnectionStrings:Movies %>"
            SelectCommand="SELECT Title FROM Movies"
            Runat="server" />

        </div>
        </form>
</body>
</html>
```

Summary

In this chapter, you learned how to use the Repeater control and the DataList controls to display a set of database records. First, you learned how to use the Repeater control to display and edit database records. For example, you learned how to use the Repeater control to enable users to edit, delete, and insert database records.

In the second half of this chapter, you learned how to work with the DataList control. You learned how to render both single and multi-column tables with the DataList control. You also learned how to selected rows with the DataList control. Finally, you learned how to edit records using the DataList control.

PART IV

Building Components

IN THIS PART

Building Components

Components enable you to reuse application logic across multiple pages or even across multiple applications. For example, you can write a method named `GetProducts()` once and use the method in all the pages in your website. By taking advantage of components, you can make your applications easier to maintain and extend.

For simple applications, there is no reason to take advantage of components. However, as soon as your application contains more than a few pages, you'll discover that you are repeating the same work over and over again. Whenever you discover that you need to write the same method more than once, you should immediately rip the method out of your page and add the method to a component.

CLASSIC ASP NOTE

In classic ASP, programmers often used massive and difficult to maintain #INCLUDE files to create libraries of reusable subroutines and functions. In ASP.NET, you use components to build these libraries.

In this chapter, you learn how to build components in the .NET framework. First, you are provided with an overview of writing components: You learn how to create simple components and use them in the pages in your application. In particular, you learn how to define component methods, properties, and constructors. You also learn how to take advantage of overloading, inheritance, and interfaces.

Next, you learn how to build component libraries that can be shared across multiple applications. Different methods of compiling a set of components into assemblies are examined. You also learn how you can add a component library to the Global Assembly Cache.

Finally, architectural issues involved in using components are discussed. The final section of this chapter shows you how to build a simple three-tiered application that is divided into distinct User Interface, Business Logic, and Data Access layers.

Building Basic Components

Let's start by building a super simple component. The HelloWorld component is contained in Listing 14.1.

LISTING 14.1   HelloWorld.vb

```
Public Class HelloWorld

    Public Function SayMessage() As String
        Return "Hello World!"
    End Function

End Class
```

VISUAL WEB DEVELOPER NOTE

When using Visual Web Developer, you create a component by selecting the menu option Website, Add New Item, and then selecting the Class item (see Figure 14.1). The first time you add a component to a project, Visual Web Developer prompts you to create a new folder named App_Code. You want your new component to be added to this folder.

The HelloWorld component consists of a single method named SayMessage() which returns the string Hello World!.

Make sure that you save the HelloWorld.vb file to your application's App_Code folder. If you don't save the component to this folder, then you won't be able to use the component in your pages.

Next, you need to create a page that uses the new component. This page is contained in Listing 14.2.

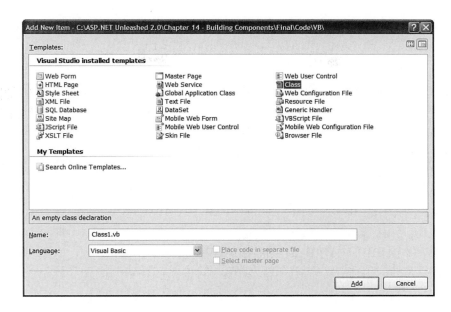

FIGURE 14.1   Creating a new component with Visual Web Developer.

LISTING 14.2   ShowHelloWorld.aspx

```
<%@ Page Language="VB" %>
<!DOCTYPE html PUBLIC "-//W3C//DTD XHTML 1.1//EN"
 "http://www.w3.org/TR/xhtml11/DTD/xhtml11.dtd">
<script runat="server">

    Sub Page_Load()
        Dim objHelloWorld As New HelloWorld()
        lblMessage.Text = objHelloWorld.SayMessage()
    End Sub

</script>
<html xmlns="http://www.w3.org/1999/xhtml" >
<head id="Head1" runat="server">
    <title>Show Hello World</title>
</head>
<body>
    <form id="form1" runat="server">
    <div>

    <asp:Label
        id="lblMessage"
        Runat="server" />
```

LISTING 14.2   Continued

```
    </div>
    </form>
</body>
</html>
```

In the `Page_Load()` event handler, an instance of the `HelloWorld` component is created. Next, the result returned by a call to the `SayMessage()` method is assigned to a `Label` control. When you open the page in your browser, you'll see the message `Hello World!`.

Notice how simple this process of creating the component is. You don't need to perform any special registration and you don't need to compile anything explicitly. Everything just works magically.

Components and Dynamic Compilation

You are not required to explicitly compile (build) the component because the ASP.NET Framework automatically compiles the component for you. Any component that you add to the App_Code folder is compiled dynamically in the same way as an ASP.NET page. If you add a new component to the App_Code folder and request any page from your website, the contents of the App_Code folder are compiled into a new assembly and saved to the Temporary ASP.NET Files folder, located at the following path:

```
C:\WINDOWS\Microsoft.NET\Framework\[version]\
Temporary ASP.NET Files\[application name]
```

Whenever you modify the component, the existing assembly in the Temporary ASP.NET Files folder is deleted. The App_Code folder is compiled again when you make a new page request.

> **NOTE**
>
> An assembly is the dll file (or dll files) in which components are stored.

You can add as many subfolders to the App_Code folder as you need to organize your components. The ASP.NET Framework finds your component no matter how deeply you nest the component in a subfolder.

One significant drawback of this process of dynamic compilation is that any errors in any component contained in the App_Code folder prevent any pages from executing. Even if a page does not use a particular component, any syntax errors in the component raise an exception when you request the page.

> **TIP**
>
> If a component contains an error, and you want to temporarily hide the component from the ASP.NET Framework, change the file extension to an extension that the ASP.NET Framework

does not recognize, such as `HelloWorld.vb.exclude`. Visual Web Developer uses this method to hide a component when you right-click a component and select the menu option Exclude From Project.

Mixing Different Language Components in the App_Code Folder

You don't have to do anything special, just as long as all the components in the App_Code folder are written in the same language. For example, if you use Visual Basic .NET to create all your components, then the ASP.NET Framework automatically infers the language of your components and everything just works.

However, if you mix components written in more than one language in the App_Code folder—for example, Visual Basic .NET, and C#—then you must perform some extra steps.

First, you need to place components written in different languages in different subfolders. You can name the subfolders anything you want. The point is to not mix different language components in the same folder.

Furthermore, you need to modify your web configuration file to recognize the different subfolders. For example, if you create two subfolders in the App_Code folder named VBCode and CSCode, then you can use the web configuration file in Listing 14.3 to use components written in both VB.NET and C#.

LISTING 14.3 Web.Config

```xml
<?xml version="1.0"?>
<configuration>
  <system.web>
    <compilation>
    <codeSubDirectories>
      <add directoryName="VBCode" />
      <add directoryName="CSCode" />
    </codeSubDirectories>
    </compilation>
  </system.web>
</configuration>
```

When the contents of the App_Code folder are compiled, two assemblies are created: one that corresponds to the VBCode folder and one that corresponds to the CSCode folder. Notice that you don't need to indicate the language used for each folder—the ASP.NET Framework infers the language for you.

There is nothing wrong with mixing components written in different languages in the same ASP.NET page. After a component is compiled, the .NET Framework treats VB.NET and C# components in the same way.

Declaring Methods

The simple `HelloWorld` component in Listing 14.1 contains a single method named `SayMessage()`, which returns a string value. When writing components with Visual Basic .NET, you create methods by creating either a subroutine or a function. Use a subroutine when a method does not return a value, and use a function when a method does return a value.

The `SayMessage()` method in Listing 14.1 is an instance method. In other words, you must create a new instance of the `HelloWorld` class before you can call the `SayMessage()`, method like this:

```
Dim objHelloWorld As New HelloWorld()
lblMessage.Text = objHelloWorld.SayMessage()
```

In the first line, a new instance of the `HelloWorld` component is created. The `SayMessage()` method is called from this instance. For this reason, the `SayMessage()` method is an instance method.

As an alternative to creating an instance method, you can create a shared method. The advantage of a shared method is that you do not need to create an instance of a component before calling it. For example, the `SayMessage()` method in the modified `HelloWorld` component in Listing 14.4 is a shared method.

> **NOTE**
>
> Shared methods are called *static methods* in other languages such as C# and Java.

LISTING 14.4   SharedHelloWorld.vb

```
Public Class SharedHelloWorld

    Public Shared Function SayMessage() As String
        Return "Hello World!"
    End Function

End Class
```

The `SharedHelloWorld` component defined in Listing 14.3 is exactly the same as the `HelloWorld` component created in Listing 14.1 with one change: The `SayMessage()` method includes a Shared modifier.

The page in Listing 14.5 uses the `SharedHelloWorld` component to display the `Hello World!` message.

LISTING 14.5   ShowSharedHelloWorld.aspx

```
<%@ Page Language="VB" %>
<!DOCTYPE html PUBLIC "-//W3C//DTD XHTML 1.1//EN"
"http://www.w3.org/TR/xhtml11/DTD/xhtml11.dtd">
<script runat="server">

    Sub Page_Load()
        lblMessage.Text = SharedHelloWorld.SayMessage()
    End Sub

</script>
<html xmlns="http://www.w3.org/1999/xhtml" >
<head id="Head1" runat="server">
    <title>Show Shared Hello World</title>
</head>
<body>
    <form id="form1" runat="server">
    <div>

    <asp:Label
        id="lblMessage"
        Runat="server" />

    </div>
    </form>
</body>
</html>
```

Notice that the page in Listing 14.5 does not create an instance of the SharedHelloWorld component. The SayMessage() method is called directly from the SharedHelloWorld class.

The advantage of using shared methods is that they save you typing. You don't have to go through the pain of instantiating a component before calling the method. Many classes in the .NET Framework include shared methods. For example, the String.Format() method, the Int32.Parse() method, and the DateTime.DaysInMonth() method are all shared methods.

There is nothing wrong with mixing both shared and instance methods in the same component. For example, you might want to create a Product component that has a shared GetProducts() method and an instance SaveProduct() method.

The one significant limitation of using a shared method is that a shared method cannot refer to an instance field or property. In other words, shared methods should be stateless.

Declaring Fields and Properties

You can define a property for a component in two ways: the lazy way and the virtuous way.

The lazy way to create a property is to create a public field. If you declare any field with the Public access modifier, then the field can be accessed from outside the component.

For example, the component in Listing 14.6 contains a public field named Message.

LISTING 14.6   FieldHelloWorld.vb

```
Public Class FieldHelloWorld

    Public Message As String

    Public Function SayMessage() As String
        Return Message
    End Function

End Class
```

The Message field is declared near the top of the FieldHelloWorld class definition. Notice that the Message field is returned by the SayMessage() method.

The page in Listing 14.7 uses the FieldHelloWorld component to display a message.

LISTING 14.7   ShowFieldHelloWorld.aspx

```
<%@ Page Language="VB" %>
<!DOCTYPE html PUBLIC "-//W3C//DTD XHTML 1.1//EN"
    "http://www.w3.org/TR/xhtml11/DTD/xhtml11.dtd">
<script runat="server">

    Sub Page_Load()
        Dim objFieldHelloWorld As New FieldHelloWorld()
        objFieldHelloWorld.Message = "Good Day!"
        lblMessage.Text = objFieldHelloWorld.SayMessage()
    End Sub

</script>
<html xmlns="http://www.w3.org/1999/xhtml" >
<head id="Head1" runat="server">
    <title>Show Field Hello World</title>
</head>
<body>
    <form id="form1" runat="server">
    <div>
```

LISTING 14.7   Continued

```
    <asp:Label
        id="lblMessage"
        Runat="server" />

    </div>
    </form>
</body>
</html>
```

In the `Page_Load()` event handler in Listing 14.7, an instance of the `FieldHelloWorld` class is created, a value is assigned to the `Message` field, and the `SayMessage()` method is called.

There are a couple of serious disadvantages to creating properties by creating public fields. First, the .NET Framework recognizes properties as separate entities. Several methods in the .NET Framework recognize properties but not fields.

For example, you can refer to component properties and not fields when using the `Eval()` method in a databinding expression. If you want to bind a collection of `Product` objects to a `GridView` control, then you should expose the properties of the Product component as true properties and not as fields.

The other disadvantage of fields is that they do not provide you with a chance to validate the value being assigned to the field. For example, imagine that a property represents a database column and the column accepts no more than five characters. In that case, you should check whether the value being assigned to the property is less than five characters.

The component in Listing 14.8 uses a property instead of a field. (It does things the virtuous way.)

LISTING 14.8   PropertyHelloWorld.vb

```
Imports System

Public Class PropertyHelloWorld

    Private _message As String

    Public Property Message() As String
        Get
            Return _message
        End Get
        Set(ByVal Value As String)
            If Value.Length > 5 Then
                Throw New Exception("Message too long!")
            End If
```

LISTING 14.8   Continued

```
            _message = Value
        End Set
    End Property

    Public Function SayMessage() As String
        Return _message
    End Function

End Class
```

Notice that the component in Listing 14.8 contains a property named Message and a private backing field named _message. The Message property contains both a Get() and a Set() function. The Get() function is called when you read the value of the Message property, and the Set() function is called when you assign a value to the Message property.

The Get() function simply returns the value of the private _message field. The Set() function assigns a value to the private _message field. The Set() function throws an exception if the length of the value being assigned to the _message field exceeds five characters.

> **NOTE**
>
> In Listing 14.8, the private field is named _message. The underscore character (_) has no programmatic significance. By convention, private members of a class are named with a leading underscore, but there is nothing wrong with following some other convention.

The page in Listing 14.9 uses the PropertyHelloWorld component.

LISTING 14.9   ShowPropertyHelloWorld.aspx

```
<%@ Page Language="VB" %>
<!DOCTYPE html PUBLIC "-//W3C//DTD XHTML 1.1//EN"
    "http://www.w3.org/TR/xhtml11/DTD/xhtml11.dtd">
<script runat="server">
    Sub Page_Load()
        Dim objPropertyHelloWorld As New PropertyHelloWorld()
        objPropertyHelloWorld.Message = "Hello World!"
        lblMessage.Text = objPropertyHelloWorld.SayMessage()
    End Sub
</script>
<html xmlns="http://www.w3.org/1999/xhtml" >
<head id="Head1" runat="server">
    <title>Show Property Hello World</title>
</head>
```

LISTING 14.9   Continued

```
<body>
    <form id="form1" runat="server">
    <div>

    <asp:Label
        id="lblMessage"
        Runat="server" />

    </div>
    </form>
</body>
</html>
```

If you open the page in Listing 14.9 in your web browser, you will get a big, fat error message (see Figure 14.2). Because a string longer than 5 characters is assigned to the Message property in the `Page_Load()` method, the Message property raises an exception.

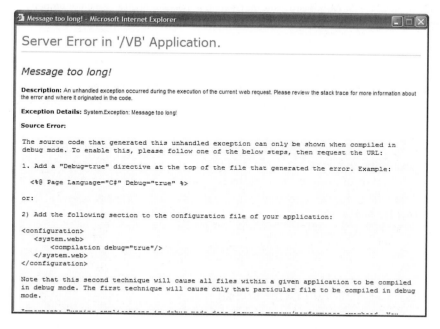

FIGURE 14.2   Assigning more than five characters.

You can also create read-only properties when the situation warrants it. For example, the component in Listing 14.10 returns the current server time. It would not make sense to assign a value to this property, so the property is declared as read-only.

14

LISTING 14.10   ServerTime.vb

```
Public Class ServerTime

    Public ReadOnly Property CurrentTime() As String
        Get
            Return DateTime.Now.ToString()
        End Get
    End Property

End Class
```

> **NOTE**
>
> You can create shared fields and properties in the same way as you create shared methods, by using the Shared keyword. Any value you assign to a shared field or property is shared among all instances of a component.
>
> I recommend that you avoid using shared fields and properties when building ASP.NET applications. Using shared fields and properties raises nasty concurrency issues in a multi-threaded environment such as ASP.NET. If you insist on creating a shared property, make the property read-only.

Declaring Constructors

A constructor is a special class method that is called automatically when you create a new instance of a class. Typically, you use the constructor to initialize private fields contained in the class.

When creating a constructor in Visual Basic .NET, you create a public subroutine named New(). For example, the class in Listing 14.11 displays a random quotation (see Figure 14.3). The collection of random quotations is created in the component's constructor.

LISTING 14.11   Quote.vb

```
Imports System.Collections.Generic

Public Class Quote

    Private _quotes As New List(Of String)

    Public Function GetQuote() As String
        Dim rnd As New Random()
        Return _quotes(rnd.Next(_quotes.Count))
    End Function

    Public Sub New()
```

LISTING 14.11   Continued

```
        _quotes.Add("All paid jobs absorb and degrade the mind -- Aristotle")
        _quotes.Add("No evil can happen to a good man, either
➥in life or after death -- Plato")
        _quotes.Add("The only good is knowledge and the only evil
➥is ignorance -- Plato")
    End Sub

End Class
```

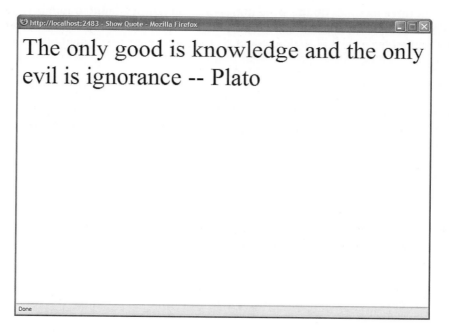

FIGURE 14.3   Displaying a random quotation.

Notice that the collection named _quotes is declared in the body of the class. That way, you can refer to the _quotes field in both the constructor and the GetQuote() method.

> **NOTE**
>
> You can create shared constructors by using the Shared keyword when declaring a constructor. A shared constructor is called once before any instance constructors.

Overloading Methods and Constructors

When a method is overloaded, a component contains two methods with exactly the same name. Many methods in the .NET Framework are overloaded, including the

`String.Replace()` method, the `Random.Next()` method, and the `Page.FindControl()` method.

For example, here is a list of the three overloaded versions of the `Random.Next()` method:

- `Next()`—Returns a random number between 0 and 2,147,483,647.

- `Next(upperbound)`—Returns a number between 0 and the upper bound.

- `Next(lowerbound, upperbound)`—Returns a number between the lower bound and the upper bound.

Because all three methods do the same thing—they all return a random number—it makes sense to overload the `Next()` method. The methods differ only in their *signatures*. A method signature consists of the order and type of parameters that a method accepts. For example, you can't overload two methods that have exactly the same set of parameters (even if the names of the parameters differ).

Overloading is useful when you want to associate related methods. Overloading is also useful when you want to provide default values for parameters. For example, the `StoreProduct` component in Listing 14.12 contains three overloaded versions of its `SaveProduct()` method.

LISTING 14.12   `StoreProduct.vb`

```vb
Public Class StoreProduct

    Public Sub SaveProduct(ByVal name As String)
        SaveProduct(name, 0, String.Empty)
    End Sub

    Public Sub SaveProduct(ByVal name As String, ByVal price As Decimal)
        SaveProduct(name, price, String.Empty)
    End Sub

    Public Sub SaveProduct(ByVal name As String, ByVal price As Decimal,
➥ByVal description As String)
        ' Save name, price, description to database
    End Sub

End Class
```

You can call any of the three `SaveProduct()` methods in Listing 14.12 to save a new product. You can supply the new product with a name, a name and a price, or a name and a price and a description.

When typing an overloaded method in Source view, the Intellisense pops up with all the different sets of parameters that you can use with the overloaded method. See Figure 14.4.

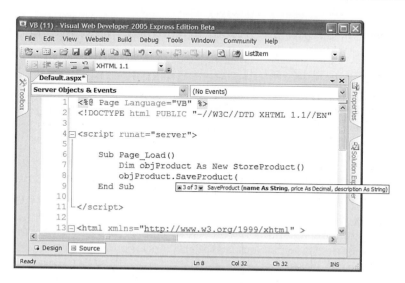

FIGURE 14.4   Typing an overloaded method in Visual Web Developer.

Because a constructor is just a special method, you also can use overloading when declaring constructors for a class. For example, the ProductConstructor class in Listing 14.13 contains three overloaded constructors that can be used to initialize the Product class.

LISTING 14.13   ProductConstructor.vb

```
Public Class ProductConstructor

    Public Sub New(ByVal name As String)
        Me.New(name, 0, String.Empty)
    End Sub

    Public Sub New(ByVal name As String, ByVal price As Decimal)
        Me.New(name, price, String.Empty)
    End Sub

    Public Sub New(ByVal name As String, ByVal price As Decimal,
➥ByVal description As String)
        ' Use name, price, and description
    End Sub

End Class
```

When you instantiate the component in Listing 14.13, you can instantiate it in any of the following ways:

```
Dim objProduct As New ProductConstructor("Milk")

Dim objProduct As New ProductConstructor("Milk", 2.99D)

Dim objProduct As New ProductConstructor("Milk", 2.99D, "Whole Milk")
```

Declaring Namespaces

A namespace enables you to group logically related classes. You are not required to provide a class with a namespace. To this point, all the components that we have created have been members of the global namespace. However, several advantages result from grouping components into namespaces.

First, namespaces prevent naming collisions. If two companies produce a component with the same name, then namespaces provide you with a method of distinguishing the components.

Second, namespaces make it easier to understand the purpose of a class. If you group all your data access components into a DataAccess namespace and all your business logic components in a BusinessLogic namespace, then you can immediately understand the function of a particular class.

In an ASP.NET page, you import a namespace like this:

```
<%@ Import Namespace="System.Collections" %>
```

In a Visual Basic component, on the hand, you import a namespace like this:

```
Imports System.Collections
```

You can create your own custom namespaces and group your components into namespaces by using the Namespace statement. For example, the component in Listing 14.13 is contained in the AspUnleashed.SampleCode namespace.

LISTING 14.14   Namespaced.vb

```
Namespace AspNetUnleashed.SampleCode

    Public Class Namespaced

        Public Function SaySomething() As String
            Return "Something"
        End Function

    End Class

End Namespace
```

The file in Listing 14.14 uses the Namespace statement to group the Namespaced component into the AspUnleashed.SampleCode namespace. Components in different files can share the same namespace, and different components in the same file can occupy different namespaces.

The periods in a namespace name have no special significance. The periods are used to break up the words in the namespace, but you could use another character, such as an underscore character, instead.

Microsoft recommends a certain naming convention when creating namespaces:

```
CompanyName.TechnologyName[.Feature][.Design]
```

So, if your company is named Acme Consulting and you are building a data access component, you might add your component to the following namespace:

```
AcmeConsulting.DataAccess
```

Of course this is simply a naming convention. No serious harm will come to you if you ignore it.

Creating Partial Classes

You can define a single component that spans multiple files by taking advantage of a new feature of the .NET 2.0 Framework called *partial classes*.

For example, the files in Listings 14.15 and 14.16 contain two halves of the same component.

LISTING 14.15 FirstHalf.vb

```
Partial Public Class Tweedle

    Private _message As String = "THEY were standing under a tree," _
        & "each with an arm round the other's neck, and Alice knew" _
        & "which was which in a moment, because one of them had" _
        & """DUM"" embroidered on his collar, and the other ""DEE""."

End Class
```

LISTING 14.16 SecondHalf.vb

```
Partial Public Class Tweedle

    Public Function GetMessage() As String
        Return _message
    End Function

End Class
```

Notice that the `private` `_message` field is defined in the first file, but this private field is used in the `GetMessage()` method in the second file. When the `GetMessage()` method is called, it returns the value of the private field from the other class.

Both files define a class with the same name. The class declaration includes the keyword `Partial`. The `Partial` keyword marks the classes as partial classes.

> **NOTE**
>
> Partial classes are the basis for code-behind pages in the ASP.NET Framework. The code-behind file and the presentation page are two partial classes that get compiled into the same class.

Inheritance and `MustInherit` Classes

When one class inherits from a second class, the inherited class automatically includes all the non-private methods and properties of its parent class. In other words, what's true of the parent is true of the child, but not the other way around.

Inheritance is used throughout the .NET Framework. For example, every ASP.NET page inherits from the base `System.Web.UI.Page` class. The only reason that you can use properties such as the `IsPostback` property in an ASP.NET page is that the page derives from the base `Page` class.

All classes in the .NET Framework derive from the base `System.Object` class. The `Object` class is the great-grandmother of every other class. This means that any methods or properties of the `Object` class, such as the `ToString()` method, are shared by all classes in the Framework.

You can take advantage of inheritance when building your own components. You indicate that one class inherits from a second class by using the `Inherits` keyword.

For example, the file in Listing 14.17 includes three components: a `BaseProduct` class, a `ComputerProduct` class, and a `TelevisionProduct` class.

LISTING 14.17   `Inheritance.vb`

```
Public Class BaseProduct

    Private _price As Decimal

    Public Property Price() As Decimal
        Get
            Return _price
        End Get
        Set(ByVal Value As Decimal)
            _price = Value
        End Set
    End Property
```

LISTING 14.17   Continued

```
End Class


Public Class ComputerProduct
    Inherits BaseProduct

    Private _processor As String

    Public Property Processor() As String
        Get
            Return _processor
        End Get
        Set(ByVal Value As String)
            _processor = value
        End Set
    End Property

End Class


Public Class TelevisionProduct
    Inherits BaseProduct

    Private _isHDTV As Boolean

    Public Property IsHDTV() As Boolean
        Get
            Return _isHDTV
        End Get
        Set(ByVal Value As Boolean)
            _isHDTV = value
        End Set
    End Property

End Class
```

Notice that both the ComputerProduct and TelevisionProduct components inherit from the BaseProduct component. Because the BaseProduct class includes a Price property, both inherited components automatically inherit this property.

When inheriting one class from another, you also can override methods and properties of the base class. Overriding a method or property is useful when you want to modify the behavior of an existing class.

To override a property or method of a base class, the property or method must be marked with the Visual Basic .NET Overridable or MustOverride keyword. Only methods or properties marked with the Overridable or MustOverride keyword can be overridden.

For example, the file in Listing 14.18 contains two components: a `ProductBase` class and a `OnSaleProduct` class. The second class inherits from the first class and overrides its `Price` property. The `Price` property of the `OnSaleProduct` component divides the price by half.

LISTING 14.18   OnSaleProduct.vb

```
Public Class ProductBase

    Private _price As Decimal

    Public Overridable Property Price() As Decimal
        Get
            Return _price
        End Get
        Set(ByVal Value As Decimal)
            _price = value
        End Set
    End Property

End Class


Public Class OnSaleProduct
    Inherits ProductBase

    Public Overrides Property Price() As Decimal
        Get
            Return MyBase.Price / 2
        End Get
        Set(ByVal Value As Decimal)
            MyBase.Price = value
        End Set
    End Property

End Class
```

Notice that the `MyBase` keyword is used in Listing 14.18 to refer to the base class (the `ProductBase` class).

Finally, you can use the `MustInherit` keyword when declaring a class to mark the class as an abstract class. You cannot instantiate a `MustInherit` class. To use a `MustInherit` class, you must derive a new class from the `MustInherit` class and instantiate the derived class.

`MustInherit` classes are the foundation for the ASP.NET 2.0 Provider Model. Personalization, Membership, Roles, Session State, and Site Maps all use the Provider Model.

For example, the `MembershipProvider` class is the base class for all Membership Providers. The `SqlMembershipProvider` and `ActiveDirectoryMembershipProvider` classes both derive from the base `MembershipProvider` class.

NOTE

Chapter 21, "Using ASP.NET Membership," discusses the `MembershipProvider` classes in detail. The `MembershipProvider` is responsible for saving and loading membership information such as application usernames and passwords.

The base `MembershipProvider` class is a `MustInherit` class. You cannot use this class directly in your code. Instead, you must use one of its derived classes. However, the base `MembershipProvider` class provides a common set of methods and properties that all `MembershipProvider`-derived classes inherit.

The base `MembershipProvider` class includes a number of methods and properties marked as `MustOverride`. A derived `MembershipProvider` class is required to override these properties and methods.

The file in Listing 14.18 contains two components. The first component, the `BaseEmployee` component, is a `MustInherit` class that contains a `MustOverride` property named `Salary`. The second component, the `SalesEmployee`, inherits the `BaseEmployee` component and overrides the `Salary` property.

LISTING 14.18   Employees.vb

```
Public MustInherit Class BaseEmployee

    Public MustOverride ReadOnly Property Salary() As Decimal

    Public ReadOnly Property Company() As String
        Get
            Return "Acme Software"
        End Get
    End Property

End Class


Public Class SalesEmployee
    Inherits BaseEmployee

    Public Overrides ReadOnly Property Salary() As Decimal
        Get
            Return 67000.23D
        End Get
    End Property

End Class
```

Declaring Interfaces

An interface is a list of properties and methods that a class must implement. If a class implements an interface, then you know that the class includes all the properties and methods contained in the interface.

For example, the file in Listing 14.19 contains an interface named IProduct and two components named MusicProduct and BookProduct.

LISTING 14.19   Products.vb

```vb
Public Interface IProduct

    ReadOnly Property Price() As Decimal

    Sub SaveProduct()

End Interface



Public Class MusicProduct
    Implements IProduct

    Public ReadOnly Property Price() As Decimal Implements IProduct.Price
        Get
            Return 12.99D
        End Get
    End Property

    Public Sub SaveProduct() Implements IProduct.SaveProduct
        ' Save Music Product
    End Sub

End Class


Public Class BookProduct
    Implements IProduct

    Public ReadOnly Property Price() As Decimal Implements IProduct.Price
        Get
            Return 23.99D
        End Get
    End Property
```

LISTING 14.19   Continued

```
Public Sub SaveProduct() Implements IProduct.SaveProduct
    ' Save Book Product
End Sub

End Class
```

The declaration of both components in Listing 14.17 includes the `Implements` keyword. Both components implement the `IProduct` interface. Notice, furthermore, that both the `SaveProduct()` method and the `Price` property include an `Implements` clause. The `Implements` clause associates a method or property in the derived class with a method or property contained in the interface.

Interfaces are similar to `MustInherit` classes with two important differences. First, a component can inherit from only one class. On the other hand, a component can implement many different interfaces.

Second, a `MustInherit` class can contain application logic. You can add methods to a `MustInherit` class that all derived classes inherit and can use. An interface, on the other hand, cannot contain any logic. An interface is nothing more than a list of methods and properties.

Using Access Modifiers

Visual Basic .NET supports the following access modifiers (also called *access levels*), which you can use when declaring a class, method, or property:

- Public—A Public class, method, or property has no access restrictions.

- Protected—A Protected method or property can be accessed only within the class itself or a derived class.

- Friend—A Friend class, method, or property can be accessed only by a component within the same assembly (dll file). Because ASP.NET pages are compiled into different assemblies than the contents of the App_Code folder, you cannot access a Friend member of a class outside of the App_Code folder.

- Protected Friend—A Protected Friend method or property can be accessed within the class itself or a derived class, or any other class located in the same assembly.

- Private—A Private class, method, or property can be accessed only within the class itself.

Using access modifiers is useful when you are developing a component library that might be used by other members of your development team (or your future self). For example, you should mark all methods that you don't want to expose from your component as private.

Intellisense and Components

Visual Web Developer automatically pops up with Intellisense when you type the names of classes, properties, or methods in Source view. You can add Intellisense to your custom components to make it easier for other developers to use your components.

If you add XML comments to a component, then the contents of the XML comments appear automatically in Intellisense. For example, the component in Listing 14.20 includes XML comments for its class definition, property definitions, and method definition (see Figure 14.5).

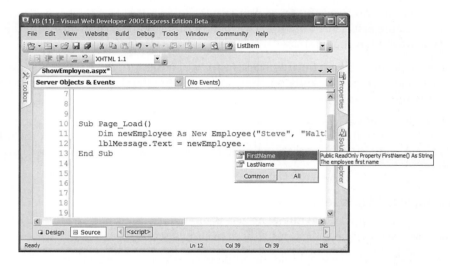

FIGURE 14.5   Adding comments to a component.

LISTING 14.20   Employee.vb

```vb
''' <summary>
''' Represents an employee of Acme.com
''' </summary>
Public Class Employee

    Private _firstName As String
    Private _lastName As String

    ''' <summary>
    ''' The employee first name
    ''' </summary>
    Public ReadOnly Property FirstName() As String
        Get
```

LISTING 14.20   Continued

```
        Return _firstName
    End Get
End Property


''' <summary>
''' The employee last name
''' </summary>
Public ReadOnly Property LastName() As String
    Get
        Return _lastName
    End Get
End Property



''' <summary>
''' Returns an employee from the database
''' </summary>
''' <param name="id">The unique employee identifier</param>
''' <returns>An instance of the Employee class</returns>
Public Shared Function getEmployee(ByVal id As Integer) As Employee
    Return Nothing
End Function

''' <summary>
''' Initializes an employee
''' </summary>
''' <param name="firstName">First Name</param>
''' <param name="lastName">Last Name</param>
Public Sub New(ByVal firstName As String, ByVal lastName As String)
    _firstName = firstName
    _lastName = lastName
End Sub

End Class
```

> **NOTE**
>
> You can generate an XML documentation file—a file that contains all the XML comments—for the components contained in a folder by using the `/doc` switch with the Visual Basic command-line compiler. The Visual Basic command-line compiler is discussed in the second part of this chapter, "Building Component Libraries."

Using ASP.NET Intrinsics in a Component

When you add code to an ASP.NET page, you are adding code to an instance of the Page class. The Page class exposes several ASP.NET intrinsic objects such as the Request, Response, Cache, Session, and Trace objects.

If you want to use these objects within a component, then you need to do a little more work. Realize that when you create a component, you are not creating an ASP.NET component. In this chapter, we are creating .NET components, and a .NET component can be used by any type of .NET application, including a Console application or Windows Forms application.

To use the ASP.NET instrinsics in a component, you need to get a reference to the current HtppContext. The HttpContext object is the one object that is available behind the scenes through the entire page processing lifecycle. You can access the HttpContext object from any user control, custom control, or component contained in a page.

> **NOTE**
>
> The HttpContext object includes an Items collection. You can add anything to the Items collection and share the thing among all the elements contained in a page.

To get a reference to the current HttpContext object, you can use the shared Current property included in the HttpContext class. For example, the component in Listing 14.21 uses the HttpContext object to use both the Session and Trace objects.

LISTING 14.21   Preferences.vb

```vb
Imports System.Web

Public Class Preferences

    Public Shared Property FavoriteColor() As String
        Get
            Dim context As HttpContext = HttpContext.Current
            context.Trace.Warn("Getting FavoriteColor")
            If context.Session("FavoriteColor") Is Nothing Then
                Return "Blue"
            Else
                Return CType(context.Session("FavoriteColor"), String)
            End If
        End Get
        Set(ByVal Value As String)
            Dim context As HttpContext = HttpContext.Current
            context.Trace.Warn("Setting FavoriteColor")
            context.Session("FavoriteColor") = value
```

LISTING 14.21   Continued

```
        End Set
    End Property


End Class
```

The `Preferences` component contains a single property named `FavoriteColor`. The value of this property is stored in `Session` state. Anytime this property is modified, the `Trace` object writes a warning.

You can use the `Preferences` component in the page contained in Listing 14.22.

LISTING 14.22   ShowPreferences.aspx

```
<%@ Page Language="VB" trace="true" %>
<!DOCTYPE html PUBLIC "-//W3C//DTD XHTML 1.1//EN"
    "http://www.w3.org/TR/xhtml11/DTD/xhtml11.dtd">
<script runat="server">

    Sub Page_PreRender()
        body1.Style("background-color") = Preferences.FavoriteColor
    End Sub

    Protected Sub btnSelect_Click(ByVal sender As Object, ByVal e As EventArgs)
        Preferences.FavoriteColor = ddlFavoriteColor.SelectedItem.Text
    End Sub
</script>

<html xmlns="http://www.w3.org/1999/xhtml" >
<head id="Head1" runat="server">
    <style type="text/css">
        .content
        {
            width:80%;
            padding:20px;
            background-color:white;
        }
    </style>
    <title>Show Preferences</title>
</head>
<body id="body1" runat="server">
    <form id="form1" runat="server">
    <div class="content">

    <h1>Show Preferences</h1>
```

LISTING 14.22   Continued

```
    <asp:DropDownList
        id="ddlFavoriteColor"
        Runat="server">
        <asp:ListItem Text="Blue" />
        <asp:ListItem Text="Red" />
        <asp:ListItem Text="Green" />
    </asp:DropDownList>
    <asp:Button
        id="btnSelect"
        Text="Select"
        Runat="server" OnClick="btnSelect_Click" />

    </div>
    </form>
</body>
</html>
```

After you open the page in Listing 14.22, you can select your favorite color from the
DropDownList control. Your favorite color is stored in the Preferences object (see
Figure 14.6).

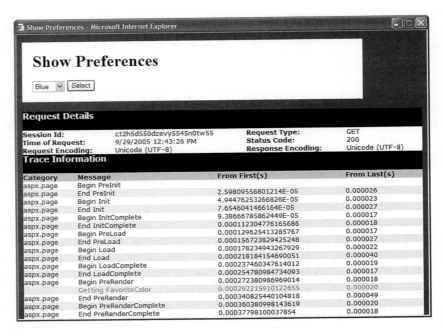

FIGURE 14.6   Selecting a favorite color.

Building Component Libraries

One of the advertised benefits of using components is code reuse. You write a method once, and then you never need to write the same method ever again.

One problem with the components that have been created to this point is that they have all been application specific. In other words, you cannot reuse the components across multiple websites without copying all the source code from one App_Code folder to another.

If you want to share components among multiple websites, then you can no longer take advantage of dynamic compilation. To share components, you need to compile the components explicitly in a separate assembly.

Compiling Component Libraries

You can use a number of methods to compile a set of components into an assembly:

- Use the command-line compiler
- Use Visual Basic Express
- Use Visual Studio .NET 2005

These options are explored in turn.

Using the Visual Basic .NET Command-Line Compiler

You can use the Visual Basic command-line compiler to compile a source code file, or set of source code files, into an assembly. The Visual Basic command-line compiler is located at the following path:

```
C:\WINDOWS\Microsoft.NET\Framework\[version]\vbc.exe
```

> **NOTE**
>
> If you have installed the .NET Framework 2.0 SDK, then you can open the SDK Command Prompt from the Microsoft .NET Framework SDK v2.0 program group. When the command prompt opens, the path to the Visual Basic .NET compiler is added to the environment automatically.

You can use the vbc.exe tool to compile any Visual Basic source file like this:

```
vbc /t:library SomeFile.vb
```

The /t (target) option causes the compiler to create a component library and not a Console or Windows application. When you execute this command, a new file named SomeFile.dll is created, which is the compiled assembly.

As an alternative to compiling a single file, you can compile all the source code files in a folder (and every subfolder) like this:

```
vbc /t:library /recurse:*.vb /out:MyLibrary.dll
```

The /recurse option causes the compiler to compile the contents of all the subfolders. The /out option provides a name for the resulting assembly.

You need to know about two other compiler options:

- /imports—Enables you to provide a comma-delimited list of namespaces to import.

- /reference—Enables you to provide a comma-delimited list of assemblies to reference.

When the source code files are compiled dynamically in the App_Code folder, several imports and references are used by default. For example, the System.Collections, System.Web, and System.Web.UI.WebControls namespaces are imported automatically. When compiling from the command line, you need to either add Imports statements to your source code files or list these namespaces, using the /imports compiler option.

Furthermore, several assembly references are added automatically during dynamic compilation, including System.Web.dll and System.Data.dll. When compiling from the command line, you need to add these references explicitly if you are using a class from one of these assemblies.

> **NOTE**
> You can determine the assembly and namespace associated with any class in the .NET Framework by looking up the main entry for the class in the .NET Framework SDK Documentation.

> **VISUAL WEB DEVELOPER TIP**
> You can add the vbc command-line compiler as an external tool to Visual Web Developer. That way, you can simply select a menu option to compile the contents of the App_Code folder automatically into an assembly. To add a new external tool, select the menu option Tools, External Tools (see Figure 14.7).

Using Visual Basic .NET Express

You can download a trial edition of Visual Basic .NET Express from the MSDN website (http://msdn.microsoft.com). Visual Basic .NET Express enables you to build Windows applications, Console applications, and class libraries.

To create a class library that you can use with an ASP.NET application, you create a Class Library project in Visual Basic .NET Express (see Figure 14.8). When you build the project, a new assembly is created.

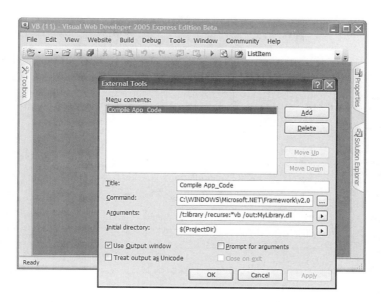

FIGURE 14.7   Adding the Visual Basic Compiler to External Tools.

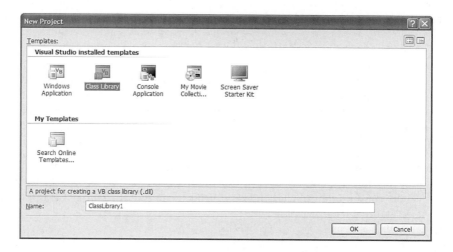

FIGURE 14.8   Creating a Class Library in Visual Basic .NET Express.

If you need to use ASP.NET classes in your class library, such as the HttpContext class, then you need to add a reference to the System.Web.dll assembly to your Class Library project. Select the menu option Project, Add Reference and add the System.Web.dll from beneath the .NET tab (see Figure 14.9).

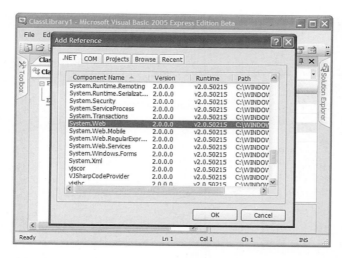

FIGURE 14.9   Adding a reference to `System.Web.dll`.

NOTE

If you are a C# developer, then you can download Visual C# Express from the MSDN Website
(http://msdn.microsoft.com).

Using Visual Studio .NET 2005

The easiest way to create a class library that you can share among multiple ASP.NET applications is to use Visual Studio .NET 2005 instead of Visual Web Developer. Visual Studio .NET 2005 was designed to enable you to easily build enterprise applications. Building class libraries is one of the features you get in Visual Studio .NET 2005 that you don't get in Visual Web Developer Express.

Visual Studio .NET 2005 enables you to add multiple projects to a single solution. For example, you can add both an ASP.NET project and a Class Library project to the same solution. When you update the Class Library project, the ASP.NET project is updated automatically (see Figure 14.10).

Adding a Reference to a Class Library

Now that you understand how you can create a class library in a separate assembly, you need to know how you can use this class library in another project. In other words, how do you use the components contained in an assembly within an ASP.NET page?

There are two ways to make an assembly available to an ASP.NET application. You can add the assembly to the application's /Bin folder or you can add the assembly to the Global Assembly Cache.

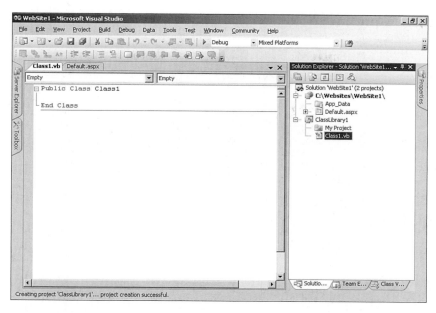

FIGURE 14.10   A solution that contains multiple projects.

Adding an Assembly to the Bin Folder

In general, the best way to use an assembly in an ASP.NET application is to add the assembly to the application's root Bin folder. There is nothing magical about this folder. The ASP.NET Framework automatically checks this folder for any assemblies. If the folder contains an assembly, the assembly is referenced automatically by the ASP.NET application when it is compiled dynamically.

If you are using Visual Web Developer, then you can select the menu option Website, Add Reference to add a new assembly to your application's Bin folder (see Figure 14.11). Alternatively, you can simply copy an assembly into this folder. (If the folder doesn't exist, just create it.)

When you add an assembly to an ASP.NET application's Bin folder, the assembly is scoped to the application. This means that you can add different versions of the same assembly to different applications without worrying about any conflicts.

Furthermore, if you add an assembly to the Bin folder, then you can take advantage of XCopy deployment. In other words, if you need to move your website to a new server, then you can simply copy all the files in your website from one server to another. As long as you copy your Bin folder, the assembly is available at the new location.

Adding an Assembly to the Global Assembly Cache

All the assemblies that make up the .NET Framework class library are contained in the Global Assembly Cache. For example, the Random class is located in the System.dll assembly, and the System.dll assembly is contained in the Global Assembly Cache. Any assembly located in the Global Assembly Cache can be referenced by any application running on a server.

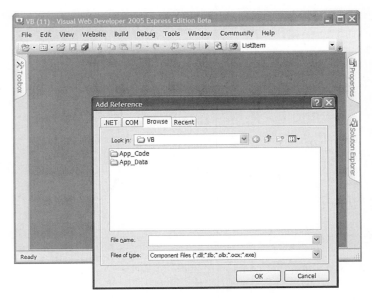

FIGURE 14.11   Adding an assembly reference with Visual Web Developer.

The Global Assembly Cache's physical location is at the following path:

```
C:\WINDOWS\assembly
```

Before you can add an assembly to the Global Assembly Cache, you must add a strong name to the assembly. A strong name is similar to a GUID. You use a strong name to provide your assembly with a universally unique identifier.

> **NOTE**
>
> Technically, a strong name consists of the name, version number, and culture of the assembly. The strong name also includes the public key from a public/private key pair. Finally, the strong name includes a hash of the assembly's contents so that you know whether the assembly has been modified.

You can generate a strong name by using the `sn.exe` command-line tool like this:

```
sn.exe -k KeyPair.snk
```

Executing this command creates a new file named `KeyPair.snk`, which includes a new random public/private key pair.

> **WARNING**
>
> Protect your key file. You should not reveal the private key to anyone.

You can compile an assembly that includes a strong name by executing the Visual Basic .NET command-line compiler like this:

```
vbc /t:library /keyfile:KeyPair.snk /recurse:*.vb /out:MyLibrary.dll
```

The resulting assembly is strongly named with the public key from the KeyPair.snk file. The /keyfile option associates the key file with the assembly. In this case, the name of the resulting assembly is MyLibrary.dll.

An alternative method of associating a strong name with an assembly is to use the <Assembly: AssemblyKeyFile> attribute. You can add this attribute to any of the source files that get compiled into the assembly. For example, you can drop the file in Listing 14.23 into the folder that you are compiling and it associates the public key from the KeyPair.snk file with the compiled assembly.

LISTING 14.23   AssemblyInfo.vb

```
Imports System.Reflection

<Assembly: AssemblyKeyFile("KeyPair.snk")>
<Assembly: AssemblyVersion("0.0.0.0")>
```

The file in Listing 14.23 actually includes two attributes. The first attribute associates the KeyPair.snk public key with the assembly. The second attribute associates a version number with the assembly. The version number consists of four sets of numbers: the major version, minor version, build number, and the revision number.

After you add the file in Listing 14.23 to a folder that contains the source code for your components, use the following command to compile the folder:

```
vbc /t:library /recurse:*.vb /out:MyLibrary.dll
```

After you associate a strong name with an assembly, you can use the GacUtil.exe command-line tool to add the assembly to the Global Assembly Cache. Executing the following statement from a command prompt adds the MyLibrary.dll assembly to the Global Assembly Cache:

```
GacUtil.exe /i MyLibrary.dll
```

You can verify that the MyLibrary.dll assembly has been added successfully to the Global Assembly Cache by opening your Global Assembly Cache folder located at the following path:

```
C:\WINDOWS\assembly
```

14

You should see the `MyLibrary.dll` assembly listed in the Assembly Name column (see Figure 14.12). Note the Version and the PublicKeyToken columns. You need to know the values of these columns to use the assembly in an application.

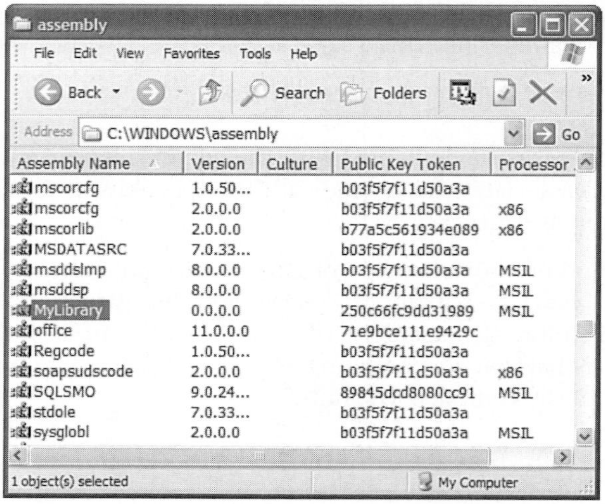

FIGURE 14.12   Viewing the Global Assembly Cache.

After you install an assembly in the Global Assembly Cache, you can use the assembly in your ASP.NET Pages and `App_Code` components by adding a reference to the assembly in your web configuration file. The web configuration file in Listing 14.24 adds the `MyLibrary.dll` assembly to your application.

LISTING 14.24   Web.Config

```
<?xml version="1.0"?>
<configuration>
  <system.web>
    <compilation>
      <assemblies>
        <add assembly="MyLibrary,Version=0.0.0.0,Culture=neutral,
          PublicKeyToken=250c66fc9dd31989"/>
      </assemblies>
    </compilation>
  </system.web>
</configuration>
```

The web configuration file in Listing 14.24 adds the `MyLibrary` assembly. Notice that you must supply the Version, Culture, and PublicKeyToken associated with the assembly. You need to substitute the correct values for these properties in Listing 14.24 before you use the file with an assembly that you have compiled. (Remember that you can get these values by opening the c:\WINDOWS\assembly folder.)

> **NOTE**
>
> When using Visual Basic Express or Visual Studio .NET 2005, you can create a strong name automatically and associate the strong name with an assembly. Right-click the name of your project in the Solution Explorer window and select Properties. Next, select the tab labeled Signing.

In general, you should avoid adding your assemblies to the Global Assembly Cache because using the Global Assembly Cache defeats XCopy deployment. Using the Global Assembly Cache makes it more difficult to back up an application. It also makes it more difficult to move an application from one server to another.

Architectural Considerations

If you embark on a large ASP.NET project, you'll quickly discover that you spend more time writing code for components than writing code for your pages. This is not a bad thing. Placing as much of your application logic as possible in components makes it easier to maintain and extend your application.

However, the process of organizing the components itself can become time consuming. In other words, you start to run into architectural issues concerning the best way to design your web application.

The topic of architecture, like the topics of politics and religion, should not be discussed in polite company. People have passionate opinions about architecture and discussions on this topic quickly devolve into people throwing things. Be aware that any and all statements about proper architecture are controversial.

With these disclaimers out of the way, in this section I provide you with an overview of one of the most common architectures for ASP.NET applications. In this section, you learn how to build a three-tiered ASP.NET application.

Building Multi-tier Applications

One very common architecture for an application follows an n-tier design model. When using an n-tier architecture, you encapsulate your application logic into separate layers.

In particular, it is recommended that an application should be divided into the following three application layers:

- User Interface Layer
- Business Logic Layer
- Data Access Layer

The idea is that the User Interface layer should contain nothing but user interface elements such as HTML and ASP.NET controls. The User Interface layer should not contain any business logic or data access code.

The Business Logic layer contains all your business rules and validation code. It manages all data access for the User Interface Layer.

Finally, the Data Access Layer contains all the code for interacting with a database. For example, all the code for interacting with Microsoft SQL Server should be encapsulated in this layer.

The advantage of encapsulating your application logic into different layers is that it makes it easier to modify your application without requiring you to rewrite your entire application. Changes in one layer can be completely isolated from the other layers.

For example, imagine that (one fine day) your company decides to switch from using Microsoft SQL Server to using Oracle as their database server. If you have been careful to create an isolated Data Access Layer, then you would need to rewrite only your Data Access Layer. It might be a major project, but you would not need to start from scratch.

Or, imagine that your company decides to create a Windows Forms version of an existing ASP.NET application. Again, if you have been careful to isolate your User Interface Layer from your Business Logic Layer, then you can extend your application to support a Windows Forms Interface without rewriting your entire application. The Windows Forms application can use your existing Business Logic and Data Access layers.

> **NOTE**
>
> I spend my working life training companies on implementing ASP.NET applications. Typically, a company is migrating a web application written in some other language such as Java or ASP Classic to the ASP.NET Framework. It always breaks my heart to see how much code is wasted in these transitions (thousands of man hours of work lost). If you are careful in the way that you design your ASP.NET application now, you can avoid this sorry fate in the future.

I realize that this is all very abstract, so let's examine a particular sample. We'll create a simple product management system that enables you to select, insert, update, and delete products. However, we'll do it the right way by dividing the application into distinct User Interface, Business Logic, and Data Access layers.

Creating the User Interface Layer

The User Interface layer is contained in Listing 14.25. Notice that the User Interface layer consists of a single ASP.NET page. This page contains no code whatsoever.

LISTING 14.25   Products.aspx

```
<%@ Page Language="VB" %>
<!DOCTYPE html PUBLIC "-//W3C//DTD XHTML 1.1//EN"
  "http://www.w3.org/TR/xhtml11/DTD/xhtml11.dtd">
```

LISTING 14.25   Continued

```html
<html xmlns="http://www.w3.org/1999/xhtml" >
<head id="Head1" runat="server">
    <style type="text/css">
    html
    {
        background-color:silver;
    }
    .content
    {
        padding:10px;
        background-color:white;
    }
    .products
    {
        margin-bottom:20px;
    }
    .products td,.products th
    {
        padding:5px;
        border-bottom:solid 1px blue;
    }
    a
    {
        color:blue;
    }
    </style>
    <title>Products</title>
</head>
<body>
    <form id="form1" runat="server">
    <div class="content">

    <asp:GridView
        id="grdProducts"
        DataSourceID="srcProducts"
        DataKeyNames="Id"
        AutoGenerateEditButton="true"
        AutoGenerateDeleteButton="true"
        AutoGenerateColumns="false"
        CssClass="products"
        GridLines="none"
        Runat="server">
        <Columns>
        <asp:BoundField
```

LISTING 14.25   Continued

```
            DataField="Id"
            ReadOnly="true"
            HeaderText="Id" />
        <asp:BoundField
            DataField="Name"
            HeaderText="Name" />
        <asp:BoundField
            DataField="Price"
            DataFormatString="{0:c}"
            HeaderText="Price" />
        <asp:BoundField
            DataField="Description"
            HeaderText="Description" />
        </Columns>
    </asp:GridView>

    <fieldset>
    <legend>Add Product</legend>
    <asp:DetailsView
        id="dtlProduct"
        DataSourceID="srcProducts"
        DefaultMode="Insert"
        AutoGenerateInsertButton="true"
        AutoGenerateRows="false"
        Runat="server">
        <Fields>
        <asp:BoundField
            DataField="Name"
            HeaderText="Name:" />
        <asp:BoundField
            DataField="Price"
            HeaderText="Price:"/>
        <asp:BoundField
            DataField="Description"
            HeaderText="Description:" />
        </Fields>
    </asp:DetailsView>
    </fieldset>


    <asp:ObjectDataSource
        id="srcProducts"
        TypeName="AcmeStore.BusinessLogicLayer.Product"
        SelectMethod="SelectAll"
```

LISTING 14.25   Continued

```
            UpdateMethod="Update"
            InsertMethod="Insert"
            DeleteMethod="Delete"
            Runat="server" />

        </div>
        </form>
    </body>
    </html>
```

The page in Listing 14.25 contains a GridView, DetailsView, and ObjectDataSource control. The GridView control enables you to view, update, and delete the products contained in the Products database table (see Figure 14.13). The DetailsView enables you to add new products to the database. Both controls use the ObjectDataSource as their data source.

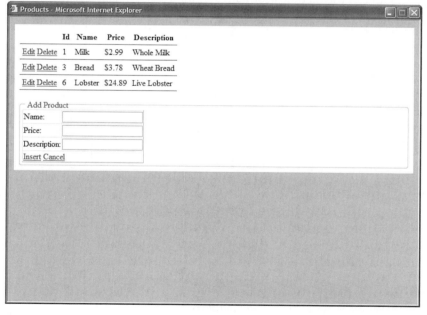

FIGURE 14.13   The Products.aspx page.

14

> **NOTE**
>
> The next chapter is entirely devoted to the ObjectDataSource control.

The page in Listing 14.25 does not interact with a database directly. Instead, the `ObjectDataSource` control is used to bind the `GridView` and `DetailsView` controls to a component named `AcmeStore.BusinessLogicLayer.Product`. The `Product` component is contained in the Business Logic layer.

> **NOTE**
>
> The page in Listing 14.25 does not contain any validation controls. I omitted adding validation controls for reasons of space. In a real application, you would want to toss some `RequiredFieldValidator` and `CompareValidator` controls into the page.

Creating the Business Logic Layer

The ASP.NET pages in your application should contain a minimum amount of code. All your application logic should be pushed into separate components contained in either the Business Logic or Data Access layers.

Your ASP.NET pages should not communicate directly with the Data Access layer. Instead, the pages should call the methods contained in the Business Logic layer.

The Business Logic layer consists of a single component named Product, which is contained in Listing 14.26. (A real-world application might contain dozens or even hundreds of components in its Business Logic layer.)

LISTING 14.26   BLL/Product.vb

```vb
Imports System
Imports System.Collections.Generic
Imports AcmeStore.DataAccessLayer


Namespace AcmeStore.BusinessLogicLayer

    ''' <summary>
    ''' Represents a store product and all the methods
    ''' for selecting, inserting, and updating a product
    ''' </summary>
    Public Class Product

        Private _id As Integer = 0
        Private _name As String = String.Empty
        Private _price As Decimal = 0
        Private _description As String = String.Empty


        ''' <summary>
        ''' Product Unique Identifier
        ''' </summary>
        Public ReadOnly Property Id() As Integer
```

LISTING 14.26 Continued

```vb
        Get
            Return _id
        End Get
    End Property

    ''' <summary>
    ''' Product Name
    ''' </summary>
    Public ReadOnly Property Name() As String
        Get
            Return _name
        End Get
    End Property

    ''' <summary>
    ''' Product Price
    ''' </summary>
    Public ReadOnly Property Price() As Decimal
        Get
            Return _price
        End Get
    End Property

    ''' <summary>
    ''' Product Description
    ''' </summary>
    Public ReadOnly Property Description() As String
        Get
            Return _description
        End Get
    End Property

    ''' <summary>
    ''' Retrieves all products
    ''' </summary>
    Public Shared Function SelectAll() As List(Of Product)
        Dim dataAccessLayer As SqlDataAccessLayer = New SqlDataAccessLayer()
        Return dataAccessLayer.ProductSelectAll()
    End Function

    ''' <summary>
    ''' Updates a particular product
    ''' </summary>
    ''' <param name="id">Product Id</param>
```

14

LISTING 14.26   Continued

```
        ''' <param name="name">Product Name</param>
        ''' <param name="price">Product Price</param>
        ''' <param name="description">Product Description</param>
        Public Shared Sub Update(ByVal id As Integer,
➥ByVal name As String, ByVal price As Decimal, ByVal description As String)
            If id < 1 Then
                Throw New ArgumentException("Product Id must be greater than 0",
➥ "id")
            End If

            Dim productToUpdate As Product =
➥New Product(id, name, price, description)
            productToUpdate.Save()
        End Sub

        ''' <summary>
        ''' Inserts a new product
        ''' </summary>
        ''' <param name="name">Product Name</param>
        ''' <param name="price">Product Price</param>
        ''' <param name="description">Product Description</param>
        Public Shared Sub Insert(ByVal name As String, ByVal price As Decimal,
➥ByVal description As String)
            Dim NewProduct As Product = New Product(name, price, description)
            NewProduct.Save()
        End Sub

        ''' <summary>
        ''' Deletes an existing product
        ''' </summary>
        ''' <param name="id">Product Id</param>
        Public Shared Sub Delete(ByVal id As Integer)
            If id < 1 Then
                Throw New ArgumentException("Product Id must be greater than 0",
➥ "id")
            End If

            Dim dataAccessLayer As SqlDataAccessLayer = New SqlDataAccessLayer()
            dataAccessLayer.ProductDelete(id)
        End Sub

        ''' <summary>
        ''' Validates product information before saving product
        ''' properties to the database
```

LISTING 14.26   Continued

```
        ''' </summary>
        Private Sub Save()
            If String.IsNullOrEmpty(_name) Then
                Throw New ArgumentException("Product Name not supplied", "name")
            End If
            If _name.Length > 50 Then
                Throw New ArgumentException("Product Name must be less
➡than 50 characters", "name")
            End If
            If String.IsNullOrEmpty(_description) Then
                Throw New ArgumentException("Product Description not supplied",
➡ "description")
            End If

            Dim dataAccessLayer As SqlDataAccessLayer = New SqlDataAccessLayer()
            If _id > 0 Then
                dataAccessLayer.ProductUpdate(Me)
            Else
                dataAccessLayer.ProductInsert(Me)
            End If
        End Sub


        ''' <summary>
        ''' Initializes Product
        ''' </summary>
        ''' <param name="name">Product Name</param>
        ''' <param name="price">Product Price</param>
        ''' <param name="description">Product Description</param>
        Public Sub New(ByVal name As String, ByVal price As Decimal,
➡ByVal description As String)
            Me.New(0, name, price, description)
        End Sub


        ''' <summary>
        ''' Initializes Product
        ''' </summary>
        ''' <param name="id">Product Id</param>
        ''' <param name="name">Product Name</param>
        ''' <param name="price">Product Price</param>
        ''' <param name="description">Product Description</param>
        Public Sub New(ByVal id As Integer, ByVal name As String,
➡ByVal price As Decimal, ByVal description As String)
            _id = id
```

LISTING 14.26   Continued

```
            _name = name
            _price = price
            _description = description
        End Sub


    End Class
End namespace
```

The Product component contains four public methods named SelectAll(), Update(), Insert(), and Delete(). All four of these methods use the SqlDataAccessLayer component to interact with the Products database table. The SqlDataAccessLayer is contained in the Data Access Layer.

For example, the SelectAll() method returns a collection of Product objects. This collection is retrieved from the SqlDataAccessLayer component.

The Insert(), Update(), and Delete() methods validate their parameters before passing the parameters to the Data Access layer. For example, when you call the Insert() method, the length of the Name parameter is checked to verify that it is less than 50 characters.

Notice that the Business Logic layer does not contain any data access logic. All this logic is contained in the Data Access layer.

Creating the Data Access Layer

The Data Access layer contains all the specialized code for interacting with a database. The Data Access layer consists of the single component in Listing 14.27. (A real-world application might contain dozens or even hundreds of components in its Data Access Layer.)

LISTING 14.27   SqlDataAccessLayer.vb

```
Imports System
Imports System.Data
Imports System.Data.SqlClient
Imports System.Web.Configuration
Imports System.Collections.Generic
Imports AcmeStore.BusinessLogicLayer


Namespace AcmeStore.DataAccessLayer


    ''' <summary>
    ''' Data Access Layer for interacting with Microsoft
    ''' SQL Server 2005
    ''' </summary>
```

LISTING 14.27 Continued

```vb
Public Class SqlDataAccessLayer
    Private Shared ReadOnly _connectionString As String = String.Empty

    ''' <summary>
    ''' Selects all products from the database
    ''' </summary>
    Public Function ProductSelectAll() As List(Of Product)
        ' Create Product collection
        Dim colProducts As New List(Of Product)()

        ' Create connection
        Dim con As SqlConnection = New SqlConnection(_connectionString)

        ' Create command
        Dim cmd As SqlCommand = New SqlCommand()
        cmd.Connection = con
        cmd.CommandText = "SELECT Id,Name,Price,Description FROM Products"

        ' Execute command
        Using con
            con.Open()
            Dim reader As SqlDataReader = cmd.ExecuteReader()
            While reader.Read()
                colProducts.Add(New Product( _
                    CType(reader("Id"), Integer), _
                    CType(reader("Name"), String), _
                    CType(reader("Price"), Decimal), _
                    CType(reader("Description"), String)))
            End While
        End Using
        Return colProducts
    End Function

    ''' <summary>
    ''' Inserts a new product into the database
    ''' </summary>
    ''' <param name="newProduct">Product</param>
    Public Sub ProductInsert(ByVal NewProduct As Product)
        ' Create connection
        Dim con As SqlConnection = New SqlConnection(_connectionString)

        ' Create command
        Dim cmd As SqlCommand = New SqlCommand()
        cmd.Connection = con
```

LISTING 14.27   Continued

```vb
            cmd.CommandText = "INSERT Products (Name,Price,Description)
➡VALUES (@Name,@Price,@Description)"

        ' Add parameters
        cmd.Parameters.AddWithValue("@Name", NewProduct.Name)
        cmd.Parameters.AddWithValue("@Price", NewProduct.Price)
        cmd.Parameters.AddWithValue("@Description", NewProduct.Description)

        ' Execute command
        Using con
            con.Open()
            cmd.ExecuteNonQuery()
        End Using
    End Sub


    ''' <summary>
    ''' Updates an existing product into the database
    ''' </summary>
    ''' <param name="productToUpdate">Product</param>
    Public Sub ProductUpdate(ByVal productToUpdate As Product)
        ' Create connection
        Dim con As SqlConnection = New SqlConnection(_connectionString)

        ' Create command
        Dim cmd As SqlCommand = New SqlCommand()
        cmd.Connection = con
        cmd.CommandText = "UPDATE Products SET
➡ Name=@Name,Price=@Price,Description=@Description WHERE Id=@Id"

        ' Add parameters
        cmd.Parameters.AddWithValue("@Name", productToUpdate.Name)
        cmd.Parameters.AddWithValue("@Price", productToUpdate.Price)
        cmd.Parameters.AddWithValue("@Description",
productToUpdate.Description)
        cmd.Parameters.AddWithValue("@Id", productToUpdate.Id)

        ' Execute command
        Using con
            con.Open()
            cmd.ExecuteNonQuery()
        End Using
    End Sub


    ''' <summary>
```

LISTING 14.27 Continued

```
            ''' Deletes an existing product in the database
            ''' </summary>
            ''' <param name="id">Product Id</param>
        Public Sub ProductDelete(ByVal Id As Integer)
                ' Create connection
                Dim con As SqlConnection = New SqlConnection(_connectionString)

                ' Create command
                Dim cmd As SqlCommand = New SqlCommand()
                cmd.Connection = con
                cmd.CommandText = "DELETE Products WHERE Id=@Id"

                ' Add parameters
                cmd.Parameters.AddWithValue("@Id", Id)

                ' Execute command
                Using con
                    con.Open()
                    cmd.ExecuteNonQuery()
                End Using
        End Sub


            ''' <summary>
            ''' Initialize the data access layer by
            ''' loading the database connection string from
            ''' the Web.Config file
            ''' </summary>
        Shared Sub New()
            _connectionString =
➥ WebConfigurationManager.ConnectionStrings("Store").ConnectionString
            If String.IsNullOrEmpty(_connectionString) Then
                Throw New Exception("No connection String configured
➥ in Web.Config file")
            End If
        End Sub
    End Class
End Namespace
```

The SqlDataAccessLayer component in Listing 14.27 grabs the database connection string that it uses when communicating with Microsoft SQL Server in its constructor. The connection string is assigned to a private field so that it can be used by all the component's methods.

The SqlDataAccessLayer component has four public methods: ProductSelectAll(), ProductInsert(), ProductUpdate(), and ProductDelete(). These methods use the ADO.NET classes from the System.Data.SqlClient namespace to communicate with Microsoft SQL Server.

NOTE

We discuss ADO.NET in Chapter 16, "Building Data Access Components."

Notice that the SqlDataAccessLayer component is not completely isolated from the components in the Business Logic Layer. The ProductSelectAll() method builds a collection of Product objects, which the method returns to the Business Logic layer. You should strive to isolate each layer as much as possible. However, in some cases, you cannot completely avoid mixing objects from different layers.

Summary

In this chapter, you learned how to build components in the .NET Framework. In the first part, you were given an overview of component building. You learned how to take advantage of dynamic compilation by using the App_Code folder. You also learned how to create component properties, methods, and constructors. You also examined several advanced topics related to components such as overloading, inheritance, MustInherit classes, and interfaces.

In the second half of this chapter, you learned how to build component libraries. You saw different methods for compiling a set of components into an assembly. You also examined how you can add components to both an application's Bin folder and the Global Assembly Cache.

Finally, you had a chance to consider architectural issues related to building applications with components. You learned how to build a three-tiered application, divided into isolated User Interface, Business Logic, and Data Access layers.

CHAPTER 15

Using the ObjectDataSource Control

The ObjectDataSource control enables you to bind DataBound controls such as the GridView, DetailsView, and FormView controls to a component. You can use the ObjectDataSource control to easily build multi-tier applications with the ASP.NET Framework. Unlike the SqlDataSource control, which mixes data access logic in the User Interface Layer, the ObjectDataSource control enables you to cleanly separate your User Interface Layer from your Business Logic and Data Access Layers.

In this chapter, you learn how to use the ObjectDataSource control to represent different types of objects. For example, you learn how to use the ObjectDataSource control with components that represent database data. You also learn how to use the ObjectDataSource control to represent different types of method parameters.

In the course of this chapter, we tackle a number of advanced topics. For example, you learn how to page, sort, and filter database records represented by the ObjectDataSource control. You learn how to page and sort through large database tables efficiently.

In the final section of this chapter, you learn how to extend the ObjectDataSource control to represent specialized data sources. You also learn how to extend the ObjectDataSource control with custom parameters.

Representing Objects with the `ObjectDataSource` Control

The `ObjectDataSource` control includes five main properties:

- `TypeName`—The name of the type of object that the `ObjectDataSource` control represents.

- `SelectMethod`—The name of a method that the `ObjectDataSource` calls when selecting data.

- `UpdateMethod`—The name of a method that the `ObjectDataSource` calls when updating data.

- `InsertMethod`—The name of a method that the `ObjectDataSource` calls when inserting data.

- `DeleteMethod`—The name of a method that the `ObjectDataSource` calls when deleting data.

An `ObjectDataSource` control can represent any type of object in the .NET Framework. This section discusses several types of objects you might want to represent. For example, you learn how to use the `ObjectDataSource` control with components that represent collections, ADO.NET DataReaders, DataSets, and web services.

> **NOTE**
>
> You can use the `ObjectDataSource` control to represent any object (any class that derives from the `System.Object` class). If the object does not support the `IEnumerable` interface, the `ObjectDataSource` control automatically wraps the object in a new object that supports the IEnumerable interface. You can even represent an ASP.NET ListBox control with an `ObjectDataSource` (not that a ListBox has any interesting methods).

Binding to a Component

Let's start with a really simple component. The component in Listing 15.1 is named `MovieCollection`. It contains one method named `GetMovies()`, which returns a collection of movie titles.

LISTING 15.1   `MovieCollection.vb`

```vb
Imports System
Imports System.Web.Configuration
Imports System.Collections.Generic


Public Class MovieCollection

    Public Function GetMovies() As List(Of String)
        Dim movies As New List(Of String)()
```

LISTING 15.1   Continued

```
        movies.Add("Star Wars")
        movies.Add("Independence Day")
        movies.Add("War of the Worlds")
        Return movies
    End Function

End Class
```

You can use the page in Listing 15.2 to display the list of movies returned by the `GetMovies()` method in a GridView control. The page contains an `ObjectDataSource` control that represents the `MovieCollection` component.

LISTING 15.2   ShowMovieCollection.aspx

```
<%@ Page Language="VB" %>
<!DOCTYPE html PUBLIC "-//W3C//DTD XHTML 1.1//EN"
    "http://www.w3.org/TR/xhtml11/DTD/xhtml11.dtd">
<html xmlns="http://www.w3.org/1999/xhtml" >
<head id="Head1" runat="server">
    <title>Show Movie Collection</title>
</head>
<body>
    <form id="form1" runat="server">
    <div>

    <asp:GridView
        id="grdMovies"
        DataSourceID="srcMovies"
        Runat="server" />

    <asp:ObjectDataSource
        id="srcMovies"
        TypeName="MovieCollection"
        SelectMethod="GetMovies"
        Runat="server" />

    </div>
    </form>
</body>
</html>
```

In Listing 15.2, the `ObjectDataSource` control includes two properties named `TypeName` and `SelectMethod`. The `TypeName` property contains the name of the component that you want to represent with the `ObjectDataSource` control. The `SelectMethod` property represents the method of the component that you want to call when selecting data.

Notice that the `GridView` control is bound to the `ObjectDataSource` control through its `DataSourceID` property. When you open the page in Listing 15.2, the list of movies is retrieved from the `MovieCollection` component and displayed in the `GridView`.

The `MovieCollection` component contains instance methods. The `ObjectDataSource` automatically creates a new instance of the `MovieCollection` component before calling its `GetMovies()` method. It automatically destroys the object after it is finished using the object.

You also can use the `ObjectDataSource` control to call shared (static) methods. In that case, the `ObjectDataSource` doesn't need to instantiate a component before calling the method.

Binding to a DataReader

Typically, you use the `ObjectDataSource` control to represent database data. The .NET Framework provides you with multiple ways of representing data. This section discusses how you can use an `ObjectDataSource` to represent a `DataReader`.

> **NOTE**
> The different ADO.NET objects are compared and contrasted in the next chapter, "Building Data Access Components."

The ADO.NET `DataReader` object provides you with a fast, read-only representation of database data. If you need to retrieve database records in the fastest possible way, then you should use a `DataReader` object.

For example, the component in Listing 15.3, the `MovieDataReader` component, returns all the movies from the Movies database table by using the `SqlDataReader` object. Notice that the component imports the `System.Data.SqlClient` namespace to use this Microsoft SQL Server–specific ADO.NET object.

LISTING 15.3　MovieDataReader.vb

```vb
Imports System
Imports System.Data
Imports System.Data.SqlClient
Imports System.Web.Configuration

Public Class MovieDataReader

    Private ReadOnly _conString As String

    Public Function GetMovies() As SqlDataReader
```

LISTING 15.3   Continued

```
        ' Create Connection
        Dim con As New SqlConnection(_conString)

        ' Create Command
        Dim cmd As New SqlCommand()
        cmd.Connection = con
        cmd.CommandText = "SELECT Id,Title,Director FROM Movies"

        ' Return DataReader
        con.Open()
        Return cmd.ExecuteReader(CommandBehavior.CloseConnection)
    End Function


    Public Sub New()
        _conString = WebConfigurationManager.ConnectionStrings("Movies").
➥ConnectionString
    End Sub

End Class
```

The component in Listing 15.3 actually uses three ADO.NET objects: the `Connection`, `Command`, and `DataReader` object. The `SqlCommand` object uses the `SqlConnection` object to connect to the database. The records are returned from the `SqlCommand` object and represented by the `SqlDataReader` object.

Notice that the `WebConfigurationManager` class is used to retrieve the database connection string from the web configuration file. To use this class, you need to import the `System.Web.Confiugration` namespace (and have a reference to the `System.Web.dll` assembly).

The `ObjectDataSource` control in Listing 15.4 represents the `MovieDataReader` object. It binds the movies to a `GridView` control.

LISTING 15.4   ShowMovieDataReader.aspx

```
<%@ Page Language="VB" %>
<!DOCTYPE html PUBLIC "-//W3C//DTD XHTML 1.1//EN"
  "http://www.w3.org/TR/xhtml11/DTD/xhtml11.dtd">
<html xmlns="http://www.w3.org/1999/xhtml" >
<head id="Head1" runat="server">
    <title>Show Movie DataReader</title>
</head>
<body>
    <form id="form1" runat="server">
```

15

LISTING 15.4   Continued

```
    <div>

    <asp:GridView
        id="grdMovies"
        DataSourceID="srcMovies"
        Runat="server" />

    <asp:ObjectDataSource
        id="srcMovies"
        TypeName="MovieDataReader"
        SelectMethod="GetMovies"
        Runat="server" />

    </div>
    </form>
</body>
</html>
```

Binding to a DataSet

You also can use the `ObjectDataSource` when you need to represent an ADO.NET `DataSet`. Using a `DataSet` is slower than using a `DataReader`. However, you can perform advanced operations, such as filtering and sorting, on data represented with a `DataSet`.

The component in Listing 15.5 returns all the records from the Movies database table. However, it uses a `DataSet` instead of a `DataReader` object.

LISTING 15.5   MovieDataSet.vb

```
Imports System
Imports System.Data
Imports System.Data.SqlClient
Imports System.Web.Configuration

Public Class MovieDataSet

    Private ReadOnly _conString As String

    Public Function GetMovies() As DataSet
        ' Create DataAdapter
        Dim commandText As String = "SELECT Id,Title,Director FROM Movies"
        Dim dad As New SqlDataAdapter(commandText, _conString)

        ' Return DataSet
        Dim dstMovies As New DataSet()
```

LISTING 15.5   Continued

```
        Using dad
            dad.Fill(dstMovies)
        End Using
        Return dstMovies
    End Function

    Public Sub New()
        _conString = WebConfigurationManager.ConnectionStrings("Movies").
➥ConnectionString
    End Sub

End Class
```

The component in Listing 15.5 uses two ADO.NET objects: a `DataAdapter` and a `DataSet`. The `SqlDataAdapter` is used to represent the SQL `select` command, and it populates the `DataSet` with the results of executing the command. Notice that the `WebConfigurationManager` class is used to read the database connection string from the web configuration file.

The page in Listing 15.6 binds the list of movies to a `DropDownList` control.

LISTING 15.6   ShowMovieDataSet.aspx

```
<%@ Page Language="VB" %>
<!DOCTYPE html PUBLIC "-//W3C//DTD XHTML 1.1//EN"
  "http://www.w3.org/TR/xhtml11/DTD/xhtml11.dtd">
<html xmlns="http://www.w3.org/1999/xhtml" >
<head id="Head1" runat="server">
    <title>Show Movie DataSet</title>
</head>
<body>
    <form id="form1" runat="server">
    <div>

    <asp:GridView
        id="grdMovies"
        DataSourceID="srcMovies"
        Runat="server" />

    <asp:ObjectDataSource
        id="srcMovies"
        TypeName="MovieDataReader"
        SelectMethod="GetMovies"
```

15

LISTING 15.6   Continued

```
            Runat="server" />

    </div>
    </form>
</body>
</html>
```

Binding to a Web Service

Web services enable you to share information across the Internet. When you communicate with a remote web service, you use a local proxy class to represent the web service located on the remote machine. You can use the `ObjectDataSource` to represent this proxy class.

For example, the file in Listing 15.7 contains a simple web service that returns the current server time. You can create this file in Visual Web Developer by selecting the menu option Website, Add New Item, and selecting the Web Service item.

LISTING 15.7   `TimeService.asmx`

```
<%@ WebService Language="VB" Class="TimeService" %>
Imports System
Imports System.Web
Imports System.Web.Services
Imports System.Web.Services.Protocols

<WebService(Namespace:="http://tempuri.org/")> _
<WebServiceBinding(ConformsTo:=WsiProfiles.BasicProfile1_1)> _
Public Class TimeService
    Inherits System.Web.Services.WebService

    <WebMethod()> _
    Public Function GetServerTime() As DateTime
        Return DateTime.Now
    End Function

End Class
```

After you create the web service in Listing 15.7, you can communicate with the service from anywhere in the world (or the galaxy, or the universe). Just as long as a computer is connected to the Internet, the computer can call the `GetServerTime()` method.

Before you can call the web service, you need to create a web service proxy class. If you are using Visual Web Developer, select the menu option Web Site, Add Web Reference and enter the URL of the `TimeService.asmx` file (You can click the `Web services in this solution` link to list all the web services in your current project.) Change the name of the web reference to LocalServices and click Add Reference (see Figure 15.1).

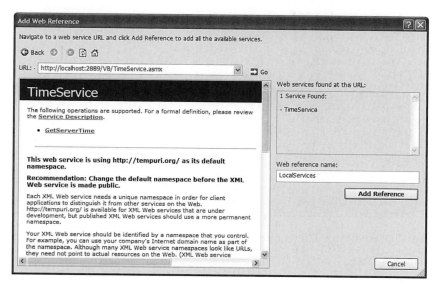

FIGURE 15.1   Adding a Web Reference in Visual Web Developer.

> **NOTE**
>
> If you are not using Visual Web Developer, you can create a web service proxy class from the command line by using the `Wsdl.exe` (Web Services Description Language) tool.

When you click Add Reference, a new folder is added to your project named App_WebReferences. The App_WebReferences folder contains a subfolder named LocalServices. Finally, your web configuration file is updated to include the URL to the TimeService web service.

Now that we have a consumable web service, we can represent the Web service using the `ObjectDataSource` control. The page in Listing 15.8 displays the server time using a FormView control bound to an `ObjectDataSource` control (see Figure 15.2).

15

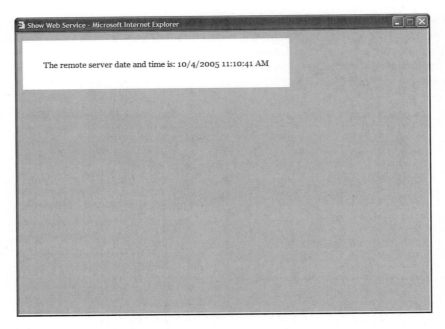

FIGURE 15.2   Retrieving the time from a web service.

LISTING 15.8   ShowWebService.aspx

```
<%@ Page Language="VB" %>
<html xmlns="http://www.w3.org/1999/xhtml" >
<head id="Head1" runat="server">
    <style type="text/css">
        html
        {
            background-color:silver;
        }
        .serverTime
        {
            background-color:white;
            font:16px Georgia,Serif;
        }
        .serverTime td
        {
            padding:40px;
        }
    </style>
    <title>Show Web Service</title>
</head>
```

LISTING 15.8   Continued

```
<body>
    <form id="form1" runat="server">
    <div>

    <asp:FormView
        id="frmServerTime"
        DataSourceID="srcServerTime"
        CssClass="serverTime"
        Runat="server">
        <ItemTemplate>
        The remote server date and time is: <%# Container.DataItem %>
        </ItemTemplate>
    </asp:FormView>

    <asp:ObjectDataSource
        id="srcServerTime"
        TypeName="LocalServices.TimeService"
        SelectMethod="GetServerTime"
        Runat="server" />

    </div>
    </form>
</body>
</html>
```

Notice that the `ObjectDataSource` control's `TypeName` property contains both the name-space and name of the web service proxy class (the web reference). In other words, it contains the fully qualified name of the proxy class. The `SelectMethod` property contains the name of the web method represented by the proxy class.

> **NOTE**
>
> If you open the `ShowWebService.aspx` page from the CD that accompanies this book, you receive an error. Before the page will work correctly, you need to update the web configuration file with the correct path to the web service on your computer.

Using Parameters with the `ObjectDataSource` Control

You can use parameters when calling a method with the `ObjectDataSource` control. The `ObjectDataSource` control includes five parameter collections:

- `SelectParameters`—Collection of parameters passed to the method represented by the `SelectMethod` property

- `InsertParameters`—Collection of parameters passed to the method represented by the `InsertMethod` property

- `UpdateParameters`—Collection of parameters passed to the method represented by the `UpdateMethod` property

- `DeleteParameters`—Collection of parameters passed to the method represented by the `DeleteParameters` property

- `FilterParameters`—Collection of parameters used by the `FilterExpression` property

DataBound controls—such as the `GridView`, `DetailsView`, and `FormView` controls—can build the necessary parameter collections for you automatically.

For example, the component in Listing 15.9 enables you select movies and update a particular movie in the Movies database table. The `UpdateMovie()` method has four parameters: id, title, director, and dateReleased.

LISTING 15.9   `Movies.vb`

```vb
Imports System
Imports System.Data
Imports System.Data.SqlClient
Imports System.Web.Configuration

Public Class Movies

    Private ReadOnly _conString As String

    Public Sub UpdateMovie(ByVal id As Integer, ByVal title As String,
➥ByVal director As String, ByVal dateReleased As DateTime)
        ' Create Command
        Dim con As New SqlConnection(_conString)
        Dim cmd As New SqlCommand()
        cmd.Connection = con
        cmd.CommandText = "UPDATE Movies SET Title=@Title,Director=@Director,
➥DateReleased=@DateReleased WHERE Id=@Id"

        ' Add parameters
        cmd.Parameters.AddWithValue("@Title", title)
        cmd.Parameters.AddWithValue("@Director", director)
        cmd.Parameters.AddWithValue("@DateReleased", dateReleased)
        cmd.Parameters.AddWithValue("@Id", id)

        ' Execute command
        Using con
            con.Open()
```

LISTING 15.9   Continued

```vb
            cmd.ExecuteNonQuery()
        End Using
    End Sub

    Public Function GetMovies() As SqlDataReader
        ' Create Connection
        Dim con As New SqlConnection(_conString)

        ' Create Command
        Dim cmd As SqlCommand = New SqlCommand()
        cmd.Connection = con
        cmd.CommandText = "SELECT Id,Title,Director,DateReleased FROM Movies"

        ' Return DataReader
        con.Open()
        Return cmd.ExecuteReader(CommandBehavior.CloseConnection)
    End Function

    Public Sub New()
        _conString = WebConfigurationManager.ConnectionStrings("Movies").
ConnectionString
    End Sub
End Class
```

The page in Listing 15.10 contains a `GridView` and `ObjectDataSource` control. Notice that the `ObjectDataSource` control includes an `UpdateMethod` property that points to the `UpdateMovie()` method.

LISTING 15.10   `ShowMovies.aspx`

```vb
<%@ Page Language="VB" %>
<!DOCTYPE html PUBLIC "-//W3C//DTD XHTML 1.1//EN"
  "http://www.w3.org/TR/xhtml11/DTD/xhtml11.dtd">
<html xmlns="http://www.w3.org/1999/xhtml" >
<head id="Head1" runat="server">
    <title>Show Movies</title>
</head>
<body>
    <form id="form1" runat="server">
    <div>

    <asp:GridView
        id="grdMovies"
        DataSourceID="srcMovies"
```

LISTING 15.10   Continued

```
            DataKeyNames="Id"
            AutoGenerateEditButton="true"
            Runat="server" />

        <asp:ObjectDataSource
            id="srcMovies"
            TypeName="Movies"
            SelectMethod="GetMovies"
            UpdateMethod="UpdateMovie"
            Runat="server"/>

        </div>
        </form>
    </body>
    </html>
```

In Listing 15.10, the GridView automatically adds the update parameters to the `ObjectDataSource` control's `UpdateParameters` collection. As an alternative, you can declare the parameters used by the `ObjectDataSource` control explicitly. For example, the page in Listing 15.11 declares all the parameters passed to the `UpdateMovie()` method.

LISTING 15.11   ExplicitShowMovies.aspx

```
<%@ Page Language="VB" %>
<!DOCTYPE html PUBLIC "-//W3C//DTD XHTML 1.1//EN"
 "http://www.w3.org/TR/xhtml11/DTD/xhtml11.dtd">
<html xmlns="http://www.w3.org/1999/xhtml" >
<head id="Head1" runat="server">
    <title>Show Movies</title>
</head>
<body>
    <form id="form1" runat="server">
    <div>

    <asp:GridView
        id="grdMovies"
        DataSourceID="srcMovies"
        DataKeyNames="Id"
        AutoGenerateEditButton="true"
        Runat="server" />

    <asp:ObjectDataSource
        id="srcMovies"
```

LISTING 15.11   Continued

```
             TypeName="Movies"
             SelectMethod="GetMovies"
             UpdateMethod="UpdateMovie"
             Runat="server">
             <UpdateParameters>
             <asp:Parameter Name="title" />
             <asp:Parameter Name="director" />
             <asp:Parameter Name="dateReleased" Type="DateTime" />
             <asp:Parameter Name="id" Type="Int32" />
             </UpdateParameters>
        </asp:ObjectDataSource>

        </div>
        </form>
</body>
</html>
```

The ObjectDataSource uses reflection to match its parameters against the parameters of the method that it calls. The order of the parameters does not matter and the case of the parameters does not matter. However, the one thing that does matter is the names of the parameters.

You specify the type of a parameter with the Type property, which represents a member of the TypeCode enumeration. The TypeCode enumeration represents an enumeration of common .NET Framework data types such as Int32, Decimal, and DateTime. If the enumeration does not include a data type that you need, then you can use the TypeCode.Object member from the enumeration.

Using Different Parameter Types

You can use all the same types of parameters with the ObjectDataSource control that you can use with the SqlDataSource control:

- Parameter—Represents an arbitrary static value

- ControlParameter—Represents the value of a control or page property

- CookieParameter—Represents the value of a browser cookie

- FormParameter—Represents the value of an HTML form field

- ProfileParameter—Represents the value of a Profile property

- QueryStringParameter—Represents the value of a query string field

- SessionParameter—Represents the value of an item stored in Session state

For example, the page in Listing 15.12 contains a `DropDownList` control and a `GridView` control, which enables you to view movies that match a selected category (see Figure 15.3).

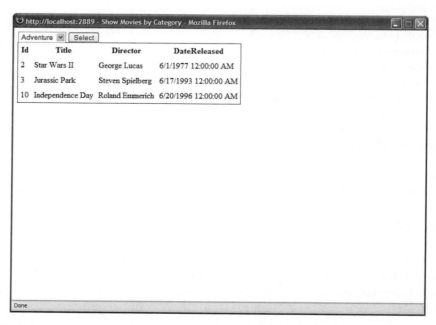

FIGURE 15.3   Displaying movies by category.

LISTING 15.12   ShowMoviesByCategory.aspx

```
<%@ Page Language="VB" %>
<!DOCTYPE html PUBLIC "-//W3C//DTD XHTML 1.1//EN"
  "http://www.w3.org/TR/xhtml11/DTD/xhtml11.dtd">
<html xmlns="http://www.w3.org/1999/xhtml" >
<head id="Head1" runat="server">
    <style type="text/css">
    .movies
    {
        border:Solid 1px black;
    }
    .movies td,.movies th
    {
        padding:5px;
    }
    </style>
    <title>Show Movies by Category</title>
</head>
<body>
```

LISTING 15.12   Continued

```
    <form id="form1" runat="server">
    <div>

    <asp:DropDownList
        id="ddlMovieCategory"
        DataSourceID="srcMovieCategories"
        DataTextField="Name"
        DataValueField="Id"
        ToolTip="Movie Category"
        Runat="server" />
    <asp:Button
        id="btnSelect"
        Text="Select"
        Runat="server" />

    <asp:GridView
        id="grdMovies"
        DataSourceID="srcMovies"
        CssClass="movies"
        GridLines="None"
        Runat="server" />

    <asp:ObjectDataSource
        id="srcMovieCategories"
        TypeName="MovieCategories"
        SelectMethod="GetCategories"
        Runat="server" />

    <asp:ObjectDataSource
        id="srcMovies"
        TypeName="MovieCategories"
        SelectMethod="GetMovies"
        Runat="server">
        <SelectParameters>
        <asp:ControlParameter
            Name="CategoryId"
            ControlID="ddlMovieCategory" />
    </SelectParameters>
    </asp:ObjectDataSource>

    </div>
    </form>
</body>
</html>
```

The ObjectDataSource control in Listing 15.12 is bound to the component contained in Listing 15.13. Notice that the ObjectDataSource control includes a SelectParameters collection. The SelectParameters collection contains a ControlParameter, which represents the current value of the ddlMovieCategory DropDownList control.

LISTING 15.13   MovieCategories.vb

```
Imports System
Imports System.Data
Imports System.Data.SqlClient
Imports System.Web.Configuration

Public Class MovieCategories

    Private ReadOnly _conString As String

    Public Function GetMovies(ByVal categoryId As Integer) As SqlDataReader
        ' Create Connection
        Dim con As New SqlConnection(_conString)

        ' Create Command
        Dim cmd As New SqlCommand()
        cmd.Connection = con
        cmd.CommandText = "SELECT Id,Title,Director,DateReleased
➥FROM Movies WHERE CategoryId=@CategoryId"

        ' Add parameters
        cmd.Parameters.AddWithValue("@CategoryId", categoryId)

        ' Return DataReader
        con.Open()
        Return cmd.ExecuteReader(CommandBehavior.CloseConnection)
    End Function

    Public Function GetCategories() As SqlDataReader
        ' Create Connection
        Dim con As New SqlConnection(_conString)

        ' Create Command
        Dim cmd As SqlCommand = New SqlCommand()
        cmd.Connection = con
        cmd.CommandText = "SELECT Id,Name FROM MovieCategories"

        ' Return DataReader
        con.Open()
        Return cmd.ExecuteReader(CommandBehavior.CloseConnection)
```

LISTING 15.13   Continued

```
    End Function

    Public Sub New()
        _conString = WebConfigurationManager.ConnectionStrings("Movies").
➥ConnectionString
    End Sub

End Class
```

Passing Objects as Parameters

Passing long lists of parameters to methods can make it difficult to maintain an application. If the list of parameters changes, you need to update every method that accepts the list of parameters.

Rather than pass a list of parameters to a method, you can pass a particular object. For example, you can pass an `Employee` object to a method used to update an employee, rather than a list of parameters that represent employee properties.

If you specify a value for an `ObjectDataSource` control's `DataObjectTypeName` property, then you can pass an object rather than a list of parameters to the methods that an `ObjectDataSource` represents. In that case, the `ObjectDataSource` parameters represent properties of the object.

For example, the `EmployeeData` component in Listing 15.14 contains an `InsertEmployee()` method for creating a new employee. This method is passed an instance of the `Employee` object that represents a particular employee. The `Employee` class also is included in Listing 15.14.

LISTING 15.14   EmployeeData.vb

```
Imports System
Imports System.Data
Imports System.Data.SqlClient
Imports System.Collections.Generic
Imports System.Web.Configuration

Public Class EmployeeData

    Dim _connectionString As String

    Public Sub UpdateEmployee(ByVal employeeToUpdate As Employee)
        ' Initialize ADO.NET objects
        Dim con As SqlConnection = New SqlConnection(_connectionString)
        Dim cmd As SqlCommand = New SqlCommand()
        cmd.CommandText = "UPDATE Employees SET FirstName=@FirstName,
```

LISTING 15.14   Continued

```vb
➥LastName=@LastName,Phone=@Phone WHERE Id=@Id"
        cmd.Connection = con

        ' Create parameters
        cmd.Parameters.AddWithValue("@Id", employeeToUpdate.Id)
        cmd.Parameters.AddWithValue("@FirstName", employeeToUpdate.FirstName)
        cmd.Parameters.AddWithValue("@LastName", employeeToUpdate.LastName)
        cmd.Parameters.AddWithValue("@Phone", employeeToUpdate.Phone)

        ' Execute command
        Using con
            con.Open()
            cmd.ExecuteNonQuery()
        End Using
    End Sub

    Public Function GetEmployees() As List(Of Employee)
        Dim employees As New List(Of Employee)()

        Dim con As SqlConnection = New SqlConnection(_connectionString)
        Dim cmd As SqlCommand = New SqlCommand()
        cmd.CommandText = "SELECT Id,FirstName,LastName,Phone FROM Employees"
        cmd.Connection = con
        Using con
            con.Open()
            Dim reader As SqlDataReader = cmd.ExecuteReader()
            While reader.Read()
                Dim NewEmployee As New Employee()
                NewEmployee.Id = CType(reader("Id"), Integer)
                NewEmployee.FirstName = CType(reader("FirstName"), String)
                NewEmployee.LastName = CType(reader("LastName"), String)
                NewEmployee.Phone = CType(reader("Phone"), String)
                employees.Add(NewEmployee)
            End While
        End Using
        Return employees
    End Function

    Public Sub New()
        _connectionString =
➥WebConfigurationManager.ConnectionStrings("Employees").ConnectionString
    End Sub

End Class
```

LISTING 15.14   Continued

```vb
Public Class Employee
    Private _id As Integer
    Private _firstName As String
    Private _lastName As String
    Private _phone As String

    Public Property Id() As Integer
        Get
            Return _id
        End Get
        Set(ByVal Value As Integer)
            _id = value
        End Set
    End Property

    Public Property FirstName() As String
        Get
            Return _firstName
        End Get
        Set(ByVal Value As String)
            _firstName = value
        End Set
    End Property

    Public Property LastName() As String
        Get
            Return _lastName
        End Get
        Set(ByVal Value As String)
            _lastName = value
        End Set
    End Property

    Public Property Phone() As String
        Get
            Return _phone
        End Get
        Set(ByVal Value As String)
            _phone = value
        End Set
    End Property

End Class
```

15

The page in Listing 15.15 contains a DetailsView control and an ObjectDataSource control. The DetailsView control enables you to update existing employees in the Employees database table.

LISTING 15.15   UpdateEmployees.aspx

```
<%@ Page Language="VB" %>
<!DOCTYPE html PUBLIC "-//W3C//DTD XHTML 1.1//EN"
  "http://www.w3.org/TR/xhtml11/DTD/xhtml11.dtd">
<html xmlns="http://www.w3.org/1999/xhtml" >
<head id="Head1" runat="server">
    <title>Update Employees</title>
</head>
<body>
    <form id="form1" runat="server">
    <div>

    <asp:DetailsView ID="DetailsView1"
        DataSourceID="srcEmployees"
        DataKeyNames="Id"
        AutoGenerateRows="True"
        AutoGenerateEditButton="True"
        AllowPaging="true"
        Runat="server" />

    <asp:ObjectDataSource
        id="srcEmployees"
        TypeName="EmployeeData"
        DataObjectTypeName="Employee"
        SelectMethod="GetEmployees"
        UpdateMethod="UpdateEmployee"
        Runat="server" />

    </div>
    </form>
</body>
</html>
```

Notice that the ObjectDataSource control includes a DataObjectTypeName property. This property contains the name of an object that is used with the UpdateEmployee() method. When the UpdateEmployee() method is called, an instance of the Employee component is created and passed to the method.

> **NOTE**
>
> The DataObjectTypeName property has an effect on only the methods represented by the InsertMethod, UpdateMethod, and DeleteMethod properties. It does not have an effect on the method represented by the SelectMethod property.

There is one important limitation when using the DataObjectTypeName property. The object represented by this property must have a parameterless constructor. For example, you could not use the following Employee class with the DataObjectTypeName property:

```
Public Class Employee

    Private _firstName As String

    Public ReadOnly Property FirstName() As String
        Get
            Return _firstName
        End Get
    End Property

    Public Sub New(ByVal firstName As String)
        _firstName = firstName
    End Sub

End Class
```

The problem with this class is that it initializes its FirstName property in its constructor. Its constructor requires a firstName parameter. Instead, you need to use a class that looks like this:

```
Public Class Employee

    Private _firstName As String

    Public Property FirstName() As String
        Get
            Return _firstName
        End Get
        Set(ByVal value As String)
            _firstName = value
        End Set
    End Property

    Public Sub New()
    End Sub

End Class
```

This class has a parameterless constructor. The `FirstName` property is a read/write property.

If you really have the need, you can get around this limitation by handling the `Inserting`, `Updating`, or `Deleting` event. When you handle one of these events, you can pass any object that you need to a method. These events are discussed later in this chapter in the section entitled "Handling `ObjectDataSource` Events."

Paging, Sorting, and Filtering Data with the `ObjectDataSource` **Control**

The `ObjectDataSource` control provides you with two options for paging and sorting database data. You can take advantage of either user interface or data source paging and sorting. The first option is easy to configure and the second option has much better performance. In this section, you learn how to take advantage of both options.

You also learn how to take advantage of the `ObjectDataSource` control's support for filtering. When you combine filtering with caching, you can improve the performance of your data-driven web pages dramatically.

User Interface Paging

Imagine that you want to use a `GridView` control to display the results of a database query in multiple pages. The easiest way to do this is to take advantage of user interface paging.

For example, the page in Listing 15.16 uses a `GridView` and `ObjectDataSource` control to display the records from the Movies database table in multiple pages (see Figure 15.4).

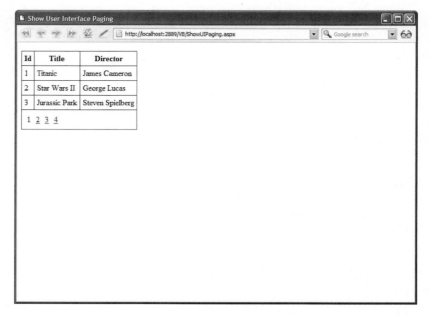

FIGURE 15.4   Displaying multiple pages with user interface paging.

LISTING 15.16   ShowUIPaging.aspx

```
<%@ Page Language="VB" %>
<!DOCTYPE html PUBLIC "-//W3C//DTD XHTML 1.1//EN"
    "http://www.w3.org/TR/xhtml11/DTD/xhtml11.dtd">
<html xmlns="http://www.w3.org/1999/xhtml" >
<head id="Head1" runat="server">
    <style type="text/css">
        .movies td,.movies th
        {
            padding:5px;
        }
    </style>
    <title>Show User Interface Paging</title>
</head>
<body>
    <form id="form1" runat="server">
    <div>

    <asp:GridView
        id="grdMovies"
        DataSourceID="srcMovies"
        AllowPaging="true"
        PageSize="3"
        CssClass="movies"
        Runat="server" />

    <asp:ObjectDataSource
        id="srcMovies"
        TypeName="MovieUIPaging"
        SelectMethod="GetMoviesDataSet"
        Runat="server" />

    </div>
    </form>
</body>
</html>
```

The GridView control in Listing 15.16 includes an AllowPaging property that is set to the value True. Setting this property enables user interface paging.

The ObjectDataSource control in Listing 15.16 represents the MovieUIPaging component in Listing 15.17. This component includes a GetMoviesDataSet() method that returns an ADO.NET DataSet object.

To take advantage of user interface paging, you must bind the `GridView` control to the right type of data source. The right type of data source includes a collection, a `DataSet`, a `DataTable`, and a `DataView`. The right type of data source does not include, for example, a `DataReader`.

LISTING 15.17   `MovieUIPaging.vb`

```vb
Imports System
Imports System.Data
Imports System.Data.SqlClient
Imports System.Web.Configuration

Public Class MovieUIPaging

    Private ReadOnly _conString As String

    Public Function GetMoviesDataSet() As DataSet
        ' Create DataAdapter
        Dim commandText As String = "SELECT Id,Title,Director FROM Movies"
        Dim dad As SqlDataAdapter = New SqlDataAdapter(commandText, _conString)

        ' Return DataSet
        Dim dstMovies As DataSet = New DataSet()
        Using dad
            dad.Fill(dstMovies)
        End Using
        Return dstMovies
    End Function

    Public Sub New()
        _conString = WebConfigurationManager.ConnectionStrings("Movies").
➡ConnectionString
    End Sub

End Class
```

User interface paging is convenient because you can enable it by setting a single property. However, there is a significant drawback to this type of paging. When user interface paging is enabled, all the movie records must be loaded into server memory. If the Movies database table contains 3 billion records, and you are displaying 3 records a page, then all 3 billion records must be loaded to display the 3 records. This places an incredible burden on both the web server and database server. In the next section, you learn how to use data source paging, which enables you to work efficiently with large sets of records.

Data Source Paging

Data source paging enables you to write custom logic for retrieving pages of database records. You can perform the paging in a component or you can perform the paging in a stored procedure.

If you want the best performance then you should write your paging logic in a stored procedure. That's the approach taken in this section.

The page in Listing 15.18 contains an ObjectDataSource control with data source paging enabled.

LISTING 15.18   ShowDSPaging.aspx

```
<%@ Page Language="VB" %>
<!DOCTYPE html PUBLIC "-//W3C//DTD XHTML 1.1//EN"
    "http://www.w3.org/TR/xhtml11/DTD/xhtml11.dtd">
<html xmlns="http://www.w3.org/1999/xhtml" >
<head id="Head1" runat="server">
    <style type="text/css">
        .movies td,.movies th
        {
            padding:5px;
        }
    </style>
    <title>Show Data Source Paging</title>
</head>
<body>
    <form id="form1" runat="server">
    <div>

    <asp:GridView
        id="grdMovies"
        DataSourceID="srcMovies"
        AllowPaging="true"
        PageSize="3"
        CssClass="movies"
        Runat="server" />

    <asp:ObjectDataSource
        id="srcMovies"
        TypeName="MoviesDSPaging"
        SelectMethod="GetMovies"
        SelectCountMethod="GetMovieCount"
        EnablePaging="True"
```

LISTING 15.18   Continued

```
        Runat="server" />

    </div>
    </form>
</body>
</html>
```

Notice that the ObjectDataSource control includes an EnablePaging property that has the value True. The ObjectDataSource also includes a SelectCountMethod property that represents the name of a method that retrieves a record count from the data source.

Notice, furthermore, that the GridView control includes both an AllowPaging and PageSize property. Even when using data source paging, you need to enable the AllowPaging property for the GridView so that the GridView can render its paging user interface.

When an ObjectDataSource control has its EnablePaging property set to the value True, the ObjectDataSource passes additional parameters when calling the method represented by its SelectMethod property. The two additional parameters are named StartRowIndex and MaximumRows.

The ObjectDataSource in Listing 15.18 represents a component named MoviesDSPaging. The control calls the component's GetMovies() and GetMovieCount() methods. The MoviesDSPaging component is contained in Listing 15.19.

LISTING 15.19   MoviesDSPaging.vb

```
Imports System
Imports System.Data
Imports System.Data.SqlClient
Imports System.Web.Configuration

Public Class MoviesDSPaging

    Private Shared ReadOnly _conString As String

    Public Shared Function GetMovies(ByVal startRowIndex As Integer,
➥ByVal maximumRows As Integer) As SqlDataReader
        ' Initialize connection
        Dim con As SqlConnection = New SqlConnection(_conString)

        ' Initialize command
        Dim cmd As SqlCommand = New SqlCommand()
        cmd.Connection = con
        cmd.CommandText = "GetPagedMovies"
```

LISTING 15.19   Continued

```
        cmd.CommandType = CommandType.StoredProcedure

        ' Add ADO.NET parameters
        cmd.Parameters.AddWithValue("@StartRowIndex", startRowIndex)
        cmd.Parameters.AddWithValue("@MaximumRows", maximumRows)

        ' Execute command
        con.Open()
        Return cmd.ExecuteReader(CommandBehavior.CloseConnection)
    End Function

    Public Shared Function GetMovieCount() As Integer
        Dim context As HttpContext = HttpContext.Current
        If context.Cache("MovieCount") Is Nothing Then
            context.Cache("MovieCount") = GetMovieCountFromDB()
        End If
        Return CType(context.Cache("MovieCount"), Integer)
    End Function

    Private Shared Function GetMovieCountFromDB() As Integer
        Dim result As Integer = 0

        ' Initialize connection
        Dim con As SqlConnection = New SqlConnection(_conString)

        ' Initialize command
        Dim cmd As SqlCommand = New SqlCommand()
        cmd.Connection = con
        cmd.CommandText = "SELECT Count(*) FROM Movies"

        ' Execute command
        Using con
            con.Open()
            result = CType(cmd.ExecuteScalar(), Integer)
        End Using
        Return result
    End Function

    Shared Sub New()
        _conString = WebConfigurationManager.ConnectionStrings("Movies").
➥ConnectionString
    End Sub
End Class
```

15

To improve performance, the `GetMovieCount()` method attempts to retrieve the total count of movie records from the server cache. If the record count cannot be retrieved from the cache, the count is retrieved from the database.

The `GetMovies()` method calls a stored procedure named `GetPagedMovies` to retrieve a particular page of movies. The `StartRowIndex` and `MaximumRows` parameters are passed to the stored procedure. The `GetPagedMovies` stored procedure is contained in Listing 15.20.

LISTING 15.20 GetPagedMovies.sql

```
CREATE PROCEDURE dbo.GetPagedMovies
(
    @StartRowIndex INT,
    @MaximumRows INT
)
AS

-- Create a temp table to store the select results
CREATE TABLE #PageIndex
(
    IndexId INT IDENTITY (1, 1) NOT NULL,
    RecordId INT
)

-- INSERT into the temp table
INSERT INTO #PageIndex (RecordId)
SELECT Id FROM Movies

-- Get a page of movies
SELECT
    Id,
    Title,
    Director,
    DateReleased
FROM
    Movies
    INNER JOIN #PageIndex WITH (nolock)
    ON Movies.Id = #PageIndex.RecordId
WHERE
    #PageIndex.IndexID > @startRowIndex
    AND #PageIndex.IndexID < (@startRowIndex + @maximumRows + 1)
ORDER BY
    #PageIndex.IndexID
```

The GetPagedMovies stored procedure returns a particular page of database records. The stored procedure creates a temporary table named #PageIndex that contains two columns: an identity column and a column that contains the primary key values from the Movies database table. The temporary table fills in any holes in the primary key column that might result from deleting records.

Next, the stored procedure retrieves a certain range of records from the #PageIndex table and joins the results with the Movies database table. The end result is that only a single page of database records is returned.

When you open the page in Listing 15.18, the GridView displays its paging interface, which you can use to navigate between different pages of records (see Figure 15.5).

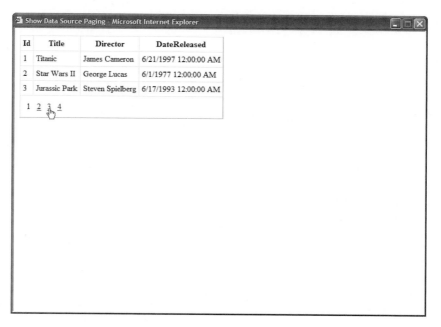

FIGURE 15.5   Displaying multiple pages with data source paging.

If temporary tables make you anxious, you have an alternative when working with Microsoft SQL Server 2005. You can take advantage of the new ROW_NUMBER() function to select a range of rows. The `ROW_NUMBER()` function automatically calculates the sequential number of a row within a resultset.

The modified stored procedure in Listing 15.21 does the same thing as the stored procedure in Listing 15.20. However, the modified stored procedure avoids any temporary tables.

LISTING 15.21   `GetPagedMovies2005.sql`

```
CREATE PROCEDURE dbo.GetPagedMovies2005
(
        @StartRowIndex INT,
        @MaximumRows INT
)
AS

WITH OrderedMovies AS
(
SELECT
        Id,
        ROW_NUMBER() OVER (ORDER BY Id) AS RowNumber
FROM Movies
)

SELECT
        OrderedMovies.RowNumber,
        Movies.Id,
        Movies.Title,
        Movies.Director
FROM
        OrderedMovies
        JOIN Movies
        ON OrderedMovies.Id = Movies.Id
WHERE
        RowNumber BETWEEN (@StartRowIndex + 1) AND (@startRowIndex + @maximumRows +
1)
```

User Interface Sorting

If you need to sort the records displayed by the `GridView` control, then the easiest type of sorting to enable is user interface sorting. When you take advantage of user interface sorting, the records are sorted in the server's memory.

For example, the page in Listing 15.22 contains a `GridView` that has its `AllowSorting` property set to the value `True`. The `GridView` is bound to an `ObjectDataSource` that represents the Employees database table (see Figure 15.6).

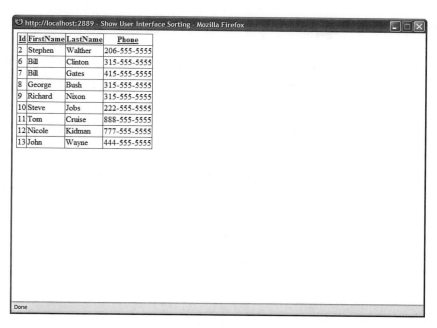

FIGURE 15.6   Sorting records with user interface sorting.

LISTING 15.22   ShowUISorting.aspx

```
<%@ Page Language="VB" %>
<!DOCTYPE html PUBLIC "-//W3C//DTD XHTML 1.1//EN"
    "http://www.w3.org/TR/xhtml11/DTD/xhtml11.dtd">
<html xmlns="http://www.w3.org/1999/xhtml" >
<head id="Head1" runat="server">
    <title>Show User Interface Sorting</title>
</head>
<body>
    <form id="form1" runat="server">
    <div>

    <asp:GridView
        id="grdEmployees"
        DataSourceID="srcEmployees"
        AllowSorting="True"
        Runat="server" />

    <asp:ObjectDataSource
        id="srcEmployees"
        TypeName="EmployeesUISorting"
        SelectMethod="GetEmployees"
```

LISTING 15.22   Continued

```
        Runat="server" />

    </div>
    </form>
</body>
</html>
```

The `ObjectDataSource` control in Listing 15.22 is bound to the component in Listing 15.23. Notice that the `GetEmployees()` method returns an ADO.NET `DataSet` object. When taking advantage of user interface sorting, the `ObjectDataSource` control must represent the right type of data source. The right type of data source includes a `DataSet`, a `DataTable`, a `DataView`, and a collection.

LISTING 15.23   EmployeesUISorting.vb

```vb
Imports System
Imports System.Data
Imports System.Data.SqlClient
Imports System.Web.Configuration


Public Class EmployeesUISorting

    Private Shared ReadOnly _conString As String

    Public Shared Function GetEmployees() As DataSet
        ' Initialize ADO.NET objects
        Dim selectText As String = "SELECT Id,FirstName,LastName,Phone
➥FROM Employees"
        Dim dad As New SqlDataAdapter(selectText, _conString)
        Dim dstEmployees As New DataSet()

        ' Fill the DataSet
        Using dad
            dad.Fill(dstEmployees)
        End Using
        Return dstEmployees
    End Function


    Shared Sub New()
        _conString = WebConfigurationManager.ConnectionStrings("Employees").
➥ConnectionString
    End Sub

End Class
```

User interface sorting is convenient. You can enable this type of sorting by setting a single property of the GridView control. Unfortunately, just as with user interface paging, some serious performance drawbacks result from user interface sorting. All the records from the underlying database must be loaded and sorted in memory. This is a particular problem when you want to enable both sorting and paging at the same time. In the next section, you learn how to implement data source sorting, which avoids this performance issue.

Data Source Sorting

Imagine that you are working with a database table that contains 3 billion records and you want to enable users to both sort the records contained in this table and page through the records contained in this table. In that case, you'll want to implement both data source sorting and paging.

The page in Listing 15.24 contains a GridView and ObjectDataSource control. The GridView has both its AllowSorting and AllowPaging properties enabled (see Figure 15.7).

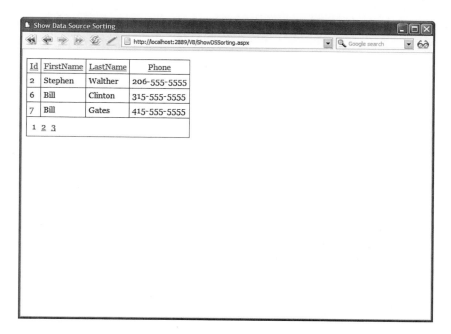

FIGURE 15.7   Paging and sorting database records.

LISTING 15.24   ShowDSSorting.aspx

```
<%@ Page Language="VB" %>
<!DOCTYPE html PUBLIC "-//W3C//DTD XHTML 1.1//EN"
 "http://www.w3.org/TR/xhtml11/DTD/xhtml11.dtd">
<html xmlns="http://www.w3.org/1999/xhtml" >
```

LISTING 15.24 Continued

```
<head id="Head1" runat="server">
    <style type="text/css">
    .employees td,.employees th
    {
        font:16px Georgia,Serif;
        padding:5px;
    }
    a
    {
        color:blue;
    }
    </style>
    <title>Show Data Source Sorting</title>
</head>
<body>
    <form id="form1" runat="server">
    <div>

    <asp:GridView
        id="grdEmployees"
        DataSourceID="srcEmployees"
        AllowSorting="true"
        AllowPaging="true"
        PageSize="3"
        CssClass="employees"
        Runat="server" />

    <asp:ObjectDataSource
        id="srcEmployees"
        TypeName="EmployeesDSSorting"
        SelectMethod="GetEmployees"
        SelectCountMethod="GetEmployeeCount"
        EnablePaging="true"
        SortParameterName="sortExpression"
        Runat="server" />

    </div>
    </form>
</body>
</html>
```

The `ObjectDataSource` control in Listing 15.24 represents the `EmployeesDSSorting`
component in Listing 15.25. Notice that the `ObjectDataSource` control includes a

SortParameterName property. When this property is present, the ObjectDataSource control uses data source sorting instead of user interface sorting.

LISTING 15.25   EmployeesDSSorting.vb

```vb
Imports System
Imports System.Data
Imports System.Data.SqlClient
Imports System.Web.Configuration


Public Class EmployeesDSSorting

    Private Shared ReadOnly _conString As String

    Public Shared Function GetEmployees(ByVal sortExpression As String, ByVal
➥startRowIndex As Integer, ByVal maximumRows As Integer) As SqlDataReader
        ' Initialize connection
        Dim con As New SqlConnection(_conString)

        ' Initialize command
        Dim cmd As New SqlCommand()
        cmd.Connection = con
        cmd.CommandText = "GetSortedEmployees"
        cmd.CommandType = CommandType.StoredProcedure

        ' Create parameters
        cmd.Parameters.AddWithValue("@SortExpression", sortExpression)
        cmd.Parameters.AddWithValue("@StartRowIndex", startRowIndex)
        cmd.Parameters.AddWithValue("@MaximumRows", maximumRows)

        ' Execute command
        con.Open()
        Return cmd.ExecuteReader(CommandBehavior.CloseConnection)
    End Function


    Public Shared Function GetEmployeeCount() As Integer
        Dim context As HttpContext = HttpContext.Current
        If context.Cache("EmployeeCount") Is Nothing Then
            context.Cache("EmployeeCount") = GetEmployeeCountFromDB()
        End If
        Return CType(context.Cache("EmployeeCount"), Integer)
    End Function

    Private Shared Function GetEmployeeCountFromDB() As Integer
        Dim result As Integer = 0
```

LISTING 15.25   Continued

```
        ' Initialize connection
        Dim con As SqlConnection = New SqlConnection(_conString)

        ' Initialize command
        Dim cmd As SqlCommand = New SqlCommand()
        cmd.Connection = con
        cmd.CommandText = "SELECT Count(*) FROM Employees"

        ' Execute command
        Using con
            con.Open()
            result = CType(cmd.ExecuteScalar(), Integer)
        End Using
        Return result
    End Function

    Shared Sub New()
        _conString = WebConfigurationManager.ConnectionStrings("Employees").
➡ConnectionString
    End Sub

End Class
```

The `GetEmployees()` method in the component in Listing 15.25 calls a stored procedure to sort and page records. The stored procedure, named `GetSortedEmployees`, returns a sorted page of records from the Employees database table. This stored procedure is contained in Listing 15.26.

LISTING 15.26   GetSortedEmployees.sql

```
CREATE PROCEDURE GetSortedEmployees
(
    @SortExpression NVarChar(100),
    @StartRowIndex INT,
    @MaximumRows INT
)
AS

-- Create a temp table to store the select results
CREATE TABLE #PageIndex
(
    IndexId INT IDENTITY (1, 1) NOT NULL,
    RecordId INT
)
```

LISTING 15.26   Continued

```
-- INSERT into the temp table
INSERT INTO #PageIndex (RecordId)
SELECT Id FROM Employees
ORDER BY
CASE WHEN @SortExpression='Id' THEN Id END ASC,
CASE WHEN @SortExpression='Id DESC' THEN Id END DESC,
CASE WHEN @SortExpression='FirstName' THEN FirstName END ASC,
CASE WHEN @SortExpression='FirstName DESC' THEN FirstName END DESC,
CASE WHEN @SortExpression='LastName' THEN LastName END ASC,
CASE WHEN @SortExpression='LastName DESC' THEN LastName END DESC,
CASE WHEN @SortExpression='Phone' THEN Phone END ASC,
CASE WHEN @SortExpression='Phone DESC' THEN Phone END DESC

-- Get a page of records
SELECT
    Id,
    FirstName,
    LastName,
    Phone
FROM
    Employees
    INNER JOIN #PageIndex WITH (nolock)
    ON Employees.Id = #PageIndex.RecordId
WHERE
    #PageIndex.IndexID > @StartRowIndex
    AND #PageIndex.IndexID < (@StartRowIndex + @MaximumRows + 1)
ORDER BY
    #PageIndex.IndexID
```

Notice that the stored procedure in Listing 15.26 uses SQL CASE functions to sort the records before they are added to the temporary table. Unfortunately, you can't use a parameter with an ORDER BY clause, so the sort columns must be hard-coded in the CASE functions. Next, a page of records is selected from the temporary table.

Filtering Data

You can supply the ObjectDataSource control with a filter expression. The filter expression is applied to the data returned by the control's select method. A filter is particularly useful when used in combination with caching. You can load all the data into the cache and then apply different filters to the cached data.

> **NOTE**
>
> You learn how to cache data with the ObjectDataSource control in Chapter 23, "Caching Application Pages and Data."

15

For example, the page in Listing 15.27 contains a `DropDownList` and `GridView` control. The `DropDownList` displays a list of movie categories, and the `GridView` displays matching movies (see Figure 15.8).

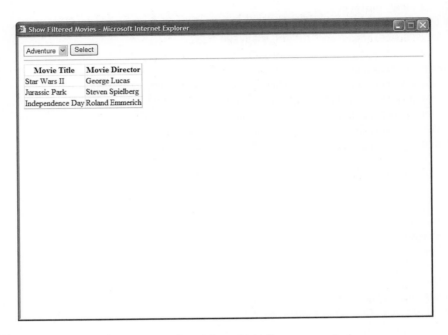

FIGURE 15.8   Filtering movies with the `ObjectDataSource` control.

LISTING 15.27   ShowFilteredMovies.aspx

```
<%@ Page Language="VB" %>
<!DOCTYPE html PUBLIC "-//W3C//DTD XHTML 1.1//EN"
    "http://www.w3.org/TR/xhtml11/DTD/xhtml11.dtd">
<html xmlns="http://www.w3.org/1999/xhtml" >
<head id="Head1" runat="server">
    <title>Show Filtered Movies</title>
</head>
<body>
    <form id="form1" runat="server">
    <div>

    <asp:DropDownList
        id="ddlMovieCategory"
        DataSourceID="srcMovieCategories"
        DataTextField="Name"
        DataValueField="Id"
```

LISTING 15.27   Continued

```
            Runat="server" />
    <asp:Button
        id="btnSelect"
        Text="Select"
        Runat="server" />

    <hr />

    <asp:GridView
        id="grdMovies"
        DataSourceID="srcMovies"
        AutoGenerateColumns="false"
        Runat="server">
        <Columns>
        <asp:BoundField
            DataField="Title"
            HeaderText="Movie Title" />
        <asp:BoundField
            DataField="Director"
            HeaderText="Movie Director" />
        </Columns>
    </asp:GridView>

    <asp:ObjectDataSource
        id="srcMovieCategories"
        TypeName="FilterMovies"
        SelectMethod="GetMovieCategories"
        EnableCaching="true"
        CacheDuration="Infinite"
        Runat="server" />

    <asp:ObjectDataSource
        id="srcMovies"
        TypeName="FilterMovies"
        SelectMethod="GetMovies"
        EnableCaching="true"
        CacheDuration="Infinite"
        FilterExpression="CategoryID={0}"
        Runat="server">
        <FilterParameters>
        <asp:ControlParameter
            Name="Category"
            ControlID="ddlMovieCategory" />
        </FilterParameters>
```

15

LISTING 15.27   Continued

```
</asp:ObjectDataSource>


    </div>
    </form>
</body>
</html>
```

Both `ObjectDataSource` controls in Listing 15.27 have caching enabled. Furthermore, the second `ObjectDataSource` control includes a `FilterExpression` property that filters the cached data, using the selected movie category from the `DropDownList` control.

Both `ObjectDataSource` controls represent the component in Listing 15.28.

LISTING 15.28   `FilterMovies.vb`

```vb
Imports System
Imports System.Web
Imports System.Data
Imports System.Data.SqlClient
Imports System.Web.Configuration


Public Class FilterMovies

    Private ReadOnly _conString As String

    Public Function GetMovies() As DataSet
        ' Initialize DataAdapter
        Dim commandText As String = "SELECT Title,Director,CategoryId FROM Movies"
        Dim dad As SqlDataAdapter = New SqlDataAdapter(commandText, _conString)

        ' Return DataSet
        Dim dstMovies As New DataSet()
        Using dad
            dad.Fill(dstMovies)
        End Using
        Return dstMovies
    End Function


    Public Function GetMovieCategories() As DataSet
        ' Initialize DataAdapter
```

LISTING 15.28 Continued

```
        Dim commandText As String = "SELECT Id,Name FROM MovieCategories"
        Dim dad As New SqlDataAdapter(commandText, _conString)

        ' Return DataSet
        Dim dstCategories As New DataSet()
        Using dad
            dad.Fill(dstCategories)
        End Using
        Return dstCategories
    End Function

    Public Sub New()
        _conString = WebConfigurationManager.ConnectionStrings("Movies").
➡ConnectionString
    End Sub
End Class
```

The ObjectDataSource enables you to filter data only when the data is represented by a DataSet, DataTable, or DataView object. This means that if you use filtering, the data must be returned as one of these objects.

> **NOTE**
>
> Behind the scenes, the ObjectDataSource control uses the DataView.RowFilter property to filter database rows. You can find detailed documentation on proper filter syntax by looking up the DataColumn.Expression property in the .NET Framework SDK 2.0 Documentation.

Handling ObjectDataSource **Control Events**

The ObjectDataSource control supports the following events:

- Deleting—Occurs immediately before the method represented by the DeleteMethod property is called

- Deleted—Occurs immediately after the method represented by the DeleteMethod property is called

- Inserting—Occurs immediately before the method represented by the InsertMethod property is called

- Inserted—Occurs immediately after the method represented by the InsertMethod property is called

- Selecting—Occurs immediately before the method represented by the SelectMethod property is called

- `Selected`—Occurs immediately after the method represented by the `InsertMethod` property is called

- `Updating`—Occurs immediately before the method represented by the `InsertMethod` property is called

- `Updated`—Occurs immediately after the method represented by the `InsertMethod` property is called

- `Filtering`—Occurs immediately before the filter expression is evaluated

- `ObjectCreating`—Occurs immediately before the object represented by the `ObjectDataSource` control is created

- `ObjectCreated`—Occurs immediately after the object represented by the `ObjectDataSource` control is created

- `ObjectDisposing`—Occurs before the object represented by the `ObjectDataSource` control is destroyed

Notice that most of these events come in pairs. One event happens immediately before a method is called, and one event happens immediately after a method is called.

You can handle these events to modify the parameters and objects represented by an `ObjectDataSource` control. You can also handle these events to handle any errors that might result from calling methods with the `ObjectDataSource` control.

Adding and Modifying Parameters

You can handle the `Selecting`, `Inserting`, `Updating`, and `Deleting` events to modify the parameters that are passed to the methods called by the `ObjectDataSource` control. There are several situations in which you might want to do this.

First, if you are working with an existing component, you might need to change the names of the parameters passed to the component. For example, instead of passing a parameter named `id` to an update method, you might want to rename the parameter to `movieId`.

Second, you might want to pass additional parameters to the method being called. For example, you might need to pass the current username, the current IP address, or the current date and time as a parameter to a method.

For example, imagine that you want to create a guestbook and automatically associate the IP address of the user making an entry with each entry in the guestbook. The page in Listing 15.29 illustrates how you can do this with the help of a `FormView` control and an `ObjectDataSource` control (see Figure 15.9).

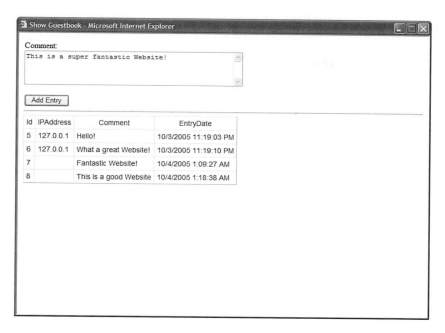

FIGURE 15.9   Displaying a guestbook.

LISTING 15.29   ShowGuestbook.aspx

```
<%@ Page Language="VB" %>
<!DOCTYPE html PUBLIC "-//W3C//DTD XHTML 1.1//EN"
    "http://www.w3.org/TR/xhtml11/DTD/xhtml11.dtd">
<script runat="server">

    Protected  Sub srcGuestbook_Inserting(ByVal sender As Object,
➥ByVal e As ObjectDataSourceMethodEventArgs)
        e.InputParameters.Add("IPAddress", Request.UserHostAddress)
    End Sub
</script>
<html xmlns="http://www.w3.org/1999/xhtml">
<head id="Head1" runat="server">
    <style type="text/css">
        .guestbook td,.guestbook th
        {
            padding:5px;
            font:14px Arial,Sans-Serif;
        }
    </style>
```

LISTING 15.29 Continued

```
    <title>Show Guestbook</title>
</head>
<body>
    <form id="form1" runat="server">
    <div>

    <asp:FormView
        id="frmGuestbook"
        DataSourceID="srcGuestbook"
        DefaultMode="Insert"
        Runat="server">
        <InsertItemTemplate>
        <asp:Label
            ID="lblComment"
            Text="Comment:"
            AssociatedControlID="txtComment"
            Runat="server" />
        <br />
        <asp:TextBox
            id="txtComment"
            Text='<%# Bind("comment") %>'
            TextMode="MultiLine"
            Columns="50"
            Rows="4"
            Runat="server" />
        <br />
        <asp:Button
            id="btnInsert"
            Text="Add Entry"
            CommandName="Insert"
            Runat="server" />
        </InsertItemTemplate>
    </asp:FormView>

    <hr />

    <asp:GridView
        id="grdGuestbook"
        DataSourceID="srcGuestbook"
        CssClass="guestbook"
        Runat="server" />

    <asp:ObjectDataSource
        id="srcGuestbook"
```

LISTING 15.29 Continued

```
            TypeName="Guestbook"
            SelectMethod="GetEntries"
            InsertMethod="AddEntry"
            OnInserting="srcGuestbook_Inserting"
            Runat="server" />

    </div>
    </form>
</body>
</html>
```

The page in Listing 15.29 includes an `Inserting` event handler. When the `insert` method is called, the IP address of the current user is added to the parameters collection.

The `ObjectDataSource` control in Listing 15.29 is bound to the `Guestbook` component in Listing 15.30.

LISTING 15.30 Guestbook.vb

```vb
Imports System
Imports System.Data
Imports System.Data.SqlClient
Imports System.Web.Configuration

Public Class Guestbook

    Private _conString As String

    Public Function GetEntries() As SqlDataReader
        ' Initialize connection
        Dim con As New SqlConnection(_conString)

        ' Initialize command
        Dim cmd As New SqlCommand()
        cmd.Connection = con
        cmd.CommandText = "SELECT Id,IPAddress,Comment,EntryDate FROM Guestbook"

        ' Execute command
        con.Open()
        Return cmd.ExecuteReader(CommandBehavior.CloseConnection)
    End Function

    Public Sub AddEnTry(ByVal IPAddress As String, ByVal comment As String)
        ' Initialize connection
```

LISTING 15.30   Continued

```vb
        Dim con As New SqlConnection(_conString)

        ' Initialize command
        Dim cmd As New SqlCommand()
        cmd.Connection = con
        cmd.CommandText = "INSERT Guestbook (IPAddress,Comment)" _
            + " VALUES (@IPAddress, @Comment)"

        ' Add ADO.NET parameters
        cmd.Parameters.AddWithValue("@IPAddress", IPAddress)
        cmd.Parameters.AddWithValue("@Comment", comment)

        ' Execute command
        Using con
            con.Open()
            cmd.ExecuteNonQuery()
        End Using
    End Sub

    Public Sub New()
        _conString = WebConfigurationManager.ConnectionStrings("Guestbook").
➡ConnectionString
    End Sub

End Class
```

Realize that you can manipulate the parameters collection in any way that you need. You can change the names, types, or values of any of the parameters.

Handling Method Errors

You can handle the `Selected`, `Inserted`, `Updated`, or `Deleted` events in order to handle any errors that might result from calling a method. For example, the page in Listing 15.31 handles the `Inserting` event to capture any errors raised when the method represented by the `ObjectDataSource` control's `InsertMethod` property is called.

LISTING 15.31   `HandleErrors.aspx`

```aspx
<%@ Page Language="VB" %>
<!DOCTYPE html PUBLIC "-//W3C//DTD XHTML 1.1//EN"
    "http://www.w3.org/TR/xhtml11/DTD/xhtml11.dtd">
<script runat="server">
```

LISTING 15.31   Continued

```
      Protected  Sub srcMovies_Inserted(ByVal sender As Object,
➡ByVal e As ObjectDataSourceStatusEventArgs)
        If Not e.Exception Is Nothing Then
            e.ExceptionHandled = True
            lblError.Text = "Could not insert movie"
        End If
    End Sub
</script>
<html xmlns="http://www.w3.org/1999/xhtml" >
<head id="Head1" runat="server">
    <style type="text/css">
        html
        {
            background-color:silver;
        }
        .insertForm
        {
            background-color:white;
        }
        .insertForm td,.insertForm th
        {
            padding:10px;
        }
        .error
        {
            color:red;
            font:bold 14px Arial,Sans-Serif;
        }
    </style>
    <title>Handle Errors</title>
</head>
<body>
    <form id="form1" runat="server">
    <div>

    <asp:Label
        id="lblError"
        EnableViewState="false"
        CssClass="error"
        Runat="server" />

    <h1>Insert Movie</h1>
    <asp:DetailsView
```

15

LISTING 15.31   Continued

```
            id="dtlMovies"
            DataSourceID="srcMovies"
            DefaultMode="Insert"
            AutoGenerateInsertButton="true"
            AutoGenerateRows="false"
            CssClass="insertForm"
            GridLines="None"
            Runat="server">
            <Fields>
            <asp:BoundField
                DataField="Title"
                HeaderText="Title:"/>
            <asp:BoundField
                DataField="Director"
                HeaderText="Director:" />
            </Fields>
        </asp:DetailsView>

        <asp:ObjectDataSource
            id="srcMovies"
            TypeName="InsertMovie"
            InsertMethod="Insert"
            Runat="server" OnInserted="srcMovies_Inserted" />

        </div>
        </form>
    </body>
</html>
```

In Listing 15.31, the `Inserted` event handler checks for an exception. If an exception exists, then the exception is handled and an error message is displayed (see Figure 15.10).

The page in Listing 15.31 is bound to the component in Listing 15.32.

LISTING 15.32   `InsertMovie.vb`

```
Imports System
Imports System.Web
Imports System.Data
Imports System.Data.SqlClient
Imports System.Web.Configuration

Public Class InsertMovie
```

LISTING 15.32 Continued

```vb
    Private Shared ReadOnly _conString As String

    Public Shared Function GetMovies() As SqlDataReader
        ' Initialize connection
        Dim con As New SqlConnection(_conString)

        ' Initialize command
        Dim cmd As New SqlCommand()
        cmd.Connection = con
        cmd.CommandText = "SELECT Id,Title,Director FROM Movies"

        ' Execute command
        con.Open()
        Return cmd.ExecuteReader(CommandBehavior.CloseConnection)
    End Function

    Public Shared Sub Insert(ByVal title As String, ByVal director As String)
        ' Initialize connection
        Dim con As New SqlConnection(_conString)

        ' Initialize command
        Dim cmd As New SqlCommand()
        cmd.Connection = con
        cmd.CommandText = "INSERT Movies (Title,Director)" _
            + " VALUES (@Title,@Director)"

        ' Add ADO.NET parameters
        cmd.Parameters.AddWithValue("@Title", title)
        cmd.Parameters.AddWithValue("@Director", director)

        ' Execute command
        Using con
            con.Open()
            cmd.ExecuteNonQuery()
        End Using
    End Sub

    Shared Sub New()
        _conString = WebConfigurationManager.ConnectionStrings("Movies").
➥ConnectionString
    End Sub

End Class
```

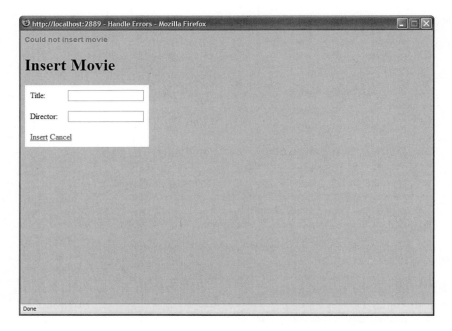

FIGURE 15.10   Handling method errors gracefully.

You can create an exception by entering a new movie record and not supplying a value for one of the fields. For example, the Title column in the Movies database table does not accept null values.

> **NOTE**
>
> Instead of handling errors at the level of the DataSource control, you can handle errors at the level of the `DataBound` control. For example, the `DetailsView` control supports an `ItemInserted` event.

Handling the `ObjectCreating` Event

By default, the `ObjectDataSource` control can represent only components that have a constructor that does not require any parameters. If you are forced to use a component that does require parameters for its constructor, then you can handle the `ObjectDataSource` control's `ObjectCreating` event.

For example, the component in Listing 15.33 must be initialized with a movie category parameter. The component returns only movies in the specified category.

LISTING 15.33   `MoviesByCategory.vb`

```
Imports System
Imports System.Web
```

LISTING 15.33   Continued

```vb
Imports System.Data
Imports System.Data.SqlClient
Imports System.Web.Configuration

Public Class MoviesByCategory

    Private ReadOnly _conString As String
    Private ReadOnly _movieCategory As String

    Public Function GetMovies() As SqlDataReader
        ' Initialize connection
        Dim con As New SqlConnection(_conString)

        ' Initialize command
        Dim cmd As New SqlCommand()
        cmd.Connection = con
        cmd.CommandText = "SELECT Title,Director,DateReleased FROM Movies" _
            + " JOIN MovieCategories ON Movies.CategoryId=MovieCategories.Id" _
            + " WHERE MovieCategories.Name=@CategoryName"

        ' Create ADO.NET parameters
        cmd.Parameters.AddWithValue("@CategoryName", _movieCategory)

        ' Execute command
        con.Open()
        Return cmd.ExecuteReader(CommandBehavior.CloseConnection)
    End Function

    Public Sub New(ByVal movieCategory As String)
        _movieCategory = movieCategory
        _conString = WebConfigurationManager.ConnectionStrings("Movies"). _
➥ConnectionString
    End Sub
End Class
```

The page in Listing 15.34 contains an `ObjectDataSource` control that represents the
`MoviesByCategory` component. The page includes a handler for the `ObjectCreating` event
so that it can assign an initialized instance of the `MoviesByCategory` component to the
`ObjectDataSource` control.

LISTING 15.34   ShowAdventureMovies.aspx

```aspx
<%@ Page Language="VB" %>
<!DOCTYPE html PUBLIC "-//W3C//DTD XHTML 1.1//EN"
```

15

LISTING 15.34   Continued

```
  "http://www.w3.org/TR/xhtml11/DTD/xhtml11.dtd">
<script runat="server">

    Protected Sub srcMovies_ObjectCreating(ByVal sender As Object,
➥ByVal e As ObjectDataSourceEventArgs)
        Dim movies As New MoviesByCategory("Adventure")
        e.ObjectInstance = movies
    End Sub
</script>
<html xmlns="http://www.w3.org/1999/xhtml" >
<head id="Head1" runat="server">
    <title>Adventure Movies</title>
</head>
<body>
    <form id="form1" runat="server">
    <div>

    <h1>Adventure Movies</h1>

    <asp:GridView
        id="grdMovies"
        DataSourceID="srcMovies"
        Runat="server" />

    <asp:ObjectDataSource
        id="srcMovies"
        TypeName="MoviesByCategory"
        SelectMethod="GetMovies"
        OnObjectCreating="srcMovies_ObjectCreating"
        Runat="server" />

    </div>
    </form>
</body>
</html>
```

Notice that even though the `MoviesByCategory` component is initialized in the
`ObjectCreating` event handler, you still must assign the name of the component to the
`ObjectDataSource` control's `TypeName` property. The `ObjectDataSource` control needs to
know what type of object it is representing when it calls its methods.

> **NOTE**
>
> The `ObjectCreating` event is not raised when a shared method is called.

Concurrency and the ObjectDataSource **Control**

Imagine that two users open the same page for editing the records in the movies database table at the same time. By default, if the first user submits changes before the second user, then the first user's changes are overwritten. In other words, the last user to submit changes wins.

This default behavior of the ObjectDataSource control can be problematic in an environment in which a lot of users are working with the same set of data. You can modify this default behavior by modifying the ObjectDataSource control's ConflictDetection property. This property accepts the following two values:

- CompareAllValues—Causes the ObjectDataSource control to track both the original and new values of its parameters

- OverwriteChanges—Causes the ObjectDataSource to overwrite the original values of its parameters with new values (the default value)

When you set the ConflictDetection property to the value CompareAllValues, you should add an OldValuesParameterFormatString property to the ObjectDataSource control. You use this property to indicate how the original values the database columns should be named.

The page in Listing 15.35 contains a GridView and ObjectDataSource control, which you can use to edit the movies in the Movies database table. The ObjectDataSource control includes a ConflictDetection property with the value CompareAllValues and an OldValuesParameterFormatString property with the value original_{0}.

LISTING 15.35   ShowConflictDetection.aspx

```
<%@ Page Language="VB" %>
<!DOCTYPE html PUBLIC "-//W3C//DTD XHTML 1.1//EN"
   "http://www.w3.org/TR/xhtml11/DTD/xhtml11.dtd">
<script runat="server">

    Protected Sub srcMovies_Updated(ByVal sender As Object,
➥ByVal e As ObjectDataSourceStatusEventArgs)
        If Not e.Exception Is Nothing Then
            e.ExceptionHandled = True
            lblError.Text = "Could not update record"
        End If
    End Sub
</script>
<html xmlns="http://www.w3.org/1999/xhtml" >
<head id="Head1" runat="server">
    <style type="text/css">
        .error
```

15

LISTING 15.35   Continued

```
        {
            color:red;
            font:bold 16px Arial,Sans-Serif;
        }
        a
        {
            color:blue;
        }
    </style>
    <title>Show Conflict Detection</title>
</head>
<body>
    <form id="form1" runat="server">
    <div>

    <asp:Label
        id="lblError"
        EnableViewState="false"
        CssClass="error"
        Runat="server" />

    <asp:GridView
        id="grdMovies"
        DataSourceID="srcMovies"
        DataKeyNames="Id"
        AutoGenerateEditButton="true"
        Runat="server" />

    <asp:ObjectDataSource
        id="srcMovies"
        ConflictDetection="CompareAllValues"
        OldValuesParameterFormatString="original_{0}"
        TypeName="ConflictedMovies"
        SelectMethod="GetMovies"
        UpdateMethod="UpdateMovie"
        OnUpdated="srcMovies_Updated"
        Runat="server" />

    </div>
    </form>
</body>
</html>
```

The `ObjectDataSource` control in Listing 15.35 is bound to the component in Listing 15.36.

LISTING 15.36   `ConflictedMovies.vb`

```
Imports System
Imports System.Data
Imports System.Data.SqlClient
Imports System.Web.Configuration


Public Class ConflictedMovies

    Private Shared ReadOnly _conString As String

    Public Shared Function GetMovies() As SqlDataReader
        ' Initialize connection
        Dim con As New SqlConnection(_conString)

        ' Initialize command
        Dim cmd As New SqlCommand()
        cmd.Connection = con
        cmd.CommandText = "SELECT Id,Title,Director FROM Movies"

        ' Execute command
        con.Open()
        Return cmd.ExecuteReader(CommandBehavior.CloseConnection)
    End Function

    Public Shared Sub UpdateMovie(ByVal title As String, ByVal director As String,
➥ByVal original_title As String, ByVal original_director As String,
➥ByVal original_id As Integer)
        ' Initialize connection
        Dim con As New SqlConnection(_conString)

        ' Initialize command
        Dim cmd As New SqlCommand()
        cmd.Connection = con
        cmd.CommandText = "UPDATE Movies SET Title=@Title,Director=@Director
➥WHERE Id=@original_Id AND Title=@original_Title
➥AND Director=@original_Director"

        ' Create parameters
        cmd.Parameters.AddWithValue("@Title", title)
        cmd.Parameters.AddWithValue("@Director", director)
        cmd.Parameters.AddWithValue("@original_Id", original_id)
        cmd.Parameters.AddWithValue("@original_Title", original_title)
```

15

LISTING 15.36   Continued

```
        cmd.Parameters.AddWithValue("@original_Director", original_director)

        Using con
            con.Open()
            Dim rowsAffected As Integer = cmd.ExecuteNonQuery()
            If rowsAffected = 0 Then
                Throw New Exception("Could not update movie record")
            End If
        End Using
    End Sub

    Shared Sub New()
        _conString = WebConfigurationManager.ConnectionStrings("Movies").
➡ConnectionString
    End Sub
End Class
```

The component in Listing 15.36 includes an `UpdateMovie()` method. Notice that this method accepts five parameters: the `original_title`, `title`, `original_director`, `director`, and `original_id` parameters.

The `UpdateMovie()` method raises an exception when the original parameter values don't match the current values in the Movies database table. Notice that the command executed by the `Command` object looks like this:

```
UPDATE Movies SET Title=@Title, Director=@Director
WHERE Id=@original_id AND Title=@original_Title AND Director=@original_Director
```

This statement updates a row in the database only when the current values from the row match the original values selected from the row. If the original and current values don't match, no records are affected and the `UpdateMovie()` method raises an exception.

Extending the `ObjectDataSource` Control

In this final section, we examine two methods of extending the `ObjectDataSource` control. You learn how to create a custom data source control by deriving a new control from the `ObjectDataSource` control. You also learn how to create custom parameters that can be used with the `ObjectDataSource` (and other `DataSource` controls).

Creating a Custom `ObjectDataSource` Control

If you discover that you are declaring an `ObjectDataSource` control with the same properties on multiple pages, then it makes sense to derive a new control from the `ObjectDataSource` control that has these properties by default. That way, you can simply declare the derived control in a page.

For example, if you are displaying a list of movies in multiple pages in your website, then it would make sense to create a specialized `MovieDataSource` control.

The control in Listing 15.37, named the `MovieDataSource` control, derives from the base `ObjectDataSource` control class. The `MovieDataSource` control represents the `MoviesComponent`, which is also contained in Listing 15.37.

LISTING 15.37   MovieDataSource.vb

```vb
Imports System
Imports System.Data
Imports System.Data.SqlClient
Imports System.Web.Configuration
Imports System.Web.UI.WebControls

Namespace AspNetUnleashed.Samples

    Public Class MovieDataSource
        Inherits ObjectDataSource

        Public Sub New()
            Me.TypeName = "AspNetUnleashed.Samples.MoviesComponent"
            Me.SelectMethod = "GetMovies"
        End Sub
    End Class

    Public Class MoviesComponent

        Private ReadOnly _conString As String

        Public Function GetMovies() As SqlDataReader
            ' Initialize connection
            Dim con As New SqlConnection(_conString)

            ' Initialize command
            Dim cmd As New SqlCommand()
            cmd.Connection = con
            cmd.CommandText = "SELECT Title,Director,DateReleased FROM Movies"

            ' Execute command
            con.Open()
            Return cmd.ExecuteReader(CommandBehavior.CloseConnection)
        End Function

        Sub New()
            _conString = WebConfigurationManager.ConnectionStrings("Movies").
```

LISTING 15.37   Continued

```
➥ConnectionString
        End Sub
    End Class
End Namespace
```

The `MovieDataSource` control initializes the base `ObjectDataSource` control's `TypeName` and `SelectMethod` properties in its constructor. The `TypeName` is assigned the fully quali-fied name of the `MoviesComponent`.

The page in Listing 15.38 illustrates how you can use the `MovieDataSource` control in a page (see Figure 15.11).

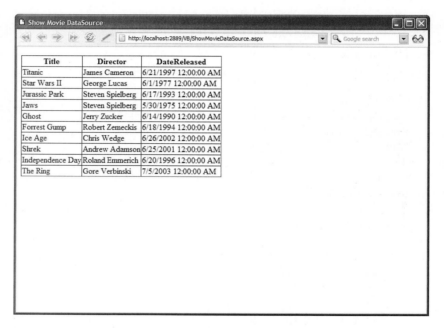

FIGURE 15.11   Using the `MovieDataSource` control to display movies.

LISTING 15.38   ShowMovieDataSource.aspx

```
<%@ Page Language="VB" %>
<%@ Register TagPrefix="custom" Namespace="AspNetUnleashed.Samples" %>
<!DOCTYPE html PUBLIC "-//W3C//DTD XHTML 1.1//EN"
    "http://www.w3.org/TR/xhtml11/DTD/xhtml11.dtd">
<html xmlns="http://www.w3.org/1999/xhtml" >
<head id="Head1" runat="server">
    <title>Show Movie DataSource</title>
```

LISTING 15.38   Continued

```
</head>
<body>
    <form id="form1" runat="server">
    <div>

    <asp:GridView
        id="grdMovies"
        DataSourceID="srcMovies"
        Runat="server" />

    <custom:MovieDataSource
        id="srcMovies"
        Runat="server" />

    </div>
    </form>
</body>
</html>
```

Notice that the custom control must be registered with a <%@ Register %> directive at the top of Listing 15.38. After you register the control, you can simply declare the MovieDataSource control in the page to represent the contents of the Movies database table.

> **NOTE**
>
> As an alternative to registering the MovieDataSource control in a page, you can register the control for an entire application in the web configuration file within the <pages> element.

Creating Custom Parameter Objects

The standard DataSource Parameter objects included in the ASP.NET Framework enable you to represent objects such as query string values, items from Session state, and the values of control properties. If none of the standard Parameter objects satisfy your requirements, you always have the option of creating a custom Parameter object.

You create a custom Parameter object by deriving a new class from the base Parameter class. In this section, we create two custom parameters. The first is a UsernameParameter that automatically represents the current username. Next is a PagePropertyParameter that represents the current value of a property contained in the page.

Creating a Username Parameter

The UsernameParameter class is contained in Listing 15.39. Notice that the class in Listing 15.39 derives from the Parameter class and overrides the Evaluate() method of the base class. The Evaluate() method determines what the parameter represents.

LISTING 15.39   UsernameParameter.vb

```
Imports System
Imports System.Web
Imports System.Web.UI
Imports System.Web.UI.WebControls

Namespace MyControls

    Public Class UsernameParameter
        Inherits Parameter
        Protected Overrides Function Evaluate(ByVal context As HttpContext,
➥ByVal control As Control) As Object
            If Not context Is Nothing Then
                Return context.User.Identity.Name
            Else
                Return Nothing
            End If
        End Function

    End Class

End Namespace
```

The UsernameParameter returns the current username. The parameter retrieves this information from the current HttpContext passed to the Evaluate() method. The UsernameParameter is used in the page in Listing 15.40.

LISTING 15.40   ShowUsernameParameter.aspx

```
<%@ Page Language="VB" %>
<%@ Register TagPrefix="custom" Namespace="MyControls" %>
<!DOCTYPE html PUBLIC "-//W3C//DTD XHTML 1.1//EN"
    "http://www.w3.org/TR/xhtml11/DTD/xhtml11.dtd">
<html xmlns="http://www.w3.org/1999/xhtml" >
<head id="Head1" runat="server">
    <style type="text/css">
        .guestbook td,.guestbook th
        {
            padding:5px;
            font:14px Arial,Sans-Serif;
        }
    </style>
    <title>Show Username Parameter</title>
</head>
<body>
```

LISTING 15.40   Continued

```
<form id="form1" runat="server">
<div>
<asp:FormView
    id="frmGuestbook"
    DataSourceID="srcGuestbook"
    DefaultMode="Insert"
    Runat="server">
    <InsertItemTemplate>
    <asp:Label
        ID="lblComment"
        Text="Comment:"
        AssociatedControlID="txtComment"
        Runat="server" />
    <br />
    <asp:TextBox
        id="txtComment"
        Text='<%# Bind("comment") %>'
        TextMode="MultiLine"
        Columns="50"
        Rows="4"
        Runat="server" />
    <br />
    <asp:Button
        id="btnInsert"
        Text="Add Entry"
        CommandName="Insert"
        Runat="server" />
    </InsertItemTemplate>
</asp:FormView>

<hr />

<asp:GridView
    id="grdGuestbook"
    DataSourceID="srcGuestbook"
    CssClass="guestbook"
    Runat="server" />

<asp:ObjectDataSource
    id="srcGuestbook"
    TypeName="GuestbookComponent"
    SelectMethod="GetEntries"
    InsertMethod="AddEntry"
    Runat="server">
```

LISTING 15.40   Continued

```
        <InsertParameters>
            <custom:UsernameParameter name="username" />
        </InsertParameters>
    </asp:ObjectDataSource>

    </div>
    </form>
</body>
</html>
```

The UsernameParameter is declared in the ObjectDataSource control's InsertParameters collection. When you add a new entry to the guestbook, your username is added automatically (see Figure 15.12).

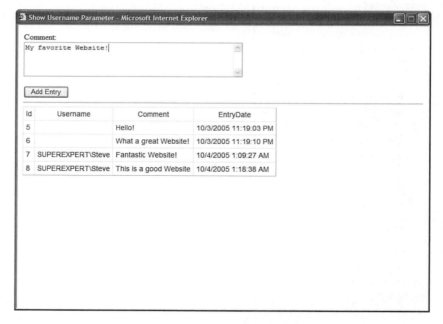

FIGURE 15.12   Inserting records with the UsernameParameter.

Creating a Page Property Parameter

The PagePropertyParameter enables you to represent an arbitrary property of the current page. The property being represented can return whatever type of value you want. The code for the PagePropertyParameter is contained in Listing 15.41.

LISTING 15.41   PagePropertyParameter.vb

```vb
Imports System
Imports System.Web
Imports System.Web.UI
Imports System.Web.UI.WebControls

Namespace MyControls

    Public Class PagePropertyParameter
        Inherits Parameter

        Private _propertyName As String

        Protected Overrides Function Evaluate(ByVal context As HttpContext,
➥ByVal control As Control) As Object
            Return DataBinder.Eval(control.Page, PropertyName)
        End Function

        Public Property PropertyName() As String
            Get
                Return _propertyName
            End Get
            Set(ByVal Value As String)
                _propertyName = value
            End Set
        End Property


    End Class
End Namespace
```

The component in Listing 15.41 overrides the `Evaluate` method of the base `Parameter` class. The `DataBinder.Eval()` method is used to return the value of a property of the current page.

The page in Listing 15.42 uses the `PagePropertyParameter` to represent a property of the page named `CurrentUsername`. This property returns the current username.

LISTING 15.42   ShowPagePropertyParameter.aspx

```aspx
<%@ Page Language="VB" %>
<%@ Register TagPrefix="custom" Namespace="MyControls" %>
<!DOCTYPE html PUBLIC "-//W3C//DTD XHTML 1.1//EN"
  "http://www.w3.org/TR/xhtml11/DTD/xhtml11.dtd">
<script runat="server">
```

LISTING 15.42   Continued

```
    Public ReadOnly Property CurrentUsername() As String
        Get
            Return User.Identity.Name
        End Get
    End Property

</script>
<html xmlns="http://www.w3.org/1999/xhtml">
<head id="Head1" runat="server">
    <style type="text/css">
        .guestbook td,.guestbook th
        {
            padding:5px;
            font:14px Arial,Sans-Serif;
        }
    </style>
    <title>Show Page Property Parameter</title>
</head>
<body>
    <form id="form1" runat="server">
    <div>

    <asp:FormView
        id="frmGuestbook"
        DataSourceID="srcGuestbook"
        DefaultMode="Insert"
        Runat="server">
        <InsertItemTemplate>
        <asp:Label
            ID="lblComment"
            Text="Comment:"
            AssociatedControlID="txtComment"
            Runat="server" />
        <br />
        <asp:TextBox
            id="txtComment"
            Text='<%# Bind("comment") %>'
            TextMode="MultiLine"
            Columns="50"
            Rows="4"
            Runat="server" />
        <br />
        <asp:Button
            id="btnInsert"
```

LISTING 15.42   Continued

```
                Text="Add Entry"
                CommandName="Insert"
                Runat="server" />
        </InsertItemTemplate>
    </asp:FormView>

    <hr />

    <asp:GridView
        id="grdGuestbook"
        DataSourceID="srcGuestbook"
        CssClass="guestbook"
        Runat="server" />

    <asp:ObjectDataSource
        id="srcGuestbook"
        TypeName="GuestbookComponent"
        SelectMethod="GetEntries"
        InsertMethod="AddEntry"
        Runat="server">
        <InsertParameters>
        <custom:PagePropertyParameter
            Name="Username"
            PropertyName="CurrentUsername" />
        </InsertParameters>
    </asp:ObjectDataSource>

    </div>
    </form>
</body>
</html>
```

In Listing 15.42, the PagePropertyParameter is used to represent the current username. Because the PagePropertyParameter can represent any page property, the parameter could represent any type of value.

Summary

In this chapter, you learned how to use the ObjectDataSource control to represent different types of objects. In the first section, you were provided with sample code that demonstrated how you can use the ObjectDataSource control to represent a collection, a DataReader, and a DataSet.

We also discussed how you can use the ObjectDataSource control to page, sort, and filter data. You learned how to implement both user interface paging and data source paging, which enables you to efficiently work with very large sets of records.

Next, we examined how you can handle ObjectDataSource control events. You learned how to add and modify the parameters represented by the ObjectDataSource control. You also learned how to gracefully handle errors raised when executing an ObjectDataSource control method.

Finally, we discussed two methods of extending the ObjectDataSource control. You learned how to derive a new control from the base ObjectDataSource control to represent specialized data sources such as a Product data source. We also discussed how you can create custom Parameter objects that can be used with the ObjectDataSource control.

Building Data Access Components

In the previous chapter, you learned how to use the ObjectDataSource control to bind data controls—such as the GridView or DetailsView controls—to a data access component. In this chapter, we shift focus from the ObjectDataSource control to the topic of building data access components.

This chapter provides you with an overview of ADO.NET. ADO.NET is the main set of classes included in the .NET Framework for working with database data. For example, under the covers, the SqlDataSource control uses ADO.NET classes to retrieve data from a SQL Server database.

The classes in the ADO.NET framework support two models of data access: a connected and disconnected model. In the first part of this chapter, you learn how to take advantage of the connected model of data access. You learn how to use the ADO.NET Connection, Command, and DataReader classes to retrieve and modify database data.

In the next part of this chapter, you learn how to take advantage of the disconnected model of data access represented by the ADO.NET DataAdapter, DataTable, DataView, and DataSet classes. You can use these classes to build an in-memory representation of database data.

Finally, at the end of this chapter, we explore two advanced topics. You learn how to take advantage of two important new features included in ADO.NET 2.0. First, you learn how to improve the performance of your database access code by executing asynchronous database commands. You learn how to build asynchronous ASP.NET pages that execute asynchronous ADO.NET commands.

You also learn how to build Microsoft SQL Server database objects, such as stored procedures and user-defined types, by using the .NET Framework. For example, you learn how to write a Microsoft SQL Server stored procedure, using the Visual Basic .NET programming language.

Connected Data Access

The ADO.NET Framework encompasses a huge number of classes. However, at its heart, it really consists of the following three classes:

- `Connection`—Enables you to represent a connection to a data source.

- `Command`—Enables you to execute a command against a data source.

- `DataReader`—Enables you to represent data retrieved from a data source.

Most of the other classes in the ADO.NET Framework are built from these three classes. These three classes provide you with the fundamental methods of working with database data. They enable you to connect to a database, execute commands against a database, and represent the data returned from a database.

Now that you understand the importance of these three classes, it's safe to tell you that they don't really exist. ADO.NET uses the Provider model. You use different sets of ADO.NET classes for communicating with different data sources.

For example, there is no such thing as the `Connection` class. Instead, there is the `SqlConnection` class, the `OracleConnection` class, the `OleDbConnection` class, and the `ODBCConnection` class. You use different `Connection` classes to connect to different data sources.

The different implementations of the `Connection`, `Command`, and `DataReader` classes are grouped into the following namespaces:

- `System.Data.SqlClient`—Contains ADO.NET classes for connecting to Microsoft SQL Server version 7.0 or higher.

- `System.Data.OleDb`—Contains ADO.NET classes for connecting to a data source with an OLEDB provider.

- `System.Data.Odbc`—Contains ADO.NET classes for connecting to a data source with an ODBC driver.

- `System.Data.OracleClient`—Contains ADO.NET classes for connecting to an Oracle database (requires Oracle 8i Release 3 [8.1.7] Client or later).

- `System.Data.SqlServerCe`—Contains ADO.NET classes for connecting to SQL Server Mobile.

If you are connecting to Microsoft SQL Server 7.0 or higher, you should always use the classes from the `SqlClient` namespace. These classes provide the best performance because they connect directly to SQL Server at the level of the Tabular Data Stream (the low-level protocol that Microsoft SQL Server uses to communicate with applications).

Of course, there are other databases in the world than Microsoft SQL Server. If you are communicating with an Oracle database, you should use the classes from the OracleClient namespace. If you are communicating with another type of database, you need to use the classes from either the OleDb or Odbc namespaces. Just about every database ever created by man has either an OLEDB provider or an ODBC driver.

Because ADO.NET follows the Provider model, all implementations of the Connection, Command, and DataReader classes inherit from a set of base classes. Here is a list of these base classes:

- DbConnection—The base class for all Connection classes.

- DbCommand—The base class for all Command classes.

- DbDataReader—The base class for all DataReader classes.

These base classes are contained in the System.Data.Common namespace.

All the sample code in this chapter assumes that you are working with Microsoft SQL Server. Therefore, all the sample code uses the classes from the SqlClient namespace. However, because ADO.NET uses the Provider model, the methods that you would use to work with another database are very similar to the methods described in this chapter.

> **NOTE**
>
> Before you can use the classes from the SqlClient namespaces in your components and pages, you need to import the System.Data.SqlClient namespace.

Before we examine the Connection, Command, and DataReader classes in detail, let's look at how you can build a simple data access component with these classes. The component in Listing 16.1, named Movie1, includes a method named GetAll() that returns every record from the Movies database table.

LISTING 16.1   App_Code\Movie1.vb

```
Imports System
Imports System.Data
Imports System.Data.SqlClient
Imports System.Web.Configuration
Imports System.Collections.Generic

Public Class Movie1
    Private Shared ReadOnly _connectionString As String

    Private _title As String
    Private _director As String
```

16

LISTING 16.1   Continued

```
    Public Property Title() As String
        Get
            Return _title
        End Get
        Set(ByVal Value As String)
            _title = value
        End Set
    End Property

    Public Property Director() As String
        Get
            Return _director
        End Get
        Set(ByVal Value As String)
            _director = value
        End Set
    End Property

    Public Function GetAll() As List(Of Movie1)
        Dim results As New List(Of Movie1)
        Dim con As New SqlConnection(_connectionString)
        Dim cmd As New SqlCommand("SELECT Title,Director FROM Movies", con)
        Using con
            con.Open()
            Dim reader As SqlDataReader = cmd.ExecuteReader()
            While reader.Read()
                Dim NewMovie As New Movie1()
                NewMovie.Title = CType(reader("Title"), String)
                NewMovie.Director = CType(reader("Director"), String)
                results.Add(NewMovie)
            End While
        End Using
        Return results
    End Function

    Shared Sub New()
        _connectionString = WebConfigurationManager.
➥ConnectionStrings("Movies").ConnectionString
    End Sub
End Class
```

In Listing 16.1, a `SqlConnection` object is used to represent a connection to a Microsoft SQL Server database. A `SqlCommand` object is used to represent a SQL `SELECT` command. The results of executing the command are represented with a `SqlDataReader`.

Each row returned by the `SELECT` command is retrieved by a call to the `SqlDataReader.Read()` method from within a `While` loop. When the last row is retrieved from the `SELECT` command, the `SqlDataReader.Read()` method returns `False` and the `While` loop ends.

Each row retrieved from the database is added to a List collection. An instance of the `Movie1` class is used to represent each record.

The page in Listing 16.2 uses a `GridView` and `ObjectDataSource` control to display the records returned by the `Movie1` data access component (see Figure 16.1).

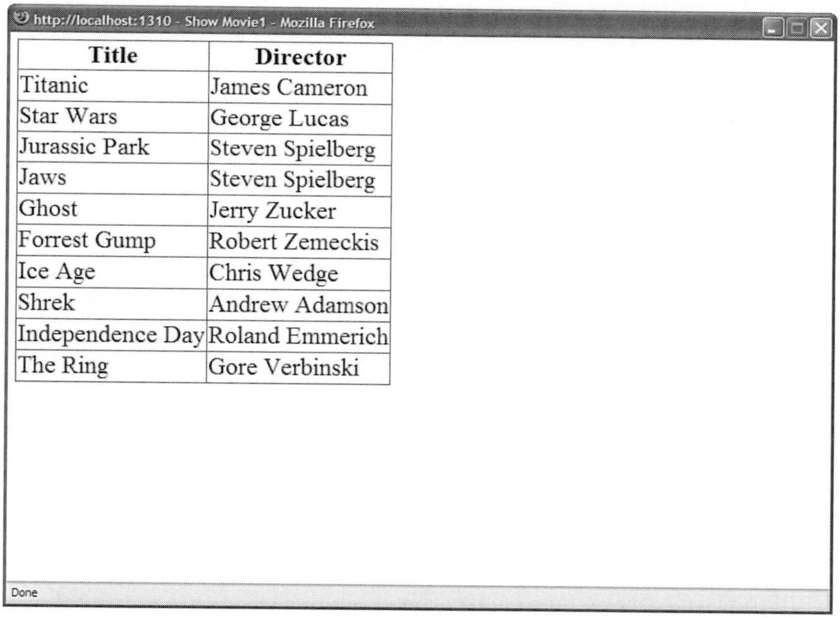

Title	Director
Titanic	James Cameron
Star Wars	George Lucas
Jurassic Park	Steven Spielberg
Jaws	Steven Spielberg
Ghost	Jerry Zucker
Forrest Gump	Robert Zemeckis
Ice Age	Chris Wedge
Shrek	Andrew Adamson
Independence Day	Roland Emmerich
The Ring	Gore Verbinski

FIGURE 16.1 Displaying movie records.

LISTING 16.2 ShowMovie1.aspx

```
<%@ Page Language="VB" %>
<!DOCTYPE html PUBLIC "-//W3C//DTD XHTML 1.0 Transitional//EN"
"http://www.w3.org/TR/xhtml1/DTD/xhtml1-transitional.dtd">
<html xmlns="http://www.w3.org/1999/xhtml" >
<head id="Head1" runat="server">
    <title>Show Movie1</title>
</head>
<body>
```

LISTING 16.2 Continued

```
    <form id="form1" runat="server">
    <div>

    <asp:GridView
        id="grdMovies"
        DataSourceID="srcMovies"
        Runat="server" />

    <asp:ObjectDataSource
        id="srcMovies"
        TypeName="Movie1"
        SelectMethod="GetAll"
        Runat="server" />

    </div>
    </form>
</body>
</html>
```

Using the `Connection` Object

The `Connection` object represents a connection to a data source. When you instantiate a `Connection`, you pass a connection string to the constructor, which contains information about the location and security credentials required for connecting to the data source.

For example, the following statement creates a `SqlConnection` that represents a connection to a Microsoft SQL Server database named Pubs that is located on the local machine:

```
Dim con As New SqlConnection("Data Source=localhost;Integrated Security=True;
➥Initial Catalog=Pubs")
```

For legacy reasons, there are a number of ways to write a connection string that does exactly the same thing. For example, the keywords `Data Source`, `Server`, `Address`, `Addr`, and `Network Address` are all synonyms. You can use any of these keywords to specify the location of the database server.

> **NOTE**
>
> You can use the `SqlConnectionStringBuilder` class to convert any connection string into canonical syntax. For example, this class replaces the keyword `Server` with the keyword `Data Source` in a connection string.

Before you execute any commands against the data source, you first must open the connection. After you finish executing commands, you should close the connection as quickly as possible.

A database connection is a valuable resource. Strive to open database connections as late as possible and close database connections as early as possible. Furthermore, always include error handling code to make sure that a database connection gets closed even when there is an exception.

For example, you can take advantage of the Using statement to force a connection to close even when an exception is raised, like this:

```
Dim con As New SqlConnection("Data Source=localhost;Integrated Security=True;
➥Initial Catalog=Pubs")
Dim cmd As New SqlCommand("INSERT Titles (Title) VALUES ('Some Title')", con)
Using con
   con.Open()
   cmd.ExecuteNonQuery()
End Using
```

The Using statement forces the connection to close, regardless of whether or not there is an error when a command is executed against the database. The Using statement also disposes of the Connection object. (If you need to reuse the Connection, then you need to reinitialize it.)

Alternatively, you can use a Try...Catch statement to force a connection to close like this:

```
Dim con As New SqlConnection("Data Source=localhost;Integrated Security=True;
➥Initial Catalog=Pubs")
Dim cmd As New SqlCommand("INSERT Titles (Title) VALUES ('Some Title')", con)
Try
   con.Open()
   cmd.ExecuteNonQuery()
Catch
Finally
   con.Close()
End Try
```

The Finally clause in this Try...Catch statement forces the database connection to close both when there are no errors and when there are errors.

Retrieving Provider Statistics

When you use the SqlConnection object, you can retrieve statistics about the database commands executed with the connection. For example, you can retrieve statistics on total execution time.

The GetAll() method exposed by the component in Listing 16.3 includes a parameter named executionTime. After the database command executes, the value of executionTime is retrieved from the Connection statistics.

LISTING 16.3   App_Code\Movie2.vb

```vb
Imports System
Imports System.Data
Imports System.Data.SqlClient
Imports System.Web.Configuration
Imports System.Collections
Imports System.Collections.Generic

Public Class Movie2
    Private Shared ReadOnly _connectionString As String

    Private _title As String
    Private _director As String

    Public Property Title() As String
        Get
            Return _title
        End Get
        Set(ByVal Value As String)
            _title = value
        End Set
    End Property

    Public Property Director() As String
        Get
            Return _director
        End Get
        Set(ByVal Value As String)
            _director = value
        End Set
    End Property

    Public Function GetAll(ByRef executionTime As Long) As List(Of Movie2)
        Dim results As New List(Of Movie2)()
        Dim con As New SqlConnection(_connectionString)
        Dim cmd As New SqlCommand("WAITFOR DELAY '0:0:03';SELECT Title,Director
➥FROM Movies", con)
        con.StatisticsEnabled = True
        Using con
            con.Open()
            Dim reader As SqlDataReader = cmd.ExecuteReader()
            While reader.Read()
                Dim NewMovie As New Movie2()
```

LISTING 16.3   Continued

```
                NewMovie.Title = CType(reader("Title"), String)
                NewMovie.Director = CType(reader("Director"), String)
                results.Add(NewMovie)
            End While
        End Using
        Dim stats As IDictionary = con.RetrieveStatistics()
        executionTime = CType(stats("ExecutionTime"), Long)
        Return results
    End Function

    Shared Sub New()
        _connectionString = WebConfigurationManager
➡.ConnectionStrings("Movies").ConnectionString
    End Sub
End Class
```

In Listing 16.3, the `SqlConnection.StatisticsEnabled` property is set to the value `True`. You must enable statistics before you can gather statistics. After the command executes, a dictionary of statistics is retrieved with the `SqlConnection.RetrieveStatistics()` method. Finally, you retrieve the `executionTime` by looking up the `ExecutionTime` key in the dictionary.

> **NOTE**
>
> In Listing 16.3, the SQL WAITFOR statement is used to pause the execution of the SELECT command for three seconds so that a more interesting execution time is retrieved from the ExecutionTime statistic. Because the SELECT command is such a simple command, if you don't add a delay, you often receive an execution time of 0 milliseconds.

The page in Listing 16.4 illustrates how you can use this component to display both the results of a database query and the database query execution time (see Figure 16.2).

LISTING 16.4   ShowMovie2.aspx

```
<%@ Page Language="VB" %>
<!DOCTYPE html PUBLIC "-//W3C//DTD XHTML 1.0 Transitional//EN"
  "http://www.w3.org/TR/xhtml1/DTD/xhtml1-transitional.dtd">
<script runat="server">

    Sub srcMovies_Selected(ByVal sender As Object,
➡ByVal e As ObjectDataSourceStatusEventArgs)
        lblExecutionTime.Text = e.OutputParameters("executionTime").ToString()
    End Sub
</script>
```

16

LISTING 16.4   Continued

```
<html xmlns="http://www.w3.org/1999/xhtml" >
<head id="Head1" runat="server">
    <title>Show Movie2</title>
</head>
<body>
    <form id="form1" runat="server">
    <div>

    <asp:GridView
        id="grdMovies"
        DataSourceID="srcMovies"
        Runat="server" />

    <asp:ObjectDataSource
        id="srcMovies"
        TypeName="Movie2"
        SelectMethod="GetAll"
        Runat="server" OnSelected="srcMovies_Selected">
        <SelectParameters>
        <asp:Parameter Name="executionTime" Type="Int64" Direction="Output" />
        </SelectParameters>
    </asp:ObjectDataSource>

    <br />

    Execution time was
    <asp:Label
        id="lblExecutionTime"
        Runat="server" />
    milliseconds

    </div>
    </form>
</body>
</html>
```

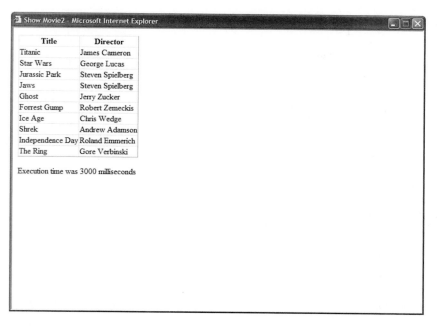

FIGURE 16.2 Displaying execution time statistics.

The `SqlConnection` object supports the following properties and methods related to gathering statistics:

- `StatisticsEnabled`—Enables you to turn on statistics gathering.
- `RetrieveStatistics()`—Enables you to retrieve statistics represented with an `IDictionary` collection.
- `ResetStatistics()`—Resets all statistics to 0.

You can call the `RetrieveStatistics()` method multiple times on the same `SqlConnection`. Each time you call the method, you get another snapshot of the `Connection` statistics.

Here's a list of the statistics that you can gather:

- `BuffersReceived`—Returns the number of TDS packets received.
- `BuffersSent`—Returns the number of TDS packets sent.
- `BytesReceived`—Returns the number of bytes received.
- `BytesSent`—Returns the number of bytes sent.
- `ConnectionTime`—Returns the total amount of time that the connection has been opened.
- `CursorsOpen`—Returns the number of cursors opened.

- `ExecutionTime`—Returns the connection execution time in milliseconds.
- `IduCount`—Returns the number of `INSERT`, `DELETE`, and `UPDATE` commands executed.
- `IduRows`—Returns the number of rows modified by `INSERT`, `DELETE`, and `UPDATE` commands.
- `NetworkServerTime`—Returns the amount of time spent waiting for a reply from the database server.
- `PreparedExecs`—Returns the number of prepared commands executed.
- `Prepares`—Returns the number of statements prepared.
- `SelectCount`—Returns the number of `SELECT` commands executed.
- `SelectRows`—Returns the number of rows selected.
- `ServerRoundtrips`—Returns the number of commands sent to the database that received a reply.
- `SumResultSets`—Returns the number of resultsets retrieved.
- `Transactions`—Returns the number of user transactions created.
- `UnpreparedExecs`—Returns the number of unprepared commands executed.

The page in Listing 16.5 displays the values of all these statistics in a `GridView` control (see Figure 16.3).

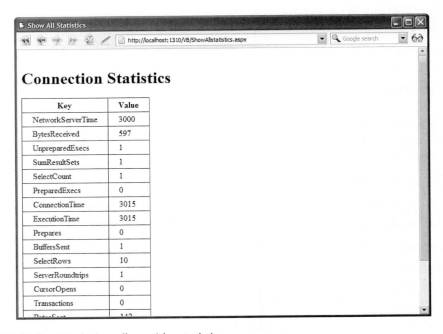

FIGURE 16.3   Displaying all provider statistics.

LISTING 16.5   ShowAllStatistics.aspx

```
<%@ Page Language="VB" %>
<%@ Import Namespace="System.Data.SqlClient" %>
<%@ Import Namespace="System.Web.Configuration" %>
<!DOCTYPE html PUBLIC "-//W3C//DTD XHTML 1.0 Transitional//EN"
"http://www.w3.org/TR/xhtml1/DTD/xhtml1-transitional.dtd">
<script runat="server">

    Sub Page_Load()
        Dim connectionString As String =
➥WebConfigurationManager.ConnectionStrings("Movies").ConnectionString
        Dim con As New SqlConnection(connectionString)
        Dim cmd As New SqlCommand("WAITFOR DELAY '0:0:03';SELECT Title,Director
➥FROM Movies", con)
        con.StatisticsEnabled = True
        Using con
            con.Open()
            Dim reader As SqlDataReader = cmd.ExecuteReader()
        End Using
        grdStats.DataSource = con.RetrieveStatistics()
        grdStats.DataBind()
    End Sub
</script>
<html xmlns="http://www.w3.org/1999/xhtml" >
<head id="Head1" runat="server">
    <style type="text/css">
        td,th
        {
            padding:4px 20px;
        }
    </style>
    <title>Show All Statistics</title>
</head>
<body>
    <form id="form1" runat="server">
    <div>

    <h1>Connection Statistics</h1>

    <asp:GridView
        id="grdStats"
        AutoGenerateColumns="false"
        Runat="server">
        <Columns>
        <asp:BoundField DataField="Key" HeaderText="Key" />
```

16

LISTING 16.5   Continued

```
            <asp:BoundField DataField="Value" HeaderText="Value" />
            </Columns>
        </asp:GridView>

        </div>
        </form>
</body>
</html>
```

Improving Performance with Connection Pooling

Database connections are precious resources. If you want your ASP.NET application to scale to handle the demands of thousands of users, then you need to do everything in your power to prevent database connections from being wasted.

Opening a database connection is a slow operation. Rather than open a new database connection each time you need to connect to a database, you can create a pool of connections that can be reused for multiple database queries.

When connection pooling is enabled, closing a connection does not really close the connection to the database server. Instead, closing the connection releases the database connection back into the pool. That way, the next time a database query is performed, a new connection to the database does not need to be opened.

When you use the SqlConnection object, connection pooling is enabled by default. By default, the ADO.NET framework keeps a maximum of 100 connections opened in a connection pool.

You need to be warned about two things in regard to connection pooling. First, when taking advantage of connection pooling, it is still very important to close your connections by calling the SqlConnection.Close() method. If you don't close a connection, the connection is not returned to the pool. It might take a very long time for an unclosed connection to be reclaimed by ADO.NET.

Second, different connection pools are created for different connection strings. In particular, a different connection pool is created for each unique combination of connection string, process, application domain, and Windows identity.

An exact character-by-character match is performed on the connection string. For this reason, you should always store your connection strings in the web configuration file. Don't hardcode connection strings inside your components. If there is a slight variation between two connection strings, then separate connection pools are created, which defeats the performance gains that you get from connection pooling.

The SqlConnection object supports two methods for clearing connection pools programmatically:

- ClearAllPools—Enables you to clear all database connections from all connection pools.

- ClearPool—Enables you to clear all database connections associated with a particular SqlConnection object.

These methods are useful when you are working with a cluster of database servers. For example, if you take a database server down, you can programmatically clear the connection pool to the database server that no longer exists.

You can control how connections are pooled by using the following attributes in a connection string:

- Connection Timeout—Enables you to specify the maximum lifetime of a connection in seconds. (The default value is 0, which indicates that connections are immortal.)

- Connection Reset—Enables you to reset connections automatically when retrieved from the connection pool (default value is True).

- Enlist—Enables you to enlist a connection in the current transaction context (default value is True).

- Load Balance Timeout—Same as Connection Timeout.

- Max Pool Size—Enables you to specify the maximum number of connections kept in the connection pool (default value is 100).

- Min Pool Size—Enables you to specify the minimum number of connections kept in the connection pool (default value is 0).

- Pooling—Enables you to turn on or off connection pooling (default value is True).

The page in Listing 16.6 displays a list of all the current user connections to a database in a GridView (see Figure 16.4). Notice that the connection string used when connecting to the database creates a minimum connection pool size of 10 connections. (You'll have to refresh the page at least once to see the 10 connections.)

LISTING 16.6   ShowUserConnections.aspx

```
<%@ Page Language="VB" %>
<%@ Import Namespace="System.Data.SqlClient" %>
<%@ Import Namespace="System.Web.Configuration" %>
<!DOCTYPE html PUBLIC "-//W3C//DTD XHTML 1.0 Transitional//EN"
"http://www.w3.org/TR/xhtml1/DTD/xhtml1-transitional.dtd">
<script runat="server">

    Private Sub Page_Load()
        Dim connectionString As String = "Min Pool Size=10;
➥Data Source=.\SQLExpress;Integrated Security=True;
➥AttachDbFileName=¦DataDirectory¦MyDatabase.mdf;User Instance=True"
```

16

LISTING 16.6   Continued

```
        Dim con As New SqlConnection(connectionString)
        Dim cmd As New SqlCommand("SELECT * FROM master..sysprocesses
➥WHERE hostname<>''", con)
        Using con
            con.Open()
            grdStats.DataSource = cmd.ExecuteReader()
            grdStats.DataBind()
        End Using
    End Sub
</script>
<html xmlns="http://www.w3.org/1999/xhtml" >
<head id="Head1" runat="server">
    <style type="text/css">
        td,th
        {
            padding:2px;
        }
    </style>
    <title>Show User Connections</title>
</head>
<body>
    <form id="form1" runat="server">
    <div>

    <h1>User Connections</h1>

    <asp:GridView
        id="grdStats"
        Runat="server" />

    </div>
    </form>
</body>
</html>
```

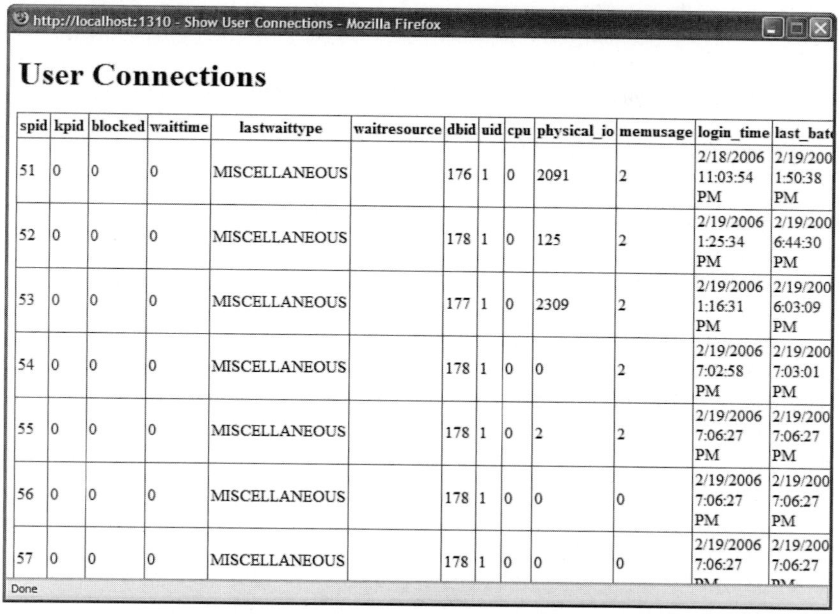

spid	kpid	blocked	waittime	lastwaittype	waitresource	dbid	uid	cpu	physical_io	memusage	login_time	last_bat
51	0	0	0	MISCELLANEOUS		176	1	0	2091	2	2/18/2006 11:03:54 PM	2/19/200 1:50:38 PM
52	0	0	0	MISCELLANEOUS		178	1	0	125	2	2/19/2006 1:25:34 PM	2/19/200 6:44:30 PM
53	0	0	0	MISCELLANEOUS		177	1	0	2309	2	2/19/2006 1:16:31 PM	2/19/200 6:03:09 PM
54	0	0	0	MISCELLANEOUS		178	1	0	0	2	2/19/2006 7:02:58 PM	2/19/200 7:03:01 PM
55	0	0	0	MISCELLANEOUS		178	1	0	2	2	2/19/2006 7:06:27 PM	2/19/200 7:06:27 PM
56	0	0	0	MISCELLANEOUS		178	1	0	0	0	2/19/2006 7:06:27 PM	2/19/200 7:06:27 PM
57	0	0	0	MISCELLANEOUS		178	1	0	0	0	2/19/2006 7:06:27	2/19/200 7:06:27

FIGURE 16.4 Displaying user database connections.

Using the `Command` Object

The `Command` object represents a command that can be executed against a data source. In this section, you learn how to use the `SqlCommand` object to execute different types of database commands against Microsoft SQL Server.

Executing a Command

You can use the `SqlCommand.ExecuteNonQuery()` method to execute a SQL command that does not return a set of rows. You can use this method when executing `SQL UPDATE`, `DELETE`, and `INSERT` commands. You can also use this method when executing more specialized commands, such as a `CREATE TABLE` or `DROP DATABASE` command.

For example, the component in Listing 16.7 includes `Update()` and `Delete()` methods that update and delete movie records.

LISTING 16.7 `App_Code\Movie3.vb`

```
Imports System
Imports System.Data
Imports System.Data.SqlClient
Imports System.Web.Configuration
Imports System.Collections.Generic
```

LISTING 16.7   Continued

```
Public Class Movie3
    Private Shared ReadOnly _connectionString As String

    Private _id As Integer
    Private _title As String
    Private _director As String

    Public Property Id() As Integer
        Get
            Return _id
        End Get
        Set(ByVal Value As Integer)
            _id = value
        End Set
    End Property

    Public Property Title() As String
        Get
            Return _title
        End Get
        Set(ByVal Value As String)
            _title = value
        End Set
    End Property

    Public Property Director() As String
        Get
            Return _director
        End Get
        Set(ByVal Value As String)
            _director = value
        End Set
    End Property

    Public Sub Update(ByVal id As Integer, ByVal title As String,
➥ByVal director As String)
        Dim con As New SqlConnection(_connectionString)
        Dim cmd As New SqlCommand("UPDATE MOVIES SET Title=@Title,
➥Director=@Director WHERE Id=@Id", con)
        cmd.Parameters.AddWithValue("@Title", title)
        cmd.Parameters.AddWithValue("@Director", director)
        cmd.Parameters.AddWithValue("@Id", id)
        Using con
            con.Open()
```

LISTING 16.7   Continued

```
                cmd.ExecuteNonQuery()
        End Using
    End Sub

    Public Sub Delete(ByVal id As Integer)
        Dim con As New SqlConnection(_connectionString)
        Dim cmd As New SqlCommand("DELETE MOVIES WHERE Id=@Id", con)
        cmd.Parameters.AddWithValue("@Id", id)
        Using con
            con.Open()
            cmd.ExecuteNonQuery()
        End Using
    End Sub

    Public Function GetAll() As List(Of Movie3)
        Dim results As New List(Of Movie3)()
        Dim con As New SqlConnection(_connectionString)
        Dim cmd As New SqlCommand("SELECT Id,Title,Director FROM Movies", con)
        Using con
            con.Open()
            Dim reader As SqlDataReader = cmd.ExecuteReader()
            While reader.Read()
                Dim NewMovie As New Movie3()
                NewMovie.Id = CType(reader("Id"), Integer)
                NewMovie.Title = CType(reader("Title"), String)
                NewMovie.Director = CType(reader("Director"), String)
                results.Add(NewMovie)
            End While
        End Using
        Return results
    End Function

    Shared Sub New()
        _connectionString = WebConfigurationManager.ConnectionStrings("Movies")
➥.ConnectionString
    End Sub
End Class
```

The page in Listing 16.8 contains a `GridView` that binds to the data access component in Listing 16.7. The `GridView` enables you to display, update, and delete database records (see Figure 16.5).

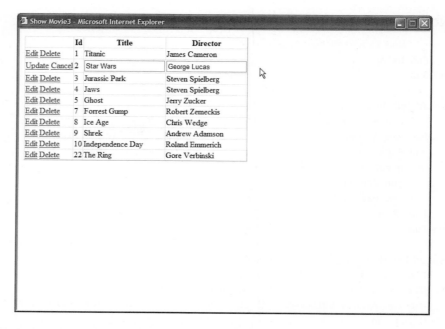

FIGURE 16.5   Updating and deleting database records.

LISTING 16.8   ShowMovie3.aspx

```
<%@ Page Language="VB" %>
<!DOCTYPE html PUBLIC "-//W3C//DTD XHTML 1.0 Transitional//EN"
 "http://www.w3.org/TR/xhtml1/DTD/xhtml1-transitional.dtd">
<html xmlns="http://www.w3.org/1999/xhtml" >
<head id="Head1" runat="server">
    <title>Show Movie3</title>
</head>
<body>
    <form id="form1" runat="server">
    <div>

    <asp:GridView
        id="grdMovies"
        DataSourceID="srcMovies"
        DataKeyNames="Id"
        AutoGenerateEditButton="true"
        AutoGenerateDeleteButton="true"
        Runat="server" />

    <asp:ObjectDataSource
        id="srcMovies"
```

LISTING 16.8   Continued

```
            TypeName="Movie3"
            SelectMethod="GetAll"
            UpdateMethod="Update"
            DeleteMethod="Delete"
            Runat="server" />

    </div>
    </form>
</body>
</html>
```

Executing a Command with Parameters

Most database commands that you execute include parameters. For example, when updating a database record, you need to supply parameters that represent the new values of the database record columns.

> **WARNING**
>
> Never build command parameters through string concatenation because concatenating strings is an open invitation for SQL injection attacks. If a user enters the proper sequence of characters in a form field, and a SQL command is built through concatenation, then a user can execute an arbitrary SQL command.
>
> Always explicitly create parameters by creating instances of the SqlParameter object. When a SQL command is executed with explicit parameters, the parameters are passed individually to a SQL Server stored procedure named sp_executesql.

You represent a parameter with the SqlParameter object. You can create a new SqlParameter in multiple ways. The easiest way is to call the SqlCommand.AddWithValue() method like this:

```
Dim cmd As New SqlCommand("INSERT Titles (Title) VALUES (@Title)", con)
cmd.Parameters.AddWithValue("@Title", "ASP.NET 2.0 Unleashed")
```

The first statement creates a SqlCommand object that represents a SQL INSERT command. Notice that the command includes a parameter named @Title.

The second statement adds a SqlParameter to the SqlCommand object's Parameters collection. The AddWithValue() method enables you to add a parameter with a certain name and value. In this case, the method is used to supply the value for the @Title parameter.

When you execute the SqlCommmand, the following command is sent to Microsoft SQL Server:

```
exec sp_executesql N'INSERT Titles (Title) VALUES (@Title)',
➥N'@Title nvarchar(17)', @Title = N'ASP.NET Unleashed'
```

The SqlCommand object calls the sp_executesql stored procedure when it executes a command. In this case, it passes the type, size, and value of the @Title parameter to the sp_executesql stored procedure.

When you use AddWithValue(), the SqlCommand object infers the type and size of the parameter for you. The method assumes that string values are SQL NVarChar values, integer values are SQL Int values, decimal values are SQL decimal values, and so on.

As an alternative to using the AddWithValue() method, you can create a SqlParameter explicitly and add the SqlParameter to a SqlCommand object's Parameters collection. The advantage of creating a parameter explicitly is that you can specify parameter properties explicitly, such as its name, type, size, precision, scale, and direction.

For example, the following code creates a parameter named @Title with a particular data type, size, and value:

```
Dim cmd As New SqlCommand("INSERT Titles (Title) VALUES (@Title)", con)
Dim paramTitle As New SqlParameter()
paramTitle.ParameterName = "@Title"
paramTitle.SqlDbType = SqlDbType.NVarChar
paramTitle.Size = 50
paramTitle.Value = "ASP.NET 2.0 Unleashed"
cmd.Parameters.Add(paramTitle)
```

If this seems like a lot of code to do something simple, then you can use one of the overloads of the Add() method to create a new SqlParameter like this:

```
Dim cmd As New SqlCommand("INSERT Test (Title) VALUES (@Title)", con)
cmd.Parameters.Add("@Title", SqlDbType.NVarChar,50).Value
➥= "ASP.NET 2.0 Unleashed";
```

In general, in this book and in the code that I write, I use the AddWithValue() method to create parameters.

I like the AddWithValue() method because it involves the least typing.

Executing a Command That Represents a Stored Procedure

You can use a SqlCommand object to represent a Microsoft SQL Server stored procedure. For example, you can use the following two statements to create a SqlCommand object that represents a stored procedure named GetTitles:

```
Dim cmd As New SqlCommand("GetTitles", con)
cmd.CommandType = CommandType.StoredProcedure
```

When you execute this SqlCommand, the GetTitles stored procedure is executed.

When you create SqlParameters for a SqlCommand that represents a stored procedure, the SqlParameters represent stored procedure parameters. The modified Movie component in Listing 16.9 uses stored procedures to retrieve and update movie records.

LISTING 16.9   App_Code\Movie4.vb

```vb
Imports System
Imports System.Data
Imports System.Data.SqlClient
Imports System.Web.Configuration
Imports System.Collections.Generic

Public Class Movie4

    Private Shared ReadOnly _connectionString As String

    Private _id As Integer
    Private _title As String
    Private _director As String

    Public Property Id() As Integer
        Get
            Return _id
        End Get
        Set(ByVal Value As Integer)
            _id = value
        End Set
    End Property

    Public Property Title() As String
        Get
            Return _title
        End Get
        Set(ByVal Value As String)
            _title = value
        End Set
    End Property

    Public Property Director() As String
        Get
            Return _director
        End Get
        Set(ByVal Value As String)
            _director = value
        End Set
    End Property

    Public Sub Update(ByVal id As Integer, ByVal title As String,
➥ByVal director As String)
        Dim con As New SqlConnection(_connectionString)
```

LISTING 16.9   Continued

```
        Dim cmd As New SqlCommand("MovieUpdate", con)
        cmd.CommandType = CommandType.StoredProcedure
        cmd.Parameters.AddWithValue("@Id", id)
        cmd.Parameters.AddWithValue("@Title", title)
        cmd.Parameters.AddWithValue("@Director", director)
        Using con
            con.Open()
            cmd.ExecuteNonQuery()
        End Using
    End Sub

    Public Function GetAll() As List(Of Movie4)
        Dim results As New List(Of Movie4)()
        Dim con As New SqlConnection(_connectionString)
        Dim cmd As New SqlCommand("MovieSelect", con)
        cmd.CommandType = CommandType.StoredProcedure
        Using con
            con.Open()
            Dim reader As SqlDataReader = cmd.ExecuteReader()
            While reader.Read()
                Dim NewMovie As New Movie4()
                NewMovie.Id = CType(reader("Id"), Integer)
                NewMovie.Title = CType(reader("Title"), String)
                NewMovie.Director = CType(reader("Director"), String)
                results.Add(NewMovie)
            End While
        End Using
        Return results
    End Function

    Shared Sub New()
        _connectionString =
➥WebConfigurationManager.ConnectionStrings("Movies").ConnectionString
    End Sub
End Class
```

The component in Listing 16.9 uses the MovieSelect and MovieUpdate stored procedures contained in Listing 16.10.

LISTING 16.10   MovieStoredProcedures.sql

```
CREATE PROCEDURE dbo.MovieSelect
AS
SELECT Id, Title, Director FROM Movies
```

LISTING 16.10   Continued

```
CREATE PROCEDURE dbo.MovieUpdate
(
    @Id int,
    @Title NVarchar(100),
    @Director NVarchar(100)
)
AS
UPDATE Movies SET
    Title = @Title,
    Director = @Director
WHERE Id = @Id
```

The ASP.NET page in Listing 16.11 contains a GridView that is bound to the modified Movie component. This GridView enables you to display and update movie records.

LISTING 16.11   ShowMovie4.aspx

```
<%@ Page Language="VB" %>
<!DOCTYPE html PUBLIC "-//W3C//DTD XHTML 1.0 Transitional//EN"
  "http://www.w3.org/TR/xhtml1/DTD/xhtml1-transitional.dtd">
<html xmlns="http://www.w3.org/1999/xhtml" >
<head id="Head1" runat="server">
    <title>Show Movie4</title>
</head>
<body>
    <form id="form1" runat="server">
    <div>

    <asp:GridView
        id="grdMovies"
        DataSourceID="srcMovies"
        DataKeyNames="Id"
        AutoGenerateEditButton="true"
        Runat="server" />

    <asp:ObjectDataSource
        id="srcMovies"
        TypeName="Movie4"
        SelectMethod="GetAll"
        UpdateMethod="Update"
        Runat="server" />

    </div>
```

16

LISTING 16.11   Continued

```
    </form>
</body>
</html>
```

You can use a `SqlParameter` to represent not only stored procedure input parameters, but to represent stored procedure return values and output parameters. If you need to return an integer value from a stored procedure, then you can create a `SqlParameter` that represents a return value. For example, the stored procedure in Listing 16.12 returns the number of rows in the Movies database table.

LISTING 16.12   GetMovieCount.sql

```
CREATE PROCEDURE dbo.GetMovieCount
AS
RETURN (SELECT COUNT(*) FROM Movies)
```

The page in Listing 16.13 displays the return value from the `GetMovieCount` stored procedure with a `Label` control (see Figure 16.6).

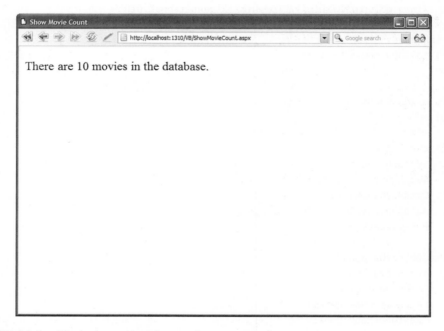

FIGURE 16.6   Displaying a stored procedure return value.

LISTING 16.13   ShowMovieCount.aspx

```
<%@ Page Language="VB" %>
<%@ Import Namespace="System.Data" %>
<%@ Import Namespace="System.Data.SqlClient" %>
<%@ Import Namespace="System.Web.Configuration" %>
<!DOCTYPE html PUBLIC "-//W3C//DTD XHTML 1.0 Transitional//EN"
  "http://www.w3.org/TR/xhtml1/DTD/xhtml1-transitional.dtd">
<script runat="server">

    Private Sub Page_Load()
        lblMovieCount.Text = GetMovieCount().ToString()
    End Sub


    Private Function GetMovieCount() As Integer
        Dim result As Integer = 0
        Dim connectionString As String = WebConfigurationManager.
➥ConnectionStrings("Movies").ConnectionString
        Dim con As New SqlConnection(connectionString)
        Dim cmd As New SqlCommand("GetMovieCount", con)
        cmd.CommandType = CommandType.StoredProcedure
        cmd.Parameters.Add("@ReturnVal", SqlDbType.Int).Direction =
➥ParameterDirection.ReturnValue
        Using con
            con.Open()
            cmd.ExecuteNonQuery()
            result = CType(cmd.Parameters("@ReturnVal").Value, Integer)
        End Using
        Return result
    End Function
</script>
<html xmlns="http://www.w3.org/1999/xhtml" >
<head id="Head1" runat="server">
    <title>Show Movie Count</title>
</head>
<body>
    <form id="form1" runat="server">
    <div>

    There are
    <asp:Label
        id="lblMovieCount"
        Runat="server" />
    movies in the database.
```

LISTING 16.13   Continued

```
      </div>
      </form>
</body>
</html>
```

In Listing 16.13, a SqlParameter is created that has the name ReturnVal. The name of the SqlParameter is not important. However, notice that the SqlParameter.Direction property is set to the value ReturnValue. After the SqlCommand is executed, the return value can be retrieved by reading the value of this parameter.

A stored procedure has only one return value, and it must be an integer value. If you need to return more than one value, or values of a different data type than an integer, then you need to use stored procedure output parameters.

For example, the stored procedure in Listing 16.14 returns movie titles and box office totals. Notice that the stored procedure includes an output parameter named @SumBoxOfficeTotals. This output parameter represents a sum of all box office totals.

LISTING 16.14   GetBoxOfficeTotals.sql

```
CREATE PROCEDURE dbo.GetBoxOfficeTotals
(
  @SumBoxOfficeTotals Money OUTPUT
)
AS
-- Assign Sum Box Office Totals
SELECT @SumBoxOfficeTotals = SUM(BoxOfficeTotals) FROM Movies

-- Return all rows
SELECT Title, BoxOfficeTotals FROM Movies
```

The data access component in Listing 16.15 contains a method named GetBoxOffice() that calls the GetBoxOfficeTotals stored procedure. The method adds an output parameter to the SqlCommand object.

LISTING 16.15   App_Code\Movie5.vb

```
Imports System
Imports System.Data
Imports System.Data.SqlClient
Imports System.Web.Configuration
Imports System.Collections.Generic

Public Class Movie5
    Private Shared ReadOnly _connectionString As String
```

LISTING 16.15   Continued

```
    Private _title As String
    Private _boxOfficeTotals As Decimal

    Public Property Title() As String
        Get
            Return _title
        End Get
        Set(ByVal Value As String)
            _title = value
        End Set
    End Property

    Public Property BoxOfficeTotals() As Decimal
        Get
            Return _boxOfficeTotals
        End Get
        Set(ByVal Value As Decimal)
            _boxOfficeTotals = value
        End Set
    End Property

    Public Function GetBoxOffice(ByRef SumBoxOfficeTotals As Decimal)
➥As List(Of Movie5)
        Dim results As New List(Of Movie5)()
        Dim con As New SqlConnection(_connectionString)
        Dim cmd As New SqlCommand("GetBoxOfficeTotals", con)
        cmd.CommandType = CommandType.StoredProcedure
        cmd.Parameters.Add("@SumBoxOfficeTotals", SqlDbType.Money).Direction
➥= ParameterDirection.Output
        Using con
            con.Open()
            Dim reader As SqlDataReader = cmd.ExecuteReader()
            While reader.Read()
                Dim NewMovie As New Movie5()
                NewMovie.Title = CType(reader("Title"), String)
                NewMovie.BoxOfficeTotals =
➥CType(reader("BoxOfficeTotals"), Decimal)
                results.Add(NewMovie)
            End While
            reader.Close()
            SumBoxOfficeTotals =
➥CType(cmd.Parameters("@SumBoxOfficeTotals").Value, Decimal)

        End Using
```

16

LISTING 16.15 Continued

```
        Return results
    End Function

    Shared Sub New()
        _connectionString = WebConfigurationManager.
➥ConnectionStrings("Movies").ConnectionString
    End Sub
End Class
```

In Listing 16.15, notice that the `SqlDataReader` is explicitly closed before the output parameter is read. If you do not close the `SqlDataReader` first, then attempting to read the value of the output parameter raises an exception.

Finally, the page in Listing 16.16 displays the movie box office totals in a `GridView`. In addition, it displays the value of the output parameter in a `Label` control (see Figure 16.7).

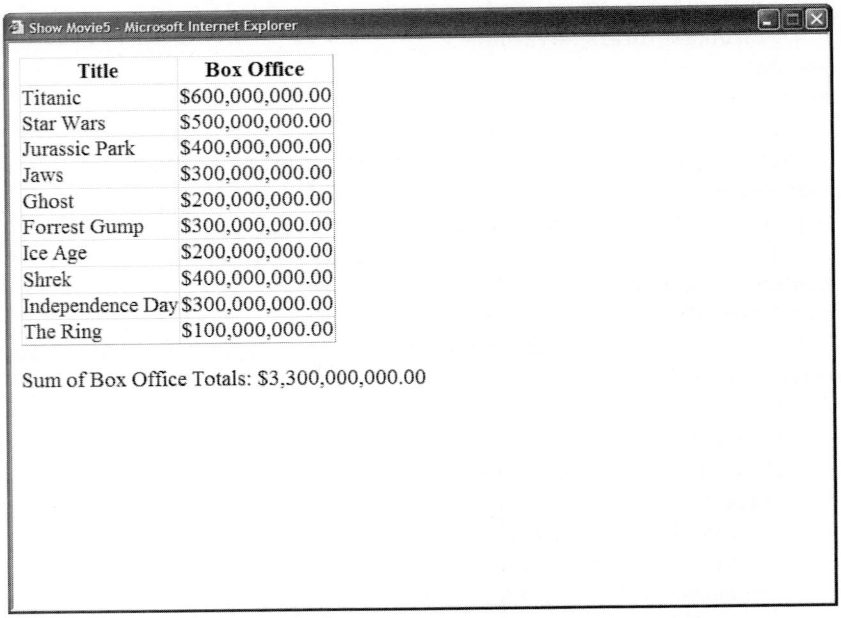
Show Movie5 - Microsoft Internet Explorer
Title
Box Office
Titanic $600,000,000.00
Star Wars $500,000,000.00
Jurassic Park $400,000,000.00
Jaws $300,000,000.00
Ghost $200,000,000.00
Forrest Gump $300,000,000.00
Ice Age $200,000,000.00
Shrek $400,000,000.00
Independence Day $300,000,000.00
The Ring $100,000,000.00
Sum of Box Office Totals: $3,300,000,000.00

FIGURE 16.7 Displaying an output parameter.

LISTING 16.16 ShowMovie5.aspx

```
<%@ Page Language="VB" %>
<!DOCTYPE html PUBLIC "-//W3C//DTD XHTML 1.0 Transitional//EN"
  "http://www.w3.org/TR/xhtml1/DTD/xhtml1-transitional.dtd">
```

LISTING 16.16   Continued

```
<script runat="server">

  Sub srcMovies_Selected(sender As object,e As ObjectDataSourceStatusEventArgs)
    Dim sum As Decimal = CType(e.OutputParameters("SumBoxOfficeTotals"), Decimal)
    lblSum.Text = sum.ToString("c")
  End Sub
</script>
<html xmlns="http://www.w3.org/1999/xhtml" >
<head id="Head1" runat="server">
    <title>Show Movie5</title>
</head>
<body>
    <form id="form1" runat="server">
    <div>

    <asp:GridView
        id="grdMovies"
        DataSourceID="srcMovies"
        AutoGenerateColumns="false"
        Runat="server">
        <Columns>
        <asp:BoundField DataField="Title" HeaderText="Title" />
        <asp:BoundField
            DataField="BoxOfficeTotals"
            HeaderText="Box Office"
            HtmlEncode="false"
            DataFormatString="{0:c}" />
        </Columns>
    </asp:GridView>
    <br />
    Sum of Box Office Totals:
    <asp:Label
        id="lblSum"
        Runat="server" />

    <asp:ObjectDataSource
        id="srcMovies"
        TypeName="Movie5"
        SelectMethod="GetBoxOffice"
        Runat="server" OnSelected="srcMovies_Selected">
        <SelectParameters>
        <asp:Parameter
            Name="SumBoxOfficeTotals"
            Type="Decimal"
```

LISTING 16.16   Continued

```
            Direction="Output" />
        </SelectParameters>
    </asp:ObjectDataSource>

    </div>
    </form>
</body>
</html>
```

Returning a Single Value

If you need to return a single value from a database query, you can use the `SqlCommand.ExecuteScalar()` method. This method always returns the value of the first column from the first row of a resultset. Even when a query returns hundreds of columns and billions of rows, everything is ignored except for the value of the first column from the first row.

For example, the page in Listing 16.17 contains a lookup form. If you enter the title of a movie, the movie's total box office returns are displayed in a `Label` control (see Figure 16.8).

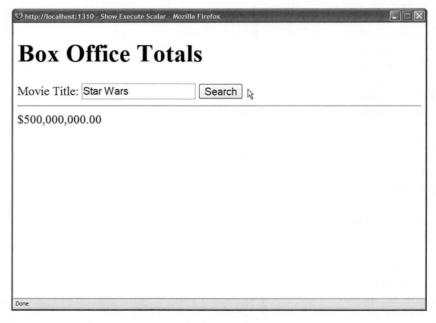

FIGURE 16.8   Retrieving a value with `ExecuteScalar()`.

LISTING 16.17   ShowExecuteScalar.aspx

```
<%@ Page Language="VB" %>
<%@ Import Namespace="System.Data" %>
<%@ Import Namespace="System.Data.SqlClient" %>
<%@ Import Namespace="System.Web.Configuration" %>
<!DOCTYPE html PUBLIC "-//W3C//DTD XHTML 1.0 Transitional//EN"
  "http://www.w3.org/TR/xhtml1/DTD/xhtml1-transitional.dtd">
<script runat="server">

    Protected Sub btnSearch_Click(ByVal sender As Object, ByVal e As EventArgs)
        Dim connectionString As String =
➥WebConfigurationManager.ConnectionStrings("Movies").ConnectionString
        Dim con As New SqlConnection(connectionString)
        Dim cmd As New SqlCommand("SELECT BoxOfficeTotals
➥FROM Movies WHERE Title=@Title", con)
        cmd.Parameters.AddWithValue("@Title", txtTitle.Text)
        Using con
            con.Open()
            Dim result As Object = cmd.ExecuteScalar()
            If Not IsNothing(result) Then
                lblResult.Text = String.Format("{0:c}", result)
            Else
                lblResult.Text = "No match!"
            End If
        End Using
    End Sub
</script>
<html xmlns="http://www.w3.org/1999/xhtml" >
<head id="Head1" runat="server">
    <title>Show Execute Scalar</title>
</head>
<body>
    <form id="form1" runat="server">
    <div>

    <h1>Box Office Totals</h1>

    <asp:Label
        id="lblTitle"
        Text="Movie Title:"
        AssociatedControlID="txtTitle"
        Runat="server" />

    <asp:TextBox
        id="txtTitle"
```

16

LISTING 16.17 Continued

```
        Runat="server" />

    <asp:Button
        id="btnSearch"
        Text="Search"
        OnClick="btnSearch_Click"
        Runat="server" />

    <hr />

    <asp:Label
        id="lblResult"
        Runat="server" />

    </div>
    </form>
</body>
</html>
```

The ExecuteScalar() method returns a value of type Object. This means that you must cast the value returned from ExecuteScalar() to a particular type before you do anything with the value. In Listing 16.17, after verifying that a value is returned, the value is cast to a decimal.

Notice that you have a choice here. Rather than use the ExecuteScalar() method, you can use an output parameter. You can use either method to return a single value from a database. There is no real difference in performance between using the ExecuteScalar() method with a stored procedure or using an output parameter. The approach you take is largely a matter of preference.

> **NOTE**
>
> For performance comparisons between ExecuteScalar and output parameters, see Priya Dhawan's article at the Microsoft MSDN website (msdn.Microsoft.com), entitled "Performance Comparison: Data Access Techniques."

Returning a Resultset

If you need to return multiple rows of data with a SqlCommand object, then you can call the SqlCommand.ExecuteReader() method. This method returns a SqlDataReader that you can use to fetch each row of records from the database.

For example, the data access component in Listing 16.18 contains a method named GetAll() that returns all the movies from the Movies database table. After the

`ExecuteReader()` method is called, each row is retrieved from the `SqlDataReader` and dumped into a generic List collection.

LISTING 16.18   App_Code\Movie6.vb

```
Imports System
Imports System.Data
Imports System.Data.SqlClient
Imports System.Web.Configuration
Imports System.Collections.Generic

Public Class Movie6
    Private Shared ReadOnly _connectionString As String

    Private _title As String
    Private _director As String

    Public Property Title() As String
        Get
            Return _title
        End Get
        Set(ByVal Value As String)
            _title = value
        End Set
    End Property

    Public Property Director() As String
        Get
            Return _director
        End Get
        Set(ByVal Value As String)
            _director = value
        End Set
    End Property

    Public Function GetAll() As List(Of Movie6)
        Dim results As New List(Of Movie6)()
        Dim con As New SqlConnection(_connectionString)
        Dim cmd As New SqlCommand("SELECT Title,Director FROM Movies", con)
        Using con
            con.Open()
            Dim reader As SqlDataReader = cmd.ExecuteReader()
            While reader.Read()
                Dim NewMovie As New Movie6()
                NewMovie.Title = CType(reader("Title"), String)
                NewMovie.Director = CType(reader("Director"), String)
```

16

LISTING 16.18   Continued

```
            results.Add(NewMovie)
        End While
    End Using
    Return results
End Function

Shared Sub New()
    _connectionString = WebConfigurationManager
➥.ConnectionStrings("Movies").ConnectionString
    End Sub
End Class
```

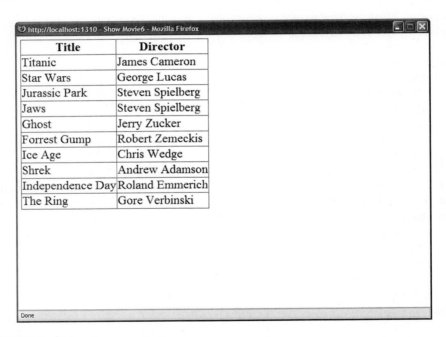

FIGURE 16.9   Returning a resultset.

LISTING 16.19   ShowMovie6.aspx

```
<%@ Page Language="VB" %>
<!DOCTYPE html PUBLIC "-//W3C//DTD XHTML 1.0 Transitional//EN"
  "http://www.w3.org/TR/xhtml1/DTD/xhtml1-transitional.dtd">
<html xmlns="http://www.w3.org/1999/xhtml" >
<head id="Head1" runat="server">
  <title>Show Movie6</title>
</head>
```

LISTING 16.19   Continued

```
<body>
    <form id="form1" runat="server">
    <div>

    <asp:GridView
        id="grdMovies"
        DataSourceID="srcMovies"
        Runat="server" />

    <asp:ObjectDataSource
        id="srcMovies"
        TypeName="Movie6"
        SelectMethod="GetAll"
        Runat="server" />

    </div>
    </form>
</body>
</html>
```

The component in Listing 16.18 copies all the records from the SqlDataReader to a collection before returning the results of the query.

If you want to skip the copying step, and not add the records to a collection, then you can pass a CommandBehavior.CloseConnection parameter to the ExecuteReader() method. This parameter causes the database connection associated with the SqlDataReader to close automatically after all the records have been fetched from the SqlDataReader.

The component in Listing 16.20 illustrates how you can use CommandBehavior.CloseConnection with the ExecuteReader() method.

LISTING 16.20   App_Code\Movie7.vb

```
Imports System
Imports System.Data
Imports System.Data.SqlClient
Imports System.Web.Configuration
Imports System.Collections.Generic

Public Class Movie7
    Private Shared ReadOnly _connectionString As String

    Public Function GetAll() As SqlDataReader
        Dim con As New SqlConnection(_connectionString)
        Dim cmd As New SqlCommand("SELECT Title,Director FROM Movies", con)
```

16

LISTING 16.20   Continued

```
        con.Open()
        Return cmd.ExecuteReader(CommandBehavior.CloseConnection)
    End Function

    Shared Sub New()
        _connectionString = WebConfigurationManager
➡.ConnectionStrings("Movies").ConnectionString
    End Sub
End Class
```

The page in Listing 16.21 displays the records returned from the component in Listing 16.20 in a GridView.

LISTING 16.21   ShowMovie7.aspx

```
<%@ Page Language="VB" %>
<!DOCTYPE html PUBLIC "-//W3C//DTD XHTML 1.0 Transitional//EN"
  "http://www.w3.org/TR/xhtml1/DTD/xhtml1-transitional.dtd">
<html xmlns="http://www.w3.org/1999/xhtml" >
<head id="Head1" runat="server">
    <title>Show Movie7</title>
</head>
<body>
    <form id="form1" runat="server">
    <div>

    <asp:GridView
        id="grdMovies"
        DataSourceID="srcMovies"
        Runat="server" />

    <asp:ObjectDataSource
        id="srcMovies"
        TypeName="Movie7"
        SelectMethod="GetAll"
        Runat="server" />

    </div>
    </form>
</body>
</html>
```

The CommandBehavior.CloseConnection parameter enables you to return a SqlDataReader from a method. When all the records are read from the SqlDataReader, the

CommandBehavior.CloseConnection parameter causes the SqlConnection object associated with the SqlDataReader to close automatically.

The big disadvantage of using the CommandBehavior.CloseConnection parameter is that it prevents you from adding any exception handling code. You can't use a Using statement or Try...Catch statement with the SqlConnection created in the component in Listing 16.19. A Using statement or Try...Catch statement would force the SqlConnection to close before the SqlDataReader is returned from the method.

Using the DataReader Object

The DataReader object represents the results of a database query. You get a DataReader by calling a Command object's ExecuteReader() method.

You can verify whether a DataReader represents any rows by checking the HasRows property or calling the Read() method. The Read() method returns true when the DataReader can advance to a new row. (Calling this method also advances you to the next row.)

The DataReader represents a single row of data at a time. To get the next row of data, you need to call the Read() method. When you get to the last row, the Read() method returns False.

There are multiple ways to refer to the columns returned by a DataReader. For example, imagine that you are using a SqlDataReader named reader to represent the following query:

```
SELECT Title, Director FROM Movies
```

If you want to retrieve the value of the Title column for the current row represented by a DataReader, then you can use any of the following methods:

```
Dim Title As String = CType(reader("Title"), String)
Dim Title As String = CType(reader(0), String)
Dim Title As String = reader.GetString(0)
Dim Title As String = reader.GetSqlString(0)
```

The first method returns the Title column by name. The value of the Title column is returned as an Object. Therefore, you must cast the value to a string before you can assign the value to a string variable.

The second method returns the Title column by position. It also returns the value of the Title column as an Object, so you must cast the value before using it.

The third method returns the Title column by position. However, it retrieves the value as a String value. You don't need to cast the value in this case.

Finally, the last method returns the Title column by position. However, it returns the value as a SqlString rather than a normal String. A SqlString represents the value as a Microsoft SQL Server 2005 String.

NOTE

SqlTypes is a new feature of ADO.NET 2.0. There is a SqlType that corresponds to each of the types supported by Microsoft SQL Server 2005. For example, there is a SqlDecimal, SqlBinary, and SqlXml type.

There are tradeoffs between the different methods of returning a column value. Retrieving a column by its position rather than its name is faster. However, this technique also makes your code more brittle. If the order of your columns changes in your query, your code no longer works.

Returning Multiple Resultsets

A single database query can return multiple resultsets. For example, the following query returns the contents of both the MovieCategories and Movies tables as separate resultsets:

```
SELECT * FROM MoviesCategories;SELECT * FROM Movies
```

Notice that a semicolon is used to separate the two queries.

Executing multiple queries in one shot can result in better performance. When you execute multiple queries with a single command, you don't tie up multiple database connections.

The component in Listing 16.22 illustrates how you can retrieve multiple resultsets with a single query when using a `SqlDataReader`. The `GetMovieData()` method returns two collections: a collection representing MovieCategories and a collection representing Movies.

LISTING 16.22   App_Code\DataLayer1.vb

```
Imports System
Imports System.Data
Imports System.Data.SqlClient
Imports System.Web.Configuration
Imports System.Collections.Generic

Public Class DataLayer1
    Private Shared ReadOnly _connectionString As String

    Public Class MovieCategory
        Private _id As Integer
        Private _name As String

        Public Property Id() As Integer
            Get
                Return _id
            End Get
```

LISTING 16.22   Continued

```
                Set(ByVal Value As Integer)
                    _id = value
                End Set
            End Property


        Public Property Name() As String
            Get
                    Return _name
            End Get
            Set(ByVal Value As String)
                    _name = value
            End Set
        End Property
    End Class


    Public Class Movie
        Private _title As String
        Private _categoryId As Integer

        Public Property Title() As String
            Get
                    Return _title
            End Get
            Set(ByVal Value As String)
                    _title = value
            End Set
        End Property


        Public Property CategoryId() As Integer
            Get
                    Return _categoryId
            End Get
            Set(ByVal Value As Integer)
                    _categoryId = value
            End Set
        End Property
    End Class


    Public Shared Sub GetMovieData(
➥ByVal movieCategories As List(Of DataLayer1.MovieCategory),
➥ByVal movies As List(Of DataLayer1.Movie))
        Dim commandText As String = "SELECT Id,Name FROM MovieCategories;
➥SELECT Title,CategoryId FROM Movies"
```

LISTING 16.22   Continued

```
        Dim con As New SqlConnection(_connectionString)
        Dim cmd As New SqlCommand(commandText, con)
        Using con
            ' Execute command
            con.Open()
            Dim reader As SqlDataReader = cmd.ExecuteReader()

            ' Create movie categories
            While reader.Read()
                Dim NewCategory As New DataLayer1.MovieCategory()
                NewCategory.Id = CType(reader("Id"), Integer)
                NewCategory.Name = CType(reader("Name"), String)
                movieCategories.Add(NewCategory)
            End While

            ' Move to next resultset
            reader.NextResult()

            ' Create movies
            While reader.Read()
                Dim NewMovie As DataLayer1.Movie = New DataLayer1.Movie()
                NewMovie.Title = CType(reader("Title"), String)
                NewMovie.CategoryId = CType(reader("CategoryID"), Integer)
                movies.Add(NewMovie)
            End While
        End Using
    End Sub

    Shared Sub New()
        _connectionString = WebConfigurationManager.
➥ConnectionStrings("Movies").ConnectionString
    End Sub
End Class
```

The SqlDataReader.NextResult() method is called to advance to the next resultset. This method returns either True or False depending on whether a next resultset exists. In Listing 16.22, it is assumed that there is both a movies category and movies resultset.

The page in Listing 16.23 displays the contents of the two database tables in two GridView controls (see Figure 16.10).

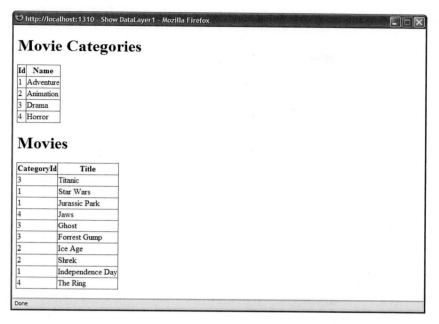

FIGURE 16.10 Displaying two resultsets.

LISTING 16.23 ShowDataLayer1.aspx

```vb
<%@ Page Language="VB" %>
<%@ Import Namespace="System.Collections.Generic" %>
<!DOCTYPE html PUBLIC "-//W3C//DTD XHTML 1.0 Transitional//EN"
  "http://www.w3.org/TR/xhtml1/DTD/xhtml1-transitional.dtd">
<script runat="server">

    Private Sub Page_Load()
        ' Get database data
        Dim categories As New List(Of DataLayer1.MovieCategory)()
        Dim movies As New List(Of DataLayer1.Movie)()
        DataLayer1.GetMovieData(categories, movies)

        ' Bind the data
        grdCategories.DataSource = categories
        grdCategories.DataBind()
        grdMovies.DataSource = movies
        grdMovies.DataBind()
    End Sub
</script>
<html xmlns="http://www.w3.org/1999/xhtml" >
```

LISTING 16.23   Continued

```
<head id="Head1" runat="server">
    <title>Show DataLayer1</title>
</head>
<body>
    <form id="form1" runat="server">
    <div>

    <h1>Movie Categories</h1>
    <asp:GridView
        id="grdCategories"
        Runat="server" />

    <h1>Movies</h1>
    <asp:GridView
        id="grdMovies"
        Runat="server" />

    </div>
    </form>
</body>
</html>
```

Working with Multiple Active Resultsets

ADO.NET 2.0 includes a new feature named Multiple Active Results Sets (MARS). In the previous version of ADO.NET, a database connection could represent only a single result-set at a time. If you take advantage of MARS, you can represent multiple resultsets with a single database connection.

Using MARS is valuable in scenarios in which you need to iterate through a resultset and perform an additional database operation for each record in the resultset.

MARS is disabled by default. To enable MARS, you must include a MultipleActiveResultSets=True attribute in a connection string.

For example, the page in Listing 16.24 programmatically builds the nodes in a TreeView control. The page displays a list of movie categories and, beneath each movie category, it displays a list of matching movies (see Figure 16.11).

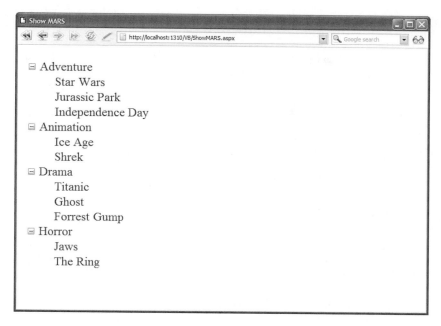

FIGURE 16.11   Fetching database records with MARS enabled.

LISTING 16.24   ShowMARS.aspx

```
<%@ Page Language="VB" %>
<%@ Import Namespace="System.Data" %>
<%@ Import Namespace="System.Data.SqlClient" %>
<!DOCTYPE html PUBLIC "-//W3C//DTD XHTML 1.0 Transitional//EN"
  "http://www.w3.org/TR/xhtml1/DTD/xhtml1-transitional.dtd">
<script runat="server">

    Private  Sub Page_Load()
        If Not Page.IsPostBack Then
            BuildTree()
        End If
    End Sub

    Sub BuildTree()
        ' Create MARS connection
        Dim connectionString As String = "MultipleActiveResultSets=True;" _
            & "Data Source=.\SQLExpress;Integrated Security=True;" _
            & "AttachDBFileName=¦DataDirectory¦MyDatabase.mdf;User Instance=True"
        Dim con As New SqlConnection(connectionString)
```

LISTING 16.24   Continued

```
          ' Create Movie Categories command
          Dim cmdCategoriesText As String =  "SELECT Id,Name FROM MovieCategories"
          Dim cmdCategories As New SqlCommand(cmdCategoriesText,con)

          ' Create Movie command
          Dim cmdMoviesText As String = "SELECT Title FROM Movies " _
              & "WHERE CategoryId=@CategoryID"
          Dim cmdMovies As New SqlCommand(cmdMoviesText, con)
          cmdMovies.Parameters.Add("@CategoryId", SqlDbType.Int)

          Using con
              con.Open()

              ' Iterate through categories
              Dim categories As SqlDataReader = cmdCategories.ExecuteReader()
              While categories.Read()
                  ' Add category node
                  Dim id As Integer = categories.GetInt32(0)
                  Dim name As String = categories.GetString(1)
                  Dim catNode As New TreeNode(name)
                  TreeView1.Nodes.Add(catNode)

                  ' Iterate through matching movies
                  cmdMovies.Parameters("@CategoryId").Value = id
                  Dim movies As SqlDataReader = cmdMovies.ExecuteReader()
                  While movies.Read()
                      ' Add movie node
                      Dim title As String = movies.GetString(0)
                      Dim movieNode As New TreeNode(title)
                      catNode.ChildNodes.Add(movieNode)
                  End While
                  movies.Close()
              End While
          End Using
      End Sub
</script>
<html xmlns="http://www.w3.org/1999/xhtml" >
<head id="Head1" runat="server">
    <title>Show MARS</title>
</head>
<body>
    <form id="form1" runat="server">
    <div>
```

LISTING 16.24   Continued

```
    <asp:TreeView
        id="TreeView1"
        Runat="server" />

    </div>
    </form>
</body>
</html>
```

Notice that the `MultipleActiveResultSets` attribute is included in the connection string used to open the database connection. If MARS were not enabled, then you would not be able to loop through the interior `SqlDataReader` that represents the matching movies while the containing `SqlDataReader` that represents the movie categories is open.

Disconnected Data Access

The ADO.NET Framework supports two models of data access. In the first part of this chapter, you saw how you can use the `SqlConnection`, `SqlCommand`, and `SqlDataReader` objects to connect to a database and retrieve data. When you read data from a database by using a `SqlDataReader` object, an open connection must be maintained between your application and the database.

In this section, we examine the second model of data access supported by ADO.NET: the disconnected model. When you use the objects discussed in this section, you do not need to keep a connection to the database open.

This section discusses four new ADO.NET objects:

- `DataAdapter`—Enables you to transfer data from the physical database to the in-memory database and back again.

- `DataTable`—Represents an in-memory database table.

- `DataView`—Represents an in-memory database view.

- `DataSet`—Represents an in-memory database.

The ADO.NET objects discussed in this section are built on top of the ADO.NET objects discussed in the previous section. For example, behind the scenes, the `DataAdapter` uses a `DataReader` to retrieve data from a database.

The advantage of using the objects discussed in this section is that they provide you with more functionality. For example, you can filter and sort the rows represented by a `DataView`. Furthermore, you can use the `DataTable` object to track changes made to records and accept or reject the changes.

The big disadvantage of using the objects discussed in this section is that they tend to be slower and more resource intensive. Retrieving 500 records with a DataReader is much faster than retrieving 500 records with a DataAdapter.

> **NOTE**
>
> For detailed performance comparisons between the DataReader and DataAdapter, see Priya Dhawan's article at the Microsoft MSDN website (msdn.Microsoft.com), entitled "Performance Comparison: Data Access Techniques."

Therefore, unless you need to use any of the specialized functionality supported by these objects, my recommendation is that you stick with the objects discussed in the first part of this chapter when accessing a database. In other words, DataReaders are good and DataAdapters are bad.

Using the DataAdapter Object

The DataAdapter acts as the bridge between an in-memory database table and a physical database table. You use the DataAdapter to retrieve data from a database and populate a DataTable. You also use a DataAdapter to push changes that you have made to a DataTable back to the physical database.

The component in Listing 16.25 illustrates how you can use a SqlDataAdapter to populate a DataTable.

LISTING 16.25   App_Code\Movie8.vb

```vb
Imports System
Imports System.Data
Imports System.Data.SqlClient
Imports System.Web.Configuration
Imports System.Collections.Generic


Public Class Movie8
    Private Shared ReadOnly _connectionString As String

    Public Function GetAll() As DataTable
        ' Initialize the DataAdapter
        Dim dad As New SqlDataAdapter("SELECT Title,Director FROM Movies", _
➥connectionString)

        ' Create a DataTable
        Dim dtblMovies As New DataTable()

        ' Populate the DataTable
        dad.Fill(dtblMovies)
```

LISTING 16.25   Continued

```
        ' Return results
        Return dtblMovies
    End Function

    Shared Sub New()
        _connectionString = WebConfigurationManager
➥.ConnectionStrings("Movies").ConnectionString
    End Sub
End Class
```

The page in Listing 16.26 contains a GridView that is bound to an ObjectDataSource that represents the component in Listing 16.25 (see Figure 16.12).

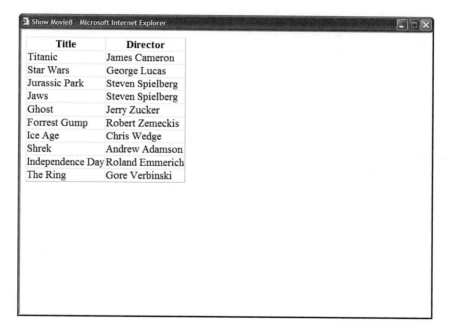

Title	Director
Titanic	James Cameron
Star Wars	George Lucas
Jurassic Park	Steven Spielberg
Jaws	Steven Spielberg
Ghost	Jerry Zucker
Forrest Gump	Robert Zemeckis
Ice Age	Chris Wedge
Shrek	Andrew Adamson
Independence Day	Roland Emmerich
The Ring	Gore Verbinski

FIGURE 16.12   Displaying data with a DataAdapter.

LISTING 16.26   ShowMovie8.aspx

```
<%@ Page Language="VB" %>
<!DOCTYPE html PUBLIC "-//W3C//DTD XHTML 1.0 Transitional//EN"
  "http://www.w3.org/TR/xhtml1/DTD/xhtml1-transitional.dtd">
<html xmlns="http://www.w3.org/1999/xhtml" >
<head id="Head1" runat="server">
```

LISTING 16.26   Continued

```
    <title>Show Movie8</title>
</head>
<body>
    <form id="form1" runat="server">
    <div>

    <asp:GridView
        id="grdMovies"
        DataSourceID="srcMovies"
        Runat="server" />

     <asp:ObjectDataSource
        id="srcMovies"
        TypeName="Movie8"
        SelectMethod="GetAll"
        Runat="server" />

    </div>
    </form>
</body>
</html>
```

Notice that a SqlConnection is never explicitly created in the component in Listing 16.25. When you call the SqlDataAdapter object's Fill() method, the SqlDataAdapter automatically creates and opens a connection. After the data is fetched from the database, the Fill() method automatically closes the connection.

You don't need to wrap the call to the Fill() method within a Using or Try...Catch statement. Internally, the SqlDataAdapter uses a Try...Catch statement to ensure that its connection gets closed.

Opening and closing a database connection is a slow operation. If you know that you will need to perform another database operation after using the SqlDataAdapter, then you should explicitly create a SqlConnection and open it like this:

```
Dim con As New SqlConnection(...connection string...)
Dim dad As New SqlDataAdapter("SELECT Title,Director FROM Movies", con)
Using con
  con.Open()
  dad.Fill(dtblMovies)
  ... Perform other database operations with connection ...
End Using
```

If a SqlConnection is already open when you call the Fill() method, the Fill() method doesn't close it. In other words, the Fill() method maintains the state of the connection.

Performing Batch Updates

You can think of a SqlDataAdapter as a collection of four SqlCommand objects:

- SelectCommand—Represents a SqlCommand used for selecting data from a database.

- UpdateCommand—Represents a SqlCommand used for updating data in a database.

- InsertCommand—Represents a SqlCommand used for inserting data into a database.

- DeleteCommand—Represents a SqlCommand used for deleting data from a database.

You can use a DataAdapter not only when retrieving data from a database. You can also use a DataAdapter when updating, inserting, and deleting data from a database.

If you call a SqlDataAdapter object's Update() method, and pass the method a DataTable, then the SqlDataAdapter calls its UpdateCommand, InsertCommand, and DeleteCommand to make changes to the database.

You can assign a SqlCommand object to each of the four properties of the SqlDataAdapter. Alternatively, you can use the SqlCommandBuilder object to create the UpdateCommand, InsertCommand, and DeleteCommand for you. The SqlCommandBuilder class takes a SqlDataAdapter that has a SELECT command and generates the other three commands automatically.

For example, the page in Listing 16.27 displays all the records from the Movies database table in a spreadsheet created with a Repeater control (see Figure 16.13). If you make changes to the data and click the Update button, then the Movies database table is updated with the changes.

16

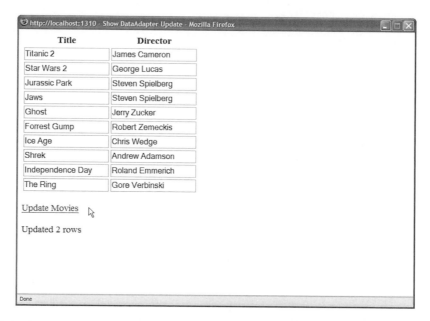

FIGURE 16.13   Batch updating database records.

LISTING 16.27   ShowDataAdapterUpdate.aspx

```
<%@ Page Language="VB" %>
<%@ Import Namespace="System.Data" %>
<%@ Import Namespace="System.Data.SqlClient" %>
<%@ Import Namespace="System.Web.Configuration" %>
<!DOCTYPE html PUBLIC "-//W3C//DTD XHTML 1.0 Transitional//EN"
  "http://www.w3.org/TR/xhtml1/DTD/xhtml1-transitional.dtd">
<script runat="server">

    Private dad As SqlDataAdapter
    Private dtblMovies As DataTable

    Sub Page_Load()
        ' Create connection
        Dim connectionString As String =
➥WebConfigurationManager.ConnectionStrings("Movies").ConnectionString
        Dim con As New SqlConnection(connectionString)

        ' Create Select command
        dad = New SqlDataAdapter("SELECT Id,Title,Director FROM Movies", con)

        ' Create Update, Insert, and Delete commands with SqlCommandBuilder
        Dim builder As New SqlCommandBuilder(dad)

        ' Add data to DataTable
        dtblMovies = New DataTable()
        dad.Fill(dtblMovies)

        ' Bind data to Repeater
        rptMovies.DataSource = dtblMovies
        rptMovies.DataBind()
    End Sub

    Protected  Sub lnkUpdate_Click(ByVal sender As Object, ByVal e As EventArgs)
        ' Update DataTable with changes
        For  i as integer = 0 To rptMovies.Items.Count- 1
            Dim item As RepeaterItem =  rptMovies.Items(i)
            Dim txtTitle As TextBox = CType(item.FindControl("txtTitle"), TextBox)
            Dim txtDirector As TextBox =
➥CType(item.FindControl("txtDirector"), TextBox)
            If dtblMovies.Rows(i)("Title") <> txtTitle.Text Then
                dtblMovies.Rows(i)("Title") = txtTitle.Text
            End If
            If dtblMovies.Rows(i)("Director") <> txtDirector.Text Then
                dtblMovies.Rows(i)("Director") = txtDirector.Text
```

LISTING 16.27   Continued

```
                End If
        Next

        ' Set batch size to maximum size
        dad.UpdateBatchSize = 0

        ' Perform update
        Dim numUpdated As Integer = dad.Update(dtblMovies)
        lblResults.Text = String.Format("Updated {0} rows", numUpdated)
    End Sub
</script>
<html xmlns="http://www.w3.org/1999/xhtml" >
<head id="Head1" runat="server">
    <title>Show DataAdapter Update</title>
</head>
<body>
    <form id="form1" runat="server">
    <div>

    <asp:Repeater
        id="rptMovies"
        EnableViewState="false"
        Runat="server">
        <HeaderTemplate>
        <table>
        <tr>
            <th>Title</th><th>Director</th>
        </tr>
        </HeaderTemplate>
        <ItemTemplate>
        <tr>
        <td>
        <asp:TextBox
            id="txtTitle"
            Text='<%#Eval("Title")%>'
            Runat="server" />
        </td>
        <td>
        <asp:TextBox
            id="txtDirector"
            Text='<%#Eval("Director")%>'
            Runat="server" />
        </td>
        </tr>
```

LISTING 16.27   Continued

```
            </ItemTemplate>
            <FooterTemplate>
            </table>
            </FooterTemplate>
        </asp:Repeater>
        <br />

        <asp:LinkButton
            id="lnkUpdate"
            Text="Update Movies"
            Runat="server" OnClick="lnkUpdate_Click" />

        <br /><br />

        <asp:Label
            id="lblResults"
            EnableViewState="false"
            Runat="server" />

    </div>
    </form>
</body>
</html>
```

The SqlDataAdapter in Listing 16.27 performs a batch update. When a SqlDataAdapter object's UpdateBatchSize property is set to the value 0, the SqlDataAdapter performs all its updates in a single batch. If you want to perform updates in smaller batches, then you can set the UpdateBatchSize to a particular size.

> **NOTE**
>
> Performing batch updates is a new feature of ADO.NET 2.0.

Using the DataTable Object

The DataTable object represents an in-memory database table. You can add rows to a DataTable with a SqlDataAdapter, with a SqlDataReader, with an XML file, or programmatically.

For example, the page in Listing 16.28 builds a new DataTable programmatically. The contents of the DataTable are then displayed in a GridView control (see Figure 16.14).

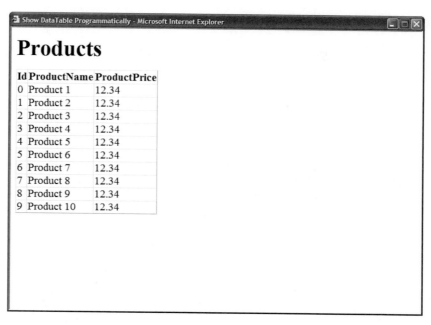

FIGURE 16.14   Displaying a `DataTable` that was built programmatically.

LISTING 16.28   ShowDataTableProgram.aspx

```
<%@ Page Language="VB" %>
<%@ Import Namespace="System.Data" %>
<!DOCTYPE html PUBLIC "-//W3C//DTD XHTML 1.0 Transitional//EN"
  "http://www.w3.org/TR/xhtml1/DTD/xhtml1-transitional.dtd">
<script runat="server">

    Sub Page_Load()
        ' Create the DataTable columns
        Dim NewDataTable As New DataTable()
        NewDataTable.Columns.Add("Id", GetType(Integer))
        NewDataTable.Columns.Add("ProductName", GetType(String))
        NewDataTable.Columns.Add("ProductPrice", GetType(Decimal))

        ' Mark the Id column as an autoincrement column
        NewDataTable.Columns("Id").AutoIncrement = True

        ' Add some data rows
        For i As Integer = 1 To 10
            Dim NewRow As DataRow = NewDataTable.NewRow()
            NewRow("ProductName") = "Product " & i.ToString()
            NewRow("ProductPrice") = 12.34
```

LISTING 16.28   Continued

```
            NewDataTable.Rows.Add(NewRow)
        Next

        ' Bind DataTable to GridView
        grdProducts.DataSource = NewDataTable
        grdProducts.DataBind()
    End Sub
</script>
<html xmlns="http://www.w3.org/1999/xhtml" >
<head id="Head1" runat="server">
    <title>Show DataTable Programmatically</title>
</head>
<body>
    <form id="form1" runat="server">
    <div>

    <h1>Products</h1>

    <asp:GridView
        id="grdProducts"
        Runat="server" />

    </div>
    </form>
</body>
</html>
```

In Listing 16.28, a `DataTable` with the following three columns is created: Id, ProductName, and ProductPrice. The data type of each column is specified with a .NET Framework type. For example, the `ProductPrice` column is created as a decimal column. Alternatively, you could create each column with a `SqlType`. For example, you could use `System.Data.SqlTypes.SqlDecimal` for the type of the ProductPrice column.

Notice that the Id column is created as an autoincrement column. When you add new rows to the `DataTable`, the column increments its value automatically.

Selecting DataRows

You can retrieve particular rows from a `DataTable` by using the `DataTable` object's `Select()` method. The `Select()` method accepts a filter parameter. You can use just about anything that you would use in a SQL `WHERE` clause with the filter parameter.

When you retrieve an array of rows with the `Select()` method, you can also specify a sort order for the rows. When specifying a sort order, you can use any expression that you would use with a SQL `ORDER BY` clause.

For example, the page in Listing 16.29 caches a DataTable in memory with the ASP.NET Cache object. The page contains a TextBox control. When you enter a partial movie title into the TextBox control, a list of matching movies is displayed in a GridView control. The rows are sorted in order of the movie title (see Figure 16.15).

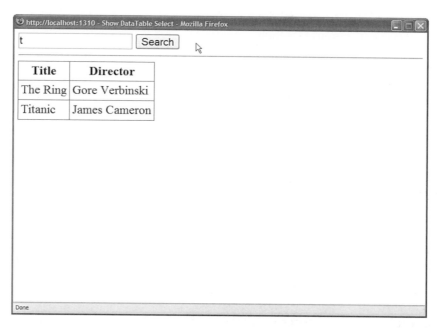

FIGURE 16.15   Selecting matching rows from a cached DataTable.

LISTING 16.29   ShowDataTableSelect.aspx

```vb
<%@ Page Language="VB" %>
<%@ Import Namespace="System.Data" %>
<%@ Import Namespace="System.Data.SqlClient" %>
<%@ Import Namespace="System.Web.Configuration" %>
<!DOCTYPE html PUBLIC "-//W3C//DTD XHTML 1.0 Transitional//EN"
 "http://www.w3.org/TR/xhtml1/DTD/xhtml1-transitional.dtd">
<script runat="server">

    Protected Sub btnSearch_Click(ByVal sender As Object, ByVal e As EventArgs)
        ' Get movies DataTable from Cache
        Dim dtblMovies As DataTable = CType(Cache("MoviesToFilter"), DataTable)
        If IsNothing(dtblMovies) Then
            dtblMovies = GetMoviesFromDB()
            Cache("MoviesToFilter") = dtblMovies
        End If
```

LISTING 16.29   Continued

```
        ' Select matching rows
        Dim filter As String = String.Format("Title LIKE '{0}*'", txtTitle.Text)
        Dim rows() As DataRow = dtblMovies.Select(filter, "Title")

        ' Bind to GridView
        grdMovies.DataSource = rows
        grdMovies.DataBind()
    End Sub

    Private Function GetMoviesFromDB() As DataTable
        Dim connectionString As String =
➥WebConfigurationManager.ConnectionStrings("Movies").ConnectionString
        Dim dad As New SqlDataAdapter("SELECT Title, Director FROM Movies",
➥connectionString)
        Dim dtblMovies As New DataTable()
        dad.Fill(dtblMovies)
        Return dtblMovies
    End Function
</script>
<html xmlns="http://www.w3.org/1999/xhtml" >
<head id="Head1" runat="server">
    <style type="text/css">
        th, td
        {
            padding:5px;
        }
    </style>
    <title>Show DataTable Select</title>
</head>
<body>
    <form id="form1" runat="server">
    <div>

    <asp:TextBox
        id="txtTitle"
        Tooltip="Search"
        Runat="server" />
    <asp:Button
        id="btnSearch"
        Text="Search"
        Runat="server" OnClick="btnSearch_Click" />

    <hr />
```

LISTING 16.29 Continued

```
<asp:GridView
    id="grdMovies"
    AutoGenerateColumns="false"
    Runat="server">
    <Columns>
    <asp:TemplateField HeaderText="Title">
    <ItemTemplate>
        <%# CType(Container.DataItem,DataRow)("Title") %>
    </ItemTemplate>
    </asp:TemplateField>
    <asp:TemplateField HeaderText="Director">
    <ItemTemplate>
        <%#CType(Container.DataItem, DataRow)("Director")%>
    </ItemTemplate>
    </asp:TemplateField>
    </Columns>
    </asp:GridView>

    </div>
    </form>
</body>
</html>
```

The `DataTable` `Select()` method returns an array of `DataRow` objects. Notice that there is nothing wrong with binding an array of `DataRow` objects to a `GridView` control. However, you must explicitly cast each data item to a `DataRow` and read within a `GridView` `TemplateField`.

DataRow States and DataRow Versions

When you modify the rows in a `DataTable`, the `DataTable` keeps track of the changes that you make. A `DataTable` maintains both the original and modified version of each row.

Each row in a `DataTable` has a particular `RowState` that has one of the following values:

- `Unchanged`—The row has not been changed.
- `Added`—The row has been added.
- `Modified`—The row has been modified.
- `Deleted`—The row has been deleted.
- `Detached`—The row has been created but not added to the `DataTable`.

Each row in a `DataTable` can have more than one version. Each version is represented by one of the following values of the `DataRowVersion` enumeration:

- Current—The current version of the row.

- Default—The default version of the row.

- Original—The original version of the row.

- Proposed—The version of a row that exists during editing.

You can use the DataTable.AcceptChanges() method to copy the current versions of all the rows to the original versions of all the rows. And you can use the DataTable. RejectChanges() method to copy the original versions of all the rows to the current versions of all the rows.

For example, the component in Listing 16.30 includes an AcceptChanges() and RejectChanges() method. The component maintains a DataTable in Session state. If you update a row in the DataTable, the row is updated in memory. If the RejectChanges() method is called, any changes made to the DataTable are rejected. If the AcceptChanges() method is called, the database is updated and all changes are accepted.

LISTING 16.30   App_Code\Movie9.vb

```vb
Imports System
Imports System.Data
Imports System.Data.SqlClient
Imports System.Web
Imports System.Web.Configuration

Public Class Movie9

    Private dad As New SqlDataAdapter()

    Public Function GetAll() As DataTable
        Return CType(HttpContext.Current.Session("MoviesToEdit"), DataTable)
    End Function

    Public Sub Update(ByVal id As Integer, ByVal title As String,
➡ByVal director As String)
        Dim movies As DataTable = CType(HttpContext.Current.
➡Session("MoviestoEdit"), DataTable)
        Dim rowToEdit As DataRow = movies.Rows.Find(id)
        rowToEdit("title") = title
        rowToEdit("director") = director
    End Sub

    Public Sub RejectChanges()
        Dim movies As DataTable = CType(HttpContext.Current.
➡Session("MoviestoEdit"), DataTable)
        movies.RejectChanges()
```

LISTING 16.30   Continued

```
    End Sub


    Public Sub AcceptChanges()
        Dim movies As DataTable = CType(HttpContext.Current.
➥Session("MoviestoEdit"), DataTable)
        dad.Update(movies)
        movies.AcceptChanges()
    End Sub


    Public Sub New()
        ' Create Data Adapter
        Dim connectionString As String = WebConfigurationManager.
➥ConnectionStrings("Movies").ConnectionString
        dad = New SqlDataAdapter("SELECT Id,Title,Director FROM Movies",
➥connectionString)
        Dim builder As New SqlCommandBuilder(dad)
        dad.UpdateBatchSize = 0

        Dim context As HttpContext = HttpContext.Current
        If IsNothing(context.Session("MoviesToEdit")) Then
            ' Add data to DataTable
            Dim dtblMovies As New DataTable()
            dad.Fill(dtblMovies)
            dtblMovies.PrimaryKey = New DataColumn() {dtblMovies.Columns("Id")}

            context.Session("MoviesToEdit") = dtblMovies
        End If
    End Sub
End Class
```

The page in Listing 16.31 contains a GridView that is bound to the component in Listing 16.30. The GridView includes a column that indicates whether each row has been changed. The column displays the value of the corresponding DataRow object's RowState property (see Figure 16.16).

LISTING 16.31   ShowMovie9.aspx

```
<%@ Page Language="VB" %>
<%@ Import Namespace="System.Data" %>
<!DOCTYPE html PUBLIC "-//W3C//DTD XHTML 1.0 Transitional//EN"
"http://www.w3.org/TR/xhtml1/DTD/xhtml1-transitional.dtd">
<script runat="server">

    Protected Sub btnReject_Click(ByVal sender As Object, ByVal e As EventArgs)
```

16

LISTING 16.31   Continued

```
        Dim movie As New Movie9()
        movie.RejectChanges()
        grdMovies.DataBind()
    End Sub

    Protected Sub btnAccept_Click(ByVal sender As Object, ByVal e As EventArgs)
        Dim movie As New Movie9()
        movie.AcceptChanges()
        grdMovies.DataBind()
    End Sub
</script>
<html xmlns="http://www.w3.org/1999/xhtml" >
<head id="Head1" runat="server">
    <title>Show Movie9</title>
</head>
<body>
    <form id="form1" runat="server">
    <div>

    <h1>Edit Movies</h1>

    <asp:GridView
        id="grdMovies"
        DataSourceID="srcMovies"
        DataKeyNames="Id"
        AutoGenerateEditButton="true"
        Runat="server">
        <Columns>
        <asp:TemplateField>
        <ItemTemplate>
        <%#CType(Container.DataItem, DataRowView).Row.RowState.ToString()%>
        </ItemTemplate>
        </asp:TemplateField>
        </Columns>
    </asp:GridView>

    <br />

    <asp:Button
        id="btnReject"
        Text="Reject Changes"
        OnClick="btnReject_Click"
        Runat="server" />

    <asp:Button
```

LISTING 16.31   Continued

```
            id="btnAccept"
            Text="Accept Changes"
            OnClick="btnAccept_Click"
            Runat="server" />

    <asp:ObjectDataSource
            id="srcMovies"
            TypeName="Movie9"
            SelectMethod="GetAll"
            UpdateMethod="Update"
            Runat="server" />

    </div>
    </form>
</body>
</html>
```

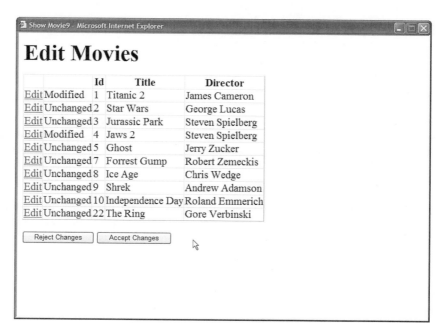

FIGURE 16.16   Tracking data row changes.

If you click the Accept Changes button, all the changes made to the rows in the GridView are sent to the database. If you click the Reject Changes button, all the rows revert to their original values.

Using the `DataView` Object

The `DataView` object represents an in-memory database view. You can use a `DataView` object to create a sortable, filterable view of a `DataTable`.

The `DataView` object supports three important properties:

- `Sort`—Enables you to sort the rows represented by the `DataView`.

- `RowFilter`—Enables you to filter the rows represented by the `DataView`.

- `RowStateFilter`—Enables you to filter the rows represented by the `DataView` according to the row state (for example, `OriginalRows`, `CurrentRows`, `Unchanged`).

The easiest way to create a new `DataView` is to use the `DefaultView` property exposed by the `DataTable` class like this:

```
Dim dataView1 As DataView = dataTable1.DefaultView;
```

The `DefaultView` property returns an unsorted, unfiltered view of the data contained in a `DataTable`.

You also can directly instantiate a new `DataView` object by passing a `DataTable`, filter, sort order, and `DataViewRowState` filter to the `DataView` object's constructor, like this:

```
Dim dataView1 As New DataView(dataTable1, _
    "BoxOfficeTotals > 100000", _
    "Title ASC", _
    DataViewRowState.CurrentRows)
```

This statement creates a new `DataView` from a `DataTable` that represents the Movies database table. The rows are filtered to include only the movies that have a box office total greater than 100,000 dollars. Also, the rows are sorted by the movie title in ascending order. Finally, all the current rows are represented from the `DataTable` (as opposed, for instance, to rows that have been deleted).

The page in Listing 16.30 illustrates one way that you can use a `DataView`. In Listing 16.32, a `DataView` is cached in `Session` state. You can sort the cached `DataView` by clicking on the header links rendered by the `GridView` control (see Figure 16.17).

LISTING 16.32   `ShowDataView.aspx`

```
<%@ Page Language="VB" %>
<%@ Import Namespace="System.Data" %>
<%@ Import Namespace="System.Data.SqlClient" %>
<%@ Import Namespace="System.Web.Configuration" %>
<!DOCTYPE html PUBLIC "-//W3C//DTD XHTML 1.0 Transitional//EN"
   "http://www.w3.org/TR/xhtml1/DTD/xhtml1-transitional.dtd">
<script runat="server">

    Sub Page_Load()
        If IsNothing(Session("MoviesToSort")) Then
```

LISTING 16.32   Continued

```
            Dim connectionString As String =
➡WebConfigurationManager.ConnectionStrings("Movies").ConnectionString
            Dim dad As New SqlDataAdapter("SELECT Id,Title,Director FROM Movies",
➡connectionString)
            Dim dtblMovies As New DataTable()
            dad.Fill(dtblMovies)
            Session("MoviesToSort") = dtblMovies.DefaultView
        End If


        If Not Page.IsPostBack Then
            BindMovies()
        End If
    End Sub


    Private  Sub BindMovies()
        grdMovies.DataSource = Session("MoviesToSort")
        grdMovies.DataBind()
    End Sub


    Protected  Sub grdMovies_Sorting(ByVal sender As Object,
➡ByVal e As GridViewSortEventArgs)
        Dim dvwMovies As DataView = CType(Session("MoviesToSort"), DataView)
        dvwMovies.Sort = e.SortExpression
        BindMovies()
    End Sub
</script>
<html xmlns="http://www.w3.org/1999/xhtml" >
<head id="Head1" runat="server">
    <title>Show DataView</title>
</head>
<body>
    <form id="form1" runat="server">
    <div>

    <asp:GridView
        id="grdMovies"
        AllowSorting="true"
        OnSorting="grdMovies_Sorting"
        Runat="server" />

    </div>
    </form>
</body>
</html>
```

16

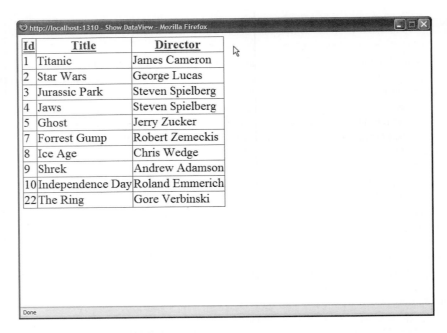

FIGURE 16.17   Sorting a cached `DataView`.

Using the `DataSet` Object

The `DataSet` object represents an in-memory database. A single `DataSet` can contain one or many `DataTable` objects. You can define parent/child relationships between the `DataTable` objects contained in a `DataSet`.

For example, the page in Listing 16.33 contains a `TreeView` control. The `TreeView` displays a list of movie categories and, beneath each movie category, a list of matching movies (see Figure 16.18).

LISTING 16.33   `ShowDataSet.aspx`

```vb
<%@ Page Language="VB" %>
<%@ Import Namespace="System.Data" %>
<%@ Import Namespace="System.Data.SqlClient" %>
<%@ Import Namespace="System.Web.Configuration" %>
<!DOCTYPE html PUBLIC "-//W3C//DTD XHTML 1.0 Transitional//EN"
    "http://www.w3.org/TR/xhtml1/DTD/xhtml1-transitional.dtd">
<script runat="server">

    Private Sub Page_Load()
        If Not Page.IsPostBack Then
            BuildTree()
        End If
```

LISTING 16.33   Continued

```
    End Sub

    Sub BuildTree()
        ' Create Connection
        Dim connectionString As String =
➥WebConfigurationManager.ConnectionStrings("Movies").ConnectionString
        Dim con As New SqlConnection(connectionString)

        ' Create Movie Categories DataAdapter
        Dim dadCategories As New SqlDataAdapter("SELECT Id,Name
➥FROM MovieCategories", con)

        ' Create Movies DataAdapter
        Dim dadMovies As New SqlDataAdapter("SELECT Title,CategoryId
➥FROM Movies", con)

        ' Add the DataTables to the DataSet
        Dim dstMovies As New DataSet()
        Using con
            con.Open()
            dadCategories.Fill(dstMovies, "Categories")
            dadMovies.Fill(dstMovies, "Movies")
        End Using

        ' Add a DataRelation
        dstMovies.Relations.Add("Children",
➥dstMovies.Tables("Categories").Columns("Id"),
➥dstMovies.Tables("Movies").Columns("CategoryId"))

        ' Add the Movie Category nodes
        For Each categoryRow As DataRow In dstMovies.Tables("Categories").Rows
            Dim name As String = CType(categoryRow("Name"), String)
            Dim catNode As New TreeNode(name)
            TreeView1.Nodes.Add(catNode)

            ' Get matching movies
            Dim movieRows() As DataRow = categoryRow.GetChildRows("Children")
            For Each movieRow As DataRow In movieRows
                Dim title As String = CType(movieRow("Title"), String)
                Dim movieNode As New TreeNode(title)
                catNode.ChildNodes.Add(movieNode)
            Next
        Next
    End Sub
```

LISTING 16.33   Continued

```
</script>
<html xmlns="http://www.w3.org/1999/xhtml" >
<head id="Head1" runat="server">
    <title>Show DataSet</title>
</head>
<body>
    <form id="form1" runat="server">
    <div>

    <asp:TreeView
        id="TreeView1"
        Runat="server" />

    </div>
    </form>
</body>
</html>
```

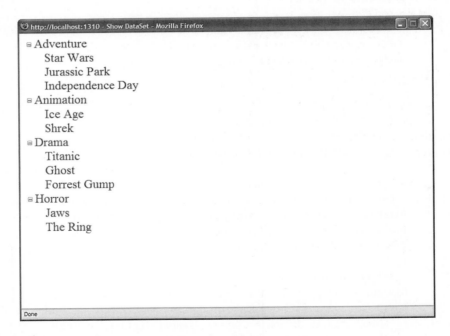

FIGURE 16.18   Building a TreeView from a DataSet.

The TreeView is built programmatically. In the BuildTree() method, a DataSet is created that contains two DataTable objects. The first DataTable represents the MovieCategories database table and the second `DataTable` represents the Movies database table. A parent/child relationship is created between the two `DataTable` objects with the help of a `DataRelation`.

The `DataRelation` is used to get the movies that match each movie category. The `DataRow.GetChildRows()` method is called to retrieve the movies that match a particular movie category.

Executing Asynchronous Database Commands

ADO.NET 2.0 supports asynchronous database commands. Normally, when you execute a database command, the thread that is executing the command must wait until the command is finished before executing any additional code. In other words, normally, when you execute a database command, the thread is blocked.

When you take advantage of asynchronous commands, on the other hand, the database command is executed on another thread so that the current thread can continue performing other work. For example, you can use the current thread to execute yet another database command.

There are two reasons that you might want to use asynchronous database commands when building an ASP.NET page. First, executing multiple database commands simultaneously can significantly improve your application's performance. This is especially true when the database commands are executed against different database servers.

Second, the ASP.NET Framework uses a limited thread pool to service page requests. When the ASP.NET Framework receives a request for a page, it assigns a thread to handle the request. If the ASP.NET Framework runs out of threads, the request is queued until a thread becomes available. If too many threads are queued, then the framework rejects the page request with a 503—Server Too Busy response code.

If you execute a database command asynchronously, then the current thread is released back into the thread pool so that it can be used to service another page request. While the asynchronous database command is executing, the ASP.NET framework can devote its attention to handling other page requests. When the asynchronous command completes, the framework reassigns a thread to the original request and the page finishes executing.

> **NOTE**
>
> You can configure the ASP.NET thread pool with the `httpRuntime` element in the web configuration file. You can modify the `appRequestQueueLimit`, `minFreeThreads`, and `minLocalRequestFreeThreads` attributes to control how many requests the ASP.NET Framework queues before giving up and sending an error.

There are two parts to this task undertaken in this section. A data access component that supports asynchronous ADO.NET methods must be created, as well as an ASP.NET page that executes asynchronously.

Using Asynchronous ADO.NET Methods

ADO.NET 2.0 introduces asynchronous versions of several of its methods. These methods come in pairs: a Begin and End method. For example, the SqlCommand object supports the following asynchronous methods:

- BeginExecuteNonQuery()

- EndExecuteNonQuery()

- BeginExecuteReader()

- EndExecuteReader()

- BeginExecuteXmlReader()

- EndExecuteXmlReader()

The idea is that when you execute the Begin method, the asynchronous task is started on a separate thread. When the method finishes executing, you can use the End method to get the results.

To use these asynchronous methods, you must use a special attribute in your connection string: the Asynchronous Processing=true attribute.

The data access component in Listing 16.34 contains a BeginGetMovies() and EndGetMovies() method that fetches movies from the Movies database table asynchronously. These methods use the ADO.NET BeginExecuteReader() and EndExecuteReader() to fetch a DataReader asynchronously.

LISTING 16.34   App_Code\AsyncDataLayer.vb

```
Imports System
Imports System.Data
Imports System.Data.SqlClient
Imports System.Web.Configuration
Imports System.Collections.Generic


Public Class AsyncDataLayer

    Private Shared ReadOnly _connectionString As String
    Private _cmdMovies As SqlCommand

    Public Function BeginGetMovies(ByVal callback As AsyncCallback,
➥ByVal state As Object) As IAsyncResult
        Dim con As New SqlConnection(_connectionString)
        _cmdMovies = New SqlCommand("SELECT Title,Director FROM Movies", con)
        con.Open()
        Return _cmdMovies.BeginExecuteReader(callback, state,
➥CommandBehavior.CloseConnection)
```

LISTING 16.34   Continued

```
    End Function

    Public Function EndGetMovies(ByVal result As IAsyncResult)
➡As List(Of AsyncDataLayer.Movie)
        Dim results As New List(Of AsyncDataLayer.Movie)()
        Dim reader As SqlDataReader = _cmdMovies.EndExecuteReader(result)
        While reader.Read()
            Dim NewMovie As New AsyncDataLayer.Movie()
            NewMovie.Title = CType(reader("Title"), String)
            NewMovie.Director = CType(reader("Director"), String)
            results.Add(NewMovie)
        End While
        Return results
    End Function

    Shared Sub New()
        _connectionString = WebConfigurationManager.
➡ConnectionStrings("Movies").ConnectionString
        _connectionString &= ";Asynchronous Processing=true"
    End Sub

    Public Class Movie
        Private _title As String
        Private _director As String

        Public Property Title() As String
            Get
                Return _title
            End Get
            Set(ByVal Value As String)
                _title = Value
            End Set
        End Property

        Public Property Director() As String
            Get
                Return _director
            End Get
            Set(ByVal Value As String)
                _director = Value
            End Set
        End Property
    End Class
End Class
```

Using Asynchronous ASP.NET Pages

When you take advantage of asynchronous ADO.NET methods, you must also enable asynchronous ASP.NET page execution. You enable an asynchronous ASP.NET page by adding the following two attributes to a page directive:

```
<%@ Page Async="true" AsyncTimeout="8" %>
```

The first attribute enables asynchronous page execution. The second attribute specifies a timeout value in seconds. The timeout value specifies the amount of time that the page gives a set of asynchronous tasks to complete before the page continues execution.

After you enable asynchronous page execution, you must set up the asychronous tasks and register the tasks with the page. You represent each asynchronous task with an instance of the PageAsyncTask object. You register an asynchronous task for a page by calling the Page.RegisterAsyncTask() method.

For example, the page in Listing 16.35 displays the records from the Movies database table in a GridView control. The database records are retrieved asynchronously from the AsyncDataLayer component created in the previous section.

LISTING 16.35 ShowPageAsyncTask.aspx

```vb
<%@ Page Language="VB" Async="true" AsyncTimeout="5" Trace="true" %>
<%@ Import Namespace="System.Threading" %>
<!DOCTYPE html PUBLIC "-//W3C//DTD XHTML 1.0 Transitional//EN"
  "http://www.w3.org/TR/xhtml1/DTD/xhtml1-transitional.dtd">
<script runat="server">

    Private dataLayer As New AsyncDataLayer()

    Private Sub Page_Load()
        ' Setup asynchronous data execution
        Dim task As PageAsyncTask = New PageAsyncTask(AddressOf BeginGetData,
➥AddressOf EndGetData, AddressOf TimeoutData, Nothing, True)
        Page.RegisterAsyncTask(task)

        ' Fire off asynchronous tasks
        Page.ExecuteRegisteredAsyncTasks()
    End Sub

    Private Function BeginGetData(ByVal sender As Object, ByVal e As EventArgs,
➥ByVal callback As AsyncCallback, ByVal state As Object) As IAsyncResult
        ' Show Page Thread ID
        Trace.Warn("BeginGetData: " & Thread.CurrentThread.GetHashCode())

        ' Execute asynchronous command
        Return dataLayer.BeginGetMovies(callback, state)
```

LISTING 16.35   Continued

```
    End Function

    Private Sub EndGetData(ByVal ar As IAsyncResult)
        ' Show Page Thread ID
        Trace.Warn("EndGetDate: " & Thread.CurrentThread.GetHashCode())

        ' Bind results
        grdMovies.DataSource = dataLayer.EndGetMovies(ar)
        grdMovies.DataBind()
    End Sub

    Private Sub TimeoutData(ByVal ar As IAsyncResult)
        ' Display error message
        lblError.Text = "Could not retrieve data!"
    End Sub

</script>
<html xmlns="http://www.w3.org/1999/xhtml" >
<head id="Head1" runat="server">
    <title>Show Page AsyncTask</title>
</head>
<body>
    <form id="form1" runat="server">
    <div>

    <asp:Label
        id="lblError"
        Runat="server" />

    <asp:GridView
        id="grdMovies"
        Runat="server" />

    </div>
    </form>
</body>
</html>
```

The page in Listing 16.35 creates an instance of the PageAsyncTask object that represents the asynchronous task. Next, the PageAsyncTask object is registered for the page with the Page.RegisterAsyncTask() method. Finally, a call to the Page.ExecuteRegisteredAsyncTasks() method executes the task. (If you don't call this method, any asynchronous tasks registered for the page are executed during the PreRender event automatically.)

The constructor for the `PageAsyncTask` object accepts the following parameters:

- `beginHandler`—The method that executes when the asynchronous task begins.
- `endHandler`—The method that executes when the asynchronous task ends.
- `timoutHandler`—The method that executes when the asynchronous task runs out of time according to the `Page` directive's `AsyncTimeout` attribute.
- `state`—An arbitrary object that represents state information.
- `executeInParallel`—A Boolean value that indicates whether multiple asynchronous tasks should execute at the same time or execute in sequence.

You can create multiple `PageAsyncTask` objects and register them for the same page. When you call the `ExecuteRegisteredAsyncTasks()` method, all the registered tasks are executed.

If an asynchronous task does not complete within the time alloted by the `AsyncTimeout` attribute, then the `timoutHandler` method executes. For example, the page in Listing 16.36 gives the asynchronous tasks 5 seconds to execute. If the database `SELECT` command does not return a record within the 5 seconds, then the `TimeoutData()` method executes.

It is important to understand that the asynchronous task continues to execute even when the task executes longer than the interval of time specified by the `AsyncTimeout` attribute. The `AsyncTimeout` attribute specifies the amount of time that a page is willing to wait before continuing execution. An asynchronous task is not canceled if takes too long.

The page in Listing 16.36 has tracing enabled and it is sprinkled liberally with calls to `Trace.Warn()` so that you can see when different events happen. The `Trace.Warn()` statements writes out the ID of the current `Page` thread. The `Page` thread ID can change between the `BeginGetData()` and `EndGetData()` methods (see Figure 16.19).

You can force the asynchronous task in Listing 16.35 to time out by adding a delay to the database command executed by the `AsyncDataLayer.BeginGetMovies()` method. For example, the following `SELECT` statement waits 15 seconds before returning results:

```
WAITFOR DELAY '0:0:15';SELECT Title,Director FROM Movies
```

If you use this modified `SELECT` statement, then the asychronous task times out and the `TimeoutData()` method executes. The `TimeoutData()` method simply displays a message in a `Label` control.

NOTE

As an alternative to using the `Page.RegisterAsyncTask()` method to register an asynchronous task, you can use the `Page.AddOnPreRenderCompleteAsync()` method. However, this latter method does not provide you with as many options.

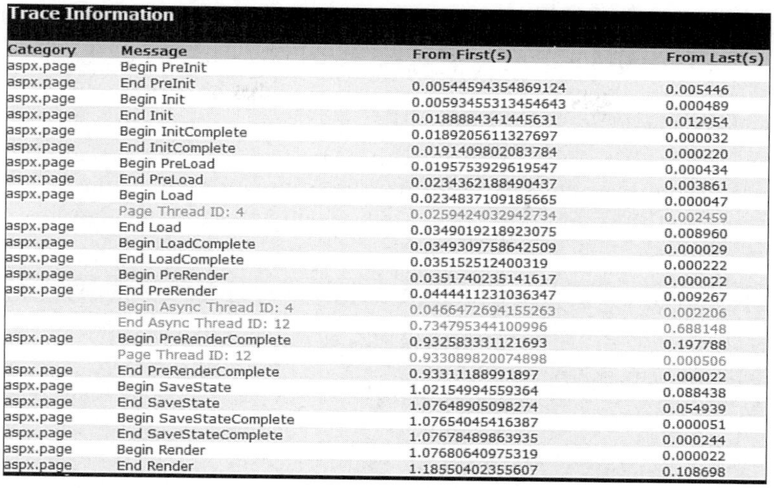

Category	Message	From First(s)	From Last(s)
aspx.page	Begin PreInit		
aspx.page	End PreInit	0.00544594354869124	0.005446
aspx.page	Begin Init	0.00593455313454643	0.000489
aspx.page	End Init	0.0188884341445631	0.012954
aspx.page	Begin InitComplete	0.0189205611327697	0.000032
aspx.page	End InitComplete	0.0191409802083784	0.000220
aspx.page	Begin PreLoad	0.0195753929619547	0.000434
aspx.page	End PreLoad	0.0234362188490437	0.003861
aspx.page	Begin Load	0.0234837109185665	0.000047
	Page Thread ID: 4	0.025942403294273	0.002459
aspx.page	End Load	0.0349019218923075	0.008960
aspx.page	Begin LoadComplete	0.0349309758642509	0.000029
aspx.page	End LoadComplete	0.035152512400319	0.000222
aspx.page	Begin PreRender	0.0351740235141617	0.000022
aspx.page	End PreRender	0.0444411231036347	0.009267
	Begin Async Thread ID: 4	0.0466472694155263	0.002206
	End Async Thread ID: 12	0.734795344100996	0.688148
aspx.page	Begin PreRenderComplete	0.932583331121693	0.197788
	Page Thread ID: 12	0.933089820074898	0.000506
aspx.page	End PreRenderComplete	0.93311188991897	0.000022
aspx.page	Begin SaveState	1.02154994559364	0.088438
aspx.page	End SaveState	1.07648905098274	0.054939
aspx.page	Begin SaveStateComplete	1.07654045416387	0.000051
aspx.page	End SaveStateComplete	1.07678489863935	0.000244
aspx.page	Begin Render	1.07680640975319	0.000022
aspx.page	End Render	1.18550402355607	0.108698

FIGURE 16.19   Trace information for a page executed asynchronously.

Building Database Objects with the .NET Framework

Microsoft SQL Server 2005 (including Microsoft SQL Server Express) supports building database objects with the .NET Framework. For example, you can create user-defined types, stored procedures, user-defined functions, and triggers written with the Visual Basic .NET or C# programming language.

The SQL language is optimized for retrieving database records. However, it is a crazy language that doesn't look like any other computer language on earth. Doing basic string parsing with SQL, for example, is a painful experience. Doing complex logic in a stored procedure is next to impossible (although many people do it).

When you work in the .NET Framework, on the other hand, you have access to thousands of classes. You can perform complex string matching and manipulation by using the Regular expression classes. You can implement business logic, no matter how complex.

By taking advantage of the .NET framework when writing database objects, you no longer have to struggle with the SQL language when implementing your business logic. In this section, you learn how to build both user-defined types and stored procedures by using the .NET Framework.

Enabling CLR Integration

By default, support for building database objects with the .NET Framework is disabled. You must enable CLR integration by executing the following SQL Server command:

```
sp_configure 'clr enabled', 1
RECONFIGURE
```

When using SQL Express, you can execute these two commands by right-clicking a database in the Database Explorer window and selecting the New Query menu option. Enter the following string:

```
sp_configure 'clr enabled', 1; RECONFIGURE
```

Select Query Designer, Execute SQL to execute the commands (see Figure 16.20). You'll receive warnings that the query can't be parsed, which you can safely ignore.

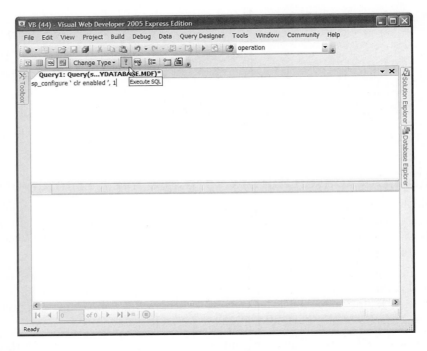

FIGURE 16.20   Executing a database query in Visual Web Developer.

Creating User-Defined Types with the .NET Framework

You can create a new user-defined type by creating either a .NET class or .NET structure. After you create a user-defined type, you can use it in exactly the same way as the built-in SQL types such as the Int, NVarChar, or Decimal types. For example, you can create a new type and use the type to define a column in a database table.

To create a user-defined type with the .NET Framework, you must complete each of the following steps:

1. Create an assembly that contains the new type.

2. Register the assembly with SQL Server.

3. Create a type based on the assembly.

We'll go through each of these steps and walk through the process of creating a new user-defined type. We'll create a new user-defined type named DBMovie. The DBMovie type represents information about a particular movie. The type includes properties for the Title, Director, and BoxOfficeTotals for the movie.

After we create the DBMovie type, we can use the new type to define a column in a database table. Next, we write ADO.NET code that inserts and retrieves DBMovie objects from the database.

Creating the User-Defined Type Assembly

You can create a new user-defined type by creating either a class or a structure. We create the DBMovie type by creating a new .NET class.

When creating a class that will be used as a user-defined type, you must meet certain requirements:

- The class must be decorated with a SqlUserDefinedType attribute.

- The class must be able to equal NULL.

- The class must be serializable to/from a byte array.

- The class must be serialisable to/from a string.

If you plan to use a class as a user-defined type, then you must add the SqlUserDefinedType attribute to the class. This attribute supports the following properties:

- Format—Enables you to specify how a user-defined type is serialized in SQL Server. Possible values are Native and UserDefined.

- IsByteOrdered—Enables you to cause the user-defined type to be ordered in the same way as its byte representation.

- IsFixedLength—Enables you to specify that all instances of this type have the same length.

- MaxByteSize—Enables you to specify the maximum size of the user-defined type in bytes.

- Name—Enables you to specify a name for the user-defined type.

- ValidationMethodName—Enables you to specify the name of a method that is called to verify whether a user-defined type is valid (useful when retrieving a user-defined type from an untrusted source).

The most important of these properties is the Format property. You use this property to specify how the user-defined type is serialized. The easiest option is to pick Native. In that case, SQL Server handles all the serialization issues and you don't need to perform any additional work.

16

Unfortunately, you can take advantage of native serialization only for simple classes. If your class exposes a non-value type property such as a `String`, then you can't use native serialization.

Because the `DBMovie` class includes a `Title` and `Director` property, it's necessary to use `UserDefined` serialization. This means that it's also necessary to implement the `IBinarySerialize` interface to specify how the class gets serialized.

The `DBMovie` class is contained in Listing 16.36.

LISTING 16.36   DBMovie.vb

```vb
Imports System
Imports System.Text
Imports Microsoft.SqlServer.Server
Imports System.Data.SqlTypes
Imports System.Runtime.InteropServices
Imports System.IO

<SqlUserDefinedType(Format.UserDefined, MaxByteSize:=512, IsByteOrdered:=True)> _
Public Class DBMovie
    Implements INullable
    Implements IBinarySerialize

    Private _isNull As Boolean
    Private _title As String
    Private _director As String
    Private _boxOfficeTotals As Decimal

    Public ReadOnly Property IsNull() As Boolean Implements INullable.IsNull
        Get
            Return _isNull
        End Get
    End Property

    Public Shared ReadOnly Property Null() As DBMovie
        Get
            Dim movie As New DBMovie()
            movie._isNull = True
            Return movie
        End Get
    End Property

    Public Property Title() As String
        Get
            Return _title
        End Get
```

LISTING 16.36   Continued

```
        Set(ByVal Value As String)
            _title = Value
        End Set
    End Property



    Public Property Director() As String
        Get
            Return _director
        End Get
        Set(ByVal Value As String)
            _director = Value
        End Set
    End Property

    <SqlFacet(Precision:=38, Scale:=2)> _
    Public Property BoxOfficeTotals() As Decimal
        Get
            Return _boxOfficeTotals
        End Get
        Set(ByVal Value As Decimal)
            _boxOfficeTotals = Value
        End Set
    End Property



    <SqlMethod(OnNullCall:=False)> _
    Public Shared Function Parse(ByVal s As SqlString) As DBMovie
        If (s.IsNull) Then
            Return Null
        End If
        Dim movie As New DBMovie()
        Dim parts() As String = s.Value.Split(New Char() {","c})
        movie.Title = parts(0)
        movie.Director = parts(1)
        movie.BoxOfficeTotals = Decimal.Parse(parts(2))
        Return movie
    End Function

    Public Overrides Function ToString() As String
        If Me.IsNull Then
            Return "NULL"
        End If
        Dim builder As New StringBuilder()
```

LISTING 16.36   Continued

```
        builder.Append(_title)
        builder.Append(",")
        builder.Append(_director)
        builder.Append(",")
        builder.Append(_boxOfficeTotals.ToString())
        Return builder.ToString()
    End Function

    Public Sub Write(ByVal w As BinaryWriter) Implements IBinarySerialize.Write
        w.Write(_title)
        w.Write(_director)
        w.Write(_boxOfficeTotals)
    End Sub

    Public Sub Read(ByVal r As BinaryReader) Implements IBinarySerialize.Read
        _title = r.ReadString()
        _director = r.ReadString()
        _boxOfficeTotals = r.ReadDecimal()
    End Sub

    Public Sub New()
    End Sub
End Class
```

The class in Listing 16.36 exposes three properties: the movie `Title`, `Director`, and `BoxOfficeTotals` properties. Notice that the `BoxOfficeTotals` property is decorated with a `SqlFacet` attribute that indicates the precision and scale of the property value. You must include this attribute if you want to perform SQL queries that use comparison operators with this property.

The class in Listing 16.36 also includes both an `IsNull` and `Null` property. SQL Server uses a three-valued logic (`True`,`False`,`Null`). All SQL Server types must be nullable.

The `DBMovie` class also includes both a `Parse()` and a `ToString()` method. These methods are required for converting the `DBMovie` class back and forth to a string representation.

Finally, the `DBMovie` class includes both a `Write()` and `Read()` method. These methods are required by the `IBinarySerialize` interface. The `Write()` method serializes the class. The `Read()` method deserializes the class. These methods must be implemented because the class uses `UserDefined` serialization.

You need to compile the `DBMovie` class into a separate assembly (`.dll` file). After you create (and debug) the class, move the class from your App_Code folder to another folder in your application, such as the root folder. Next, open the SDK Command prompt and execute the following command:

```
vbc /t:library DBMovie.vb
```

This command uses the Visual Basic command-line compiler to compile the DBMovie class into an assembly.

Registering the User-Defined Type Assembly with SQL Server

After you create the assembly that contains your user-defined type, you must register the assembly in SQL Server. You can register the DBMovie assembly by executing the following command:

```
CREATE ASSEMBLY DBMovie
FROM 'C:\DBMovie.dll'
```

You need to provide the right path for the DBMovie.dll file on your hard drive.

After you complete this step, the assembly is added to Microsoft SQL Server. When using Visual Web Developer, you can see the assembly by expanding the Assemblies folder in the Database Explorer window. Alternatively, you can view a list of all the assemblies installed on SQL Server by executing the following query:

```
SELECT * FROM sys.assemblies
```

You can drop any assembly by executing the DROP Assembly command. For example, the following command removes the DBMovie assembly from SQL Server:

```
DROP Assembly DBMovie
```

Creating the User-Defined Type

After you have loaded the DBMovie assembly, you can create a new user-defined type from the assembly. Execute the following command:

```
CREATE TYPE dbo.DBMovie EXTERNAL NAME DBMovie.DBMovie
```

If you need to delete the type, you can execute the following command:

```
DROP TYPE DBMovie
```

After you have added the type, you can use it just like any other SQL Server native type. For example, you can create a new database table with the following command:

```
CREATE TABLE DBMovies(Id INT IDENTITY, Movie DBMovie)
```

You can insert a new record into this table with the following command:

```
INSERT DBMovies (Movie)
VALUES ('Star Wars,George Lucas,12.34')
```

Finally, you can perform queries against the table with queries like the following:

```
SELECT Id, Movie FROM DBMovies WHERE  Movie.BoxOfficeTotals > 13.23
SELECT  MAX(Movie.BoxOfficeTotals) FROM DBMovies
SELECT  Movie FROM DBMovies WHERE Movie.Director LIKE 'g%'
```

I find the fact that you can execute queries like this truly amazing.

Building a Data Access Layer with a User-Defined Type

In this final section, let's actually do something with our new user-defined type. We'll create a new data access component that uses the DBMovie class and an ASP.NET page that interfaces with the component.

Before we can do anything with the DBMovie type, we need to add a reference to the DBMovie.dll assembly to our application. In Visual Web Developer, select the menu option Website, Add Reference, and browse to the DBMovie.dll. Alternatively, you can create an application root Bin folder and copy the DBMovie.dll into the Bin folder.

Our new data access component is contained in Listing 16.37.

LISTING 16.37   App_Code\DBDataLayer.vb

```
Imports System
Imports System.Data
Imports System.Data.SqlClient
Imports System.Web.Configuration
Imports System.Collections.Generic


Public Class DBDataLayer
    Private Shared ReadOnly _connectionString As String

    Public Function GetAll() As List(Of DBMovie)
        Dim results As New List(Of DBMovie)()
        Dim con As New SqlConnection(_connectionString)
        Dim cmd As New SqlCommand("SELECT Movie FROM DBMovies", con)
        Using con
            con.Open()
            Dim reader As SqlDataReader = cmd.ExecuteReader()
            While reader.Read()
                Dim NewMovie As DBMovie = CType(reader("Movie"), DBMovie)
                results.Add(NewMovie)
            End While
        End Using
        Return results
    End Function
```

LISTING 16.37   Continued

```
    Public Sub Insert(ByVal movieToAdd As DBMovie)
        Dim con As New SqlConnection(_connectionString)
        Dim cmd As New SqlCommand("INSERT DBMovies (Movie) VALUES (@Movie)", con)
        cmd.Parameters.Add("@Movie", SqlDbType.Udt)
        cmd.Parameters("@Movie").UdtTypeName = "DBMovie"
        cmd.Parameters("@Movie").Value = movieToAdd
        Using con
            con.Open()
            cmd.ExecuteNonQuery()
        End Using
    End Sub


    Shared Sub New()
        _connectionString = WebConfigurationManager.
➥ConnectionStrings("Movies").ConnectionString
    End Sub
End Class
```

The component in Listing 16.37 contains two methods: `GetAll()` and `Insert()`. The `GetAll()` method retrieves all the `Movie` objects from the DBMovies database table. Notice that you can cast the object represented by the `DataReader` directly to a `DBMovie`.

The `Insert()` method adds a new `DBMovie` to the DBMovies database table. The method creates a normal ADO.NET `Command` object. However, notice that a special parameter is added to the command that represents the `DBMovie` object.

When you create a parameter that represents a user-defined type, you must specify a `UdtTypeName` property that represents the name of the user-defined type. In Listing 16.38, the value `DBMovie` is assigned to the `UdtTypeName` property. When the command executes, a new `DBMovie` object is added to the DBMovies database table.

The page in Listing 16.38 contains a `GridView`, `DetailsView`, and `ObjectDataSource` control. The `GridView` displays all the movies from the DBMovies database table. The `DetailsView` control enables you to insert a new `DBMovie` into the database (see Figure 16.21).

LISTING 16.38   ShowDBDataLayer.aspx

```
<%@ Page Language="VB" %>
<!DOCTYPE html PUBLIC "-//W3C//DTD XHTML 1.0 Transitional//EN"
  "http://www.w3.org/TR/xhtml1/DTD/xhtml1-transitional.dtd">
<html xmlns="http://www.w3.org/1999/xhtml" >
<head id="Head1" runat="server">
    <title>Show DBDataLayer</title>
</head>
```

16

LISTING 16.38   Continued

```
<body>
    <form id="form1" runat="server">
    <div>

    <asp:GridView
        id="grdMovies"
        DataSourceID="srcMovies"
        Runat="server" />

    <br />

    <fieldset>
    <legend>Add Movie</legend>
    <asp:DetailsView
        id="dtlMovie"
        DataSourceID="srcMovies"
        DefaultMode="Insert"
        AutoGenerateInsertButton="true"
        AutoGenerateRows="false"
        Runat="server">
        <Fields>
        <asp:BoundField DataField="Title" HeaderText="Title" />
        <asp:BoundField DataField="Director" HeaderText="Director" />
        <asp:BoundField DataField="BoxOfficeTotals"
            HeaderText="Box Office Totals" />
        </Fields>
    </asp:DetailsView>
    </fieldset>

    <asp:ObjectDataSource
        id="srcMovies"
        TypeName="DBDataLayer"
        DataObjectTypeName="DBMovie"
        SelectMethod="GetAll"
        InsertMethod="Insert"
        Runat="server" />

    </div>
    </form>
</body>
</html>
```

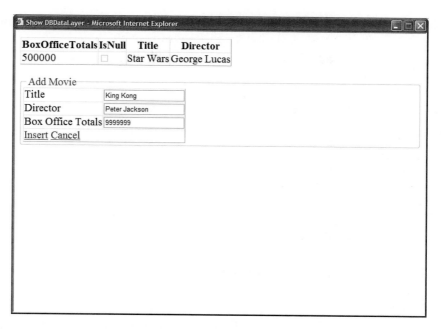

FIGURE 16.21 Displaying and inserting `DBMovie` objects.

Creating Stored Procedures with the .NET Framework

You can use the .NET Framework to build a SQL stored procedure by mapping a stored procedure to a method defined in a class. You must complete the following steps:

- Create an assembly that contains the stored procedure method.
- Register the assembly with SQL Server.
- Create a stored procedure based on the assembly.

In this section, we create two stored procedures with the .NET Framework. The first stored procedure, named `GetRandomRow()`, randomly returns a single row from a database table. The second stored procedure, `GetRandomRows()`, randomly returns a set of rows from a database table.

Creating the Stored Procedure Assembly

Creating a stored procedure with the .NET Framework is easy. All you need to do is decorate a method with the `SqlProcedure` attribute.

The method used for the stored procedure must satisfy two requirements. The method must be a shared (static) method. Furthermore, the method must be implemented either as a subroutine or as a function that returns an integer value.

Within your method, you can take advantage of the `SqlPipe` class to send results back to your application. The `SqlPipe` class supports the following methods:

- `Send()`—Enables you to send a `DataReader`, single-row resultset, or string.
- `ExecuteAndSend()`—Enables you to execute a `SqlCommand` and send the results.
- `SendResultsStart()`—Enables you to initiate the sending of a resultset.
- `SendResultsRow()`—Enables you to send a single row of a resultset.
- `SendResultsEnd()`—Enables you to end the sending of a resultset.

Within the method used for creating the stored procedure, you can use ADO.NET objects such as the `SqlCommand`, `SqlDataReader`, and `SqlDataAdapter` objects in the normal way. However, rather than connect to the database by using a normal connection string, you can create something called a *context connection*. A context connection enables you to connect to the same database server as the stored procedure without authenticating.

Here's how you can initialize a SqlConnection to use a context connection:

```
Dim con As New SqlConnection("context connection=true")
```

Notice that you don't specify credentials or the location of the database in the connection string. Remember that the method actually executes within SQL Server. Therefore, you don't need to connect to SQL Server in the normal way.

The class in Listing 16.39 contains two methods named `GetRandomRow()` and `GetRandomRows()`. Both methods use a `SqlDataAdapter` to fill a `DataTable` with the contents of the Movies database table. The `GetRandomRow()` method grabs a single row from the `DataTable` and sends it back to the client. The `GetRandomRows()` method sends multiple rows back to the client.

LISTING 16.39   RandomRows.vb

```
Imports System
Imports System.Data
Imports System.Data.SqlClient
Imports Microsoft.SqlServer.Server

Public Class RandomRows
    <SqlProcedure()> _
    Public Shared Sub GetRandomRow()
        ' Dump all records from Movies into a DataTable
        Dim dad As New SqlDataAdapter("SELECT Id,Title FROM Movies",
➥"context connection=true")
        Dim dtblMovies As New DataTable()
        dad.Fill(dtblMovies)
```

LISTING 16.39   Continued

```vb
        ' Grab a random row
        Dim rnd As New Random()
        Dim ranRow As DataRow = dtblMovies.Rows(rnd.Next(dtblMovies.Rows.Count))

        ' Build a SqlDataRecord that represents the row
        Dim result As New SqlDataRecord( _
                New SqlMetaData("Id", SqlDbType.Int), _
                New SqlMetaData("Title", SqlDbType.NVarChar, 100))
        result.SetSqlInt32(0, CType(ranRow("Id"), Integer))
        result.SetSqlString(1, CType(ranRow("Title"), String))

        ' Send result
        SqlContext.Pipe.Send(result)
    End Sub

    <SqlProcedure> _
    Public Shared Sub GetRandomRows(ByVal rowsToReturn As Integer)
        ' Dump all records from Movies into a DataTable
        Dim dad As New SqlDataAdapter("SELECT Id,Title FROM Movies",
➥"context connection=true")
        Dim dtblMovies As New DataTable()
        dad.Fill(dtblMovies)

        ' Send start record
        Dim result As New SqlDataRecord( _
                New SqlMetaData("Id", SqlDbType.Int), _
                New SqlMetaData("Title", SqlDbType.NVarChar, 100))
        SqlContext.Pipe.SendResultsStart(result)

        Dim rnd As Random = New Random()
        For i As integer = 0 To rowsToReturn - 1
            ' Grab a random row
            Dim ranRow As DataRow = dtblMovies.Rows(rnd.Next(
➥dtblMovies.Rows.Count))

            ' Set the record
            result.SetSqlInt32(0, CType(ranRow("Id"), Integer))
            result.SetSqlString(1, CType(ranRow("Title"), String))

            ' Send record
            SqlContext.Pipe.SendResultsRow(result)
        Next
```

16

LISTING 16.39   Continued

```
         ' Send end record
         SqlContext.Pipe.SendResultsEnd()
     End Sub
End Class
```

You need to compile the `RandomRows` class into a separate assembly (`.dll` file). After you create (and debug) the class, move the class from your App_Code folder to another folder in your application, such as the root folder. Next, open the SDK Command prompt and execute the following command:

```
vbc /t:library RandomRows.vb
```

This command uses the Visual Basic command-line compiler to compile the `RandomRows` class into an assembly.

Registering the Stored Procedure Assembly with SQL Server

After you compile the `RandomRows` assembly, you are ready to deploy the assembly to SQL Server. You can load the assembly into SQL Server by executing the following command:

```
CREATE ASSEMBLY RandomRows
FROM 'C:\RandomRows.dll'
```

You need to supply the proper path to the `RandomRows.dll` assembly on your hard drive.

If you need to remove the assembly, you can execute the following command:

```
DROP Assembly RandomRows
```

Creating the Stored Procedures

Now that the assembly is loaded, you can create two stored procedures that correspond to the two methods defined in the assembly. Execute the following two SQL commands:

```
CREATE PROCEDURE GetRandomRow AS
EXTERNAL NAME RandomRows.RandomRows.GetRandomRow

CREATE PROCEDURE GetRandomRows(@rowsToReturn Int) AS
EXTERNAL NAME RandomRows.RandomRows.GetRandomRows
```

After you execute these two commands, you'll have two new stored procedures named `GetRandomRow` and `GetRandomRows`. You can treat these stored procedures just like normal stored procedures. For example, executing the following command displays three random movies from the Movies database:

```
GetRandomRows 3
```

If you need to delete these stored procedures, you can execute the following two commands:

```
DROP PROCEDURE GetRandomRow
DROP PROCEDURE GetRandomRows
```

Executing a .NET Stored Procedure from an ASP.NET Page

After the two stored procedures have been created, you can use the stored procedures with an ASP.NET page. For example, the component in Listing 16.40 contains two methods that call the two stored procedures.

LISTING 16.40   App_Code\RandomDataLayer.vb

```
Imports System
Imports System.Data
Imports System.Data.SqlClient
Imports System.Web.Configuration
Imports System.Collections.Generic


Public Class RandomDataLayer
    Private Shared ReadOnly _connectionString As String

    Public Function GetRandomMovies() As List(Of String)
        Dim results As New List(Of String)()
        Dim con As New SqlConnection(_connectionString)
        Dim cmd As New SqlCommand("GetRandomRows", con)
        cmd.CommandType = CommandType.StoredProcedure
        cmd.Parameters.AddWithValue("@rowsToReturn", 5)
        Using con
            con.Open()
            Dim reader As SqlDataReader = cmd.ExecuteReader()
            While reader.Read()
                results.Add(CType(reader("Title"), String))
            End While
        End Using
        Return results
    End Function



    Public Shared Function GetRandomMovie() As String
        Dim result As String = String.Empty
        Dim con As New SqlConnection(_connectionString)
        Dim cmd As New SqlCommand("GetRandomRow", con)
        cmd.CommandType = CommandType.StoredProcedure
        Using con
            con.Open()
            Dim reader As SqlDataReader = cmd.ExecuteReader()
            If reader.Read() Then
```

LISTING 16.40   Continued

```
            result = CType(reader("Title"), String)
        End If
    End Using
    Return result
End Function

Shared Sub New()
    _connectionString = WebConfigurationManager.
➥ConnectionStrings("Movies").ConnectionString
    End Sub

End Class
```

In Listing 16.40, the `GetRandomRow` and `GetRandomRows` stored procedures are executed with the help of `SqlCommand` objects.

The page in Listing 16.41 contains a `GridView` and `ObjectDataSource` control. The `ObjectDataSource` control represents the `RandomDataLayer` component. When you request the page, a single random movie title is displayed in a `Label` control. Furthermore, a list of five random movie titles is displayed in the `GridView` control (see Figure 16.22).

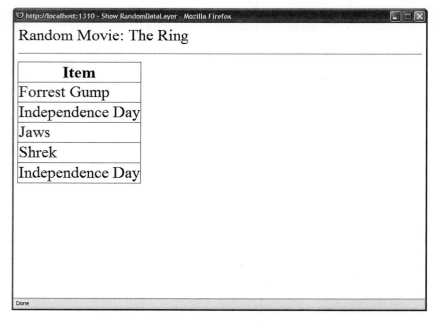

FIGURE 16.22   Calling a .NET stored procedure from an ASP.NET page.

LISTING 16.41   ShowRandomDataLayer.aspx

```
<%@ Page Language="VB" %>
<!DOCTYPE html PUBLIC "-//W3C//DTD XHTML 1.0 Transitional//EN"
"http://www.w3.org/TR/xhtml1/DTD/xhtml1-transitional.dtd">
<script runat="server">

    Sub Page_Load()
        lblRandomMovie.Text = RandomDataLayer.GetRandomMovie()
    End Sub
</script>
<html xmlns="http://www.w3.org/1999/xhtml" >
<head id="Head1" runat="server">
    <title>Show RandomDataLayer</title>
</head>
<body>
    <form id="form1" runat="server">
    <div>

    Random Movie:
    <asp:Label
        id="lblRandomMovie"
        Runat="server" />

    <hr />

    <asp:GridView
        id="grdMovies"
        DataSourceID="srcMovies"
        Runat="server" />
    <asp:ObjectDataSource
        id="srcMovies"
        TypeName="RandomDataLayer"
        SelectMethod="GetRandomMovies"
        Runat="server" />


    </div>
    </form>
</body>
</html>
```

16

Summary

This chapter provided you with an overview of ADO.NET. It described how you can use ADO.NET to represent database data with both a connected and disconnected model of data access.

In the first part of this chapter, you learned how to use the Connection, Command, and DataReader objects to connect to a database, execute commands, and represent the results of a database query. You learned how to retrieve provider statistics such as command execution times. You also learned how to represent stored procedures with the Command object. Finally, you learned how to work with multiple active resultsets (MARS).

In the second part of this chapter, you learned how to work with the DataAdapter, DataTable, DataView, and DataSet objects. You learned how you can perform batch updates with the DataAdapter object. You also learned how to use the DataTable object to represent and edit database rows.

Next, you learned how to improve the data access performance of your ASP.NET pages by executing asynchronous database commands within asynchronous ASP.NET pages.

Finally, you got a chance to tackle the advanced topic of building database objects with the .NET Framework. You learned how you can use the .NET Framework to build both user-defined types and stored procedures. For example, you learned how to insert and select a custom class from a database table by creating a user-defined type with the .NET Framework.

PART V

Site Navigation

IN THIS PART

CHAPTER **17**

Using the Navigation Controls

In this chapter, you learn how to use the SiteMapPath, Menu, and TreeView controls. All three of these controls can be used to enable users to navigate your website. Furthermore, the Menu and TreeView controls can be used independently of website navigation. You can bind these two controls to other data sources such as XML documents or database data.

This chapter explores different methods of binding the Menu and TreeView controls to different data sources and shows you how to format the rendered output of both of these controls. You also learn how to take advantage of AJAX when working with the TreeView control.

In the final section of this chapter, we build a SqlHierarchicalDataSource control, which enables you to bind controls such as the TreeView and Menu controls to hierarchical database data.

Understanding Site Maps

Before you learn about the navigation controls, you first need to understand Site Maps. All three navigation controls use Site Maps to retrieve navigation information. A Site Map enables you to represent the navigational relationships between the pages in an application, independent of the actual physical relationship between pages as stored in the file system.

Site Maps use the provider model. In the next chapter, you learn how to create custom Site Map providers to store Site Maps in custom data stores such as database tables. The examples in this chapter take advantage of the default XML Site Map provider, which enables you to store a Site Map in an XML file.

By default, the navigation controls assume the existence of an XML file named Web.sitemap, which is located in the root of your application.

For example, Listing 17.1 contains a simple Site Map.

LISTING 17.1   Web.sitemap

```xml
<?xml version="1.0" encoding="utf-8" ?>
<siteMap xmlns="http://schemas.microsoft.com/AspNet/SiteMap-File-1.0" >

<siteMapNode
  url="~/Default.aspx"
  title="Home"
  description="The home page of the Website">

  <!-- Product Nodes -->
  <siteMapNode
    title="Products"
    description="Website products">
    <siteMapNode
      url="~/Products/FirstProduct.aspx"
      title="First Product"
      description="The first product" />
    <siteMapNode
      url="~/Products/SecondProduct.aspx"
      title="Second Product"
      description="The second product" />
  </siteMapNode>

  <!-- Services Nodes -->
  <siteMapNode
    title="Services"
    description="Website services">
    <siteMapNode
      url="~/Service/FirstService.aspx"
      title="First Service"
      description="The first service" />
    <siteMapNode
      url="~/Products/SecondService.aspx"
      title="Second Service"
      description="The second service" />
  </siteMapNode>
  </siteMapNode>

</siteMapNode>

</siteMap>
```

A Site Map file contains `<siteMapNode>` elements. There can be only one top-level node. In the case of Listing 17.1, the top-level node represents the website's homepage.

A `<siteMapNode>` supports three main attributes:

- `title`—A brief title that you want to associate with a node.
- `description`—A longer description that you want to associate with a node.
- `url`—A URL that points to a page or other resource.

Notice that the `url` attribute is not required. Both the Products and Services nodes do not include a `url` attribute because these nodes do not represent pages to which you can navigate.

Each `<siteMapNode>` can contain any number of child nodes. In Listing 17.1, both the Products and Services nodes include two child nodes.

The Site Map in Listing 17.1 represents a website that has the following folder and page structure:

```
Default.aspx
Products
  FirstProduct.aspx
  SecondProduct.aspx
Services
  FirstService.aspx
  SecondService.aspx
```

The navigational structure of a website as represented by a Site Map is not required to have any relationship to the navigational structure of a website as stored in the file system. You can create any relationship between the nodes in a Site Map that you want.

Using the `SiteMapPath` Control

The `SiteMapPath` control enables you to navigate easily to any parent page of the current page. It displays the standard bread crumb trail that you see on many popular websites (see Figure 17.1).

You can use the `SiteMapPath` control simply by declaring the control in a page. The control automatically uses the `Web.sitemap` file located in the root of your application. For example, the page in Listing 17.2 includes the `SiteMapPath` control (see Figure 17.2).

17

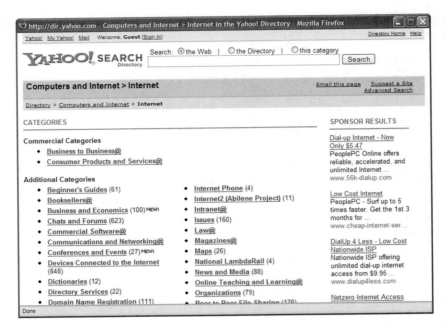

FIGURE 17.1   Bread crumb trail at Yahoo.com.

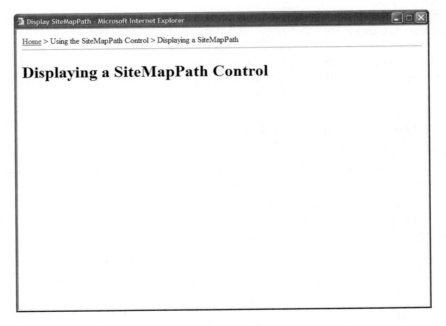

FIGURE 17.2   Displaying the `SiteMapPath` control.

LISTING 17.2   UsingSiteMapPath/DisplaySiteMapPath.aspx

```
<%@ Page Language="VB" %>
<!DOCTYPE html PUBLIC "-//W3C//DTD XHTML 1.1//EN"
 "http://www.w3.org/TR/xhtml11/DTD/xhtml11.dtd">
<html xmlns="http://www.w3.org/1999/xhtml" >
<head id="Head1" runat="server">
    <title>Display SiteMapPath</title>
</head>
<body>
    <form id="form1" runat="server">
    <div>

    <asp:SiteMapPath
        id="SiteMapPath1"
        Runat="server" />

    <hr />

    <h1>Displaying a SiteMapPath Control</h1>

    </div>
    </form>
</body>
</html>
```

Notice that you can click the Home link rendered by the `SiteMapPath` control to navigate to the website's home page.

The `SiteMapPath` uses both the `title` and `description` attributes from the `<siteMapNode>` elements contained in the `Web.sitemap` file. The `title` attribute is used for the node (link) text, and the `description` attribute is used for the node tool tip.

> **NOTE**
>
> Typically, you do not add a `SiteMapPath` control to individual pages in your website. If you add a `SiteMapPath` control to a Master Page, then you can display the `SiteMapPath` control automatically on every page. To learn more about Master Pages, see Chapter 5, "Designing Websites with Master Pages."

The `SiteMapPath` control supports the following properties:

- `ParentLevelsDisplay`—Enables you to limit the number of parent nodes displayed. By default, a `SiteMapPath` control displays all the parent nodes.

17

- PathDirection—Enables you to reverse the order of the links displayed by the SiteMapPath control. Possible values are RootToCurrent (the default) or CurrentToRoot.

- PathSeparator—Enables you to specify the character used to separate the nodes displayed by the SiteMapPath control. The default value is >.

- RenderCurrentNodeAsLink—Enables you to render the SiteMapPath node that represents the current page as a link. By default, the current node is not rendered as a link.

- ShowToolTips—Enables you to disable the display of tool tips.

- SiteMapProvider—Enables you to specify the name of an alternate Site Map provider to use with the SiteMapPath control.

- SkipLinkText—Enables you to specify more specific text for skipping the links displayed by the SiteMapPath control. The default value for this property is Skip Navigation Links.

WEB STANDARDS NOTE

All the navigation controls automatically render a skip navigation link to meet accessibility requirements. The skip navigation link is read by a screen reader, but it is not displayed in a normal browser.

If you are interacting with a web page through a screen reader, you don't want to hear the list of navigation links each and every time you open a page. (It is the equivalent of listening to a phone menu every time you open a page.) The skip navigation link enables users of screen readers to skip the repetitive reading of links.

Formatting the SiteMapPath Control

You can use either styles or templates to format the SiteMapPath control.

The control supports the following Style objects:

- CurrentNodeStyle—Formats the SiteMapPath node that represents the current page.

- NodeStyle—Formats every node rendered by the SiteMapPath control.

- PathSeparatorStyle—Formats the text displayed between each SiteMapPath node.

- RootNodeStyle—Formats the root (first) node rendered by the SiteMapPath control.

For example, the page in Listing 17.3 takes advantage of all four Style properties to modify the default appearance of the SiteMapPath control (see Figure 17.3).

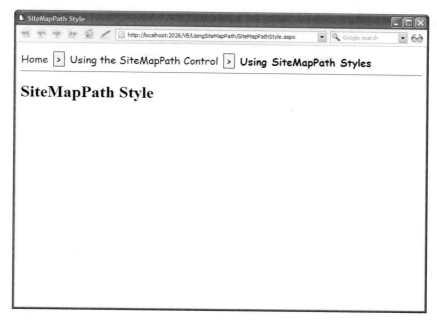

FIGURE 17.3   Using styles with the SiteMapPath control.

LISTING 17.3   UsingSiteMapPath/SiteMapPathStyle.aspx

```
<%@ Page Language="VB" %>
<!DOCTYPE html PUBLIC "-//W3C//DTD XHTML 1.1//EN"
    "http://www.w3.org/TR/xhtml11/DTD/xhtml11.dtd">
<html xmlns="http://www.w3.org/1999/xhtml" >
<head id="Head1" runat="server">
    <style type="text/css">
        .siteMapPath
        {
            font:20px Comic Sans MS,Serif;
        }
        .currentNodeStyle
        {
            font-weight:bold;
        }
        .nodeStyle
        {
            text-decoration:none;
        }
        .pathSeparatorStyle
        {
            background-color:yellow;
```

17

LISTING 17.3   Continued

```
                margin:10px;
                border:Solid 1px black;
            }
            .rootNodeStyle
            {
                text-decoration:none;
            }
        </style>
        <title>SiteMapPath Style</title>
</head>
<body>
        <form id="form1" runat="server">
        <div>

        <asp:SiteMapPath
            id="SiteMapPath1"
            CssClass="siteMapPath"
            CurrentNodeStyle-CssClass="currentNodeStyle"
            NodeStyle-CssClass="nodeStyle"
            PathSeparatorStyle-CssClass="pathSeparatorStyle"
            RootNodeStyle-CssClass="rootNodeStyle"
            Runat="server" />

        <hr />

        <h1>SiteMapPath Style</h1>

        </div>
        </form>
</body>
</html>
```

Furthermore, you can use templates with the SiteMapPath control to format the appearance of the control (and change its behavior). The SiteMapPath control supports the following templates:

- CurrentNodeTemplate—Template for the SiteMapPath node that represents the current page.

- NodeTemplate—Template for each SiteMapPath node that is not the current or root node.

- PathSeparatorTemplate—Template for the text displayed between each SiteMapPath node.

- RootNodeTemplate—Template for the root (first) node rendered by the SiteMapPath control.

For example, the SiteMapPath control in Listing 17.4 includes a NodeTemplate. The NodeTemplate includes a HyperLink control that displays the current SiteMapPath node. The template also displays a count of the child nodes of the current node (see Figure 17.4).

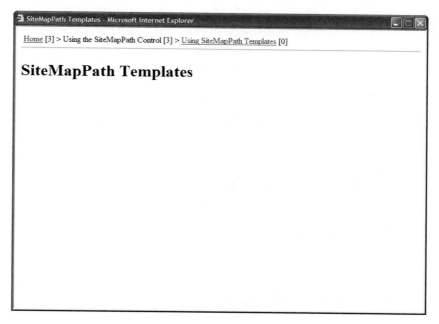

FIGURE 17.4   Using a template with the SiteMapPath control.

LISTING 17.4   UsingSiteMapPath/SiteMapPathTemplates.aspx

```
<%@ Page Language="VB" %>
<!DOCTYPE html PUBLIC "-//W3C//DTD XHTML 1.1//EN"
  "http://www.w3.org/TR/xhtml11/DTD/xhtml11.dtd">
<html xmlns="http://www.w3.org/1999/xhtml" >
<head id="Head1" runat="server">
    <title>SiteMapPath Templates</title>
</head>
<body>
    <form id="form1" runat="server">
    <div>

    <asp:SiteMapPath
```

LISTING 17.4   Continued

```
        id="SiteMapPath1"
        Runat="server">
        <NodeTemplate>
        <asp:HyperLink
            id="lnkPage"
            Text='<%# Eval("Title") %>'
            NavigateUrl='<%# Eval("Url") %>'
            ToolTip='<%# Eval("Description") %>'
            Runat="server" />
        [<%# Eval("ChildNodes.Count") %>]
        </NodeTemplate>
    </asp:SiteMapPath>

    <hr />

    <h1>SiteMapPath Templates</h1>


    </div>
    </form>
</body>
</html>
```

Within a template, the data item represents a `SiteMapNode`. Therefore, you can refer to any of the properties of the `SiteMapNode` class in a databinding expression.

Using the `Menu` Control

The `Menu` control enables you to create two types of menus. You can use the `Menu` control to create the left-column menu that appears in many websites. In other words, you can use the `Menu` control to display a vertical list of links.

You also can use the `Menu` control to create a menu that more closely resembles the drop-down menus that appear in traditional desktop applications. In this case, the `Menu` control renders a horizontal list of links.

Unlike the `SiteMapPath` control, the `Menu` control can represent other types of data than Site Map data. Technically, you can bind a `Menu` control to any data source that implements the `IHiearchicalDataSource` or `IHiearchicalEnumerable` interface.

In this section, you learn how to create different types of menus with the `Menu` control. First, you learn how to add menu items declaratively to a `Menu` control. Next, we discuss how the `Menu` control can be used with the `MultiView` control to display a tabbed page.

You also examine how you can bind the Menu control to different types of data sources. You learn how to use the Menu control with Site Map data, XML data, and database data.

Declaratively Adding Menu Items

You can display a menu with the Menu control by adding one or more MenuItem objects to its Items property. For example, the page in Listing 17.5 uses a Menu control to create a simple vertical menu (see Figure 17.5).

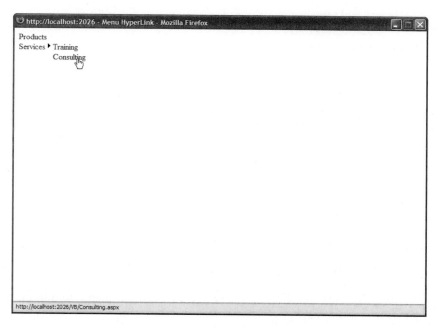

FIGURE 17.5   Displaying a menu with the Menu control.

LISTING 17.5   MenuHyperLink.aspx

```
<%@ Page Language="VB" %>
<!DOCTYPE html PUBLIC "-//W3C//DTD XHTML 1.1//EN"
 "http://www.w3.org/TR/xhtml11/DTD/xhtml11.dtd">
<html xmlns="http://www.w3.org/1999/xhtml" >
<head id="Head1" runat="server">
    <title>Menu HyperLink</title>
</head>
<body>
    <form id="form1" runat="server">
    <div>
```

LISTING 17.5   Continued

```
<asp:Menu
    id="Menu1"
    Runat="server">
    <Items>
        <asp:MenuItem
            Text="Products"
            NavigateUrl="Products.aspx" />
        <asp:MenuItem
            Text="Services"
            NavigateUrl="Services.aspx">
            <asp:MenuItem
                Text="Training"
                NavigateUrl="Training.aspx" />
            <asp:MenuItem
                Text="Consulting"
                NavigateUrl="Consulting.aspx" />
        </asp:MenuItem>
    </Items>
</asp:Menu>

    </div>
    </form>
</body>
</html>
```

The Menu in Listing 17.5 is created from MenuItem objects. Each menu item in Listing 17.5 contains a link to another page.

Notice that MenuItem objects can be nested. The second MenuItem object—Services— includes two child MenuItem objects. When you hover your mouse over a parent menu item, the child menu items are displayed.

Each MenuItem in Listing 17.5 includes a Text and NavigateUrl property. Rather than use a MenuItem to link to a new page, you also can use a MenuItem to link back to the same page. In other words, each MenuItem can act like a Linkbutton control instead of a HyperLink control.

For example, each MenuItem object in Listing 17.6 includes a Text and Value property. When you click a menu item, the same page is reloaded and the value of the selected menu item is displayed (see Figure 17.6).

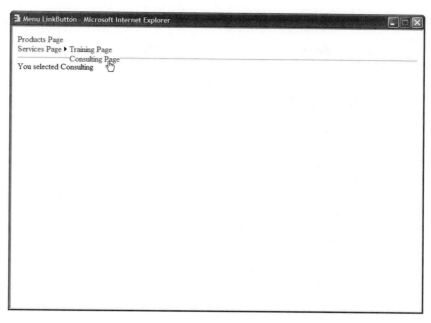

FIGURE 17.6   Selecting menu items.

LISTING 17.6   MenuLinkButton.aspx

```
<%@ Page Language="VB" %>
<!DOCTYPE html PUBLIC "-//W3C//DTD XHTML 1.1//EN"
   "http://www.w3.org/TR/xhtml11/DTD/xhtml11.dtd">
<script runat="server">

    Protected  Sub Menu1_MenuItemClick(ByVal sender As Object,
➥ByVal e As MenuEventArgs)
        lblMessage.Text = "You selected " & Menu1.SelectedValue
    End Sub

</script>
<html xmlns="http://www.w3.org/1999/xhtml" >
<head id="Head1" runat="server">
    <title>Menu LinkButton</title>
</head>
<body>
    <form id="form1" runat="server">
    <div>

    <asp:Menu
```

LISTING 17.6   Continued

```
            id="Menu1"
            OnMenuItemClick="Menu1_MenuItemClick"
            Runat="server">
            <Items>
                <asp:MenuItem
                    Text="Products Page"
                    Value="Products" />
                <asp:MenuItem
                    Text="Services Page"
                    Value="Services">
                    <asp:MenuItem
                        Text="Training Page"
                        Value="Training" />
                    <asp:MenuItem
                        Text="Consulting Page"
                        Value="Consulting" />
                </asp:MenuItem>
            </Items>
        </asp:Menu>

        <hr />

        <asp:Label
            id="lblMessage"
            EnableViewState="false"
            Runat="server" />

    </div>
    </form>
</body>
</html>
```

Notice that the page includes a MenuItemClick event handler. When you click a MenuItem (and the MenuItem does not have a NavigateUrl property), the MenuItemClick event is raised.

In Listing 17.6, the MenuItemClick handler displays the value of the selected MenuItem in a Label control.

Using the Menu Control with the MultiView Control

When the Menu control is used with the MultiView control, you can create tabbed pages. You use the Menu control to display the tabs, and the MultiView control to display the content that corresponds to the selected tab.

For example, the page in Listing 17.7 displays three tabs (see Figure 17.7).

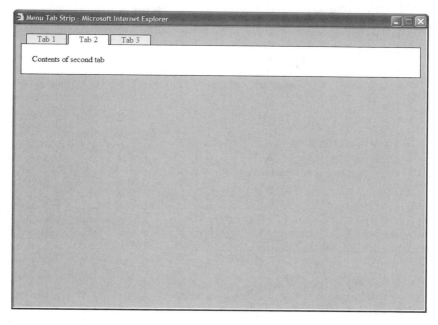

FIGURE 17.7   Displaying a tabbed page.

LISTING 17.7   MenuTabStrip.aspx

```
<%@ Page Language="VB" %>
<!DOCTYPE html PUBLIC "-//W3C//DTD XHTML 1.1//EN"
    "http://www.w3.org/TR/xhtml11/DTD/xhtml11.dtd">
<script runat="server">

    Protected  Sub menuTabs_MenuItemClick(ByVal sender As Object,
➥ByVal e As MenuEventArgs)
        multiTabs.ActiveViewIndex = Int32.Parse(menuTabs.SelectedValue)
    End Sub

</script>
<html xmlns="http://www.w3.org/1999/xhtml" >
<head id="Head1" runat="server">
    <style type="text/css">
        html
        {
            background-color:silver;
        }
```

LISTING 17.7   Continued

```
        .menuTabs
        {
            position:relative;
            top:1px;
            left:10px;
        }
        .tab
        {
            border:Solid 1px black;
            border-bottom:none;
            padding:0px 10px;
            background-color:#eeeeee;
        }
        .selectedTab
        {
            border:Solid 1px black;
            border-bottom:Solid 1px white;
            padding:0px 10px;
            background-color:white;
        }
        .tabBody
        {
            border:Solid 1px black;
            padding:20px;
            background-color:white;
        }
    </style>
    <title>Menu Tab Strip</title>
</head>
<body>
    <form id="form1" runat="server">
    <div>

    <asp:Menu
        id="menuTabs"
        CssClass="menuTabs"
        StaticMenuItemStyle-CssClass="tab"
        StaticSelectedStyle-CssClass="selectedTab"
        Orientation="Horizontal"
        OnMenuItemClick="menuTabs_MenuItemClick"
        Runat="server">
        <Items>
```

LISTING 17.7   Continued

```
        <asp:MenuItem
            Text="Tab 1"
            Value="0"
            Selected="true" />
        <asp:MenuItem
            Text="Tab 2"
            Value="1"/>
        <asp:MenuItem
            Text="Tab 3"
            Value="2" />

    </Items>
</asp:Menu>


<div class="tabBody">
<asp:MultiView
    id="multiTabs"
    ActiveViewIndex="0"
    Runat="server">
    <asp:View ID="view1" runat="server">

    Contents of first tab

    </asp:View>
    <asp:View ID="view2" runat="server">

    Contents of second tab

    </asp:View>
    <asp:View ID="view3" runat="server">

    Contents of third tab

    </asp:View>
</asp:MultiView>
</div>

</div>
</form>
</body>
</html>
```

After you open the page in Listing 17.7 and click a tab, the `MenuItemClick` event is raised. The `MenuItemClick` event handler changes the `ActiveViewIndex` property of the `MultiView` control to display the content of the selected tab.

WEB STANDARDS NOTE

The `Menu` control in Listing 17.7 is pushed down one pixel and pushed right 10 pixels to hide the border between the selected tab and the contents of the tab. (The `Menu` control has a relative position.) Notice that the style rule for the selected tab includes a white bottom border. This trick works in Internet Explorer 6, Firefox 1, and Opera 8.

Binding to a Site Map

Like the `SiteMapPath` control, you can use the `Menu` control with a Site Map. Users can click menu items to navigate to particular pages in your website.

Unlike the `SiteMapPath` control, however, the `Menu` control does not automatically bind to a Site Map. You must explicitly bind the `Menu` control to a `SiteMapDataSource` control to display nodes from a Site Map.

For example, the page in Listing 17.8 contains a menu that contains links to all the pages in a website (see Figure 17.8).

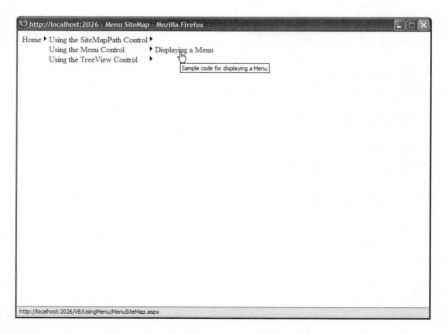

FIGURE 17.8   Displaying a Site Map with a `Menu` control.

LISTING 17.8   UsingMenu/MenuSiteMap.aspx

```
<%@ Page Language="VB" %>
<!DOCTYPE html PUBLIC "-//W3C//DTD XHTML 1.1//EN"
    "http://www.w3.org/TR/xhtml11/DTD/xhtml11.dtd">
<html xmlns="http://www.w3.org/1999/xhtml" >
<head id="Head1" runat="server">
    <title>Menu SiteMap</title>
</head>
<body>
    <form id="form1" runat="server">
    <div>

    <asp:Menu
        id="Menu1"
        DataSourceID="srcSiteMap"
        Runat="server" />

    <asp:SiteMapDataSource
        id="srcSiteMap"
        Runat="server" />

    </div>
    </form>
</body>
</html>
```

When you initially open the page in Listing 17.8, the only menu item that appears is the link to the Home page. If you hover your mouse over this link, links to additional pages are displayed.

Normally, you do not want the Home link to be displayed in a navigation menu. Instead, you want to display the second level of menu items. You can use the ShowStartingNode property of the SiteMapDataSource control to hide the topmost node in a Site Map.

For example, the page in Listing 17.9 uses a Menu control that renders a standard left-column navigational menu (see Figure 17.9).

LISTING 17.9   UsingMenu/MenuNavigate.aspx

```
<%@ Page Language="VB" %>
<!DOCTYPE html PUBLIC "-//W3C//DTD XHTML 1.1//EN"
    "http://www.w3.org/TR/xhtml11/DTD/xhtml11.dtd">
<html xmlns="http://www.w3.org/1999/xhtml" >
<head id="Head1" runat="server">
    <style type="text/css">
        html
```

17

LISTING 17.9   Continued

```
        {
            background-color:silver;
        }
        .navigation
        {
            float:left;
            width:280px;
            height:500px;
            padding:20px;
            background-color:#eeeeee;
        }
        .content
        {
            float:left;
            width:550px;
            height:500px;
            padding:20px;
            background-color:white;
        }
        .menuItem
        {
            border:Outset 1px black;
            background-color:Gray;
            font:14px Arial;
            color:White;
            padding:8px;
        }
    </style>
    <title>Menu Navigate</title>
</head>
<body>
    <form id="form1" runat="server">


    <div class="navigation">

    <asp:Menu
        id="Menu1"
        DataSourceID="srcSiteMap"
        StaticMenuItemStyle-CssClass="menuItem"
        DynamicMenuItemStyle-CssClass="menuItem"
        Runat="server" />
```

LISTING 17.9   Continued

```
<asp:SiteMapDataSource
    id="srcSiteMap"
    ShowStartingNode="false"
    Runat="server" />

</div>

<div class="content">

<h1>Displaying a Website menu with the Menu control</h1>

</div>


</form>
</body>
</html>
```

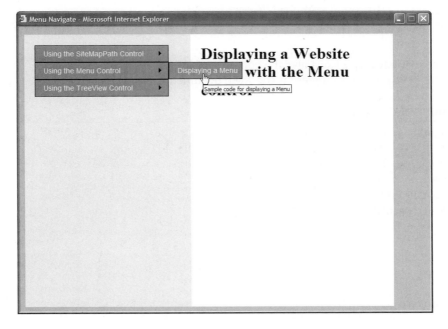

FIGURE 17.9   Displaying a navigation menu.

When you open the page in Listing 17.9, the second-level nodes from the Site Map are initially displayed. Furthermore, the Menu control is styled to appear more like a traditional website navigation menu.

Binding to an XML File

As an alternative to binding a Menu control to a SiteMapDataSource control, you can bind the control to an XML document by using the XmlDataSource control. For example, suppose that you have the XML file in Listing 17.10.

LISTING 17.10   Menu.xml

```xml
<?xml version="1.0" encoding="utf-8" ?>
<menu>
  <appetizer>
    <soup />
    <cheese />
  </appetizer>
  <entree>
    <duck />
    <chicken />
  </entree>
  <dessert>
    <cake />
    <pie />
  </dessert>
</menu>
```

The page in Listing 17.11 displays the contents of Listing 17.10 by using an XmlDataSource control to represent the XML document.

LISTING 17.11   MenuXML.aspx

```asp
<%@ Page Language="VB" %>
<!DOCTYPE html PUBLIC "-//W3C//DTD XHTML 1.1//EN"
    "http://www.w3.org/TR/xhtml11/DTD/xhtml11.dtd">
<html xmlns="http://www.w3.org/1999/xhtml" >
<head id="Head1" runat="server">
    <title>Menu XML</title>
</head>
<body>
    <form id="form1" runat="server">
    <div>

    <asp:Menu
        id="Menu1"
        DataSourceID="srcMenu"
        Runat="server" />
```

LISTING 17.11   Continued

```
    <asp:XmlDataSource
        id="srcMenu"
        DataFile="Menu.xml"
        Runat="server" />

    </div>
    </form>
</body>
</html>
```

When using the XmlDataSource control, you can use the XPath property to supply an xpath query that restricts the nodes returned by the XmlDataSource. You also can use either the Transform or TransformFile property to apply an XSLT Style Sheet to the XML document and transform the nodes returned by the XmlDataSource.

The XML file in Listing 17.10 is very simple. The nodes do not contain any attributes. When you bind the Menu control to the XML file, the ToString() method is called on each XML file node.

You also can bind the Menu control to more complex XML documents. For example, the item nodes in the XML document in Listing 17.12 include two attributes: text and price.

LISTING 17.12   MenuComplex.xml

```
<?xml version="1.0" encoding="utf-8" ?>
<menu>
  <category text="appetizer">
    <item text="soup" price="12.56" />
    <item text="cheese" price="17.23" />
  </category>
  <category text="entree">
    <item text="duck" price="89.21" />
    <item text="chicken" price="34.56" />
  </category>
  <category text="dessert">
    <item text="cake" price="23.43" />
    <item text="pie" price="115.46" />
  </category>
</menu>
```

When you bind to the XML document in Listing 17.12, you must specify one or more menu item bindings. The menu item bindings specify the relationship between node attributes and the menu items displayed by the Menu control.

The Menu control in Listing 17.13 includes MenuItemBinding subtags (see Figure 17.10).

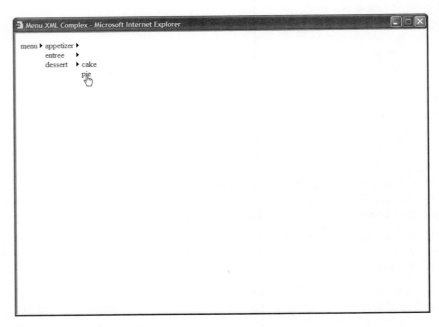

FIGURE 17.10   Displaying an XML document with the Menu control.

LISTING 17.13   MenuXMLComplex.aspx

```
<%@ Page Language="VB" %>
<!DOCTYPE html PUBLIC "-//W3C//DTD XHTML 1.1//EN"
    "http://www.w3.org/TR/xhtml11/DTD/xhtml11.dtd">
<html xmlns="http://www.w3.org/1999/xhtml" >
<head id="Head1" runat="server">
    <title>Menu XML Complex</title>
</head>
<body>
    <form id="form1" runat="server">
    <div>

    <asp:Menu
        id="Menu1"
        DataSourceID="srcMenu"
        Runat="server">
        <DataBindings>
        <asp:MenuItemBinding
            DataMember="category"
```

LISTING 17.13 Continued

```
            TextField="text" />
        <asp:MenuItemBinding
            DataMember="item"
            TextField="text"
            ValueField="price" />
        </DataBindings>
    </asp:Menu>

    <asp:XmlDataSource
        id="srcMenu"
        DataFile="MenuComplex.xml"
        Runat="server" />

    </div>
    </form>
</body>
</html>
```

Notice that the Menu control includes a <DataBindings> element. This element includes two MenuItemBinding subtags. The first subtag represents the relationship between the category nodes in the XML file and the menu items. The second subtag represents the relationship between the item nodes in the XML file and the menu items.

Binding to Database Data

You can't bind a Menu control directly to database data. Neither the SqlDataSource nor ObjectDataSource controls implement the IHierachicalDataSource interface. Therefore, if you want to represent database data with the Menu control, then you need to perform some more work.

One option is to create your own SqlHiearachicalDataSource control. You can do this either by deriving from the base HiearchicalDataSourceControl class or implementing the IHierachicalDataSource interface. We'll take this approach in the final section of this chapter, when we create a custom SqlHierarchicalDataSource control.

A second option is to build the menu items programmatically in the Menu control. This is the approach that is followed here.

Imagine that you want to represent the contents of the following database table with a Menu control:

CategoryId	ParentId	Name
1	null	Beverages
2	null	Fruit
3	1	Milk
4	1	Juice

CategoryId	ParentId	Name
5	4	Apple Juice
6	4	Orange Juice
7	2	Apples
8	2	Pears

This database table represents product categories. The categories are nested with the help of the ParentId column. For example, the Orange Juice category is nested below the Juice category, and the Juice category is nested below the Beverages category.

The page in Listing 17.14 illustrates how you can display this database table with a Menu control (see Figure 17.11).

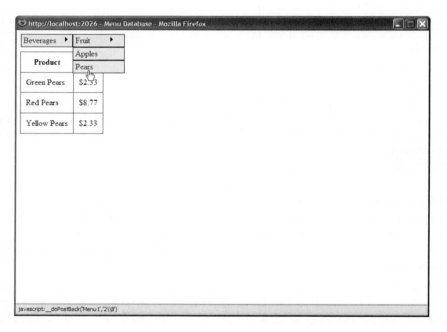

FIGURE 17.11   Displaying database data with the Menu control.

LISTING 17.14   MenuDatabase.aspx

```
<%@ Page Language="VB" %>
<%@ Import Namespace="System.Web.Configuration" %>
<%@ Import Namespace="System.Data" %>
<%@ Import Namespace="System.Data.SqlClient" %>
<!DOCTYPE html PUBLIC "-//W3C//DTD XHTML 1.1//EN"
    "http://www.w3.org/TR/xhtml11/DTD/xhtml11.dtd">
<script runat="server">
```

LISTING 17.14   Continued

```
''' <summary>
''' Only populate the menu when the page first loads
''' </summary>
Private Sub Page_Load()
    If Not Page.IsPostBack Then
        PopulateMenu()
    End If
End Sub


''' <summary>
''' Get the data from the database and create the top-level
''' menu items
''' </summary>
Private Sub PopulateMenu()
    Dim menuData As DataTable = GetMenuData()
    AddTopMenuItems(menuData)
End Sub


''' <summary>
''' Use a DataAdapter and DataTable to grab the database data
''' </summary>
''' <returns></returns>
Private Function GetMenuData() As DataTable
    ' Get Categories table
    Dim selectCommand As String = "SELECT CategoryId,ParentId,Name
➡FROM Categories"
    Dim conString As String =
➡ WebConfigurationManager.ConnectionStrings("Categories").ConnectionString
    Dim dad As SqlDataAdapter = New SqlDataAdapter(selectCommand, conString)
    Dim dtblCategories As DataTable = New DataTable()
    dad.Fill(dtblCategories)
    Return dtblCategories
End Function


''' <summary>
''' Filter the data to get only the rows that have a
''' null ParentID (these are the top-level menu items)
''' </summary>
Private Sub AddTopMenuItems(ByVal menuData As DataTable)
    Dim view As DataView = New DataView(menuData)
    view.RowFilter = "ParentID IS NULL"
    Dim row As DataRowView
    For Each row In view
```

LISTING 17.14   Continued

```
        Dim NewMenuItem As MenuItem = New MenuItem(row("Name").ToString(),
➡ row("CategoryId").ToString())
        Menu1.Items.Add(NewMenuItem)
        AddChildMenuItems(menuData, NewMenuItem)
    Next

End Sub

''' <summary>
''' Recursively add child menu items by filtering by ParentID
''' </summary>
Private Sub AddChildMenuItems(ByVal menuData As DataTable, _
➡ByVal parentMenuItem As MenuItem)
    Dim view As DataView = New DataView(menuData)
    view.RowFilter = "ParentID=" + parentMenuItem.Value
    Dim row As DataRowView
    For Each row In view
        Dim NewMenuItem As MenuItem = New MenuItem(row("Name").ToString(),
➡ row("CategoryId").ToString())
        parentMenuItem.ChildItems.Add(NewMenuItem)
        AddChildMenuItems(menuData, NewMenuItem)
    Next
End Sub

</script>
<html xmlns="http://www.w3.org/1999/xhtml" >
<head id="Head1" runat="server">
    <style type="text/css">
        .menuItem
        {
            border:Solid 1px black;
            width:100px;
            padding:2px;
            background-color:#eeeeee;
        }
        .menuItem a
        {
            color:blue;
        }
        .grid
        {
            margin-top:10px;
        }
```

LISTING 17.14   Continued

```
        .grid td, .grid th
        {
            padding:10px;
        }
    </style>
    <title>Menu Database</title>
</head>
<body>
    <form id="form1" runat="server">
    <div>

    <asp:Menu
        id="Menu1"
        Orientation="horizontal"
        StaticMenuItemStyle-CssClass="menuItem"
        DynamicMenuItemStyle-CssClass="menuItem"
        Runat="server" />

    <asp:GridView
        id="grdProducts"
        DataSourceID="srcProducts"
        CssClass="grid"
        AutoGenerateColumns="false"
        Runat="server">
        <Columns>
        <asp:BoundField
            DataField="ProductName"
            HeaderText="Product" />
        <asp:BoundField
            DataField="Price"
            HeaderText="Price"
            DataFormatString="{0:c}" />
        </Columns>
    </asp:GridView>

    <asp:SqlDataSource
        id="srcProducts"
        ConnectionString="<%$ ConnectionStrings:Categories %>"
        SelectCommand="SELECT ProductName,Price FROM Products
            WHERE CategoryId=@CategoryId"
        Runat="server">
        <SelectParameters>
        <asp:ControlParameter
            Name="CategoryId"
```

17

LISTING 17.14   Continued

```
            ControlID="Menu1" />
        </SelectParameters>
    </asp:SqlDataSource>


    </div>
    </form>
</body>
</html>
```

The menu items are added to the Menu control in the PopulateMenu() method. This method first grabs a DataTable that contains the contents of the Categories database table. Next, it creates a menu item for each row that does not have a parent row (each row where the ParentId column has the value null).

The child menu items for each menu item are added recursively. The ParentId column is used to filter the contents of the Categories DataTable.

The page in Listing 17.14 also includes a GridView control that displays a list of products that match the category selected in the menu. The GridView is bound to a SqlDataSource control, which includes a ControlParameter that filters the products based on the selected menu item.

Formatting the Menu Control

The Menu control supports an abundance of properties that can be used to format the appearance of the control. Many of these properties have an effect on static menu items, and many of these properties have an effect on dynamic menu items. Static menu items are menu items that always appear. Dynamic menu items are menu items that appear only when you hover your mouse over another menu item.

First, the Menu control supports the following general properties related to formatting:

- DisappearAfter—Enables you to specify the amount of time, in milliseconds, that a dynamic menu item is displayed after a user moves the mouse away from the menu item.

- DynamicBottomSeparatorImageUrl—Enables you to specify the URL to an image that appears under each dynamic menu item.

- DynamicEnableDefaultPopOutImage—Enables you to disable the image (triangle) that indicates that a dynamic menu item has child menu items.

- DynamicHorizontalOffset—Enables you to specify the number of pixels that a dynamic menu item is shifted relative to its parent menu item.

- DynamicItemFormatString—Enables you to format the text displayed in a dynamic menu item.

- DynamicPopOutImageTextFormatString—Enables you to format the alt text displayed for the popout image.

- DynamicPopOutImageUrl—Enables you to specify the URL for the dynamic popout image. (By default, a triangle is displayed.)

- DynamicTopSeparatorImageUrl—Enables you to specify the URL to an image that appears above each dynamic menu item.

- DynamicVerticalOffset—Enables you to specify the number of pixels that a dynamic menu item is shifted relative to its parent menu item.

- ItemWrap—Enables you to specify whether the text in menu items should wrap.

- MaximumDynamicDisplayLevels—Enables you to specify the maximum number of levels of dynamic menu items to display.

- Orientation—Enables you to display a menu horizontally or vertically (the default value is Vertical).

- ScollDownImageUrl—Enables you to specify the URL to an image that is displayed and that enables you to scroll down through menu items.

- ScrollDownText—Enables you to specify alt text for the ScrollDown image.

- ScrollUpImageUrl—Enables you to specify the URL to an image that is displayed and that enables you to scroll up through menu items.

- ScrollUpText—Enables you to specify alt text for the ScrollUp image.

- SkipLinkText—Enables you to modify the text displayed by the skip link. (The skip link enables blind users to skip past the contents of a menu.)

- StaticBottomSeparatorImageUrl—Enables you to specify the URL to an image that appears below each static menu item.

- StaticDisplayLevels—Enables you to specify the number of static levels of menu items to display.

- StaticEnableDefaultPopOutImage—Enables you to disable the default popout image that indicates that a menu item has child menu items.

- StaticItemFormatString—Enables you to format the text displayed in each static menu item.

- StaticImagePopOutFormatString—Enables you to specify the alt text displayed by the popout image.

- StaticPopOutImageUrl—Enables you to specify the URL for the popout image.

17

- StaticSubMenuIndent—Enables you to specify the number of pixels that a static menu item is indented relative to its parent menu item.

- StaticTopSeparatorImageUrl—Enables you to specify the URL to an image that appears above each static menu item.

- Target—Enables you to specify the window in which a new page opens when you click a menu item.

This list includes several interesting properties. For example, notice that you can specify images for scrolling up and down through a list of menu items. These images appear when you constrain the height of either the static or dynamic menu.

The Menu control also exposes several Style objects. You can use these Style objects as hooks to which you can attach Cascading Style Sheet classes:

- DynamicHoverStyle—Style applied to a dynamic menu item when you hover your mouse over it.

- DynamicMenuItemStyle—Style applied to each dynamic menu item.

- DynamicMenuStyle—Style applied to the container tag for the dynamic menu.

- DynamicSelectedStyle—Style applied to the selected dynamic menu item.

- StaticHoverStyle—Style applied to a static menu item when you hover your mouse over it.

- StaticMenuItemStyle—Style applied to each static menu item.

- StaticMenuStyle—Style applied to the container tag for the static menu.

- StaticSelectedStyle—Style applied to the selected static menu item.

Furthermore, you can apply styles to menu items based on their level in the menu. For example, you might want the font size to get progressively smaller depending on how deeply nested a menu item is within a menu. You can use three properties of the Menu control to format menu items, depending on their level:

- LevelMenuItemStyles—Contains a collection of MenuItemStyle controls, which correspond to different menu levels.

- LevelSelectedStyles—Contains a collection of MenuItemStyle controls, which correspond to different menu levels of selected menu items.

- LevelSubMenuStyles—Contains a collection of MenuItemStyle controls, which correspond to different menu levels of static menu items.

For example, the page in Listing 17.15 illustrates how you can apply different formatting to menu items that appear at different menu levels (see Figure 17.12).

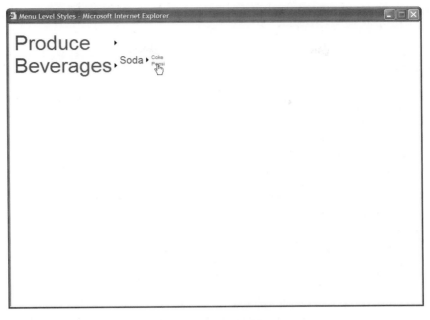

FIGURE 17.12 Applying styles to different menu levels.

LISTING 17.15 MenuLevelStyles.aspx

```
<%@ Page Language="VB" %>
<!DOCTYPE html PUBLIC "-//W3C//DTD XHTML 1.1//EN"
  "http://www.w3.org/TR/xhtml11/DTD/xhtml11.dtd">
<html xmlns="http://www.w3.org/1999/xhtml" >
<head id="Head1" runat="server">
    <style type="text/css">
        .menuLevel1
        {
            font:40px Arial,Sans-Serif;
        }
        .menuLevel2
        {
            font:20px Arial,Sans-Serif;
        }
        .menuLevel3
        {
            font:10px Arial,Sans-Serif;
        }
    </style>
    <title>Menu Level Styles</title>
```

LISTING 17.15   Continued

```
</head>
<body>
    <form id="form1" runat="server">
    <div>

    <asp:Menu
        id="Menu1"
        Runat="server">
        <LevelMenuItemStyles>
            <asp:MenuItemStyle CssClass="menuLevel1" />
            <asp:MenuItemStyle CssClass="menuLevel2" />
            <asp:MenuItemStyle CssClass="menuLevel3" />
        </LevelMenuItemStyles>
        <Items>
        <asp:MenuItem Text="Produce">
            <asp:MenuItem Text="Apples" />
            <asp:MenuItem Text="Oranges" />
        </asp:MenuItem>
        <asp:MenuItem Text="Beverages">
            <asp:MenuItem Text="Soda">
                <asp:MenuItem Text="Coke" />
                <asp:MenuItem Text="Pepsi" />
            </asp:MenuItem>
        </asp:MenuItem>
        </Items>
    </asp:Menu>

    </div>
    </form>
</body>
</html>
```

The `MenuItemStyle` controls are applied to the menu level that corresponds to their order of declaration. The first `MenuItemStyle` is applied to the first menu level, the second `MenuItemStyle` is applied to the second menu level, and so on.

Finally, the `MenuItem` class itself includes several useful formatting properties:

- `ImageUrl`—Enables you to specify the URL for an image that is displayed next to a menu item.

- `PopOutImageUrl`—Enables you to specify the URL for an image that is displayed when a menu item contains child menu items.

- `SeparatorImageUrl`—Enables you to specify the URL for an image that appears below a menu item.

- Selectable—Enables you to prevent users from selecting (clicking) a menu item.

- Selected—Enables you to specify whether a menu item is selected.

- Target—Enables you to specify the name of the window that opens when you click a menu item.

For example, the page in Listing 17.16 displays a menu that resembles a traditional desktop application menu (see Figure 17.13).

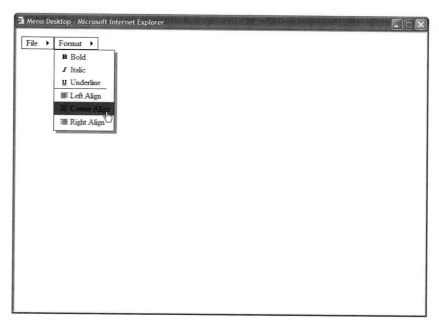

FIGURE 17.13   Displaying a desktop application menu.

LISTING 17.16   MenuDesktop.aspx

```
<%@ Page Language="VB" %>
<!DOCTYPE html PUBLIC "-//W3C//DTD XHTML 1.1//EN"
    "http://www.w3.org/TR/xhtml11/DTD/xhtml11.dtd">
<html xmlns="http://www.w3.org/1999/xhtml" >
<head id="Head1" runat="server">
    <style type="text/css">
        .staticMenuItem
        {
            color:black;
            border:solid 1px black;
            padding:2px 4px;
        }
```

LISTING 17.16   Continued

```
        .menuHover
        {
            color:white;
            background-color:blue;
        }
        .dynamicMenuItem
        {
            color:black;
            padding:2px 4px;
        }
        .dynamicMenu
        {
            border:Solid 1px black;
            filter:progid:DXImageTransform.Microsoft.dropshadow(OffX=5, OffY=5,
 Color='gray', Positive='true')"
        }
    </style>
    <title>Menu Desktop</title>
</head>
<body>
    <form id="form1" runat="server">
    <div>

    <asp:Menu
        id="Menu1"
        Orientation="Horizontal"
        StaticMenuItemStyle-CssClass="staticMenuItem"
        StaticHoverStyle-CssClass="menuHover"
        DynamicHoverStyle-CssClass="menuHover"
        DynamicMenuItemStyle-CssClass="dynamicMenuItem"
        DynamicMenuStyle-CssClass="dynamicMenu"
        Runat="server">
        <Items>
        <asp:MenuItem
            Text="File"
            Selectable="false">
            <asp:MenuItem
                Text="Save" />
            <asp:MenuItem
                Text="Open" />
        </asp:MenuItem>
        <asp:MenuItem
            Text="Format"
```

LISTING 17.16   Continued

```
                    Selectable="false">
                    <asp:MenuItem
                        Text="Bold"
                        ImageUrl="Images/Bold.gif" />
                    <asp:MenuItem
                        Text="Italic"
                        ImageUrl="Images/Italic.gif" />
                    <asp:MenuItem
                        Text="Underline"
                        ImageUrl="Images/Underline.gif"
                        SeparatorImageUrl="Images/Divider.gif" />
                    <asp:MenuItem
                        Text="Left Align"
                        ImageUrl="Images/JustifyLeft.gif" />
                    <asp:MenuItem
                        Text="Center Align"
                        ImageUrl="Images/JustifyCenter.gif" />
                    <asp:MenuItem
                        Text="Right Align"
                        ImageUrl="Images/JustifyRight.gif" />
                </asp:MenuItem>
                </Items>
            </asp:Menu>

        </div>
        </form>
</body>
</html>
```

Using Templates with the Menu Control

The Menu control supports templates. You can use templates to completely customize the appearance of the Menu control.

The Menu control supports the following two templates:

- DynamicItemTemplate—Template applied to dynamic menu items.
- StaticItemTemplate—Template applied to static menu items.

The page in Listing 17.17 uses both templates to display menu items. The templates display a count of child items for each menu item (see Figure 17.14).

17

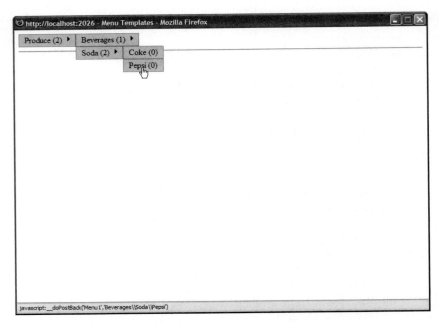

FIGURE 17.14   Using templates with the Menu control.

LISTING 17.17   MenuTemplates.aspx

```
<%@ Page Language="VB" %>
<!DOCTYPE html PUBLIC "-//W3C//DTD XHTML 1.1//EN"
 "http://www.w3.org/TR/xhtml11/DTD/xhtml11.dtd">
<script runat="server">

    Protected  Sub Menu1_MenuItemClick(ByVal sender As Object,
➥ByVal e As MenuEventArgs)
        lblMessage.Text = Menu1.SelectedValue
    End Sub
</script>
<html xmlns="http://www.w3.org/1999/xhtml" >
<head id="Head1" runat="server">
    <style type="text/css">
        .menuItem
        {
            color:black;
            border:Solid 1px Gray;
            background-color:#c9c9c9;
            padding:2px 5px;
        }
```

LISTING 17.17   Continued

```
    </style>
    <title>Menu Templates</title>
</head>
<body>
    <form id="form1" runat="server">
    <div>

    <asp:Menu
        id="Menu1"
        OnMenuItemClick="Menu1_MenuItemClick"
        Orientation="Horizontal"
        StaticMenuItemStyle-CssClass="menuItem"
        DynamicMenuItemStyle-CssClass="menuItem"
        Runat="server">
        <StaticItemTemplate>
        <%# Eval("Text") %>
        (<%# Eval("ChildItems.Count") %>)
        </StaticItemTemplate>
        <DynamicItemTemplate>
        <%# Eval("Text") %>
        (<%# Eval("ChildItems.Count") %>)
        </DynamicItemTemplate>
        <Items>
        <asp:MenuItem Text="Produce">
            <asp:MenuItem Text="Apples" />
            <asp:MenuItem Text="Oranges" />
        </asp:MenuItem>
        <asp:MenuItem Text="Beverages">
            <asp:MenuItem Text="Soda">
                <asp:MenuItem Text="Coke" />
                <asp:MenuItem Text="Pepsi" />
            </asp:MenuItem>
        </asp:MenuItem>
        </Items>
    </asp:Menu>

    <hr />

    <asp:Label
        id="lblMessage"
        EnableViewState="false"
        Runat="server" />
```

17

LISTING 17.17   Continued

```
        </div>
        </form>
</body>
</html>
```

Notice that you do not need to create LinkButton controls in the templates. The content of the template is wrapped in a link automatically when it is appropriate.

Using the `TreeView` Control

The TreeView control is very similar to the Menu control. Like the Menu control, you can use the TreeView control to display hierarchical data. The TreeView control binds to any data source that implements the IHierarchicalDataSource or IHierarchicalEnumerable interface.

In this section, you learn how to add items declaratively to the TreeView control. You also learn how to bind a TreeView control to hierarchical data sources such as the SiteMapDataSource and XmlDataSource controls.

You also see how you can use the TreeView control with database data. A TreeView is built programmatically from database data.

Finally, you learn how you can use AJAX with the TreeView control to display large sets of data efficiently. By taking advantage of AJAX, you can update a TreeView without posting a page back to the server.

Declaratively Adding Tree Nodes

A TreeView control is made up of TreeNode objects. You can build a TreeView control by declaring TreeNode objects in the TreeView control's Items collection.

For example, Listing 17.18 contains a TreeView which renders a nested set of links to pages (see Figure 17.15).

LISTING 17.18   TreeViewDeclare.aspx

```
<%@ Page Language="VB" %>
<!DOCTYPE html PUBLIC "-//W3C//DTD XHTML 1.1//EN"
    "http://www.w3.org/TR/xhtml11/DTD/xhtml11.dtd">
<html xmlns="http://www.w3.org/1999/xhtml" >
<head id="Head1" runat="server">
    <title>TreeView Declare</title>
</head>
<body>
    <form id="form1" runat="server">
    <div>
```

LISTING 17.18   Continued

```
<asp:TreeView
    id="TreeView1"
    Runat="server">
    <Nodes>
    <asp:TreeNode
        Text="Home"
        NavigateUrl="~/Default.aspx">
        <asp:TreeNode
            Text="Products">
            <asp:TreeNode
                Text="First Product"
                NavigateUrl="~/Products/FirstProduct.aspx" />
            <asp:TreeNode
                Text="Second Product"
                NavigateUrl="~/Products/SecondProduct.aspx" />
        </asp:TreeNode>
        <asp:TreeNode
            Text="Services">
            <asp:TreeNode
                Text="First Service"
                NavigateUrl="~/Services/FirstService.aspx" />
            <asp:TreeNode
                Text="Second Service"
                NavigateUrl="~/Services/SecondService.aspx" />
        </asp:TreeNode>
    </asp:TreeNode>
    </Nodes>
    </asp:TreeView>


    </div>
    </form>
</body>
</html>
```

Some of the TreeNodes in Listing 17.18 include a Text property, and some of the TreeNodes include both a Text and NavigateUrl property. You can click the TreeNodes that include a NavigateUrl property to link to a new page.

You also can associate a Value property with a TreeNode. This is useful when you want to post back to the same page. For example, the page in Listing 17.19 enables you to display the value of the selected TreeNode in a Label control (see Figure 17.16).

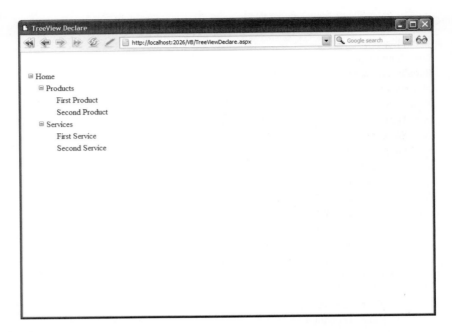

FIGURE 17.15 Displaying a TreeView control.

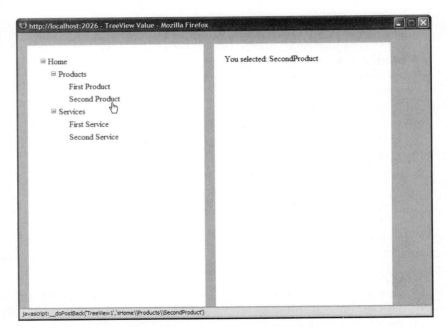

FIGURE 17.16 Selecting a TreeView node.

LISTING 17.19   TreeViewValue.aspx

```
<%@ Page Language="VB" %>
<!DOCTYPE html PUBLIC "-//W3C//DTD XHTML 1.1//EN"
 "http://www.w3.org/TR/xhtml11/DTD/xhtml11.dtd">
<script runat="server">

    Protected Sub TreeView1_SelectedNodeChanged(ByVal sender As Object,
➥ByVal e As EventArgs)
        lblMessage.Text = TreeView1.SelectedValue
    End Sub
</script>
<html xmlns="http://www.w3.org/1999/xhtml" >
<head id="Head1" runat="server">
    <style type="text/css">
        html
        {
            background-color:silver;
        }
        .content
        {
            float:left;
            width:350px;
            height:500px;
            padding:20px;
            margin:10px;
            background-color:white;
        }
    </style>
    <title>TreeView Value</title>
</head>
<body>
    <form id="form1" runat="server">

    <div class="content">
    <asp:TreeView
        id="TreeView1"
        OnSelectedNodeChanged="TreeView1_SelectedNodeChanged"
        Runat="server" >
        <Nodes>
        <asp:TreeNode
            Text="Home"
            Value="Home">
            <asp:TreeNode
                Text="Products">
                <asp:TreeNode
```

17

LISTING 17.19   Continued

```
                         Text="First Product"
                         Value="FirstProduct" />
                    <asp:TreeNode
                         Text="Second Product"
                         Value="SecondProduct" />
                </asp:TreeNode>
                <asp:TreeNode
                    Text="Services">
                    <asp:TreeNode
                         Text="First Service"
                         Value="FirstService" />
                    <asp:TreeNode
                         Text="Second Service"
                         Value="SecondService" />
                </asp:TreeNode>
            </asp:TreeNode>
            </Nodes>
        </asp:TreeView>
        </div>

        <div class="content">
        You selected:
        <asp:Label
            id="lblMessage"
            EnableViewState="false"
            Runat="server" />
        </div>

        </form>
</body>
</html>
```

Notice that the page in Listing 17.19 includes a SelectedNodeChanged event handler. When you select a new node, the SelectedNodeChanged event handler displays the value of the selected TreeNode in a Label control.

Displaying Check Boxes with the TreeView Control

You can display check boxes next to each node in a TreeView control by assigning a value to the ShowCheckBoxes property. This property accepts the following values:

- All

- Leaf

- None

- Parent

- Root

You can use a bitwise combination of these values when specifying the nodes to display with check boxes.

The page in Listing 17.20 illustrates the ShowCheckBoxes property (see Figure 17.17).

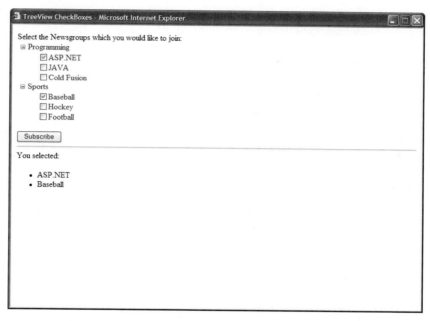

FIGURE 17.17   Displaying TreeView check boxes.

LISTING 17.20   TreeViewCheckBoxes.aspx

```
<%@ Page Language="VB" %>
<!DOCTYPE html PUBLIC "-//W3C//DTD XHTML 1.1//EN"
  "http://www.w3.org/TR/xhtml11/DTD/xhtml11.dtd">
<script runat="server">

    Protected Sub btnSubscribe_Click(ByVal sender As Object,
➥ByVal e As EventArgs)
        For Each node As TreeNode In TreeView1.CheckedNodes
            bltSubscribed.Items.Add(node.Text)
        Next
    End Sub
</script>
```

LISTING 17.20   Continued

```
<html xmlns="http://www.w3.org/1999/xhtml" >
<head id="Head1" runat="server">
    <title>TreeView CheckBoxes</title>
</head>
<body>
    <form id="form1" runat="server">
    <div>

    Select the Newsgroups which you
    would like to join:

    <br />

    <asp:TreeView
        id="TreeView1"
        ShowCheckBoxes="Leaf"
        Runat="server">
        <Nodes>
        <asp:TreeNode
            Text="Programming">
            <asp:TreeNode Text="ASP.NET" />
            <asp:TreeNode Text="JAVA" />
            <asp:TreeNode Text="Cold Fusion" />
        </asp:TreeNode>
        <asp:TreeNode
            Text="Sports">
            <asp:TreeNode Text="Baseball" />
            <asp:TreeNode Text="Hockey" />
            <asp:TreeNode Text="Football" />
        </asp:TreeNode>
        </Nodes>
    </asp:TreeView>

    <br />

    <asp:Button
        id="btnSubscribe"
        Text="Subscribe"
        OnClick="btnSubscribe_Click"
        Runat="server" />

    <hr />

    You selected:
```

LISTING 17.20   Continued

```
    <asp:BulletedList
        id="bltSubscribed"
        EnableViewState="false"
        Runat="server" />

    </div>
    </form>
</body>
</html>
```

The page in Listing 17.20 displays nested newsgroups. You can subscribe to the news-groups by clicking the Subscribe button.

When you click the Subscribe button, the CheckedNodes property is used to return a list of all of the checked TreeNodes. This list is displayed in a BulletedList control.

Binding to a Site Map

You can use a TreeView control as a navigation element in your pages by binding the TreeView to a Site Map. The page in Listing 17.21 demonstrates how you can bind a TreeView to a SiteMapDataSource control (see Figure 17.18).

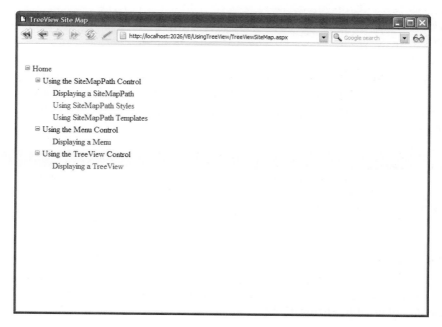

FIGURE 17.18   Displaying a Site Map with a TreeView control.

LISTING 17.21   `UsingTreeView/TreeViewSiteMap.aspx`

```
<%@ Page Language="VB" %>
<!DOCTYPE html PUBLIC "-//W3C//DTD XHTML 1.1//EN"
 "http://www.w3.org/TR/xhtml11/DTD/xhtml11.dtd">
<html xmlns="http://www.w3.org/1999/xhtml" >
<head id="Head1" runat="server">
    <title>TreeView Site Map</title>
</head>
<body>
    <form id="form1" runat="server">
    <div>

    <asp:TreeView
        id="TreeView1"
        DataSourceID="srcSiteMap"
        Runat="server" />

    <asp:SiteMapDataSource
        id="srcSiteMap"
        Runat="server" />

    </div>
    </form>
</body>
</html>
```

When you open the page in Listing 17.21, all the nodes from the Site Map are displayed automatically in the TreeView control. By default, the SiteMapDataSource uses the XmlSiteMapProvider, which represents a file named Web.sitemap located at the root of an application.

> **NOTE**
>
> You can add a TreeView and SiteMapDataSource control to a Master Page to show the TreeView in multiple pages. To learn more about Master Pages, see Chapter 5, "Designing Websites with Master Pages."

Binding to an XML File

Because an XmlDataSource control returns hierarchical data, you can bind a TreeView directly to an XmlDataSource. For example, imagine that you need to display the XML document contained in Listing 17.22.

LISTING 17.22   Movies.xml

```xml
<?xml version="1.0" encoding="utf-8" ?>
<movies>
  <action>
    <StarWars />
    <IndependenceDay />
  </action>
  <horror>
    <Jaws />
    <NightmareBeforeChristmas />
  </horror>
</movies>
```

The page in Listing 17.23 illustrates how you can display the contents of this XML document with a TreeView control.

LISTING 17.23   TreeViewXml.aspx

```asp
<%@ Page Language="VB" %>
<!DOCTYPE html PUBLIC "-//W3C//DTD XHTML 1.1//EN"
 "http://www.w3.org/TR/xhtml11/DTD/xhtml11.dtd">
<html xmlns="http://www.w3.org/1999/xhtml" >
<head id="Head1" runat="server">
    <title>TreeView XML</title>
</head>
<body>
    <form id="form1" runat="server">
    <div>

    <asp:TreeView
        id="TreeView1"
        DataSourceID="srcMovies"
        Runat="server" />

     <asp:XmlDataSource
        id="srcMovies"
        DataFile="~/Movies.xml"
        Runat="server" />

    </div>
    </form>
</body>
</html>
```

17

The Movies.xml document in Listing 17.22 is extremely simple. The elements do not include any attributes. You can display more complicated XML documents with the TreeView control by declaring one or more TreeNodeBinding elements.

For example, the nodes in the XML document in Listing 17.24 include id and text attributes.

LISTING 17.24   MoviesComplex.xml

```
<?xml version="1.0" encoding="utf-8" ?>
<movies>
  <category id="category1" text="Action">
    <movie id="movie1" text="Star Wars" />
    <movie id="movie2" text="Independence Day" />
  </category>
  <category id="category2" text="Horror">
    <movie id="movie3" text="Jaws" />
    <movie id="movie4" text="Nightmare Before Christmas" />
  </category>
</movies>
```

The page in Listing 17.25 displays the contents of the XML document in Listing 17.24.

LISTING 17.25   TreeViewXMLComplex.aspx

```
<%@ Page Language="VB" %>
<!DOCTYPE html PUBLIC "-//W3C//DTD XHTML 1.1//EN"
  "http://www.w3.org/TR/xhtml11/DTD/xhtml11.dtd">
<html xmlns="http://www.w3.org/1999/xhtml" >
<head id="Head1" runat="server">
    <title>TreeView XML Complex</title>
</head>
<body>
    <form id="form1" runat="server">
    <div>

    <asp:TreeView
        id="TreeView1"
        DataSourceID="srcMovies"
        Runat="server">
        <DataBindings>
        <asp:TreeNodeBinding
            DataMember="category"
            TextField="text"
            ValueField="id" />
        <asp:TreeNodeBinding
            DataMember="movie"
```

LISTING 17.25 Continued

```
            TextField="text"
            ValueField="id" />
        </DataBindings>
    </asp:TreeView>

    <asp:XmlDataSource
        id="srcMovies"
        DataFile="~/MoviesComplex.xml"
        Runat="server" />

    </div>
    </form>
</body>
</html>
```

The TreeView in Listing 17.25 includes a DataBindings subtag. This tag includes two TreeNodeBinding elements. The first TreeNodeBinding specifies the relationship between <category> nodes in the XML document and TreeView nodes. The second TreeNodeBinding specifies the relationship between <movie> nodes and TreeView nodes.

Binding to Database Data

You cannot bind a TreeView control directly to a SqlDataSource or ObjectDataSource control because neither of these two controls expose hierarchical data. If you want to display database data with the TreeView control then you have a choice: create a custom SqlHierarchicalDataSource control or programmatically bind the TreeView to the database data.

The hard option is to build a SQL hierarchical DataSource control. You can do this by deriving a new control from the base HierarchicalDataSourceControl class or by implementing the IHierarchicalDataSource interface. We explore this option in the final section of this chapter.

The second option is to build the TreeView control programmatically from a set of database records. This is the approach that we will follow in this section.

Imagine that you have a database table that looks like this:

MessageId	ParentId	Subject
1	null	How do you use the Menu control?
2	null	What is the TreeView control?
3	1	RE:How do you use the Menu control?
4	1	RE:How do you use the Menu control?
5	2	RE:What is the TreeView control?
6	5	RE:RE:What is the TreeView control?

17

This database table represents a discussion forum. The relationship between the messages is determined by the `ParentId` column. The messages that have a null `ParentID` represent the threads, and the other messages represent replies to the threads.

The page in Listing 17.26 uses a `TreeView` control to display the contents of the Discuss database table (see Figure 17.19).

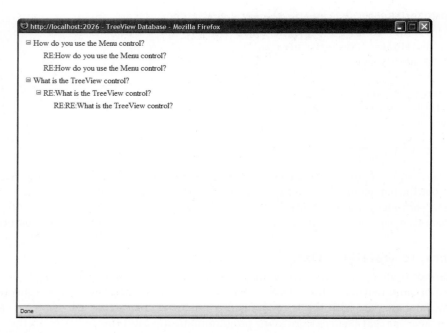

FIGURE 17.19   Displaying database data with a `TreeView` control.

LISTING 17.26   `TreeViewDatabase.aspx`

```
<%@ Page Language="VB" %>
<%@ Import Namespace="System.Web.Configuration" %>
<%@ Import Namespace="System.Data" %>
<%@ Import Namespace="System.Data.SqlClient" %>
<!DOCTYPE html PUBLIC "-//W3C//DTD XHTML 1.1//EN"
  "http://www.w3.org/TR/xhtml11/DTD/xhtml11.dtd">
<script runat="server">

    ''' <summary>
    ''' Only populate the TreeView when the page first loads
    ''' </summary>
    Private Sub Page_Load()
        If Not Page.IsPostBack Then
```

LISTING 17.26   Continued

```
                PopulateTreeView()
        End If
    End Sub


    ''' <summary>
    ''' Get the data from the database and create the top-level
    ''' TreeView items
    ''' </summary>
    Private Sub PopulateTreeView()
        Dim treeViewData As DataTable = GetTreeViewData()
        AddTopTreeViewNodes(treeViewData)
    End Sub


    ''' <summary>
    ''' Use a DataAdapter and DataTable to grab the database data
    ''' </summary>
    ''' <returns></returns>
    Private Function GetTreeViewData() As DataTable
        ' Get Discuss table
        Dim selectCommand As String = "SELECT MessageId,ParentId,Subject
➥FROM Discuss"
        Dim conString As String =
➥ WebConfigurationManager.ConnectionStrings("Discuss").ConnectionString
        Dim dad As SqlDataAdapter = New SqlDataAdapter(selectCommand, conString)
        Dim dtblDiscuss As DataTable = New DataTable()
        dad.Fill(dtblDiscuss)
        Return dtblDiscuss
    End Function


    ''' <summary>
    ''' Filter the data to get only the rows that have a
    ''' null ParentID (these are the top-level TreeView items)
    ''' </summary>
    Private Sub AddTopTreeViewNodes(ByVal treeViewData As DataTable)
        Dim view As DataView = New DataView(treeViewData)
        view.RowFilter = "ParentID IS NULL"
        Dim row As DataRowView
        For Each row In view
            Dim NewNode As TreeNode = New TreeNode(row("Subject").ToString(),
➥ row("MessageId").ToString())
            TreeView1.Nodes.Add(NewNode)
            AddChildTreeViewNodes(treeViewData, NewNode)
        Next
```

17

LISTING 17.26   Continued

```
    End Sub

    ''' <summary>
    ''' Recursively add child TreeView items by filtering by ParentID
    ''' </summary>
    Private Sub AddChildTreeViewNodes(ByVal treeViewData As DataTable,
➡ByVal parentTreeViewNode As TreeNode)
        Dim view As DataView = New DataView(treeViewData)
        view.RowFilter = "ParentID=" + parentTreeViewNode.Value
        Dim row As DataRowView
        For Each row In view
            Dim NewNode As TreeNode = New TreeNode(row("Subject").ToString(),
➡ row("MessageId").ToString())
            parentTreeViewNode.ChildNodes.Add(NewNode)
            AddChildTreeViewNodes(treeViewData, NewNode)
        Next
    End Sub

</script>
<html xmlns="http://www.w3.org/1999/xhtml" >
<head id="Head1" runat="server">
    <style type="text/css">
    </style>
    <title>TreeView Database</title>
</head>
<body>
    <form id="form1" runat="server">
    <div>

    <asp:TreeView
        id="TreeView1"
        Runat="server" />

    </div>
    </form>
</body>
</html>
```

The page in Listing 17.26 filters the contents of the Discuss database table by its ParentID column. First, the top-level nodes are added to the TreeView. Next, the child nodes are recursively added to the TreeView with the help of the AddChildTreeViewNodes() method.

Using Populate On Demand and AJAX

You can use the TreeView control even when working with a large set of data. For example, the Microsoft MSDN website (msdn.Microsoft.com) has links to thousands of articles. This website uses a tree view to display the nested links to the articles.

Because thousands of articles are hosted at the MSDN website, not all the tree nodes are downloaded to the browser when you open a page. Instead, additional nodes are downloaded to your browser only when you expand a particular node.

You can use a feature named Populate On Demand with the TreeView control. When you enable the PopulateOnDemand property for a Tree node, child nodes are not added to the parent node until the parent node is expanded.

For example, the page in Listing 17.27 contains an infinitely expanding TreeView. Each time you expand a Tree node, five new child nodes are displayed. Each time you expand a child node, five more child nodes are displayed, and so on (see Figure 17.20).

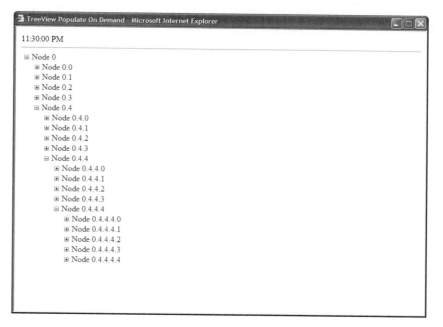

FIGURE 17.20   An infinitely expanding TreeView control.

LISTING 17.27   TreeViewPopulateOnDemand.aspx

```
<%@ Page Language="VB" %>
<!DOCTYPE html PUBLIC "-//W3C//DTD XHTML 1.1//EN"
  "http://www.w3.org/TR/xhtml11/DTD/xhtml11.dtd">
<script runat="server">
```

LISTING 17.27   Continued

```
    Private Sub TreeView1_TreeNodePopulate(ByVal s As Object,
➡ByVal e As TreeNodeEventArgs)
        For i As Integer = 0 To 4
            Dim NewNode As New TreeNode()
            NewNode.Text = String.Format("{0}.{1}", e.Node.Text, i)
            NewNode.PopulateOnDemand = True
            e.Node.ChildNodes.Add(NewNode)
        Next
    End Sub
</script>
<html xmlns="http://www.w3.org/1999/xhtml" >
<head id="Head1" runat="server">
    <title>TreeView Populate On Demand</title>
</head>
<body>
    <form id="form1" runat="server">
    <div>

    <%=DateTime.Now.ToString("T") %>

    <hr />

    <asp:TreeView
        ID="TreeView1"
        ExpandDepth="0"
        OnTreeNodePopulate="TreeView1_TreeNodePopulate"
        Runat="server">
        <Nodes>
        <asp:TreeNode
            PopulateOnDemand="true"
            Text="Node 0" />
        </Nodes>
    </asp:TreeView>

    </div>
    </form>
</body>
</html>
```

The TreeView in Listing 17.27 includes a single statically declared TreeNode. Notice that this TreeNode includes a PopulateOnDemand property that is set to the value True.

Additionally, the TreeView control itself includes a TreeNodePopulate event handler. When you expand a TreeNode that has its PopulateOnDemand property enabled, the

TreeNodePopulate event handler executes. In the case of Listing 17.27, the event handler adds five new TreeNodes to the TreeNode that was expanded.

When you use the Populate On Demand feature with a modern browser (Internet Explorer 6, Firefox 1, Opera 8), the page containing the TreeView is not posted back to the server when you expand a TreeNode. Instead, the browser uses AJAX (Asynchronous JavaScript and XML) to communicate with the web server. The additional TreeNodes are retrieved from the server, without performing a postback.

The page in Listing 17.27 displays the current time when you open the page. Notice that the time is not updated when you expand a particular TreeNode. The time is not updated because the only content in the page that is updated when you expand a node is the TreeView content. AJAX can have a dramatic impact on performance because it does not require the entire page to be re-rendered each time you expand a TreeNode.

> **NOTE**
>
> If, for some reason, you don't want to use AJAX with Populate On Demand, you can assign the value False to the TreeView control's PopulateNodesFromClient property.

The page in Listing 17.28 contains a more realistic sample of using Populate On Demand and AJAX. This page uses a TreeView control to display the contents of the Discuss database table (see Figure 17.21).

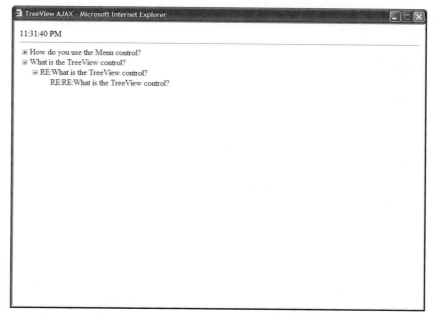

FIGURE 17.21   Displaying database data with AJAX.

LISTING 17.28   TreeViewAJAX.aspx

```
<%@ Page Language="VB" %>
<%@ Import Namespace="System.Web.Configuration" %>
<%@ Import Namespace="System.Data" %>
<%@ Import Namespace="System.Data.SqlClient" %>
<!DOCTYPE html PUBLIC "-//W3C//DTD XHTML 1.1//EN"
 "http://www.w3.org/TR/xhtml11/DTD/xhtml11.dtd">
<script runat="server">

    ''' <summary>
    ''' Only populate the TreeView when the page first loads
    ''' </summary>
    Private Sub Page_Load()
        If Not Page.IsPostBack Then
            PopulateTopNodes()
        End If
    End Sub


    ''' <summary>
    ''' Get the top-level nodes (nodes with a null ParentId)
    ''' </summary>
    Private Sub PopulateTopNodes()
        Dim selectCommand As String = "SELECT MessageId,ParentId,Subject
➥FROM Discuss WHERE ParentId IS NULL"
        Dim conString As String =
➥ WebConfigurationManager.ConnectionStrings("Discuss").ConnectionString
        Dim dad As New SqlDataAdapter(selectCommand, conString)
        Dim dtblMessages As New DataTable()
        dad.Fill(dtblMessages)

        For Each row As DataRow In dtblMessages.Rows
            Dim NewNode As New TreeNode(row("Subject").ToString(),
➥ row("MessageId").ToString())
            NewNode.PopulateOnDemand = True
            TreeView1.Nodes.Add(NewNode)
        Next
    End Sub


    ''' <summary>
    ''' Get the child nodes of the expanded node
    ''' </summary>
    Protected Sub TreeView1_TreeNodePopulate(ByVal sender As Object,
➥ByVal e As TreeNodeEventArgs)
```

LISTING 17.28   Continued

```
            Dim selectCommand As String = "SELECT MessageId,ParentId,Subject
➡FROM Discuss WHERE ParentId=@ParentId"
            Dim conString As String =
➡ WebConfigurationManager.ConnectionStrings("Discuss").ConnectionString
            Dim dad As New SqlDataAdapter(selectCommand, conString)
            dad.SelectCommand.Parameters.AddWithValue("@ParentId", e.Node.Value)
            Dim dtblMessages As New DataTable()
            dad.Fill(dtblMessages)

            For Each row As DataRow In dtblMessages.Rows
                Dim NewNode As New TreeNode(row("Subject").ToString(),
➡ row("MessageId").ToString())
                NewNode.PopulateOnDemand = True
                e.Node.ChildNodes.Add(NewNode)
            Next
        End Sub
</script>
<html xmlns="http://www.w3.org/1999/xhtml" >
<head id="Head1" runat="server">
    <style type="text/css">
    </style>
    <title>TreeView AJAX</title>
</head>
<body>
    <form id="form1" runat="server">
    <div>

    <%= DateTime.Now.ToString("T") %>

    <hr />

    <asp:TreeView
        id="TreeView1"
        ExpandDepth="0"
        OnTreeNodePopulate="TreeView1_TreeNodePopulate"
        Runat="server" />

    </div>
    </form>
</body>
</html>
```

When the page in Listing 17.28 first opens, only the first-level message subjects are displayed. These messages are retrieved by the PopulateTopNodes() method.

When you expand a thread, the matching replies are retrieved for the thread. These replies are retrieved in the `TreeView1_TreeNodePopulate()` event handler.

The `TreeView` in Listing 17.28 performs well even when working with a large set of data. At any time, only the child messages of a message are retrieved from the database. At no time are all the messages retrieved from the database.

When the page is used with a modern browser, AJAX is used to retrieve the messages from the web server. The page does not need to be posted back to the web server when you expand a particular message thread.

Formatting the `TreeView` Control

The `TreeView` control supports an abundance of properties that have an effect on how the `TreeView` is formatted.

Here are some of the more useful properties of a `TreeView` control, which modify its appearance (this is not a complete list):

- `CollapseImageToolTip`—Enables you to specify the title attribute for the collapse image.

- `CollapseImageUrl`—Enables you to specify a URL to an image for the collapse image.

- `ExpandDepth`—Enables you to specify the number of `TreeNode` levels to display initially.

- `ExpandImageToolTip`—Enables you to specify the title attribute for the expand image.

- `ExpandImageUrl`—Enables you to specify the URL to an image for the expand image.

- `ImageSet`—Enables you to specify a set of images to use with the `TreeView` control.

- `LineImagesFolder`—Enables you to specify a folder that contains line images.

- `MaxDataBindDepth`—Enables you to specify the maximum levels of `TreeView` levels to display when binding to a data source.

- `NodeIndent`—Enables you to specify the number of pixels to indent a child Tree node.

- `NodeWrap`—Enables you to specify whether or not text is wrapped in a Tree node.

- `NoExpandImageUrl`—Enables you to specify the URL to an image for the `NoExpand` image (typically, an invisible spacer image).

- `ShowCheckBoxes`—Enables you to display check boxes next to each Tree node. Possible values are `All`, `Leaf`, `None`, `Parent`, and `Root`.

- `ShowExpandCollapse`—Enables you to disable the expand and collapse icons that appear next to each expandable node.

- `ShowLines`—Enables you to show connecting lines between Tree nodes.

- `SkipLinkText`—Enables you to specify the text used for skipping the contents of the `TreeView` control. (The Skip Link contains hidden text that is accessible only to users of assistive devices.)

- `Target`—Enables you to specify the name of the window that opens when you navigate to a URL with the `TreeView` control.

The two most interesting properties in this list are the `ImageSet` and the `ShowLines` properties. You can set the `ImageSet` property to any of the following values to modify the images displayed by the `TreeView` control:

- `Arrows`

- `BulletedList`

- `BulletedList2`

- `BulletedList3`

- `BulletedList4`

- `Contacts`

- `Custom`

- `Events`

- `Faq`

- `Inbox`

- `Msdn`

- `News`

- `Simple`

- `Simple2`

- `WindowsHelp`

- `XPFileExplorer`

The `ShowLines` property causes connecting line images to be rendered between `TreeView` nodes. Displaying lines between Tree nodes can make it easier to visually discern the nested relationships between nodes. If you want to create custom lines, you can specify a value for the `LinesImagesFolder` property.

VISUAL WEB DEVELOPER NOTE

Visual Web Developer includes a `TreeView` Line Image Generator that enables you to create custom connecting lines. You can open this tool in Design view by selecting the `TreeView` control and opening the Tasks dialog box and selecting Customize Line Images.

The page in Listing 17.29 illustrates how to use both the `ImageSet` and `ShowLines` properties (see Figure 17.22).

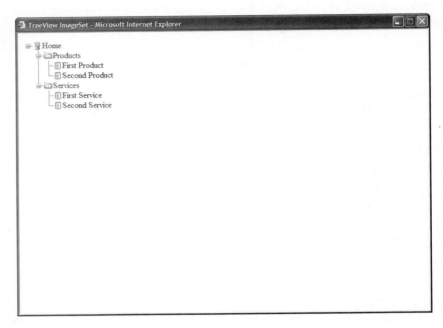

FIGURE 17.22   Formatting a `TreeView` with an image set and lines.

LISTING 17.29   `TreeViewImageSet.aspx`

```
<%@ Page Language="VB" %>
<!DOCTYPE html PUBLIC "-//W3C//DTD XHTML 1.1//EN"
    "http://www.w3.org/TR/xhtml11/DTD/xhtml11.dtd">
<html xmlns="http://www.w3.org/1999/xhtml" >
<head id="Head1" runat="server">
    <title>TreeView ImageSet</title>
</head>
<body>
    <form id="form1" runat="server">
    <div>

    <asp:TreeView
        id="TreeView1"
        ImageSet="XPFileExplorer"
        ShowLines="true"
        Runat="server">
```

LISTING 17.29 Continued

```
            <Nodes>
            <asp:TreeNode
                Text="Home">
                <asp:TreeNode Text="Products">
                    <asp:TreeNode Text="First Product" />
                    <asp:TreeNode Text="Second Product" />
                </asp:TreeNode>
                <asp:TreeNode Text="Services">
                    <asp:TreeNode Text="First Service" />
                    <asp:TreeNode Text="Second Service" />
                </asp:TreeNode>
            </asp:TreeNode>
            </Nodes>
        </asp:TreeView>


        </div>
        </form>
</body>
</html>
```

The TreeNode object itself also supports several properties that have an effect on the appearance of its containing TreeView. Here is a list of the most useful properties of the TreeNode object:

- Checked—Enables you to check the check box that appears next to the Tree node.

- Expanded—Enables you to initially expand a node.

- ImageToolTip—Enables you to associate alt text with a Tree node image.

- ImageUrl—Enables you to specify an image that appears next to a Tree node.

- NavigateUrl—Enables you to specify the URL to which the current Tree node links.

- SelectAction—Enables you to specify the action that occurs when you click a Tree node. Possible values are Expand, None, Select, or SelectExpand.

- Selected—Enables you to specify whether the current Tree node is selected.

- ShowCheckBox—Enables you to display a check box for the current Tree node.

- Target—Enables you to specify the name of the window that opens when you navigate to a URL.

- ToolTip—Enables you to specify a title attribute for the current Tree node.

17

You can style the `TreeView` control by attaching Cascading Style Sheet classes to the `Style` object exposed by the `TreeView` control. The `TreeView` control supports the following `Style` objects:

- `HoverNodeStyle`—Style applied to a Tree node when you hover your mouse over a node.

- `LeafNodeStyle`—Style applied to leaf Tree nodes (Tree nodes without child nodes).

- `NodeStyle`—Style applied to Tree nodes by default.

- `ParentNodeStyle`—Style applied to parent nodes (Tree nodes with child nodes).

- `RootNodeStyle`—Style applied to root nodes (Tree nodes with no parent nodes).

- `SelectedNodeStyle`—Style applied to the selected node.

For example, the page in Listing 17.30 uses several of these Style objects to format a `TreeView` control (see Figure 17.23).

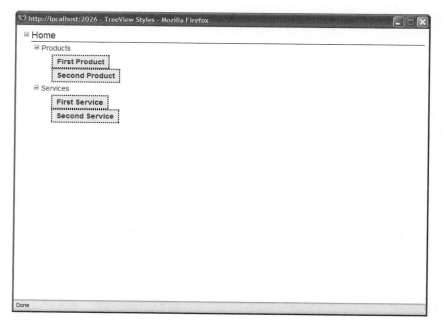

FIGURE 17.23   Using Styles with the `TreeView` control.

LISTING 17.30   TreeViewStyles.aspx

```
<%@ Page Language="VB" %>
<!DOCTYPE html PUBLIC "-//W3C//DTD XHTML 1.1//EN"
  "http://www.w3.org/TR/xhtml11/DTD/xhtml11.dtd">
```

LISTING 17.30   Continued

```
<html xmlns="http://www.w3.org/1999/xhtml" >
<head id="Head1" runat="server">
    <style type="text/css">
        .treeNode
        {
            color:blue;
            font:14px Arial, Sans-Serif;
        }
        .rootNode
        {
            font-size:18px;
            width:100%;
            border-bottom:Solid 1px black;
        }
        .leafNode
        {
            border:Dotted 2px black;
            padding:4px;
            background-color:#eeeeee;
            font-weight:bold;
        }
    </style>
    <title>TreeView Styles</title>
</head>
<body>
    <form id="form1" runat="server">
    <div>

    <asp:TreeView
        id="TreeView1"
        NodeStyle-CssClass="treeNode"
        RootNodeStyle-CssClass="rootNode"
        LeafNodeStyle-CssClass="leafNode"
        Runat="server">
        <Nodes>
        <asp:TreeNode
            Text="Home">
            <asp:TreeNode Text="Products">
                <asp:TreeNode Text="First Product" />
                <asp:TreeNode Text="Second Product" />
            </asp:TreeNode>
            <asp:TreeNode Text="Services">
                <asp:TreeNode Text="First Service" />
```

LISTING 17.30   Continued

```
                <asp:TreeNode Text="Second Service" />
            </asp:TreeNode>
        </asp:TreeNode>
        </Nodes>
    </asp:TreeView>

    </div>
    </form>
</body>
</html>
```

Furthermore, you can apply styles to particular Tree node levels by taking advantage of the `TreeView` control's `LevelStyles` property. The page in Listing 17.31 uses the `LevelStyles` property to format first level nodes differently than second level nodes and third level nodes (see Figure 17.24).

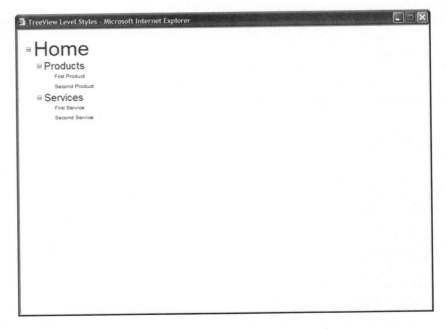

FIGURE 17.24   Applying styles to different `TreeView` node levels.

LISTING 17.31   `TreeViewLevelStyles.aspx`

```
<%@ Page Language="VB" %>
<!DOCTYPE html PUBLIC "-//W3C//DTD XHTML 1.1//EN"
    "http://www.w3.org/TR/xhtml11/DTD/xhtml11.dtd">
```

LISTING 17.31   Continued

```
<html xmlns="http://www.w3.org/1999/xhtml" >
<head id="Head1" runat="server">
    <style type="text/css">
        .nodeLevel1
        {
            font:40px Arial,Sans-Serif;
        }
        .nodeLevel2
        {
            font:20px Arial,Sans-Serif;
        }
        .nodeLevel3
        {
            font:10px Arial,Sans-Serif;
        }
    </style>
    <title>TreeView Level Styles</title>
</head>
<body>
    <form id="form1" runat="server">
    <div>

    <asp:TreeView
        id="TreeView1"
        Runat="server">
        <LevelStyles>
        <asp:TreeNodeStyle CssClass="nodeLevel1" />
        <asp:TreeNodeStyle CssClass="nodeLevel2" />
        <asp:TreeNodeStyle CssClass="nodeLevel3" />
        </LevelStyles>
        <Nodes>
        <asp:TreeNode
            Text="Home">
            <asp:TreeNode Text="Products">
                <asp:TreeNode Text="First Product" />
                <asp:TreeNode Text="Second Product" />
            </asp:TreeNode>
            <asp:TreeNode Text="Services">
                <asp:TreeNode Text="First Service" />
                <asp:TreeNode Text="Second Service" />
            </asp:TreeNode>
        </asp:TreeNode>
        </Nodes>
```

17

LISTING 17.31   Continued

```
    </asp:TreeView>

    </div>
    </form>
</body>
</html>
```

Building a SQL Hierarchical Data Source Control

In this final section of this chapter, we build a SqlHierarchicalDataSource control. This custom control enables you to declaratively and (thus) easily bind controls such as the Menu and TreeView controls to data retrieved from a database.

> **NOTE**
>
> The code samples in this section can be found in the SqlHierarchicalDataSourceVB and SqlHierarchicalDataSourceCS applications on the CD.

The page in Listing 17.32 illustrates how you can use the SqlHierarchicalDataSource control to bind a Menu control to a database table that contains nested categories.

LISTING 17.32   ShowMenu.aspx

```
<%@ Page Language="VB" %>
<%@ Register TagPrefix="custom" Namespace="AspNetUnleashed" %>
<!DOCTYPE html PUBLIC "-//W3C//DTD XHTML 1.1//EN"
    "http://www.w3.org/TR/xhtml11/DTD/xhtml11.dtd">
<script runat="server">

    Sub Menu1_MenuItemClick(sender As Object, e As MenuEventArgs)
        lblSelected.Text = Menu1.SelectedValue
    End Sub
</script>
<html xmlns="http://www.w3.org/1999/xhtml" >
<head id="Head1" runat="server">
    <style type="text/css">
        .menu
        {
            border:solid 1px black;
            padding:4px;
        }
    </style>
    <title>Show Menu</title>
```

LISTING 17.32   Continued

```
</head>
<body>
    <form id="form1" runat="server">
    <div>

    <asp:Menu
        id="Menu1"
        DataSourceId="srcCategories"
        OnMenuItemClick="Menu1_MenuItemClick"
        Orientation="Horizontal"
        DynamicMenuStyle-CssClass="menu"
        Runat="server">
        <DataBindings>
            <asp:MenuItemBinding TextField="Name" ValueField="Name" />
        </DataBindings>
    </asp:Menu>

    <custom:SqlHierarchicalDataSource
        id="srcCategories"
        ConnectionString='<%$ ConnectionStrings:Categories %>'
        DataKeyName="CategoryId"
        DataParentKeyName="ParentId"
        SelectCommand="SELECT CategoryId, ParentId, Name FROM Categories"
        Runat="server" />

    <hr />

    <asp:Label
        id="lblSelected"
        Runat="server" />

    </div>
    </form>
</body>
</html>
```

When you open the page in Listing 17.32, all the rows from the Categories table are displayed in the Menu control.

Notice that the SqlHierarchicalDataSource control includes two properties: DataKeyName and DataParentKeyName. The DataKeyName property represents the name of a database column that contains a unique value for each database table row. The DataParentKeyName column represents the name of a database column that relates each row to its parent row.

Furthermore, notice that the Menu control includes a MenuItemBinding, which associates the database Name column with the Menu item Text property, and the Name column with the Menu item Value property.

You also can use the SqlHierarchicalDataSource control when working with the TreeView control. The page in Listing 17.33 displays all the rows from the Discuss database table in a TreeView control.

LISTING 17.33   ShowTreeView.aspx

```
<%@ Page Language="VB" %>
<%@ Register TagPrefix="custom" Namespace="AspNetUnleashed" %>
<!DOCTYPE html PUBLIC "-//W3C//DTD XHTML 1.1//EN"
 "http://www.w3.org/TR/xhtml11/DTD/xhtml11.dtd">
<script runat="server">

    Sub TreeView1_SelectedNodeChanged(sender As object, e As EventArgs)
        lblSelected.Text = TreeView1.SelectedValue
    End Sub
</script>
<html xmlns="http://www.w3.org/1999/xhtml" >
<head id="Head1" runat="server">
    <title>Show TreeView</title>
</head>
<body>
    <form id="form1" runat="server">
    <div>

    <asp:TreeView
        id="TreeView1"
        DataSourceID="srcDiscuss"
        OnSelectedNodeChanged="TreeView1_SelectedNodeChanged"
        ImageSet="News"
        Runat="server">
        <DataBindings>
            <asp:TreeNodeBinding
                TextField="Subject"
                ValueField="MessageId" />
        </DataBindings>
    </asp:TreeView>

    <custom:SqlHierarchicalDataSource
        id="srcDiscuss"
        ConnectionString='<%$ ConnectionStrings:Discuss %>'
        DataKeyName="MessageId"
        DataParentKeyName="ParentId"
```

LISTING 17.33   Continued

```
        SelectCommand="SELECT MessageId,ParentId,Subject FROM Discuss"
        Runat="server" />

    <hr />

    You selected message number:
    <asp:Label
        id="lblSelected"
        Runat="server" />

    </div>
    </form>
</body>
</html>
```

When you open the page in Listing 17.33, the contents of the Discuss database table are displayed in the TreeView control.

All the code for the SqlHierarchicalDataSource control is included on the CD that accompanies this book. The control is composed out of five separate classes:

- SqlHierarchicalDataSource—This class represents the actual control. It inherits from the base SqlDataSource control and implements the IHierarchicalDataSource interface.

- SqlHierarchicalDataSourceView—This class represents the hierarchical data returned by the control. It inherits from the base HierarchicalDataSourceView class.

- SqlHierarchicalEnumerable—This class represents a collection of SqlNodes.

- SqlNode—This class represents a particular database row from the data source. It includes methods for retrieving child and parent rows.

- SqlNodePropertyDescriptor—This class inherits from the base PropertyDescriptor class. It converts the database columns represented by a SqlNode into class properties so that you can bind to the columns using TreeView and Menu control DataBindings.

> **NOTE**
>
> The Microsoft .NET Framework SDK Documentation includes a sample of a FileSystemDataSource control that implements the IHierarchicalDataSource interface. Look up the IHearchicalDataSource topic in the documentation index.

Summary

In this chapter, you learned how to use the SiteMapPath, Menu, and TreeView Controls. First, you learned how to use the SiteMapPath control to display a breadcrumb trail. You learned how to format the SiteMapPath control with styles and templates.

Next, you explored the Menu control. You learned how to create both vertical and horizontal menus. You also learned how you can bind a Menu control to different data sources such as Site Maps, XML documents, and database data.

The TreeView control was also discussed. You learned how to display check boxes with a TreeView control. You also learned how to bind a TreeView control to different data sources such as Site Maps, XML documents, and database data. You also learned how to display a large set of Tree nodes efficiently by using AJAX and the TreeView control.

Finally, we created a custom SqlHierarchicalDataSource control that enables you to easily bind controls such as the Menu and TreeView controls to hierarchical database data.

CHAPTER 18

Using Site Maps

This chapter jumps into the details of Site Maps. First, you learn how to use the `SiteMapDataSource` control to represent a Site Map on a page. For example, you learn how to use the `SiteMapDataSource` control to display a list of all the pages contained in a folder.

Next, you'll explore the `SiteMap` and `SiteMapNode` classes. You learn how to create new Site Map nodes dynamically. You also learn how to programmatically retrieve Site Map nodes and display the properties of a node in a page.

This chapter also examines several advanced features of Site Maps. For example, you learn how to show different Site Maps to different users depending on their roles. You also learn how you can extend Site Maps with custom attributes.

You also learn how to create custom Site Map providers. The first custom Site Map provider—the AutoSiteMapProvider—automatically builds a Site Map based on the folder and page structure of your website. The second custom Site Map provider—the SqlSiteMapProvider—enables you to store a Site Map in a Microsoft SQL Server database table.

Finally, you learn how to generate Google SiteMaps from ASP.NET Site Maps automatically. You can use a Google SiteMap to improve the way that your website is indexed by the Google search engine.

Using the `SiteMapDataSource` **Control**

The `SiteMapDataSource` control enables you to represent a Site Map declaratively in a page. You can bind navigation controls such as the `TreeView` and `Menu` controls to a `SiteMapDataSource` control. You also can bind other controls such as the `GridView` or `DropDownList` control to a `SiteMapDataSource` control.

Imagine, for example, that your website contains the `Web.sitemap` file in Listing 18.1. Because the default `SiteMapProvider` is the `XmlSiteMapProvider`, the `SiteMapDataSource` control automatically represents the contents of this XML file.

> **NOTE**
>
> The code samples in this section are located in the `SiteMaps` application on the CD that accompanies this book.

LISTING 18.1   `Web.sitemap`

```xml
<?xml version="1.0" encoding="utf-8" ?>
<siteMap xmlns="http://schemas.microsoft.com/AspNet/SiteMap-File-1.0" >
<siteMapNode
  url="Default.aspx"
  title="Home"
  description="The Home Page">
  <siteMapNode
    url="Products/Default.aspx"
    title="Our Products"
    description="Products that we offer">
    <siteMapNode
      url="Products/FirstProduct.aspx"
      title="First Product"
      description="The description of the First Product" />
    <siteMapNode
      url="Products/SecondProduct.aspx"
      title="Second Product"
      description="The description of the Second Product" />
  </siteMapNode>
  <siteMapNode
    url="Services/Default.aspx"
    title="Our Services"
    description="Services that we offer">
    <siteMapNode
      url="Services/FirstService.aspx"
      title="First Service"
      description="The description of the First Service"
      metaDescription="The first service" />
    <siteMapNode
      url="Services/SecondService.aspx"
      title="Second Service"
      description="The description of the Second Service" />
  </siteMapNode>
</siteMapNode>
</siteMap>
```

The Site Map file in Listing 18.1 represents a website with the following folder and page structure:

```
Default.aspx
Products
    FirstProduct.aspx
    SecondProduct.aspx
Services
    FirstService.aspx
    SecondService.aspx
```

The page in Listing 18.2 illustrates how you can represent a Site Map by binding a `TreeView` control to the `SiteMapDataSource` control.

LISTING 18.2   `Default.aspx`

```
<%@ Page Language="VB" %>
<!DOCTYPE html PUBLIC "-//W3C//DTD XHTML 1.1//EN" "http://www.w3.org/TR/
➥xhtml11/DTD/xhtml11.dtd">
<html xmlns="http://www.w3.org/1999/xhtml" >
<head id="Head1" runat="server">
    <title>Home</title>
</head>
<body>
    <form id="form1" runat="server">
    <div>

    <asp:SiteMapPath
        id="SiteMapPath1"
        Runat="server" />

    <hr />

    <asp:TreeView
        id="TreeView1"
        DataSourceID="srcSiteMap"
        Runat="server" />

    <asp:SiteMapDataSource
        id="srcSiteMap"
        Runat="server" />

    </div>
    </form>
</body>
</html>
```

18

When you open the page in Listing 18.2, all the elements from the Web.sitemap file are displayed in the TreeView control with the help of the SiteMapDataSource control (see Figure 18.1).

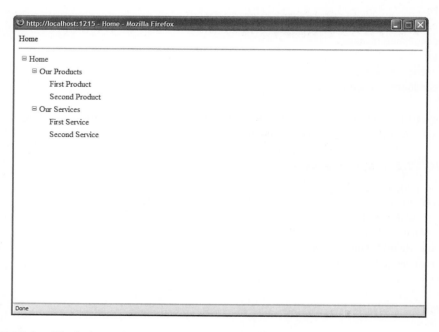

FIGURE 18.1   Displaying a Site Map with a TreeView control.

Setting SiteMapDataSource Properties

The SiteMapDataSource control includes several valuable properties that you can set to modify the nodes that the control returns:

- ShowStartingNode—Enables you to hide the starting node.

- StartFromCurrentNode—Enables you to return all nodes starting from the current node.

- StartingNodeOffset—Enables you to specify a positive or negative offset from the current node.

- StartingNodeUrl—Enables you to return all nodes, starting at a node associated with a specified URL.

The most useful of these properties is the ShowStartingNode property. Normally, when you display a list of nodes with a Menu or TreeView control, you do not want to display the starting node (the link to the home page). The page in Listing 18.3 illustrates how you can bind a Menu control to a SiteMapDataSource that has the value False assigned to its ShowStartingNode property.

LISTING 18.3   Services/Default.aspx

```
<%@ Page Language="VB" %>
<!DOCTYPE html PUBLIC "-//W3C//DTD XHTML 1.1//EN" "http://www.w3.org/TR/
➥xhtml11/DTD/xhtml11.dtd">
<html xmlns="http://www.w3.org/1999/xhtml" >
<head id="Head1" runat="server">
    <style type="text/css">
        .menuItem
        {
            border:solid 1px black;
            background-color:#eeeeee;
            padding:4px;
            margin:1px 0px;
        }
    </style>
    <title>Our Services</title>
</head>
<body>
    <form id="form1" runat="server">
    <div>

    <asp:SiteMapPath
        id="SiteMapPath1"
        Runat="server" />

    <hr />

    <asp:Menu
        id="Menu1"
        DataSourceID="srcSiteMap"
        StaticMenuItemStyle-CssClass="menuItem"
        DynamicMenuItemStyle-CssClass="menuItem"
        Runat="server" />

    <asp:SiteMapDataSource
        id="srcSiteMap"
        ShowStartingNode="false"
        Runat="server" />

    </div>
    </form>
</body>
</html>
```

18

When you open the page in Listing 18.3, only the second-level nodes and descendent nodes are displayed (see Figure 18.2).

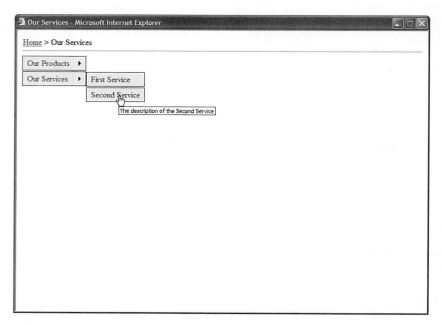

FIGURE 18.2   Hiding the starting node.

The StartFromCurrentNode property is useful when you want to display a list of all nodes below the current node. For example, the page in Listing 18.4 is the Default.aspx page contained in the Products folder. It displays a list of all the product pages contained in the folder.

LISTING 18.4   Products/Default.aspx

```
<%@ Page Language="VB" %>
<!DOCTYPE html PUBLIC "-//W3C//DTD XHTML 1.1//EN" "http://www.w3.org/TR/
➥xhtml11/DTD/xhtml11.dtd">
<html xmlns="http://www.w3.org/1999/xhtml" >
<head id="Head1" runat="server">
    <style type="text/css">
        html
        {
            font:16px Georgia,Serif;
        }
        .productList li
        {
            margin:5px;
```

LISTING 18.4   Continued

```
        }
    </style>
    <title>Our Products</title>
</head>
<body>
    <form id="form1" runat="server">
    <div>

    <h1>Products</h1>

    <asp:BulletedList
        id="bltProducts"
        DisplayMode="HyperLink"
        DataTextField="Title"
        DataValueField="Url"
        DataSourceID="srcSiteMap"
        CssClass="productList"
        Runat="server" />

    <asp:SiteMapDataSource
        id="srcSiteMap"
        ShowStartingNode="false"
        StartFromCurrentNode="true"
        Runat="server" />

    </div>
    </form>
</body>
</html>
```

The page in Listing 18.4 contains a `BulletedList` control bound to a `SiteMapDataSource` control. Because the `SiteMapDataSource` control has its `StartFromCurrentNode` property set to the value `True` and its `ShowStartingNode` property set to the value `False`, all immediate child nodes of the current node are displayed (see Figure 18.3).

Using the `SiteMap` Class

Under the covers, the `SiteMapDataSource` control represents the contents of the `SiteMap` class. The `SiteMap` class represents an application's Site Map regardless of whether the Site Map is stored in an XML file, a database, or some other data source. The class is a memory-resident representation of Site Map data.

18

FIGURE 18.3   Displaying the contents of a folder.

All the properties exposed by the SiteMap class are shared (static) properties:

- CurrentNode—Enables you to retrieve the SiteMapNode that corresponds to the current page.

- Enabled—Enables you to determine whether the Site Map is enabled.

- Provider—Enables you to retrieve the default SiteMapProvider.

- Providers—Enables you to retrieve all the configured SiteMapProvders.

- RootNode—Enables you to retrieve the root SiteMapNode.

The CurrentNode and RootNode properties return a SiteMapNode object. Because a Site Map can contain only one root node, and the root node contains all the other nodes as children, the RootNode property enables you to iterate through all the nodes in a Site Map.

The Provider property returns the default SiteMapProvider. You can use this property to access all the properties and methods of the SiteMapProvider class, such as the FindSiteMapNode() and GetParentNode() methods.

The SiteMap class also supports a single event:

- SiteMapResolve—Raised when the current node is accessed.

You can handle this event to modify the node returned when the current node is retrieved. For example, the Global.asax file in Listing 18.5 automatically adds a new node when the current page does not include a node in the Site Map.

LISTING 18.5   Global.asax

```
<%@ Application Language="VB" %>
<%@ Import Namespace="System.IO" %>
<script runat="server">

    Private Sub Application_Start(ByVal sender As Object, ByVal e As EventArgs)
        AddHandler SiteMap.SiteMapResolve, AddressOf SiteMap_SiteMapResolve
    End Sub

    Private Function SiteMap_SiteMapResolve(ByVal sender As Object, ByVal e
➥As SiteMapResolveEventArgs) As SiteMapNode
        If SiteMap.CurrentNode Is Nothing Then
            Dim url As String = e.Context.Request.Path
            Dim title As String = Path.GetFileNameWithoutExtension(url)
            Dim NewNode As New SiteMapNode(e.Provider, url, url, title)
            NewNode.ParentNode = SiteMap.RootNode
            Return NewNode
        End If
        Return SiteMap.CurrentNode
    End Function
</script>
```

The Application_Start() event handler in Listing 18.5 executes only once when the application first starts. The handler adds a SiteMapResolve event handler to the SiteMap class.

Whenever any control retrieves the current node, the SiteMap_SiteMapResolve() method executes. If there is no node that corresponds to a page, then the method creates a new node and returns it.

The About.aspx page in Listing 18.6 is not included in the Web.sitemap file. However, this page includes a SiteMapPath control. The SiteMapPath control works correctly because the About.aspx page is dynamically added to the Site Map when you access the page (see Figure 18.4).

LISTING 18.6   About.aspx

```
<%@ Page Language="VB" %>
<!DOCTYPE html PUBLIC "-//W3C//DTD XHTML 1.1//EN" "http://www.w3.org/TR/
➥xhtml11/DTD/xhtml11.dtd">
<html xmlns="http://www.w3.org/1999/xhtml" >
<head id="Head1" runat="server">
    <title>About</title>
</head>
<body>
    <form id="form1" runat="server">
```

18

LISTING 18.6   Continued

```
    <div>

    <asp:SiteMapPath
        id="SiteMapPath1"
        Runat="server" />

    <hr />

    <h1>About Our Company</h1>

    </div>
    </form>
</body>
</html>
```

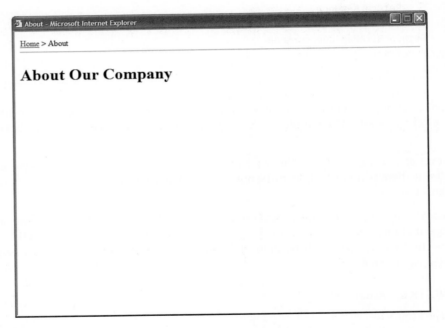

FIGURE 18.4   Adding nodes to a Site Map dynamically.

Using the SiteMapNode Class

All pages and folders in a Site Map are represented by instances of the SiteMapNode class. The SiteMapNode class contains the following properties:

- ChildNodes—Returns the child nodes of the current node.

- Description—Returns the description of the current node.

- HasChildNodes—Returns True when the current node has child nodes.

- Item—Returns a custom attribute (or resource string).

- Key—Returns a unique identifier for the current node.

- NextSibling—Returns the next sibling of the current node.

- ParentNode—Returns the parent node of the current node.

- PreviousSibling—Returns the previous sibling of the current node.

- Provider—Returns the SiteMapProvider associated with the current node.

- ReadOnly—Returns true when a node is read-only.

- ResourceKey—Returns the resource key associated with the current node (enables localization).

- Roles—Returns the user roles associated with the current node.

- RootNode—Returns the Site Map root node.

- Title—Returns the title associated with the current node.

- Url—Returns the URL associated with the current node.

The SiteMapNode class also supports the following methods:

- Clone()—Returns a clone of the current node.

- GetAllNodes()—Returns all descendent nodes of the current node.

- GetDataSourceView()—Returns a SiteMapDataSourceView object.

- GetHierarchicalDataSourceView()—Returns a SiteMapHierarchicalDataSourceView.

- IsAccessibleToUser()—Returns True when the current user has permissions to view the current node.

- IsDescendantOf()—Returns True when the current node is a descendant of a particular node.

By taking advantage of the SiteMap and SiteMapNode classes, you can work directly with Site Maps in a page. For example, imagine that you want to display the value of the SiteMapNode title attribute in both the browser's title bar and in the body of the page. Listing 18.7 demonstrates how you can retrieve the value of the Title property associated with the current page programmatically.

18

LISTING 18.7   Products/FirstProduct.aspx

```
<%@ Page Language="VB" %>
<!DOCTYPE html PUBLIC "-//W3C//DTD XHTML 1.1//EN" "http://www.w3.org/TR/
➥xhtml11/DTD/xhtml11.dtd">
<script runat="server">

    Private Sub Page_Load()
        If Not Page.IsPostBack Then
            Dim currentNode As SiteMapNode = SiteMap.CurrentNode
            Me.Title = currentNode.Title
            ltlBodyTitle.Text = currentNode.Title
            lblDescription.Text = currentNode.Description
        End If
    End Sub
</script>
<html xmlns="http://www.w3.org/1999/xhtml" >
<head id="Head1" runat="server">
    <title>First Product</title>
</head>
<body>
    <form id="form1" runat="server">
    <div>

    <h1><asp:Literal ID="ltlBodyTitle" runat="server" /></h1>

    <asp:Label
        id="lblDescription"
        Runat="server" />

    </div>
    </form>
</body>
</html>
```

When you open the page in Listing 18.7, the Page_Load() event handler grabs the current SiteMapNode and modifies the Page Title property. The handler also assigns the value of the Title property to a Literal control contained in the body of the page. Finally, the value of the SiteMapNode's Description property is assigned to a Label control (see Figure 18.5).

NOTE

It would make sense to place the code in Listing 18.7 in a Master Page. To learn more about Master Pages, see Chapter 5, "Designing Web Sites with Master Pages."

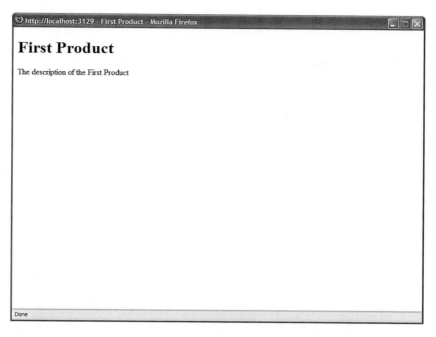

FIGURE 18.5   Retrieving Site Map node properties.

Advanced Site Map Configuration

This section explores several advanced features of Site Maps. For example, you learn how to display different SiteMap nodes, depending on the roles associated with the current user. You also learn how to create multiple Site Maps for a single application. Finally, you learn how you can extend Site Maps with custom attributes.

Using Security Trimming

You might want to display different navigation links to different users, depending on their roles. For example, if a user is a member of the Administrators role, you might want to display links to pages for administrating the website. However, you might want to hide these links from other users.

To display different links to different users depending on their roles, you must enable a feature of Site Maps named Security Trimming. This feature is disabled by default. The web configuration file in Listing 18.8 enables Security Trimming.

LISTING 18.8   Web.Config

```
<?xml version="1.0"?>
<configuration>
  <system.web>
```

LISTING 18.8   Continued

```
    <authentication mode="Windows" />
    <roleManager enabled="true" />

    <siteMap defaultProvider="MySiteMapProvider">
      <providers>
        <add
          name="MySiteMapProvider"
          type="System.Web.XmlSiteMapProvider"
          securityTrimmingEnabled="true"
          siteMapFile="Web.sitemap" />

      </providers>
    </siteMap>

  </system.web>
</configuration>
```

Notice that the configuration file in Listing 18.8 includes a <siteMap> element that configures a new SiteMapProvider named MySiteMapProvider. The new provider enables Security Trimming with its securityTrimmingEnabled property.

After you enable Security Trimming, any pages a user is not allowed to view are automatically hidden. For example, imagine that your website includes a folder named Admin that contains the web configuration file in Listing 18.9.

LISTING 18.9   Web.Config

```
<?xml version="1.0"?>
<configuration xmlns="http://schemas.microsoft.com/.NetConfiguration/v2.0">
<system.web>

  <authorization>
    <allow users="WebAdmin" />
    <deny users="*" />
  </authorization>

</system.web>
</configuration>
```

The configuration file in Listing 18.9 prevents anyone who is not a member of the WebAdmin role from viewing pages in the same folder (and below) as the configuration file. Even if the Web.sitemap file includes nodes that represent pages in the Admin folder, the links don't appear for anyone except members of the WebAdmin role.

Another option is to explicitly associate roles with nodes in a Site Map. This is useful in two situations. First, if your website contains links to another website, then you can hide or display these links based on the user role. Second, if you explicitly associate roles with pages, then you hide page links even when a user has permission to view a page.

The Web.sitemap file in Listing 18.10 contains links to the Microsoft, Google, and Yahoo! websites. A different set of roles is associated with each link.

LISTING 18.10   Web.sitemap

```
<?xml version="1.0" encoding="utf-8" ?>
<siteMap xmlns="http://schemas.microsoft.com/AspNet/SiteMap-File-1.0" >
  <siteMapNode
    title="External Links"
    description="Links to external Websites"
    roles="RoleA,RoleB,RoleC">
    <siteMapNode
      title="Google"
      url="http://www.Google.com"
      description="The Google Website"
      roles="RoleA" />
    <siteMapNode
      title="Microsoft"
      url="http://www.Microsoft.com"
      description="The Microsoft Website"
      roles="RoleB" />
    <siteMapNode
      title="Yahoo"
      url="http://www.Yahoo.com"
      description="The Yahoo Website"
      roles="RoleC" />
  </siteMapNode>
</siteMap>
```

The page in Listing 18.11 enables you to add yourself and remove yourself from different roles. Notice that different links appear in the TreeView control, depending on which roles you select.

LISTING 18.11   ShowSecurityTrimming.aspx

```
<%@ Page Language="VB" %>
<!DOCTYPE html PUBLIC "-//W3C//DTD XHTML 1.1//EN" "http://www.w3.org/TR/
➥xhtml11/DTD/xhtml11.dtd">
<script runat="server">

    Sub Page_Load()
        If Not Page.IsPostBack Then
```

18

LISTING 18.11   Continued

```vb
            For Each item As ListItem In cblSelectRoles.Items
                If Not Roles.RoleExists(item.Text) Then
                    Roles.CreateRole(item.Text)
                    Roles.AddUserToRole(User.Identity.Name, item.Text)
                End If
            Next
        End If
    End Sub

    Sub btnSelect_Click(ByVal sender As Object, ByVal e As EventArgs)
        For Each item As ListItem In cblSelectRoles.Items
            If item.Selected Then
                If Not User.IsInRole(item.Text) Then
                    Roles.AddUserToRole(User.Identity.Name, item.Text)
                End If
            Else
                If User.IsInRole(item.Text) Then
                    Roles.RemoveUserFromRole(User.Identity.Name, item.Text)
                End If
            End If
        Next
        Response.Redirect(Request.Path)
    End Sub

    Sub Page_PreRender()
        For Each item As ListItem In cblSelectRoles.Items
            item.Selected = User.IsInRole(item.Text)
        Next
    End Sub

</script>
<html xmlns="http://www.w3.org/1999/xhtml" >
<head id="Head1" runat="server">
    <style type="text/css">
        html
        {
            background-color:silver;
        }
        .column
        {
            float:left;
            width:300px;
            border:Solid 1px black;
```

LISTING 18.11   Continued

```
            background-color:white;
            padding:10px;
        }
    </style>
    <title>Show Security Trimming</title>
</head>
<body>
    <form id="form1" runat="server">

    <div class="column">

    <asp:Label
        id="lblSelectRoles"
        Text="Select Roles:"
        AssociatedControlID="cblSelectRoles"
        Runat="server" />

    <br />

    <asp:CheckBoxList
        id="cblSelectRoles"
        Runat="server">
        <asp:ListItem Text="RoleA" />
        <asp:ListItem Text="RoleB" />
        <asp:ListItem Text="RoleC" />
    </asp:CheckBoxList>

    <asp:Button
        id="btnSelect"
        Text="Select"
        OnClick="btnSelect_Click"
        Runat="server" />

    </div>

    <div class="column">

    <asp:TreeView
        id="TreeView1"
        DataSourceID="srcSiteMap"
        Runat="server" />

    <asp:SiteMapDataSource
```

18

LISTING 18.11   Continued

```
        id="srcSiteMap"
        Runat="server" />

    </div>
    </form>
</body>
</html>
```

When you first open the page in Listing 18.11, the `Page_Load()` handler creates three roles—RoleA, RoleB, and RoleC—and adds the current user to each role.

The `CheckBoxList` control in the body of the page enables you to select the roles that you want to join. Notice that different links to external websites appear, depending on which roles you select (see Figure 18.6).

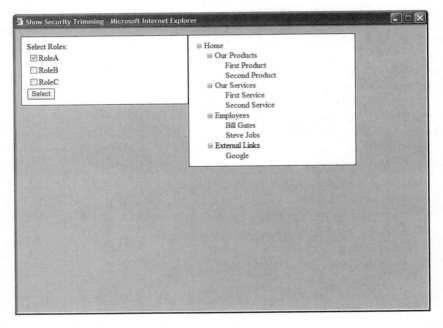

FIGURE 18.6   Hiding Site Map nodes by user role.

Merging Multiple Site Maps

To make it easier to manage a large application, you can store Site Maps in more than one location and merge the Site Maps at runtime. For example, if you are using the default `SiteMapProvider`—the `XmlSiteMapProvider`—then you can create multiple sitemap files that describe the navigation structure of different sections of your website.

For example, the Web.sitemap file in Listing 18.12 includes a node that points to another sitemap file.

LISTING 18.12   Web.sitemap

```xml
<?xml version="1.0" encoding="utf-8" ?>
<siteMap xmlns="http://schemas.microsoft.com/AspNet/SiteMap-File-1.0" >
<siteMapNode
  url="Default.aspx"
  title="Home"
  description="The Home Page">
  <siteMapNode
    url="Products/Default.aspx"
    title="Our Products"
    description="Products that we offer">
    <siteMapNode
      url="Products/FirstProduct.aspx"
      title="First Product"
      description="The description of the First Product" />
    <siteMapNode
      url="Products/SecondProduct.aspx"
      title="Second Product"
      description="The description of the Second Product" />
  </siteMapNode>
  <siteMapNode
    url="Services"
    title="Our Services"
    description="Services that we offer">
    <siteMapNode
      url="Services/FirstService.aspx"
      title="First Service"
      description="The description of the First Service"
      metaDescription="The first service" />
    <siteMapNode
      url="Services/SecondService.aspx"
      title="Second Service"
      description="The description of the Second Service" />
  </siteMapNode>
  <siteMapNode
    siteMapFile="Employees/Employees.sitemap" />
</siteMapNode>
</siteMap>
```

The sitemap in Listing 18.12 includes the following node:

```xml
<siteMapNode siteMapFile="Employees/Employees.sitemap" />
```

18

This node includes a `siteMapFile` attribute that points to a sitemap located in the Employees subdirectory of the current application. The contents of the `Employees.sitemap` are automatically merged with the default `Web.sitemap`.

The `Employees.sitemap` is contained in Listing 18.13.

LISTING 18.13   `Employees/Employees.sitemap`

```xml
<?xml version="1.0" encoding="utf-8" ?>
<siteMap xmlns="http://schemas.microsoft.com/AspNet/SiteMap-File-1.0" >
  <siteMapNode
    url="Employees/Default.aspx"
    title="Employees"
    description="Contains descriptions of employees">
    <siteMapNode
      url="Employees/BillGates.aspx"
      title="Bill Gates"
      description="Bill Gates Page" />
    <siteMapNode
      url="Employees/SteveJobs.aspx"
      title="Steve Jobs"
      description="Steve Jobs Page" />
  </siteMapNode>
</siteMap>
```

Notice that there is nothing special about the sitemap in Listing 18.13. It contains a description of the two pages in the Employees subdirectory.

This is a great feature for working with large websites. Each section of the website can be managed by a different developer. When the website is accessed by a user, the contents of the different sitemaps are seamlessly stitched together.

> **NOTE**
>
> You also can associate different `SiteMapProviders` with different nodes in a sitemap file by taking advantage of the `provider` attribute. For example, a Site Map might be stored in a database table for one section of your website and stored in an XML file for another section of your website.

Creating Custom Site Map Attributes

You can extend a Site Map with your own custom attributes. You can use a custom attribute to represent any type of information that you want.

For example, imagine that you want to associate `<meta>` Description tags with each page in your web application to make it easier for search engines to index your website. In that case, you can add a `metaDescription` attribute to the nodes in a `Web.sitemap` file.

The `Web.sitemap` file in Listing 18.14 includes `metaDescription` attributes for the two Services pages.

LISTING 18.14   `Web.sitemap`

```xml
<?xml version="1.0" encoding="utf-8" ?>
<siteMap xmlns="http://schemas.microsoft.com/AspNet/SiteMap-File-1.0" >
  <siteMapNode
    url="Default.aspx"
    title="Home"
    description="The Home Page">
    <siteMapNode
      url="Products/Default.aspx"
      title="Our Products"
      description="Products that we offer">
      <siteMapNode
        url="Products/FirstProduct.aspx"
        title="First Product"
        description="The description of the First Product" />
      <siteMapNode
        url="Products/SecondProduct.aspx"
        title="Second Product"
        description="The description of the Second Product" />
    </siteMapNode>
    <siteMapNode
      url="Services/Default.aspx"
      title="Our Services"
      description="Services that we offer">
      <siteMapNode
        url="Services/FirstService.aspx"
        title="First Service"
        description="The description of the First Service"
        metaDescription="The first service" />
      <siteMapNode
        url="Services/SecondService.aspx"
        title="Second Service"
        description="The description of the Second Service"
        metaDescription="The second service"  />
    </siteMapNode>
  </siteMapNode>
</siteMap>
```

18

VISUAL WEB DEVELOPER NOTE

Visual Web Developer displays blue squiggles (warning messages) under any custom attributes in a SiteMap file. You can safely ignore these warnings.

Any custom attributes that you add to a Site Map are exposed by instances of the SiteMapNode class. For example, the page in Listing 18.15 retrieves the value of the metaDescription attribute from the current node and displays the value in an actual <meta> tag.

LISTING 18.15   Services/FirstService.aspx

```
<%@ Page Language="VB" %>
<!DOCTYPE html PUBLIC "-//W3C//DTD XHTML 1.1//EN" "http://www.w3.org/TR/
➥xhtml11/DTD/xhtml11.dtd">
<script runat="server">

    Private Sub Page_Load()
        Dim meta As HtmlMeta = New HtmlMeta()
        meta.Name = "Description"
        meta.Content = SiteMap.CurrentNode("metaDescription")
        head1.Controls.Add(meta)
    End Sub
</script>
<html xmlns="http://www.w3.org/1999/xhtml" >
<head id="head1" runat="server">
    <title>First Service</title>
</head>
<body>
    <form id="form1" runat="server">
    <div>

    <h1>The First Service</h1>

    </div>
    </form>
</body>
</html>
```

After you open the page in Listing 18.15 in a web browser, you can select View, Source to see the <meta> tag added to the source of the page (see Figure 18.7).

It is important emphasize that you can do anything you want with custom SiteMapNode attributes. You can represent page titles, section titles, product icons, or anything else with a custom attribute.

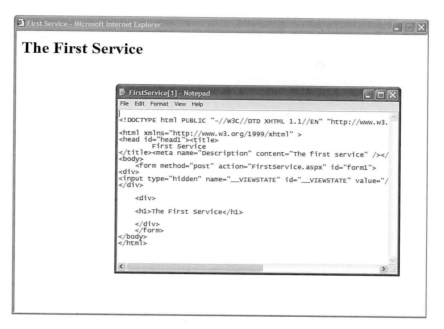

FIGURE 18.7   Extending a Site Map with a `<meta>` tag.

Creating Custom Site Map Providers

Site Maps use the provider model. This means that you can easily modify or extend the way Site Maps work by creating your own Site Map provider.

In this section, we create two custom Site Map providers. First, we create the `AutoSiteMapProvider`. This provider automatically builds a Site Map based on the file and folder structure of a website.

Next, we create a `SqlSiteMapProvider`. This provider enables you to store a Site Map in a Microsoft SQL Server database table instead of an XML file.

Creating the `AutoSiteMapProvider`

All Site Map providers inherit from the base `SiteMapProvider` class. If you want to create your own Site Map provider, then you can override the methods of this base class.

However, in most cases it makes more sense to derive a custom Site Map provider from the base `StaticSiteMapProvider` class. This is the base class for the default Site Map provider—the `XmlSiteMapProvider`—and this class includes default implementations of many of the `SiteMapProvider` methods.

This AutoSiteMapProvider derives from the StaticSiteMapProvider class. It overrides two methods of the base class: GetRootNodeCore() and BuildSiteMap().

The GetRootNodeCore() method returns the root node of the Site Map. The BuildSiteMap() method is the method that is actually responsible for building the Site Map.

The AutoSiteMapProvider is contained in Listing 18.16.

LISTING 18.16   App_Code/AutoSiteMapProvider.vb

```
Imports System
Imports System.Collections.Generic
Imports System.IO
Imports System.Web
Imports System.Web.Caching


Namespace AspNetUnleashed

    Public Class AutoSiteMapProvider
        Inherits StaticSiteMapProvider

        Private _rootNode As SiteMapNode
        Private Shared _excluded As New List(Of String)()
        Private _dependencies As New List(Of String)()

        ''' <summary>
        ''' These folders and pages won't be added
        ''' to the Site Map
        ''' </summary>
        Shared Sub New()
            _excluded.Add("app_code")
            _excluded.Add("app_data")
            _excluded.Add("app_themes")
            _excluded.Add("bin")
        End Sub

        ''' <summary>
        ''' Return the root node of the Site Map
        ''' </summary>
        Protected Overrides Function GetRootNodeCore() As SiteMapNode
            Return BuildSiteMap()
        End Function

        ''' <summary>
        ''' Where all the work of building the Site Map happens
```

LISTING 18.16   Continued

```vb
''' </summary>
Public Overrides Function BuildSiteMap() As SiteMapNode
    ' Allow the Site Map to be created by only a single thread
    SyncLock Me
        ' Attempt to get Root Node from Cache
        Dim context As HttpContext = HttpContext.Current
        _rootNode = CType(context.Cache("RootNode"), SiteMapNode)
        If _rootNode Is Nothing Then
            ' Clear current Site Map
            Clear()

            ' Create root node
            Dim folderUrl As String = HttpRuntime.AppDomainAppVirtualPath
            Dim defaultUrl As String = folderUrl + "/Default.aspx"
            _rootNode = New SiteMapNode(Me, folderUrl, defaultUrl, "Home")
            AddNode(_rootNode)

            ' Create child nodes
            AddChildNodes(_rootNode)
            _dependencies.Add(HttpRuntime.AppDomainAppPath)

            ' Add root node to cache with file dependencies
            Dim fileDependency As CacheDependency =
➥New CacheDependency(_dependencies.ToArray())
            context.Cache.Insert("RootNode", _rootNode, fileDependency)
        End If
        Return _rootNode
    End SyncLock
End Function


''' <summary>
''' Add child folders and pages to the Site Map
''' </summary>
Private Sub AddChildNodes(ByVal parentNode As SiteMapNode)
    AddChildFolders(parentNode)
    AddChildPages(parentNode)
End Sub

''' <summary>
''' Add child folders to the Site Map
''' </summary>
Private Sub AddChildFolders(ByVal parentNode As SiteMapNode)
    Dim context As HttpContext = HttpContext.Current
    Dim parentFolderPath As String = context.Server.MapPath(parentNode.Key)
```

LISTING 18.16   Continued

```
            Dim folderInfo As DirectoryInfo = New DirectoryInfo(parentFolderPath)

            ' Get sub folders
            Dim folders() As DirectoryInfo = folderInfo.GetDirectories()
            For Each folder As DirectoryInfo In folders
                If Not _excluded.Contains(folder.Name.ToLower()) Then
                    Dim folderUrl As String = parentNode.Key + "/" + folder.Name
                    Dim folderNode As SiteMapNode = New SiteMapNode(Me, folderUrl,
➡Nothing, GetName(folder.Name))
                    AddNode(folderNode, parentNode)
                    AddChildNodes(folderNode)
                    _dependencies.Add(folder.FullName)
                End If
            Next
        End Sub

        ''' <summary>
        ''' Add child pages to the Site Map
        ''' </summary>
        Private Sub AddChildPages(ByVal parentNode As SiteMapNode)
            Dim context As HttpContext = HttpContext.Current
            Dim parentFolderPath As String = context.Server.MapPath(parentNode.Key)
            Dim folderInfo As DirectoryInfo = New DirectoryInfo(parentFolderPath)

            Dim pages() As FileInfo = folderInfo.GetFiles("*.aspx")
            For Each page As FileInfo In pages
                If Not _excluded.Contains(page.Name.ToLower()) Then
                    Dim pageUrl As String = parentNode.Key + "/" + page.Name
                    If String.Compare(pageUrl, _rootNode.Url, True) <> 0 Then
                        Dim pageNode As SiteMapNode = New SiteMapNode(Me, pageUrl,
➡pageUrl, GetName(page.Name))
                        AddNode(pageNode, parentNode)
                    End If
                End If
            Next
        End Sub

        ''' <summary>
        ''' Fix the name of the page or folder
        ''' by removing the extension and replacing
        ''' underscores with spaces
        ''' </summary>
        Private Function GetName(ByVal name As String) As String
            name = Path.GetFileNameWithoutExtension(name)
```

LISTING 18.16 Continued

```
            Return Name.Replace("_", " ")
        End Function

    End Class
End Namespace
```

Almost all of the work in Listing 18.16 happens in the `BuildSiteMap()` method. This method recursively iterates through all the folders and pages in the current web application creating `SiteMapNodes`. When the method completes its work, a Site Map that reflects the folder and page structure of the website is created.

You should notice two special aspects of the code in Listing 18.16. First, file dependencies are created for each folder. If you add a new folder or page to your website, the `BuildSiteMap()` method is automatically called the next time you request a page.

Second, notice that the constructor for the `AutoSiteMapProvider` class creates a list of excluded files. For example, this list includes the App_Code and Bin folders. You do not want these files to appear in a Site Map. If there are other special files that you want to hide, then you need to add the filenames to the list of excluded files in the constructor.

After you create the `AutoSiteMapProvider` class, you need to configure your application to use the custom Site Map provider. You can use the configuration file in Listing 18.17 to enable the `AutoSiteMapProvider`.

LISTING 18.17 Web.Config

```
<?xml version="1.0"?>
<configuration xmlns="http://schemas.microsoft.com/.NetConfiguration/v2.0">
    <system.web>

        <siteMap defaultProvider="MyAutoSiteMapProvider">
            <providers>
              <add
                name="MyAutoSiteMapProvider"
                type="AspNetUnleashed.AutoSiteMapProvider" />
            </providers>
        </siteMap>

    </system.web>
</configuration>
```

The configuration file in Listing 18.17 configures the `AutoSiteMapProvider` as the application's default provider.

You can try out the `AutoSiteMapProvider` by requesting the `Default.aspx` page from the `AutoSiteMapProviderApp` Web application contained on the CD that accompanies this book. This application does not include a `Web.sitemap` file. The Site Map is automatically generated from the structure of the website.

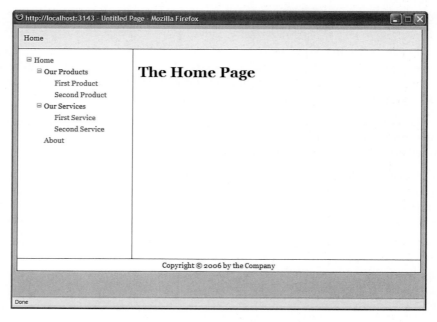

FIGURE 18.8   Displaying an automatically generated Site Map.

Creating the `SqlSiteMapProvider`

For certain applications it makes more sense to store a Site Map in a database table than an XML file. In this section, you can see the creation of the `SqlSiteMapProvider`, which stores a Site Map in a Microsoft SQL Server database.

To use the `SqlSiteMapProvider` class, you must create a SQL database table named SiteMap. Furthermore, the SiteMap database table must look like this:

Id	ParentId	Url	Title	Description
1	null	Default.aspx	Home	The Home Page
2	1		Products	Products
3	2	Products/FirstProduct.aspx	First Product	The First Product
4	2	Products/SecondProduct.aspx	Second Product	The Second Product
6	1		Services	Services
7	6	Services/FirstService.aspx	First Service	The First Service

Each row in the SiteMap table represents a particular Site Map node. The relationship between the nodes is represented by the ParentId column. The row that represents the root node has a ParentId column with the value null. Every other row is either a child of the root node or the child of some other node.

The code for the SqlSiteMapProvider is contained in Listing 18.18.

LISTING 18.18   App_Code\SqlSiteMapProvider.vb

```vb
Imports System
Imports System.Collections.Specialized
Imports System.Web.Configuration
Imports System.Data
Imports System.Data.SqlClient
Imports System.Web
Imports System.Web.Caching


Namespace AspNetUnleashed

    ''' <summary>
    ''' Summary description for SqlSiteMapProvider
    ''' </summary>
    Public Class SqlSiteMapProvider
        Inherits StaticSiteMapProvider

        Private _isInitialized As Boolean = False
        Private _connectionString As String
        Private _rootNode As SiteMapNode

        ''' <summary>
        ''' Initialize provider with database
        ''' connection string
        ''' </summary>
        Public Overrides Sub Initialize(ByVal name As String, ByVal attributes
➥As NameValueCollection)
            If _isInitialized Then
                Return
            End If

            MyBase.Initialize(name, attributes)

            Dim connectionStringName As String = attributes("connectionStringName")
            If String.IsNullOrEmpty(connectionStringName) Then
                Throw New Exception("You must provide a connectionStringName
➥attribute")
            End If
```

18

LISTING 18.18   Continued

```
            _connectionString =
➥WebConfigurationManager.ConnectionStrings(connectionStringName).
➥ConnectionString
            If String.IsNullOrEmpty(_connectionString) Then
                Throw New Exception("Could not find connection String " &
[ic;ccc] connectionStringName)
            End If

            _isInitialized = True
        End Sub

        ''' <summary>
        ''' Return root node by calling
        ''' BuildSiteMap
        ''' </summary>
        Protected Overrides Function GetRootNodeCore() As SiteMapNode
            Return BuildSiteMap()
        End Function

        ''' <summary>
        ''' Build the Site Map and
        ''' create SQL Cache Dependency
        ''' </summary>
        ''' <returns></returns>
        ''' <remarks></remarks>
        Public Overrides Function BuildSiteMap() As SiteMapNode
            ' Only allow the Site Map to be created by a single thread
            SyncLock Me
                ' Attempt to get Root Node from Cache
                Dim context As HttpContext = HttpContext.Current
                _rootNode = CType(context.Cache("RootNode"), SiteMapNode)

                If _rootNode Is Nothing Then
                    HttpContext.Current.Trace.Warn("Loading from database")

                    ' Clear current Site Map
                    Clear()

                    ' Load the database data
                    Dim tblSiteMap As DataTable = GetSiteMapFromDB()

                    ' Get the root node
                    _rootNode = GetRootNode(tblSiteMap)
                    AddNode(_rootNode)
```

LISTING 18.18   Continued

```vb
                      ' Build the child nodes
                      BuildSiteMapRecurse(tblSiteMap, _rootNode)

                      ' Add root node to cache with database dependency
                      Dim sqlDepend As SqlCacheDependency =
➥New SqlCacheDependency("SiteMapDB", "SiteMap")
                      context.Cache.Insert("RootNode", _rootNode, sqlDepend)
                End If
                Return _rootNode
            End SyncLock
        End Function

        ''' <summary>
        ''' Loads Site Map from Database
        ''' </summary>
        Private Function GetSiteMapFromDB() As DataTable
            Dim selectCommand As String = "SELECT Id,ParentId,Url,Title,Description
➥FROM SiteMap"
            Dim dad As New SqlDataAdapter(selectCommand, _connectionString)
            Dim tblSiteMap As New DataTable()
            dad.Fill(tblSiteMap)
            Return tblSiteMap
        End Function

        ''' <summary>
        ''' Gets the root node by returning row
        ''' with null ParentId
        ''' </summary>
        Private Function GetRootNode(ByVal siteMapTable As DataTable)
➥As SiteMapNode
            Dim results() As DataRow = siteMapTable.Select("ParentId IS NULL")
            If results.Length = 0 Then
                Throw New Exception("No root node in database")
            End If
            Dim rootRow As DataRow = results(0)
            Return New SiteMapNode(Me, rootRow("Id").ToString(),
➥rootRow("url").ToString(), rootRow("title").ToString(),
➥rootRow("description").ToString())
        End Function

        ''' <summary>
        ''' Recursively builds a Site Map by iterating ParentId
        ''' </summary>
```

18

LISTING 18.18   Continued

```
        Private Sub BuildSiteMapRecurse(ByVal siteMapTable As DataTable,
➥ByVal parentNode As SiteMapNode)
            Dim results() As DataRow = siteMapTable.Select("ParentId=" +
➥parentNode.Key)
            For Each row As DataRow In results
                Dim node As SiteMapNode = New SiteMapNode(Me, row("Id").ToString(),
➥ row("url").ToString(), row("title").ToString(),
➥row("description").ToString())
                AddNode(node, parentNode)
                BuildSiteMapRecurse(siteMapTable, node)
            Next
        End Sub


    End Class
End Namespace
```

Like the custom Site Map provider that was created in the previous section, the
SqlSiteMapProvider derives from the base StaticSiteMapProvider class. The
SqlSiteMapProvider class overrides three methods of the base class: Initialize(),
GetRootNodeCore(), and BuildSiteMap().

The Initialize() method retrieves a database connection string from the web configuration file. If a database connection string cannot be retrieved, then the method throws a
big, fat exception.

Almost all the work happens in the BuildSiteMap() method. This method loads the
contents of the SiteMap database table into an ADO.NET DataTable. Next, it recursively
builds the Site Map nodes from the DataTable.

There is one special aspect of the code in Listing 18.18. It uses a SQL cache dependency to
automatically rebuild the Site Map when the contents of the SiteMap database table are
changed.

To enable SQL cache dependencies for a database, you must configure the database with
either the enableNotifications tool or the aspnet_regsql tool. Use the
enableNotifications tool when enabling SQL cache dependencies for a SQL Express
database table, and use the aspnet_regsql tool when enabling SQL cache dependencies
for the full version of Microsoft SQL Server.

> **NOTE**
>
> To learn more about configuring SQL cache dependencies, see Chapter 23, "Caching
> Application Pages and Data."

To enable SQL cache dependencies for a SQL Express database named SiteMapDB that contains a table named SiteMap, browse to the folder that contains the SiteMapDB.mdf file and execute the following command from a Command Prompt:

```
enableNotifications "SiteMapDB.mdf" "SiteMap"
```

You can configure your website to use the SqlSiteMapProvider class with the Web configuration file in Listing 18.19.

LISTING 18.19   Web.Config

```
<?xml version="1.0"?>
<configuration>
  <connectionStrings>
    <add
      name="conSiteMap"
      connectionString="Data Source=.\SQLExpress;Integrated
 Security=True;AttachDbFileName=¦DataDirectory¦SiteMapDB.mdf;User Instance=True"/>
  </connectionStrings>

    <system.web>
      <siteMap defaultProvider="myProvider">
        <providers>
          <add
            name="myProvider"
            type="AspNetUnleashed.SqlSiteMapProvider"
            connectionStringName="conSiteMap" />

        </providers>
      </siteMap>

      <caching>
      <sqlCacheDependency enabled = "true" pollTime = "5000" >
        <databases>
          <add name="SiteMapDB"
               connectionStringName="conSiteMap"
          />
        </databases>
      </sqlCacheDependency>
      </caching>

    </system.web>
</configuration>
```

The configuration file in Listing 18.19 accomplishes several tasks. First, it configures the SqlSiteMapProvider as the default Site Map provider. Notice that the provider includes a connectionStringName attribute that points to the connection string for the local SQL Express database named SiteMapDB.

The configuration file also enables SQL cache dependency polling. The application is configured to poll the SiteMapDB database for changes every five seconds. In other words, if you make a change to the SiteMap database table, the Site Map is updated to reflect the change within five seconds.

You can try out the SqlSiteMapProvider by opening the Default.aspx page included in the SqlSiteMapProviderApp web application on the CD that accompanies this book. If you modify the SiteMap database table, the changes are automatically reflected in the Site Map (see Figure 18.9).

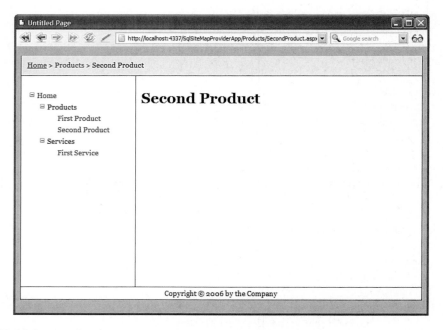

FIGURE 18.9   Displaying a Site Map from a Microsoft SQL database.

Generating a Google SiteMap File

Google provides a free service, named Google SiteMaps, that you can use to monitor and improve the way that Google indexes the pages on your website. For example, you can use Google SiteMaps to discover which Google search queries have returned pages from your website and the ranking of your pages in Google search results. You also can use Google SiteMaps to view any problems that the Google crawler encounters when indexing your site.

You can sign up for Google SiteMaps by visiting the following URL:

```
http://www.google.com/webmasters/sitemaps
```

To use Google SiteMaps, you must provide Google with the URL of a Google SiteMap file hosted on your website. The Google SiteMap file is an XML file that contains a list of URLs you want Google to index.

The Google SiteMap XML file has the following format:

```
<?xml version="1.0" encoding="UTF-8"?>
<urlset xmlns="http://www.google.com/schemas/sitemap/0.84">
  <url>
    <loc>http://www.example.com/</loc>
    <lastmod>2005-01-01</lastmod>
  </url>
  <url>
    <loc>http://www.example.com/sample.html/</loc>
    <lastmod>2006-03-11</lastmod>
  </url>
</urlset>
```

The Google SiteMap file contains a simple list of `<url>` elements that contain `<loc>` elements representing the location of the URL and `<lastmod>` elements representing the last modified date of the URL.

> **NOTE**
>
> The Google SiteMap file also can contain `<changefreq>` and `<priority>` elements. The `<changefreq>` element indicates how frequently a URL changes, and the `<priority>` element represents the priority of a URL relative to other URLs in your site. These elements are optional and are ignored here.

You can generate a Google SiteMap file automatically from an ASP.NET SiteMap. The HTTP Handler in Listing 18.20 generates a Google SiteMap that conforms to Google's requirements for a valid SiteMap file.

LISTING 18.20   PublicSiteMap.ashx

```
<%@ WebHandler Language="VB" Class="PublicSiteMap" %>
Imports System
Imports System.Web
Imports System.Xml
Imports System.Text
Imports System.IO


Public Class PublicSiteMap
    Implements IHttpHandler
```

18

LISTING 18.20   Continued

```
    Private _xmlWriter As XmlWriter

    Public Sub ProcessRequest(ByVal context As HttpContext)
➥Implements IHttpHandler.ProcessRequest
        context.Response.ContentType = "text/xml"

        Dim settings As New XmlWriterSettings()
        settings.Encoding = Encoding.UTF8
        settings.Indent = True
        _xmlWriter = XmlWriter.Create(context.Response.OutputStream, settings)
        _xmlWriter.WriteStartDocument()
        _xmlWriter.WriteStartElement("urlset",
➥"http://www.google.com/schemas/sitemap/0.84")

        ' Add root node
        AddUrl(SiteMap.RootNode)

        ' Add all other nodes
        Dim nodes As SiteMapNodeCollection = SiteMap.RootNode.GetAllNodes()
        For Each node As SiteMapNode In nodes
            AddUrl(node)
        Next

        _xmlWriter.WriteEndElement()
        _xmlWriter.WriteEndDocument()
        _xmlWriter.Flush()
    End Sub

    Private  Sub AddUrl(ByVal node As SiteMapNode)
        ' Skip empty Urls
        If String.IsNullOrEmpty(node.Url) Then
            Return
        End If
        ' Skip remote nodes
        If node.Url.StartsWith("http",True,Nothing) Then
            Return
        End If
        ' Open url tag
        _xmlWriter.WriteStartElement("url")
        ' Write location
        _xmlWriter.WriteStartElement("loc")
        _xmlWriter.WriteString(GetFullUrl(node.Url))
        _xmlWriter.WriteEndElement()
        ' Write last modified
```

LISTING 18.20   Continued

```
        _xmlWriter.WriteStartElement("lastmod")
        _xmlWriter.WriteString(GetLastModified(node.Url))
        _xmlWriter.WriteEndElement()
        ' Close url tag
        _xmlWriter.WriteEndElement()
    End Sub


    Private Function GetFullUrl(ByVal url As String) As String
        Dim context As HttpContext =  HttpContext.Current
        Dim server As String =  context.Request.Url.GetComponents(
➥UriComponents.SchemeAndServer,UriFormat.UriEscaped)
        Return Combine(server,url)
    End Function


    Private Function Combine(ByVal baseUrl As String, ByVal url As String)
➥As String
        baseUrl = baseUrl.TrimEnd(New Char() {"/"c})
        url = url.TrimStart(New Char() {"/"c})
        Return baseUrl + "/" + url
    End Function


    Private Function GetLastModified(ByVal url As String) As String
        Dim context As HttpContext =  HttpContext.Current
        Dim physicalPath As String =  context.Server.MapPath(url)
        Return File.GetLastWriteTimeUtc(physicalPath).ToString("s")
    End Function


    Public ReadOnly Property IsReusable() As Boolean
➥Implements IHttpHandler.IsReusable
        Get
            Return True
        End Get
    End Property
End Class
```

The HTTP Handler in Listing 18.20 generates an XML file by iterating through each of the nodes in an ASP.NET Site Map. The XML file is created with the help of the XmlWriter class. This class is used to generate each of the XML tags.

> **NOTE**
>
> You can think of an HTTP Handler is a lightweight ASP.NET page. You learn about HTTP Handlers in Chapter 25, "Working with the HTTP Runtime."

18

The file in Listing 18.21 contains the XML file returned by the `PublicSiteMap.ashx` handler when the Handler is called from the sample application contained on the CD that accompanies this book. (The file has been abridged for reasons of space.)

LISTING 18.21   `PublicSiteMap.ashx` Results

```
<?xml version="1.0" encoding="utf-8"?>
<urlset xmlns="http://www.google.com/schemas/sitemap/0.84">
  <url>
    <loc>http://localhost:2905/SiteMaps/Default.aspx</loc>
    <lastmod>2005-10-30T03:13:58</lastmod>
  </url>
  <url>
    <loc>http://localhost:2905/SiteMaps/Products/Default.aspx</loc>
    <lastmod>2005-10-28T21:48:04</lastmod>
  </url>
  <url>
    <loc>http://localhost:2905/SiteMaps/Services</loc>
    <lastmod>2005-10-30T04:31:57</lastmod>
  </url>
  <url>
    <loc>http://localhost:2905/SiteMaps/Employees/Default.aspx</loc>
    <lastmod>1601-01-01T00:00:00</lastmod>
  </url>
  <url>
    <loc>http://localhost:2905/SiteMaps/Products/FirstProduct.aspx</loc>
    <lastmod>2005-10-30T03:43:52</lastmod>
  </url>
</urlset>
```

When you sign up at the Google SiteMaps website, submit the URL of the `PublicSiteMap.ashx` file when you are asked to enter your SiteMap URL. The Google service retrieves your SiteMap from the handler automatically.

Summary

In this chapter, you learned how to work with Site Maps. The first section discussed the `SiteMapDataSource` control. You learned how to declaratively represent different sets of nodes in a Site Map with this control.

Next, the `SiteMap` and `SiteMapNode` classes were examined. You learned how to create new Site Map nodes dynamically by handling the `SiteMapResolve` event. You also learned how to programmatically retrieve the current Site Map node in a page.

The next section discussed several advanced features of Site Maps. You learned how to display different Site Map nodes to different users depending on their roles. You also learned how to merge SiteMap files located in different subfolders. Finally, you learned how to extend Site Maps with custom attributes.

We also built two custom Site Map providers. We created an `AutoSiteMapProvider` that automatically builds a Site Map that reflects the folder and page structure of a website. We also created a `SqlSiteMapProvider` that stores a Site Map in a Microsoft SQL Server database table.

Finally, you learned how to use ASP.NET Site Maps with Google SiteMaps. In the final section of this chapter, you learned how to create a custom HTTP Handler that converts an ASP.NET Site Map into a Google SiteMap so that you can improve the way that Google indexes your website's pages.

18

Advanced Navigation

Websites tend to be organic—they grow and change over time. This can create problems when other applications link to your application. You need some way of modifying your website without breaking all the existing links to your website.

In this chapter, you learn how to remap URLs. In other words, you learn how to serve a different page than the page a user requests. In the first section of the chapter, you learn how to remap URLs in the web configuration file.

Next, you learn how to remap URLs by creating a custom HTTP module. Using a module is useful when you need to support wildcard matches and other types of pattern matching when remapping a URL.

Finally, you learn how to use the VirtualPathProvider class to remap URLs. You learn how you can store all your website pages in a database. In the last section of this chapter, a simple CMS (Content Management System) is built with the VirtualPathProvider class.

Remapping URLs

The simplest way to remap a URL is to specify the remapping in your application's web configuration file. For example, the web configuration file in Listing 19.1 remaps the Home.aspx page to the Default.aspx page.

LISTING 19.1   Web.Config

```
<?xml version="1.0"?>
<configuration>
<system.web>
  <urlMappings>
    <add
      url="~/Home.aspx"
      mappedUrl="~/Default.aspx"/>
  </urlMappings>
</system.web>
</configuration>
```

The configuration file in Listing 19.1 contains a <urlMappings> element. This element can contain one or more elements that remap a page from a URL to a mapped Url.

> **CD NOTE**
>
> The code samples in this section can be found in the UrlMappingsApp application on the CD that accompanies this book.

The mappedUrl attribute can contain query strings. However, it cannot contain wildcards. You can use the <urlMappings> element only when performing simple page-to-page mappings.

After you add the web configuration file in Listing 19.1 to your application, any requests for the Home.aspx page are modified automatically to requests for the Default.aspx page. It doesn't matter whether the Home.aspx page actually exists. If the Home.aspx page does exist, you can never open the page.

> **NOTE**
>
> The tilde character (~) has a special meaning when used with a path. It represents the current application root. A forward slash (/) at the start of a URL, on the other hand, represents the website root.
>
> You can use the tilde only with properties of ASP.NET controls. For example, you can use it with the ASP.NET Image control's ImageUrl property, but you cannot use it with the HTML <img> src attribute.
>
> In code, you can use the tilde character with a path by using the Page.ResolveUrl() method. This method automatically expands the tilde to the application root.

When working with remapped URLs, you often need to determine the original URL that a user requested. For example, you might want to display a message that tells users to update their bookmarks (favorites) to point to the new URL.

There are three properties you can use to determine the current URL:

- `Request.RawUrl`—Returns the original URL (before being remapped).

- `Request.Path`—Returns the current URL (after being remapped).

- `Request.AppRelativeCurrentExecutionFilePath`—Returns the application relative URL (after being remapped).

The last property automatically replaces the name of the web application with a tilde (~) character.

For example, the `Default.aspx` page in Listing 19.2 illustrates all three properties.

LISTING 19.2   `Default.aspx`

```
<%@ Page Language="VB" %>
<!DOCTYPE html PUBLIC "-//W3C//DTD XHTML 1.1//EN" "http://www.w3.org/TR/
➥xhtml11/DTD/xhtml11.dtd">
<script runat="server">

    Private Sub Page_Load()
        If String.Compare(Request.Path, Request.RawUrl, True) <> 0 Then
            lblMessage.Text = "The URL to this page has changed, " _
                & "please update your bookmarks."
        End If
    End Sub
</script>
<html xmlns="http://www.w3.org/1999/xhtml" >
<head id="Head1" runat="server">
    <style type="text/css">
        html
        {
            font:14px Georgia,Serif;
        }
        .message
        {
            border:Dotted 2px red;
            background-color:yellow;
        }
    </style>
    <title>Default Page</title>
</head>
<body>
    <form id="form1" runat="server">
    <div>
```

LISTING 19.2   Continued

```
<h1>The Default Page</h1>

<p>
<asp:Label
    id="lblMessage"
    CssClass="message"
    Runat="server" />
</p>

The original request was for:
<blockquote>
    <%=Request.RawUrl%>
</blockquote>
which got remapped to:
<blockquote>
    <%= Request.Path %>
</blockquote>
and the application relative version is:
<blockquote>
    <%= Request.AppRelativeCurrentExecutionFilePath %>
</blockquote>

    </div>
    </form>
</body>
</html>
```

If you request the Home.aspx page, the request is remapped to the Default.aspx page by the web configuration file in Listing 19.1. The Page_Load() event handler displays a message asking users to update their bookmarks when the RawUrl does not match the path (see Figure 19.1).

Each property displayed in the body of the page displays a different value:

```
Request.RawUrl = /UrlMappingsApp/Home.aspx
Request.Path = /UrlMappingsApp/Default.aspx
Request.AppRelativeCurrentExecutionFilePath = ~/Default.aspx
```

Creating a Custom UrlRemapper Module

The <urlMappings> configuration element discussed in the previous section performs a very simple task. It remaps one page to another. However, you'll quickly discover that you need to perform more complex remappings.

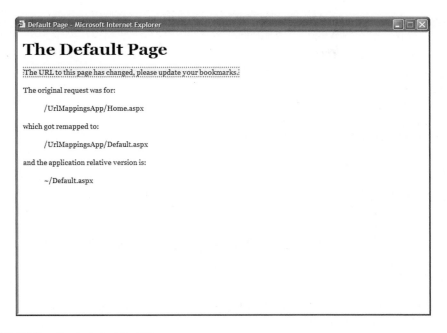

FIGURE 19.1   Remapping the Home page.

For example, imagine that you have a database that contains a table of product categories and a table of products. You want your website's users to request a URL that contains a product category and be able to see matching products. For example, if someone requests the /Products/Soda.aspx page, you want to display all the products in the Soda category. If someone requests the /Products/Milk.aspx page, you want to display all the products in the Milk category.

In that case, you need to use a wildcard when matching URLs. When someone requests any path that matches the pattern /Products/*, you want to redirect the user to a page where you can display matching products for the category specified in the path.

In this section, we create a custom HTTP module that remaps one URL to another. The module supports regular expression matching. Therefore it supports wildcard matches.

> **CD NOTE**
>
> The code samples in this section are located in the UrlRemapperApp application on the CD that accompanies this book.

The code for the custom module—named `UrlRemapper`—is contained in Listing 19.3.

LISTING 19.3   UrlRemapper.vb

```vb
Imports System
Imports System.Web
Imports System.Xml
Imports System.Web.Caching
Imports System.Text.RegularExpressions

Namespace AspNetUnleashed

    Public Class UrlRemapper
        Implements IHttpModule

        Public Sub Init(ByVal app As HttpApplication) Implements IHttpModule.Init
            AddHandler app.BeginRequest, AddressOf app_BeginRequest
        End Sub

        Public Sub app_BeginRequest(ByVal s As Object, ByVal e As EventArgs)
            ' Get HTTP Context
            Dim app As HttpApplication = CType(s, HttpApplication)
            Dim context As HttpContext = app.Context

            ' Get current URL
            Dim currentUrl As String = context.Request.AppRelativeCurrent
➥ExecutionFilePath

            ' Get URL Mappings
            Dim urlMappings As XmlDocument = GetUrlMappings(context)

            ' Compare current URL against each URL from mappings file
            Dim nodes As XmlNodeList = urlMappings.SelectNodes("//add")
            For Each node As XmlNode In nodes
                Dim url As String = node.Attributes("url").Value
                Dim mappedUrl As String = node.Attributes("mappedUrl").Value
                If Regex.Match(currentUrl, url, RegexOptions.IgnoreCase).Success
➥Then
                    context.RewritePath(mappedUrl)
                End If
            Next
        End Sub


        Private Function GetUrlMappings(ByVal context As HttpContext)
➥As XmlDocument
```

LISTING 19.3 Continued

```
        Dim urlMappings As XmlDocument =
➥CType(context.Cache("UrlMappings"), XmlDocument)
        If urlMappings Is Nothing Then
            urlMappings = New XmlDocument()
            Dim path As String = context.Server.MapPath("~/UrlMappings.config")
            urlMappings.Load(path)
            Dim fileDepend As CacheDependency = New CacheDependency(path)
            context.Cache.Insert("UrlMappings", urlMappings, fileDepend)
        End If
        Return urlMappings
    End Function


    Public Sub Dispose() Implements System.Web.IHttpModule.Dispose
    End Sub


  End Class
End Namespace
```

Notice that the class in Listing 19.3 implements the `IHttpModule` interface. An HTTP module is a special class that executes whenever you make a page request. HTTP Modules are discussed in detail in Chapter 25, "Working with the HTTP Runtime."

The module in Listing 19.3 includes an `Init()` method. This method adds an event handler for the Application `BeginRequest` event. The `BeginRequest` event is the first event that is raised when you request a page.

The `BeginRequest` handler gets a list of URL remappings from an XML file named `UrlMappings.config`. The contents of this XML file are cached in memory until the `UrlMappings.config` file is changed on the hard drive.

Next, the module iterates through each remapping from the XML file and performs a regular expression match against the current URL. If the match is successful, then the `Context.RewritePath()` method is used to change the current path to the remapped path.

Before you can use the module in Listing 19.3 in an application, you must first register the module in your application's web configuration file. The web configuration file in Listing 19.4 contains an `<httpModules>` element that includes the `UrlRemapper` module.

LISTING 19.4 Web.Config

```
<?xml version="1.0"?>
<configuration xmlns="http://schemas.microsoft.com/.NetConfiguration/v2.0">
<system.web>

  <httpModules>
    <add
```

19

LISTING 19.4   Continued

```
        name="UrlRemapper"
        type="AspNetUnleashed.UrlRemapper" />
  </httpModules>

</system.web>
</configuration>
```

A sample `UrlMappings.config` file is contained in Listing 19.5.

LISTING 19.5   UrlMappings.config

```xml
<?xml version="1.0"?>
<urlMappings>
  <add
    url="~/Home.aspx"
    mappedUrl="~/Default.aspx" />
  <add
    url="/Products/.*"
    mappedUrl="~/Products/Default.aspx" />
</urlMappings>
```

The XML file in Listing 19.5 contains two remappings. First, it remaps any request for the `Home.aspx` page to the `Default.aspx` page. Second, it remaps any request for any page in the Products directory to the `Default.aspx` page located in the Products folder.

The second mapping uses a regular expression to match the incoming URL. The `.*` expression matches any sequence of characters.

The `Default.aspx` page in the Products folder is contained in Listing 19.6.

LISTING 19.6   Products/Default.aspx

```vbnet
<%@ Page Language="VB" %>
<%@ Import Namespace="System.IO" %>
<!DOCTYPE html PUBLIC "-//W3C//DTD XHTML 1.1//EN"
➥"http://www.w3.org/TR/xhtml11/DTD/xhtml11.dtd">
<script runat="server">

    Private  Sub Page_Load()
        If Not Page.IsPostBack Then
            Dim category As String =
➥Path.GetFileNameWithoutExtension(Request.RawUrl)
            ltlCategory.Text = category
            srcProducts.SelectParameters("Category").DefaultValue = category
        End If
```

LISTING 19.6   Continued

```
      End Sub
</script>
<html xmlns="http://www.w3.org/1999/xhtml" >
<head id="Head1" runat="server">
    <style type="text/css">
        .grid td,.grid th
        {
            padding:4px;
            border-bottom:solid 1px black;
        }
    </style>
    <title>Products</title>
</head>
<body>
    <form id="form1" runat="server">
    <div>

    <h1>
    <asp:Literal
        ID="ltlCategory"
        runat="server" />
    </h1>

    <asp:GridView
        id="grdProducts"
        DataSourceID="srcProducts"
        CssClass="grid"
        GridLines="None"
        AutoGenerateColumns="false"
        Runat="server">
        <Columns>
        <asp:BoundField
            HeaderText="Product Name"
            DataField="Name" />
        <asp:BoundField
            HeaderText="Price"
            DataField="Price"
            DataFormatString="{0:c}" />
        </Columns>
    </asp:GridView>

    <asp:SqlDataSource
        id="srcProducts"
        ConnectionString="<%$ ConnectionStrings:Products %>"
        SelectCommand="SELECT Products.* FROM Products
```

LISTING 19.6   Continued

```
            JOIN Categories ON Products.CategoryId=Categories.Id
            WHERE Categories.Name=@Category"
        Runat="server">
        <SelectParameters>
        <asp:Parameter Name="Category" />
        </SelectParameters>
    </asp:SqlDataSource>

    </div>
    </form>
</body>
</html>
```

The Page_Load() event handler in Listing 19.6 grabs the path of the original request, using the Request.RawUrl property. Next, it extracts the filename from the path, using the System.IO.Path.GetFileNameWithoutExtension() method. Finally, it assigns the name of the page (the category name) to a Label and SqlDataSource control. Products that match the category are displayed in a GridView control.

For example, if you request the /Products/Soda.aspx page, then all the products in the Soda category are displayed (see Figure 19.2). If you request the /Products/Milk.aspx page, then all products in the Milk category are displayed.

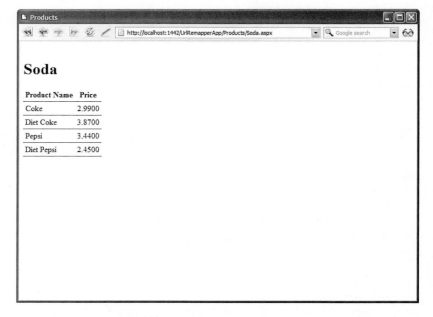

FIGURE 19.2   Displaying matching products.

Using the `VirtualPathProvider` Class

The `VirtualPathProvider` class enables you to abstract the pages in a web application from the file system. In other words, it enables you to store your ASP.NET pages any way you please.

For example, you can use the `VirtualPathProvider` class to store all the pages in your application in a database. This would be an appropriate choice when you need to build a Content Management System. If you store pages in a database, then users can update the pages easily in an application through an HTML form interface and save the changes to the database.

In this section, you learn how to store the pages in an ASP.NET application in a Microsoft SQL Server 2005 Express database. But first, it's a good idea to examine the classes related to the `VirtualPathProvider` class in more detail.

Limitations of the `VirtualPathProvider` Class

Unfortunately, you can't use the `VirtualPathProvider` with every type of file. In particular, the following types of files must always be located on the file system:

- The `Global.asax` file
- `Web.Config` files
- The App_Data folder
- The App_Code folder
- The App_GlobalResources folder
- App_LocalResource folders
- The Bin folder

Every other type of file is fair game. This includes ASP.NET pages, User Controls, Themes, and Master Pages.

Understanding the `VirtualPathProvider` Class

The `VirtualPathProvider` class is a `MustInherit` (abstract) class. It contains the following methods, which you can override:

- `CombineVirtualPaths()`—Returns a combined path from two paths.
- `DirectoryExists()`—Returns `true` when a directory exists.
- `FileExists()`—Returns `true` when a file exists.
- `GetCacheDependency()`—Returns a cache dependency object that indicates when a file has been changed.
- `GetCacheKey()`—Returns the key used by the cache dependency.
- `GetDirectory()`—Returns a VirtualDirectory.

19

- `GetFile()`—Returns a VirtualFile.

- `GetFileHash()`—Returns a hash of the files used by the cache dependency.

- `OpenFile()`—Returns the contents of a file.

Typically, you override the `FileExists()` and `GetFile()` methods to retrieve a file from your data store. If you want to represent directories, then you also need to override the `DirectoryExists()` and `GetDirectory()` methods.

Notice that several of these methods are related to caching. The `VirtualPathProvider` needs to know when a file has been modified so that it can retrieve the new version of the file and compile it. By default, the ASP.NET Framework uses a file dependency to determine when a file has been modified on the hard drive. However, in this situation a `SqlCacheDependency` is used because the files will be stored in a database.

The `VirtualPathProvider` also includes a very useful property:

- `Previous`—Returns the previously registered VirtualPathProvider.

The `Previous` property enables you to use the default `VirtualPathProvider`. For example, if you want to store some files in the file system and other files in the database, then you can use the `Previous` property to avoid rewriting all of the logic for working with files in the file system.

The `GetFile()` method returns an instance of the `VirtualFile` class. When using the `VirtualPathProvider`, you must create a new class that inherits from the `VirtualFile` class. This class contains the following properties:

- `IsDirectory`—Always returns False.

- `Name`—Returns the name of the file.

- `VirtualPath`—Returns the virtual path of the file.

The `VirtualFile` class also contains the following method:

- `Open()`—Returns the contents of the file.

Typically, when creating a class that inherits from the `VirtualFile` class, you override the `Open()` method. For example, we'll override this method to get the contents of a file from a database table in the code sample built in this section.

The `GetDirectory()` method returns an instance of the `VirtualDirectory` class. This class contains the following properties:

- `Children`—Returns all the files and directories that are children of the current directory.

- `Directories`—Returns all the directories that are children of the current directory.

- `Files`—Returns all the files that are children of the current directory.

- `IsDirectory`—Always returns `True`.
- `Name`—Returns the name of the directory.
- `VirtualPath`—Returns the virtual path of the directory.

There is another class in the ASP.NET Framework that you'll want to use when working with the `VirtualPathProvider` class. The `VirtualPathUtility` class contains several useful methods for working with virtual paths:

- `AppendTrailingSlash()`—Returns a path with at most one forward slash appended to the end of the path.
- `Combine()`—Returns the combination of two virtual paths.
- `GetDirectory()`—Returns the directory portion of a path.
- `GetExtension()`—Returns the file extension of a path.
- `GetFileName()`—Returns the file name from a path.
- `IsAbsolute()`—Returns `True` when a path starts with a forward slash.
- `IsAppRelative()`—Returns `True` when a path starts with a tilde (~).
- `MakeRelative()`—Returns a relative path from an application-relative path.
- `RemoveTrailingSlash()`—Removes trailing slash from the end of a path.
- `ToAbsolute()`—Returns a path that starts with a forward slash.
- `ToAppRelative()`—Returns a path that starts with a tilde (~).

By taking advantage of the `VirtualPathUtility` class, you can avoid doing a lot of tedious string parsing on paths.

Registering a `VirtualPathProvider` Class

Before you can use an instance of the `VirtualPathProvider` class, you must register it for your application. You can register a `VirtualPathProvider` instance with the `HostingEnvironment.RegisterVirtualPathProvider()` method.

You need to register the `VirtualPathProvider` when an application first initializes. You can do this by creating a shared method named `AppInitialize()` and adding the method to any class contained in the App_Code folder. The `AppInitialize()` method is automatically called by the ASP.NET Framework when an application starts.

For example, the following `AppInitialize` method registers a `VirtualPathProvider` named `MyVirtualPathProvider`:

```
Public Shared Sub AppInitialize()
  Dim myProvider As New MyVirtualPathProvider()
  HostingEnvironment.RegisterVirtualPathProvider(myProvider)
End Sub
```

19

In our `VirtualPathProvider` application, we'll include the `AppInitialize()` method in the `VirtualPathProvider` class itself.

Storing a Website in Microsoft SQL Server

In this section, we'll create a `VirtualPathProvider` that stores files and directories in two Microsoft SQL Server database tables named `VirtualFiles` and `VirtualDirectories`. The VirtualFiles table looks like this:

Path	Name	Content
~/	Test.aspx	The time is now <%= DateTime.Now.ToString() %>
~/Products/	FirstProduct.aspx	The first product
~/Products/	SecondProduct.aspx	The second product

The Path column represents the directory that contains the file. The Name column contains the name of the file. Finally, the Content column contains the actual file content.

Notice that the file can contain scripts. The `Test.aspx` page displays the current date and time. You can place anything that you would place in a normal ASP.NET page, including ASP.NET controls, in the Content column.

The VirtualDirectories table looks like this:

Path	ParentPath
~/	NULL
~/Products	~/

The Path column represents the entire directory path. The ParentPath column represents the entire directory path of the directory that contains the directory.

The `VirtualPathProvider` class in Listing 19.7—named `SqlVirtualPathProvider`—uses both database tables.

LISTING 19.7   `SqlVirtualPathProvider`

```
Imports System
Imports System.Web
Imports System.Web.Caching
Imports System.Collections
Imports System.Collections.Generic
Imports System.Web.Hosting

Namespace AspNetUnleashed

    Public Class SqlVirtualPathProvider
        Inherits VirtualPathProvider
```

LISTING 19.7   Continued

```
''' <summary>
''' Register VirtualPathProvider for the application
''' </summary>
Public Shared Sub AppInitialize()
    Dim sqlProvider As New SqlVirtualPathProvider()
    HostingEnvironment.RegisterVirtualPathProvider(sqlProvider)
End Sub

Public Sub New()
    MyBase.New()
End Sub

''' <summary>
''' Returns true when the file is a virtual file
''' instead of a normal filesystem file
''' </summary>
Private Function IsVirtualFile(ByVal virtualPath As String) As Boolean
    Dim appVirtualPath As String =
➥VirtualPathUtility.ToAppRelative(virtualPath)
    Return Not appVirtualPath.StartsWith("~/admin/",
➥ StringComparison.InvariantCultureIgnoreCase)
End Function

''' <summary>
''' Returns true when a file exists
''' </summary>
Public Overrides Function FileExists(ByVal virtualPath As String)
➥As Boolean
    If IsVirtualFile(virtualPath) Then
        Return VirtualFiles.FileExists(virtualPath)
    Else
        Return Previous.FileExists(virtualPath)
    End If
End Function

''' <summary>
''' Gets a SqlVirtualFile that corresponds
''' to a file with a certain path
''' </summary>
Public Overrides Function GetFile(ByVal virtualPath As String)
➥As VirtualFile
    If IsVirtualFile(virtualPath) Then
        Return New SqlVirtualFile(virtualPath)
    Else
        Return Previous.GetFile(virtualPath)
```

19

LISTING 19.7   Continued

```
            End If
        End Function


        ''' <summary>
        ''' Returns true when a directory exists
        ''' </summary>
        Public Overrides Function DirectoryExists(ByVal virtualPath As String)
➥As Boolean
            If IsVirtualFile(virtualPath) Then
                Return VirtualFiles.DirectoryExists(virtualPath)
            Else
                Return Previous.DirectoryExists(virtualPath)
            End If
        End Function


        ''' <summary>
        ''' Returns a SqlVirtualDirectory that corresponds
        ''' to a virtual path
        ''' </summary>
        Public Overrides Function GetDirectory(ByVal virtualPath As String)
➥As VirtualDirectory
            If IsVirtualFile(virtualPath) Then
                Return New SqlVirtualDirectory(virtualPath)
            Else
                Return Previous.GetDirectory(virtualPath)
            End If
        End Function


        ''' <summary>
        ''' Gets the SqlCacheDependency object for the VirtualFilesDB
        ''' database
        ''' </summary>
        Public Overrides Function GetCacheDependency(ByVal virtualPath As String,
➥ByVal virtualPathDependencies As IEnumerable, ByVal utcStart As DateTime)
➥As CacheDependency
            If IsVirtualFile(virtualPath) Then
                Return New SqlCacheDependency("VirtualFiles", "VirtualFiles")
            Else
                Return Previous.GetCacheDependency(virtualPath,
➥virtualPathDependencies, utcStart)
            End If
        End Function


    End Class
End Namespace
```

The class in Listing 19.7 overrides the FileExists(), GetFile(), DirectoryExists(), and GetDirectory() methods of the base VirtualPathProvider class.

The class also includes a private method named IsVirtualFile(). This method returns the value True when a file is not contained in the Admin folder. The Admin directory contains a normal file system file. You'll notice that each method, such as the FileExists() method, checks the IsVirtualFile() method. If the method returns False, the Previous property is used to pass the handling of the file to the file system.

The SqlVirtualPathProvider class also overrides the GetCacheDependency() method. This method returns a SqlCacheDependency. The SQL cache dependency is configured with the Web configuration file in Listing 19.8.

LISTING 19.8 Web.Config

```
<?xml version="1.0"?>
<configuration xmlns="http://schemas.microsoft.com/.NetConfiguration/v2.0">
  <connectionStrings>
    <add
      name="VirtualFiles"
      connectionString="Data Source=.\SQLExpress;Integrated
  Security=True;AttachDbFileName=¦DataDirectory¦VirtualFilesDB.mdf;
  User Instance=True"/>
  </connectionStrings>
    <system.web>
      <caching>
        <sqlCacheDependency enabled="true">
          <databases>
            <add
              name="VirtualFiles"
              connectionStringName="VirtualFiles"
              pollTime="5000"/>
          </databases>
        </sqlCacheDependency>
      </caching>
    </system.web>
</configuration>
```

To use the SQL cache dependency, you must configure the SQL database to support the cache dependency. You can enable SQL cache dependencies for the VirtualFilesDB database and the two database tables contained in the database by executing the following two commands from a Command Prompt after navigating to the application's App_Data folder:

```
enableNotifications "VirtualFilesDB.mdf", "VirtualDirectories"
enableNotifications "VirtualFilesDB.mdf", "VirtualFiles"
```

NOTE

SQL cache dependencies are discussed in detail in Chapter 23, "Caching Application Pages and Data."

The GetFile() method in the SqlVirtualPathProvider class returns an instance of the SqlVirtualFile class. This class is contained in Listing 19.9.

LISTING 19.9   SqlVirtualFile.vb

```vb
Imports System
Imports System.Data
Imports System.Data.SqlClient
Imports System.Web.Hosting
Imports System.IO
Imports System.Web

Namespace AspNetUnleashed

    Public Class SqlVirtualFile
        Inherits VirtualFile

        Public Sub New(ByVal virtualPath As String)
            MyBase.New(virtualPath)
        End Sub

        Public Overrides Function Open() As Stream
            ' Get content from database
            Dim content As String = VirtualFiles.FileContentSelect(Me.VirtualPath)

            ' return results as stream
            Dim mem As MemoryStream = New MemoryStream()
            Dim writer As StreamWriter = New StreamWriter(mem)
            writer.Write(content)
            writer.Flush()
            mem.Seek(0, SeekOrigin.Begin)
            Return mem
        End Function

        Public ReadOnly Property Content() As String
            Get
                Return VirtualFiles.FileContentSelect(Me.VirtualPath)
            End Get
        End Property

    End Class
End Namespace
```

The `SqlVirtualFile` class overrides the `Open()` method of the base `VirtualFile` class. The `Open()` method grabs the contents of the file from the Content column of the VirtualFiles database table.

The `GetDirectory()` method returns an instance of the `SqlVirtualDirectory` class. This class is contained in Listing 19.10.

LISTING 19.10   `SqlVirtualDirectory.vb`

```vbnet
Imports System
Imports System.Collections
Imports System.Web.Hosting
Imports System.Web

Namespace AspNetUnleashed

    Public Class SqlVirtualDirectory
    Inherits VirtualDirectory

        Public  Sub New(ByVal virtualPath As String)
            MyBase.New(virtualPath)
        End Sub

        Public ReadOnly Property AppPath() As String
        Get
            Return VirtualPathUtility.ToAppRelative(VirtualPath)
        End Get
        End Property

        Public Overrides ReadOnly Property Children() As IEnumerable
        Get
            Return VirtualFiles.DirectorySelectChildren(VirtualPath)
        End Get
        End Property

        Public Overrides ReadOnly Property Directories() As IEnumerable
        Get
            Return VirtualFiles.DirectorySelectDirectories(VirtualPath)
        End Get
        End Property

        Public Overrides ReadOnly Property Files() As IEnumerable
        Get
            Return VirtualFiles.DirectorySelectFiles(VirtualPath)
        End Get
        End Property
    End Class
End Namespace
```

19

The SqlVirtualDirectory class overrides three properties of the base VirtualDirectory class: the Children, Directories, and Files properties. These properties return files and subfolders from the VirtualFiles and VirtualDirectories database tables.

The VirtualPathProvider classes use the VirtualFiles class to interact with the SQL database. The VirtualFiles class acts as the data access layer. The code for this class is contained in Listing 19.11.

LISTING 19.11   VirtualFiles.vb

```vb
Imports System
Imports System.Web
Imports System.Web.Configuration
Imports System.Data
Imports System.Data.SqlClient
Imports System.Collections
Imports System.Collections.Generic

Namespace AspNetUnleashed

    Public Class VirtualFiles

        Shared ReadOnly _connectionString As String

        ''' <summary>
        ''' Get the connection string from Web.Config
        ''' </summary>
        Shared Sub New()
            _connectionString = WebConfigurationManager.
➥ConnectionStrings("VirtualFiles").ConnectionString
        End Sub


        ''' <summary>
        ''' Check whether file exists in database
        ''' </summary>
        Public Shared Function FileExists(ByVal virtualPath As String) As Boolean
            ' Relativize path
            virtualPath = VirtualPathUtility.ToAppRelative(virtualPath)

            ' Break virtual path
            Dim fileName As String = VirtualPathUtility.GetFileName(virtualPath)
            Dim path As String = VirtualPathUtility.GetDirectory(virtualPath)

            ' Initialize command
            Dim con As New SqlConnection(_connectionString)
```

LISTING 19.11   Continued

```
            Dim commandText As String = "SELECT Name FROM VirtualFiles
➥WHERE Path=@Path AND Name=@Name"
            Dim cmd As New SqlCommand(commandText, con)

            ' Create parameter
            cmd.Parameters.AddWithValue("@Path", path)
            cmd.Parameters.AddWithValue("@Name", fileName)

            ' Execute command
            Dim result As Boolean
            Using con
                con.Open()
                Dim reader As SqlDataReader = cmd.ExecuteReader()
                result = reader.HasRows
            End Using
            Return result
        End Function

        ''' <summary>
        ''' Add new file to database
        ''' </summary>
        Public Shared Sub FileInsert(ByVal virtualPath As String,
➥ByVal name As String, ByVal content As String)
            ' Relativize path
            virtualPath = VirtualPathUtility.ToAppRelative(virtualPath)

            ' Initialize command
            Dim con As New SqlConnection(_connectionString)
            Dim commandText As String = "INSERT VirtualFiles (Path,Name,Content)
➥VALUES (@Path,@Name,@Content)"
            Dim cmd As New SqlCommand(commandText, con)

            ' Create parameters
            cmd.Parameters.AddWithValue("@Path", virtualPath)
            cmd.Parameters.AddWithValue("@Name", name)
            cmd.Parameters.AddWithValue("@Content", content)

            ' Execute command
            Using con
                con.Open()
                cmd.ExecuteNonQuery()
            End Using
        End Sub
```

LISTING 19.11   Continued

```vb
        ''' <summary>
        ''' Get contents of file
        ''' </summary>
        Public Shared Function FileContentSelect(ByVal virtualPath As String)
➥As String
            ' Relativize path
            virtualPath = VirtualPathUtility.ToAppRelative(virtualPath)

            ' Break virtualPath
            Dim path As String = VirtualPathUtility.GetDirectory(virtualPath)
            Dim fileName As String = VirtualPathUtility.GetFileName(virtualPath)

            ' Initialize command
            Dim con As New SqlConnection(_connectionString)
            Dim commandText As String = "SELECT Content FROM VirtualFiles
➥WHERE Path=@Path AND Name=@Name"
            Dim cmd As New SqlCommand(commandText, con)

            ' Create parameter
            cmd.Parameters.AddWithValue("@Path", path)
            cmd.Parameters.AddWithValue("@Name", fileName)

            ' Execute command
            Dim content As String
            Using con
                con.Open()
                content = CType(cmd.ExecuteScalar(), String)
            End Using
            Return content
        End Function



        ''' <summary>
        ''' Update File content
        ''' </summary>
        Public Shared Sub FileContentUpdate(ByVal virtualPath As String,
➥ByVal content As String)
            ' Relativize path
            virtualPath = VirtualPathUtility.ToAppRelative(virtualPath)

            ' Break virtualPath
            Dim path As String = VirtualPathUtility.GetDirectory(virtualPath)
            Dim fileName As String = VirtualPathUtility.GetFileName(virtualPath)
```

LISTING 19.11   Continued

```
            ' Initialize command
            Dim con As New SqlConnection(_connectionString)
            Dim commandText As String = "UPDATE VirtualFiles SET Content=@Content
➥WHERE Path=@Path AND Name=@Name"
            Dim cmd As New SqlCommand(commandText, con)

            ' Create parameter
            cmd.Parameters.AddWithValue("@Path", path)
            cmd.Parameters.AddWithValue("@Name", fileName)
            cmd.Parameters.AddWithValue("@Content", content)

            ' Execute command
            Using con
                con.Open()
                cmd.ExecuteScalar()
            End Using
        End Sub


        ''' <summary>
        ''' Returns a single virtual file
        ''' </summary>
        Public Shared Function FileSelect(ByVal virtualPath As String)
➥As SqlVirtualFile
            Return New SqlVirtualFile(virtualPath)
        End Function

        ''' <summary>
        ''' Deletes a file from the database
        ''' </summary>
        Public Shared Sub FileDelete(ByVal virtualPath As String)
            ' Relativize path
            virtualPath = VirtualPathUtility.ToAppRelative(virtualPath)

            ' Break virtualPath
            Dim path As String = VirtualPathUtility.GetDirectory(virtualPath)
            Dim fileName As String = VirtualPathUtility.GetFileName(virtualPath)

            ' Initialize command
            Dim con As New SqlConnection(_connectionString)
            Dim commandText As String = "DELETE VirtualFiles
➥WHERE Path=@Path AND Name=@Name"
            Dim cmd As New SqlCommand(commandText, con)

            ' Create parameters
```

19

LISTING 19.11   Continued

```vb
            cmd.Parameters.AddWithValue("@Path", path)
            cmd.Parameters.AddWithValue("@Name", fileName)

            ' Execute command
            Using con
                con.Open()
                cmd.ExecuteNonQuery()
            End Using
        End Sub


        ''' <summary>
        ''' Check whether directory exists in database
        ''' </summary>
        Public Shared Function DirectoryExists(ByVal virtualPath As String)
➥As Boolean
            ' Relativize path
            virtualPath = VirtualPathUtility.ToAppRelative(virtualPath)

            ' Initialize command
            Dim con As New SqlConnection(_connectionString)
            Dim commandText As String = "SELECT Path FROM VirtualDirectories
➥WHERE Path=@Path"
            Dim cmd As New SqlCommand(commandText, con)

            ' Create parameter
            cmd.Parameters.AddWithValue("@Path", virtualPath)

            ' Execute command
            Dim result As Boolean
            Using con
                con.Open()
                Dim reader As SqlDataReader = cmd.ExecuteReader()
                result = reader.HasRows
            End Using
            Return result
        End Function


        ''' <summary>
        ''' Create a new directory
        ''' </summary>
        Public Shared Sub DirectoryInsert(ByVal virtualPath As String,
➥ByVal path As String)
            ' Relativize path
```

LISTING 19.11   Continued

```vb
            virtualPath = VirtualPathUtility.ToAppRelative(virtualPath)

            ' Initialize command
            Dim con As New SqlConnection(_connectionString)
            Dim commandText As String = "INSERT VirtualDirectories
➥(Path,ParentPath) VALUES (@Path,@ParentPath)"
            Dim cmd As New SqlCommand(commandText, con)

            ' Create parameters
            cmd.Parameters.AddWithValue("@Path", VirtualPathUtility.Combine(
➥virtualPath, path))
            cmd.Parameters.AddWithValue("@ParentPath", virtualPath)

            ' Execute command
            Using con
                con.Open()
                cmd.ExecuteNonQuery()
            End Using
        End Sub


        ''' <summary>
        ''' Deletes a directory
        ''' </summary>
        Public Shared Sub DirectoryDelete(ByVal virtualPath As String)
            ' Relativize path
            virtualPath = VirtualPathUtility.ToAppRelative(virtualPath)

            ' Initialize command
            Dim con As New SqlConnection(_connectionString)
            Dim commandText As String = "DELETE VirtualDirectories
➥WHERE Path + '/'=@Path OR ParentPath=@Path"
            Dim cmd As New SqlCommand(commandText, con)

            ' Create parameters
            cmd.Parameters.AddWithValue("@Path", virtualPath)

            ' Execute command
            Using con
                con.Open()
                cmd.ExecuteNonQuery()
            End Using
        End Sub


        ''' <summary>
```

LISTING 19.11 Continued

```
        ''' Get a directory
        ''' </summary>
        Public Shared Function DirectorySelect() As List(Of SqlVirtualDirectory)
            Dim dirs As New List(Of SqlVirtualDirectory)()

            ' Initialize command
            Dim con As New SqlConnection(_connectionString)
            Dim commandText As String = "SELECT Path FROM VirtualDirectories"
            Dim cmd As New SqlCommand(commandText, con)

            Using con
                con.Open()
                Dim reader As SqlDataReader = cmd.ExecuteReader()
                While reader.Read()
                    dirs.Add(New SqlVirtualDirectory(CType(reader("Path"),
➥String)))
                End While
            End Using
            Return dirs
        End Function


        ''' <summary>
        ''' Get all files in a directory
        ''' </summary>
        Public Shared Function DirectorySelectFiles(ByVal virtualPath As String)
➥As List(Of SqlVirtualFile)
            ' Relativize path
            virtualPath = VirtualPathUtility.ToAppRelative(virtualPath)

            ' Initialize command
            Dim con As SqlConnection = New SqlConnection(_connectionString)
            Dim commandText As String = "SELECT Path,Name FROM VirtualFiles " _
                & "WHERE Path=@Path ORDER BY Path"
            Dim cmd As New SqlCommand(commandText, con)

            ' Create parameter
            cmd.Parameters.AddWithValue("@Path", virtualPath)

            ' Execute command
            Dim files As New List(Of SqlVirtualFile)()
            Using con
                con.Open()
                Dim reader As SqlDataReader = cmd.ExecuteReader()
                While reader.Read()
```

LISTING 19.11   Continued

```
                Dim fullName As String = VirtualPathUtility.Combine(
➥reader("Path").ToString(), reader("Name").ToString())
                    files.Add(New SqlVirtualFile(fullName))
                End While
            End Using

            Return files
        End Function

        ''' <summary>
        ''' Retrieves all subdirectories for a directory
        ''' </summary>
        Public Shared Function DirectorySelectDirectories(ByVal virtualPath _
➥As String) As List(Of SqlVirtualDirectory)
            ' Relativize path
            virtualPath = VirtualPathUtility.ToAppRelative(virtualPath)

            ' Initialize command
            Dim con As SqlConnection = New SqlConnection(_connectionString)
            Dim commandText As String = "SELECT Path FROM VirtualDirectories " _
                & "WHERE ParentPath=@Path ORDER BY Path"
            Dim cmd As New SqlCommand(commandText, con)

            ' Create parameters
            cmd.Parameters.AddWithValue("@Path", virtualPath)

            ' Execute command
            Dim dirs As New List(Of SqlVirtualDirectory)()
            Using con
                con.Open()
                Dim reader As SqlDataReader = cmd.ExecuteReader()
                While reader.Read()
                    dirs.Add(New SqlVirtualDirectory(reader("Path").ToString()))
                End While
            End Using
            Return dirs
        End Function

        ''' <summary>
        ''' Returns all files and subdirectories from a directory
        ''' </summary>
        Public Shared Function DirectorySelectChildren(ByVal virtualPath As String)
➥As ArrayList
            Dim filesAndDirs As ArrayList = New ArrayList()
```

19

LISTING 19.11   Continued

```
            Dim dirs As List(Of SqlVirtualDirectory) =
➥DirectorySelectDirectories(virtualPath)
            For Each dir As SqlVirtualDirectory In dirs
                filesAndDirs.Add(dir)
            Next

            Dim files As List(Of SqlVirtualFile) = DirectorySelectFiles(
➥virtualPath)
            For Each file As SqlVirtualFile In files
                filesAndDirs.Add(file)
            Next
            Return filesAndDirs
        End Function


    End Class
End Namespace
```

The CD that accompanies this book includes an application named
SqlVirtualPathProviderApp, which contains all the files discussed in this section. The
application also includes an Admin folder with a Default.aspx page which enables you
to add, edit, and delete virtual directories and files (see Figure 19.3 and Figure 19.4). You
can use this page to build an entire application that is stored in the database.

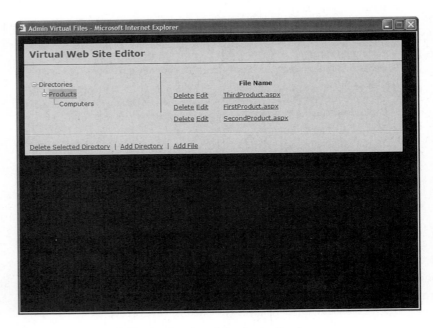

FIGURE 19.3   Listing virtual files in the virtual Products directory.

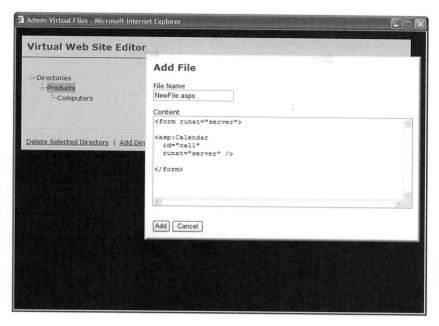

FIGURE 19.4   Adding a new virtual file.

Summary

This chapter explored several advanced topics related to website navigation. In the first two sections, you learned how to map URLs from one path to another. In the first section, you learned how to configure remappings in the Web configuration file. In the second section, you learned how to build a custom HTTP module, which enables you to use wildcard matches when remapping a URL.

In the final section of this chapter, you learned how to abstract pages in your application from the file system by using the `VirtualPathProvider` class. You saw the creation of an application that enables you to store application files in a Microsoft SQL Server database table.

Summary

PART VI

Security

IN THIS PART

Using the Login Controls

You can use the ASP.NET Login controls to build a user registration system for your website easily. You can use the Login controls to display user registration forms, login forms, change password forms, and password reminder forms.

By default, the Login controls use ASP.NET Membership to authenticate users, create new users, and change user properties. When you use the Login controls, you are not required to write any code when performing these tasks.

> **NOTE**
>
> ASP.NET Membership is discussed in detail in the following chapter.

In the first part of this chapter, you are provided with an overview of the Login controls. You learn how to password-protect a section of your website and enable users to register and log in to your website.

In the remainder of this chapter, you learn how to use each of the following Login controls in detail:

- Login—Enables you to display a user login form.

- CreateUserWizard—Enables you to display a user registration form.

- LoginStatus—Enables you to display either a log in or log out link, depending on a user's authentication status.

- LoginName—Enables you to display the current user's registered username.

- ChangePassword—Enables you to display a form that allows users to change their passwords.

- PasswordRecovery—Enables you to display a form that allows a user to receive an email containing his or her password.

- LoginView—Enables you to display different content to different users depending on the user's authentication status or role.

Overview of the Login Controls

You won't have any fun using the Login controls unless you have confidential information to protect. Therefore, let's start by creating a page that needs password protection.

Create a new folder in your application named SecretFiles and add the page in Listing 20.1 to the SecretFiles folder.

LISTING 20.1   SecretFiles\Secret.aspx

```
<%@ Page Language="VB" %>
<!DOCTYPE html PUBLIC "-//W3C//DTD XHTML 1.0 Transitional//EN"
  "http://www.w3.org/TR/xhtml1/DTD/xhtml1-transitional.dtd">
<html xmlns="http://www.w3.org/1999/xhtml" >
<head id="Head1" runat="server">
    <title>Secret</title>
</head>
<body>
    <form id="form1" runat="server">
    <div>

    <h1>This Page is Secret!</h1>

    </div>
    </form>
</body>
</html>
```

There is nothing special about the page in Listing 20.1. It just displays the message This Page is Secret!.

To password-protect the Secret.aspx page, you need to make two configuration changes to your application: You need to configure both authentication and authorization.

First, you need to enable the proper type of authentication for your application. By default, Windows authentication is enabled. To use the Login controls, you need enable Forms authentication by adding the web configuration file in Listing 20.2 to the root of your application.

LISTING 20.2   Web.Config

```
<?xml version="1.0" encoding="utf-8"?>
<configuration>
  <system.web>
    <authentication mode="Forms" />
  </system.web>
</configuration>
```

The web configuration file in Listing 20.2 contains an authentication element that includes a mode attribute. The mode attribute has the value Forms.

> **NOTE**
>
> Authentication and authorization is discussed in more detail in Chapter 21, "Using ASP.NET Membership."

By default, all users have access to all pages in an application. If you want to restrict access to the pages in a folder, then you need to configure authorization for the folder.

If you add the web configuration file in Listing 20.3 to the SecretFiles folder, then anonymous users are prevented from accessing any pages in the folder.

LISTING 20.3   SecretFiles\Web.Config

```
<?xml version="1.0"?>
<configuration>
  <system.web>
    <authorization>
      <deny users="?" />
    </authorization>
  </system.web>
</configuration>
```

The web configuration file in Listing 20.3 contains an authorization element. This element contains a list of authorization rules for the folder. The single authorization rule in Listing 20.3 prevents anonymous users from accessing pages in the folder (the ? represents anonymous users).

> **VISUAL WEB DEVELOPER NOTE**
>
> If you prefer, you can use the Web Site Administration Tool to configure authentication and authorization. This tool provides you with a form interface for performing these configuration changes. When using Visual Web Developer, you can open the Web Site Administration Tool by selecting the menu option Website, ASP.NET Configuration.

20

If you attempt to request the Secret.aspx page after adding the web configuration file in Listing 20.3, then you are redirected to a page named Login.aspx automatically. Therefore, the next page that we need to create is the Login.aspx page. (By default, this page must be located in the root of your application.)

The Login.aspx page in Listing 20.4 contains a Login control. The Login control automatically generates a login form (see Figure 20.1).

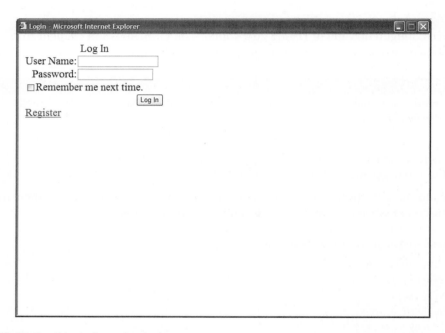

FIGURE 20.1   Displaying a Login form.

LISTING 20.4   Login.aspx

```
<%@ Page Language="VB" %>
<!DOCTYPE html PUBLIC "-//W3C//DTD XHTML 1.0 Transitional//EN"
  "http://www.w3.org/TR/xhtml1/DTD/xhtml1-transitional.dtd">
<html xmlns="http://www.w3.org/1999/xhtml" >
<head id="Head1" runat="server">
    <title>Login</title>
</head>
<body>
    <form id="form1" runat="server">
    <div>

    <asp:Login
```

LISTING 20.4   Continued

```
            id="Login1"
            CreateUserText="Register"
            CreateUserUrl="~/Register.aspx"
            Runat="server" />

      </div>
      </form>
</body>
</html>
```

Notice that the Login control includes a CreateUserText and CreateUserUrl property. Adding these properties to the Login control causes the control to display a link to a page that enables a new user to register for your application. The Login control in Listing 20.4 links to a page named Register.aspx. This page is contained in Listing 20.5.

LISTING 20.5   Register.aspx

```
<%@ Page Language="VB" %>
<!DOCTYPE html PUBLIC "-//W3C//DTD XHTML 1.0 Transitional//EN"
  "http://www.w3.org/TR/xhtml1/DTD/xhtml1-transitional.dtd">
<html xmlns="http://www.w3.org/1999/xhtml" >
<head id="Head1" runat="server">
    <title>Register</title>
</head>
<body>
    <form id="form1" runat="server">
    <div>

    <asp:CreateUserWizard
        id="CreateUserWizard1"
        ContinueDestinationPageUrl="~/SecretFiles/Secret.aspx"
        Runat="server" />

    </div>
    </form>
</body>
</html>
```

The Register.aspx page contains a CreateUserWizard control. This control automatically generates a user registration form (see Figure 20.2). After you submit the form, a new user is created and you are redirected back to the Secret.aspx page.

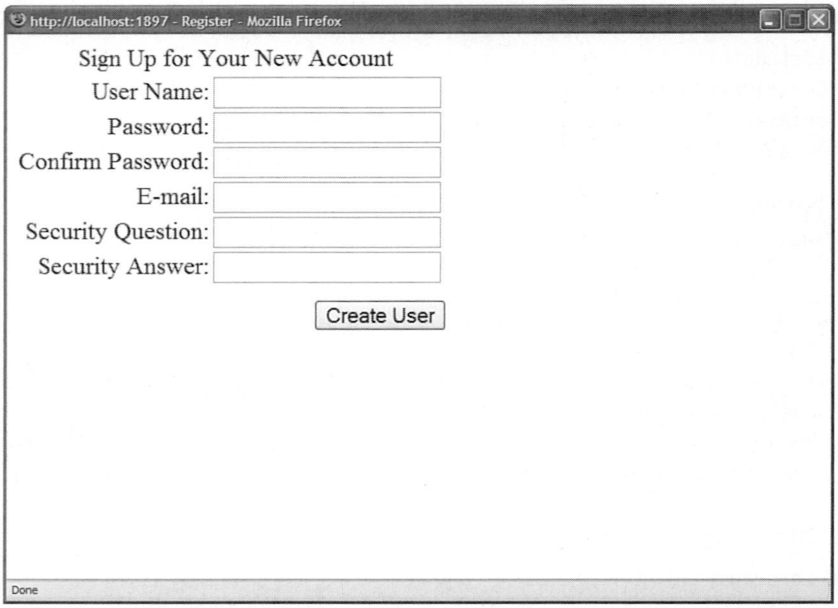

FIGURE 20.2   Displaying a registration form.

> **WARNING**
>
> The default ASP.NET Membership provider requires you to create a password that contains at
> least seven characters, and at least one of the characters must be non-alphanumeric (not a letter
> and not a number). So, secret_ is a valid password, but not secret9. In the next chapter, you
> learn how to change these default passwords requirements.

That's all there is to it. Notice that we have created a complete user registration system
without writing a single line of code. All the messy details of storing usernames and passwords are taken care of by the ASP.NET Framework in the background.

Using the Login **Control**

The Login control renders a standard user login form. By default, the Login control uses
ASP.NET Membership to authenticate users. However, as you'll see in a moment, you can
customize how the Login control authenticates users.

The Login control supports a large number of properties that enable you to customize the
appearance and behavior of the control (too many properties to list here). The page in
Listing 20.6 illustrates how you can modify several of the Login control's properties to
customize the form rendered by the control (see Figure 20.3).

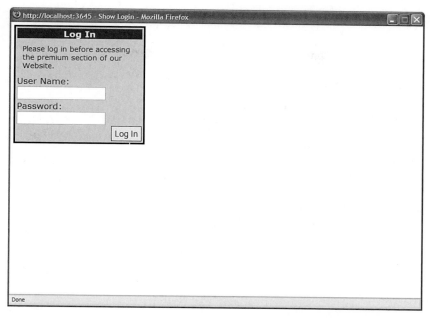

FIGURE 20.3   Customizing the Login form.

LISTING 20.6   ShowLogin.aspx

```
<%@ Page Language="VB" %>
<!DOCTYPE html PUBLIC "-//W3C//DTD XHTML 1.0 Transitional//EN"
  "http://www.w3.org/TR/xhtml1/DTD/xhtml1-transitional.dtd">
<html xmlns="http://www.w3.org/1999/xhtml" >
<head id="Head1" runat="server">
    <style type="text/css">
        .login
        {
            width:250px;
            font:14px Verdana,Sans-Serif;
            background-color:lightblue;
            border:solid 3px black;
            padding:4px;
        }
        .login_title
        {
            background-color:darkblue;
            color:white;
            font-weight:bold;
        }
        .login_instructions
```

LISTING 20.6   Continued

```
            {
                font-size:12px;
                text-align:left;
                padding:10px;
            }
            .login_button
            {
                border:solid 1px black;
                padding:3px;
            }
        </style>
        <title>Show Login</title>
</head>
<body>
    <form id="form1" runat="server">
    <div>

    <asp:Login
        id="Login1"
        InstructionText="Please log in before
            accessing the premium section of our Website."
        TitleText="Log In"
        TextLayout="TextOnTop"
        LoginButtonText="Log In"
        DisplayRememberMe="false"
        CssClass="login"
        TitleTextStyle-CssClass="login_title"
        InstructionTextStyle-CssClass="login_instructions"
        LoginButtonStyle-CssClass="login_button"
        Runat="server" />

    </div>
    </form>
</body>
</html>
```

The page in Listing 20.6 uses Cascading Style Sheets to change the appearance of the login form rendered by the Login control. By taking advantage of Cascading Style Sheets, you can customize the appearance of the Login control in any way that you can imagine.

NOTE

For the complete list of properties supported by the Login control, see the Microsoft .NET Framework SDK 2.0 documentation.

Automatically Redirecting a User to the Referring Page

If you request a page that you are not authorized to view, then the ASP.NET Framework automatically redirects you to the Login.aspx page. After you log in successfully, you are redirected back to the original page that you requested.

When you are redirected to the Login.aspx page, a query string parameter named ReturnUrl is automatically added to the page request. This query string parameter contains the path of the page that you originally requested. The Login control uses the ReturnUrl parameter when redirecting you back to the original page.

You need to be aware of two special circumstances. First, if you request the Login.aspx page directly, then a ReturnUrl parameter is not passed to the Login.aspx page. In that case, after you successfully log in, you are redirected to the Default.aspx page.

Second, if you add the Login control to a page other than the Login.aspx page, then the ReturnUrl query string parameter is ignored. In this case, you need to set the Login control's DestinationPageUrl property. When you successfully log in, you are redirected to the URL represented by this property. If you don't supply a value for the DestinationPageUrl property, the same page is reloaded.

Automatically Hiding the Login Control from Authenticated Users

Some websites display a login form at the top of every page. That way, registered users can log in at any time to view additional content. The easiest way to add a Login control to all the pages in an application is to take advantage of Master Pages. If you add a Login control to a Master Page, then the Login control is included in every content page that uses the Master Page.

You can change the layout of the Login control by modifying the Login control's Orientation property. If you set this property to the value Horizontal, then the Username and Password text boxes are rendered in the same row.

If you include a Login control in all your pages, you should also modify the Login control's VisibleWhenLoggedIn property. If you set this property to the value False, then the Login control is not displayed when a user has already authenticated.

For example, the Master Page in Listing 20.7 contains a Login control that has both its Orientation and VisibleWhenLoggedIn properties set.

LISTING 20.7   LoginMaster.master

```
<%@ Master Language="VB" %>
<!DOCTYPE html PUBLIC "-//W3C//DTD XHTML 1.0 Transitional//EN"
  "http://www.w3.org/TR/xhtml1/DTD/xhtml1-transitional.dtd">
<html xmlns="http://www.w3.org/1999/xhtml" >
<head id="Head1" runat="server">
    <style type="text/css">
        html
        {
            background-color:silver;
```

LISTING 20.7   Continued

```
            }
            .content
            {
                margin:auto;
                width:650px;
                border:solid 1px black;
                background-color:white;
                padding:10px;
            }
            .login
            {
                font:10px Arial,Sans-Serif;
                margin-left:auto;
            }
            .login input
            {
                font:10px Arial,Sans-Serif;
            }
        </style>
        <title>My Website</title>
    </head>
    <body>
        <form id="form1" runat="server">
        <div class="content">
        <asp:Login
            id="Login1"
            Orientation="Horizontal"
            VisibleWhenLoggedIn="false"
            DisplayRememberMe="false"
            TitleText=""
            CssClass="login"
            Runat="server" />
            <hr />
            <asp:contentplaceholder
                id="ContentPlaceHolder1"
                runat="server">
            </asp:contentplaceholder>
        </div>
        </form>
    </body>
</html>
```

The content page in Listing 20.8 uses the Master Page in Listing 20.7 (see Figure 20.4).
When you open the page in a browser, the Login control is hidden after you successfully
log in to the application.

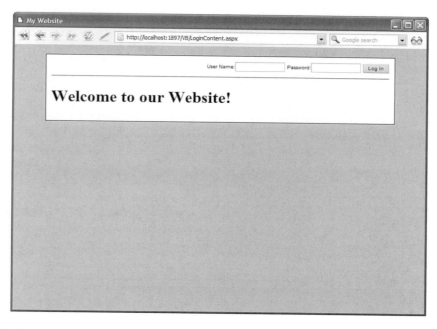

FIGURE 20.4   Adding the Login control to a Master Page.

LISTING 20.8   LoginContent.aspx

```
<%@ Page Language="VB" MasterPageFile="~/LoginMaster.master" %>
<asp:Content
    ID="Content1"
    ContentPlaceHolderID="ContentPlaceHolder1"
    Runat="Server">

    <h1>Welcome to our Website!</h1>

</asp:Content>
```

Using a Template with the Login Control

If you need to completely customize the appearance of the Login control, then you can use a template. The Login control includes a LayoutTemplate property that enables you to customize the layout of the controls rendered by the Login control.

When you create a Layout template, you can add controls to the template that have the following IDs:

- UserName
- Password

- RememberMe
- FailureText

You also need to add a Button control that includes a CommandName property with the value Login.

The page in Listing 20.9 illustrates how you can use a LayoutTemplate to customize the appearance of the Login control (see Figure 20.5).

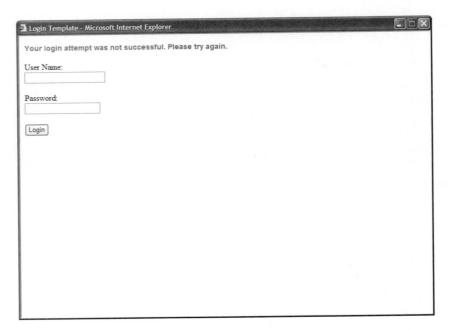

FIGURE 20.5   Using a template with the Login control.

LISTING 20.9   LoginTemplate.aspx

```
<%@ Page Language="VB" %>
<!DOCTYPE html PUBLIC "-//W3C//DTD XHTML 1.0 Transitional//EN"
  "http://www.w3.org/TR/xhtml1/DTD/xhtml1-transitional.dtd">
<html xmlns="http://www.w3.org/1999/xhtml" >
<head id="Head1" runat="server">
    <style type="text/css">
        .loginError
        {
            color:red;
            font:bold 14px Arial,Sans-Serif;
        }
```

LISTING 20.9 Continued

```
    </style>
    <title>Login Template</title>
</head>
<body>
    <form id="form1" runat="server">
    <div>

    <asp:Login
        id="Login1"
        Runat="server">
        <LayoutTemplate>
        <asp:Label
            id="FailureText"
            EnableViewState="false"
            CssClass="loginError"
            Runat="server" />

        <br />
        <asp:Label
            id="lblUserName"
            AssociatedControlID="UserName"
            Text="User Name:"
            Runat="server" />
        <br />
        <asp:TextBox
            id="UserName"
            Runat="server" />

        <br /><br />
        <asp:Label
            id="lblPassword"
            AssociatedControlID="Password"
            Text="Password:"
            Runat="server" />
        <br />
        <asp:TextBox
            id="Password"
            TextMode="Password"
            Runat="server" />

        <br /><br />
        <asp:Button
            id="btnLogin"
            Text="Login"
```

LISTING 20.9   Continued

```
            CommandName="Login"
            Runat="server" />
        </LayoutTemplate>
    </asp:Login>

    </div>
    </form>
</body>
</html>
```

WEB STANDARDS NOTE

The Login control renders an HTML table for layout even when you use a LayoutTemplate.

Performing Custom Authentication with the Login Control

By default, the Login control uses ASP.NET Membership to authenticate a username and password. If you need to change this default behavior, then you can handle the Login control's Authenticate event.

Imagine, for example, that you are building a simple application and you want to store a list of usernames and passwords in the web configuration file. The web configuration file in Listing 20.10 contains the credentials for two users named Bill and Ted.

LISTING 20.10   Web.Config

```
<?xml version="1.0" encoding="utf-8"?>
<configuration>
  <system.web>
    <authentication mode="Forms">
      <forms>
        <credentials passwordFormat="Clear">
          <user name="Bill" password="secret" />
          <user name="Ted" password="secret" />
        </credentials>
      </forms>
    </authentication>
  </system.web>
</configuration>
```

The page in Listing 20.11 contains a Login control that authenticates users against the list of usernames and passwords stored in the web configuration file.

LISTING 20.11   LoginCustom.aspx

```
<%@ Page Language="VB" %>
<!DOCTYPE html PUBLIC "-//W3C//DTD XHTML 1.0 Transitional//EN"
  "http://www.w3.org/TR/xhtml1/DTD/xhtml1-transitional.dtd">
<script runat="server">
    Sub Login1_Authenticate(ByVal sender As Object,
(ByVal e As AuthenticateEventArgs)
        Dim userName As String = Login1.UserName
        Dim password As String = Login1.Password
        e.Authenticated = FormsAuthentication.Authenticate(userName, password)
    End Sub
</script>
<html xmlns="http://www.w3.org/1999/xhtml" >
<head id="Head1" runat="server">
    <title>Login Custom</title>
</head>
<body>
    <form id="form1" runat="server">
    <div>

    <asp:Login
        id="Login1"
        OnAuthenticate="Login1_Authenticate"
        Runat="server" />

    </div>
    </form>
</body>
</html>
```

Notice that the page in Listing 20.11 includes a method that handles the Login control's Authenticate event. The second parameter passed to the Authenticate event handler is an instance of the AuthenticateEventArgs class. This class includes the following property:

- Authenticated

If you assign the value True to this property, then the Login control authenticates the user.

In Listing 20.11, the FormsAuthentication.Authenticate() method is called to check for a username and password in the web configuration file that matches the username and password entered into the login form. The value returned from this method is assigned to the AuthenticateEventArgs.Authenticated property.

Using the `CreateUserWizard` Control

The `CreateUserWizard` control renders a user registration form. If a user successfully submits the form, then a new user is added to your website. In the background, the `CreateUserWizard` control uses ASP.NET membership to create the new user.

The `CreateUserWizard` control supports a large number of properties (too many to list here) that enable you to modify the appearance and behavior of the control. For example, the page in Listing 20.12 uses several of the `CreateUserWizard` properties to customize the appearance of the form rendered by the control.

LISTING 20.12   ShowCreateUserWizard.aspx

```
<%@ Page Language="VB" %>
<!DOCTYPE html PUBLIC "-//W3C//DTD XHTML 1.0 Transitional//EN"
  "http://www.w3.org/TR/xhtml1/DTD/xhtml1-transitional.dtd">
<html xmlns="http://www.w3.org/1999/xhtml" >
<head id="Head1" runat="server">
    <style type="text/css">
        .createUser
        {
            width:350px;
            font:14px Verdana,Sans-Serif;
            background-color:lightblue;
            border:solid 3px black;
            padding:4px;
        }
        .createUser_title
        {
            background-color:darkblue;
            color:white;
            font-weight:bold;
        }
        .createUser_instructions
        {
            font-size:12px;
            text-align:left;
            padding:10px;
        }
        .createUser_button
        {
            border:solid 1px black;
            padding:3px;
        }
    </style>
    <title>Show CreateUserWizard</title>
</head>
<body>
```

LISTING 20.12   Continued

```
<form id="form1" runat="server">
<div>

<asp:CreateUserWizard
    id="CreateUserWizard1"
    ContinueDestinationPageUrl="~/Default.aspx"
    InstructionText="Please complete the following form
        to register at this Website."
    CompleteSuccessText="Your new account has been
        created. Thank you for registering."
    CssClass="createUser"
    TitleTextStyle-CssClass="createUser_title"
    InstructionTextStyle-CssClass="createUser_instructions"
    CreateUserButtonStyle-CssClass="createUser_button"
    ContinueButtonStyle-CssClass="createUser_button"
    Runat="server" />


    </div>
    </form>
</body>
</html>
```

The CreateUserWizard control in Listing 20.12 is formatted with Cascading Style Sheets (see Figure 20.6). Notice that the control's ContinueDestinationPageUrl property is set to the value "~/Default.aspx". After you successfully register, you are redirected to the Default.aspx page.

> **NOTE**
>
> For the complete list of properties supported by the CreateUserWizard control, see the Microsoft .NET Framework SDK 2.0 documentation.

Configuring Create User Form Fields

By default, the CreateUserWizard control displays the following form fields:

- Username

- Password

- Confirm Password

- Email

- Security Question

- Security Answer

These are the default form fields. The last three fields are optional.

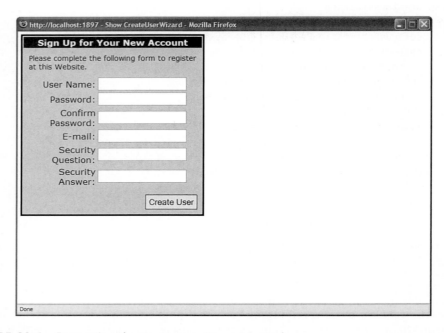

FIGURE 20.6   Formatting the `CreateUserWizard` control.

If you don't want to require a user to enter either an email address or a security question and answer, then you need to modify the configuration of the default membership provider. The web configuration file in Listing 20.13 makes both an email address and security question and answer optional.

LISTING 20.13   Web.Config

```
<?xml version="1.0" encoding="utf-8"?>
<configuration>
  <system.web>

    <authentication mode="Forms" />

    <membership defaultProvider="MyMembership">
      <providers>
        <add
          name="MyMembership"
          type="System.Web.Security.SqlMembershipProvider"
```

LISTING 20.13   Continued

```
            connectionStringName="LocalSqlServer"
            requiresQuestionAndAnswer="false"
            requiresUniqueEmail="false" />
        </providers>
    </membership>

    </system.web>
</configuration>
```

If you add the web configuration file in Listing 20.13 to your application, then the `CreateUserWizard` control does not render fields for a security question and answer. However, the `CreateUserWizard` control still renders an email field. If you don't want the email form field to be rendered, then you must perform an additional step. You must set the `CreateUserWizard` control's `RequireEmail` property to the value `False`.

If you add the page in Listing 20.14 to an application that contains the web configuration file in Listing 20.13, then the email, security question, and security answer form fields are not displayed (see Figure 20.7).

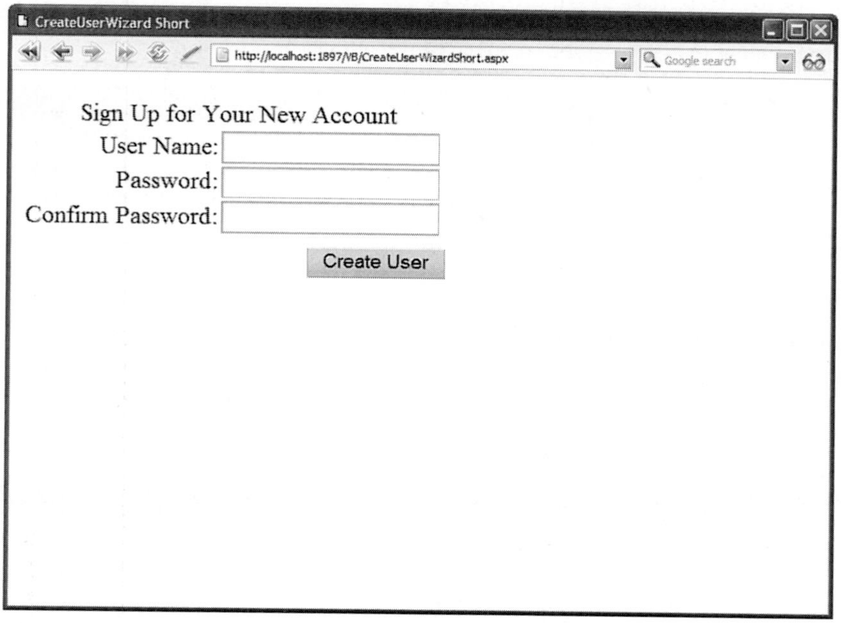

FIGURE 20.7   An abbreviated registration form.

LISTING 20.14 CreateUserWizardShort.aspx

```
<%@ Page Language="C#" %>
<!DOCTYPE html PUBLIC "-//W3C//DTD XHTML 1.0 Transitional//EN"
  "http://www.w3.org/TR/xhtml1/DTD/xhtml1-transitional.dtd">
<html xmlns="http://www.w3.org/1999/xhtml" >
<head id="Head1" runat="server">
    <title>CreateUserWizard Short</title>
</head>
<body>
    <form id="form1" runat="server">
    <div>

    <asp:CreateUserWizard
        id="CreateUserWizard1"
        RequireEmail="false"
        Runat="server" />

    </div>
    </form>
</body>
</html>
```

> **WARNING**
>
> Don't set the CreateUserWizard control's RequireEmail property to the value False when the membership provider's requiresUniqueEmail property is set to the value True. In other words, don't require an email address when you haven't provided a user with a method for entering an email address.

Sending a Create User Email Message

You can set up the CreateUserWizard control so that it automatically sends an email when a new user registers. For example, you can send an email that contains the new user's registered username and password to that user's email account.

> **WARNING**
>
> Sending an unencrypted email across the Internet with a user's password is dangerous. However, it also is a very common practice to include a password in a registration confirmation email.

The page in Listing 20.15 includes a MailDefinition property that specifies the properties of the email that is sent to a user after the user successfully registers.

LISTING 20.15   CreateUserWizardEmail.aspx

```
<%@ Page Language="VB" %>
<!DOCTYPE html PUBLIC "-//W3C//DTD XHTML 1.0 Transitional//EN"
   "http://www.w3.org/TR/xhtml1/DTD/xhtml1-transitional.dtd">
<html xmlns="http://www.w3.org/1999/xhtml" >
<head id="Head1" runat="server">
    <title>CreateUserWizard Email</title>
</head>
<body>
    <form id="form1" runat="server">
    <div>

    <asp:CreateUserWizard
        id="CreateUserWizard1"
        Runat="server">
        <MailDefinition
            BodyFileName="Register.txt"
            Subject="Registration Confirmation"
            From="Admin@YourSite.com" />
    </asp:CreateUserWizard>

    </div>
    </form>
</body>
</html>
```

The `MailDefinition` class supports the following properties:

- `BodyFileName`—Enables you to specify the path to the email message.

- `CC`—Enables you to send a carbon copy of the email message.

- `EmbeddedObjects`—Enables you to embed objects, such as images, in the email message.

- `From`—Enables you to specify the FROM email address.

- `IsBodyHtml`—Enables you to send an HTML email message.

- `Priority`—Enables you to specify the priority of the email message. Possible values are High, Low, and Normal.

- `Subject`—Enables you to specify the subject of the email message.

The `MailDefinition` associated with the `CreateUserWizard` control in Listing 20.15 sends the contents of the text file in Listing 20.16.

LISTING 20.16   Register.txt

```
Thank you for registering!

Here is your new username and password:

  username: <% UserName %>
  password: <% Password %>
```

Notice that the email message in Listing 20.16 includes two special expressions: <% UserName %> and <% Password %>. When the email is sent, the user's registered username and password are substituted for these expressions (see Figure 20.8).

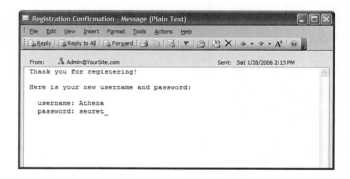

FIGURE 20.8   Receiving a registration email.

> **NOTE**
>
> You can send a user's password in an email message even when password is encrypted or hashed by the Membership provider.

The MailDefinition class uses the email server configured by the smtp element in the web configuration file. For example, the web configuration file in Listing 20.17 illustrates how you can configure the MailDefinition class to use the local SMTP server included with Internet Information Services. (You can enable the local SMTP Server by opening Internet Information Services from the Administrative Tools folder.)

LISTING 20.17   Web.Config

```xml
<?xml version="1.0" encoding="utf-8"?>
<configuration>
  <system.net>
    <mailSettings>
      <smtp deliveryMethod="PickupDirectoryFromIis"/>
    </mailSettings>
```

LISTING 20.17   Continued

```
    </system.net>
    <system.web>
      <authentication mode="Forms" />
    </system.web>
</configuration>
```

If you need to connect to a mail server located on another machine, you can use the web configuration file in Listing 20.18. In Listing 20.18, the `smtp` element includes a network element that specifies a mail host, username, and password.

LISTING 20.18   Web.Config

```
<?xml version="1.0" encoding="utf-8"?>
<configuration>
  <system.net>
    <mailSettings>
      <smtp>
        <network
            host="mail.YourServer.com"
            userName="admin"
            password="secret" />
      </smtp>
    </mailSettings>
  </system.net>
  <system.web>
    <authentication mode="Forms" />
  </system.web>
</configuration>
```

> **NOTE**
>
> If you need to customize the email message sent by the `CreateUserWizard` control, then you can handle the `CreateUserWizard` control's `SendingMail` event. See the `CreateUserWizardCodeConfirmation.aspx` page in the next section.

Automatically Redirecting a User to the Referring Page

When you successfully log in from the `Login.aspx` page, you automatically are redirected back to the original page you requested. The `CreateUserWizard` control, on the other hand, does not redirect you back anywhere. If you want the `CreateUserWizard` control to work in the same way as the `Login` control, you need to write some code.

The Login control in Listing 20.19 includes a link to a user registration page named CreateUserWizardReturn.aspx. In the Page_Load() event handler, the value of the ReturnUrl query string parameter is added to the link to the registration page.

LISTING 20.19   LoginReturn.aspx

```
<%@ Page Language="VB" %>
<!DOCTYPE html PUBLIC "-//W3C//DTD XHTML 1.0 Transitional//EN"
  "http://www.w3.org/TR/xhtml1/DTD/xhtml1-transitional.dtd">
<script runat="server">

    Sub Page_Load(ByVal sender As Object, ByVal e As EventArgs)
        If Not Page.IsPostBack Then
            Dim dest As String = Request.QueryString("ReturnUrl")
            Login1.CreateUserUrl = "~/CreateUserWizardReturn.aspx?ReturnUrl="
➥& Server.UrlEncode(dest)
        End If
    End Sub
</script>
<html xmlns="http://www.w3.org/1999/xhtml" >
<head id="Head1" runat="server">
    <title>Login Return</title>
</head>
<body>
    <form id="form1" runat="server">
    <div>

    <asp:Login
        id="Login1"
        CreateUserText="Register"
        CreateUserUrl="~/CreateUserWizardReturn.aspx"
        Runat="server" />

    </div>
    </form>
</body>
</html>
```

Before you use the page in Listing 20.19, you need to rename the page to Login.aspx. If a user requests a page that the user is not authorized to access, then the user is automatically redirected to the Login.aspx page. The ReturnUrl parameter is automatically added to the request for Login.aspx.

The page in Listing 20.20 contains a CreateUserWizard control. This page also contains a Page_Load() event handler. The value of the ReturnUrl query string parameter is used to redirect the user back to the originally requested page.

LISTING 20.20   CreateUserWizardReturn.aspx

```
<%@ Page Language="VB" %>
<!DOCTYPE html PUBLIC "-//W3C//DTD XHTML 1.0 Transitional//EN"
   "http://www.w3.org/TR/xhtml1/DTD/xhtml1-transitional.dtd">
<script runat="server">

    Sub Page_Load()
        If Not Page.IsPostBack Then
            Dim dest As String = "~/Default.aspx"
            If Not String.IsNullOrEmpty(Request.QueryString("ReturnURL")) Then
                dest = Request.QueryString("ReturnURL")
                CreateUserWizard1.ContinueDestinationPageUrl = dest
            End If
        End If
    End Sub
</script>
<html xmlns="http://www.w3.org/1999/xhtml" >
<head id="Head1" runat="server">
    <title>CreateUserWizard Return</title>
</head>
<body>
    <form id="form1" runat="server">
    <div>

    <asp:CreateUserWizard
        id="CreateUserWizard1"
        Runat="server" />

    </div>
    </form>
</body>
</html>
```

Automatically Generating a Password

Some websites require you to complete multiple steps when registering. For example, you must complete the following steps when registering for a new account at eBay:

1. Complete the registration form.

2. Receive an email with a confirmation code.

3. Enter the confirmation code into a form.

This method of registration enables you to verify a user's email address. If someone enters an invalid email address, then the confirmation code is never received.

If you need to implement this registration scenario, then you need to know about the following three properties of the CreateUserWizard control:

- AutoGeneratePassword—Enables the CreateUserWizard control to generate a new password automatically.

- DisableCreatedUser—Enables you to disable the new user account created by the CreateUserWizard control.

- LoginCreatedUser—Enables you to prevent a new user from being logged in automatically.

You can send two types of confirmation email messages. First, you can generate a new password automatically and send the password to the user. In that case, you'll want to enable the AutoGeneratePassword property and disable the LoginCreatedUser properties.

Alternatively, you can allow a new user to enter her own password and send a distinct confirmation code in the confirmation email message. In that case, you'll want to enable the DisableCreatedUser property and disable the LoginCreatedUser property. Let's examine each of these scenarios in turn.

The page in Listing 20.21 contains a CreateUserWizard control that does not render a password form field. The control has its AutoGeneratePassword property enabled and its LoginCreatedUser property disabled. After you complete the form rendered by the CreateUserWizard control, you can click the Continue button to open the Login.aspx page.

LISTING 20.21   CreateUserWizardPasswordConfirmation.aspx

```
<%@ Page Language="VB" %>
<!DOCTYPE html PUBLIC "-//W3C//DTD XHTML 1.0 Transitional//EN"
  "http://www.w3.org/TR/xhtml1/DTD/xhtml1-transitional.dtd">
<html xmlns="http://www.w3.org/1999/xhtml" >
<head id="Head1" runat="server">
    <title>CreateUserWizard Password Confirmation</title>
</head>
<body>
    <form id="form1" runat="server">
    <div>

    <asp:CreateUserWizard
        id="CreateUserWizard1"
        CompleteSuccessText="A confirmation email
            containing your new password has been
            sent to your email address."
        AutoGeneratePassword="true"
        LoginCreatedUser="false"
        ContinueDestinationPageUrl="~/Login.aspx"
        Runat="server">
        <MailDefinition
```

LISTING 20.21   Continued

```
            From="Admin@YourSite.com"
            BodyFileName="PasswordConfirmation.htm"
            IsBodyHtml="true"
            Subject="Registration Confirmation" />
    </asp:CreateUserWizard>

    </div>
    </form>
</body>
</html>
```

> **WARNING**
>
> Don't set the membership provider's `passwordStrengthRegularExpression` attribute when enabling the `CreateUserWizard` control's `AutoGeneratePassword` property.

The `CreateUserWizard` control in Listing 20.21 sends the email message contained in Listing 20.22.

LISTING 20.22   `PasswordConfirmation.htm`

```
<!DOCTYPE html PUBLIC "-//W3C//DTD XHTML 1.0 Transitional//EN"
    "http://www.w3.org/TR/xhtml1/DTD/xhtml1-transitional.dtd">
<html xmlns="http://www.w3.org/1999/xhtml" >
<head>
    <title>Password Confirmation</title>
</head>
<body>

    Your new password is <% Password %>.

</body>
</html>
```

The email message in Listing 20.22 includes the automatically generated password. When the new user receives the automatically generated password in her inbox, she can enter the password in the `Login.aspx` page.

In the second scenario, the user gets to choose his password. However, the user's account is disabled until he enters his confirmation code.

The `CreateUserWizard` control in Listing 20.23 has its `DisableCreateUser` property enabled and its `LoginCreatedUser` property disabled.

20

LISTING 20.23   CreateUserWizardCodeConfirmation.aspx

```
<%@ Page Language="VB" %>
<!DOCTYPE html PUBLIC "-//W3C//DTD XHTML 1.0 Transitional//EN"
  "http://www.w3.org/TR/xhtml1/DTD/xhtml1-transitional.dtd">
<script runat="server">

    Sub CreateUserWizard1_SendingMail(sender As object, e As MailMessageEventArgs)
        Dim user As MembershipUser = Membership.GetUser(CreateUserWizard1.UserName)
        Dim code As String = user.ProviderUserKey.ToString()
        e.Message.Body = e.Message.Body.Replace("<%ConfirmationCode%>", code)
    End Sub
</script>
<html xmlns="http://www.w3.org/1999/xhtml" >
<head id="Head1" runat="server">
    <title>CreateUserWizard Code Confirmation</title>
</head>
<body>
    <form id="form1" runat="server">
    <div>

    <asp:CreateUserWizard
        id="CreateUserWizard1"
        CompleteSuccessText="A confirmation email
            containing your new password has been
            sent to your email address."
        DisableCreatedUser="true"
        ContinueDestinationPageUrl="~/ConfirmCode.aspx"
        OnSendingMail="CreateUserWizard1_SendingMail"
        Runat="server">
        <MailDefinition
            From="Admin@YourSite.com"
            BodyFileName="CodeConfirmation.htm"
            IsBodyHtml="true"
            Subject="Registration Confirmation" />
    </asp:CreateUserWizard>

    </div>
    </form>
</body>
</html>
```

Notice that the page in Listing 20.23 includes a SendingMail event handler. The confirmation code is the unique key assigned to the new user by the membership provider (a GUID). The confirmation code is substituted into the email message before the message is sent. The email message is contained in Listing 20.24.

LISTING 20.24   CodeConfirmation.htm

```
<!DOCTYPE html PUBLIC "-//W3C//DTD XHTML 1.0 Transitional//EN"
  "http://www.w3.org/TR/xhtml1/DTD/xhtml1-transitional.dtd">
<html xmlns="http://www.w3.org/1999/xhtml" >
<head>
    <title>Code Confirmation</title>
</head>
<body>

<%UserName%>,
your confirmation code is <%ConfirmationCode%>

</body>
</html>
```

After you complete the form rendered by the CreateUserWizard control, you can click the Continue button to open the ConfirmCode.aspx page (see Figure 20.9).

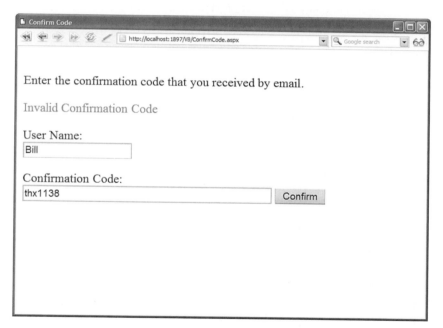

FIGURE 20.9   Entering a confirmation code.

LISTING 20.25   ConfirmCode.aspx

```
<%@ Page Language="VB" %>
<!DOCTYPE html PUBLIC "-//W3C//DTD XHTML 1.0 Transitional//EN"
    "http://www.w3.org/TR/xhtml1/DTD/xhtml1-transitional.dtd">
<script runat="server">

    Sub btnConfirm_Click(ByVal sender As Object, ByVal e As EventArgs)
        Dim user As MembershipUser = Membership.GetUser(txtUserName.Text)
        If IsNothing(user) Then
            lblError.Text = "Invalid User Name"
        Else
            Dim providerCode As String = user.ProviderUserKey.ToString()
            Dim userCode As String = txtConfirmationCode.Text.Trim()
            If providerCode <> userCode Then
                lblError.Text = "Invalid Confirmation Code"
            Else
                user.IsApproved = True
                Membership.UpdateUser(user)
                Response.Redirect("~/SecretFiles/Secret.aspx")
            End If
        End If
    End Sub
</script>
<html xmlns="http://www.w3.org/1999/xhtml" >
<head id="Head1" runat="server">
    <title>Confirm Code</title>
</head>
<body>
    <form id="form1" runat="server">
    <div>

    <p>
    Enter the confirmation code that you received by email.
    </p>

    <asp:Label
        id="lblError"
        EnableViewState="false"
        ForeColor="Red"
        Runat="server" />

    <br /><br />
    <asp:Label
        id="lblUserName"
        Text="User Name:"
```

LISTING 20.25   Continued

```
            AssociatedControlID="txtUserName"
            Runat="server" />
        <br />
        <asp:TextBox
            id="txtUserName"
            Runat="server" />

        <br /><br />
        <asp:Label
            id="lblConfirmationCode"
            Text="Confirmation Code:"
            AssociatedControlID="txtConfirmationCode"
            Runat="server" />
        <br />
        <asp:TextBox
            id="txtConfirmationCode"
            Columns="50"
            Runat="server" />
        <asp:Button
            id="btnConfirm"
            Text="Confirm"
            OnClick="btnConfirm_Click"
            Runat="server" />


    </div>
    </form>
</body>
</html>
```

If the user enters the correct username and confirmation code, then his account is enabled. The `MembershipUser.IsApproved` property is assigned the value `True` and the updated user information is saved with the `Membership.UpdateUser()` method.

Using Templates with the `CreateUserWizard` Control

If you need to customize the appearance of the form rendered by the `CreateUserWizard` control, then you can create templates for the `CreateUserWizardStep` and the `CompleteWizardStep`. For example, the page in Listing 20.26 displays a drop-down list to display options for the security question (see Figure 20.10).

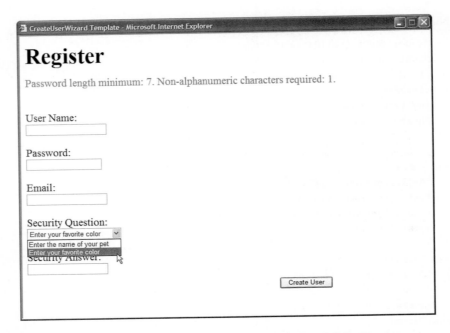

FIGURE 20.10   Customizing the `CreateUserWizard` control with templates.

LISTING 20.26   `CreateUserWizardTemplate.aspx`

```
<%@ Page Language="VB" %>
<!DOCTYPE html PUBLIC "-//W3C//DTD XHTML 1.0 Transitional//EN"
  "http://www.w3.org/TR/xhtml1/DTD/xhtml1-transitional.dtd">
<html xmlns="http://www.w3.org/1999/xhtml" >
<head id="Head1" runat="server">
    <title>CreateUserWizard Template</title>
</head>
<body>
    <form id="form1" runat="server">
    <div>

    <asp:CreateUserWizard
        id="CreateUserWizard1"
        Runat="server">
        <WizardSteps>
        <asp:CreateUserWizardStep>
        <ContentTemplate>
        <h1>Register</h1>

        <asp:Label
            id="ErrorMessage"
```

LISTING 20.26   Continued

```
        ForeColor="Red"
        Runat="server" />

    <br /><br />
    <asp:Label
        id="lblUserName"
        Text="User Name:"
        AssociatedControlID="UserName"
        Runat="server" />
    <br />
    <asp:TextBox
        id="UserName"
        Runat="server" />

    <br /><br />
    <asp:Label
        id="lblPassword"
        Text="Password:"
        AssociatedControlID="Password"
        Runat="server" />
    <br />
    <asp:TextBox
        id="Password"
        TextMode="Password"
        Runat="server" />

    <br /><br />
    <asp:Label
        id="lblEmail"
        Text="Email:"
        AssociatedControlID="Email"
        Runat="server" />
    <br />
    <asp:TextBox
        id="Email"
        Runat="server" />

    <br /><br />
    <asp:Label
        id="lblQuestion"
        Text="Security Question:"
        AssociatedControlID="Question"
        Runat="server" />
    <br />
```

20

LISTING 20.26   Continued

```
            <asp:DropDownList
                id="Question"
                Runat="server">
                <asp:ListItem
                    Text="Enter the name of your pet"
                    Value="Pet Name" />
                <asp:ListItem
                    Text="Enter your favorite color"
                    Value="Favorite Color" />
            </asp:DropDownList>

            <br /><br />
            <asp:Label
                id="lblAnswer"
                Text="Security Answer:"
                AssociatedControlID="Answer"
                Runat="server" />
            <br />
            <asp:TextBox
                id="Answer"
                Runat="server" />
            </ContentTemplate>
            </asp:CreateUserWizardStep>
            <asp:CompleteWizardStep>
            <ContentTemplate>
                Your account was successfully created.
            </ContentTemplate>
            </asp:CompleteWizardStep>
            </WizardSteps>
        </asp:CreateUserWizard>

    </div>
    </form>
</body>
</html>
```

In the CreateUserWizardStep, you can add controls with the following IDs:

- UserName

- Password

- Email

- ConfirmPassword

- Question

- Answer

- ErrorMessage

Of course, you can add any other controls that you need. For example, you can request additional information when a new user registers and store the information in a separate database table (see the next section).

In the `CreateUserWizardStep`, you also can add `Button` controls that contain `CommandName` properties with the following values:

- CreateUser

- Cancel

Adding Steps to the `CreateUserWizard` Control

The `CreateUserWizard` control inherits from the base `Wizard` control. That means that you can use all the properties supported by the `Wizard` control when using the `CreateUserWizard` control. In particular, you can extend the `CreateUserWizard` control with additional wizard steps.

For example, imagine that you want to require new users to enter their first and last names. The page in Listing 20.27 contains an additional `WizardStep` that includes both first and last name form fields.

LISTING 20.27   CreateUserWizardExtra.aspx

```
<%@ Page Language="VB" %>
<%@ Import Namespace="System.Data.SqlClient" %>
<%@ Import Namespace="System.Web.Configuration" %>
<!DOCTYPE html PUBLIC "-//W3C//DTD XHTML 1.0 Transitional//EN"
  "http://www.w3.org/TR/xhtml1/DTD/xhtml1-transitional.dtd">

<script runat="server">

    Sub CreateUserWizard1_CreatedUser(ByVal sender As Object, ByVal e As EventArgs)
        CreateUserProfile(CreateUserWizard1.UserName, txtFirstName.Text,
➥ txtLastName.Text)
    End Sub

    Private Sub CreateUserProfile(ByVal userName As String,
➥ByVal firstName As String, ByVal lastName As String)
        Dim conString As String =
➥WebConfigurationManager.ConnectionStrings("UserProfiles").ConnectionString
        Dim con As New SqlConnection(conString)
        Dim cmd As New SqlCommand("INSERT UserProfiles
```

20

LISTING 20.27   Continued

```
➥(UserName,FirstName,LastName) VALUES (@UserName,@FirstName,@LastName)", con)
        cmd.Parameters.AddWithValue("@UserName", userName)
        cmd.Parameters.AddWithValue("@FirstName", firstName)
        cmd.Parameters.AddWithValue("@LastName", lastName)
        Using con
            con.Open()
            cmd.ExecuteNonQuery()
        End Using
    End Sub

</script>

<html xmlns="http://www.w3.org/1999/xhtml" >
<head id="Head1" runat="server">
    <title>CreateUserWizard Extra</title>
</head>
<body>
    <form id="form1" runat="server">
    <div>

    <asp:CreateUserWizard
        id="CreateUserWizard1"
        OnCreatedUser="CreateUserWizard1_CreatedUser"
        Runat="server" >
        <WizardSteps>
        <asp:WizardStep>
            <asp:Label
                id="lblFirstName"
                Text="First Name:"
                AssociatedControlID="txtFirstName"
                Runat="server" />
            <br />
            <asp:TextBox
                id="txtFirstName"
                Runat="server" />

            <br /><br />
            <asp:Label
                id="lblLastName"
                Text="Last Name:"
                AssociatedControlID="txtLastName"
                Runat="server" />
            <br />
            <asp:TextBox
                id="txtLastName"
```

LISTING 20.27   Continued

```
                Runat="server" />
        </asp:WizardStep>
        <asp:CreateUserWizardStep />
        </WizardSteps>
    </asp:CreateUserWizard>

    </div>
    </form>
</body>
</html>
```

The page in Listing 20.27 includes a CreatedUser event handler that executes after the new user is created. This handler adds the new user's first and last name to a database named UserProfilesDB.

Using the LoginStatus Control

The LoginStatus control displays either a Login link or a Logout link, depending on your authentication status. When you click the Login link, you are transferred to the Login.aspx page. When you click the Logout link, you are logged out of the website.

The page in Listing 20.28 contains a LoginStatus control (see Figure 20.11).

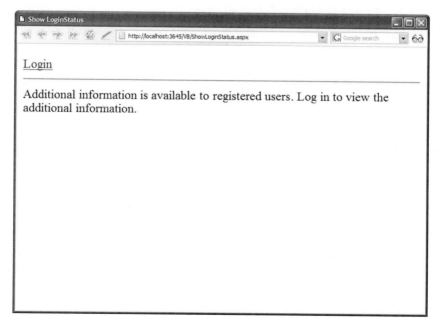

FIGURE 20.11   Displaying a Login link with the LoginStatus control.

LISTING 20.28   ShowLoginStatus.aspx

```
<%@ Page Language="VB" %>
<!DOCTYPE html PUBLIC "-//W3C//DTD XHTML 1.0 Transitional//EN"
  "http://www.w3.org/TR/xhtml1/DTD/xhtml1-transitional.dtd">
<html xmlns="http://www.w3.org/1999/xhtml" >
<head id="Head1" runat="server">
    <title>Show LoginStatus</title>
</head>
<body>
    <form id="form1" runat="server">
    <div>

    <asp:LoginStatus
        id="LoginStatus1"
        Runat="server" />

    <hr />

    Additional information is available to registered users. Log in to view
    the additional information.


    </div>
    </form>
</body>
</html>
```

After you open the page in Listing 20.28, if you click the Login link, you are redirected to the Login page. If you enter a valid username and password, you are redirected back to the ShowLoginStatus.aspx page.

The LoginStatus control supports the following properties:

- LoginImageUrl—Enables you to specify an image for the Login link.

- LoginText—Enables you to specify the text for the Login link.

- LogoutAction—Enables you to control what happens when the Logout link is clicked. Possible values are Redirect, RedirectToLoginPage, and Refresh.

- LogoutImageUrl—Enables you to specify an image for the Logout link.

- LogoutPageUrl—Enables you to specify a page to which the user is redirected when the user logs out. This property is ignored unless the LogoutAction property is set to the value Redirect.

- LogoutText—Enables you to specify the text for the Logout link.

The LoginStatus control also supports the following two events:

- LoggingOut—Raised before the user is logged out.

- LoggedOut—Raised after the user is logged out.

Using the LoginName Control

The LoginName control displays the current user's registered username. If the current user is not authenticated, the LoginName control renders nothing.

The page in Listing 20.28 contains both a LoginName and LoginStatus control.

LISTING 20.28   ShowLoginName.aspx

```
<%@ Page Language="VB" %>
<!DOCTYPE html PUBLIC "-//W3C//DTD XHTML 1.0 Transitional//EN"
  "http://www.w3.org/TR/xhtml1/DTD/xhtml1-transitional.dtd">
<html xmlns="http://www.w3.org/1999/xhtml" >
<head id="Head1" runat="server">
    <title>Show LoginName</title>
</head>
<body>
    <form id="form1" runat="server">
    <div>

    <asp:LoginName
        id="LoginName1"
        FormatString="{0} /"
        Runat="server" />

    <asp:LoginStatus
        id="LoginStatus1"
        Runat="server" />

    <hr />

    Additional information is available to registered users. Log in to view
    the additional information.

    </div>
    </form>
</body>
</html>
```

When you first open the page in Listing 20.28, the LoginName control displays nothing. However, if you login by clicking the Login link, then the LoginName control displays your username (see Figure 20.12).

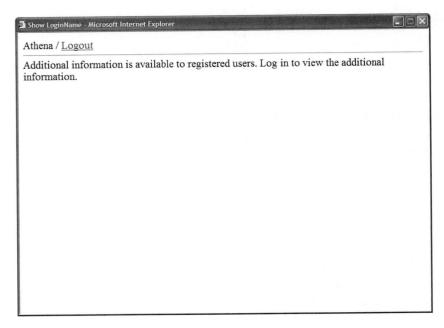

FIGURE 20.12   Displaying the current username with the LoginName control.

The LoginName control supports the following property:

- FormatString—Enables you to format the user name when the user name is rendered

Using the ChangePassword Control

The ChangePassword control enables a user (or administrator) to change a user password. The page in Listing 20.29 illustrates how you can use this control.

LISTING 20.29   ShowChangePassword.aspx

```
<%@ Page Language="VB" %>
<!DOCTYPE html PUBLIC "-//W3C//DTD XHTML 1.0 Transitional//EN"
 "http://www.w3.org/TR/xhtml1/DTD/xhtml1-transitional.dtd">
<html xmlns="http://www.w3.org/1999/xhtml" >
<head id="Head1" runat="server">
    <style type="text/css">
        .changePassword
        {
            font:14px Verdana,Sans-Serif;
            background-color:lightblue;
            border:solid 3px black;
            padding:4px;
        }
        .changePassword_title
```

LISTING 20.29   Continued

```
        {
            background-color:darkblue;
            color:white;
            font-weight:bold;
        }
        .changePassword_instructions
        {
            font-size:12px;
            text-align:left;
            padding:10px;
        }
        .changePassword_button
        {
            border:solid 1px black;
            padding:3px;
        }
    </style>
    <title>Show ChangePassword</title>
</head>
<body>
    <form id="form1" runat="server">
    <div>

    <asp:LoginName ID="LoginName1" runat="server" />

    <asp:ChangePassword
        id="ChangePassword1"
        InstructionText="Complete this form to create
            a new password."
        DisplayUserName="true"
        ContinueDestinationPageUrl="~/Default.aspx"
        CancelDestinationPageUrl="~/Default.aspx"
        CssClass="changePassword"
        TitleTextStyle-CssClass="changePassword_title"
        InstructionTextStyle-CssClass="changePassword_instructions"
        ChangePasswordButtonStyle-CssClass="changePassword_button"
        CancelButtonStyle-CssClass="changePassword_button"
        ContinueButtonStyle-CssClass="changePassword_button"
        Runat="server" />

    </div>
    </form>
</body>
</html>
```

The form in Listing 20.29 includes form fields for entering your username, old password, and new password (see Figure 20.13). After you submit the form, your old password is changed to the new password.

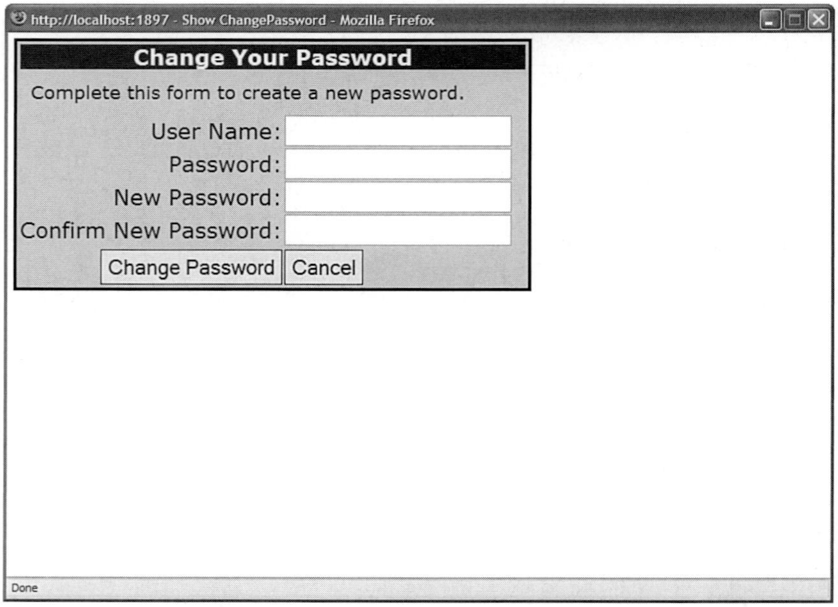

FIGURE 20.13   Changing your password with the ChangePassword control.

Notice that the ChangePassword control in Listing 20.29 includes a DisplayUserName property. When this property is enabled, the username form field is rendered. You don't need to include the DisplayUserName property when you place the page within a password-protected section of your web application. In that case, the ChangePassword control uses the name of the current user automatically.

Sending a Change Password Email

After the user changes his password, you can use the ChangePassword control to automatically send an email message that contains the new password. The page in Listing 20.30 contains a ChangePassword control that automatically sends an email.

> **NOTE**
>
> You can send a user's password in an email message even when password is encrypted or hashed by the membership provider.

LISTING 20.30   ChangePasswordEmail.aspx

```
<%@ Page Language="VB" %>
<!DOCTYPE html PUBLIC "-//W3C//DTD XHTML 1.0 Transitional//EN"
   "http://www.w3.org/TR/xhtml1/DTD/xhtml1-transitional.dtd">
<html xmlns="http://www.w3.org/1999/xhtml" >
<head id="Head1" runat="server">
    <title>ChangePassword Email</title>
</head>
<body>
    <form id="form1" runat="server">
    <div>

    <asp:ChangePassword
        id="ChangePassword1"
        DisplayUserName="true"
        Runat="server">
        <MailDefinition
            From="Admin@YourSite.com"
            BodyFileName="ChangePassword.txt"
            Subject="Your New Password" />
    </asp:ChangePassword>

    </div>
    </form>
</body>
</html>
```

Notice that the ChangePassword control in Listing 20.30 includes a MailDefinition property that defines the email sent by the control. The ChangePassword control emails the message contained in Listing 20.31.

LISTING 20.31   ChangePassword.txt

```
<%UserName%>,
your new password is <%Password%>.
```

The email message in Listing 20.31 includes two special expressions: <% UserName %> and <% Password %>. When the email is sent, the user's existing username and new password are substituted for these expressions.

> **NOTE**
>
> The MailDefinition class uses the email server configured by the smtp element in the web configuration file. For more information on configuring the smtp element, see the earlier section of this chapter, "Sending a Create User Email Message."

Using Templates with the ChangePassword Control

If you need to completely modify the appearance of the ChangePassword control, then you can use templates to format the control. The ChangePassword control supports both a ChangePasswordTemplate and a SuccessTemplate.

The page in Listing 20.32 illustrates how you can use both the templates supported by the ChangePassword control (see Figure 20.14).

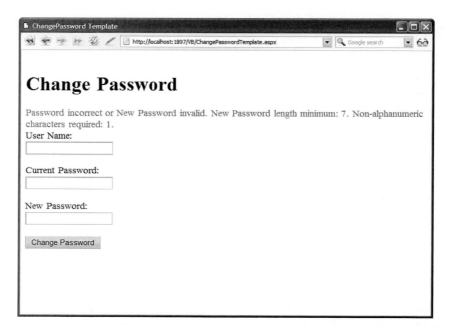

FIGURE 20.14   Customizing the ChangePassword control with templates.

LISTING 20.32   ChangePasswordTemplate.aspx

```
<%@ Page Language="VB" %>
<!DOCTYPE html PUBLIC "-//W3C//DTD XHTML 1.0 Transitional//EN"
    "http://www.w3.org/TR/xhtml1/DTD/xhtml1-transitional.dtd">
<html xmlns="http://www.w3.org/1999/xhtml" >
<head id="Head1" runat="server">
    <title>ChangePassword Template</title>
</head>
<body>
    <form id="form1" runat="server">
    <div>

    <asp:ChangePassword
        id="ChangePassword1"
```

LISTING 20.32   Continued

```
        DisplayUserName="true"
        Runat="server">
        <ChangePasswordTemplate>
            <h1>Change Password</h1>
            <asp:Label
                id="FailureText"
                EnableViewState="false"
                ForeColor="Red"
                Runat="server" />
            <br />
            <asp:Label
                id="lblUserName"
                Text="User Name:"
                AssociatedControlID="UserName"
                Runat="server" />
            <br />
            <asp:TextBox
                id="UserName"
                Runat="server" />
            <br /><br />
            <asp:Label
                id="lblCurrentPassword"
                Text="Current Password:"
                AssociatedControlID="CurrentPassword"
                Runat="server" />
            <br />
            <asp:TextBox
                id="CurrentPassword"
                TextMode="Password"
                Runat="server" />
            <br /><br />
            <asp:Label
                id="lblNewPassword"
                Text="New Password:"
                AssociatedControlID="NewPassword"
                Runat="server" />
            <br />
            <asp:TextBox
                id="NewPassword"
                TextMode="Password"
                Runat="server" />
            <br /><br />
            <asp:Button
                id="btnChangePassword"
```

20

LISTING 20.32   Continued

```
                Text="Change Password"
                CommandName="ChangePassword"
                Runat="server" />
        </ChangePasswordTemplate>
        <SuccessTemplate>
            Your password has been changed!
        </SuccessTemplate>
    </asp:ChangePassword>

    </div>
    </form>
</body>
</html>
```

You can use controls with the following IDs in the ChangePasswordTemplate template:

- UserName

- CurrentPassword

- ConfirmPassword

- NewPassword

- FailureText

You also can add Button controls with the following values for the CommandName property:

- ChangePassword

- Cancel

- Continue

Using the PasswordRecovery **Control**

If a user forgets her password, then she can use the PasswordRecovery control to email herself her password. The PasswordRecovery control either sends the user's original password or resets the password and sends the new password.

The page in Listing 20.33 contains a PasswordRecovery control.

LISTING 20.33   ShowPasswordRecovery.aspx

```
<%@ Page Language="VB" %>
<!DOCTYPE html PUBLIC "-//W3C//DTD XHTML 1.0 Transitional//EN"
    "http://www.w3.org/TR/xhtml1/DTD/xhtml1-transitional.dtd">
<html xmlns="http://www.w3.org/1999/xhtml" >
```

LISTING 20.33   Continued

```
<head id="Head1" runat="server">
    <style type="text/css">
        .passwordRecovery
        {
            font:14px Verdana,Sans-Serif;
            background-color:lightblue;
            border:solid 3px black;
            padding:4px;
        }
        .passwordRecovery_title
        {
            background-color:darkblue;
            color:white;
            font-weight:bold;
        }
        .passwordRecovery_instructions
        {
            font-size:12px;
            text-align:left;
            padding:10px;
        }
        .passwordRecovery_button
        {
            border:solid 1px black;
            padding:3px;
        }
    </style>
    <title>Show PasswordRecovery</title>
</head>
<body>
    <form id="form1" runat="server">
    <div>

    <asp:PasswordRecovery
        id="PasswordRecovery1"
        CssClass="passwordRecovery"
        TitleTextStyle-CssClass="passwordRecovery_title"
        InstructionTextStyle-CssClass="passwordRecovery_instructions"
        SubmitButtonStyle-CssClass="passwordRecovery_button"
        Runat="server">
        <MailDefinition
            From="Admin@YourSite.com"
            Subject="Password Reminder" />
    </asp:PasswordRecovery>
```

20

LISTING 20.33   Continued

```
    </div>
    </form>
</body>
</html>
```

After you open the page in Listing 20.33 in your web browser, you are first asked to enter your username (see Figure 20.15). Next, you are asked to enter the answer to the security question that you entered when registering. Finally, a password is emailed to your registered email account.

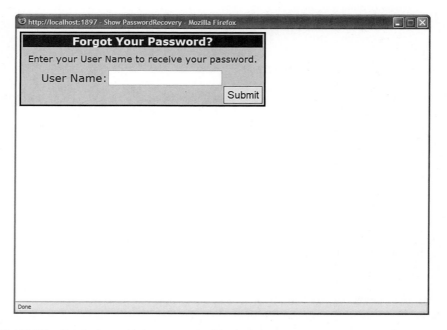

FIGURE 20.15   Retrieving a lost password with the `PasswordRecovery` control.

NOTE

Before you use the `PasswordRecovery` control, you must specify your mail server settings in your application's web configuration file. See the earlier section in this chapter, "Sending a Create User Email Message."

By default, the `PasswordRecovery` control first resets your password before sending you the password. In the next section, you learn how to send a user's original password.

Sending the Original Password

By default, the PasswordRecovery control does not send a user's original password. If you don't want the PasswordRecovery control to reset a user's password before sending it, then you must change the configuration of the membership provider. Three configuration settings matter: passwordFormat, enablePasswordRetrieval, and enablePasswordReset.

By default, the passwordFormat attribute has the value Hashed. When passwords are hashed, the PasswordRecovery control cannot send a user's original password. This limitation makes sense because when passwords are hashed, the actual passwords are never stored anywhere. If you want to send a user his original password, then you need to set the passwordFormat attribute to either the value Clear or Encrypted.

By default, the enablePasswordRetrieval attribute has the value False. Therefore, if you want to send a user his original password, you must enable this property in the web configuration file.

Finally, by default, the enablePasswordReset attribute has the value True. Regardless of the value of the passwordFormat or enablePasswordRetrieval attributes, you can always reset a user's password and email the new password to the user.

The web configuration file in Listing 20.34 contains the necessary configuration settings to enable a user's original password to be sent.

LISTING 20.34 Web.Config

```
<?xml version="1.0" encoding="utf-8"?>
<configuration>
  <system.web>
    <authentication mode="Forms" />

    <membership defaultProvider="MyMembership">
      <providers>
        <add
          name="MyMembership"
          type="System.Web.Security.SqlMembershipProvider"
          connectionStringName="LocalSqlServer"
          passwordFormat="Clear"
          enablePasswordRetrieval="true"
          />
      </providers>
    </membership>

  </system.web>
</configuration>
```

The configuration file in Listing 20.34 causes passwords to be stored in plain text rather than hashed. Furthermore, password retrieval is enabled.

Requiring a Security Question and Answer

When you use the `CreateUserWizard` control to register, you are required to select a security question and answer. The `PasswordRecovery` control displays a form that contains the security question. If you cannot enter the correct security answer, then your password is not sent.

If you do not want to require users to answer a security question before receiving their passwords, then you can modify the configuration of the membership provider. The web configuration file in Listing 20.35 assigns the value `false` to the `requiresQuestionAndAnswer` attribute.

LISTING 20.35   Web.Config

```
<?xml version="1.0" encoding="utf-8"?>
<configuration>
  <system.web>
    <authentication mode="Forms" />

    <membership defaultProvider="MyMembership">
      <providers>
        <add
          name="MyMembership"
          type="System.Web.Security.SqlMembershipProvider"
          connectionStringName="LocalSqlServer"
          requiresQuestionAndAnswer="false"
          />
      </providers>
    </membership>

  </system.web>
</configuration>
```

Using Templates with the `PasswordRecovery` Control

If you need to completely customize the appearance of the `PasswordRecovery` control, you can use templates. The `PasswordRecovery` control supports the following three types of templates:

- `UserNameTemplate`
- `QuestionTemplate`
- `SuccessTemplate`

The page in Listing 20.36 illustrates how you can use all three of these templates.

LISTING 20.36   PasswordRecoveryTemplate.aspx

```
<%@ Page Language="C#" %>
<!DOCTYPE html PUBLIC "-//W3C//DTD XHTML 1.0 Transitional//EN"
  "http://www.w3.org/TR/xhtml1/DTD/xhtml1-transitional.dtd">
<html xmlns="http://www.w3.org/1999/xhtml" >
<head id="Head1" runat="server">
    <style type="text/css">
        html
        {
            font:12px Arial,Sans-Serif;
        }
        h1
        {
            font:bold 16px Arial,Sans-Serif;
            color:DarkGray;
        }
    </style>
    <title>PasswordRecovery Template</title>
</head>
<body>
    <form id="form1" runat="server">
    <div>

    <asp:PasswordRecovery
        id="PasswordRecovery1"
        Runat="server">
        <MailDefinition
            From="Admin@YourSite.com"
            Subject="Password Reminder"
            BodyFileName="PasswordRecovery.txt" />
        <UserNameTemplate>
        <h1>User Name</h1>
        <asp:Label
            id="FailureText"
            EnableViewState="false"
            ForeColor="Red"
            Runat="server" />
        <br />
        <asp:Label
            id="lblUserName"
            Text="Enter your user name:"
            AssociatedControlID="UserName"
            Runat="server" />
        <br />
        <asp:TextBox
```

LISTING 20.36   Continued

```
                id="UserName"
                Runat="server" />
        <br />
        <asp:Button
            id="btnSubmit"
            Text="Next"
            CommandName="Submit"
            Runat="server" />
        </UserNameTemplate>
        <QuestionTemplate>
        <h1>Security Question</h1>
        <asp:Label
            id="FailureText"
            EnableViewState="false"
            ForeColor="Red"
            Runat="server" />
        <br />
        <asp:Label
            id="Question"
            Text="Enter your user name:"
            AssociatedControlID="Answer"
            Runat="server" />
        <br />
        <asp:TextBox
            id="Answer"
            Runat="server" />
        <br />
        <asp:Button
            id="btnSubmit"
            Text="Next"
            CommandName="Submit"
            Runat="server" />
        </QuestionTemplate>
        <SuccessTemplate>
        <h1>Success</h1>
        An email has been sent to your registered
        email account that contains your user name
        and password.
        </SuccessTemplate>
    </asp:PasswordRecovery>

    </div>
    </form>
</body>
</html>
```

The `UserNameTemplate` must contain a control with an ID of `UserName`. You also can include a control with an ID of `FailureText` when you want to display error messages. This template also must contain a `Button` control with a `CommandName` that has the value `Submit`.

The `QuestionTemplate` must contain a control with an ID of `Question` and a control with an ID of `Answer`. Optionally, you can include a `FailureText` control when you want to display error messages. It also must have a `Button` control with a `CommandName` that has the value `Submit`.

The `SuccessTemplate`, on the other hand, does not require any special controls.

Notice that the `PasswordRecovery` control in Listing 20.36 includes a `MailDefinition` property that references a custom email message. The message is contained in Listing 20.37.

LISTING 20.37   `PasswordRecovery.txt`

```
Here's your login information:

  user name: <%UserName%>
   password: <%Password%>
```

The email message in Listing 20.37 contains substitution expressions for both the username and password.

Using the `LoginView` Control

The `LoginView` control enables you to display different content to different users depending on their authentication status. For example, the page in Listing 20.38 displays different content for authenticated users and anonymous users (see Figure 20.16).

LISTING 20.38   `ShowLoginView.aspx`

```
<%@ Page Language="VB" %>
<!DOCTYPE html PUBLIC "-//W3C//DTD XHTML 1.0 Transitional//EN"
    "http://www.w3.org/TR/xhtml1/DTD/xhtml1-transitional.dtd">
<html xmlns="http://www.w3.org/1999/xhtml" >
<head id="Head1" runat="server">
    <title>Show LoginView</title>
</head>
<body>
    <form id="form1" runat="server">
    <div>

    <asp:LoginStatus
        id="LoginStatus"
        Runat="server" />
```

20

LISTING 20.38   Continued

```
    <hr />

    <asp:LoginView
        id="LoginView1"
        Runat="server">
        <AnonymousTemplate>
        This content is displayed to anonymous users.
        </AnonymousTemplate>
        <LoggedInTemplate>
        This content is displayed to authenticated users.
        </LoggedInTemplate>
    </asp:LoginView>

    </div>
    </form>
</body>
</html>
```

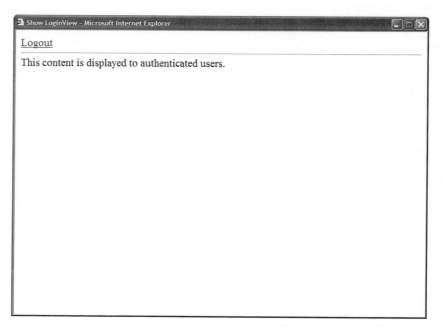

FIGURE 20.16   Displaying content to authenticated users with the LoginView control.

The LoginView control in Listing 20.38 contains two templates: an AnonymousTemplate and a LoggedInTemplate. Only one of the two templates is displayed at a time.

The page also includes a `LoginStatus` control. You can use this control to log in and log out quickly.

> **NOTE**
>
> You can use the `LoginView` control with Windows authentication as well as Forms authentication.

Using Roles with the `LoginView` Control

You also can use the `LoginView` control to display different content to users who belong to different roles. The page in Listing 20.39 contains a `LoginView` that contains two `RoleGroup` controls. The first `RoleGroup` contains content that is displayed to members of the Administrator role. The second `RoleGroup` contains content that is displayed to members of the Manager and Worker roles.

LISTING 20.39   `LoginViewRoles.aspx`

```
<%@ Page Language="VB" %>
<!DOCTYPE html PUBLIC "-//W3C//DTD XHTML 1.0 Transitional//EN"
   "http://www.w3.org/TR/xhtml1/DTD/xhtml1-transitional.dtd">
<script runat="server">

    Sub Page_Load(ByVal sender As Object, ByVal e As EventArgs)
        Dim status As MembershipCreateStatus
        ' Create Bill
        Membership.CreateUser("Bill", "secret_", "bill@somewhere.com",
➥"dog", "rover", True, status)
        ' Create Ted
        Membership.CreateUser("Ted", "secret_", "ted@somewhere.com",
➥"dog", "rover", True, status)
        ' Create Fred
        Membership.CreateUser("Fred", "secret_", "fred@somewhere.com",
➥"dog", "rover", True, status)
        ' Create Administrator Role
        If Not Roles.RoleExists("Administrator") Then
            Roles.CreateRole("Administrator")
            Roles.AddUserToRole("Bill", "Administrator")
        End If
        ' Create Manager Role
        If Not Roles.RoleExists("Manager") Then
            Roles.CreateRole("Manager")
            Roles.AddUserToRole("Bill", "Manager")
            Roles.AddUserToRole("Ted", "Manager")
        End If
        ' Create Worker Role
        If Not Roles.RoleExists("Worker") Then
```

LISTING 20.39   Continued

```
            Roles.CreateRole("Worker")
            Roles.AddUserToRole("Fred", "Worker")
        End If
    End Sub
</script>
<html xmlns="http://www.w3.org/1999/xhtml" >
<head id="Head1" runat="server">
    <title>LoginView Roles</title>
</head>
<body>
    <form id="form1" runat="server">
    <div>

    <asp:LoginStatus
        id="LoginStatus"
        Runat="server" />
    <hr />

    <asp:LoginView
        id="LoginView1"
        Runat="server">
        <RoleGroups>
        <asp:RoleGroup Roles="Administrator">
        <ContentTemplate>
        This content is displayed to Administrators.
        </ContentTemplate>
        </asp:RoleGroup>
        <asp:RoleGroup Roles="Manager,Worker">
        <ContentTemplate>
        This content is displayed to Managers
        and Workers.
        </ContentTemplate>
        </asp:RoleGroup>
        </RoleGroups>
    </asp:LoginView>

    </div>
    </form>
</body>
</html>
```

The Page_Load() handler in Listing 20.39 creates three users named Bill, Ted, and Fred. Bill is added to both the Administrator and Manager roles, Ted is added to the Manager role, and Fred is added to the Worker role.

The content of only one RoleGroup is displayed by the LoginView control at a time. If a user matches more than one RoleGroup, then the content of the first RoleGroup matched is displayed and the other RoleGroups are ignored.

Before you can use the page in Listing 20.39, you must enable roles in the web configuration file. The file in Listing 20.40 contains the necessary roleManager element.

LISTING 20.40   Web.Config

```
<?xml version="1.0" encoding="utf-8"?>
<configuration>
  <system.web>

    <authentication mode="Forms" />

    <roleManager enabled="true" />

  </system.web>
</configuration>
```

Summary

This chapter was devoted to the ASP.NET Login controls. In the first section, you were provided with an overview of the Login controls. You learned how to create both a Login and Registration page.

Next, we examined each of the Login controls one by one. You learned how to use the Login control to authenticate users and the CreateUserWizard control to register new users. You also learned how to send an email to new users automatically.

We also examined the LoginStatus and LoginView controls. You learned how to display either a Login or Logout link with the LoginStatus control. You learned how to display the current user's name with the LoginName control.

You also learned how to change passwords and send password reminders by using the ChangePassword and PasswordRecovery controls. You learned how to customize both of these controls by using templates.

Finally, you learned how to use the LoginView control to display different content to different users, depending on their authentication status. We also discussed how you can use roles with the LoginView control.

20

Using ASP.NET Membership

In the previous chapter, you learned how to use the Login controls to create an entire user registration system. This chapter looks under the covers and examines the security frameworks on which the Login controls are built.

The ASP.NET Framework includes four frameworks related to security:

- **ASP.NET Authentication**—Enables you to identify users.

- **ASP.NET Authorization**—Enables you to authorize users to request particular resources.

- **ASP.NET Membership**—Enables you to represent users and modify their properties.

- **Role Manager**—Enables you to represent user roles and modify their properties.

In this chapter, you learn how to configure authentication, authorization, ASP.NET Membership, and the Role Manager. You learn how to enable Forms authentication and configure advanced Forms authentication features such as cookieless authentication and cross-application authentication.

You learn how to configure authorization to control access to resources. We explore several advanced features of authorization. For example, you learn how to password-protect images and ASP classic pages.

You also learn how to configure different Membership providers, create custom Membership providers, and work with the properties and methods of the Membership class.

For example, you learn how to build a custom `XmlMembershipProvider` that stores membership information in an XML file.

Finally, we examine the Role Manager. You learn how to create user roles and add and remove users from a particular role. You also learn how to configure the different Role providers included in the ASP.NET Framework.

Configuring Authentication

Authentication refers to the process of identifying who you are. The ASP.NET Framework supports three types of authentication:

- Windows Authentication
- .NET Passport Authentication
- Forms Authentication

A particular application can have only one type of authentication enabled. You can't, for example, enable both Windows and Forms authentication at the same time.

Windows authentication is enabled by default. When Windows authentication is enabled, users are identified by their Microsoft Windows account names. Roles correspond to Microsoft Windows groups.

Windows authentication delegates the responsibility of identifying users to Internet Information Server. Internet Information Server can be configured to use Basic, Integrated Windows, or Digest authentication.

.NET Passport authentication is the same type of authentication used at Microsoft websites such as MSN and Hotmail. If you want to enable users to log in to your application by using their existing Hotmail usernames and passwords, then you can enable .NET Passport authentication.

> **NOTE**
>
> You must download and install the Microsoft .NET Passport SDK, register with Microsoft, and pay Microsoft a fee before you can use .NET Passport authentication. For more information, see the MSDN website (msdn.microsoft.com).

The final type of authentication is Forms authentication. When Forms authentication is enabled, users are typically identified by a cookie (but see the next section). When a user is authenticated, an encrypted cookie is added to the user's browser. As the user moves from page to page, the user is identified by the cookie.

When Forms authentication is enabled, user and role information is stored in a custom data store. You can store user information anywhere that you want. For example, you can store usernames and passwords in a database, an XML file, or even a plain text file.

In the previous version of ASP.NET, after enabling Forms authentication, you had to write all the code for storing and retrieving user information. When building an ASP.NET 2.0 application, on the other hand, you can let ASP.NET Membership do all this work for you. ASP.NET Membership can handle all the details of storing and retrieving user and role information.

You enable a particular type of authentication for an application in an application's root web configuration file. The file in Listing 21.1 enables Forms authentication.

LISTING 21.1   Web.Config

```
<?xml version="1.0"?>
<configuration>
    <system.web>

        <authentication mode="Forms" />

    </system.web>
</configuration>
```

In Listing 21.1, the authentication element's mode attribute is set to the value Forms. The possible values for the mode attribute are None, Windows, Forms, and Passport.

> **NOTE**
>
> Windows, Forms, and Passport authentication are implemented with HTTP Modules. If you need to implement a custom authentication scheme, then you can create a custom HTTP Module. For more information on HTTP Module, see Chapter 25, "Working with the HTTP Runtime."

> **VISUAL WEB DEVELOPER NOTE**
>
> If you prefer, you can enable a particular type of authentication by using the Web Site Administration Tool. This tool provides you with a form interface for modifying the web configuration file. You can open the Web Site Administration Tool by selecting the menu option Website, ASP.NET Configuration.

Configuring Forms Authentication

Several configuration options are specific to Forms authentication:

- cookieless—Enables you to use Forms authentication even when a browser does not support cookies. Possible values are UseCookies, UseUri, AutoDetect, and UseDeviceProfile. The default value is UseDeviceProfile.

- defaultUrl—Enables you to specify the page to which a user is redirected after being authenticated. The default value is Default.aspx.

- domain—Enables you to specify the domain associated with the authentication cookie. The default value is an empty string.

- enableCrossAppRedirects—Enables you to authenticate users across applications by passing an authentication ticket in a query string. The default value is false.

- loginUrl—Enables you to specify the path to the Login page. The default value is Login.aspx.

- name—Enables you to specify the name of the authentication cookie. The default value is .ASPXAUTH.

- path—Enables you to specify the path associated with the authentication cookie. The default value is /.

- protection—Enables you to specify how the authentication cookie is encrypted. Possible values are All, Encryption, None, and Validation. The default value is All.

- requiresSSL—Enables you to require a SSL (Secure Sockets Layer) connection when transmitting the authentication cookie. The default value is false.

- slidingExpiration—Enables you to prevent the authentication cookie from expiring as long as a user continues to make requests within an interval of time. Possible values are True and False. The default value is True.

- timeout—Enables you to specify the amount of time in minutes before the authentication cookie expires. The default value is 30.

Several of these configuration settings are related to the authentication cookie. For example, you can use the web configuration file in Listing 21.2 to change the name of the authentication cookie.

LISTING 21.2   Web.Config

```
<?xml version="1.0"?>
<configuration>

    <system.web>
      <authentication mode="Forms">
        <forms name="MyApp" />
      </authentication>

    </system.web>
</configuration>
```

Several of these options require additional explanation. In the following sections, you learn how to enable cookieless authentication, modify the cookie expiration policy, and enable authentication across applications.

Using Cookieless Forms Authentication

Normally, Forms authentication uses a cookie to identify a user. However, Forms authentication also supports a feature named cookieless authentication. When cookieless authentication is enabled, a user can be identified without a browser cookie.

By taking advantage of cookieless authentication, you can use Forms Authentication and ASP.NET Membership to authenticate users even when someone is using a browser that does not support cookies or a browser with cookies disabled.

When cookieless authentication is enabled, a user can be identified by a unique token added to a page's URL. If a user uses relative URLs to link from one page to another, then the token is passed from page to page automatically and the user can be identified across multiple page requests.

When you request a page that requires authentication and cookieless authentication is enabled, the URL in the browser address bar looks like this:

```
http://localhost:2500/Original/(F(WfAnevWxFyuN4SpenRclAEh_lY6OKWVllOKdQkRk
tOqV7cfcrgUJ2NKxNhH9dTA7fgzZ-cZwyr4ojyU6EnarC-bbf8g4sl6m4k5kk6Nmcsg1))/
SecretFiles/Secret2.aspx
```

That long, ugly code in the URL is the user's encoded authentication ticket.

You configure cookieless authentication by assigning a value to the cookieless attribute of the forms element in the web configuration file. The cookieless attribute accepts any of the following four values:

- UseCookies—Always use an authentication cookie.

- UseUri—Never use an authentication cookie.

- AutoDetect—Automatically detect when to use an authentication cookie.

- UseDeviceProfile—Use the device profile to determine when to use an authentication cookie.

The default value is UseDeviceProfile. By default, the ASP.NET Framework issues a cookie only when a particular type of device supports cookies. The ASP.NET Framework maintains a database of device capabilities in a set of files contained in the following folder:

```
\WINDOWS\Microsoft.NET\Framework\[version]\CONFIG\Browsers
```

By default, the ASP.NET Framework never uses cookieless authentication with a browser such as Microsoft Internet Explorer. According to the device profile for Internet Explorer, Internet Explorer supports cookies, so cookieless authentication is not used. The Framework doesn't use cookieless authentication even when cookies are disabled in a browser.

If you want the ASP.NET Framework to automatically detect whether or not a browser supports cookies, then you need to set the cookieless attribute to the value AutoDetect. When AutoDetect is enabled, the ASP.NET Framework checks whether a browser sends an

HTTP COOKIE header. If the COOKIE header is present, then an authentication cookie is assigned to the browser. Otherwise, the ASP.NET Framework uses cookieless authentication.

The web configuration file in Listing 21.3 enables AutoDetect.

LISTING 21.3   Web.Config

```
<?xml version="1.0"?>
<configuration>
    <system.web>
      <authentication mode="Forms">
        <forms cookieless="AutoDetect"/>
      </authentication>
    </system.web>
</configuration>
```

Using Sliding Expiration with Forms Authentication

By default, Forms authentication uses a sliding expiration policy. As long as a user lets no more than 30 minutes pass without requesting a page, the user continues to be authenticated. However, if the user does not request a page for 30 minutes, then the user is logged out automatically.

If you have strict security requirements, you can use an absolute expiration policy rather than a sliding expiration policy. In other words, you can force a user to log in again after a particular interval of time.

The web configuration file in Listing 21.4 forces a user to log in again every minute.

LISTING 21.4   Web.Config

```
<?xml version="1.0"?>
<configuration>
    <system.web>
      <authentication mode="Forms">
        <forms slidingExpiration="false" timeout="1" />
      </authentication>
    </system.web>
</configuration>
```

Using Forms Authentication Across Applications

By default, Forms authentication is application relative. In other words, if you log in to one application, you aren't logged in to any other application—even when the other application is located on the same web server.

This creates problems in two situations. First, you don't want to require the employees of your company to log in multiple times as they move between different applications hosted by your company. An employee should be able to log in once and use any application provided by your company automatically.

Second, if you are hosting a web farm, you don't want to force a user to log in whenever a request is served by a different web server. From the perspective of a user, a web farm should seem just like a single server.

By default, the Forms authentication cookie is encrypted and signed. Furthermore, by default, each application generates a unique decryption and validation key. Therefore, by default, you can't share the same authentication cookie across applications.

You specify encryption and validation options with the machineKey element in the web configuration file. Here are the default settings for this element:

```
<machineKey
  decryption="Auto"
  validation="SHA1"
  decryptionKey="AutoGenerate,IsolateApps"
  validationKey="AutoGenerate,IsolateApps" />
```

The decryption attribute specifies the algorithm used to encrypt and decrypt the forms authentication cookie. Possible values are Auto, AES (the government standard encryption algorithm), and 3DES (Triple DES). By default, the decryption attribute is set to Auto, which causes the ASP.NET Framework to select the encryption algorithm based on the capabilities of the web server.

The validation attribute specifies the hash or encryption algorithm used when an authentication cookie is signed. Possible values are AES, MD5, SHA1, and TripleDES.

The decryptionKey attribute represents the key used to encrypt and decrypt the authentication cookie. The validationKey represents the key used when the authentication cookie is signed. By default, both attributes are set to the value AutoGenerate, which causes the ASP.NET Framework to generate a random key and store it in the LSA (your web server's Local Security Authority).

Notice that both the decryptionKey and validationKey attributes include an IsolateApps modifier. When the IsolateApps modifier is present, a unique key is created for each application on the same web server.

If you want to share the same authentication cookie across every application hosted on the same web server, then you can override the default machineKey element in the machine root web configuration file and remove the IsolateApps attribute from both the decryptionKey and validationKey attributes. You can add the following machineKey element anywhere within the system.web section in the web configuration file:

```
<machineKey
  decryption="Auto"
  validation="SHA1"
  decryptionKey="AutoGenerate"
  validationKey="AutoGenerate" />
```

21

The root web configuration file is located at the following path:

```
C:\WINDOWS\Microsoft.NET\Framework\[version]\CONFIG\Web.Config
```

On the other hand, if you need to share the same authentication cookie across separate web servers, then you need to specify the `decryptionKey` and `validationKey` manually. You cannot allow the ASP.NET Framework to generate these keys automatically because you need to share the keys across the different web servers.

For example, the following `machineKey` element contains explicit decryption and validation keys:

```
<machineKey
  decryption="AES"
  validation="SHA1"
  decryptionKey="306C1FA852AB3B0115150DD8BA30821CDFD125538A0C606DACA53DBB3C3E0AD2"
  validationKey="61A8E04A146AFFAB81B6AD19654F99EA7370807F18F5002725DAB98B8EFD19C711
➥337E26948E26D1D174B159973EA0BE8CC9CAA6AAF513BF84E44B2247792265" />
```

When using AES, you need to set the decryption key to a random sequence of 64 hex characters. When using SHA1, you need to set the decryption key to a random sequence of 128 hex characters. You can use the page in Listing 21.4 to generate these random character sequences for you (see Figure 21.1).

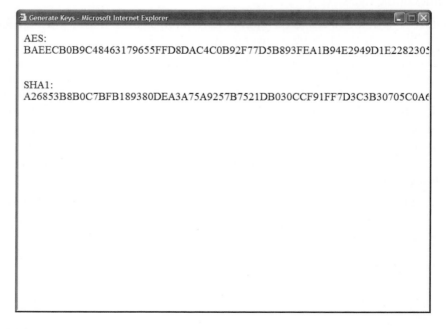

FIGURE 21.1 Generating cryptographically strong keys.

LISTING 21.5   GenerateKeys.aspx

```
<%@ Page Language="VB" %>
<%@ Import Namespace="System.Security.Cryptography" %>
<!DOCTYPE html PUBLIC "-//W3C//DTD XHTML 1.0 Transitional//EN"
   "http://www.w3.org/TR/xhtml1/DTD/xhtml1-transitional.dtd">
<script runat="server">

    Sub Page_Load()
        lblAES.Text = GetSequence(64)
        lblSHA1.Text = GetSequence(128)
    End Sub

    Private Function GetSequence(ByVal length As Integer) As String
        Dim buff(length / 2) As Byte
        Dim provider As New RNGCryptoServiceProvider()
        provider.GetBytes(buff)
        Dim builder As New StringBuilder(length)
        For i As Integer = 0 To buff.Length - 1
            builder.Append(String.Format("{0:X2}", buff(i)))
        Next
        Return builder.ToString()
    End Function
</script>
<html xmlns="http://www.w3.org/1999/xhtml" >
<head id="Head1" runat="server">
    <title>Generate Keys</title>
</head>
<body>
    <form id="form1" runat="server">
    <div>

    AES:
    <asp:Label
        id="lblAES"
        Runat="server" />
    <br /><br />
    SHA1:
    <asp:Label
        id="lblSHA1"
        Runat="server" />

    </div>
    </form>
</body>
</html>
```

21

The page in Listing 21.4 uses the `RNGCryptoServiceProvider` to generate the random sequence of characters. The `GetBytes()` method returns a cryptographically strong sequence of random values.

> **NOTE**
>
> The `GenerateKeys.aspx` page is based on a code sample from an article entitled "How To: Configure MachineKey in ASP.NET 2.0," located at the Microsoft MSDN website (msdn.microsoft.com).

You can add a `machineKey` element with explicit keys to either the machine root web configuration file or to particular application web configuration files. If you don't want to share the same keys across all the applications on a web server, then you should add the `machineKey` element only to the applications that you need to share.

Using Forms Authentication Across Domains

In the previous section, you learned how to share the same authentication cookie across applications located on the same server or a different server. But how do you share the same authentication cookie across domains?

A browser cookie is always domain relative. For example, the Amazon website cannot read cookies set by the Barnes and Noble website, which is a good thing. However, you might discover that you need to share authentication information across websites with different domains.

You can work around this problem by passing an authentication ticket in a query string parameter rather than in a cookie. There is nothing to prevent you from passing query strings between domains.

To enable this scenario, you must configure your applications to accept authentication tickets passed in a query string. The web configuration file in Listing 21.6 includes an `enableCrossAppRedirects` attribute that enables sharing authentication tickets across domains.

LISTING 21.6   `Web.config`

```
<?xml version="1.0"?>
<configuration>
  <system.web>
    <authentication mode="Forms">
      <forms enableCrossAppRedirects="true" />
    </authentication>

    <machineKey
      decryption="AES"
      validation="SHA1"
      decryptionKey="306C1FA852AB3B0115150DD8BA30821CDFD125538A0C606DACA5
```

LISTING 21.6   Continued

➡3DBB3C3E0AD2"
        validationKey="61A8E04A146AFFAB81B6AD19654F99EA7370807F18F5002725DAB98B8E
➡FD19C711337E26948E26D1D174B159973EA0BE8CC9CAA6AAF513BF84E44B2247792265" />

```
  </system.web>
</configuration>
```

If you add the web configuration file in Listing 21.6 to two applications located in different domains, the two applications can share the same authentication ticket.

> **WARNING**
>
> Make sure that you change the validation and encryption keys in Listing 21.6. You can use the
> `GenerateKeys.aspx` page discussed in the previous section to generate new random keys.

When you link or redirect from one application to another, you must pass the authentication ticket in a query string parameter. The page in Listing 21.7 adds the necessary query string parameter to a hyperlink.

LISTING 21.7   QueryStringAuthenticate.aspx

```
<%@ Page Language="VB" %>
<!DOCTYPE html PUBLIC "-//W3C//DTD XHTML 1.0 Transitional//EN"
"http://www.w3.org/TR/xhtml1/DTD/xhtml1-transitional.dtd">
<script runat="server">

    Sub Page_Load()
        Dim cookieName As String = FormsAuthentication.FormsCookieName
        Dim cookieValue As String =
➡FormsAuthentication.GetAuthCookie(User.Identity.Name, False).Value
        lnkOtherDomain.NavigateUrl &= String.Format("?{0}={1}", cookieName,
➡cookieValue)
    End Sub
</script>
<html xmlns="http://www.w3.org/1999/xhtml" >
<head id="Head1" runat="server">
    <title>Query String Authenticate</title>
</head>
<body>
    <form id="form1" runat="server">
    <div>

    <asp:HyperLink
        id="lnkOtherDomain"
        Text="Link to Other Domain"
```

21

LISTING 21.7   Continued

```
            NavigateUrl="http://www.OtherDomain.com/Secret.aspx"
            Runat="server" />

    </div>
    </form>
</body>
</html>
```

Using the FormsAuthentication Class

The main application programming interface for interacting with Forms authentication is the FormsAuthentication class. This class supports the following properties:

- CookieDomain—Returns the domain associated with the authentication cookie.

- CookieMode—Returns the cookieless authentication mode. Possible values are AutoDetect, UseCookies, UseDeviceProfile, and UseUri.

- CookiesSupported—Returns true when a browser supports cookies and Forms authentication is configured to use cookies.

- DefaultUrl—Returns the URL of the page to which a user is redirected after being authenticated.

- EnableCrossAppRedirects—Returns true when an authentication ticket can be removed from a query string.

- FormsCookieName—Returns the name of the authentication cookie.

- FormsCookiePath—Returns the path associated with the authentication cookie.

- LoginUrl—Returns the URL of the page to which a user is redirected when being authenticated.

- RequireSSL—Returns True when the authentication cookie must be transmitted with SSL (the Secure Sockets Layer).

- SlidingExpiration—Returns True when the authentication cookie uses a sliding expiration policy.

These properties return the configuration settings for Forms authentication from the web configuration file.

The FormsAuthentication class supports the following methods:

- Authenticate—Enables you to validate a username and password against a list of usernames and passwords stored in the web configuration file.

- Decrypt—Enables you to decrypt an authentication cookie.

- GetAuthCookie—Enables you to retrieve an authentication cookie.

- GetRedirectUrl—Enables you to retrieve the path to the original page that caused the redirect to the Login page.

- HashPasswordForStoringInConfigFile—Enables you to hash a password so that it can be stored in the web configuration file.

- RedirectFromLoginPage—Enables you to redirect a user back to the original page requested before the user was redirected to the Login page.

- RedirectToLoginPage—Enables you to redirect the user to the Login page.

- RenewTicketIfOld—Enables you to update the expiration time of an authentication cookie.

- SetAuthCookie—Enables you to create and issue an authentication cookie.

- SignOut—Enables you to remove an authentication cookie and log out a user.

You can use the methods and properties of the FormsAuthentication class to build a user registration and authentication system without using ASP.NET Membership. For example, the web configuration file in Listing 21.8 contains a list of usernames and passwords.

LISTING 21.8   Web.Config

```
<?xml version="1.0"?>
<configuration>
  <system.web>

    <authentication mode="Forms">
      <forms>
        <credentials passwordFormat="Clear">
          <user name="Bill" password="secret" />
          <user name="Jane" password="secret" />
          <user name="Fred" password="secret" />
        </credentials>
      </forms>
    </authentication>

  </system.web>
</configuration>
```

The web configuration file in Listing 21.8 contains a forms element that contains a credentials element. The credentials element includes a list of usernames and passwords.

Notice that the credentials element includes a passwordFormat attribute that is set to the value Clear. If you prefer, rather than store passwords in clear text, you can store password hash values. That way, anyone working on the web server can't see everyone else's passwords. The other two possible values for the passwordFormat attribute are MD5 and SHA1.

> **NOTE**
>
> If you need to hash a password so you can store it in the web configuration file, you can use the (appropriately named) `FormsAuthentication.HashPasswordForStoringInConfigFile()` method. This method accepts a clear text password and the name of a hash algorithm, and it returns a hashed version of the password.

The Login page in Listing 21.9 contains a User Name and a Password text box (see Figure 21.2).

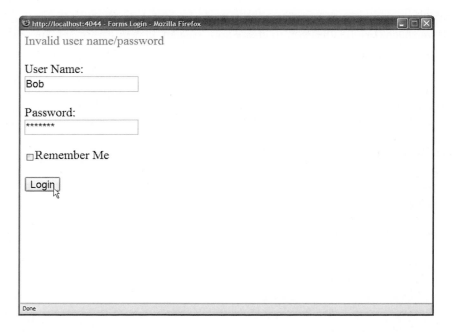

FIGURE 21.2   Authenticating against web configuration credientials.

LISTING 21.9   FormsLogin.aspx

```
<%@ Page Language="VB" %>
<!DOCTYPE html PUBLIC "-//W3C//DTD XHTML 1.0 Transitional//EN"
  "http://www.w3.org/TR/xhtml1/DTD/xhtml1-transitional.dtd">
<script runat="server">

    Sub btnLogin_Click(ByVal sender As Object, ByVal e As EventArgs)
        If (FormsAuthentication.Authenticate(txtUserName.Text, txtPassword.Text))
➥Then

            FormsAuthentication.RedirectFromLoginPage(txtUserName.Text,
➥chkRememberMe.Checked)
        Else
```

LISTING 21.9   Continued

```
                lblError.Text = "Invalid user name/password"
        End If
    End Sub
</script>
<html xmlns="http://www.w3.org/1999/xhtml" >
<head id="Head1" runat="server">
    <title>Forms Login</title>
</head>
<body>
    <form id="form1" runat="server">
    <div>

    <asp:Label
        id="lblError"
        EnableViewState="false"
        ForeColor="Red"
        Runat="server" />

    <br /><br />
    <asp:Label
        id="lblUserName"
        Text="User Name:"
        AssociatedControlID="txtUserName"
        Runat="server" />
    <br />
    <asp:TextBox
        id="txtUserName"
        Runat="server" />
    <br /><br />
    <asp:Label
        id="lblPassword"
        Text="Password:"
        AssociatedControlID="txtPassword"
        Runat="server" />
    <br />
    <asp:TextBox
        id="txtPassword"
        TextMode="Password"
        Runat="server" />
    <br /><br />
    <asp:CheckBox
        id="chkRememberMe"
        Text="Remember Me"
        Runat="server" />
    <br /><br />
```

21

LISTING 21.9   Continued

```
    <asp:Button
        id="btnLogin"
        Text="Login"
        OnClick="btnLogin_Click"
        Runat="server" />

    </div>
    </form>
</body>
</html>
```

When you click the Login button, the btnLogin_Click() handler executes and the FormsAuthentication.Authenticate() method is used to check whether the username and password entered into the TextBox controls match a username and password in the web configuration file. If the user successfully authenticates, the FormsAuthentication. RedirectFromLoginPage() method is called.

The RedirectFromLoginPage() method does two things. The method adds an authentication cookie to the user's browser. The method also redirects the user back to whatever page the user originally requested. If the user requests the Login page directly, then the user is redirected to the Default.aspx page.

The second parameter passed to the RedirectFromLoginPage() method indicates whether you want to create a session or persistent cookie. If you create a persistent cookie, then a user does not need to log in when the user returns to the website in the future.

Using the User Class

You can use the Page.User or the HttpContext.User property to retrieve information about the current user. The Page.User property exposes a Principal object that supports the following method:

- IsInRole—Enables you to check whether a user is a member of a particular role.

For example, when Windows authentication is enabled, you can use the IsInRole() method to check whether a user is a member of a particular Microsoft Windows group such as the BUILTIN\Administrators group:

```
If User.IsInRole("BUILTIN\Administrators") Then
    ' Do some Administrator only operation
End If
```

> **NOTE**
>
> If the Role Manager is enabled, then you must configure the Role Manager to use the WindowsTokenRoleProvider before you can use the User.IsInRole() method with Windows groups.

The `Principal` object also includes an `Identity` property that enables you to get information about the current user's identity. The `Identity` object supports the following three properties:

- `AuthenticationType`—Enables you to determine how the user was authenticated. Examples of possible values are `Forms`, `Basic`, and `NTLM`.

- `IsAuthenticated`—Enables you to determine whether a user is authenticated.

- `Name`—Enables you to retrieve the user's name.

If you want to get the name of the current user, then you can use logic that looks like this:

```
Dim name As String = User.Identity.Name
```

If a user is not authenticated, the `User.Identity.Name` property returns an empty string.

Configuring Authorization

Authorization refers to the process of identifying the resources that you are allowed to access. You control authorization by adding an authorization element to a web configuration file.

Authorization works the same way regardless of the type of authentication that is enabled. In other words, you configure authorization in the same way when using Forms, Windows, and .NET Passport authentication.

Typically, you place all the pages that you want to password-protect in a separate folder. If you add a web configuration file to the folder, then the settings in the web configuration file apply to all pages in the folder and all subfolders.

For example, if you add the web configuration file in Listing 21.10 to a folder, then unauthenticated users are blocked from accessing pages in the folder.

LISTING 21.10   SecretFiles\Web.Config

```xml
<?xml version="1.0"?>
<configuration>
    <system.web>

        <authorization>
          <deny users="?" />
        </authorization>

    </system.web>
</configuration>
```

If you add the file in Listing 21.10 to a folder, then unauthenticated users cannot access any pages in the folder. When Forms authentication is enabled, unauthenticated users are automatically redirected to the Login page.

The web configuration file in Listing 21.9 contains an authorization element that contains a single authorization rule. The configuration file denies access to anonymous users. The ? symbol represents anonymous (unauthenticated) users.

You can use the following two special symbols with the users attribute:

- ?—Represents unauthenticated users.

- *—Represents all users (unauthenticated or authenticated).

You also can assign a particular username, or comma-delimited list of usernames, to the deny element. For example, the authorization element in Listing 21.11 allows access for a user named Jane, but denies access to anyone else (even authenticated users).

LISTING 21.11   SecretFiles\Web.Config

```
<?xml version="1.0"?>
<configuration>
    <system.web>

      <authorization>
        <allow users="Jane" />
        <deny users="*" />
      </authorization>

    </system.web>
</configuration>
```

The order of the authorization rules is important. The ASP.NET Framework uses a first-match algorithm. If you switched the allow and deny rules in Listing 21.11, then no one, not event Jane, would be allowed to access the pages in the folder.

> **NOTE**
>
> You can prevent anonymous users from accessing any page in an application by adding an authorization element to the application root web configuration file. In that case, anonymous users are still allowed to access the Login page. (Otherwise, no one would ever be able to log in when using Forms authentication.)

> **VISUAL WEB DEVELOPER NOTE**
>
> If you prefer, you can configure authorization rules by using the Web Site Administration Tool. This tool provides you with a form interface for configuring authorization rules for different folders. You can open the Web Site Administration Tool by selecting the menu option Website, ASP.NET Configuration.

Authorizing by Role

When creating authorization rules, you can authorize by user role. For example, the web configuration file in Listing 21.12 prevents access to any pages in a folder by anyone except members of the Administrators role.

LISTING 21.12   SecretFiles\Web.Config

```
<?xml version="1.0"?>
<configuration>
    <system.web>

      <authorization>
        <allow roles="Administrator"/>
        <deny users="*"/>

      </authorization>

    </system.web>
</configuration>
```

When Forms authentication is enabled, the role refers to a custom role. In the final section of this chapter, "Using the Role Manager," you learn how to configure and create custom roles. When Windows authentication is enabled, the role refers to a Microsoft Windows group.

Authorizing Files by Location

By default, authorization rules are applied to all pages in a folder and all subfolders. However, you also have the option of using the location element with the authorization element. The location element enables you to apply a set of authorization rules to a folder or page at a particular path.

For example, imagine that you want to password-protect one, and only one, page in a folder. In that case, you can use the location element to specify the path of the single page. The web configuration file in Listing 21.13 password-protects a page named Secret.aspx.

LISTING 21.13   Web.Config

```
<?xml version="1.0"?>
<configuration>

  <system.web>
    <authentication mode="Forms" />
  </system.web>

  <location path="Secret.aspx">
    <system.web>
```

21

LISTING 21.13   Continued

```
      <authorization>
        <deny users="?"/>
      </authorization>
    </system.web>
  </location>

</configuration>
```

You also can use the location element to apply configuration settings to a particular subfolder. For example, the web configuration file in Listing 21.14 password-protects a folder named SecretFiles.

LISTING 21.14   **WEB.CONFIG**

```
<?xml version="1.0"?>
<configuration>

  <system.web>
    <authentication mode="Forms" />
  </system.web>

  <location path="SecretFiles">
    <system.web>
      <authorization>
        <deny users="?"/>
      </authorization>
    </system.web>
  </location>

</configuration>
```

Using Authorization with Images and Other File Types

Authorization rules are applied only to files mapped into the ASP.NET Framework. The Visual Web Developer web server maps all file types to the ASP.NET Framework. Internet Information Server, on the other hand, maps only particular file types to the ASP.NET Framework.

If you are using Internet Information Server, and you add an image to a password-protected folder, then users aren't blocked from requesting the image. By default, authorization rules apply only to ASP.NET file types such as ASP.NET pages. Files such as images, Microsoft Word documents, and classic ASP pages are ignored by the ASP.NET Framework.

If you need to password-protect a particular type of static file, such as an image or Microsoft Word document, then you need to map the file's extension to the ASP.NET ISAPI extension.

For example, follow these steps to enable authorization for .gif image files:

1. Open Internet Information Services by selecting Start, Control Panel, Administrative Tools, Internet Information Services.

2. Open the property sheet for a particular website or virtual directory.

3. Open the Application Configuration dialog box by selecting the Directory tab and clicking the Configuration button.

4. Select the Mappings tab (see Figure 21.3).

5. Click the Add button to open the Add/Edit Application Extension Mapping dialog box.

6. In the Executable field, enter the path to the ASP.NET ISAPI DLL. (You can copy and paste this path from the Application Mapping for the .aspx extension.)

7. In the Extension field, enter **.gif**.

FIGURE 21.3   The Mappings tab in Internet Information Services (Windows XP).

After you complete these steps, requests for .gif images are passed to the ASP.NET Framework. You can then use authentication and authorization rules with .gif images.

You can complete the same sequence of steps to password-protect other static file types, such as Microsoft Word documents, Excel spreadsheets, or video files.

Using Authorization with ASP Classic Pages

You can mix ASP.NET pages and ASP classic pages in the same application. However, normally ASP.NET pages and ASP classic pages live in parallel but separate universes. In particular, ASP.NET authentication and authorization is not applied to ASP classic pages.

If you are using Internet Information Server 6 (available with Windows Server 2003), then you can map ASP classic pages into the ASP.NET Framework. In that case, you can apply ASP.NET authorization rules to ASP classic pages.

Internet Information Server 6 supports a feature named *wildcard application mappings*. You can use a wildcard mapping to intercept requests for ASP classic pages and process the requests with the ASP.NET Framework. The ASP.NET Framework can then pass the request back to be executed by ASP classic.

To enable wildcard mapping for ASP.NET, follow these steps:

1. Open Internet Information Services by selecting Start, Control Panel, Administrative Tools, Internet Information Services.

2. Open the property sheet for a particular website or virtual directory.

3. Open the Application Configuration dialog box by selecting the Directory tab and clicking the Configuration button.

4. Select the Mappings tab.

5. Click the Insert button at the bottom of the Mappings tab to open the Add/Edit Application Extension Mapping dialog box (see Figure 21.4).

6. In the Executable field, enter the path to the ASP.NET ISAPI DLL. (You can copy and paste this path from the Application Mapping for the .aspx extension.)

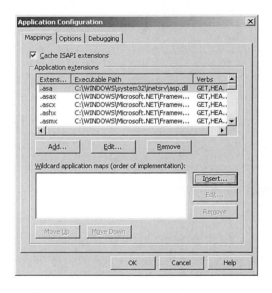

FIGURE 21.4 Enabling wildcard mappings in Internet Information Services (Windows Server 2003).

After you complete these steps, then all files, not only ASP classic files, are mapped to the ASP.NET Framework. You can use ASP.NET authorization rules to password-protect ASP classic pages in the same way that you can use these rules to password-protect ASP.NET pages. The authorization rules also work with image files, Microsoft Word documents, and any other type of file.

Using ASP.NET Membership

ASP.NET Membership enables you to create new users, delete users, and edit user properties. It's the framework that is used behind the scenes by the Login controls.

ASP.NET Membership picks up where Forms authentication leaves off. Forms authentication provides you with a way of identifying users. ASP.NET Membership is responsible for representing the user information.

ASP.NET Membership uses the provider model. The ASP.NET Framework includes two Membership providers:

- SqlMembershipProvider—Stores user information in a Microsoft SQL Server database.

- ActiveDirectoryMembershipProvider—Stores user information in the Active Directory or an Active Directory Application Mode server.

In this section, you learn how to use the ASP.NET Membership application programming interface. You learn how to use the Membership class to modify membership information programmatically.

You also learn how to configure both the SqlMembershipProvider and the ActiveDirectoryMembershipProvider. For example, you learn how to modify the requirements for a valid membership password.

Finally, we build a custom Membership provider. It is an XmlMembershipProvider that stores membership information in an XML file.

Using the Membership Application Programming Interface

The main application programming interface for ASP.NET Membership is the Membership class. This class supports the following methods:

- CreateUser—Enables you to create a new user.

- DeleteUser—Enables you to delete an existing user.

- FindUsersByEmail—Enables you to retrieve all users who have a particular email address.

- FindUsersByName—Enables you to retrieve all users who have a particular username.

- GeneratePassword—Enables you to generate a random password.

- GetAllUsers—Enables you to retrieve all users.

- GetNumberOfUsersOnline—Enables you to retrieve a count of all users online.

21

- `GetUser`—Enables you to retrieve a user by username.

- `GetUserNameByEmail`—Enables you to retrieve the username for a user with a particular email address.

- `UpdateUser`—Enables you to update a user.

- `ValidateUser`—Enables you to validate a username and password.

This class also supports the following event:

- `ValidatingPassword`—Raised when a user password is validated. You can handle this event to implement a custom validation algorithm.

You can use the methods of the Membership class to administer the users of your website. For example, the page in Listing 21.15 displays a list of every registered user (see Figure 21.5).

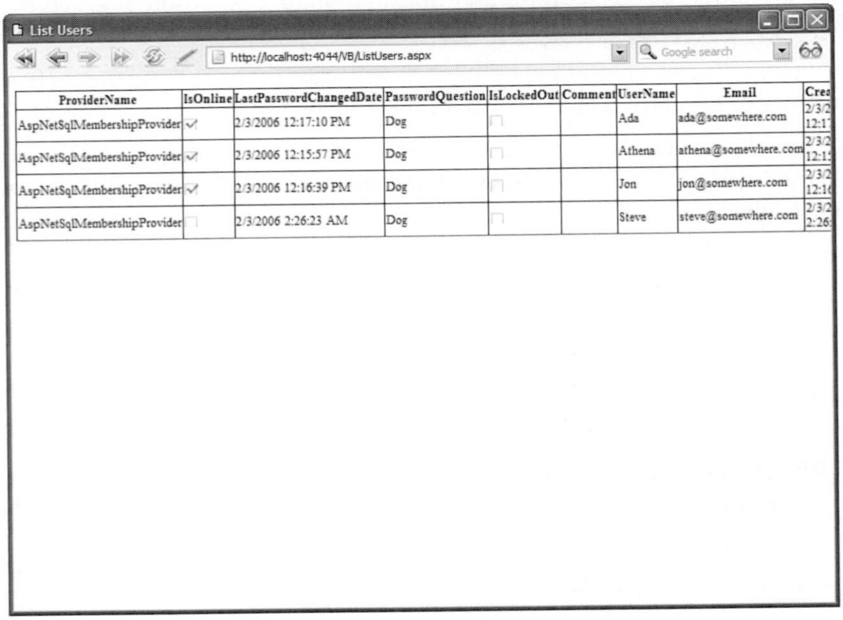

FIGURE 21.5   Displaying registered users.

LISTING 21.15   ListUsers.aspx

```
<%@ Page Language="VB" %>
<!DOCTYPE html PUBLIC "-//W3C//DTD XHTML 1.0 Transitional//EN"
   "http://www.w3.org/TR/xhtml1/DTD/xhtml1-transitional.dtd">
<html xmlns="http://www.w3.org/1999/xhtml" >
```

LISTING 21.5   Continued

```
<head id="Head1" runat="server">
    <title>List Users</title>
</head>
<body>
    <form id="form1" runat="server">
    <div>

    <asp:GridView
        id="grdUsers"
        DataSourceID="srcUsers"
        Runat="server" />

    <asp:ObjectDataSource
        id="srcUsers"
        TypeName="System.Web.Security.Membership"
        SelectMethod="GetAllUsers"
        Runat="server" />

    </div>
    </form>
</body>
</html>
```

In Listing 21.15, an `ObjectDataSource` control is used to represent the `Membership` class. The `GetAllUsers()` method is called to get the list of users.

You also can use the methods of the `Membership` class to create custom `Login` controls. For example, notice that you can retrieve the number of users currently online by calling the `GetNumberOfUsersOnline()` method. The custom control in Listing 21.16 displays the value returned by this method.

> **NOTE**
>
> Chapter 31, "Building Custom Controls," discusses custom control building.

LISTING 21.16   UsersOnline.vb

```
Imports System.Web.Security
Imports System.Web.UI
Imports System.Web.UI.WebControls

Namespace myControls

    ''' <summary>
    ''' Displays Number of Users Online
```

21

LISTING 21.16   Continued

```
''' </summary>
Public Class UsersOnline
    Inherits WebControl

    Protected Overrides Sub RenderContents(ByVal writer As HtmlTextWriter)
        writer.Write(Membership.GetNumberOfUsersOnline())
    End Sub

End Class
End namespace
```

The page in Listing 21.17 uses the UsersOnline control to display the number of users currently online (see Figure 21.6).

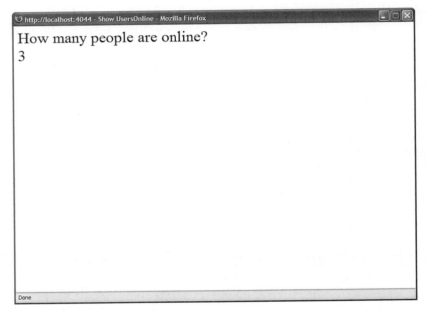

FIGURE 21.6   Display number of users online.

LISTING 21.17   ShowUsersOnline.aspx

```
<%@ Page Language="VB" %>
<%@ Register TagPrefix="custom" Namespace="myControls" %>
<!DOCTYPE html PUBLIC "-//W3C//DTD XHTML 1.0 Transitional//EN"
  "http://www.w3.org/TR/xhtml1/DTD/xhtml1-transitional.dtd">
<html xmlns="http://www.w3.org/1999/xhtml" >
```

LISTING 21.17   Continued

```
<head id="Head1" runat="server">
    <title>Show UsersOnline</title>
</head>
<body>
    <form id="form1" runat="server">
    <div>

    How many people are online?
    <br />
    <custom:UsersOnline
        id="UsersOnline1"
        Runat="server" />

    </div>
    </form>
</body>
</html>
```

> **NOTE**
>
> A user is considered online if his username was used in a call to the ValidateUser(),
> UpdateUser(), or GetUser() method in the last 15 minutes. You can modify the default time
> interval of 15 minutes by modifying the userIsOnlineTimeWindow attribute of the membership
> element in the web configuration file.

Several of the methods of the Membership class return one or more MembershipUser
objects. The MembershipUser object is used to represent a particular website member. This
class supports the following properties:

- Comment—Enables you to associate a comment with the user.

- CreationDate—Enables you to get the date when the user was created.

- Email—Enables you to get or set the user's email address.

- IsApproved—Enables you to get or set whether or not the user is approved and her
  account is active.

- IsLockedOut—Enables you to get the user's lockout status.

- IsOnline—Enables you to determine whether the user is online.

- LastActivityDate—Enables you to get or set the date of the user's last activity. This
  date is updated automatically with a call to CreateUser(), ValidateUser(), or
  GetUser().

- LastLockoutDate—Enables you to get the date that the user was last locked out.

- LastLoginDate—Enables you to get the date that the user last logged in.

- `LastPasswordChangedDate`—Enables you to get the date that the user last changed her password.

- `PasswordQuestion`—Enables you to get the user's password question.

- `ProviderName`—Enables you to retrieve the name of the Membership provider associated with this user.

- `ProviderUserKey`—Enables you to retrieve a unique key associated with the user. In the case of the `SqlMembershipProvider`, this is the value of a GUID column.

- `UserName`—Enables you to get the name of the user.

Notice that the `MembershipUser` class does not contain a property for the user's password or password answer. This is intentional. If you need to change a user's password, then you need to call a method.

The `MembershipUser` class supports the following methods:

- `ChangePassword`—Enables you to change a user's password.

- `ChangePasswordQuestionAndAnswer`—Enables you to change a user's password question and answer.

- `GetPassword`—Enables you to get a user's password.

- `ResetPassword`—Enables you to reset a user's password to a randomly generated password.

- `UnlockUser`—Enables you to unlock a user account that has been locked out.

Encrypting and Hashing User Passwords

Both of the default Membership providers included in the ASP.NET Framework enable you to store user passwords in three ways:

- **Clear**—Passwords are stored in clear text.

- **Encrypted**—Passwords are encrypted before they are stored.

- **Hashed**—Passwords are not stored. Only the hash values of passwords are stored. (This is the default value.)

You configure how passwords are stored by setting the `passwordFormat` attribute in the web configuration file. For example, the web configuration file in Listing 21.18 configures the `SqlMembershipProvider` to store passwords in plain text.

LISTING 21.18   Web.Config

```
<?xml version="1.0"?>
<configuration>
    <system.web>
      <authentication mode="Forms" />
```

LISTING 21.18   Continued

```
    <membership defaultProvider="MyProvider">
      <providers>
        <add
          name="MyProvider"
          type="System.Web.Security.SqlMembershipProvider"
          passwordFormat="Clear"
          connectionStringName="LocalSqlServer"/>
      </providers>

    </membership>
  </system.web>
</configuration>
```

The default value of the `passwordFormat` attribute is `Hashed`. By default, actual passwords are not stored anywhere. A hash value is generated for a password and the hash value is stored.

> **NOTE**
>
> A hash algorithm generates a unique value for each input. The distinctive thing about a hash algorithm is that it works in only one direction. You can easily generate a hash value from any value. However, you cannot easily determine the original value from a hash value.

The advantage of storing hash values is that even if your website is compromised by a hacker, the hacker cannot steal anyone's passwords. The disadvantage of using hash values is that you also cannot retrieve user passwords. For example, you cannot use the `PasswordRecovery` control to email a user his original password.

Instead of hashing passwords, you can encrypt the passwords. The disadvantage of encrypting passwords is that it is more processor intensive than hashing passwords. The advantage of encrypting passwords is that you can retrieve user passwords.

The web configuration file in Listing 21.19 configures the `SqlMembershipProvider` to encrypt passwords. Notice that the web configuration file includes a `machineKey` element. You must supply an explicit `decryptionKey` when encrypting passwords.

> **NOTE**
>
> For more information on the `machineKey` element, see the "Using Forms Authentication Across Applications" section, earlier in this chapter.

LISTING 21.19   Web.Config

```
<?xml version="1.0"?>
<configuration>
  <system.web>
```

21

LISTING 21.19   Continued

```
    <authentication mode="Forms" />

    <membership defaultProvider="MyProvider">
      <providers>
        <add
          name="MyProvider"
          type="System.Web.Security.SqlMembershipProvider"
          passwordFormat="Encrypted"
          connectionStringName="LocalSqlServer"/>
      </providers>
    </membership>

    <machineKey
        decryption="AES"
        decryptionKey="306C1FA852AB3B0115150DD8BA30821CDFD1
➥25538A0C606DACA53DBB3C3E0AD2" />

  </system.web>
</configuration>
```

> **WARNING**
>
> Make sure that you change the value of the decryptionKey attribute before using the web
> configuration file in Listing 21.19. You can generate a new decryptionKey with the
> GenerateKeys.aspx page described in the "Using Forms Authentication Across Applications"
> section, earlier in this chapter.

Modifying User Password Requirements

By default, passwords are required to contain at least 7 characters and 1 non-alphanumeric character (a character that is not a letter or a number such as *,_, or !). You can set
three Membership provider attributes that determine password policy:

- minRequiredPasswordLength—The minimum required password length (the default
  value is 7).

- minRequiredNonalphanumericCharacters—The minimum number of non-alphanumeric characters (the default value is 1).

- passwordStrengthRegularExpression—The regular expression pattern that a valid
  password must match (the default value is an empty string).

The minRequiredNonAlphanumericCharacters attribute confuses everyone. Website users
are not familiar with the requirement that they must enter a non-alphanumeric character.
The web configuration file in Listing 21.20 illustrates how you can disable this require-

ment when using the `SqlMembershipProvider`.

LISTING 21.20   Web.Config

```xml
<?xml version="1.0"?>
<configuration>
  <system.web>
    <authentication mode="Forms" />

    <membership defaultProvider="MyProvider">
      <providers>
        <add
          name="MyProvider"
          type="System.Web.Security.SqlMembershipProvider"
          minRequiredNonalphanumericCharacters="0"
          connectionStringName="LocalSqlServer"/>
      </providers>
    </membership>

  </system.web>
</configuration>
```

Locking Out Bad Users

By default, if you enter a bad password more than five times within 10 minutes, your account is automatically locked out. In other words, it is disabled.

Also, if you enter the wrong answer for the password answer more than five times in a 10-minute interval, your account is locked out. You get five attempts at your password and five attempts at your password answer. (These two things are tracked independently.)

Two configuration settings control when an account gets locked out:

- `maxInvalidPasswordAttempts`—The maximum number of bad passwords or bad password answers that you are allowed to enter (default value is 5).

- `passwordAttemptWindow`—The time interval in minutes in which entering bad passwords or bad password answers results in being locked out.

For example, the web configuration file in Listing 21.21 modifies the default settings to enable you to enter a maximum of three bad passwords or bad password answers in one hour.

LISTING 21.21   Web.Config

```xml
<?xml version="1.0"?>
<configuration>
  <system.web>
    <authentication mode="Forms" />
```

21

LISTING 21.21   Continued

```
<membership defaultProvider="MyProvider">
  <providers>
    <add
      name="MyProvider"
      type="System.Web.Security.SqlMembershipProvider"
      maxInvalidPasswordAttempts="3"
      passwordAttemptWindow="60"
      connectionStringName="LocalSqlServer"/>
  </providers>
</membership>

  </system.web>
</configuration>
```

After a user has been locked out, you must call the `MembershipUser.UnlockUser()` method to re-enable the user account. The page in Listing 21.22 enables you to enter a username and remove a lock (see Figure 21.7).

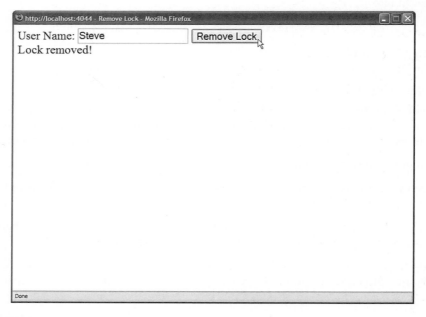

FIGURE 21.7   Removing a user lock.

LISTING 21.22   RemoveLock.aspx

```
<%@ Page Language="VB" %>
<!DOCTYPE html PUBLIC "-//W3C//DTD XHTML 1.0 Transitional//EN"
  "http://www.w3.org/TR/xhtml1/DTD/xhtml1-transitional.dtd">
<script runat="server">

    Sub btnRemove_Click(ByVal sender As Object, ByVal e As EventArgs)
        Dim userToUnlock As MembershipUser = Membership.GetUser(txtUserName.Text)
        If IsNothing(userToUnlock) Then
            lblMessage.Text = "User not found!"
        Else
            userToUnlock.UnlockUser()
            lblMessage.Text = "Lock removed!"
        End If
    End Sub
</script>
<html xmlns="http://www.w3.org/1999/xhtml" >
<head id="Head1" runat="server">
    <title>Remove Lock</title>
</head>
<body>
    <form id="form1" runat="server">
    <div>

    <asp:Label
        id="lblUserName"
        Text="User Name:"
        AssociatedControlID="txtUserName"
        Runat="server" />
    <asp:TextBox
        id="txtUserName"
        Runat="server" />
    <asp:Button
        id="btnRemove"
        Text="Remove Lock"
        OnClick="btnRemove_Click"
        Runat="server" />
    <br />
    <asp:Label
        id="lblMessage"
        EnableViewState="false"
        Runat="server" />

    </div>
    </form>
</body>
</html>
```

21

Configuring the SQLMembershipProvider

The SqlMembershipProvider is the default Membership provider. Unless otherwise configured, it stores membership information in the local ASPNETDB.mdf Microsoft SQL Server Express database located in your application's App_Data folder. This database is created for you automatically the first time that you use Membership.

If you want to store membership information in some other Microsoft SQL Server database, then you need to perform the following two tasks:

- Add the necessary database objects to the Microsoft SQL Server database.

- Configure your application to use the new database.

To complete the first task, you can use the aspnet_regiis command-line tool. This tool is located in the following folder:

\WINDOWS\Microsoft.NET\Framework\v2.0.50727

> **NOTE**
>
> If you open the SDK Command Prompt, then you don't need to navigate to the Microsoft.NET folder before using the aspnet_regsql tool.

If you execute the aspnet_regsql tool without supplying any parameters, then the ASP.NET SQL Server Setup Wizard appears (see Figure 21.8). You can use this wizard to select a database and install the Membership objects automatically.

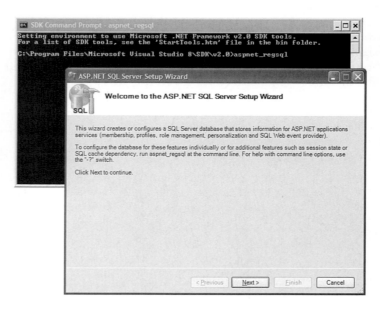

FIGURE 21.8   Using the ASP.NET SQL Setup Wizard.

If you prefer, rather than use the `aspnet_reqsql` tool, you can execute the following two SQL batch files to install Membership:

```
\WINDOWS\Microsoft.NET\Framework\v2.0.50727\InstallCommon.sql
\WINDOWS\Microsoft.NET\Framework\v2.0.50727\InstallMembership.sql
```

If you don't want to install the .NET Framework on your database server, then you can execute these SQL batch files.

After you have configured your database to support ASP.NET Membership, you must configure your application to connect to your database when using Membership. The web configuration file in Listing 21.23 connects to a database named MyDatabase located on a server named MyServer.

LISTING 21.23   `Web.Config`

```
<?xml version="1.0"?>
<configuration>
  <connectionStrings>
    <add name="MyConnection" connectionString="Data Source=MyServer;Integrated
➥Security=True;Initial Catalog=MyDatabase"/>
  </connectionStrings>

  <system.web>
    <authentication mode="Forms" />

    <membership defaultProvider="MyMembershipProvider" >
      <providers>
        <add
          name="MyMembershipProvider"
          type="System.Web.Security.SqlMembershipProvider"
          connectionStringName="MyConnection" />
      </providers>
    </membership>
  </system.web>
</configuration>
```

In Listing 21.23, a new default Membership provider named `MyMembershipProvider` is configured. The new Membership provider uses a connection string name that has the value `MyConnection`. The `MyConnection` connection string is defined in the `connectionStrings` element near the top of the configuration file. This connection string represents a connection to a database named `MyDatabase` located on a server named `MyServer`.

Configuring the `ActiveDirectoryMembershipProvider`

The other Membership provider included in the ASP.NET Framework is the `ActiveDirectoryMembershipProvider`. You can use this provider to store user information in Active Directory or ADAM (Active Directory Application Mode).

ADAM is a lightweight version of Active Directory. You can download ADAM from the Microsoft website (www.microsoft.com/adam). ADAM is compatible with both Microsoft Windows Server 2003 and Microsoft Windows XP Professional (Service Pack 1).

If you want to use ASP.NET Membership with ADAM, then you need to complete the following two steps:

1. Create an ADAM instance and create the required classes.

2. Configure your application to use the `ActiveDirectoryMembershipProvider` and connect to the ADAM instance.

The following sections examine each of these steps in turn.

Configuring ADAM

First, you need to set up a new instance of ADAM. After downloading and installing ADAM, follow these steps:

1. Launch the Active Directory Application Mode Setup Wizard by selecting Create an ADAM Instance from the ADAM program group (see Figure 21.9).

2. In the Setup Options step, select the option to create a unique instance.

3. In the Instance Name step, enter the name **WebUsersInstance**.

4. In the Ports step, use the default LDAP and SSL port numbers (389 and 636).

5. In the Application Directory Partition step, create a new directory application partition named `O=WebUsersDirectory`.

6. In the File Locations step, use the default data file locations.

7. In the Service Account Selection step, select Network Service Account.

8. In the ADAM Administrators step, select Currently Logged on User for the administrator account.

9. In the Importing LDIF Files step, select `MS-AZMan.ldf`, `MS-InetOrgPerson.ldf`, `MS-User.ldf`, `MS-UserProxy.ldf`.

After you have completed the preceding steps, a new ADAM instance named `WebUsersInstance` is created. The next step is to configure an ADAM administrator account. Follow these steps:

> **WARNING**
>
> If you are using Windows XP, and you don't have an SSL certificate installed, then you need to perform an additional configuration step. Otherwise, you'll receive an error when you attempt to reset a user password.
>
> By default, you are not allowed to perform password operations over a non-secured connection to an ADAM instance. You can disable this requirement by using the `dsmgmt.exe` tool included with ADAM. Open the ADAM Tools Command Prompt and type the following series of commands:

1. Type **dsmgmt**.

2. Type **ds behavior**.

3. Type **connections**.

4. Type **connect to server localhost:389**.

5. Type **quit**.

6. Type **allow passwd op on unsecured connection**.

7. Type **quit**.

If you don't use an SSL connection, then passwords are transmitted in plain text. Don't do this in the case of a production application.

FIGURE 21.9   Creating a new ADAM instance.

1. Open the ADAM ADSI Edit application from the ADAM program group (see Figure 21.10).

2. Open the Connection Settings dialog box by selecting the menu option Action, Connect To.

3. In the Connection Settings dialog box, select the option to connect to a node by using a distinguished name and enter the name **O=WebUsersDirectory**. Click OK.

4. Expand the new connection and select the **O=WebUsersDirectory** node.

5. Select the menu option Action, New, Object.

6. In the Create Object dialog box, select the organizationalUnit class and name the new class WebUsers.

7. Select the OU=WebUsers node and select the menu option Action, New, Object.

8. In the Create Object dialog box, select the user class and name the new class
   ADAMAdministrator.

9. Select CN=ADAMAdministrator and select the menu option Action, Reset Password
   and enter the password **secret_**.

10. Select the CN=Roles node and double-click the CN-Administrators node.

11. Double-click the Member attribute and add the distinguished name for the
    ADAMAdministrator ADAM account (CN=ADAMAdministrator,OU=WebUsers,
    O=WebUsersDirectory).

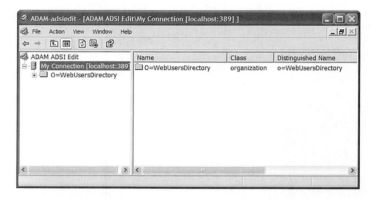

FIGURE 21.10   Using ADAM ADSI Edit.

After you complete this series of steps, an ADAMAdministrator account is configured. You
need to use this account when connecting to the ADAM instance from the
ActiveDirectoryMembershipProvider.

Configuring the ActiveDirectoryMembershipProvider
The next step is to configure your application to use the ActiveDirectoryMembership
provider. You can use the web configuration file in Listing 21.24.

LISTING 21.24   Web.Config

```
<?xml version="1.0"?>
<configuration>

  <connectionStrings>
    <add
      name="ADAMConnection"
      connectionString="LDAP://localhost:389/OU=WebUsers,O=WebUsersDirectory"/>
  </connectionStrings>

  <system.web>
    <authentication mode="Forms" />
```

LISTING 21.24   Continued

```
<membership defaultProvider="MyMembershipProvider">
  <providers>
    <add
      name="MyMembershipProvider"
      type="System.Web.Security.ActiveDirectoryMembershipProvider"
      connectionStringName="ADAMConnection"
      connectionProtection="None"
      connectionUsername="CN=ADAMAdministrator,OU=WebUsers,O=WebUsersDirectory"
      connectionPassword="secret_"
      enableSearchMethods="true" />

  </providers>
  </membership>
</system.web>
</configuration>
```

The web configuration file in Listing 21.24 configures a new default Membership provider named `MyMembershipProvider`. This provider is an instance of the `ActiveDirectoryMembershipProvider`.

Several of the attributes used with the `ActiveDirectoryMembershipProvider` require additional explanation. The `connectionStringName` attribute points to the connection string defined in the `connectionStrings` section. This connection string connects to a local ADAM instance that listens on port 389.

Notice that the `connectionProtection` attribute is set to the value `None`. If you don't modify this attribute, then you are required to use an SSL connection. If you do use an SSL connection, you need to change the port used in the connection string (typically port 636).

The `connectionUsername` and `connectionPassword` attributes use the `ADAMAdministrator` account that you configured in the previous section. When you don't use an SSL connection, you must provide both a `connectionUsername` and `connectionPassword` attribute.

Finally, notice that the provider declaration includes an `enableSearchMethods` attribute. If you want to be able to configure users by using the Web Site Administration Tool, then you must include this attribute.

The `ActiveDirectoryMembershipProvider` class supports several attributes specific to working with Active Directory:

- `connectionStringName`—Enables you to specify the name of the connection to the Active Directory Server in the `connectionStrings` section.

- `connectionUsername`—Enables you to specify the Active Directory account used to connect to Active Directory.

21

- `connectionPassword`—Enables you to specify the Active Directory password used to connect to Active Directory.

- `connectionProtection`—Enables you to specify whether or not the connection is encrypted. Possible values are `None` and `Secure`.

- `enableSearchMethods`—Enables the `ActiveDirectoryMembershipProvider` class to use additional methods. You must enable this attribute when using the Web Site Administration Tool.

- `attributeMapPasswordQuestion`—Enables you to map the Membership security question to an Active Directory attribute.

- `attributeMapPasswordAnswer`—Enables you to map the Membership security answer to an Active Directory attribute.

- `attributeMapFailedPasswordAnswerCount`—Enables you to map the Membership `MaxInvalidPasswordAttempts` property to an Active Directory attribute.

- `attributeMapFailedPasswordAnswerTime`—Enables you to map the Membership `PasswordAttemptWindow` property to an Active Directory attribute.

- `attributeMapFailedPasswordAnswerLockoutTime`—Enables you to map the Membership `PasswordAnswerAttemptLockoutDuration` property to an Active Directory attribute.

After you finish these configuration steps, you can use the `ActiveDirectoryMembershipProvider` in precisely the same way that you can use the `SqlMembershipProvider`. When you use the `Login` control, users are validated against Active Directory. When you use the `CreateUserWizard` control, new users are created in Active Directory.

Creating a Custom Membership Provider

Because ASP.NET Membership uses the provider model, you can easily extend ASP.NET membership by creating a custom Membership provider. There are two main situations in which you might need to create a custom Membership provider.

First, imagine that you have an existing ASP.NET 1.x or ASP classic application. You are currently storing membership information in your own custom set of database tables. Furthermore, your table schemas don't easily map to the table schemas used by the `SqlMembershipProvider`.

In this situation, it makes sense to create a custom Membership provider that reflects your existing database schema. If you create a custom Membership provider, you can use your existing database tables with ASP.NET Membership.

Second, imagine that you need to store membership information in a data store other than Microsoft SQL Server or Active Directory. For example, your organization might be committed to Oracle or DB2. In that case, you need to create a custom Membership provider to work with the custom data store.

In this section, we create a simple custom Membership provider: an XmlMembershipProvider that stores membership information in an XML file.

Unfortunately, the code for the XmlMembershipProvider is too long to place here. The code is included on the CD that accompanies this book in a file named XmlMembershipProvider.vb, located in the App_Code folder.

The XmlMembershipProvider class inherits from the abstract MembershipProvider class. This class has over 25 properties and methods that you are required to implement.

For example, you are required to implement the ValidateUser() method. The Login control calls this method when it validates a username and password.

You also are required to implement the CreateUser() method. This method is called by the CreateUserWizard control when a new user is created.

The web configuration file used to set up the XmlMembershipProvider is contained in Listing 21.25.

LISTING 21.25   Web.Config

```
<?xml version="1.0"?>
<configuration>
    <system.web>

      <authentication mode="Forms" />

      <membership defaultProvider="MyMembershipProvider">
        <providers>
          <add
            name="MyMembershipProvider"
            type="AspNetUnleashed.XmlMembershipProvider"
            dataFile="~/App_Data/Membership.xml"
            requiresQuestionAndAnswer="false"
            enablePasswordRetrieval="true"
            enablePasswordReset="true"
            passwordFormat="Clear" />
        </providers>
      </membership>

    </system.web>
</configuration>
```

Notice that the XmlMembershipProvider supports a number of attributes. For example, it supports a passwordFormat attribute that enables you to specify whether passwords are stored as hash values or as plain text. (It does not support encrypted passwords.)

The `XmlMembershipProvider` stores membership information in an XML file named `Membership.xml`, located in the `App_Data` folder. If you want, you can add users to the file by hand. Alternatively, you can use the `CreateUserWizard` control or the Web Site Administration Tool to create new users.

A sample of the `Membership.xml` file is contained in Listing 21.26.

LISTING 21.26   App_Data\Membership.xml

```
<credentials>
  <user name="Steve" password="secret" email="steve@somewhere.com" />
  <user name="Andrew" password="secret" email="andrew@somewhere.com" />
</credentials>
```

The sample code folder on the CD includes a `Register.aspx`, `Login.aspx`, and `ChangePassword.aspx` page. You can use these pages to try out different features of the `XmlMembershipProvider`.

WARNING

Dynamic XPath queries are open to XPath Injection Attacks in the same way that dynamic SQL queries are open to SQL Injection Attacks. When writing the `XmlMembershipProvider` class, I avoided using methods such as the `SelectSingleNode()` method to avoid XPath Injection Attack issues, even though using this method would result in leaner and faster code. Sometimes, it is better to be safe than fast.

Using the Role Manager

Instead of configuring authorization for particular users, you can group users into roles and assign authorization rules to the roles. For example, you might want to password-protect a section of your website so that only members of the Administrators role can access the pages in that section.

Like ASP.NET Membership, the Role Manager is built on the existing ASP.NET authentication framework. You configure role authorization rules by adding an authorization element to one or more web configuration files.

Furthermore, like ASP.NET Membership, the Role Manager uses the provider model. You can customize where role information is stored by configuring a particular Role provider.

The ASP.NET Framework includes three role providers:

- `SqlRoleProvider`—Enables you to store role information in a Microsoft SQL Server database.

- `WindowsTokenRoleProvider`—Enables you to use Microsoft Windows groups to represent role information.

- AuthorizationStoreRoleProvider—Enables you to use Authorization Manager to store role information in an XML file, Active Directory, or Activity Directory Application Mode (ADAM).

In the following sections, you learn how to configure each of these Role providers. You also learn how to manage role information programmatically by working with the Roles application programming interface.

Configuring the SqlRoleProvider

The SqlRoleProvider is the default role provider. You can use the SqlRoleProvider to store role information in a Microsoft SQL Server database. The SqlRoleProvider enables you to create custom roles. You can make up any roles that you need.

You can use the SqlRoleProvider with either Forms authentication or Windows authentication. When Forms authentication is enabled, you can use ASP.NET Membership to represent users and assign the users to particular roles. When Windows authentication is enabled, you assign particular Windows user accounts to custom roles. I assume, in this section, that you are using Forms authentication.

> **WARNING**
>
> The Web Site Administration Tool does not support assigning users to roles when Windows authentication is enabled. When Windows authentication is enabled, you must assign users to roles programmatically.

The web configuration file in Listing 21.27 enables the SqlRoleProvider.

LISTING 21.27   Web.Config

```
<?xml version="1.0" encoding="utf-8"?>
<configuration>
    <system.web>
        <roleManager enabled="true" />
        <authentication mode="Forms" />
    </system.web>
</configuration>
```

The Role Manager is disabled by default. The configuration file in Listing 21.27 simply enables the Role Manager. Notice that the configuration file also enables Forms authentication.

If you don't want to type the file in Listing 21.27, you can let the Web Site Administration Tool create the file for you. Open the Web Site Administration Tool in Visual Web Developer by selecting the menu option Website, ASP.NET Configuration. Next, click the Security tab and click the Enable roles link (see Figure 21.11).

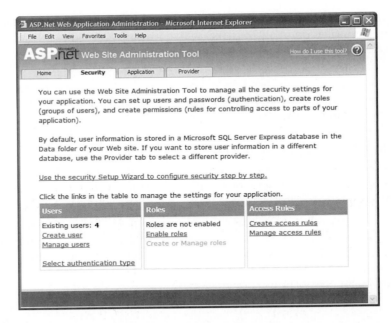

FIGURE 21.11   Enabling Roles with the Web Site Administration Tool.

After you enable the Role Manager, you need to create some roles. You can create roles in two ways. You can use the Web Site Administration Tool or you can create the roles programmatically.

Open the Web Site Administration Tool and click the Create or Manage Roles link located under the Security tab. At this point, you can start creating roles. I'll assume that you have created a role named Managers.

After you create a set of roles, you need to assign users to the roles. Again, you can do this by using the Web Site Administration Tool or you can assign users to roles programmatically.

If you have not created any users for your application, create a user now by clicking the Create User link under the Security tab. Notice that you can assign a user to one or more roles when you create the user (see Figure 21.12). You can click the Create or Manage Roles link to assign roles to users at a later date.

After you finish creating your roles and assigning users to the roles, you can use the roles in the authentication section of a web configuration file. For example, imagine that your web site includes a folder named SecretFiles and you want only members of the Managers role to be able to access the pages in that folder. The web configuration file in Listing 21.28 blocks access to anyone except members of the Managers role to the SecretFiles folder.

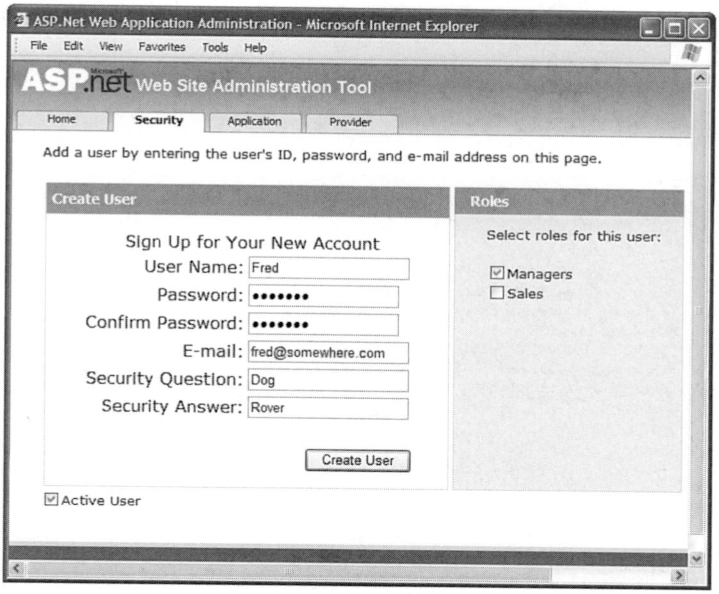

FIGURE 21.12   Assigning a new user to a role.

LISTING 21.28   Web.Config

```xml
<?xml version="1.0"?>
<configuration>
    <system.web>

        <authorization>
          <allow roles="Managers"/>
          <deny users="*"/>
        </authorization>

    </system.web>
</configuration>
```

The configuration file in Listing 21.28 authorizes Managers and denies access to everyone else.

If you prefer, you can manage authorization with the Web Site Administration Tool. Behind the scenes, this tool creates web configuration files that contain authorization elements (in other words, it does the same thing as we just did).

Under the Security tab, click the Create Access Rules link. Select the SecretFiles folder from the tree view, select the Managers role, and select Allow (see Figure 21.13). Click the OK button to create the rule. Next, create a second access rule to deny access to users not in the Managers role. Select the SecretFiles folder, select All Users, and select Deny. Click the OK button to add the new rule.

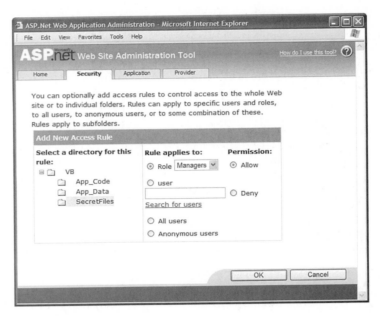

FIGURE 21.13   Creating authorization rules.

Using a Different Database with the `SqlRoleProvider`

By default, the SqlRoleProvider uses the same Microsoft SQL Server Express database as ASP.NET Membership: the `AspNetDB.mdf` database. This database is created for you automatically in your application's root App_Data folder.

If you want to store role information in another Microsoft SQL Server database, then you must perform the following two configuration steps.

- Configure the database so that it contains the necessary database objects.

- Configure your application to use the new database.

Before you can store role information in a database, you need to add the necessary tables and stored procedures to the database. The easiest way to add these objects is to use the `aspnet_regsql` command-line tool. This tool is located in the following folder:

`\WINDOWS\Microsoft.NET\Framework\[version]`

NOTE

You don't need to navigate to the Microsoft.NET folder when you open the SDK Command Prompt.

If you execute aspnet_regsql without any parameters, then the ASP.NET SQL Server Setup Wizard opens (see Figure 21.14). You can use this wizard to connect to a database and add the necessary database objects automatically.

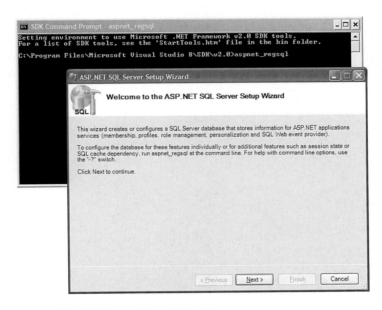

FIGURE 21.14   Using the SQL Server Setup Wizard.

Alternatively, you can set up a database by executing the following two SQL batch files.

- InstallCommon.sql

- InstallRoles.sql

These batch files are located in the same folder as the aspnet_regsql tool.

After you set up your database, you need to configure a new SqlRoleProvider that includes the proper connection string for your database. The web configuration file in Listing 21.29 configures a new provider named MyRoleProvider that connects to a database named MyDatabase located on a server named MyServer.

LISTING 21.29   Web.Config

```
<?xml version="1.0" encoding="utf-8"?>
<configuration>
  <connectionStrings>
    <add
      name="MyConnection"
      connectionString="Data Source=MyServer;
➥Integrated Security=True;Initial Catalog=MyDatabase"/>
```

nued

```
  ...b>
    <authentication mode="Forms" />

    <roleManager enabled="true" defaultProvider="MyRoleProvider">
      <providers>
        <add
          name="MyRoleProvider"
          type="System.Web.Security.SqlRoleProvider"
          connectionStringName="MyConnection"/>
      </providers>
    </roleManager>

  </system.web>
</configuration>
```

The configuration file in Listing 21.29 creates a new default `RoleManager` named `MyRoleProvider`. Notice that the `MyRoleProvider` provider includes a `connectionStringName` attribute that points to the `MyConnection` connection.

Configuring the `WindowsTokenRoleProvider`

When you use the `WindowsTokenRoleProvider`, roles correspond to Microsoft Windows groups. You must enable Windows authentication when using the `WindowsTokenRoleProvider`. You cannot use Forms authentication or ASP.NET Membership with the `WindowsTokenRoleProvider`.

The configuration file in Listing 21.30 configures the `WindowsTokenRoleProvider` as the default provider.

LISTING 21.30 `Web.Config`

```
<?xml version="1.0" encoding="utf-8"?>
<configuration>
    <system.web>
      <authentication mode="Windows" />

      <roleManager enabled="true" defaultProvider="MyRoleProvider">
        <providers>
          <add
            name="MyRoleProvider"
            type="System.Web.Security.WindowsTokenRoleProvider" />
        </providers>
```

LISTING 2130   Continued

```
    </roleManager>

  </system.web>
</configuration>
```

The page in Listing 21.31 contains a `LoginView` control. The `LoginView` control displays different content to the members of the Windows Administrators group than it displays to everyone else (see Figure 21.15).

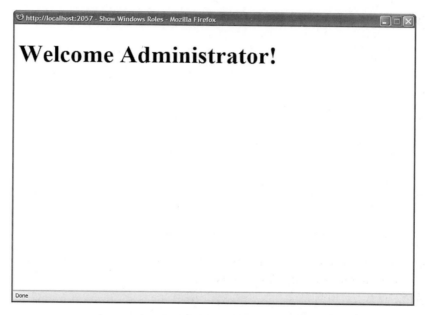

FIGURE 21.15   Displaying different content to members of the Windows Administrators group.

LISTING 21.31   ShowWindowsRoles.aspx

```
<%@ Page Language="VB" %>
<!DOCTYPE html PUBLIC "-//W3C//DTD XHTML 1.0 Transitional//EN"
  "http://www.w3.org/TR/xhtml1/DTD/xhtml1-transitional.dtd">
<html xmlns="http://www.w3.org/1999/xhtml" >
<head id="Head1" runat="server">
    <title>Show Windows Roles</title>
</head>
<body>
    <form id="form1" runat="server">
    <div>
```

LISTING 21.31   Continued

```
    <asp:LoginView
        id="LoginView1"
        Runat="server">
        <RoleGroups>
        <asp:RoleGroup Roles="BUILTIN\Administrators">
            <ContentTemplate>
            <h1>Welcome Administrator!</h1>
            </ContentTemplate>
        </asp:RoleGroup>
        </RoleGroups>
        <LoggedInTemplate>
            <h1>Welcome Average User!</h1>
        </LoggedInTemplate>
    </asp:LoginView>

    </div>
    </form>
</body>
</html>
```

If you request the page in Listing 21.31 after enabling the `WindowsTokenRoleProvider`, then you see the content displayed by the `LoginView` control only when you are a member of the Windows Administrators group.

Configuring the `AuthorizationStoreRoleProvider`

Authorization Manager (AzMan) is a component of Windows Server 2003. You can use Authorization Manager to define roles, tasks, and operations.

Authorization Manager supports more features than the authorization framework included in the ASP.NET Framework. For example, Authorization Manager supports role inheritance, which enables you to easily define new roles based on existing roles.

> **NOTE**
>
> You can use Authorization Manager with Windows XP Professional. However, you must install it first. You need to download the Windows Server 2003 Administrative Tools Pack from the Microsoft MSDN website (msdn.microsoft.com).

Authorization Manager can store role information in three different ways. You can create an authorization store by using an XML file, by using Active Directory, or by using Active Directory Application Mode (ADAM).

Before you use Authorization Manager with the ASP.NET Framework, you need to create an authorization store. Role information is stored in an XML file local to the application. Follow these steps:

1. Launch Authorization Manager by executing the command AzMan.msc from a command prompt (see Figure 21.16).

2. Switch Authorization Manager into Developer mode by selecting the menu option Action, Options and selecting Developer mode.

3. Open the New Authorization Store dialog box by selecting the menu option Action, New Authorization Store.

4. Select the XML file option and enter the path to your application's App_Data folder for the Store Name field. For example:

```
c:\Websites\MyWebsite\App_Data\WebRoles.xml
```

5. Create a new Authorization Manager application by right-clicking the name of your authorization store and selecting New Application. Enter the name WebRoles for your application (you can leave the other fields blank).

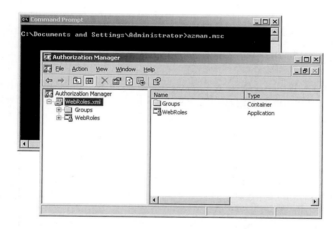

FIGURE 21.16   Using Authorization Manager.

After you complete these steps, a new XML file is added to your application. This XML file contains the authorization store.

Next, you need to configure the ASP.NET Role Manager to use the authorization store. The web configuration file in Listing 21.32 uses the WebRoles.xml authorization store.

LISTING 21.32   Web.Config

```
<?xml version="1.0" encoding="utf-8"?>
<configuration>
  <connectionStrings>
    <add
      name="AZConnection"
      connectionString="msxml://~/App_Data/WebRoles.xml"/>
```

LISTING 21.32   Continued

```
  </connectionStrings>

  <system.web>
    <authentication mode="Windows" />

    <roleManager enabled="true" defaultProvider="MyRoleProvider">
      <providers>
        <add
          name="MyRoleProvider"
          type="System.Web.Security.AuthorizationStoreRoleProvider"
          connectionStringName="AZConnection"
          applicationName="WebRoles"
          />
      </providers>
    </roleManager>

  </system.web>
</configuration>
```

You should notice a couple of things about the configuration file in Listing 21.32. First, notice that the connection string uses the prefix msxml: to indicate that the connection string represents a connection to an XML file.

Second, notice that the AuthorizationStoreRoleProvider includes an applicationName attribute. This attribute must contain the name of the Authorization Manager application that you created in the preceding steps.

After you complete these configuration steps, you can use the Authorization Manager just as you do the default SqlMembershipProvider. You can define new roles by using either the Web Site Administration Tool or the Authorization Manager interface (see Figure 21.17).

Caching Roles in a Browser Cookie

To improve your application's performance, you can cache user roles in a browser cookie. That way, the Role Manager does not have to perform a query against the Role provider each and every time a user visits a page.

Caching roles in cookies is disabled by default. You can enable this feature with the web configuration file in Listing 21.33.

LISTING 21.33   Web.Config

```
<?xml version="1.0" encoding="utf-8"?>
<configuration>
    <system.web>
      <roleManager
```

LISTING 21.33   Continued

```
        enabled="true"
        cacheRolesInCookie="true"
        createPersistentCookie="true" />
    </system.web>
</configuration>
```

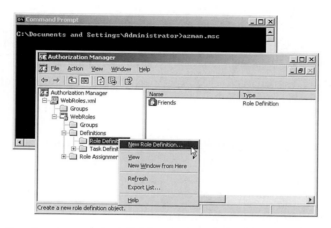

FIGURE 21.17   Creating a new role definition with Authorization Manager.

The web configuration in Listing 21.33 enables role caching. Furthermore, it causes the roles to be cached in a persistent cookie rather than a session cookie.

> **WARNING**
>
> When you cache roles in a cookie, there is the potential that a user's cached roles can become out of sync with a user's actual roles. If you update a user's roles on the server, they don't get updated on the browser. You can call the `Roles.DeleteCookie()` method to delete the cached cookies.

You can set a number of attributes that are related to the roles cookie:

- `cacheRolesInCookie`—Enables you to cache user roles in a browser cookie (the default value is `false`).

- `cookieName`—Enables you to specify the name for the roles cookie (the default value is `.ASPXROLES`).

- `cookiePath`—Enables you to specify the path associated with the cookie (the default value is `/`).

- `cookieProtection`—Enables you to encrypt and validate the roles cookie. Possible values are `All`, `Encryption`, `None`, and `Validation` (the default value is `All`).

21

- cookieRequireSSL—Enables you to require that the roles cookie be transmitted over a Secure Sockets Layer connection (the default value is false).

- cookieSlidingExpiration—Enables you to prevent a cookie from expiring just as long as a user continues to request pages (the default value is true).

- cookieTimeout—Enables you to specify the amount of time in minutes before a cookie times out (the default value is 30).

- createPersistentCookie—Enables you to create a persistent rather than a session cookie (the default value is false).

- domain—Enables you to specify the domain associated with the cookie (the default value is an empty string).

- maxCachedResults—Enables you to specify the maximum number of roles that are cached in a cookie (the default is 25).

Using the Roles Application Programming Interface

The Roles class exposes the main application programming interface for manipulating roles. If you need to create roles programmatically, delete roles, or assign users to roles, then you use the methods of the Roles class.

The Roles class includes the following methods:

- AddUsersToRole—Enables you to add an array of users to a role.

- AddUsersToRoles—Enables you to add an array of users to an array of roles.

- AddUserToRole—Enables you to add a user to a role.

- AddUserToRoles—Enables you to add a user to an array of roles.

- CreateRole—Enables you to create a new role.

- DeleteCookie—Enables you to delete the roles cookie.

- DeleteRole—Enables you to delete a particular role.

- FindUsersInRole—Enables you to return a list of users in a role that has a particular username.

- GetAllRoles—Enables you to retrieve a list of all roles.

- GetRolesForUser—Enables you to get a list of all roles to which a user belongs.

- GetUsersInRole—Enables you to get a list of users in a particular role.

- IsUserInRole—Enables you to determine whether a particular user is a member of a particular role.

- RemoveUserFromRole—Enables you to remove a particular user from a particular role.

- RemoveUserFromRoles—Enables you to remove a particular user from an array of roles.

- RemoveUsersFromRole—Enables you to remove an array of users from a particular role.

- RemoveUsersFromRoles—Enables you to remove an array of users from an array of roles.

- RoleExists—Enables you to determine whether a particular role exists.

The page in Listing 21.34 illustrates how you can use the methods of the Roles class. The Page_Load() method creates two roles named Sales and Managers (if they don't already exist). Next, it assigns the current user to both roles. The body of the page contains a GridView that displays all the roles to which the current user belongs (see Figure 21.18).

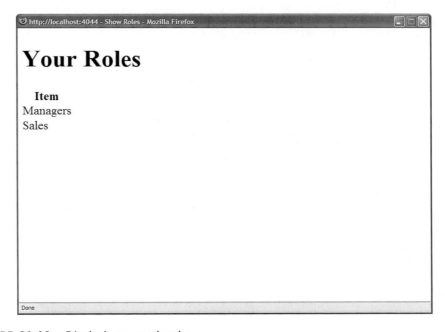

FIGURE 21.18   Displaying a user's roles.

LISTING 21.34   ShowRoles.aspx

```
<%@ Page Language="VB" %>
<!DOCTYPE html PUBLIC "-//W3C//DTD XHTML 1.0 Transitional//EN"
  "http://www.w3.org/TR/xhtml1/DTD/xhtml1-transitional.dtd">
<script runat="server">
    Sub Page_Load()
        ' If user is not authenticated, redirect to Login page
        If Not Request.IsAuthenticated Then
            FormsAuthentication.RedirectToLoginPage()
            Response.End()
        End If
```

LISTING 21.34   Continued

```
        ' Create two roles
        If Not Roles.RoleExists("Managers") Then
            Roles.CreateRole("Managers")
        End If
        If Not Roles.RoleExists("Sales") Then
            Roles.CreateRole("Sales")
        End If

        ' Add current user to both roles
        If Not Roles.IsUserInRole("Managers") Then
            Roles.AddUserToRole(User.Identity.Name, "Managers")
        End If
        If Not Roles.IsUserInRole("Sales") Then
            Roles.AddUserToRole(User.Identity.Name, "Sales")
        End If
    End Sub
</script>
<html xmlns="http://www.w3.org/1999/xhtml" >
<head id="Head1" runat="server">
    <title>Show Roles</title>
</head>
<body>
    <form id="form1" runat="server">
    <div>

    <h1>Your Roles</h1>

    <asp:GridView
        id="grdRoles"
        DataSourceID="srcRoles"
        EmptyDataText="You are not a member of any roles"
        GridLines="none"
        Runat="server" />

    <asp:ObjectDataSource
        id="srcRoles"
        TypeName="System.Web.Security.Roles"
        SelectMethod="GetRolesForUser"
        Runat="server" />

    </div>
    </form>
</body>
</html>
```

Summary

In this chapter, you learned about the four security frameworks included in the ASP.NET Framework. In the first part of the chapter, you learned how to authenticate users by enabling both Forms and Windows authentication. You learned how to take advantage of several advanced features of authentication such as cookieless authentication and cross-application authentication.

You also learn how to authorize users to access particular resources. You not only learned how to control access to ASP.NET pages, but how you can control access to image files and ASP classic pages.

Next, you learned how to use ASP.NET Membership to represent user information. You learned how to use the `Membership` class to create users, delete users, and modify user properties programmatically. You also explored the two Membership providers included with the ASP.NET Framework: the `SqlMembershipProvider` and the `ActiveDirectoryMembershipProvider`. Finally, we created a custom `MembershipProvider`: the `XmlMembershipProvider`.

The final section of this chapter was devoted to the Role Manager. You learned how to configure the three Role providers included in the ASP.NET Framework: the `SqlRoleProvider`, `WindowsTokenRoleProvider`, and the `AuthorizationStoreRoleProvider`. You also learned how to take advantage of the `Roles` class to create roles, delete roles, and assign users to roles programmatically.

21

PART VII

Building ASP.NET Applications

IN THIS PART

Maintaining Application State

Developers who are new to programming for the web always have difficulty understanding the problem of maintaining state. The HTTP protocol, the fundamental protocol of the World Wide Web, is a stateless protocol. What this means is that from a web server's perspective, every request is from a new user. The HTTP protocol does not provide you with any method of determining whether any two requests are made by the same person.

However, maintaining state is important in just about any web application. The paradigmatic example is a shopping cart. If you want to associate a shopping cart with a user over multiple page requests, then you need some method of maintaining state.

This chapter looks at three methods included in the ASP.NET 2.0 Framework for associating data with a particular user over multiple page requests. In the first section, you learn how to create and manipulate browser cookies. A browser cookie enables you to associate a little bit of text with each website user.

Next, you learn how to take advantage of Session state. Session state enables you to associate an arbitrary object with any user. For example, you can store a shipping cart object in Session state.

You learn how to take advantage of cookieless Session state so that you can use Session state even when a browser has cookies disabled. You also learn how to make Session state more robust by enabling out-of-process Session state.

Finally, we examine a new feature introduced with the ASP.NET 2.0 framework: the Profile object. The Profile object provides you with a method of creating a strongly typed and persistent form of session state.

You learn different methods of defining a profile. You also learn how to use the `Profile` object from within a component. Finally, you learn how to implement a custom `Profile` provider.

Using Browser Cookies

Cookies were introduced into the world with the first version of the Netscape browser. The developers at Netscape invented cookies to solve a problem that plagued the Internet at the time. There was no way to make money because there was no way to create a shopping cart.

> **NOTE**
>
> You can read Netscape's original cookie specification at http://home.netscape.com/newsref/std/cookie_spec.html.

Here's how cookies work. When a web server creates a cookie, an additional HTTP header is sent to the browser when a page is served to the browser. The HTTP header looks like this:

```
Set-Cookie: message=Hello
```

This `Set-Cookie` header causes the browser to create a cookie named `message` that has the value `Hello`.

After a cookie has been created on a browser, whenever the browser requests a page from the same application in the future, the browser sends a header that looks like this:

```
Cookie: message=Hello
```

The `Cookie` header contains all the cookies that have been set by the web server. The cookies are sent back to the web server each time a request is made from the browser.

Notice that a cookie is nothing more than a little bit of text. You can store only string values when using a cookie.

You actually can create two types of cookies: session cookies and persistent cookies. A session cookie exists only in memory. If a user closes the web browser, the session cookie disappears forever.

A persistent cookie, on the other hand, can last for months or even years. When you create a persistent cookie, the cookie is stored permanently by the user's browser on the user's computer. Internet Explorer, for example, stores cookies in a set of text files contained in the following folder:

```
\Documents and Settings\[user]\Cookies
```

The Mozilla Firefox browser, on the other hand, stores cookies in the following file:

```
\Documents and Settings\[user]\Application Data\Mozilla\Firefox\Profiles\
➥[random folder name]\Cookies.txt
```

Because different browsers store cookies in different locations, cookies are browser relative. If you request a page that creates a cookie when using Internet Explorer, the cookie doesn't exist when you open Firefox or Opera.

Furthermore, notice that both Internet Explorer and Firefox store cookies in clear text. You should never store sensitive information—such as social security numbers or credit card numbers—in a cookie.

> **NOTE**
>
> Where does the name *cookie* come from? According to the original Netscape cookie specification, the term cookie was selected "for no compelling reason." However, the name most likely derives from the UNIX world in which a "magic cookie" is an opaque token passed between programs.

Cookie Security Restrictions

Cookies raise security concerns. When you create a persistent cookie, you are modifying a file on a visitor's computer. There are people who sit around all day dreaming up evil things that they can do to your computer. To prevent cookies from doing horrible things to people's computers, browsers enforce a number of security restrictions on cookies.

First, all cookies are domain relative. If the Amazon website sets a cookie, then the Barnes and Noble website cannot read the cookie. When a browser creates a cookie, the browser records the domain associated with the cookie and doesn't send the cookie to another domain.

> **NOTE**
>
> An image contained in a web page might be served from another domain than the web page itself. Therefore, when the browser makes a request for the image, a cookie can be set from the other domain. Companies, such as DoubleClick, that display and track advertisements on multiple websites take advantage of this loophole to track advertisement statistics across multiple web sites. This type of cookie is called a third-party cookie.

The other important restriction that browsers place on cookies is a restriction on size. A single domain cannot store more than 4096 bytes. This size restriction encompasses the size of both the cookie names and the cookie values.

> **NOTE**
>
> Internet Explorer, version 5.0 or higher, supports a feature named the userData behavior. The userData behavior enables you to persist far more data than a cookie (10240KB for an intranet site and 1024 for an Internet site). To learn more about the userData behavior, visit the Microsoft MSDN website (msdn.microsoft.com).

Finally, most browsers restrict the number of cookies that can be set by a single domain to no more than 20 cookies (but not Internet Explorer). If you attempt to set more than 20 cookies, the oldest cookies are automatically deleted.

> **NOTE**
>
> The White House's Office of Management and Budget bans all federal websites from creating persistent cookies unless there is a "compelling need." See http://www.whitehouse.gov/omb/memoranda/m00-13.html.
>
> The National Security Agency web site (www.nsa.gov) recently got into trouble for creating persistent cookies. They stopped using persistent cookies after they received a barrage of complaints from privacy advocates.
>
> Personally, I think that this cookie paranoia is crazy, but you need to be aware of it.

Because of all the security concerns related to cookies, all modern browsers provide users with the option of disabling cookies. This means that unless you are building an Intranet application and you control every user's browser, you should attempt to not rely on cookies. Strive to use cookies only when storing non-crucial information.

That said, many parts of the ASP.NET Framework rely on cookies. For example, Web Parts, Forms Authentication, Session state, and anonymous Profiles all depend on cookies by default. If you are depending on one of these features anyway, then there is no reason not to use cookies.

Furthermore, many websites rely on cookies. There are many sections of the Yahoo! and MSDN websites that you cannot visit without having cookies enabled. In other words, requiring visitors to have cookies enabled to use your website is not an entirely unreasonable requirement.

Creating Cookies

You create a new cookie by adding a cookie to the Response.Cookies collection. The Response.Cookies collection contains all the cookies sent from the web server to the web browser.

For example, the page in Listing 22.1 enables you to create a new cookie named Message. The page contains a form that enables you to enter the value of the Message cookie (see Figure 22.1).

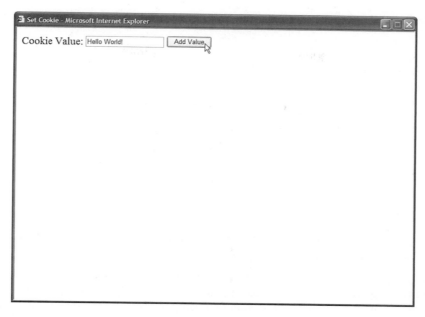

FIGURE 22.1   Creating a new cookie.

LISTING 22.1   SetCookie.aspx

```
<%@ Page Language="VB" %>
<!DOCTYPE html PUBLIC "-//W3C//DTD XHTML 1.0 Transitional//EN"
  "http://www.w3.org/TR/xhtml1/DTD/xhtml1-transitional.dtd">
<script runat="server">

    Sub btnAdd_Click(ByVal sender As Object, ByVal e As EventArgs)
        Response.Cookies("message").Value = txtCookieValue.Text
    End Sub
</script>
<html xmlns="http://www.w3.org/1999/xhtml" >
<head id="Head1" runat="server">
    <title>Set Cookie</title>
</head>
<body>
    <form id="form1" runat="server">
    <div>

    <asp:Label
        id="lblCookieValue"
        Text="Cookie Value:"
        AssociatedControlID="txtCookieValue"
        Runat="server" />
    <asp:TextBox
```

LISTING 22.1   Continued

```
            id="txtCookieValue"
            Runat="server" />
        <asp:Button
            id="btnAdd"
            Text="Add Value"
            OnClick="btnAdd_Click"
            Runat="server" />

        </div>
        </form>
</body>
</html>
```

Be warned that cookie names are case sensitive. Setting a cookie named message is different from setting a cookie named Message.

If you want to modify the value of the cookie created by the page in Listing 22.1, then you can open the page and enter a new value for the message cookie. When the web server sends its response to the browser, the modified value of the cookie is set on the browser.

The page in Listing 22.1 creates a session cookie. The cookie disappears when you close your web browser. If you want to create a persistent cookie, then you need to specify an expiration date for the cookie.

The page in Listing 22.2 creates a persistent cookie.

LISTING 22.2   SetPersistentCookie.aspx

```
<%@ Page Language="VB" %>
<!DOCTYPE html PUBLIC "-//W3C//DTD XHTML 1.0 Transitional//EN"
  "http://www.w3.org/TR/xhtml1/DTD/xhtml1-transitional.dtd">
<script runat="server">

    Private Sub Page_Load()
        ' Get current value of cookie
        Dim counter As Integer = 0
        If Not IsNothing(Request.Cookies("counter")) Then
            counter = Int32.Parse(Request.Cookies("counter").Value)
        End If

        ' Increment counter
        counter = counter + 1

        ' Add persistent cookie to browser
        Response.Cookies("counter").Value = counter.ToString()
        Response.Cookies("counter").Expires = DateTime.Now.AddYears(2)

        ' Display value of counter cookie
```

LISTING 22.2   Continued

```
            lblCounter.Text = counter.ToString()
    End Sub
</script>
<html xmlns="http://www.w3.org/1999/xhtml" >
<head id="Head1" runat="server">
    <title>Set Persistent Cookie</title>
</head>
<body>
    <form id="form1" runat="server">
    <div>

    You have visited this page
    <asp:Label
        id="lblCounter"
        Runat="server" />
    times!

    </div>
    </form>
</body>
</html>
```

The page in Listing 22.2 tracks the number of times that you have requested the page. A persistent cookie named counter is used to track page requests. Notice that the counter cookie's Expires property is set to two years in the future. When you set a particular expiration date for a cookie, the cookie is stored as a persistent cookie.

Reading Cookies

You use the Response.Cookies collection to create and modify cookies. You use the Request.Cookies collection to retrieve a cookie's value.

For example, the page in Listing 22.3 retrieves the message cookie's value.

LISTING 22.3   GetCookie.aspx

```
<%@ Page Language="VB" %>
<!DOCTYPE html PUBLIC "-//W3C//DTD XHTML 1.0 Transitional//EN"
  "http://www.w3.org/TR/xhtml1/DTD/xhtml1-transitional.dtd">
<script runat="server">

    Sub Page_Load()
        If Not IsNothing(Request.Cookies("message")) Then
            lblCookieValue.Text = Request.Cookies("message").Value
        End If
    End Sub
</script>
```

LISTING 22.3   Continued

```
<html xmlns="http://www.w3.org/1999/xhtml" >
<head id="Head1" runat="server">
    <title>Get Cookie</title>
</head>
<body>
    <form id="form1" runat="server">
    <div>

    The value of the message cookie is:
    <asp:Label
        id="lblCookieValue"
        Runat="server" />

    </div>
    </form>
</body>
</html>
```

In Listing 22.3, the IsNothing() function is used to check whether the cookie exists before reading its value. If you don't include this check, you might get a null reference exception. Also, don't forget that cookie names are case sensitive.

The page in Listing 22.4 lists all cookies contained in the Request.Cookies collection (see Figure 22.2).

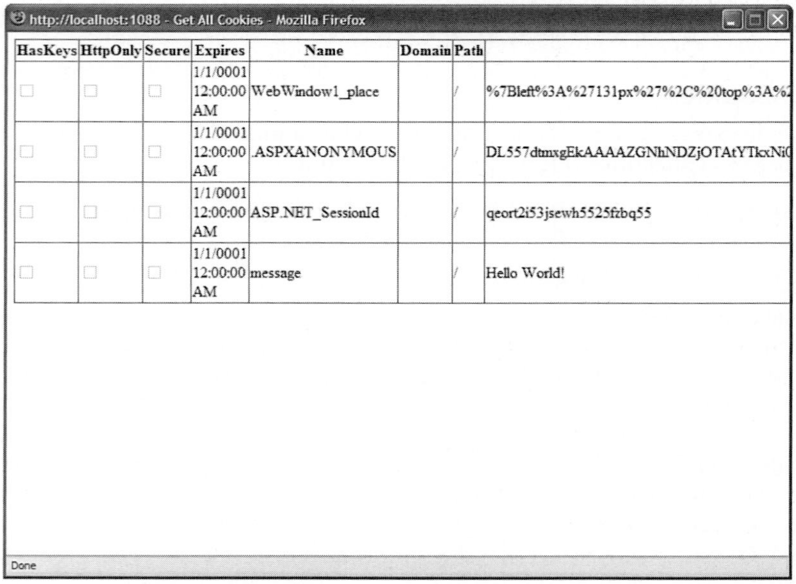

HasKeys	HttpOnly	Secure	Expires	Name	Domain	Path	
☐	☐	☐	1/1/0001 12:00:00 AM	WebWindow1_place		/	%7Bleft%3A%27131px%27%2C%20top%3A%2
☐	☐	☐	1/1/0001 12:00:00 AM	.ASPXANONYMOUS		/	DL557dtmxgEkAAAAZGNhNDZjOTAtYTkxNi(
☐	☐	☐	1/1/0001 12:00:00 AM	ASP.NET_SessionId		/	qeort2i53jsewh5525fzbq55
☐	☐	☐	1/1/0001 12:00:00 AM	message		/	Hello World!

FIGURE 22.2   Displaying a list of all cookies.

LISTING 22.4   GetAllCookies.aspx

```
<%@ Page Language="VB" %>
<!DOCTYPE html PUBLIC "-//W3C//DTD XHTML 1.0 Transitional//EN"
   "http://www.w3.org/TR/xhtml1/DTD/xhtml1-transitional.dtd">
<script runat="server">

    Sub Page_Load()
        Dim colCookies As New ArrayList()
        For i As Integer = 0 To Request.Cookies.Count - 1
            colCookies.Add(Request.Cookies(i))
        Next

        grdCookies.DataSource = colCookies
        grdCookies.DataBind()
    End Sub
</script>
<html xmlns="http://www.w3.org/1999/xhtml" >
<head id="Head1" runat="server">
    <title>Get All Cookies</title>
</head>
<body>
    <form id="form1" runat="server">
    <div>

    <asp:GridView
        id="grdCookies"
        Runat="server"/>

    </div>
    </form>
</body>
</html>
```

Notice that the only meaningful information that you get back from iterating through the Request.Cookies collection is the HasKeys, Name, and Value properties. The other columns show incorrect information. For example, the Expires column always displays a minimal date. Browsers don't communicate these additional properties with page requests, so you can't retrieve these property values.

When using the Request.Cookies collection, it is important to understand that a For...Each loop returns different values than a For...Next loop. If you iterate through the Request.Cookies collection with a For...Each loop, you get the cookie names. If you iterate through the collection with a For...Next loop, then you get instances of the HttpCookie class (described in the next section).

Setting Cookie Properties

Cookies are represented with the `HttpCookie` class. When you create or read a cookie, you can use any of the properties of this class:

- `Domain`—Enables you to specify the domain associated with the cookie. The default value is the current domain.

- `Expires`—Enables you to create a persistent cookie by specifying an expiration date.

- `HasKeys`—Enables you to determine whether a cookie is a multi-valued cookie (see the section "Working with Multi-Valued Cookies" later in this chapter).

- `HttpOnly`—Enables you to prevent a cookie from being accessed by JavaScript.

- `Name`—Enables you to specify a name for a cookie.

- `Path`—Enables you to specify the path associated with a cookie. The default value is /.

- `Secure`—Enables you to require a cookie to be transmitted across a Secure Sockets Layer (SSL) connection.

- `Value`—Enables you to get or set a cookie value.

- `Values`—Enables you to get or set a particular value when working with a multi-valued cookie (see the section "Working with Multi-Valued Cookies" later in this chapter).

A couple of these properties require additional explanation. For example, you might find the `Domain` property confusing because you can't change the domain associated with a cookie.

The `Domain` property is useful when your organization includes subdomains. If you want to set a cookie that can be read by the Sales.MyCompany.com, Managers.MyCompany.com, and Support.MyCompany.com domains, then you can set the `Domain` property to the value `.MyCompany.com` (notice the leading period). You can't, however, use this property to associate a cookie with an entirely different domain.

The `HttpOnly` property enables you to specify whether a cookie can be accessed from JavaScript code. This property works only with Internet Explorer 6 (Service Pack 1) and above. The property was introduced to help prevent cross-site scripting attacks.

The `Path` property enables you to scope cookies to a particular path. For example, if you are hosting multiple applications in the same domain, and you do not want the applications to share the same cookies, then you can use the `Path` property to prevent one application from reading another application's cookies.

The `Path` property sounds really useful. Unfortunately, you should never use it. Internet Explorer performs a case-sensitive match against the path. If a user uses a different case when typing the path to a page into the address bar, then the cookie isn't sent. In other words, the following two paths don't match:

```
http://localhost/original/GetAllCookies.aspx
http://localhost/ORIGINAL/GetAllCookies.aspx
```

Deleting Cookies

The method for deleting cookies is not intuitive. To delete an existing cookie, you must set its expiration date to a date in the past.

The page in Listing 22.5 illustrates how you can delete a single cookie. The page contains a form field for the cookie name. When you submit the form, the cookie with the specified name is deleted.

LISTING 22.5   DeleteCookie.aspx

```
<%@ Page Language="VB" %>
<!DOCTYPE html PUBLIC "-//W3C//DTD XHTML 1.0 Transitional//EN"
  "http://www.w3.org/TR/xhtml1/DTD/xhtml1-transitional.dtd">
<script runat="server">

    Sub btnDelete_Click(ByVal sender As Object, ByVal e As EventArgs)
        Response.Cookies(txtCookieName.Text).Expires = DateTime.Now.AddDays(-1)
    End Sub
</script>
<html xmlns="http://www.w3.org/1999/xhtml" >
<head id="Head1" runat="server">
    <title>Delete Cookie</title>
</head>
<body>
    <form id="form1" runat="server">
    <div>

    <asp:Label
        id="lblCookieName"
        Text="Cookie Name:"
        AssociatedControlID="txtCookieName"
        Runat="server" />
    <asp:TextBox
        id="txtCookieName"
        Runat="server" />
    <asp:Button
        id="btnDelete"
        Text="Delete Cookie"
        OnClick="btnDelete_Click"
        Runat="server" />

    </div>
    </form>
</body>
</html>
```

22

The particular date that you specify when deleting a cookie doesn't really matter as long as it is in the past. In Listing 22.5, the expiration date is set to one day ago.

The page in Listing 22.6 deletes all cookies sent from the browser to the current domain (and path).

LISTING 22.6   DeleteAllCookies.aspx

```
<%@ Page Language="VB" %>
<!DOCTYPE html PUBLIC "-//W3C//DTD XHTML 1.0 Transitional//EN"
  "http://www.w3.org/TR/xhtml1/DTD/xhtml1-transitional.dtd">
<script runat="server">

    Sub Page_Load()
        Dim cookies As String() = Request.Cookies.AllKeys
        for each cookie As String in cookies
            BulletedList1.Items.Add("Deleting " & cookie)
            Response.Cookies(cookie).Expires = DateTime.Now.AddDays(-1)
        Next
    End Sub
</script>
<html xmlns="http://www.w3.org/1999/xhtml" >
<head id="Head1" runat="server">
    <title>Delete All Cookies</title>
</head>
<body>
    <form id="form1" runat="server">
    <div>

    <h1>Delete All Cookies</h1>

    <asp:BulletedList
        id="BulletedList1"
        EnableViewState="false"
        Runat="server" />

    </div>
    </form>
</body>
</html>
```

The page in Listing 22.6 loops through all the cookie names from the `Request.Cookies` collection and deletes each cookie.

Working with Multi-Valued Cookies

According to the cookie specifications, browsers should not store more than 20 cookies from a single domain. You can work around this limitation by creating multi-valued cookies.

A multi-valued cookie is a single cookie that contains subkeys. You can create as many subkeys as you need.

For example, the page in Listing 22.7 creates a multi-valued cookie named preferences. The preferences cookie is used to store a first name, last name, and favorite color (see Figure 22.3).

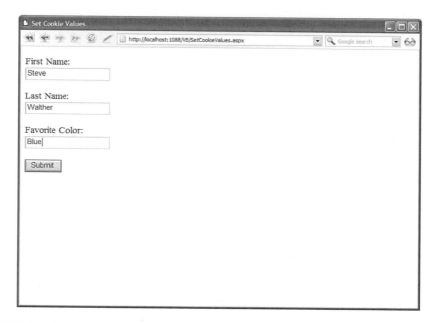

FIGURE 22.3   Creating a multi-valued cookie.

LISTING 22.7   SetCookieValues.aspx

```
<%@ Page Language="VB" %>
<!DOCTYPE html PUBLIC "-//W3C//DTD XHTML 1.0 Transitional//EN"
  "http://www.w3.org/TR/xhtml1/DTD/xhtml1-transitional.dtd">
<script runat="server">

    Sub btnSubmit_Click(ByVal s As Object, ByVal e As EventArgs)
        Response.Cookies("preferences")("firstName") = txtFirstName.Text
        Response.Cookies("preferences")("lastName") = txtLastName.Text
        Response.Cookies("preferences")("favoriteColor") = txtFavoriteColor.Text
        Response.Cookies("preferences").Expires = DateTime.MaxValue
```

22

LISTING 22.7   Continued

```
    End Sub
</script>
<html xmlns="http://www.w3.org/1999/xhtml" >
<head id="Head1" runat="server">
    <title>Set Cookie Values</title>
</head>
<body>
    <form id="form1" runat="server">
    <div>

    <asp:Label
        id="lblFirstName"
        Text="First Name:"
        AssociatedControlID="txtFirstName"
        Runat="server" />
    <br />
    <asp:TextBox
        id="txtFirstName"
        Runat="server" />
    <br /><br />
    <asp:Label
        id="lblLastName"
        Text="Last Name:"
        AssociatedControlID="txtFirstName"
        Runat="server" />
    <br />
    <asp:TextBox
        id="txtLastName"
        Runat="server" />
    <br /><br />
    <asp:Label
        id="lblFavoriteColor"
        Text="Favorite Color:"
        AssociatedControlID="txtFavoriteColor"
        Runat="server" />
    <br />
    <asp:TextBox
        id="txtFavoriteColor"
        Runat="server" />
    <br /><br />
    <asp:Button
        id="btnSubmit"
        Text="Submit"
        OnClick="btnSubmit_Click"
        Runat="server" />
```

LISTING 22.7   Continued

```
        </div>
        </form>
    </body>
    </html>
```

When you submit the page in Listing 22.7, the following HTTP header is sent to the browser:

```
Set-Cookie: preferences=firstName=Steve&lastName=Walther&favoriteColor=green;

expires=Fri, 31-Dec-9999 23:59:59 GMT; path=/
```

The page in Listing 22.8 reads the values from the preferences cookie.

LISTING 22.8   GetCookieValues.aspx

```
<%@ Page Language="VB" %>
<!DOCTYPE html PUBLIC "-//W3C//DTD XHTML 1.0 Transitional//EN"
  "http://www.w3.org/TR/xhtml1/DTD/xhtml1-transitional.dtd">
<script runat="server">

    Sub Page_Load()
        If Not IsNothing(Request.Cookies("preferences")) Then
            lblFirstName.Text = Request.Cookies("preferences")("firstName")
            lblLastName.Text = Request.Cookies("preferences")("lastName")
            lblFavoriteColor.Text = Request.Cookies("preferences")("favoriteColor")
        End If
    End Sub
</script>
<html xmlns="http://www.w3.org/1999/xhtml" >
<head id="Head1" runat="server">
    <title>Get Cookie Values</title>
</head>
<body>
    <form id="form1" runat="server">
    <div>

    First Name:
    <asp:Label
        id="lblFirstName"
        Runat="server" />
    <br />
    Last Name:
    <asp:Label
        id="lblLastName"
        Runat="server" />
    <br />
    Favorite Color:
```

LISTING 22.8   Continued

```
        <asp:Label
            id="lblFavoriteColor"
            Runat="server" />

    </div>
    </form>
</body>
</html>
```

You can use the `HttpCookie.HasKeys` property to detect whether a cookie is a normal cookie or a multi-valued cookie.

Using Session State

You can't really use a cookie to store a shopping cart. A cookie is just too small and too simple. To enable you to work around the limitations of cookies, the ASP.NET Framework supports a feature called `Session` state.

Like cookies, items stored in `Session` state are scoped to a particular user. You can use `Session` state to store user preferences or other user-specific data across multiple page requests.

Unlike cookies, `Session` state has no size limitations. If you had a compelling need, you could store gigabytes of data in `Session` state.

Furthermore, unlike cookies, `Session` state can represent more complex objects than simple strings of text. You can store any object in `Session` state. For example, you can store a `DataSet` or a custom shopping cart object in `Session` state.

You add items to `Session` state by using the `Session` object. For example, the page in Listing 22.9 adds a new item named `message` to `Session` state that has the value `Hello World!`.

LISTING 22.9   `SessionSet.aspx`

```
<%@ Page Language="VB" %>
<!DOCTYPE html PUBLIC "-//W3C//DTD XHTML 1.0 Transitional//EN"
  "http://www.w3.org/TR/xhtml1/DTD/xhtml1-transitional.dtd">
<script runat="server">

    Sub Page_Load()
        Session("message") = "Hello World!"
    End Sub
</script>
<html xmlns="http://www.w3.org/1999/xhtml" >
<head id="Head1" runat="server">
    <title>Session Set</title>
</head>
```

LISTING 22.9   Continued

```
<body>
    <form id="form1" runat="server">
    <div>

    <h1>Session item added!</h1>

    </div>
    </form>
</body>
</html>
```

In the `Page_Load()` event handler in Listing 22.9, a new item is added to the `Session` object. Notice that you can use the `Session` object just as you would use a `Hashtable` collection.

The page in Listing 22.10 illustrates how you can retrieve the value of an item that you have stored in `Session` state.

LISTING 22.10   `SessionGet.aspx`

```
<%@ Page Language="VB" %>
<!DOCTYPE html PUBLIC "-//W3C//DTD XHTML 1.0 Transitional//EN"
  "http://www.w3.org/TR/xhtml1/DTD/xhtml1-transitional.dtd">
<script runat="server">

    Sub Page_Load()
        lblMessage.Text = Session("message").ToString()
    End Sub
</script>
<html xmlns="http://www.w3.org/1999/xhtml" >
<head id="Head1" runat="server">
    <title>Session Get</title>
</head>
<body>
    <form id="form1" runat="server">
    <div>

    <asp:Label
        id="lblMessage"
        Runat="server" />

    </div>
    </form>
</body>
</html>
```

When you use Session state, a session cookie named ASP.NET_SessionId is added to your browser automatically. This cookie contains a unique identifier. It is used to track you as you move from page to page.

When you add items to the Session object, the items are stored on the web server and not the web browser. The ASP.NET_SessionId cookie is used to associate the correct data with the correct user.

By default, if cookies are disabled, Session state does not work. You don't receive an error, but items that you add to Session state aren't available when you attempt to retrieve them in later page requests. (You learn how to enable cookieless Session state later in this section.)

> **WARNING**
>
> Be careful not to abuse Session state by overusing it. A separate copy of each item added to Session state is created for each user who requests the page. If you place a DataSet with 400 records into Session state in a page, and 500 users request the page, then you'll have 500 copies of that DataSet in memory.

By default, the ASP.NET Framework assumes that a user has left the website when the user has not requested a page for more than 20 minutes. At that point, any data stored in Session state for the user is discarded.

Storing Database Data in Session State

You can use Session state to create a user-relative cache. For example, you can load data for a user and enable the user to sort or filter the data.

The page in Listing 22.11 loads a DataView into Session state. The user can sort the contents of the DataView by using a GridView control (see Figure 22.4).

LISTING 22.11   SessionDataView.aspx

```
<%@ Page Language="VB" %>
<%@ Import Namespace="System.Data" %>
<%@ Import Namespace="System.Data.SqlClient" %>
<%@ Import Namespace="System.Web.Configuration" %>
<!DOCTYPE html PUBLIC "-//W3C//DTD XHTML 1.0 Transitional//EN"
  "http://www.w3.org/TR/xhtml1/DTD/xhtml1-transitional.dtd">
<script runat="server">

    Dim dvMovies As DataView

    ''' <summary>
    ''' Load the Movies
    ''' </summary>
    Private Sub Page_Load()
        dvMovies = CType(Session("Movies"), DataView)
        If IsNothing(dvMovies) Then
```

LISTING 22.11   Continued

```
            Dim conString As String =
➥WebConfigurationManager.ConnectionStrings("Movies").ConnectionString
            Dim dad As New SqlDataAdapter("SELECT Id,Title,Director
➥FROM Movies", conString)
            Dim dtblMovies As New DataTable()
            dad.Fill(dtblMovies)
            dvMovies = New DataView(dtblMovies)
            Session("Movies") = dvMovies
        End If
    End Sub


    ''' <summary>
    ''' Sort the Movies
    ''' </summary>
    Protected Sub grdMovies_Sorting(ByVal sender As Object,
➥ByVal e As GridViewSortEventArgs)
        dvMovies.Sort = e.SortExpression
    End Sub


    ''' <summary>
    ''' Render the Movies
    ''' </summary>
    Private Sub Page_PreRender()
        grdMovies.DataSource = dvMovies
        grdMovies.DataBind()
    End Sub
</script>
<html xmlns="http://www.w3.org/1999/xhtml" >
<head id="Head1" runat="server">
    <title>Session DataView</title>
</head>
<body>
    <form id="form1" runat="server">
    <div>

    <asp:GridView
        id="grdMovies"
        AllowSorting="true"
        EnableViewState="false"
        OnSorting="grdMovies_Sorting"
        Runat="server" />
    <br />
    <asp:LinkButton
        id="lnkReload"
        Text="Reload Page"
        Runat="server" />
```

22

LISTING 22.XX   Continued

```
      </div>
      </form>
</body>
</html>
```

FIGURE 22.4   Sorting a `DataView` stored in `Session` state.

In Listing 22.11, a `DataView` object is stored in `Session` state. When you sort the `GridView` control, the `DataView` is sorted.

The page in Listing 22.11 includes a link that enables you to reload the page. Notice that the sort order of the records displayed by the `GridView` is remembered across page requests. The sort order is remembered even if you navigate to another page before returning to the page.

Using the `Session` Object

The main application programming interface for working with `Session` state is the `HttpSessionState` class. This object is exposed by the `Page.Session`, `Context.Session`, `UserControl.Session`, `WebService.Session`, and `Application.Session` properties. This means that you can access `Session` state from just about anywhere.

This `HttpSessionState` class supports the following properties (this is not a complete list):

- CookieMode—Enables you to specify whether cookieless sessions are enabled. Possible values are AutoDetect, UseCookies, UseDeviceProfile, and UseUri.

- Count—Enables you to retrieve the number of items in Session state.

- IsCookieless—Enables you to determine whether cookieless sessions are enabled.

- IsNewSession—Enables you to determine whether a new user session was created with the current request.

- IsReadOnly—Enables you to determine whether the Session state is read-only.

- Keys—Enables you to retrieve a list of item names stored in Session state.

- Mode—Enables you to determine the current Session state store provider. Possible values are Custom, InProc, Off, SqlServer, and StateServer.

- SessionID—Enables you to retrieve the unique session identifier.

- Timeout—Enables you to specify the amount of time in minutes before the web server assumes that the user has left and discards the session. The maximum value is 525,600 (1 year).

The HttpSessionState object also supports the following methods:

- Abandon—Enables you to end a user session.

- Clear—Enables you to clear all items from Session state.

- Remove—Enables you to remove a particular item from Session state.

The Abandon() method enables you to end a user session programmatically. For example, you might want to end a user session automatically when a user logs out from your application to clear away all of a user's session state information.

Handling Session Events

There are two events related to Session state that you can handle in the Global.asax file: the Session Start and Session End events.

The Session Start event is raised whenever a new user session begins. You can handle this event to load user information from the database. For example, you can handle the Session Start event to load the user's shopping cart.

The Session End event is raised when a session ends. A session comes to an end when it times out because of user inactivity or when it is explicitly ended with the Session.Abandon() method. You can handle the Session End event, for example, when you want to automatically save the user's shopping cart to a database table.

The Global.asax file in Listing 22.12 demonstrates how you can handle both the Session Start and End events.

LISTING 22.12   Global.asax

```vb
<%@ Application Language="VB" %>

<script runat="server">

    Private Sub Application_Start(ByVal sender As Object, ByVal e As EventArgs)
        Application("SessionCount") = 0
    End Sub

    Private Sub Session_Start(ByVal sender As Object, ByVal e As EventArgs)
        Application.Lock()
        Dim count As Integer = CType(Application("SessionCount"), Integer)
        Application("SessionCount") = count + 1
        Application.UnLock()
    End Sub

    Private Sub Session_End(ByVal sender As Object, ByVal e As EventArgs)
        Application.Lock()
        Dim count As Integer = CType(Application("SessionCount"), Integer)
        Application("SessionCount") = count - 1
        Application.UnLock()
    End Sub
</script>
```

In Listing 22.12, the Global.asax file is used to track the number of active sessions. Whenever a new session begins, the Session Start event is raised and the SessionCount variable is incremented by one. When a session ends, the Session End event is raised and the SessionCount variable is decremented by one.

The SessionCount variable is stored in Application state. Application state contains items that are shared among all users of a web application. Notice that the Application object is locked before it is modified. You must lock and unlock the Application object because multiple users could potentially access the same item in Application state at the same time.

> **NOTE**
>
> Application state is little used in ASP.NET applications. In most cases, you should use the Cache object instead of Application state because the Cache object is designed to manage memory automatically.

The page in Listing 22.13 displays the number of active sessions with a Label control (see Figure 22.5).

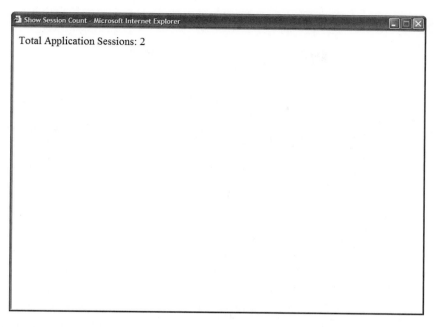

FIGURE 22.5   Displaying a count of user sessions.

LISTING 22.13   ShowSessionCount.aspx

```
<%@ Page Language="VB" %>
<!DOCTYPE html PUBLIC "-//W3C//DTD XHTML 1.0 Transitional//EN"
  "http://www.w3.org/TR/xhtml1/DTD/xhtml1-transitional.dtd">
<script runat="server">

    Sub Page_Load()
        lblSessionCount.Text = Application("SessionCount").ToString()
    End Sub
</script>
<html xmlns="http://www.w3.org/1999/xhtml" >
<head id="Head1" runat="server">
    <title>Show Session Count</title>
</head>
<body>
    <form id="form1" runat="server">
    <div>

    Total Application Sessions:
    <asp:Label
        id="lblSessionCount"
        Runat="server" />
```

LISTING 22.13   Continued

```
    </div>
    </form>
</body>
</html>
```

> **WARNING**
>
> The Session End event is not raised by all session store providers. The event is raised by the InProc session store provider (the default provider), but it is not raised by the StateServer or SQLServer state providers.

Controlling When a Session Times Out

By default, the ASP.NET Framework assumes that a user has left an application after 20 minutes have passed without the user requesting a page. In some situations, you'll want to modify the default timeout value.

For example, imagine that you are creating a college admissions website and the website includes a form that enables an applicant to enter a long essay. In that situation, you would not want the user session to timeout after 20 minutes. Please, give the poor college applicants at least an hour to write their essays.

The disadvantage of increasing the Session timeout is that more memory is consumed by your application. The longer the Session timeout, the more server memory is potentially consumed.

You can specify the Session timeout in the web configuration file or you can set the Session timeout programmatically. For example, the web configuration file in Listing 22.14 changes the Session timeout value to 60 (one hour).

LISTING 22.14   Web.Config

```
<?xml version="1.0"?>
<configuration>
<system.web>

  <sessionState timeout="60" />

</system.web>
</configuration>
```

You can modify the Session timeout value programmatically with the Timeout property of the Session object. For example, the following statement changes the timeout value from the default of 20 minutes to 60 minutes.

```
Session.Timeout = 60
```

After you execute this statement, the timeout value is modified for the remainder of the user session. This is true even when the user visits other pages.

Using Cookieless Session State

By default, Session state depends on cookies. The ASP.NET Framework uses the ASP.NET_SessionId cookie to identity a user across page requests so that the correct data can be associated with the correct user. If a user disables cookies in the browser, then Session state doesn't work.

If you want Session state to work even when cookies are disabled, then you can take advantage of cookieless sessions. When cookieless sessions are enabled, a user's session ID is added to the page URL.

Here's a sample of what a page URL looks like when cookieless sessions are enabled:

```
http://localhost:4945/Original/(S(5pnh11553sszre45oevthxnn))/SomePage.aspx
```

The strange-looking code in this URL is the current user's Session ID. It is the same value as the one you get from the Session.SessionID property.

You enable cookieless sessions by modifying the sessionState element in the web configuration file. The sessionState element includes a cookieless attribute that accepts the following values:

- AutoDetect—The Session ID is stored in a cookie when a browser has cookies enabled. Otherwise, the cookie is added to the URL.

- UseCookies—The Session ID is always stored in a cookie (the default value).

- UseDeviceProfile—The Session ID is stored in a cookie when a browser supports cookies. Otherwise, the cookie is added to the URL.

- UseUri—The Session ID is always added to the URL.

When you set cookieless to the value UseDeviceProfile, the ASP.NET Framework determines whether the browser supports cookies by looking up the browser's capabilities from a set of files contained in the following folder:

```
\WINDOWS\Microsoft.NET\Framework\[version]\CONFIG\Browsers
```

If, according to these files, a browser supports cookies, then the ASP.NET Framework uses a cookie to store the Session ID. The Framework attempts to add a cookie even when a user has disabled cookies in the browser.

When cookieless is set to the value AutoDetect, the framework checks for the existence of the HTTP Cookie header. If the Cookie header is detected, then the framework stores the Session ID in a cookie. Otherwise, the framework falls back to storing the Session ID in the page URL.

The web configuration file in Listing 22.15 enables cookieless sessions by assigning the value AutoDetect to the cookieless attribute.

LISTING 22.15   `Web.Config`

```
<?xml version="1.0"?>
<configuration>
<system.web>

  <sessionState
    cookieless="AutoDetect"
    regenerateExpiredSessionId="true" />

</system.web>
</configuration>
```

> **NOTE**
>
> The easiest way to test cookieless sessions is to use the Mozilla Firefox browser because this browser enables you to disable cookies easily. Select the menu option Tools, Options. Select the Privacy tab and uncheck Allow Sites to Set Cookies.

Notice that the configuration file in Listing 22.16 also includes a `regenerateExpiredSessionId` attribute. When you enable cookieless session state, you should also enable this attribute because it can help prevent users from inadvertently sharing session state.

For example, imagine that someone posts a link in a discussion forum to an ASP.NET website that has cookieless sessions enabled. The link includes the Session ID. If someone follows the link after the original session has timed out, then a new Session is started automatically. However, if multiple people follow the link at the same time, then all the people will share the same Session ID and, therefore, they will share the same `Session` state, which is a major security problem.

On the other hand, when `regenerateExpiredSessionId` is enabled and a session times out, the Session ID in the URL is regenerated when a person requests the page. A redirect back to the same page is performed to change the Session ID in the URL. If a link is posted in a discussion forum, or sent to multiple users in an email, then each user who follows the link is assigned a new Session ID.

When you enable cookieless sessions, you need to be careful to use relative URLs when linking between pages in your application. If you don't use a relative URL, then the Session ID cannot be added to the URL automatically.

For example, when linking to another page in your website, use a URL that looks like this (a relative URL):

`/SomeFolder/SomePage.aspx`

Do not use a URL that looks like this (an absolute URL):

`http://SomeSite.com/SomeFolder/SomePage.aspx`

If, for some reason, you really need to use an absolute URL, you can add the Session ID to the URL by using the `Response.ApplyAppPathModifier()` method. This method takes an absolute URL and returns the URL with a Session ID embedded in it.

Configuring a Session State Store

By default, `Session` state is stored in memory in the same process as the ASP.NET process. There are two significant disadvantages to storing `Session` state in the ASP.NET process.

First, in-process `Session` state is fragile. If your application restarts, then all `Session` state is lost. A number of different events can cause an application restart. For example, modifying the web configuration file or errors in your application both can cause an application restart.

Second, in-process `Session` state is not scalable. When `Session` state is stored in-process, it is stored on a particular web server. In other words, you can't use in-process `Session` state with a web farm.

If you need to implement a more robust version of `Session` state, then the ASP.NET Framework supplies you with a number of options. You can configure the ASP.NET Framework to store `Session` state in an alternate location by modifying the `Session` state mode.

You can set the `Session` state mode to any of the following values:

- `Off`—Disables `Session` state.
- `InProc`—Stores `Session` state in the same process as the ASP.NET process.
- `StateServer`—Stores `Session` state in a Windows NT process, which is distinct from the ASP.NET process.
- `SQLServer`—Stores `Session` state in a SQL Server database.
- `Custom`—Stores `Session` state in a custom location.

By default, the `Session` state mode is set to the value `InProc`. This is done for performance reasons. In-process `Session` state results in the best performance. However, it sacrifices robustness and scalability.

When you set the `Session` state mode to either `StateServer` or `SQLServer`, you get robustness and scalability at the price of performance. Storing `Session` state out-of-process results in worse performance because `Session` state information must be passed back and forth over your network.

Finally, you can create a custom `Session` state store provider by inheriting a new class from the `SessionStateStoreProviderBase` class. In that case, you can store `Session` state any place that you want. For example, you can create a `Session` state store provider that stores `Session` state in an Oracle or FoxPro database.

Configuring State Server Session State

When you enable State Server Session state, Session state information is stored in a separate Windows NT Service. The Windows NT Service can be located on the same server as your web server, or it can be located on another server in your network.

If you store Session state in the memory of a separate Windows NT Service, then Session state information survives even when your ASP.NET application doesn't. For example, if your ASP.NET application crashes, then your Session state information is not lost because it is stored in a separate process.

Furthermore, you can create a web farm when you store state information by using a Windows NT Service. You can designate one server in your network as your state server. All the web servers in your web farm can use the central state server to store Session state.

You must complete the following two steps to use State Server Session state:

- Start the ASP.NET State Service.

- Configure your application to use the ASP.NET State Service.

You can start the ASP.NET State Service by opening the Services applet located at Start, Control Panel, Administrative Tools (see Figure 22.6). After you open the Services applet, double-click the ASP.NET State Service and click Start to run the service. You also should change the Startup type of the service to the value Automatic so that the service starts automatically every time that you reboot your machine.

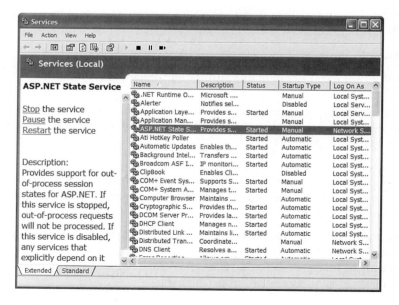

FIGURE 22.6   Starting the ASP.NET State service.

If you want to run the ASP.NET State Service on a separate server on your network, then you must edit a Registry setting on the server that hosts the ASP.NET State Service. By default, the ASP.NET State Service does not accept remote connections. To allow remote connections, execute RegEdit from a command prompt and set the following Registry key to the value 1:

```
HKEY_LOCAL_MACHINE\SYSTEM\CurrentControlSet\Services\aspnet_state\
➥Parameters\AllowRemoteConnection
```

After you start the ASP.NET State Service, you need to configure your ASP.NET application to use it. The web configuration file in Listing 22.16 enables State Server Session State.

LISTING 22.16   Web.Config

```
<?xml version="1.0"?>
<configuration>
    <system.web>

      <sessionState
        mode="StateServer"
        stateConnectionString="tcpip=localhost:42424"
        stateNetworkTimeout="10"   />

      <machineKey
        decryption="AES"
        validation="SHA1"
        decryptionKey="306C1FA852AB3B0115150DD8BA30821
➥CDFD125538A0C606DACA53DBB3C3E0AD2"
        validationKey="61A8E04A146AFFAB81B6AD19654F
➥99EA7370807F18F5002725DAB98B8EFD19C711337E2
➥6948E26D1D174B159973EA0BE8CC9CAA6AAF513BF84E44B2247792265" />

    </system.web>
</configuration>
```

The web configuration file in Listing 22.16 modifies three attributes of the sessionState element. First, the mode attribute is set to the value StateServer. Next, the stateConnectionString attribute is used to specify the location of the ASP.NET State Server. In Listing 22.16, a connection is created to the local server on port 42424. Finally, the stateNetworkTimeout attribute is used to specify a connection timeout in seconds.

> **NOTE**
>
> You can configure the ASP.NET State Server to use a different port by modifying the following Registry value:
>
> ```
> HKEY_LOCAL_MACHINE\SYSTEM\CurrentControlSet\Services\aspnet_state\
> ➥Parameters\Port
> ```
>
> You need to stop and restart the ASP.NET State Service with the Services applet after making this modification.

Notice that the web configuration in Listing 22.17 includes a `machineKey` element. If you are setting up a web farm, and you need to use the same State Server to store `Session` state for multiple servers, then you are required to specify explicit encryption and validation keys. On the other hand, you don't need to include a `machineKey` element when the ASP.NET State Server is hosted on the same machine as your ASP.NET application.

> **WARNING**
>
> Don't use the web configuration file in Listing 22.17 without modifying the values of both the `decryptionKey` and `validationKey` attributes. Those values must be secret. You can use the `GenerateKeys.aspx` page discussed in the previous chapter (Chapter 21, "Using ASP.NET Membership") to generate new values for these attributes.

After you complete these configuration steps, `Session` state information is stored in the ASP.NET State Server automatically. You don't need to modify any of your application code when you switch to out-of-process `Session` state.

Configuring SQL Server Session State

If you want to store `Session` state in the most reliable way possible, then you can store `Session` state in a Microsoft SQL Server database. Because you can set up failover SQL Server clusters, `Session` state stored in SQL Server should be able to survive just anything, including a major nuclear war.

You must complete the following two steps to enable SQL Server `Session` state:

- Configure your database to support SQL Server `Session` state.

- Configure your application to use SQL Server `Session` state.

You can use the `aspnet_regsql` tool to add the necessary tables and stored procedures to your database to support SQL Server Session state. The `aspnet_regsql` tool is located in the following path:

```
\WINDOWS\Microsoft.NET\Framework\[version]\aspnet_regsql.exe
```

> **NOTE**
>
> If you open the SDK Command Prompt, you don't need to navigate to the Microsoft.NET folder to use the `aspnet_regsql` tool.

Executing the following command enables SQL Server Session state for a database server named YourServer.

```
aspnet_regsql -C "Data Source=YourServer;Integrated Security=True" -ssadd
```

When you execute this command, a new database is created on your database server named ASPState. The ASPState database contains all the stored procedures used by `Session` state. However, by default, Session state information is stored in the TempDB database. When your database server restarts, the TempDB database is cleared automatically.

If you want to use SQL Server Session state with a failover cluster of SQL Servers, then you can't store Session state in the TempDB database. Also, if you want Session state to survive database restarts, then you can't store the state information in the TempDB database.

If you execute the following command, then Session state is stored in the ASPState database instead of the TempDB database:

```
aspnet_regsql -C "Data Source=YourServer;Integrated Security=True" -ssadd -sstype p
```

Notice that this command includes a -sstype p switch. The p stands for persistent. Session state that is stored in the ASPState database is called persistent Session state because it survives database server restarts.

Finally, you can store Session state in a custom database. The following command stores Session state in a database named MySessionDB:

```
aspnet_regsql -C "Data Source=YourServer;Integrated Security=True"
➥-ssadd -sstype c -d MySessionDB
```

Executing this command creates a new database named MySessionDB that contains both the tables and stored procedures for storing Session state. Notice that the -sstype switch has the value c for custom. The command also includes a -d switch that enables you to specify the name of the new database.

If you want to remove the Session state tables and stored procedures from a server, then you can execute the following command:

```
aspnet_regsql -C "Data Source=YourServer;Integrated Security=True" -ssremove
```

Executing this command removes the ASPState database. It does not remove a custom Session state database. You must remove a custom database manually.

After you configure your database server to support Session state, you must configure your ASP.NET application to connect to your database. You can use the web configuration file in Listing 22.17 to connect to a database named YourServer.

LISTING 22.17   Web.Config

```
<?xml version="1.0"?>
<configuration>
    <system.web>

        <sessionState
          mode="SQLServer"
          sqlConnectionString="Data Source=YourServer;Integrated Security=True"
          sqlCommandTimeout="30" />

        <machineKey
```

LISTING 22.17   Continued

```
        decryption="AES"
        validation="SHA1"
        decryptionKey="306C1FA852AB3B0115150DD8BA30821CDFD125538A0C606DACA
➥53DBB3C3E0AD2"
        validationKey="61A8E04A146AFFAB81B6AD19654F99EA7370807F18F5002725D
➥AB98B8EFD19C711337E26948E26D1D174B159973EA0BE8CC9CAA6AAF513BF84E44
➥B2247792265" />

    </system.web>
</configuration>
```

The sessionState element includes three attributes. The mode attribute is set to the value SQLServer to enable SQL Server Session state. The second attribute, sqlConnectionString, contains the connection string to the Session state database. Finally, the sqlCommandTimeout specifies the maximum amount of time in seconds before a command that retrieves or stores Session state times out.

Notice that the configuration file in Listing 22.18 includes a machineKey element. If your Session state database is located on a different machine than your ASP.NET application, then you are required to include a machineKey element that contains explicit encryption and validation keys.

> **WARNING**
>
> Don't use the web configuration file in Listing 22.17 without modifying the values of both the decryptionKey and validationKey attributes. Those values must be secret. You can use the GenerateKeys.aspx page discussed in the previous chapter (Chapter 21, "Using ASP.NET Membership") to generate new values for these attributes.

If you select the option to store Session state in a custom database when executing the aspnet_regsql tool, then you need to specify the name of the custom database in your configuration file. You can use the web configuration file in Listing 22.18.

LISTING 22.18   Web.config

```
<?xml version="1.0"?>
<configuration>
    <system.web>

      <sessionState
        mode="SQLServer"
        sqlConnectionString="Data Source=YourServer;
Integrated Security=True;database=MySessionDB"
        sqlCommandTimeout="30"
        allowCustomSqlDatabase="true"/>

      <machineKey
```

LISTING 22.18   Continued

```
          decryption="AES"
          validation="SHA1"
          decryptionKey="306C1FA852AB3B0115150DD8BA30821CDFD125538A0C606DACA
➥53DBB3C3E0AD2"
          validationKey="61A8E04A146AFFAB81B6AD19654F99EA7370807F18F5002725D
➥AB98B8EFD19C711337E26948E26D1D174B159973EA0BE8CC9CAA6AAF513BF84E44
➥B2247792265" />

    </system.web>
</configuration>
```

The `sessionState` element in the configuration file in Listing 22.18 includes an `allowCustomSqlDatabase` attribute. Furthermore, the `sqlConnectionString` attribute contains the name of the custom database.

Enabling SQL Server session state has no effect on how you write your application code. You can initially build your application using in-process `Session` state and, when you have the need, you can switch to SQL Server `Session` state.

Using Profiles

The ASP.NET 2.0 Framework provides you with an alternative to using cookies or `Session` state to store user information: the `Profile` object. The `Profile` object provides you with a strongly typed, persistent form of session state.

You create a `Profile` by defining a list of `Profile` properties in your application root web configuration file. The ASP.NET Framework dynamically compiles a class that contains these properties in the background.

For example, the web configuration file in Listing 22.19 defines a `Profile` that contains three properties: `firstName`, `lastName`, and `numberOfVisits`.

LISTING 22.19   Web.Config

```
<?xml version="1.0"?>
<configuration>
<system.web>

  <profile>
    <properties>
      <add name="firstName" />
      <add name="lastName" />
      <add name="numberOfVisits" type="Int32" defaultValue="0" />
    </properties>
  </profile>

</system.web>
</configuration>
```

When you define a `Profile` property, you can use any of the following attributes:

- `name`—Enables you to specify the name of the property.
- `type`—Enables you to specify the type of the property. The type can be any custom type, including a custom component that you define in the `App_Code` folder. (The default type is string.)
- `defaultValue`—Enables you to specify a default value for the property.
- `readOnly`—Enables you to create a read-only property. (The default value is `false`.)
- `serializeAs`—Enables you to specify how a property is persisted into a static representation. Possible values are `Binary`, `ProviderSpecific`, `String`, and `Xml`. (The default value is `ProviderSpecific`.)
- `allowAnonymous`—Enables you to allow anonymous users to read and set the property. (The default value is false.)
- `provider`—Enables you to associate the property with a particular Profile provider.
- `customProviderData`—Enables you to pass custom data to a Profile provider.

After you define a `Profile` in the web configuration file, you can use the `Profile` object to modify the `Profile` properties. For example, the page in Listing 22.20 enables you to modify the `firstName` and `lastName` properties with a form. Furthermore, the page automatically updates the `numberOfVisits` property each time the page is requested (see Figure 22.7).

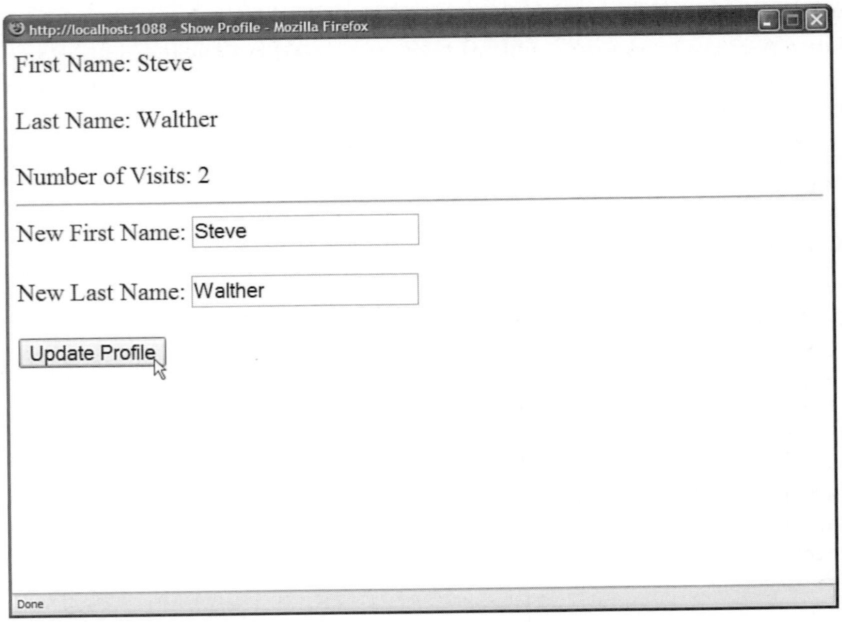

FIGURE 22.7   Displaying `Profile` information.

LISTING 22.20 ShowProfile.aspx

```
<%@ Page Language="VB" %>
<!DOCTYPE html PUBLIC "-//W3C//DTD XHTML 1.0 Transitional//EN"
  "http://www.w3.org/TR/xhtml1/DTD/xhtml1-transitional.dtd">
<script runat="server">

    Private Sub Page_PreRender()
        lblFirstname.Text = Profile.firstName
        lblLastName.Text = Profile.lastName

        Profile.numberOfVisits = Profile.numberOfVisits + 1
        lblNumberOfVisits.Text = Profile.numberOfVisits.ToString()
    End Sub

    Protected Sub btnUpdate_Click(ByVal sender As Object, ByVal e As EventArgs)
        Profile.firstName = txtNewFirstName.Text
        Profile.lastName = txtNewLastName.Text
    End Sub
</script>
<html xmlns="http://www.w3.org/1999/xhtml" >
<head id="Head1" runat="server">
    <title>Show Profile</title>
</head>
<body>
    <form id="form1" runat="server">
    <div>

    First Name:
    <asp:Label
        id="lblFirstname"
        Runat="server" />
    <br /><br />
    Last Name:
    <asp:Label
        id="lblLastName"
        Runat="server" />
    <br /><br />
    Number of Visits:
    <asp:Label
        id="lblNumberOfVisits"
        Runat="server" />

    <hr />

    <asp:Label
        id="lblNewFirstName"
        Text="New First Name:"
```

22

LISTING 22.20   Continued

```
            AssociatedControlID="txtNewFirstName"
            Runat="server" />
      <asp:TextBox
            id="txtNewFirstName"
            Runat="server" />
      <br /><br />
      <asp:Label
            id="lblNewLastName"
            Text="New Last Name:"
            AssociatedControlID="txtNewLastName"
            Runat="server" />
      <asp:TextBox
            id="txtNewLastName"
            Runat="server" />
      <br /><br />
      <asp:Button
            id="btnUpdate"
            Text="Update Profile"
            OnClick="btnUpdate_Click"
            Runat="server" />

      </div>
      </form>
</body>
</html>
```

Notice that `Profile` properties are exposed as strongly typed properties. The `numberOfVisits` property, for example, is exposed as an integer property because you defined it as an integer property.

It is important to understand that `Profile` properties are persistent. If you set a `Profile` property for a user, and that user does not return to your web site for 500 years, the property retains its value. Unlike `Session` state, when you assign a value to a `Profile` property, the value does not evaporate after a user leaves your website.

The `Profile` object uses the Provider model. The default `Profile` provider is the `SqlProfileProvider`. By default, this provider stores the `Profile` data in a Microsoft SQL Server 2005 Express database named `ASPNETDB.mdf`, located in your application's App_Code folder. If the database does not exist, it is created automatically the first time that you use the `Profile` object.

By default, you cannot store `Profile` information for an anonymous user. The ASP.NET Framework uses your authenticated identity to associate `Profile` information with you. You can use the `Profile` object with any of the standard types of authentication supported by the ASP.NET Framework, including both Forms and Windows authentication. (Windows authentication is enabled by default.)

> **NOTE**
>
> Later in this section, you learn how to store Profile information for anonymous users.

Creating Profile Groups

If you need to define a lot of Profile properties, then you can make the properties more manageable by organizing the properties into groups. For example, the web configuration file in Listing 22.21 defines two groups named Preferences and ContactInfo.

LISTING 22.21   Web.Config

```
<?xml version="1.0"?>
<configuration>
<system.web>

  <profile>
    <properties>
      <group name="Preferences">
        <add name="BackColor" defaultValue="lightblue"/>
        <add name="Font" defaultValue="Arial"/>
      </group>
      <group name="ContactInfo">
        <add name="Email" defaultValue="Your Email"/>
        <add name="Phone" defaultValue="Your Phone"/>
      </group>
    </properties>
  </profile>

</system.web>
</configuration>
```

The page in Listing 22.22 illustrates how you can set and read properties in different groups.

LISTING 22.22   ShowProfileGroups.aspx

```
<%@ Page Language="VB" %>
<%@ Import Namespace="System.Drawing" %>
<!DOCTYPE html PUBLIC "-//W3C//DTD XHTML 1.0 Transitional//EN"
  "http://www.w3.org/TR/xhtml1/DTD/xhtml1-transitional.dtd">
<script runat="server">

    Private  Sub Page_Load()
        ' Display Contact Info
        lblEmail.Text = Profile.ContactInfo.Email
```

22

LISTING 22.22   Continued

```
            lblPhone.Text = Profile.ContactInfo.Phone


            ' Apply Preferences
            Dim pageStyle As New Style()
            pageStyle.BackColor = ColorTranslator.FromHtml(
➥Profile.Preferences.BackColor)
            pageStyle.Font.Name = Profile.Preferences.Font
            Header.StyleSheet.CreateStyleRule(pageStyle, Nothing, "html")
        End Sub


    </script>
    <html xmlns="http://www.w3.org/1999/xhtml" >
    <head id="Head1" runat="server">
        <title>Untitled Page</title>
    </head>
    <body>
        <form id="form1" runat="server">
        <div>

        Email:
        <asp:Label
            id="lblEmail"
            Runat="server" />
        <br /><br />
        Phone:
        <asp:Label
            id="lblPhone"
            Runat="server" />

        </div>
        </form>
    </body>
    </html>
```

Supporting Anonymous Users

By default, anonymous users cannot modify Profile properties. The problem is that the ASP.NET Framework has no method of associating Profile data with a particular user unless the user is authenticated.

If you want to enable anonymous users to modify Profile properties, you must enable a feature of the ASP.NET Framework called Anonymous Identification. When Anonymous Identification is enabled, a unique identifier (a GUID) is assigned to anonymous users and stored in a persistent browser cookie.

> **NOTE**
>
> You can enable cookieless anonymous identifiers. Cookieless anonymous identifier cookieless sessions: The anonymous identifier is added to the page URL instead of enable cookieless anonymous identifiers by setting the cookieless attribute of the `anonymousIdentification` element in the web configuration file to the value UseU. `AutoDetect`.

Furthermore, you must mark all `Profile` properties that you want anonymous users to be able to modify with the `allowAnonymous` attribute. For example, the web configuration file in Listing 22.23 enables Anonymous Identification and defines a `Profile` property that can be modified by anonymous users.

LISTING 22.23   Web.Config

```
<?xml version="1.0"?>
<configuration>
<system.web>

  <authentication mode="Forms" />

  <anonymousIdentification enabled="true" />

  <profile>
    <properties>
      <add
        name="numberOfVisits"
        type="Int32"
        defaultValue="0"
        allowAnonymous="true" />
    </properties>
  </profile>

</system.web>
</configuration>
```

The `numberOfVisits` property defined in Listing 22.23 includes the `allowAnonymous` attribute. Notice that the web configuration file also enables Forms authentication. When Forms authentication is enabled, and you don't log in, then you are an anonymous user.

The page in Listing 22.24 illustrates how you modify a `Profile` property when Anonymous Identification is enabled.

LISTING 22.24   ShowAnonymousIdentification.aspx

```
<%@ Page Language="VB" %>
<!DOCTYPE html PUBLIC "-//W3C//DTD XHTML 1.0 Transitional//EN"
```

LISTING 22.24   Continued

```
    "http://www.w3.org/TR/xhtml1/DTD/xhtml1-transitional.dtd">
<script runat="server">

    Private Sub Page_PreRender()
        lblUserName.Text = Profile.UserName
        lblIsAnonymous.Text = Profile.IsAnonymous.ToString()
        Profile.numberOfVisits = Profile.numberOfVisits + 1
        lblNumberOfVisits.Text = Profile.numberOfVisits.ToString()
    End Sub

    Protected Sub btnLogin_Click(ByVal sender As Object, ByVal e As EventArgs)
        FormsAuthentication.SetAuthCookie("Bob", False)
        Response.Redirect(Request.Path)
    End Sub

    Protected Sub btnLogout_Click(ByVal sender As Object, ByVal e As EventArgs)
        FormsAuthentication.SignOut()
        Response.Redirect(Request.Path)
    End Sub
</script>
<html xmlns="http://www.w3.org/1999/xhtml" >
<head id="Head1" runat="server">
    <title>Show Anonymous Identification</title>
</head>
<body>
    <form id="form1" runat="server">
    <div>

    User Name:
    <asp:Label
        id="lblUserName"
        Runat="server" />
    <br />
    Is Anonymous:
    <asp:Label
        id="lblIsAnonymous"
        Runat="server" />
    <br />
    Number Of Visits:
    <asp:Label
        id="lblNumberOfVisits"
        Runat="server" />

    <hr />
    <asp:Button
        id="btnReload"
        Text="Reload"
```

LISTING 22.24   Continued

```
            Runat="server" />

        <asp:Button
            id="btnLogin"
            Text="Login"
            OnClick="btnLogin_Click"
            Runat="server" />

        <asp:Button
            id="btnLogout"
            Text="Logout"
            OnClick="btnLogout_Click"
            Runat="server" />

    </div>
    </form>
</body>
</html>
```

Each time that you request the page in Listing 22.24, the `numberOfVisits` Profile property is incremented and displayed. The page includes three buttons: Reload, Login, and
Logout (see Figure 22.8).

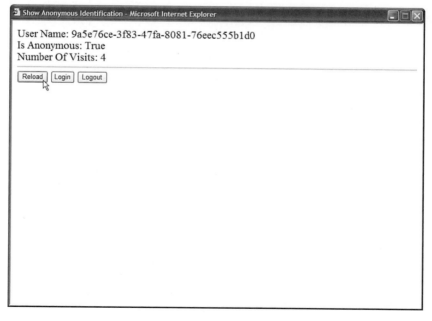

FIGURE 22.8   Creating an anonymous profile.

22

The page also displays the value of the Profile.UserName property. This property represents either the current username or the anonymous identifier. The value of the numberOfVisits Profile property is tied to the value of the Profile.UserName property.

You can click the Reload button to quickly reload the page and increment the value of the numberOfVisits property.

If you click the Login button, then the Profile.UserName property changes to the value Bob. The numberOfVisits property is reset.

If you click the Logout button, then the Profile.UserName property switches back to your anonymous identifier. The numberOfVisits property reverts to its previous value.

Migrating Anonymous Profiles

In the previous section, you saw that all profile information is lost when a user transitions from anonymous to authenticated. For example, if you store a shopping cart in the Profile object and a user logs in, then all the shopping cart items are lost.

You can preserve the value of Profile properties when a user transitions from anonymous to authenticated by handling the MigrateAnonymous event in the Global.asax file. This event is raised when an anonymous user that has a profile logs in.

For example, the MigrateAnonymous event handler in Listing 22.25 automatically copies the values of all anonymous Profile properties to the user's current authenticated profile.

LISTING 22.25   Global.asax

```
<%@ Application Language="VB" %>

<script runat="server">

    Public Sub Profile_OnMigrateAnonymous(ByVal sender As Object,
➥ByVal args As ProfileMigrateEventArgs)
        ' Get anonymous profile
        Dim anonProfile As ProfileCommon = Profile.GetProfile(args.AnonymousID)

        ' Copy anonymous properties to authenticated
        For Each prop As SettingsProperty In ProfileBase.Properties
            Profile(prop.Name) = anonProfile(prop.Name)
        Next

        ' Kill the anonymous profile
        ProfileManager.DeleteProfile(args.AnonymousID)
        AnonymousIdentificationModule.ClearAnonymousIdentifier()
    End Sub
</script>
```

The anonymous `Profile` associated with the user is retrieved when the user's anonymous identifier is passed to the `Profile.GetProfile()` method. Next, each `Profile` property is copied from the anonymous `Profile` to the current `Profile`. Finally, the anonymous `Profile` is deleted and the anonymous identifier is destroyed. (If you don't destroy the anonymous identifier, then the `MigrateAnonymous` event continues to be raised with each page request after the user authenticates.)

Inheriting a Profile from a Custom Class

Instead of defining a list of `Profile` properties in the web configuration file, you can define `Profile` properties in a separate class. For example, the class in Listing 22.26 contains two properties named `FirstName` and `LastName`.

LISTING 22.26   App_Code\SiteProfile.vb

```vb
Imports SystemSiteProfile.vb
Imports System.Web.Profile

Public Class SiteProfile
    Inherits ProfileBase

    Private _firstName As String = "Your First Name"
    Private _lastName As String = "Your Last Name"

    <SettingsAllowAnonymous(True)> _
    Public Property FirstName() As String
        Get
            Return _firstName
        End Get
        Set(ByVal Value As String)
            _firstName = value
        End Set
    End Property

    <SettingsAllowAnonymous(True)> _
    Public Property LastName() As String
        Get
            Return _lastName
        End Get
        Set(ByVal Value As String)
            _lastName = value
        End Set
    End Property
End Class
```

Notice that the class in Listing 22.26 inherits from the `BaseProfile` class.

22

After you declare a class, you can use it to define a profile by inheriting the `Profile` object from the class in the web configuration file. The web configuration file in Listing 22.27 uses the `inherits` attribute to inherit the `Profile` from the `SiteProfile` class.

LISTING 22.27   Web.Config

```
<?xml version="1.0"?>
<configuration>
<system.web>

  <anonymousIdentification enabled="true" />

  <profile inherits="SiteProfile" />

</system.web>
</configuration>
```

After you inherit a `Profile` in the web configuration file, you can use the `Profile` in the normal way. You can set or read any of the properties that you defined in the `SiteProfile` class by accessing the properties through the `Profile` object.

> **NOTE**
>
> The CD that accompanies this book includes a page named `ShowSiteProfile.aspx`, which displays the `Profile` properties defined in Listing 22.27.

> **NOTE**
>
> If you inherit `Profile` properties from a class and define `Profile` properties in the web configuration file, then the two sets of `Profile` properties are merged.

When you define `Profile` properties in a class, you can decorate the properties with the following attributes:

- `SettingsAllowAnonymous`—Enables you to allow anonymous users to read and set the property.

- `ProfileProvider`—Enables you to associate the property with a particular `Profile` provider.

- `CustomProviderData`—Enables you to pass custom data to a `Profile` provider.

For example, both properties declared in the `SiteProfile` class in Listing 22.28 include the `SettingsAllowAnonymous` attribute, which allows anonymous users to read and modify the properties.

Creating Complex Profile Properties

To this point, we've used the `Profile` properties to represent simple types such as strings and integers. You can use `Profile` properties to represent more complex types such as a custom `ShoppingCart` class.

For example, the class in Listing 22.28 represents a simple shopping cart.

LISTING 22.28   App_Code\ShoppingCart.vb

```
Imports System
Imports System.Collections.Generic
Imports System.Web.Profile

Namespace AspNetUnleashed
    Public Class ShoppingCart

        Private _items As New List(Of CartItem)()

        Public ReadOnly Property Items() As List(Of CartItem)
            Get
                Return _items
            End Get
        End Property
    End Class

    Public Class CartItem
        Private _name As String
        Private _price As Decimal
        Private _description As String

        Public Property Name() As String
            Get
                Return _name
            End Get
            Set(ByVal Value As String)
                _name = value
            End Set
        End Property

        Public Property Price() As Decimal
            Get
                Return _price
            End Get
            Set(ByVal Value As Decimal)
                _price = value
            End Set
        End Property
```

22

LISTING 22.28   Continued

```
        Public Property Description() As String
            Get
                Return _description
            End Get
            Set(ByVal Value As String)
                _description = value
            End Set
        End Property

        Public Sub New()
        End Sub

        Public Sub New(ByVal name As String, ByVal price As Decimal,
➥ByVal description As String)
            _name = name
            _price = price
            _description = description
        End Sub
    End Class
End Namespace
```

The file in Listing 22.28 actually contains two classes: the ShoppingCart class and the CartItem class. The ShoppingCart class exposes a collection of CartItem objects.

The web configuration file in Listing 22.29 defines a Profile property named ShoppingCart that represents the ShoppingCart class. The type attribute is set to the fully qualified name of the ShoppingCart class.

LISTING 22.29   Web.Config

```
<?xml version="1.0"?>
<configuration>
<system.web>

  <profile>
    <properties>
      <add name="ShoppingCart" type="AspNetUnleashed.ShoppingCart" />
    </properties>
  </profile>

</system.web>
</configuration>
```

Finally, the page in Listing 22.30 uses the Profile.ShoppingCart property. The contents of the ShoppingCart are bound and displayed in a GridView control. The page also contains a form that enables you to add new items to the ShoppingCart (see Figure 22.9).

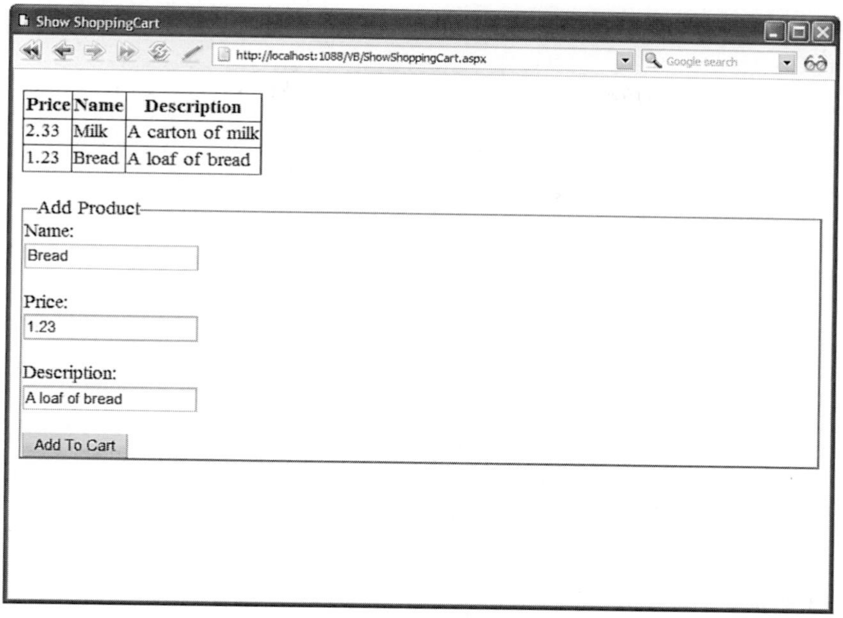

FIGURE 22.9   Storing a shopping cart in a profile.

LISTING 22.30   ShowShoppingCart.aspx

```
<%@ Page Language="VB" %>
<%@ Import Namespace="AspNetUnleashed" %>
<!DOCTYPE html PUBLIC "-//W3C//DTD XHTML 1.0 Transitional//EN"
  "http://www.w3.org/TR/xhtml1/DTD/xhtml1-transitional.dtd">
<script runat="server">

    Private Sub Page_PreRender()
        grdShoppingCart.DataSource = Profile.ShoppingCart.Items
        grdShoppingCart.DataBind()
    End Sub

    Protected Sub btnAdd_Click(ByVal sender As Object, ByVal e As EventArgs)
        Dim NewItem As New CartItem(txtName.Text, Decimal.Parse(txtPrice.Text),
➥txtDescription.Text)
        Profile.ShoppingCart.Items.Add(NewItem)
    End Sub
</script>
<html xmlns="http://www.w3.org/1999/xhtml" >
<head id="Head1" runat="server">
    <title>Show ShoppingCart</title>
</head>
<body>
```

LISTING 22.30   Continued

```
<form id="form1" runat="server">
<div>

<asp:GridView
    id="grdShoppingCart"
    EmptyDataText="There are no items in your shopping cart"
    Runat="server" />

<br />

<fieldset>
<legend>Add Product</legend>
<asp:Label
    id="lblName"
    Text="Name:"
    AssociatedControlID="txtName"
    Runat="server" />
<br />
<asp:TextBox
    id="txtName"
    Runat="server" />
<br /><br />
<asp:Label
    id="lblPrice"
    Text="Price:"
    AssociatedControlID="txtPrice"
    Runat="server" />
<br />
<asp:TextBox
    id="txtPrice"
    Runat="server" />
<br /><br />
<asp:Label
    id="lblDescription"
    Text="Description:"
    AssociatedControlID="txtDescription"
    Runat="server" />
<br />
<asp:TextBox
    id="txtDescription"
    Runat="server" />
<br /><br />
<asp:Button
    id="btnAdd"
    Text="Add To Cart"
```

LISTING 22.30   Continued

```
        Runat="server" OnClick="btnAdd_Click" />
    </fieldset>

    </div>
    </form>
</body>
</html>
```

If you want to take control over how complex properties are stored, you can modify the value of the serializeAs attribute associated with a Profile property. The serializeAs attribute accepts the following four values:

- Binary

- ProviderSpecific

- String

- Xml

The default value, when using the SqlProfileProvider, is ProviderSpecific. In other words, the SqlProfileProvider decides on the best method for storing properties. In general, simple types are serialized as strings and complex types are serialized with the XML Serializer.

One disadvantage of the XML Serializer is that it produces a more bloated representation of a property than the Binary Serializer. For example, the results of serializing the ShoppingCart class with the XML Serializer are contained in Listing 22.31:

LISTING 22.31   Serialized Shopping Cart

```
<?xml version="1.0" encoding="utf-16"?>
<ShoppingCart xmlns:xsi=http://www.w3.org/2001/XMLSchema-instance
 xmlns:xsd="http://www.w3.org/2001/XMLSchema">
  <Items>
    <CartItem>
      <Name>First Product</Name>
      <Price>2.99</Price>
      <Description>The First Product</Description>
    </CartItem>
    <CartItem>
      <Name>Second Product</Name>
      <Price>2.99</Price>
      <Description>The Second Product</Description>
    </CartItem>
  </Items>
</ShoppingCart>
```

22

If you want to serialize a `Profile` property with the Binary Serializer (and save some database space) then you need to do two things. First, you need to indicate in the web configuration file that the `Profile` property should be serialized with the Binary Serializer. Furthermore, you need to mark the class that the `Profile` property represents as serializable.

The modified `ShoppingClass` (named `BinaryShoppingCart`) in Listing 22.32 includes a `Serializable` attribute. Notice that both the `BinaryShoppingCart` and `BinaryCartItem` classes are decorated with the `Serializable` attribute.

LISTING 22.32   App_Code\BinaryShoppingCart.vb

```
Imports System
Imports System.Collections.Generic
Imports System.Web.Profile

Namespace AspNetUnleashed

    <Serializable()> _
    Public Class BinaryShoppingCart
        Private _items As New List(Of BinaryCartItem)()

        Public ReadOnly Property Items() As List(Of BinaryCartItem)
            Get
                Return _items
            End Get
        End Property
    End Class

    <Serializable()> _
    Public Class BinaryCartItem
        Private _name As String
        Private _price As Decimal
        Private _description As String

        Public Property Name() As String
            Get
                Return _name
            End Get
            Set(ByVal Value As String)
                _name = Value
            End Set
        End Property

        Public Property Price() As Decimal
            Get
                Return _price
            End Get
            Set(ByVal Value As Decimal)
                _price = Value
```

LISTING 22.32   Continued

```vbnet
            End Set
        End Property

        Public Property Description() As String
            Get
                Return _description
            End Get
            Set(ByVal Value As String)
                _description = Value
            End Set
        End Property

        Public Sub New()
        End Sub

        Public Sub New(ByVal name As String, ByVal price As Decimal,
➥ByVal description As String)
            _name = name
            _price = price
            _description = description
        End Sub
    End Class
End Namespace
```

The Profile in the web configuration file in Listing 22.33 includes a property that represents the BinaryShoppingCart class. Notice that the property includes a serializeAs attribute that has the value Binary. If you don't include this attribute, the BinaryShoppingCart will be serialized as XML.

LISTING 22.33   Web.Config

```xml
<?xml version="1.0"?>
<configuration>
<system.web>

  <profile>
    <properties>
      <add
        name="ShoppingCart"
        type="AspNetUnleashed.BinaryShoppingCart"
        serializeAs="Binary" />
    </properties>
  </profile>

</system.web>
</configuration>
```

22

> **NOTE**
>
> The CD that accompanies this book includes a page named `ShowBinaryShoppingCart.aspx` that displays the `BinaryShoppingCart`.

Saving Profiles Automatically

A profile is loaded from its profile provider the first time that a property from the profile is accessed. For example, if you use a `Profile` property in a `Page_Load()` handler, then the profile is loaded during the Page Load event. If you use a `Profile` property in a `Page_PreRender()` handler, then the `Profile` is loaded during the page `PreRender` event.

If a `Profile` property is modified, then the `Profile` is saved automatically at the end of page execution. The ASP.NET Framework can detect automatically when certain types of properties are changed but not others. In general, the ASP.NET Framework can detect changes made to simple types but not to complex types.

For example, if you access a property that exposes a simple type such as a string, integer, or Datetime, then the ASP.NET Framework can detect when the property has been changed. In that case, the framework sets the `Profile.IsDirty` property to the value `true`. At the end of page execution, if a profile is marked as dirty, then the profile is saved automatically.

The ASP.NET Framework cannot detect when a `Profile` property that represents a complex type has been modified. For example, if your profile includes a property that represents a custom `ShoppingCart` class, then the ASP.NET Framework has no way of determining when the contents of the `ShoppingCart` class have been changed.

The ASP.NET Framework errs on the side of caution. If you access a complex `Profile` property at all—even if you simply read the property—the ASP.NET Framework sets the `Profile.IsDirty` property to the value `true`. In other words, if you read a complex property, the profile is always saved at the end of page execution.

Because storing a profile at the end of each page execution can be an expensive operation, the ASP.NET Framework provides you with two methods of controlling when a profile is saved.

First, you can take the responsibility of determining when a profile is saved. The web configuration file in Listing 22.34 disables the automatic saving of profiles by setting the `autoSaveEnabled` property to the value `false`.

LISTING 22.34   Web.Config

```
<?xml version="1.0"?>
<configuration>
  <system.web>

    <profile automaticSaveEnabled="false">
      <properties>
```

LISTING 22.34   Continued

```
            <add name="ShoppingCart" type="AspNetUnleashed.ShoppingCart"/>
        </properties>
    </profile>


</system.web>
</configuration>
```

After you disable the automatic saving of profiles, you must explicitly call the `Profile.Save()` method to save a profile after you modify it. For example, the `btnAdd_Click()` method in Listing 22.35 explicitly calls the `Profile.Save()` method when a new item has been added to the shopping cart.

LISTING 22.35   ShowExplicitSave.aspx

```
<%@ Page Language="VB" %>
<%@ Import Namespace="AspNetUnleashed" %>
<!DOCTYPE html PUBLIC "-//W3C//DTD XHTML 1.0 Transitional//EN"
  "http://www.w3.org/TR/xhtml1/DTD/xhtml1-transitional.dtd">
<script runat="server">

    Sub Page_PreRender()
        grdShoppingCart.DataSource = Profile.ShoppingCart.Items
        grdShoppingCart.DataBind()
    End Sub

    Sub btnAdd_Click(sender As object, e As EventArgs)
        Dim newItem as new CartItem(txtName.Text, decimal.Parse(txtPrice.Text),
➥txtDescription.Text)
        Profile.ShoppingCart.Items.Add(newItem)

        ' Explicitly Save Shopping Cart
        Profile.Save()
    End Sub
</script>
<html xmlns="http://www.w3.org/1999/xhtml" >
<head id="Head1" runat="server">
    <title>Show Explicit Save</title>
</head>
<body>
    <form id="form1" runat="server">
    <div>

    <asp:GridView
        id="grdShoppingCart"
        EmptyDataText="There are no items in your shopping cart"
        Runat="server" />
```

LISTING 22.35   Continued

```
    <br />

    <fieldset>
    <legend>Add Product</legend>
    <asp:Label
        id="lblName"
        Text="Name:"
        AssociatedControlID="txtName"
        Runat="server" />
    <br />
    <asp:TextBox
        id="txtName"
        Runat="server" />
    <br /><br />
    <asp:Label
        id="lblPrice"
        Text="Price:"
        AssociatedControlID="txtPrice"
        Runat="server" />
    <br />
    <asp:TextBox
        id="txtPrice"
        Runat="server" />
    <br /><br />
    <asp:Label
        id="lblDescription"
        Text="Description:"
        AssociatedControlID="txtDescription"
        Runat="server" />
    <br />
    <asp:TextBox
        id="txtDescription"
        Runat="server" />
    <br /><br />
    <asp:Button
        id="btnAdd"
        Text="Add To Cart"
        OnClick="btnAdd_Click"
        Runat="server" />
    </fieldset>

    </div>
    </form>
</body>
</html>
```

As an alternative to disabling the automatic saving of profiles, you can write custom logic to control when a profile is saved by handling the `ProfileAutoSaving` event in the `Global.asax` file. For example, the `Global.asax` file in Listing 22.36 saves a profile only when the `Profile.ShoppingCart.HasChanged` property has been assigned the value `True`.

LISTING 22.36   `Global.asax`

```
<%@ Application Language="VB" %>

<script runat="server">

    Public Sub Profile_ProfileAutoSaving(ByVal s As Object,
➡ByVal e As ProfileAutoSaveEventArgs)
        If Profile.ShoppingCart.HasChanged Then
            e.ContinueWithProfileAutoSave = True
        Else
            e.ContinueWithProfileAutoSave = False
        End If
    End Sub

</script>
```

> **NOTE**
>
> The CD that accompanies this book includes the shopping cart class and ASP.NET page that accompany the `Global.asax` file in Listing 22.37. The class is named `ShoppingCartHasChanged.vb` and the page is named `ShowShoppingCartHasChanged.aspx`. You'll need to modify the web configuration file so that the profile inherits from the `ShoppingCartHasChanged` class.

Accessing Profiles from Components

You can access the `Profile` object from within a component by referring to the `HttpContext.Profile` property. However, you must cast the value of this property to an instance of the `ProfileCommon` object before you access its properties.

For example, the web configuration file in Listing 22.37 defines a `Profile` property named `firstName`.

LISTING 22.37   `Web.Config`

```
<?xml version="1.0"?>
<configuration>
  <system.web>

  <profile>
    <properties>
```

LISTING 22.37   Continued

```
        <add name="firstName" defaultValue="Steve" />
    </properties>
  </profile>


</system.web>
</configuration>
```

The component in Listing 22.38 grabs the value of the `firstName` `Profile` property. Notice that the `Profile` object retrieved from the current `HttpContext` object must be case to a `ProfileCommon` object.

LISTING 22.38   App_Code\ProfileComponent.vb

```
Imports System
Imports System.Web
Imports System.Web.Profile

''' <summary>
''' Retrieves first name from Profile
''' </summary>
Public Class ProfileComponent
    Public Shared Function GetFirstNameFromProfile() As String
        Dim profile As ProfileCommon = CType(HttpContext.Current.Profile,
➥ProfileCommon)
        Return profile.firstName
    End Function
End Class
```

> **WARNING**
>
> To avoid conflicts with other code samples in this chapter, the component in Listing 22.38 is named `ProfileComponent.vb_listing38` on the CD that accompanies this book. You'll need to rename the file to `ProfileComponent.vb` before you use the component.

Finally, the page in Listing 22.39 illustrates how you can call the `ProfileComponent` from within an ASP.NET page to retrieve and display the `firstName` attribute.

LISTING 22.39   ShowProfileComponent.aspx

```
<%@ Page Language="VB" %>
<!DOCTYPE html PUBLIC "-//W3C//DTD XHTML 1.0 Transitional//EN"
  "http://www.w3.org/TR/xhtml1/DTD/xhtml1-transitional.dtd">
<script runat="server">
```

LISTING 22.39   Continued

```
Sub Page_Load()
    lblFirstName.Text = ProfileComponent.GetFirstNameFromProfile()
End Sub

</script>
<html xmlns="http://www.w3.org/1999/xhtml" >
<head id="Head1" runat="server">
    <title>Show Profile Component</title>
</head>
<body>
    <form id="form1" runat="server">
    <div>

    First Name:
    <asp:Label
        id="lblFirstName"
        Runat="server" />

    </div>
    </form>
</body>
</html>
```

Using the Profile Manager

Unlike Session state, profile data does not evaporate when a user leaves your application. Over time, as more users visit your application, the amount of data stored by the Profile object can become huge. If you allow anonymous profiles, the situation becomes even worse.

The ASP.NET Framework includes a class named the ProfileManager class that enables you to delete old profiles. This class supports the following methods:

- DeleteInactiveProfiles—Enables you to delete profiles that have not been used since a specified date.

- DeleteProfile—Enables you to delete a profile associated with a specified username.

- DeleteProfiles—Enables you to delete profiles that match an array of usernames or collection of ProfileInfo objects.

- FindInactiveProfilesByUserName—Enables you to retrieve all profiles associated with a specified username that have been inactive since a specified date.

- FindProfilesByUserName—Enables you to retrieve all profiles associated with a specified user.

- `GetAllInactiveProfiles`—Enables you to retrieve all profiles that have been inactive since a specified date.

- `GetAllProfiles`—Enables you to retrieve every profile.

- `GetNumberOfInactiveProfiles`—Enables you to retrieve a count of profiles that have been inactive since a specified date.

- `GetNumberOfProfiles`—Enables you to retrieve a count of the total number of profiles.

You can use the `ProfileManager` class from within a console application and execute the `DeleteInactiveProfiles()` method on a periodic basis to delete inactive profiles. Alternatively, you can create an administrative page in your web application that enables you to manage profile data.

The page in Listing 22.40 illustrates how you can use the `ProfileManager` class to remove inactive profiles (see Figure 22.10).

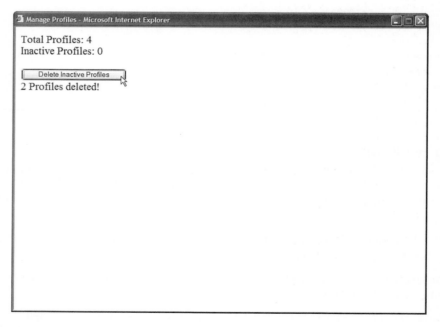

FIGURE 22.10   Deleting inactive profiles.

LISTING 22.40   ManageProfiles.aspx

```
<%@ Page Language="VB" %>
<!DOCTYPE html PUBLIC "-//W3C//DTD XHTML 1.0 Transitional//EN"
  "http://www.w3.org/TR/xhtml1/DTD/xhtml1-transitional.dtd">
<script runat="server">
```

LISTING 22.40   Continued

```
    Dim inactiveDate As DateTime = DateTime.Now.AddMonths(-3)

    Private Sub Page_PreRender()
        lblProfiles.Text =
➥ProfileManager.GetNumberOfProfiles(ProfileAuthenticationOption.All).ToString()
        lblInactiveProfiles.Text = ProfileManager.GetNumberOfInactiveProfiles(
➥ProfileAuthenticationOption.All, inactiveDate).ToString()
    End Sub

    Protected Sub btnDelete_Click(ByVal sender As Object, ByVal e As EventArgs)
        Dim results As Integer = ProfileManager.DeleteInactiveProfiles(
➥ProfileAuthenticationOption.All, inactiveDate)
        lblResults.Text = String.Format("{0} Profiles deleted!", results)
    End Sub
</script>
<html xmlns="http://www.w3.org/1999/xhtml" >
<head id="Head1" runat="server">
    <title>Manage Profiles</title>
</head>
<body>
    <form id="form1" runat="server">
    <div>

    Total Profiles:
    <asp:Label
        id="lblProfiles"
        Runat="server" />
    <br />
    Inactive Profiles:
    <asp:Label
        id="lblInactiveProfiles"
        Runat="server" />
    <br /><br />

    <asp:Button
        id="btnDelete"
        Text="Delete Inactive Profiles"
        Runat="server" OnClick="btnDelete_Click" />
    <br />
    <asp:Label
        id="lblResults"
        EnableViewState="false"
        Runat="server" />
```

22

LISTING 22.40   Continued

```
    </div>
    </form>
</body>
</html>
```

The page in Listing 22.40 displays the total number of profiles and the total number of inactive profiles. An inactive profile is a profile that has not been accessed for more than three months. The page also includes a Delete Inactive Profiles button that enables you to remove the old profiles.

Configuring the Profile Provider

By default, profile data is stored in a Microsoft SQL Server Express database named ASPNETDB.mdf, located in your application's root App_Data folder. If you want to store profile data in another database in your network, then you need to perform the following two tasks:

- Add the necessary database objects required by the profile object to the database.

- Configure your application to connect to the database.

You can add the necessary database tables and stored procedures required by the Profile object to a database by executing the aspnet_regsql command-line tool. The aspnet_regsql tool is located at the following path:

```
\WINDOWS\Microsoft.NET\Framework\[version]\aspnet_regsql.exe
```

> **NOTE**
>
> If you open the SDK Command Prompt, then you do not need to navigate to the Microsoft.NET directory to execute the aspnet_regsql tool.

If you execute this tool without supplying any parameters, then the ASP.NET SQL Server Setup Wizard launches. This wizard guides you through the process of connecting to a database and adding the necessary database objects.

As an alternative to using the aspnet_regsql tool, you can install the necessary database objects by executing the following two SQL batch files:

```
\WINDOWS\Microsoft.NET\Framework\[version]\InstallCommon.sql
\WINDOWS\Microsoft.NET\Framework\[version]\InstallProfile.sql
```

After you have set up your database, you need to configure the default profile provider to connect to the database. The web configuration file in Listing 22.41 connects to a database named MyDatabase on a server named MyServer

LISTING 22.41   Web.Config

```
<?xml version="1.0"?>
<configuration>
  <connectionStrings>
    <add
      name="conProfile"
      connectionString="Data Source=MyServer;
Integrated Security=true;database=MyDatabase"/>
  </connectionStrings>
  <system.web>

    <profile defaultProvider="MyProfileProvider">
      <properties>
        <add name="firstName" />
        <add name="lastName" />
      </properties>
      <providers>
        <add
          name="MyProfileProvider"
          type="System.Web.Profile.SqlProfileProvider"
          connectionStringName="conProfile"/>
      </providers>
    </profile>

  </system.web>
</configuration>
```

After you complete these configuration steps, all profile data is stored in a custom database.

Creating a Custom Profile Provider

The Profile object uses the Provider Model. The ASP.NET Framework includes a single profile provider, the SqlProfileProvider, that stores profile data in a Microsoft SQL Server database. In this section, you learn how to build a custom profile provider.

One problem with the default SqlProfileProvider is that it serializes an entire profile into a single blob and stores the blob in a database table column. This means that you can't execute SQL queries against the properties in a profile. In other words, the default SqlProfileProvider makes it extremely difficult to generate reports off the properties stored in a profile.

In this section, we create a new profile provider that is modestly named the BetterProfileProvider. The BetterProfileProvider stores each Profile property in a separate database column.

Unfortunately, the code for the BetterProfileProvider is too long to place in this book. However, the entire source code is included on the CD that accompanies this book.

The BetterProfileProvider inherits from the base ProfileProvider class. The two most important methods that must be overridden in the base ProfileProvider class are the GetPropertyValues() and SetPropertyValues() methods. These methods are responsible for loading and saving a profile for a particular user.

Imagine that you want to use the BetterProfileProvider to represent a profile that contains the following three properties: FirstName, LastName, and NumberOfVisits. Before you can use the BetterProfileProvider, you must create a database table that contains three columns that correspond to these Profile properties. In addition, the database table must contain an int column named ProfileID.

You can create the necessary database table with the following SQL command:

```
CREATE TABLE ProfileData
{
  ProfileID Int,
  FirstName NVarChar(50),
  LastName NVarChar(50),
  NumberOfVisits Int
}
```

Next, you need to create a database table named Profiles. This table is used to describe the properties of each profile. You can create the Profiles table with the following SQL command:

```
CREATE TABLE Profiles
(
  UniqueID IDENTITY NOT NULL PRIMARY KEY,
  UserName NVarchar(255) NOT NULL,
  ApplicationName NVarchar(255) NOT NULL,
  IsAnonymous BIT,
  LastActivityDate DateTime,
  LastUpdatedDate DateTime,
)
```

After you create these two database tables, you are ready to use the BetterProfileProvider. The web configuration file in Listing 22.42 configures the BetterProfileProvider as the default profile provider.

LISTING 22.42   Web.Config

```
<?xml version="1.0"?>
<configuration>
  <connectionStrings>
    <add
```

LISTING 22.42   Continued

```
       name="conProfile"
       connectionString="Data Source=.\SQLExpress;
Integrated Security=true;AttachDBFileName=¦DataDirectory¦ProfilesDB.mdf;User
Instance=true" />
  </connectionStrings>
  <system.web>

    <profile defaultProvider="MyProfileProvider">
      <properties>
        <add name="FirstName" />
        <add name="LastName" />
        <add name="NumberOfVisits" type="Int32" />
      </properties>
      <providers>
        <add
          name="MyProfileProvider"
          type="AspNetUnleashed.BetterProfileProvider"
          connectionStringName="conProfile"
          profileTableName="ProfileData" />
      </providers>
    </profile>

  </system.web>
</configuration>
```

Notice that the `BetterProfileProvider` is configured with both a `connectionStringName` and `profileTableName` attribute. The `connectionStringName` points to the database that contains the two database tables that were created earlier. The `profileTableName` property contains the name of the table that contains the profile data. (This attribute defaults to the value `ProfileData`, so it really isn't necessary here.)

After you configure the `BetterProfileProvider`, you can use it in a similar manner to the default `SqlProfileProvider`. For example, the page in Listing 22.43 displays the values of the `FirstName`, `LastName`, and `NumberOfVisits` profile properties and enables you to modify the `FirstName` and `LastName` properties.

> **WARNING**
>
> The `BetterProfileProvider` has several important limitations. It does not support serialization, so you cannot use it with complex types such as a custom shopping cart class. It also does not support default values for `Profile` properties.

LISTING 22.43   ShowBetterProfileProvider.aspx

```
<%@ Page Language="VB" %>
<!DOCTYPE html PUBLIC "-//W3C//DTD XHTML 1.0 Transitional//EN"
  "http://www.w3.org/TR/xhtml1/DTD/xhtml1-transitional.dtd">
<script runat="server">

    Sub Page_PreRender()
        Profile.NumberOfVisits = Profile.NumberOfVisits + 1
        lblNumberOfVisits.Text = Profile.NumberOfVisits.ToString()

        lblFirstName.Text = Profile.FirstName
        lblLastName.Text = Profile.LastName
    End Sub

    Sub btnUpdate_Click(ByVal sender As Object, ByVal e As EventArgs)
        Profile.FirstName = txtNewFirstName.Text
        Profile.LastName = txtNewLastName.Text
    End Sub
</script>
<html xmlns="http://www.w3.org/1999/xhtml" >
<head id="Head1" runat="server">
    <title>Show BetterProfileProvider</title>
</head>
<body>
    <form id="form1" runat="server">
    <div>

    Number of Visits:
    <asp:Label
        id="lblNumberOfVisits"
        Runat="server" />
    <br />
    First Name:
    <asp:Label
        id="lblFirstName"
        Runat="server" />
    <br />
    Last Name:
    <asp:Label
        id="lblLastName"
        Runat="server" />
```

LISTING 22.43   Continued

```
        <hr />

        <asp:Label
            id="lblNewFirstName"
            Text="First Name:"
            AssociatedControlID="txtNewFirstName"
            Runat="server" />
        <asp:TextBox
            id="txtNewFirstName"
            Runat="server" />
        <br />
        <asp:Label
            id="lblNewLastname"
            Text="Last Name:"
            AssociatedControlID="txtNewLastName"
            Runat="server" />
        <asp:TextBox
            id="txtNewLastName"
            Runat="server" />
        <br />
        <asp:Button
            id="btnUpdate"
            Text="Update"
            OnClick="btnUpdate_Click"
            Runat="server" />

    </div>
    </form>
</body>
</html>
```

The main advantage of the BetterProfileProvider is that you can perform SQL queries against the data stored in the ProfileData table. For example, the page in Listing 22.44 displays the contents of the ProfileData table in a GridView control (see Figure 22.11). You can't do this when using the default SqlProfileProvider because the SqlProfileProvider stores profile data in a blob.

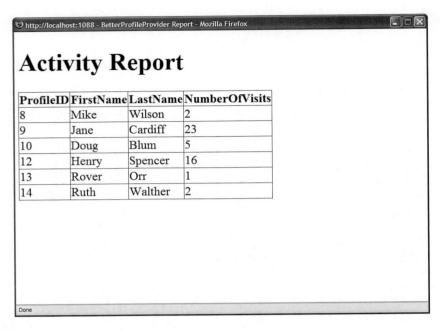

FIGURE 22.11   Displaying a profile report.

LISTING 22.44   BetterProfileProviderReport.aspx

```
<%@ Page Language="VB" %>
<!DOCTYPE html PUBLIC "-//W3C//DTD XHTML 1.0 Transitional//EN"
  "http://www.w3.org/TR/xhtml1/DTD/xhtml1-transitional.dtd">
<html xmlns="http://www.w3.org/1999/xhtml" >
<head id="Head1" runat="server">
    <title>BetterProfileProvider Report</title>
</head>
<body>
    <form id="form1" runat="server">
    <div>

    <h1>Activity Report</h1>

    <asp:GridView
        id="grdProfiles"
        DataSourceID="srcProfiles"
        Runat="server" />

    <asp:SqlDataSource
        id="srcProfiles"
        ConnectionString="<%$ ConnectionStrings:conProfile %>"
```

LISTING 22.44   Continued

```
        SelectCommand="SELECT ProfileID,FirstName,LastName,NumberOfVisits
            FROM ProfileData"
        Runat="server" />

    </div>
    </form>
</body>
</html>
```

Summary

In this chapter, you learned how to maintain state in your ASP.NET applications. In the first section, you learned how to create, modify, and delete browser cookies. You learned how you can take advantage of cookies when you need to add a small amount of data to a browser. You also learned how to preserve precious cookie space by creating multi-valued cookies.

Next, we examined the topic of Session state. You learned how to take advantage of Session state to store larger amounts of data than can be stored in a cookie. You also learned how to configure cookieless Session state so that Session state works even when a browser has cookies disabled. We also discussed how to make Session state more robust by storing Session state data in a Windows NT Service or a Microsoft SQL Server database table.

Finally, you learned how to use the Profile object to create a typed and persistent form of Session state. You learned how to enable anonymous profiles. In the final section of this chapter, we built a custom Profile provider that enables you to store Profile properties in separate database table columns.

CHAPTER **23**

Caching Application Pages and Data

If someone put a gun to my head and told me that I had 5 minutes to improve the performance of a website, then I would immediately think of caching. By taking advantage of caching, you can dramatically improve the performance of your web applications.

The slowest operation that you can perform in an ASP.NET page is database access. Opening a database connection and retrieving data is a slow operation. The best way to improve the performance of your data access code is not to access the database at all.

By taking advantage of caching, you can cache your database records in memory. Retrieving data from a database is dog slow. Retrieving data from the cache, on the other hand, is lightning fast.

In this chapter, you learn about the different caching mechanisms supported by the ASP.NET Framework. The ASP.NET 2.0 Framework provides you with an (almost) overwhelming number of caching options. I attempt to clarify all these caching options over the course of this chapter.

In the final section of this chapter, you learn how to use SQL Cache Dependencies. A SQL Cache Dependency enables you to reload cached data automatically when data changes in a database table. You learn how to use both polling and push SQL Cache Dependencies.

Overview of Caching

The ASP.NET 2.0 Framework supports the following types of caching:

- Page Output Caching
- Partial Page Caching
- DataSource Caching
- Data Caching

Page Output Caching enables you to cache the entire rendered contents of a page in memory (everything that you see when you select View Source in your web browser). The next time that any user requests the same page, the page is retrieved from the cache.

Page Output Caching caches an entire page. In some situations, this might create problems. For example, if you want to display different banner advertisements randomly in a page, and you cache the entire page, then the same banner advertisement is displayed with each page request.

> **NOTE**
>
> The `AdRotator` control included in the ASP.NET Framework takes advantage of a feature called post-cache substitution to randomly display different advertisements even when a page is cached. Post-cache substitution is described later in this chapter.

Partial Page Caching enables you to get around this problem by enabling you to cache only particular regions of a page. By taking advantage of Partial Page Caching, you can apply different caching policies to different areas of a page.

You use DataSource Caching with the different ASP.NET `DataSource` controls such as the `SqlDataSource` and `ObjectDataSource` controls. When you enable caching with a `DataSource` control, the `DataSource` control caches the data that it represents.

Finally, Data Caching is the fundamental caching mechanism. Behind the scenes, all the other types of caching use Data Caching. You can use Data Caching to cache arbitrary objects in memory. For example, you can use Data Caching to cache a DataSet across multiple pages in a web application.

In the following sections, you learn how to use each of these different types of caching in detail.

> **NOTE**
>
> When configuring and debugging caching, having a tool that enables you to monitor the HTTP traffic between web server and browser is extremely helpful. You can download the free Fiddler tool, which enables you to view the raw request and response HTTP traffic, from http://www.FiddlerTool.com.

Using Page Output Caching

You enable Page Output Caching by adding an `<%@ OutputCache %>` directive to a page. For example, the page in Listing 23.1 caches its contents for 15 seconds.

LISTING 23.1   CachePageOutput.aspx

```
<%@ Page Language="VB" %>
<%@ OutputCache Duration="15" VaryByParam="none" %>
<!DOCTYPE html PUBLIC "-//W3C//DTD XHTML 1.0 Transitional//EN"
  "http://www.w3.org/TR/xhtml1/DTD/xhtml1-transitional.dtd">
<script runat="server">

    Sub Page_Load()
        lblTime.Text = DateTime.Now.ToString("T")
    End Sub
</script>
<html xmlns="http://www.w3.org/1999/xhtml" >
<head id="Head1" runat="server">
    <title>Cache Page Output</title>
</head>
<body>
    <form id="form1" runat="server">
    <div>

    <asp:Label
        id="lblTime"
        Runat="server" />

    </div>
    </form>
</body>
</html>
```

The page in Listing 23.1 displays the current server time in a Label control. The page also includes an `<%@ OutputCache %>` directive. If you refresh the page multiple times, you will notice that the time is not updated until at least 15 seconds have passed.

When you cache a page, the contents of the page are not regenerated each time you request the page. The .NET class that corresponds to the page is not executed with each page request. The rendered contents of the page are cached for every user that requests the page.

The page is cached in multiple locations. By default, the page is cached on the browser, any proxy servers, and on the web server.

In Listing 23.1, the page is cached for 15 seconds. You can assign a much larger number to the duration attribute. For example, if you assign the value 86400 to the duration parameter, then the page is cached for a day.

Varying the Output Cache by Parameter

Imagine that you need to create a separate master and details page. The master page displays a list of movies. When you click a movie title, the details page displays detailed information on the movie selected.

When you create a master/details page, you typically pass a query string parameter between the master and details page to indicate the particular movie to display in the details page. If you cache the output of the details page, however, then everyone will see the first movie selected.

You can get around this problem by using the `VaryByParam` attribute. The `VaryByParam` attribute causes a new instance of a page to be cached when a different parameter is passed to the page. (The parameter can be either a query string parameter or a form parameter.)

For example, the page in Listing 23.2 contains a master page that displays a list of movie titles as links.

LISTING 23.2   Master.aspx

```
<%@ Page Language="VB" %>
<!DOCTYPE html PUBLIC "-//W3C//DTD XHTML 1.0 Transitional//EN"
 "http://www.w3.org/TR/xhtml1/DTD/xhtml1-transitional.dtd">
<html xmlns="http://www.w3.org/1999/xhtml" >
<head id="Head1" runat="server">
    <title>Master</title>
</head>
<body>
    <form id="form1" runat="server">
    <div>

    <asp:GridView
        id="grdMovies"
        DataSourceID="srcMovies"
        AutoGenerateColumns="false"
        ShowHeader="false"
        GridLines="none"
        Runat="server">
        <Columns>
        <asp:HyperLinkField
            DataTextField="Title"
```

LISTING 23.2   Continued

```
            DataNavigateUrlFields="Id"
            DataNavigateUrlFormatString="~/Details.aspx?id={0}" />
        </Columns>
    </asp:GridView>

    <asp:SqlDataSource
        id="srcMovies"
        ConnectionString="<%$ ConnectionStrings:Movies %>"
        SelectCommand="SELECT Id,Title FROM Movies"
        Runat="server" />

    </div>
    </form>
</body>
</html>
```

If you hover your mouse over the links displayed in Listing 23.2, you can see the query string parameter passed by each link in the browser status bar (see Figure 23.1). For example, the first movie link includes a query string parameter with the value 1, the second link includes a query string parameter with the value 2, and so on. When you click a movie link, this query string parameter is passed to the details page in Listing 23.3.

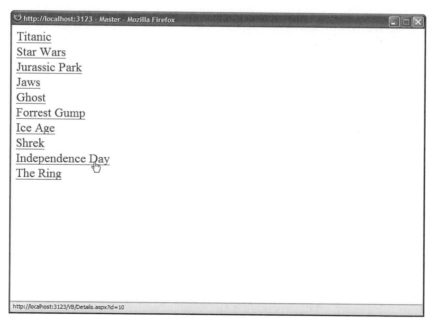

FIGURE 23.1   Displaying the Master page.

LISTING 23.3   Details.aspx

```
<%@ Page Language="VB" %>
<%@ OutputCache Duration="3600" VaryByParam="id" %>
<!DOCTYPE html PUBLIC "-//W3C//DTD XHTML 1.0 Transitional//EN"
  "http://www.w3.org/TR/xhtml1/DTD/xhtml1-transitional.dtd">
<html xmlns="http://www.w3.org/1999/xhtml" >
<head id="Head1" runat="server">
    <title>Details</title>
</head>
<body>
    <form id="form1" runat="server">
    <div>

    <%= DateTime.Now.ToString("T") %>

    <hr />

    <asp:DetailsView
        id="dtlMovie"
        DataSourceID="srcMovies"
        Runat="server" />

    <asp:SqlDataSource
        id="srcMovies"
        ConnectionString="<%$ ConnectionStrings:Movies %>"
        SelectCommand="SELECT * FROM Movies
            WHERE Id=@Id"
        Runat="server">
        <SelectParameters>
            <asp:QueryStringParameter
                Name="Id"
                Type="int32"
                QueryStringField="Id" />
        </SelectParameters>
    </asp:SqlDataSource>

    </div>
    </form>
</body>
</html>
```

The page in Listing 23.3 uses a DetailsView to display detailed information on the movie selected from the master page (see Figure 23.2). The DetailsView is bound to a SqlDataSource control that includes a QueryStringParameter SELECT parameter that represents the id query string parameter.

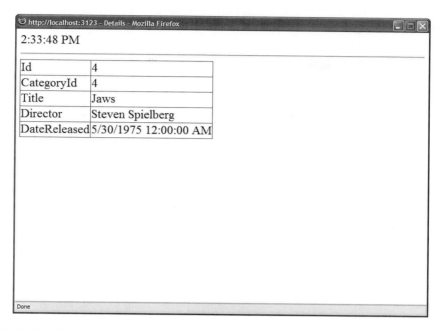

FIGURE 23.2   Displaying the Details page.

Notice that the Details.aspx page includes an <%@ OutputCache %> directive. The VaryByParam attribute in the <%@ OutputCache %> directive has the value id. If you request the Details.aspx page with a different value for the id query string parameter, then a different cached version of the page is created.

It is important to understand that using VaryByParam results in more caching and not less caching. Each time a different id parameter is passed to the Details.aspx page, another version of the same page is cached in memory.

The Details.aspx page displays the current time. Notice that the time does not change when you request the Details.aspx page with the same query string parameter.

You can assign two special values to the VaryByParam attribute:

- none—Causes any query string or form parameters to be ignored. Only one version of the page is cached.

- *—Causes a new cached version of the page to be created whenever there is a change in any query string or form parameter passed to the page.

You also can assign a semicolon-delimited list of parameters to the VaryByParam attribute when you want to create different cached versions of a page, depending on the values of more than one parameter.

Varying the Output Cache by Control

The VaryByControl attribute enables you to generate different cached versions of a page depending on the value of a particular control in the page. This attribute is useful when you need to create a single-page Master/Details form.

For example, the page in Listing 23.4 contains both a DropDownList and GridView control. When you select a new movie category from the DropDownList, a list of matching movies is displayed in the GridView (see Figure 23.3).

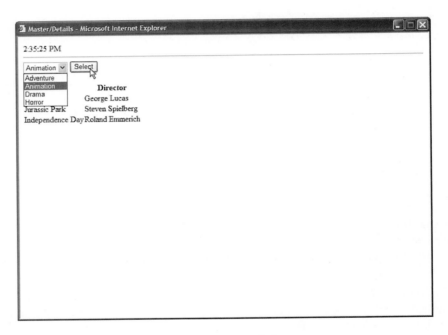

FIGURE 23.3   Displaying a single-page Master/Details form.

LISTING 23.4   MasterDetails.aspx

```
<%@ Page Language="VB" %>
<%@ OutputCache Duration="3600" VaryByControl="dropCategories" %>
<!DOCTYPE html PUBLIC "-//W3C//DTD XHTML 1.0 Transitional//EN"
    "http://www.w3.org/TR/xhtml1/DTD/xhtml1-transitional.dtd">
<html xmlns="http://www.w3.org/1999/xhtml" >
<head id="Head1" runat="server">
    <title>Master/Details</title>
</head>
<body>
    <form id="form1" runat="server">
    <div>
```

LISTING 23.4   Continued

```
    <%= DateTime.Now.ToString("T") %>
    <hr />

    <asp:DropDownList
        id="dropCategories"
        DataSourceID="srcCategories"
        DataTextField="Name"
        DataValueField="Id"
        Runat="server" />
    <asp:Button
        id="btnSelect"
        Text="Select"
        Runat="server" />

    <br /><br />

    <asp:GridView
        id="grdMovies"
        DataSourceID="srcMovies"
        GridLines="none"
        Runat="server" />

    <asp:SqlDataSource
        id="srcCategories"
        ConnectionString="<%$ ConnectionStrings:Movies %>"
        SelectCommand="SELECT Id,Name FROM MovieCategories"
        Runat="server" />

    <asp:SqlDataSource
        id="srcMovies"
        ConnectionString="<%$ ConnectionStrings:Movies %>"
        SelectCommand="SELECT Title,Director FROM Movies
            WHERE CategoryId=@CategoryId"
        Runat="server">
        <SelectParameters>
        <asp:ControlParameter
            Name="CategoryId"
            ControlID="dropCategories" />
        </SelectParameters>
    </asp:SqlDataSource>

    </div>
    </form>
</body>
</html>
```

The page in Listing 23.4 contains an `<%@ OutputCache %>` directive. This directive includes a `VaryByControl` parameter. The ID of the `DropDownList` control is assigned to this parameter.

If you neglected to add the `VaryByControl` attribute, then the same list of movies would be displayed in the `GridView` regardless of which movie category is selected. The `VaryByControl` attribute causes different cached versions of the page to be created whenever the `DropDownList` represents a different value.

Varying the Output Cache by Header

Another option is to use the `VaryByHeader` attribute to create different cached versions of a page when the value of a particular browser header changes. Several standard browser headers are transmitted with each page request, including

- `Accept-Language`—Represents a prioritized list of languages that represent the preferred human language of the user making the request.
- `User-Agent`—Represents the type of device making the request.
- `Cookie`—Represents the browser cookies created in the current domain.

For example, the page in Listing 23.5 includes an `<%@ OutputCache %>` directive that has a `VaryByHeader` attribute with the value `User-Agent`. When you request the page with different browsers, different versions of the page are cached.

LISTING 23.5   `VaryByHeader.aspx`

```
<%@ Page Language="VB" %>
<%@ OutputCache Duration="3600" VaryByParam="none" VaryByHeader="User-Agent"  %>
<!DOCTYPE html PUBLIC "-//W3C//DTD XHTML 1.0 Transitional//EN"
   "http://www.w3.org/TR/xhtml1/DTD/xhtml1-transitional.dtd">
<html xmlns="http://www.w3.org/1999/xhtml" >
<head id="Head1" runat="server">
    <title>Vary By Header</title>
</head>
<body>
    <form id="form1" runat="server">
    <div>

    <%= DateTime.Now.ToString("T") %>

    <hr />

    <%= Request.UserAgent %>

    </div>
    </form>
</body>
</html>
```

I don't recommend using the `VaryByHeader` attribute with the `User-Agent` header. The problem with this attribute is that it is too fine-grained. If there is any variation in the `User-Agent` header, then a different cached version of a page is generated.

Consider the `User-Agent` header sent by the Internet Explorer browser installed on my computer. It looks like this:

```
Mozilla/4.0 (compatible; MSIE 6.0; Windows NT 5.1; SV1; .NET CLR 1.1.4322;
.NET CLR 2.0.50727)
```

This header includes the major and minor version of the browser, the platform (Windows XP), a string indicating that Service Pack 2 has been installed (SV1), and the versions of the .NET framework installed on my machine. If someone else requests the same page with a slight difference in the `User-Agent` header, then a different cached version of the page is generated. In other words, the web server must do more work rather than less, which defeats the point of caching.

Instead of using the `VaryByHeader` attribute, I recommend that you use the `VaryByCustom` attribute described in the next two sections.

Varying the Output Cache by Browser

A better way to create different cached versions of a page that depend on the type of browser being used to request the page is to use the `VaryByCustom` attribute. This attribute accepts the special value `browser`. When `VaryByCustom` has the value `browser`, only two attributes of the browser are considered important: the type of browser and its major version.

For example, a page request from Internet Explorer results in a different cached version of the page than does one from FireFox. A page request from Internet Explorer 5 rather than Internet Explorer 6.5 also results in a different cached version. Any other variations in the `User-Agent` header are ignored.

The page in Listing 23.6 illustrates how you can use the `VaryByCustom` attribute with the value browser. The page displays the current time and the value of the `User-Agent` header. If you request the page with Internet Explorer and request the page with Firefox, different cached versions of the page are created.

LISTING 23.6 `VaryByBrowser.aspx`

```
<%@ Page Language="VB" %>
<%@ OutputCache Duration="3600" VaryByParam="none" VaryByCustom="browser"  %>
<!DOCTYPE html PUBLIC "-//W3C//DTD XHTML 1.0 Transitional//EN"
    "http://www.w3.org/TR/xhtml1/DTD/xhtml1-transitional.dtd">
<html xmlns="http://www.w3.org/1999/xhtml" >
<head id="Head1" runat="server">
    <title>Vary By Browser</title>
</head>
<body>
```

23

LISTING 23.6 Continued

```
    <form id="form1" runat="server">
    <div>

    <%= DateTime.Now.ToString("T") %>

    <hr />

    <%= Request.UserAgent %>

    </div>
    </form>
</body>
</html>
```

Varying the Output Cache by a Custom Function

The VaryByCustom attribute is named the VaryByCustom attribute for a reason. You can specify a custom function that determines when a different cached version of a page is generated.

You can use any criteria that you please with the custom function. You can create different cached versions of a page depending on the browser minor version, the browser DOM support, the time of day, or even the weather.

You create the custom function in the Global.asax file by overriding the GetVaryByCustomString() method. For example, the Global.asax file in Listing 23.7 illustrates how you can override the GetVaryByCustomString() method to create different cached versions of a page depending on a particular feature of a browser. If the VaryByCustom attribute in a page has the value css, then the function returns a string representing whether or not the current browser supports Cascading Style Sheets.

LISTING 23.7 Global.asax

```
<%@ Application Language="VB" %>
<script runat="server">

    Public Overrides Function GetVaryByCustomString(ByVal context
➥As HttpContext, ByVal custom As String) As String
        If String.Compare(custom, "css") = 0 Then
            Return Request.Browser.SupportsCss.ToString()
        End If
        Return MyBase.GetVaryByCustomString(context, custom)
    End Function
</script>
```

The page in Listing 23.8 displays one of two `Panel` controls. The first `Panel` contains text formatted with a Cascading Style Sheet style and the second `Panel` contains text formatted with (outdated) HTML. Depending on whether a browser supports CSS, either the first or second `Panel` is displayed.

LISTING 23.8   `VaryByCustom.aspx`

```
<%@ Page Language="VB" %>
<%@ OutputCache Duration="3600" VaryByParam="none" VaryByCustom="css" %>
<!DOCTYPE html PUBLIC "-//W3C//DTD XHTML 1.0 Transitional//EN"
    "http://www.w3.org/TR/xhtml1/DTD/xhtml1-transitional.dtd">
<script runat="server">

    Sub Page_Load()
        If Request.Browser.SupportsCss Then
            pnlCss.Visible = True
        Else
            pnlNotCss.Visible = True
        End If
    End Sub
</script>
<html xmlns="http://www.w3.org/1999/xhtml" >
<head id="Head1" runat="server">
    <title>Vary By Custom</title>
</head>
<body>
    <form id="form1" runat="server">
    <div>

    <asp:Panel
        id="pnlCss"
        Visible="false"
        Runat="server">
        <span style="font-weight:bold">Hello!</span>
    </asp:Panel>

    <asp:Panel
        id="pnlNotCss"
        Visible="false"
        Runat="server">
        <b>Hello!</b>
    </asp:Panel>

    </div>
    </form>
</body>
</html>
```

23

> **NOTE**
>
> You can detect browser capabilities by using the HttpBrowserCapabilities class exposed by the Request.Browser property. This class includes dozens of properties that enable you to detect the features of the browser being used to request a page.

The page contains an <%@ OutputCache %> directive with a VaryByCustom attribute set to the value css. Two different cached versions of the same page are generated: one version for CSS browsers and another version for non-CSS browsers.

Specifying the Cache Location

You can use the Location attribute of the <%@ OutputCache %> directive to specify where a page is cached. This attribute accepts the following values:

- Any—The page is cached on the browser, proxy servers, and web server (the default value).
- Client—The page is cached only on the browser.
- Downstream—The page is cached on the browser and any proxy servers, but not the web server.
- None—The page is not cached.
- Server—The page is cached on the web server, but not the browser or any proxy servers.
- ServerAndClient—The page is cached on the browser and web server, but not on any proxy servers.

By default, when you use Page Output Caching, a page is cached in three locations: the web server, any proxy servers, and the browser. There are situations in which you might need to modify this default behavior. For example, if you are caching private information, then you don't want to cache the information on the web server or any proxy servers.

> **NOTE**
>
> When Windows authentication is enabled in the web configuration file (the default), the Cache-Control header is automatically set to the value private, and the setting of the Location attribute is ignored.

For example, the page in Listing 23.9 caches a page only on the browser and not on any proxy servers or the web server. The page displays a random number (see Figure 23.4).

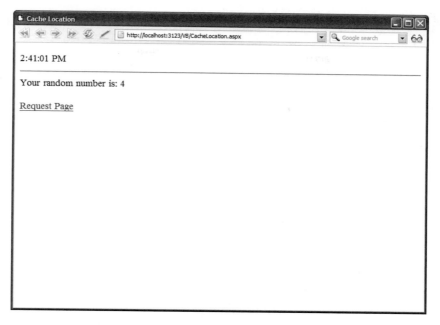

FIGURE 23.4   Caching a page on the browser.

LISTING 23.9   CacheLocation.aspx

```
<%@ Page Language="VB" %>
<%@ OutputCache Duration="3600" VaryByParam="none" Location="Client" %>
<!DOCTYPE html PUBLIC "-//W3C//DTD XHTML 1.0 Transitional//EN"
  "http://www.w3.org/TR/xhtml1/DTD/xhtml1-transitional.dtd">
<script runat="server">

    Sub Page_Load()
        Dim rnd As New Random()
        lblRandom.Text = rnd.Next(10).ToString()
    End Sub
</script>
<html xmlns="http://www.w3.org/1999/xhtml" >
<head id="Head1" runat="server">
    <title>Cache Location</title>
</head>
<body>
    <form id="form1" runat="server">
    <div>
```

LISTING 23.9 Continued

```
    <%= DateTime.Now.ToString("T") %>
    <hr />

    Your random number is:
    <asp:Label
        id="lblRandom"
        Runat="server" />

    <br /><br />
    <a href="CacheLocation.aspx">Request Page</a>

    </div>
    </form>
</body>
</html>
```

If you click the link located at the bottom of the page in Listing 23.9 and request the same page, then the page is retrieved from the browser cache and the same random number is displayed. If you reload the page in your web browser by clicking your browser's Reload button, then the page is reloaded from the web server and a new random number is displayed. The page is cached only in your local browser cache and nowhere else.

> **NOTE**
>
> Behind the scenes, the ASP.NET Framework uses the Cache-Control HTTP header to specify where a page is cached. This header is defined in RFC 2616, "Hypertext Transfer Protocol—HTTP/1.1."

Creating a Page Output Cache File Dependency

You can create a dependency between a cached page and a file (or set of files) on your hard drive. When the file is modified, the cached page is automatically dropped and regenerated with the next page request.

For example, the page in Listing 23.10 displays the contents of an XML file in a GridView. The page is cached until the XML file is modified (see Figure 23.5).

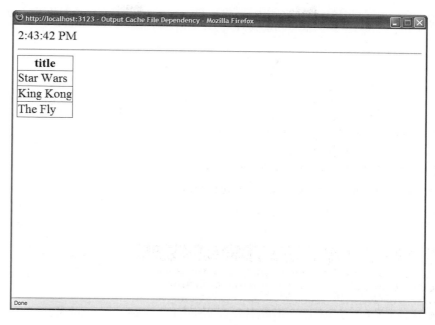

FIGURE 23.5   Caching a page with a file dependency.

LISTING 23.10   `OutputCacheFileDependency.aspx`

```
<%@ Page Language="VB" %>
<%@ OutputCache Duration="9999" VaryByParam="none" %>
<!DOCTYPE html PUBLIC "-//W3C//DTD XHTML 1.0 Transitional//EN"
  "http://www.w3.org/TR/xhtml1/DTD/xhtml1-transitional.dtd">
<script runat="server">

    Sub Page_Load()
        Response.AddFileDependency(MapPath("Movies.xml"))
    End Sub
</script>
<html xmlns="http://www.w3.org/1999/xhtml" >
<head id="Head1" runat="server">
    <title>Output Cache File Dependency</title>
</head>
<body>
    <form id="form1" runat="server">
    <div>

    <%= DateTime.Now.ToString("T") %>
    <hr />
```

LISTING 23.10   Continued

```
    <asp:GridView
        id="grdMovies"
        DataSourceID="srcMovies"
        Runat="server" />

    <asp:XmlDataSource
        id="srcMovies"
        DataFile="Movies.xml"
        Runat="server" />

    </div>
    </form>
</body>
</html>
```

The page in Listing 23.10 displays the current time. Notice that the time does not change until you modify the `Movies.xml` XML file.

The page in Listing 23.10 uses the `Response.AddFileDependency()` method to create a dependency between the cached page and a single file on disk. If you need to create a dependency on multiple files, then you can use the `AddFileDependencies()` method instead.

Expiring the Page Output Cache Programmatically

You can remove a page from the cache programmatically by using the `Response.RemoveOutputCacheItem()` method. For example, imagine that you are caching a page that displays a list of products. Furthermore, imagine that your website includes a separate page for adding a new product. In that case, you'll want to remove the first page programmatically from the cache when the list of products is updated.

The page in Listing 23.11 uses a GridView control to display a list of movies. The page is cached for one hour with an `<%@ OutputCache %>` directive.

LISTING 23.11   MovieList.aspx

```
<%@ Page Language="VB" %>
<%@ OutputCache Duration="3600" VaryByParam="none" %>
<!DOCTYPE html PUBLIC "-//W3C//DTD XHTML 1.0 Transitional//EN"
    "http://www.w3.org/TR/xhtml1/DTD/xhtml1-transitional.dtd">
<html xmlns="http://www.w3.org/1999/xhtml" >
<head id="Head1" runat="server">
    <title>Movie List</title>
</head>
<body>
    <form id="form1" runat="server">
```

LISTING 23.11 Continued

```
    <div>

    <%= DateTime.Now.ToString("T") %>
    <hr />

    <asp:GridView
        id="grdMovies"
        DataSourceID="srcMovies"
        Runat="server" />

    <asp:SqlDataSource
        id="srcMovies"
        ConnectionString="<%$ ConnectionStrings:Movies %>"
        SelectCommand="SELECT Title, Director FROM Movies"
        Runat="server" />

    <br /><br />
    <a href="AddMovie.aspx">Add Movie</a>

    </div>
    </form>
</body>
</html>
```

The page in Listing 23.12 contains a DetailsView control that enables you to add a new movie. When you insert a new movie into the database, the Response. RemoveOutputCacheItem() method is called to remove the MovieList.aspx page from the cache. Because this method accepts only a "virtual absolute" path, the Page.ResolveUrl() method is used to convert the tilde into the application root path.

LISTING 23.12 AddMovie.aspx

```
<%@ Page Language="VB" %>
<!DOCTYPE html PUBLIC "-//W3C//DTD XHTML 1.0 Transitional//EN"
  "http://www.w3.org/TR/xhtml1/DTD/xhtml1-transitional.dtd">
<script runat="server">

    Sub dtlMovie_ItemInserted(sender as object, e as DetailsViewInsertedEventArgs)
        HttpResponse.RemoveOutputCacheItem(Page.ResolveUrl("~/MovieList.aspx"))
        Response.Redirect("~/MovieList.aspx")
    End Sub
</script>
<html xmlns="http://www.w3.org/1999/xhtml" >
<head id="Head1" runat="server">
```

LISTING 23.12   Continued

```
    <title>Add Movie</title>
</head>
<body>
    <form id="form1" runat="server">
    <div>

    <h1>Add Movie</h1>

    <asp:DetailsView
        id="dtlMovie"
        DefaultMode="Insert"
        DataSourceID="srcMovies"
        AutoGenerateRows="false"
        AutoGenerateInsertButton="true"
        Runat="server" OnItemInserted="dtlMovie_ItemInserted">
        <Fields>
        <asp:BoundField
            DataField="Title"
            HeaderText="Title:" />
        <asp:BoundField
            DataField="Director"
            HeaderText="Director:" />
        </Fields>
    </asp:DetailsView>

    <asp:SqlDataSource
        id="srcMovies"
        ConnectionString="<%$ ConnectionStrings:Movies %>"
        InsertCommand="INSERT Movies (Title, Director)
            VALUES (@Title, @Director)"
        Runat="server" />

    </div>
    </form>
</body>
</html>
```

The `Response.RemoveOutputCacheItem()` method enables you to remove only one page from the cache at a time. If you need to remove multiple pages, then you can create something called a *key dependency*. A key dependency enables you to create a dependency between one item in the cache and another item. When the second item is removed from the cache, the first item is removed automatically.

For example, the page in Listing 23.13 also displays a list of movies. However, the page is cached with a dependency on an item in the cache named Movies.

LISTING 23.13   MovieListKeyDependency.aspx

```
<%@ Page Language="VB" %>
<%@ OutputCache Duration="3600" VaryByParam="none" %>
<!DOCTYPE html PUBLIC "-//W3C//DTD XHTML 1.0 Transitional//EN"
   "http://www.w3.org/TR/xhtml1/DTD/xhtml1-transitional.dtd">
<script runat="server">

    Sub Page_Load(ByVal sender As Object, ByVal e As EventArgs)
        Cache.Insert("Movies", DateTime.Now)
        Response.AddCacheItemDependency("Movies")
    End Sub
</script>
<html xmlns="http://www.w3.org/1999/xhtml" >
<head id="Head1" runat="server">
    <title>Movie List Key Dependency</title>
</head>
<body>
    <form id="form1" runat="server">
    <div>

    <%= DateTime.Now.ToString("T") %>
    <hr />

    <asp:GridView
        id="grdMovies"
        DataSourceID="srcMovies"
        Runat="server" />

    <asp:SqlDataSource
        id="srcMovies"
        ConnectionString="<%$ ConnectionStrings:Movies %>"
        SelectCommand="SELECT Title, Director FROM Movies"
        Runat="server" />

    <br /><br />
    <a href="AddMovieKeyDependency.aspx">Add Movie</a>

    </div>
    </form>
</body>
</html>
```

The page in Listing 23.14 enables you to add a new movie to the Movies database table. When the new movie is inserted, the Movies item is removed and any pages that are dependent on the Movies item are dropped from the cache automatically.

LISTING 23.14   AddMovieKeyDependency.aspx

```
<%@ Page Language="VB" %>
<!DOCTYPE html PUBLIC "-//W3C//DTD XHTML 1.0 Transitional//EN"
  "http://www.w3.org/TR/xhtml1/DTD/xhtml1-transitional.dtd">
<script runat="server">

    Sub dtlMovie_ItemInserted(ByVal sender As Object,
➥ByVal e As DetailsViewInsertedEventArgs)
        Cache.Remove("Movies")
        Response.Redirect("~/MovieListKeyDependency.aspx")
    End Sub
</script>
<html xmlns="http://www.w3.org/1999/xhtml" >
<head id="Head1" runat="server">
    <title>Add Movie Key Dependency</title>
</head>
<body>
    <form id="form1" runat="server">
    <div>

    <h1>Add Movie</h1>

    <asp:DetailsView
        id="dtlMovie"
        DefaultMode="Insert"
        DataSourceID="srcMovies"
        AutoGenerateRows="false"
        AutoGenerateInsertButton="true"
        Runat="server" OnItemInserted="dtlMovie_ItemInserted">
        <Fields>
        <asp:BoundField
            DataField="Title"
            HeaderText="Title:" />
        <asp:BoundField
            DataField="Director"
            HeaderText="Director:" />
        </Fields>
    </asp:DetailsView>

    <asp:SqlDataSource
        id="srcMovies"
        ConnectionString="<%$ ConnectionStrings:Movies %>"
        InsertCommand="INSERT Movies (Title, Director)
            VALUES (@Title, @Director)"
        Runat="server" />
```

LISTING 23.14   Continued

```
        </div>
        </form>
</body>
</html>
```

Manipulating the Page Output Cache Programmatically

If you need more control over how the ASP.NET Framework caches pages, then you can work directly with the `HttpCachePolicy` class. This class is exposed by the `Response.Cache` property.

The `HttpCachePolicy` class includes properties and methods that enable you to perform programmatically all the tasks that you can perform with the `<%@ OutputCache %>` directive. You also can use the methods of this class to manipulate the HTTP cache headers that are sent to proxy servers and browsers.

This class supports the following properties:

- `VaryByHeaders`—Gets the list of headers that are used to vary cache output.

- `VaryByParams`—Gets the list of query string and form parameters that are used to vary cache output.

The `HttpCachePolicy` class also supports the following methods:

- `AddValidationCallback`—Enables you to create a method that is called automatically before a page is retrieved from the cache.

- `AppendCacheExtension`—Enables you to add custom text to the `Cache-Control` HTTP header.

- `SetAllowResponseInBrowserHistory`—Enables you to prevent a page from appearing in the browser history cache.

- `SetCacheability`—Enables you to set the `Cache-Control` header and the server cache.

- `SetETag`—Enables you to set the `ETag` HTTP header.

- `SetETagFromFileDependencies`—Enables you to set the `ETag` HTTP header from the time stamps of all files on which the page is dependent.

- `SetExpires`—Enables you to set the `Expires` HTTP header.

- `SetLastModified`—Enables you to set the `Last-Modified` HTTP header.

- `SetLastModifiedFromFileDependencies`—Enables you to set the `Last-Modified` HTTP header from the time stamps of all files on which the page is dependent.

- `SetMaxAge`—Enables you to set the `Cache-Control:max-age` HTTP header.

- `SetNoServerCaching`—Enables you to disable web server caching.

23

- SetNoStore—Enables you to send a `Cache-Control:no-store` HTTP header.

- SetNoTransform—Enables you to send a `Cache-Control:no-transform` HTTP header.

- SetOmitVaryStar—Enables you to not send the `vary:*` HTTP header.

- SetProxyMaxAge—Enables you to set the `Cache-Control:s-maxage` HTTP header.

- SetRevalidation—Enables you to set the `Cache-Control` HTTP header to either `must-revalidation` or `proxy-revalidate`.

- SetSlidingExpiration—Enables you to set a sliding expiration policy.

- SetValidUntilExpires—Enables you to prevent a page from expiring from the web server cache when a browser sends a `Cache-Control` header.

- SetVaryByCustom—Enables you to set the string passed to the `GetVaryByCustomString()` method in the `Global.asax` file.

For example, the page in Listing 23.15 programmatically places a page in the output cache. The page is cached on the browser, proxy servers, and web server for 15 seconds.

LISTING 23.15   ProgramOutputCache.aspx

```
<%@ Page Language="VB" %>
<!DOCTYPE html PUBLIC "-//W3C//DTD XHTML 1.0 Transitional//EN"
    "http://www.w3.org/TR/xhtml1/DTD/xhtml1-transitional.dtd">
<script runat="server">

    Sub Page_Load()
        Response.Cache.SetCacheability(HttpCacheability.Public)
        Response.Cache.SetExpires(DateTime.Now.AddSeconds(15))
        Response.Cache.SetMaxAge(TimeSpan.FromSeconds(15))
        Response.Cache.SetValidUntilExpires(True)
        Response.Cache.SetLastModified(DateTime.Now)
        Response.Cache.SetOmitVaryStar(True)
    End Sub
</script>
<html xmlns="http://www.w3.org/1999/xhtml" >
<head id="Head1" runat="server">
    <title>Program OutputCache</title>
</head>
<body>
    <form id="form1" runat="server">
    <div>

    <%= DateTime.Now.ToString("T") %>

    <br /><br />
    <a href="ProgramOutputCache.aspx">Request this Page</a>
```

LISTING 23.15   Continued

```
    </div>
    </form>
</body>
</html>
```

Clearly, it is more difficult to enable Page Output Caching programmatically than declaratively. You need to call many methods to cache a page in the same way as you can with a single <%@ OutputCache %> directive. However, programmatically manipulating the cache provides you with fine-grained control over the HTTP headers sent to proxy servers and browsers.

Creating Page Output Cache Profiles

Instead of configuring Page Output Caching for each page in an application, you can configure Page Output Caching in a web configuration file and apply the settings to multiple pages. You can create something called a Cache Profile. Creating Cache Profiles makes your website easier to manage.

For example, the web configuration file in Listing 23.16 contains the definition for a Cache Profile named Cache1Hour that caches a page for one hour.

LISTING 23.16   Web.Config

```
<?xml version="1.0"?>
<configuration>
  <system.web>
    <caching>
      <outputCacheSettings>
        <outputCacheProfiles>
          <add name="Cache1Hour" duration="3600" varyByParam="none" />
        </outputCacheProfiles>
      </outputCacheSettings>
    </caching>
  </system.web>
</configuration>
```

The page in Listing 23.17 uses the Cache1Hour profile. This profile is set with the <%@ OutputCache %> directive's CacheProfile attribute.

LISTING 23.17   OutputCacheProfile.aspx

```
<%@ Page Language="VB" %>
<%@ OutputCache CacheProfile="Cache1Hour" %>
<!DOCTYPE html PUBLIC "-//W3C//DTD XHTML 1.0 Transitional//EN"
  "http://www.w3.org/TR/xhtml1/DTD/xhtml1-transitional.dtd">
<html xmlns="http://www.w3.org/1999/xhtml" >
```

LISTING 23.17   Continued

```
<head id="Head1" runat="server">
    <title>Output Cache Profile</title>
</head>
<body>
    <form id="form1" runat="server">
    <div>

    <%= DateTime.Now.ToString("T") %>

    </div>
    </form>
</body>
</html>
```

You can set the same caching properties in a Cache Profile as you can set in an individual page's <%@ OutputCache %> directive. For example, you can set varyByParam, varyByControl, varyByHeader, and even varyByCustom attributes in a Cache Profile.

Using Partial Page Caching

In the previous section of this chapter, you learned how to cache the entire output of a page. In this section, you learn how to take advantage of Partial Page Caching to cache particular regions of a page.

Partial Page Caching makes sense when a page contains both dynamic and static content. For example, you might want to cache a set of database records displayed in a page, but not cache a random list of news items displayed in the same page.

In this section, you learn about two methods for enabling Partial Page Caching. You can use post-cache substitution to cache an entire page except for a particular region. You can use User Controls to cache particular regions in a page, but not the entire page.

Using Post-Cache Substitution

In some cases, you might want to cache an entire page except for one small area. For example, you might want to display the current username dynamically at the top of a page, but cache the remainder of a page. In these cases, you can take advantage of a feature of the ASP.NET Framework called *post-cache substitution*.

Post-cache substitution is used internally by the AdRotator control. Even when you use Page Output Caching to cache a page that contains an AdRotator control, the content rendered by the AdRotator control is not cached.

You can use post-cache substitution either declaratively or programmatically. If you want to use post-cache substitution declaratively, then you can use the ASP.NET Substitution control. For example, the page in Listing 23.18 uses the Substitution control to display the current time on a page that has been output cached (see Figure 23.6).

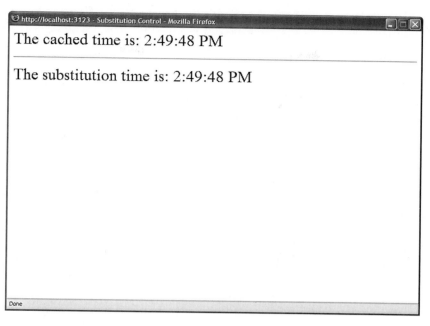

FIGURE 23.6   Using the Substitution control.

LISTING 23.18   SubstitutionControl.aspx

```
<%@ Page Language="VB" %>
<%@ OutputCache Duration="15" VaryByParam="none" %>
<!DOCTYPE html PUBLIC "-//W3C//DTD XHTML 1.0 Transitional//EN"
    "http://www.w3.org/TR/xhtml1/DTD/xhtml1-transitional.dtd">
<script runat="server">

    Public Shared Function GetTime(ByVal context As HttpContext) As String
        Return DateTime.Now.ToString("T")
    End Function
</script>
<html xmlns="http://www.w3.org/1999/xhtml" >
<head id="Head1" runat="server">
    <title>Substitution Control</title>
</head>
<body>
    <form id="form1" runat="server">
    <div>

    The cached time is: <%= DateTime.Now.ToString("T") %>
    <hr />
    The substitution time is:
```

LISTING 23.18   Continued

```
    <asp:Substitution
        id="Substitution1"
        MethodName="GetTime"
        Runat="server" />

    </div>
    </form>
</body>
</html>
```

In Listing 23.18, the time is displayed twice. The time displayed in the body of the page is output cached. The time displayed by the Substitution control is not cached.

The Substitution control has one important property: MethodName. The MethodName property accepts the name of a method defined in the page. The method must be a shared (static) method because an instance of the class is not created when the page is output cached.

Alternatively, you can use post-cache substitution programmatically by using the Response.WriteSubstitution() method. This method is illustrated in the page in Listing 23.19.

LISTING 23.19   ShowWriteSubstitution.aspx

```
<%@ Page Language="VB" %>
<%@ OutputCache Duration="15" VaryByParam="none" %>
<!DOCTYPE html PUBLIC "-//W3C//DTD XHTML 1.0 Transitional//EN"
  "http://www.w3.org/TR/xhtml1/DTD/xhtml1-transitional.dtd">
<script runat="server">

    Public Shared Function GetTime(ByVal context As HttpContext) As String
        Return DateTime.Now.ToString("T")
    End Function
</script>
<html xmlns="http://www.w3.org/1999/xhtml" >
<head id="Head1" runat="server">
    <title>Show WriteSubstitution</title>
</head>
<body>
    <form id="form1" runat="server">
    <div>

    The cached time is: <%= DateTime.Now.ToString("T") %>
    <hr />
    The substitution time is:
    <% Response.WriteSubstitution(AddressOf GetTime)%>
```

LISTING 23.19   Continued

```
        </div>
        </form>
</body>
</html>
```

There are two advantages to using the WriteSubstitution() method. First, the method referenced by the WriteSubstitution() method does not have to be a method of the current class. The method can be either an instance or shared method on any class.

The second advantage of the WriteSubstitution() method is that you can use it within a custom control to perform post-cache substitutions. For example, the NewsRotator control in Listing 23.20 uses the WriteSubstitution() method when displaying a random news item. If you use this control in a page that has been output cached, the NewsRotator control continues to display news items randomly.

LISTING 23.20   NewsRotator.vb

```
Imports System
Imports System.Data
Imports System.Web
Imports System.Web.UI
Imports System.Web.UI.WebControls
Imports System.Collections.Generic

Namespace myControls
    Public Class NewsRotator
        Inherits WebControl

        Public Shared Function GetNews(ByVal context As HttpContext) As String
            Dim News As New List(Of String)()
            News.Add("Martians attack!")
            News.Add("Moon collides with earth!")
            News.Add("Life on Jupiter!")

            Dim rnd As Random = New Random()
            Return News(rnd.Next(News.Count))
        End Function

        Protected Overrides Sub RenderContents(ByVal writer As HtmlTextWriter)
            Context.Response.WriteSubstitution(AddressOf GetNews)
        End Sub

    End Class
End Namespace
```

23

> **NOTE**
>
> Building custom controls is discussed in detail in Chapter 31, "Building Custom Controls."

The CD that accompanies this book includes a page named ShowNewsRotator.aspx. If you open this page, all the content of the page is cached except for the random news item displayed by the NewsRotator control (see Figure 23.7).

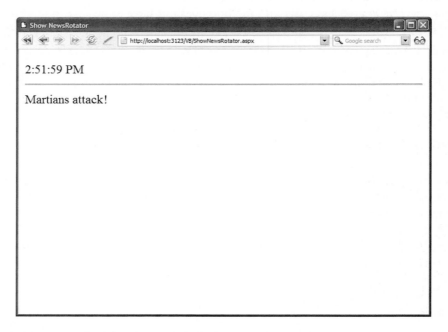

FIGURE 23.7   Displaying dynamic news items in a cached page.

When you use post-cache substitution (declaratively or programmatically) then caching no longer happens beyond the web server. Using post-cache substitution causes a Cache-Control:no-cache HTTP header to be included in the HTTP response, which disables caching on proxy servers and browsers. This limitation is understandable because the substitution content must be generated dynamically with each page request.

Caching with a User Control

Using post-cache substitution is appropriate only when working with a string of text or HTML. If you need to perform more complex partial page caching, then you should take advantage of User Controls.

You can cache the rendered contents of a User Control in memory in the same way as you can cache an ASP.NET page. When you add an `<%@ OutputCache %>` directive to a User Control, the rendered output of the User Control is cached.

> **NOTE**
>
> When you cache a User Control, the content is cached on the web server and not on any proxy servers or web browsers. When a web browser or proxy server caches a page, it always caches an entire page.

For example, the Movies User Control in Listing 23.21 displays all the rows from the Movies database table. Furthermore, it includes an `OutputCache` directive, which causes the contents of the User Control to be cached in memory for a maximum of 10 minutes (600 seconds).

LISTING 23.21 `Movies.ascx`

```
<%@ Control Language="VB" ClassName="Movies" %>
<%@ OutputCache Duration="600" VaryByParam="none" %>

User Control Time:
<%= DateTime.Now.ToString("T") %>

<asp:GridView
    id="grdMovies"
    DataSourceID="srcMovies"
    Runat="server" />

<asp:SqlDataSource
    id="srcMovies"
    ConnectionString="<%$ ConnectionStrings:Movies %>"
    SelectCommand="SELECT Title,Director FROM Movies"
    Runat="server" />
```

The User Control in Listing 23.21 displays the records from the Movies database table with a `GridView` control. It also displays the current time. Because the control includes an `OutputCache` directive, the entire rendered output of the control is cached in memory.

The page in Listing 23.22 includes the Movies User Control in the body of the page. It also displays the current time at the top of the page. When you refresh the page, the time displayed by the Movies control changes, but not the time displayed in the body of the page (see Figure 23.8).

23

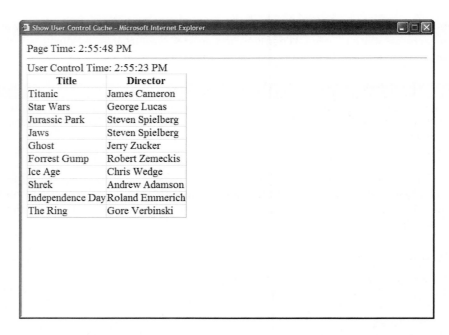

FIGURE 23.8   Caching the output of a User Control.

LISTING 23.22   ShowUserControlCache.aspx

```
<%@ Page Language="VB" %>
<%@ Register TagPrefix="user" TagName="Movies" Src="~/Movies.ascx" %>
<!DOCTYPE html PUBLIC "-//W3C//DTD XHTML 1.1//EN"
 "http://www.w3.org/TR/xhtml11/DTD/xhtml11.dtd">
<html xmlns="http://www.w3.org/1999/xhtml" >
<head id="Head1" runat="server">
    <title>Show User Control Cache</title>
</head>
<body>
    <form id="form1" runat="server">
    <div>

    Page Time:
    <%= DateTime.Now.ToString("T") %>
    <hr />

    <user:Movies
        id="Movies1"
        Runat="server" />

    </div>
```

LISTING 23.22   Continued

```
    </form>
</body>
</html>
```

You can use the following attributes with an `<%@ OutputCache %>` directive declared in a User Control:

- `Duration`—The amount of time in seconds that the rendered content of the User Control is cached.

- `Shared`—Enables you to share the same cached version of the User Control across multiple pages.

- `VaryByParam`—Enables you to create different cached versions of a User Control, depending on the values of one or more query string or form parameters. You can specify multiple parameters by supplying a semicolon-delimited list of query string or form parameter names.

- `VaryByControl`—Enables you to create different cached versions of a User Control, depending on the value of a control. You can specify multiple controls by supplying a semicolon-delimited list of control IDs.

- `VaryByCustom`—Enables you to specify a custom string used by a custom cache policy. (You also can supply the special value browser, which causes different cached versions of the control to be created when the type and major version of the browser differs.)

Because each User Control that you add to a page can have different caching policies, and because you can nest User Controls with different caching policies, you can build pages that have fiendishly complex caching policies. There is nothing wrong with doing this. In fact, you should take advantage of this caching functionality whenever possible to improve the performance of your applications.

> **WARNING**
>
> Be careful when setting properties of a cached User Control. If you attempt to set the property of a User Control programmatically when the content of the control is served from the cache, you get a `NullReference` exception. Before setting a property of a cached control, first check whether the control actually exists like this:
>
> ```
> If Not IsNothing(myControl) Then
>   myControl.SomeProperty = "some value"
> End If
> ```

Sharing a User Control Output Cache

By default, instances of the same User Control located on different pages do not share the same cache. For example, if you add the same `Movies` User Control to more than one page, then the contents of each user control is cached separately.

If you want to cache the same User Control content across multiple pages, then you need to include the `Shared` attribute when adding the `<%@ OutputCache %>` directive to a User Control. For example, the modified `Movies` User Control in Listing 23.23 includes the `Shared` attribute.

LISTING 23.23   SharedMovies.ascx

```
<%@ Control Language="VB" ClassName="SharedMovies" %>
<%@ OutputCache Duration="600" VaryByParam="none" Shared="true" %>

User Control Time:
<%= DateTime.Now.ToString() %>

<asp:GridView
    id="grdMovies"
    DataSourceID="srcMovies"
    Runat="server" />

<asp:SqlDataSource
    id="srcMovies"
    ConnectionString="<%$ ConnectionStrings:Movies %>"
    SelectCommand="SELECT Title,Director FROM Movies"
    Runat="server" />
```

Using the `Shared` attribute is almost always a good idea. You can save a significant amount of server memory by taking advantage of this attribute.

Manipulating a User Control Cache Programmatically

When you include an `<%@ OutputCache %>` directive in a User Control, you can modify programmatically how the User Control is cached. The User Control `CachePolicy` property exposes an instance of the `ControlCachePolicy` class, which supports the following properties:

- `Cached`—Enables you to enable or disable caching.
- `Dependency`—Enables you to get or set a cache dependency for the User Control.
- `Duration`—Enables you to get or set the amount of time (in seconds) that content is cached.

- SupportsCaching—Enables you to check whether the control supports caching.

- VaryByControl—Enables you to create different cached versions of the control, depending on the value of a control.

- VaryByParams—Enables you to create different cached versions of the control, depending on the value of a query string or form parameter.

The ControlCachePolicy class also supports the following methods:

- SetExpires—Enables you to set the expiration time for the cache.

- SetSlidingExpiration—Enables you to set a sliding expiration cache policy.

- SetVaryByCustom—Enables you to specify a custom string used by a custom cache policy. (You also can supply the special value browser, which causes different cached versions of the control to be created when the type and major version of the browser differs.)

For example, the User Control in Listing 23.24 uses a sliding expiration policy of one minute. When you specify a sliding expiration policy, a User Control is cached just as long as you continue to request the User Control within the specified interval of time.

LISTING 23.24   SlidingUserCache.ascx

```
<%@ Control Language="VB" ClassName="SlidingUserCache" %>
<%@ OutputCache Duration="10" VaryByParam="none" %>
<script runat="server">

    Sub Page_Load()
        CachePolicy.SetSlidingExpiration(true)
        CachePolicy.Duration = TimeSpan.FromMinutes(1)
    End Sub
</script>


User Control Time:
<%= DateTime.Now.ToString("T") %>
```

The CD that accompanies this book includes a page named ShowSlidingUserCache.aspx, which contains the SlidingUserCache control. If you keep requesting this page, and do not let more than one minute pass between requests, then the User Control isn't dropped from the cache.

Creating a User Control Cache File Dependency

You can use the CacheControlPolicy.Dependency property to create a dependency between a cached User Control and a file (or set of files) on the file system. When the file is modified, the User Control is dropped from the cache automatically and reloaded with the next page request.

For example, the User Control in Listing 23.25 displays all the movies from the Movies.xml file in a GridView control. Notice that the User Control includes a Page_Load() handler that creates a dependency on the Movies.xml file.

LISTING 23.25   MovieFileDependency.ascx

```
<%@ Control Language="VB" ClassName="MovieFileDependency" %>
<%@ OutputCache Duration="9999" VaryByParam="none" %>
<script runat="server">

    Sub Page_Load()
        Dim depend As New CacheDependency(MapPath("~/Movies.xml"))
        Me.CachePolicy.Dependency = depend
    End Sub
</script>
User Control Time:
<%= DateTime.Now.ToString("T") %>
<hr />

<asp:GridView
    id="grdMovies"
    DataSourceID="srcMovies"
    Runat="server" />

<asp:XmlDataSource
    id="srcMovies"
    DataFile="Movies.xml"
    Runat="server" />
```

The CD that accompanies this book includes a page named ShowMovieFileDependency, which displays the MovieFileDependency User Control (see Figure 23.9). If you open the page, then the User Control is automatically cached until you modify the Movies.xml file.

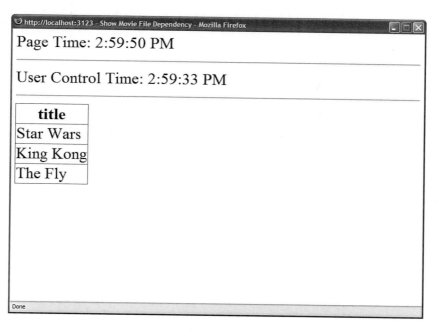

FIGURE 23.9 Displaying a User Control with a file dependency.

Caching Dynamically Loaded User Controls

You can load a User Control dynamically by using the `Page.LoadControl()` method. You can cache dynamically loaded User Controls in the same way that you can cache User Controls declared in a page. If a User Control includes an `<%@ OutputCache %>` directive, then the User Control will be cached regardless of whether the control was added to a page declaratively or programmatically.

However, you need to be aware that when a cached User Control is loaded dynamically, the ASP.NET Framework automatically wraps the User Control in an instance of the `PartialCachingControl` class. Therefore, you need to cast the control returned by the `Page.LoadControl()` method to an instance of the `PartialCachingControl` class.

For example, the page in Listing 23.26 dynamically adds the `Movies` User Control in its `Page_Load()` event handler. The `Page_Load()` method overrides the default cache duration specified in the User Control's `<%@ OutputCache %>` directive. The cache duration is changed to 15 seconds (see Figure 23.10).

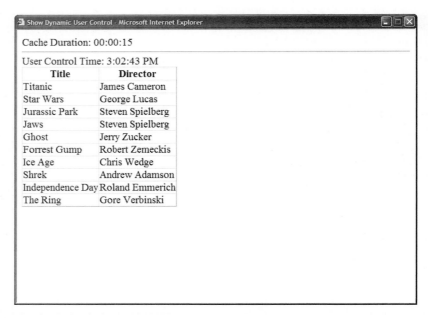

FIGURE 23.10   Programmatically caching a User Control.

LISTING 23.26   ShowDynamicUserControl.aspx

```
<%@ Page Language="VB" %>
<!DOCTYPE html PUBLIC "-//W3C//DTD XHTML 1.1//EN"
  "http://www.w3.org/TR/xhtml11/DTD/xhtml11.dtd">
<script runat="server">

    Sub Page_Load()
        ' Load the control
        Dim cacheMe As PartialCachingControl =
➥CType(Page.LoadControl("Movies.ascx"), PartialCachingControl)

        ' Change cache duration to 15 seconds
        cacheMe.CachePolicy.SetExpires(DateTime.Now.AddSeconds(15))

        ' Add control to page
        PlaceHolder1.Controls.Add(cacheMe)

        ' Display control cache duration
        lblCacheDuration.Text = cacheMe.CachePolicy.Duration.ToString()
    End Sub
</script>
<html xmlns="http://www.w3.org/1999/xhtml" >
<head id="Head1" runat="server">
    <title>Show Dynamic User Control</title>
```

LISTING 23.26   Continued

```
  </head>
  <body>
      <form id="form1" runat="server">
      <div>

      Cache Duration:
      <asp:Label
          id="lblCacheDuration"
          Runat="server" />
      <hr />

      <asp:PlaceHolder
          id="PlaceHolder1"
          Runat="server" />

      </div>
      </form>
  </body>
  </html>
```

In Listing 23.26, the default cache duration is modified by modifying the
PartialCachingControl's CachePolicy property. This property returns an instance of the
same ControlCachePolicy class described in the two previous sections of this chapter.

You can refer to the User Control contained with an instance of the
PartialCachingControl class by using the class's CachedControl property. Normally, this
property returns the value Nothing (null) because when the User Control is cached, it is
never actually created.

Using DataSource Caching

Instead of caching at the page or User Control level, you can cache at the level of a
DataSource control. All three of the standard ASP.NET DataSource controls—the
SqlDataSource, ObjectDataSource, and XmlDataSource controls—include properties that
enable you to cache the data that the DataSource control represents.

One advantage of using the DataSource controls when caching is that the DataSource
controls can reload data automatically when the data is updated. For example, if you use
a SqlDataSource control to both select and update a set of database records, then the
SqlDataSource control is smart enough to reload the cached data after an update.

The DataSource controls are also smart enough to share the same data across multiple
pages. For example, when using the SqlDataSource control, a unique entry is created in
the Cache object for each combination of the following SqlDataSource properties:
SelectCommand, SelectParameters, and ConnectionString. If these properties are identical
for two SqlDataSource controls located on two different pages, then the two controls
share the same cached data.

In this section, you learn how to use the `SqlDataSource`, `ObjectDataSource`, and `XmlDataSource` controls to cache data. You learn how to set either an absolute or sliding expiration policy. Finally, you learn how to create a cache key dependency that you can use to expire the cache programmatically.

Using an Absolute Cache Expiration Policy

When you use an absolute cache expiration policy, the data that a `DataSource` represents is cached in memory for a particular duration of time. Using an absolute cache expiration policy is useful when you know that your data does not change that often. For example, if you know that the records contained in a database table are modified only once a day, then there is no reason to keep grabbing the same records each and every time someone requests a web page.

> **WARNING**
>
> When caching with the `SqlDataSource` control, the `SqlDataSource` control's `DataSourceMode` property must be set to the value `DataSet` (the default value) rather than `DataReader`.

The page in Listing 23.27 displays a list of movies that are cached in memory. The page uses a `SqlDataSource` control to cache the data.

LISTING 23.27   DataSourceAbsoluteCache.aspx

```
<%@ Page Language="VB" %>
<!DOCTYPE html PUBLIC "-//W3C//DTD XHTML 1.1//EN"
  "http://www.w3.org/TR/xhtml11/DTD/xhtml11.dtd">
<html xmlns="http://www.w3.org/1999/xhtml" >
<head id="Head1" runat="server">
    <title>DataSource Absolute Cache</title>
</head>
<body>
    <form id="form1" runat="server">
    <div>

    <asp:GridView
        id="grdMovies"
        DataSourceID="srcMovies"
        Runat="server" />

    <asp:SqlDataSource
        id="srcMovies"
        EnableCaching="True"
        CacheDuration="3600"
        SelectCommand="SELECT * FROM Movies"
        ConnectionString="<%$ ConnectionStrings:Movies %>"
        Runat="server" />
```

LISTING 23.27   Continued

```
      </div>
      </form>
</body>
</html>
```

In Listing 23.27, two properties of the SqlDataSource control related to caching are set. First, the EnableCaching property is set to the value True. Next, the CacheDuration property is set to the value 3,600 seconds (1 hour). The movies are cached in memory for a maximum of one hour. If you don't supply a value for the CacheDuration property, the default value is Infinite.

It is important to understand that there is no guarantee that the SqlDataSource control will cache data for the amount of time specified by its CacheDuration property. Behind the scenes, DataSource controls use the Cache object for caching. This object supports scavenging. When memory resources become low, the Cache object automatically removes items from the cache.

You can test whether the page in Listing 23.27 is working by opening the page and temporarily turning off your database server. You can turn off SQL Server Express by opening the SQL Configuration Manager located in the Microsoft SQL Server 2005 program group and stopping the SQL Server service (see Figure 23.11). If you refresh the page, the data is displayed even though the database server is unavailable.

23

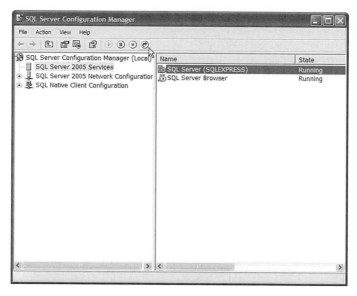

FIGURE 23.11   The SQL Configuration Manager.

Using a Sliding Cache Expiration Policy

If you need to cache a lot of data, then it makes more sense to use a sliding expiration policy rather than an absolute expiration policy. When you use a sliding expiration policy, data remains in the cache as long as the data continues to be requested within a certain interval.

For example, imagine that you have been asked to rewrite the Amazon website with ASP.NET 2.0. The Amazon website displays information on billions of books. You couldn't cache all this book information in memory. However, if you use a sliding expiration policy, then you can cache the most frequently requested books automatically.

The page in Listing 23.28 illustrates how you can enable a sliding cache expiration policy. The cache duration is set to 15 seconds. As long as no more than 15 seconds pass before you request the page, the movies are kept cached in memory.

LISTING 23.28   DataSourceSlidingCache.aspx

```
<%@ Page Language="VB" %>
<!DOCTYPE html PUBLIC "-//W3C//DTD XHTML 1.1//EN"
    "http://www.w3.org/TR/xhtml11/DTD/xhtml11.dtd">
<script runat="server">

    Sub srcMovies_Selecting(ByVal sender As Object,
➥ByVal e As SqlDataSourceSelectingEventArgs)
        lblMessage.Text = "Selecting data from database"
    End Sub
</script>
<html xmlns="http://www.w3.org/1999/xhtml" >
<head id="Head1" runat="server">
    <title>DataSource Sliding Cache</title>
</head>
<body>
    <form id="form1" runat="server">
    <div>

    <p>
    <asp:Label
        id="lblMessage"
        EnableViewState="false"
        Runat="server" />
    </p>

    <asp:GridView
        id="grdMovies"
        DataSourceID="srcMovies"
        Runat="server" />
```

LISTING 23.28   Continued

```
<asp:SqlDataSource
    id="srcMovies"
    EnableCaching="True"
    CacheExpirationPolicy="Sliding"
    CacheDuration="15"
    SelectCommand="SELECT * FROM Movies"
    ConnectionString="<%$ ConnectionStrings:Movies %>"
    OnSelecting="srcMovies_Selecting"
    Runat="server" />

    </div>
    </form>
</body>
</html>
```

Notice that the page in Listing 23.28 includes a srcMovies_Selecting() event handler. This handler is called only when the movies are retrieved from the database rather than from memory. In other words, you can use this event handler to detect when the movies are dropped from the cache (see Figure 23.12).

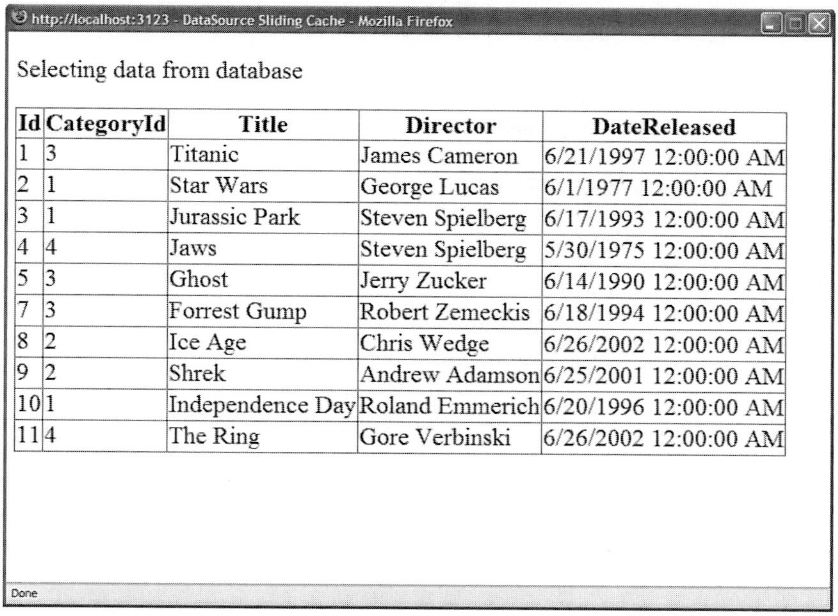

Id	CategoryId	Title	Director	DateReleased
1	3	Titanic	James Cameron	6/21/1997 12:00:00 AM
2	1	Star Wars	George Lucas	6/1/1977 12:00:00 AM
3	1	Jurassic Park	Steven Spielberg	6/17/1993 12:00:00 AM
4	4	Jaws	Steven Spielberg	5/30/1975 12:00:00 AM
5	3	Ghost	Jerry Zucker	6/14/1990 12:00:00 AM
7	3	Forrest Gump	Robert Zemeckis	6/18/1994 12:00:00 AM
8	2	Ice Age	Chris Wedge	6/26/2002 12:00:00 AM
9	2	Shrek	Andrew Adamson	6/25/2001 12:00:00 AM
10	1	Independence Day	Roland Emmerich	6/20/1996 12:00:00 AM
11	4	The Ring	Gore Verbinski	6/26/2002 12:00:00 AM

FIGURE 23.12   Using a sliding expiration policy with a DataSource control.

Caching with the `ObjectDataSource` Control

The `ObjectDataSource` control supports the same caching properties as the `SqlDataSource` control. You can cache the data that an `ObjectDataSource` control represents by setting its `EnableCaching`, `CacheDuration`, and (optionally) `CacheExpirationPolicy` properties.

> **NOTE**
>
> Multiple `ObjectDataSource` controls can share the same cached data. To share the same cache, the `ObjectDataSource` controls must have identical `TypeName`, `SelectMethod`, and `SelectParameters` properties.

For example, the page in Listing 23.29 uses an `ObjectDataSource` control to represent the `Movies` database table. The `ObjectDataSource` is bound to a component named `Movie` that includes a method named `GetMovies()` that returns all of the records from the `Movies` database table.

LISTING 23.29   ShowObjectDataSourceCaching.aspx

```
<%@ Page Language="VB" %>
<!DOCTYPE html PUBLIC "-//W3C//DTD XHTML 1.0 Transitional//EN"
 "http://www.w3.org/TR/xhtml1/DTD/xhtml1-transitional.dtd">
<script runat="server">

    Sub srcMovies_Selecting(ByVal sender As Object,
➥ByVal e As ObjectDataSourceSelectingEventArgs)
        lblMessage.Text = "Selecting data from component"
    End Sub
</script>
<html xmlns="http://www.w3.org/1999/xhtml" >
<head id="Head1" runat="server">
    <title>Show ObjectDataSource Caching</title>
</head>
<body>
    <form id="form1" runat="server">
    <div>

    <asp:Label
        id="lblMessage"
        EnableViewState="false"
        Runat="server" />
    <br /><br />

    <asp:GridView
        id="grdMovies"
        DataSourceID="srcMovies"
        Runat="server" />
```

LISTING 23.29   Continued

```
    <asp:ObjectDataSource
        id="srcMovies"
        EnableCaching="true"
        CacheDuration="15"
        TypeName="Movie"
        SelectMethod="GetMovies"
        OnSelecting="srcMovies_Selecting"
        Runat="server" />

    </div>
    </form>
</body>
</html>
```

The `ObjectDataSource` control in Listing 23.29 includes an event handler for its `Selecting` event. The event handler displays a message in a `Label` control. Because the `Selecting` event is not raised when data is retrieved from the cache, you can use this method to determine when data is retrieved from the cache or the `Movie` component.

The `Movie` component is contained in Listing 23.30.

LISTING 23.30   `Movie.vb`

```
Imports System
Imports System.Data
Imports System.Data.SqlClient
Imports System.Web.Configuration

Public Class Movie
    Public Shared Function GetMovies() As DataTable
        Dim conString As String =
➥WebConfigurationManager.ConnectionStrings("Movies").ConnectionString
        Dim dad As New SqlDataAdapter("SELECT Title,Director FROM Movies",
➥conString)
        Dim movies As New DataTable()
        dad.Fill(movies)
        Return movies
    End Function
End Class
```

Notice that the `GetMovies()` method returns a `DataTable`. When using the `ObjectDataSource` control, you can cache certain types of data but not others. For example, you can cache data represented with a `DataSet`, `DataTable`, `DataView`, or collection. However, you cannot cache data represented by a `DataReader`. If you attempt to bind to a method that returns a `DataReader`, then an exception is thrown.

Caching with the `XmlDataSource` Control

Unlike the `SqlDataSource` and `ObjectDataSource` controls, the `XmlDataSource` control has caching enabled by default. The `XmlDataSource` automatically creates a file dependency on the XML file that it represents. If the XML file is modified, the `XmlDataSource` control automatically reloads the modified XML file.

For example, the page in Listing 23.31 contains an `XmlDataSource` control that represents the `Movies.xml` file. If you modify the `Movies.xml` file, then the contents of the files are automatically reloaded.

LISTING 23.31   ShowXmlDataSourceCaching.aspx

```
<%@ Page Language="VB" %>
<!DOCTYPE html PUBLIC "-//W3C//DTD XHTML 1.0 Transitional//EN"
 "http://www.w3.org/TR/xhtml1/DTD/xhtml1-transitional.dtd">
<html xmlns="http://www.w3.org/1999/xhtml" >
<head id="Head1" runat="server">
    <title>Show XmlDataSource Caching</title>
</head>
<body>
    <form id="form1" runat="server">
    <div>

    <asp:GridView
        id="grdMovies"
        DataSourceID="srcMovies"
        Runat="server" />

    <asp:XmlDataSource
        id="srcMovies"
        DataFile="Movies.xml"
        Runat="server" />

    </div>
    </form>
</body>
</html>
```

Creating a `DataSource` Control Key Dependency

Imagine that your web application has multiple pages that display different sets of records from the Movies database table. However, you have one page that enables a user to enter a new movie. In that case, you need some method of signaling to all your `DataSource` controls that the Movies database table has changed.

You can create a key dependency between the DataSource controls in your application and an item in the cache. That way, if you remove the item from the cache, all the DataSource controls will reload their data.

The page in Listing 23.32 contains a SqlDataSource control that displays the contents of the Movies database table. The SqlDataSource caches its data for an infinite duration.

LISTING 23.32   DataSourceKeyDependency.aspx

```
<%@ Page Language="VB" %>
<!DOCTYPE html PUBLIC "-//W3C//DTD XHTML 1.1//EN"
  "http://www.w3.org/TR/xhtml11/DTD/xhtml11.dtd">
<script runat="server">

    Sub srcMovies_Selecting(ByVal sender As Object,
➥ByVal e As SqlDataSourceSelectingEventArgs)
        lblMessage.Text = "Selecting data from database"
    End Sub
</script>

<html xmlns="http://www.w3.org/1999/xhtml" >
<head id="Head1" runat="server">
    <title>DataSource Key Dependency</title>
</head>
<body>
    <form id="form1" runat="server">
    <div>

    <p>
    <asp:Label
        id="lblMessage"
        EnableViewState="false"
        Runat="server" />
    </p>

    <asp:GridView
        id="grdMovies"
        DataSourceID="srcMovies"
        Runat="server" />

    <asp:SqlDataSource
        id="srcMovies"
        EnableCaching="True"
        CacheDuration="Infinite"
        CacheKeyDependency="MovieKey"
        SelectCommand="SELECT * FROM Movies"
```

23

LISTING 23.32   Continued

```
            ConnectionString="<%$ ConnectionStrings:Movies %>"
            OnSelecting="srcMovies_Selecting"
            Runat="server" />

    <br /><br />
    <a href="AddMovieDataSourceKeyDependency.aspx">Add Movie</a>

    </div>
    </form>
</body>
</html>
```

Notice that the `SqlDataSource` control in Listing 23.32 includes a `CacheKeyDependency` property that has the value `MovieKey`. This property creates a dependency between the DataSource control's cached data and an item in the cache named `MovieKey`.

The `Global.asax` file in Listing 23.33 creates the initial `MovieKey` cache item. The value of the cache item doesn't really matter. In Listing 23.33, the `MovieKey` cache item is set to the current date and time.

LISTING 23.33   `Global.asax`

```
<%@ Application Language="VB" %>
<script runat="server">
    Private Sub Application_Start(ByVal sender As Object, ByVal e As EventArgs)
        Dim context As HttpContext = HttpContext.Current
        context.Cache.Insert( _
            "MovieKey", _
            DateTime.Now, _
            Nothing, _
            DateTime.MaxValue, _
            Cache.NoSlidingExpiration, _
            CacheItemPriority.NotRemovable, _
            Nothing)
    End Sub
</script>
```

The page in Listing 23.34 contains a `DetailsView` control that enables you to insert a new record. Notice that the `DetailsView` control's `ItemInserted` event is handled. When you insert a new record, the `MovieKey` item is reinserted into the cache and every `DataSource` control that is dependent on this key is reloaded automatically.

LISTING 23.34 AddMovieDataSourceKeyDependency.aspx

```
<%@ Page Language="VB" %>
<!DOCTYPE html PUBLIC "-//W3C//DTD XHTML 1.0 Transitional//EN"
  "http://www.w3.org/TR/xhtml1/DTD/xhtml1-transitional.dtd">
<script runat="server">

    Sub dtlMovie_ItemInserted(ByVal sender As Object,
➥ByVal e As DetailsViewInsertedEventArgs)
        Cache.Insert("MovieKey", DateTime.Now)
        Response.Redirect("~/DataSourceKeyDependency.aspx")
    End Sub
</script>
<html xmlns="http://www.w3.org/1999/xhtml" >
<head id="Head1" runat="server">
    <title>Add Movie Key Dependency</title>
</head>
<body>
    <form id="form1" runat="server">
    <div>

    <h1>Add Movie</h1>

    <asp:DetailsView
        id="dtlMovie"
        DefaultMode="Insert"
        DataSourceID="srcMovies"
        AutoGenerateRows="false"
        AutoGenerateInsertButton="true"
        OnItemInserted="dtlMovie_ItemInserted"
        Runat="server">
        <Fields>
        <asp:BoundField
            DataField="Title"
            HeaderText="Title:" />
        <asp:BoundField
            DataField="Director"
            HeaderText="Director:" />
        </Fields>
    </asp:DetailsView>

    <asp:SqlDataSource
        id="srcMovies"
        ConnectionString="<%$ ConnectionStrings:Movies %>"
        InsertCommand="INSERT Movies (Title, Director)
            VALUES (@Title, @Director)"
```

LISTING 23.34   Continued

```
        Runat="server" />

    </div>
    </form>
</body>
</html>
```

Using Data Caching

Behind the scenes, all the various caching mechanisms included in the ASP.NET Framework use the Cache object. In other words, the Cache object is the fundamental mechanism for all caching in the ASP.NET Framework.

One instance of the Cache object is created for each ASP.NET application. Any items you add to the cache can be accessed by any other page, control, or component contained in the same application (virtual directory).

In this section, you learn how to use the properties and methods of the Cache object. You learn how to add items to the cache, set cache expiration policies, and create cache item dependencies.

Using the Cache Application Programming Interface

The Cache object exposes the main application programming interface for caching. This object supports the following properties:

- Count—Represents the number of items in the cache.

- EffectivePrivateBytesLimit—Represents the size of the cache in kilobytes.

The Cache object also supports the following methods:

- Add—Enables you to add a new item to the cache. If the item already exists, this method fails.

- Get—Enables you to return a particular item from the cache.

- GetEnumerator—Enables you to iterate through all the items in the cache.

- Insert—Enables you to insert a new item into the cache. If the item already exists, this method replaces it.

- Remove—Enables you to remove an item from the cache.

For example, the page in Listing 23.35 displays all the items currently contained in the cache (see Figure 23.13).

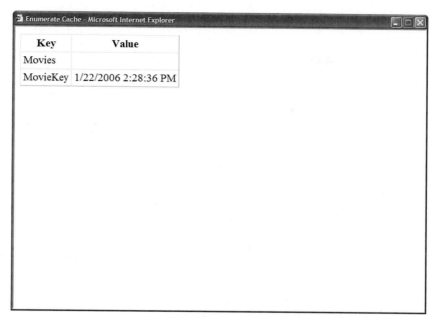

FIGURE 23.13   Displaying the cache's contents.

LISTING 23.35   EnumerateCache.aspx

```vb
<%@ Page Language="VB" %>
<!DOCTYPE html PUBLIC "-//W3C//DTD XHTML 1.0 Transitional//EN"
    "http://www.w3.org/TR/xhtml1/DTD/xhtml1-transitional.dtd">
<script runat="server">

    Public Class CacheItem
        Private _key As String
        Private _value As Object

        Public ReadOnly Property Key() As String
            Get
                Return _key
            End Get
        End Property

        Public ReadOnly Property Value() As String
            Get
                Return _value.ToString()
            End Get
        End Property
```

LISTING 23.35   Continued

```
        Public Sub New(ByVal key As String, ByVal value As Object)
            _key = key
            _value = value
        End Sub
    End Class

    Private Sub Page_Load()
        Dim items As New ArrayList()
        For Each item As DictionaryEntry In Cache
            items.Add(New CacheItem(item.Key.ToString(), item.Value))
        Next

        grdCache.DataSource = items
        grdCache.DataBind()
    End Sub

</script>
<html xmlns="http://www.w3.org/1999/xhtml" >
<head id="Head1" runat="server">
    <style type="text/css">
        .grid td, .grid th
        {
            padding:5px;
        }
    </style>
    <title>Enumerate Cache</title>
</head>
<body>
    <form id="form1" runat="server">
    <div>

    <asp:GridView
        id="grdCache"
        CssClass="grid"
        Runat="server" />

    </div>
    </form>
</body>
</html>
```

The page in Listing 23.35 displays only items that have been added to the cache by the methods of the Cache object. For example, it does not display a list of pages that have been output cached. Output cached pages are stored in the internal cache (the secret cache maintained by the ASP.NET framework).

Adding Items to the Cache

You can add items to the cache by using the `Insert()` method. There are several over-loaded versions of the `Insert()` method. The maximally overloaded version of the `Insert()` method accepts the following parameters:

- `key`—Enables you to specify the name of the new item.

- `value`—Enables you to specify the value of the new item.

- `dependencies`—Enables you to specify one or more cache dependencies, such as a file, key, or SQL dependency.

- `absoluteExpiration`—Enables you to specify an absolute expiration time for the cached item. If you don't need to specify a value for this property, use the static field `Cache.NoAbsoluteExpiration`.

- `slidingExpiration`—Enables you to specify a sliding expiration interval for the cached item. If you don't need to specify a value for this property, use the static field `Cache.NoSlidingExpiration`.

- `priority`—Enables you to specify the priority of the cached item. Possible values are `AboveNormal`, `BelowNormal`, `Default`, `High`, `Low`, `Normal`, and `NotRemovable`.

- `onRemoveCallback`—Enables you to specify a method that is called automatically before the item is removed from the cache.

When using the cache, it is important to understand that items that you add to the cache might not be there when you attempt to retrieve the item in the future. The cache supports scavenging. When memory resources become low, items are automatically evicted from the cache.

Before using any item that you retrieve from the cache, you should always check whether the item is `Nothing` (null). If an item has been removed, then you'll retrieve `Nothing` when you attempt to retrieve it from the cache in the future.

You can add almost any object to the cache. For example, you can add custom components, `DataSets`, `DataTables`, `ArrayLists`, and `Lists` to the cache.

You shouldn't add items to the cache that depend on an external resource. For example, it does not make sense to add a `SqlDataReader` or a `FileStream` to the cache. When using a `SqlDataReader`, you need to copy the contents of the `SqlDataReader` into a static representation such as an `ArrayList` or `List` collection.

Adding Items with an Absolute Expiration Policy

When you insert items in the cache, you can specify a time when the item will expire. If you want an item to remain in the cache for an extended period of time, then you should always specify an expiration time for the item.

The page in Listing 23.36 illustrates how you can add an item to the cache with an absolute expiration policy. The item is added to the cache for one hour.

LISTING 23.36   ShowAbsoluteExpiration.aspx

```
<%@ Page Language="VB" Trace="true" %>
<%@ Import Namespace="System.Data" %>
<%@ Import Namespace="System.Data.SqlClient" %>
<%@ Import Namespace="System.Web.Configuration" %>
<!DOCTYPE html PUBLIC "-//W3C//DTD XHTML 1.0 Transitional//EN"
    "http://www.w3.org/TR/xhtml1/DTD/xhtml1-transitional.dtd">
<script runat="server">

    Private Sub Page_Load()
        ' Get movies from Cache
        Dim movies As DataTable = CType(Cache("Movies"), DataTable)

        ' If movies not in cache, recreate movies
        If IsNothing(movies) Then
            movies = GetMoviesFromDB()
            Cache.Insert("Movies", movies, Nothing,
➥DateTime.Now.AddHours(1), Cache.NoSlidingExpiration)
        End If

        grdMovies.DataSource = movies
        grdMovies.DataBind()
    End Sub

    Private Function GetMoviesFromDB() As DataTable
        Trace.Warn("Getting movies from database")
        Dim conString As String =
➥WebConfigurationManager.ConnectionStrings("Movies").ConnectionString
        Dim dad As New SqlDataAdapter("SELECT Title,Director FROM Movies",
➥conString)
        Dim movies As New DataTable()
        dad.Fill(movies)
        Return movies
    End Function
</script>
<html xmlns="http://www.w3.org/1999/xhtml" >
<head id="Head1" runat="server">
    <title>Show Absolute Expiration</title>
</head>
<body>
    <form id="form1" runat="server">
    <div>

    <asp:GridView
        id="grdMovies"
```

LISTING 23.36   Continued

```
            Runat="server" />

    </div>
    </form>
</body>
</html>
```

The first time the page in Listing 23.36 is requested, nothing is retrieved from the cache. In that case, a new `DataTable` is created that represents the Movies database table. The `DataTable` is inserted into the cache. The next time the page is requested, the `DataTable` can be retrieved from the cache and there is no need to access the database.

The `DataTable` will remain in the cache for one hour, or until memory pressures force the `DataTable` to be evicted from the cache. In either case, the logic of the page dictates that the `DataTable` will be added back to the cache when the page is next requested.

Tracing is enabled for the page in Listing 23.36 so that you can see when the Movies database table is loaded from the cache and when the table is loaded from the database. The `GetMoviesFromDB()` method writes a `Trace` message whenever it executes (see Figure 23.14).

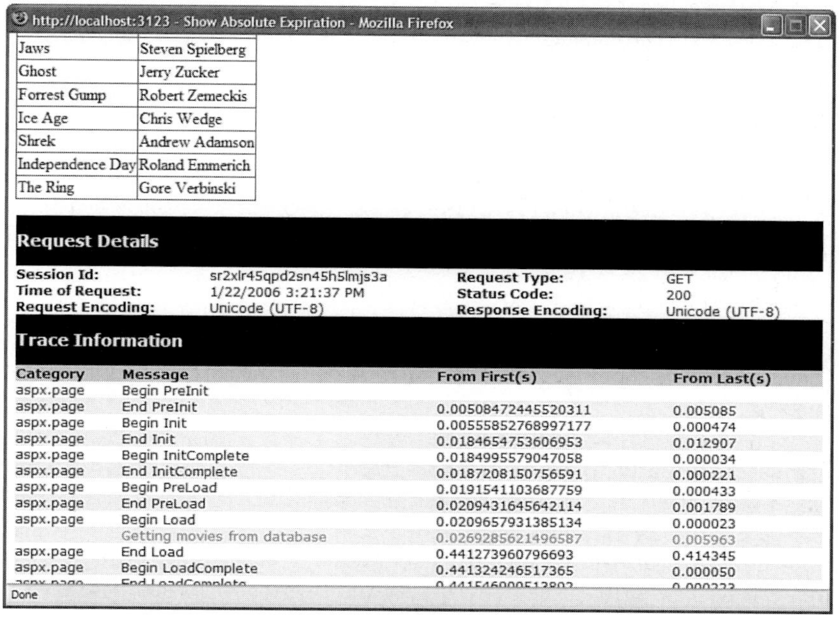

FIGURE 23.14   Adding an item to the cache with an absolute expiration policy.

Adding Items with a Sliding Expiration Policy

When you specify a sliding expiration policy, items remain in the cache just as long as they continue to be requested within a specified interval of time. For example, if you specify a sliding expiration policy of 5 minutes, then the item remains in the Cache just as long as no more than 5 minutes pass without the item being requested.

Using a sliding expiration policy makes sense when you have too many items to add to the cache. A sliding expiration policy keeps the most requested items in memory and the remaining items are dropped from memory automatically.

The page in Listing 23.37 illustrates how you can add a DataSet to the cache with a sliding expiration policy of 5 minutes.

LISTING 23.37   ShowSlidingExpiration.aspx

```
<%@ Page Language="VB" Trace="true" %>
<%@ Import Namespace="System.Data" %>
<%@ Import Namespace="System.Data.SqlClient" %>
<%@ Import Namespace="System.Web.Configuration" %>
<!DOCTYPE html PUBLIC "-//W3C//DTD XHTML 1.0 Transitional//EN"
   "http://www.w3.org/TR/xhtml1/DTD/xhtml1-transitional.dtd">
<script runat="server">

    Private Sub Page_Load()
        ' Get movies from Cache
        Dim movies As DataSet = CType(Cache("Movies"), DataSet)

        ' If movies not in cache, re-create movies
        If IsNothing(movies) Then
            movies = GetMoviesFromDB()
            Cache.Insert("Movies", movies, Nothing, Cache.NoAbsoluteExpiration,
➥TimeSpan.FromMinutes(5))
        End If

        grdMovies.DataSource = movies
        grdMovies.DataBind()
    End Sub

    Private Function GetMoviesFromDB() As DataSet
        Trace.Warn("Getting movies from database")
        Dim conString As String =
➥WebConfigurationManager.ConnectionStrings("Movies").ConnectionString
        Dim dad As New SqlDataAdapter("SELECT Title,Director FROM Movies",
➥conString)
        Dim movies As New DataSet()
        dad.Fill(movies)
        Return movies
```

LISTING 23.37   Continued

```
    End Function
</script>
<html xmlns="http://www.w3.org/1999/xhtml" >
<head id="Head1" runat="server">
    <title>Show Sliding Expiration</title>
</head>
<body>
    <form id="form1" runat="server">
    <div>

    <asp:GridView
        id="grdMovies"
        Runat="server" />

    </div>
    </form>
</body>
</html>
```

In Listing 23.37, when the DataSet is added to the cache with the Insert() method, its absoluteExpiration parameter is set to the value Cache.NoAbsoluteExpiration and its slidingExpiration parameter is set to an interval of 5 minutes.

Adding Items with Dependencies

When you add an item to the Cache object, you can make the item dependent on an external object. If the external object is modified, then the item is automatically dropped from the cache.

The ASP.NET Framework includes three cache dependency classes:

- CacheDependency—Enables you to create a dependency on a file or other cache key.

- SqlCacheDependency—Enables you to create a dependency on a Microsoft SQL Server database table or the result of a SQL Server 2005 query.

- AggregateCacheDependency—Enables you to create a dependency using multiple CacheDependency objects. For example, you can combine file and SQL dependencies with this object.

The CacheDependency class is the base class. The other two classes derive from this class. The CacheDependency class supports the following properties:

- HasChanged—Enables you to detect when the dependency object has changed.

- UtcLastModified—Enables you to retrieve the time when the dependency object last changed.

The CacheDependency object also supports the following method:

- GetUniqueID—Enables you to retrieve a unique identifier for the dependency object.

> **NOTE**
>
> You can create a custom cache dependency class by deriving a new class from the base CacheDependency class.

The SqlCacheDependency class is discussed in detail in the final section of this chapter. In this section, I want to show you how you can use the base CacheDependency class to create a file dependency on an XML file.

The page in Listing 23.38 creates a dependency on an XML file named Movies.xml. If you modify the Movies.xml file, the cache is reloaded with the modified file automatically.

LISTING 23.38   ShowFileDependency.aspx

```
<%@ Page Language="VB" Trace="true" %>
<%@ Import Namespace="System.Data" %>
<%@ Import Namespace="System.Data.SqlClient" %>
<!DOCTYPE html PUBLIC "-//W3C//DTD XHTML 1.0 Transitional//EN"
    "http://www.w3.org/TR/xhtml1/DTD/xhtml1-transitional.dtd">
<script runat="server">

    Private Sub Page_Load()
        Dim movies As DataSet = CType(Cache("Movies"), DataSet)
        If IsNothing(movies) Then
            Trace.Warn("Retrieving movies from file system")
            movies = New DataSet()
            movies.ReadXml(MapPath("~/Movies.xml"))
            Dim fileDepend As New CacheDependency(MapPath("~/Movies.xml"))
            Cache.Insert("Movies", movies, fileDepend)
        End If
        grdMovies.DataSource = movies
        grdMovies.DataBind()
    End Sub
</script>
<html xmlns="http://www.w3.org/1999/xhtml" >
<head id="Head1" runat="server">
    <title>Show File Dependency</title>
</head>
```

LISTING 23.38   Continued

```
<body>
    <form id="form1" runat="server">
    <div>

    <asp:GridView
        id="grdMovies"
        Runat="server" />

    </div>
    </form>
</body>
</html>
```

Specifying Cache Item Priorities

When you add an item to the Cache, you can specify a particular priority for the item. Specifying a priority provides you with some control over when an item gets evicted from the Cache. For example, you can indicate that one cached item is more important than other cache items so that when memory resources become low, the important item is not evicted as quickly as other items.

You can specify any of the following values of the CacheItemPriority enumeration to indicate the priority of a cached item:

- AboveNormal

- BelowNormal

- Default

- High

- Low

- Normal

- NotRemovable

For example, the following line of code adds an item to the cache with a maximum absolute expiration time and a cache item priority of NotRemovable:

```
Cache.Insert("ImportantItem", DateTime.Now, Nothing, DateTime.MaxValue,
➥ Cache.NoSlidingExpiration, CacheItemPriority.NotRemovable, Nothing)
```

Configuring the Cache

You can configure the size of the cache by using the web configuration file. You specify cache settings with the cache element. This element supports the following attributes:

- disableMemoryCollection—Enables you to prevent items from being removed from the cache when memory resources become low.

- disableExpiration—Enables you to prevent items from being removed from the cache when the items expire.

- privateBytesLimit—Enables you to specify the total amount of memory that can be consumed by your application and its cache before items are removed.

- percentagePhysicalMemoryUsedLimit—Enables you to specify the total percentage of memory that can be consumed by your application and its cache before items are removed.

- privateBytesPollTime—Enables you to specify the time interval for checking the application's memory usage.

Notice that you can't set the size of the cache directly. However, you can specify limits on the overall memory that your application consumes, which indirectly limits the size of the cache.

By default, both the privateBytesLimit and percentPhysicalMemoryUsedLimit attributes have the value 0, which indicates that the ASP.NET Framework should determine the correct values for these attributes automatically.

The web configuration file in Listing 23.39 changes the memory limit of your application to 100,000 kilobytes and disables the expiration of items in the cache.

LISTING 23.39   Web.Config

```
<?xml version="1.0"?>
<configuration>
    <system.web>
      <caching>
        <cache privateBytesLimit="100000" disableExpiration="true"/>
      </caching>
    </system.web>
</configuration>
```

The page in Listing 23.40 displays your application's current private bytes limit (see Figure 23.15):

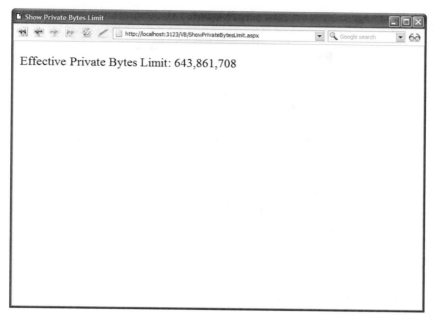

FIGURE 23.15   Displaying the maximum application and cache size.

LISTING 23.40   ShowPrivateBytesLimit.aspx

```
<%@ Page Language="VB" %>
<!DOCTYPE html PUBLIC "-//W3C//DTD XHTML 1.0 Transitional//EN"
   "http://www.w3.org/TR/xhtml1/DTD/xhtml1-transitional.dtd">
<script runat="server">

    Sub Page_Load()
        lblPrivateBytes.Text = Cache.EffectivePrivateBytesLimit.ToString("n0")
    End Sub
</script>
<html xmlns="http://www.w3.org/1999/xhtml" >
<head id="Head1" runat="server">
    <title>Show Private Bytes Limit</title>
</head>
<body>
    <form id="form1" runat="server">
    <div>

    Effective Private Bytes Limit:
    <asp:Label
        id="lblPrivateBytes"
        Runat="server" />
```

LISTING 23.40   Continued

```
    </div>
    </form>
</body>
</html>
```

Using SQL Cache Dependencies

One of the most powerful new features added to the ASP.NET 2.0 Framework is SQL cache dependencies. This feature enables you to reload cached database data automatically whenever the data in the underlying databases changes.

There is a tradeoff when you use either an absolute or sliding cache expiration policy. The tradeoff is between performance and stale data. For example, if you cache data in memory for 20 seconds, then the data that is displayed on your web pages might be 20 seconds out of date.

In the case of most applications, displaying slightly stale data does not really matter. For example, if you are building a discussion forum, then everyone can live with the fact that new posts might not appear immediately.

However, there are certain types of applications in which you cannot afford to display any stale data at all. For example, if you are creating a stock trading website or an auction website, then every second might count.

The ASP.NET Framework's support for SQL cache dependencies enables you to take advantage of caching but minimize stale data. When you use a SQL cache dependency, you can automatically detect when data has changed in the underlying database and refresh the data in the cache.

The ASP.NET Framework supports two types of SQL cache dependencies: Polling and Push. You can use Polling SQL cache dependencies with any recent version of Microsoft SQL Server, including Microsoft SQL Server 2005 Express, Microsoft SQL Server 2000, and Microsoft SQL Server 7.0. The second type of cache dependency, Push SQL cache dependencies, works with only Microsoft SQL Server 2005 or Microsoft SQL Server 2005 Express because it requires the SQL Server 2005 Service Broker.

You can use either type of SQL cache dependencies with Page Output Caching, DataSource Control Caching, and Data Caching. The following sections examine each scenario.

Using Polling SQL Cache Dependencies

A Polling SQL cache dependency is the most flexible type of SQL cache dependency, and I recommend that you use Polling rather than Push SQL cache dependencies for most applications. You can use a Polling SQL cache dependency to detect any type of modification to a database table.

Behind the scenes, a Polling SQL cache dependency uses a database trigger. When a table is modified, the trigger fires and a row in a database table named AspNet_ SqlCacheTablesForChangeNotification is updated to record the fact that the table has been changed.

The ASP.NET Framework uses a background thread to poll this database table for changes on a periodic basis. If there has been a change, then any item in the cache that is dependent on the database table is dropped from the cache.

If you use a Polling SQL cache dependency, then you can eliminate the majority of your database traffic. Unless a database table changes, the only traffic between your web server and the database server is the query that checks for changes in the AspNet_ SqlCacheTablesForChangeNotification table.

Because a Polling SQL cache dependency must poll the database for changes, an item cached with a SQL Polling cache dependency won't be dropped from the cache immediately after there is a change in the database. The polling interval determines the staleness of your cached data. You can configure the polling interval to be any value you need.

Configuring Polling SQL Cache Dependencies

Before you can use a Polling SQL cache dependency, you must perform two configuration steps:

1. You must enable SQL cache dependencies for a database and one or more database tables.

2. You must configure SQL cache dependencies in your web configuration file.

Let's examine each of these steps.

Configuring a Database for Polling SQL Cache Dependencies

You can configure a SQL Server database to support Polling SQL cache dependencies by using a class in the Framework named the SqlCacheDependencyAdmin class. This class has the following methods:

- DisableNotifications—Enables you to disable a database for Polling SQL cache dependencies. Removes all tables and stored procedures used by Polling SQL cache dependencies.

- DisableTableForNotification—Enables you to disable a particular database table for Polling SQL cache dependencies.

- EnableNotifications—Enables a database for Polling SQL cache dependencies by adding all the necessary database objects.

- EnableTableForNotifications—Enables a particular database table for Polling SQL cache dependencies.

- GetTablesEnabledForNotifications—Enables you to retrieve all tables enabled for Polling SQL cache dependencies.

23

You should not use the `SqlCacheDependencyAdmin` class in an ASP.NET page because calling the methods of this class requires database permissions to create tables, stored procedures, and triggers. For security reasons, the ASP.NET process should not be given these permissions. Instead, you should use the `SqlCacheDependencyAdmin` class in a command-line tool.

The ASP.NET Framework includes a command-line tool named `aspnet_regsql` that enables you to configure a database to support Polling SQL cache dependencies. This tool works with Microsoft SQL Server 7.0, Microsoft SQL Server 2000, and Microsoft SQL Server 2005. Unfortunately, the `aspnet_regsql` command-line tool does not work with a local instance of Microsoft SQL Server 2005 (but we'll fix this limitation in a moment).

The `aspnet_regsql` tool is located in the following folder:

```
c:\Windows\Microsoft.NET\Framework\[version]
```

> **NOTE**
>
> If you open the SDK Command Prompt from the Microsoft .NET Framework SDK Program group, then you do not need to navigate to the Microsoft.NET folder to execute the `aspnet_regsql` command-line tool.

Executing the following command enables the Pubs database for SQL cache dependencies:

```
aspnet_regsql -C "Data Source=localhost;Integrated Security=True;
➥Initial Catalog=Pubs" -ed
```

This command creates the `AspNet_SqlCacheTablesForChangeNotification` database table and adds a set of stored procedures to the database specified in the connection string.

After you enable a database, you can enable a particular table for SQL cache dependencies with the following command:

```
aspnet_regsql -C "Data Source=localhost;Integrated Security=True;
➥Initial Catalog=Pubs" -et -t Titles
```

This command enables the Titles database table for SQL cache dependencies. It creates a new trigger for the Titles database table and adds a new entry in the `AspNet_SqlCacheTablesForChangeNotification` table.

Unfortunately, you cannot use the standard `aspnet_regsql` tool to enable a local SQL Server 2005 Express database for Polling SQL cache dependencies. The aspnet_regsql tool does not allow you to use the `AttachDBFileName` parameter in the connection string.

To get around this limitation, I've written a custom command-line tool named `enableNotifications` that works with a local SQL Express database. This tool is included on the CD that accompanies this book.

To use the `enableNotifications` tool, you need to open a command prompt and navigate to the folder that contains your local SQL Express database table. Next, execute the command with the name of the database file and the name of the database table that you want to enable for Polling SQL cache dependencies. For example, the following command enables the Movies database table located in the `MyDatabase.mdf` database:

```
enableNotifications "MyDatabase.mdf" "Movies"
```

The `enableNotifications` tool works only with a local instance of Microsoft SQL Server Express 2005. You cannot use the tool with other versions of Microsoft SQL Server.

> **WARNING**
>
> When using the `enableNotifications` tool, you must navigate to the same folder as the database that you want to enable for Polling SQL cache dependencies.

Configuring an Application for Polling SQL Cache Dependencies

After you set up a database to support Polling SQL cache dependencies, you must configure your application to poll the database. You configure Polling SQL cache dependencies with the `sqlCacheDependency` sub-element of the caching element in the web configuration file.

For example, the file in Listing 23.41 causes your application to poll the `AspNet_SqlCacheTablesForChangeNotification` table every 5 seconds (5000 milliseconds) for changes.

LISTING 23.41   Web.Config

```
<?xml version="1.0"?>
<configuration>

  <connectionStrings>
    <add name="Movies" connectionString="Data Source=.\SQLEXPRESS;
      AttachDbFilename=¦DataDirectory¦MyDatabase.mdf;Integrated Security=True;
User Instance=True" />
  </connectionStrings>

  <system.web>
    <caching>
      <sqlCacheDependency enabled="true" pollTime="5000">
        <databases>
          <add
            name="MyDatabase"
            connectionStringName="Movies" />
        </databases>
      </sqlCacheDependency>
    </caching>
  </system.web>
</configuration>
```

23

Using Polling SQL Cache Dependencies with Page Output Caching

After you configure Polling SQL cache dependencies, you can use a SQL dependency with Page Output Caching. For example, the page in Listing 23.42 is output cached until you modify the Movies database table.

LISTING 23.42   PollingSQLOutputCache.aspx

```
<%@ Page Language="VB" %>
<%@ OutputCache Duration="9999" VaryByParam="none"
  SqlDependency="MyDatabase:Movies" %>
<!DOCTYPE html PUBLIC "-//W3C//DTD XHTML 1.0 Transitional//EN"
  "http://www.w3.org/TR/xhtml1/DTD/xhtml1-transitional.dtd">
<html xmlns="http://www.w3.org/1999/xhtml" >
<head id="Head1" runat="server">
    <title>Polling SQL Output Cache</title>
</head>
<body>
    <form id="form1" runat="server">
    <div>

    <%= DateTime.Now.ToString("T") %>
    <hr />

    <asp:GridView
        id="grdMovies"
        DataSourceID="srcMovies"
        Runat="server" />

    <asp:SqlDataSource
        id="srcMovies"
        ConnectionString="<%$ ConnectionStrings:Movies %>"
        SelectCommand="SELECT Title, Director FROM Movies"
        Runat="server" />

    </div>
    </form>
</body>
</html>
```

The page in Listing 23.42 includes an `<%@ OutputCache %>` directive with a `SqlDependency` attribute. The value of the `SqlDependency` attribute is the name of the database enabled for SQL dependencies in the web configuration file, followed by the name of a database table.

If you open the page in Listing 23.42 in your browser and click your browser's Reload button multiple times, then you'll notice that the time displayed does not change. The page is output cached (see Figure 23.16).

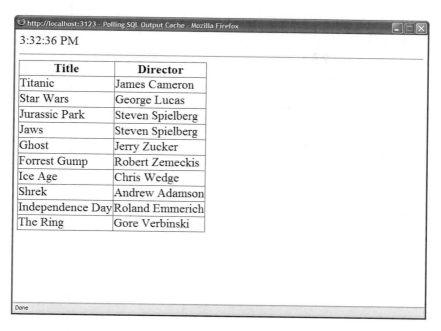

FIGURE 23.16   Using Page Output Caching with a Polling SQL cache dependency.

However, if you modify the Movies database, then the page is dropped from the cache automatically (within 5 seconds). The next time you click the Reload button, the modified data is displayed.

If you want to make a page dependent on multiple database tables, then you can assign a semicolon-delimited list of database and table names to the SqlDependency attribute.

> **NOTE**
>
> You also can use Polling SQL cache dependencies with an <%@ OutputCache %> directive included in a User Control. In other words, you can use Polling SQL cache dependencies with Partial Page Caching.

Using Polling SQL Cache Dependencies with DataSource Caching

You can use Polling SQL cache dependencies with both the SqlDataSource and ObjectDataSource controls by setting the SqlCacheDependency property. For example, the page in Listing 23.43 caches the output of a SqlDataSource control until the Movies database table is modified.

23

LISTING 23.43   PollingSQLDataSourceCache.aspx

```
<%@ Page Language="VB" %>
<!DOCTYPE html PUBLIC "-//W3C//DTD XHTML 1.0 Transitional//EN"
 "http://www.w3.org/TR/xhtml1/DTD/xhtml1-transitional.dtd">
<script runat="server">

    Sub srcMovies_Selecting(ByVal sender As Object,
➥ByVal e As SqlDataSourceSelectingEventArgs)
        lblMessage.Text = "Retrieving data from database"
    End Sub
</script>
<html xmlns="http://www.w3.org/1999/xhtml" >
<head id="Head1" runat="server">
    <title>Polling SQL DataSource Cache</title>
</head>
<body>
    <form id="form1" runat="server">
    <div>

    <asp:Label
        id="lblMessage"
        EnableViewState="false"
        Runat="server" />
    <hr />

    <asp:GridView
        id="grdMovies"
        DataSourceID="srcMovies"
        Runat="server" />

    <asp:SqlDataSource
        id="srcMovies"
        ConnectionString="<%$ ConnectionStrings:Movies %>"
        SelectCommand="SELECT Title, Director FROM Movies"
        EnableCaching="true"
        SqlCacheDependency="MyDatabase:Movies"
        OnSelecting="srcMovies_Selecting"
        Runat="server" />

    </div>
    </form>
</body>
</html>
```

In Listing 23.43, the SqlDataSource control includes both an EnableCaching property and a SqlCacheDependency property. A database name and table name are assigned to the SqlCacheDependency property. (The database name must correspond to the database name configured in the <sqlCacheDependency> section of the web configuration file.)

If you need to monitor multiple database tables, then you can assign a semicolon-delimited list of database and table names to the SqlCacheDependency property.

Using Polling SQL Cache Dependencies with Data Caching

You also can use Polling SQL cache dependencies when working with the Cache object. You represent a Polling SQL cache dependency with the SqlCacheDependency object.

For example, the page in Listing 23.44 creates a SqlCacheDependency object that represents the Movies database table. When a DataTable is added to the Cache object, the DataTable is added with the SqlCacheDependency object.

LISTING 23.44   PollingSQLDataCache.aspx

```
<%@ Page Language="VB" Trace="true" %>
<%@ Import Namespace="System.Data" %>
<%@ Import Namespace="System.Data.SqlClient" %>
<%@ Import Namespace="System.Web.Configuration" %>
<!DOCTYPE html PUBLIC "-//W3C//DTD XHTML 1.0 Transitional//EN"
 "http://www.w3.org/TR/xhtml1/DTD/xhtml1-transitional.dtd">
<script runat="server">

    Private Sub Page_Load()
        Dim movies As DataTable = CType(Cache("Movies"), DataTable)
        If IsNothing(movies) Then
            movies = GetMoviesFromDB()
            Dim sqlDepend As New SqlCacheDependency("MyDatabase", "Movies")
            Cache.Insert("Movies", movies, sqlDepend)
        End If
        grdMovies.DataSource = movies
        grdMovies.DataBind()
    End Sub


    Private Function GetMoviesFromDB() As DataTable
        Trace.Warn("Retrieving data from database")
        Dim conString As String =
➥WebConfigurationManager.ConnectionStrings("Movies").ConnectionString
        Dim dad As New SqlDataAdapter("SELECT Title,Director FROM Movies",
➥conString)
        Dim movies As New DataTable()
        dad.Fill(movies)
        Return movies
    End Function
</script>
```

LISTING 23.44   Continued

```html
<html xmlns="http://www.w3.org/1999/xhtml" >
<head id="Head1" runat="server">
    <title>Polling SQL Data Cache</title>
</head>
<body>
    <form id="form1" runat="server">
    <div>

    <asp:GridView
        id="grdMovies"
        Runat="server" />

    </div>
    </form>
</body>
</html>
```

In Listing 23.44, an instance of the `SqlCacheDependency` class is created. A database name and table name are passed to the constructor for the `SqlCacheDependency` class. This class is used as a parameter with the `Cache.Insert()` method when the `DataTable` is added to the `Cache`.

> **NOTE**
>
> If you need to create dependencies on multiple database tables, then you need to create multiple `SqlCacheDependency` objects and represent the multiple dependencies with an instance of the `AggregateCacheDependency` class.

Using Push SQL Cache Dependencies

When using Microsoft SQL Server 2005, you have the option of using Push SQL cache dependencies rather than Polling SQL cache dependencies. Microsoft SQL Server 2005 includes a feature called query notifications, which use the Microsoft SQL Server 2005 Service Broker in the background. The Service Broker can automatically send a message to an application when data changes in the database.

> **WARNING**
>
> You can create two types of databases with SQL Server Express: a Local or a Server database. You should not use Push dependencies with a Local database. You should use Push dependencies only with a Server database.
>
> You cannot create new Server databases when using Visual Web Developer. You can create a Server database by using the full version of Visual Studio .NET 2005 or by downloading Microsoft SQL Server Management Studio Express from the Microsoft MSDN website (msdn.microsoft.com).

The advantage of using Push dependencies rather than Polling dependencies is that your ASP.NET application does not need to continuously poll your database for changes. When a change happens, your database is responsible for notifying your application of the change.

Now the bad news. There are significant limitations on the types of queries that you can use with Push dependencies. Here are some of the more significant limitations:

- The query must use two-part table names (for example, dbo.Movies instead of Movies) to refer to tables.

- The query must contain an explicit list of column names (you cannot use *).

- The query cannot reference a view, derived table, temporary table, or table variable.

- The query cannot reference large object types such as Text, NText, and Image columns.

- The query cannot contain a subquery, outer join, or self join.

- The query cannot use the DISTINCT, COMPUTE, COMPUTE BY, or INSERT keywords.

- The query cannot use many aggregate functions including AVG, COUNT(*), MAX, and MIN.

This is not a complete list of query limitations. For the complete list, refer to the Creating a Query for Notification topic in the SQL Server 2005 Books Online or the MSDN website (msdn.Microsoft.com).

For example, the following simple query won't work:

```
SELECT * FROM Movies
```

This query won't work for two reasons. First, you cannot use the asterisk (*) to represent columns. Second, you must supply a two-part table name. The following query, on the other hand, will work:

```
SELECT Title, Director FROM dbo.Movies
```

You can use Push SQL cache dependencies with stored procedures. However, each SELECT statement in the stored procedure must meet all the requirements just listed.

Configuring Push SQL Cache Dependencies

You must perform two configuration steps to enable Push SQL cache dependencies:

- You must configure your database by enabling the SQL Server 2005 Service Broker.

- You must configure your application by starting the notification listener.

In this section, you learn how to perform both of these configuration steps.

23

WARNING

Unfortunately, when a Push SQL cache dependency fails, it fails silently, without adding an error message to the Event Log. This makes the situation especially difficult to debug. I recommend that after you make the configuration changes discussed in this section that you restart both your web server and database server.

Configuring a Database for Push SQL Cache Dependencies

Before you can use Push SQL cache dependencies, you must enable the Microsoft SQL Server 2005 Service Broker. You can check whether the Service Broker is activated for a particular database by executing the following SQL query:

```
SELECT name, is_broker_enabled FROM sys.databases
```

If the Service Broker is not enabled for a database, then you can enable it by executing an `ALTER DATABASE` command. For example, the following SQL command enables the Service Broker for a database named MyMovies:

```
ALTER DATABASE MyMovies SET ENABLE_BROKER
```

Finally, the ASP.NET process must be supplied with adequate permissions to subscribe to query notifications. When an ASP.NET page is served from Internet Information Server, the page executes in the context of the `NETWORK SERVICE` account (in the case of Microsoft Windows Server 2003) or the `ASPNET` account (in the case of other operating systems such as Windows XP).

Executing the following SQL command provides the local `ASPNET` account on a server named YOURSERVER with the required permissions:

```
GRANT SUBSCRIBE QUERY NOTIFICATIONS TO "YOURSERVER\ASPNET"
```

When you request an ASP.NET page when using the Visual Web Developer web server, an ASP.NET page executes in the security context of your current user account. Therefore, when using a file system website, you'll need to grant `SUBSCRIBE QUERY NOTIFICATIONS` permissions to your current account.

NOTE

Push SQL cache dependencies do not use the SQL Server 2005 Notification Services.

Configuring an Application for Push SQL Cache Dependencies

Before you can receive change notifications in your application, you must enable the query notification listener. You can enable the listener with the `Global.asax` file in Listing 23.45.

LISTING 23.45   Global.asax

```
<%@ Application Language="VB" %>
<%@ Import Namespace="System.Data.SqlClient" %>
<%@ Import Namespace="System.Web.Configuration" %>
<script runat="server">
    Private Sub Application_Start(ByVal sender As Object,
➥ByVal e As EventArgs)
        ' Enable Push SQL cache dependencies
        Dim conString As String =
➥ WebConfigurationManager.ConnectionStrings("MyMovies").ConnectionString
        SqlDependency.Start(conString)
    End Sub
</script>
```

The `Application_Start` handler executes once when your application first starts. In Listing 23.45, the `SqlDependency.Start()` method is called with a connection string to a SQL Express server database named MyMovies.

> **WARNING**
>
> The code in Listing 23.45 is commented out in the `Global.asax` file on the CD that accompanies this book so that it won't interfere with all the previous code samples discussed in this chapter. You'll need to remove the comments to use the code samples in the following sections.

Using Push SQL Cache Dependencies with Page Output Caching

You can use Push SQL cache dependencies when caching an entire ASP.NET page. If the results of any SQL command contained in the page changes, then the page is dropped automatically from the cache.

The `SqlCommand` object includes a property named the `NotificationAutoEnlist` property. This property has the value `True` by default. When `NotificationAutoEnlist` is enabled, a Push cache dependency is created between the page and the command automatically.

For example, the page in Listing 23.46 includes an `<%@ OutputCache %>` directive that includes a `SqlDependency` attribute. This attribute is set to the special value `CommandNotification`.

LISTING 23.46   PushSQLOutputCache.aspx

```
<%@ Page Language="C#" %>
<%@ OutputCache Duration="9999" VaryByParam="none"
  SqlDependency="CommandNotification" %>
<!DOCTYPE html PUBLIC "-//W3C//DTD XHTML 1.0 Transitional//EN"
  "http://www.w3.org/TR/xhtml1/DTD/xhtml1-transitional.dtd">
<html xmlns="http://www.w3.org/1999/xhtml" >
```

23

LISTING 23.46 Continued

```
<head id="Head1" runat="server">
    <title>Push SQL Output Cache</title>
</head>
<body>
    <form id="form1" runat="server">
    <div>

    <%= DateTime.Now.ToString("T") %>
    <hr />

    <asp:GridView
        id="grdMovies"
        DataSourceID="srcMovies"
        Runat="server" />

    <asp:SqlDataSource
        id="srcMovies"
        ConnectionString="<%$ ConnectionStrings:MyMovies %>"
        SelectCommand="SELECT Title, Director FROM dbo.Movies"
        Runat="server" />

    </div>
    </form>
</body>
</html>
```

The page in Listing 23.46 includes a `SqlDataSource` control that retrieves all the records from the Movies database table. Notice that the `SqlDataSource` control uses a SQL query that explicitly lists column names and uses a two-part table name. These are requirements when using Push dependencies.

The page in Listing 23.46 displays the current time. If you request the page in your browser, and refresh the page, the time does not change. The time does not change until you modify the Movies database table.

> **WARNING**
>
> The page in Listing 23.46 connects to a Server database named MyMovies. You should not use Push dependencies with a Local SQL Express database. The page uses a database table named Movies, which was created with the following SQL command:
>
> ```
> CREATE TABLE Movies
> (
>   Id int IDENTITY NOT NULL,
>   Title nvarchar(100) NOT NULL,
> ```

```
    Director nvarchar(50) NOT NULL,
    EntryDate datetime NOT NULL DEFAULT GetDate()
)
```

WARNING

You cannot use Push SQL cache dependencies with an `<%@ OutputCache %>` directive included in a User Control. In other words, you cannot use Push SQL cache dependencies with Partial Page Caching.

Using Push SQL Cache Dependencies with DataSource Caching

You also can use Push SQL cache dependencies with both the `SqlDataSource` and `ObjectDataSource` controls by setting the `SqlCacheDependency` property. When using Push rather than Polling dependencies, you need to set the `SqlCacheDependency` property to the value `CommandNotification`.

For example, the page in Listing 23.47 contains a `SqlDataSource` control that has both its `EnableCaching` and `SqlDependency` properties set.

LISTING 23.47   PushSQLDataSourceCache.aspx

```
<%@ Page Language="VB" %>
<!DOCTYPE html PUBLIC "-//W3C//DTD XHTML 1.0 Transitional//EN"
 "http://www.w3.org/TR/xhtml1/DTD/xhtml1-transitional.dtd">
<script runat="server">

    Sub srcMovies_Selecting(ByVal sender As Object,
➥ByVal e As SqlDataSourceSelectingEventArgs)
        lblMessage.Text = "Retrieving data from database"
    End Sub
</script>
<html xmlns="http://www.w3.org/1999/xhtml" >
<head id="Head1" runat="server">
    <title>Push SQL DataSource Cache</title>
</head>
<body>
    <form id="form1" runat="server">
    <div>

    <asp:Label
        id="lblMessage"
        EnableViewState="false"
        Runat="server" />
    <hr />
```

23

LISTING 23.47   Continued

```
<asp:GridView
    id="grdMovies"
    DataSourceID="srcMovies"
    Runat="server" />

<asp:SqlDataSource
    id="srcMovies"
    ConnectionString="<%$ ConnectionStrings:MyMovies %>"
    SelectCommand="SELECT Title, Director FROM dbo.Movies"
    EnableCaching="true"
    SqlCacheDependency="CommandNotification"
    OnSelecting="srcMovies_Selecting"
    Runat="server" />

</div>
</form>
</body>
</html>
```

In Listing 23.47, the SqlDataSource control includes a Selecting event handler. Because this event is raised when the data cannot be retrieved from the cache, you can use this event to determine when the data is retrieved from the cache or the database server (see Figure 23.17).

> **WARNING**
>
> The page in Listing 23.47 connects to a Server database named MyMovies. You should not use Push dependencies with a Local SQL Express database. The page uses a database table named Movies, which was created with the following SQL command:
>
> ```
> CREATE TABLE Movies
> (
>   Id int IDENTITY NOT NULL,
>   Title nvarchar(100) NOT NULL,
>   Director nvarchar(50) NOT NULL,
>   EntryDate datetime NOT NULL DEFAULT GetDate()
> )
> ```

Using Push SQL Cache Dependencies with Data Caching

You can use Push SQL cache dependencies when working with the Cache object. You represent a Push SQL cache dependency with an instance of the SqlCacheDependency class.

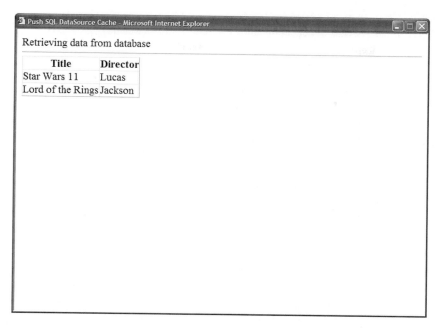

FIGURE 23.17   Using Push SQL cache dependencies with a `DataSource` control.

For example, in the `Page_Load()` handler in Listing 23.48, a `DataTable` is added to the cache that represents the contents of the Movies database table. The `DataTable` is displayed in a `GridView` control.

LISTING 23.48   PushSQLDataCache.aspx

```
<%@ Page Language="VB" Trace="true" %>
<%@ Import Namespace="System.Data" %>
<%@ Import Namespace="System.Data.SqlClient" %>
<%@ Import Namespace="System.Web.Configuration" %>
<!DOCTYPE html PUBLIC "-//W3C//DTD XHTML 1.0 Transitional//EN"
  "http://www.w3.org/TR/xhtml1/DTD/xhtml1-transitional.dtd">
<script runat="server">

    Private  Sub Page_Load()
        Dim movies As DataTable = CType(Cache("Movies"), DataTable)
        If IsNothing(movies) Then
            Trace.Warn("Retrieving data from database")
            Dim conString As String =
➥WebConfigurationManager.ConnectionStrings("MyMovies").ConnectionString
            Dim dad As New SqlDataAdapter("SELECT Title,Director FROM dbo.Movies",
➥conString)
```

LISTING 23.48   Continued

```
                Dim sqlDepend As New SqlCacheDependency(dad.SelectCommand)
                movies = New DataTable()
                dad.Fill(movies)

                Cache.Insert("Movies", movies, sqlDepend)
        End If
        grdMovies.DataSource = movies
        grdMovies.DataBind()
    End Sub
</script>
<html xmlns="http://www.w3.org/1999/xhtml" >
<head id="Head1" runat="server">
    <title>Push SQL Data Cache</title>
</head>
<body>
    <form id="form1" runat="server">
    <div>

    <asp:GridView
        id="grdMovies"
        Runat="server" />

    </div>
    </form>
</body>
</html>
```

Notice that an instance of the SqlCacheDependency class is created. A SqlCommand object is passed to the constructor for the SqlCacheDependency class. If the results of the SqlCommand changes, then the DataTable will be dropped automatically from the cache.

The order of the commands here is important. You need to create the SqlCacheDependency object before you execute the command. If you call the Fill() method before you create the SqlCacheDependency object, then the dependency is ignored.

> **WARNING**
>
> The page in Listing 23.48 connects to a Server database named MyMovies. You should not use Push dependencies with a Local SQL Express database. The page uses a database table named Movies, which was created with the following SQL command:

```
CREATE TABLE Movies
(
    Id int IDENTITY NOT NULL,
    Title nvarchar(100) NOT NULL,
    Director nvarchar(50) NOT NULL,
    EntryDate datetime NOT NULL DEFAULT GetDate()
)
```

Summary

In this chapter, you learned how to improve the performance of your ASP.NET applications by taking advantage of caching. In the first part of this chapter, you learned how to use each of the different types of caching technologies supported by the ASP.NET Framework.

First, you learned how to use Page Output Caching to cache the entire rendered contents of a page. You learned how to create different cached versions of the same page when the page is requested with different parameters, headers, and browsers. You also learned how to remove pages programmatically from the Page Output Cache. Finally, we discussed how you can define Cache Profiles in a web configuration file.

Next, you learned how to use Partial Page Caching to apply different caching policies to different regions in a page. You learned how to use post-cache substitution to dynamically inject content into a page that has been output cached. You also learned how to use User Controls to cache different areas of a page.

We also discussed how you can cache data by using the different DataSource controls. You learned how to enable caching when working with the SqlDataSource, ObjectDataSource, and XmlDataSource controls.

Next, you learned how to use the Cache object to cache items programmatically. You learned how to add items to the cache with different expiration policies and dependencies. You also learned how to configure the maximum size of the cache in the web configuration file.

Finally, we discussed SQL cache dependencies. You learned how to use SQL cache dependencies to reload database data in the cache automatically when the data in the underlying database changes. You learned how to use both Polling and Push SQL cache dependencies with Page Output Caching, DataSource Caching, and the Cache object.

CHAPTER 24

Localizing Applications for Multiple Languages

You can localize an ASP.NET website so that it supports multiple languages and cultures. For example, you might need to create both an English language and Spanish language version of the same website.

One approach to localization is to simply create multiple copies of the same website and translate each copy into a different language. This is a common approach when building ASP Classic (or even ASP.NET 1.1) websites. The problem with this approach is it creates a website maintenance nightmare. Whenever you need to make a change to the website—no matter how simple—you must make the change in each copy of the website.

When building ASP.NET 2.0 applications, you do not need to create multiple copies of a website to support multiple languages. Instead, you can take advantage of resource files. A resource file contains language-specific content. For example, one resource file might contain a Spanish version of all the text in your website, and a second resource file might contain the Indonesian version of all the text in your website.

In this chapter, you learn how to localize ASP.NET applications. First, you learn how to set the culture of the current page. You learn how to use both the Culture and UICulture properties. You also learn how to detect users' preferred languages automatically through their browser settings.

Next, local resources are explored. A local resource contains content that is scoped to a particular file such as an ASP.NET page. You learn how to use both implicit and explicit resource expressions.

This chapter also examines global resources. A global resource contains content that can be used in any page within an application. For example, you can place the title of your website in a global resource file.

Finally, the ASP.NET Localize control is discussed. You learn how to use this control in your pages to localize big chunks of page text.

Setting the Current Culture

Two main properties of the Page class have an effect on localization:

- UICulture
- Culture

The UICulture property is used to specify which resource files are loaded for the page. The resource files can contain all the text content of your pages translated into a particular language. You can set this property to any standard culture name. This property is discussed in detail during the discussion of using local and global resources later in this chapter.

The Culture property, on the other hand, determines how strings such as dates, numerals, and currency amounts are formatted. It also determines how values are compared and sorted. For example, by modifying the Culture property, you can display dates with language-specific month names such as January (English), Januar (German), or Enero (Spanish).

Both the UICulture and Culture properties accept standard culture names for their values. Culture names follow the RFC 1766 and RFC 3066 standards maintained by the Internet Engineering Task Force (IETF). The IETF website is located at http://www.IETF.org.

Here are some common culture names:

- de-DE = German (Germany)
- en-US = English (United States)
- en-GB = English (United Kingdom)
- es-MX = Spanish (Mexico)
- id-ID = Indonesian (Indonesia)
- zh-CN = Chinese (China)

Notice that each culture name consists of two parts. The first part represents the language code and the second part represents the country/region code. If you specify a culture name and do not provide a country/region code—for example, en—then you have specified something called a *neutral culture*. If you provide both a language code and a country/region code—for example, en-US—then you have specified something called a *specific culture*.

The `Culture` property must always be set to a specific culture. This makes sense because, for example, different English speakers use different currency symbols. The `UICulture` property, on the other hand, can be set to either a neutral or specific culture name. Text written in Canadian English is pretty much the same as text written in U.S. English.

You can set the `UICulture` and `Culture` properties to the same value or different values. For example, if you are creating an online store then you might want to set the `UICulture` property to the value de-DE to display German product descriptions. However, you might want to set the `Culture` property to the value en-US to display product prices in United State currency amounts.

Setting a Culture Manually

You can set either the `UICulture` or `Culture` properties by using the <%@ Page %> directive. For example, the page in Listing 24.1 sets both properties to the value id-ID (Indonesian).

LISTING 24.1   Bagus.aspx

```
<%@ Page Language="VB" Culture="id-ID" UICulture="id-ID" %>
<!DOCTYPE html PUBLIC "-//W3C//DTD XHTML 1.1//EN"
    "http://www.w3.org/TR/xhtml11/DTD/xhtml11.dtd">
<script runat="server">

    Sub Page_Load()
        lblDate.Text = DateTime.Now.ToString("D")
        lblPrice.Text = (512.33D).ToString("c")
    End Sub
</script>
<html xmlns="http://www.w3.org/1999/xhtml" >
<head id="Head1" runat="server">
    <title>Bagus</title>
</head>
<body>
    <form id="form1" runat="server">
    <div>

    Today's date is:
    <br />
    <asp:Label
        id="lblDate"
        Runat="server" />
```

LISTING 24.1   Continued

```
    <hr />
    The price of the product is:
    <br />
    <asp:Label
        id="lblPrice"
        Runat="server" />

    </div>
    </form>
</body>
</html>
```

The page in Listing 24.1 displays a date and a currency amount. Because the `Culture` property is set to the value `id-ID` in the `<%@ Page %>` directive, both the date and currency amount are formatted with Indonesian cultural conventions (see Figure 24.1).

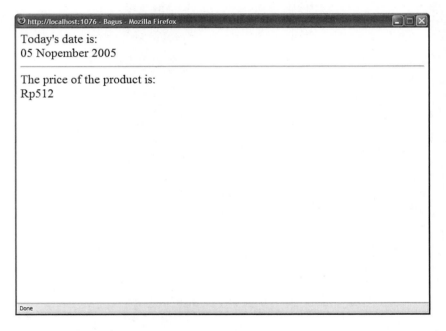

FIGURE 24.1   Displaying a localized date and price.

The date is displayed like this:

05 Nopember 2005

The currency amount is displayed as an Indonesian Rupiah amount like this:

Rp512

> **NOTE**
>
> Setting the Culture does not actually convert a currency amount. Setting a particular culture only formats the currency as appropriate for a particular culture. If you need to convert currency amounts, then you need to use a Web service: Conversion rates change minute by minute. See, for example, http://www.xmethods.com/.

Instead of using the <%@ Page %> directive to set the Culture or UICulture properties, you can set these properties programmatically. For example, the page in Listing 24.2 enables you to select a particular culture from a drop-down list of cultures (see Figure 24.2).

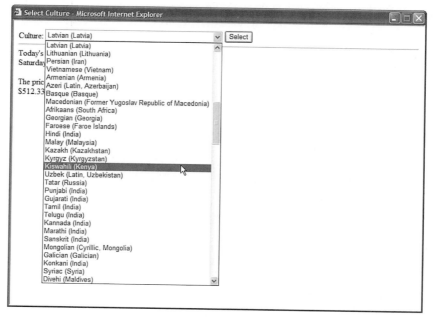

FIGURE 24.2   Selecting a culture from a DropDownList control.

LISTING 24.2 SelectCulture.aspx

```
<%@ Page Language="VB" %>
<!DOCTYPE html PUBLIC "-//W3C//DTD XHTML 1.1//EN"
    "http://www.w3.org/TR/xhtml11/DTD/xhtml11.dtd">
<script runat="server">
    Sub btnSelect_Click(ByVal sender As Object, ByVal e As EventArgs)
        Culture = ddlCulture.SelectedValue
    End Sub

    Sub Page_PreRender()
        lblDate.Text = DateTime.Now.ToString("D")
        lblPrice.Text = (512.33D).ToString("c")
    End Sub
</script>
<html xmlns="http://www.w3.org/1999/xhtml" >
<head id="Head1" runat="server">
    <title>Select Culture</title>
</head>
<body>
    <form id="form1" runat="server">
    <div>

    <asp:Label
        id="lblCulture"
        Text="Culture:"
        AssociatedControlID="ddlCulture"
        Runat="server" />

    <asp:DropDownList
        id="ddlCulture"
        DataTextField="DisplayName"
        DataValueField="Name"
        DataSourceID="srcCultures"
        Runat="server" />

    <asp:Button
        id="btnSelect"
        Text="Select"
        Runat="server" OnClick="btnSelect_Click" />


    <asp:ObjectDataSource
        id="srcCultures"
        TypeName="System.Globalization.CultureInfo"
        SelectMethod="GetCultures"
```

LISTING 24.2   Continued

```
            Runat="server">
            <SelectParameters>
                <asp:Parameter Name="types"
                    DefaultValue="SpecificCultures" />
            </SelectParameters>
        </asp:ObjectDataSource>

        <hr />

        Today's date is:
        <br />
        <asp:Label
            id="lblDate"
            Runat="server" />

        <br /><br />

        The price of the product is:
        <br />
        <asp:Label
            id="lblPrice"
            Runat="server" />

        </div>
        </form>
</body>
</html>
```

The DropDownList control in Listing 24.2 is bound to an ObjectDataSource control, which retrieves a list of all the culture names supported by the .NET Framework. The culture names are retrieved during a call to the GetCultures() method of the CultureInfo class.

When you click the button to select a culture, the btnSelect_Click() method executes and assigns the name of the selected culture to the page's Culture property. When you select a new culture, the formatting applied to the date and currency amount changes.

Several websites on the Internet display a page that requires the user to select a language before entering the main website. For example, the Federal Express website (www.FedEx.com) requires you to select a country before entering the website.

You can take advantage of the Profile object to store a user's preferred culture. That way, a user needs to select a culture only once and the culture is then used any time the user returns to your website in the future. The page in Listing 24.3 illustrates this approach.

LISTING 24.3   SelectCultureProfile.aspx

```
<%@ Page Language="VB" %>
<!DOCTYPE html PUBLIC "-//W3C//DTD XHTML 1.1//EN"
    "http://www.w3.org/TR/xhtml11/DTD/xhtml11.dtd">
<script runat="server">

    Protected Overrides Sub InitializeCulture()
        Culture = Profile.UserCulture
        UICulture = Profile.UserUICulture
    End Sub


    Protected Sub btnSelect_Click(ByVal sender As Object, ByVal e As EventArgs)
        Profile.UserCulture = ddlCulture.SelectedValue
        Profile.UserUICulture = ddlCulture.SelectedValue
        Response.Redirect(Request.Path)
    End Sub

    Private Sub Page_PreRender()
        lblDate.Text = DateTime.Now.ToString("D")
        lblPrice.Text = (512.33D).ToString("c")
    End Sub
</script>
<html xmlns="http://www.w3.org/1999/xhtml" >
<head id="Head1" runat="server">
    <title>Select Culture Profile</title>
</head>
<body>
    <form id="form1" runat="server">
    <div>

    <asp:Label
        id="lblCulture"
        Text="Culture:"
        AssociatedControlID="ddlCulture"
        Runat="server" />

    <asp:DropDownList
        id="ddlCulture"
        DataTextField="DisplayName"
        DataValueField="Name"
        DataSourceID="srcCultures"
        Runat="server" />

    <asp:Button
```

LISTING 24.3   Continued

```
            id="btnSelect"
            Text="Select"
            Runat="server" OnClick="btnSelect_Click" />


    <asp:ObjectDataSource
        id="srcCultures"
        TypeName="System.Globalization.CultureInfo"
        SelectMethod="GetCultures"
        Runat="server">
        <SelectParameters>
            <asp:Parameter Name="types" DefaultValue="SpecificCultures" />
        </SelectParameters>
    </asp:ObjectDataSource>

    <hr />

    Today's date is:
    <br />
    <asp:Label
        id="lblDate"
        Runat="server" />

    <br /><br />

    The price of the product is:
    <br />
    <asp:Label
        id="lblPrice"
        Runat="server" />

    </div>
    </form>
</body>
</html>
```

You should notice two things about the page in Listing 24.3. First, notice that the culture is set in the InitializeCulture() method. This method overrides the InitializeCulture() method of the base Page class and sets the UICulture and Culture properties by using the Profile object.

Second, notice that the btnSelect_Click() handler updates the properties of the Profile object and redirects the page back to itself. This is done so that the InitializeCulture() method executes after a user changes the selected culture.

The page in Listing 24.3 uses the `Profile` defined in the web configuration file contained in Listing 24.4.

LISTING 24.4   Web.Config

```
<?xml version="1.0"?>
<configuration xmlns="http://schemas.microsoft.com/.NetConfiguration/v2.0">
  <system.web>
    <anonymousIdentification enabled="true"/>

    <profile>
      <properties>
        <add
          name="UserCulture"
          defaultValue="en-US" />
        <add
          name="UserUICulture"
          defaultValue="en"/>
      </properties>
    </profile>
  </system.web>
</configuration>
```

Notice that the web configuration file in Listing 24.4 includes a `anonymousIdentification` element. Including this element causes a profile to be created for a user even if the user has not been authenticated.

Automatically Detecting a Culture

In the previous section, you learned how to set the `UICulture` and `Culture` properties by allowing the user to select a particular culture from a `DropDownList` control. Instead of requiring users to select their culture, you can automatically detect users' cultures through their browser settings.

Whenever a browser makes a request for a web page, the browser sends an Accept-Language header. The Accept-Language header contains a list of the user's preferred languages.

You can set your preferred languages when using Microsoft Internet Explorer or Mozilla Firefox by selecting the menu option Tools, Internet Options and clicking the Languages button. You can then create an ordered list of your preferred languages (see Figure 24.3). When using Opera, select the menu option Tools, Preferences and click the Details button (see Figure 24.4).

FIGURE 24.3   Setting your preferred language with Internet Explorer.

FIGURE 24.4   Setting your preferred language with Opera.

You can retrieve the value of the Accept-Language header by using the
Request.UserLanguages property. For example, the page in Listing 24.5 displays a list of
the languages retrieved from a browser's Accept-Language header (see Figure 24.5).

FIGURE 24.5   Displaying a browser's language settings.

LISTING 24.5   ShowAcceptLanguages.aspx

```
<%@ Page Language="VB" %>
<!DOCTYPE html PUBLIC "-//W3C//DTD XHTML 1.1//EN"
    "http://www.w3.org/TR/xhtml11/DTD/xhtml11.dtd">
<script runat="server">

    Sub Page_Load()
        bltAcceptLanguages.DataSource = Request.UserLanguages
        bltAcceptLanguages.DataBind()
    End Sub
</script>
<html xmlns="http://www.w3.org/1999/xhtml" >
<head id="Head1" runat="server">
    <title>Show Accept Languages</title>
</head>
<body>
    <form id="form1" runat="server">
    <div>

    <asp:BulletedList
        id="bltAcceptLanguages"
        Runat="server" />

    </div>
```

LISTING 24.5   Continued

```
        </form>
    </body>
</html>
```

If you want to set the `Culture` or `UICulture` properties automatically by detecting the browser's Accept-Language header, then you can set either of these properties to the value auto. For example, the page in Listing 24.6 automatically displays the date and currency amount according to the user's preferred language.

LISTING 24.6   `SelectCultureAuto.aspx`

```
<%@ Page Language="VB" Culture="auto:en-US" UICulture="auto:en-US"%>
<!DOCTYPE html PUBLIC "-//W3C//DTD XHTML 1.1//EN"
    "http://www.w3.org/TR/xhtml11/DTD/xhtml11.dtd">
<script runat="server">

    Sub Page_PreRender()
        lblDate.Text = DateTime.Now.ToString("D")
        lblPrice.Text = (512.33D).ToString("c")
    End Sub
</script>
<html xmlns="http://www.w3.org/1999/xhtml" >
<head id="Head1" runat="server">
    <title>Select Culture Auto</title>
</head>
<body>
    <form id="form1" runat="server">
    <div>

    Today's date is:
    <br />
    <asp:Label
        id="lblDate"
        Runat="server" />

    <br /><br />

    The price of the product is:
    <br />
    <asp:Label
        id="lblPrice"
        Runat="server" />

    </div>
    </form>
</body>
</html>
```

24

In the <%@ Page %> directive in Listing 24.6, both the Culture and UICulture attributes are set to the value auto:en-US. The culture name that appears after the colon enables you to specify a default culture when a language preference cannot be detected from the browser.

> **WARNING**
>
> Don't assume that all values of the Accept-Language header retrieved from a browser are valid culture names. Most browsers enable users to enter a "user-defined" language, which may or may not be valid.

Setting the Culture in the Web Configuration File

Rather than set the Culture and UICulture properties in each page, you can set these properties once in the web configuration file. Typically, you should take this approach because it makes your website easier to maintain.

The web configuration file in Listing 24.7 sets both the Culture and UICulture properties to the value de-DE (German).

LISTING 24.7   Web.Config

```
<?xml version="1.0"?>
<configuration xmlns="http://schemas.microsoft.com/.NetConfiguration/v2.0">
<system.web>

  <globalization
    culture="de-DE"
    uiCulture="de-DE" />

</system.web>
</configuration>
```

The web configuration file in Listing 24.7 sets the Culture and UICulture for all pages to the value de-DE (German).

If you prefer, you can use the value auto in the web configuration file if you want the culture to be automatically detected based on the value of the browser Accept-Language header. If you need to override the configuration settings in the web configuration file in a particular page, then you can simply set the Culture and UICulture properties in the page.

Culture and ASP.NET Controls

The value of the Culture property automatically has an effect on the rendering behavior of ASP.NET controls such as the Calendar control. For example, Listing 24.8 uses the ASP.NET Calendar controll to display a calendar (see Figure 24.6).

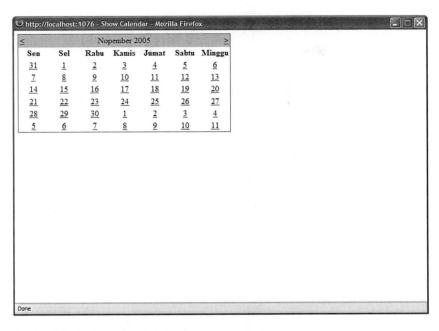

FIGURE 24.6   Displaying a localized Calendar control.

LISTING 24.8   ShowCalendar.aspx

```
<%@ Page Language="VB" Culture="id-ID" %>
<!DOCTYPE html PUBLIC "-//W3C//DTD XHTML 1.1//EN"
    "http://www.w3.org/TR/xhtml11/DTD/xhtml11.dtd">
<html xmlns="http://www.w3.org/1999/xhtml" >
<head id="Head1" runat="server">
    <title>Show Calendar</title>
</head>
<body>
    <form id="form1" runat="server">
    <div>

    <asp:Calendar
        id="Calendar1"
        Runat="server" />

    </div>
    </form>
</body>
</html>
```

The `Culture` attribute in the `<%@ Page %>` directive is set to the value `id-ID` (Indonesian). When the calendar is rendered, Indonesian month names are displayed in the calendar.

Using the `CultureInfo` Class

The `CultureInfo` class contains information about more than 150 different cultures. You can use the methods of this class in your code to retrieve information about a specific culture and use the information when formatting values such as dates, numbers, and currency amounts.

To represent a culture with the `CultureInfo` class, you can instantiate the class by passing a culture name to the class constructor like this:

```
Dim culture As New CultureInfo("de-DE")
```

You can also use any of the following methods of the `CultureInfo` class to retrieve information about a culture or cultures:

- `CreateSpecificCulture`—Enables you to create a `CultureInfo` object by supplying the name of a specific culture.

- `GetCultureInfo`—Enables you to create a `CultureInfo` object by supplying an identifier, culture name, or `CompareInfo` and `TextInfo` object.

- `GetCultureInfoByIetfLanguageTag`—Enables you to create a `CultureInfo` object efficiently by supplying a culture name.

- `GetCultures`—Enables you to retrieve an array of cultures.

The `CultureInfo` class lives in the `System.Globalization` namespace. Before you can use the `CultureInfo` class, you need to import this namespace.

Using the `CultureInfo` Class to Format String Values

To this point, the culture has been set at the level of an individual ASP.NET page or the level of an entire ASP.NET application. However, you might need to take advantage of locale-specific formatting at a more granular level. You can use the `CultureInfo` class to format a particular value independent of the `Culture` set for the page.

When you use the `ToString()` method to format dates, times, numbers, and currency amounts, you can supply an additional parameter that formats the value in accordance with a specific culture. For example, the page in Listing 24.9 formats two sets of date and time values.

LISTING 24.9 ToStringCulture.aspx

```
<%@ Page Language="VB" %>
<%@ Import Namespace="System.Globalization" %>
<!DOCTYPE html PUBLIC "-//W3C//DTD XHTML 1.1//EN"
    "http://www.w3.org/TR/xhtml11/DTD/xhtml11.dtd">
```

LISTING 24.9   Continued

```
<script runat="server">

    Private  Sub Page_Load()
        ' Get German Culture Info
        Dim gCulture As New CultureInfo("de-DE")

        ' Use culture when formatting strings
        lblGermanDate.Text = DateTime.Now.ToString("D", gCulture)
        lblGermanPrice.Text = (512.33D).ToString("c", gCulture)

        ' Get Indonesian Culture Info
        Dim iCulture As New CultureInfo("id-ID")

        ' Use culture when formatting strings
        lblIndonesianDate.Text = DateTime.Now.ToString("D", iCulture)
        lblIndonesianPrice.Text = (512.33D).ToString("c", iCulture)
    End Sub
</script>
<html xmlns="http://www.w3.org/1999/xhtml" >
<head id="Head1" runat="server">
    <title>ToString Culture</title>
</head>
<body>
    <form id="form1" runat="server">
    <div>

    <h1>German</h1>

    Today's date is:
    <br />
    <asp:Label
        id="lblGermanDate"
        Runat="server" />

    <br /><br />

    The price of the product is:
    <br />
    <asp:Label
        id="lblGermanPrice"
        Runat="server" />

    <h1>Indonesian</h1>

    Today's date is:
    <br />
    <asp:Label
```

24

LISTING 24.9 Continued

```
        id="lblIndonesianDate"
        Runat="server" />

    <br /><br />

    The price of the product is:
    <br />
    <asp:Label
        id="lblIndonesianPrice"
        Runat="server" />


    </div>
    </form>
</body>
</html>
```

The first date and time is formatted with German cultural conventions, and the second date and time is formatted with Indonesian cultural conventions (see Figure 24.7). Notice that two CultureInfo objects, corresponding to two cultures, are created in the Page_Load() method.

FIGURE 24.7 Formatting with the ToString() method.

Comparing and Sorting String Values

Different cultures follow different conventions when comparing and sorting string values. If you need to compare or sort string values in your code, then you should use the `String.Compare()` method and optionally supply the method with an instance of the `CultureInfo` object.

The `String.Compare()` method returns one of the following values:

- Negative Integer—The first string is less than the second string
- Zero—The first string is equal to the second string
- Positive Integer—The first string is greater than the second string

For example, the following conditional compares two strings, using the current culture set for the page:

```
If String.Compare("Hello", "Hello") = 0 Then
  lblResult.Text = "The strings are the same!"
End If
```

The following conditional uses a specific culture to perform a string comparison:

```
If String.Compare("Hello", "Hello", True, New CultureInfo("de-DE")) = 0 Then
  lblResult.Text = "The strings are the same!"
End If
```

In this case, the first two parameters passed to the `String.Compare()` method are the strings being compared. The third parameter indicates whether the comparison performed should be case sensitive or not. Finally, the last parameter represents a `CultureInfo` object.

Creating Local Resources

If you need to modify the text (or other content) in a page depending on a user's language, then you can take advantage of resource files. Each resource file can contain page text translated into a particular language.

The ASP.NET Framework supports two types of resource files: local and global resources. In this section, you learn how to use local resources. A local resource is scoped to a particular file such as an ASP.NET page.

Explicit Localization Expressions

The page in Listing 24.10 is a very simple page. It contains a button labeled "Click Here!" and displays the text "Thank You!" after you click the button.

LISTING 24.10   SimplePage.aspx

```
<%@ Page Language="VB" %>
<!DOCTYPE html PUBLIC "-//W3C//DTD XHTML 1.1//EN"
    "http://www.w3.org/TR/xhtml11/DTD/xhtml11.dtd">
<script runat="server">

    Sub btnSubmit_Click(ByVal sender As Object, ByVal e As EventArgs)
        lblMessage.Visible = True
    End Sub
</script>
<html xmlns="http://www.w3.org/1999/xhtml" >
<head id="Head1" runat="server">
    <title>Simple Page</title>
</head>
<body>
    <form id="form1" runat="server">
    <div>

    <asp:Button
        id="btnSubmit"
        Text="Click Here!"
        OnClick="btnSubmit_Click"
        Runat="server" />

    <br /><br />

    <asp:Label
        id="lblMessage"
        Text="Thank You!"
        Visible="false"
        Runat="server" />

    </div>
    </form>
</body>
</html>
```

The page in Listing 24.10 displays the same text regardless of the language of the user visiting the page. If you want to display text in different languages for different users, then you need to make a few modifications to the page.

The page in Listing 24.11 is a localizable version of the same page.

LISTING 24.11   LocalizablePage.aspx

```
<%@ Page Language="VB" UICulture="auto" %>
<!DOCTYPE html PUBLIC "-//W3C//DTD XHTML 1.1//EN"
    "http://www.w3.org/TR/xhtml11/DTD/xhtml11.dtd">
<script runat="server">

    Sub btnSubmit_Click(ByVal sender As Object, ByVal e As EventArgs)
        lblMessage.Visible = True
    End Sub
</script>
<html xmlns="http://www.w3.org/1999/xhtml" >
<head id="Head1" runat="server">
    <title>Localizable Page</title>
</head>
<body>
    <form id="form1" runat="server">
    <div>

    <asp:Button
        id="btnSubmit"
        Text="<%$ Resources:ClickHere %>"
        OnClick="btnSubmit_Click"
        Runat="server" />

    <br /><br />

    <asp:Label
        id="lblMessage"
        Text="<%$ Resources:ThankYou %>"
        Visible="false"
        Runat="server" />

    </div>
    </form>
</body>
</html>
```

Two types of changes were made to the page in Listing 24.11. First, notice that the
<%@ Page %> directive includes a UICulture attribute that is set to the value auto. When a
user requests the page, a resource file that matches the user's preferred browser language is
loaded automatically.

Second, notice that both the Button and Label controls have been modified. The Button control is declared like this:

```
<asp:Button
    id="btnSubmit"
    Text="<%$ Resources:ClickHere %>"
    OnClick="btnSubmit_Click"
    Runat="server" />
```

The value of the Text property is a resource expression. This resource expression retrieves the value of an entry named ClickHere from the loaded resource file. This resource expression is considered to be an *explicit* resource expression because the property is explicitly set to the value of a particular resource entry.

After you localize a page, you can associate a resource file with the page. All the resource files that you want to associate with a page must be added to a special folder named App_LocalResources. You create the App_LocalResources folder in the same folder as the page that you want to localize. For example, if the page is located in the root of your application, then you would add the App_LocalResources folder to the root folder.

You associate a resource file in the App_LocalResources folder with a particular page by using the following file naming convention:

```
page name.[culture name].resx
```

For example, all the following resource files are associated with the LocalizablePage.aspx page:

```
LocalizablePage.aspx.resx
LocalizablePage.aspx.es-PR.resx
LocalizablePage.aspx.es.resx
```

The first resource file is the default resource file. If none of the other resource files match the user's language settings, then the contents of the default resource file are used.

The second resource file name includes the specific culture name es-PR (Puerto Rican Spanish). If a user's browser is set to Puerto Rican Spanish, then the contents of this resource file are loaded.

Finally, the third resource file name includes the neutral culture name es (Spanish). If a user's preferred language is Spanish, but not Puerto Rican Spanish, then the contents of this resource file are loaded.

You create a resource file when using Visual Web Developing by right-clicking an App_LocalResources folder, selecting Add New Item, and selecting Assembly Resource file. Visual Web Developer automatically displays an editor for the resource file. The editor enables you to enter name and value pairs. For example, the `LocalizablePage.aspx.es.resx` resource file contains the two name/value pairs in Listing 24.12.

LISTING 24.12   `App_LocalResources\LocalizablePage.aspx.es.resx`

Name	Value
ClickHere	chasque aquí
ThankYou	¡Gracias!

Behind the scenes, resource files are XML files. You can open a resource file in Notepad and edit its contents. The ASP.NET Framework dynamically compiles resource files into assemblies in the background.

Implicit Localization Expressions

As an alternative to using explicit localization expressions, you can use an implicit localization expression. An implicit localization expression enables you to localize multiple control properties with one resource key.

The page in Listing 24.13 uses implicit localization expressions.

LISTING 24.13   `LocalizablePageImplicit.aspx`

```
<%@ Page Language="VB" UICulture="auto" %>
<!DOCTYPE html PUBLIC "-//W3C//DTD XHTML 1.1//EN"
    "http://www.w3.org/TR/xhtml11/DTD/xhtml11.dtd">
<script runat="server">

    Sub btnSubmit_Click(ByVal s As Object, ByVal e As EventArgs)
        lblMessage.Visible = True
    End Sub
</script>
<html xmlns="http://www.w3.org/1999/xhtml" >
<head id="Head1" runat="server">
    <title>Localizable Page Implicit</title>
</head>
<body>
    <form id="form1" runat="server">
    <div>

    <asp:Button
        id="btnSubmit"
        meta:resourceKey="btnSubmit"
        Text="Click Me!"
```

LISTING 24.13   Continued

```
            ToolTip="Click to show message"
            OnClick="btnSubmit_Click"
            Runat="server" />

    <br /><br />

    <asp:Label
        id="lblMessage"
        meta:resourceKey="lblMessage"
        Text="Thank You!"
        Visible="false"
        Runat="server" />

    </div>
    </form>
</body>
</html>
```

Notice that both the Button and Label control include a `meta:resourceKey` property. The value of this property represents a resource key in a local resource file.

For example, the resource file in Listing 24.14 contains three entries.

LISTING 24.14   `App_LocalResources\LocalizablePageImplicit.aspx.es.resx`

Name	Value
btnSubmit.Text	chasque aquí
btnSubmit.ToolTip	Chasque aquí para demostrar el mensaje
lblMessage.Text	¡Gracias!

The first two entries set the `Text` and `ToolTip` properties of the `btnSubmit` control. The third entry sets the value of the `Text` property of the `lblMessage` property.

> **WARNING**
>
> When you are ready to start localizing a page, always create a default localization file (for example, `LocalizablePageImplicit.aspx.resx`). If you don't create a default localization file, other culture-specific localization files are ignored.

There are two advantages to using implicit localization expressions over using explicit localization expressions. First, implicit expressions enable you to override multiple control properties by associating a single resource key with the control.

Second, by taking advantage of implicit localization expressions, you can more easily localize an existing website. You simply need to add the `meta:resourceKey` attribute to any control that you need to localize.

Using Local Resources with Page Properties

You can use resource expressions when setting page properties such as the page title. For example, the page in Listing 24.15 uses an explicit resource expression to set the page title.

LISTING 24.15 PageExplicit.aspx

```
<%@ Page Language="VB" UICulture="auto" %>
<!DOCTYPE html PUBLIC "-//W3C//DTD XHTML 1.1//EN"
    "http://www.w3.org/TR/xhtml11/DTD/xhtml11.dtd">
<html xmlns="http://www.w3.org/1999/xhtml" >
<head id="Head1" runat="server">
    <title><asp:Literal Text="<%$ Resources:Title %>" runat="Server" /></title>
</head>
<body>
    <form id="form1" runat="server">
    <div>


    <h1>Page Explicit Localization</h1>



    </div>
    </form>
</body>
</html>
```

In Listing 24.15, the page title is created with a `Literal` control. The `Literal` control contains an explicit resource expression for the value of its `Text` property.

You also can use implicit resource expressions when setting the page title. This approach is illustrated by the page in Listing 24.16.

LISTING 24.16 PageImplicit.aspx

```
<%@ Page Language="VB" UICulture="auto" meta:resourceKey="page" %>
<!DOCTYPE html PUBLIC "-//W3C//DTD XHTML 1.1//EN"
    "http://www.w3.org/TR/xhtml11/DTD/xhtml11.dtd">
<html xmlns="http://www.w3.org/1999/xhtml" >
<head id="Head1" runat="server">
    <title>Page Title</title>
</head>
<body>
    <form id="form1" runat="server">
    <div>


    <h1>Page Implicit Localization</h1>
```

24

LISTING 24.16   Continued

```
    </div>
    </form>
</body>
</html>
```

Notice that the <%@ Page %> directive includes a meta:resourceKey attribute. If a local resource includes a page.Title entry, then the value of this entry is used for the title displayed by the page.

Retrieving Local Resources Programmatically

If you need to retrieve a local resource in your page code, then you can use the GetLocalResourceObject() method. For example, the page in Listing 24.17 grabs a welcome message from a resource file. The welcome message is used to format some text, and then the formatted text is displayed in a Label control.

LISTING 24.17   ProgramLocal.aspx

```
<%@ Page Language="VB" %>
<!DOCTYPE html PUBLIC "-//W3C//DTD XHTML 1.1//EN"
   "http://www.w3.org/TR/xhtml11/DTD/xhtml11.dtd">
<script runat="server">

    sub Page_Load()
        Dim welcomeMessage As String =
➥CType(GetLocalResourceObject("welcomeMessage"), String)
        lblMessage.Text = String.Format(welcomeMessage, "Steve")
    end Sub

</script>
<html xmlns="http://www.w3.org/1999/xhtml" >
<head id="Head1" runat="server">
    <title>Program Local Resource</title>
</head>
<body>
    <form id="form1" runat="server">
    <div>

    <asp:Label
        id="lblMessage"
        Runat="server" />

    </div>
    </form>
</body>
</html>
```

Notice that the result returned from the `GetLocalResourceObject()` must be cast to a string value. As the method name implies, the method returns an object and not a string value.

The resource file associated with the page in Listing 24.17, named `ProgramLocal.aspx.es.resx`, is contained in Listing 24.18.

LISTING 24.18 App_LocalResources\ProgramLocal.aspx.es.resx

Name	Value
welcomeMessage	Welcome {0} to our website!

If someone's browser is set to Spanish as the preferred language, and the user requests the page, then the welcome message is retrieved from this resource file, the name Steve is added to the string, and the result is displayed in the browser (see Figure 24.8).

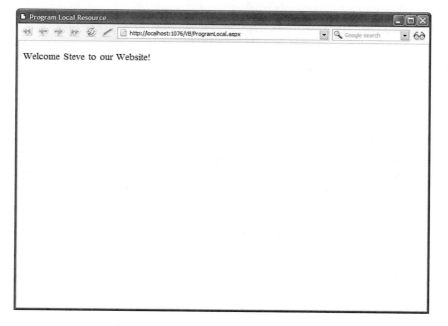

FIGURE 24.8 Retrieving a local resource programmatically.

You also can retrieve local resources in a component. Within a component, use the shared `HttpContext.GetLocalResourceObject()` method. For example, the component in Listing 24.19 grabs the entry named `ClickHere` from the local resource file that corresponds to the page named `LocalizablePage.aspx`.

24

LISTING 24.19   `LocalComponent.cs`

```
Public Class LocalComponent

    Public Shared Function getResource() As String
        Return CType(HttpContext.GetLocalResourceObject("~/LocalizablePage.aspx",
    ➥ "ClickHere"), String)
    End Function

End Class
```

Creating Global Resources

A local resource is scoped to a particular page. A global resource, on the other hand, can be used by any page in an application. Any localized content that you need to share among multiple pages in your website should be added to a global resource file.

You create global resource files by adding the files to a special folder named `App_GlobalResources`. This folder must be located in the root of your application.

For example, the file in Listing 24.20 is a global resource file.

LISTING 24.20   `App_GlobalResources\Site.resx`

Name	Value
Title	My website
Copyright	Copyright © 2006 by the Company

The page in Listing 24.21 uses the entries from the global resource file (see Figure 24.9).

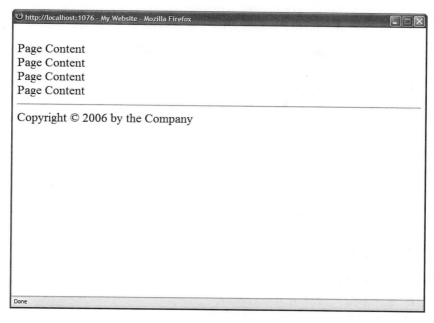

FIGURE 24.9   Displaying global resource entries.

LISTING 24.21   `ShowGlobalPage.aspx`

```
<%@ Page Language="VB" %>
<!DOCTYPE html PUBLIC "-//W3C//DTD XHTML 1.1//EN"
    "http://www.w3.org/TR/xhtml11/DTD/xhtml11.dtd">
<html xmlns="http://www.w3.org/1999/xhtml" >
<head id="Head1" runat="server">
    <title>
    <asp:Literal
        id="ltlTitle"
        Text="<%$ Resources:Site,Title %>"
        Runat="Server" />
    </title>
</head>
<body>
    <form id="form1" runat="server">
    <div>

    <br />Page Content
    <br />Page Content
    <br />Page Content
    <br />Page Content
```

LISTING 24.21   Continued

```
    <hr />
    <asp:Literal
        id="ltlCopyright"
        Text="<%$ Resources:Site,Copyright %>"
        Runat="Server" />

    </div>
    </form>
</body>
</html>
```

Just as you can with a local resource file, you can localize a global resource file by adding culture names to the file name. For example, the page in Listing 24.22 is localized to Spanish.

LISTING 24.22   App_GlobalResources\Site.es.resx

Name	Value
Title	Mi Website
Copyright	Copyright © 2006 de la compañía

If you modify the UICulture attribute contained in the <%@ Page %> directive in Listing 24.21 to the value es, then the resource file in Listing 24.22 will be used with the page. Alternatively, you can set UICulture to the value auto and change your browser's language settings.

Retrieving Global Resources Programmatically

You can retrieve a global resource entry programmatically from any page by using the GetGlobalResourceObject() method. For example, the page in Listing 24.23 grabs the Title entry from the Site resource file and displays the value of the entry in a Label control.

LISTING 24.23   ProgramGlobal.aspx

```
<%@ Page Language="VB" UICulture="auto" %>
<!DOCTYPE html PUBLIC "-//W3C//DTD XHTML 1.1//EN" "http://www.w3.org/TR/
➥xhtml11/DTD/xhtml11.dtd">
<script runat="server">

    Sub Page_Load()
        lblMessage.Text = CType(GetGlobalResourceObject("Site", "Title"), String)
    End Sub
</script>
<html xmlns="http://www.w3.org/1999/xhtml" >
```

LISTING 24.223   Continued

```
<head id="Head1" runat="server">
    <title>Program Global</title>
</head>
<body>
    <form id="form1" runat="server">
    <div>

    <asp:Label
        id="lblMessage"
        Runat="server" />

    </div>
    </form>
</body>
</html>
```

The `GetGlobalResourceObject()` method requires two parameters: the name of the resource class and the name of an entry. The resource class corresponds to the global resource filename.

Using Strongly Typed Localization Expressions

The ASP.NET Framework automatically converts global resources into compiled classes behind the scenes. This enables you to use strongly typed expressions when working with global resources in your code.

When you create a resource, a new class is added automatically to the Resources namespace. The class exposes all the entries of the resource file as properties.

For example, the page in Listing 24.24 retrieves the Title entry from the Site global resource file (`Site.resx` and its culture-specific variations).

LISTING 24.24   ProgramGlobalTyped.aspx

```
<%@ Page Language="VB" UICulture="auto" %>
<!DOCTYPE html PUBLIC "-//W3C//DTD XHTML 1.1//EN"
    "http://www.w3.org/TR/xhtml11/DTD/xhtml11.dtd">
<script runat="server">

    sub Page_Load()
        lblMessage.Text = Resources.Site.Title
    end sub
</script>
<html xmlns="http://www.w3.org/1999/xhtml" >
<head id="Head1" runat="server">
    <title>Program Global Typed</title>
```

LISTING 24.24   Continued

```
</head>
<body>
    <form id="form1" runat="server">
    <div>

    <asp:Label
        id="lblMessage"
        Runat="server" />

    </div>
    </form>
</body>
</html>
```

Notice that you can use the following expression magically to refer to the Title entry in the Site resource file:

```
lblMessage.Text = Resources.Site.Title
```

Using the Localize Control

The ASP.NET Framework includes a control named the Localize control. This control is included in the Framework to make it easier to localize big chunks of text in a page.

For example, the page in Listing 24.25 uses the Localize control in the body of the page.

LISTING 24.25   ShowLocalizeControl.aspx

```
<%@ Page Language="VB" UICulture="auto" %>
<!DOCTYPE html PUBLIC "-//W3C//DTD XHTML 1.1//EN"
    "http://www.w3.org/TR/xhtml11/DTD/xhtml11.dtd">
<html xmlns="http://www.w3.org/1999/xhtml" >
<head id="Head1" runat="server">
    <title>Show Localize Control</title>
</head>
<body>
    <form id="form1" runat="server">
    <div>

    <asp:Localize
        ID="locBodyText"
        meta:resourceKey="locBodyText"
        Runat="server">
        Here is the page body text
```

LISTING 24.25   Continued

```
    </asp:Localize>

    <br /><br />

    <asp:Literal
        ID="ltlBodyText"
        runat="server">
        Here is some literal text
    </asp:Literal>

    </div>
    </form>
</body>
</html>
```

The Localize control is very similar to the Literal control (it derives from the Literal control). In Source View, there is nothing that distinguishes the two controls. The difference between the Localize control and Literal control is apparent only in Design View. Unlike the Literal control, the contents of the Localize control can be edited directly on the Designer surface in Design View (see Figure 24.10).

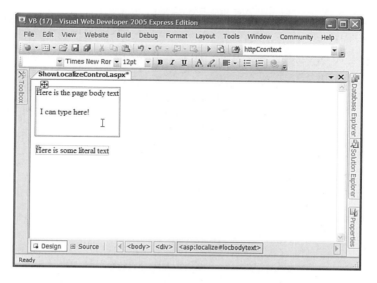

FIGURE 24.10   Using the Localize control in Design View.

Summary

In this chapter, you learned how to localize websites for different languages and culture. In the first section, you learned how to use the `Culture` and `UICulture` properties to set the current culture for the page. You also learned how to set these properties automatically by detecting a browser's preferred language settings.

Next, you learned how to create local resource files that you can apply to particular pages (and other files). You learned how to use both explicit and implicit localization expressions. You also saw how you can programmatically retrieve local resource entries in your code.

You then studied the topic of global resource files, which contain entries that can be used within any page in a website. You learned to use explicit resource expressions with global resources and how to retrieve global resource entries programmatically.

Finally, you had a brief look at the ASP.NET Localize control. You learned how to use this control to localize big chunks of text in a page.

CHAPTER 25

Working with the HTTP Runtime

This chapter tackles a number of advanced topics by digging deeper into the mechanics of how an ASP.NET page is processed. In this first section, you learn how to create a custom `BuildProvider`. A `BuildProvider` is a .NET class that generates source code from a file automatically. You learn how to create a custom `BuildProvider` that builds custom data access components automatically.

Next, you learn how to create a custom `ExpressionBuilder`. An `ExpressionBuilder` is responsible for parsing an expression into code. For example, when you use the `<%$ ConnectionStrings:MyDatabase %>` syntax to refer to a connection string, you are using the `ConnectionStringExpressionBuilder` in the background. In this chapter, you learn how to build a custom `ExpressionBuilder` that looks up values from an XML file.

You also learn how to work with HTTP Handlers. An HTTP Handler is a .NET class that executes whenever a request is made for a file at a certain path. For example, you can use a custom HTTP Handler to retrieve an image from a database table whenever someone requests a file with the extension `.gif` or `.jpeg`.

Finally, you learn how to create custom HTTP Modules. An HTTP Module is a .NET class that executes with each and every request. For example, you can implement a custom authentication system by creating a custom HTTP Module. You also can use a custom HTTP Module to create a custom logging module.

Creating a Custom `BuildProvider`

When you write an ASP.NET page and save the page to your computer's file system, the ASP.NET page gets compiled dynamically into a .NET class in the background. The page is compiled dynamically by a `BuildProvider`.

The ASP.NET Framework includes a number of `BuildProviders`. Each `BuildProvider` is responsible for compiling a file with a particular extension that is located in a particular type of folder. For example, there are `BuildProviders` for Themes, Master Pages, User Controls, and Web Services.

When a `BuildProvider` builds, it builds a new class in the Temporary ASP.NET Files folder. Any class added to the folder becomes available to your application automatically. When you use Visual Web Developer, any public properties and methods of the class appear in Intellisense.

You can create your own `BuildProviders`. This can be useful in a variety of different scenarios. For example, imagine that you find yourself building a lot of ASP.NET pages that display forms. You can tediously build each ASP.NET page by hand by adding all the necessary form and validation controls. Alternatively, you can create a new `BuildProvider` that takes an XML file and generates the form pages for you automatically.

Or, imagine that you are spending a lot of time building data access components. For example, every time you need to access a database table, you create a new component that exposes properties that correspond to each of the columns in the database table. In this case, it would make sense to create a custom `BuildProvider` that generates the data access component automatically.

Creating a Simple `BuildProvider`

Let's start by creating a really simple `BuildProvider`. The new `BuildProvider` will be named the `SimpleBuildProvider`. Whenever you create a file that has the extension `.simple`, the `SimpleBuilderProvider` builds a new class with the same name as the file in the background. The dynamically compiled class also includes a single method named `DoSomething()` that doesn't actually do anything.

The `SimpleBuildProvider` is contained in Listing 25.1.

LISTING 25.1   App_Code\CustomBuildProviders\SimpleBuildProvider.vb

```
Imports System
Imports System.Web.Compilation
Imports System.CodeDom
Imports System.IO

Namespace AspNetUnleashed
    Public Class SimpleBuildProvider
        Inherits BuildProvider
```

LISTING 25.1   Continued

```
Public Overrides Sub GenerateCode(ByVal ab As AssemblyBuilder)
    Dim fileName As String = Path.GetFileNameWithoutExtension(Me.VirtualPath)
    Dim snippet As String = "Public Class " & fileName & vbNewLine
      snippet &= "  Public Shared Sub DoSomething()" & vbNewLine
      snippet &= "  End Sub" & vbNewLine
      snippet &= "End Class"
    ab.AddCodeCompileUnit(Me, New CodeSnippetCompileUnit(snippet))
    End Sub

    End Class
End Namespace
```

All BuildProviders must inherit from the base BuildProvider class. Typically, you override the BuildProvider class GenerateCode() method. This method is responsible for generating the class that gets added to the Temporary ASP.NET Files folder.

An instance of the AssemblyBuilder class is passed to the GenerateCode() method. You add the class that you want to create to this AssemblyBuilder by calling the AssemblyBuilder.AddCodeCompileUnit() method.

In Listing 25.1, a CodeSnippetCompileUnit is used to represent the source code for the class. Any code that you represent with the CodeSnippetCompileUnit is added, verbatim, to the dynamically generated class. This approach is problematic.

Unfortunately, you can use the SimpleBuildProvider in Listing 25.1 only when building a Visual Basic .NET application. It doesn't work with a C# application. Because the code represented by the CodeSnippetCompileUnit is Visual Basic .NET code, using the SimpleBuildProvider with a C# application would result in compilation errors. The SimpleBuildProvider would inject Visual Basic .NET code into a C# assembly.

The proper way to write the SimpleBuildProvider class would be to use the CodeDom. The CodeDom enables you to represent .NET code in a language neutral manner. When you represent a block of code with the CodeDom, the code can be converted to either C# or Visual Basic .NET code automatically. You'll learn how to use the CodeDom when we build a more complicated BuildProvider in the next section. For now, just realize that we are taking a shortcut to keep things simple.

When you add the SimpleBuildProvider to your project, it is important that you add the file to a separate subfolder in your App_Code folder and you mark the folder as a separate code folder in the web configuration file. For example, in the sample code on the CD that accompanies this book, the SimpleBuildProvider is located in the App_Code\CustomBuildProviders folder.

You must add a BuildProvider to a separate subfolder because a BuildProvider must be compiled into a different assembly than the other code in the App_Code folder. This makes sense because a BuildProvider is actually responsible for compiling the other code in the App_Code folder.

The web configuration file in Listing 25.2 defines the CustomBuildProviders folder and registers the `SimpleBuildProvider`.

LISTING 25.2 Web.Config

```
<?xml version="1.0"?>
<configuration>
    <system.web>

      <compilation>
        <codeSubDirectories>
          <add directoryName="CustomBuildProviders"/>
        </codeSubDirectories>
        <buildProviders>
          <add extension=".simple" type="AspNetUnleashed.SimpleBuildProvider" />
        </buildProviders>
      </compilation>

    </system.web>
</configuration>
```

The web configuration file in Listing 25.2 associates the `SimpleBuildProvider` with the file extension `.simple`. Whenever you add a file with the `.simple` extension to the App_Code folder, the `SimpleBuildProvider` automatically compiles a new class based on the file.

For example, adding the file in Listing 25.3 to your App_Code folder causes the `SimpleBuildProvider` to create a new class named `Mike`.

LISTING 25.3 App_Code\Mike.simple

```
Hello!
Hello!
Hello!
```

The actual content of the file that you create doesn't matter. The `SimpleBuildProvider` ignores everything about the file except for the name of the file.

You can see the new file created by the `SimpleBuildProvider` by navigating to the Sources_App_Code folder contained in the folder that corresponds to your application in the Temporary ASP.NET Files folder. The contents of the auto-generated file are contained in Listing 25.4.

LISTING 25.4   `mike.simple.72cecc2a.vb`

```
#ExternalChecksum("C:\Websites\MyApp\Code\VB\App_Code\Mike.simple",
"{406ea660-64cf-4c82-b6f0-42d48172a799}","E3A7385F5DCED38D7B52DBB3CBCA0B40")
Public Class Mike
  Public Shared Sub DoSomething()
  End Sub
End Class
```

Any class added to the Temporary ASP.NET Files folder is available in your application automatically. For example, the page in Listing 25.5 uses the Mike class.

LISTING 25.5   `ShowSimpleBuildProvider.aspx`

```
<%@ Page Language="VB" %>
<!DOCTYPE html PUBLIC "-//W3C//DTD XHTML 1.0 Transitional//EN"
  "http://www.w3.org/TR/xhtml1/DTD/xhtml1-transitional.dtd">
<script runat="server">

    Sub Page_Load()
        Mike.DoSomething()
    End Sub

</script>
<html xmlns="http://www.w3.org/1999/xhtml" >
<head runat="server">
    <title>Show SimpleBuildProvider</title>
</head>
<body>
    <form id="form1" runat="server">
    <div>

    </div>
    </form>
</body>
</html>
```

The Mike class appears in Intellisense. For example, if you type **Mike** followed by a period, the DoSomething() method appears (see Figure 25.1).

25

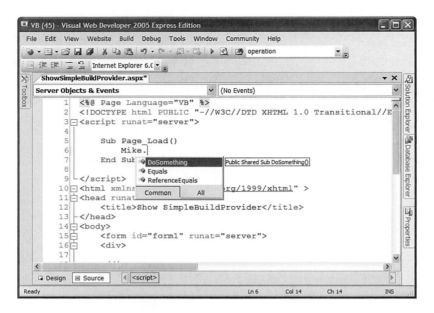

FIGURE 25.1   Using a `BuildProvider` to generate a class dynamically.

Creating a Data Access Component `BuildProvider`

In the previous section, we created a simple but useless `BuildProvider`. In this section, we create a complicated but useful `BuildProvider`.

In this section, we create a `DataBuildProvider`. The `DataBuildProvider` generates a data access component automatically from an XML file. For example, if you add the XML file in Listing 25.6 to your project, then the `DataBuildProvider` generates the class in Listing 25.7 automatically.

LISTING 25.6   App_Code\Movie.data

```
<Movies>
  <add name="Title" />
  <add name="Director" />
  <add name="BoxOfficeTotals" type="Decimal" />
</Movies>
```

LISTING 25.7   movie.data.72cecc2a.vb

```
#ExternalChecksum("C:\Websites\MyApp\App_Code\Movie.data",
"{406ea660-64cf-4c82-b6f0-42d48172a799}","E043FB9DD82756F3156AD9FC5090A8BD")
'.................................................................................
' <auto-generated>
'     This code was generated by a tool.
```

LISTING 25.7 Continued

```
'      Runtime Version:2.0.50727.42
'
'      Changes to this file may cause incorrect behavior and will be lost if
'      the code is regenerated.
' </auto-generated>
'----------------------------------------------------------------------

Option Strict Off
Option Explicit On

Imports System

Namespace Data
    Partial Public Class Movie

        Private _Title As String
        Private _Director As String
        Private _BoxOfficeTotals As [Decimal]

        Public Sub New()
            MyBase.New
        End Sub

        Public Overridable Property Title() As String
            Get
                Return Me._Title
            End Get
            Set
                Me._Title = value
            End Set
        End Property

        Public Overridable Property Director() As String
            Get
                Return Me._Director
            End Get
            Set
                Me._Director = value
            End Set
        End Property

        Public Overridable Property BoxOfficeTotals() As [Decimal]
            Get
                Return Me._BoxOfficeTotals
            End Get
```

LISTING 25.7   Continued

```
            Set
                Me._BoxOfficeTotals = value
            End Set
        End Property


        '''<summary>Returns List of Movie</summary>
        Public Overloads Shared Function [Select](ByVal con As
➥System.Data.SqlClient.SqlConnection) As
➥System.Collections.Generic.List(Of Movie)
            Dim results As System.Collections.Generic.List(Of Movie) =
➥New System.Collections.Generic.List(Of Movie)
            Dim cmd As System.Data.SqlClient.SqlCommand =
➥New System.Data.SqlClient.SqlCommand
            cmd.Connection = con
            Dim cmdText As String = "SELECT Title,Director,BoxOfficeTotals
➥FROM Movies"
            cmd.CommandText = cmdText
            Dim reader As System.Data.SqlClient.SqlDataReader = cmd.ExecuteReader
            Dim counter As Integer
            counter = 0
            Do While reader.Read
                Dim record As Movie = New Movie
                record.Title = CType(reader("Title"),String)
                record.Director = CType(reader("Director"),String)
                record.BoxOfficeTotals = CType(reader("BoxOfficeTotals"),[Decimal])
                results.Add(record)
                counter = (counter + 1)
            Loop
            Return results
        End Function


        '''<summary>Returns List of Movie</summary>
        Public Overloads Shared Function [Select](ByVal connectionStringName
➥As String) As System.Collections.Generic.List(Of Movie)
            Dim results As System.Collections.Generic.List(Of Movie) =
➥New System.Collections.Generic.List(Of Movie)
            Dim conStringSettings As System.Configuration.
➥ConnectionStringSettings = System.Web.Configuration.WebConfigurationManager.
➥ConnectionStrings(connectionStringName)
            Dim conString As String = conStringSettings.ConnectionString
            Dim con As System.Data.SqlClient.SqlConnection =
➥New System.Data.SqlClient.SqlConnection
            con.ConnectionString = conString
            Try
                con.Open
                results = Movie.Select(con)
```

LISTING 25.7 Continued

```
            Finally
                con.Close
            End Try
            Return results
        End Function
    End Class
End Namespace
```

The XML file in Listing 25.6 contains the name of a database table (Movies) and it contains a list of columns from the database table. When you add the file in Listing 25.6 to your project, the class in Listing 25.7 is generated automatically.

The data access component in Listing 25.7 contains a property that corresponds to each of the columns listed in the `Movie.data` file. Furthermore, each property has the data type specified in the `Movie.data` file.

Notice, furthermore, that the Movie data access component includes two `Select()` methods. You can retrieve all the records from the Movies database table in two ways: by passing an open `SqlConnection` object to the `Select()` method or by passing the name of a connection string defined in the web configuration file to the `Select()` method.

The page in Listing 25.8 illustrates how you can use the Movie data access component within an ASP.NET page (see Figure 25.2).

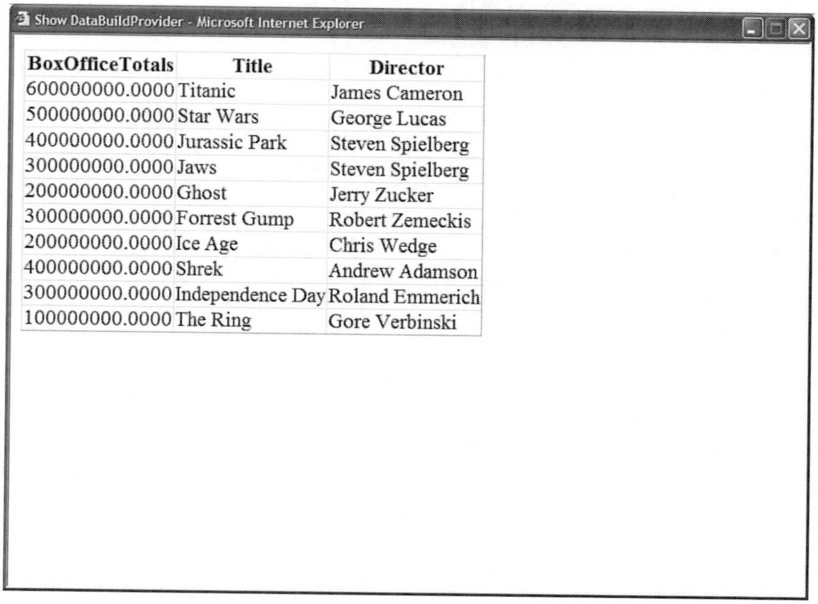
Show DataBuildProvider - Microsoft Internet Explorer
BoxOfficeTotals Title Director
600000000.0000 Titanic James Cameron
500000000.0000 Star Wars George Lucas
400000000.0000 Jurassic Park Steven Spielberg
300000000.0000 Jaws Steven Spielberg
200000000.0000 Ghost Jerry Zucker
300000000.0000 Forrest Gump Robert Zemeckis
200000000.0000 Ice Age Chris Wedge
400000000.0000 Shrek Andrew Adamson
300000000.0000 Independence Day Roland Emmerich
100000000.0000 The Ring Gore Verbinski

FIGURE 25.2 Displaying data returned by a dynamically generated data access component.

LISTING 25.8   ShowDataBuildProvider.aspx

```
<%@ Page Language="VB" %>
<!DOCTYPE html PUBLIC "-//W3C//DTD XHTML 1.0 Transitional//EN"
  "http://www.w3.org/TR/xhtml1/DTD/xhtml1-transitional.dtd">
<script runat="server">

    Sub Page_Load()
        grdMovies.DataSource = Data.Movie.Select("Movies")
        grdMovies.DataBind()
    End Sub

</script>
<html xmlns="http://www.w3.org/1999/xhtml" >
<head id="Head1" runat="server">
    <title>Show DataBuildProvider</title>
</head>
<body>
    <form id="form1" runat="server">
    <div>

    <asp:GridView
        id="grdMovies"
        Runat="server" />

    </div>
    </form>
</body>
</html>
```

Unlike the `SimpleBuildProvider` created in the previous section, the `DataBuildProvider` uses the `CodeDom` to represent code. This means that you can use the `DataBuildProvider` in both Visual Basic .NET and C# applications. The `DataBuildProvider` generates the data access component in different languages automatically. For example, if you use the `DataBuildProvider` in a C# application, the `BuildProvider` generates the code in Listing 25.6 in C#.

Unfortunately, the code for the `DataBuildProvider` is much too long to include here. The entire code is included on the CD that accompanies the book. The file in Listing 25.9 contains part of the `DataBuildProvider` code.

LISTING 25.9   DataBuildProvider.vb (Partial)

```
Namespace AspNetUnleashed

    Public Class DataBuildProvider
        Inherits BuildProvider
```

LISTING 25.9   Continued

```
Private _className As String

Public Overrides Sub GenerateCode(ByVal ab As AssemblyBuilder)
    ' Load the XML file
    Dim xmlData As New XmlDocument()
    xmlData.Load(HostingEnvironment.MapPath(Me.VirtualPath))

    ' Generate code from XML document
    Dim dataCode As CodeCompileUnit = GetDataCode(xmlData)

    ' Add the code
    ab.AddCodeCompileUnit(Me, dataCode)
End Sub

Private Function GetDataCode(ByVal xmlData As XmlDocument) _
 As CodeCompileUnit
    ' Add class
    _className = Path.GetFileNameWithoutExtension(Me.VirtualPath)
    Dim dataType As New CodeTypeDeclaration(_className)
    dataType.IsPartial = True

    ' Add constructor
    AddConstructor(dataType)

    ' Add properties
    AddProperties(dataType, xmlData)

    ' Add Select method
    AddSelect(dataType, xmlData)

    ' Add Select with conString overload
    AddSelectConString(dataType, xmlData)

    ' Create namespace
    Dim dataNS As New CodeNamespace("Data")

    ' Add class to namespace
    dataNS.Types.Add(dataType)

    ' Create code unit
    Dim dataCode As New CodeCompileUnit()

    ' Add namespace to code unit
    dataCode.Namespaces.Add(dataNS)
```

25

LISTING 25.9   Continued

```
                ' Add default namespaces
                dataNS.Imports.Add(New CodeNamespaceImport("System"))

                Return dataCode
        End Function

    End Class
End Namespace
```

The DataBuildProvider's GenerateCode() method loads a .data file into an XmlDocument. Notice that the VirtualPath property represents the path of the file that is being built. For example, if you add a file named Products.data to your project, then the VirtualPath property would represent the path to the Products.data file.

Next, the code for the data access component is created from the XML file by the GetDataCode() method. The GetDataCode() method makes heavy use of the CodeDom to generate the code in a language-neutral manner.

Working with the CodeDom is a strange and tedious experience. You must build up a block of code by building a code tree. In Listing 25.9, a CodeCompileUnit named dataCode is created. A CodeNamespace named dataNS that represents a namespace is created and added to the CodeCompileUnit. And, a CodeTypeDeclaration named datatype that represents a class is added to the namespace. After the class is created, the methods and properties are added to the class block by block.

Creating a Custom **ExpressionBuilder**

An ExpressionBuilder class generates one expression from another expression. Typically, you use an ExpressionBuilder to look up a particular value given a particular key.

The ASP.NET Framework includes the following ExpressionBuilder classes:

- AppSettingsExpressionBuilder—Retrieves values from the appSettings section of the web configuration file.

- ConnectionStringsExpressionBuilder—Retrieves values from the connectionStrings section of the web configuration file.

- ResourceExpressionBuilder—Retrieves values from resource files.

The ConnectionStringsExpressionBuilder has been used throughout this book whenever a connection string has needed to be retrieved.

You use the following syntax when working with an ExpressionBuilder:

```
<%$ ConnectionStrings:MyDatabase %>
```

The <%$ and %> tags are used to mark an expression that should be parsed by an ExpressionBuilder. The prefix ConnectionStrings is mapped to the particular ExpressionBuilder class that is responsible for parsing the expression.

ExpressionBuilders must always be used with control properties. For example, you cannot display a connection string in a page like this:

```
<%$ ConnectionStrings:MyDatabase %>
```

Instead, you must display the connection string like this:

```
<asp:Literal
  Id="ltlConnectionString"
  Text='<%$ ConnectionStrings:MyDatabase %>'
  Runat="server" />
```

You can create a custom ExpressionBuilder when none of the existing ExpressionBuilder classes do what you need. For example, you might want to store your application settings in a custom section of the web configuration file. In that case, you might want to create a custom ExpressionBuilder that grabs values from the custom configuration section.

Creating a Lookup ExpressionBuilder

In this section, you learn how to extend the ASP.NET Framework by building a custom ExpressionBuilder class. We'll create a Lookup ExpressionBuilder that looks up string values from an XML file.

The LookupExpressionBuilder class is contained in Listing 25.10.

LISTING 25.10   App_Code\LookupExpressionBuilder.vb

```
Imports System
Imports System.CodeDom
Imports System.Web.UI
Imports System.ComponentModel
Imports System.Web.Compilation
Imports System.Xml
Imports System.Web.Hosting
Imports System.Web.Caching

Namespace AspNetUnleashed
    Public Class LookupExpressionBuilder
        Inherits ExpressionBuilder

        Public Overrides Function GetCodeExpression(ByVal entry As
➥BoundPropertyEntry, ByVal parsedData As Object, ByVal context As
➥ExpressionBuilderContext) As CodeExpression
            Dim refMe As New CodeTypeReferenceExpression(MyBase.GetType())
```

LISTING 25.10   Continued

```
            Dim expression As New CodePrimitiveExpression(enTry.Expression)
            Return New CodeMethodInvokeExpression(refMe, "GetEvalData",
➥New CodeExpression() {expression})
        End Function

        Public Overrides Function EvaluateExpression(ByVal target As Object,
➥ByVal enTry As BoundPropertyEnTry, ByVal parsedData As Object, ByVal context
➥As ExpressionBuilderContext) As Object
            Return GetEvalData(enTry.Expression)
        End Function

        Public Overrides ReadOnly Property SupportsEvaluate() As Boolean
            Get
                Return True
            End Get
        End Property

        Public Shared Function GetEvalData(ByVal expression As String) As String
            Dim lookupDoc As XmlDocument =
➥CType(HostingEnvironment.Cache("Lookup"), XmlDocument)
            If IsNothing(lookupDoc) Then
                lookupDoc = New XmlDocument()
                Dim lookupFileName As String =
➥HostingEnvironment.MapPath("~/Lookup.config")
                lookupDoc.Load(lookupFileName)
                Dim fileDepend As New CacheDependency(lookupFileName)
                HostingEnvironment.Cache.Insert("Lookup", lookupDoc, fileDepend)
            End If

            Dim search As String = String.Format("//add[@key='{0}']", expression)
            Dim match As XmlNode = lookupDoc.SelectSingleNode(search)
            If Not IsNothing(match) Then
                Return match.Attributes("value").Value
            End If
            Return "[no match]"
        End Function

    End Class
End Namespace
```

Before you can use the LookupExpressionBuilder class, you need to register it in the
web configuration file. The web configuration file in Listing 25.11 includes an
<expressionBuilders> section that registers the LookupExpressionBuilder class for the
prefix lookup.

LISTING 25.11   Web.Config

```
<?xml version="1.0"?>
<configuration>
  <system.web>
    <compilation>
      <expressionBuilders>
        <add expressionPrefix="lookup"
            type="AspNetUnleashed.LookupExpressionBuilder" />
      </expressionBuilders>
    </compilation>
  </system.web>
</configuration>
```

The LookupExpressionBuilder uses an XML file named Lookup.config to contain a database of lookup values. This file contains key and value pairs. A sample Lookup.config file is contained in Listing 25.12.

LISTING 25.12   Lookup.config

```
<?xml version="1.0"?>
<lookup>
  <add key="WelcomeMessage" value="Welcome to our Web site!" />
  <add key="Copyright" value="All content copyrighted by the company." />
</lookup>
```

Finally, the page in Listing 25.13 uses the LookupExpressionBuilder. It contains a Literal control that displays the value of a lookup expression named WelcomeMessage (see Figure 25.3).

LISTING 25.13   ShowLookupExpressionBuilder.aspx

```
<%@ Page Language="VB" %>
<!DOCTYPE html PUBLIC "-//W3C//DTD XHTML 1.0 Transitional//EN"
  "http://www.w3.org/TR/xhtml1/DTD/xhtml1-transitional.dtd">
<html xmlns="http://www.w3.org/1999/xhtml" >
<head id="Head1" runat="server">
    <title>Show LookupExpressionBuilder</title>
</head>
<body>
    <form id="form1" runat="server">
    <div>

    <asp:Literal ID="Literal1"
        Text="<%$ lookup:WelcomeMessage %>"
        runat="Server" />
```

25

LISTING 25.13   Continued

```
      </div>
      </form>
</body>
</html>
```

FIGURE 25.3   Displaying text generated by an ExpressionBuilder.

You create a custom ExpressionBuilder by inheriting a new class from the base ExpressionBuilder class. The ExpressionBuilder class has the following methods:

- GetCodeExpression—Returns the code that is used to evaluate an expression.

- EvaluateExpression—Evaluates the expression in the case of no-compile ASP.NET pages.

- ParseExpression—Returns a parsed version of the expression.

The ExpressionBuilder class also supports the following property:

- SupportsEvaluate—When true, the ExpressionBuilder can be used in no-compile ASP.NET pages.

When you use an ExpressionBuilder in a normal ASP.NET page, the ExpressionBuilder returns code that is integrated into the compiled ASP.NET page. The GetCodeExpression()

method returns a block of code that is injected into the compiled ASP.NET page class that gets created in the Temporary ASP.NET Files folder.

Because an `ExpressionBuilder` might be used with either a Visual Basic .NET or C# ASP.NET page, the code returned by the `GetCodeExpression()` method must be language neutral. This means that you must represent the code that gets executed with the `CodeDom`.

In Listing 25.11, the `GetCodeExpression()` method returns an instance of the `CodeMethodInvokeExpression` class. This class represents an expression that invokes a class method. In this case, the `CodeMethodInvokeExpression` class is used to represent the expression `LookupExpressionBuilder.GetEvalData()`. In other words, the `ExpressionBuilder` adds code to the compiled ASP.NET page class that invokes the `GetEvalData()` method contained in Listing 25.10.

As an alternative to creating a normal ASP.NET page, you can create something called a *no-compile* ASP.NET page. A no-compile ASP.NET page is not compiled dynamically. You create a no-compile ASP.NET page by adding the following attribute to a `<%@ Page %>` directive:

```
<%@ Page CompilationMode="Never" %>
```

> **NOTE**
>
> No-compile ASP.NET pages are discussed in Chapter 1, "Overview of the ASP.NET Framework."

If you want an `ExpressionBuilder` to work with no-compile ASP.NET pages, then you must return the value `True` from the `ExpressionBuilder.SupportsEvaluate` property and implement the `EvaluateExpression()` method. The `EvaluateExpression` is executed at runtime when the no-compile ASP.NET page is requested. In Listing 25.11, the `EvaluateExpression()` method simply calls the `GetEvalData()` method.

Creating HTTP Handlers

An HTTP Handler is a .NET class that executes whenever you make a request for a file at a certain path. Each type of resource that you can request from an ASP.NET application has a corresponding handler.

For example, when you request an ASP.NET page, the `Page` class executes. The `Page` class is actually an HTTP Handler because it implements the `IHttpHandler` interface.

Other examples of HTTP Handlers are the `TraceHandler` class, which displays application-level trace information when you request the `Trace.axd` page, and the `ForbiddenHandler` class, which displays an Access Forbidden message when you attempt to request source code files from the browser.

You can implement your own HTTP handlers. For example, imagine that you want to store all your images in a database table. However, you want use normal HTML `<img>` tags to display images in your web pages. In that case, you can map any file that has a `.gif` or `.jpeg` extension to a custom image HTTP handler. The image HTTP handler can retrieve images from a database automatically whenever an image request is made.

Or, imagine that you want to expose an RSS feed from your website. In that case, you can create a RSS HTTP Handler that displays a list of blog entries or articles hosted on your website.

You can create an HTTP Handler in two ways. You can either create something called a Generic Handler or you can implement the `IHttpHandler` interface in a custom class. This section explores both methods of creating an HTTP Handler.

Creating a Generic Handler

The easiest way to create a new HTTP Handler is to create a Generic Handler. When you create a Generic Handler, you create a file that ends with the extension `.ashx`. Whenever you request the `.ashx` file, the Generic Handler executes.

You can think of a Generic Handler as a very lightweight ASP.NET page. A Generic Handler is like an ASP.NET page that contains a single method that renders content to the browser. You can't add any controls declaratively to a Generic Handler. A Generic Handler also doesn't support events such as the Page `Load` or Page `PreRender` events.

In this section, we create a Generic Handler that dynamically generates an image from a string of text. For example, if you pass the string `Hello World!` to the handler, the handler returns an image of the text `Hello World!`.

The Generic Handler is contained in Listing 25.14.

LISTING 25.14   `ImageTextHandler.ashx`

```vb
<%@ WebHandler Language="VB" Class="ImageTextHandler" %>

Imports System
Imports System.Web
Imports System.Drawing
Imports System.Drawing.Imaging

Public Class ImageTextHandler
    Implements IHttpHandler

    Public Sub ProcessRequest(ByVal context As HttpContext) _
    Implements IHttpHandler.ProcessRequest
        ' Get parameters from querystring
        Dim text As String = context.Request.QueryString("text")
        Dim font As String = context.Request.QueryString("font")
        Dim size As String = context.Request.QueryString("size")

        ' Create Font
```

LISTING 25.14   Continued

```
        Dim fntText As New Font(font, Single.Parse(size))

        ' Calculate image width and height
        Dim bmp As New Bitmap(10, 10)
        Dim g As Graphics = Graphics.FromImage(bmp)
        Dim bmpSize As SizeF = g.MeasureString(text, fntText)
        Dim width As Integer = CType(Math.Ceiling(bmpSize.Width), Integer)
        Dim height As Integer = CType(Math.Ceiling(bmpSize.Height), Integer)
        bmp = New Bitmap(bmp, width, height)
        g.Dispose()

        ' Draw the text
        g = Graphics.FromImage(bmp)
        g.Clear(Color.White)
        g.DrawString(text, fntText, Brushes.Black, New PointF(0, 0))
        g.Dispose()

        ' Save bitmap to output stream
        bmp.Save(context.Response.OutputStream, ImageFormat.Gif)
    End Sub

    Public ReadOnly Property IsReusable() As Boolean _
    Implements IHttpHandler.IsReusable
        Get
            Return True
        End Get
    End Property

End Class
```

The `ImageTextHandler` in Listing 25.14 includes one method and one property. The `ProcessRequest()` method is responsible for outputting any content that the handler renders to the browser.

In Listing 25.14, the image text, font, and size are retrieved from query string fields. You specify the image that you want to return from the handler by making a request that looks like this:

```
/ImageTextHandler.ashx?text=Hello&font=Arial&size=30
```

Next, a bitmap is created with the help of the classes from the System.Drawing namespace. The bitmap is actually created twice. The first one is used to measure the size of the bitmap required for generating an image that contains the text. Next, a new bitmap of the correct size is created, and the text is drawn on the bitmap.

25

After the bitmap has been created, it is saved to the `HttpResponse` object's `OutputStream` so that it can be rendered to the browser.

The handler in Listing 25.14 also includes an `IsReusable` property. The `IsReusable` property indicates whether the same handler can be reused over multiple requests. You can improve your application's performance by returning the value `True`. Because the handler isn't maintaining any state information, there is nothing wrong with releasing it back into the pool so that it can be used with a future request.

The page in Listing 25.15 illustrates how you can use the `ImageTextHandler.ashx` file. This page contains three HTML `<img>` tags that pass different query strings to the handler (see Figure 25.4).

FIGURE 25.4   Displaying text images with an HTTP Handler.

LISTING 25.15   ShowImageTextHandler.aspx

```
<%@ Page Language="VB" %>
<!DOCTYPE html PUBLIC "-//W3C//DTD XHTML 1.0 Transitional//EN"
  "http://www.w3.org/TR/xhtml1/DTD/xhtml1-transitional.dtd">
<html xmlns="http://www.w3.org/1999/xhtml" >
<head id="Head1" runat="server">
    <title>Show ImageTextHandler</title>
</head>
<body>
    <form id="form1" runat="server">
```

LISTING 25.15 Continued

```
    <div>

    <img src="ImageTextHandler.ashx?text=Some Text&font=WebDings&size=42" />
    <br />
    <img src="ImageTextHandler.ashx?text=Some Text&font=Comic Sans MS&size=42" />
    <br />
    <img src="ImageTextHandler.ashx?text=Some Text&font=Courier New&size=42" />

    </div>
    </form>
</body>
</html>
```

Implementing the `IHttpHandler` Interface

The big disadvantage of a Generic Handler is that you cannot map a Generic Handler to a particular page path. For example, you cannot execute a Generic Handler whenever someone requests a file with the extension `.gif`.

If you need more control over when an HTTP Handler executes, then you can create a class that implements the `IHttpHandler` interface.

For example, the class in Listing 25.16 represents an Image HTTP Handler. This handler retrieves an image from a database table and renders the image to the browser.

LISTING 25.16 App_Code\ImageHandler.vb

```vb
Imports System
Imports System.Web
Imports System.Data
Imports System.Data.SqlClient
Imports System.Web.Configuration

Namespace AspNetUnleashed

    Public Class ImageHandler
        Implements IHttpHandler

        Const connectionStringName As String = "Images"

        Public Sub ProcessRequest(ByVal context As HttpContext) _
        Implements IHttpHandler.ProcessRequest
            ' Don't buffer response
            context.Response.Buffer = False

            ' Get file name
            Dim fileName As String = VirtualPathUtility.GetFileName(
```

LISTING 25.16   Continued

```
➥context.Request.Path)

              ' Get image from database
              Dim conString As String = WebConfigurationManager.
➥ConnectionStrings(connectionStringName).ConnectionString
              Dim con As New SqlConnection(conString)
              Dim cmd As New SqlCommand("SELECT Image FROM Images
➥WHERE FileName=@FileName", con)
              cmd.Parameters.AddWithValue("@fileName", fileName)
              Using con
                  con.Open()
                  Dim reader As SqlDataReader = cmd.ExecuteReader(
➥CommandBehavior.SequentialAccess)
                  If reader.Read() Then
                      Dim bufferSize As Integer = 8040
                      Dim chunk(bufferSize) As Byte
                      Dim retCount As Long
                      Dim startIndex As Long = 0
                      retCount = reader.GetBytes(0, startIndex, chunk, 0, bufferSize)
                      While retCount = bufferSize
                          context.Response.BinaryWrite(chunk)
                          startIndex += bufferSize
                          retCount = reader.GetBytes(0, startIndex, chunk, 0,
➥bufferSize)
                      End While
                      Dim actualChunk() As Byte = New Byte(retCount - 1) {}
                      Buffer.BlockCopy(chunk, 0, actualChunk, 0, CType(retCount - 1,
➥Integer))
                      context.Response.BinaryWrite(actualChunk)
                  End If
              End Using
          End Sub


          Public ReadOnly Property IsReusable() As Boolean _
          Implements IHttpHandler.IsReusable
              Get
                  Return True
              End Get
          End Property
      End Class
End Namespace
```

After you create a class that implements the IHttpHandler interface, you need to register the class in the web configuration file. The web configuration file in Listing 25.17 includes an httpHandlers section that associates the .gif, .jpeg, and .jpg extensions with the Image handler.

LISTING 25.17   Web.Config

```
<?xml version="1.0"?>
<configuration>
  <connectionStrings>
    <add name="Images"
      connectionString="Data Source=.\SQLExpress;Integrated
          Security=True;AttachDBFileName=|DataDirectory|ImagesDB.mdf;
          User Instance=True"/>
  </connectionStrings>
    <system.web>

      <httpHandlers>
        <add path="*.gif" verb="*"
          type="AspNetUnleashed.ImageHandler" validate="false" />
        <add path="*.jpeg" verb="*"
          type="AspNetUnleashed.ImageHandler" validate="false" />
        <add path="*.jpg" verb="*"
          type="AspNetUnleashed.ImageHandler" validate="false" />
      </httpHandlers>

    </system.web>
</configuration>
```

When you register a handler, you specify the following four attributes:

- path—Enables you to specify the path associated with the handler. You can use wildcards in the path expression.

- verb—Enables you to specify the HTTP verbs, such as GET or POST, associated with the handler. You can specify multiple verbs in a comma-separated list. You can represent any verb with the * wildcard.

- type—Enables you to specify the name of the class that implements the handler.

- validate—Enables you to specify whether the handler is loaded during application startup. When true, the handler is loaded at startup. When false, the handler is not loaded until a request associated with the handler is made. This second option can improve your application's performance when a handler is never used.

The page in Listing 25.18 uses the ImageHandler to render its images. The page enables you to upload new images to a database named ImagesDB. The page also displays existing images (see Figure 25.5).

FIGURE 25.5 Displaying images with the `ImageHandler`.

LISTING 25.18 `ImageUpload.aspx`

```
<%@ Page Language="VB" %>
<!DOCTYPE html PUBLIC "-//W3C//DTD XHTML 1.0 Transitional//EN"
  "http://www.w3.org/TR/xhtml1/DTD/xhtml1-transitional.dtd">
<script runat="server">

    Sub btnAdd_Click(ByVal sender As Object, ByVal e As EventArgs)
        If upFile.HasFile Then
            srcImages.Insert()
        End If
    End Sub
</script>
<html xmlns="http://www.w3.org/1999/xhtml" >
<head id="Head1" runat="server">
    <style type="text/css">
        .fileList li
        {
            margin-bottom:5px;
        }
    </style>
    <title>Image Upload</title>
</head>
```

LISTING 25.18 Continued

```
<body>
    <form id="form1" runat="server">
    <div>

    <asp:Label
        id="lblFile"
        Text="Image File:"
        AssociatedControlID="upFile"
        Runat="server" />
    <asp:FileUpload
        id="upFile"
        Runat="server" />
    <asp:Button
        id="btnAdd"
        Text="Add Image"
        OnClick="btnAdd_Click"
        Runat="server" />
    <hr />

    <asp:GridView
        id="grdImages"
        DataSourceID="srcImages"
        AutoGenerateColumns="false"
        ShowHeader="false"
        GridLines="None"
        Runat="server">
        <Columns>
        <asp:ImageField
            DataImageUrlField="FileName"
            DataAlternateTextField="FileName" />
        </Columns>
    </asp:GridView>

    <asp:SqlDataSource
        id="srcImages"
        ConnectionString="<%$ ConnectionStrings:Images %>"
        SelectCommand="SELECT FileName FROM Images"
        InsertCommand="INSERT Images (FileName,Image)
          VALUES (@FileName,@FileBytes)"
        Runat="server">
        <InsertParameters>
            <asp:ControlParameter Name="FileName" ControlID="upFile"
              PropertyName="FileName" />
            <asp:ControlParameter Name="FileBytes" ControlID="upFile"
```

25

LISTING 25.18   Continued

```
            PropertyName="FileBytes" />
      </InsertParameters>
   </asp:SqlDataSource>

   </div>
   </form>
</body>
</html>
```

Registering Extensions with Internet Information Server

The web server included with Visual Web Developer maps all requests to the ASP.NET Framework. For example, if you create an HTTP Handler that handles requests for .gif files, then you don't have to do anything special when using the handler with the Visual Web Developer web server.

Internet Information Server, on the other hand, does not map all requests to the ASP.NET Framework. In particular, it does not map requests for .gif files to ASP.NET. If you want to use a special extension for a handler, then you must configure Internet Information Server to map that extension to the ASP.NET Framework.

If you are serving your pages with Internet Information Server 6.0 (included with Windows Server 2003), then you can create something called a *wildcard application mapping*. A wildcard application mapping enables you to map all page requests to an application such as the ASP.NET Framework. Follow these steps to configure a wildcard mapping for ASP.NET:

1. Open Internet Information Services by selecting Start, Control Panel, Administrative Tools, Internet Information Services.

2. Open the property sheet for a particular website or virtual directory.

3. Open the Application Configuration dialog box by selecting the Directory tab and clicking the Configuration button.

4. Select the Mappings tab.

5. Click the Insert button at the bottom of the Mappings tab to open the Add/Edit Application Extension Mapping dialog box (see Figure 25.6).

6. In the Executable field, enter the path to the ASP.NET ISAPI DLL. (You can copy and paste this path from the Application Mapping for the .aspx extension.)

After you complete these steps, all requests made for any type of file are handled by the ASP.NET Framework. If you make a request for a .gif image, then any handlers that you have registered in the web configuration file for the .gif extension will execute.

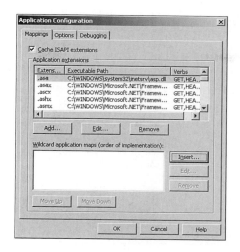

FIGURE 25.6   Adding a wildcard application mapping.

Earlier versions of Internet Information Server, such as the version included with Microsoft Windows XP, do not support wildcard application mappings. You must map each file extension that you want to associate with the ASP.NET Framework one by one. Follow these steps to map the `.gif` extension to the ASP.NET Framework:

1. Open Internet Information Services by selecting Start, Control Panel, Administrative Tools, Internet Information Services.

2. Open the property sheet for a particular website or virtual directory.

3. Open the Application Configuration dialog box by selecting the Directory tab and clicking the Configuration button.

4. Select the Mappings tab (see Figure 25.7).

5. Click the Add button to open the Add/Edit Application Extension Mapping dialog box.

6. In the Executable field, enter the path to the ASP.NET ISAPI DLL. (You can copy and paste this path from the Application Mapping for the `.aspx` extension.)

7. In the Extension field, enter **.gif**.

After you complete these steps, requests for `.gif` images are handled by the ASP.NET Framework. If you have registered an HTTP handler for the `.gif` extension in the web configuration file, then the HTTP Handler will execute whenever someone makes a request for a `.gif` file.

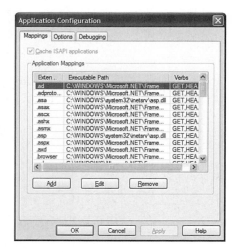

FIGURE 25.7   Adding an application mapping.

Creating an Asynchronous HTTP Handler

When you create an HTTP Handler by creating either a Generic Handler or implementing the IHttpHandler interface, you are creating a synchronous handler. In this section, you learn how to create an asynchronous handler.

The advantage of creating an asynchronous handler is scalability. The ASP.NET Framework maintains a limited pool of threads that are used to service requests. When the ASP.NET Framework receives a request for a file, it assigns a thread to handle the request. If the ASP.NET Framework runs out of threads, the request is queued until a thread becomes available. If too many threads are queued, then the framework rejects the page request with a 503—Server Too Busy response code.

If you execute an HTTP Handler asynchronously, then the current thread is released back into the thread pool so that it can be used to service another page request. While the asynchronous handler is executing, the ASP.NET framework can devote its attention to handling other requests. When the asynchronous handler completes its work, the framework reassigns a thread to the original request and the handler can render content to the browser.

> **NOTE**
>
> You can configure the ASP.NET thread pool with the httpRuntime element in the web configuration file. You can modify the appRequestQueueLimit, minFreeThreads, and minLocalRequestFreeThreads attributes to control how many requests the ASP.NET Framework queues before giving up and sending an error.

You create an asynchronous HTTP handler by implementing the `IHttpAsyncHandler` interface. This interface derives from the `IHttpHandler` interface and adds two additional methods:

- `BeginProcessRequest`—Called to start the asynchronous task.

- `EndProcessRequest`—Called when the asynchronous task completes.

For example, the file in Listing 25.19 contains an asynchronous handler that grabs an RSS feed from the Microsoft MSDN website.

LISTING 25.19   App_Code\RSSHandler.vb

```vb
Imports System
Imports System.Web
Imports System.Net
Imports System.IO

Namespace AspNetUnleashed
    Public Class RSSHandler
        Implements IHttpAsyncHandler

        Private _context As HttpContext
        Private _request As WebRequest

        Public Function BeginProcessRequest(ByVal context As HttpContext,
➥ByVal cb As AsyncCallback, ByVal extraData As Object) As IAsyncResult
➥Implements IHttpAsyncHandler.BeginProcessRequest
            ' Store context
            _context = context

            ' Initiate call to RSS feed
            _request = WebRequest.Create(
➥"http://msdn.microsoft.com/asp.net/rss.xml")
            Return _request.BeginGetResponse(cb, extraData)
        End Function

        Public Sub EndProcessRequest(ByVal result As IAsyncResult)
➥Implements IHttpAsyncHandler.EndProcessRequest
            ' Get the RSS feed
            Dim rss As String = String.Empty
            Dim response As WebResponse = _request.EndGetResponse(result)
            Using response
                Dim reader As New StreamReader(response.GetResponseStream())
                rss = reader.ReadToEnd()
            End Using
```

25

LISTING 25.19   Continued

```
            _context.Response.Write(rss)
        End Sub


        Public ReadOnly Property IsReusable() As Boolean
➥Implements IHttpHandler.IsReusable
            Get
                Throw New Exception("The IsReusable property is not implemented.")
            End Get
        End Property


        Public Sub ProcessRequest(ByVal context As HttpContext)
➥Implements IHttpHandler.ProcessRequest
            Throw New Exception("The ProcessRequest method is not implemented.")
        End Sub
    End Class
End Namespace
```

The handler in Listing 25.19 implements both the BeginProcessRequest() and
EndProcessRequest() methods required by the IHttpAsyncHandler interface.

The BeginProcessRequest() method uses the WebRequest class to request the page that
contains the RSS headlines from the MSDN website. The WebRequest.BeginGetResponse()
method is used to retrieve the remote page asynchronously.

When the BeginGetResponse() method completes, the handler's EndProcessRequest()
method is called. This method retrieves the page and renders the contents of the page to
the browser.

Before you can use the RSSHandler, you need to register it in your web configuration file.
The web configuration file in Listing 25.20 includes an <httpHandlers> section that registers the RSSHandler and associates the handler with the .rss extension.

LISTING 25.20   Web.Config

```
<?xml version="1.0"?>
<configuration>
    <system.web>


      <httpHandlers>
        <add path="*.rss" verb="*" type="AspNetUnleashed.RSSHandler"/>
      </httpHandlers>


    </system.web>
</configuration>
```

After you register the `RSSHandler`, you can execute the handler by making a request for any file that ends with the extension `.rss`. If you have a news reader, such as SharpReader, then you can enter a path like the following in the reader's address bar:

```
http://localhost:2026/YourApp/news.rss
```

The page in Listing 25.21 contains a `GridView` and `XmlDataSource` control. The `XmlDataSource` control calls the `RssHandler` to retrieve the headlines that are displayed in the `GridView` control (see Figure 25.8).

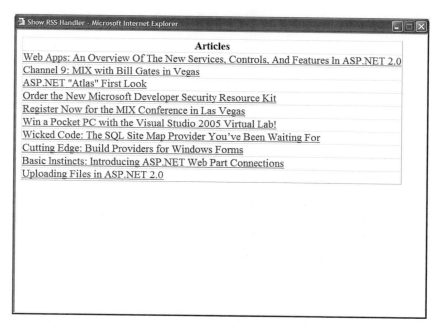

FIGURE 25.8   Retrieving an RSS feed asynchronously.

LISTING 25.21   ShowRSSHandler.aspx

```
<%@ Page Language="VB" %>
<%@ Import Namespace="System.IO" %>
<!DOCTYPE html PUBLIC "-//W3C//DTD XHTML 1.0 Transitional//EN"
  "http://www.w3.org/TR/xhtml1/DTD/xhtml1-transitional.dtd">
<script runat="server">

    Sub Page_Load()
        Dim pagePath As String = Request.Url.OriginalString
        Dim rssPath As String = Path.ChangeExtension(pagePath, ".rss")
        srcRSS.DataFile = rssPath
    End Sub
```

LISTING 25.21   Continued

```
</script>
<html xmlns="http://www.w3.org/1999/xhtml" >
<head id="Head1" runat="server">
    <title>Show RSS Handler</title>
</head>
<body>
    <form id="form1" runat="server">
    <div>

    <asp:GridView
        id="grdRSS"
        DataSourceID="srcRSS"
        AutoGenerateColumns="false"
        Runat="server">
        <Columns>
        <asp:TemplateField HeaderText="Articles">
        <ItemTemplate>
            <asp:HyperLink
                id="lnkRSS"
                Text='<%# XPath("title") %>'
                NavigateUrl='<%# XPath("link") %>'
                Runat="server" />
        </ItemTemplate>
        </asp:TemplateField>
        </Columns>
    </asp:GridView>

    <asp:XmlDataSource
        id="srcRSS"
        XPath="//item"
        Runat="server" />

    </div>
    </form>
</body>
</html>
```

Working with HTTP Applications and HTTP Modules

Whenever you request an ASP.NET page, the ASP.NET Framework assigns an instance of the HttpApplication class to the request. This class performs the following actions in the following order:

1. Raises the `BeginRequest` event.

2. Raises the `AuthenticateRequest` event.

3. Raises the `AuthorizeRequest` event.

4. Calls the `ProcessRequest()` method of the `Page` class.

5. Raises the `EndRequest` event.

> **NOTE**
>
> This is not a complete list of `HttpApplication` events. There are a lot of them!

The entire page execution lifecycle happens during the fourth step. For example, the `Page` `Init`, `Load`, and `PreRender` events all happen when the `Page` class `ProcessRequest()` method is called.

The `HttpApplication` object is responsible for raising application events. These application events happen both before and after a page is executed.

You might want to handle one of the application events for several reasons. For example, you might want to implement a custom authentication scheme. In that case, you would need to handle the `AuthenticateRequest` event to identify the user.

Or, you might want to create a custom logging module that tracks the pages that your website users visit. In that case, you might want to handle the `BeginRequest` event to record the pages being requested.

If you want to handle `HttpApplication` events, there are two ways to do it. You can create a `Global.asax` file or you can create one or more custom HTTP Modules.

Creating a `Global.asax` File

By default, the ASP.NET Framework maintains a pool of `HttpApplication` objects to service incoming page requests. A separate `HttpApplication` instance is assigned to each request.

If you prefer, you can create a custom `HttpApplication` class. That way, an instance of your custom class is assigned to each page request.

You can create custom properties in your derived class. These properties can be accessed from any page, control, or component. You also can handle any application events in your custom `HttpApplication` class.

You create a custom `HttpApplication` class by creating a special file named `Global.asax` in the root of your application. Every application can have one and only one of these files.

For example, the `Global.asax` file in Listing 25.22 can be used to track the number of page requests made for any page.

25

LISTING 25.22   Global.asax

```
<%@ Application Language="VB" %>
<%@ Import Namespace="System.Data" %>
<%@ Import Namespace="System.Data.SqlClient" %>
<%@ Import Namespace="System.Web.Configuration" %>
<script runat="server">
    Private _conString As String
    Private _con As SqlConnection
    Private _cmdSelect As SqlCommand
    Private _cmdInsert As SqlCommand

    Public Overrides  Sub Init()
        ' initialize connection
        _conString = WebConfigurationManager.ConnectionStrings("Log").
➥ConnectionString
        _con = New SqlConnection(_conString)

        ' initialize select command
        _cmdSelect = New SqlCommand("SELECT COUNT(*) FROM Log WHERE Path=@Path", _
➥con)
        _cmdSelect.Parameters.Add("@Path", SqlDbType.NVarChar, 500)

        ' initialize insert command
        _cmdInsert = New SqlCommand("INSERT Log (Path) VALUES (@Path)", _con)
        _cmdInsert.Parameters.Add("@Path", SqlDbType.NVarChar, 500)
    End Sub

    Public ReadOnly Property NumberOfRequests() As Integer
    Get
            Dim result As Integer =  0
            _cmdSelect.Parameters("@Path").Value =
➥Request.AppRelativeCurrentExecutionFilePath
            Try
                _con.Open()
                result = CType(_cmdSelect.ExecuteScalar(), Integer)
            Finally
                _con.Close()
            End Try
            Return result
    End Get
    End Property

    Private  Sub Application_BeginRequest(ByVal sender As Object, _
➥ByVal e As EventArgs)
        ' Record new request
```

LISTING 25.22   Continued

```
        _cmdInsert.Parameters("@Path").Value =
➥Request.AppRelativeCurrentExecutionFilePath
        Try
            _con.Open()
            _cmdInsert.ExecuteNonQuery()
        Finally
            _con.Close()
        End Try
    End Sub
</script>
```

The `Global.asax` page in Listing 25.23 handles the `Application BeginRequest()` event. You can handle any application event by following the naming pattern `Application_EventName` where `EventName` is the name of the `HttpApplication` event.

In Listing 25.23, the `Application_BeginRequest()` handler is used to record the path of the page being requested. A `SqlCommand` object is used to record the page path to a database table named Log.

The `Global.asax` file also extends the base `HttpApplication` class with a custom property named `NumberOfRequests`. This property retrieves the number of requests made for the page at the current path.

Finally, the `Global.asax` includes an `Init()` method that overrides the base `HttpApplication`'s `Init()` method. In Listing 25.23, the `Init()` method is used to initialize the `SqlConnection` and two `SqlCommand` objects used in the `Global.asax` file.

The `Init()` method is called when the class represented by the `Global.asax` is initialized. It is called only once, when the class is first created.

> **WARNING**
>
> The same instance of the `HttpApplication` object is re-used for multiple page requests (although never for multiple page requests at the same time). Any value that you assign to a property in a `Global.asax` file is maintained over the multiple page requests.

The page in Listing 25.23 displays the value of the custom property exposed by the `Global.asax` file (see Figure 25.9). Notice that the `ApplicationInstance` property is used to refer to the instance of the `HttpApplication` class associated with the page. Because the `Global.asax` file is compiled dynamically in the background, any properties that you declare in the `Global.asax` file are exposed as strongly typed properties.

25

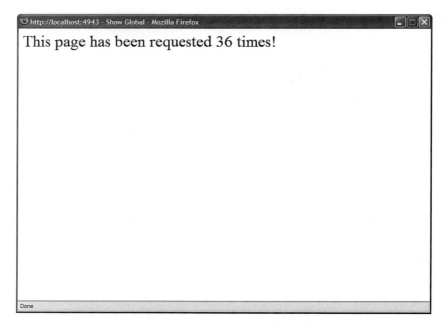

FIGURE 25.9   Displaying the NumberOfRequests property.

LISTING 25.23   ShowGlobal.aspx

```
<%@ Page Language="VB" %>
<!DOCTYPE html PUBLIC "-//W3C//DTD XHTML 1.0 Transitional//EN"
  "http://www.w3.org/TR/xhtml1/DTD/xhtml1-transitional.dtd">
<html xmlns="http://www.w3.org/1999/xhtml" >
<head id="Head1" runat="server">
    <title>Show Global</title>
</head>
<body>
    <form id="form1" runat="server">
    <div>

    This page has been requested
    <%= Me.ApplicationInstance.NumberOfRequests %>
    times!

    </div>
    </form>
</body>
</html>
```

Creating Custom HTTP Modules

An HTTP Module is a .NET class that executes with each and every page request. You can use an HTTP Module to handle any of the HttpApplication events that you can handle in the Global.asax file.

Behind the scenes, the ASP.NET Framework uses HTTP Modules to implement many of the standard features of the Framework. For example, the ASP.NET Framework uses the FormsAuthenticationModule to implement Forms authentication and the WindowsAuthenticationModule to implement Windows authentication.

Session state is implemented with an HTTP Module named the SessionStateModule. Page output caching is implemented with an HTTP Module named the OutputCacheModule, and the Profile object is implemented with an HTTP Module named the ProfileModule.

When a new instance of an HttpApplication class is created, the HttpApplication loads all of the HTTP Modules configured in the web configuration file. Each HTTP Module subscribes to one or more HttpApplication events. For example, when the HttpApplication object raises its AuthenticateRequest event, the FormsAuthenticationModule executes its code to authenticate the current user.

In this section, we create a simple authentication HTTP Module. The HTTP Module doesn't allow you to request a page unless you include the proper query string with the request. The code for the custom HTTP Module is contained in Listing 25.24.

LISTING 25.24   App_Code\QueryStringAuthenticationModule.vb

```vb
Imports System
Imports System.Web

Namespace AspNetUnleashed
    Public Class QueryStringAuthenticationModule
        Implements IHttpModule

        Public Sub Init(ByVal app As HttpApplication) Implements IHttpModule.Init
            AddHandler app.AuthorizeRequest, AddressOf AuthorizeRequest
        End Sub

        Private Sub AuthorizeRequest(ByVal sender As Object, ByVal e As EventArgs)
            ' Get context
            Dim app As HttpApplication = CType(sender, HttpApplication)
            Dim context As HttpContext = app.Context

            ' If the request is for Login.aspx, exit
            Dim path As String = _
context.Request.AppRelativeCurrentExecutionFilePath
            If String.Compare(path, "~/login.aspx", True) = 0 Then
                Return
            End If
```

LISTING 25.24   Continued

```
        ' Check for password
        Dim authenticated As Boolean = False
        If Not IsNothing(context.Request.QueryString("password")) Then
            If context.Request.QueryString("password") = "secret" Then
                authenticated = True
            End If
        End If

        ' If not authenticated, redirect to login.aspx
        If Not authenticated Then
            context.Response.Redirect("~/Login.aspx")
        End If
    End Sub

    Public Sub Dispose() Implements IHttpModule.Dispose
    End Sub
    End Class
End Namespace
```

The class in Listing 25.25 implements the IHttpModule interface. This interface includes two methods:

- Init—Enables you to subscribe to HttpApplication events.

- Dispose—Enables you to clean up any resources used by the HTTP Module.

In Listing 25.25, the Init() method adds an event handler for the HttpApplication AuthorizeRequest event. When the HttpApplication raises the AuthorizeRequest event, the HTTP Module's AuthorizeRequest() method executes.

The AuthorizeRequest() method checks for a password=secret query string. If the query string does not exist, then the user is redirected to the Login.aspx page (the method also checks whether the user is requesting the Login.aspx page to avoid a vicious circle).

Before you can use the `QueryStringAuthenticationModule`, you must register the HTTP Module in the web configuration file. The web configuration file in Listing 25.25 includes an `<httpModules>` section that registers the module.

LISTING 25.25   `Web.Config`

```xml
<?xml version="1.0"?>
<configuration>
    <system.web>

      <httpModules>
        <add name="QueryStringAuthenticationModule"
            type="AspNetUnleashed.QueryStringAuthenticationModule"/>
      </httpModules>

    </system.web>
</configuration>
```

After you register the HTTP Module, if you attempt to request any page without including the `password=secret` query string, then you are redirected to the `Login.aspx` page. (If the `Login.aspx` page doesn't exist, you receive a `404 - Not Found` error message.)

Summary

In this chapter, you learned how to extend the ASP.NET Framework by extending different parts of the HTTP Runtime. In the first section, you learned how to create a custom `BuildProvider`. For example, you learned how to create a `BuildProvider` that dynamically generates a data access component from an XML file.

Next, you explored the topic of `ExpressionBuilders`. You learned how to use an `ExpressionBuilder` to automatically replace one expression with another. For example, we created a custom `ExpressionBuilder` that enables you to look up a value from an XML file.

The topic of HTTP Handlers was also explored. You learned two methods of creating custom HTTP Handlers. You learned how to create a Generic Handler and you learned how to create an HTTP Handler by implementing the `IHttpHandler` interface. You also saw how you can improve the scalability of your ASP.NET applications by implementing asynchronous HTTP Handlers.

Finally, you learned two methods of handling application-wide events. You learned how to create a custom `HttpApplication` by creating a `Global.asax` file. You also learned how to handle application events by implementing a custom HTTP Module.

Configuring Applications

In this chapter, you learn how to configure your ASP.NET applications. In the first section, you are provided with an overview of the different sections contained in a web configuration file. You also learn how to modify web configuration files by using both the Web Site Administration Tool and the ASP.NET Microsoft Management Console Snap-In.

Next, you learn how to manipulate configuration settings programmatically with the Configuration API. We discuss how you can both retrieve and modify configuration settings. You also learn how to work with configuration settings located at a remote website.

You also learn how to add custom configuration sections to the web configuration file. You learn how to register custom configuration sections and interact with custom configuration sections with the Configuration API.

Finally, we discuss the very important topic of protecting your configuration files. You learn how to encrypt different sections of a configuration file so that they cannot be read by human eyes. You also learn how you can deploy an encrypted configuration file from one server to another.

Overview of Website Configuration

ASP.NET uses a hierarchical system of configuration. At the top of the hierarchy is the `Machine.config` file. This file contains all the default configuration settings for ASP.NET applications and all other types of applications built with the .NET Framework.

The `Machine.config` file is located at the following path:

`\WINDOWS\Microsoft.NET\Framework\[version]\CONFIG\Machine.config`

This same folder also contains a `Web.config` file. The `Web.config` file contains settings specific to ASP.NET applications. The `Web.config` file overrides particular settings in the `Machine.config` file.

NOTE

The `\CONFIG` folder includes the following six files:

- `Machine.config`—Contains the actual configuration settings.
- `Machine.config.default`—Contains the default values for all configuration settings.
- `Machine.config.comments`—Contains comments on each configuration setting.
- `Web.config`—Contains the actual configuration settings.
- `Web.config.default`—Contains the default values for all configuration settings.
- `Web.config.comments`—Contains comments on each configuration setting.

Only the `Machine.config` and `Web.config` files are actually used. The other files are there for the purpose of documentation.

You can place a `Web.config` file in the root folder of a website, such as the wwwroot folder. A `Web.config` file located in the root folder of a website contains settings that apply to all applications contained in the website.

You also can place a `Web.config` file in the root of a particular application. In that case, the `Web.config` file has application scope.

Finally, you can place a `Web.config` file in an application subfolder. In that case, the `Web.config` file applies to all pages in that folder and below.

When an ASP.NET application starts, this hierarchy of configuration files is merged and cached in memory. A file dependency is created between the cached configuration settings and the file system. If you make a change to any of the configuration files in the hierarchy, the new configuration settings are loaded into memory automatically.

When an ASP.NET page reads a configuration setting, the setting is read from memory. This means that the ASP.NET Framework can read configuration settings, such as connection strings, very efficiently.

Furthermore, when you make a change to a configuration setting, you don't need to stop and restart an application manually for the new setting to take effect. The ASP.NET Framework reloads the cached configuration settings automatically when the configuration settings are changed on the file system. (The one exception to this is modifications to the `processModel` section.)

> **WARNING**
>
> Modifying most configuration settings results in an application restart. Any data stored using the cache or in-process Session state is lost and must be reloaded. You can get around this issue by using external configuration files. See the section "Placing Configuration Settings in an External File" later in this chapter.

The configuration files are XML files. You can modify configuration settings by opening the Machine.config file or a Web.config file and modifying a setting in Notepad. Alternatively, you can change many of the configuration settings (but not all) by using either the Web Site Administration Tool or the ASP.NET Microsoft Management Console Snap-In.

Using the Web Site Administration Tool

If you are using Visual Web Developer (or Visual Studio .NET), then you can modify certain configuration settings with the Web Site Administration Tool. This tool provides you with a form interface for making configuration changes (see Figure 26.1).

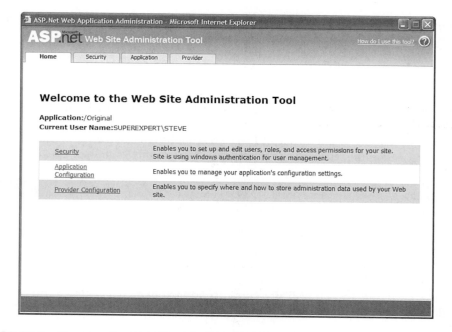

FIGURE 26.1   Opening the Web Site Administration Tool.

You open the Web Site Administration Tool by selecting the menu option Website, ASP.NET Configuration. Selecting this option opens a browser window that contains the tool.

> **WARNING**
>
> There is a bug in the first release of ASP.NET 2.0. If you open the Web Site Administration Tool, then you'll lose Intellisense when you open the `Web.config` file directly in Visual Web Developer. The Web Site Administration Tool adds an `xmlns` attribute to the opening `<configuration>` tag. If you want to get Intellisense working again, then you need to remove the `xmlns` attribute.

The Web Site Administration Tool has the following four tabs:

- **Home**—This tab contains links to the other tabs.

- **Security**—This tab enables you to configure authentication, authorization, and the Role Manager.

- **Application**—This tab enables you to create and manage application settings, configure SMTP settings, and enable application tracing, debugging, and error pages. You also can use this tab to take your application offline.

- **Provider**—This tab enables you to select a provider for Membership and the Role Manager.

Under the Application tab, you can click the link to take your application offline. When you click this link, the following `httpRuntime` element is added to your web configuration file:

```
<httpRuntime enable="false" />
```

This setting causes the Application Domain associated with the ASP.NET application to refuse any requests. When an application is offline, all requests result in a 404—Not Found error message. You might want to take your application offline, for example, to prevent people from requesting pages while you perform updates to your application.

> **NOTE**
>
> You also can take an ASP.NET application offline by adding a file with the name `app_offline.htm` to the root of your application.

The Web Site Administration Tool is implemented as an ASP.NET application. Behind the scenes, it uses the Configuration API that is discussed later in this chapter. You can view the entire source code for the Web Site Administration Tool by navigating to the following folder:

```
\WINDOWS\Microsoft.NET\Framework\[version]\ASP.NETWebAdminFiles
```

Using the ASP.NET Microsoft Management Console Snap-In

You also can make configuration changes with the ASP.NET Microsoft Management Console (MMC) Snap-In tool (see Figure 26.2). You can open the ASP.NET MMC Snap-In by following these steps:

1. Open Internet Information Services from Start, Control Panel, Administrative Tools.

2. Open the property sheet for either a website or a virtual directory.

3. Select the ASP.NET tab.

4. Click the Edit Configuration (or Edit Global Configuration) button.

The ASP.NET MMC Snap-In includes the following tabs:

- **General**—Enables you to configure connection strings and application settings.

- **Custom Errors**—Enables you to configure custom error pages.

- **Authorization**—Enables you to configure authorization rules.

- **Authentication**—Enables you to configure Forms, Windows, or Passport authentication.

- **Application**—Enables you to configure application settings such as application-wide Master Pages and Themes.

- **State Management**—Enables you to configure Session state.

- **Locations**—Enables you to apply configuration settings to a particular folder or page.

Behind the scenes, the ASP.NET MMC Snap-In uses the Configuration API to make changes to web configuration files.

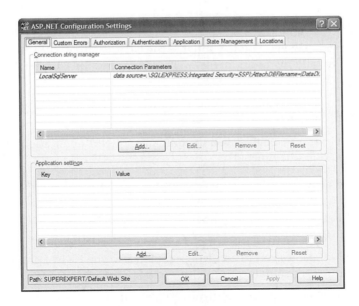

FIGURE 26.2   Using the ASP.NET Microsoft Management Console Snap-In.

ASP.NET Configuration Sections

All the configuration sections in the `Machine.config` or `Web.config` file related to
ASP.NET are contained in the `<system.web>` section group. Here is a complete list of the
36 ASP.NET configuration sections and a brief explanation of the purpose of each section:

- `anonymousIdentification`—Enables you to configure anonymous user identification, which is used, for example, by the `Profile` object. See Chapter 22, "Maintaining Application State."

- `authentication`—Enables you to configure authentication. See Chapter 21, "Using ASP.NET Membership."

- `authorization`—Enables you to configure authorization. See Chapter 21.

- `browserCaps`—Enables you to configure the lookup of browser capabilities.

- `caching`—Enables you to configure caching. See Chapter 23, "Caching Application Pages and Data."

- `clientTarget`—Enables you to configure aliases for different clients (browsers).

- `compilation`—Enables you to configure how ASP.NET applications are compiled. For example, you can specify whether or not an application is compiled in debug mode.

- `customErrors`—Enables you to configure custom error pages.

- `deployment`—Enables you to specify whether an ASP.NET application is deployed in retail mode.

- `deviceFilters`—Enables you to configure device filters.

- `globalization`—Enables you to configure the `Culture`, `UICulture`, and other attributes related to building multi-lingual web applications. See Chapter 24, "Localizing Applications for Multiple Languages."

- `healthMonitoring`—Enables you to configure Health Monitoring. See the final section of this chapter.

- `hostingEnvironment`—Enables you to configure ASP.NET application properties such as the application idle timeout.

- `httpCookies`—Enables you to configure how cookies are sent to the browser. See Chapter 22.

- `httpHandlers`—Enables you to configure HTTP Handlers. See Chapter 25, "Working with the HTTP Runtime."

- `httpRuntime`—Enables you to configure properties of the HTTP Runtime, such as the number of threads maintained in the thread pool.

- `httpModules`—Enables you to configure HTTP Modules. See Chapter 25.

- `identity`—Enables you to configure the identity of the ASP.NET application account.

- machineKey—Enables you to configure encryption keys used by Membership and Session state. See Chapter 21 and Chapter 22.

- membership—Enables you to configure ASP.NET Membership. See Chapter 21.

- mobileControls—Enables you to configure adapters used with ASP.NET mobile controls.

- pages—Enables you to configure page properties such as the website Master Page and Theme. See Chapter 5, "Designing Websites with Master Pages," and Chapter 6, Designing Websites with Themes."

- processModel—Enables you to configure the ASP.NET process.

- profile—Enables you to configure the Profile object. See Chapter 22.

- roleManager—Enables you to configure the Role Manager. See Chapter 21.

- securityPolicy—Enables you to map security policy files to trust levels.

- sessionPageState—Enables you to configure how mobile devices store Session state.

- sessionState—Enables you to configure Session state. See Chapter 22.

- siteMap—Enables you to configure Site Maps. See Chapter 18, "Using Site Maps."

- trace—Enables you to configure page and application tracing.

- trust—Enables you to configure Code Access Security (CAS) for an ASP.NET application.

- urlMappings—Enables you to remap page requests to new pages. See Chapter 19, "Advanced Navigation."

- webControls—Enables you to specify the location of client-script files used by web controls.

- webParts—Enables you to configure Web Parts. See Part VIII, "Building Applications with Web Parts."

- webServices—Enables you to configure web services.

- xhtmlConformance—Enables you to configure the level of XHTML conformance of the XHTML rendered by web controls.

Applying Configuration Settings to a Particular Path

By default, the settings in a Machine.config or Web.config file are applied to all pages in the same folder and below. However, if you have the need, you can also apply configuration settings to a particular path. For example, you can apply configuration settings to a particular subfolder or even a particular page.

You apply configuration settings to a particular path by using the `<location>` element. For example, the web configuration file in Listing 26.1 enables password-protection for a single file named `Secret.aspx`.

LISTING 26.1   Web.config

```
<?xml version="1.0"?>
<configuration >

  <system.web>
    <authentication mode="Forms" />
  </system.web>

  <location path="Secret.aspx">
    <system.web>
      <authorization>
        <deny users="?" />
      </authorization>
    </system.web>
  </location>

</configuration>
```

If you attempt to request the `Secret.aspx` page, you are redirected to the `Login.aspx` page. However, none of the other files in the same application are password protected by the configuration file.

The `<location>` element must be added as an immediate child of the `<configuration>` element. You can't, for example, add the `<location>` element within a `<system.web>` element. You must surround the `<system.web>` element with the `<location>` element.

> **NOTE**
>
> You can create the web configuration file in Listing 26.1 by selecting the menu option Website, Add New Item, and selecting the Web Configuration File template. Alternatively, you can add the `appSettings` section by using either the Web Site Administration Tool or the ASP.NET MMC Snap-In. Both tools enable you to enter values for the `appSettings` section through a user-friendly interface.

Locking Configuration Settings

You can lock configuration settings so that they cannot be overridden at a lower level in the configuration hierarchy. For example, you might want to require that no application running on your production server execute in debug mode. In that case, you can lock the debug configuration setting in a website `Web.config` file, the root `Web.config` file, or the `Machine.config` file.

You can lock a configuration setting in multiple ways. The Web.config file in Listing 26.2 illustrates how you can lock a setting by using the allowOverride="false" attribute of the <location> element.

LISTING 26.2 Web.config

```
<?xml version="1.0"?>
<configuration >

  <location allowOverride="false">
    <system.web>
      <compilation debug="false" />
    </system.web>
  </location>


</configuration>
```

The configuration file in Listing 26.2 locks the compilation element. If you attempt to add a configuration file that sets the debug attribute to the value true, and the configuration file is located below the configuration file in Listing 26.2, then an exception is raised (see Figure 26.3).

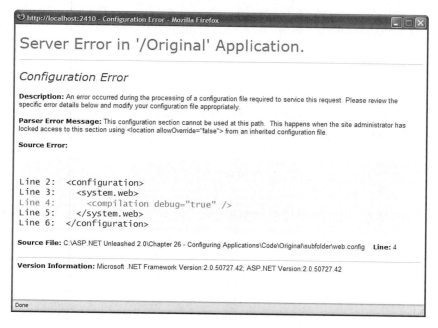

FIGURE 26.3 Attempting to override a locked configuration section.

26

One problem with the configuration file in Listing 26.2 is that it locks the entire compilation element. If you attempt to change any attribute of the compilation element at a lower level in the configuration hierarchy, then an exception is raised.

You can add any of the following attributes to a particular configuration element to lock either the entire element or one or more of its attributes:

- lockAllAttributesExcept—Enables you to lock all attributes except those listed as the value of this attribute. You can specify multiple attributes to exclude in a comma-delimited list.

- lockAllElementsExcept—Enables you to lock all child elements of the current element except those listed as the value of this attribute. You can specify multiple elements to exclude in a comma-delimited list.

- lockAttributes—Enables you to lock multiple attributes. You can specify the attributes to lock in a comma-delimited list.

- lockElement—Enables you to lock multiple child elements. You can specify the child elements to lock in a comma-delimited list.

- lockItem—Enables you to lock the current element.

For example, the web configuration file in Listing 26.3 locks the debug attribute, and only the debug attribute, of the <compilation> element.

LISTING 26.3 Web.config

```
<?xml version="1.0"?>
<configuration >

    <system.web>
      <compilation debug="false" lockAttributes="debug" />
    </system.web>

</configuration>
```

Adding Custom Application Settings

You can add custom configuration settings to the web configuration file easily by taking advantage of the appSettings section. The appSettings section contains a list of key and value pairs.

For example, the web configuration file in Listing 26.4 contains a welcome message and a copyright notice.

LISTING 26.4   Web.config

```xml
<?xml version="1.0"?>
<configuration>
  <appSettings>
    <add key="welcome" value="Welcome to our Web site!" />
    <add key="copyright" value="Copyright (c) 2007 by the company" />
  </appSettings>
</configuration>
```

You can retrieve values from the appSettings section either programmatically or declaratively. The page in Listing 26.5 illustrates both approaches (see Figure 26.4).

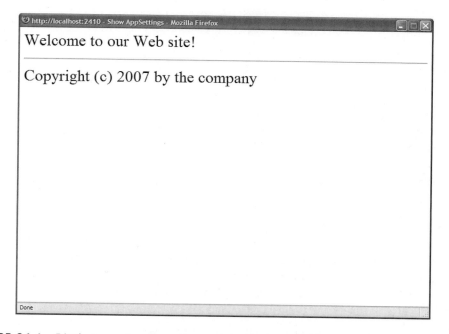

FIGURE 26.4   Displaying values from the appSettings configuration section.

LISTING 26.5   ShowAppSettings.aspx

```
<%@ Page Language="VB" %>
<%@ Import Namespace="System.Web.Configuration" %>
<!DOCTYPE html PUBLIC "-//W3C//DTD XHTML 1.0 Transitional//EN"
  "http://www.w3.org/TR/xhtml1/DTD/xhtml1-transitional.dtd">
<script runat="server">

    Sub Page_Load()
        lblWelcome.Text = WebConfigurationManager.AppSettings("welcome")
```

LISTING 26.5   Continued

```
    End Sub

</script>
<html xmlns="http://www.w3.org/1999/xhtml" >
<head id="Head1" runat="server">
    <title>Show AppSettings</title>
</head>
<body>
    <form id="form1" runat="server">
    <div>

    <asp:Label
        id="lblWelcome"
        Runat="server" />

    <hr />

    <asp:Literal
        id="ltlCopyright"
        Text="<%$ AppSettings:copyright %>"
        Runat="server" />

    </div>
    </form>
</body>
</html>
```

In Listing 26.5, the welcome message is retrieved programmatically from the
WebConfigurationManager.AppSettings property. The value retrieved is assigned to a
Label control. Notice that the System.Web.Configuration namespace must be imported
before you can use the WebConfigurationManager class.

You retrieve the copyright notice declaratively by using the
AppSettingsExpressionBuilder. The following expression is used to retrieve the value of
the copyright key:

```
<%$ AppSettings: copyright %>
```

Placing Configuration Settings in an External File

You can place particular configuration sections in an external file. You might want to do
this for a couple of reasons. First, you can make a configuration file more manageable by
dividing it into multiple files. Also, when you place configuration information in a separate file, you can prevent application restarts when you change a configuration setting.

Every configuration element includes a `configSource` attribute. You can assign a path to a file as the value of the `configSource` attribute.

For example, the web configuration file in Listing 26.6 uses the `configSource` attribute in its <appSettings> element.

LISTING 26.6 Web.config

```
<?xml version="1.0"?>
<configuration>
  <appSettings configSource="appSettings.config" />
</configuration>
```

The appSettings are stored in the external file in Listing 26.7.

LISTING 26.7 appSettings.config

```
<?xml version="1.0"?>
<appSettings>
  <add key="message" value="Hello World!" />
</appSettings>
```

Normally, modifying a web configuration file results in your ASP.NET application restarting. Any data stored in Session State or the `Cache` object is lost.

However, the `appSettings` section is declared in the `Machine.config` file with a `restartOnExternalChanges="false"` attribute. This attribute prevents your application from restarting when a change is made to the `appSettings` section in an external configuration file. If you modify the file in Listing 26.6, for example, your application won't restart.

> **NOTE**
>
> The CD that accompanies this book includes a page named `ShowAppStartTime.aspx`, which displays the time that the current ASP.NET application started. You can use this file to detect when a modification made to a web configuration file caused an application restart. (The application start time is retrieved in the `Application_Start()` event handler in the `Global.asax` file.)

Using the Configuration API

The Configuration API enables you to retrieve and modify configuration settings. You can use the Configuration API to modify web configuration files on the local machine or a remote machine.

If you are responsible for maintaining a large number of websites, the Configuration API can make your life much easier. You can build administrative tools that enable you to make configuration changes quickly to multiple applications. You can use the

Configuration API in an ASP.NET page, or you can build command-line tools or Windows Forms applications that use the Configuration API.

The Configuration API is exposed by the `WebConfigurationManager` class (located in the `System.Web.Configuration` namespace). This class supports the following properties:

- `AppSettings`—Exposes all the settings from the `appSettings` section.

- `ConnectionStrings`—Exposes all the settings from the `connectionStrings` section.

The `WebConfigurationManager` also supports the following methods:

- `GetSection`—Retrieves a configuration section relative to the current page or a supplied virtual path.

- `GetWebApplicationSection`—Retrieves a configuration section from the current web application root web configuration file.

- `OpenMachineConfiguration`—Retrieves a `Machine.config` file on either the local machine or a remote server.

- `OpenMappedMachineConfiguration`—Retrieves a `Machine.config` file by using a particular file mapping.

- `OpenMappedWebConfiguration`—Retrieves a web configuration file by using a particular file mapping.

- `OpenWebConfiguration`—Retrieves a `Web.config` file on either the local machine or a remote server.

Almost every configuration section in the web configuration file has a corresponding class in the .NET Framework that represents the configuration section. These classes provide you with a strongly typed representation of each configuration section.

For example, corresponding to the `<authentication>` section in the web configuration file, there is a `System.Web.Configuration.AuthenticationSection` class. Corresponding to the `<pages>` section in the web configuration file, there is a `System.Web.Configuration.PagesSection` class. Each of these classes expose properties that correspond to all the attributes you can set in the web configuration file.

Reading Configuration Sections from the Current Application

When an ASP.NET application starts, the application merges all the configuration settings in the configuration hierarchy to create one representation of the configuration settings. A particular configuration setting might have different values at different levels in the hierarchy. You can use the methods of the `WebConfigurationManager` class to get the value of a configuration setting at any level in the hierarchy.

The `WebConfigurationManager.GetWebApplicationSection()` method always retrieves a configuration setting from the application root `Web.config` file. For example, the page in Listing 26.8 displays whether debugging is enabled.

LISTING 26.8   ShowConfigApp.aspx

```
<%@ Page Language="VB" %>
<%@ Import Namespace="System.Web.Configuration" %>
<!DOCTYPE html PUBLIC "-//W3C//DTD XHTML 1.0 Transitional//EN"
  "http://www.w3.org/TR/xhtml1/DTD/xhtml1-transitional.dtd">
<script runat="server">

    Sub Page_Load()
        Dim section As CompilationSection = CType( WebConfigurationManager.
➥GetWebApplicationSection("system.web/compilation"), CompilationSection)
        lblDebug.Text = section.Debug.ToString()
    End Sub
</script>
<html xmlns="http://www.w3.org/1999/xhtml" >
<head id="Head1" runat="server">
    <title>Show Config App</title>
</head>
<body>
    <form id="form1" runat="server">
    <div>

    Debug Mode:
    <asp:Label
        id="lblDebug"
        Runat="server" />

    </div>
    </form>
</body>
</html>
```

The GetWebApplication() method returns an object. You must cast the value returned by
this method to a particular configuration section type. In Listing 26.8, the value returned
by this method is cast to an instance of the CompilationSection type.

Realize that you will get the same result when the page in Listing 26.8 is located in different subfolders. For example, debugging might not be enabled in a root configuration file,
but it might be enabled in a configuration file in a particular subfolder. However, if you
call the GetWebApplicationSection() method, the method always returns the configuration setting for the application root Web.config file.

If you want to get the value of a configuration setting relative to the folder in which the
page executes, then you can use the GetSection() method instead of the
GetWebApplicationSection() method. The page in Listing 26.9 is located in a subfolder.
The page displays the value of the debug setting retrieved from both the
GetWebApplicationSection() method and the GetSection() method (see Figure 26.5).

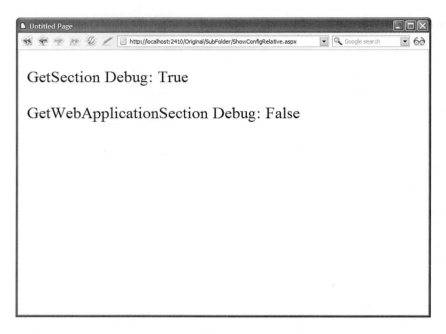

FIGURE 26.5   Retrieving a configuration setting with the `GetSection()` and
`GetWebApplicationSection()` methods.

LISTING 26.9   SubFolder\ShowConfigRelative.aspx

```
<%@ Page Language="VB" %>
<%@ Import Namespace="System.Web.Configuration" %>
<!DOCTYPE html PUBLIC "-//W3C//DTD XHTML 1.0 Transitional//EN"
  "http://www.w3.org/TR/xhtml1/DTD/xhtml1-transitional.dtd">
<script runat="server">

    Sub Page_Load()
        Dim section As CompilationSection = CType( WebConfigurationManager.
➥GetSection("system.web/compilation"), CompilationSection)
        lblDebug1.Text = section.Debug.ToString()

        section = CType(WebConfigurationManager.
➥GetWebApplicationSection("system.web/compilation"), CompilationSection)
        lblDebug2.Text = section.Debug.ToString()
    End Sub
```

LISTING 26.9   Continued

```
</script>
<html xmlns="http://www.w3.org/1999/xhtml" >
<head id="Head1" runat="server">
    <title>Show Config Relative</title>
</head>
<body>
    <form id="form1" runat="server">
    <div>

    GetSection Debug:
    <asp:Label
        id="lblDebug1"
        Runat="server" />

    <br /><br />

    GetWebApplicationSection Debug:
    <asp:Label
        id="lblDebug2"
        Runat="server" />

    </div>
    </form>
</body>
</html>
```

When you request the page in Listing 26.9, different values are displayed by the GetSection() method and GetWebApplicationSection() method. The method displays the configuration setting relative to the current directory. The second method displays the configuration setting from the application root Web.config file.

If you want to retrieve the value of a configuration setting for a particular path, then you can use the overload of the GetSection() method that accepts a path parameter. The page in Listing 26.10 iterates through all the immediate subfolders contained in the current application and displays whether debugging is enabled (see Figure 26.6).

26

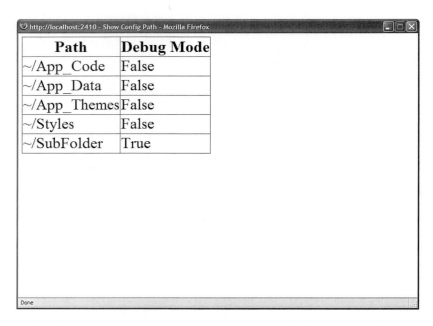

FIGURE 26.6   Displaying configuration settings for each subfolder in an application.

LISTING 26.10   ShowConfigPath.aspx

```
<%@ Page Language="VB" %>
<%@ Import Namespace="System.IO" %>
<%@ Import Namespace="System.Web.Configuration" %>
<%@ Import Namespace="System.Collections.Generic" %>
<!DOCTYPE html PUBLIC "-//W3C//DTD XHTML 1.0 Transitional//EN"
  "http://www.w3.org/TR/xhtml1/DTD/xhtml1-transitional.dtd">
<script runat="server">

    Sub Page_Load()
        Dim results As New Dictionary(Of String, Boolean)()
        Dim rootDir As New DirectoryInfo(Request.PhysicalApplicationPath)
        Dim dirs As DirectoryInfo() = rootDir.GetDirectories()
        For Each dir As DirectoryInfo In dirs
            Dim path As String = "~/" & dir.Name
            Dim section As CompilationSection = CType(WebConfigurationManager.
➥GetSection("system.web/compilation", path), CompilationSection)
            results.Add(path, section.Debug)
        Next
        grdResults.DataSource = results
        grdResults.DataBind()
    End Sub
</script>
<html xmlns="http://www.w3.org/1999/xhtml" >
```

LISTING 26.10   Continued

```
<head id="Head1" runat="server">
    <title>Show Config Path</title>
</head>
<body>
    <form id="form1" runat="server">
    <div>

    <asp:GridView
        id="grdResults"
        AutoGenerateColumns="false"
        Runat="server">
        <Columns>
        <asp:BoundField DataField="Key" HeaderText="Path" />
        <asp:BoundField DataField="Value" HeaderText="Debug Mode" />
        </Columns>
    </asp:GridView>

    </div>
    </form>
</body>
</html>
```

Opening a Configuration File

If you want to open a particular configuration file, then you can use one of the Open methods exposed by the WebConfigurationManager class. For example, the page in Listing 26.11 uses the OpenMachineConfiguration() method to open the Machine.config file and display the default value for the authentication mode setting.

LISTING 26.11   ShowConfigMachine.aspx

```
<%@ Page Language="VB" %>
<%@ Import Namespace="System.Web.Configuration" %>
<!DOCTYPE html PUBLIC "-//W3C//DTD XHTML 1.0 Transitional//EN"
  "http://www.w3.org/TR/xhtml1/DTD/xhtml1-transitional.dtd">
<script runat="server">

  Sub Page_Load()
    Dim config As Configuration =
➥WebConfigurationManager.OpenMachineConfiguration()
    Dim section As AuthenticationSection =
➥CType(config.GetSection("system.web/authentication"), AuthenticationSection)
        lblMode.Text = section.Mode.ToString()
    End Sub
</script>
<html xmlns="http://www.w3.org/1999/xhtml" >
```

26

LISTING 26.11   Continued

```
<head id="Head1" runat="server">
    <title>Show Config Machine</title>
</head>
<body>
    <form id="form1" runat="server">
    <div>

    Authentication Mode Default Value:
    <asp:Label
        id="lblMode"
        Runat="server" />

    </div>
    </form>
</body>
</html>
```

You can use the WebConfigurationManager class to display configuration information for other websites located on the same server. For example, the page in Listing 26.12 displays a list of all the virtual directories contained in the default website. You can select a virtual directory and view the authentication mode associated with the virtual directory (see Figure 26.7).

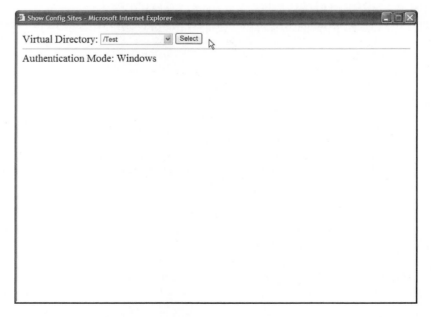

FIGURE 26.7   Displaying configuration information for any application hosted on a server.

LISTING 26.12   ShowConfigSites.aspx

```
<%@ Page Language="VB" %>
<%@ Import Namespace="System.Web.Configuration" %>
<%@ Import Namespace="System.DirectoryServices" %>
<%@ Import Namespace="System.Collections.Generic" %>
<!DOCTYPE html PUBLIC "-//W3C//DTD XHTML 1.0 Transitional//EN"
   "http://www.w3.org/TR/xhtml1/DTD/xhtml1-transitional.dtd">

<script runat="server">

    Const sitePath As String = "IIS://localhost/W3SVC/1/ROOT"

    Sub Page_Load()
        If Not Page.IsPostBack Then
            dropVDirs.DataSource = GetVirtualDirectories()
            dropVDirs.DataBind()
        End If
    End Sub

    Private Function GetVirtualDirectories() As List(Of String)
        Dim dirs As New List(Of String)()
        Dim site As New DirectoryEntry(sitePath)
        Dim vdirs As DirectoryEntries = site.Children

        For Each vdir As DirectoryEntry In vdirs
            If vdir.SchemaClassName = "IIsWebVirtualDir" Then
                Dim vPath As String = vdir.Path.Remove(0, sitePath.Length)
                dirs.Add(vPath)
            End If
        Next
        Return dirs
    End Function

    Protected Sub btnSelect_Click(ByVal sender As Object, ByVal e As EventArgs)
        Dim config As Configuration = WebConfigurationManager.
➥OpenWebConfiguration(dropVDirs.SelectedValue)
        Dim section As AuthenticationSection = CType( config.
➥GetSection("system.web/authentication"), AuthenticationSection)
        lblAuthenticationMode.Text = section.Mode.ToString()
    End Sub
</script>
<html xmlns="http://www.w3.org/1999/xhtml" >
<head id="Head1" runat="server">
    <title>Show Config Sites</title>
</head>
```

26

LISTING 26.12   Continued

```
<body>
    <form id="form1" runat="server">
    <div>

    <asp:Label
        id="lblVirtualDirectory"
        Text="Virtual Directory:"
        AssociatedControlID="dropVDirs"
        Runat="server" />
    <asp:DropDownList
        id="dropVDirs"
        Runat="server" />
    <asp:Button
        id="btnSelect"
        Text="Select"
        OnClick="btnSelect_Click"
        Runat="server" />

    <hr />

    Authentication Mode:
    <asp:Label
        id="lblAuthenticationMode"
        Runat="server" />

    </div>
    </form>
</body>
</html>ShowConfigSites
```

The list of virtual directories is retrieved with the classes from the
System.DirectoryServices namespace. When you select a virtual directory, the
OpenWebConfiguration() method is called with the path to the virtual directory to get the
configuration information.

> **WARNING**
>
> Before you can use the classes from the System.DirectoryServices namespace, you must add
> a reference to the System.DirectoryServices.dll assembly. In Visual Web Developer, select
> the menu option Website, Add Reference.

Opening a Configuration File on a Remote Server

You can use the WebConfigurationManager class to open Machine.config or Web.config
files located on remote web servers. However, before you can do this, you must perform

one configuration step. You must enable the remote server to accept remote configuration connections by executing the following command from a command prompt:

```
aspnet_regiis -config+
```

To disable remove configuration connections, execute the following command:

```
aspnet_regiis -config-
```

The `aspnet_regiis` tool is located in the following path:

```
\WINDOWS\Microsoft.NET\Framework\[version]\aspnet_regiis.exe
```

> **NOTE**
>
> If you open the SDK Command Prompt, then you don't need to navigate to the Microsoft.NET folder to execute the `aspnet_regiis` tool.

After you make this modification to a remote server, you can retrieve (and modify) configuration settings on the remote server by using one of the Open methods exposed by the `WebConfigurationManager` class. For example, the page in Listing 26.13 contains a form that enables you to enter a server, username, and password. When you submit the form, the page connects to the remote server and retrieves its `Machine.config` file. The page displays the current value of the remote server's authentication mode (see Figure 26.8).

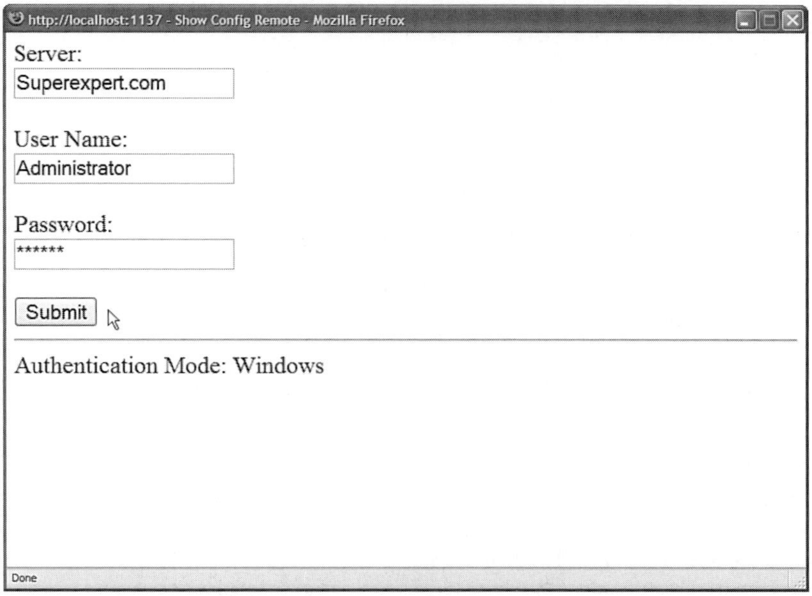

FIGURE 26.8   Changing configuration settings for a remote server.

26

LISTING 26.13   ShowConfigRemote.aspx

```
<%@ Page Language="VB" %>
<%@ Import Namespace="System.Web.Configuration" %>
<!DOCTYPE html PUBLIC "-//W3C//DTD XHTML 1.0 Transitional//EN"
  "http://www.w3.org/TR/xhtml1/DTD/xhtml1-transitional.dtd">
<script runat="server">

    Protected Sub btnSubmit_Click(ByVal sender As Object, ByVal e As EventArgs)
        Try
            Dim config As Configuration =
➥WebConfigurationManager.OpenMachineConfiguration(Nothing, txtServer.Text,
➥txtUserName.Text, txtPassword.Text)
            Dim section As AuthenticationSection =
➥CType(config.GetSection("system.web/authentication"), AuthenticationSection)
            lblAuthenticationMode.Text = section.Mode.ToString()
        Catch ex As Exception
            lblAuthenticationMode.Text = ex.Message
        End Try
    End Sub
</script>
<html xmlns="http://www.w3.org/1999/xhtml" >
<head id="Head1" runat="server">
    <title>Show Config Remote</title>
</head>
<body>
    <form id="form1" runat="server">
    <div>

    <asp:Label
        id="lblServer"
        Text="Server:"
        AssociatedControlID="txtServer"
        Runat="server" />
    <br />
    <asp:TextBox
        id="txtServer"
        Runat="server" />
    <br /><br />
    <asp:Label
        id="lblUserName"
        Text="User Name:"
        AssociatedControlID="txtUserName"
        Runat="server" />
```

LISTING 26.13   Continued

```
        <br />
        <asp:TextBox
            id="txtUserName"
            Runat="server" />
        <br /><br />
      <asp:Label
            id="lblPassword"
            Text="Password:"
            AssociatedControlID="txtPassword"
            Runat="server" />
        <br />
        <asp:TextBox
            id="txtPassword"
            TextMode="Password"
            Runat="server" />
        <br /><br />
      <asp:Button
            id="btnSubmit"
            Text="Submit"
            OnClick="btnSubmit_Click"
            Runat="server" />

        <hr />

        Authentication Mode:
        <asp:Label
            id="lblAuthenticationMode"
            Runat="server" />

        </div>
        </form>
</body>
</html>
```

You can use the page in Listing 26.13 even when the web server is located in some distant part of the Internet. You can enter a domain name or IP address in the server field.

Using the Configuration Class

When you use one of the WebConfigurationManager Open methods—such as the OpenMachineConfiguration() or OpenWebConfiguration() methods—the method returns an instance of the Configuration class. This class supports the following properties:

- AppSettings—Returns the appSettings configuration section.

- ConnectionStrings—Returns the connectionStrings configuration section.

- EvaluationContext—Returns an instance of the ContextInformation class that enables you to determine the context of the configuration information.

- FilePath—Returns the physical file path to the configuration file.

- HasFile—Returns True when there is a file that corresponds to the configuration information.

- Locations—Returns a list of locations defined by the configuration.

- NamespaceDeclared—Returns True when the configuration file includes a namespace declaration.

- RootSectionGroup—Returns the root section group.

- SectionGroups—Returns the child section groups contained by this configuration.

- Sections—Returns the child sections contained by this configuration.

The Configuration class also supports the following methods:

- GetSection—Enables you to return the specified configuration section.

- GetSectionGroup—Enables you to return the specified configuration section group.

- Save—Enables you to save any configuration changes.

- SaveAs—Enables you to save the configuration as a new file.

A configuration file contains two basic types of entities: section groups and sections. For example, the <system.web> element in a configuration file represents a section group. The <system.web> section group contains child sections such as the <authentication> and <httpRuntime> sections.

You can use the Configuration.RootSectionGroup property to get the primary section group in a configuration file. You can use the SectionGroups property to return all of a section group's child section groups and the Sections property to return all of a section group's child sections.

For example, the page in Listing 26.14 recursively displays the contents of the Machine.config file in a TreeView control (see Figure 26.9).

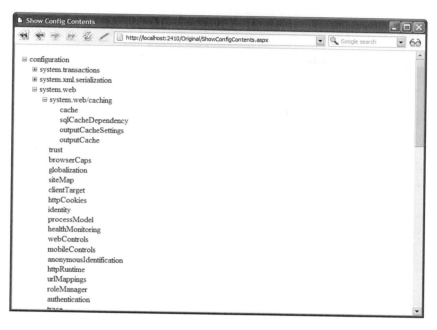

FIGURE 26.9 Displaying all configuration sections from the `system.web` configuration section group.

LISTING 26.14 ShowConfigContents.aspx

```
<%@ Page Language="VB" %>
<%@ Import Namespace="System.Web.Configuration" %>
<!DOCTYPE html PUBLIC "-//W3C//DTD XHTML 1.0 Transitional//EN"
  "http://www.w3.org/TR/xhtml1/DTD/xhtml1-transitional.dtd">
<script runat="server">

    sub Page_Load()
        ' Add first node
        Dim parentNode As New TreeNode("configuration")
        TreeView1.Nodes.Add(parentNode)

        ' Start from the root section group
        Dim config As Configuration = WebConfigurationManager.
➥OpenMachineConfiguration()

        ' Show child section groups
        AddChildSectionGroups(parentNode, config.RootSectionGroup)

        ' Show child sections
        AddChildSections(parentNode, config.RootSectionGroup)
    end sub
```

LISTING 26.14   Continued

```
    Private Sub AddChildSectionGroups(ByVal parentNode As TreeNode,
➡ByVal parentConfigSectionGroup As ConfigurationSectionGroup)
        For Each configSectionGroup As ConfigurationSectionGroup
➡In parentConfigSectionGroup.SectionGroups
            Dim childNode As New TreeNode(configSectionGroup.SectionGroupName)
            parentNode.ChildNodes.Add(childNode)
            AddChildSectionGroups(childNode, configSectionGroup)
            AddChildSections(childNode, configSectionGroup)
        Next
    End Sub

    Private Sub AddChildSections(ByVal parentNode As TreeNode,
➡ByVal parentConfigSectionGroup As ConfigurationSectionGroup)
        For Each configSection As ConfigurationSection In
➡parentConfigSectionGroup.Sections
            Dim childNode As New TreeNode(configSection.SectionInformation.Name)
            parentNode.ChildNodes.Add(childNode)
        Next
    End Sub
</script>
<html xmlns="http://www.w3.org/1999/xhtml" >
<head id="Head1" runat="server">
    <title>Show Config Contents</title>
</head>
<body>
    <form id="form1" runat="server">
    <div>

    <asp:TreeView
        id="TreeView1"
        Runat="server" />

    </div>
    </form>
</body>
</html>
```

Modifying Configuration Sections

You can use the WebConfigurationManager class not only when opening a configuration file to read the values of various configuration settings. You also can use the WebConfigurationManager class to modify existing configuration settings or add new ones.

The Configuration class supports two methods for saving configuration information: the Save() and SaveAs() methods. For example, the page in Listing 26.15 enables you to turn on and off debugging for an application (see Figure 26.10).

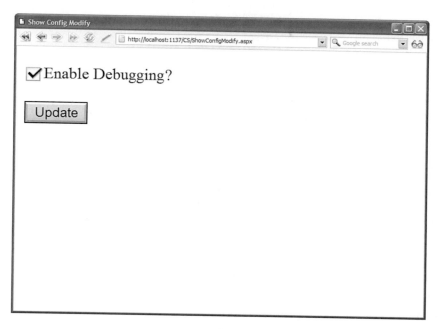

FIGURE 26.10   Modifying the value of the Debug configuration setting.

LISTING 26.15   ShowConfigModify.aspx

```
<%@ Page Language="VB" %>
<%@ Import Namespace="System.Web.Configuration" %>
<!DOCTYPE html PUBLIC "-//W3C//DTD XHTML 1.0 Transitional//EN"
  "http://www.w3.org/TR/xhtml1/DTD/xhtml1-transitional.dtd">
<script runat="server">

    sub Page_Load()
        if Not Page.IsPostBack Then
            Dim config As Configuration = WebConfigurationManager.
➡OpenWebConfiguration(Request.ApplicationPath)
            Dim section As CompilationSection = CType(config.
➡GetSection("system.web/compilation"), CompilationSection)
            chkDebug.Checked = section.Debug
        end if
    end sub

    Protected Sub btnUpdate_Click(ByVal sender As Object, ByVal e As EventArgs)
```

26

LISTING 26.15   Continued

```
        Dim config As Configuration =
➥WebConfigurationManager.OpenWebConfiguration(Request.ApplicationPath)
        Dim section As CompilationSection = CType(config.
➥GetSection("system.web/compilation"), CompilationSection)
        section.Debug = chkDebug.Checked
        config.Save(ConfigurationSaveMode.Modified)
    End Sub
</script>
<html xmlns="http://www.w3.org/1999/xhtml" >
<head id="Head1" runat="server">
    <title>Show Config Modify</title>
</head>
<body>
    <form id="form1" runat="server">
    <div>

    <asp:CheckBox
        id="chkDebug"
        Text="Enable Debugging?"
        Runat="server" />
    <br /><br />
    <asp:Button
        id="btnUpdate"
        Text="Update"
        OnClick="btnUpdate_Click"
        Runat="server" />

    </div>
    </form>
</body>
</html>
```

The page in Listing 26.15 loads the application root Web.config file with the help of the
OpenWebConfiguration() method (the Nothing parameter causes the root Web.config file
to be loaded). Next, the value of the Compilation.Debug property is modified. Finally, the
Save() method is called to save this change.

When you call the Save() method, you can pass a ConfigurationSaveMode parameter to
the method. This parameter can have the following values:

- Full—Saves all configuration settings, regardless of whether they have been modified.

- Minimal—Saves only those configuration settings that are different from their inherited value.

- Modified—Saves only those configuration settings that have been modified.

To use the Save() or SaveAs() methods, the account associated with the page must have Write permissions for the folder where the configuration file is saved. By default, when pages are served from Internet Information Server, ASP.NET pages execute in the security context of the NETWORK SERVICE account (in the case of Windows Server 2003) or the ASPNET account (in the case of other operating systems). By default, neither of these accounts have permissions to save configuration changes.

> **NOTE**
>
> To make things more confusing, when pages are served from the web server included with Visual Web Developer, the pages are always served in the security context of the current user.

There are multiple ways that you can get around this permission problem. First, remember that you can use many of the methods of the WebConfigurationManager class from a console application or a Windows Forms application. If you build this type of application, then you can sidestep these security issues.

Another option is to enable per-request impersonation for your ASP.NET application. When impersonation is enabled, an ASP.NET page executes within the security context of the user making the page request. If the user account has permissions to write to the file system, then the page has permissions to write to the file system.

The web configuration file in Listing 26.16 enables impersonation.

LISTING 26.16   Web.config

```xml
<?xml version="1.0"?>
<configuration>
    <system.web>
      <identity impersonate="true" />
    </system.web>
</configuration>
```

If you add the configuration file in Listing 26.16 to the same folder that contains the file in Listing 26.15, then you will be able to make modifications to configuration files.

> **WARNING**
>
> Most changes to a configuration file result in an application restart. When an ASP.NET application restarts, all data stored in memory is blown away. For example, all data cached in the Cache object or Session state is lost.

Provisioning a New Website

When you are provisioning new websites, you often need to create a new virtual directory. The Configuration API doesn't provide you with any help here.

However, you can create new virtual directories (and applications) by taking advantage of the classes in the `System.DirectoryServices` namespace. These classes enable you to use Active Directory Services Interface (ADSI) to modify properties of Internet Information Server.

> **NOTE**
>
> You also can manipulate Internet Information Server properties by using Windows Management Instrumentation (WMI). For more information, see the topic "Using WMI to Configure IIS" at the Microsoft MSDN website (msdn.microsoft.com).

Before you can use the classes from the `System.DirectoryServices` namespace, you need to add a reference to the `System.DirectoryServices.dll` assembly. In Visual Web Developer, select the menu option Website, Add Reference, and select `System.DirectoryServices.dll`.

For example, the page in Listing 26.17 enables you to provision a new ASP.NET application (see Figure 26.11). The page creates a new virtual directory and a new application. The page also creates a new web configuration file in the virtual directory that contains the default language and debug settings you specify.

FIGURE 26.11   Creating a new ASP.NET application.

LISTING 26.17   ProvisionSite.aspx

```vb
<%@ Page Language="VB" %>
<%@ Import Namespace="System.IO" %>
<%@ Import Namespace="System.DirectoryServices" %>
<%@ Import Namespace="System.Web.Configuration" %>
<!DOCTYPE html PUBLIC "-//W3C//DTD XHTML 1.0 Transitional//EN"
  "http://www.w3.org/TR/xhtml1/DTD/xhtml1-transitional.dtd">
<script runat="server">

    Const wwwroot As String = "c:\Inetpub"
    Const sitePath As String = "IIS://localhost/W3SVC/1/ROOT"

    Protected Sub btnSubmit_Click(ByVal sender As Object, ByVal e As EventArgs)
        Dim NewFolder As String = Path.Combine(wwwroot, txtVirtualDir.Text)

        CreateVirtualDirectory(NewFolder, txtVirtualDir.Text, txtVirtualDir.Text)
        CreateConfiguration(txtVirtualDir.Text)

        ' Show link to new site
        lnkNewSite.NavigateUrl = "http://localhost/" & txtVirtualDir.Text
        lnkNewSite.Target = "_top"
        lnkNewSite.Visible = True
    End Sub

    Private Sub CreateVirtualDirectory(ByVal folderPath As String,
➥ByVal virtualDirectoryName As String, ByVal appFriendlyName As String)
        ' Create new Folder
        Directory.CreateDirectory(folderPath)

        ' Create Virtual Directory
        Dim vRoot As New DirectoryEntry(sitePath)
        Dim vDir As DirectoryEnTry = vRoot.Children.Add(virtualDirectoryName,
➥"IIsWebVirtualDir")
        vDir.CommitChanges()
        vDir.Properties("Path").Value = folderPath
        vDir.Properties("DefaultDoc").Value = "Default.aspx"
        vDir.Properties("DirBrowseFlags").Value = 2147483648
        vDir.CommitChanges()
        vRoot.CommitChanges()

        ' Create Application (Isolated)
        vDir.Invoke("AppCreate2", 1)
        vDir.Properties("AppFriendlyName").Value = appFriendlyName
        vDir.CommitChanges()
    End Sub
```

26

LISTING 26.17   Continued

```
    Private Sub CreateConfiguration(ByVal virtualPath As String)
        ' Open configuration
        Dim config As Configuration = WebConfigurationManager.
➥OpenWebConfiguration("/" & virtualPath)

        ' Set language and debug setting
        Dim section As CompilationSection = CType(config.
➥GetSection("system.web/compilation"), CompilationSection)
        section.DefaultLanguage = rdlLanguage.SelectedItem.Text
        section.Debug = chkDebug.Checked

        ' Save configuration
        config.Save(ConfigurationSaveMode.Modified)
    End Sub
</script>
<html xmlns="http://www.w3.org/1999/xhtml" >
<head id="Head1" runat="server">
    <title>Provision Site</title>
</head>
<body>
    <form id="form1" runat="server">
    <div>

    <asp:Label
        id="lblVirtualDir"
        Text="Virtual Directory:"
        AssociatedControlID="txtVirtualDir"
        Runat="server" />
    <br />
    <asp:TextBox
        id="txtVirtualDir"
        Runat="server" />
    <br /><br />
    <asp:Label
        id="lblLanguage"
        Text="Default Language:"
        AssociatedControlID="rdlLanguage"
        Runat="server" />
    <asp:RadioButtonList
        id="rdlLanguage"
        Runat="server">
        <asp:ListItem Text="VB" Selected="True" />
        <asp:ListItem Text="C#" />
    </asp:RadioButtonList>
    <br />
```

LISTING 26.17   Continued

```
        <asp:CheckBox
            id="chkDebug"
            Text="Enable Debugging"
            Runat="server" />
        <br /><br />
        <asp:Button
            id="btnSubmit"
            Text="Submit"
            OnClick="btnSubmit_Click"
            Runat="server" />

        <hr />
        <asp:HyperLink
            id="lnkNewSite"
            Visible="false"
            Text="Go to New Site"
            Runat="server" />

    </div>
    </form>
</body>
</html>
```

To use the page in Listing 26.17, you'll need adequate permissions. You can enable per-request impersonation by adding the file in Listing 26.16 to the same folder as the page in Listing 26.17.

> **NOTE**
>
> Internet Information Server includes several sample ADSI scripts. Look in your `Inetpub\AdminScripts` folder.

Creating Custom Configuration Sections

You can add custom configuration sections to a web configuration file. You can use a custom configuration section to store whatever information you want.

For example, if you need to manage a large number of database connection strings, then you might want to create a custom database connection string configuration section. Or, if you want to follow the Provider Model and implement a custom provider, then you need to create a custom configuration section for your provider.

You create a custom configuration section by inheriting a new class from the base `ConfigurationSection` class. For example, the class in Listing 26.18 represents a simple custom configuration section.

LISTING 26.18   App_Code\DesignSection.vb

```vb
Imports System
Imports System.Configuration
Imports System.Drawing

Namespace AspNetUnleashed
    Public Class DesignSection
        Inherits ConfigurationSection

        <ConfigurationProperty("backcolor", DefaultValue:="lightblue", _
➥IsRequired:=True)> _
        Public Property BackColor() As Color
            Get
                Return CType(Me("backcolor"), Color)
            End Get
            Set(ByVal Value As Color)
                Me("backcolor") = Value
            End Set
        End Property

        <ConfigurationProperty("styleSheetUrl", DefaultValue:="~/styles/style.css", _
➥IsRequired:=True)> _
        <RegexStringValidator(".css$")> _
        Public Property StyleSheetUrl() As String
            Get
                Return CType(Me("styleSheetUrl"), String)
            End Get
            Set(ByVal Value As String)
                Me("styleSheetUrl") = Value
            End Set
        End Property

        Public Sub New(ByVal backcolor As Color, ByVal styleSheetUrl As String)
            Me.BackColor = backcolor
            Me.StyleSheetUrl = styleSheetUrl
        End Sub

        Public Sub New()
        End Sub
    End Class
End Namespace
```

The class in Listing 26.18 represents a Design configuration section. This section has two properties: BackColor and StyleSheetUrl.

Notice that both properties are decorated with `ConfigurationProperty` attributes. The `ConfigurationProperty` attribute is used to map the property to an element attribute in the configuration file. When you declare the `ConfigurationProperty` attribute, you can use the following parameters:

- `Name`—Enables you to specify the name of the attribute in the configuration file that corresponds to the property.

- `DefaultValue`—Enables you to specify the default value of the property.

- `IsDefaultCollection`—Enables you to specify whether the property represents the default collection of an element.

- `IsKey`—Enables you to specify whether the property represents a key for a collection of configuration elements.

- `IsRequired`—Enables you to specify whether this property must have a value.

- `Options`—Enables you to use flags to specify the values of the above options.

You also can use validators when defining configuration properties. For example, in Listing 26.18, the `RegexStringValidator` is used to check whether the value of the `StyleSheetUrl` property ends with a `.css` extension.

You can use the following validators with configuration properties:

- `CallbackValidator`—Enables you to specify a custom method to use to validate a property value.

- `IntegerValidator`—Enables you to validate whether a property value is an integer value (`System.Int32`).

- `LongValidator`—Enables you to validate whether a property value is a long value (`System.Int64`).

- `PositiveTimeSpanValidator`—Enables you to validate whether a property value is a valid time span.

- `RegexStringValidator`—Enables you to validate a property value against a regular expression pattern.

- `StringValidator`—Enables you to validate a property value that represents a string against a minimum length, maximum length, and list of invalid characters.

- `SubClassTypeValidator`—Enables you to validate whether the value of a property is inherited from a particular class

- `TimeSpanValidator`—Enables you to validate a property value that represents a time span against a minimum and maximum value.

After you create a custom configuration section, you need to register it in a configuration file before you can use it. The web configuration file in Listing 26.19 adds the `DesignSection` configuration section to the `system.web` section.

LISTING 26.19   Web.config

```
<configuration>
  <configSections>
    <sectionGroup name="system.web">
    <section
        name="design"
        type="AspNetUnleashed.DesignSection"
        allowLocation="true"
        allowDefinition="Everywhere"/>
    </sectionGroup>
  </configSections>
  <system.web>
    <design
      backcolor="red"
      styleSheetUrl="~/styles/style.css"/>
  </system.web>
</configuration>
```

You are not required to add a custom configuration section to any particular configuration section group. For that matter, you are not required to add a custom configuration section to any configuration section group at all.

After you register a custom configuration section, you can use it just like any of the standard configuration sections. You can use the methods of the `WebConfigurationManager` class to retrieve and modify the custom section.

For example, the page in Listing 26.20 uses the custom configuration section just created to retrieve the page background color and style sheet (see Figure 26.12).

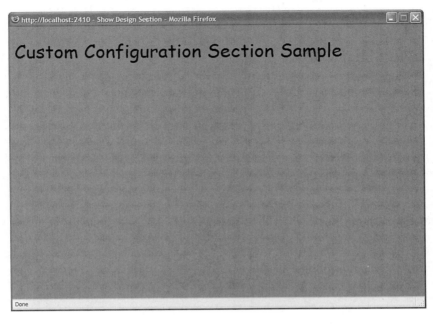

FIGURE 26.12   Using the custom configuration section to modify the page style and background color.

LISTING 26.20   ShowDesignSection.aspx

```
<%@ Page Language="VB" %>
<%@ Import Namespace="AspNetUnleashed" %>
<%@ Import Namespace="System.Web.Configuration" %>
<%@ Import Namespace="System.Drawing" %>
<!DOCTYPE html PUBLIC "-//W3C//DTD XHTML 1.0 Transitional//EN"
  "http://www.w3.org/TR/xhtml1/DTD/xhtml1-transitional.dtd">
<script runat="server">

    Sub Page_Load()
        ' Get configuration
        Dim section As DesignSection = CType(WebConfigurationManager.
➥GetWebApplicationSection("system.web/design"), DesignSection)

        ' Set Background Color
        htmlBody.Attributes("bgcolor") = ColorTranslator.ToHtml(section.BackColor)

        ' Set style sheet
        Dim link As New HtmlLink()
        link.Href = section.StyleSheetUrl
        link.Attributes.Add("rel", "stylesheet")
```

LISTING 26.20   Continued

```
            link.Attributes.Add("type", "text/css")
            Page.Header.Controls.Add(link)
        End Sub
    </script>
    <html xmlns="http://www.w3.org/1999/xhtml" >
    <head id="Head1" runat="server">
        <title>Show Design Section</title>
    </head>
    <body id="htmlBody" runat="server">
        <form id="form1" runat="server">
        <div>

        <h1>Custom Configuration Section Sample</h1>

        </div>
        </form>
    </body>
    </html>
```

Creating a Configuration Element Collection

A configuration element can contain a collection of child elements. For example, if you need to create a custom configuration section to configure a provider, then you use child elements to represent the list of providers.

The class in Listing 26.21 represents a configuration section for a ShoppingCart. The configuration section includes three properties: MaximumItems, DefaultProvider, and Providers. The Providers property represents a collection of shopping cart providers.

LISTING 26.21   App_Code\ShoppingCartSection.vb

```
Imports System
Imports System.Configuration

Namespace AspNetUnleashed
    Public Class ShoppingCartSection
        Inherits ConfigurationSection

        <ConfigurationProperty("maximumItems", DefaultValue:=100,
    ➥IsRequired:=True)> _
        Public Property MaximumItems() As Integer
            Get
                Return CType(Me("maximumItems"), Integer)
            End Get
            Set(ByVal Value As Integer)
```

LISTING 26.21   Continued

```
                    Me("maximumItems") = Value
            End Set
        End Property


        <ConfigurationProperty("defaultProvider")> _
        Public Property DefaultProvider() As String
            Get
                Return CType(Me("defaultProvider"), String)
            End Get
            Set(ByVal Value As String)
                Me("defaultProvider") = value
            End Set
        End Property


        <ConfigurationProperty("providers", IsDefaultCollection:=False)> _
        Public ReadOnly Property Providers() As ProviderSettingsCollection
            Get
                Return CType(Me("providers"), ProviderSettingsCollection)
            End Get
        End Property


        Public Sub New(ByVal maximumItems As Integer,
➥ByVal defaultProvider As String)
            Me.MaximumItems = maximumItems
            Me.DefaultProvider = defaultProvider
        End Sub


        Public Sub New()
        End Sub
    End Class
End Namespace
```

The `Providers` property returns an instance of the `ProviderSettingsCollection` class.
This class is contained in the `System.Configuration` namespace.

The web configuration file in Listing 26.22 illustrates how you can use the
`ShoppingCartSection`.

LISTING 26.22   Web.config

```
<configuration>
  <configSections>
    <sectionGroup name="system.web">
      <section
        name="shoppingCart"
```

26

LISTING 26.22   Continued

```
        type="AspNetUnleashed.ShoppingCartSection"
        allowLocation="true"
        allowDefinition="Everywhere" />
    </sectionGroup>
</configSections>
<system.web>

  <shoppingCart
    maximumItems="50"
    defaultProvider="SqlShoppingCartProvider">
    <providers>
      <add
        name="SqlShoppingCartProvider"
        type="AspNetUnleashed.SqlShoppingCartProvider" />
      <add
        name="XmlShoppingCartProvider"
        type="AspNetUnleashed.XmlShoppingCartProvider" />
    </providers>
  </shoppingCart>

</system.web>
</configuration>
```

The ShoppingCartSection class takes advantage of an existing class in the .NET Framework: the ProviderSettingsCollection class. If you have the need, you can create a custom configuration element collection class.

The AdminUsersSection class in Listing 26.23 enables you to represent a list of users. The class includes a property named Users that exposes an instance of the AdminUsersCollection class. The AdminUsersCollection represents a collection of configuration elements. The AdminUsersCollection class is also defined in Listing 26.23.

LISTING 26.23   App_Code\AdminUsersSection.vb

```
Imports System
Imports System.Configuration

Namespace AspNetUnleashed
    Public Class AdminUsersSection
        Inherits ConfigurationSection

        <ConfigurationProperty("", IsDefaultCollection:=True)> _
        Public ReadOnly Property Users() As AdminUsersCollection
            Get
                Return CType(Me(""), AdminUsersCollection)
```

LISTING 26.23   Continued

```
            End Get
        End Property

        Public Sub New()
        End Sub
    End Class

    Public Class AdminUsersCollection
        Inherits ConfigurationElementCollection

        Protected Overrides Function CreateNewElement() As ConfigurationElement
            Return New AdminUser()
        End Function

        Protected Overrides Function GetElementKey(ByVal element As
➡ConfigurationElement) As Object
            Return (CType(element, AdminUser)).Name
        End Function

        Public Sub New()
            Me.AddElementName = "user"
        End Sub
    End Class

    Public Class AdminUser
        Inherits ConfigurationElement

        <ConfigurationProperty("name", IsRequired:=True, IsKey:=True)> _
        Public Property Name() As String
            Get
                Return CType(Me("name"), String)
            End Get
            Set(ByVal Value As String)
                Me("name") = Value
            End Set
        End Property

        <ConfigurationProperty("password", IsRequired:=True)> _
        Public Property Password() As String
            Get
                Return CType(Me("password"), String)
            End Get
            Set(ByVal Value As String)
                Me("password") = Value
```

LISTING 26.23   Continued

```
            End Set
         End Property
      End Class
End Namespace
```

Notice that the ConfigurationProperty attribute that decorates the Users property sets the name of the configuration attribute to an empty string. It also marks the property as representing the section's default collection. These options enable you to avoid having to create a subtag for the user collection. The user collection appears immediately below the main <adminUsers> section tag.

The web configuration file in Listing 26.24 illustrates how you can use the AdminUsersSection class.

LISTING 26.24   Web.config

```
<configuration>
<configSections>
  <sectionGroup name="system.web">
    <section
      name="adminUsers"
      type="AspNetUnleashed.AdminUsersSection"
      allowLocation="true"
      allowDefinition="Everywhere" />
  </sectionGroup>
</configSections>
<system.web>

  <adminUsers>
    <user name="Bob" password="secret" />
    <user name="Fred" password="secret" />
  </adminUsers>

</system.web>
</configuration>
```

The ASP.NET page in Listing 26.25 displays all the users from the adminUsers section in a BulletedList control (see Figure 26.13).

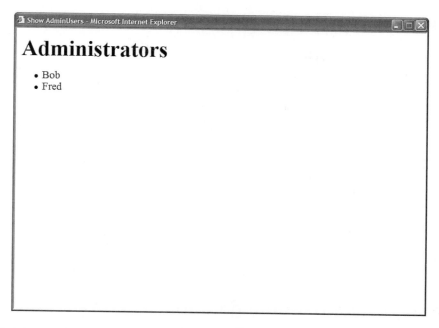

FIGURE 26.13   Displaying the contents of the `adminUsers` section in a `BulletedList` control.

LISTING 26.25   ShowAdminUsersSection.aspx

```
<%@ Page Language="VB" %>
<%@ Import Namespace="AspNetUnleashed" %>
<%@ Import Namespace="System.Web.Configuration" %>
<!DOCTYPE html PUBLIC "-//W3C//DTD XHTML 1.0 Transitional//EN"
  "http://www.w3.org/TR/xhtml1/DTD/xhtml1-transitional.dtd">
<script runat="server">

    Sub Page_Load()
        ' Get configuration
        Dim section As AdminUsersSection = CType(WebConfigurationManager.
➥GetWebApplicationSection("system.web/adminUsers"), AdminUsersSection)

        ' Bind section to GridView
        bltAdminUsers.DataSource = section.Users
        bltAdminUsers.DataBind()
    End Sub
</script>
<html xmlns="http://www.w3.org/1999/xhtml" >
<head id="Head1" runat="server">
    <title>Show AdminUsersSection</title>
```

LISTING 26.25   Continued

```
</head>
<body>
    <form id="form1" runat="server">
    <div>

    <h1>Administrators</h1>
    <asp:BulletedList
        id="bltAdminUsers"
        DataTextField="Name"
        Runat="server" />

    </div>
    </form>
</body>
</html>
```

Creating Encrypted Configuration Sections

If you need to protect sensitive information stored in a configuration file, you can encrypt the information. For example, you should always encrypt the `connectionStrings` section of a configuration file to prevent your database connection strings from being stolen by evil hackers.

You can encrypt just about any section in the web configuration file. You can encrypt any of the sections in the `system.web` section group with the sole exception of the `processModel` section. You also can encrypt a custom configuration section.

The .NET Framework uses the Provider Model for encrypting configuration sections. The Framework ships with two `ProtectedConfigurationProviders`: the `RsaProtectedConfigurationProvider` and the `DpapiProtectedConfigurationProvider`.

The `RsaProtectedConfigurationProvider` protect sensitive information stored in a configuration file, you can encrypt is the default provider. It uses the RSA algorithm to protect a configuration section. The RSA algorithm uses public key cryptography. It depends on the fact that no one has discovered an efficient method to factor large prime numbers.

The second provider, the `DpapiProtectedConfigurationProvider`, uses the Data Protection API (DPAPI) to encrypt a configuration section. The DPAPI is built into the Windows operating system (Microsoft Windows 2000 and later). It uses either Triple-DES or AES (the United States Government–standard encryption algorithm) to encrypt data.

The `RsaProtectedConfigurationProvider` is the default provider, and it is the one that you should almost always use. The advantage of the `RsaProtectedConfigurationProvider` is that this provider supports exporting and importing encryption keys. This means that you can move an application that contains an encrypted configuration file from one web server a new web server. For example, you can encrypt a configuration section on your development web server and deploy the application to a production server.

If you use the `DpapiProtectedConfigurationProvider` to encrypt a configuration section, on the other hand, then you cannot decrypt the configuration section on another web server. If you need to move the configuration file from one server to another, then you need to first decrypt the configuration file on the source server and re-encrypt the configuration file on the destination server.

> **WEB STANDARDS NOTE**
>
> The .NET Framework uses the World Wide Web Consortium (W3C) recommendation for encrypting XML files. This recommendation is located at http://www.w3.org/TR/2002/REC-xmlenc-core-20021210/.
>
> You can use encryption not only with configuration files, but also with other XML files. To learn more about encrypting XML files, look up the `EncryptedXml` class in the Microsoft .NET Framework 2.0 SDK Documentation.

Encrypting Sections with the `aspnet_regiis` tool

The easiest way to encrypt a section in the web configuration file is to use the `aspnet_regiis` command-line tool. This tool is located at the following path:

```
\WINDOWS\Microsoft.NET\Framework\[version]\aspnet_regiis.exe
```

> **NOTE**
>
> You don't need to navigate to the Microsoft.NET directory to execute the `aspnet_regiis` tool if you open the SDK Command Prompt.

If you want to encrypt a particular section of a configuration file, then you can use the -pef option when executing the `aspnet_regiis` tool. For example, the following command encrypts the `connectionStrings` section of a configuration file located in a folder named MyWebApp:

```
aspnet_regiis -pef connectionStrings c:\Websites\MyWebApp
```

If you prefer, rather than specify the location of a web application by its file system path, you can use its virtual path. The following command encrypts the `connectionStrings` section of a configuration file located in a virtual directory named /MyApp:

```
aspnet_regiis -pe connectionStrings -app /MyApp
```

Notice that the -app option is used to specify the application's virtual path.

You can decrypt a configuration section by using the -pdf option. The following command decrypts a configuration file located in a folder named MyWebApp:

```
aspnet_regiis -pdf connectionStrings c:\Websites\MyWebApp
```

You also can decrypt a configuration section by specifying a virtual directory. The following command uses the -pd option with the -app option:

```
aspnet_regiis -pd connectionStrings -app /MyApp
```

When you encrypt a configuration section, you can specify the ProtectedConfigurationProvider to use to encrypt the section. The Machine.config file configures two providers: the RsaProtectedConfigurationProvider and the DataProtectionConfigurationProvider. The RsaProtectedConfigurationProvider is used by default.

If you execute the following command, then the connectionStrings section is encrypted with the DataProtectionConfigurationProvider:

```
aspnet_regiis -pe connectionStrings -app /MyApp -prov
ProtectedConfigurationProvider
```

Notice that this command includes a -prov option that enables you to specify the ProtectedConfigurationProvider.

Encrypting Sections Programmatically

Instead of using the aspnet_regiis tool to encrypt configuration sections, you can use the Configuration API. Specifically, you can encrypt a configuration section by calling the SectionInformation.ProtectSection() method.

For example, the ASP.NET page in Listing 26.26 displays all the sections contained in the system.web section group in a GridView control. You can click Protect to encrypt a section, and you can click UnProtect to decrypt a section (see Figure 26.14).

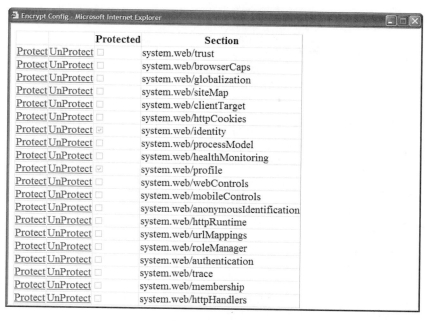

FIGURE 26.14   Encrypting and decrypting configuration sections.

LISTING 26.26   EncryptConfig.aspx

```
<%@ Page Language="VB" %>
<%@ Import Namespace="System.Web.Configuration" %>
<%@ Import Namespace="System.Collections.Generic" %>
<!DOCTYPE html PUBLIC "-//W3C//DTD XHTML 1.0 Transitional//EN"
  "http://www.w3.org/TR/xhtml1/DTD/xhtml1-transitional.dtd">
<script runat="server">

    Private Sub Page_Load()
        If Not Page.IsPostBack Then
            BindSections()
        End If
    End Sub


    Protected Sub grdSections_RowCommand(ByVal sender As Object,
➥ByVal e As GridViewCommandEventArgs)
        Dim rowIndex As Integer = Int32.Parse(CType(e.CommandArgument, String))
        Dim sectionName As String =
➥CType(grdSections.DataKeys(rowIndex).Value, String)
        If e.CommandName = "Protect" Then
```

LISTING 26.26   Continued

```
                ProtectSection(sectionName)
        End If
        If e.CommandName = "UnProtect" Then
            UnProtectSection(sectionName)
        End If
        BindSections()
    End Sub


    Private Sub ProtectSection(ByVal sectionName As String)
        Dim config As Configuration =
➥WebConfigurationManager.OpenWebConfiguration(Request.ApplicationPath)
        Dim section As ConfigurationSection = config.GetSection(sectionName)
        section.SectionInformation.
➥ProtectSection("RsaProtectedConfigurationProvider")
        config.Save(ConfigurationSaveMode.Modified)
    End Sub


    Private Sub UnProtectSection(ByVal sectionName As String)
        Dim config As Configuration =
➥WebConfigurationManager.OpenWebConfiguration(Request.ApplicationPath)
        Dim section As ConfigurationSection = config.GetSection(sectionName)
        section.SectionInformation.UnprotectSection()
        config.Save(ConfigurationSaveMode.Modified)
    End Sub


    Private Sub BindSections()
        Dim config As Configuration =
➥WebConfigurationManager.OpenWebConfiguration(Request.ApplicationPath)
        Dim colSections As New List(Of SectionInformation)()
        For Each section As ConfigurationSection In
➥config.SectionGroups("system.web").Sections
            colSections.Add(section.SectionInformation)
        Next
        grdSections.DataSource = colSections
        grdSections.DataBind()
    End Sub
</script>
<html xmlns="http://www.w3.org/1999/xhtml" >
<head id="Head1" runat="server">
    <title>Encrypt Config</title>
</head>
<body>
    <form id="form1" runat="server">
```

LISTING 26.6   Continued

```
    <div>

    <asp:GridView
        id="grdSections"
        DataKeyNames="SectionName"
        AutoGenerateColumns="false"
        OnRowCommand="grdSections_RowCommand"
        Runat="server" >
        <Columns>
        <asp:ButtonField ButtonType="Link" Text="Protect"
          CommandName="Protect" />
        <asp:ButtonField ButtonType="Link" Text="UnProtect"
          CommandName="UnProtect" />
        <asp:CheckBoxField DataField="IsProtected" HeaderText="Protected" />
        <asp:BoundField DataField="SectionName" HeaderText="Section" />
        </Columns>
    </asp:GridView>

    </div>
    </form>
</body>
</html>
```

When you click the Protect link, the grdSection_RowCommand() event handler executes
and calls the ProtectSection() method. This method calls the SectionInformation.
ProtectSection() method to encrypt the selected section. Notice that the name of a
ProtectedConfigurationProvider is passed to the ProtectSection() method.

> **WARNING**
>
> The page in Listing 26.26 saves the configuration file. By default, the ASPNET and NETWORK
> SERVICE accounts do not have permission to write to the file system. If you want the page in
> Listing 26.26 to execute within the security context of the user requesting the page, then you
> can enable per-request impersonation by adding the configuration file in Listing 26.16 to the
> root of your application.

Deploying Encrypted Web Configuration Files

If you need to copy an encrypted configuration file from one server to a new server, then
you must copy the keys used to encrypt the configuration file to the new server.
Otherwise, your application can't read encrypted sections of the configuration file on the
new server.

> **WARNING**
>
> You can't copy an encrypted configuration file from one server to another when you are using the `DpapiProtectedConfigurationProvider`. This section assumes that you are using the `RsaProtectedConfigurationProvider`.

By default, the `RsaProtectedConfigurationProvider` uses a public/private key pair stored in a key container named `NetFrameworkConfigurationKey`. This key container is located at the following path:

`\Documents and Settings\All Users\Application Data\Microsoft\Crypto\RSA\MachineKeys`

If you want to deploy an application that contains an encrypted configuration file to a new server, then you must configure a new key container and import the key container to the new server. You must complete five configuration steps:

1. Create a new key container.

2. Configure your application to use the new key container.

3. Export the keys from the origin server.

4. Import the keys on the destination server.

5. Grant access to the key container to your ASP.NET application.

You need to perform this sequence of configuration steps only once. After you have set up both servers to use the same encryption keys, you can copy ASP.NET applications back and forth between the two servers and read the encrypted configuration sections. Let's examine each of these steps one by one.

First, you need to create a new key container because the default key container, the `NetFrameworkConfigurationKey` key container, does not support exporting both the public and private encryption keys. Execute the following command from a command prompt:

`aspnet_regiis -pc "SharedKeys" -exp`

This command creates a new key container named `SharedKeys`. The `-exp` option is used to make any keys added to the container exportable.

After you create the new key container, you must configure your application to use it. The web configuration file in Listing 26.27 configures the `RsaProtectedConfigurationProvider` to use the `SharedKeys` key container.

LISTING 26.27   `Web.config`

```
<?xml version="1.0"?>
<configuration>
  <configProtectedData
```

LISTING 26.27 Continued

```
      defaultProvider="MyProtectedConfigurationProvider">
      <providers>
      <add
        name="MyProtectedConfigurationProvider"
        type="System.Configuration.RsaProtectedConfigurationProvider"
        cspProviderName=""
        useMachineContainer="true"
        useOAEP="false"
        keyContainerName="SharedKeys" />
      </providers>
  </configProtectedData>

  <connectionStrings>
    <add
      name="Movies"
      connectionString="Data Source=DataServer;Integrated Security=true;
        Initial Catalog=MyDB" />
  </connectionStrings>
</configuration>
```

Notice that the configuration file in Listing 26.27 includes a `configProtectedData` section. This section is used to configure a new `ProtectedConfigurationProvider` named `MyProtectedConfigurationProvider`. This provider includes a `keyContainerName` attribute that points to the `SharedKeys` key container.

The next step is to export the keys contained in the `SharedKeys` key container to an XML file. You can export the contents of the `SharedKeys` key container by executing the following command:

```
aspnet_regiis -px "SharedKeys" keys.xml -pri
```

Executing this command creates a new XML file named `keys.xml`. The `-pri` option causes both the private and public key—and not only the public key—to be exported to the XML file.

WARNING

The XML key file contains very secret information (the keys to the kingdom). After importing the XML file, you should immediately destroy the XML file (or stick the XML file on a CD and lock the CD away in a safe location).

26

After you create the `keys.xml` file on the origin server, you need to copy the file to the destination server and import the encryption keys. Execute the following command on the destination server to create a new key container and import the encryption keys:

```
aspnet_regiis -pi "SharedKeys" keys.xml
```

The final step is to grant access to the key container to your ASP.NET application. By default, a page served from Internet Information Server executes within the security context of either the NETWORK SERVICE account (Windows 2003 Server) or the ASPNET account (other operating systems). You can grant access to the SharedKeys key container to the ASPNET account by executing the following command:

```
aspnet_regiis -pa "SharedKeys" "ASPNET"
```

Executing this command modifies the ACLs for the SharedKeys key container so that the ASPNET account has access to the encryption keys.

After you complete this final step, you can transfer ASP.NET applications with encrypted configuration files back and forth between the two servers. An application on one server can read configuration files that were encrypted on the other server.

> **NOTE**
>
> As an alternative to using the aspnet_regiis tool, you can transfer encryption keys with the help of the RsaProtectedConfigurationProvider class. The RsaProtectedConfigurationProvider class contains methods for exporting and importing keys to and from XML files programmatically.

Summary

This chapter was devoted to the topic of configuration. In the first section, you were provided with an overview of the configuration sections used by the ASP.NET Framework. You learned how to lock configuration sections to prevent sections from being modified. You also learned how to place configuration sections in external files.

Next, we tackled the topic of the Configuration API. You learned how to read and modify configuration files programmatically. You also learned how to provision new ASP.NET applications by creating new virtual directories and configuration files.

You also learned how to create custom configuration sections. You learned how to create both simple custom configuration sections and custom configuration sections that contain custom collections of configuration elements.

Finally, we discussed the topic of encryption. You learned how to encrypt a configuration section by using the aspnet_regiis command-line tool. You also learned how to encrypt configuration sections programmatically. In the final section, you also learned how to deploy encrypted configuration files from a development server to a production server.

PART VIII

Building Applications with Web Parts

IN THIS PART

CHAPTER **27**

Introduction to Web Parts

The ASP.NET Web Part Framework enables you to build web applications that can be personalized by users at runtime. A Web Part application can be personalized by individual users or the application can be personalized by a single administrator for everyone.

You can take advantage of Web Parts to build *personalizable* portal applications like My Yahoo! (http://my.yahoo.com) or My MSN (http://my.msn.com). Users of these applications can customize both the content and appearance of the application by interacting with a web page. For example, you can select the content you want to see from categories of content such as News, Sports, and Weather (see Figure 27.1). You can also arrange the content on a page in the manner that is most relevant to you (see Figure 27.2).

Most large companies have internal website portals. You can take advantage of Web Parts to enable the individual employees of your company to customize the portal pages in the way that is most relevant to them. For example, a software tester might want a home page that displays a list of the most recent bugs. A marketing person, on the other hand, might want to see a news feed and stock ticker.

The Web Part Framework also can be used to build applications that can be customized by one or more administrators for everyone. Imagine, for example, that you want to build and sell a customized web store to your clients. If you build your application by using Web Parts, your clients can customize the application's appearance from their browsers without any technical knowledge.

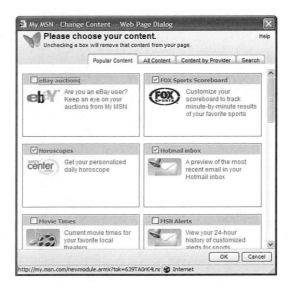

FIGURE 27.1   Selecting content at My MSN.

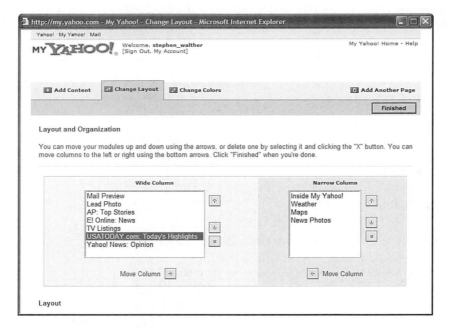

FIGURE 27.2   Arranging Content at My Yahoo!.

In this chapter, you are introduced to the Web Part Framework. You learn how to build simple Web Parts and add the Web Parts to different zones in a page. You also learn how to enable users to edit Web Part properties from a Web Form page. Finally, you learn how you can connect Web Parts to communicate information from one Web Part to another.

Overview of the Web Part Framework

A Web Part is an ASP.NET control that is contained within a Web Part Zone. Any ASP.NET control can be used as a Web Part, including any standard ASP.NET control such as the GridView, Image, or LinkButton control. You can also create a Web Part by creating a new User control or a new custom Web control.

> **NOTE**
>
> ASP.NET 2.0 Web Parts will be used in the next version of Windows Sharepoint Services (WSS) and Microsoft Office Sharepoint Portal Server (SPS). The good news is that if you develop Web Parts for the ASP.NET 2.0 Framework, then the Web Parts will work with the new versions of these products when they are released. The bad news is that ASP.NET 2.0 Web Parts are not compatible with the current implementation of Web Parts used in these two products.

Because you can create a new Web Part by creating a new control, a Web Part can do anything you want. You can create an Email Client Web Part, a Random Quotation of the Day Web Part, a Shopping Cart Web Part, or a Task List Web Part. Anything you can do in the ASP.NET Framework, you can do with Web Parts.

When you add an ASP.NET control to a Web Part Zone, the control automatically gets several special capabilities. For example, you can drag and drop a Web Part from one Web Part Zone to another. You can minimize and maximize a Web Part. You can modify the properties of a Web Part and the modifications are automatically saved.

> **NOTE**
>
> The next chapter is devoted exclusively to the topic of building Web Parts.

Web Parts are just one type of control included in the Web Part Framework. You can use several different types of parts when building a Web Part page. You can also add several different types of zones to a Web Part page.

Web Part Zones

When you build a page that contains Web Parts, you divide the page into different zones. Each zone is responsible for managing and rendering a particular type of part. There are four standard types of zones included in the Web Part Framework:

- **Web Part Zones** —This type of zone is used to render Web Parts. You can add Web Parts to a Web Part Zone and drag and drop Web Parts between different Web Part Zones.

- **Editor Zones**—This type of zone is used to render Editor Parts. Use Editor Parts to enable a user to edit Web Part properties.

- **Catalog Zones**—This type of zone is used to render Catalog Parts. Use Catalog Parts to display lists of Web Parts that a user can add to a page.

- **Connections Zones**—This type of zone is used to display an interface that enables users to connect Web Parts dynamically.

NOTE

You can extend the Web Part Framework with custom zones. We'll explore this option in Chapter 30, "Extending the Web Part Framework."

Every page that contains Web Parts contains at least one Web Part Zone. A Web Part Zone is used to lay out the Web Parts on a page.

The other types of zones are known collectively as *tool zones*. Adding a tool zone to a page is optional. If you don't want a user to add new Web Parts to a page, then don't include a Catalog Zone in the page. If you don't want a user to be able to edit or connect Web Parts, then don't add Editor or Connections Zones to a page.

Web Part Display Modes

By default, when you first open a page that contains Web Parts, the only type of zone that is rendered is Web Part Zones. To display the other types of zones, you must change the page's Display Mode.

At any time, a page can be in one of the following Display Modes:

- **Browse**—The default mode. In this mode, you cannot rearrange or edit Web Parts.

- **Design**—In this mode, you can drag and drop Web Parts from one Web Part Zone to another.

- **Edit**—In this mode, you can edit a Web Part's properties by using one or more Editor Parts.

- **Catalog**—In this mode, you can add new Web Parts to a page from one or more Catalog Parts.

- **Connect**—In this mode, you can create dynamic connections between Web Parts.

A page that contains Web Parts can be in only one Display Mode at a time. If you switch to Edit Display Mode, then the contents of any Editor Zones are rendered and you can edit Web Parts. If you switch to Catalog Display Mode, then the contents of any Catalog Zones are rendered and you can add new Web Parts. However, you cannot set a page to both Edit and Catalog Display Mode at the same time.

NOTE

You can extend the Web Part Framework with custom Display Modes. We'll explore this option in Chapter 30.

Web Part Personalization

When a user makes changes to a Web Part's properties, the Web Part Framework automatically saves these changes. For example, a user can add one or more Web Parts to a page and arrange the Web Parts with a particular layout. If the user returns to the page in the future, the Web Parts will remember the layout. This feature of the Web Part Framework is called *personalization*.

The Web Part Framework supports two types of personalization: User and Shared. By default, all changes made to a Web Parts page have User scope. Changes are scoped to a particular user, which enables each user to personalize the same page in different ways.

The Web Part Framework also supports Shared scope personalization. An administrator of a Web Part application can make changes that have an effect on everyone who uses the application. For example, an administrator might want to add a standard set of Web Parts to a page and prevent individual users from removing them.

NOTE

This chapter sticks to User scope personalization. In Chapter 29, "Personalizing Web Parts," the topic of User and Shared scope personalization is examined in detail.

For personalization to work, the Web Part Framework must have a method of identifying users. The default personalization provider included with the Web Part Framework requires that users be authenticated. If you use the default provider, then an unauthenticated user can browse, but not customize, a Web Part application. (In Chapter 29, you learn how to create a custom personalization provider.)

WARNING

You must enable authentication for your application for many of the sample pages in this chapter to work. By default, Windows Authentication is enabled. For more information about enabling authentication, see Chapter 20, "Using the Login Controls."

Creating a Simple Web Part Application

Let's get our hands dirty by building a simple Web Part application. In this section, you'll create a minimal Web Part application that consists of a single page. It illustrates how to use three of the different types of zones: Web Part Zones, Editor Zones, and Catalog Zones.

You start by creating two painfully simple Web Parts. The easiest way to create new Web Parts is to create User Controls. The User Controls contained in Listing 27.1 and Listing 27.2 serve as the Web Parts.

NOTE

To learn more about User Controls, see Chapter 7, "Creating Custom Controls with User Controls."

LISTING 27.1   FirstSimplePart.ascx

```
<%@ Control Language="VB" ClassName="FirstSimplePart" %>

<h1>First Simple Part</h1>
```

LISTING 27.2   SecondSimplePart.ascx

```
<%@ Control Language="VB" ClassName="SecondSimplePart" %>

<h1>Second Simple Part</h1>
```

These simple Web Parts both consist of nothing more than a single line of text. You can, of course, create more complicated Web Parts with User controls. For example, you can create a User control that contains a GridView control bound to some database data. Or, you can create a User Control that calls a remote web service to display the current weather. In this section, however, we keep things simple.

Next, you need to create the page that you'll use to host your Web Parts. Every page that contains Web Parts must, at a minimum, have one WebPartManager control and one or more WebPartZone controls.

Every page that contains Web Parts must include one, and only one, WebPartManager control. The WebPartManager control is responsible for tracking the state of all the Web Parts on the page. The WebPartManager control must appear before any other Web Parts on the page. For this reason, it is a good idea to place the WebPartManager control immediately after the server-side form control in the page.

The WebPartZone controls are used to mark the different areas of the page that can contain Web Parts. They are used to lay out Web Parts on a page. You can add as many WebPartZone controls to a page as you want.

TIP

You can add the WebPartManager control and the WebPartZone controls to a Master Page. This is useful when you want to automatically include a WebPartManager and WebPartZone controls in multiple content pages without explicitly declaring the controls in each page.

You'll build the page in stages. First, create a page that contains a WebPartManager control and two Web Part Zone controls (see Listing 27.3).

LISTING 27.3   SimpleWebParts1.aspx

```
<%@ Page Language="VB" %>
<%@ Register TagPrefix="user" TagName="FirstSimplePart"
Src="~/FirstSimplePart.ascx" %>
<%@ Register TagPrefix="user" TagName="SecondSimplePart"
Src="~/SecondSimplePart.ascx" %>
<!DOCTYPE html
        PUBLIC "-//W3C//DTD XHTML 1.1//EN"
"http://www.w3.org/TR/xhtml11/DTD/xhtml11.dtd">
<html xmlns="http://www.w3.org/1999/xhtml" >
<head id="Head1" runat="server">
    <style type="text/css">
        .column
        {
            float:left;
            width:40%;
            height:200px;
            margin-right:10px;
            border:solid 1px black;
            background-color: white;
        }
        html
        {
            background-color:#eeeeee;
        }
    </style>
    <title>Simple Web Parts 1</title>
</head>
<body>
    <form id="form1" runat="server">
    <asp:WebPartManager
        id="WebPartManager1"
        Runat="server" />

        <asp:WebPartZone
            id="WebPartZone1"
            CssClass="column"
            Runat="server">
            <ZoneTemplate>
            <user:FirstSimplePart
                id="FirstSimplePart1"
                Title="First Web Part"
```

27

LISTING 27.3   Continued

```
                Description="Our first simple Web Part"
                Runat="server" />
            <user:SecondSimplePart
                id="SecondSimplePart1"
                Title="Second Web Part"
                Description="Our second simple Web Part"
                Runat="server" />
            </ZoneTemplate>
        </asp:WebPartZone>

        <asp:WebPartZone
            id="WebPartZone2"
            CssClass="column"
            Runat="server" />


    </form>
</body>
</html>
```

Notice that the page in Listing 27.3 contains a WebPartManager control immediately after the server-side <form> tag. If you neglected to add the WebPartManager control to the page, you would get an exception when you opened the page.

The page also contains two Web Part Zones. The first Web Part Zone contains the two simple Web Parts that you created earlier. The Web Parts are listed in the WebPartZone control's ZoneTemplate. The second Web Part Zone is empty.

Notice that the two simple Web Parts are both provided with a Title and Description attribute. The Title attribute appears in the Web Part's title bar, and the description appears as a tool tip when you hover your mouse over a Web Part.

VISUAL WEB DEVELOPER NOTE

If you open the page in Listing 27.3 in Source View, you'll notice a green squiggle warning beneath the Title and Description attributes. You can safely ignore this warning. The warning appears because these aren't really properties of the User Controls. Technically, the Title and Description properties are expando properties that are interpreted by the Web Part Framework at runtime.

NOTE

To keep things simple, the two User controls are registered with the <%@ Register %> directive at the top of the page. Another option would be to register the User Controls in your application's Web Configuration file and make the controls automatically available in any page in your application. To learn more about User controls see Chapter 7.

When you open the page in Listing 27.3 in a browser, you see the page in Figure 27.3. At the moment, you can't do very much with the page. The only thing you can do is open each of the Web Part's menus. Each Web Part menu has two options: Minimize and Close. Minimizing a Web Part shrinks a Web Part to its title bar. If you close a Web Part, then the Web Part is no longer rendered to the page.

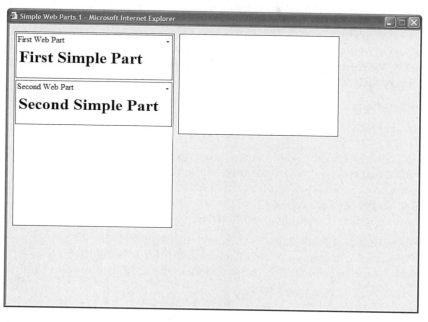

FIGURE 27.3   The Simple Parts 1 page.

WEB STANDARDS NOTE

The page in Listing 27.3 uses an internal Cascading Style Sheet to position the two Web Part Zones. The zones are positioned with a liquid layout. Both Web Part Zones are floated to the left with the help of a CSS class named *column*.

You can, of course, lay out the Web Part Zones in a page by using an HTML table. However, you should feel very guilty about even thinking about doing it because you should strive to use HTML tables only when displaying tabular data and not for layout.

NOTE

How do you open a Web Part after you close it? You use the PageCatalogPart control that is discussed later in this section.

If you prefer, you can prevent users from closing Web Parts by disabling the Close menu option. Set the CloseVerb-Visible property on the WebPartZone control to the value false.

To do anything interesting in a page that contains Web Parts, you need to add a mechanism to the page that enables users to switch between different Web Part Display Modes. The WebPartManager control is responsible for setting the Display Mode. You can set the Display Mode by taking advantage of the WebPartManager control's `DisplayMode` property like this:

```
WebPartManager1.DisplayMode = WebPartManager.DesignDisplayMode
```

This line of code sets the page to Design Display Mode. Each of the standard Web Part Display Modes is represented by a shared (static) field exposed by the WebPartManager class. (Display Modes are not represented by an enumeration because you can create custom Display Modes.)

Here's another method of setting the Display Mode:

```
WebPartManager1.DisplayMode = WebPartManager1.DisplayModes("Design")
```

This line of code also sets the page Display Mode to Design Display Mode. However, in this case, the `DisplayModes` property is used as the value of the assignment. The `DisplayModes` property exposes a collection of all the Display Modes that the WebPartManager control knows. We'll use this second method of setting the Display Mode because it makes it possible to avoid using a Visual Basic `SELECT...CASE` statement.

The page in Listing 27.4 is the same as the previous page in Listing 27.3 with one addition. This new page contains an ASP.NET menu control that enables you to switch the Display Mode of the page to Design Display Mode. (The modifications are emphasized in bold.)

LISTING 27.4   `SimpleWebParts2.aspx`

```
<%@ Page Language="VB" %>
<%@ Register TagPrefix="user" TagName="FirstSimplePart"
Src="~/FirstSimplePart.ascx" %>
<%@ Register TagPrefix="user" TagName="SecondSimplePart"
Src="~/SecondSimplePart.ascx" %>
<!DOCTYPE html PUBLIC "-//W3C//DTD XHTML 1.1//EN"
"http://www.w3.org/TR/xhtml11/DTD/xhtml11.dtd">
<script runat="server">

    Sub Menu1_MenuItemClick(sender As Object, e As MenuEventArgs)
        WebPartManager1.DisplayMode = WebPartManager1.DisplayModes(e.Item.Text)
    End Sub
</script>

<html xmlns="http://www.w3.org/1999/xhtml" >
<head id="Head1" runat="server">
    <style type="text/css">
        .column
```

LISTING 27.4   Continued

```
            {
                float:left;
                width:40%;
                height:200px;
                margin-right:10px;
                border:solid 1px black;
                background-color: white;
            }
            .menu
            {
                margin:5px 0px;
            }
            html
            {
                background-color:#eeeeee;
            }
        </style>
        <title>Simple Web Parts 2</title>
</head>
<body>
        <form id="form1" runat="server">
        <asp:WebPartManager
            id="WebPartManager1"
            Runat="server" />

            <asp:Menu
                id="Menu1"
                OnMenuItemClick="Menu1_MenuItemClick"
                Orientation="Horizontal"
                CssClass="menu"
                Runat="server">
                <Items>
                <asp:MenuItem Text="Browse" />
                <asp:MenuItem Text="Design" />
                </Items>
            </asp:Menu>

            <asp:WebPartZone
                id="WebPartZone1"
                CssClass="column"
                Runat="server">
                <ZoneTemplate>
                <user:FirstSimplePart
                    id="FirstSimplePart1"
```

LISTING 27.4   Continued

```
                Title="First Web Part"
                Description="Our first simple Web Part"
                Runat="server" />
            <user:SecondSimplePart
                id="SecondSimplePart1"
                Title="Second Web Part"
                Description="Our second simple Web Part"
                Runat="server" />
            </ZoneTemplate>
        </asp:WebPartZone>

        <asp:WebPartZone
            id="WebPartZone2"
            CssClass="column"
            Runat="server" />

    </form>
</body>
</html>
```

After you open the page in Listing 27.4, you can click the Design menu option and drag and drop the Web Parts between the two Web Part Zones (see Figure 27.4). When you set a page to be in Design Display Mode, the Web Part Framework automatically generates the necessary client-side JavaScript code for moving Web Parts.

> **WEB STANDARDS NOTE**
>
> Performing a drag-and-drop operation requires using a mouse. This requirement violates Section 508 and WCAG accessibility guidelines because a person with limited mobility might need to interact with a web page from the keyboard. You can satisfy these accessibility requirements by adding a LayoutEditorPart control to the page. The LayoutEditorPart control enables you to move Web Parts around a page without using a mouse.

It is important to understand that the Web Part Framework automatically saves the state of all the Web Parts in a page. In other words, if you rearrange the Web Parts, the Web Parts retain their new positions when you return to the page in the future.

> **NOTE**
>
> In this section, I'm assuming that Windows Authentication is enabled for your application (which is the default Authentication mode). If your Web Parts are forgetting their positions on a page after you close and re-open the page then, most likely, you are not being authenticated. For more information on configuring Authentication, see Part VI, "Security," of this book.

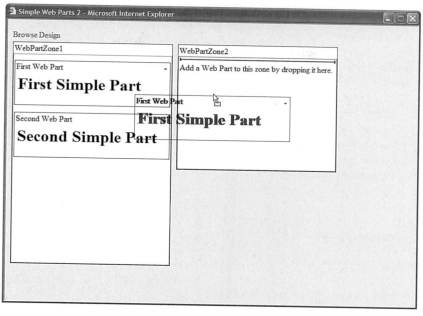

FIGURE 27.4   Dragging a Web Part between Web Part Zones.

You can also enable users to add new Web Parts to a page. To do this, you need to add a CatalogZone control that contains one or more Catalog Parts to the page. For example, the page in Listing 27.5 includes a Declarative Catalog Part which lists both the FirstSimplePart and SecondSimplePart Web Parts.

LISTING 27.5   SimpleWebParts3.aspx

```
<%@ Page Language="VB" %>
<%@ Register TagPrefix="user" TagName="FirstSimplePart"
Src="~/FirstSimplePart.ascx" %>
<%@ Register TagPrefix="user" TagName="SecondSimplePart"
Src="~/SecondSimplePart.ascx" %>
<!DOCTYPE html PUBLIC "-//W3C//DTD XHTML 1.1//EN"
"http://www.w3.org/TR/xhtml11/DTD/xhtml11.dtd">

<script runat="server">

    Sub Menu1_MenuItemClick(ByVal sender As Object, ByVal e As MenuEventArgs)
        WebPartManager1.DisplayMode = WebPartManager1.DisplayModes(e.Item.Text)
    End Sub
</script>

<html xmlns="http://www.w3.org/1999/xhtml" >
```

27

LISTING 27.5   Continued

```
<head id="Head1" runat="server">
    <style type="text/css">
        .column
        {
            float:left;
            width:30%;
            height:200px;
            margin-right:10px;
            border:solid 1px black;
            background-color: white;
        }
        .menu
        {
            margin:5px 0px;
        }
        html
        {
            background-color:#eeeeee;
        }
    </style>
    <title>Simple Web Parts 3</title>
</head>
<body>
    <form id="form1" runat="server">
    <asp:WebPartManager
        id="WebPartManager1"
        Runat="server" />

        <asp:Menu
            id="Menu1"
            OnMenuItemClick="Menu1_MenuItemClick"
            Orientation="Horizontal"
            CssClass="menu"
            Runat="server">
            <Items>
            <asp:MenuItem Text="Browse" />
            <asp:MenuItem Text="Design" />
            <asp:MenuItem Text="Catalog" />
            </Items>
        </asp:Menu>

        <asp:WebPartZone
            id="WebPartZone1"
```

LISTING 27.5   Continued

```
                CssClass="column"
                Runat="server" />

        <asp:WebPartZone
            id="WebPartZone2"
            CssClass="column"
            Runat="server" />

    <asp:CatalogZone
        id="CatalogZone1"
        CssClass="column"
        Runat="server">
        <ZoneTemplate>
        <asp:DeclarativeCatalogPart
            id="DeclarativeCatalogPart"
            Runat="server">
            <WebPartsTemplate>
            <user:FirstSimplePart
                id="FirstSimplePart1"
                Title="First Web Part"
                Description="Our first simple Web Part"
                Runat="server" />
            <user:SecondSimplePart
                id="SecondSimplePart1"
                Title="Second Web Part"
                Description="Our second simple Web Part"
                Runat="server" />
            </WebPartsTemplate>
        </asp:DeclarativeCatalogPart>
        <asp:PageCatalogPart
            id="PageCatalogPart1"
            Runat="server" />
        </ZoneTemplate>
    </asp:CatalogZone>

    </form>
</body>
</html>
```

The additions to Listing 27.5 are emphasized in bold. Notice that a new menu option has been added to the ASP.NET Menu control. The new menu option enables you to switch the page to Catalog Display Mode (see Figure 27.5).

27

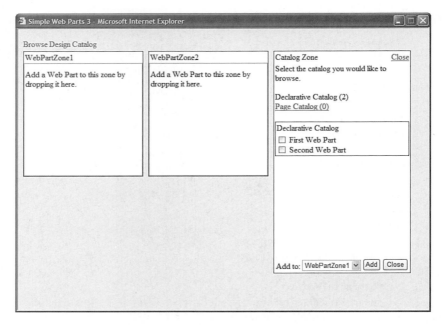

FIGURE 27.5 Opening Catalog Display mode.

Furthermore, a Catalog Zone has been added to the page. The Catalog Zone includes a DeclarativeCatalogPart which is used to list the two Web Parts that you can add to the page. The CatalogZone also includes a PageCatalogPart control, which is used to add closed Web Parts back to a page.

After you open the page in Listing 27.5 in a browser, you can click the Catalog menu option and add new instances of the two Web Parts to the page. Again, any changes you make to the page are saved automatically by the Web Part Framework.

Notice that you can now retrieve any Web Parts that you have closed on the page by taking advantage of the PageCatalogPart. If you close a Web Part by selecting a Web Part's Close menu option, you can re-open the Web Part by clicking Catalog and selecting the closed Web Part from the list of Web Parts rendered by the Page Catalog Part control.

> **NOTE**
>
> The DeclarativeCatalogPart control does not enable you to drag and drop Web Parts onto the page. If you want to add drag-and-drop support or paging and sorting support or any other custom functionality to a Catalog Part, then you need to create a custom Catalog Part. This option is discussed in Chapter 30.

Finally, you can enable users to edit Web Parts. For example, Listing 27.6 contains a new Web Part named FeaturedBookPart. This Web Part displays information about a particular book.

LISTING 27.6   FeaturedBookPart.ascx

```
<%@ Control Language="VB" ClassName="FeaturedBookPart" %>
<script runat="server">

    Private _bookTitle As String = "Untitled"
    Private _category As BookCategory = BookCategory.Computers
    Private _bookDescription As String
    Private _onSale As Boolean

    Public Enum BookCategory
        Computers
        History
        Mystery
    End Enum

    <Personalizable()> _
    <WebBrowsable()> _
    <WebDisplayName("Title")> _
    <WebDescription("The title of the book")> _
    Public Property BookTitle() As String
        Get
            Return _bookTitle
        End Get
        Set(ByVal Value As String)
            _bookTitle = value
        End Set
    End Property

    <Personalizable()> _
    <WebBrowsable()> _
    <WebDisplayName("Category")> _
    <WebDescription("The category of the book")> _
    Public Property Category() As BookCategory
        Get
            Return _category
        End Get
        Set(ByVal Value As BookCategory)
            _category = value
        End Set
    End Property

    <Personalizable()> _
    <WebBrowsable()> _
    <WebDisplayName("Description")> _
    <WebDescription("The description of the book")> _
```

27

LISTING 27.6   Continued

```
    Public Property BookDescription() As String
        Get
            Return _bookDescription
        End Get
        Set(ByVal Value As String)
            _bookDescription = value
        End Set
    End Property

    <Personalizable()> _
    <WebBrowsable()> _
    <WebDisplayName("On Sale")> _
    <WebDescription("Indicates that the book is on sale")> _
    Public Property OnSale() As Boolean
        Get
            Return _onSale
        End Get
        Set(ByVal Value As Boolean)
            _onSale = value
        End Set
    End Property

    Private Sub Page_PreRender()
        ltlBookTitle.Text = _bookTitle
        lblCategory.Text = _category.ToString()
        lblBookDescription.Text = _bookDescription
        lblOnSale.Visible = _onSale
    End Sub

</script>
<h1 class="bookTitle">
<asp:Literal
    ID="ltlBookTitle"
    runat="server"/>
</h1>
<asp:Label
    ID="lblCategory"
    CssClass="category"
    runat="server" />
<br />
<asp:Label
    ID="lblBookDescription"
    runat="server" />
<br />
```

LISTING 27.6   Continued

```
<asp:Label
    ID="lblOnSale"
    Text="On Sale!"
    Visible="false"
    CssClass="onSale"
    runat="server" />
```

You should notice several things about the Web Part in Listing 27.6. Notice that each of its properties is decorated with the following attributes: Personalizable, WebBrowsable, WebDisplayName, WebDescription. The Web Part Framework automatically detects these attributes.

The most important attribute is the Personalizable attribute. Any property marked with the Personalizable attribute is automatically saved and loaded by the Web Part Framework. Because the BookTitle, BookCategory, BookDescription, and OnSale properties are all marked as Personalizable, any changes to these properties are saved by the Web Part Framework.

The remaining three attributes—WebBrowsable, WebDisplayName, and WebDescription— are used by the PropertyGridEditorPart control. Only properties marked with the WebBrowsable attribute are displayed in the property grid rendered by the PropertyGridEditorPart control. The WebDisplayName and WebDescription attributes determine the title and description displayed for the property in the property sheet. Both the WebDisplayName and WebDescription attributes are optional.

The page in Listing 27.7 illustrates how you can edit the FeaturedBookPart by using the PropertyGridEditorPart control (changes from the previous listings are emphasized in bold).

LISTING 27.7   SimpleWebParts4.aspx

```
<%@ Page Language="VB" %>
<%@ Register TagPrefix="user" TagName="FeaturedBookPart"
Src="~/FeaturedBookPart.ascx" %>
<!DOCTYPE html PUBLIC "-//W3C//DTD XHTML 1.1//EN"
"http://www.w3.org/TR/xhtml11/DTD/xhtml11.dtd">

<script runat="server">

    Sub Menu1_MenuItemClick(ByVal sender As Object, ByVal e As MenuEventArgs)
        WebPartManager1.DisplayMode = WebPartManager1.DisplayModes(e.Item.Text)
    End Sub
</script>

<html xmlns="http://www.w3.org/1999/xhtml" >
```

27

LISTING 27.7   Continued

```
<head id="Head1" runat="server">
    <style type="text/css">
        .column
        {
            float:left;
            width:30%;
            height:200px;
            margin-right:10px;
            border:solid 1px black;
            background-color: white;
        }
        .menu
        {
            margin:5px 0px;
        }
        html
        {
            background-color:#eeeeee;
        }
        .bookTitle
        {
            font:bold 14px Arial,Sans-Serif;
            border-bottom:solid 1px black;
        }
        .category
        {
            font:italic 12px Arial,Sans-Serif;
        }
        .onSale
        {
            font:bold 14px Arial,Sans-Serif;
            background-color:yellow;
        }
    </style>
    <title>Simple Web Parts 4</title>
</head>
<body>
    <form id="form1" runat="server">
    <asp:WebPartManager
        id="WebPartManager1"
        Runat="server" />

        <asp:Menu
```

LISTING 27.7   Continued

```
            id="Menu1"
            OnMenuItemClick="Menu1_MenuItemClick"
            Orientation="Horizontal"
            CssClass="menu"
            Runat="server">
            <Items>
            <asp:MenuItem Text="Browse" />
            <asp:MenuItem Text="Design" />
            <asp:MenuItem Text="Edit" />
            </Items>
        </asp:Menu>

        <asp:WebPartZone
            id="WebPartZone1"
            CssClass="column"
            Runat="server">
            <ZoneTemplate>
            <user:FeaturedBookPart
                id="FeaturedBookPart1"
                Title="Featured Book"
                Description="Displays featured book"
                Runat="server" />
            </ZoneTemplate>
        </asp:WebPartZone>

        <asp:WebPartZone
            id="WebPartZone2"
            CssClass="column"
            Runat="server" />

        <asp:EditorZone
            id="EditorZone1"
            CssClass="column"
            Runat="server">
            <ZoneTemplate>
            <asp:PropertyGridEditorPart
                id="PropertyGridEditorPart1"
                Runat="server" />
            </ZoneTemplate>
        </asp:EditorZone>
    </form>
</body>
</html>
```

27

When you open the page in Listing 27.7 in a browser, you can click the Edit menu option to switch the page into Edit Display Mode. When a page is in Edit Display Mode, you can edit particular Web Parts by selecting the Edit menu option from a Web Part menu. Selecting a Web Part to edit causes the EditorZone to render the PropertyGridEditorPart control (see Figure 27.6).

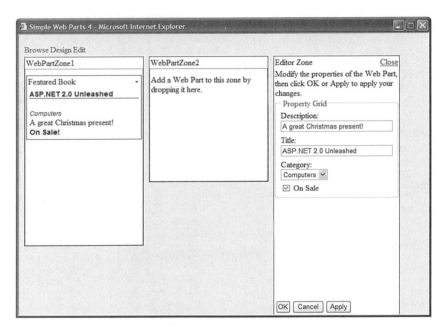

FIGURE 27.6 Opening the PropertyGridEditorPart control.

Notice that form fields are automatically generated for each of the properties that were marked as Personalizable. If you modify any of the properties and click either OK or Apply, the Web Part Framework automatically saves any changes to the properties.

> **NOTE**
>
> By default, changes to a Web Part property have User scope. In other words, each person who uses a Web Part page can customize it for his or her particular needs. You can also enable Shared scope personalization. In that case, changes to a Web Part property have an effect on all users. To learn more about personalization, see Chapter 29, "Personalizing Web Parts."

> **WEB STANDARDS NOTE**
>
> The PropertyGridEditorPart automatically generates a form that is accessible to persons with disabilities. The form is contained in a *fieldset* element. Furthermore, *label* elements with for attributes are used to explicitly associate each label with each form field.

This section has walked you through the process of creating a basic page that contains Web Parts. The remainder of this chapter examines each of the tool zones included in the Web Part Framework in more detail. You'll learn how to work with Catalog Zones, Editor Zones, and Connections Zones.

Using Catalog Zones

You use a Catalog Zone to list one or more catalogs of Web Parts that you can add to the page. The contents of a Catalog Zone appear only when a page is in Catalog Display Mode.

There are three standard types of Catalog Part controls included in the Web Part Framework: Declarative Catalog Parts, Page Catalog Parts, and Import Catalog Parts.

Using a Declarative Catalog Part

A Declarative Catalog Part contains a static list of controls that you can add to a page. You can supply the list of controls in two ways: The controls can be listed in the DeclarativeCatalogPart control's <WebPartsTemplate> tag or you can list the Web Parts in an external file.

The page in Listing 27.8 illustrates how you can list the Web Parts displayed in the Declarative Catalog Part inline.

LISTING 27.8   DeclarativeCatalogPart1.aspx

```
<%@ Page Language="VB" %>
<%@ Register TagPrefix="user" TagName="FirstSimplePart"
Src="~/FirstSimplePart.ascx" %>
<%@ Register TagPrefix="user" TagName="SecondSimplePart"
Src="~/SecondSimplePart.ascx" %>
<!DOCTYPE html PUBLIC "-//W3C//DTD XHTML 1.1//EN"
"http://www.w3.org/TR/xhtml11/DTD/xhtml11.dtd">
<script runat="server">
    Sub Menu1_MenuItemClick(ByVal sender As Object, ByVal e As MenuEventArgs)
        WebPartManager1.DisplayMode = WebPartManager1.DisplayModes(e.Item.Text)
    End Sub

</script>
<html xmlns="http://www.w3.org/1999/xhtml" >
<head id="Head1" runat="server">
    <style type="text/css">
        .column
        {
            float:left;
            width:30%;
            height:200px;
```

27

LISTING 27.8   Continued

```
            margin-right:10px;
            border:solid 1px black;
            background-color: white;
        }
        .menu
        {
            margin:5px 0px;
        }
        html
        {
            background-color:#eeeeee;
        }
    </style>
    <title>Declarative Catalog Part 1</title>
</head>
<body>
    <form id="form1" runat="server">
    <asp:WebPartManager
        id="WebPartManager1"
        Runat="server" />

        <asp:Menu
            id="Menu1"
            OnMenuItemClick="Menu1_MenuItemClick"
            Orientation="Horizontal"
            CssClass="menu"
            Runat="server">
            <Items>
            <asp:MenuItem Text="Browse" />
            <asp:MenuItem Text="Design" />
            <asp:MenuItem Text="Catalog" />
            </Items>
        </asp:Menu>

        <asp:WebPartZone
            id="WebPartZone1"
            CssClass="column"
            Runat="server" />

        <asp:WebPartZone
            id="WebPartZone2"
            CssClass="column"
            Runat="server" />
```

LISTING 27.8   Continued

```
    <asp:CatalogZone
        id="CatalogZone1"
        CssClass="column"
        Runat="server">
        <ZoneTemplate>
        <asp:DeclarativeCatalogPart
            id="DeclarativeCatalogPart"
            Runat="server">
            <WebPartsTemplate>
            <user:FirstSimplePart
                id="FirstSimplePart1"
                Title="First Web Part"
                Description="Our first simple Web Part"
                Runat="server" />
            <user:SecondSimplePart
                id="SecondSimplePart1"
                Title="Second Web Part"
                Description="Our second simple Web Part"
                Runat="server" />
            </WebPartsTemplate>
        </asp:DeclarativeCatalogPart>
        </ZoneTemplate>
    </asp:CatalogZone>

    </form>
</body>
</html>
```

The page in Listing 27.8 contains a CatalogZone control. The CatalogZone control contains a ZoneTemplate, which includes the DeclarativeCatalogPart control. Finally, the DeclarativeCatalogPart control has a WebPartsTemplate that lists two Web Parts: the FirstSimplePart and SecondSimplePart.

If you open the page in your browser and click the Catalog menu link, you can see the list of controls rendered by the DeclarativeCatalogPart control. You can add a new part to the page by selecting any of the parts in the list, selecting a Web Part Zone from the drop-down list, and clicking the Add button (see Figure 27.7).

> **NOTE**
>
> The DeclarativeCatalogPart does not support paging or sorting. In Chapter 30, "Extending the Web Part Framework," you learn how to create custom CatalogPart controls that support more functionality.

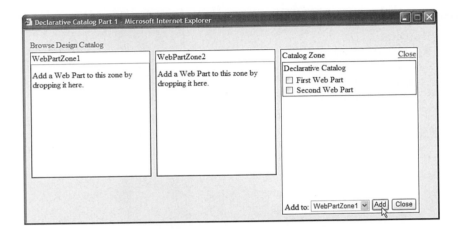

If you want to enable users to personalize multiple pages in an application, then it doesn't make sense to list the Web Parts displayed by a Declarative Catalog Part in each page. You can use the `DeclarativeCatalogPart` control's `WebPartsListUserControlPath` property to point to an external file that contains a list of Web Parts.

The `DeclarativeCatalogPart` in Listing 27.9 uses the `WebPartsListUserControlPath` property. The file that contains the list of Web Parts is contained in Listing 27.10. (Notice that the file is a User Control.)

LISTING 27.9   DeclarativeCatalogPart2.aspx

```
<%@ Page Language="VB" %>
<!DOCTYPE html PUBLIC "-//W3C//DTD XHTML 1.1//EN"
"http://www.w3.org/TR/xhtml11/DTD/xhtml11.dtd">

<script runat="server">
    Sub Menu1_MenuItemClick(ByVal sender As Object, ByVal e As MenuEventArgs)
        WebPartManager1.DisplayMode = WebPartManager1.DisplayModes(e.Item.Text)
    End Sub

</script>

<html xmlns="http://www.w3.org/1999/xhtml" >
<head id="Head1" runat="server">
    <style type="text/css">
        .column
        {
            float:left;
```

LISTING 27.9 Continued

```
                width:30%;
                height:200px;
                margin-right:10px;
                border:solid 1px black;
                background-color: white;
            }
            .menu
            {
                margin:5px 0px;
            }
            html
            {
                background-color:#eeeeee;
            }
        </style>
        <title>Declarative Catalog Part 2</title>
    </head>
<body>
    <form id="form1" runat="server">
    <asp:WebPartManager
        id="WebPartManager1"
        Runat="server" />

        <asp:Menu
            id="Menu1"
            OnMenuItemClick="Menu1_MenuItemClick"
            Orientation="Horizontal"
            CssClass="menu"
            Runat="server">
            <Items>
            <asp:MenuItem Text="Browse" />
            <asp:MenuItem Text="Design" />
            <asp:MenuItem Text="Catalog" />
            </Items>
        </asp:Menu>

        <asp:WebPartZone
            id="WebPartZone1"
            CssClass="column"
            Runat="server" />

        <asp:WebPartZone
            id="WebPartZone2"
            CssClass="column"
```

LISTING 27.9   Continued

```
                Runat="server" />


        <asp:CatalogZone
            id="CatalogZone1"
            CssClass="column"
            Runat="server">
            <ZoneTemplate>
            <asp:DeclarativeCatalogPart
                id="DeclarativeCatalogPart"
                WebPartsListUserControlPath="~/WebPartList.ascx"
                Runat="server" />
            </ZoneTemplate>
        </asp:CatalogZone>


    </form>
</body>
</html>
```

LISTING 27.10   WebPartList.ascx

```
<%@ Control Language="VB" ClassName="WebPartList" %>
<%@ Register TagPrefix="user" TagName="FirstSimplePart"
➥ Src="~/FirstSimplePart.ascx" %>
<%@ Register TagPrefix="user" TagName="SecondSimplePart"
➥ Src="~/SecondSimplePart.ascx" %>

<user:FirstSimplePart
    id="FirstSimplePart1"
    Title="First Web Part"
    Description="Our first simple Web Part"
    Runat="server" />
<user:SecondSimplePart
    id="SecondSimplePart1"
    Title="Second Web Part"
    Description="Our second simple Web Part"
    Runat="server" />
```

Notice that the FirstSimplePart and SecondSimplePart controls are not registered in the page in Listing 27.9. However, you do need to register the controls in the file in Listing 27.10.

You can mix the Web Parts retrieved from an external file and the Web Parts declared inline. The Web Parts retrieved from the two sources are combined into one list.

Using a Page Catalog Part

The `PageCatalogPart` control displays all the Web Parts in the current page that have been closed. The control enables users to add closed Web Parts back to the original page.

> **NOTE**
>
> There is a difference between closing a Web Part and deleting a Web Part. You cannot delete a Web Part that is declared in a page, but you can close it. Furthermore, when you delete a Web Part from a page, all personalization state information is lost. When you close a Web Part, on the other hand, personalization data is not lost.

The page in Listing 27.11 demonstrates how you can use the `PageCatalogPart` control in a Catalog Zone.

LISTING 27.11   ShowPageCatalogPart.aspx

```
<%@ Page Language="VB" %>
<%@ Register TagPrefix="user" TagName="FirstSimplePart"
➥ Src="~/FirstSimplePart.ascx" %>
<%@ Register TagPrefix="user" TagName="SecondSimplePart"
➥ Src="~/SecondSimplePart.ascx" %>`1
<!DOCTYPE html PUBLIC "-//W3C//DTD XHTML 1.1//EN"
"http://www.w3.org/TR/xhtml11/DTD/xhtml11.dtd">
<script runat="server">

    Sub Menu1_MenuItemClick(ByVal sender As Object, ByVal e As MenuEventArgs)
        WebPartManager1.DisplayMode = WebPartManager1.DisplayModes(e.Item.Text)
    End Sub
</script>


<html xmlns="http://www.w3.org/1999/xhtml" >
<head id="Head1" runat="server">
    <style type="text/css">
        .column
        {
            float:left;
            width:30%;
            height:200px;
            margin-right:10px;
            border:solid 1px black;
            background-color: white;
        }
        .menu
        {
            margin:5px 0px;
        }
        html
```

27

LISTING 27.11   Continued

```
        {
            background-color:#eeeeee;
        }
    </style>
    <title>Show Page Catalog Part</title>
</head>
<body>
    <form id="form1" runat="server">
    <asp:WebPartManager
        id="WebPartManager1"
        Runat="server" />

        <asp:Menu
            id="Menu1"
            OnMenuItemClick="Menu1_MenuItemClick"
            Orientation="Horizontal"
            CssClass="menu"
            Runat="server">
            <Items>
            <asp:MenuItem Text="Browse" />
            <asp:MenuItem Text="Design" />
            <asp:MenuItem Text="Catalog" />
            </Items>
        </asp:Menu>

        <asp:WebPartZone
            id="WebPartZone1"
            CssClass="column"
            Runat="server">
            <ZoneTemplate>
                <user:FirstSimplePart
                    id="FirstSimplePart1"
                    Title="First Web Part"
                    Description="Our first simple Web Part"
                    Runat="server" />
                <user:SecondSimplePart
                    id="SecondSimplePart1"
                    Title="Second Web Part"
                    Description="Our second simple Web Part"
                    Runat="server" />
            </ZoneTemplate>
        </asp:WebPartZone>

        <asp:WebPartZone
            id="WebPartZone2"
```

LISTING 27.11   Continued

```
                    CssClass="column"
                    Runat="server" />

            <asp:CatalogZone
                id="CatalogZone1"
                CssClass="column"
                Runat="server">
                <ZoneTemplate>
                <asp:PageCatalogPart
                    id="PageCatalogPart1"
                    Runat="server" />
                </ZoneTemplate>
            </asp:CatalogZone>

    </form>
</body>
</html>
```

After you open the page in Listing 27.11, you see two Web Parts in the left column Web Part Zone. You can close either Web Part by selecting Close from the Web Part's menu. If you click the Catalog link, you can open the Page Catalog and add any closed Web Parts back to the page (see Figure 27.8).

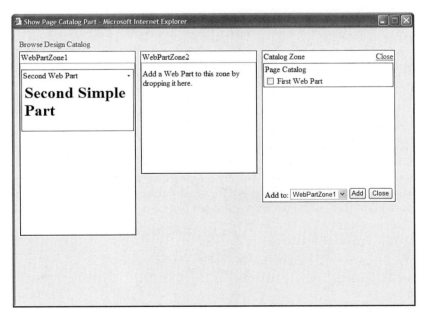

FIGURE 27.8   Adding closed Web Parts from the Page Catalog.

27

> **NOTE**
>
> You can prevent users from closing Web Parts by setting the `CloseVerb-Visible` property on a `WebPartZone` control to the value `false`.

Using the Import Catalog Part

If you need to transfer a Web Part control's settings between two different pages, or even between two different applications, you can export the Web Part from one page and import the Web Part on another page.

When you export a Web Part, an XML file that represents the Web Part's properties is generated. You can download and save the settings file to your local computer. After you export the settings file, you can import the settings to any Web Part application that includes an Import Catalog Part and knows about the type of Web Part control that you are importing. When you import a Web Part, a new instance of the Web Part control is created that contains the original settings.

> **NOTE**
>
> You can programmatically export and import Web Parts by using the `WebPartManager` control's `ExportWebPart()` and `ImportWebPart()` methods.

Before you can export any Web Parts from a page, you must enable exporting for your application. The web configuration file in Listing 27.12 contains the necessary configuration settings.

LISTING 27.12   Web.Config

```
<?xml version="1.0"?>
<configuration>
    <system.web>
      <webParts enableExport="true" />
    </system.web>
</configuration>
```

To make things more interesting, we'll create a new Web Part to illustrate how exporting a Web Part works. The new Web Part represents a user profile. It displays both sensitive and non-sensitive data. The `ProfilePart` is contained in Listing 27.13.

LISTING 27.13   ProfilePart.ascx

```
<%@ Control Language="VB" ClassName="ProfilePart" %>

<script runat="server">
    Private _firstName As String
    Private _lastName As String
```

LISTING 27.13 Continued

```vbnet
Private _socialSecurityNumber As String
Private _userProfile As String

<Personalizable()> _
<WebBrowsable()> _
Public Property FirstName() As String
    Get
        Return _firstName
    End Get
    Set(ByVal Value As String)
        _firstName = value
    End Set
End Property


<Personalizable()> _
<WebBrowsable()> _
Public Property LastName() As String
    Get
        Return _lastName
    End Get
    Set(ByVal Value As String)
        _lastName = value
    End Set
End Property


<Personalizable(PersonalizationScope.User, True)> _
<WebBrowsable()> _
Public Property SocialSecurityNumber() As String
    Get
        Return _socialSecurityNumber
    End Get
    Set(ByVal Value As String)
        _socialSecurityNumber = value
    End Set
End Property


<Personalizable()> _
<WebBrowsable()> _
Public Property UserProfile() As String
    Get
        Return _userProfile
    End Get
    Set(ByVal Value As String)
        _userProfile = value
    End Set
```

LISTING 27.13   Continued

```
    End Property

    Private Sub Page_PreRender()
        lblFirstName.Text = _firstName
        lblLastName.Text = _lastName
        lblSocialSecurityNumber.Text = _socialSecurityNumber
        lblUserProfile.Text = _userProfile
    End Sub

</script>

First Name:
<asp:Label
    id="lblFirstName"
    Runat="server" />
<br />
Last Name:
<asp:Label
    id="lblLastName"
    Runat="server" />
<br />
Social Security Number:
<asp:Label
    id="lblSocialSecurityNumber"
    Runat="server" />
<br />
User Profile:
<asp:Label
    id="lblUserProfile"
    Runat="server" />
```

The ProfilePart displays four profile properties: a person's First Name, Last Name, Social Security Number, and User Profile. The value of the Social Security Number property is considered to be sensitive data and the values of the other properties are not.

Notice that all four properties in Listing 27.13 are decorated with the Personalizable attribute. Only properties marked with this attribute can be exported.

Furthermore, notice that the Personalizable attribute associated with the SocialSecurityNumber property includes two parameters. The second parameter represents whether or not the property contains sensitive data. To prevent the Social Security Number from being exported, this parameter is set to the value True.

The page in Listing 27.14 illustrates how you can use the `ProfilePart` in a page.

LISTING 27.14   ShowImportCatalogPart.aspx

```
<%@ Page Language="VB" %>
<%@ Register TagPrefix="user" TagName="ProfilePart" Src="~/ProfilePart.ascx" %>
<%@ Register TagPrefix="user" TagName="FirstSimplePart"
➥ Src="~/FirstSimplePart.ascx" %>
<%@ Register TagPrefix="user" TagName="SecondSimplePart"
➥ Src="~/SecondSimplePart.ascx" %>
<!DOCTYPE html PUBLIC "-//W3C//DTD XHTML 1.1//EN"
"http://www.w3.org/TR/xhtml11/DTD/xhtml11.dtd">

<script runat="server">

    Sub Menu1_MenuItemClick(ByVal sender As Object, ByVal e As MenuEventArgs)
        WebPartManager1.DisplayMode = WebPartManager1.DisplayModes(e.Item.Text)
    End Sub
</script>

<html xmlns="http://www.w3.org/1999/xhtml" >
<head id="Head1" runat="server">
    <style type="text/css">
        .column
        {
            float:left;
            width:30%;
            height:200px;
            margin-right:10px;
            border:solid 1px black;
            background-color: white;
        }
        .menu
        {
            margin:5px 0px;
        }
        html
        {
            background-color:#eeeeee;
        }
    </style>
    <title>Show Import Catalog Part</title>
</head>
<body>
    <form id="form1" runat="server">
    <asp:WebPartManager
```

27

LISTING 27.14   Continued

```
        id="WebPartManager1"
        Runat="server" />

    <asp:Menu
        id="Menu1"
        OnMenuItemClick="Menu1_MenuItemClick"
        Orientation="Horizontal"
        CssClass="menu"
        Runat="server">
        <Items>
        <asp:MenuItem Text="Browse" />
        <asp:MenuItem Text="Design" />
        <asp:MenuItem Text="Catalog" />
        <asp:MenuItem Text="Edit" />
        </Items>
    </asp:Menu>

    <asp:WebPartZone
        id="WebPartZone1"
        CssClass="column"
        Runat="server">
        <ZoneTemplate>
            <user:ProfilePart
                id="ProfilePart1"
                Title="Profile Part"
                Description="Displays your profile"
                ExportMode="NonSensitiveData"
                Runat="server" />
            <user:FirstSimplePart
                id="FirstSimplePart1"
                Title="First Web Part"
                Description="Our first simple Web Part"
                Runat="server" />
            <user:SecondSimplePart
                id="SecondSimplePart1"
                Title="Second Web Part"
                Description="Our second simple Web Part"
                Runat="server" />
        </ZoneTemplate>
    </asp:WebPartZone>

    <asp:WebPartZone
        id="WebPartZone2"
```

LISTING 27.14   Continued

```
            CssClass="column"
            Runat="server" />

        <asp:CatalogZone
            id="CatalogZone1"
            CssClass="column"
            Runat="server">
            <ZoneTemplate>
            <asp:ImportCatalogPart
                id="ImportCatalogPart1"
                Runat="server" />
            </ZoneTemplate>
        </asp:CatalogZone>

        <asp:EditorZone
            id="EditorZone1"
            CssClass="column"
            Runat="server">
            <ZoneTemplate>
            <asp:PropertyGridEditorPart
                id="PropertyGridEditorPart1"
                Runat="server" />
            </ZoneTemplate>
        </asp:EditorZone>

    </form>
</body>
</html>
```

In Listing 27.14, the ProfilePart is declared in the first Web Part Zone. Notice that the ProfilePart includes an ExportMode property. This property can have three possible values:

- None—The default value is to prevent users from exporting a Web Part.
- All—This value enables users to export both sensitive and non-sensitive data.
- NonSensitiveData—This value enables users to export only data that has not been marked as sensitive.

The first thing that you should do after opening the page in Listing 27.14 is to create a user profile. Click the Edit link to switch the page to Edit Display Mode. Select the Edit menu option on the ProfilePart and enter values for the ProfilePart control's properties. Click the OK button when you are finished.

Next, you can export the ProfilePart by selecting Export from the ProfilePart control's menu (see Figure 27.9). When you export the ProfilePart, an XML file resembling the file in Listing 27.15 is downloaded to your computer.

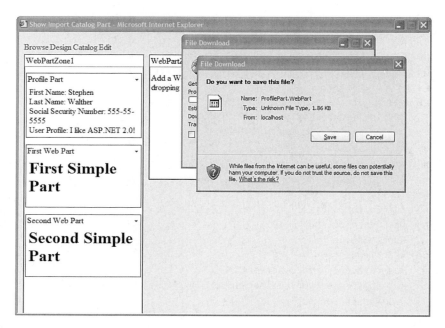

FIGURE 27.9   Exporting a Web Part.

LISTING 27.15   ProfilePart.WebPart

```
<?xml version="1.0" encoding="utf-8"?>
<webParts>
  <webPart>
    <metaData>
      <type src="~/ProfilePart.ascx" />
      <importErrorMessage>Cannot import this Web Part.</importErrorMessage>
    </metaData>
    <data>
      <properties>
        <property name="LastName" type="string">Walther</property>
        <property name="FirstName" type="string">Ruth</property>
        <property name="UserProfile" type="string">I like ASP.NET 2.0!</property>
      </properties>
```

LISTING 27.15 Continued

```xml
      <genericWebPartProperties>
        <property name="AllowClose" type="bool">True</property>
        <property name="Width" type="unit" />
        <property name="AllowMinimize" type="bool">True</property>
        <property name="AllowConnect" type="bool">True</property>
        <property name="ChromeType" type="chrometype">Default</property>
        <property name="TitleIconImageUrl" type="string" />
        <property name="Description" type="string">Displays your profile</property>
        <property name="Hidden" type="bool">False</property>
        <property name="TitleUrl" type="string" />
        <property name="AllowEdit" type="bool">True</property>
        <property name="Height" type="unit" />
        <property name="HelpUrl" type="string" />
        <property name="Title" type="string">Profile Part</property>
        <property name="CatalogIconImageUrl" type="string" />
        <property name="Direction" type="direction">NotSet</property>
        <property name="ChromeState" type="chromestate">Normal</property>
        <property name="AllowZoneChange" type="bool">True</property>
        <property name="AllowHide" type="bool">True</property>
        <property name="HelpMode" type="helpmode">Navigate</property>
        <property name="ExportMode" type="exportmode">NonSensitiveData</property>
      </genericWebPartProperties>
    </data>
  </webPart>
</webParts>
```

27

Notice that the file in Listing 27.15 does not include the Social Security Number property. However, it does include the First Name, Last Name, and User Profile properties.

After you download the XML file, you can import the Web Part represented by the XML file into another Web Part page or another Web Part application. Click the Catalog link to switch to Catalog Display Mode. The Import Catalog Part enables you to upload a Web Part settings file.

After you upload the settings file, the Web Part represented by the file is listed by the Import Catalog Part. You can add the ProfilePart to any Web Part Zone (see Figure 27.10).

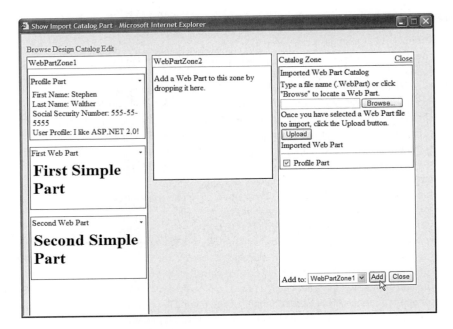

FIGURE 27.10 Importing a Web Part.

Using Editor Zones

You use an Editor Zone to enable users to edit the Web Parts contained in a page. An Editor Zone can contain one or more Editor Parts. The contents of an Editor Zone are displayed only when the page is in Edit Display Mode.

The Web Part Framework includes four standard Editor Parts: the AppearanceEditorPart, the BehaviorEditorPart, the LayoutEditorPart, and the PropertyGridEditorPart. This section discusses each of these Editor Parts.

> **NOTE**
>
> You can create your own Editor Parts. This option is explored in Chapter 30, "Extending the Web Part Framework."

Using the Appearance Editor Part

The AppearanceEditorPart control is useful for an administrator of a Web Part application, who can use the part to modify the general appearances of the Web Parts in the application (see Figure 27.11). This control enables you to modify the following properties of a Web Part:

- `Title`—The title displayed for a Web Part in the Web Part title bar.

- `ChromeType`—The type of chrome rendered around a Web Part. Possible values are Default, `TitleAndBorder`, `TitleOnly`, `BorderOnly`, and None.

- `Direction`—The direction that text is displayed in a Web Part. This property is useful when working with languages that are written from right to left, such as Arabic.

- `Height`—The pixel height of the Web Part.

- `Width`—The pixel width of the Web Part.

- `Hidden`—When true, the Web Part is not displayed in a browser. The Web Part is rendered with a `display:hidden` Cascading Style Sheet property.

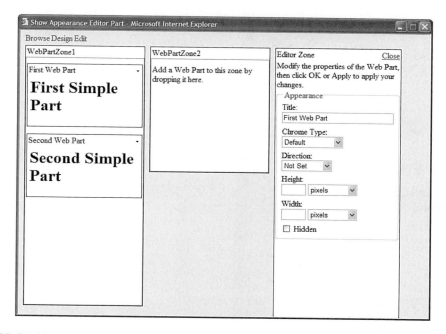

FIGURE 27.11 Using the `AppearanceEditorPart`.

The page in Listing 27.16 illustrates how you can add the `AppearanceEditorPart` to an Editor Zone.

LISTING 27.16 ShowAppearanceEditorPart.aspx

```
<%@ Page Language="VB" %>
<%@ Register TagPrefix="user" TagName="FirstSimplePart"
➥ Src="~/FirstSimplePart.ascx" %>
<%@ Register TagPrefix="user" TagName="SecondSimplePart"
➥ Src="~/SecondSimplePart.ascx" %>
```

LISTING 27.16   Continued

```
<!DOCTYPE html PUBLIC "-//W3C//DTD XHTML 1.1//EN"
"http://www.w3.org/TR/xhtml11/DTD/xhtml11.dtd">

<script runat="server">

    Sub Menu1_MenuItemClick(ByVal sender As Object, ByVal e As MenuEventArgs)
        WebPartManager1.DisplayMode = WebPartManager1.DisplayModes(e.Item.Text)
    End Sub
</script>

<html xmlns="http://www.w3.org/1999/xhtml" >
<head id="Head1" runat="server">
    <style type="text/css">
        .column
        {
            float:left;
            width:30%;
            height:200px;
            margin-right:10px;
            border:solid 1px black;
            background-color: white;
        }
        .menu
        {
            margin:5px 0px;
        }
        html
        {
            background-color:#eeeeee;
        }
    </style>
    <title>Show Appearance Editor Part</title>
</head>
<body>
    <form id="form1" runat="server">
    <asp:WebPartManager
        id="WebPartManager1"
        Runat="server" />

        <asp:Menu
            id="Menu1"
            OnMenuItemClick="Menu1_MenuItemClick"
            Orientation="Horizontal"
            CssClass="menu"
            Runat="server">
```

LISTING 27.16   Continued

```
            <Items>
            <asp:MenuItem Text="Browse" />
            <asp:MenuItem Text="Design" />
            <asp:MenuItem Text="Edit" />
            </Items>
        </asp:Menu>

        <asp:WebPartZone
            id="WebPartZone1"
            CssClass="column"
            Runat="server">
            <ZoneTemplate>
                <user:FirstSimplePart
                    id="FirstSimplePart1"
                    Title="First Web Part"
                    Description="Our first simple Web Part"
                    Runat="server" />
                <user:SecondSimplePart
                    id="SecondSimplePart1"
                    Title="Second Web Part"
                    Description="Our second simple Web Part"
                    Runat="server" />
            </ZoneTemplate>
        </asp:WebPartZone>

        <asp:WebPartZone
            id="WebPartZone2"
            CssClass="column"
            Runat="server" />

        <asp:EditorZone
            id="EditorZone1"
            CssClass="column"
            Runat="server">
            <ZoneTemplate>
            <asp:AppearanceEditorPart
                id="AppearanceEditorPart1"
                Runat="server" />
            </ZoneTemplate>
        </asp:EditorZone>

    </form>
</body>
</html>
```

27

After you open the page in Listing 27.16, you can view the Appearance Editor Part by clicking the page menu's Edit link, and then selecting Edit from either of the two Web Part control menus.

Using the Behavior Editor Part

The Behavior Editor Part can be used to modify properties of a Web Part that have Shared personalization scope. In other words, it can be used to modify the properties that appear for all users and not only the current user.

The Behavior Editor Part enables you to modify the following properties:

- Description—Enables you to set the Web Part description that appears as a tooltip when you hover your mouse over a Web Part.

- Title Link—Enables you to convert the title of a Web Part into a hyperlink to a page.

- Title Icon Image Link—Enables you to specify an image that appears in a Web Part title bar.

- Catalog Icon Image Link—Enables you to specify an image that appears when a Web Part is listed in a Catalog Part.

- Help Link—Enables you to add a Help menu item that links to a help page.

- Help Mode—Enables you to specify how the help window appears when you select a Web Part's Help menu option. Possible values are Modal, Modeless, and Navigate.

- Import Error Message—Enables you to specify the error text that appears when a Web Part is imported with an ImportCatalogPart control that fails.

- Export Mode—Enables you to specify whether a Web Part can be exported. Possible values are Do Not Allow, Export All Values, and Non-Sensitive Data Only.

- Authorization Filter—Enables you to specify a string that can be used to determine whether a Web Part can be added to a page.

- Allow Close—Enables you to prevent users from closing a Web Part.

- Allow Connect—Enables you to specify whether a user is allowed to connect the current Web Part to another Web Part.

- Allow Edit—Enables you to specify whether a Web Part can be edited.

- Allow Hide—Enables you to specify whether a user can hide a Web Part (render the Web Part, but not display it).

- Allow Minimize—Enables you to specify whether a user is allowed to minimize a Web Part.

- Allow Zone Change—Enables you to specify whether a user is allowed to drag and drop the Web Part to a new location.

The Behavior Editor Part appears only when Shared personalization scope has been enabled for the page. You'll learn the gritty details of Shared personalization scope in Chapter 29, "Personalizing Web Parts." Right now, however, it is enough to know that there are two requirements for placing a page into Shared personalization scope.

First, you need to add the web configuration file in Listing 27.17 to your application.

LISTING 27.17 Web.Config

```
<?xml version="1.0"?>
<configuration xmlns="http://schemas.microsoft.com/.NetConfiguration/v2.0">
    <system.web>
      <webParts>
        <personalization>
          <authorization>
            <allow users="*" verbs="enterSharedScope"/>
          </authorization>
        </personalization>
      </webParts>
    </system.web>
</configuration>
```

The Web Configuration file in Listing 27.17 authorizes all users to enter Shared personalization scope (the asterisk represents everyone). Normally, you want to restrict this privilege to the administrators of your application.

Next, you need to place the current page in Shared personalization scope. One way to do this is to use the Personalization property of the WebPartManager control, like this:

```
<asp:WebPartManager
    id="WebPartManager1"
    Personalization-InitialScope="Shared"
    Runat="server" />
```

The Personalization-InitialScope attribute causes the page to enter Shared personalization scope for users who are authorized by the web configuration file to enter Shared personalization scope. If a user is not authorized, the attribute is ignored.

The page in Listing 27.18 illustrates how you can add a BehaviorEditorPart control to an EditorZone.

LISTING 27.18 ShowBehaviorEditorPart.aspx

```
<%@ Page Language="VB" %>
<%@ Register TagPrefix="user" TagName="FirstSimplePart"
➥ Src="~/FirstSimplePart.ascx" %>
<%@ Register TagPrefix="user" TagName="SecondSimplePart"
➥ Src="~/SecondSimplePart.ascx" %>
```

LISTING 27.18   Continued

```
<!DOCTYPE html PUBLIC "-//W3C//DTD XHTML 1.1//EN"
"http://www.w3.org/TR/xhtml11/DTD/xhtml11.dtd">

<script runat="server">

    Sub Menu1_MenuItemClick(ByVal sender As Object, ByVal e As MenuEventArgs)
        WebPartManager1.DisplayMode = WebPartManager1.DisplayModes(e.Item.Text)
    End Sub
</script>

<html xmlns="http://www.w3.org/1999/xhtml" >
<head id="Head1" runat="server">
    <style type="text/css">
        .column
        {
            float:left;
            width:30%;
            height:200px;
            margin-right:10px;
            border:solid 1px black;
            background-color: white;
        }
        .menu
        {
            margin:5px 0px;
        }
        html
        {
            background-color:#eeeeee;
        }
    </style>
    <title>Show Behavior Editor Part</title>
</head>
<body>
    <form id="form1" runat="server">
    <asp:WebPartManager
        id="WebPartManager1"
        Personalization-InitialScope="Shared"
        Runat="server" />

        <asp:Menu
            id="Menu1"
            OnMenuItemClick="Menu1_MenuItemClick"
            Orientation="Horizontal"
            CssClass="menu"
```

LISTING 27.18   Continued

```
            Runat="server">
            <Items>
            <asp:MenuItem Text="Browse" />
            <asp:MenuItem Text="Design" />
            <asp:MenuItem Text="Edit" />
            </Items>
        </asp:Menu>

        <asp:WebPartZone
            id="WebPartZone1"
            CssClass="column"
            Runat="server">
            <ZoneTemplate>
                <user:FirstSimplePart
                    id="FirstSimplePart1"
                    Title="First Web Part"
                    Description="Our first simple Web Part"
                    Runat="server" />
                <user:SecondSimplePart
                    id="SecondSimplePart1"
                    Title="Second Web Part"
                    Description="Our second simple Web Part"
                    Runat="server" />
            </ZoneTemplate>
        </asp:WebPartZone>

        <asp:WebPartZone
            id="WebPartZone2"
            CssClass="column"
            Runat="server" />

        <asp:EditorZone
            id="EditorZone1"
            CssClass="column"
            Runat="server">
            <ZoneTemplate>
            <asp:BehaviorEditorPart
                id="BehaviorEditorPart1"
                Runat="server" />
            </ZoneTemplate>
        </asp:EditorZone>

    </form>
</body>
</html>
```

27

After you open the page in Listing 27.18 in your web browser, you can click the Edit menu link to place the page in Edit Display Mode. Next, select the Edit menu option on one of the two Web Parts, which causes the Behavior Editor Part to appear (see Figure 27.12).

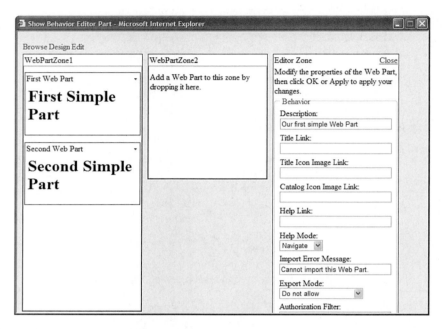

FIGURE 27.12   Using the Behavior Editor Part.

Using the Layout Editor Part

The Layout Editor Part enables you to arrange Web Parts on a page without using a mouse (see Figure 27.13). You should always include a Layout Editor Part in every Web Parts page for two reasons.

First, adding a Layout Editor Part to a page makes your web application more accessible to persons with disabilities. Many persons with disabilities must interact with websites by using the keyboard. For example, if you are blind, then you will not be using a mouse to drag Web Parts around a page.

> **WEB STANDARDS NOTE**
>
> Both the Section 508 and WCAG 1.0 standards include guidelines concerned with the impor-
> tance of creating device-independent pages.

Second, the Web Part Framework does not support drag-and-drop for browseers other than Internet Explorer. In particular, you cannot drag-and-drop Web parts when using

Firefox or Opera. The Layout Editor Part provides you with an (imperfect) method of supporting browseres other than Internet Explorer.

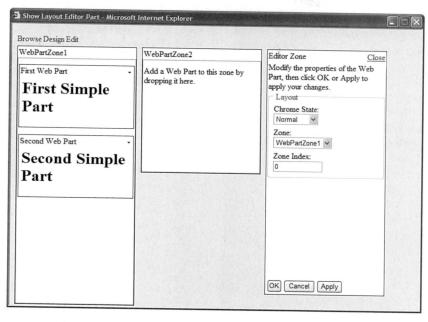

FIGURE 27.13   Using the Layout Editor Part.

The LayoutEditorPart control enables users to modify the following three properties:

- `Chrome State`—Enables users to specify whether a Web Part is minimized or maximized.

- `Zone`—Enables users to select a zone where they want a Web Part to be placed.

- `Zone Index`—Enables users to specify the location of a Web Part within a zone.

The page in Listing 27.19 illustrates how you can add a `LayoutEditorPart` control to an Editor Zone.

LISTING 27.19   ShowLayoutEditorPart.aspx

```
<%@ Page Language="VB" %>
<%@ Register TagPrefix="user" TagName="FirstSimplePart"
➥ Src="~/FirstSimplePart.ascx" %>
<%@ Register TagPrefix="user" TagName="SecondSimplePart"
➥ Src="~/SecondSimplePart.ascx" %>
<!DOCTYPE html PUBLIC "-//W3C//DTD XHTML 1.1//EN"
"http://www.w3.org/TR/xhtml11/DTD/xhtml11.dtd">
```

LISTING 27.19   Continued

```
<script runat="server">

    Sub Menu1_MenuItemClick(ByVal sender As Object, ByVal e As MenuEventArgs)
        WebPartManager1.DisplayMode = WebPartManager1.DisplayModes(e.Item.Text)
    End Sub
</script>

<html xmlns="http://www.w3.org/1999/xhtml" >
<head id="Head1" runat="server">
    <style type="text/css">
        .column
        {
            float:left;
            width:30%;
            height:200px;
            margin-right:10px;
            border:solid 1px black;
            background-color: white;
        }
        .menu
        {
            margin:5px 0px;
        }
        html
        {
            background-color:#eeeeee;
        }
    </style>
    <title>Show Layout Editor Part</title>
</head>
<body>
    <form id="form1" runat="server">
    <asp:WebPartManager
        id="WebPartManager1"
        Runat="server" />

        <asp:Menu
            id="Menu1"
            OnMenuItemClick="Menu1_MenuItemClick"
            Orientation="Horizontal"
            CssClass="menu"
            Runat="server">
            <Items>
```

LISTING 27.19   Continued

```
            <asp:MenuItem Text="Browse" />
            <asp:MenuItem Text="Design" />
            <asp:MenuItem Text="Edit" />
            </Items>
        </asp:Menu>

        <asp:WebPartZone
            id="WebPartZone1"
            CssClass="column"
            Runat="server">
            <ZoneTemplate>
            <user:FirstSimplePart
                id="FirstSimplePart1"
                Title="First Web Part"
                Description="Our first simple Web Part"
                Runat="server" />
            <user:SecondSimplePart
                id="SecondSimplePart1"
                Title="Second Web Part"
                Description="Our second simple Web Part"
                Runat="server" />
            </ZoneTemplate>
        </asp:WebPartZone>

        <asp:WebPartZone
            id="WebPartZone2"
            CssClass="column"
            Runat="server" />

        <asp:EditorZone
            id="EditorZone1"
            CssClass="column"
            Runat="server">
            <ZoneTemplate>
            <asp:LayoutEditorPart
                id="LayoutEditorPart1"
                Runat="server" />
            </ZoneTemplate>
        </asp:EditorZone>

    </form>
</body>
</html>
```

27

When you open the page in Listing 27.19 in a web browser, you can click the Edit link to place the page into Edit Display Mode. Next, select the Edit menu option from any Web Part menu to see the Layout Editor Part.

Using the Property Grid Editor

The `PropertyGridEditorPart` control enables users to modify custom properties of a Web Part control through a form interface. This control automatically generates a property sheet for a Web Part (see Figure 27.14).

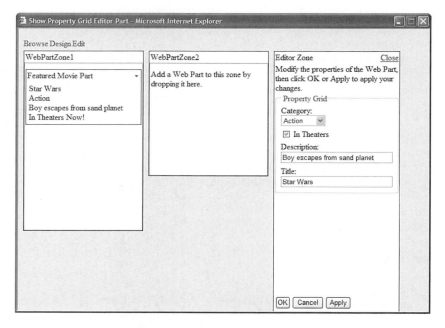

FIGURE 27.14   Using the Property Grid Editor Part.

If you want to be able to modify a particular Web Part property with the `PropertyGridEditorPart`, then you must decorate the property with two attributes. First, you must add a `Personalizable` attribute to the property. The Web Part Framework automatically saves any property decorated with the `Personalizable` attribute.

Second, you must add a `WebBrowsable` attribute to the property. The `WebBrowsable` attribute is for the benefit of the `PropertyGridEditorPart` control. The control displays only properties decorated with this attribute.

The Web Part in Listing 27.20, the `FeaturedMoviePart` illustrates how to use both of these attributes.

LISTING 27.20   FeaturedMoviePart.ascx

```
<%@ Control Language="VB" ClassName="FeaturedMoviePart" %>

<script runat="server">

    Public Enum MovieCategory
        Action
        Animation
        Drama
        Horror
    End Enum

    Private _movieTitle As String
    Private _category As MovieCategory
    Private _movieDescription As String
    Private _inTheaters As Boolean

    <Personalizable()> _
    <WebBrowsable()> _
    <WebDisplayName("Title")> _
    <WebDescription("The title of the movie")> _
    Public Property MovieTitle() As String
        Get
            Return _movieTitle
        End Get
        Set(ByVal Value As String)
            _movieTitle = value
        End Set
    End Property

    <Personalizable()> _
    <WebBrowsable()> _
    <WebDisplayName("Category")> _
    <WebDescription("The movie category")> _
    Public Property Category() As MovieCategory
        Get
            Return _category
        End Get
        Set(ByVal Value As MovieCategory)
            _category = value
        End Set
    End Property

    <Personalizable()> _
    <WebBrowsable()> _
```

LISTING 27.20   Continued

```
    <WebDisplayName("Description")> _
    <WebDescription("The movie description")> _
    Public Property MovieDescription() As String
        Get
            Return _movieDescription
        End Get
        Set(ByVal Value As String)
            _movieDescription = value
        End Set
    End Property

    <Personalizable()> _
    <WebBrowsable()> _
    <WebDisplayName("In Theaters")> _
    <WebDescription("Is the movie currently showing?")> _
    Public Property InTheaters() As Boolean
        Get
            Return _inTheaters
        End Get
        Set(ByVal Value As Boolean)
            _inTheaters = value
        End Set
    End Property

    Private Sub Page_PreRender()
        lblMovieTitle.Text = _movieTitle
        lblCategory.Text = _category.ToString()
        lblMovieDescription.Text = _movieDescription
        lblInTheaters.Visible = _inTheaters
    End Sub
</script>
<asp:Label
    id="lblMovieTitle"
    Runat="server" />
<br />
<asp:Label
    id="lblCategory"
    Runat="server" />
<br />
<asp:Label
    id="lblMovieDescription"
    Runat="server" />
<br />
```

LISTING 27.20   Continued

```
<asp:Label
    id="lblInTheaters"
    Text="In Theaters Now!"
    CssClass="inTheaters"
    Runat="server" />
```

Notice that each of the properties of the FeatureMoviePart in Listing 27.20 is marked with four attributes. Each property includes the required Personalizable and WebBrowsable attributes. In addition, the WebDisplayName and WebDescription attributes are used to provide each property with a name and description in the property sheet.

The page in Listing 27.21 demonstrates how you can use the PropertyGridEditorPart control to edit the properties of the FeaturedMoviePart.

LISTING 27.21   ShowPropertyGridEditorPart.aspx

```
<%@ Page Language="VB" %>
<%@ Register TagPrefix="user" TagName="FeaturedMoviePart"
➥ Src="~/FeaturedMoviePart.ascx" %>
<!DOCTYPE html PUBLIC "-//W3C//DTD XHTML 1.1//EN"
"http://www.w3.org/TR/xhtml11/DTD/xhtml11.dtd">
<script runat="server">

    Sub Menu1_MenuItemClick(ByVal sender As Object, ByVal e As MenuEventArgs)
        WebPartManager1.DisplayMode = WebPartManager1.DisplayModes(e.Item.Text)
    End Sub
</script>
<html xmlns="http://www.w3.org/1999/xhtml" >
<head id="Head1" runat="server">
    <style type="text/css">
        .column
        {
            float:left;
            width:30%;
            height:200px;
            margin-right:10px;
            border:solid 1px black;
            background-color: white;
        }
        .menu
        {
            margin:5px 0px;
        }
        html
```

LISTING 27.21 Continued

```
        {
             background-color:#eeeeee;
        }
    </style>
    <title>Show Property Grid Editor Part</title>
</head>
<body>
    <form id="form1" runat="server">
    <asp:WebPartManager
        id="WebPartManager1"
        Runat="server" />

        <asp:Menu
            id="Menu1"
            OnMenuItemClick="Menu1_MenuItemClick"
            Orientation="Horizontal"
            CssClass="menu"
            Runat="server">
            <Items>
            <asp:MenuItem Text="Browse" />
            <asp:MenuItem Text="Design" />
            <asp:MenuItem Text="Edit" />
            </Items>
        </asp:Menu>

        <asp:WebPartZone
            id="WebPartZone1"
            CssClass="column"
            Runat="server">
            <ZoneTemplate>
                <user:FeaturedMoviePart
                    id="FeaturedMoviePart1"
                    Title="Featured Movie Part"
                    Description="Displays movie information"
                    Runat="server" />
            </ZoneTemplate>
        </asp:WebPartZone>

        <asp:WebPartZone
            id="WebPartZone2"
            CssClass="column"
            Runat="server" />
```

LISTING 27.21   Continued

```
        <asp:EditorZone
            id="EditorZone1"
            CssClass="column"
            Runat="server">
            <ZoneTemplate>
            <asp:PropertyGridEditorPart
                id="PropertyGridEditorPart1"
                Runat="server" />
            </ZoneTemplate>
        </asp:EditorZone>
    </form>
</body>
</html>
```

After you open the page in Listing 27.21, you can click the Edit link to switch the page to Edit Display Mode. Next, select the Edit menu option on the FeaturedMoviePart and you will see the property sheet rendered by the PropertyGridEditorPart.

The PropertyGridEditorPart automatically associates certain types of properties with certain types of form fields in the property sheet:

- **Boolean Property**—Displayed with a CheckBox control.

- **Enumeration Property**—Displayed with a DropDownList control.

- **Other Properties**—Displayed with a TextBox control.

In the case of the FeaturedMoviePart, The PropertyGridEditorPart control renders a TextBox control for the MovieTitle property, a DropDownList control for the Category property, a TextBox for the Description property, and a CheckBox control for the InTheaters property.

> **NOTE**
>
> The PropertyGridEditorPart does not provide you with very much control over the appearance of the property sheet. For example, there is no way to specify the order of the form fields. If you want more control, then you need to create a custom EditorPart. This option in discussed Chapter 30, "Extending the Web Part Framework."

Using Connections Zones

You can share information between two or more Web Parts on a page by connecting the Web Parts. There are a variety of different situations in which you might want to communicate information between two Web Parts.

27

For example, imagine that you are creating a Web Part application for a human resources department. You could create one Web Part that enables you to select a current employee. Another Web Part might display insurance information for the selected employee. Yet another Web Part might display information about the selected employee's work history. If you connect all the Web Parts, then you can select a new employee from the first Web Part to see detailed information about the employee with the other two Web Parts.

Or, imagine that you are building a blog application with Web Parts. One Web Part might display a calendar. A second Web Part might display a list of blog entries. If you connect the two Web Parts, you can select a date in the calendar Web Part to see a list of matching entries in the blog Web Part.

Connecting Web Parts

When you connect two Web Parts, you create a connection between a *provider* Web Part and a *consumer* Web Part. The provider Web Part provides the information that is retrieved by the consumer Web Part. Multiple consumer Web Parts can be connected to the same provider.

You must follow a certain sequence of steps whenever you connect two Web Parts:

1. Create an interface that represents the information being shared.

2. Add the `ConnectionProvider` attribute to a method of the provider Web Part.

3. Add the `ConnectionConsumer` attribute to a method of the consumer Web Part.

Before you can communicate information between two Web Parts, you must specify an interface that describes the information being shared. An interface can contain a list of properties, methods, and events.

Next, the provider Web Part must have a method that returns a class that implements the interface. You mark the method that provides the interface by decorating the method with the `ConnectionProvider` attribute.

Finally, the consumer Web Part must have a method that retrieves the interface. This method is marked in the consumer Web Part with the `ConnectionConsumer` attribute.

Connecting Simple Web Parts

Let's go ahead and build a simple provider and consumer Web Part that you can connect. The provider Web Part will enable users to enter a ZIP code. The consumer Web Part displays the weather for the selected ZIP code (see Figure 27.15).

First, you need to create an interface which describes the information being passed between the provider and consumer Web Parts. Our interface is contained in Listing 27.22.

LISTING 27.22   App_Code\IZIPCode.vb

```
''' <summary>
''' Represents a ZIP Code
''' </summary>
Public Interface IZIPCode
    ReadOnly Property ZIPCode() As String
End Interface
```

The IZIPCode interface defines one read-only property named ZIPCode. This is the bit of information that will pass between the two Web Parts.

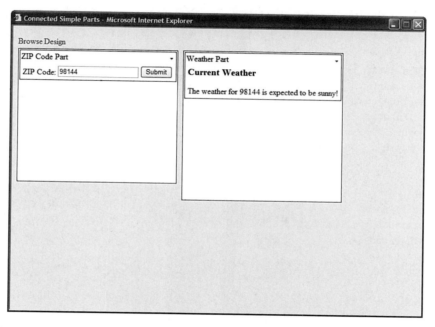

FIGURE 27.15   Connecting the ZIP Code with the weather.

> **NOTE**
>
> The IZIPCode interface must be saved in the App_Code folder or it will not be automatically compiled.

Next, you need to create the provider Web Part. This Web Part enables a user to enter a ZIP code in a text box. The ZIPCodePart is contained in Listing 27.23.

LISTING 27.23   `ZIPCodePart.ascx`

```
<%@ Control Language="VB" ClassName="ZIPCodePart" %>
<%@ Implements Interface="IZIPCode" %>
<script runat="server">

    ''' <summary>
    ''' Implements the IZIPCode interface
    ''' </summary>
    Public ReadOnly Property ZIPCode() As String Implements IZIPCode.ZIPCode
        Get
            Return txtZIPCode.Text
        End Get
    End Property

    ''' <summary>
    ''' This method is called from connected Web Parts
    ''' </summary>
    <ConnectionProvider("ZIP Code")> _
    Public Function ProvideZIPCode() As IZIPCode
        Return Me
    End Function
</script>

<asp:Label
    id="lblZIPCode"
    AssociatedControlID="txtZIPCode"
    Text="ZIP Code:"
    Runat="server" />
<asp:TextBox
    id="txtZIPCode"
    Runat="server" />
<asp:Button
    id="btnSubmit"
    Text="Submit"
    Runat="server" />
```

Notice that the ZIPCodePart includes a method named ProvideZIPCode(), which is decorated with the ConnectionProvider attribute. This method is called by any consumer Web Parts connected to the ZIPCodePart.

The ProvideZIPCode() method returns the ZIPCodePart itself when the method is called. Notice that the ZIPCodePart implements the IZIPCode interface. The Web Part includes an <%@ Implements %> directive and it implements the ZIPCode property.

The provider Web Part is not required to implement the interface it exposes. If you prefer, you could return a different class that implements the IZIPCode interface from the ProvideZIPCode() method.

Now you are ready to create the consumer Web Part. This Web Part, named WeatherPart, displays the current weather. The code for the WeatherPart is contained in Listing 27.24.

LISTING 27.24   WeatherPart.ascx

```
<%@ Control Language="VB" ClassName="WeatherPart" %>
<script runat="server">

    Private _zipCode As IZIPCode

    ''' <summary>
    ''' This method retrieves the IZIPCode interface returned
    ''' by the ProvideZIPCode method
    ''' </summary>
    <ConnectionConsumer("ZIP Code")> _
    Public  Sub ConsumeZIPCode(ByVal zipCode As IZIPCode)
        _zipCode = zipCode
    End Sub


    ''' <summary>
    ''' Display the weather
    ''' </summary>
    Private  Sub Page_PreRender()
        ' Check if we are connected
        If Not _zipCode Is Nothing Then
            If _zipCode.ZIPCode <> String.Empty Then
                lblWeather.Text = String.Format("The weather for {0} is expected to
be sunny!", _zipCode.ZIPCode)
            Else
                lblWeather.Text = "Please enter your ZIP code"
            End If
        End If
    End Sub

</script>


<h3>Current Weather</h3>
<asp:Label
    id="lblWeather"
    Runat="server" />
```

27

The `WeatherPart` contains a method named `ConsumeZIPCode()` that is decorated with the `ConnectionConsumer` attribute. This method is called when a class that implements the `IZIPCode` interface is returned from the provider Web Part.

The `ConsumeZIPCode()` method assigns the class that implements the `IZIPCode` interface to a private field. The private field is used to display the weather in the `Page_PreRender()` method.

> **NOTE**
>
> When working with connected Web Parts, it is important to know when in the page execution lifecycle the consumer Web Part actually calls the provider Web Part. This happens during the Page's `LoadComplete` event, which occurs right after the Page's Load event.
>
> For this reason, the information exposed by a provider Web Part is not available during a consumer Web Part's Load event. You should place all your logic that depends on this information in the Web Part's `PreRender` event handler.

Finally, you can create a Web Part page that hosts the `ZIPCodePart` and `WeatherPart`. This page is contained in Listing 27.25.

LISTING 27.25   `ConnectedSimpleParts.aspx`

```
<%@ Page Language="VB" %>
<%@ Register TagPrefix="user" TagName="ZIPCodePart" Src="~/ZIPCodePart.ascx" %>
<%@ Register TagPrefix="user" TagName="WeatherPart" Src="~/WeatherPart.ascx" %>
<!DOCTYPE html PUBLIC "-//W3C//DTD XHTML 1.1//EN"
"http://www.w3.org/TR/xhtml11/DTD/xhtml11.dtd">

<script runat="server">

    Sub Menu1_MenuItemClick(ByVal sender As Object, ByVal e As MenuEventArgs)
        WebPartManager1.DisplayMode = WebPartManager1.DisplayModes(e.Item.Text)
    End Sub
</script>

<html xmlns="http://www.w3.org/1999/xhtml" >
<head id="Head1" runat="server">
    <style type="text/css">
        .column
        {
            float:left;
            width:40%;
            height:200px;
            margin-right:10px;
            border:solid 1px black;
            background-color: white;
        }
```

LISTING 27.25   Continued

```
        .menu
        {
            margin:5px 0px;
        }
        html
        {
            background-color:#eeeeee;
        }
    </style>
    <title>Connected Simple Parts</title>
</head>
<body>
    <form id="form1" runat="server">
    <asp:WebPartManager
        id="WebPartManager1"
        Runat="server">
        <StaticConnections>
        <asp:WebPartConnection
            ID="WebPartConnection1"
            ProviderID="ZIPCodePart1"
            ConsumerID="WeatherPart1" />
        </StaticConnections>
     </asp:WebPartManager>

        <asp:Menu
            id="Menu1"
            OnMenuItemClick="Menu1_MenuItemClick"
            Orientation="Horizontal"
            CssClass="menu"
            Runat="server">
            <Items>
            <asp:MenuItem Text="Browse" />
            <asp:MenuItem Text="Design" />
            </Items>
        </asp:Menu>

        <asp:WebPartZone
            id="WebPartZone1"
            CssClass="column"
            Runat="server">
            <ZoneTemplate>
            <user:ZIPCodePart
                id="ZIPCodePart1"
                Title="ZIP Code Part"
```

LISTING 27.25   Continued

```
                    Description="Enables entry of ZIP code"
                    Runat="Server" />
            </ZoneTemplate>
        </asp:WebPartZone>

        <asp:WebPartZone
            id="WebPartZone2"
            CssClass="column"
            Runat="server">
            <ZoneTemplate>
            <user:WeatherPart
                id="WeatherPart1"
                Title="Weather Part"
                Description="Displays current weather"
                Runat="Server" />
            </ZoneTemplate>
        </asp:WebPartZone>


        </form>
</body>
</html>
```

The page in Listing 27.25 contains the ZIPCodePart and WeatherPart in its two Web Part Zones. The two Web Parts are statically connected by the WebPartManager control. Notice that the WebPartManager control includes a <StaticConnections> section that connects the two parts.

After you open the page in Listing 27.25 in your web browser, you can enter a ZIP code in the ZIPCodePart and see the ZIP code displayed in the WeatherPart.

> **NOTE**
>
> If you place your WebPartManager control in a Master Page, you can still create static connections between Web Parts in a content page. To do this, you need to add a ProxyWebPartManager control that lists the static connections to the content page.

Connecting Databound Web Parts

This section tackles a slightly more complicated sample of connected Web Parts. You connect two Web Parts that display database data.

The provider Web Part displays a list of movie categories, and the consumer Web Part displays a list of movies. When the Web Parts are connected, you can select a movie category and see a list of matching movies (see Figure 27.16).

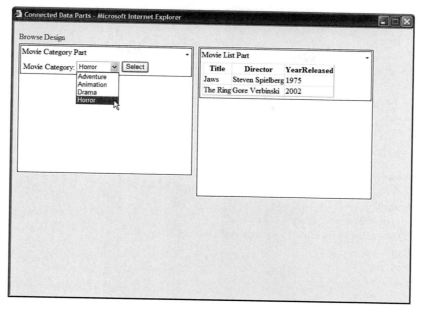

FIGURE 27.16   Connecting databound controls.

The first thing to do is define the interface that describes the information passed from the provider Web Part to the consumer Web Part. The interface is contained in Listing 27.26.

LISTING 27.26   IMovieCategory.vb

```vb
''' <summary>
''' Decribes the data exposed by
''' the MovieCategoryPart
''' </summary>
Public Interface IMovieCategory
    ReadOnly Property SelectedCategoryId() As Integer
End Interface
```

The next step is to create the provider Web Part that exposes the IMovieCategory interface. The MovieCategoryPart is contained in Listing 27.27. This Web Part enables you to select a movie from a drop-down list.

LISTING 27.27   MovieCategoryPart.ascx

```vb
<%@ Control Language="VB" ClassName="MovieCategoryPart" %>
<%@ Implements Interface="IMovieCategory" %>

<script runat="server">
    ''' <summary>
    ''' Implements IMovieCategoryPart.SelectedCategoryId
```

LISTING 27.17   Continued

```
    ''' </summary>
    Public ReadOnly Property SelectedCategoryId() As Integer Implements
➥ IMovieCategory.SelectedCategoryId
        Get
            Return CInt(dropCategories.SelectedValue)
        End Get
    End Property


    ''' <summary>
    ''' This method is called from connected Web Parts
    ''' </summary>
    <ConnectionProvider("Movie Category")> _
    Public Function ProvideCategory() As IMovieCategory
        Return Me
    End Function

</script>

<asp:Label
    id="lblCategory"
    Text="Movie Category:"
    AssociatedControlID="dropCategories"
    Runat="server" />

<asp:DropDownList
    id="dropCategories"
    DataSourceId="srcCategories"
    DataTextField="Name"
    DataValueField="Id"
    AutoPostBack="true"
    Runat="server" />

<asp:Button
    id="btnSelect"
    Text="Select"
    Runat="server" />

<asp:SqlDataSource
    id="srcCategories"
    ConnectionString="Server=.\SQLExpress;
        Integrated Security=True;AttachDbFileName=¦DataDirectory¦MyDatabase.mdf;
        User Instance=True"
    SelectCommand="SELECT Id,Name FROM MovieCategories"
    Runat="server" />
```

The MovieCategoryPart contains a DropDownList control bound to a SqlDataSource control. The SqlDataSource control represents the contents of a SQL Express database table named MovieCategories.

Notice that the Web Part includes a method named ProvideCategory(), which is decorated with the ConnectionProvider attribute. This method returns a reference to the MovieCategoryPart when a consumer Web Part connects to the MovieCategoryPart.

The next step is to create the consumer Web Part. The consumer Web Part is named MovieListPart and it is contained in Listing 27.28.

LISTING 27.28 MovieListPart.ascx

```
<%@ Control Language="VB" ClassName="MovieListPart" %>
<%@ Import Namespace="System.Data" %>
<%@ Import Namespace="System.Data.SqlClient" %>

<script runat="server">

    Private _category As IMovieCategory

    ''' <summary>
    ''' This method is called when the ProvideCategory method
    ''' returns a class that implements the IMovieCategory interface
    ''' </summary>
    <ConnectionConsumer("Movie Category")> _
    Public  Sub ConsumeCategory(ByVal category As IMovieCategory)
        _category = category
    End Sub

    ''' <summary>
    ''' Update SelectedCategoryId from Provider Web Part
    ''' </summary>
    Private  Sub Page_PreRender()
        If Not _category Is Nothing Then
            srcMovies.SelectParameters("CategoryId").DefaultValue =
_category.SelectedCategoryId.ToString()
        End If
    End Sub

</script>

<asp:GridView
    id="grdMovies"
    DataSourceId="srcMovies"
    Runat="server" />
```

27

LISTING 27.28   Continued

```
<asp:SqlDataSource
    id="srcMovies"
    ConnectionString="Server=.\SQLExpress;Integrated Security=True;
        AttachDbFileName=¦DataDirectory¦MyDatabase.mdf;User Instance=True"
    SelectCommand="SELECT Title,Director,YearReleased
        FROM Movies WHERE CategoryId=@CategoryId"
    Runat="server">
    <SelectParameters>
        <asp:Parameter Name="CategoryId" Type="int32" />
    </SelectParameters>
</asp:SqlDataSource>
```

The MovieListPart displays a list of movies in a GridView control. When you connect the MovieListPart to the MovieCategoryPart, the MovieListPart displays only those movies that match the selected movie category.

Notice that the MovieListPart includes a method named ConsumeCategory(), which is decorated with the ConnectionConsumer attribute. This method retrieves the class that implements the IMovieCategory interface (the MovieCategoryPart) from the provider Web Part.

The Page_PreRender() method updates the list of movies displayed in the GridView control. The method updates the value of the CategoryId parameter used by the SqlDataSource control.

Finally, you can create a page that hosts the provider and consumer Web Parts. The page is contained in Listing 27.29.

LISTING 27.29   ConnectedDataParts.aspx

```
<%@ Page Language="VB" %>
<%@ Register TagPrefix="user" TagName="MovieCategoryPart"
➥ Src="~/MovieCategoryPart.ascx" %>
<%@ Register TagPrefix="user" TagName="MovieListPart" Src="~/MovieListPart.ascx" %>
<!DOCTYPE html PUBLIC "-//W3C//DTD XHTML 1.1//EN"
"http://www.w3.org/TR/xhtml11/DTD/xhtml11.dtd">

<script runat="server">

    Sub Menu1_MenuItemClick(ByVal sender As Object, ByVal e As MenuEventArgs)
        WebPartManager1.DisplayMode = WebPartManager1.DisplayModes(e.Item.Text)
    End Sub

</script>
```

LISTING 27.29   Continued

```
<html xmlns="http://www.w3.org/1999/xhtml" >
<head id="Head1" runat="server">
    <style type="text/css">
        .column
        {
            float:left;
            width:45%;
            height:200px;
            margin-right:10px;
            border:solid 1px black;
            background-color: white;
        }
        .menu
        {
            margin:5px 0px;
        }
        html
        {
            background-color:#eeeeee;
        }
    </style>
    <title>Connected Data Parts</title>
</head>
<body>
    <form id="form1" runat="server">
    <asp:WebPartManager
        id="WebPartManager1"
        Runat="server">
        <StaticConnections>
        <asp:WebPartConnection
            ID="WebPartConnection1"
            ProviderID="MovieCategoryPart1"
            ConsumerID="MovieListPart1" />
        </StaticConnections>
    </asp:WebPartManager>

        <asp:Menu
            id="Menu1"
            OnMenuItemClick="Menu1_MenuItemClick"
            Orientation="Horizontal"
            CssClass="menu"
            Runat="server">
            <Items>
            <asp:MenuItem Text="Browse" />
```

27

LISTING 27.29   Continued

```
                <asp:MenuItem Text="Design" />
                </Items>
            </asp:Menu>

            <asp:WebPartZone
                id="WebPartZone1"
                CssClass="column"
                Runat="server">
                <ZoneTemplate>
                <user:MovieCategoryPart
                    id="MovieCategoryPart1"
                    Title="Movie Category Part"
                    Description="Displays movie categories"
                    Runat="Server" />
                </ZoneTemplate>
            </asp:WebPartZone>

            <asp:WebPartZone
                id="WebPartZone2"
                CssClass="column"
                Runat="server">
                <ZoneTemplate>
                <user:MovieListPart
                    id="MovieListPart1"
                    Title="Movie List Part"
                    Description="Displays list of movies"
                    Runat="Server" />
                </ZoneTemplate>
            </asp:WebPartZone>


    </form>
</body>
</html>
```

The page in Listing 27.29 statically connects the MovieCategoryPart and MovieListPart Web Parts. The static connection is created in the WebPartManager control's <StaticConnections> section.

Dynamically Connecting Web Parts

In the previous sections, you connected Web Parts by declaring a static connection between the Web Parts. Creating a static connection makes sense when the Web Parts themselves are also statically declared in the page.

There are situations, however, in which you will want to enable users of your application to form dynamic connections between Web Parts. For example, you might want to allow a user to add a new Web Part to a page from a catalog of Web Parts and connect the new Web Part to an existing Web Part.

You can enable users to create dynamic connections between Web Parts by adding a Connections Zone to a page. The page in Listing 27.30 illustrates how you can declare a Connections Zone.

LISTING 27.30   ConnectedDynamicParts.aspx

```
<%@ Page Language="VB" %>
<%@ Register TagPrefix="user" TagName="ZIPCodePart" Src="~/ZIPCodePart.ascx" %>
<%@ Register TagPrefix="user" TagName="WeatherPart" Src="~/WeatherPart.ascx" %>
<!DOCTYPE html PUBLIC "-//W3C//DTD XHTML 1.1//EN"
"http://www.w3.org/TR/xhtml11/DTD/xhtml11.dtd">
<script runat="server">

    Sub Menu1_MenuItemClick(ByVal sender As Object, ByVal e As MenuEventArgs)
        WebPartManager1.DisplayMode = WebPartManager1.DisplayModes(e.Item.Text)
    End Sub
</script>


<html xmlns="http://www.w3.org/1999/xhtml" >
<head id="Head1" runat="server">
    <style type="text/css">
        .column
        {
            float:left;
            width:30%;
            height:200px;
            margin-right:10px;
            border:solid 1px black;
            background-color: white;
        }
        .menu
        {
            margin:5px 0px;
        }
        html
        {
            background-color:#eeeeee;
        }
    </style>
    <title>Connected Dynamic Parts</title>
</head>
```

27

LISTING 27.30   Continued

```
<body>
    <form id="form1" runat="server">
    <asp:WebPartManager
        id="WebPartManager1"
        Runat="server" />

        <asp:Menu
            id="Menu1"
            OnMenuItemClick="Menu1_MenuItemClick"
            Orientation="Horizontal"
            CssClass="menu"
            Runat="server">
            <Items>
            <asp:MenuItem Text="Browse" />
            <asp:MenuItem Text="Design" />
            <asp:MenuItem Text="Catalog" />
            <asp:MenuItem Text="Connect" />
            </Items>
        </asp:Menu>

        <asp:WebPartZone
            id="WebPartZone1"
            CssClass="column"
            Runat="server" />

        <asp:WebPartZone
            id="WebPartZone2"
            CssClass="column"
            Runat="server" />

        <asp:CatalogZone
            id="CatalogZone1"
            CssClass="column"
            Runat="server">
            <ZoneTemplate>
            <asp:DeclarativeCatalogPart
                id="DeclarativeCatalogPart1"
                Runat="server">
                <WebPartsTemplate>
                <user:ZIPCodePart
                    id="ZIPCodePart1"
                    Title="ZIP Code Part"
                    Description="Enables entry of ZIP code"
                    Runat="Server" />
```

LISTING 27.30   Continued

```
                <user:WeatherPart
                    id="WeatherPart1"
                    Title="Weather Part"
                    Description="Displays current weather"
                    Runat="Server" />
                </WebPartsTemplate>
            </asp:DeclarativeCatalogPart>
            </ZoneTemplate>
        </asp:CatalogZone>

        <asp:ConnectionsZone
            id="ConnectionsZone"
            CssClass="column"
            Runat="server" />

    </form>
</body>
</html>
```

Notice that, unlike other tool zones, the Connections Zone does not include any parts. In Listing 27.30, a `<ConnectionsZone>` tag is declared in the page without any child elements.

If you open the page in Listing 27.30 in your browser, you can click the Catalog link to display the contents of the Declarative Catalog. Next, you can add an instance of both the `ZIPCodePart` and `WeatherPart` to the page. At this point, the two Web Parts are not connected.

Next, you can connect the Web Parts by clicking the Connect link and selecting Connect from either of the two Web Part control's menus. For example, if you select Connect from the `WeatherPart` control's menu and click the Create a Connection to a Provider link, the connection interface in Figure 27.17 appears.

You can select the ZIP Code Part from the drop-down list to connect the two Web Parts. After the Web Parts are connected, entering a ZIP code causes the Weather Part to display the weather for that ZIP code.

Using Transformers with Connected Web Parts

For two Web Parts to communicate, the two Web Parts must agree on a common interface. With careful planning, a single developer can build a set of Web Parts and interfaces that enable all the Web Parts contained in an application to communicate cleanly.

However, imagine that you need to connect Web Parts created by different developers in your organization. Or imagine that you need to connect Web Parts sold by different companies. It is unlikely that the Web Parts will share exactly the same interfaces.

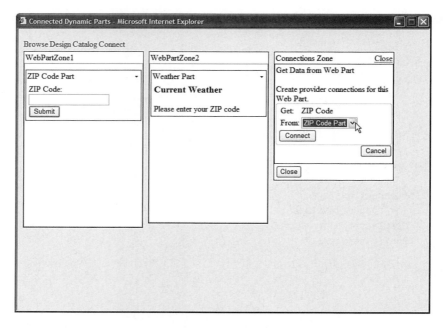

FIGURE 27.17   Dynamically connecting two Web Parts.

In situations in which you do not have control over the interface exposed by a Web Part, you can take advantage of a Transformer to modify the interface. A Transformer enables you to transform the data passed between a provider Web Part and a consumer Web Part.

Imagine, for example, that you buy a new Web Part—named the LocalNewsPart—that displays a list of local news headlines. You want to use this new Web Part with your existing ZIPCodePart and WeatherPart in an application.

Unfortunately, you quickly discover that you cannot connect the LocalNewsPart to the ZIPCodePart control. The two Web Parts expect different interfaces. To solve this problem, you need to create a *Transformer*.

The LocalNewsPart Web Part is contained in Listing 27.31.

LISTING 27.31   LocalNewsPart.ascx

```
<%@ Control Language="VB" ClassName="LocalNewsPart" %>

<script runat="server">

    Private _zipCode As INewsZIPCode

    ''' <summary>
    ''' This method retrieves the INewsZIPCode interface returned
```

LISTING 27.31   Continued

```
    ''' by the provider Web Part
    ''' </summary>
    <ConnectionConsumer("News ZIP Code")> _
    Public  Sub ConsumeZIPCode(ByVal zipCode As INewsZIPCode)
        _zipCode = zipCode
    End Sub


    ''' <summary>
    ''' Display the news
    ''' </summary>
    Private  Sub Page_PreRender()
        ' Check if we are connected
        If Not _zipCode Is Nothing Then
            If _zipCode.ZIPCode <> String.Empty Then
                lblNews.Text = String.Format("Everything looks terrific for {0}!",
_zipCode.ZIPCode)
            Else
                lblNews.Text = "Please enter your ZIP code"
            End If
        End If
    End Sub
</script>

<h3>Current News</h3>
<asp:Label
    id="lblNews"
    Runat="server" />
```

The LocalNewsPart Web Part uses the interface defined in Listing 27.32—the INewsZIPCode interface—to represent a ZIP code.

LISTING 27.32   App_Code\INewsZIPCode.vb

```
''' <summary>
''' Represents a ZIP code
''' </summary>
Public Interface INewsZIPCode
    ReadOnly Property ZIPCode() As String
End Interface
```

The INewsZIPCode interface represents a ZIP code in exactly the same way as the IZIPCode interface used by the ZIPCodePart and WeatherPart Web Parts. Unfortunately, however, it is a different interface. Therefore, before you can connect the `LocalNewsPart` Web Part to the `ZIPCodePart`, you must first define a Transformer.

The Transformer in Listing 27.33 converts an instance of the `IZIPCode` interface to an instance of the `INewsZIPCode` interface.

LISTING 27.33   App_Code\ZIPCodeTransformer.vb

```
Imports System
Imports System.Web.UI.WebControls.WebParts

Namespace myControls

    ''' <summary>
    ''' This class transforms an IZIPCode to
    ''' an INewsZIPCode
    ''' </summary>
    <WebPartTransformer(GetType(IZIPCode), GetType(INewsZIPCode))> _
    Public Class ZIPCodeTransformer
        Inherits WebPartTransformer
        Public Overrides Function Transform(ByVal providerData As Object) As Object
            Return New TempZIP((CType(providerData, IZIPCode)).ZIPCode)
        End Function
    End Class


    Public Class TempZIP
        Implements INewsZIPCode
        Private _zipCode As String

        Public ReadOnly Property ZIPCode() As String Implements
➡ INewsZIPCode.ZIPCode
            Get
                Return _zipCode
            End Get
        End Property

        Friend Sub New(ByVal zipCode As String)
            _zipCode = zipCode
        End Sub
    End Class
End Namespace
```

After you create the file in Listing 27.33, you need to add it to your application's App_Code folder to automatically compile the Transformer class.

There are a number of things that you should notice about the code for the Transformer. First, notice that the ZIPCodeTransformer class is decorated with a WebPartTransformer attribute. This attribute has two parameters: the provider interface and the consumer interface.

Next, you should notice that the ZIPCodeTransformer class derives from the base WebPartTransformer class. The ZIPCodeTransformer class overrides the base class's Transform() method. The Transform() method takes the instance of the interface provided by the provider Web Part and transforms it into an instance of an interface appropriate for the consumer Web Part.

> **NOTE**
>
> The WebPartTransformer class includes another useful method that you can override: the CreateConfigurationControl() method. You can use this method to return an editor for configuring a Transformer. The Transformer editor appears when you click the Edit button in the Connections Zone.

Before you can use a Transformer in an application, you must register the Transformer in your application's web configuration file. The file in Listing 27.34 contains the necessary configuration settings.

LISTING 27.34   Web.Config

```
<?xml version="1.0"?>
<configuration xmlns="http://schemas.microsoft.com/.NetConfiguration/v2.0">
    <system.web>
      <webParts>
        <transformers>
          <add
              name="ZIPCodeTransformer"
              type="myControls.ZIPCodeTransformer"/>
        </transformers>
      </webParts>
    </system.web>
</configuration>
```

After you are finished setting up the Transformer, you can use the Transformer when creating either a static or dynamic connection between Web Parts. The page in Listing 27.35 demonstrates how you can declare a Transformer when creating a static connection between the ZIPCodePart and the LocalNewsPart Web Parts.

27

LISTING 27.35   ConnectedTransformerParts.aspx

```
<%@ Page Language="VB" %>
<%@ Register TagPrefix="user" TagName="ZIPCodePart" Src="~/ZIPCodePart.ascx" %>
<%@ Register TagPrefix="user" TagName="WeatherPart" Src="~/WeatherPart.ascx" %>
<%@ Register TagPrefix="user" TagName="LocalNewsPart" Src="~/LocalNewsPart.ascx" %>
<%@ Register TagPrefix="custom" Namespace="myControls" %>
<!DOCTYPE html PUBLIC "-//W3C//DTD XHTML 1.1//EN"
"http://www.w3.org/TR/xhtml11/DTD/xhtml11.dtd">
<script runat="server">

    Sub Menu1_MenuItemClick(ByVal sender As Object, ByVal e As MenuEventArgs)
        WebPartManager1.DisplayMode = WebPartManager1.DisplayModes(e.Item.Text)
    End Sub

</script>
<html xmlns="http://www.w3.org/1999/xhtml" >
<head id="Head1" runat="server">
    <style type="text/css">
        .column
        {
            float:left;
            width:45%;
            height:200px;
            margin-right:10px;
            border:solid 1px black;
            background-color: white;
        }
        .menu
        {
            margin:5px 0px;
        }
        html
        {
            background-color:#eeeeee;
        }
    </style>
    <title>Connected Transformer Parts</title>
</head>
<body>
    <form id="form1" runat="server">
    <asp:WebPartManager
        id="WebPartManager1"
        Runat="server">
        <StaticConnections>
        <asp:WebPartConnection
```

LISTING 27.35   Continued

```
                ID="WebPartConnection1"
                ProviderID="ZIPCodePart1"
                ConsumerID="WeatherPart1" />
        <asp:WebPartConnection
                ID="WebPartConnection2"
                ProviderID="ZIPCodePart1"
                ConsumerID="LocalNewsPart1">
                <custom:ZIPCodeTransformer
                    Runat="Server" />
        </asp:WebPartConnection>
        </StaticConnections>
    </asp:WebPartManager>

        <asp:Menu
            id="Menu1"
            OnMenuItemClick="Menu1_MenuItemClick"
            Orientation="Horizontal"
            CssClass="menu"
            Runat="server">
            <Items>
            <asp:MenuItem Text="Browse" />
            <asp:MenuItem Text="Design" />
            </Items>
        </asp:Menu>

        <asp:WebPartZone
            id="WebPartZone1"
            CssClass="column"
            Runat="server">
            <ZoneTemplate>
            <user:ZIPCodePart
                id="ZIPCodePart1"
                Title="ZIP Code Part"
                Description="Enables entry of ZIP code"
                Runat="Server" />
            </ZoneTemplate>
        </asp:WebPartZone>

        <asp:WebPartZone
            id="WebPartZone2"
            CssClass="column"
            Runat="server">
            <ZoneTemplate>
            <user:WeatherPart
```

27

LISTING 27.35   Continued

```
                id="WeatherPart1"
                Title="Weather Part"
                Description="Displays current weather"
                Runat="Server" />
            <user:LocalNewsPart
                id="LocalNewsPart1"
                Title="Local News Part"
                Description="Displays current news"
                Runat="Server" />
            </ZoneTemplate>
        </asp:WebPartZone>
    </form>
</body>
</html>
```

The ZIPCodeTransformer is registered at the top of the page in Listing 27.35. The page uses the ZIPCodeTransformer in the declaration of the static connection between the ZIPCodePart and the LocalNewsPart Web Parts.

After you configure a Transformer in an application's web configuration file, you don't need to do anything special to use the Transformer in a page in which you are dynamically connecting Web Parts.

For example, the page in Listing 27.35 contains a catalog that lists the ZIPCodePart, the WeatherPart, and the LocalNewsPart. You can add all three Web Parts to a page and then connect the Web Parts by clicking the Connect link and selecting the Connect menu option included in each Web Part menu. If you connect the LocalNewsPart to the ZIPCodePart, the connection will automatically use the ZIPCodeTransformer.

Summary

This chapter introduced you to the Web Part Framework. You learned how to use each of the different types of zones that you can add to a Web Part page.

You learned how to use Web Part Zones to mark the areas in a page that can contain Web Parts. You also saw how you can take advantage of Catalog Zones to enable users to add new Web Parts to a page at runtime. You learned how to use Editor Zones to enable users to edit Web Part properties. Finally, you learned how to use Connections Zones to enable users to create dynamic connections between Web Parts.

CHAPTER 28

Building Web Parts

T his chapter is devoted exclusively to the topic of building Web Parts. You learn how to create Web Parts by creating User controls and by creating custom controls that derive from the base WebPart class.

We also examine the important topic of authorization filters. You learn how to display different sets of Web Parts to different users. For example, you learn how to create Web Parts that only members of the Administrator role can view.

Later in this chapter, custom Web Part verbs are discussed. You learn how to add custom menu items to a Web Part and execute server-side and client-side code when a user selects the menu item.

This chapter also explores how you can add help to Web Parts. You learn how to open a modal dialog box that displays a help page.

WARNING

For many of the samples to work in this chapter, you must enable authentication for your application. Windows authentication is enabled by default. For more information about authentication, see Chapter 20, "Using the Login Controls."

Finally, the WebPartManager class is examined. You learn how to take advantage of this class to programmatically manipulate the Web Parts contained in a page.

Creating Simple Web Parts

Technically, there are two types of Web Parts. You can create a Web Part by adding any ASP.NET control—including any custom control or User control—to a Web

Part Zone. Alternatively, you can create a Web Part by building a custom control that derives from the base `WebPart` class.

The Web Part Framework handles these two types of Web Parts differently. When you add a standard ASP.NET control to a Web Part Zone, the Web Part Framework wraps the control in a `GenericWebPart` control. Wrapping a standard control in a `GenericWebPart` adds all the standard Web Part properties to the control.

For example, if you add an Image control to a Web Part Zone, the Web Part Framework automatically creates a new `GenericWebPart` control that includes the Image control as its only child control.

If, on the other hand, you create a Web Part by building a custom control that derives from the base `WebPart` class, the Web Part Framework doesn't need to do anything special with the control. The control is already a Web Part.

Because the `GenericWebPart` class itself derives from the base `WebPart` class, you can do anything with a generic Web Part that you can do with a "True" Web Part with one important limitation. Because a control gets wrapped in a `GenericWebPart` at runtime, there are a number of Web Part properties that you cannot set declaratively when working with a generic Web Part.

In this section, you learn how to create simple Web Parts. You also learn how to take advantage of both the core and extended properties supported by Web Part controls.

The Hello World Web Part

All authors of programming books are contractually obligated to include at least one Hello World sample in every book that they write. In this section, two Hello World Web Parts illustrate how to create a Web Part with a User control and a custom control derived from the base `WebPart` class. In other words, both a Generic Web Part and a True Web Part are created.

The Generic Hello World Web Part is contained in Listing 28.1.

LISTING 28.1   `HelloWorldPart.ascx`

```
<%@ Control Language="VB" ClassName="HelloWorldPart" %>

Hello World!
```

Notice how simple the Generic Hello World Web Part is. The control simply renders a single line of text.

Creating a True Web Part that does the same thing isn't that much more difficult. The Web Part in Listing 28.2 inherits from the base `WebPart` class, making it a True Web Part.

LISTING 28.2   App_Code\HelloWorldPart.vb

```vb
Imports System
Imports System.Web.UI
Imports System.Web.UI.WebControls.WebParts

Namespace myControls

    ''' <summary>
    ''' True Web Part
    ''' </summary>
    Public Class HelloWorldPart
        Inherits WebPart

        Protected Overrides Sub RenderContents(ByVal writer As HtmlTextWriter)
            writer.Write("Hello World!")
        End Sub

    End Class
End Namespace
```

The class in Listing 28.2 inherits from the base WebPart class and overrides the RenderContents() method to display the single line of text.

> **NOTE**
>
> You must add the file in Listing 28.2 to the App_Code folder for the control to be automatically compiled.

The page in Listing 28.3 displays both the Generic and True Web Parts.

LISTING 28.3   ShowHelloWorldPart.aspx

```aspx
<%@ Page Language="VB" %>
<%@ Register TagPrefix="custom" Namespace="myControls" %>
<%@ Register TagPrefix="user" TagName="HelloWorldPart"
➥ Src="~/HelloWorldPart.ascx" %>
<!DOCTYPE html PUBLIC "-//W3C//DTD XHTML 1.1//EN"
  "http://www.w3.org/TR/xhtml11/DTD/xhtml11.dtd">
<html xmlns="http://www.w3.org/1999/xhtml" >
<head id="Head1" runat="server">
    <style type="text/css">
        .column
        {
            float:left;
            width:45%;
```

28

LISTING 28.3   Continued

```
            height:200px;
            margin-right:10px;
            border:solid 1px black;
            background-color: white;
        }
        html
        {
            background-color:#eeeeee;
        }
    </style>
    <title>Show Hello World Part</title>
</head>
<body>
    <form id="form1" runat="server">
    <asp:WebPartManager
        id="WebPartManager1"
        Runat="server" />
        <asp:WebPartZone
            id="WebPartZone1"
            CssClass="column"
            Runat="server">
            <ZoneTemplate>
            <user:HelloWorldPart
                id="HelloWorldPart1"
                Runat="server" />
            </ZoneTemplate>
        </asp:WebPartZone>

        <asp:WebPartZone
            id="WebPartZone2"
            CssClass="column"
            Runat="server">
            <ZoneTemplate>
            <custom:HelloWorldPart
                id="HelloWorldPart2"
                Runat="server" />
            </ZoneTemplate>
        </asp:WebPartZone>

    </form>
</body>
</html>
```

After you open the page in Listing 28.3, you'll see two Web Part Zones. The Generic Hello World Web Part is contained in the first zone and the True Web Part is contained in the second zone (see Figure 28.1).

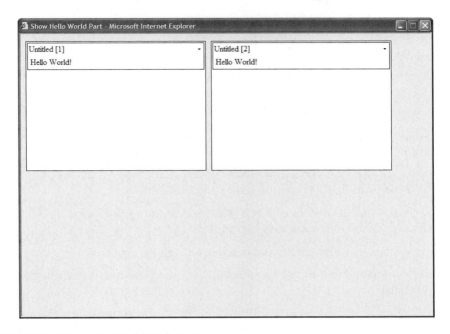

FIGURE 28.1   The Hello World Web Parts.

Notice that both Web Parts are registered at the top of the page. As an alternative to registering Web Parts in each page, you can register the Web Parts once in an application's web configuration file, as is shown in Listing 28.4.

LISTING 28.4   Web.Config

```
<?xml version="1.0"?>
<configuration>
    <system.web>
    <pages>
      <controls>
        <add tagPrefix="custom" namespace="myControls" />
        <add tagPrefix="user" tagName="HelloWorldPart"
             src="~/WebParts/HelloWorldPart.ascx"/>
      </controls>
    </pages>
    </system.web>
</configuration>
```

When you register a User control in the web configuration file, you must place the User control in a different folder than any page that uses it (otherwise, you'll get an exception). Typically, you should locate all your user controls in a subfolder in your application. In the web configuration file in Listing 28.4, the `HelloWorldPart.ascx` file has been moved to a folder named WebParts.

Standard Web Part Properties

As mentioned earlier, both Generic and True Web Parts support a core set of properties:

- `AuthorizationFilter`—Enables you to specify a string that the Web Part Manager can check before adding a Web Part to a page.

- `CatalogIconImageUrl`—Enables you to specify the icon displayed for the Web Part when the Web Part is listed in a Catalog Part.

- `Description`—Enables you to specify the description displayed for the Web Part as a tooltip when you hover your mouse over the Web Part.

- `ExportMode`—Enables you to export a Web Part control's settings to an XML file. Possible values are `All`, `None`, and `NonSensitiveData`.

- `Height`—Enables you to specify the height of a Web Part control.

- `Subtitle`—Enables you to add an additional string to the end of the title displayed in a Web Part.

- `Title`—Enables you to specify the title of the Web Part displayed, for example, in the title bar.

- `TitleIconImageUrl`—The title icon image is displayed next to the title in the title bar.

- `TitleUrl`—Enables you to convert the title into a hyperlink that links to a page with more information about the Web Part.

- `Width`—Enables you to specify the width of the Web Part.

You can set any of these properties declaratively on any control that you add to a Web Part Zone. For example, you can set the Title and Description properties like this:

```
<user:HelloWorldPart
  id="HelloWorldPart1"
  Title="Hello World"
  Description="Displays Hello World"
  Runat="server" />
```

VISUAL WEB DEVELOPER NOTE

When working in Source view in Visual Web Developer, you get a green squiggle warning when setting Web Part properties such as the `Title` or `Description` property for a User control. Technically, you are setting expando properties because the `UserControl` class doesn't know anything about the specialized Web Part properties. You can safely ignore the warning messages.

Alternatively, you can supply any of these properties with default values in the Web Part control itself. You set these properties in different ways depending on whether you are working with a Generic Web Part control or a True Web Part control.

When setting default Web Part property values for a Generic Web Part control, you need to implement the IWebPart interface. For example, Listing 28.5 contains the code for a Random Quote Web Part.

LISTING 28.5   RandomQuotePart.ascx

```
<%@ Control Language="VB" ClassName="RandomQuotePart" %>
<%@ Implements Interface="System.Web.UI.WebControls.WebParts.IWebPart" %>
<%@ Import Namespace="System.Collections.Generic" %>
<script runat="server">

    Private _title As String = "Random Quote"
    Private _titleUrl As String = "~/Help.aspx"
    Private _description As String = "Displays a random quote"
    Private _subTitle As String = "User Control Version"
    Private _catalogIconImageUrl As String = "~/Images/BigRandomQuote.gif"
    Private _titleIconImageUrl As String = "~/Images/SmallRandomQuote.gif"

    Public Property Title() As String Implements IWebPart.Title
        Get
            Return _title
        End Get
        Set(ByVal Value As String)
            _title = Value
        End Set
    End Property


    Public Property TitleUrl() As String Implements IWebPart.TitleUrl
        Get
            Return _titleUrl
        End Get
        Set(ByVal Value As String)
            _titleUrl = Value
        End Set
    End Property
```

28

LISTING 28.5   Continued

```
    Public Property Description() As String Implements IWebPart.Description
        Get
            Return _description
        End Get
        Set(ByVal Value As String)
            _description = Value
        End Set
    End Property

    Public ReadOnly Property Subtitle() As String Implements IWebPart.Subtitle
        Get
            Return _subTitle
        End Get
    End Property

    Public Property CatalogIconImageUrl() As String
➥Implements IWebPart.CatalogIconImageUrl
        Get
            Return _catalogIconImageUrl
        End Get
        Set(ByVal Value As String)
            _catalogIconImageUrl = Value
        End Set
    End Property

    Public Property TitleIconImageUrl() As String
➥Implements IWebPart.TitleIconImageUrl
        Get
            Return _titleIconImageUrl
        End Get
        Set(ByVal Value As String)
            _titleIconImageUrl = Value
        End Set
    End Property


    Private Sub Page_PreRender()
        Dim quotes As New List(Of String)
        quotes.Add("All paid jobs absorb and degrade the mind -- Aristotle")
        quotes.Add("No evil can happen to a good man,
➥either in life or after death -- Plato")
        quotes.Add("The only good is knowledge and the
➥only evil is ignorance -- Plato")
        Dim rnd As New Random()
        lblQuote.Text = quotes(rnd.Next(quotes.Count))
```

LISTING 28.5   Continued

```
      End Sub
</script>

<asp:Label
    id="lblQuote"
    runat="server" />
```

Notice that the User control in Listing 28.5 implements the IWebPart interface. It includes an <%@ Implements %> directive at the top of the file. Default values are provided for each of the standard Web Part properties.

When working with a True Web Part control, you do not need to implement the IWebPart interface. Because a True Web Part control derives from the base WebPart class, and the WebPart class contains all the properties of the IWebPart interface, you simply need to override the Web Part properties that you want to modify.

The Web Part in Listing 28.6 also displays a random quotation. However, this control is a True Web Part control.

LISTING 28.6   App_Code\RandomQuotePart.vb

```
Imports System
Imports System.Collections.Generic
Imports System.Web.UI
Imports System.Web.UI.WebControls.WebParts

Namespace myControls

    ''' <summary>
    ''' Displays a random quotation
    ''' </summary>
    Public Class RandomQuotePart
        Inherits WebPart

        Private _title As String = "Random Quote"
        Private _titleUrl As String = "~/Help.aspx"
        Private _description As String = "Displays a random quote"
        Private _subTitle As String = "True Web Part Version"
        Private _catalogIconImageUrl As String = "~/Images/BigRandomQuote.gif"
        Private _titleIconImageUrl As String = "~/Images/SmallRandomQuote.gif"

        Public Overrides Property Title() As String
            Get
                Return _title
            End Get
            Set(ByVal Value As String)
```

28

LISTING 28.6 Continued

```
            _title = value
        End Set
    End Property

    Public Overrides Property TitleUrl() As String
        Get
            Return _titleUrl
        End Get
        Set(ByVal Value As String)
            _titleUrl = value
        End Set
    End Property

    Public Overrides Property Description() As String
        Get
            Return _description
        End Get
        Set(ByVal Value As String)
            _description = value
        End Set
    End Property

    Public Overrides ReadOnly Property Subtitle() As String
        Get
            Return _subTitle
        End Get
    End Property

    Public Overrides Property CatalogIconImageUrl() As String
        Get
            Return _catalogIconImageUrl
        End Get
        Set(ByVal Value As String)
            _catalogIconImageUrl = value
        End Set
    End Property

    Public Overrides Property TitleIconImageUrl() As String
        Get
            Return _titleIconImageUrl
        End Get
        Set(ByVal Value As String)
            _titleIconImageUrl = value
        End Set
```

LISTING 28.6   Continued

```
        End Property

        Protected Overrides Sub RenderContents(ByVal writer As HtmlTextWriter)
            Dim quotes As New List(Of String)()
            quotes.Add("All paid jobs absorb and degrade the mind -- Aristotle")
            quotes.Add("No evil can happen to a good man,
⇒either in life or after death -- Plato")
            quotes.Add("The only good is knowledge and
⇒the only evil is ignorance -- Plato")
            Dim rnd As New Random()
            writer.Write(quotes(rnd.Next(quotes.Count)))
        End Sub

    End Class
End Namespace
```

Notice that the class in Listing 28.6 overrides the properties of the base WebPart class. For example, the RandomQuotePart class overrides the Title property of the base WebPart class to display a default title for the Web Part (see Figure 28.2).

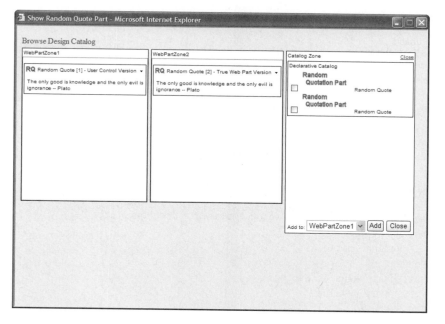

FIGURE 28.2   Displaying random quotations.

Creating a User Control Web Part Base Class

Implementing the `IWebPart` interface in a User Control every time you want to supply a default value for a Web Part property quickly gets tedious. Because the `IWebPart` interface is an interface, you are obligated to implement all the properties included in the interface even if you need to supply a value for only one of the properties.

To make your life easier, you can create a custom base class for every Web Part that you create with a User control. The `UserControlWebPartBase` class in Listing 28.7 creates default values for all the core Web Part properties.

LISTING 28.7   `App_Code\UserControlWebPartBase.vb`

```vb
Imports System
Imports System.Web.UI
Imports System.Web.UI.WebControls.WebParts

''' <summary>
''' Base Class for User Control Web Parts
''' </summary>
Public Class UserControlWebPartBase
    Inherits UserControl
    Implements IWebPart

    Private _title As String = "Untitled"
    Private _titleUrl As String = String.Empty
    Private _description As String = String.Empty
    Private _subTitle As String = String.Empty
    Private _catalogIconImageUrl As String = String.Empty
    Private _titleIconImageUrl As String = String.Empty

    Public Property Title() As String Implements IWebPart.Title
        Get
            Return _title
        End Get
        Set(ByVal Value As String)
            _title = Value
        End Set
    End Property

    Public Property TitleUrl() As String Implements IWebPart.TitleUrl
```

LISTING 28.7   Continued

```
        Get
            Return _titleUrl
        End Get
        Set(ByVal Value As String)
            _titleUrl = Value
        End Set
    End Property

    Public Property Description() As String Implements IWebPart.Description
        Get
            Return _description
        End Get
        Set(ByVal Value As String)
            _description = Value
        End Set
    End Property

    Public ReadOnly Property Subtitle() As String Implements IWebPart.Subtitle
        Get
            Return _subTitle
        End Get
    End Property

    Public Property CatalogIconImageUrl() As String
➥Implements IWebPart.CatalogIconImageUrl
        Get
            Return _catalogIconImageUrl
        End Get
        Set(ByVal Value As String)
            _catalogIconImageUrl = Value
        End Set
    End Property

    Public Property TitleIconImageUrl() As String
➥Implements IWebPart.TitleIconImageUrl
        Get
            Return _titleIconImageUrl
        End Get
        Set(ByVal Value As String)
            _titleIconImageUrl = Value
        End Set
    End Property

End Class
```

28

After you create the class in Listing 28.7, you can derive all your User Control Web Parts from this class. For example, the `MinimalPart` Web Part in Listing 28.8 inherits from the `UserControlWebPartBase` class.

LISTING 28.8   `MinimalPart.ascx`

```
<%@ Control Language="VB" ClassName="MinimalPart"
  Inherits="UserControlWebPartBase" %>

<script runat="server">

    Sub Page_Load()
        Me.Title = "Minimal Part"
        Me.Description = "Displays hardly anything at all"
    End Sub

</script>

Minimal
```

The `<%@ Control %>` directive includes an `Inherits` attribute that causes the User Control to inherit from the base `UserControlWebPartBase` class. Notice that you are not obligated to implement all the properties of the `IWebPart` interface in the `MinimalPart`. Only the `Title` and `Description` properties are set.

> **CD NOTE**
>
> You can view the `MinimalPart` with the `ShowMinimalPart.aspx` page included on the CD that accompanies this book.

Using Extended Web Part Properties

True Web Parts are slightly more powerful than Generic Web Parts. Not all Web Part properties are exposed through the `IWebPart` interface.

When deriving a Web Part from the base `WebPart` class, you can take advantage of any of the following properties:

- `AllowClose`—Enables you to prevent users from closing a Web Part.
- `AllowConnect`—Enables you to prevent users from connecting a Web Part.
- `AllowEdit`—Enables you to prevent users from editing a Web Part.
- `AllowHide`—Enables you to prevent users from hiding a Web Part.
- `AllowMinimize`—Enables you to prevent users from minimizing (collapsing) a Web Part.

- `AllowZoneChange`—Enables you to prevent users from moving a Web Part.

- `AuthorizationFilter`—Enables you to specify a string that the Web Part Manager can check before adding a Web Part to a page.

- `CatalogIconImageUrl`—Enables you to specify the icon displayed for the Web Part when the Web Part is listed in a Catalog Part.

- `ChromeState`—Enables you to get or set whether a Web Part is currently minimized or maximized. Possible values are `Minimized` and `Normal`.

- `ChromeType`—Enables you to get or set the appearance of a Web Part's chrome. Possible values are `BorderOnly`, `Default`, `None`, `TitleAndBorder`, and `TitleOnly`.

- `ConnectErrorMessage`—Enables you to get the error message displayed when errors happen while Web Parts are connected.

- `CreateEditorParts`—Enables you to associate particular Editor Parts with a Web Part.

- `Description`—Enables you to specify the description displayed for the Web Part as a tooltip when you hover your mouse over the Web Part.

- `ExportMode`—Enables you to specify whether a Web Part's settings can be exported to an XML file.

- `HasSharedData`—Enables you to determine whether a Web Part has Shared Personalization data.

- `HasUserData`—Enables you to determine whether a Web Part has User Personalization data.

- `Height`—Enables you to specify the height of a Web Part control.

- `HelpMode`—Enables you to specify the type of user interface displayed for help. Possible values are `Modal`, `Modeless`, and `Navigate`.

- `HelpUrl`—Enables you to get or set the URL for a help page associated with the Web Part.

- `Hidden`—Enables you to get or set whether a Web Part is hidden. When a Web Part is hidden, the Web Part is rendered with the Cascading Style Sheet attribute `display:none`.

- `ImportErrorMessage`—Enables you to get or set the message displayed when an error occurs during the import process.

- `IsClosed`—Enables you to determine whether a Web Part is closed.

- `IsShared`—Enables you to determine whether a Web Part is visible to all users of a Web Part page.

- `IsStandalone`—Enables you to determine whether a Web Part is visible to only certain users of a Web Part page.

- IsStatic—Enables you to determine whether a Web Part is declared in a Web Part Zone (as opposed to being added from a Catalog Zone).

- Subtitle—Enables you to add an additional string to the end of the title displayed in a Web Part.

- Title—Enables you to specify the title of the Web Part displayed, for example, in the title bar.

- TitleIconImageUrl—The title icon image is displayed next to the title in the title bar.

- TitleUrl—Enables you to convert the title into a hyperlink that links to a page with more information about the Web Part.

- WebBrowsableObject—Enables you to retrieve the object that is edited by an Editor Part.

- WebPartManager—Enables you to get the WebPartManager control responsible for tracking a Web Part.

- Width—Enables you to specify the width of the Web Part.

- Verbs—Enables you to retrieve the collection of menu items displayed by a Web Part.

- Zone—Enables you to get the zone that contains a Web Part.

- ZoneIndex—Enables you to get the position of a Web Part in a zone.

You can override any of these properties when building a True Web Part control. For example, Listing 28.9 contains a Web Part named the IrritatingPart. The IrritatingPart control is hidden and cannot be closed or minimized.

LISTING 28.9   App_Code\IrritatingPart.vb

```
Imports System
Imports System.Web.UI
Imports System.Web.UI.WebControls.WebParts

Namespace myControls

    ''' <summary>
    ''' Hidden Part that cannot be closed
    ''' or minimized.
    ''' </summary>
    Public Class IrritatingPart
        Inherits WebPart
        Private _title As String = "Irritating Part"
        Private _description As String = "This Web Part is irritating"
        Private _hidden As Boolean = True
        Private _allowClose As Boolean = False
```

LISTING 28.9   Continued

```
        Private _allowMinimize As Boolean = False

        Public Overrides Property Title() As String
            Get
                Return _title
            End Get
            Set(ByVal Value As String)
                _title = Value
            End Set
        End Property


        Public Overrides Property Description() As String
            Get
                Return _description
            End Get
            Set(ByVal Value As String)
                _description = Value
            End Set
        End Property



        Public Overrides Property Hidden() As Boolean
            Get
                Return _hidden
            End Get
            Set(ByVal Value As Boolean)
                _hidden = Value
            End Set
        End Property

        Public Overrides Property AllowClose() As Boolean
            Get
                Return _allowClose
            End Get
            Set(ByVal Value As Boolean)
                _allowClose = Value
            End Set
        End Property

        Public Overrides Property AllowMinimize() As Boolean
            Get
                Return _allowMinimize
            End Get
            Set(ByVal Value As Boolean)
                _allowMinimize = False
```

28

LISTING 28.9   Continued

```
        End Set
    End Property


    Protected Overrides Sub RenderContents(ByVal writer As HtmlTextWriter)
        writer.Write("<h1>You can't get rid of me!</h1>")
    End Sub

End Class


End Namespace
```

If you add the Web Part in Listing 28.9 to a page, then you won't be able to see the Web Part in Browse Display mode because the Web Part overrides the Hidden property to hide itself. You can only see the IrritatingPart when a page is in Design or Catalog Display mode. You also cannot close or minimize the Web Part because both these properties are also overridden (see Figure 28.3).

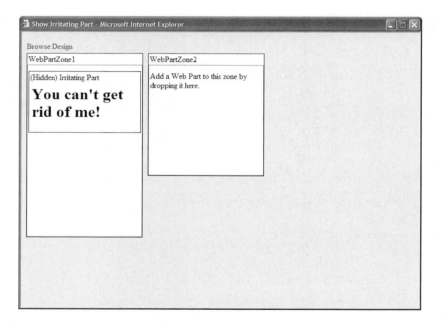

FIGURE 28.3   An Irritating Web Part.

CD NOTE

You can view the IrritatingPart with the ShowIrritatingPart.aspx page included on the CD that accompanies this book.

NOTE

Of course, the IrritatingPart Web Part is not a very realistic sample of when you would use the Hidden property. When a Web Part is hidden, the Web Part is rendered but not visible. The Cascading Style Sheet display:none property is set. Using the Hidden property is useful when you want to add a non-visual Web Part to a page such as a data source Web Part that exposes all the records from the Movies database table. The Hidden Web Part can be connected to Web Parts that aren't hidden.

You cannot set any of the properties discussed in this section declaratively in the case of a Generic Web Part. Because the controls in a Web Part Zone do not get wrapped in the GenericWebPart class until runtime, a Generic Web Part is not a Web Part until a page is actually executed.

However, you can set any of these properties programmatically in the case of either a Generic or True Web Part. The GenericWebPart class derives from the base WebPart class, so you can do anything with a Generic Web Part that you can do with a True Web Part. The only requirement is that you do it programmatically rather than declaratively.

For example, the page in Listing 28.10 contains three links for minimizing the Web Parts contained in the page (see Figure 28.4).

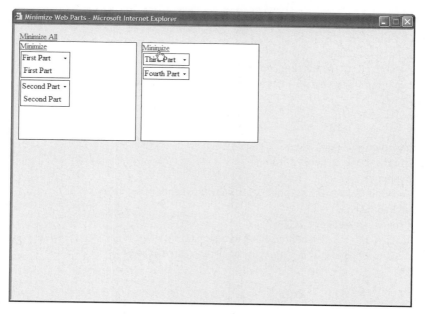

FIGURE 28.4   Minimizing Web Parts.

28

LISTING 28.10   MinimizeWebParts.aspx

```
<%@ Page Language="VB" %>
<!DOCTYPE html PUBLIC "-//W3C//DTD XHTML 1.1//EN"
 "http://www.w3.org/TR/xhtml11/DTD/xhtml11.dtd">

<script runat="server">

    ''' <summary>
    ''' Minimize All Web Parts
    ''' </summary>
    Protected Sub lnkMinimizeAll_Click(ByVal sender As Object,
➥ByVal e As EventArgs)
        Dim part As WebPart
        For Each part In WebPartManager1.WebParts
            part.ChromeState = PartChromeState.Minimized
        Next
    End Sub

    ''' <summary>
    ''' Minimize Zone 1 Web Parts
    ''' </summary>
    Protected Sub lnkMinimizeZone1_Click(ByVal sender As Object,
➥ByVal e As EventArgs)
        Dim part As WebPart
        For Each part In WebPartZone1.WebParts
            part.ChromeState = PartChromeState.Minimized
        Next
    End Sub

    ''' <summary>
    ''' Minimize Zone 2 Web Parts
    ''' </summary>
    Protected Sub lnkMinimizeZone2_Click(ByVal sender As Object,
➥ByVal e As EventArgs)
        Dim part As WebPart
        For Each part In WebPartZone2.WebParts
            part.ChromeState = PartChromeState.Minimized
        Next
    End Sub

</script>

<html xmlns="http://www.w3.org/1999/xhtml" >
<head id="Head1" runat="server">
    <style type="text/css">
```

LISTING 28.10   Continued

```
        .column
        {
            float:left;
            width:30%;
            height:200px;
            margin-right:10px;
            border:solid 1px black;
            background-color: white;
        }
        html
        {
            background-color:#eeeeee;
        }
    </style>
    <title>Minimize Web Parts</title>
</head>
<body>
    <form id="form1" runat="server">
    <asp:WebPartManager
        id="WebPartManager1"
        Runat="server" />

    <asp:LinkButton
        id="lnkMinimizeAll"
        Text="Minimize All"
        Runat="server" OnClick="lnkMinimizeAll_Click" />

    <div class="column">
    <asp:LinkButton
        id="lnkMinimizeZone1"
        Text="Minimize"
        OnClick="lnkMinimizeZone1_Click"
        Runat="server" />
    <asp:WebPartZone
        id="WebPartZone1"
        Runat="server">
        <ZoneTemplate>
        <asp:Label
            id="Label1"
            Title="First Part"
            Text="First Part"
            Runat="server" />
        <asp:Label
            id="Label2"
```

LISTING 28.10   Continued

```
                Title="Second Part"
                Text="Second Part"
                Runat="server" />
        </ZoneTemplate>
    </asp:WebPartZone>
    </div>

    <div class="column">
    <asp:LinkButton
        id="lnkMinimizeZone2"
        Text="Minimize"
        OnClick="lnkMinimizeZone2_Click"
        Runat="server" />
    <asp:WebPartZone
        id="WebPartZone2"
        Runat="server">
        <ZoneTemplate>
        <asp:Label
            id="Label3"
            Title="Third Part"
            Text="Third Part"
            Runat="server" />
        <asp:Label
            id="Label4"
            Title="Fourth Part"
            Text="Fourth Part"
            Runat="server" />
        </ZoneTemplate>
    </asp:WebPartZone>
    </div>

    </form>
</body>
</html>
```

When you click the Minimize All link, the collection of all the Web Parts in the page is retrieved from the WebPartManager control, and the ChromeState property for each Web Part is set to the value Minimized. If you click the Minimize link associated with a particular zone, then the Web Parts are retrieved from the Zone's WebParts property and the Web Parts in the selected zone are minimized.

Notice that the ChromeState property can be set, even for the Generic Web Parts (Labels) in the page. Because the Generic Web Parts are being retrieved from the WebPartManager and WebPartZone WebParts collection, the controls in the Web Part Zones have already been wrapped in the GenericWebPart class that includes all the properties of a True Web Part.

By taking advantage of the WebParts property exposed by both the WebPartManager and WebPartZone controls, you can retrieve information about the Web Parts contained in a page. For example, the User control in Listing 28.11—the WebPartInfo control—displays several properties of the Web Parts contained in the page.

LISTING 28.11   WebPartInfo.ascx

```
<%@ Control Language="VB" ClassName="WebPartInfo" %>
<script runat="server">

    Sub Page_PreRender()
        Dim wpm As WebPartManager = WebPartManager.GetCurrentWebPartManager(Page)
        grdInfo.DataSource = wpm.WebParts
        grdInfo.DataBind()
    End Sub

</script>

<asp:GridView
    id="grdInfo"
    AutoGenerateColumns="false"
    Runat="server">
    <Columns>
    <asp:BoundField HeaderText="Title" DataField="Title" />
    <asp:BoundField HeaderText="IsShared" DataField="IsShared" />
    <asp:BoundField HeaderText="IsStatic" DataField="IsStatic" />
    <asp:BoundField HeaderText="IsClosed" DataField="IsClosed" />
    <asp:BoundField HeaderText="HasUserData" DataField="HasUserData" />
    <asp:BoundField HeaderText="HasSharedData" DataField="HasSharedData" />
    </Columns>
</asp:GridView>
```

You can add the User Control in Listing 28.11 to any page to view the properties of the Web Parts in the page (see Figure 28.5).

CD NOTE

You can view the information displayed by the WebPartInfo control by opening the ShowWebPartInfo.aspx page located on the CD that accompanies this book.

28

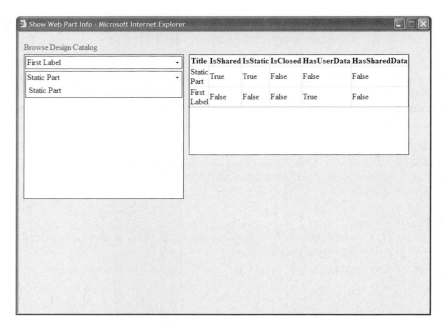

FIGURE 28.5   Displaying Information about Web Parts.

Filtering Web Parts

When building a Web Part application, you might want to allow different users of the application to see different sets of Web Parts. For example, you might want the president of the company to be able to view the World Domination Plans Web Part, but you wouldn't want a lowly temporary employee to see the contents of this particular Web Part. On the other hand, you might want everyone in the company to be able to see the Copying Machine Locations Web Part.

You can filter the Web Parts that a user can see on a Web Part page. When you create an authorization filter, only the Web Parts that a person is authorized to view will appear in Web Part Zones and Web Part Catalogs.

You can create an authorization filter in either of two ways. First, you can handle the AuthorizeWebPart event of the WebPartManager control class. This event is raised every time that a Web Part is added to the page while the Web Part Framework builds the page. The event argument passed to the event handler for the AuthorizeWebPart event includes an IsAuthorized property. You can set this property to the value True or False to indicate whether a Web Part is authorized to be displayed.

You can also create an authorization filter by creating a custom WebPartManager control that inherits from the WebPartManager control and overrides its IsAuthorized() method. The IsAuthorized() method returns a Boolean value. If you return the value False, then a Web Part fails authorization and it is not added to the page. Using this second way of creating an authorization filter makes sense when you want to apply the same authorization logic to multiple Web Part pages in an application.

Regardless of whether you handle the AuthorizeWebPart event or you override the IsAuthorized() method, it is up to you to write the logic for the authorization filter. In the following sections, you'll learn three ways of filtering Web Parts, depending on the role of the user.

Filtering by Authorization Filter

One of the core properties shared by every Web Part is the AuthorizationFilter property. This property represents a string that you can use when filtering Web Parts. You can assign any string value to this property.

For example, you can use the AuthorizationFilter property to represent a user role. In that case, in your AuthorizeWebPart event handler, you can prevent users who are not in the correct role from seeing a Web Part.

In this section, we create three Web Parts: the MissionStatementPart, the CopyingMachinesLocationPart, and the WorldDominationPlanPart. These Web Parts are contained in Listings 28.12, 13, and 14.

LISTING 28.12 MissionStatementPart.ascx

```
<%@ Control Language="VB" ClassName="MissionStatementPart" %>


<h3>Mission Statement</h3>
The purpose of this company is...
```

LISTING 28.13 CopyingMachinesLocationPart.ascx

```
<%@ Control Language="VB" ClassName="CopyingMachinesLocationPart" %>


<h3>Copying Machines Location</h3>
The copying machines are located on the 5th floor...
```

LISTING 28.14 WorldDominationPlansPart.ascx

```
<%@ Control Language="VB" ClassName="WorldDominationPlansPart" %>


<h3>World Domination Plans</h3>
Start by placing secret messages in every Unleashed book...
```

Notice that there is nothing special about these Web Parts. They are simply User controls.

Next, because the Web Parts are filtered by user role, roles need to be enabled for the application. One option would be to use Windows Authentication and local Windows groups. This is the default type of authentication enabled for an ASP.NET application and there is nothing wrong with this option. However, this sample uses Forms Authentication and custom roles. It is easier to switch between users when using Forms Authentication, which makes it easier to test the page.

Forms Authentication and custom roles can be enabled with the Web configuration file in Listing 28.15.

LISTING 28.15   Web.Config

```
<?xml version="1.0"?>
<configuration xmlns="http://schemas.microsoft.com/.NetConfiguration/v2.0">
    <system.web>
      <authentication mode="Forms" />
      <roleManager enabled="true" />
      <membership defaultProvider="MyMembershipProvider">
      <providers>
      <add name="MyMembershipProvider"
        type="System.Web.Security.SqlMembershipProvider"
        connectionStringName="LocalSqlServer"
        requiresQuestionAndAnswer="false"
        minRequiredNonalphanumericCharacters="0"
        minRequiredPasswordLength="1"
        requiresUniqueEmail="false" />
      </providers>
      </membership>
    </system.web>
</configuration>
```

CD NOTE

The configuration file in Listing 28.15 is included on the CD with the name Web.Config_ Disabled so that the configuration file doesn't interfere with the other samples in this chapter.

The web configuration file in Listing 28.15 enables Forms Authentication and the Role Manager. It also configures the Membership provider so that email addresses and strong passwords are not required when creating a new user. (This makes it easier to create new users in the page.)

Finally, the page in Listing 28.16 uses an authorization filter to display the three Web Parts (see Figure 28.6).

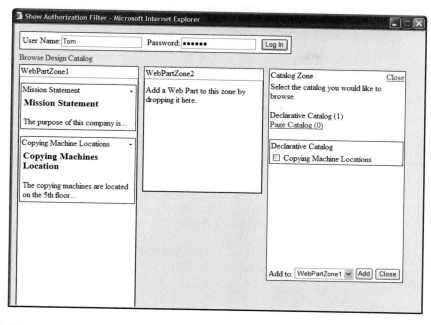

FIGURE 28.6   Filtering Web Parts.

LISTING 28.16   ShowAuthorizationFilter.aspx

```
<%@ Page Language="VB" %>
<%@ Register TagPrefix="user" TagName="MissionStatementPart"
  Src="~/MissionStatementPart.ascx" %>
<%@ Register TagPrefix="user" TagName="WorldDominationPlansPart"
  Src="~/WorldDominationPlansPart.ascx" %>
<%@ Register TagPrefix="user" TagName="CopyingMachineLocationsPart"
  Src="~/CopyingMachinesLocationPart.ascx" %>
<!DOCTYPE html PUBLIC "-//W3C//DTD XHTML 1.1//EN"
  "http://www.w3.org/TR/xhtml11/DTD/xhtml11.dtd">

<script runat="server">

    ''' <summary>
    ''' Create the Administrator and Serf roles and
    ''' create two users named Bill and Tom.
    ''' </summary>
    Private  Sub Page_Load()
        If Not Roles.RoleExists("Administrator") Then
            Roles.CreateRole("Administrator")
            Roles.CreateRole("Serf")
```

LISTING 28.16   Continued

```
            Membership.CreateUser("Bill", "secret")
            Membership.CreateUser("Tom", "secret")
            Roles.AddUserToRoles("Bill", New String(){"Administrator", "Serf"})
            Roles.AddUserToRole("Tom", "Serf")
        End If
    End Sub


    ''' <summary>
    ''' Only add a Web Part when the AuthorizationFilter
    ''' property contains the current user's role or the
    ''' AuthorizationFilter property is empty.
    ''' </summary>
    Protected Sub WebPartManager1_AuthorizeWebPart(ByVal sender As Object,
➥ByVal e As WebPartAuthorizationEventArgs)
        e.IsAuthorized = User.IsInRole(e.AuthorizationFilter)
➥Or e.AuthorizationFilter = String.Empty
    End Sub


    ''' <summary>
    ''' Hide the menu for unauthorized users
    ''' </summary>
    Private  Sub Page_PreRender()
        Menu1.Visible = Request.IsAuthenticated
    End Sub


    Protected  Sub Menu1_MenuItemClick(ByVal sender As Object,
➥ByVal e As MenuEventArgs)
        WebPartManager1.DisplayMode = WebPartManager1.DisplayModes(e.Item.Text)
    End Sub


</script>

<html xmlns="http://www.w3.org/1999/xhtml" >
<head id="Head1" runat="server">
    <style type="text/css">
        .login
        {
            border:solid 1px black;
            background-color:white;
        }
        .column
        {
            float:left;
            width:30%;
```

LISTING 28.16   Continued

```
                height:200px;
                margin-right:10px;
                border:solid 1px black;
                background-color: white;
            }
            .menu
            {
                margin:5px 0px;
            }
            html
            {
                background-color:#eeeeee;
            }
        </style>
        <title>Show Authorization Filter</title>
</head>
<body>
    <form id="form1" runat="server">
    <asp:WebPartManager
        id="WebPartManager1"
        OnAuthorizeWebPart="WebPartManager1_AuthorizeWebPart"
        Runat="server" />

    <asp:Login
        id="Login1"
        CssClass="login"
        TitleText=""
        Orientation="horizontal"
        DisplayRememberMe="false"
        Runat="server" />

    <asp:Menu
        id="Menu1"
        OnMenuItemClick="Menu1_MenuItemClick"
        Orientation="Horizontal"
        CssClass="menu"
        Runat="server">
        <Items>
        <asp:MenuItem Text="Browse" />
        <asp:MenuItem Text="Design" />
        <asp:MenuItem Text="Catalog" />
        </Items>
    </asp:Menu>
```

LISTING 28.16   Continued

```
<asp:WebPartZone
    id="WebPartZone1"
    CssClass="column"
    Runat="server">
    <ZoneTemplate>
    <user:MissionStatementPart
        id="MissionStatementPart1"
        title="Mission Statement"
        runat="server" />
    <user:CopyingMachineLocationsPart
        id="CopyingMachineLocationsPart1"
        title="Copying Machine Locations"
        AuthorizationFilter="Serf"
        runat="server" />
    <user:WorldDominationPlansPart
        id="WorldDominationPart1"
        title="World Domination Plans"
        AuthorizationFilter="Administrator"
        runat="server" />
    </ZoneTemplate>
</asp:WebPartZone>

<asp:WebPartZone
    id="WebPartZone2"
    CssClass="column"
    Runat="server" />

<asp:CatalogZone
    id="CatalogZone1"
    CssClass="column"
    Runat="server">
    <ZoneTemplate>
    <asp:DeclarativeCatalogPart
        id="DeclarativeCatalogPart"
        Runat="server">
        <WebPartsTemplate>
        <user:CopyingMachineLocationsPart
            id="CopyingMachineLocationsPart1"
            title="Copying Machine Locations"
            AuthorizationFilter="Serf"
            runat="server" />
        <user:WorldDominationPlansPart
            id="WorldDominationPart1"
            title="World Domination Plans"
```

LISTING 28.16   Continued

```
                AuthorizationFilter="Administrator"
                runat="server" />
            </WebPartsTemplate>
        </asp:DeclarativeCatalogPart>
        <asp:PageCatalogPart
            id="PageCatalogPart1"
            Runat="server" />
        </ZoneTemplate>
    </asp:CatalogZone>

    </form>
</body>
</html>
```

The `Page_Load()` method in Listing 28.16 automatically creates two roles named Administrator and Serf. The method also creates two users named Bill and Tom. Bill is associated with both the Administrator and Serf role and Tom is associated with the Serf role.

After you open the page in Listing 28.16, you'll see only the `MissionStatementPart` Web Part because this is the only Web Part that anonymous users can view.

If you log in with the username **Tom** and password **secret**, then you can see both the `MissionStatementPart` and `CopyingMachineLocationsPart` Web Parts. Both these Web Parts are visible in both the Web Part Zone and Catalog Zone contained in the page.

Finally, if you log in with the username **Bill** and the password **secret**, you can see all three Web Parts. All three Web Parts are displayed in both the Web Part Zone and the Catalog Zone.

Notice that the `CopyingMachinesLocationPart` and `WorldDominationPlansPart` Web Parts are declared with an `AuthorizationFilter` attribute. The `CopyingMachinesLocationPart` is associated with the Serf user role. The `WorldDominiationPlansPart` is associated with the Administrator user role.

The `WebPartManager` control has an `AuthorizeWebPart` event handler associated with it. The event handler consists of the following line of code:

```
e.IsAuthorized = User.IsInRole(e.AuthorizationFilter)
➥Or e.AuthorizationFilter = String.Empty
```

This line of code checks whether the current user is a member of the role represented by a Web Part's `AuthorizationFilter` property. If the user is in the role associated with the Web Part or the Web Part has no role associated with it, then the user is authorized to see the Web Part.

28

Filtering by User Control Path

Using the `AuthorizationFilter` property is potentially dangerous when you use the property with Generic Web Parts. The problem is that you might forget to add the `AuthorizationFilter` attribute when adding a Generic Web Part to a zone. Because the `AuthorizationFilter` property is not a member of the `IWebPart` interface, you cannot set this property in the User Control itself.

This section explores an alternate method of creating an authorization filter. This method works only with Web Parts created as User Controls. Web Parts will be filtered depending on their paths.

The idea is that to place every Web Part that a member of the Administrator role can see in a folder named Administrator. Furthermore, every Web Part that a member of the Serf role can see will be located in a folder named Serf.

Let's start by creating the two User Controls contained in Listing 28.17 and 18.

LISTING 28.17   Serf\SerfPart.ascx

```
<%@ Control Language="VB" ClassName="SerfPart" %>


<h3>Serf Part</h3>
```

LISTING 28.18   Administrator\AdministratorPart.ascx

```
<%@ Control Language="VB" ClassName="AdministratorPart" %>


<h3>Administrator Part</h3>
```

The `SerfPart` Web Part is located in the Serf folder and the `AdministratorPart` Web Part is located in the Administrator folder.

The page in Listing 28.19 filters the two Web Parts. Different Web Parts are displayed, depending on the role of the current user.

LISTING 28.19   ShowAuthorizationPath.aspx

```
<%@ Page Language="VB" %>
<%@ Register TagPrefix="user" TagName="AdministratorPart"
 Src="~/Administrator/AdministratorPart.ascx" %>
<%@ Register TagPrefix="user" TagName="SerfPart" Src="~/Serf/SerfPart.ascx" %>
<!DOCTYPE html PUBLIC "-//W3C//DTD XHTML 1.1//EN"
 "http://www.w3.org/TR/xhtml11/DTD/xhtml11.dtd">
<script runat="server">

    ''' <summary>
    ''' Create the Administrator and Serf roles and
```

LISTING 28.19   Continued

```
''' the Bill and Tom user accounts
''' </summary>
Private  Sub Page_Load()
    If Not Roles.RoleExists("Administrator") Then
        Roles.CreateRole("Administrator")
        Roles.CreateRole("Serf")
        Membership.CreateUser("Bill", "secret")
        Membership.CreateUser("Tom", "secret")
        Roles.AddUserToRoles("Bill", New String(){"Administrator", "Serf"})
        Roles.AddUserToRole("Tom", "Serf")
    End If
End Sub


''' <summary>
''' Filter based on the Web Part User Control path
''' </summary>
Protected  Sub WebPartManager1_AuthorizeWebPart(ByVal sender As Object,
➥ByVal e As WebPartAuthorizationEventArgs)
    e.IsAuthorized = User.IsInRole(GetFolder(e.Path))
End Sub


''' <summary>
''' Gets the name of the folder that contains
''' the User Control
''' </summary>
Private Function GetFolder(ByVal path As String) As String
    Dim baseFolder As String = String.Empty
    Dim parts As String() = path.Split("/"c)
    If parts.Length > 2 Then
        baseFolder = parts(1)
    End If
    Return baseFolder
End Function



Private  Sub Page_PreRender()
    Menu1.Visible = Request.IsAuthenticated
End Sub



Protected  Sub Menu1_MenuItemClick(ByVal sender As Object,
➥ByVal e As MenuEventArgs)
    WebPartManager1.DisplayMode = WebPartManager1.DisplayModes(e.Item.Text)
End Sub
```

28

LISTING 28.19   Continued

```
</script>

<html xmlns="http://www.w3.org/1999/xhtml" >
<head id="Head1" runat="server">
    <style type="text/css">
        .login
        {
            border:solid 1px black;
            background-color:white;
        }
        .column
        {
            float:left;
            width:30%;
            height:200px;
            margin-right:10px;
            border:solid 1px black;
            background-color: white;
        }
        .menu
        {
            margin:5px 0px;
        }
        html
        {
            background-color:#eeeeee;
        }
    </style>
    <title>Show Authorization Path</title>
</head>
<body>
    <form id="form1" runat="server">
    <asp:WebPartManager
        id="WebPartManager1"
        OnAuthorizeWebPart="WebPartManager1_AuthorizeWebPart"
        Runat="server" />

    <asp:Login
        id="Login1"
        CssClass="login"
        TitleText=""
        Orientation="horizontal"
        DisplayRememberMe="false"
        Runat="server" />
```

LISTING 28.19   Continued

```
<asp:Menu
    id="Menu1"
    OnMenuItemClick="Menu1_MenuItemClick"
    Orientation="Horizontal"
    CssClass="menu"
    Runat="server">
    <Items>
    <asp:MenuItem Text="Browse" />
    <asp:MenuItem Text="Design" />
    <asp:MenuItem Text="Catalog" />
    </Items>
</asp:Menu>

<asp:WebPartZone
    id="WebPartZone1"
    CssClass="column"
    Runat="server">
    <ZoneTemplate>
    <user:AdministratorPart
        id="AdministratorPart1"
        title="Administrator Part"
        runat="server" />
    <user:SerfPart
        id="SerfPart1"
        title="Serf Part"
        runat="server" />
    </ZoneTemplate>
</asp:WebPartZone>

<asp:WebPartZone
    id="WebPartZone2"
    CssClass="column"
    Runat="server" />

<asp:CatalogZone
    id="CatalogZone1"
    CssClass="column"
    Runat="server">
    <ZoneTemplate>
    <asp:DeclarativeCatalogPart
        id="DeclarativeCatalogPart"
        Runat="server">
        <WebPartsTemplate>
    <user:AdministratorPart
```

28

LISTING 28.19   Continued

```
                id="AdministratorPart1"
                title="Administrator Part"
                runat="server" />
        <user:SerfPart
                id="SerfPart1"
                title="Serf Part"
                runat="server" />
                </WebPartsTemplate>
        </asp:DeclarativeCatalogPart>
        <asp:PageCatalogPart
                id="PageCatalogPart1"
                Runat="server" />
        </ZoneTemplate>
    </asp:CatalogZone>

    </form>
</body>
</html>
```

After you open the page in Listing 28.19, you won't see any Web Parts. If you log in with the username **Tom** and password **secret**, you'll see the `SerfPart` Web Part. If you log in with the user name **Bill** and password **secret**, you'll see both the `SerfPart` and `AdministratorPart` Web Part (Bill is a member of both the Administrator and Serf roles).

The `AuthorizeWebPart` event handler consists of the following single line of code:

```
e.IsAuthorized = User.IsInRole( GetFolder(e.Path) )
```

The `GetFolder()` method returns the root folder of the Web Part being authorized. In other words, it returns the name of the folder where the User Control that corresponds to the Web Part is located. If the name of the root folder matches one of the current user's roles, then the Web Part is authorized and it is displayed in the page.

Filtering by Custom Control Type

You can't filter a True Web Part by its path because a True Web Part doesn't have a path. However, you can do something similar. Rather than filter a True Web Part by its path, you can filter a True Web Part by its type.

In this section, two Web Part base classes are created, named `AdministratorWebPartBase` and `SerfWebPartBase`. Anyone who is a member of the Administrator role can see any Web Part that inherits directly from the `AdministratorWebPartBase` class, and anyone who is a member of the Serf role can see any Web Part that inherits directly from the `SerfWebPartBase` class.

The `AdministratorWebPartBase` and `SerfWebPartBase` classes are contained in Listing 28.20 and Listing 28.21.

LISTING 28.20   App_Code\AdministratorWebPartBase.cs

```
Imports System
Imports System.Web.UI.WebControls.WebParts

Namespace myControls

    ''' <summary>
    ''' Base class for all Web Parts that
    ''' an Administrator is authorized to see
    ''' </summary>
    Public MustInherit Class AdministratorWebPartBase
        Inherits WebPart
    End Class
End Namespace
```

LISTING 28.21   App_Code\SerfWebPartBase.cs

```
Imports System
Imports System.Web.UI.WebControls.WebParts

Namespace myControls

    ''' <summary>
    ''' Base class for all Web Parts that
    ''' a member of the Serf role is authorized
    ''' to see.
    ''' </summary>
    Public MustInherit Class SerfWebPartBase
        Inherits WebPart
    End Class
End Namespace
```

Now that we have the base classes, we can inherit any number of Administrator and Serf Web Parts from the base classes. Listing 28.22 and Listing 28.23 contain an Administrator Web Part and a Serf Web Part.

LISTING 28.22   App_Code\AdministratorPart.cs

```
Imports System
Imports System.Web.UI
Imports System.Web.UI.WebControls.WebParts
```

28

LISTING 28.22   Continued

```
Namespace myControls
    ''' <summary>
    ''' A Web Part that only an Administrator can see
    ''' </summary>
    Public Class AdministratorPart
        Inherits AdministratorWebPartBase
        Private _title As String = "Administrator Part"

        Public Overrides Property Title() As String
            Get
                Return _title
            End Get
            Set(ByVal Value As String)
                _title = value
            End Set
        End Property

        Protected Overrides Sub RenderContents(ByVal writer As HtmlTextWriter)
            writer.RenderBeginTag(HtmlTextWriterTag.H3)
            writer.Write("Administrator Part")
            writer.RenderEndTag()
        End Sub
    End Class
End Namespace
```

LISTING 28.23   App_Code\SerfPart.cs

```
Imports System
Imports System.Web.UI
Imports System.Web.UI.WebControls.WebParts

Namespace myControls
    ''' <summary>
    ''' A Web Part that only a Serf can see
    ''' </summary>
    Public Class SerfPart
        Inherits SerfWebPartBase
        Private _title As String = "Serf Part"

        Public Overrides Property Title() As String
            Get
                Return _title
            End Get
```

LISTING 28.23   Continued

```
                Set(ByVal Value As String)
                    _title = value
                End Set
            End Property

            Protected Overrides Sub RenderContents(ByVal writer As HtmlTextWriter)
                writer.RenderBeginTag(HtmlTextWriterTag.H3)
                writer.Write("Serf Part")
                writer.RenderEndTag()
            End Sub
        End Class
    End Namespace
```

Notice that the `AdministratorPart` inherits from the `AdministratorWebPartBase` class, and the `SerfPart` inherits from the `SerfWebPartBase` class. The authorization filter in Listing 28.24 takes advantage of that fact.

LISTING 28.24   ShowAuthorizationType.aspx

```
<%@ Page Language="VB" %>
<%@ Register TagPrefix="custom" Namespace="myControls" %>
<!DOCTYPE html PUBLIC "-//W3C//DTD XHTML 1.1//EN"
    "http://www.w3.org/TR/xhtml11/DTD/xhtml11.dtd">
<script runat="server">

    ''' <summary>
    ''' Create the Administrator and Serf roles and
    ''' the Bill and Tom user accounts.
    ''' </summary>
    Private  Sub Page_Load()
        If Not Roles.RoleExists("Administrator") Then
            Roles.CreateRole("Administrator")
            Roles.CreateRole("Serf")
            Membership.CreateUser("Bill", "secret")
            Membership.CreateUser("Tom", "secret")
            Roles.AddUserToRoles("Bill", New String(){"Administrator", "Serf"})
            Roles.AddUserToRole("Tom", "Serf")
        End If
    End Sub

    ''' <summary>
    ''' Authorizes a user to see a Web Part when the base type of the Web Part
    ''' matches one of the user's roles
    ''' </summary>
```

28

LISTING 28.24   Continued

```
    Protected  Sub WebPartManager1_AuthorizeWebPart(ByVal sender As Object,
➡ByVal e As WebPartAuthorizationEventArgs)
        e.IsAuthorized = User.IsInRole(GetRoleFromType(e.Type))
    End Sub


    ''' <summary>
    ''' Returns the name of the base class from a type
    ''' after stripping the text WebPartBase
    ''' </summary>
    Private Function GetRoleFromType(ByVal partType As Type) As String
        Dim typeName As String = partType.BaseType.Name
        Return typeName.Replace("WebPartBase", String.Empty)
    End Function


    Private  Sub Page_PreRender()
        Menu1.Visible = Request.IsAuthenticated
    End Sub


    Protected  Sub Menu1_MenuItemClick(ByVal sender As Object,
➡ByVal e As MenuEventArgs)
        WebPartManager1.DisplayMode = WebPartManager1.DisplayModes(e.Item.Text)
    End Sub



</script>

<html xmlns="http://www.w3.org/1999/xhtml" >
<head id="Head1" runat="server">
    <style type="text/css">
        .login
        {
            border:solid 1px black;
            background-color:white;
        }
        .column
        {
            float:left;
            width:30%;
            height:200px;
            margin-right:10px;
            border:solid 1px black;
            background-color: white;
        }
        .menu
```

LISTING 28.24   Continued

```
        {
            margin:5px 0px;
        }
        html
        {
            background-color:#eeeeee;
        }
    </style>
    <title>Show Authorization Type</title>
</head>
<body>
    <form id="form1" runat="server">
    <asp:WebPartManager
        id="WebPartManager1"
        OnAuthorizeWebPart="WebPartManager1_AuthorizeWebPart"
        Runat="server" />

    <asp:Login
        id="Login1"
        CssClass="login"
        TitleText=""
        Orientation="horizontal"
        DisplayRememberMe="false"
        Runat="server" />

    <asp:Menu
        id="Menu1"
        OnMenuItemClick="Menu1_MenuItemClick"
        Orientation="Horizontal"
        CssClass="menu"
        Runat="server">
        <Items>
        <asp:MenuItem Text="Browse" />
        <asp:MenuItem Text="Design" />
        <asp:MenuItem Text="Catalog" />
        </Items>
    </asp:Menu>

    <asp:WebPartZone
        id="WebPartZone1"
        CssClass="column"
        Runat="server">
        <ZoneTemplate>
        <custom:AdministratorPart
```

28

LISTING 28.24   Continued

```
                id="AdministratorPart1"
                runat="Server" />
        <custom:SerfPart
                id="SerfPart1"
                runat="server" />
        </ZoneTemplate>
    </asp:WebPartZone>

    <asp:WebPartZone
        id="WebPartZone2"
        CssClass="column"
        Runat="server" />

    <asp:CatalogZone
        id="CatalogZone1"
        CssClass="column"
        Runat="server">
        <ZoneTemplate>
        <asp:DeclarativeCatalogPart
            id="DeclarativeCatalogPart"
            Runat="server">
            <WebPartsTemplate>
            <custom:AdministratorPart
                id="AdministratorPart1"
                runat="Server" />
            <custom:SerfPart
                id="SerfPart1"
                runat="server" />
            </WebPartsTemplate>
        </asp:DeclarativeCatalogPart>
        </ZoneTemplate>
    </asp:CatalogZone>

    </form>
</body>
</html>
```

Once again, Tom only can see the `SerfPart` Web Part, and Bill can see both the `SerfPart` and `AdministratorPart` Web Parts. The `AuthorizeWebPart` event handler consists of the following single line of code:

```
e.IsAuthorized = User.IsInRole(GetRoleFromType(e.Type))
```

The `GetRoleFromType()` method returns the name of the base type of the current Web Part (and strips the string `"WebPartBase"` from the name). If the current user is a member of the role represented by the base type, then the user can see the Web Part.

Creating Custom Web Part Verbs

In the terminology of the Web Part Framework, a menu item displayed by a Web Part is called a *verb*. In this section, you'll learn how to extend the standard set of verbs displayed by a Web Part with your own custom verbs. You'll learn how to create verbs that execute both server-side and client-side code. You'll also learn how to add verbs to every Web Part that appears in a particular Web Part Zone.

Creating Server-Side Verbs

Adding new verbs to a Web Part is easy. You simply need to provide the Web Part with a Verbs property that returns the collection of verbs that you want the Web Part to display.

Listing 28.25 contains a Generic Web Part that contains a custom `Add to Cart` verb.

LISTING 28.25   ProductPart.ascx

```
<%@ Control Language="VB" ClassName="ProductPart" %>
<%@ Implements Interface="System.Web.UI.WebControls.WebParts.IWebActionable" %>
<%@ Import Namespace="System.Collections.Generic" %>
<script runat="server">

    Private _productName As String
    Private _productPrice As Decimal

    Public ReadOnly Property Verbs() As WebPartVerbCollection Implements
➥IWebActionable.Verbs
        Get
            Dim menu As New List(Of WebPartVerb)
            Dim menuItem As New WebPartVerb("AddToCart", AddressOf AddToCart)
            menuItem.Text = "Add To Cart"
            menuItem.Description = "Adds item to shopping cart"
            menuItem.ImageUrl = "~/Images/AddToCart.gif"
            menu.Add(menuItem)
            Return New WebPartVerbCollection(menu)
        End Get
    End Property


    Public  Sub AddToCart(ByVal s As Object, ByVal e As WebPartEventArgs)
        Dim wpm As WebPartManager =  WebPartManager.GetCurrentWebPartManager(Page)
        wpm.MoveWebPart(e.WebPart, wpm.Zones("ShoppingCartZone"), 0)
    End Sub
```

28

LISTING 28.25   Continued

```
    Public Property ProductName() As String
    Get
        Return _productName
    End Get
    Set (ByVal Value As String)
        productName = value
    End Set
    End Property

    Public Property ProductPrice() As Decimal
    Get
      Return _productPrice
    End Get
    Set (ByVal Value As Decimal)
      productPrice = value
    End Set
    End Property

</script>

<h3><%= _productName %></h3>
Price: <%= _productPrice.ToString("c") %>
```

Notice that the Web Part in Listing 28.25 implements the IWebActionable interface. It includes an <%@ Implements %> directive at the top of the file. This interface contains one member: the Verbs property.

The Verbs property returns the verbs (menu items) displayed by the Web Part. In the case of the ProductPart Web Part, a new verb is created, which displays the text Add to Cart. The verb also displays an image and it is associated with a server-side method named AddToCart().

The AddToCart() method moves the current Web Part into a Web Part Zone named the ShoppingCartZone. When you select the Add to Cart menu option on the ProductPart, the Web Part is moved to the Shopping Cart Zone.

Listing 28.26 contains the same ProductPart implemented as a True Web part.

LISTING 28.26   App_Code\ProductPart.vb

```
Imports System
Imports System.Collections.Generic
Imports System.Web.UI
Imports System.Web.UI.WebControls.WebParts

Namespace myControls
```

LISTING 28.26   Continued

```
Public Class ProductPart
    Inherits WebPart
    Private _title As String = "Product Part"
    Private _productName As String
    Private _productPrice As Decimal

    Public Overrides Property Title() As String
        Get
            Return _title
        End Get
        Set(ByVal Value As String)
            _title = value
        End Set
    End Property

    Public Overrides ReadOnly Property Verbs() As WebPartVerbCollection
        Get
            Dim menu As New List(Of WebPartVerb)()
            Dim menuItem As New WebPartVerb("AddToCart", AddressOf AddToCart)
            menuItem.Text = "Add To Cart"
            menuItem.Description = "Adds item to shopping cart"
            menuItem.ImageUrl = "~/Images/AddToCart.gif"
            menu.Add(menuItem)
            Return New WebPartVerbCollection(menu)
        End Get
    End Property

    Public Sub AddToCart(ByVal s As Object, ByVal e As WebPartEventArgs)
        Dim wpm As WebPartManager =
➥WebPartManager.GetCurrentWebPartManager(Page)
        wpm.MoveWebPart(e.WebPart, wpm.Zones("ShoppingCartZone"), 0)
    End Sub

    Public Property ProductName() As String
        Get
            Return _productName
        End Get
        Set(ByVal Value As String)
            _productName = value
        End Set
    End Property

    Public Property ProductPrice() As Decimal
        Get
            Return _productPrice
```

28

LISTING 28.26   Continued

```
            End Get
            Set(ByVal Value As Decimal)
                _productPrice = value
            End Set
        End Property

        Protected Overrides Sub RenderContents(ByVal writer As HtmlTextWriter)
            writer.RenderBeginTag(HtmlTextWriterTag.H3)
            writer.Write(_productName)
            writer.RenderEndTag()
            writer.Write("Price: {0:c}", _productPrice)
        End Sub

    End Class
End Namespace
```

Notice that the class in Listing 28.26 does not implement the IWebActionable interface. It doesn't need to implement this interface because the base WebPart class already includes a Verbs property.

You can view both versions of the ProductPart with the page in Listing 28.27 (see Figure 28.7).

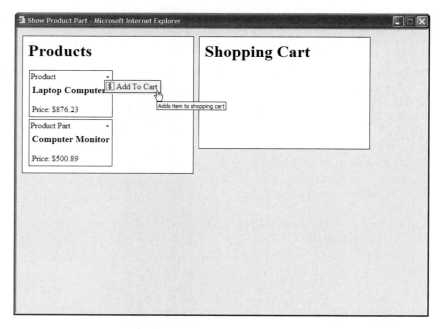

FIGURE 28.7   Displaying custom menu items.

LISTING 28.27 ShowProductPart.aspx

```
<%@ Page Language="VB" %>
<%@ Register TagPrefix="user" TagName="ProductPart" Src="~/ProductPart.ascx" %>
<%@ Register TagPrefix="custom" Namespace="myControls" %>
<!DOCTYPE html PUBLIC "-//W3C//DTD XHTML 1.1//EN"
    "http://www.w3.org/TR/xhtml11/DTD/xhtml11.dtd">
<script runat="server">

    Protected  Sub lnkClear_Click(ByVal sender As Object, ByVal e As EventArgs)
        Dim part As WebPart
        For Each part In ShoppingCartZone.WebParts
            WebPartManager1.MoveWebPart(part, ProductZone, 0)
        Next
    End Sub


    Private  Sub Page_PreRender()
        lnkClear.Visible = (ShoppingCartZone.WebParts.Count > 0)
    End Sub

</script>

<html xmlns="http://www.w3.org/1999/xhtml" >
<head id="Head1" runat="server">
    <style type="text/css">
        .column
        {
            float:left;
            width:40%;
            padding:10px;
            height:200px;
            margin-right:10px;
            border:solid 1px black;
            background-color: white;
        }
        html
        {
            background-color:#eeeeee;
        }
    </style>
    <title>Show Product Part</title>
</head>
<body>
    <form id="form1" runat="server">
    <asp:WebPartManager
        id="WebPartManager1"
```

28

LISTING 28.27   Continued

```
    Runat="server" />

    <div class="column">
    <h1>Products</h1>
    <asp:WebPartZone
        id="ProductZone"
        HeaderText="Products"
        MenuPopupStyle-BackColor="aliceBlue"
        MenuPopupStyle-BorderStyle="solid"
        MenuPopupStyle-BorderWidth="1px"
        MenuPopupStyle-BorderColor="black"
        MenuPopupStyle-ShadowColor="lightgray"
        AllowLayoutChange="false"
        Runat="server">
        <ZoneTemplate>
        <user:ProductPart
            id="ProductPart1"
            Title="Product"
            ProductName="Laptop Computer"
            ProductPrice="876.23"
            Runat="server" />
        <custom:ProductPart
            id="ProductPart2"
            ProductName="Computer Monitor"
            ProductPrice="500.89"
            Runat="server" />
        </ZoneTemplate>
    </asp:WebPartZone>
    </div>

    <div class="column">
    <h1>Shopping Cart</h1>
    <asp:WebPartZone
        id="ShoppingCartZone"
        HeaderText="Shopping Cart"
        VerbStyle-CssClass="verbs"
        AllowLayoutChange="false"
        Runat="server"/>
    <asp:LinkButton
        id="lnkClear"
        Text="Clear Cart"
        OnClick="lnkClear_Click"
        runat="server" />
```

LISTING 28.27   Continued

```
      </div>
   </form>
</body>
</html>
```

After you open the page in Listing 28.27, you can select the Add to Cart menu option from either of the two Web Parts to add the Web Part to the Shopping Cart Zone. Notice that the page also contains a Clear Cart link. Clicking this link moves all the Web Parts back from the Shopping Cart Zone to the Web Part Zone.

Creating Client-Side Verbs

A Web Part verb can execute client-side code as well as server-side code. The client-side code can do anything you want. For example, you can call any JavaScript function that you have defined in your page.

In this section, the ProductPart Web Part is modified so that it displays a confirmation dialog box before adding a Web Part to the Shopping Cart Zone. The modified ProductPart, named ConfirmProductPart, is contained in Listing 28.28.

LISTING 28.28   ConfirmProductPart.ascx

```
<%@ Control Language="VB" ClassName="ConfirmProductPart" %>
<%@ Implements Interface="System.Web.UI.WebControls.WebParts.IWebActionable" %>
<%@ Import Namespace="System.Collections.Generic" %>
<script runat="server">
    Private _productName As String
    Private _productPrice As Decimal


    Public ReadOnly Property Verbs() As WebPartVerbCollection
➥Implements IWebActionable.Verbs
        Get
            Dim menu As New List(Of WebPartVerb)()
            Dim menuItem As New WebPartVerb("AddToCart", AddressOf AddToCart,
➥"return confirm('Are You Sure?');")
            menuItem.Text = "Add To Cart"
            menuItem.Description = "Adds item to shopping cart"
            menuItem.ImageUrl = "~/Images/AddToCart.gif"
            menu.Add(menuItem)
            Return New WebPartVerbCollection(menu)
        End Get
    End Property
```

28

LISTING 28.28 Continued

```
Public  Sub AddToCart(ByVal s As Object, ByVal e As WebPartEventArgs)
    Dim wpm As WebPartManager = WebPartManager.GetCurrentWebPartManager(Page)
    wpm.MoveWebPart(e.WebPart, wpm.Zones("ShoppingCartZone"), 0)
End Sub

Public Property ProductName() As String
    Get
            Return _productName
    End Get
    Set (ByVal Value As String)
            _productName = value
    End Set
End Property

Public Property ProductPrice() As Decimal
    Get
            Return _productPrice
    End Get
    Set (ByVal Value As Decimal)
            _productPrice = value
    End Set
End Property

</script>

<h3><%= _productName %></h3>
Price: <%= _productPrice.ToString("c") %>
```

The `ConfirmProductPart` is identical to the `ProductPart` that was created in the previous section, except for the one line of code that is highlighted in bold in Listing 28.28. A little bit of JavaScript code has been added, which opens a confirmation dialog box whenever someone selects the Add to Cart menu option (see Figure 28.8).

> **CD NOTE**
>
> You can view the `ConfirmProductPart` by opening the `ShowConfirmProductPart.aspx` page included on the CD that accompanies this book.

If your JavaScript code returns the value `false`, then the server-side code has not executed. Therefore, if you click the Cancel button in the JavaScript confirmation dialog box, the server-side `AddToCart()` method is not executed.

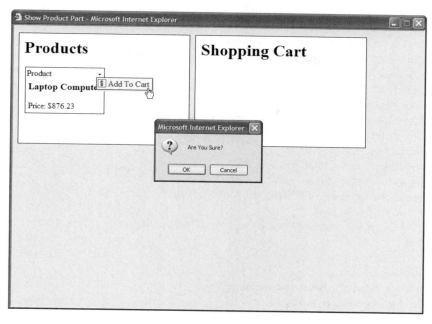

FIGURE 28.8   Displaying a Confirmation dialog box.

Creating Zone Verbs

One problem with the `ProductPart` Web Part is that it displays the Add to Cart menu item no matter in what zone the Web Part is displayed. In particular, the Web Part displays this menu option even when the Web Part is already located in the Shopping Cart Zone.

There is a way to fix this problem. Rather than create a custom verb at the level of an individual Web Part, you can create a custom verb at the level of a Web Part Zone. When you create a zone verb, every Web Part contained in the zone gets the additional verb automatically.

The page in Listing 28.29 handles the `CreateVerbs` event associated with the Product Zone to add a verb to every Web Part in the zone.

LISTING 28.29   ShowZoneVerbs.aspx

```
<%@ Page Language="VB" %>
<%@ Import Namespace="System.Collections.Generic" %>
<!DOCTYPE html PUBLIC "-//W3C//DTD XHTML 1.1//EN"
  "http://www.w3.org/TR/xhtml11/DTD/xhtml11.dtd">
<script runat="server">

    ''' <summary>
```

28

LISTING 28.29   Continued

```
''' Create the verbs that will appear for every
''' Web Part in the Product Zone
''' </summary>
Protected Sub ProductZone_CreateVerbs(ByVal sender As Object,
➥ByVal e As WebPartVerbsEventArgs)
    Dim menu As New List(Of WebPartVerb)()
    Dim menuItem As New WebPartVerb("AddToCart", AddressOf AddToCart,
➥"return confirm('Are You Sure?');")
    menuItem.Text = "Add To Cart"
    menuItem.Description = "Adds item to shopping cart"
    menuItem.ImageUrl = "~/Images/AddToCart.gif"
    menu.Add(menuItem)
    e.Verbs = New WebPartVerbCollection(e.Verbs, menu)
End Sub


''' <summary>
''' Move a Web Part from the Product Zone
''' to the Shopping Cart Zone
''' </summary>
Public  Sub AddToCart(ByVal s As Object, ByVal e As WebPartEventArgs)
    Dim wpm As WebPartManager =  WebPartManager.GetCurrentWebPartManager(Page)
    wpm.MoveWebPart(e.WebPart, wpm.Zones("ShoppingCartZone"), 0)
End Sub


Protected  Sub lnkClear_Click(ByVal sender As Object, ByVal e As EventArgs)
    Dim part As WebPart
    For Each part In ShoppingCartZone.WebParts
        WebPartManager1.MoveWebPart(part, ProductZone, 0)
    Next
End Sub


Private  Sub Page_PreRender()
    lnkClear.Visible = (ShoppingCartZone.WebParts.Count > 0)
End Sub


</script>

<html xmlns="http://www.w3.org/1999/xhtml" >
<head id="Head1" runat="server">
    <style type="text/css">
        .column
        {
            float:left;
            width:40%;
```

LISTING 28.29   Continued

```
            padding:10px;
            height:200px;
            margin-right:10px;
            border:solid 1px black;
            background-color: white;
        }
        html
        {
            background-color:#eeeeee;
        }
    </style>
    <title>Show Zone Verbs</title>
</head>
<body>
    <form id="form1" runat="server">
    <asp:WebPartManager
        id="WebPartManager1"
        Runat="server" />

        <div class="column">
        <h1>Products</h1>
        <asp:WebPartZone
            id="ProductZone"
            OnCreateVerbs="ProductZone_CreateVerbs"
            HeaderText="Products"
            MenuPopupStyle-BackColor="aliceBlue"
            MenuPopupStyle-BorderStyle="solid"
            MenuPopupStyle-BorderWidth="1px"
            MenuPopupStyle-BorderColor="black"
            MenuPopupStyle-ShadowColor="lightgray"
            AllowLayoutChange="false"
            Runat="server">
            <ZoneTemplate>
            <asp:Label
                id="Label1"
                Title="Product"
                Text="Laptop Computer -- $900.00"
                Runat="server" />
            <asp:Label
                id="Label2"
                Title="Product"
                Text="Computer Monitor -- $900.00"
                Runat="server" />
            <asp:Label
```

28

LISTING 28.29   Continued

```
                id="Label3"
                Title="Product"
                Text="Network Card -- $64.20"
                Runat="server" />
        </ZoneTemplate>
    </asp:WebPartZone>
    </div>

    <div class="column">
    <h1>Shopping Cart</h1>
    <asp:WebPartZone
        id="ShoppingCartZone"
        HeaderText="Shopping Cart"
        VerbStyle-CssClass="verbs"
        AllowLayoutChange="false"
        Runat="server"/>
    <asp:LinkButton
        id="lnkClear"
        Text="Clear Cart"
        OnClick="lnkClear_Click"
        runat="server" />
    </div>
    </form>
</body>
</html>
```

After you open the page in Listing 28.29, you should notice that each of the Web Parts displayed in the Product Zone includes the Add to Cart menu option. However, as soon as you move a Web Part to the Shopping Cart Zone, this menu option goes away.

Displaying Web Part Help

When you create True Web Parts, you have the option of adding a help menu option to the Web Part. You can set two properties related to help:

- HelpUrl—The URL of the help page to display.

- HelpMode—The user interface used when displaying the help page. Possible values are Modal, Modeless, and Navigate.

If you set HelpMode to the value Modal, then the help page opens in a modal window that you must close before returning to the original Web Part page. This option works only with Internet Explorer because it uses the Microsoft proprietary ShowModalDialog() statement.

The Web Part in Listing 28.30 displays a modal help page (see Figure 28.9).

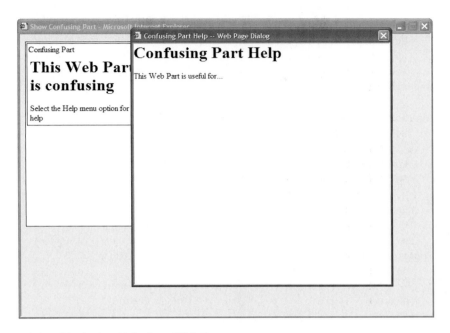

FIGURE 28.9   Displaying Help for a Web Part.

LISTING 28.30   App_Code\ConfusingPart.vb

```
Imports System
Imports System.Web.UI
Imports System.Web.UI.WebControls.WebParts

Namespace myControls
    ''' <summary>
    ''' This Web Part illustrates how to
    ''' use the HelpUrl and HelpMode properties
    ''' </summary>
    Public Class ConfusingPart
        Inherits WebPart

        Private _title As String = "Confusing Part"
        Private _helpUrl As String = "~/ConfusingPartHelp.aspx"
        Private _helpMode As WebPartHelpMode = WebPartHelpMode.Modal

        Public Overrides Property Title() As String
            Get
```

LISTING 28.30   Continued

```
                Return _title
        End Get
        Set(ByVal Value As String)
            _title = value
        End Set
    End Property

    Public Overrides Property HelpUrl() As String
        Get
            Return _helpUrl
        End Get
        Set(ByVal Value As String)
            _helpUrl = value
        End Set
    End Property

    Public Overrides Property HelpMode() As WebPartHelpMode
        Get
            Return _helpMode
        End Get
        Set(ByVal Value As WebPartHelpMode)
            _helpMode = value
        End Set
    End Property

    Protected Overrides Sub RenderContents(ByVal writer As HtmlTextWriter)
        writer.RenderBeginTag(HtmlTextWriterTag.H1)
        writer.Write("This Web Part is confusing")
        writer.RenderEndTag()
        writer.Write("Select the Help menu option for help")
    End Sub

    End Class
End Namespace
```

Notice that the Web Part in Listing 28.30 overrides both the HelpUrl and HelpMode
properties.

> **NOTE**
>
> You can't use the HelpUrl and HelpMode properties with a Generic Web Part. However, you can
> simulate the same user experience by adding a custom Help verb, which opens a new browser
> window, to the Generic Web Part.

Managing Web Parts with the WebPartManager Control

This final section of this chapter takes a closer look at the WebPartManager control. The WebPartManager control is responsible for tracking all the Web Parts in a page. It exposes the primary application programming interface for working with Web Parts.

The WebPartManager control supports the following particularly useful properties (this is not a complete list):

- AvailableTransformers—Represents all the transformers available on the page. Transformers are used when you connect incompatible Web Parts.

- Connections—Represents all the connections between Web Parts in a page.

- DisplayMode—Represents the current Display mode.

- DisplayModes—Returns a collection of all the Display modes associated with the WebPartManager.

- Personalization—Represents the WebPartPersonalization class, which tracks personalization data.

- SelectedWebPart—Represents the Web Part that is currently selected on the page. For example, when you select a Web Part control's Edit menu option, the Web Part becomes the selected Web Part.

- SupportedDisplayModes—Represents all the Display modes supported by the current page,

- WebParts—Represents all the Web Parts on the page,

- Zones—Represents of the Web Part Zones on the page,

Some of these properties require additional explanation. Both the DisplayModes and the SupportedDisplayModes properties return a collection of Web Part Display Modes. However, in some situations, the DisplayModes property returns more Display Modes than the SupportedDisplayModes property. For example, if a page does not include a Catalog Zone, then the SupportedDisplayModes property doesn't return CatalogDisplayMode as one of its values.

You can take advantage of the SupportDisplayModes property to automatically populate a Menu control with the list of available Display Modes like this:

```
Sub Page_Load()
  If Not Page.IsPostBack Then
    For Each mode As WebPartDisplayMode in WebPartManager1.SupportedDisplayModes
      Menu1.Items.Add(new MenuItem(mode.Name))
    Next
  End If
End Sub
```

The Zones property represents all the `WebPartZone` controls on a page. However, it does not include tool zones such as Catalog or Editor Zones.

The `WebPartManager` control also supports a number of useful methods:

- `AddWebPart`—Enables you to add a new Web Part to a Web Part Zone.
- `CanConnectWebParts`—Enables you to determine whether two Web Parts can be connected in a page. This method optionally enables you to specify a Transformer for the connection.
- `CloseWebPart`—Enables you to close a Web Part.
- `ConnectWebParts`—Enables you to connect two Web Parts in a page. This method optionally enables you to specify a Transformer for the connection.
- `CreateWebPart`—Enables you to create a new Generic Web Part from a control.
- `DeleteWebPart`—Enables you to delete a Web Part from a page.
- `DisconnectWebParts`—Enables you to break the connection between two Web Parts.
- `ExportWebPart`—Enables you to export Web Part settings to XML.
- `GetConsumerConnectionPoints`—Enables you to get all the consumer connection points exposed by a Web Part.
- `GetCurrentWebPartManager`—Enables you to get a reference to a page's `WebPartManager` control from any user control or component used in a page. This is a shared (static) method.
- `GetGenericWebPart`—Enables you to retrieve an existing Web Part as a Generic Web Part.
- `GetProviderConnectionPoints`—Enables you to get all the provider connection points exposed by a Web Part.
- `ImportWebPart`—Enables you to import Web Part settings from XML.
- `IsAuthorized`—Enables you to create an authorization filter.
- `MoveWebPart`—Enables you to move a Web Part between Web Part Zones, or change the position of a Web Part in a Web Part Zone.

Notice that everything that you can do from particular tool zones—such as Editor and Catalog Zones—you can do using the methods of the `WebPartManager` control.

For example, the page in Listing 28.31 illustrates how you can dynamically rearrange the Web Parts in a Web Part Zone every time the page is requested.

LISTING 28.31 `DynamicWebParts.aspx`

```
<%@ Page Language="VB" %>
<!DOCTYPE html PUBLIC "-//W3C//DTD XHTML 1.1//EN"
  "http://www.w3.org/TR/xhtml11/DTD/xhtml11.dtd">
```

LISTING 28.31   Continued

```
<script runat="server">

    Private  Sub Page_PreRender()
        Dim rnd As Random =  New Random()
        Dim webPartToMove As WebPart =
➥ WebPartManager1.WebParts(rnd.Next(WebPartManager1.WebParts.Count))
        Dim NewZoneIndex As Integer =  rnd.Next(webPartToMove.Zone.WebParts.Count)
        WebPartManager1.MoveWebPart(webPartToMove, webPartToMove.Zone,
➥NewZoneIndex)
    End Sub

</script>
<html xmlns="http://www.w3.org/1999/xhtml" >
<head id="Head1" runat="server">
    <style type="text/css">
        .column
        {
            width:400px;
            height:200px;
            margin-right:10px;
            border:solid 1px black;
            background-color: white;
        }
        html
        {
            background-color:#eeeeee;
        }
    </style>
    <title>Dynamic Web Parts</title>
</head>
<body>
    <form id="form1" runat="server">
    <asp:WebPartManager
        id="WebPartManager1"
        Runat="server" />

        <asp:WebPartZone
            id="FeaturedProductsZone"
            CssClass="column"
            Runat="server">
            <ZoneTemplate>
            <asp:Panel
                id="FeaturedBooks"
                Title="Featured Books"
```

28

LISTING 28.31   Continued

```
                    Runat="server">
                    <ul>
                        <li>Blink</li>
                        <li>A Theory of Justice</li>
                    </ul>
                </asp:Panel>
                <asp:Panel
                    id="FeaturedMovies"
                    Title="Featured Movies"
                    Runat="server">
                    <ul>
                        <li>Star Wars: Episode III</li>
                        <li>Blade Runner</li>
                    </ul>
                </asp:Panel>
                <asp:Panel
                    id="FeaturedMusic"
                    Title="Featured Music"
                    Runat="server">
                    <ul>
                        <li>Black Eyed Peas</li>
                        <li>Coldplay</li>
                    </ul>
                </asp:Panel>

            </ZoneTemplate>
        </asp:WebPartZone>

    </form>
</body>
</html>
```

In Listing 28.31, the MoveWebPart() method called in the Page_Load() event handler is used to randomly move one of the Web Parts in the Featured Products Zone to a new position (see Figure 28.10).

Finally, the WebPartManager control supports a number of useful events:

- AuthorizeWebPart—Raised when the WebPartManager control adds each Web Part to a page (and Web Parts are displayed in the Catalog Zone).

- ConnectionsActivated—Raised after a connection between two Web Parts is activated.

- ConnectionsActivating—Raised before a connection between two Web Parts is activated.

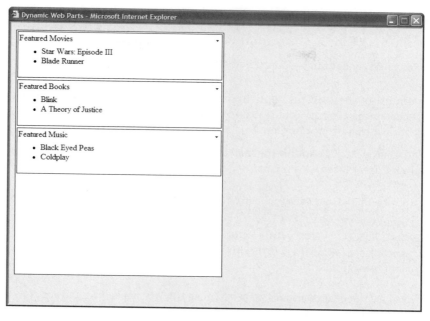

FIGURE 28.10   Randomly Positioning Web Parts.

- DisplayModeChanged—Raised after the Web Part Display Mode is changed.

- DisplayModeChanging—Raised before the Web Part Display Mode is changed.

- SelectedWebPartChanged—Raised after a Web Part is selected (for example, selected for editing).

- SelectedWebPartChanging—Raised before a Web Part is selected (for example, selected for editing).

- WebPartAdded—Raised after a new Web Part is added to the page.

- WebPartAdding—Raised before a new Web Part is added to the page.

- WebPartClosed—Raised after a Web Part is closed.

- WebPartClosing—Raised before a Web Part is closed.

- WebPartDeleted—Raised after a Web Part is deleted.

- WebPartDeleting—Raised before a Web Part is deleted.

- WebPartMoved—Raised after a Web Part is moved.

- WebPartMoving—Raised before a Web Part is moved.

- WebPartsConnected—Raised after a Web Part is connected.

28

- WebPartsConnecting—Raised before a Web Part is connected.

- WebPartsDisconnected—Raised after a Web Part is disconnected.

- WebPartsDisconnecting—Raised before a Web Part is disconnected .

Notice that most of these events come in pairs. There is a DisplayModeChang*ing* event and a DisplayModeChang*ed* event. You can cancel the action associated with most of these events within the ing event handler.

The page in Listing 28.32 handles the WebPartClosed event to display an informational message after a user closes a Web Part.

LISTING 28.32   ShowCloseWarning.aspx

```
<%@ Page Language="VB" %>
<!DOCTYPE html PUBLIC "-//W3C//DTD XHTML 1.1//EN"
  "http://www.w3.org/TR/xhtml11/DTD/xhtml11.dtd">
<script runat="server">

    Protected Sub WebPartManager1_WebPartClosed(ByVal sender As Object,
➥ByVal e As WebPartEventArgs)
        divCloseWarning.Visible = True
    End Sub

    Protected Sub Menu1_MenuItemClick(ByVal sender As Object,
➥ByVal e As MenuEventArgs)
        WebPartManager1.DisplayMode = WebPartManager1.DisplayModes(e.Item.Text)
    End Sub

</script>
<html xmlns="http://www.w3.org/1999/xhtml" >
<head id="Head1" runat="server">
    <style type="text/css">
        .divCloseWarning
        {
            position:absolute;
            background-color:#eeeeee;
            padding:15px;
            left:200px;
            top:50px;
            border:double 3px red;
            width:200px;
        }
        .column
        {
            float:left;
```

LISTING 28.32   Continued

```
            width:40%;
            height:200px;
            margin-right:10px;
            border:solid 1px black;
            background-color: white;
        }
        .menu
        {
            margin:5px 0px;
        }
        html
        {
            background-color:#eeeeee;
        }
    </style>
    <title>Show Close Warning</title>
</head>
<body>
    <form id="form1" runat="server">
    <asp:WebPartManager
        id="WebPartManager1"
        OnWebPartClosed="WebPartManager1_WebPartClosed"
        Runat="server" />

    <asp:Menu
        id="Menu1"
        OnMenuItemClick="Menu1_MenuItemClick"
        Orientation="Horizontal"
        CssClass="menu"
        Runat="server">
        <Items>
        <asp:MenuItem Text="Browse" />
        <asp:MenuItem Text="Design" />
        <asp:MenuItem Text="Catalog" />
        </Items>
    </asp:Menu>

    <asp:WebPartZone
        id="FeaturedProductsZone"
        CssClass="column"
        Runat="server">
        <ZoneTemplate>
        <asp:Label
```

28

LISTING 28.32   Continued

```
            id="Label1"
            Title="First Web Part"
            Text="Contents of First Web Part"
            Runat="server" />
        <asp:Label
            id="Label2"
            Title="Second Web Part"
            Text="Contents of Second Web Part"
            Runat="server" />
        </ZoneTemplate>
    </asp:WebPartZone>

    <div
        id="divCloseWarning"
        class="divCloseWarning"
        Visible="false"
        Enableviewstate="false"
        Runat="server">
        You have closed a Web Part. You
        can reopen the Web Part by opening
        the Page Catalog.
        <br /><br />
        <asp:Button
            id="btnOK"
            Text="OK"
            Runat="server" />
    </div>

    <asp:CatalogZone
        id="CatalogZone1"
        CssClass="column"
        runat="server">
        <ZoneTemplate>
        <asp:PageCatalogPart
            id="PageCatalogPart1"
            Runat="server" />
        </ZoneTemplate>
    </asp:CatalogZone>

    </form>
</body>
</html>
```

After you open the page in Listing 28.32, you can close a Web Part by selecting a Web Part control's Close menu option. When you close a Web Part, an informational message appears (see Figure 28.11).

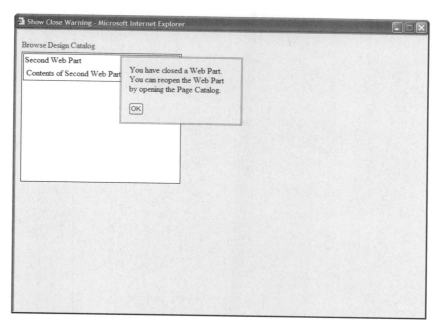

FIGURE 28.11   Displaying a Close warning.

Summary

In this chapter, you learned how to build Web Parts. We started by creating two Hello World Web Parts. One Web Part was created with a User Control, and the other Web Part was created with a control that inherits from the base WebPart class.

Next, you learned how to create authorization filters for Web Parts. You learned different methods of filtering Web Parts so that different users can view different sets of Web Parts on the same page.

You also learned how to add custom verbs (menu items) to a Web Part. You learned how to associate both server-side and client-side code with a verb.

We also discussed the important topic of adding help to a Web Part. You learned how to open a modal dialog box that displays help information for a particular Web Part.

Finally, the Web Part application programming interface exposed by the WebPartManager control was explored in detail. You learned how to manipulate the Web Parts contained in a page through the methods of the WebPartManager class.

28

Personalizing Web Parts

The heart of the Web Part Framework is personalization. When users interact with a website built with Web Parts, individual users can customize the website according to their personal preferences. They can pick and choose the Web Parts that they want to display in their pages, rearrange the layout of Web Parts to their hearts' desires, and they can customize the properties of particular Web Parts.

This chapter leaps into the details of personalization. You learn how to enable users to personalize both Web Part pages and individual Web Parts. You also learn how to administer a Web Parts application by pruning stale personalization data. Finally, you learn how to create custom personalization providers. At the end of this chapter, we create both a custom query string personalization provider and an anonymous personalization provider.

Overview of Personalization

When a user modifies the layout or content of a page that contains Web Parts, the personalization changes are scoped to two things: the page and the user. Each page in an application can have different personalization data associated with it. If you change the name of a page, all personalization data that was associated with the page is lost and you must personalize the page again from scratch.

> **NOTE**
>
> Personalization data is scoped to a page's application relative path. If you move a Web Part application from one server to another, personalization data is not lost. However, if you rename an application, the personalization data is lost.

Personalization is also scoped to the user. The Web Part Framework supports two types of personalization: User and Shared. By default, when a user customizes a Web Part page, the changes have User scope. Each user of a Web Part application can personalize the same application in different ways.

You can also make Shared scoped hanges to a Web Part application. A Shared scope change, unlike a User scope change, has an effect on all users of a Web Part application. Typically, you want to enable only a select group of administrators to make Shared scope changes to an application.

Shared and User scoped personalization data is merged when a user requests a page. For example, an administrator can add a standard set of Web Parts to a page. A particular user can add an additional set of Web Parts. When the page is displayed, both sets of Web Parts are displayed.

So how is all this personalization data stored? The Web Part framework uses the provider model, so it is really up to you. Later in this chapter, we'll extend the ASP.NET Framework with our own custom personalization providers.

The default and only personalization provider included in the ASP.NET framework is the SqlPersonalizationProvider. This provider stores personalization data in two database tables: aspnet_PersonalizationAllUsers and aspnet_PersonalizationPerUser. The first table contains the personalization data that is scoped to all users, and the second table contains the personalization data that is scoped to a particular user. By default, these database tables are located in the ASPNETDB.mdf SQL Server 2005 Express database, located in your application's APP_Data folder.

Using the WebPartPersonalization Class

Under the covers, the WebPartPersonalization class is responsible for all of the low-level operations related to personalization. This class acts as a bridge between the WebPartManager control and a particular personalization provider.

The WebPartPersonalization class is exposed by the WebPartManager control's Personalization property. You access the properties and methods of the WebPartPersonalization class through the WebPartManager control.

The WebPartPersonalization class has a number of useful properties:

- CanEnterSharedScope—Use this property to determine whether the current user can make changes to the page that have Shared personalization scope (has an effect on all users).

- Enabled—Use this property to disable personalization for the current page.

- HasPersonalizationState—Use this property to determine whether any personalization data is associated with the current page and the current user, given the current personalization scope.

- InitialScope—Use this property to place a page in either Shared or User personalization scope.

- IsEnabled—Use this property to determine whether personalization is currently enabled for this page.

- IsModified—Use this property to determine whether the current user can make changes to personalization data.

- ProviderName—Use this property to retrieve or set the name of the personalization provider.

- Scope—Use this property to determine the current personalization scope (User or Shared).

Furthermore, the WebPartPersonalization class has two important methods:

- ResetPersonalizationState—Deletes personalization data associated with the current page and the current user, given the current personalization scope.

- ToggleScope—Toggles the current personalization scope between User personalization scope and Shared personalization scope (or vice versa).

Creating a Personalization Manager

When working with personalization, it helps to see exactly how personalization data is being stored. In the examples in this section, we take advantage of the properties and methods of the WebPartPersonalization class to create a Personalization Manager. The Personalization Manager is contained in Listing 29.1.

LISTING 29.1   PersonalizationManager.ascx

```
<%@ Control Language="VB" ClassName="PersonalizationManager" %>
<script runat="server">

    ''' <summary>
    ''' Display Personalization Information
    ''' </summary>
    Private Sub Page_PreRender()
        Dim wpm As WebPartManager = WebPartManager.GetCurrentWebPartManager(Page)
        lblCurrentScope.Text = wpm.Personalization.Scope.ToString()
        lblIsModifiable.Text = wpm.Personalization.IsModifiable.ToString()
        lblCanEnterSharedScope.Text =
➥wpm.Personalization.CanEnterSharedScope.ToString()
        lblHasPersonalizationState.Text =
➥ wpm.Personalization.HasPersonalizationState.ToString()
        lnkToggleScope.Visible = wpm.Personalization.CanEnterSharedScope
    End Sub

    ''' <summary>
    ''' Switches to Shared Scope
```

29

LISTING 29.1 Continued

```
    ''' </summary>
    Protected Sub lnkToggleScope_Click(ByVal sender As Object,
➥ByVal e As EventArgs)
        Dim wpm As WebPartManager = WebPartManager.GetCurrentWebPartManager(Page)
        wpm.Personalization.ToggleScope()
    End Sub

    ''' <summary>
    ''' Deletes Personalization data
    ''' </summary>
    Protected Sub lnkReset_Click(ByVal sender As Object, ByVal e As EventArgs)
        Dim wpm As WebPartManager = WebPartManager.GetCurrentWebPartManager(Page)
        wpm.Personalization.ResetPersonalizationState()
    End Sub
</script>
<div class="personalizationManager">
Current Scope:
<asp:Label
    id="lblCurrentScope"
    Runat="server" />
Can Modify State:
<asp:Label
    id="lblIsModifiable"
    Runat="server" />
Can Enter Shared Scope:
<asp:Label
    id="lblCanEnterSharedScope"
    Runat="server" />
Has Personalization State:
<asp:Label
    id="lblHasPersonalizationState"
    Runat="server" />
<span>
<asp:LinkButton
    id="lnkToggleScope"
    Text="Toggle Scope"
    OnClick="lnkToggleScope_Click"
    Runat="server" />
</span>
<asp:LinkButton
    id="lnkReset"
    Text="Reset Personalization"
    Runat="server" OnClick="lnkReset_Click" />
</div>
```

The Personalization Manager displays an information bar across the top of a page (see Figure 29.1). The bar displays the values of the following properties:

- `Current Scope`—Displays whether the page is in User or Shared scope personalization mode.

- `Can Modify State`—Displays whether the user can modify the personalization state associated with the page.

- `Can Enter Shared Scope`—Displays whether the user can enter Shared Personalization scope.

- `Has Personalization State`—Displays whether the current page, given the current personalization scope, has personalization data associated with it.

The Personalization Manager includes links to invoke the following methods:

- `Toggle Scope`—Clicking this link switches the page from User to Shared personalization scope (or back again). This link appears only when the user can enter Shared personalization scope.

- `Reset Personalization`—Clicking this link removes the personalization data associated with the current personalization scope. Clicking this link in User scope personalization mode removes all User scoped personalization data, and clicking the link in Shared scope personalization mode removes all Shared scoped personalization data.

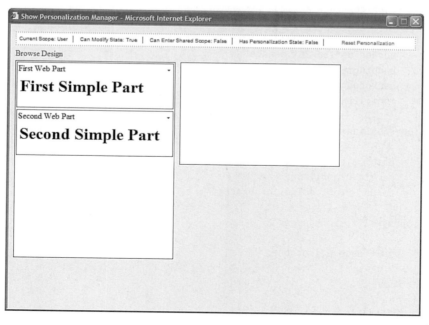

FIGURE 29.1   Viewing the Personalization Manager.

You can use the Personalization Manager in any Web Part page. For example, you can experiment with the Personalization Manager with the page in Listing 29.2.

LISTING 29.2   ShowPersonalizationManager.aspx

```
<%@ Page Language="VB" %>
<%@ Register TagPrefix="user" TagName="PersonalizationManager"
    Src="~/PersonalizationManager.ascx" %>
<%@ Register TagPrefix="user" TagName="FirstSimplePart"
    Src="~/FirstSimplePart.ascx" %>
<%@ Register TagPrefix="user" TagName="SecondSimplePart"
    Src="~/SecondSimplePart.ascx" %>
<!DOCTYPE html PUBLIC "-//W3C//DTD XHTML 1.1//EN"
    "http://www.w3.org/TR/xhtml11/DTD/xhtml11.dtd">
<script runat="server">

    Protected  Sub Menu1_MenuItemClick(ByVal sender As Object,
➥ByVal e As MenuEventArgs)
        WebPartManager1.DisplayMode = WebPartManager1.DisplayModes(e.Item.Text)
    End Sub
</script>

<html xmlns="http://www.w3.org/1999/xhtml" >
<head id="Head1" runat="server">
    <style type="text/css">
        .personalizationManager
        {
            border:dotted 2px orange;
            padding:5px;
            background-color:White;
            font:12px Arial, Sans-Serif;
        }
        .personalizationManager span
        {
            padding-right:10px;
            margin-right:10px;
            border-right:solid 1px black;
        }
        .personalizationManager a
        {
            text-decoration:none;
        }
        .column
        {
            float:left;
            width:40%;
            height:200px;
```

LISTING 29.2 Continued

```
                margin-right:10px;
                border:solid 1px black;
                background-color: white;
            }
            .menu
            {
                margin:5px 0px;
            }
            html
            {
                background-color:#eeeeee;
            }
        </style>
        <title>Show Personalization Manager</title>
</head>
<body>
        <form id="form1" runat="server">
        <user:PersonalizationManager
            id="PersonalizationManager1"
            Runat="Server" />

        <asp:WebPartManager
            id="WebPartManager1"
            Runat="server" />

            <asp:Menu
                id="Menu1"
                OnMenuItemClick="Menu1_MenuItemClick"
                Orientation="Horizontal"
                CssClass="menu"
                Runat="server">
                <Items>
                <asp:MenuItem Text="Browse" />
                <asp:MenuItem Text="Design" />
                </Items>
            </asp:Menu>

            <asp:WebPartZone
                id="WebPartZone1"
                CssClass="column"
                Runat="server">
                <ZoneTemplate>
                <user:FirstSimplePart
                    id="FirstSimplePart1"
                    Title="First Web Part"
```

LISTING 29.2 Continued

```
                Description="Our first simple Web Part"
                Runat="server" />
            <user:SecondSimplePart
                id="SecondSimplePart1"
                Title="Second Web Part"
                Description="Our second simple Web Part"
                Runat="server" />
            </ZoneTemplate>
        </asp:WebPartZone>

        <asp:WebPartZone
            id="WebPartZone2"
            CssClass="column"
            Runat="server" />

    </form>
</body>
</html>
```

When you first open the page in Listing 29.2, the Personalization Manager displays the fact that no personalization data is associated with the page. If you click the Design link, and re-arrange the Web Parts in the page, you create new personalization data. You can click the Reset Personalization link at any time to clear away any personalization data associated with the page.

Configuring Personalization

To this point, we have relied on User scoped personalization exclusively. All personalization data has been scoped to a particular user. In this section, you'll learn how to enable Shared personalization scope so that you can enable administrators to make changes to an application for everyone.

You'll also learn how to configure the SqlPersonalization provider to store personalization data in a particular database in your computer network.

Configuring User and Shared Scope Personalization

To enable User and Shared scope personalization, you must authorize the group of users allowed to make personalization changes. By default, all users are allowed to make User personalization changes and no users are allowed to make Shared personalization changes.

The default personalization configuration settings are contained in the root Web.Config file located at the following path:

```
Windows\Microsoft.NET\Framework\v2.0.xxxxx\config\
```

The default authorization section is contained in Listing 29.3.

LISTING 29.3   Web.Config

```
<webParts>
  <personalization>
  <authorization>
    <deny users="*" verbs="enterSharedScope" />
    <allow users="*" verbs="modifyState" />
  </authorization>
  </personalization>
</webParts>
```

The first authorization rule prevents any user from entering Shared authorization scope. The second authorization rule enables any user to personalize Web Part pages.

To authorize an administrator to make Shared personalization changes, you need to override these settings in the default Web configuration file. If you add the configuration file in Listing 29.4 to the root of your application, then anyone who is a member of the Administrators role can make Shared personalization changes.

LISTING 29.4   Web.Config

```
<?xml version="1.0" encoding="utf-8"?>
<configuration xmlns="http://schemas.microsoft.com/.NetConfiguration/v2.0">
  <system.web>
    <webParts>
     <personalization>
       <authorization>
         <allow users="*" verbs="modifyState" />
         <allow roles="Administrators" verbs="enterSharedScope" />
       </authorization>
     </personalization>
    </webParts>
  </system.web>
</configuration>
```

> **CD NOTE**
>
> The Web.Config file in Listing 29.4 is saved with the name Web.Config_listing4 on the CD so that it does not interfere with the other code samples in this chapter.

After you authorize a user or role to enter Shared personalization scope, you can place a page into Shared personalization mode in either of two ways. First, you can take advantage of the InitialScope property of the WebPartPersonalization class. If you want a page to open in Shared personalization mode by default, then you can declare the WebPartManager control in the page like this:

```
<asp:WebPartManager
  id="WebPartManager1"
  Personalization-InitialScope="Shared"
  Runat="server" />
```

This WebPartManager control declaration causes the page to enter Shared scope personalization mode by default. If a user requests the page and the user is authorized to enter Shared scope, then changes made to the page have Shared scope. If the user is not authorized to make Shared scope changes, then the page remains in User scope personalization mode (no exception is thrown).

> **NOTE**
>
> You cannot modify the IntialScope property after the Page PreInit event. What this means, in practice, is that you need to set this property declaratively. The ToggleScope() method gets around this limitation by automatically performing a Server.Transfer() back to the same page.

An alternate and in many situations better way to change personalization scope is to take advantage of the ToggleScope() method. Calling this method switches the page between User and Shared personalization scope.

The Personalization Manager created in Listing 29.1 includes a link that invokes the ToggleScope() method. If you want to experiment with Shared personalization scope, you can add the Personalization Manager to a Web Part Page and toggle between User and Shared scope.

Configuring the Personalization Database

By default, all personalization data is saved in a SQL Server 2005 Express database named ASPNETDB.mdf, located in your application's APP_Data folder. If you want to store personalization data in another SQL Server database on your network (for example, a SQL Server 2000 or SQL Server 2005 database) then you need to do two things:

1. You need to set up the new database.

2. You need to modify your application's web configuration file.

First, you need to add the necessary database objects for personalization to the new database. The ASP.NET Framework includes a command-line tool named aspnet_regsql, which automatically installs the necessary objects. This tool is located at the following path:

```
Windows\Microsoft.NET\Framework\v2.0.xxxxx\aspnet_regsql.exe
```

If you run the tool without any parameters, the tool displays a wizard that walks you through the steps required for configuring a database for personalization (see Figure 29.2).

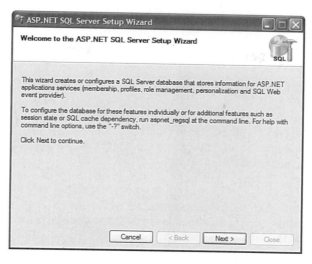

FIGURE 29.2   The ASP.NET SQL Server Setup Wizard.

Alternatively, you can execute a set of SQL Server batch files directly against a database. This is useful when you don't want to set up the .NET Framework on the server hosting your database. The same folder that contains the `aspnet_regsql.exe` tool contains the following four scripts:

- `InstallCommon.sql`—Installs the database objects that are used by several ASP.NET services such as the aspnet_Users table. Run this script first.

- `InstallPersonalization.sql`—Installs the database objects particular to Web Part personalization. Run this script after executing `InstallCommon.sql`.

- `UninstallCommon.sql`—Removes the objects added by `InstallCommon.sql`.

- `UninstallPersonalization.sql`—Removes the objects added by `InstallPersonalization.sql`.

After you add the necessary database objects for personalization, you can point any of your ASP.NET applications at the new database. For example, the Web configuration file in Listing 29.5 causes an application to store personalization data in a SQL Server database named AppData located on a server named DataServer.

LISTING 29.5   `Web.Config`

```
<?xml version="1.0" encoding="utf-8"?>
<configuration xmlns="http://schemas.microsoft.com/.NetConfiguration/v2.0">
  <connectionStrings>
    <add
      name="DataServer"
      connectionString="Server=DataServer;Trusted_Connection=true;
      Database=AppData"/>
  </connectionStrings>
```

29

LISTING 29.5 Continued

```
  <system.web>
    <webParts>
      <personalization defaultProvider="MyPersonalizationProvider">
        <providers>
          <add
            name="MyPersonalizationProvider"
            type="System.Web.UI.WebControls.WebParts.SqlPersonalizationProvider"
            connectionStringName="DataServer" />
        </providers>
        <authorization>
          <allow users="*" verbs="modifyState" />
          <allow roles="Administrators" verbs="enterSharedScope" />
        </authorization>
      </personalization>
    </webParts>
  </system.web>
</configuration>
```

> **CD NOTE**
>
> The Web.Config file in Listing 29.5 is saved with the name Web.Config_listing5 on the CD so
> that it does not interfere with the other code samples in this chapter.

The web configuration file in Listing 29.5 contains a `<webParts>` section that contains a
`<personalization>` sub-section. The `defaultProvider` attribute points to a provider named
`MyPersonalizationProvider` defined in the `<providers>` section. This provider uses the
`SqlPersonalization` provider and uses a database connection string named `DataServer`.

The `DataServer` connection string is defined in the `<connectionStrings>` configuration
section at the top of the configuration file. This connection string points to a server
named `DataServer` and a database named `AppData`. You can, of course, provide a connection string for any database in your network.

Creating Personalizable Web Parts

Users can edit Web Part properties at runtime. For example, you might want to create a
Web Part that displays database data. You can enable users to modify the SQL select query
that returns the database records.

The Web Part Framework automatically saves the value of any property marked with the
Personalizable attribute. By default, a personalizable property is scoped to a particular
user. In other words, each user can personalize a property in different ways. However, you
also have the option of creating a personalizable property that can be modified only in
Shared user scope.

The Web Part in Listing 29.6, the DataPart Web Part, enables you to display records from any database table. The Web Part includes one personalizable property that has User scope—the SelectCommand property—and one property that has Shared scope—the ConnectionString property.

LISTING 29.6   DataPart.ascx

```
<%@ Control Language="VB" ClassName="DataPart" %>
<%@ Import Namespace="System.Data" %>
<%@ Import Namespace="System.Data.SqlClient" %>
<script runat="server">

    Private _connectionString As String =  String.Empty
    Private _selectCommand As String =  String.Empty

    <Personalizable(PersonalizationScope.Shared)> _
    <WebBrowsable> _
    Public Property ConnectionString() As String
        Get
                Return _connectionString
        End Get
        Set (ByVal Value As String)
                _connectionString = value
        End Set
    End Property

    <Personalizable> _
    <WebBrowsable> _
    Public Property SelectCommand() As String
        Get
                Return _selectCommand
        End Get
        Set (ByVal Value As String)
                _selectCommand = value
        End Set
    End Property

    Private  Sub Page_PreRender()
        If _connectionString <> String.Empty ➥
And_selectCommand <> String.Empty Then
            Try
                Dim dad As SqlDataAdapter =
➥New SqlDataAdapter(_selectCommand,_connectionString)
                Dim dst As DataSet =  New DataSet()
                dad.Fill(dst)
                grdData.DataSource = dst
```

29

LISTING 29.6 Continued

```
                grdData.DataBind()
            Catch e As Exception
                lblError.Text = e.Message
            End Try
        End If
    End Sub

</script>

<asp:Label
    id="lblError"
    EnableViewState="false"
    Runat="server" />

<asp:GridView
    id="grdData"
    Runat="server" />
```

Notice that the first property in Listing 29.6, the ConnectionString property, is decorated with a Personalizable attribute that includes a PersonalizationScope.Shared parameter. This property can be edited only by an administrator who can enter Shared personalization mode.

The second property, SelectCommand, is also decorated with the Personalizable attribute. This property can be modified in either Shared or User personalization mode. Modifying the property in Shared personalization mode provides the property with a default value for everyone. (Individual users can override the default value.)

You can experiment with the DataPart Web Part with the page in Listing 29.7. This page includes the Personalization Manager so you can toggle between User and Shared scope.

LISTING 29.7   ShowDataPart.aspx

```
<%@ Page Language="VB" %>
<%@ Register TagPrefix="user" TagName="DataPart" Src="~/DataPart.ascx" %>
<%@ Register TagPrefix="user" TagName="PersonalizationManager"
    Src="~/PersonalizationManager.ascx" %>
<!DOCTYPE html PUBLIC "-//W3C//DTD XHTML 1.1//EN"
    "http://www.w3.org/TR/xhtml11/DTD/xhtml11.dtd">
<script runat="server">

    Protected  Sub Menu1_MenuItemClick(ByVal sender As Object,
➥ByVal e As MenuEventArgs)
        WebPartManager1.DisplayMode = WebPartManager1.DisplayModes(e.Item.Text)
    End Sub
</script>
```

LISTING 29.7 Continued

```html
<html xmlns="http://www.w3.org/1999/xhtml" >
<head id="Head1" runat="server">
    <style type="text/css">
        .personalizationManager
        {
            border:dotted 2px orange;
            padding:5px;
            background-color:White;
            font:12px Arial, Sans-Serif;
        }
        .personalizationManager span
        {
            padding-right:10px;
            margin-right:10px;
            border-right:solid 1px black;
        }
        .personalizationManager a
        {
            text-decoration:none;
        }
        .column
        {
            float:left;
            width:30%;
            height:200px;
            margin-right:10px;
            border:solid 1px black;
            background-color: white;
        }
        .menu
        {
            margin:5px 0px;
        }
        html
        {
            background-color:#eeeeee;
        }
    </style>
    <title>Show Data Part</title>
</head>
<body>
    <form id="form1" runat="server">
    <user:PersonalizationManager
        id="PersonalizationManager1"
        Runat="Server" />

    <asp:WebPartManager
```

LISTING 29.7 Continued

```
          id="WebPartManager1"
          Runat="server" />

      <asp:Menu
          id="Menu1"
          OnMenuItemClick="Menu1_MenuItemClick"
          Orientation="Horizontal"
          CssClass="menu"
          Runat="server">
          <Items>
          <asp:MenuItem Text="Browse" />
          <asp:MenuItem Text="Design" />
          <asp:MenuItem Text="Edit" />
          </Items>
      </asp:Menu>

      <asp:WebPartZone
          id="WebPartZone1"
          CssClass="column"
          Runat="server">
          <ZoneTemplate>
          <user:DataPart
              id="DataPart1"
              Title="Data Part"
              Description="Displays database records"
              Runat="server" />
          </ZoneTemplate>
      </asp:WebPartZone>

      <asp:WebPartZone
          id="WebPartZone2"
          CssClass="column"
          Runat="server" />

      <asp:EditorZone
          id="EditorZone1"
          CssClass="column"
          Runat="server">
          <ZoneTemplate>
          <asp:PropertyGridEditorPart
              id="PropertyGridEditorPart1"
              Runat="server" />
          </ZoneTemplate>
      </asp:EditorZone>
  </form>
</body>
</html>
```

After you open the page in Listing 29.7, you can edit the properties of the DataPart Web Part by clicking the Edit link. The PropertyGridEditorPart control automatically renders a property sheet, which enables you to modify the values of the ConnectionString and SelectCommand properties (see Figure 29.3).

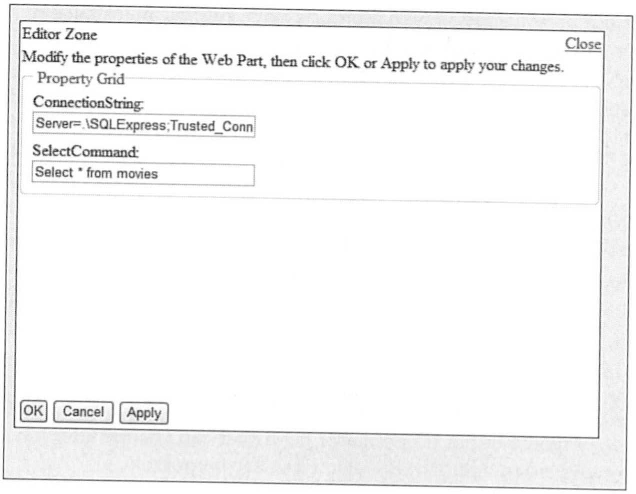

FIGURE 29.3   Editing the ConnectionString and SelectCommmand properties.

The ConnectionString property appears only when you enter Shared personalization scope by clicking the Toggle Scope link in the Personalization Manager control's information bar. The SelectCommand property, on the other hand, can be altered in either Shared or User personalization mode.

CD NOTE

The CD includes a sample database in the App_Data folder named MyDatabase.mdf, which includes a Movie database table. You can connect to this database with the following connection string:

```
Server=.\SQLExpress;Trusted_Connection=true;
AttachDbFileName=¦DataDirectory¦MyDatabase.mdf;User Instance=true
```

And execute the following SQL SELECT statement:

```
SELECT * FROM Movies
```

Working with Complex Personalizable Properties

In the previous section, you learned how to use the Personalizable attribute with properties that represent simple types such as Strings and Integers. You also can use the Web Part Framework to automatically persist the values of properties that represent more complex types such as ArrayLists or custom classes.

Behind the scenes, the Web Part Framework uses the `ObjectStateFormatter` class to serialize and deserialize the values of Web Part properties. This is a powerful class. It can serialize the state of any class that can be represented statically.

> **NOTE**
>
> You should not use personalization with a property that returns an instance of a class defined in the App_Code folder. If you make changes to the App_Code folder, the contents of the folder are automatically recompiled into a new assembly. Because the assembly name changes with each recompilation, the Web Part Framework cannot automatically serialize and deserialize classes defined in the assembly.

However, one important limitation of the Web Part Framework relates to complex properties. The Web Part Framework can detect changes to simple properties automatically, but the framework cannot detect changes made to more complex properties automatically. In general, the Web Part Framework can detect changes to immutable properties, but not changes made to mutable properties.

> **NOTE**
>
> A mutable type is a type that has properties or fields that can change after it is instantiated. Most reference types are mutable. Most value types are immutable.

For example, if you attempt to use the `Personalizable` attribute with a property that returns an ArrayList, you don't get an exception, but the state of the ArrayList is not saved. The Web Part Framework fails to save the state of the property because the Web Part Framework cannot detect when the ArrayList has changed.

There are two ways around this limitation. The next section in this chapter discusses how you can take advantage of the `IPersonalizable` interface to take a more hands-on approach to personalization state management. When you implement the `IPersonalizable` interface, you can indicate exactly when you want the Web Part Framework to save changes to a Web Part's properties.

This section, however, explores a simpler option. The `WebPart` class includes a method named the `SetPersonalizationDirty()` method. There is both a shared (static) and an instance version of this method, so you can use it either when working with a Web Part created from a User Control or when working with a "True" Web Part derived from the base `WebPart` class.

For example, the Web Part in Listing 29.8—the `FirstTaskListPart` Web Part—enables you to create and save a task list (see Figure 29.4). The list of tasks is represented by an ArrayList.

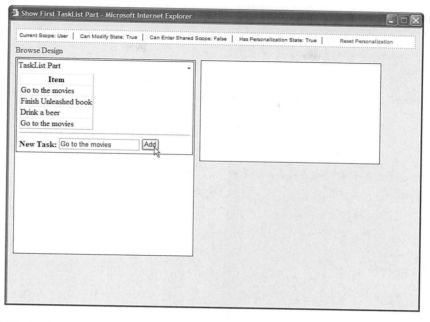

FIGURE 29.4   A personalizable task list.

LISTING 29.8   FirstTaskListPart.ascx

```
<%@ Control Language="VB" ClassName="FirstTaskListPart" %>
<script runat="server">

    Private _tasks As ArrayList = Nothing

    <Personalizable()> _
    Public Property Tasks() As ArrayList
        Get
            Return _tasks
        End Get
        Set(ByVal Value As ArrayList)
            _tasks = value
        End Set
    End Property


    Private Sub Page_PreRender()
```

LISTING 29.8 Continued

```
        grdTasks.DataSource = _tasks
        grdTasks.DataBind()
    End Sub

    Protected Sub btnAdd_Click(ByVal sender As Object, ByVal e As EventArgs)
        If _tasks Is Nothing Then
            _tasks = New ArrayList()
        End If
        _tasks.Add(txtNewTask.Text)
        WebPart.SetPersonalizationDirty(Me)
    End Sub
</script>

<asp:GridView
    id="grdTasks"
    Runat="server" />

<hr>
<b>New Task:</b>
<asp:TextBox
    id="txtNewTask"
    Runat="server" />
<asp:Button
    id="btnAdd"
    Text="Add"
    OnClick="btnAdd_Click"
    Runat="server" />
```

Notice that the WebPart.SetPersonalizationDirty() method is called after a new item is added to the ArrayList. If you neglected to call this method, then you would never be able to add more than a single item to the Task List.

Also, it is important to notice that the _tasks variable used to represent the tasks is initially set to Nothing (null). The variable is initialized like this:

```
Private _tasks As ArrayList = Nothing
```

It is important that you initialize a personalizable property that represents a reference type with the value Nothing. The very first value assigned to a personalizable property is considered the default value. The Web Part Framework compares the current value against the default value and if there are no changes, the framework does not update the saved personalization data.

Imagine that you had initialized the property like this:

```
Private _tasks As ArrayList = New ArrayList()
```

In that case, because an ArrayList is a reference type, the Web Part Framework would never detect a change in the property even when new items have been added to the ArrayList. (This is true even when you use the `WebPart.SetPersonalizationDirty()` method to warn the framework that there have been changes.)

Using the `IPersonalizable` Interface

In most cases, using the `Personalizable` attribute to mark the Web Part properties that you want to save automatically works fine. However, the Personalizable attribute does have some limitations:

- A Personalizable property must be public.

- A Personalizable property must have both a public get and set accessor.

- A Personalizable property cannot have an indexer or parameter.

- A Personalizable property is ignored in a nested control.

If you encounter one of these limitations, then you have no choice but to implement the `IPersonalizable` interface. When you implement this interface, you are responsible for selecting the data that you want to save.

The `IPersonalizable` interface includes one property and two methods that you must implement:

- `IsDirty`—Return the value `True` from this property when the Web Part Framework calls the `Save()` method.

- `Load()`—This method loads personalization state information.

- `Save()`—This method saves personalization state information.

For example, Listing 29.9 contains a task list Web Part that implements the `IPersonalizable` interface named `SecondTaskListPart.ascx`.

LISTING 29.9   SecondTaskListPart.ascx

```
<%@ Control Language="VB" ClassName="SecondTaskListPart" %>
<%@ Implements Interface="System.Web.UI.WebControls.WebParts.IPersonalizable" %>
<script runat="server">

    Private _tasks As ArrayList = New ArrayList()
    Private _isDirty As Boolean = False

    Public Property Tasks() As ArrayList
        Get
            Return _tasks
        End Get
        Set(ByVal Value As ArrayList)
            _tasks = value
        End Set
```

LISTING 29.9 Continued

```
    End Property

    Public ReadOnly Property IsDirty() As Boolean
➥Implements IPersonalizable.IsDirty
        Get
            Return _isDirty
        End Get
    End Property

    Public Sub Save(ByVal state As PersonalizationDictionary)
➥Implements IPersonalizable.Save
        Dim wpm As WebPartManager = WebPartManager.GetCurrentWebPartManager(Page)
        state.Add("tasks",
➥New PersonalizationEntry(_tasks, wpm.Personalization.Scope))
    End Sub

    Public Sub Load(ByVal state As PersonalizationDictionary)
➥Implements IPersonalizable.Load
        _tasks = CType(state("tasks").Value, ArrayList)
    End Sub

    Private Sub Page_PreRender()
        grdTasks.DataSource = _tasks
        grdTasks.DataBind()
    End Sub

    Protected Sub btnAdd_Click(ByVal sender As Object, ByVal e As EventArgs)
        _tasks.Add(txtNewTask.Text)
        _isDirty = True
    End Sub
</script>
<asp:GridView
    id="grdTasks"
    Runat="server" />

<hr>
<b>New Task:</b>
<asp:TextBox
    id="txtNewTask"
    Runat="server" />
<asp:Button
    id="btnAdd"
    Text="Add"
    OnClick="btnAdd_Click"
    Runat="server" />
```

You can view the `SecondTaskListPart` Web Part with the `ShowSecondTaskList.aspx` page on the CD that accompanies this book.

Notice that the Web Part in Listing 29.9 includes an `<%@ Implements %>` directive and that the Web Part implements the `IPersonalizable` interface.

The body of the Web Part contains a `GridView` control, a `TextBox` control, and a `Button` control. When a user enters a new task description in the `TextBox` and clicks the button, the `btnAdd_Click()` method executes. This method adds the new task to the ArrayList and marks the Web Part as dirty.

Each time the Web Part is loaded in the page, the `Load()` method is called and the task list is returned from the underlying personalization data store. Whenever the Web Part is marked as dirty—after a user enters a new task—the `Save()` method is called. The Web Part framework calls this method before saving the personalization data.

Notice that both the `Load()` and `Save()` methods use a PersonalizationDictionary, which contains instances of the `PersonalizationEntry` class. Each PersonalizationEntry represents the information being saved and the personalization scope associated with the information being saved (User or Shared). In the `Save()` method, the current `WebPartManager` control is used to determine the page's current personalization scope.

Administrating Personalization

A public website that uses Web Parts might have thousands of members. Each member, potentially, could personalize multiple pages in the website.

Most public websites experience significant churn. A person registers at the website, plays around with it for a few minutes, and then leaves without ever being seen again. Saving personalization data for inactive users could be a huge waste of resources.

The Web Part Framework includes a `PersonalizationAdministration` class. This class includes several valuable methods for identifying and pruning inactive personalization data. Here is a list of the methods supported by this class:

- `FindInactiveUserState`—Returns a collection of User personalization state information when supplied with path, username, and date parameters. This method supports wildcards in its parameters.

- `FindSharedState`—Returns a collection of Shared personalization state information when supplied with a path. This method supports wildcards in its path parameter.

- `FindUserState`—Returns a collection of User personalization state information when supplied with a path and username. This method supports wildcards in its parameters.

- `GetAllInactiveUserState`—Returns a collection of User personalization state information when supplied with a date.

- GetAllState—Returns a collection of personalization state information when supplied with a personalization scope.

- GetCountOfInactiveUserState—Returns the number of user personalization items older than the supplied date parameter.

- GetCountOfState—Returns the number of user personalization items matching a particular personalization scope.

- GetCountOfUserState—Returns the number of user personalization items matching a certain username. This method supports wildcards in the username parameter.

- ResetAllState—Deletes personalization information matching a particular personalization scope.

- ResetInactiveUserState—Deletes User personalization data older than the supplied date parameter.

- ResetSharedState—Deletes Shared state information that matches the supplied path parameter.

- ResetState—Deletes state information that matches the contents of the supplied parameter, which represents a collection of state information.

- ResetUserState—Deletes state information that matches either the supplied username or path parameters.

The ResetAllState() method is the nuclear bomb of personalization administration methods. You can use this method to blow away all User and Shared state information for all users.

The other methods are useful for pruning stale state information. The page in Listing 29.10 illustrates how you can retrieve personalization state information for a particular user.

LISTING 29.10   AdministerPersonalization.aspx

```
<%@ Page Language="VB" %>
<!DOCTYPE html PUBLIC "-//W3C//DTD XHTML 1.1//EN"
    "http://www.w3.org/TR/xhtml11/DTD/xhtml11.dtd">
<script runat="server">

    Protected  Sub btnSubmit_Click(ByVal sender As Object, ByVal e As EventArgs)
        GridView1.DataSource =
➥PersonalizationAdministration.FindUserState(Nothing, txtUsername.Text)
        GridView1.DataBind()
    End Sub
</script>

<html xmlns="http://www.w3.org/1999/xhtml" >
<head id="Head1" runat="server">
    <style type="text/css">
```

LISTING 29.10 Continued

```
            .grid
            {
                font: 14px Arial, Sans-Serif;
            }
            .grid td
            {
                padding:10px;
            }
            .grid th
            {
                padding:10px;
                background-color:orange;
                text-align:left;
            }
        </style>

        <title>Administer Personalization</title>
</head>
<body>
        <form id="form1" runat="server">
        <div>

        <asp:Label
            id="lblUsername"
            AssociatedControlID="txtUsername"
            Text="Username:"
            Runat="server" />
        <asp:TextBox
            id="txtUsername"
            Runat="server" />
        <asp:Button
            id="btnSubmit"
            Text="Submit"
            OnClick="btnSubmit_Click"
            Runat="server" />

        <hr />
        <asp:GridView
            id="GridView1"
            CssClass="grid"
            Runat="server" />

        </div>
        </form>
</body>
</html>
```

If you enter a username in the form contained in Listing 29.10 and click the Submit button, matching personalization items are displayed by the GridView control (see Figure 29.5). The FindUserState() method is used to retrieve the matching personalization items.

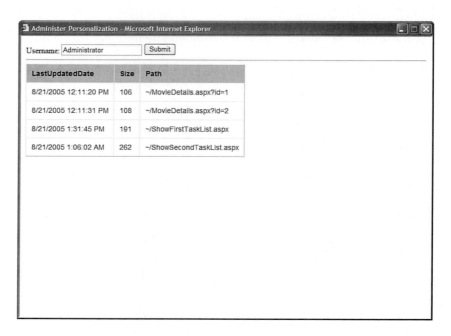

FIGURE 29.5   Displaying personalization data.

Creating Custom Personalization Providers

The Web Part Framework uses the Provider Model to save personalization information. The default and only Personalization Provider included with the framework is the SqlPersonalizationProvider. The beautiful thing about the Provider Model is that if you don't like anything about the default provider, then you can easily create your own custom provider.

In this section, we create two custom personalization providers: a Query String Personalization Provider and a Anonymous Personalization Provider.

Building a Query String Personalization Provider

Personalization information, by default, is scoped against a particular page path. A user can personalize two different pages in two different ways. However, a user cannot personalize the same page in two different ways.

For some applications, this limitation might present a problem. For example, imagine that you are creating an online store that includes a Product.aspx page. This page displays information on different products, depending on the value of a Query String passed to the page.

> **NOTE**
>
> Another approach to solving the problem discussed in this section is to create a VirtualPathProvider. This option is discussed in Chapter 19, "Advanced Navigation."

The SqlPersonalization provider does not enable you to customize the page differently, depending on the product ID passed to the page. To enable users to personalize different versions of the same product page, you need to create a custom Query String Personalization Provider.

This project contains the following two pages:

- `MovieList.aspx`—This page displays a list of movies. Clicking a movie links to the `MovieDetails.aspx` page, with the movie ID passed as a query string parameter.

- `MovieDetails.aspx`—This Web Part page displays information on a particular movie.

The project also includes the following two Web Parts:

- `MoviePart.ascx`—Displays details for a particular movie.

- `TextPart.ascx`—Displays a block of text.

Finally, the project contains the following two support files:

- `QueryStringPersonalizationProvider`—This class implements the custom personalization provider.

- `Web.Config`—This configuration file configures the custom personalization provider.

All the files listed here are contained on the CD that accompanies the book. In this section, we concentrate on the `QueryStringPersonalizationProvider` class, which is contained in Listing 29.11.

LISTING 29.11   QueryStringPersonalizationProvider.vb

```
Imports System
Imports System.Web
Imports System.Web.UI.WebControls.WebParts

Namespace myControls

    ''' <summary>
    ''' Custom personalization provider which takes into account the
    ''' id query string parameter.
    ''' </summary>
```

29

LISTING 29.11 Continued

```
Public Class QueryStringPersonalizationProvider
    Inherits SqlPersonalizationProvider

    ''' <summary>
    ''' Called when data is saved to the database
    ''' </summary>
    Protected Overrides Sub SavePersonalizationBlob(ByVal webPartManager As
➥ WebPartManager, ByVal path As String, ByVal userName As String,
➥ByVal dataBlob() As Byte)
        Dim queryStringId As String = HttpContext.Current.Request("id")
        If Not queryStringId Is Nothing Then
            path += "?id=" + queryStringId
        End If
        MyBase.SavePersonalizationBlob(webPartManager, path, userName,
➥dataBlob)
    End Sub

    ''' <summary>
    ''' Called when data is loaded from the database
    ''' </summary>
    Protected Overrides Sub LoadPersonalizationBlobs(ByVal webPartManager
➥As WebPartManager, ByVal path As String, ByVal userName As String,
➥ByRef sharedDataBlob() As Byte, ByRef userDataBlob() As Byte)
        Dim queryStringId As String = HttpContext.Current.Request("id")
        If Not queryStringId Is Nothing Then
            path += "?id=" + queryStringId
        End If
        MyBase.LoadPersonalizationBlobs(webPartManager, path, userName,
➥ sharedDataBlob, userDataBlob)
    End Sub

    ''' <summary>
    ''' Called when a user's personalization data is reset
    ''' </summary>
    Protected Overrides Sub ResetPersonalizationBlob(ByVal webPartManager As
➥ WebPartManager, ByVal path As String, ByVal userName As String)
        Dim queryStringId As String = HttpContext.Current.Request("id")
        If Not queryStringId Is Nothing Then
            path += "?id=" + queryStringId
        End If
        MyBase.ResetPersonalizationBlob(webPartManager, path, userName)
    End Sub

End Class
End Namespace
```

The class in Listing 29.11 overrides three methods of the base
SqlPersonalizationProvider class: the SavePersonalizationBlob(),
LoadPersonalizationBlob(), and ResetPersonalizationBlob() methods. The Blob, in
this context, refers to the serialized blob of personalization data.

In each of these methods, the value of the query string parameter named ID is added to
the path associated with the state data being saved. In other words, the state data is
scoped to the path and ID query string parameter.

After you add the class in Listing 29.11 to your application's App_Code folder, you need
to configure the custom personalization provider. The Web configuration file in Listing
29.12 configures the QueryStringPersonalizationProvider as the application's default
personalization provider.

LISTING 29.12   Web.Config

```
<?xml version="1.0"?>
<configuration xmlns="http://schemas.microsoft.com/.NetConfiguration/v2.0">
  <connectionStrings>
    <add
      name="Northwind"
      connectionString="Server=localhost;Trusted_Connection=true;
Database=Northwind"/>
  </connectionStrings>
    <system.web>
      <webParts>
        <personalization
          defaultProvider="QueryStringPersonalizationProvider">
          <providers>
            <add
              name="QueryStringPersonalizationProvider"
              type="myControls.QueryStringPersonalizationProvider"
              connectionStringName="localSQLServer" />
          </providers>
        </personalization>
      </webParts>
    </system.web>
</configuration>
```

CD NOTE

The Web.Config file in this section is named Web.Config_listing12 on the CD so that it does
not interfere with the other code samples in this chapter.

You can test the QueryStringPersonalizatonProvider by opening the MovieList.aspx page
on the CD that accompanies this book in your browser. When you click on a movie title,
you are linked to the MovieDetails.aspx page, which displays a particular movie. Notice
that you can personalize each version of the MovieDetails.aspx page differently. For
example, you can enter different text in the TextPart control for each movie (see Figure
29.6 and Figure 29.7), even though the different movies are displayed by the same page.

29

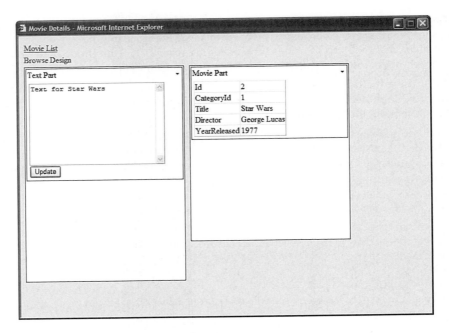

FIGURE 29.6   Displaying Star Wars movie details.

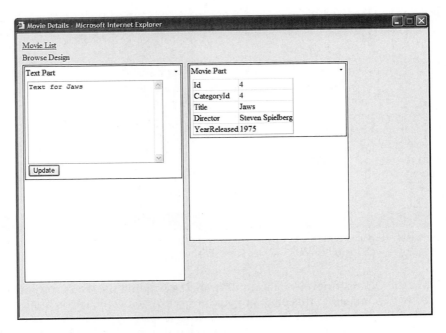

FIGURE 29.7   Displaying Jaws movie details.

Building an Anonymous Personalization Provider

The default SqlPersonalizationProvider stores personalization data for a user only when the user is authenticated. This requirement makes sense. Typically, you do not want to store personalization data for every random stranger who visits your website.

However, there are situations in which you might want to enable anonymous users to personalize a Web Part application. For example, you might want to create a customizable portal page, such as those used for My MSN or My Yahoo, and not require users to register at your website prior to performing the customization.

Fortunately, modifying the existing SqlPersonalizationProvider to support anonymous users is not that difficult because another part of the ASP.NET Framework already includes the infrastructure for identifying anonymous users. The ASP.NET Framework supports a feature called Anonymous Identification, which is used to support anonymous ASP.NET Profiles.

> **NOTE**
>
> The Profile class is discussed in Chapter 22, "Maintaining Application State."

In this section, you learn how to create an Anonymous Personalization Provider. To create this custom personalization provider, you need to modify three of the standard classes used by the Web Part Framework.

First, you need to create the Anonymous Personalization Provider class itself. This class is contained in Listing 29.13.

LISTING 29.13   AnonSqlPersonalizationProvider.vb

```
Imports System
Imports System.Web
Imports System.Web.UI.WebControls.WebParts

Namespace myControls

    ''' <summary>
    ''' Custom Personalizaton Provider which enables
    ''' anonymous personalization
    ''' </summary>
    Public Class AnonSqlPersonalizationProvider
        Inherits SqlPersonalizationProvider
        ''' <summary>
        ''' Saves personalization data to the database
        ''' </summary>
        Protected Overrides Sub SavePersonalizationBlob(ByVal webPartManager As
➥ WebPartManager, ByVal path As String, ByVal userName As String,
➥ByVal dataBlob() As Byte)
            If Not HttpContext.Current.Request.IsAuthenticated Then
```

LISTING 29.13 Continued

```
                userName = HttpContext.Current.Request.AnonymousID
            End If
            MyBase.SavePersonalizationBlob(webPartManager, path, userName,
➥dataBlob)
        End Sub


        ''' <summary>
        ''' Loads personalization data from the database
        ''' </summary>
        Protected Overrides Sub LoadPersonalizationBlobs(ByVal webPartManager As
➥ WebPartManager, ByVal path As String, ByVal userName As String,
➥ByRef sharedDataBlob() As Byte, ByRef userDataBlob() As Byte)
            If Not HttpContext.Current.Request.IsAuthenticated Then
                userName = HttpContext.Current.Request.AnonymousID
            End If
            MyBase.LoadPersonalizationBlobs(webPartManager, path, userName,
➥ sharedDataBlob, userDataBlob)
        End Sub


        ''' <summary>
        ''' Deletes personalization data from the database
        ''' </summary>
        Protected Overrides Sub ResetPersonalizationBlob(ByVal webPartManager As
➥ WebPartManager, ByVal path As String, ByVal userName As String)
            If Not HttpContext.Current.Request.IsAuthenticated Then
                userName = HttpContext.Current.Request.AnonymousID
            End If
            MyBase.ResetPersonalizationBlob(webPartManager, path, userName)
        End Sub


        ''' <summary>
        ''' Determines whether the page opens in User or Shared
        ''' personalization scope
        ''' </summary>
        Public Overrides Function DetermineInitialScope(ByVal webPartManager As
➥WebPartManager, ByVal loadedState As PersonalizationState) As PersonalizationScope
            Return webPartManager.Personalization.InitialScope
        End Function

    End Class
End Namespace
```

The AnonPersonalizationProvider overrides four methods of the base
SqlPersonalizationProvider class. If a user is anonymous, then the

LoadPersonalizationBlob(), SavePersonalizationBlob(), and
ResetPersonalizationBlob() methods use the anonymous ID associated with the user
rather than the normal username. The DetermineInitialScope() method is also overridden because the default implementation of this method automatically puts anonymous
users into Shared personalization scope.

Next, you need to modify the standard WebPartPersonalization class. The standard
version of this class prevents anonymous users from modifying state information. The
updated AnonWebPartPersonalization class is contained in Listing 29.14.

LISTING 29.14   AnonWebPartPersonalization.vb

```vb
Imports System
Imports System.Collections
Imports System.Web
Imports System.Web.UI.WebControls.WebParts

Namespace myControls

    ''' <summary>
    ''' Overrides the standard WebPartPersonalization class
    ''' to enable anonymous users to modify state.
    ''' </summary>
    Public Class AnonWebPartPersonalization
        Inherits WebPartPersonalization

        Public Sub New(ByVal webPartManager As WebPartManager)
            MyBase.New(webPartManager)
        End Sub

        Protected Overrides ReadOnly Property UserCapabilities() As IDictionary
            Get
                If HttpContext.Current.Request.IsAuthenticated = True Then
                    Return MyBase.UserCapabilities
                Else
                    Dim capabilities As Hashtable = New Hashtable()
                    capabilities.Add(WebPartPersonalization.ModifyStateUserCapability,
➥ WebPartPersonalization.ModifyStateUserCapability)
                    Return capabilities
                End If
            End Get
        End Property
    End Class
End Namespace
```

In Listing 29.14, the UserCapabilities property is overridden. The new version of this property ensures that all users, even anonymous users, have the capability to modify state information.

Next, because a custom WebPartPersonalization class has been created, the standard WebPartManager control has to be modified before you can use it. The updated WebPartManager control is contained in Listing 29.15.

LISTING 29.15   AnonWebPartManager.vb

```
Imports System
Imports System.Web.UI.WebControls.WebParts

Namespace myControls
    ''' <summary>
    ''' Modifies the base WebPartManager control
    ''' to use the AnonWebPartPersonalization class
    ''' </summary>
    Public Class AnonWebPartManager
        Inherits WebPartManager
        Protected Overrides Function CreatePersonalization()
➥As WebPartPersonalization
            Return New AnonWebPartPersonalization(Me)
        End Function
    End Class
End Namespace
```

In Listing 29.15, the base CreatePersonalization() method of the WebPartManager control is overridden to use the custom AnonWebPartPersonalization class.

Next, you are ready to enable the Anonymous Personalization Provider. The web configuration file in Listing 29.16 contains the necessary configuration settings.

> **WARNING**
>
> You might need to restart your application to load the new personalization provider.

LISTING 29.16   Web.Config

```
<?xml version="1.0"?>
<configuration xmlns="http://schemas.microsoft.com/.NetConfiguration/v2.0">
        <system.web>
                <anonymousIdentification enabled="True"/>
                <authentication mode="None" />
                <webParts>
                        <personalization defaultProvider="AnonProvider">
                                <providers>
                                        <add
```

LISTING 29.16 Continued

```
                name="AnonProvider"
                type="myControls.AnonSqlPersonalizationProvider"
                connectionStringName="localSQLServer"/>
                            </providers>
                            <authorization>
            <allow users="Administrators" verbs="enterSharedScope"/>
                            </authorization>
                        </personalization>
                    </webParts>
                    </system.web>
</configuration>
```

CD NOTE

The configuration file in Listing 29.16 is saved with the name Web.Config_listing16 on the CD so that it does not interfere with the other code samples in this chapter.

The Web configuration file in Listing 29.16 does three things. First, it enables Anonymous Identification. When this feature is enabled, a GUID is generated automatically for each user and stored in a browser cookie. Second, the configuration file disables authentication by setting the Authentication Mode to the value None. Finally, the configuration file configures the AnonPersonalizationProvider as the default personalization provider for the application.

WARNING

You might need to restart your application to load the new personalization provider.

At this point, it's finally time to try out the Anonymous Personalization Provider. The Web Form page in Listing 29.17 can be customized by strangers.

LISTING 29.17   TestAnonymous.aspx

```
<%@ Page Language="VB" %>
<%@ Register TagPrefix="custom" Namespace="myControls" %>
<%@ Register TagPrefix="user" TagName="PersonalizationManager"
    Src="~/PersonalizationManager.ascx" %>
<%@ Register TagPrefix="user" TagName="TextPart" Src="~/TextPart.ascx" %>
<!DOCTYPE html PUBLIC "-//W3C//DTD XHTML 1.1//EN"
    "http://www.w3.org/TR/xhtml11/DTD/xhtml11.dtd">

<script runat="server">

    Protected Sub Menu1_MenuItemClick(ByVal sender As Object,
➥ByVal e As MenuEventArgs)
```

29

LISTING 29.17 Continued

```
            WebPartManager1.DisplayMode = WebPartManager1.DisplayModes(e.Item.Text)
        End Sub

    </script>

    <html xmlns="http://www.w3.org/1999/xhtml" >
    <head id="Head1" runat="server">
        <style type="text/css">
            .personalizationManager
            {
                border:dotted 2px orange;
                padding:5px;
                background-color:White;
                font:12px Arial, Sans-Serif;
            }
            .personalizationManager span
            {
                padding-right:10px;
                margin-right:10px;
                border-right:solid 1px black;
            }
            .personalizationManager a
            {
                text-decoration:none;
            }
            .column
            {
                float:left;
                width:30%;
                height:200px;
                margin-right:10px;
                border:solid 1px black;
                background-color: white;
            }
            .menu
            {
                margin:5px 0px;
            }
            html
            {
                background-color:#eeeeee;
            }
        </style>
        <title>Anonymous Personalization</title>
```

LISTING 29.17 Continued

```
</head>
<body>
    <form id="form1" runat="server">
    <custom:AnonWebPartManager
        id="WebPartManager1"
        Runat="server" />

    <user:PersonalizationManager
        id="PersonalizationManager1"
        runat="server" />

        <asp:Menu
            id="Menu1"
            OnMenuItemClick="Menu1_MenuItemClick"
            Orientation="Horizontal"
            CssClass="menu"
            Runat="server">
            <Items>
            <asp:MenuItem Text="Browse" />
            <asp:MenuItem Text="Design" />
            </Items>
        </asp:Menu>

        <asp:WebPartZone
            id="WebPartZone1"
            CssClass="column"
            Runat="server">
            <ZoneTemplate>
            <user:TextPart
                id="TextPart1"
                Title="Text Part"
                Description="Displays block of text"
                Runat="server" />
            </ZoneTemplate>
        </asp:WebPartZone>

        <asp:WebPartZone
            id="WebPartZone2"
            CssClass="column"
            Runat="server" />
    </form>
</body>
</html>
```

29

After you open the page in Listing 29.17, you can update the text displayed by the TextPart Web Part (see Figure 29.8). If you close your browser and return to the website in two years, the same text will appear.

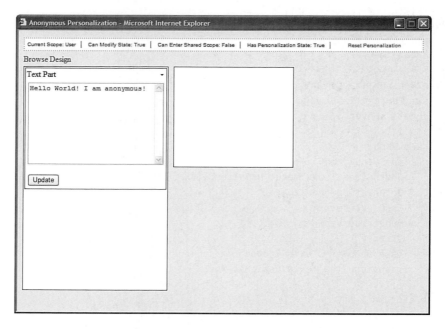

FIGURE 29.8   Using the Anonymous Personalization Provider.

If you want to simulate two anonymous users, then you need to open two different types of browsers (opening multiple instances of Internet Explorer doesn't work because they all share the same browser cookies). For example, you can open the Default.aspx page in both Internet Explorer and Mozilla Firefox and make different changes to the same page.

WARNING

There is one undesirable consequence of the way that the Anonymous Personalization Provider was implemented in this chapter. Anonymous users are added to the aspnet_Users database table without being marked as anonymous. To fix this problem you need to modify the following line in the aspnet_PersonalizationPerUser_SetPageSettings stored procedure:

EXEC dbo.aspnet_Users_CreateUser @ApplicationId, @UserName, 0,
➥@CurrentTimeUtc, @UserId OUTPUT

The 0 parameter hard codes all users as authenticated.

Summary

This chapter leapt into the details of Web Part personalization. First, you learned how to enable a user to make both User and Shared scoped personalization changes to a page. Next, you learned how to mark different properties of a Web Part as personalizable. You learned how to use the IPersonalizable interface for advanced personalization scenarios.

You also learned how to administer a Web Part application. In particular, you learned methods of pruning stale personalization data from a Web Part application. You also learned to generate a report of how much personalization data is being stored for each application user.

Finally, you studied the advanced topic of creating custom personalization providers. You learned how to create both a custom Query String Personalization Provider and a custom Anonymous Personalization Provider.

29

Summary

Extending the Web Part Framework

The standard parts included in the Web Part Framework are fine for building simple Web Part applications, but you'll quickly run into some of their limitations when your needs become more complex.

For example, the Web Part Framework includes the DeclarativeCatalogPart control, which you can use to add new Web Parts to a page. However, this control is quite limited. Because it does not support paging or sorting, you cannot use the DeclarativeCatalogPart control to display a catalog that contains more than a small number of Web Parts. It also does not support drag-and-drop functionality.

The PropertyGridEditorPart included with the framework enables you to edit custom Web Part properties easily. However, when you use this control, you cannot customize the appearance of the form displayed by the editor. In particular, the form generated by this control does not support validation.

Don't worry. The Web Part Framework can be extended easily. In this chapter, you learn how to create custom Web Part Zones, custom Catalog Zones, custom Editor Zones, and custom Display Modes. By the end of this chapter, you will be able to extend the Web Part Framework so it does just about anything you want.

Creating Custom Web Part Zones

The WebPartZone control is responsible for rendering all the Web Parts contained in a zone. Therefore, if you want to modify the appearance of a Web Part Zone, or modify the appearance of the Web Parts that appear in a Web Part Zone, then you need to create a custom Web Part Zone.

In this section, we create three custom Web Part Zones: a Photo Web Part Zone, a Multi-Column Web Part Zone, and a Menu Web Part Zone.

How Web Part Zones Work

Three types of parts included in the Web Part Framework are related to Web Part Zones: the WebPartZone, WebPartChrome, and WebPart controls.

The WebPartZone control is derived from the WebPartZoneBase class. This class includes one important MustOverride (abstract) method named GetInitialWebParts(). The GetInitialWebParts() method returns the Web Parts that the Web Part Zone initially displays before a user personalizes the zone.

For example, the standard WebPartZone control overrides the GetInitialWebParts() method and returns the collection of Web Parts contained in its ZoneTemplate. In other words, the WebPartZone control overrides the WebPartZoneBase control to support declaratively listing a set of initial Web Parts in a ZoneTemplate.

You can override the GetInitialWebParts() method and return any set of Web Parts that you please. For example, you could get the initial list of Web Parts from a database table, a Web service, or generate a random collection of Web Parts.

Before a Web Part Zone renders its Web Parts, the Web Part Zone creates an instance of the WebPartChrome class. The Web Part Chrome contains the standard elements which appear around each Web Part in a Web Part Zone. The default chrome includes the Web Part title bar and menu.

If you want to modify the Web Part Chrome, then you need to derive a new class from the base WebPartChrome class and associate your new chrome with a Web Part Zone. You can associate a custom WebPartChrome class with a Web Part Zone by overriding the WebPartZoneBase class's CreateWebPartChrome() method.

After the Web Part Zone gets an instance of the WebPartChrome class from its CreateWebPartChrome() method, the Web Part Zone uses the class to render each of its Web Parts. The WebPartChrome class includes a method named RenderWebPart(), which renders a particular Web Part that uses the chrome.

When all is said and done, you must interact with three classes to modify the appearance of a Web Part Zone. The WebPartZone control uses the WebPartChrome class to render individual WebPart controls.

Creating a Photo Web Part Zone

In this section, we create a custom Web Part Zone, which automatically displays a list of photos from a folder. Each photo is converted automatically into a Web Part so that you can re-arrange the photos on a page (see Figure 30.1).

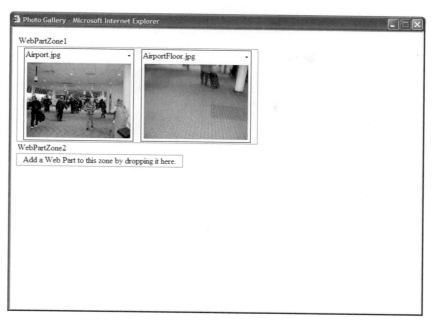

FIGURE 30.1   The Photo Web Part Zone.

To create a Photo Web Part Zone, you need to override the `GetInitialWebParts()` method. By default, this method retrieves a list of initial Web Parts from the ZoneTemplate contained in a Web Part Zone. In the modified version of this method, the list of Web Parts is obtained from a Photo folder.

The `PhotoWebPartZone` control is contained in Listing 30.1.

LISTING 30.1   PhotoWebPartZone.vb

```vb
Imports System
Imports System.IO
Imports System.Collections.Generic
Imports System.Web.UI.WebControls
Imports System.Web.UI.WebControls.WebParts

Namespace myControls

    Public Class PhotoWebPartZone
        Inherits WebPartZoneBase
        Dim _photoFolderUrl As String = "~/Photos"

        ''' <summary>
        ''' Represents the URL for the folder that
        ''' contains the photos.
        ''' </summary>
```

LISTING 30.1   Continued

```vbnet
        Public Property PhotoFolderUrl() As String
            Get
                Return _photoFolderUrl
            End Get
            Set(ByVal Value As String)
                _photoFolderUrl = Value
            End Set
        End Property

        ''' <summary>
        ''' Get the initial Web Parts from the Photo Folder
        ''' </summary>
        Protected Overrides Function GetInitialWebParts() As WebPartCollection
            ' Don't do anything when displayed in Designer
            If (Me.DesignMode) Then
                Return New WebPartCollection()
            End If

            ' Get the WebPartManager control
            Dim wpm As WebPartManager = WebPartManager.
➥GetCurrentWebPartManager(Page)

            ' Create a WebPart collection
            Dim photos As New List(Of WebPart)()

            ' Get the list of photos
            Dim photoDir As DirectoryInfo = New
➥DirectoryInfo(Page.MapPath(_photoFolderUrl))
            Dim files() As FileInfo = photoDir.GetFiles()
            Dim file As FileInfo
            For Each file In files
                Dim photo As Image = New Image()
                photo.ID = Path.GetFileNameWithoutExtension(file.Name)
                photo.ImageUrl = Path.Combine(_photoFolderUrl, file.Name)
                photo.Width = Unit.Pixel(200)
                photo.Attributes.Add("Title", file.Name)
                photo.AlternateText = file.Name + " Photo"
                photos.Add(wpm.CreateWebPart(photo))
            Next

            ' Return WebPartCollection
            Return New WebPartCollection(photos)
        End Function

    End Class
End Namespace
```

The bulk of the code in Listing 30.1 is contained in the GetInitialWebParts() method. This method grabs a list of all the files located in the Photo folder. Next, the method creates a new ASP.NET Image control for each of the photos. Each Image control is wrapped in a Generic Web Part with the help of the WebPartManager control's CreateWebPart() method. Finally, the collection of Web Parts is returned.

The page in Listing 30.2 includes the PhotoWebPartZone control.

LISTING 30.2   PhotoGallery.aspx

```
<%@ Page Language="VB" %>
<%@ Register TagPrefix="custom" Namespace="myControls" %>
<!DOCTYPE html PUBLIC "-//W3C//DTD XHTML 1.1//EN"
  "http://www.w3.org/TR/xhtml11/DTD/xhtml11.dtd">
<script runat="server">

    Sub Page_Load()
        WebPartManager1.DisplayMode = WebPartManager.DesignDisplayMode
    End Sub
</script>
<html xmlns="http://www.w3.org/1999/xhtml" >
<head id="Head1" runat="server">
    <title>Photo Gallery</title>
</head>
<body>
    <form id="form1" runat="server">
    <div>
    <asp:WebPartManager
        id="WebPartManager1"
        Runat="server" />

    <custom:PhotoWebPartZone
        id="WebPartZone1"
        PhotoFolderUrl="~/Photos"
        LayoutOrientation="Horizontal"
        runat="server" />

    <asp:WebPartZone
        id="WebPartZone2"
        LayoutOrientation="Horizontal"
        runat="server" />
    </div>
    </form>
</body>
</html>
```

The page in Listing 30.2 contains two Web Part Zones. The first Web Part Zone is the custom Photo Web Part Zone. The second zone is a standard Web Part Zone.

When you first open the page, all the photos contained in the Photos folder are displayed in the Photo Web Part Zone. Because the page is set to be in Design Display Mode by default in the Page_Load() method, you can rearrange the photos immediately after opening the page.

The GetInitialWebParts() method returns the list of Web Parts that a zone displays before the page has been personalized. You can re-arrange the photos in any way that you please and the Web Part Framework automatically saves your personalization data.

Notice that you can move photos between the custom Photo Web Part Zone and the standard Web Part Zone. If you close the page and return in the future, all the photos will retain their positions.

Creating a Multi-Column Web Part Zone

By default, a Web Part Zone displays the Web Parts that it contains in only one of two orientations: Horizontal or Vertical. You can select a particular orientation with the WebPartZone control's LayoutOrientation property.

However, there are situations in which you might want to display Web Parts with a more complicated layout. For example, in the previous section, we created a Photo Web Part Zone. It would be nice if we could display the photos in a certain number of repeating columns.

In this section, we build a Multi-Column Web Part Zone. This Web Part Zone includes a RepeatColumns property. When you declare the Web Part Zone, you can use this property to set the number of columns of Web Parts to display (see Figure 30.2).

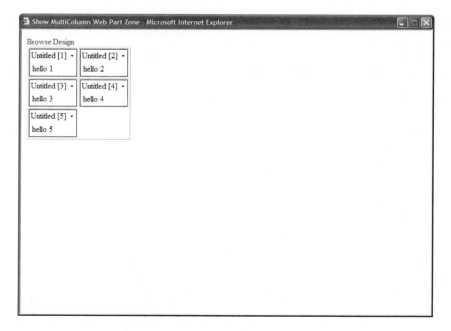

FIGURE 30.2   Displaying Web Parts in multiple columns.

To create this custom Web Part Zone, you need to override the default rendering behavior of the WebPartZone class. The WebPartZone class includes several methods related to rendering its content including:

- RenderContents()—Renders the entire contents of the Web Part Zone.
- RenderHeader()—Renders the header of the Web Part Zone.
- RenderBody()—Renders the body of the Web Part Zone.
- RenderDropCue()—Renders the drop cues that appear when you move Web Parts.
- RenderFooter()—Renders the footer of the Web Part Zone.

> **WEB STANDARDS NOTE**
>
> In an ideal world, Web Part Zones and Web Parts would not use HTML tables for layout. We would use Cascading Style Sheets for layout and use HTML tables only for their intended purpose: displaying tabular information. Unfortunately, we do not live in an ideal world. Microsoft is committed to supporting older browsers and older browsers do not provide good support for Cascading Style Sheets. So we're stuck with HTML tables.

To create a Multi-Column Web Part Zone, you need to override the RenderBody() method. The code for the MultiColumnWebPartZone control is contained in Listing 30.3.

LISTING 30.3   MultiColumnWebPartZone.vb

```vb
Imports System
Imports System.Web.UI
Imports System.Web.UI.WebControls.WebParts

Namespace myControls

    ''' <summary>
    ''' Displays Web Parts in multiple columns
    ''' </summary>
    Public Class MultiColumnWebPartZone
        Inherits WebPartZone

        Private _repeatColumns As Integer = 2

        ''' <summary>
        ''' The number of columns to display
        ''' </summary>
        Public Property RepeatColumns() As Integer
            Get
                Return _repeatColumns
            End Get
            Set(ByVal Value As Integer)
```

30

LISTING 30.3   Continued

```vb
                    _repeatColumns = Value
            End Set
        End Property


        ''' <summary>
        ''' Overrides default Web Part Zone rendering
        ''' in Browse Display Mode
        ''' </summary>
        Protected Overrides Sub RenderBody(ByVal writer As HtmlTextWriter)
            If Me.DesignMode Then
                MyBase.RenderBody(writer)
            ElseIf Me.WebPartManager.DisplayMode Is WebPartManager.
➥BrowseDisplayMode Then
                RenderMultiColumnBody(writer)
            Else
                MyBase.RenderBody(writer)
            End If
        End Sub


        ''' <summary>
        ''' Renders Web Parts in multiple columns by iterating
        ''' through the Web Parts collection
        ''' </summary>
        Private Sub RenderMultiColumnBody(ByVal writer As HtmlTextWriter)
            ' Create the Web Part Chrome
            Dim chrome As WebPartChrome = Me.CreateWebPartChrome()

            ' Create the opening Table Tag
            writer.AddAttribute("border", "1")
            writer.RenderBeginTag(HtmlTextWriterTag.Table)
            writer.RenderBeginTag(HtmlTextWriterTag.Tr)

            ' Render each Web Part
            Dim counter As Integer = 1
            Dim part As WebPart
            For Each part In Me.WebParts
                writer.RenderBeginTag(HtmlTextWriterTag.Td)
                chrome.RenderWebPart(writer, part)
                writer.RenderEndTag()

                ' Add a Tr when counter = RepeatColumns
                If counter = _repeatColumns Then
                    writer.RenderEndTag() ' Close Tr
                    writer.RenderBeginTag(HtmlTextWriterTag.Tr)
                    counter = 0
                End If
```

LISTING 30.3   Continued

```
                counter = counter + 1
          Next

            ' Close Table Tag
            writer.RenderEndTag()
            writer.RenderEndTag()
        End Sub
     End Class
End Namespace
```

The class contained in Listing 30.3 inherits from the base WebPartZone class. The MultiColumnWebPartZone control overrides the base class's RenderBody() method to render the zone's Web Parts in a multi-column table.

Notice that a multi-column table is rendered only when the page is in Browse Display mode. When the page is in any other display mode or the control is displayed in a designer, the base RenderBody() method is called and the Web Parts are rendered the normal way.

> **NOTE**
>
> It would be nice if the Web Parts could be rendered in a multi-column table in Design Mode as well as in Browse Mode. Unfortunately, the JavaScript that renders the drop cues for moving Web Parts assumes that a Web Part Zone is rendered either vertically or horizontally. To fix this problem, you would have to rewrite the JavaScript library used by the Web Part Framework.

The RenderMultiColumnBody() method performs all the work of rendering the multi-column table. First, the method grabs the Web Part Chrome that is used when rendering each Web Part. Each of the Web Parts contained in the zone are rendered by calling the RenderWebPart() method of the WebPartChrome class (otherwise, the Web Parts would appear without their title bars and menus).

The actual list of Web Parts that the zone renders is retrieved from the base WebPartZone control's WebParts property. Be aware that this property, unlike the GetInitialWebParts() method, returns the list of Web Parts that the Web Part Zone displays *after personalization.*

You can experiment with the MultiPartWebPartZone control with the page in Listing 30.4.

LISTING 30.4   ShowMultiColumnWebPartZone.aspx

```
<%@ Page Language="VB" %>
<%@ Register TagPrefix="custom" Namespace="myControls" Assembly="__code" %>
<!DOCTYPE html PUBLIC "-//W3C//DTD XHTML 1.1//EN"
   "http://www.w3.org/TR/xhtml11/DTD/xhtml11.dtd">
<script runat="server">
```

LISTING 30.4   Continued

```
    Protected Sub Menu1_MenuItemClick(ByVal sender As Object, ByVal e
➥As MenuEventArgs)
        WebPartManager1.DisplayMode = WebPartManager1.DisplayModes(e.Item.Text)
    End Sub

</script>
<html xmlns="http://www.w3.org/1999/xhtml" >
<head id="Head1" runat="server">
    <title>Show MultiColumn Web Part Zone</title>
</head>
<body>
    <form id="form1" runat="server">
    <asp:WebPartManager
        id="WebPartManager1"
        Runat="server" />

    <asp:Menu
        id="Menu1"
        OnMenuItemClick="Menu1_MenuItemClick"
        Orientation="Horizontal"
        CssClass="menu"
        Runat="server">
        <Items>
        <asp:MenuItem Text="Browse" />
        <asp:MenuItem Text="Design" />
        </Items>
    </asp:Menu>

    <custom:MultiColumnWebPartZone
        id="WebPartZone1"
        RepeatColumns="2"
        runat="server">
        <ZoneTemplate>
        <asp:Label
            id="Label1"
            Text="hello 1"
            runat="server" />
        <asp:Label
            id="Label2"
            Text="hello 2"
            runat="server" />
        <asp:Label
            id="Label3"
            Text="hello 3"
            runat="server" />
```

LISTING 30.4 Continued

```
            <asp:Label
                id="Label4"
                Text="hello 4"
                runat="server" />
            <asp:Label
                id="Label5"
                Text="hello 5"
                runat="server" />
        </ZoneTemplate>
    </custom:MultiColumnWebPartZone>

    </form>
</body>
</html>
```

The page in Listing 30.4 uses the `MultiColumnWebPartZone` control to render its one and only Web Part Zone. The `MultiColumnWebPartZone` control's `RepeatColumns` property is set to display a two-column table. When you open the page in your browser, you will see the page in Figure 30.2.

Creating a Menu Web Part Zone

By default, Web Part controls display very simple menus. You can use the `WebPartVerbRenderMode` property of the `WebPartZone` class to display one of two types of menus: a menu that appears in a single drop-down list or a menu that appears as a list of static links in the title bar.

In this section, we create fancier menus for Web Parts. We add the necessary functionality to the Web Part Framework to make it possible to create mulltiple drop-down menus for a single Web Part. We also add support for creating dividers between menu items (see Figure 30.3).

To create fancy menus, three of the standard classes in the Web Part Framework must be modified:

- `WebPartVerb`—This class represents a menu item. It needs to be extended to support nested menus and menu dividers.

- `WebPartChrome`—This class represents the chrome that is rendered around a Web Part. To create fancy menus, you have to completely override the default rendering behavior of this class.

- `WebPartZone`—This class represents the Web Part Zone which hosts a set of Web Parts. You need to modify this class so you can display a custom Web Part Chrome.

Let's start by modifying the `WebPartVerb` class. The modified version of this class, named `MenuWebPartVerb`, is contained in Listing 30.5.

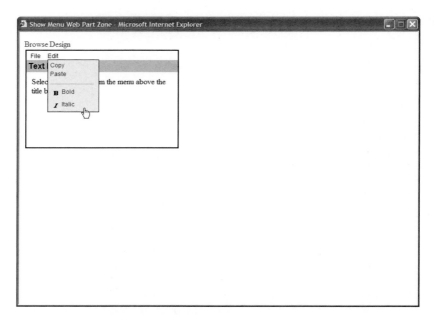

FIGURE 30.3   Displaying fancy Web Part menus.

LISTING 30.5   MenuWebPartVerb.vb

```vb
Imports System
Imports System.Web.UI.WebControls.WebParts

''' <summary>
''' Extends the base WebPartVerb class
''' with support for nested menus and menu
''' dividers.
''' </summary>
Public Class MenuWebPartVerb
    Inherits WebPartVerb

    Private _parentVerbId As String = String.Empty
    Private _hasDivider As Boolean = False

    ''' <summary>
    ''' Enables you to nest one menu beneath another
    ''' </summary>
    Public Property parentVerbId() As String
        Get
            Return _parentVerbId
        End Get
        Set(ByVal Value As String)
```

LISTING 30.5 Continued

```vb
                _parentVerbId = Value
            End Set
        End Property


        ''' <summary>
        ''' This property enables you to render a divider
        ''' above the menu item.
        ''' </summary>
        Public Property hasDivider() As Boolean
            Get
                Return _hasDivider
            End Get
            Set(ByVal Value As Boolean)
                _hasDivider = Value
            End Set
        End Property


        ''' <summary>
        ''' We need to call the base class constructors
        ''' in our derived class
        ''' </summary>
        Public Sub New(ByVal id As String, ByVal clientClickHandler As String)
            MyBase.New(id, clientClickHandler)
        End Sub


        Public Sub New(ByVal id As String, ByVal serverClickHandler
    ➥As WebPartEventHandler)
            MyBase.New(id, serverClickHandler)
        End Sub


        Public Sub New(ByVal id As String, ByVal serverClickHandler
    ➥As WebPartEventHandler, ByVal clientClickHandler As String)
            MyBase.New(id, serverClickHandler, clientClickHandler)
        End Sub
End Class
```

In Listing 30.5, the base WebPartVerb class is extended with two new properties: ParentId and HasDivider. The parentId property enables you to nest menu items. For example, all the menu items that appear beneath the File menu will have the ID of the File menu as their ParentId.

The HasDivider property enables you to display a menu divider above a menu item. When you set this property to the value True, an HTML <hr> tag is rendered above the current menu item.

30

The bulk of the code for the fancy menus is contained in Listing 30.6, which contains the custom Web Part Chrome that renders the fancy menus.

LISTING 30.6   MenuWebPartChrome.vb

```vb
Imports System
Imports System.Collections.Generic
Imports System.Web.UI
Imports System.Web.UI.WebControls.WebParts

Namespace myControls

    ''' <summary>
    ''' WebPartChrome, which includes multiple drop-down
    ''' menus and menu dividers
    ''' </summary>
    Public Class MenuWebPartChrome
        Inherits WebPartChrome

        ''' <summary>
        ''' Required Constructor
        ''' </summary>
        Public Sub New(ByVal zone As WebPartZone, ByVal manager As WebPartManager)
            MyBase.New(zone, manager)
        End Sub


        ''' <summary>
        ''' The main method for rendering a Web Part.
        ''' Here, we take over responsibility for rendering
        ''' the title and menu
        ''' </summary>
        Public Overrides Sub RenderWebPart(ByVal writer As HtmlTextWriter, _
➥ByVal webPart As WebPart)
            ' Render an enclosing Div
            writer.AddAttribute(HtmlTextWriterAttribute.Id, _
➥ Me.GetWebPartChromeClientID(webPart))
            writer.AddAttribute(HtmlTextWriterAttribute.Class, _
➥"menuWebPartZone_chrome")
            writer.RenderBeginTag(HtmlTextWriterTag.Div)

            ' Render the title bar
            RenderTitleBar(writer, webPart)

            ' Render the Web Part
            MyBase.RenderPartContents(writer, webPart)
```

LISTING 30.6 Continued

```
                ' Close the enclosing Div
                writer.RenderEndTag() ' Close main DIV
          End Sub


          ''' <summary>
          ''' Renders the title bar area of the chrome.
          ''' This is the part that a user can drag
          ''' </summary>
          Private Sub RenderTitleBar(ByVal writer As HtmlTextWriter,
➥ByVal webPart As WebPart)
                ' Render the menu
                RenderMenu(writer, webPart)

                ' Create a break
                writer.AddStyleAttribute("clear", "all")
                writer.RenderBeginTag(HtmlTextWriterTag.Br)

                ' Render the title bar
                writer.AddAttribute(HtmlTextWriterAttribute.Id,
➥Me.GetWebPartTitleClientID(webPart))
                writer.AddAttribute(HtmlTextWriterAttribute.Class,
➥ "menuWebPartZone_chromeTitle")
                writer.RenderBeginTag(HtmlTextWriterTag.Div)
                writer.Write(webPart.DisplayTitle)
                writer.RenderEndTag() ' Close title DIV
          End Sub


          ''' <summary>
          ''' Renders the menus (possibly nested)
          ''' </summary>
          Private Sub RenderMenu(ByVal writer As HtmlTextWriter,
➥ByVal webPart As WebPart)
                writer.AddStyleAttribute("display", "inline")
                writer.AddAttribute(HtmlTextWriterAttribute.Class,
➥"menuWebPartZone_menu")
                writer.RenderBeginTag(HtmlTextWriterTag.Ul)

                ' Get the top-level menu items that are not hidden
                Dim topLevelVerbs As WebPartVerbCollection =
➥GetChildVerbs(webPart.Verbs, String.Empty)
                For Each verb As MenuWebPartVerb In topLevelVerbs
                    writer.AddStyleAttribute("float", "left")
                    writer.AddAttribute("onmouseover",
➥"menuWebPartZone.showMenu(this)")
                    writer.RenderBeginTag(HtmlTextWriterTag.Li)
```

LISTING 30.6   Continued

```
            RenderMenuRecurse(writer, verb, webPart)
            writer.RenderEndTag()
        Next
        writer.RenderEndTag() ' Close Ul
    End Sub


    ''' <summary>
    ''' The main method for rendering the subMenus.
    ''' This method is called recursively so you
    ''' can show infinitely nested menus.
    ''' </summary>
    Private Sub RenderMenuRecurse(ByVal writer As HtmlTextWriter,
➥ByVal verb As MenuWebPartVerb, ByVal webPart As WebPart)
        Dim childVerbs As WebPartVerbCollection =
➥GetChildVerbs(WebPart.Verbs, verb.ID)
        If (childVerbs.Count > 0) Then
            ' Renders a menu item that is not a link
            RenderHeaderMenuItem(writer, verb)

            writer.AddAttribute(HtmlTextWriterAttribute.Class,
➥ "menuWebPartZone_popupMenu")
            writer.AddStyleAttribute("position", "absolute")
            writer.AddStyleAttribute(HtmlTextWriterStyle.Display, "none")
            writer.RenderBeginTag(HtmlTextWriterTag.Ul)

            For Each childVerb As MenuWebPartVerb In childVerbs
                writer.AddAttribute("onmouseover",
➥"menuWebPartZone.showMenu(this)")
                writer.RenderBeginTag(HtmlTextWriterTag.Li)
                RenderMenuRecurse(writer, childVerb, webPart)
                writer.RenderEndTag()
            Next
            writer.RenderEndTag() ' Close UL
        Else
            ' Renders a link menu item
            RenderLinkMenuItem(writer, verb, webPart)
        End If
    End Sub


    ''' <summary>
    ''' Renders a menu item that is not a link.
    ''' When a user clicks this menu item, it
    ''' expands sub-menu items.
    ''' </summary>
    Private Sub RenderHeaderMenuItem(ByVal writer As HtmlTextWriter,
➥ByVal verb As MenuWebPartVerb)
```

LISTING 30.6   Continued

```
                ' Render divider
                RenderMenuDivider(writer, verb)

                ' Render encloding Div
                writer.AddAttribute(HtmlTextWriterAttribute.Class,
➥ "menuWebPartZone_menuItem")
                writer.RenderBeginTag(HtmlTextWriterTag.Div)

                ' Render verb icon
                RenderMenuIcon(writer, verb)

                ' Render the verb text
                writer.Write(verb.Text)

                writer.RenderEndTag() ' Close Div
        End Sub

        ''' <summary>
        ''' Renders a menu item that causes a postback.
        ''' </summary>
        Private Sub RenderLinkMenuItem(ByVal writer As HtmlTextWriter,
➥ByVal verb As MenuWebPartVerb, ByVal webPart As WebPart)
                ' Render divider
                RenderMenuDivider(writer, verb)

                ' Render Enclosing Div
                writer.AddAttribute(HtmlTextWriterAttribute.Class,
➥"menuWebPartZone_menuItem")
                writer.RenderBeginTag(HtmlTextWriterTag.Div)

                ' Render verb icon
                RenderMenuIcon(writer, verb)

                ' Render the verb link
                Dim eventArg As String = String.Format("partverb:{0}:{1}",
➥verb.ID, WebPart.ID)
                Dim eventRef As String =
➥Me.Zone.Page.ClientScript.GetPostBackClientHyperlink(Me.Zone, eventArg)
                writer.AddAttribute(HtmlTextWriterAttribute.Href, eventRef)
                writer.RenderBeginTag(HtmlTextWriterTag.A)
                writer.Write(verb.Text)
                writer.RenderEndTag()

                writer.RenderEndTag() ' Close Div
        End Sub

        ''' <summary>
```

30

LISTING 30.6   Continued

```
''' If a menu item has an icon then show it.
''' </summary>
''' <remarks>
''' Notice that we set empty ALT text for
''' accessibility reasons.
''' </remarks>
Private Sub RenderMenuIcon(ByVal writer As HtmlTextWriter, ByVal verb
➡As WebPartVerb)
    If verb.ImageUrl <> String.Empty Then
        writer.AddAttribute(HtmlTextWriterAttribute.Src,
➡Me.Zone.Page.ResolveUrl(verb.ImageUrl))
        writer.AddAttribute(HtmlTextWriterAttribute.Alt, String.Empty)
        writer.AddAttribute(HtmlTextWriterAttribute.Align, "middle")
        writer.RenderBeginTag(HtmlTextWriterTag.Img)
        writer.RenderEndTag()
    End If
End Sub


''' <summary>
''' If a menu should display a divider above it,
''' then show it with an hr tag.
''' </summary>
Private Sub RenderMenuDivider(ByVal writer As HtmlTextWriter, ByVal verb
➡As MenuWebPartVerb)
    If verb.hasDivider Then
        writer.RenderBeginTag(HtmlTextWriterTag.Hr)
        writer.RenderEndTag()
    End If
End Sub


''' <summary>
''' Returns all the verbs that have a certain
''' parent verb
''' </summary>
Private Function GetChildVerbs(ByVal verbs As WebPartVerbCollection,
➡ByVal parentId As String) As WebPartVerbCollection
    Dim children As New List(Of WebPartVerb)()
    For Each verb As MenuWebPartVerb In verbs
        If verb.parentVerbId = parentId Then
            children.Add(verb)
        End If
    Next
    Return New WebPartVerbCollection(children)
End Function

End Class
End Namespace
```

The WebPartChrome class is responsible for rendering the outer chrome displayed around each Web Part in a Web Part Zone. This outer chrome includes the title bar and menu rendered for each Web Part.

In Listing 30.6, we override the RenderWebPart() method. When you override this method, you must take complete responsibility for rendering the entire contents of the Web Part Chrome.

The RenderWebPart() method does two things. First, it renders the chrome's title bar. The title bar contains the area that a user selects when dragging a Web Part from one zone to another when a page is in Design Display mode. The custom Web Part Chrome gets this functionality for free because the base WebPartChrome class's GetWebPartTitleClientID() is used to render the right ID for the title bar. The JavaScript library used by the Web Part Framework automatically detects this ID and enables drag-and-drop support.

WEB STANDARDS NOTE

The default WebPartChrome class renders an HTML table to create the chrome around a Web Part. In the custom MenuWebPartChrome class, we use a <div> tag instead. This choice makes sense from a standards perspective and requires less code. Unfortunately, using a div element instead of a table element breaks all the default formatting properties included with the WebPartZone control. If you want to format the custom MenuWebPartChrome class, you need to use Cascading Style Sheets.

Next, in the RenderWebPart() method, the Web Part contained within the Web Part Chrome is rendered. The Web Part is rendered with the help of the base WebPartChrome class's RenderPartContents() method.

The bulk of the code in Listing 30.6 is devoted to rendering the fancy menus. The RenderTitleBar() method calls the RenderMenu() method to build the custom menu.

The fancy menus are created with a set of nested unordered lists (HTML <ul> tags). The second-level menus are hidden by default with the display:none Cascading Style Sheet rule. A client-side onmouseover event handler is added to each list item so that a submenu is displayed when you hover your mouse over a list item.

The links rendered in the menu require additional explanation. The menu links are rendered by the RenderLinkMenuItem() method. When you click a menu item link, the server-side method that corresponds to the menu item is executed by the Web Part.

The GetPostBackClientHyperlink() method is called to retrieve the necessary JavaScript for invoking the server-side menu event. This method returns a string that contains JavaScript code for posting an argument back to the server. The argument must be in a special format to invoke the correct server-side menu click handler in the Web Part.

The argument passed back to the server must have three parts, separated by colons:

- partverb—This string indicates that a Web Part verb has been clicked.
- Verb ID—The ID of the Web Part verb that a user clicked.

- Web Part ID—The ID of the Web Part that contains the server-side method to execute.

By following this special format, you can leverage the existing Web Part Framework support for firing off the correct server-side method when you click a particular menu item.

To use a custom Web Part Chrome, you need to create a custom Web Part Zone. The MenuWebPartZone is contained in Listing 30.7.

LISTING 30.7   MenuWebPartZone.vb

```
Imports System
Imports System.Web.UI.WebControls.WebParts

Namespace myControls

    ''' <summary>
    ''' Web Part Zone that displays fancy nested menus
    ''' </summary>
    Public Class MenuWebPartZone
        Inherits WebPartZone
        ''' <summary>
        ''' Register the client-script for the menus.
        ''' </summary>
        Protected Overrides Sub OnPreRender(ByVal e As EventArgs)
            If Not Page.ClientScript.IsClientScriptIncludeRegistered(
➥"MenuWebPartZone") Then
                Page.ClientScript.RegisterClientScriptInclude(
➥"MenuWebPartZone", Page.ResolveUrl("~/ClientScripts/MenuWebPartZone.js"))
            End If
            MyBase.OnPreRender(e)
        End Sub

        ''' <summary>
        ''' Create special Web Part chrome that contains the menus
        ''' </summary>
        Protected Overrides Function CreateWebPartChrome() As WebPartChrome
            Return New MenuWebPartChrome(Me, Me.WebPartManager)
        End Function

    End Class
End Namespace
```

The custom Menu Web Part Zone overrides two methods of the base WebPartZone class.

First, it overrides the CreateWebPartChrome() method to substitute the custom Web Part Chrome. In this method, what's returned is simply an instance of the MenuWebPartChrome class.

Second, the `OnPreRender()` method is overridden so that you can include a link to a JavaScript library, named `MenuWebPartZone.js`, which contains the client-side code for the fancy menus. The `MenuWebPartZone.js` library is contained in Listing 30.8.

LISTING 30.8 MenuWebPartZone.js

```
var menuWebPartZone = new function()
    {
        this.showMenu = menuWebPartZone_showMenu;
    }


function menuWebPartZone_showMenu(el)
{
    // Get ul elements
    var subMenus = el.getElementsByTagName('UL');

    // If there are ul elements, show the first one
    if (subMenus.length > 0)
    {
        subMenus[0].style.display = '';

        // Set up function to hide ul element again
        el.onmouseout = function(e)
            {
                subMenus[0].style.display = 'none';
            }
    }
}
```

When you hover your mouse over a menu item, the `menuWebPartZone_showMenu()` method is called. This JavaScript method finds the first HTML `<ul>` tag contained under the current list item and displays it. Next, the method adds a `onmouseout` handler to hide the submenu when the user moves the mouse away from the menu item.

WEB STANDARDS NOTE

The JavaScript menu library works well in the case of Internet Explorer 6 and Opera 8. Unfortunately, it doesn't work so well with Firefox 1. Firefox does not reliably fire the `onmouseout` handler, so open menus tend to get stuck.

We are finally in a position to try out the fancy menus. First, a new Web Part needs to be created that takes advantage of them. The `TextEditorPart` in Listing 30.9 displays both a File and Edit menu.

LISTING 30.9   TextEditorPart.ascx

```
<%@ Control Language="VB" ClassName="TextEditorPart" %>
<%@ Implements Interface="System.Web.UI.WebControls.WebParts.IWebActionable" %>
<%@ Import Namespace="System.Collections.Generic" %>

<script runat="server">

    ''' <summary>
    ''' Create the menu
    ''' </summary>
    Public ReadOnly Property Verbs() As WebPartVerbCollection
➡Implements IWebActionable.Verbs
        Get
            Dim myVerbs As New List(Of WebPartVerb)()

            ' Create File menu
            Dim fileVerb As New MenuWebPartVerb("file", AddressOf doMenuAction)
            fileVerb.Text = "File"
            myVerbs.Add(fileVerb)

            Dim NewVerb As New MenuWebPartVerb("new", AddressOf doMenuAction)
            NewVerb.Text = "New"
            NewVerb.parentVerbId = fileVerb.ID
            myVerbs.Add(NewVerb)

            ' Create Edit menu
            Dim editVerb As New MenuWebPartVerb("edit", AddressOf doMenuAction)
            editVerb.Text = "Edit"
            myVerbs.Add(editVerb)

            Dim copyVerb As New MenuWebPartVerb("copy", AddressOf doMenuAction)
            copyVerb.Text = "Copy"
            copyVerb.parentVerbId = editVerb.ID
            myVerbs.Add(copyVerb)

            Dim pasteVerb As New MenuWebPartVerb("pasted", AddressOf doMenuAction)
            pasteVerb.Text = "Paste"
            pasteVerb.parentVerbId = editVerb.ID
            myVerbs.Add(pasteVerb)

            Dim boldVerb As New MenuWebPartVerb("bold", AddressOf doMenuAction)
            boldVerb.Text = "Bold"
            boldVerb.ImageUrl = "~/Icons/Bold.gif"
            boldVerb.hasDivider = True
            boldVerb.parentVerbId = editVerb.ID
            myVerbs.Add(boldVerb)
```

LISTING 30.9   Continued

```
        Dim italicVerb As New MenuWebPartVerb("italic", AddressOf doMenuAction)
        italicVerb.Text = "Italic"
        italicVerb.ImageUrl = "~/Icons/Italic.gif"
        italicVerb.parentVerbId = editVerb.ID
        myVerbs.Add(italicVerb)


        ' Return the menu
        Return New WebPartVerbCollection(myVerbs)
    End Get
End Property


''' <summary>
''' The server-side method that is invoked when you
''' click a menu item
''' </summary>
Public Sub doMenuAction(ByVal s As Object, ByVal e As WebPartEventArgs)
    Dim verb As MenuWebPartVerb = CType(s, MenuWebPartVerb)
    lblAction.Text = String.Format("{0} clicked!", verb.Text)
End Sub

</script>

<div style="padding:10px">

Select a menu item from the menu above the title bar.
<br />
<asp:Label
    id="lblAction"
    EnableViewState="false"
    Runat="server" />
</div>
```

The menu is created by the TextEditorPart control's Verbs property. This property is a member of the IWebActionable interface (notice that the user control implements this interface with the directive at the top of the file).

All the menu items are wired to the same server-side method. If you click any of the menu items, the doMenuAction() method executes and reports the ID of the menu item clicked. You could, of course, wire each menu item to a different server-side method.

You can use the TextEditorPart in the page in Listing 30.10.

LISTING 30.10   ShowMenuWebPartZone.aspx

```
<%@ Page Language="VB" %>
<%@ Register TagPrefix="custom" Namespace="myControls" Assembly="__code" %>
<%@ Register TagPrefix="user" TagName="TextEditorPart"
  Src="~/TextEditorPart.ascx" %>
<!DOCTYPE html PUBLIC "-//W3C//DTD XHTML 1.1//EN"
    "http://www.w3.org/TR/xhtml11/DTD/xhtml11.dtd">
<script runat="server">

    Protected Sub Menu1_MenuItemClick(ByVal sender As Object, ByVal e
➥As MenuEventArgs)
        WebPartManager1.DisplayMode = WebPartManager1.DisplayModes(e.Item.Text)
    End Sub

</script>
<html xmlns="http://www.w3.org/1999/xhtml" >
<head id="Head1" runat="server">
    <title>Show Menu Web Part Zone</title>
    <style type="text/css">
        .menuWebPartZone_chrome
        {
            border:solid 2px black;
            width:300px;
            height:200px;
        }
        .menuWebPartZone_chromeTitle
        {
            background-color:silver;
            padding:3px;
            font:bold 16px Arial,sans-serif;
        }
        .menuWebPartZone_menuItem
        {
            cursor:hand;
        }

        .menuWebPartZone_menu
        {
            font:12px Arial, sans-serif;
        }

        .menuWebPartZone_menu li
        {
            margin-left:4px;
            margin-right:10px;
            margin-top:3px;
```

LISTING 30.10   Continued

```
                list-style-type:none;
        }

        .menuWebPartZone_menu ul
        {
            padding:0px;
            margin:0px;
            background-color:#eeeeee;
            border:solid 1px black;
            width:100px;
        }

        .menuWebPartZone_menu a
        {
            color:blue;
            text-decoration:none;
        }

    </style>

</head>
<body>
    <form id="form1" runat="server">
    <asp:WebPartManager
        id="WebPartManager1"
        runat="server" />

    <asp:Menu
        id="Menu1"
        OnMenuItemClick="Menu1_MenuItemClick"
        Orientation="Horizontal"
        CssClass="menu"
        Runat="server">
        <Items>
        <asp:MenuItem Text="Browse" />
        <asp:MenuItem Text="Design" />
        </Items>
    </asp:Menu>

    <custom:MenuWebPartZone
        id="WebPartZone1"
        Runat="server">
        <ZoneTemplate>
        <user:TextEditorPart
            id="TextEditorPart1"
```

LISTING 30.10   Continued

```
            Title="Text Editor Part"
            Description="Enables you to edit text"
            runat="server" />
        </ZoneTemplate>
    </custom:MenuWebPartZone>

    <custom:MenuWebPartZone
        id="WebPartZone2"
        Runat="server" />

    </form>
</body>
</html>
```

After you open the page in Listing 30.10 in your Web browser, you can hover your mouse over the File and Edit menu items displayed by the TextEditorWebPart and see the sub-menus. If you select a menu option, the page posts back to the server and executes the doMenuAction() method. This method simply reports the name of the menu item clicked in a Label control.

Notice that the ShowMenuWebPartZone.aspx page contains several style sheet rules. These rules are used to define the background color, size, and general appearance of the menus. The page also includes style sheet rules that determine several aspects of the appearance of the Web Part Chrome, such as the style of the chrome's title bar and border.

Creating Custom Catalog Zones

As previously mentioned, the default functionality of a Web Part Catalog is pretty limited. By default, Web Part Catalogs do not support paging or sorting. You also cannot drag and drop new Web Parts from a catalog into a Web Part Zone.

This section explores several methods of creating fancier catalogs. We'll create a catalog that automatically displays all the Web Parts available in the current application, a catalog that supports drag-and-drop, and a catalog that supports templates.

How Catalog Zones Work

Three types of parts in the Web Part Framework are related to catalogs: the CatalogZone class, the CatalogPartChrome class, and the CatalogPart class. All three parts participate in the rendering of a catalog. The CatalogZone class creates an instance of the CatalogPartChrome class, and the CatalogPartChrome class renders each CatalogPart control contained in the Catalog Zone.

It is important to understand that individual CatalogPart controls, such as the DeclarativeCatalogPart or PageCatalogPart control, don't render anything. They merely act as databases of available catalog items.

The `CatalogPart` class has two important methods:

- `GetAvailableWebPartDescriptions`—Returns the list of descriptions of Web Parts contained in the catalog.

- `GetWebPart`—Returns an actual Web Part.

For example, the `DeclarativeCatalogPart` control derives from the CatalogPart class. This control overrides the `GetAvailableWebPartDescriptions()` method and returns the list of catalog parts that have been listed in its template. The `DeclarativeCatalogPart` also overrides the `GetWebPart()` method to return one of the Web Parts declared in its template.

The individual Catalog Part controls contained in a Catalog Zone do not render anything. The `CatalogZone` control creates an instance of the `CatalogPartChrome` control and uses this instance to render each of the `CatalogPart` controls.

The `CatalogPartChrome` control has four important methods:

- `CreateCatalogPartChromeStyle()`—If you override this method, you can modify the properties of the `Style` object used when rendering the chrome and catalog part.

- `PerformPreRender()`—If you override this method, you can execute code before a `CatalogPart` control is rendered.

- `RenderCatalogPart()`—If you override this method, then you modify the entire rendering behavior of the chrome.

- `RenderPartContents()`—If you override this method, then you can render additional content inside the chrome.

The `CatalogZone` class creates an instance of the `CatalogPartChrome` class and calls its `RenderCatalogPart()` method to render the selected `CatalogPart` control. The `CatalogZone` control itself includes several valuable methods:

- `CreateCatalogParts()`—Returns the list of catalog parts that the Catalog Zone displays.

- `InvalidateCatalogParts()`—Resets the collection of catalog parts associated with the Catalog Zone.

- `RenderContents()`—Renders the entire Catalog Zone.

- `RenderHeader()`—Renders the header area of a catalog zone.

- `RenderBody()`—Renders the body area of a catalog zone.

- `RenderFooter()`—Renders the footer area of a catalog zone.

- `RenderCatalogPartLinks()`—Renders the list of links to the particular Catalog Parts contained in the Catalog Zone.

- `RenderVerbs()`—Renders the verbs that appear at the bottom of a catalog zone.

30

The `CatalogZoneBase` class also includes the following properties:

- `CatalogParts`—This property automatically calls the `CreateCatalogParts()` method to create a list of catalog parts.

- `SelectedCatalogPartID`—This property enables you to get or set the current Catalog Part.

If you want to modify the appearance of any Catalog Part, then you must modify the rendering behavior of the Catalog Zone or Catalog Part Chrome that contains the Catalog Part.

Creating a Reflection Catalog Part

Let's start by creating a new Catalog Part that automatically lists all the Web Part controls contained in the App_Code folder. Because the custom Catalog Part will take advantage of reflection to determine the list of available Web Parts, we'll name this custom Catalog Part the Reflect Catalog Part.

> **NOTE**
>
> Reflection refers to the process of retrieving information about .NET Framework types—such as classes, methods, properties, and attributes—at runtime. Two namespaces in the .NET Framework are devoted to reflection: `System.Reflection` and `System.Reflection.Emit`.

The ReflectCatalogPart control is contained in Listing 30.11.

LISTING 30.11   ReflectCatalogPart.cs

```
Imports System
Imports System.Reflection
Imports System.Collections.Generic
Imports System.Web.UI.WebControls.WebParts

Namespace myControls

    ''' <summary>
    ''' Catalog Part that automatically displays all
    ''' Web Parts defined in the App_Code folder
    ''' </summary>
    Public Class ReflectCatalogPart
        Inherits CatalogPart

        Private _catalog As New Dictionary(Of String, WebPart)

        ''' <summary>
        ''' We create the list of available Web Parts
        ''' during the Init event since we use this list
```

LISTING 30.11   Continued

```
''' with both the GetAvailableWebPartDescriptions()
''' and GetWebPart() methods
''' </summary>
Protected Overrides Sub OnInit(ByVal e As EventArgs)
    ' Get the list of Web Parts through reflection
    Dim moduleArray As Reflection.Module() =
➥Assembly.GetExecutingAssembly().GetModules(False)
    Dim webPartTypes As Type() = moduleArray(0).
➥FindTypes(AddressOf WebPartFilter, Nothing)

    ' Create and instance of each Web Part and add to catalog
    For i As Integer = 0 To webPartTypes.Length - 1
        Dim newPart As WebPart = CType(Activator.CreateInstance(
➥webPartTypes(i)), WebPart)
        newPart.ID = "part" + i.ToString()
        _catalog.Add(newPart.ID, newPart)
    Next
    MyBase.OnInit(e)
End Sub


''' <summary>
''' Returns a collection of descriptions of Web Parts
''' in the App_Code folder
''' </summary>
Public Overrides Function GetAvailableWebPartDescriptions()
➥As WebPartDescriptionCollection
    Dim descriptions As New List(Of WebPartDescription)()
    For Each NewPart As WebPart In _catalog.Values
        descriptions.Add(New WebPartDescription(NewPart))
    Next
    Return New WebPartDescriptionCollection(descriptions)
End Function


''' <summary>
''' Because you already instantiated all the Web Parts
''' in the OnInit() method, you simply return a
''' Web Part from the catalog collection
''' </summary>
Public Overrides Function GetWebPart(ByVal description
➥As WebPartDescription) As WebPart
    Return _catalog(description.ID)
End Function


''' <summary>
''' You don't want a list of all classes in the App_Code folder,
''' only those classes that derive from the WebPart class
```

30

LISTING 30.11   Continued

```
    ''' </summary>
    Private Function WebPartFilter(ByVal t As Type, ByVal s As Object)
➥As Boolean
        Return GetType(WebPart).IsAssignableFrom(t)
    End Function


    End Class
End Namespace
```

The list of Web Parts defined in the App_Code folder is retrieved in the `OnInit()` method. The current module is retrieved by grabbing the first module in the currently executing assembly. Next, the `FindTypes()` method is called with a filter that returns only classes derived from the Web Part class (the filter used by `FindTypes()` is created with the `WebPartFilter()` method).

The `GetAvailableWebPartDescriptions()` method returns a collection of `WebPartDescription` classes. The Catalog Zone calls this method to get the list of Web Parts that it displays. In our implementation of this method, we simply copy the list of Web Parts that we retrieved in the `OnInit()` method into a `WebPartDescriptionCollection` class.

Finally, the `GetWebPart()` method returns a Web Part that matches a description. This method is called by the Catalog Zone when a Web Part is added to a Web Part Zone. Again, we take advantage of the collection built in the `OnInit()` method to return a Web Part that matches the description parameter.

You can use the custom `ReflectCatalogPart` in the page in Listing 30.12. You'll need to switch to Catalog Display Mode by clicking the Catalog link to see the Reflect Catalog Part.

LISTING 30.12   ShowReflectCatalogPart.aspx

```
<%@ Page Language="VB" %>
<%@ Register TagPrefix="custom" Namespace="myControls" %>
<!DOCTYPE html PUBLIC "-//W3C//DTD XHTML 1.1//EN"
    "http://www.w3.org/TR/xhtml11/DTD/xhtml11.dtd">
<script runat="server">

    Protected Sub Menu1_MenuItemClick(ByVal sender As Object, ByVal e
➥As MenuEventArgs)
        WebPartManager1.DisplayMode = WebPartManager1.DisplayModes(e.Item.Text)
    End Sub

</script>
<html xmlns="http://www.w3.org/1999/xhtml" >
<head id="Head1" runat="server">
    <style type="text/css">
```

LISTING 30.12   Continued

```
        .column
        {
            float:left;
            width:30%;
            height:200px;
            margin-right:10px;
            border:solid 1px black;
            background-color: white;
        }
        .menu
        {
            margin:5px 0px;
        }
        html
        {
            background-color:#eeeeee;
        }
    </style>
    <title>Show Reflect Catalog Part</title>
</head>
<body>
    <form id="form1" runat="server">
    <asp:WebPartManager
        id="WebPartManager1"
        Runat="server" />

        <asp:Menu
            id="Menu1"
            OnMenuItemClick="Menu1_MenuItemClick"
            Orientation="Horizontal"
            CssClass="menu"
            Runat="server">
            <Items>
            <asp:MenuItem Text="Browse" />
            <asp:MenuItem Text="Design" />
            <asp:MenuItem Text="Catalog" />
            </Items>
        </asp:Menu>

        <asp:WebPartZone
            id="WebPartZone1"
            CssClass="column"
            Runat="server" />

        <asp:WebPartZone
            id="WebPartZone2"
```

LISTING 30.12   Continued

```
            CssClass="column"
            Runat="server" />

        <asp:CatalogZone
            id="CatalogZone1"
            CssClass="column"
            Runat="server">
            <ZoneTemplate>
                <custom:ReflectCatalogPart
                    id="ReflectCatalogPart1"
                    Runat="server" />
            </ZoneTemplate>
        </asp:CatalogZone>

    </form>
</body>
</html>
```

When you open the page in Listing 30.12 and click the Catalog link, you'll see all of the Web Parts defined in your App_Code folder listed (see Figure 30.4). The Reflect Catalog Part doesn't display anything unless you add some Web Parts to your App_Code folder. In particular, the control doesn't show Web Parts that you have created with User Controls because these Web Parts are contained in a different assembly.

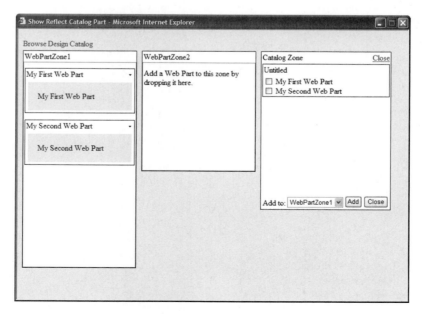

FIGURE 30.4   Automatically displaying available Web Parts.

Creating a Drag-and-Drop Catalog Zone

Although the Web Part Framework supports drag-and-drop functionality when you move Web Parts between Web Part Zones, the Web Part Framework does not support drag-and-drop when you want to add new Web Parts to a Web Part Zone from a Catalog Zone. In this section, we'll fix this limitation of the Web Part Framework by creating a custom DragDropCatalogZone control.

To create the custom Catalog Zone, you won't have to do as much work as you might expect. You can leverage the existing JavaScript library included with the Web Part Framework. We'll tweak this library so it will work the same way with Catalog Zones as it works with Web Part Zones.

First, we need to create a custom Catalog Zone. Listing 30.13 contains the code for the custom DragDropCatalogZone class.

LISTING 30.13   DragDropCatalogZone.vb

```
Imports System
Imports System.Web.UI
Imports System.Web.UI.WebControls.WebParts

Namespace myControls

    ''' <summary>
    ''' CatalogZone that supports drag-and-drop
    ''' adding of Web Parts
    ''' </summary>
    Public Class DragDropCatalogZone
        Inherits CatalogZone

        ''' <summary>
        ''' Adds the client-side script for drag-and-drop
        ''' </summary>
        Protected Overrides Sub OnPreRender(ByVal e As EventArgs)
            EnsureID()
            Dim startupScript As String = String.Format(
➥"dragDropCatalogZone.start('{0}');", Me.ClientID)

            If Not Page.ClientScript.IsClientScriptIncludeRegistered(
➥"DragDropCatalogZone") Then
                Page.ClientScript.RegisterClientScriptInclude(
➥"DragDropCatalogZone", Page.ResolveUrl("~/ClientScripts/
➥DragDropCatalogZone.js"))
                Page.ClientScript.RegisterStartupScript(
➥GetType(DragDropCatalogZone), "DragDropCatalogZone", startupScript, True)
            End If
            MyBase.OnPreRender(e)
        End Sub
```

LISTING 30.13   Continued

```vb
''' <summary>
''' Utility method to return currently
''' selected Catalog Part
''' </summary>
Public ReadOnly Property SelectedCatalogPart() As CatalogPart
    Get
        Return Me.CatalogParts(Me.SelectedCatalogPartID)
    End Get
End Property

''' <summary>
''' Override the default postback handler to
''' add support for adding a Web Part to a
''' Web Part Zone
''' </summary>
Protected Overrides Sub RaisePostBackEvent(ByVal eventArgument As String)
    If eventArgument.StartsWith("Add:") Then
        Dim args() As String = eventArgument.Split(":"c)
        AddWebPart(args(1), args(2), Int32.Parse(args(3)))
    End If
    MyBase.RaisePostBackEvent(eventArgument)
End Sub

''' <summary>
''' Use the WebPartManager control to
''' actually add the Web Part
''' </summary>
Private Sub AddWebPart(ByVal webPartId As String, ByVal zoneId As String,
➥ByVal zoneIndex As Integer)
    ' Get Web Part
    Dim desc As WebPartDescription =
➥SelectedCatalogPart.GetAvailableWebPartDescriptions()(webPartId)
    Dim webPart As WebPart = SelectedCatalogPart.GetWebPart(desc)

    ' Get Zone
    Dim zone As WebPartZoneBase = Me.WebPartManager.Zones(zoneId)

    ' Add Web Part
    Me.WebPartManager.AddWebPart(webPart, zone, zoneIndex)
End Sub

''' <summary>
''' This Web Part Zone uses the specialized
''' DragDropWebPartChrome
''' </summary>
```

LISTING 30.13   Continued

```
        Protected Overrides Function CreateCatalogPartChrome()
➥As CatalogPartChrome
            Return New DragDropCatalogPartChrome(Me)
        End Function
    End Class


    ''' <summary>
    ''' This class extends the base CatalogPartChrome
    ''' class by adding a div element to mark the
    ''' area of draggable images.
    ''' </summary>
    Public Class DragDropCatalogPartChrome
        Inherits CatalogPartChrome

        ''' <summary>
        ''' Add the DIV tag
        ''' </summary>
        Public Overrides Sub RenderCatalogPart(ByVal writer As HtmlTextWriter,
➥ByVal catalogPart As CatalogPart)
            writer.AddAttribute(HtmlTextWriterAttribute.Id, GenerateId())
            writer.RenderBeginTag(HtmlTextWriterTag.Div)
            MyBase.RenderCatalogPart(writer, catalogPart)
            writer.RenderEndTag()
        End Sub

        ''' <summary>
        ''' Create a unique ID for the DIV tag
        ''' so we can grab the DIV tag in our
        ''' client script
        ''' </summary>
        Private Function GenerateId() As String
            Return String.Format("{0}_draggable", Me.Zone.ID)
        End Function

        Public Sub New(ByVal zone As CatalogZoneBase)
            MyBase.New(zone)
        End Sub
    End Class

End Namespace
```

The custom Catalog Zone does three things. First, the OnPreRender() method adds a reference to an external JavaScript file named DragDropCatalogZone.js. This file contains the JavaScript code used to support the client-side drag-and-drop functionality. This file is discussed in a moment.

The custom Catalog Zone also overrides the base `CatalogZone` control's
`RaisePostBackEvent()` method. This method is called after a user drops a catalog item
into a Web Part Zone. The method adds the new Web Part to the zone with the help of
the `WebPartManager` control's `AddWebPart()` method.

Finally, the custom Catalog Zone overrides the base `CreateCatalogPartChrome()` method.
Notice that the file in Listing 30.13 actually defines two classes: `DragDropCatalogZone` and
`DragDropCatalogPartChrome`. The `DragDropCatalogZone` control renders a catalog part by
using the custom chrome defined by the `DragDropCatalogPartChrome` class. This class
simply adds a <div> tag around the contents of the CatalogPart. This <div> tag is used in
the JavaScript code to identify the draggable catalog items.

The JavaScript code used by the custom DragDropCatalogZone control is contained in
Listing 30.14.

LISTING 30.14   DragDropCatalogZone.js

```
var dragDropCatalogZone = new function()
    {
        this.start = dragDropCatalogZone_start;
        this.addWebPart = dragDropCatalogZone_addWebPart;
    }


function dragDropCatalogZone_start(catalogZoneId)
    {
        // Get Catalog Zone
        var catalogZone = document.getElementById(catalogZoneId);

        // Find Element with Draggable Class
        var draggable = document.getElementById(catalogZoneId + '_draggable');

        // Get Images contained in Draggable
        var images = draggable.getElementsByTagName('img');

        // Get Inputs contained in Draggable
        var inputs = draggable.getElementsByTagName('input');

        // Check that Images == Inputs
        if (images.length != inputs.length)
        {
            alert('DragDropCatalogZone:Each catalog item must
➥have a catalog icon');
            return;
        }

        // Convert images into Web Parts
        for (var i=0;i<images.length;i++)
        {
```

LISTING 30.14   Continued

```
            var catItem = new WebPart(images[i],images[i]);
            images[i].webPartId = inputs[i].value;
            images[i].detachEvent("ondragend", WebPart_OnDragEnd);
            images[i].attachEvent("ondragend", dragDropCatalogZone.addWebPart);
        }

        // Add Drop Handler to WebPartManager
        __wpm.xCatalogZoneId = catalogZoneId;
        __wpm.xCompleteAddWebPartDragDrop =
➥dragDropCatalogZone_CompleteAddWebPartDragDrop;
    }


function dragDropCatalogZone_addWebPart()
    {
        __wpm.xCompleteAddWebPartDragDrop();
    }


function dragDropCatalogZone_CompleteAddWebPartDragDrop() {
    var dragState = this.dragState;
    this.dragState = null;
    if (dragState.dropZoneElement != null) {
        dragState.dropZoneElement.__zone.ToggleDropCues(false,
➥dragState.dropIndex, false);
    }
    document.body.detachEvent("ondragover", Zone_OnDragOver);
    for (var i = 0; i < __wpm.zones.length; i++) {
        __wpm.zones[i].allowDrop = false;
    }
    this.overlayContainerElement.removeChild(
➥this.overlayContainerElement.firstChild);
    this.overlayContainerElement.style.display = "none";
    if ((dragState != null) && (dragState.dropped == true)) {
        var currentZone = dragState.webPartElement.__webPart.zone;
        var currentZoneIndex = dragState.webPartElement.__webPart.zoneIndex;
        if ((currentZone != dragState.dropZoneElement.__zone) ||
            ((currentZoneIndex != dragState.dropIndex) &&
             (currentZoneIndex != (dragState.dropIndex - 1)))) {

            var eventTarget = this.xCatalogZoneId;
            var eventArgument = 'Add:' + dragState.webPartElement.webPartId +
➥':' + dragState.dropZoneElement.__zone.uniqueID + ':' + dragState.dropIndex;
            this.SubmitPage(eventTarget, eventArgument);
        }
    }
}
```

30

The dragDropCatalogZone_start() method is called immediately after the DragDropCatalogZone control is rendered. This method takes advantage of the <div> tag added to the Catalog Zone by the DragDropCatalogPartChrome class to identify the images and input elements associated with the catalog items.

The method converts each of the images in the catalog zone into a Web Part by calling the WebPart() constructor defined in the Web Part Framework JavaScript library. Next, the method overrides the default JavaScript function that is called when a Web Part is dropped into a Web Part Zone. When a user drops a catalog item into a Web Part Zone, the dragDropCatalogZone_CompleteAddWebPartDragDrop() method is called.

The dragDropCatalogZone_CompleteAddWebPartDragDrop() method posts the page back to the server by calling the SubmitPage() method. An eventArgument that represents the Web Part ID, Web Part Zone ID, and Web Part Zone index is posted back to the server and processed by the RaisePostBackEventHandler() method. This server method actually adds the Web Part to the selected zone.

Listing 30.15 illustrates how you can use the DragDropCatalogZone control in a page.

LISTING 30.15   ShowDragDropCatalogZone.aspx

```
<%@ Page Language="VB" %>
<%@ Register TagPrefix="custom" Namespace="myControls" %>
<!DOCTYPE html PUBLIC "-//W3C//DTD XHTML 1.1//EN"
  "http://www.w3.org/TR/xhtml11/DTD/xhtml11.dtd">
<script runat="server">

    Protected Sub Menu1_MenuItemClick(ByVal sender As Object,
➥ByVal e As MenuEventArgs)
        WebPartManager1.DisplayMode = WebPartManager1.DisplayModes(e.Item.Text)
    End Sub

</script>
<html xmlns="http://www.w3.org/1999/xhtml" >
<head id="Head1" runat="server">
    <style type="text/css">
        .column
        {
            float:left;
            width:30%;
            height:200px;
            margin-right:10px;
            border:solid 1px black;
            background-color: white;
        }
        .menu
        {
            margin:5px 0px;
        }
```

LISTING 30.15   Continued

```
        html
        {
            background-color:#eeeeee;
        }
    </style>
    <title>Show Drag-and-Drop Catalog Zone</title>
</head>
<body>
    <form id="form1" runat="server">
    <asp:WebPartManager
        id="WebPartManager1"
        Runat="server" />

        <asp:Menu
            id="Menu1"
            OnMenuItemClick="Menu1_MenuItemClick"
            Orientation="Horizontal"
            CssClass="menu"
            Runat="server">
            <Items>
            <asp:MenuItem Text="Browse" />
            <asp:MenuItem Text="Design" />
            <asp:MenuItem Text="Catalog" />
            </Items>
        </asp:Menu>

        <asp:WebPartZone
            id="WebPartZone1"
            CssClass="column"
            Runat="server" />

        <asp:WebPartZone
            id="WebPartZone2"
            CssClass="column"
            Runat="server" />

        <custom:DragDropCatalogZone
            id="CatalogZone1"
            CssClass="column"
            Runat="server">
            <ZoneTemplate>
                <asp:DeclarativeCatalogPart
                    id="DeclarativeCatalogPart1"
                    Runat="server">
                    <WebPartsTemplate>
```

LISTING 30.15   Continued

```
                    <asp:Label
                        id="Label1"
                        CatalogIconImageUrl="~/Images/FirstSimplePart.gif"
                        Title="First Simple Part"
                        Description="The first Web Part"
                        Runat="server" />
                    <asp:Label
                        id="Label2"
                        CatalogIconImageUrl="~/Images/SecondSimplePart.gif"
                        Title="Second Simple Part"
                        Description="The second Web Part"
                        Runat="server" />
                    </WebPartsTemplate>
                </asp:DeclarativeCatalogPart>
                <asp:PageCatalogPart
                    id="PageCatalogPart1"
                    Runat="server" />
            </ZoneTemplate>
        </custom:DragDropCatalogZone>
    </form>
</body>
</html>
```

After you open the page in Listing 30.15, you can view the custom Catalog Zone by clicking the Catalog link. Notice that you can add items from the catalog to the page by dragging the catalog icons onto particular Web Part Zones (see Figure 30.5).

> **WEB STANDARDS NOTE**
>
> The `DragDropCatalogZone` control still renders the normal check boxes for adding items. This is good from an accessibility standpoint. When you implement fancy JavaScript drag-and-drop functionality, you should always implement an equivalent way of doing the same thing from the keyboard.

Creating a Templated Catalog Zone

The default `CatalogZone` control has a certain appearance and there is nothing you can do about it. The `CatalogZone` control does not support paging or sorting. It doesn't even display the descriptions with Web Parts.

In this section, we'll fix this limitation of the Web Part Framework by building a custom Templated Catalog Zone. The custom `CatalogZone` control supports an `ItemTemplate`. You can take advantage of the `ItemTemplate` to display catalog items in any way that you please.

For example, you can use a `GridView` control in the `ItemTemplate` to enable users to sort and page through catalog items. You can also take advantage of the `ItemTemplate` to modify the default appearance of the Catalog Part menu. Rather than display a list of links to individual Catalog Parts, you can display a drop-down list of Catalog Parts (see Figure 30.6).

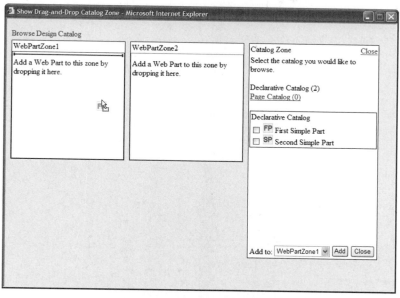

FIGURE 30.5   Dragging and dropping from a catalog.

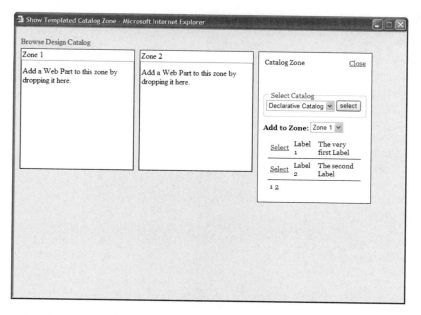

FIGURE 30.6   Displaying a drop-down list of catalog parts.

The custom Templated Catalog Zone control is contained in Listing 30.16.

LISTING 30.16   TemplatedCatalogZone.vb

```vb
Imports System
Imports System.Web.UI
Imports System.Web.UI.WebControls.WebParts

Namespace myControls

    ''' <summary>
    ''' This control enables you to lay out a
    ''' Catalog Zone with a template
    ''' </summary>
    Public Class TemplatedCatalogZone
        Inherits CatalogZone

        Private _itemTemplate As ITemplate
        Private _item As ItemContainer

        ''' <summary>
        ''' Represents the Item Template
        ''' </summary>
        <TemplateContainer(GetType(TemplatedCatalogZone))> _
        Public Property ItemTemplate() As ITemplate
            Get
                Return _itemTemplate
            End Get
            Set(ByVal Value As ITemplate)
                _itemTemplate = Value
            End Set
        End Property


        ''' <summary>
        ''' Utility method that returns the currently
        ''' selected Catalog Part
        ''' </summary>
        Public ReadOnly Property SelectedCatalogPart() As CatalogPart
            Get
                Return CatalogParts(SelectedCatalogPartID)
            End Get
        End Property

        ''' <summary>
        ''' Returns list of Web Web Part descriptions
        ''' so that you can use Container.Descriptions
```

LISTING 30.16   Continued

```vb
''' in the ItemTemplate
''' </summary>
Public ReadOnly Property Descriptions() As WebPartDescriptionCollection
    Get
        Return SelectedCatalogPart.GetAvailableWebPartDescriptions()
    End Get
End Property


''' <summary>
''' Returns list of Web Part Zones so that you
''' can use Container.Zones in the ItemTemplate
''' </summary>
Public ReadOnly Property Zones() As WebPartZoneCollection
    Get
        Return Me.WebPartManager.Zones
    End Get
End Property


''' <summary>
''' Adds a new Web Part to a Web Part Zone
''' </summary>
Public Sub AddWebPart(ByVal webPartID As String, ByVal zoneID As String)
    ' Get Web Part
    Dim descs As WebPartDescriptionCollection =
➥SelectedCatalogPart.GetAvailableWebPartDescriptions()
    Dim NewWebPart As WebPart = SelectedCatalogPart.GetWebPart(
➥descs(webPartID))

    ' Get Zone
    Dim zones As WebPartZoneCollection = Me.WebPartManager.Zones
    Dim selectedZone As WebPartZoneBase = zones(zoneID)

    ' Add the Web Part
    Me.WebPartManager.AddWebPart(NewWebPart, selectedZone, 0)
End Sub


''' <summary>
''' Extends base method to support the ItemTemplate
''' </summary>
Protected Overrides Sub CreateChildControls()
    MyBase.CreateChildControls()
    _item = New ItemContainer()
    ItemTemplate.InstantiateIn(_item)
    Controls.Add(_item)
End Sub
```

30

LISTING 30.16   Continued

```vb
    ''' <summary>
    ''' Render the contents of the ItemTemplate
    ''' </summary>
    Protected Overrides Sub RenderBody(ByVal writer As HtmlTextWriter)
        _item.RenderControl(writer)
    End Sub

    ''' <summary>
    ''' Suppress the footer since the same content
    ''' is contained in our ItemTemplate
    ''' </summary>
    Protected Overrides Sub RenderFooter(ByVal writer As HtmlTextWriter)
    End Sub
End Class

''' <summary>
''' This class does nothing but hold the contents
''' of the ItemTemplate so we can render it.
''' </summary>
Public Class ItemContainer
    Inherits Control
End Class

End Namespace
```

The `TemplatedCatalogZone` control in Listing 30.16 inherits from the base `CatalogZone` class. The derived class exposes an `ItemTemplate` property that you can use to customize the control's appearance. The `ItemTemplate` is created in the `CreateChildControls()` method, and the contents of the `ItemTemplate` are rendered in the `RenderBody()` method.

Notice that the `TemplatedCatalogZone` class includes a public `AddWebPart()` method. This method adds a Web Part with a particular ID to a particular Web Part Zone. The Web Part is added with the help of the `WebPartManager` class's `AddWebPart()` method.

The page in Listing 30.17 contains the `TemplatedCatalogZone` control.

LISTING 30.17   ShowTemplatedCatalogZone.aspx

```aspx
<%@ Page Language="VB" %>
<%@ Register TagPrefix="custom" Namespace="myControls" %>
<!DOCTYPE html PUBLIC "-//W3C//DTD XHTML 1.1//EN"
 "http://www.w3.org/TR/xhtml11/DTD/xhtml11.dtd">

<script runat="server">
```

LISTING 30.17 Continued

```
''' <summary>
''' Whenever the CatalogZone is opened, we need to
''' rebind to the datasource
''' </summary>
Protected Sub WebPartManager1_DisplayModeChanged(ByVal sender As Object,
➥ByVal e As WebPartDisplayModeEventArgs)
    If WebPartManager1.DisplayMode Is WebPartManager.CatalogDisplayMode Then
        CatalogZone1.SelectedCatalogPartID = CatalogZone1.CatalogParts(0).ID
        CatalogZone1.DataBind()
    End If
End Sub


''' <summary>
''' When a user selects a new Catalog Part,
''' we need to rebind the GridView
''' </summary>
Protected Sub btnSelectCatalog_Click(ByVal sender As Object,
➥ByVal e As EventArgs)
    ' Update selected catalog
    Dim dropCatalogs As DropDownList =
ICType(CatalogZone1.FindControl("dropCatalogs"), DropDownList)
    CatalogZone1.SelectedCatalogPartID = dropCatalogs.SelectedValue
End Sub


''' <summary>
''' When a user selects a new page, we
''' must rebind the GridView
''' </summary>
Protected Sub grdDesc_PageIndexChanging(ByVal sender As Object,
➥ByVal e As GridViewPageEventArgs)
    Dim grdDesc As GridView = CType(sender, GridView)
    grdDesc.PageIndex = e.NewPageIndex
End Sub


''' <summary>
''' When a user selects a Web Part from a Catalog, we
''' add the new Web Part to the page
''' </summary>
Protected Sub grdDesc_SelectedIndexChanged(ByVal sender As Object,
➥ByVal e As EventArgs)
    ' Rebind the GridView to reload the DataKeys
    Dim grdDesc As GridView = CType(sender, GridView)
    grdDesc.DataBind()

    ' Get Selected Web Part
```

30

LISTING 30.17   Continued

```
        Dim webPartID As String = CType(grdDesc.SelectedValue, String)

        ' Get Selected Zone
        Dim dropZones As DropDownList = CType(CatalogZone1.
➥FindControl("dropZones"), DropDownList)
        Dim zoneID As String = dropZones.SelectedValue

        ' Add the Web Part to the Page
        CatalogZone1.AddWebPart(webPartID, zoneID)
    End Sub

    ''' <summary>
    ''' If in Catalog Display Mode, bind GridView
    ''' </summary>
    Protected Overrides Sub OnPreRenderComplete(ByVal e As EventArgs)
        If WebPartManager1.DisplayMode Is WebPartManager.CatalogDisplayMode Then
            Dim grdDesc As GridView = CType(CatalogZone1.
➥FindControl("grdDesc"), GridView)
            grdDesc.DataBind()
        End If
        MyBase.OnPreRenderComplete(e)
    End Sub

    Protected Sub Menu1_MenuItemClick(ByVal sender As Object, ByVal e
➥As MenuEventArgs)
        WebPartManager1.DisplayMode = WebPartManager1.DisplayModes(e.Item.Text)
    End Sub

</script>
<html xmlns="http://www.w3.org/1999/xhtml" >
<head id="Head1" runat="server">
    <style type="text/css">
        .catalogPartStyle
        {
            padding:10px;
            font:14px Georgia,serif;
        }
        .catalogPartStyle fieldset
        {
            padding-top:30px;
            padding-bottom:10px;
            margin-bottom:10px;
        }
        .catalogPartStyle label
        {
```

LISTING 30.17   Continued

```
            font-weight:bold;
        }
        .catalogGrid
        {
            margin:10px;
        }
        .catalogRow td
        {
            padding:5px;
            border-bottom:solid 1px black;
        }

        .column
        {
            float:left;
            width:30%;
            height:200px;
            margin-right:10px;
            border:solid 1px black;
            background-color: white;
        }
        .menu
        {
            margin:5px 0px;
        }
        html
        {
            background-color:#eeeeee;
        }
    </style>
    <title>Show Templated Catalog Zone</title>
</head>
<body>
    <form id="form1" runat="server">
    <asp:WebPartManager
        id="WebPartManager1"
        Runat="server" OnDisplayModeChanged="WebPartManager1_DisplayModeChanged" />

        <asp:Menu
            id="Menu1"
            OnMenuItemClick="Menu1_MenuItemClick"
            Orientation="Horizontal"
            CssClass="menu"
            Runat="server">
            <Items>
```

LISTING 30.17   Continued

```
            <asp:MenuItem Text="Browse" />
            <asp:MenuItem Text="Design" />
            <asp:MenuItem Text="Catalog" />
            </Items>
    </asp:Menu>

    <asp:WebPartZone
        id="WebPartZone1"
        HeaderText="Zone 1"
        CssClass="column"
        Runat="server" />

    <asp:WebPartZone
        id="WebPartZone2"
        HeaderText="Zone 2"
        CssClass="column"
        Runat="server"/>

    <custom:TemplatedCatalogZone
        id="CatalogZone1"
        CssClass="column catalogPartStyle"
        Runat="server">
        <ItemTemplate>
        <fieldset>
        <legend>Select Catalog</legend>
        <asp:DropDownList
            id="dropCatalogs"
            DataTextField="Title"
            DataValueField="ID"
            DataSource='<%# Container.CatalogParts %>'
            runat="server"/>
        <asp:Button
            id="btnSelectCatalog"
            Text="select"
            Tooltip="Select Catalog"
            OnClick="btnSelectCatalog_Click"
            runat="server"/>
        </fieldset>

        <asp:Label
            id="lblZone"
            Text="Add to Zone:"
            AssociatedControlID="dropZones"
            Runat="server"/>
        <asp:DropDownList
```

LISTING 30.17   Continued

```
            id="dropZones"
            DataTextField="HeaderText"
            DataValueField="ID"
            DataSource='<%# Container.Zones %>'
            runat="server" />
        <asp:GridView
            id="grdDesc"
            GridLines="none"
            CssClass="catalogGrid"
            RowStyle-CssClass="catalogRow"
            DataKeyNames="ID"
            AllowPaging="true"
            PageSize="2"
            ShowHeader="false"
            EmptyDataText="This catalog is empty"
            AutoGenerateColumns="false"
            AutoGenerateSelectButton="true"
            DataSource='<%# Container.Descriptions %>'
            OnPageIndexChanging="grdDesc_PageIndexChanging"
            OnSelectedIndexChanged="grdDesc_SelectedIndexChanged"
            runat="server">
            <Columns>
                <asp:BoundField DataField="Title" />
                <asp:BoundField DataField="Description" />
            </Columns>
        </asp:GridView>
    </ItemTemplate>
    <ZoneTemplate>
    <asp:DeclarativeCatalogPart
        id="DeclarativeCatalogPart1"
        Title="Declarative Catalog"
        Runat="server">
        <WebPartsTemplate>
            <asp:Label
                id="Label1"
                Title="Label 1"
                Description="The very first Label"
                Runat="server" />
            <asp:Label
                id="Label2"
                Title="Label 2"
                Description="The second Label"
                Runat="server" />
            <asp:Label
                id="Label3"
```

30

LISTING 30.17 Continued

```
                        Title="Label 3"
                        Description="The very last Label"
                        Runat="server" />
                </WebPartsTemplate>
            </asp:DeclarativeCatalogPart>
            <asp:PageCatalogPart
                id="PageCatalogPart1"
                Title="Page Catalog"
                Runat="server"/>
            </ZoneTemplate>
        </custom:TemplatedCatalogZone>
    </form>
</body>
</html>
```

If you open the page in Listing 30.17 in your browser and click the Catalog link, you can
see the custom Templated Catalog Zone. Notice that the custom Catalog Zone supports
paging. Furthermore, notice that unlike the default CatalogZone control, the list of
Catalog Parts is displayed in a drop-down list.

In Listing 30.17, the `TemplatedCatalogZone` control contains an `ItemTemplate` that
includes two `DropDownList` controls and a `GridView` control. The `DropDownList` controls
are used to display a list of Catalog Parts and a list of Web Part Zones. The `GridView`
control is used to display the list of catalog items (the Web Part descriptions).

Each of these three controls is bound to a datasource with a databinding expression. For
example, the `DropDownList` control that displays the list of Catalog Parts is declared like
this:

```
<asp:DropDownList
    id="dropCatalogs"
    DataTextField="Title"
    DataValueField="ID"
    DataSource='<%# Container.CatalogParts %>'
    runat="server"/>
```

In this control declaration, `Container.CatalogParts` refers to the `CatalogParts` property
exposed by the `TemplateCatalogControl` class. Because this class also exposes a
Descriptions and Zones property, you can also use `Container.Descriptions` and
`Container.Zones` in a databinding expression within the `TemplateCatalogZone` control's
`ItemTemplate`.

Because the controls in the `ItemTemplate` do not take advantage of declarative databinding, you must undertake the responsibility of binding the controls to their respective data
sources. Notice, for instance, that the GridView control is bound to its data source in the
`OnPreRenderComplete()` method defined near the top of the file in Listing 30.17.

The advantage of using the `TemplatedCatalogZone` control is that you can make a Catalog Zone look like anything you want. However, as Spiderman says, "With great power comes great responsibility." The disadvantage is that you are forced to write all sorts of additional code to bind the data controls to their data sources.

Creating Custom Editor Zones

Editor Zones contain the Editor Parts you can use to edit the properties of your Web Parts. The Web Part Framework contains a standard set of Editor Part controls that can be used to edit the standard properties of a Web Part: the `AppearanceEditorPart`, the `BehaviorEditorPart`, and the `LayoutEditorPart` controls.

If your Web Part has custom properties, and you want to edit these properties with an Editor Part, then you have two choices. You can use the `PropertyGridEditorPart` control or build your own custom Editor Part. In most cases, you won't want to use the `PropertyGridEditorPart` because it does not provide any support for form validation or advanced layout. When using the `PropertyGridEditorPart`, for any property other than a Boolean or Enum property, you get a single-line text box and there isn't anything you can do about it.

This section explores two methods of creating custom Editor Parts. First, to clarify the concepts involved, we'll create a simple Editor Part designed to edit the properties of a particular Web Part. Next, you'll learn how to create a templated Editor Part you can use when editing any Web Part control regardless of the types of properties that it contains.

How Editor Zones Work

As in other types of Web Zones, three types of objects are involved in rendering an Editor Zone: the `EditorZone` control, the `EditorPartChrome` class, and the `EditorPart` control.

The EditorZone control appears only when a page is in Edit Display Mode. When the page is in Edit Display Mode, the Editor Zone still does not display any Editor Parts until you select the Edit menu option on a particular Web Part.

When you select a Web Part to edit, two types of Editor Parts are displayed. First, any Editor Parts declared in the Editor Zone are displayed. Second, if the Web Part implements the IWebEditable interface or derives from the base WebPart class, then any Editor Parts returned from the Web Part's CreateEditorParts() method are displayed.

> **NOTE**
>
> The BehaviorEditorPart appears only when a page is in Shared Personalization scope and the Web Part being edited is shared among all users.

Finally, the EditorPartChrome class is actually responsible for rendering each Editor Part. An instance of the EditorPartChrome class is created by an Editor Zone, and then the Editor Zone calls the EditorPartChrome control's RenderEditorPart() method to render each Editor Part.

If you want to modify the appearance of an Editor Zone or the chrome that appears around each Editor Part, then you need to modify the EditorZone and EditorPartChrome classes. If you want to modify the appearance of the Editor Parts themselves, then you need to modify the properties of a particular Editor Part control.

Creating a Simple Custom Editor Part

Let's start by creating the Web Part that we will edit. The FeaturedBookPart is contained in Listing 30.18.

LISTING 30.18   FeaturedBookPart.ascx

```
<%@ Control Language="VB" ClassName="FeaturedBookPart" %>
<%@ Implements Interface="System.Web.UI.WebControls.WebParts.IWebEditable" %>
<%@ Implements Interface="myControls.IFeaturedBook" %>
<%@ Import Namespace="System.Collections.Generic" %>
<%@ Import Namespace="myControls" %>
<script runat="server">

    Private _bookTitle As String
    Private _datePublished As DateTime
    Private _price As Decimal

    Public ReadOnly Property WebBrowsableObject() As Object
➥Implements IWebEditable.WebBrowsableObject
        Get
            Return Me
        End Get
    End Property
```

LISTING 30.18   Continued

```
    Public Function CreateEditorParts() As EditorPartCollection
➥Implements IWebEditable.CreateEditorParts
        Dim editorParts As New List(Of EditorPart)()
        Dim editor As New FeaturedBookEditorPart()
        editor.ID = "FeaturedEditor1"
        editorParts.Add(editor)
        Return New EditorPartCollection(editorParts)
    End Function

    <Personalizable()> _
    Public Property BookTitle() As String Implements IFeaturedBook.BookTitle
        Get
            Return _bookTitle
        End Get
        Set(ByVal Value As String)
            _bookTitle = Value
        End Set
    End Property

    <Personalizable()> _
    Public Property DatePublished() As DateTime
➥Implements IFeaturedBook.DatePublished
        Get
            Return _datePublished
        End Get
        Set(ByVal Value As DateTime)
            _datePublished = Value
        End Set
    End Property

    <Personalizable()> _
    Public Property Price() As Decimal Implements IFeaturedBook.Price
        Get
            Return _price
        End Get
        Set(ByVal Value As Decimal)
            _price = Value
        End Set
    End Property

    Private Sub Page_PreRender()
        lblBookTitle.Text = _bookTitle
        lblDatePublished.Text = _datePublished.ToString("D")
        lblPrice.Text = _price.ToString("c")
    End Sub
```

30

LISTING 30.18   Continued

```
</script>

Title:
<asp:Label
    id="lblBookTitle"
    Runat="server" />

<br />
Published:
<asp:Label
    id="lblDatePublished"
    Runat="server" />
<br />
Price:
<asp:Label
    id="lblPrice"
    Runat="server" />
```

Notice that the FeaturedBookPart control implements two interfaces: the IWebEditable and the IFeaturedBook interfaces. Implementing the first interface enables you to associate the FeaturedBookPart with a custom EditorPart control. The IWebEditable interface has two members:

- WebBrowsableObject—This property represents the object that is edited. Normally, the property should just return a reference to the current control.

- CreateEditorParts—This method returns the collection of EditorPart controls associated with the current Web Part.

The FeaturedBookPart also implements the IFeaturedBook interface that we create in a moment. The custom EditorPart control needs some method of identifying the properties exposed by the FeaturedBookPart. The IFeaturedBook interface provides the EditorPart with this information. (You don't need to create an interface when creating a Web Part with a custom control rather than a User Control.)

The custom Editor Part is contained in Listing 30.19.

LISTING 30.19   FeaturedBookEditorPart.vb

```
Imports System
Imports System.Web.UI
Imports System.Web.UI.WebControls
Imports System.Web.UI.WebControls.WebParts

Namespace myControls
```

LISTING 30.19 Continued

```
''' <summary>
''' Describes the properties of the
''' FeaturedWebPart control
''' </summary>
Public Interface IFeaturedBook
    Property BookTitle() As String
    Property DatePublished() As DateTime
    Property Price() As Decimal
End Interface


''' <summary>
''' Custom Editor for FeaturedBookPart
''' </summary>
Public Class FeaturedBookEditorPart
    Inherits EditorPart

    Private _txtBookTitle As TextBox
    Private _calDatePublished As Calendar
    Private _txtPrice As TextBox
    Private _valPrice As CompareValidator

    Private _title As String = "Featured Book Editor"

    ''' <summary>
    ''' Create standard title
    ''' </summary>
    Public Overrides Property Title() As String
        Get
            Return _title
        End Get
        Set(ByVal Value As String)
            _title = Value
        End Set
    End Property

    ''' <summary>
    ''' Utility method that returns the child control
    ''' in the case of a GenericWebPart
    ''' </summary>
    Private ReadOnly Property ControlToEdit() As Control
        Get
            If TypeOf (Me.WebPartToEdit) Is GenericWebPart Then
                Return (CType(WebPartToEdit, GenericWebPart)).ChildControl
            Else
```

LISTING 30.19   Continued

```
                Return Me.WebPartToEdit
            End If
        End Get
    End Property


        ''' <summary>
        ''' Called when you click OK or Apply to
        ''' apply the Web Part property changes
        ''' </summary>
        Public Overrides Function ApplyChanges() As Boolean
            Dim success As Boolean = False
            EnsureChildControls()
            Page.Validate()
            If Page.IsValid Then
                CType(ControlToEdit, IFeaturedBook).BookTitle = _txtBookTitle.Text
                CType(ControlToEdit, IFeaturedBook).DatePublished =
➥calDatePublished.SelectedDate
                CType(ControlToEdit, IFeaturedBook).Price =
➥Decimal.Parse(_txtPrice.Text)
                success = True
            End If
            Return success
        End Function


        ''' <summary>
        ''' Called when the Web Part Framework
        ''' has initialized the Web Part being edited
        ''' </summary>
        Public Overrides Sub SyncChanges()
            EnsureChildControls()
            _txtBookTitle.Text = (CType(ControlToEdit, IFeaturedBook)).BookTitle
            _calDatePublished.SelectedDate = (CType(ControlToEdit,
➥IFeaturedBook)).DatePublished
            _txtPrice.Text = (CType(ControlToEdit, IFeaturedBook)).
➥Price.ToString()
        End Sub


        ''' <summary>
        ''' Adds the controls rendered by this Editor Part
        ''' to the controls collection.
        ''' </summary>
        Protected Overrides Sub CreateChildControls()
            ' Add Book Title
            _txtBookTitle = New TextBox()
```

LISTING 30.19   Continued

```
        _txtBookTitle.ID = "txtBookTitle"
        Controls.Add(_txtBookTitle)

        ' Add Date Published
        _calDatePublished = New Calendar()
        _calDatePublished.ID = "calDatePublished"
        Controls.Add(_calDatePublished)

        ' Add Price
        _txtPrice = New TextBox()
        _txtPrice.ID = "txtPrice"
        _txtPrice.Columns = 5
        Controls.Add(_txtPrice)

        ' Add Price Validator
        _valPrice = New CompareValidator()
        _valPrice.ID = "valPrice"
        _valPrice.ControlToValidate = _txtPrice.ID
        _valPrice.Operator = ValidationCompareOperator.DataTypeCheck
        _valPrice.Type = ValidationDataType.Currency
        _valPrice.Text = "(Must be currency)"
        Controls.Add(_valPrice)
    End Sub

    ''' <summary>
    ''' Renders the User Interface for the Editor Part
    ''' </summary>
    ''' <param name="writer"></param>
    Protected Overrides Sub RenderContents(ByVal writer As HtmlTextWriter)
        ' Render Book Title
        RenderLabel(writer, "Book Title:", _txtBookTitle.ClientID)
        writer.WriteBreak()
        _txtBookTitle.RenderControl(writer)

        writer.WriteBreak()
        writer.WriteBreak()

        ' Render Date Published
        RenderLabel(writer, "Date Published:", _calDatePublished.ClientID)
        writer.WriteBreak()
        _calDatePublished.RenderControl(writer)

        writer.WriteBreak()
        writer.WriteBreak()
```

30

LISTING 30.19 Continued

```
            ' Render Price
            RenderLabel(writer, "Price:", _txtPrice.ClientID)
            _valPrice.RenderControl(writer)
            writer.WriteBreak()
            _txtPrice.RenderControl(writer)
            writer.WriteBreak()
        End Sub


        ''' <summary>
        ''' Renders an accessible Label for the
        ''' form fields
        ''' </summary>
        Private Sub RenderLabel(ByVal writer As HtmlTextWriter,
➥ByVal labelText As String, ByVal associatedControlId As String)
            writer.AddAttribute(HtmlTextWriterAttribute.For, associatedControlId)
            writer.RenderBeginTag(HtmlTextWriterTag.Label)
            writer.Write(labelText)
            writer.RenderEndTag()
        End Sub


    End Class
End Namespace
```

The class in Listing 30.19 inherits from the base EditorPart class. It overrides two methods from the base class: SyncChanges() and ApplyChanges().

The SyncChanges() method is called automatically when the EditorPart is displayed and the Web Part being edited has been initialized. Listing 30.19 takes advantage of this method to synchronize the editor form with the current property values of the Web Part being edited.

The ApplyChanges() method is automatically called when the user clicks the Apply or OK button in the Editor Zone. This method updates the properties of the Web Part being edited with the values from the editor form.

> **NOTE**
>
> The ApplyChanges() and SyncChanges() methods are executed during the processing of post-back data after the Page Load event and before the PreRender event.

Notice that both the SyncChanges() and ApplyChanges() methods take advantage of a property named ControlToEdit, which also is defined in the class in Listing 30.19. This property returns a different control depending on whether the Web Part being edited is a GenericWebPart or a "true" Web Part. When you create a Web Part by using a User Control or any control that does not derive from the WebPart class, the Web Part

Framework automatically wraps the control in a `GenericWebPart` control. In the case of a `GenericWebPart` control, you want to edit the properties of the first child control of the Web Part and not the properties of the Web Part itself.

The bulk of the work in Listing 30.19 is devoted to building the custom editor form. Two `TextBox` controls and one `Calendar` control are created in the `CreateChildControls()` method. These controls are actually rendered in the `RenderContents()` method.

Finally, Listing 30.20 contains a page that displays the `FeaturedBookPart` and `FeaturedBookEditorPart` controls.

LISTING 30.20 ShowFeaturedBookEditorPart.aspx

```
<%@ Page Language="VB" %>
<%@ Register TagPrefix="custom" Namespace="myControls" %>
<%@ Register TagPrefix="user" TagName="FeaturedBookPart"
  Src="~/FeaturedBookPart.ascx" %>
<!DOCTYPE html PUBLIC "-//W3C//DTD XHTML 1.1//EN"
  "http://www.w3.org/TR/xhtml11/DTD/xhtml11.dtd">
<script runat="server">


    Protected Sub Menu1_MenuItemClick(ByVal sender As Object, ByVal e
➥As MenuEventArgs)
        WebPartManager1.DisplayMode = WebPartManager1.DisplayModes(e.Item.Text)
    End Sub

</script>
<html xmlns="http://www.w3.org/1999/xhtml" >
<head id="Head1" runat="server">
    <style type="text/css">
        .column
        {
            float:left;
            width:30%;
            height:200px;
            margin-right:10px;
            border:solid 1px black;
            background-color: white;
        }
        .menu
        {
            margin:5px 0px;
        }
        html
        {
            background-color:#eeeeee;
        }
    </style>
```

30

LISTING 30.20   Continued

```
    <title>Show Help Display Mode</title>
</head>
<body>
    <form id="form1" runat="server">
    <asp:WebPartManager
        id="WebPartManager1"
        Runat="server" />

        <asp:Menu
            id="Menu1"
            OnMenuItemClick="Menu1_MenuItemClick"
            Orientation="Horizontal"
            CssClass="menu"
            Runat="server">
            <Items>
            <asp:MenuItem Text="Browse" />
            <asp:MenuItem Text="Design" />
            <asp:MenuItem Text="Edit" />
            </Items>
        </asp:Menu>

        <asp:WebPartZone
            id="WebPartZone1"
            CssClass="column"
            Runat="server">
            <ZoneTemplate>
            <user:FeaturedBookPart
                id="FeaturedBookPart1"
                Title="Featured Book"
                runat="Server" />
            </ZoneTemplate>
        </asp:WebPartZone>

        <asp:WebPartZone
            id="WebPartZone2"
            CssClass="column"
            Runat="server"/>

        <asp:EditorZone
            id="EditorZone1"
            CssClass="column"
            runat="server">
            <ZoneTemplate>
            <asp:LayoutEditorPart
                id="LayoutEditorPart1"
                runat="server" />
```

LISTING 30.20   Continued

```
            </ZoneTemplate>
          </asp:EditorZone>
      </form>
  </body>
</html>
```

After you open the page in Listing 30.20, you can click the Edit link and then select the Edit menu option on the FeaturedBookPart. When you edit the FeaturedBookPart, both our custom FeaturedBookEditorPart and the standard LayoutEditorPart will appear in the Editor Zone (see Figure 30.7). Notice that an instance of the LayoutEditorPart control was declared in the Editor Zone contained in the page.

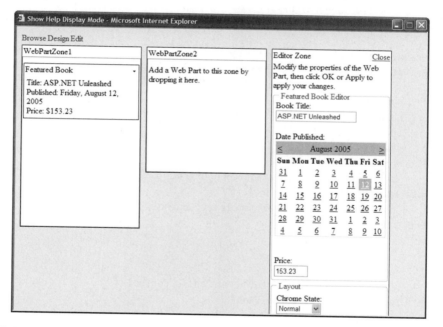

FIGURE 30.7   Displaying a custom editor.

It took a lot of work to create the custom Editor Part control. Too much work to simply display an editor form. In the next section, you'll learn how to avoid doing any of this work in the future. In the next section, we create a templated Editor Part.

Creating a Templated Editor Part

In this section, we create the last Editor Part that you'll ever need to make. We will create a Templated Editor Part, which will enable you to easily build any type of editor form that you need. You can create the custom form for the Templated Editor Part with a form defined in a user control file.

The Templated Editor Part is contained in Listing 30.21.

LISTING 30.21   TemplatedEditorPart.vb

```vb
Imports System
Imports System.Web.UI
Imports System.Web.UI.WebControls.WebParts

Namespace myControls

    ''' <summary>
    ''' Enables you to use templates when
    ''' editing Web Parts
    ''' </summary>
    Public Class TemplatedEditorPart
        Inherits EditorPart

        Private _editTemplateUrl As String
        Private _editTemplate As ITemplatedEditorPart

        ''' <summary>
        ''' Loads the user control that contains
        ''' the Edit Template
        ''' </summary>
        Protected Overrides Sub CreateChildControls()
            _editTemplate = CType(Page.LoadControl(_
➥editTemplateUrl), ITemplatedEditorPart)
            Controls.Add(CType(_editTemplate, Control))
        End Sub


        ''' <summary>
        ''' Utility method that returns the child control
        ''' in the case of a GenericWebPart
        ''' </summary>
        Private ReadOnly Property ControlToEdit() As Control
            Get
                If TypeOf Me.WebPartToEdit Is GenericWebPart Then
                    Return (CType(WebPartToEdit, GenericWebPart)).ChildControl
                Else
                    Return Me.WebPartToEdit
                End If
            End Get
        End Property

        ''' <summary>
```

LISTING 30.21   Continued

```
        ''' Called when the user clicks Apply or OK
        ''' in the Editor Zone
        ''' </summary>
        ''' <returns></returns>
        Public Overrides Function ApplyChanges() As Boolean
            EnsureChildControls()
            Return _editTemplate.ApplyChanges(ControlToEdit)
        End Function

        ''' <summary>
        ''' Called when the Editor Template
        ''' displays current Web Part property
        ''' values.
        ''' </summary>
        Public Overrides Sub SyncChanges()
            EnsureChildControls()
            _editTemplate.SyncChanges(ControlToEdit)
        End Sub

        ''' <summary>
        ''' Pass the Editor Part Title and Template
        ''' URL to the constructor
        ''' </summary>
        Public Sub New(ByVal title As String, ByVal editTemplateUrl As String)
            Me.Title = title
            _editTemplateUrl = editTemplateUrl
        End Sub
    End Class

    ''' <summary>
    ''' Defines the contract that any Edit Template
    ''' must satisfy
    ''' </summary>
    Public Interface ITemplatedEditorPart

        Function ApplyChanges(ByVal controlToEdit As Control) As Boolean
        Sub SyncChanges(ByVal controlToEdit As Control)
    End Interface
End Namespace
```

The constructor for the TemplatedEditorPart class takes a title and editTemplateUrl parameter. The editTemplateUrl parameter specifies the location of a user control that contains the edit form used by the TemplatedEditorPart control. The user control is loaded in the CreateChildControls() method.

Notice that the `TemplatedEditorPart` control derives from the base `EditorPart` class. It implements the `ApplyChanges()` and `SyncChanges()` from the base class. In this case, however, the control simply calls methods with the same name in the user control that it loads.

The Web Part in Listing 30.22 uses the `TemplatedEditorPart` control.

LISTING 30.22   FeaturedVideoPart.ascx

```
<%@ Control Language="VB" ClassName="FeaturedVideoPart" %>
<%@ Implements Interface="System.Web.UI.WebControls.WebParts.IWebEditable" %>
<%@ Import Namespace="System.Collections.Generic" %>
<%@ Import Namespace="myControls" %>
<script runat="server">

    Private _videoTitle As String
    Private _director As String
    Private _price As Decimal

    Public ReadOnly Property WebBrowsableObject() As Object
➥Implements IWebEditable.WebBrowsableObject
        Get
            Return Me
        End Get
    End Property


    Public Function CreateEditorParts() As EditorPartCollection
➥Implements IWebEditable.CreateEditorParts
        Dim editorParts As New List(Of EditorPart)()
        Dim editor As New TemplatedEditorPart("Featured Video Editor",
➥"~/FeaturedVideoEditTemplate.ascx")
        editor.ID = "Editor1"
        editorParts.Add(editor)
        Return New EditorPartCollection(editorParts)
    End Function

    <Personalizable> _
    Public Property VideoTitle() As String
    Get
        Return _videoTitle
    End Get
    Set (ByVal Value As String)
        _videoTitle = value
    End Set
    End Property
```

LISTING 30.22   Continued

```
    <Personalizable> _
    Public Property Director() As String
    Get
            Return _director
    End Get
    Set (ByVal Value As String)
        _director = value
    End Set
    End Property

    <Personalizable> _
    Public Property Price() As Decimal
    Get
            Return _price
    End Get
    Set (ByVal Value As Decimal)
        _price = value
    End Set
    End Property

    Private  Sub Page_PreRender()
        lblVideoTitle.Text = _videoTitle
        lblDirector.Text = _director
        lblPrice.Text = _price.ToString("c")
    End Sub

</script>

Title:
<asp:Label
    id="lblVideoTitle"
    Runat="server" />

<br />
Director:
<asp:Label
    id="lblDirector"
    Runat="server" />
<br />
Price:
<asp:Label
    id="lblPrice"
    Runat="server" />
```

30

The Web Part in Listing 30.22 displays a featured video. Notice that the Web Part implements the IWebActionable interface with its CreateEditorParts() method and WebBrowsableObject property.

The CreateEditorParts() method returns an instance of the TemplatedEditorPart control. The TemplatedEditorPart is initialized with the path to a user control named FeaturedVideoEditTemplate. This user control contains the template for editing the Web Part, and it is contained in Listing 30.23.

LISTING 30.23   FeaturedVideoEditTemplate.ascx

```
<%@ Control Language="VB" ClassName="FeaturedVideoEditTemplate" %>
<%@ Reference Control="~/FeaturedVideoPart.ascx" %>
<%@ Implements Interface="myControls.ITemplatedEditorPart" %>
<%@ Import Namespace="myControls" %>

<script runat="server">

    Public Sub SyncChanges(ByVal controlToEdit As Control)
➥Implements ITemplatedEditorPart.SyncChanges
        Dim part As ASP.FeaturedVideoPart = CType(controlToEdit,
➥ASP.FeaturedVideoPart)
        txtVideoTitle.Text = part.VideoTitle
        txtDirector.Text = part.Director
        txtPrice.Text = part.Price.ToString()
    End Sub


    Public Function ApplyChanges(ByVal controlToEdit As Control)
➥As Boolean Implements ITemplatedEditorPart.ApplyChanges
        Dim success As Boolean = False
        Page.Validate()
        If Page.IsValid Then
            Dim part As ASP.FeaturedVideoPart = CType(controlToEdit,
➥ASP.FeaturedVideoPart)
            part.VideoTitle = txtVideoTitle.Text
            part.Director = txtDirector.Text
            part.Price = Decimal.Parse(txtPrice.Text)
            success = True
        End If
        Return success
    End Function

</script>

<asp:Label
    id="lblVideoTitle"
```

LISTING 30.23   Continued

```
        Text="Video Title:"
        AssociatedControlID="txtVideoTitle"
        Runat="server" />
<br />
<asp:TextBox
        id="txtVideoTitle"
        Runat="server" />

<br /><br />

<asp:Label
        id="lblDirector"
        Text="Director:"
        AssociatedControlID="txtDirector"
        Runat="server" />
<br />
<asp:TextBox
        id="txtDirector"
        Runat="server" />

<br /><br />

<asp:Label
        id="lblPrice"
        Text="Price:"
        AssociatedControlID="txtPrice"
        Runat="server" />
<br />
<asp:TextBox
        id="txtPrice"
        Runat="server" />
<asp:CompareValidator
        id="valprice"
        ControlToValidate="txtPrice"
        Display="dynamic"
        Text="(Must be Currency)"
        Type="Currency"
        Operator="DataTypeCheck"
        Runat="server" />
<asp:RequiredFieldValidator ID="RequiredFieldValidator1"
        ControlToValidate="txtPrice"
        Display="dynamic"
        Text="(Required)"
        Runat="server" />
```

Notice that the user control in Listing 30.23 implements the `ITemplatedEditorPart` interface with its `SyncChanges()` and `ApplyChanges()` methods. The `SyncChanges()` method initializes the form fields in the user control with the current values of the properties of the Web Part being edited. The `ApplyChanges()` method updates the Web Part being edited with changes made in the edit form.

The page in Listing 30.24 uses the `TemplatedEditorPart` control to edit the `FeaturedVideoPart` control.

LISTING 30.24   ShowTemplatedEditorPart.aspx

```
<%@ Page Language="VB" %>
<%@ Register TagPrefix="custom" Namespace="myControls" %>
<%@ Register TagPrefix="user" TagName="FeaturedVideoPart"
  Src="~/FeaturedVideoPart.ascx" %>
<!DOCTYPE html PUBLIC "-//W3C//DTD XHTML 1.1//EN"
   "http://www.w3.org/TR/xhtml11/DTD/xhtml11.dtd">
<script runat="server">

    Protected Sub Menu1_MenuItemClick(ByVal sender As Object,
➥ByVal e As MenuEventArgs)
        WebPartManager1.DisplayMode = WebPartManager1.DisplayModes(e.Item.Text)
    End Sub
</script>
<html xmlns="http://www.w3.org/1999/xhtml" >
<head id="Head1" runat="server">
    <style type="text/css">
        .column
        {
            float:left;
            width:30%;
            height:200px;
            margin-right:10px;
            border:solid 1px black;
            background-color: white;
        }
        .menu
        {
            margin:5px 0px;
        }
        html
        {
            background-color:#eeeeee;
        }
    </style>
    <title>Show Templated Editor Part</title>
</head>
```

LISTING 30.24   Continued

```
<body>
    <form id="form1" runat="server">
    <asp:WebPartManager
        id="WebPartManager1"
        Runat="server" />

        <asp:Menu
            id="Menu1"
            OnMenuItemClick="Menu1_MenuItemClick"
            Orientation="Horizontal"
            CssClass="menu"
            Runat="server">
            <Items>
            <asp:MenuItem Text="Browse" />
            <asp:MenuItem Text="Design" />
            <asp:MenuItem Text="Edit" />
            </Items>
        </asp:Menu>

        <asp:WebPartZone
            id="WebPartZone1"
            CssClass="column"
            Runat="server">
            <ZoneTemplate>
            <user:FeaturedVideoPart
                id="FeaturedVideoPart1"
                Title="Featured Video"
                runat="server" />
            </ZoneTemplate>
        </asp:WebPartZone>

        <asp:WebPartZone
            id="WebPartZone2"
            CssClass="column"
            Runat="server" />

        <asp:EditorZone
            id="EditorZone1"
            CssClass="column"
            Runat="server" />

    </form>
</body>
</html>
```

30

After you open the page in Listing 30.24, you can view the `TemplatedEditorPart` by clicking the Edit link and selecting a Web Part to edit (see Figure 30.8).

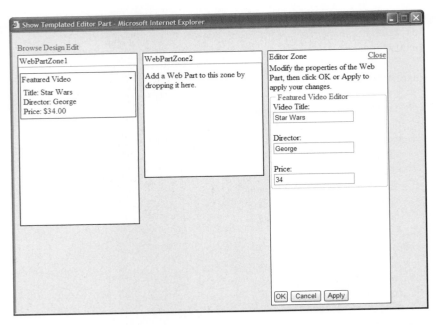

FIGURE 30.8   Using the Templated Editor Part.

The nice thing about the `TemplatedEditorPart` control is that you can associate a different edit template with each of the different types of Web Parts in a page. Just pass the path to a different template when initializing the `TemplatedEditorPart` in each Web Part's `CreateEditorParts()` method.

Creating Custom Web Part Display Modes

By default, the Web Part Framework supports the following Display Modes:

- `BrowseDisplayMode`—The default mode.
- `DesignDisplayMode`—Enables you to drag and drop Web Parts between Web Part Zones.
- `EditDisplayMode`—Enables you to select a Web Part for editing. Associated with Editor Zones.
- `CatalogDisplayMode`—Enables you to add new Web Parts to a page. Associated with Catalog Zones.
- `ConnectDisplayMode`—Enables you to connect Web Parts. Associated with Connections Zones.

Notice that the last three display modes are associated with particular tool zones. For example, when you select a Web Part for editing, the contents of the Editor Zone are displayed.

Like most other aspects of the Web Part Framework, this list of Display Modes is not written in stone. You can extend the Web Part Framework with your own custom display modes.

In this section, we'll create a custom Display Mode and an associated custom tool zone. We'll create a Help Display Mode. When a Web Parts page is in Help Display Mode, a help box appears above each Web Part. Furthermore, detailed help can be accessed from a HelpZone (see Figure 30.9).

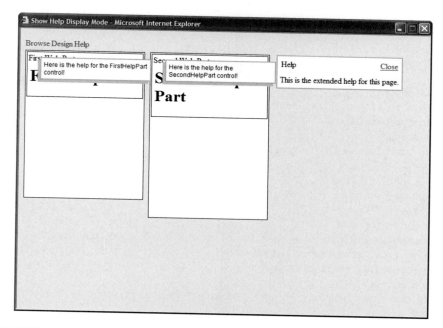

FIGURE 30.9   A page in Help Display Mode.

Let's start by creating the Web Part Help Display Mode itself. The custom `HelpDisplayMode` class is contained in Listing 30.25.

LISTING 30.25   `HelpDisplayMode.vb`

```
Imports System
Imports System.Web.UI.WebControls.WebParts

''' <summary>
''' Defines custom Help Display Mode
''' </summary>
Public Class HelpDisplayMode
```

LISTING 30.25   Continued

```vb
Inherits WebPartDisplayMode

Public Sub New(ByVal name As String)
    MyBase.New(name)
End Sub

''' <summary>
''' When true, users can move Web Parts
''' </summary>
Public Overrides ReadOnly Property AllowPageDesign() As Boolean
    Get
        Return False
    End Get
End Property

''' <summary>
''' When true, a HelpZone must be added
''' to the page.
''' </summary>
Public Overrides ReadOnly Property AssociatedWithToolZone() As Boolean
    Get
        Return False
    End Get
End Property

''' <summary>
''' When true, an error is raised when
''' personalization is disabled.
''' </summary>
Public Overrides ReadOnly Property RequiresPersonalization() As Boolean
    Get
        Return False
    End Get
End Property

''' <summary>
''' When true, hidden Web Parts
''' are displayed.
''' </summary>
Public Overrides ReadOnly Property ShowHiddenWebParts() As Boolean
    Get
        Return True
    End Get
End Property

End Class
```

The HelpDisplayMode class overrides a number of properties from its base WebPartDisplayMode class. For example, you prevent users from dragging Web Parts between zones when Help Display Mode is enabled by setting the AllowPageDesign property to the value False.

To use the custom Web Part Display Mode, you must modify the WebPartManager control. The modified WebPartManager control, named CustomWebPartManager, is contained in Listing 30.26.

LISTING 30.26   CustomWebPartManager.vb

```
Imports System
Imports System.Web.UI.WebControls.WebParts

Namespace myControls

    ''' <summary>
    ''' Extends WebPartManager control with support for
    ''' HelpDisplayMode
    ''' </summary>
    Public Class CustomWebPartManager
        Inherits WebPartManager

        Public Shared ReadOnly HelpDisplayMode As HelpDisplayMode =
➥New HelpDisplayMode("Help")

        Protected Overrides Function CreateDisplayModes()
➥As WebPartDisplayModeCollection
            Dim modes As WebPartDisplayModeCollection = MyBase.CreateDisplayModes()
            modes.Add(HelpDisplayMode)
            Return modes
        End Function

    End Class
End Namespace
```

In Listing 30.26, the CreateDisplayModes() method is overridden and the HelpDisplayMode class is added. Notice that the HelpDisplayMode class is exposed as a public field of the CustomWebPartManager. That way, you can use CustomWebPartManager.HelpDisplayMode in your code to refer to the custom Display Mode.

Next, we need to create the Web Parts that displays in the page. These Web Parts will display a floating help box. They are contained in Listing 30.27 and Listing 30.28.

30

LISTING 30.27   FirstHelpPart.ascx

```
<%@ Control Language="VB" ClassName="FirstHelpPart" %>
<%@ Import Namespace="myControls" %>
<script runat="server">

    Sub Page_PreRender()
        Dim wpm As CustomWebPartManager =
➥CType(WebPartManager.GetCurrentWebPartManager(Page), CustomWebPartManager)
        divHelp.Visible = (wpm.DisplayMode Is CustomWebPartManager.HelpDisplayMode)
    End Sub

</script>

<div id="divHelp" class="divHelp" runat="server">
Here is the help for the FirstHelpPart control!
</div>

<h1>First Help Part</h1>
```

LISTING 30.28   SecondHelpPart.ascx

```
<%@ Control Language="VB" ClassName="SecondHelpPart" %>
<%@ Import Namespace="myControls" %>
<script runat="server">

    Sub Page_PreRender()
        Dim wpm As CustomWebPartManager =
➥CType(WebPartManager.GetCurrentWebPartManager(Page), CustomWebPartManager)
        divHelp.Visible = (wpm.DisplayMode Is CustomWebPartManager.HelpDisplayMode)
    End Sub

</script>

<div id="divHelp" class="divHelp" runat="server">
Here is the help for the SecondHelpPart control!
</div>

<h1>Second Help Part</h1>
```

Both Web Parts contain a <div> tag that has a brief help message. The contents of the <div> tag are hidden or displayed in the Page_PreRender() method, depending on the current Web Part Display Mode.

Next, we need to create the custom HelpZone control. This control can be used to display extended help for the page. The HelpZone control is contained in Listing 30.29.

LISTING 30.29   HelpZone.vb

```vb
Imports System
Imports System.Web.UI
Imports System.Web.UI.WebControls.WebParts

Namespace myControls

    ''' <summary>
    ''' Displays extended page help when a page
    ''' is in Help Display Mode
    ''' </summary>
    Public Class HelpZone
        Inherits ToolZone
        Private _contents As String = "Help Contents"
        Private _headerText As String = "Help"

        Public Sub New()
            MyBase.New(CustomWebPartManager.HelpDisplayMode)
        End Sub

        ''' <summary>
        ''' Text displayed in title bar
        ''' </summary>
        Public Overrides Property HeaderText() As String
            Get
                Return _headerText
            End Get
            Set(ByVal Value As String)
                _headerText = Value
            End Set
        End Property

        ''' <summary>
        ''' Represents the help text displayed in the
        ''' Help Zone
        ''' </summary>
        <PersistenceMode(PersistenceMode.InnerProperty)> _
        Public Property Contents() As String
            Get
                Return _contents
            End Get
            Set(ByVal Value As String)
                _contents = Value
            End Set
        End Property
```

30

LISTING 30.29 Continued

```
        ''' <summary>
        ''' Renders the help text
        ''' </summary>
        Protected Overrides Sub RenderBody(ByVal writer As HtmlTextWriter)
            writer.Write(_contents)
        End Sub


        ''' <summary>
        ''' When the user clicks Close, switch
        ''' back to Browse Display Mode
        ''' </summary>
        Protected Overrides Sub Close()
            Me.WebPartManager.DisplayMode = WebPartManager.BrowseDisplayMode
        End Sub
    End Class
End Namespace
```

The HelpZone control takes whatever text is contained in its <Contents> tag and renders it. The text appears only when the page is in Help Display Mode.

Finally, we can create the page that hosts all of the custom controls. The page in Listing 30.30 contains the CustomWebPartManager control, the custom HelpZone control, and the two custom Web Parts.

LISTING 30.30 ShowHelpDisplayMode.aspx

```
<%@ Page Language="VB" %>
<%@ Register TagPrefix="custom" Namespace="myControls" %>
<%@ Register TagPrefix="user" TagName="FirstHelpPart" Src="~/FirstHelpPart.ascx" %>
<%@ Register TagPrefix="user" TagName="SecondHelpPart"
  Src="~/SecondHelpPart.ascx" %>
<!DOCTYPE html PUBLIC "-//W3C//DTD XHTML 1.1//EN"
    "http://www.w3.org/TR/xhtml11/DTD/xhtml11.dtd">
<script runat="server">

    Protected Sub Menu1_MenuItemClick(ByVal sender As Object,
➥ByVal e As MenuEventArgs)
        CustomWebPartManager1.DisplayMode =
➥CustomWebPartManager1.DisplayModes(e.Item.Text)
    End Sub

</script>
<html xmlns="http://www.w3.org/1999/xhtml" >
<head id="Head1" runat="server">
    <style type="text/css">
```

LISTING 30.30   Continued

```
        .divHelp
        {
            position:absolute;
            width:200px;
            top:10px;
            left:20px;
            border:solid 2px orange;
            background-color:#FFFFE0;
            padding:5px;
            font:12px Arial,sans-serif;
            filter:progid:DXImageTransform.Microsoft.dropshadow(OffX=-5,
OffY=5, Color=#cccccc)
        }
        .helpZone
        {
            border:solid 2px orange;
            background-color:#FFFFE0;
            padding:5px;
        }
        .column table
        {
            position:relative;
        }
        .column
        {
            float:left;
            width:30%;
            height:200px;
            margin-right:10px;
            border:solid 1px black;
            background-color: white;
        }
        .menu
        {
            margin:5px 0px;
        }
        html
        {
            background-color:#eeeeee;
        }
    </style>
    <title>Show Help Display Mode</title>
</head>
<body>
```

LISTING 30.30   Continued

```
<form id="form1" runat="server">
<custom:CustomWebPartManager
    id="CustomWebPartManager1"
    Runat="server" />

    <asp:Menu
        id="Menu1"
        OnMenuItemClick="Menu1_MenuItemClick"
        Orientation="Horizontal"
        CssClass="menu"
        Runat="server">
        <Items>
        <asp:MenuItem Text="Browse" />
        <asp:MenuItem Text="Design" />
        <asp:MenuItem Text="Help" />
        </Items>
    </asp:Menu>

    <asp:WebPartZone
        id="WebPartZone1"
        CssClass="column"
        Runat="server">
        <ZoneTemplate>
        <user:FirstHelpPart
            id="FirstHelpPart1"
            Title="First Web Part"
            runat="Server" />
        </ZoneTemplate>
    </asp:WebPartZone>

    <asp:WebPartZone
        id="WebPartZone2"
        CssClass="column"
        Runat="server">
        <ZoneTemplate>
        <user:SecondHelpPart
            id="SecondHelpPart1"
            Title="Second Web Part"
            runat="Server" />
        </ZoneTemplate>
    </asp:WebPartZone>

    <custom:HelpZone
        id="HelpZone1"
```

LISTING 30.30   Continued

```
            CssClass="helpZone"
            runat="Server">
            <Contents>
            This is the extended help for this page.
            </Contents>
        </custom:HelpZone>
    </form>
</body>
</html>
```

After you open the page in Listing 30.30, you can click the Help link to switch the page into Help Display Mode. When you switch to Help Display Mode, you should see help messages pop up above each Web Part. Furthermore, the contents of the HelpZone are displayed.

The page in Listing 30.30 takes advantage of its style sheet to perform most of the formatting. For example, the floating help boxes are created with the help of the divHelp CSS class.

Summary

In this chapter, you learned how you easily can extend the power of the Web Part Framework. The first section explored different types of Web Part Zones that you can create. For example, we created a custom Photo Web Part Zone that automatically displays the photos contained in a folder. We also created a multi-column Web Part Zone that displays Web Parts in a configurable number of repeating columns. Finally, we created a Web Part Zone that supports fancy drop-down menus.

Next, you learned about several methods of extending Catalog Zones. We created a custom Catalog Part that automatically displays all the Web Part controls contained in an application's App_Code folder. We also created a custom Catalog Zone that supports drag-and-drop functionality. Finally, you explored a method for creating a templated Catalog Zone that enables you to customize the appearance of a catalog in any way that you please.

Next, we tackled the subject of Editor Zones. First, we created a simple custom Editor Part that renders a custom form for editing the properties of a Web Part. Next, we created a templated Editor Zone that enables you to easily associate custom editor forms with any Web Part.

Finally, we built a custom Web Part Display Mode and Tool Zone. By taking advantage of a custom Help Display Mode, you can display help messages easily to the users of a Web Part page.

PART IX

Custom Control Building

IN THIS PART

CHAPTER **31**

Building Custom Controls

In this chapter, you learn how to extend the ASP.NET Framework by building custom controls. You learn how to create controls in exactly the same way as Microsoft developed the standard ASP.NET controls such as the TextBox and Button controls.

Overview of Custom Control Building

You must answer two questions before writing a custom control:

- What type of control do I want to write?

- From what class do I inherit?

The two basic types of controls are fully rendered and composite controls. When you build a fully rendered control, you start from scratch. You specify all the HTML content that the control renders to the browser.

When you create a composite control, on the other hand, you build a new control from existing controls. For example, you can create a composite AddressForm control from existing TextBox and RequiredFieldValidator controls. When you create a composite control, you bundle together existing controls as a new control.

The second question that you must address is the choice of the base control for your new control. You can inherit a new control from any existing ASP.NET control. For example, if you want to create a better GridView control, then you can inherit a new control from the GridView control and add additional properties and methods to your custom GridView control.

Typically, when building a basic control, you inherit your new control from one of the following base classes:

- System.Web.UI.Control

- System.Web.UI.WebControls.WebControl

- System.Web.UI.WebControls.CompositeControl

The CompositeControl class inherits from the WebControl class, which inherits from the Control class. Each of these base classes adds additional functionality.

The base class for all controls in the ASP.NET Framework is the System.Web.UI.Control class. Every control, including the TextBox and GridView controls, ultimately derives from this control. This means that all the properties, methods, and events of the System.Web.UI.Control class are shared by all controls in the Framework.

All Web controls inherit from the base System.Web.UI.WebControls.WebControl class. The difference between the Control class and WebControl class is that controls that derive from the WebControl class always have opening and closing tags. Because a WebControl has an opening and closing tag, you also get more formatting options. For example, the WebControl class includes BackColor, Font, and ForeColor properties.

For example, the ASP.NET Literal control inherits from the base Control class, whereas the Label control inherits from the base WebControl class. The Repeater control inherits from the base Control class, whereas the GridView control (ultimately) inherits from the WebControl class.

Finally, the System.Web.UI.WebControls.CompositeControl is new in the ASP.NET 2.0 Framework. You should use this class as the base class for any composite control. The CompositeControl automatically creates a naming container for its child controls. It also includes an overridden Controls property that forces child controls to appear in Design view.

Building Fully Rendered Controls

Let's start by creating a simple fully rendered control. When you create a fully rendered control, you take on the responsibility of specifying all the HTML content that the control renders to the browser.

The file in Listing 31.1 contains a fully rendered control that derives from the base Control class.

LISTING 31.1   FullyRenderedControl.vb

```
Imports System.Web.UI

Namespace myControls
    Public Class FullyRenderedControl
```

LISTING 31.1   Continued

```
        Inherits Control

        Private _Text As String

        Public Property Text() As String
            Get
                Return _Text
            End Get
            Set(ByVal Value As String)
                _Text = value
            End Set
        End Property

        Protected Overrides Sub Render(ByVal writer As HtmlTextWriter)
            writer.Write(_Text)
        End Sub


    End Class
End Namespace
```

> **NOTE**
>
> Add the control in Listing 31.1 to your App_Code folder. Any code added to the App_Code folder is compiled dynamically.

The control in Listing 31.1 inherits from the base `Control` class, overriding the base class `Render()` method. The control simply displays whatever value that you assign to its `Text` property. The value of the `Text` property is written to the browser with the `HtmlTextWriter` class's `Write()` method.

The file in Listing 31.2 illustrates how you can use the new control in a page.

LISTING 31.2   ShowFullyRenderedControl.aspx

```
<%@ Page Language="VB" %>
<%@ Register TagPrefix="custom" Namespace="myControls" %>
<!DOCTYPE html PUBLIC "-//W3C//DTD XHTML 1.0 Transitional//EN"
➥"http://www.w3.org/TR/xhtml1/DTD/xhtml1-transitional.dtd">
<html xmlns="http://www.w3.org/1999/xhtml" >
<head id="Head1" runat="server">
    <title>Show Fully Rendered Control</title>
</head>
<body>
    <form id="form1" runat="server">
    <div>
```

LISTING 31.2   Continued

```
<custom:FullyRenderedControl
    ID="FullyRenderedControl1"
    Text="Hello World!"
    runat="Server" />

    </div>
    </form>
</body>
</html>
```

> **NOTE**
>
> In Listing 31.2, the custom control is registered in the page through use of the <%@ Register
> %> directive. Alternatively, you can register the control for an entire website by registering the
> control in the <pages> section of the web configuration file.

If you open the page in Listing 31.2 in a browser and select View Source, you can see the HTML rendered by the control. The control simply renders the string "Hello World!".

Rather than inherit from the base Control class, you can create a fully rendered control by inheriting a new control from the base WebControl class. When inheriting from the WebControl class, you override the RenderContents() method instead of the Render() method.

For example, the control in Listing 31.3 contains a simple fully rendered control that inherits from the WebControl class.

LISTING 31.3   FullyRenderedWebControl.vb

```
Imports System.Web.UI
Imports System.Web.UI.WebControls

Namespace myControls
    Public Class FullyRenderedWebControl
        Inherits WebControl

        Private _Text As String

        Public Property Text() As String
            Get
                Return _Text
            End Get
            Set(ByVal Value As String)
                _Text = value
            End Set
        End Property
```

LISTING 31.3   Continued

```
    Protected Overrides Sub RenderContents(ByVal writer As HtmlTextWriter)
        writer.Write(_Text)
    End Sub

  End Class
End Namespace
```

The page in Listing 31.4 illustrates how you can use the new control (see Figure 31.1). Notice that the `BackColor`, `BorderStyle`, and `Font` properties are set. Because the control in Listing 31.3 derives from the base `WebControl` class, you get these properties for free.

FIGURE 31.1   Displaying a fully rendered `WebControl`.

LISTING 31.4   ShowFullyRenderedWebControl.aspx

```
<%@ Page Language="VB" %>
<%@ Register TagPrefix="custom" Namespace="myControls" %>
<!DOCTYPE html PUBLIC "-//W3C//DTD XHTML 1.0 Transitional//EN"
➡"http://www.w3.org/TR/xhtml1/DTD/xhtml1-transitional.dtd">
<html xmlns="http://www.w3.org/1999/xhtml" >
<head id="Head1" runat="server">
    <title>Show Fully Rendered WebControl</title>
</head>
```

31

LISTING 31.4   Continued

```
<body>
    <form id="form1" runat="server">
    <div>

    <custom:FullyRenderedWebControl
        ID="FullyrenderedWebControl1"
        Text="Hello World"
        BackColor="Yellow"
        BorderStyle="Dashed"
        Font-Size="32px"
        Runat="Server" />

    </div>
    </form>
</body>
</html>
```

After opening the page in Listing 31.4, if you select View Source in your browser, you can see the rendered output of the control. It looks like this:

```
<span id="FullyrenderedWebControl1" style="display:inline-block;
➥background-color:Yellow;border-style:Dashed;
➥font-size:32px;">Hello World</span>
```

A WebControl, unlike a control, renders an enclosing <span> tag by default.

Understanding the HtmlTextWriter Class

When you create a fully rendered control, you use the HtmlTextWriter class to write the HTML content to the browser. The HtmlTextWriter class was specifically designed to make it easier to render HTML. Here is a partial list of the methods supported by this class:

- AddAttribute()—Adds an HTML attribute to the tag rendered by calling RenderBeginTag().

- AddStyleAttribute()—Adds a CSS attribute to the tag rendered by a call to RenderBeginTag().

- RenderBeginTag()—Renders an opening HTML tag.

- RenderEndTag()—Renders a closing HTML tag.

- Write()—Renders a string to the browser.

- WriteBreak()—Renders a <br /> tag to the browser.

You can call the AddAttribute() or the AddStyleAttribute() method as many times as you please before calling RenderBeginTag(). When you call RenderBeginTag(), all the attributes are added to the opening HTML tag.

The methods of the `HtmlTextWriter` class can use the following enumerations:

- `HtmlTextWriterTag`—Contains a list of the most common HTML tags.
- `HtmlTextWriterAttribute`—Contains a list of the most common HTML attributes.
- `HtmlTextWriterStyle`—Contains a list of the most Cascading Style Sheet attributes.

When using the methods of the `HtmlTextWriter` class, you should strive to use these enumerations to represent HTML tags and attributes. If a particular tag or attribute is missing from one of the enumerations, you can pass a string value instead.

For example, the control in Listing 31.5 renders a table of HTML colors by using an HTML table (see Figure 31.2). Notice that the `RenderContents()` method takes advantage of the methods of the `HtmlTextWriter` class to render the HTML table.

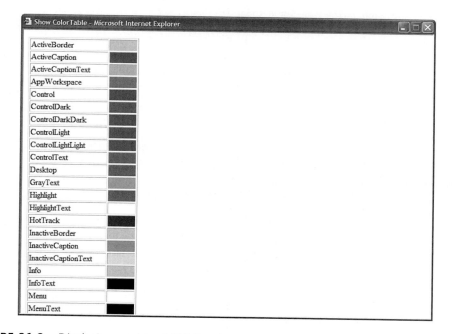

FIGURE 31.2   Displaying a table of HTML colors.

LISTING 31.5   `ColorTable.vb`

```vb
Imports System
Imports System.Web.UI
Imports System.Web.UI.WebControls
Imports System.Drawing

Namespace myControls
    Public Class ColorTable
```

LISTING 31.5   Continued

```
        Inherits WebControl

        Protected Overrides Sub RenderContents(ByVal writer As HtmlTextWriter)
            ' Get list of colors
            Dim colors() As KnownColor =
➥CType(System.Enum.GetValues(GetType(KnownColor)), KnownColor())

            ' Render opening table tag
            writer.AddAttribute(HtmlTextWriterAttribute.Border, "1")
            writer.RenderBeginTag(HtmlTextWriterTag.Table)

            ' Render table body
            Dim colorName As KnownColor
            For Each colorName In colors
                writer.RenderBeginTag(HtmlTextWriterTag.Tr)

                ' Render first column
                writer.RenderBeginTag(HtmlTextWriterTag.Td)
                writer.Write(colorName.ToString())
                writer.RenderEndTag()

                ' Render second column
                writer.AddAttribute(HtmlTextWriterAttribute.Width, "50px")
                writer.AddAttribute(HtmlTextWriterAttribute.Bgcolor,
➥ colorName.ToString())
                writer.RenderBeginTag(HtmlTextWriterTag.Td)
                writer.Write(" ")
                writer.RenderEndTag()

                writer.RenderEndTag()
            Next

            ' close table
            writer.RenderEndTag()
        End Sub

    End Class
End Namespace
```

You should notice a number of things about the control in Listing 31.5. First, notice that
the AddAttribute() method is called to add the table border attribute. When the
RenderBeginTag() method is called, the table border attribute is added to the opening
table tag.

Furthermore, notice that you do not specify the tag when calling the `RenderEndTag()` method. This method automatically closes the last tag opened with the `RenderBeginTag()` method.

NOTE

The CD that accompanies this book includes a `ShowColorTable.aspx` page that you can open in your browser to view the rendered output of the `ColorTable` control.

The control in Listing 31.6, the DropShadow control, illustrates how you can use the `AddStyleAttribute()` method of the `HtmlTextWriter` class to add Cascading Style Sheet attributes to an HTML tag.

LISTING 31.6   DropShadow.vb

```
Imports System.Web.UI
Imports System.Web.UI.WebControls

Namespace myControls
    Public Class DropShadow
        Inherits WebControl

        Private _Text As String

        Public Property Text() As String
            Get
                Return _Text
            End Get
            Set(ByVal Value As String)
                _Text = value
            End Set
        End Property

        Protected Overrides Sub RenderContents(ByVal writer As HtmlTextWriter)
            writer.AddStyleAttribute(HtmlTextWriterStyle.Filter,
➥"dropShadow(color=#AAAAAA,offX=3,offY=3);width:500px")
            writer.RenderBeginTag(HtmlTextWriterTag.Div)
            writer.Write(_Text)
            writer.RenderEndTag()
        End Sub

    End Class
End Namespace
```

The control in Listing 31.6 renders a drop shadow behind whatever text you assign to the control's `Text` property (see Figure 31.3). The drop shadow is created with the help of an Internet Explorer `DropShadow` filter.

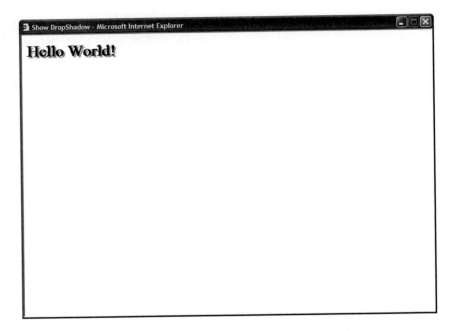

FIGURE 31.3   Displaying a drop shadow with the `DropShadow` control.

Notice that the `Filter` attribute is added to the `<div>` tag with a call to the `AddStyleAttribute()` method. The `AddStyleAttribute()` method works just like the `AddAttribute()` method, except that the `AddStyleAttribute()` method adds a CSS attribute instead of an HTML attribute.

WEB STANDARDS NOTE

Filters are an Internet Explorer extension to the Cascading Style Sheet standard. They don't work with Firefox or Opera. Firefox has its own extensions to Cascading Style Sheets with its `-moz` style rules.

Specifying the Containing `WebControl` Tag
By default, a `WebControl` renders an HTML `<span>` tag around its contents. You can specify a different tag by overriding the `WebControl`'s `TagKey` property.

For example, the control in Listing 31.7 renders its contents within an HTML `<div>` tag.

LISTING 31.7   Glow.vb

```
Imports System.Web.UI
Imports System.Web.UI.WebControls


Namespace myControls
    Public Class Glow
```

LISTING 31.7   Continued

```vb
        Inherits WebControl
        Private _Text As String

        Public Property Text() As String
            Get
                Return _Text
            End Get
            Set(ByVal Value As String)
                _Text = value
            End Set
        End Property

        Protected Overrides ReadOnly Property TagKey() As HtmlTextWriterTag
            Get
                Return HtmlTextWriterTag.Div
            End Get
        End Property

        Protected Overrides Sub AddAttributesToRender(ByVal writer
➥As HtmlTextWriter)
            writer.AddStyleAttribute(HtmlTextWriterStyle.Filter,
➥"glow(Color=#ffd700,Strength=10)")
            MyBase.AddAttributesToRender(writer)
        End Sub

        Protected Overrides Sub RenderContents(ByVal writer As HtmlTextWriter)
            writer.Write(_Text)
        End Sub

        Public Sub New()
            Me.Width = Unit.Parse("500px")
        End Sub

    End Class
End Namespace
```

The control in Listing 31.7 displays a glowing effect around any text that you assign to its Text property. The control takes advantage of the Internet Explorer Glow filter to create the glow effect (see Figure 31.4).

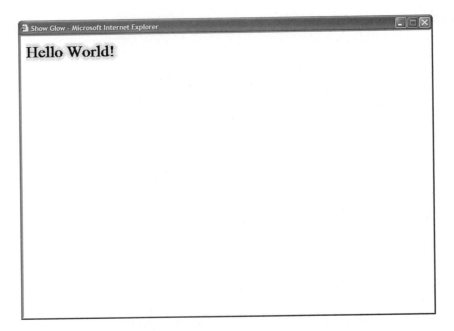

FIGURE 31.4   Displaying glowing text with the Glow control.

Notice that the control overrides the base WebControl's TagKey property. Because the over-ridden property returns a <div> tag, the WebControl renders a <div> tag.

> **NOTE**
>
> There are several methods you can use to modify the tag rendered by a WebControl. You can override the TagName property instead of the TagKey property. The TagName property enables you to specify an arbitrary string for the tag. (It doesn't limit you to the HtmlTextWriterTag enumeration.) You also can specify the tag rendered by a WebControl in the WebControl's constructor. Finally, you can override a WebControl's RenderBeginTag() and RenderEndTag() methods and completely customize the opening and closing tags.

Furthermore, you should notice that the control in Listing 31.7 overrides the AddAttributesToRender() method. If you override this method, then you can add HTML or CSS attributes to the opening HTML tag rendered by the control. When overriding this method, be careful to call the base AddAttributesToRender() method or the standard control attributes, such as the control ID, won't be rendered.

Building Composite Controls

If you don't want to start from scratch when building a custom control, you can build a composite control. When you create a composite control, you create a new control from existing controls.

Every ASP.NET control has a `Controls` property that represents all of its child controls. If you add child controls to a control, then the child controls are automatically rendered when the parent control is rendered.

When you create a composite control, you typically override a control's `CreateChildControls()` method. This method is called when a control builds its collection of child controls.

For example, the control in Listing 31.8 combines a `TextBox` control and `RequiredFieldValidator` control.

LISTING 31.8   RequiredTextBox.vb

```
Imports System
Imports System.Web.UI.WebControls

Namespace myControls
    Public Class RequiredTextBox
        Inherits CompositeControl

        Private input As TextBox

        Private validator As RequiredFieldValidator

        Public Property Text() As String
            Get
                EnsureChildControls()
                Return input.Text
            End Get
            Set(ByVal Value As String)
                EnsureChildControls()
                input.Text = value
            End Set
        End Property

        Protected Overrides Sub CreateChildControls()
            input = New TextBox()
            input.ID = "input"
            Me.Controls.Add(input)

            validator = New RequiredFieldValidator()
            validator.ID = "valInput"
            validator.ControlToValidate = input.ID
            validator.ErrorMessage = "(Required)"
            validator.Display = ValidatorDisplay.Dynamic
            Me.Controls.Add(validator)
        End Sub

    End Class
End Namespace
```

31

Notice that the control in Listing 31.8 inherits from the base `CompositeControl` class. Furthermore, rather than override the base control's `RenderContents()` method, the control overrides the base control's `CreateChildControls()` method.

You should notice one other special thing in Listing 31.8. Notice that the `EnsureChildControls()` method is called in both the `Get` and `Set` methods of the `Text` property. The `EnsureChildControls()` method forces the `CreateChildControls()` method to be called. However, it prevents the `CreateChildControls()` method from being called more than once.

The Text property gets or sets a property of a child control (the TextBox control). If you attempt to use the Text property before the `CreateChildControls()` method is called, then you receive a null reference exception. The child controls must be created before you can access any of the child control properties.

The page in Listing 31.9 illustrates how you can use the `RequiredTextBox` control in a page.

LISTING 31.9   ShowRequiredTextBox.aspx

```
<%@ Page Language="VB" Trace="true" %>
<%@ Register TagPrefix="custom" Namespace="myControls" %>
<!DOCTYPE html PUBLIC "-//W3C//DTD XHTML 1.0 Transitional//EN"
➥"http://www.w3.org/TR/xhtml1/DTD/xhtml1-transitional.dtd">
<script runat="server">

    Sub btnSubmit_Click(ByVal sender As Object, ByVal e As EventArgs)
        lblResults.Text = txtUserName.Text
    End Sub
</script>
<html xmlns="http://www.w3.org/1999/xhtml" >
<head id="Head1" runat="server">
    <title>Show RequiredTextBox</title>
</head>
<body>
    <form id="form1" runat="server">
    <div>

    <asp:Label
        ID="lblUserName"
        Text="User Name:"
        AssociatedControlID="txtUserName"
        Runat="server" />

    <custom:RequiredTextBox
        ID="txtUserName"
        Runat="Server" />
```

LISTING 31.9   Continued

```
        <br />

        <asp:Button
            ID="btnSubmit"
            Text="Submit"
            OnClick="btnSubmit_Click"
            Runat="server" />

        <hr />

        <asp:Label
            id="lblResults"
            Runat="server" />

    </div>
    </form>
</body>
</html>
```

The page in Listing 31.9 has tracing enabled. If you look at the control tree for the page, you'll see that the RequiredTextBox control includes both a TextBox and RequiredFieldValidator control as child controls.

Building Hybrid Controls

In practice, you very rarely build pure composite controls. In most cases in which you override a control's CreateChildControls() method, you also override the control's RenderContents() method to specify the layout of the child controls.

For example, the control in Listing 31.10 represents a Login control. In the control's CreateChildControls() method, two TextBox controls are added to the control's collection of child controls.

LISTING 31.10   Login.vb

```
Imports System
Imports System.Web.UI
Imports System.Web.UI.WebControls

Namespace myControls

    Public Class Login
        Inherits CompositeControl
        Private txtUserName As TextBox
```

LISTING 31.10   Continued

```vbnet
    Private txtPassword As TextBox

    Public Property UserName() As String
        Get
            EnsureChildControls()
            Return txtUserName.Text
        End Get
        Set(ByVal Value As String)
            EnsureChildControls()
            txtUserName.Text = value
        End Set
    End Property

    Public Property Password() As String
        Get
            EnsureChildControls()
            Return txtPassword.Text
        End Get
        Set(ByVal Value As String)
            EnsureChildControls()
            txtPassword.Text = value
        End Set
    End Property

    Protected Overrides Sub CreateChildControls()
        txtUserName = New TextBox()
        txtUserName.ID = "txtUserName"
        Me.Controls.Add(txtUserName)

        txtPassword = New TextBox()
        txtPassword.ID = "txtPassword"
        txtPassword.TextMode = TextBoxMode.Password
        Me.Controls.Add(txtPassword)
    End Sub

    Protected Overrides Sub RenderContents(ByVal writer As HtmlTextWriter)
        writer.RenderBeginTag(HtmlTextWriterTag.Tr)

        ' Render UserName Label
        writer.RenderBeginTag(HtmlTextWriterTag.Td)
        writer.AddAttribute(HtmlTextWriterAttribute.For, txtUserName.ClientID)
        writer.RenderBeginTag(HtmlTextWriterTag.Label)
        writer.Write("User Name:")
```

LISTING 31.10   Continued

```
            writer.RenderEndTag() ' Label
            writer.RenderEndTag() ' TD

            ' Render UserName TextBox
            writer.RenderBeginTag(HtmlTextWriterTag.Td)
            txtUserName.RenderControl(writer)
            writer.RenderEndTag() ' TD

            writer.RenderEndTag()
            writer.RenderBeginTag(HtmlTextWriterTag.Tr)

            ' Render Password Label
            writer.RenderBeginTag(HtmlTextWriterTag.Td)
            writer.AddAttribute(HtmlTextWriterAttribute.For, txtPassword.ClientID)
            writer.RenderBeginTag(HtmlTextWriterTag.Label)
            writer.Write("Password:")
            writer.RenderEndTag() ' Label
            writer.RenderEndTag() ' TD

            ' Render Password TextBox
            writer.RenderBeginTag(HtmlTextWriterTag.Td)
            txtPassword.RenderControl(writer)
            writer.RenderEndTag() ' TD

            writer.RenderEndTag() ' TR
        End Sub

        Protected Overrides ReadOnly Property TagKey() As HtmlTextWriterTag
            Get
                Return HtmlTextWriterTag.Table
            End Get
        End Property

    End Class
End Namespace
```

In Listing 31.10, the `RenderContents()` method is overridden in order to layout the two TextBox controls. The TextBox controls are rendered within an HTML table (see Figure 31.5). Notice that each TextBox is rendered by calling the `RenderControl()` method.

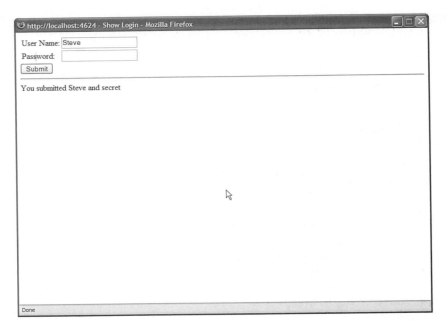

FIGURE 31.5 Performing layout with an HTML table.

The default `RenderContents()` method simply calls the `RenderControl()` method for each child control. If you override the `RenderContents()` method, you have more control over the layout of the control.

The `Login` control in Listing 31.10 uses an HTML table for layout. From a web standards perspective, using HTML tables for layout is frowned upon. The modified `Login` control in Listing 31.11 uses `<div>` tags instead of a `<table>` tag for layout.

LISTING 31.11 LoginStandards.vb

```
Imports System
Imports System.Web.UI
Imports System.Web.UI.WebControls

Namespace myControls
    Public Class LoginStandards
        Inherits CompositeControl

        Private txtUserName As TextBox
        Private txtPassword As TextBox

        Public Property UserName() As String
            Get
                EnsureChildControls()
```

LISTING 31.11   Continued

```
            Return txtUserName.Text
        End Get
        Set(ByVal Value As String)
            EnsureChildControls()
            txtUserName.Text = Value
        End Set
    End Property

    Public Property Password() As String
        Get
            EnsureChildControls()
            Return txtPassword.Text
        End Get
        Set(ByVal Value As String)
            EnsureChildControls()
            txtPassword.Text = Value
        End Set
    End Property

    Protected Overrides Sub CreateChildControls()
        txtUserName = New TextBox()
        txtUserName.ID = "txtUserName"
        Me.Controls.Add(txtUserName)

        txtPassword = New TextBox()
        txtPassword.ID = "txtPassword"
        txtPassword.TextMode = TextBoxMode.Password
        Me.Controls.Add(txtPassword)
    End Sub

    Protected Overrides Sub RenderContents(ByVal writer As HtmlTextWriter)
        writer.AddStyleAttribute("float", "left")
        writer.RenderBeginTag(HtmlTextWriterTag.Div)
        writer.AddStyleAttribute(HtmlTextWriterStyle.Padding, "3px")
        writer.RenderBeginTag(HtmlTextWriterTag.Div)
        writer.AddAttribute(HtmlTextWriterAttribute.For, txtUserName.ClientID)
        writer.RenderBeginTag(HtmlTextWriterTag.Label)
        writer.Write("User Name:")
        writer.RenderEndTag()
        writer.RenderEndTag()

        writer.AddStyleAttribute(HtmlTextWriterStyle.Padding, "3px")
        writer.RenderBeginTag(HtmlTextWriterTag.Div)
        writer.AddAttribute(HtmlTextWriterAttribute.For, txtPassword.ClientID)
```

31

LISTING 31.11   Continued

```
            writer.RenderBeginTag(HtmlTextWriterTag.Label)
            writer.Write("Password:")
            writer.RenderEndTag()
            writer.RenderEndTag()
            writer.RenderEndTag()

            writer.AddStyleAttribute("float", "left")
            writer.RenderBeginTag(HtmlTextWriterTag.Div)
            writer.AddStyleAttribute(HtmlTextWriterStyle.Padding, "3px")
            writer.RenderBeginTag(HtmlTextWriterTag.Div)
            txtUserName.RenderControl(writer)
            writer.RenderEndTag()

            writer.AddStyleAttribute(HtmlTextWriterStyle.Padding, "3px")
            writer.RenderBeginTag(HtmlTextWriterTag.Div)
            txtPassword.RenderControl(writer)
            writer.RenderEndTag()
            writer.RenderEndTag()

            writer.Write("<br style='clear:left' />")
        End Sub

        Protected Overrides ReadOnly Property TagKey() As HtmlTextWriterTag
            Get
                Return HtmlTextWriterTag.Div
            End Get
        End Property


    End Class
End Namespace
```

The control in Listing 31.11 works quite nicely in all recent browsers (Internet Explorer 6, Firefox 1, Opera 8) without requiring an HTML table for layout (see Figure 31.6).

> **NOTE**
>
> Microsoft does not have the luxury of using <div> tags for layout. Because Microsoft must support very old browsers that have limited or no support for Cascading Style Sheets (HTML 3.2 browsers), the standard controls must rely on HTML tables for layout.

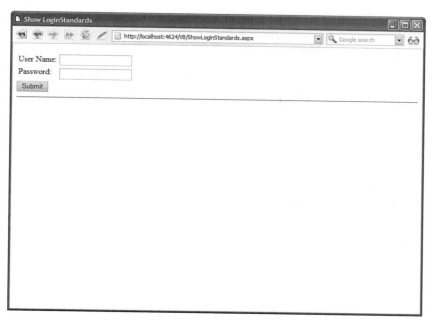

FIGURE 31.6   Performing CSS layout.

View State and Control State

The standard ASP.NET controls retain the values of their properties across postbacks. For example, if you change the text displayed by a Label control, the Label control will continue to display the new text even if you repeatedly post the page containing the Label control back to the server.

The ASP.NET Framework takes advantage of a hidden form field named __VIEWSTATE to preserve the state of control properties across postbacks. If you want your controls to preserve the values of their properties, then you need to add the values of your control properties to this hidden form field.

The ASP.NET 2.0 Framework supports two methods of preserving values across postbacks. You can take advantage of either View State or Control State.

Supporting View State

You can use the ViewState property of the Control or Page class to add values to View State. The ViewState property exposes a dictionary of key and value pairs. For example, the following statement adds the string Hello World! to View State:

```
ViewState("message") = "Hello World!"
```

Technically, you can add an instance of any serializable class to View State. In practice, however, you should add only simple values to View State, such as Strings, DateTimes, and `Integers`. Remember that anything that you add to View State must be added to the hidden `__VIEWSTATE` form field. If this field gets too big, it can have a significant impact on your page's performance.

The control in Listing 31.12 has two properties, named `Text` and `ViewStateText`. The first property does not use View State, and the second property does use View State. The value of the `ViewStateText` property is preserved across postbacks automatically.

LISTING 31.12   ViewStateControl.vb

```vb
Imports System
Imports System.Web
Imports System.Web.UI
Imports System.Web.UI.WebControls

Namespace myControls
    Public Class ViewStateControl
        Inherits WebControl

        Private _text As String

        Public Property Text() As String
            Get
                Return _text
            End Get
            Set(ByVal Value As String)
                _text = value
            End Set
        End Property

        Public Property ViewStateText() As String
            Get
                If IsNothing(ViewState("ViewStateText")) Then
                    Return String.Empty
                Else
                    Return CType(ViewState("ViewStateText"), String)
                End If
            End Get
            Set(ByVal Value As String)
                ViewState("ViewStateText") = value
            End Set
        End Property

        Protected Overrides Sub RenderContents(ByVal writer As HtmlTextWriter)
            writer.Write("Text: " & Text)
            writer.WriteBreak()
            writer.Write("ViewStateText: " & ViewStateText)
```

LISTING 31.12   Continued

```
            writer.WriteBreak()
        End Sub


    End Class
End Namespace
```

Notice that the ViewStateText property uses the Control's ViewState collection to preserve whatever value is assigned to the ViewStateText property across postbacks. When you add a value to the ViewState collection, the value is stuffed into the hidden __VIEWSTATE form field automatically.

> **WARNING**
>
> View State is loaded after the Page InitComplete event, and View State is saved after the Page PreRenderComplete event. This means that you should not attempt to retrieve a value from View State before or during the InitComplete event. You also should not attempt to add a value to View State after the PreRenderComplete event.

The page in Listing 31.13 includes the ViewStateControl. The text Hello World! is assigned to both control properties in the Page_Load() handler. However, if you post the page back to itself by clicking the button, only the value of the ViewStateText property is preserved across postbacks.

LISTING 31.13   ShowViewState.aspx

```
<%@ Page Language="VB" %>
<%@ Register TagPrefix="custom" Namespace="myControls" %>
<!DOCTYPE html PUBLIC "-//W3C//DTD XHTML 1.0 Transitional//EN"
  "http://www.w3.org/TR/xhtml1/DTD/xhtml1-transitional.dtd">
<script runat="server">

    sub Page_Load()
        If Not Page.IsPostBack Then
            ViewStateControl1.Text = "Hello World!"
            ViewStateControl1.ViewStateText = "Hello World!"
        End If
    end sub

</script>
<html xmlns="http://www.w3.org/1999/xhtml" >
<head id="Head1" runat="server">
    <title>Show View State</title>
</head>
<body>
```

LISTING 31.13   Continued

```
    <form id="form1" runat="server">
    <div>

    <custom:ViewStateControl
        id="ViewStateControl1"
        Runat="server" />

    <asp:Button
        id="btnSubmit"
        Text="Submit"
        Runat="server" />

    </div>
    </form>
</body>
</html>
```

Supporting Control State

The ASP.NET 2.0 Framework introduces a new feature named Control State. Control State is very similar to View State. Just like View State, any values that you add to Control State are preserved in the hidden __VIEWSTATE form field. However, unlike View State, Control State cannot be disabled. Control State is intended to be used only for storing crucial information across postbacks.

Control State was introduced to address a problem that developers encountered in the first version of the ASP.NET Framework. You can disable View State for any control by assigning the value False to a control's EnableViewState property. Often, this is a very good idea for performance reasons. However, disabling View State also made several controls non-functional.

For example, by default a GridView control retains the values of all the records that it displays in View State. If you display 500 database records with a GridView control, then by default all 500 records are stuffed into the hidden __VIEWSTATE form field. To improve performance, you might want to disable View State for the GridView.

However, a GridView uses the __VIEWSTATE form field to remember crucial information required for the proper functioning of the control, such as the current page number and the currently selected row. You don't want the GridView to forget this critical information even when View State is disabled.

The ASP.NET 2.0 Framework introduces the concept of Control State to enable you to save critical information in the hidden __VIEWSTATE form field even when View State is disabled. Microsoft makes it slightly more difficult to use Control State because they don't want you to overuse this feature. You should use it only when storing super critical information.

For example, the control in Listing 31.14 includes two properties named `ViewStateText` and `ControlStateText`. View State is used to preserve the value of the first property, and Control State is used to preserve the value of the second property.

LISTING 31.14   `ControlStateControl.vb`

```
Imports System
Imports System.Web
Imports System.Web.UI
Imports System.Web.UI.WebControls

Namespace myControls

    Public Class ControlStateControl
        Inherits WebControl

        Private _controlStateText As String

        Public Property ViewStateText() As String
            Get
                If IsNothing(ViewState("ViewStateText")) Then
                    Return String.Empty
                Else
                    Return CType(ViewState("ViewStateText"), String)
                End If
            End Get
            Set(ByVal Value As String)
                ViewState("ViewStateText") = Value
            End Set
        End Property

        Public Property ControlStateText() As String
            Get
                Return _controlStateText
            End Get
            Set(ByVal Value As String)
                _controlStateText = Value
            End Set
        End Property

        Protected Overrides Sub OnInit(ByVal e As EventArgs)
            Page.RegisterRequiresControlState(Me)
            MyBase.OnInit(e)
        End Sub

        Protected Overrides Function SaveControlState() As Object
```

31

LISTING 31.14   Continued

```
            Return _controlStateText
        End Function

        Protected Overrides Sub LoadControlState(ByVal savedState As Object)
            _controlStateText = CType(savedState, String)
        End Sub

        Protected Overrides Sub RenderContents(ByVal writer As HtmlTextWriter)
            writer.Write("ViewStateText: " + ViewStateText)
            writer.WriteBreak()
            writer.Write("ControlStateText: " + ControlStateText)
            writer.WriteBreak()
        End Sub


    End Class
End Namespace
```

Notice that the control in Listing 31.14 overrides the base Control class's `OnInit()`, `SaveControlState()`, and `LoadControlState()` methods. In the `OnInit()` method, the `RegisterRequiresControlState()` method is called to indicate that the control needs to take advantage of Control State.

The `SaveControlState()` and `LoadControlState()` methods are responsible for saving and loading the Control State. Notice that Control State is saved as an object. The object is serialized by the ASP.NET Framework into the hidden __VIEWSTATE form field automatically.

The page in Listing 31.15 illustrates the difference between View State and Control State. In the `Page_Load()` handler, the value `Hello World!` is assigned to both properties of the `ControlStateControl`. Notice that the control has View State disabled. However, if you click the button and post the page back to itself, the value of the `ControlStateText` property is not lost.

LISTING 31.15   ShowControlState.aspx

```
<%@ Page Language="VB" %>
<%@ Register TagPrefix="custom" Namespace="myControls" %>
<!DOCTYPE html PUBLIC "-//W3C//DTD XHTML 1.0 Transitional//EN"
 "http://www.w3.org/TR/xhtml1/DTD/xhtml1-transitional.dtd">
<script runat="server">

    sub Page_Load()
        If Not Page.IsPostBack Then
            ControlStateControl1.ViewStateText = "Hello World!"
            ControlStateControl1.ControlStateText = "Hello World!"
        End If
```

LISTING 31.15   Continued

```
        end sub

</script>
<html xmlns="http://www.w3.org/1999/xhtml" >
<head id="Head1" runat="server">
    <title>Show Control State</title>
</head>
<body>
    <form id="form1" runat="server">
    <div>

    <custom:ControlStateControl
        id="ControlStateControl1"
        EnableViewState="false"
        Runat="server" />

    <asp:Button
        id="btnSubmit"
        Text="Submit"
        Runat="server" />

    </div>
    </form>
</body>
</html>
```

Processing Postback Data and Events

The ASP.NET Framework is built around web forms. ASP.NET controls pass information from the browser to the server by submitting a form to the server. This process of posting a form back to the server is called a *postback*.

When an ASP.NET page processes a form that has been posted back to the server, two types of information can be passed to the controls in the page. First, if a control initiates a postback, then a server-side event can be raised when the form is posted to the server. For example, if you click a Button control, then a Click event is raised on the server when the form containing the Button is posted back to the server. This event is called a *postback event*.

Second, the form data contained in the web form can be passed to a control. For example, when you submit a form that contains a TextBox control, the form data is passed to the TextBox control when the web form is submitted to the server. This form data is called the *postback data*.

When building a custom control, you might need to process either postback data or a postback event. In this section, you learn how to implement the required control interfaces for processing postbacks.

Handling Postback Data

If your control needs to process form data submitted to the server, then you need to implement the IPostbackDataHandler interface. This interface includes the following two methods:

- LoadPostData()—Receives the form fields posted from the browser.

- RaisePostDataChangedEvent()—EnablesReceives the form fields posted from the browser. you to raise an event indicating that the value of a form field has been changed.

For example, the control in Listing 31.16 is a simple TextBox control. It implements the IPostbackDataHandler interface to preserve the state of an input field across postbacks.

LISTING 31.16   CustomTextBox.vb

```vb
Imports System
Imports System.Web.UI
Imports System.Web.UI.WebControls
Imports System.Collections.Specialized

Namespace myControls
    Public Class CustomTextBox
        Inherits WebControl
        Implements IPostBackDataHandler

        Public Event TextChanged As EventHandler

        Public Property Text() As String
            Get
                If ViewState("Text") Is Nothing Then
                    Return String.Empty
                Else
                    Return CType(ViewState("Text"), String)
                End If
            End Get
            Set(ByVal Value As String)
                ViewState("Text") = value
            End Set
        End Property

        Protected Overrides Sub AddAttributesToRender(ByVal writer
➥As HtmlTextWriter)
            writer.AddAttribute(HtmlTextWriterAttribute.Type, "text")
```

LISTING 31.16   Continued

```
                writer.AddAttribute(HtmlTextWriterAttribute.Value, Text)
                writer.AddAttribute(HtmlTextWriterAttribute.Name, Me.UniqueID)
                MyBase.AddAttributesToRender(writer)
            End Sub


            Protected Overrides ReadOnly Property TagKey() As HtmlTextWriterTag
                Get
                        Return HtmlTextWriterTag.Input
                End Get
            End Property


            Public Function LoadPostData(ByVal postDataKey As String,
➥ByVal postCollection As NameValueCollection) As Boolean
➥Implements IPostBackDataHandler.LoadPostData
                If postCollection(postDataKey) <> Text Then
                    Text = postCollection(postDataKey)
                    Return True
                End If
                Return False
            End Function


            Public Sub RaisePostDataChangedEvent()
➥Implements IPostBackDataHandler.RaisePostDataChangedEvent
                RaiseEvent TextChanged(Me, EventArgs.Empty)
            End Sub
        End Class
End Namespace
```

The LoadPostData()Receives the form fields posted from the browser. method in Listing
31.16 is passed a collection of all the form fields posted to the server. The postDataKey
represents the name of the field that corresponds to the current control.

> **NOTE**
>
> If the name of a form field rendered by a control does not match the name of the control, then
> you need to notify the page containing the control to pass the form data to the control. You can
> call the Page.RegisterRequiresPostBack() method inside (or before) the control's
> PreRender() event to notify the page that the control is interested in receiving the postback
> data. In other words, if you discover that your control's LoadPostData() method is never being
> called, then call the Page.RegisterRequiresPostBack() method in your control.

If the value of the form field has changed—in other words, it does not match the current
value of the control's Text property—then the Text property is updated and the method
returns the value True. Otherwise, the method returns the value False.

When the `LoadPostData()` method returns `True`, the `RaisePostDataChangedEvent()` method is executed. Typically, you implement this method to raise a change event. In Listing 31.16, this method is used to raise the `TextChanged` event, indicating that the contents of the `TextBox` have been changed.

The page in Listing 31.17 illustrates how you can use the custom `TextBox` control in a page (see Figure 31.7).

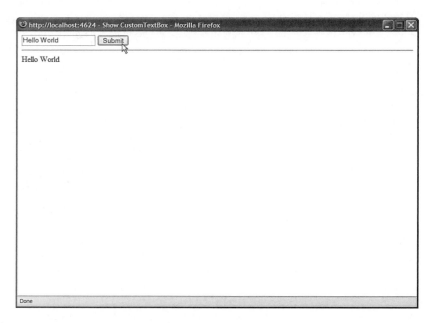

FIGURE 31.7   Handling postback data.

LISTING 31.17   ShowCustomTextBox.aspx

```
<%@ Page Language="VB" %>
<%@ Register TagPrefix="custom" Namespace="myControls" %>
<!DOCTYPE html PUBLIC "-//W3C//DTD XHTML 1.0 Transitional//EN"
➥"http://www.w3.org/TR/xhtml1/DTD/xhtml1-transitional.dtd">
<script runat="server">

    Sub CustomTextBox1_TextChanged(ByVal sender As Object, ByVal e As EventArgs)
        lblResults.Text = CustomTextBox1.Text
    End Sub
</script>
<html xmlns="http://www.w3.org/1999/xhtml" >
<head id="Head1" runat="server">
    <title>Show CustomTextBox</title>
</head>
```

LISTING 31.17   Continued

```
<body>
    <form id="form1" runat="server">
    <div>

    <custom:CustomTextBox
        id="CustomTextBox1"
        OnTextChanged="CustomTextBox1_TextChanged"
        Runat="server" />

    <asp:Button id="btnSubmit"
        Text="Submit"
        Runat="server" />

    <hr />

    <asp:Label
        id="lblResults"
        Runat="server" />

    </div>
    </form>
</body>
</html>
```

The custom `TextBox` control works in a very similar manner as the standard ASP.NET `TextBox` control. The control preserves its state across postbacks and it raises a `TextChanged` event when its contents have been modified.

> **NOTE**
>
> You will discover that you'll need to implement the `IPostbackDataHandler` interface quite often when building custom JavaScript controls. A common method of passing data from a JavaScript control back to the server is to use a hidden form field. You can process the contents of the hidden form field by using the `IPostBackDataHandler` interface. You'll see this, for example, when the `ClientTabs` control is built in the next chapter.

Handling Postback Events

Only one control in a page at a time can cause a form to be submitted back to the server. When a control initiates a postback, the control can raise a postback event.

To process a postback event, you need to implement the `IPostBackEventHandler` interface. This interface includes a single method:

- `RaisePostBackEvent()`—Called on the server when a control initiates a postback.

The control in Listing 31.18 illustrates how you can implement the
IPostBackEventHandler interface.

LISTING 31.18   CustomLinkButton.vb

```
Imports System
Imports System.Web.UI
Imports System.Web.UI.WebControls

Namespace myControls
    Public Class CustomLinkButton
        Inherits WebControl
        Implements IPostBackEventHandler

        Public Event Click As EventHandler

        Private _Text As String

        Public Property Text() As String
            Get
                Return _Text
            End Get
            Set(ByVal Value As String)
                _Text = value
            End Set
        End Property

        Protected Overrides Sub AddAttributesToRender(ByVal writer
➥As HtmlTextWriter)
            Dim eRef As String = Page.ClientScript.GetPostBackClientHyperlink(Me,
➥String.Empty)
            writer.AddAttribute(HtmlTextWriterAttribute.Href, eRef)
            MyBase.AddAttributesToRender(writer)
        End Sub

        Protected Overrides ReadOnly Property TagKey() As HtmlTextWriterTag
            Get
                Return HtmlTextWriterTag.A
            End Get
        End Property

        Protected Overrides Sub RenderContents(ByVal writer As HtmlTextWriter)
            writer.Write(_Text)
        End Sub
```

LISTING 31.18   Continued

```
        Public Sub RaisePostBackEvent(ByVal eventArgument As String)
➥Implements IPostBackEventHandler.RaisePostBackEvent
            RaiseEvent Click(Me, EventArgs.Empty)
        End Sub
    End Class
End Namespace
```

The control in Listing 31.18 is a simple custom `LinkButton` control. It works very much like the standard ASP.NET `LinkButton` control. When you click the link rendered by the control on the browser, the form containing the control is posted back to the server and the `RaisePostBackEvent()` method is called. In Listing 31.18, the `RaisePostBackEvent()` method simply raises the `Click` event.

Notice that the `Page.ClientScript.GetPostBackClientHyperlink()` method is called in the control's `AddAttributesToRender()` method. The `GetPostBackClientHyperLink()` method returns the JavaScript that initiates the form postback in the browser. When this method is called in Listing 31.18, it returns the following JavaScript:

```
javascript:__doPostBack('CustomLinkButton1','')
```

The `__doPostBack()` JavaScript method calls the client-side form `submit()` method, which causes the form to be submitted back to the web server. (You can see all this by selecting View Source in your web browser.)

> **NOTE**
>
> There is a closely related method to the `GetPostBackClientHyperLink()` method named the `GetPostBackEventReference()` method. The `GetPostBackClientHyperLink()` method includes the `"JavaScript:"` prefix, whereas the `GetPostBackEventReference()` does not.

The page in Listing 31.19 demonstrates how you can use the custom `LinkButton` in an ASP.NET page.

LISTING 31.19   ShowCustomLinkButton.aspx

```
<%@ Page Language="VB" %>
<%@ Register TagPrefix="custom" Namespace="myControls" %>
<!DOCTYPE html PUBLIC "-//W3C//DTD XHTML 1.0 Transitional//EN"
➥"http://www.w3.org/TR/xhtml1/DTD/xhtml1-transitional.dtd">
<script runat="server">

    Sub CustomLinkButton1_Click(ByVal sender As Object, ByVal e As EventArgs)
        lblResults.Text = txtUserName.Text
    End Sub
</script>
```

31

LISTING 31.19   Continued

```
<html xmlns="http://www.w3.org/1999/xhtml" >
<head id="Head1" runat="server">
    <title>Show CustomLinkButton</title>
</head>
<body>
    <form id="form1" runat="server">
    <div>

    <asp:Label
        id="lblUserName"
        Text="User Name:"
        AssociatedControlID="txtUserName"
        Runat="server" />
    <asp:TextBox
        id="txtUserName"
        Runat="server" />

    <br /><br />

    <custom:CustomLinkButton
        id="CustomLinkButton1"
        Text="Submit"
        OnClick="CustomLinkButton1_Click"
        runat="server" />

    <hr />

    <asp:Label
        id="lblResults"
        EnableViewState="false"
        Runat="server" />

    </div>
    </form>
</body>
</html>
```

The page in Listing 31.19 contains a TextBox control and the custom LinkButton control. When you click the LinkButton, the form is posted back to the server. The Click handler displays the value of the TextBox control's Text property in a Label control (see Figure 31.8).

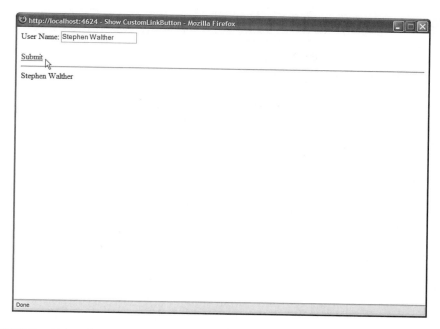

FIGURE 31.8   Using the `CustomLinkButton` control.

Passing Postback Event Arguments

When you call the `GetPostBackClientHyperLink()` method, you can supply the method with an optional argument. The argument is passed from the browser to the server when a postback is initiated. The value of the argument is passed to the `RaisePostBackEvent()` method on the server.

Imagine, for example, that you want to create a custom pager control that you could use with the `GridView` control. You want the custom control to display a list of page numbers you can click to navigate to a particular page of records displayed by a `GridView`.

To create this control, you need to render multiple links that initiate a postback event. Each link needs to pass the correct page number.

Listing 31.20 contains the custom pager control.

LISTING 31.20   Pager.vb

```
Imports System
Imports System.Web.UI
Imports System.Web.UI.WebControls

Namespace myControls
    Public Class Pager
        Inherits WebControl
        Implements IPostBackEventHandler
```

LISTING 31.20   Continued

```
        Private _controlToPage As String

        Public Property ControlToPage() As String
            Get
                Return _controlToPage
            End Get
            Set(ByVal Value As String)
                _controlToPage = value
            End Set
        End Property

        Protected Overrides Sub RenderContents(ByVal writer As HtmlTextWriter)
            Dim grid As GridView = GetControlToPage()

            Dim i As Integer
            For i = 0 To grid.PageCount - 1 Step i + 1
                Dim eRef As String = Page.ClientScript.GetPostBackClientHyperlink(
➥Me, i.ToString())
                writer.Write("[")
                If i = grid.PageIndex Then
                    writer.AddStyleAttribute(HtmlTextWriterStyle.FontWeight,
➥"bold")
                End If
                writer.AddAttribute(HtmlTextWriterAttribute.Href, eRef)
                writer.RenderBeginTag(HtmlTextWriterTag.A)
                writer.Write("{0}", i + 1)
                writer.RenderEndTag()
                writer.Write("] ")
            Next
        End Sub

        Private Function GetControlToPage() As GridView
            If String.IsNullOrEmpty(_controlToPage) Then
                Throw New Exception("Must set ControlToPage property")
            End If
            Return CType(Page.FindControl(_controlToPage), GridView)
        End Function

        Public Sub RaisePostBackEvent(ByVal eventArgument As String)
➥Implements IPostBackEventHandler.RaisePostBackEvent
            Dim grid As GridView = GetControlToPage()
            grid.PageIndex = Int32.Parse(eventArgument)
        End Sub
    End Class
End Namespace
```

In Listing 31.20, the RenderContents() method renders the page numbers. Each page number is rendered as a link. When you click a link, the associated GridView control changes the page that it displays (see Figure 31.9).

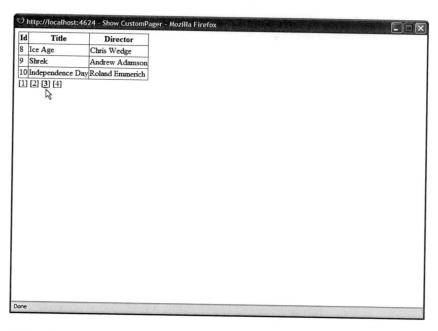

FIGURE 31.9   Using the Pager control.

The href attribute for each link is created by calling the GetPostBackClientHyperLink() method. The page number is passed as an argument to this method. When the pager is rendered to the browser, the following series of links is rendered:

```
[<a href="javascript:__doPostBack('Pager1','0')" style="font-weight:bold;">1</a>]
[<a href="javascript:__doPostBack('Pager1','1')">2</a>]
[<a href="javascript:__doPostBack('Pager1','2')">3</a>]
[<a href="javascript:__doPostBack('Pager1','3')">4</a>]
```

When you click a page number link, the corresponding page number is posted back to the server. The RaisePostBackEvent() method receives the page number and changes the page displayed by its associated GridView.

The page in Listing 31.21 illustrates how you can use the pager control to navigate to different pages of records displayed by a GridView control.

LISTING 31.21   ShowPager.aspx

```
<%@ Page Language="VB" %>
<%@ Register TagPrefix="custom" Namespace="myControls" %>
<!DOCTYPE html PUBLIC "-//W3C//DTD XHTML 1.0 Transitional//EN"
➥"http://www.w3.org/TR/xhtml1/DTD/xhtml1-transitional.dtd">
<html xmlns="http://www.w3.org/1999/xhtml" >
<head id="Head1" runat="server">
    <title>Show CustomPager</title>
</head>
<body>
    <form id="form1" runat="server">
    <div>

    <asp:GridView
        id="GridView1"
        DataSourceID="srcMovies"
        AllowPaging="true"
        PageSize="3"
        PagerSettings-Visible="false"
        Runat="server" />

    <custom:Pager
        id="Pager1"
        ControlToPage="GridView1"
        Runat="server" />

    <asp:SqlDataSource
        id="srcMovies"
        ConnectionString="Data Source=.\SQLExpress;Integrated Security=True;
            AttachDbFileName=|DataDirectory|MyDatabase.mdf;User Instance=True"
        SelectCommand="SELECT Id,Title,Director FROM Movies"
        Runat="server" />

    </div>
    </form>
</body>
</html>
```

Using Postback Options

Postbacks are more complicated in the ASP.NET 2.0 Framework than they were in the previous version of the Framework. For example, the ASP.NET 2.0 Framework supports cross-page posts, validation groups, and programmatic control of control focus. To implement these advanced features in a custom control, you need to be able to specify advanced postback options.

You specify advanced postback options by taking advantage of the `PostBackOptions` class. This class has the following properties:

- `ActionUrl`—Enables you to specify the page where form data is posted.

- `Argument`—Enables you to specify a postback argument.

- `AutoPostBack`—Enables you to add JavaScript necessary for implementing an `AutoPostBack` event.

- `ClientSubmit`—Enables you to initiate the postback through client-side script.

- `PerformValidation`—Enables you to specify whether validation is performed (set by the `CausesValidation` property).

- `RequiresJavaScriptProtocol`—Enables you to generate the `JavaScript:` prefix.

- `TargetControl`—Enables you to specify the control responsible for initiating the postback.

- `TrackFocus`—Enables you to scroll the page back to its current position and return focus to the control after a postback.

- `ValidationGroup`—Enables you to specify the validation group associated with the control.

Imagine that you need to create a form that enables users to place a product order. However, imagine that you want to create an advanced options check box. When someone clicks the advanced options check box, the current form data is submitted to a new page that includes a more complex form.

The `AdvancedCheckBox` control in Listing 31.22 supports cross-page posts. When you click the check box, the form data is submitted to the page indicated by its `PostBackUrl` property.

> **NOTE**
>
> Cross-page posts are covered during the discussion of `Button` controls in Chapter 2, "Using the Standard Controls."

LISTING 31.22   AdvancedCheckBox.vb

```vb
Imports System
Imports System.Web.UI
Imports System.Web.UI.WebControls

Namespace myControls
    Public Class AdvancedCheckBox
        Inherits WebControl

        Private _Text As String
        Private _PostBackUrl As String
```

LISTING 31.22   Continued

```vb
        Public Property Text() As String
            Get
                Return _Text
            End Get
            Set(ByVal Value As String)
                _Text = Value
            End Set
        End Property


        Public Property PostBackUrl() As String
            Get
                Return _PostBackUrl
            End Get
            Set(ByVal Value As String)
                _PostBackUrl = Value
            End Set
        End Property


        Protected Overrides Sub AddAttributesToRender(ByVal writer
➥As HtmlTextWriter)
            Dim options As PostBackOptions = New PostBackOptions(Me)
            options.ActionUrl = _PostBackUrl
            Dim eRef As String = Page.ClientScript.
➥GetPostBackEventReference(options)
            writer.AddAttribute(HtmlTextWriterAttribute.Onclick, eRef)
            writer.AddAttribute(HtmlTextWriterAttribute.Name, Me.UniqueID)
            writer.AddAttribute(HtmlTextWriterAttribute.Type, "checkbox")
            MyBase.AddAttributesToRender(writer)
        End Sub


        Protected Overrides Sub RenderContents(ByVal writer As HtmlTextWriter)
            If Not String.IsNullOrEmpty(_Text) Then
                writer.AddAttribute(HtmlTextWriterAttribute.For, Me.ClientID)
                writer.RenderBeginTag(HtmlTextWriterTag.Label)
                writer.Write(_Text)
                writer.RenderEndTag()
            End If
        End Sub


        Protected Overrides ReadOnly Property TagKey() As HtmlTextWriterTag
            Get
                Return HtmlTextWriterTag.Input
            End Get
```

LISTING 31.22   Continued

```
        End Property
    End Class
End Namespace
```

In the AddAttributesToRender() method in Listing 31.22, an instance of the PostBackOptions class is created. The ActionUrl property is modified to support cross-page posts. The instance of the PostBackOptions class is passed to the GetPostBackEventReference() method to generate the JavaScript for initiating the postback.

The page in Listing 31.23 illustrates how you can use the AdvancedCheckBox control to submit form data to a new page when you click the check box (see Figure 31.10). Notice that the AdvancedCheckBox control's PostBackUrl property is set to the value ShowAdvancedOptions.aspx. When you click the check box, the form data is posted to this page.

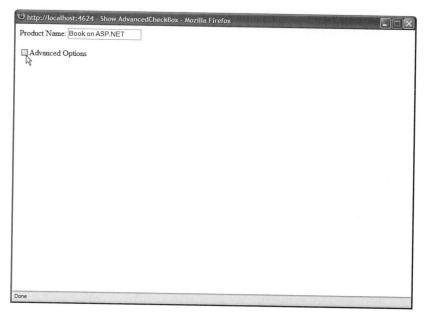

FIGURE 31.10   Using the AdvancedCheckBox control.

LISTING 31.23   ShowAdvancedCheckBox.aspx

```
<%@ Page Language="VB" %>
<%@ Register TagPrefix="custom" Namespace="myControls" %>
<!DOCTYPE html PUBLIC "-//W3C//DTD XHTML 1.0 Transitional//EN"
➥"http://www.w3.org/TR/xhtml1/DTD/xhtml1-transitional.dtd">
```

LISTING 31.23   Continued

```
<script runat="server">

    Public ReadOnly Property ProductName() As String
        Get
            Return txtProductName.Text
        End Get
    End Property
</script>
<html xmlns="http://www.w3.org/1999/xhtml" >
<head id="Head1" runat="server">
    <title>Show AdvancedCheckBox</title>
</head>
<body>
    <form id="form1" runat="server">
    <div>

    <asp:Label
        id="lblProductName"
        Text="Product Name:"
        AssociatedControlID="txtProductName"
        Runat="server" />

    <asp:TextBox
        id="txtProductName"
        Runat="server" />

    <br /><br />

    <custom:AdvancedCheckBox
        id="AdvancedCheckBox1"
        Text="Advanced Options"
        PostBackUrl="AdvancedOptions.aspx"
        Runat="server" />

    </div>
    </form>
</body>
</html>
```

Working with Control Property Collections

When you build more complex controls, you often need to represent a collection of items. For example, the standard ASP.NET DropDownList control contains one or more ListItem controls that represent individual options in the DropDownList. The GridView control can contain one or more DataBoundField controls that represent particular columns to display.

In this section, we build several controls that represent a collection of items. We build multiple content rotator controls that randomly display HTML content, as well as a server-side tab control that renders a tabbed view of content.

Using the ParseChildren **Attribute**

When building a control that contains a collection of child controls, you need to be aware of an attribute named the ParseChildren attribute. This attribute determines how the content contained in a control is parsed.

When the ParseChildren attribute has the value True, then content contained in the control is parsed as properties of the containing control. If the control contains child controls, then the child controls are parsed as properties of the containing control. (The attribute really should have been named the ParseChildrenAsProperties attribute.)

When the ParseChildren attribute has the value False, then no attempt is made to parse a control's child controls as properties. The content contained in the control is left alone.

The default value of the ParseChildren attribute is False. However, the WebControl class overrides this default value and sets the ParseChildren attribute to the value to True. Therefore, you should assume that ParseChildren is False when used with a control that inherits directly from the System.Web.UI.Control class, but assume that ParseChildren is True when used with a control that inherits from the System.Web.UI.WebControls.WebControl class.

Imagine, for example, that you need to create a content rotator control that randomly displays content in a page. There are two ways of creating this control, depending on whether ParseChildren has the value True or False.

The control in Listing 31.24 illustrates how you can create a content rotator control when ParseChildren has the value False.

LISTING 31.24   ContentRotator.vb

```
Imports System
Imports System.Web.UI
Imports System.Web.UI.WebControls

Namespace myControls
    <ParseChildren(False)> _
    Public Class ContentRotator
        Inherits WebControl

        Protected Overrides Sub AddParsedSubObject(ByVal obj As Object)
            If TypeOf obj Is Content Then
                MyBase.AddParsedSubObject(obj)
            End If
        End Sub

        Protected Overrides Sub RenderContents(ByVal writer As HtmlTextWriter)
```

LISTING 31.24   Continued

```
            Dim rnd As Random = New Random()
            Dim index As Integer = rnd.Next(Me.Controls.Count)
            Me.Controls(index).RenderControl(writer)
        End Sub
    End Class

    Public Class Content
        Inherits Control
    End Class
End Namespace
```

The file in Listing 31.24 actually contains two controls: a `ContentRotator` control and a `Content` control. The `ContentRotator` control randomly selects a single `Content` control from its child controls and renders the `Content` control to the browser. This all happens in the control's `RenderContents()` method.

Notice that the `ParseChildren` attribute has the value `False` in Listing 31.24. If you neglected to add this attribute, then the `Content` controls would be parsed as properties of the `ContentRotator` control and you would get an exception.

> **NOTE**
>
> The `AddParsedSubObject()` method is discussed in the next section.

The page in Listing 31.25 illustrates how you can use the `ContentRotator` and `Content` controls (see Figure 31.11).

LISTING 31.25   ShowContentRotator.aspx

```
<%@ Page Language="VB" %>
<%@ Register TagPrefix="custom" Namespace="myControls" %>
<!DOCTYPE html PUBLIC "-//W3C//DTD XHTML 1.0 Transitional//EN"
➥"http://www.w3.org/TR/xhtml1/DTD/xhtml1-transitional.dtd">
<html xmlns="http://www.w3.org/1999/xhtml" >
<head id="Head1" runat="server">
    <title>Show ContentRotator</title>
</head>
<body>
    <form id="form1" runat="server">
    <div>

    <custom:ContentRotator
        id="ContentRotator1"
        Runat="server">
        <custom:Content
            id="Content1"
```

LISTING 31.25   Continued

```
            Runat="server">
            First Content Item
        </custom:Content>
        <custom:Content
            id="Content2"
            Runat="server">
            Second Content Item
            <asp:Calendar
                id="Calendar1"
                Runat="server" />
        </custom:Content>
        <custom:Content
            id="Content3"
            Runat="server">
            Third Content Item
        </custom:Content>
    </custom:ContentRotator>

    </div>
    </form>
</body>
</html>
```

31

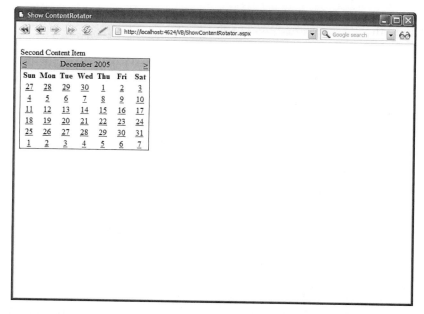

FIGURE 31.11   Randomly displaying content with the ContentRotator control.

If ParseChildren is not set to the value False, then you need to add a property to your control that corresponds to the child controls contained in the control. For example, the control in Listing 31.26 includes an Items property that represents the Item controls contained in the control.

LISTING 31.26   ItemRotator.vb

```vb
Imports System
Imports System.Collections
Imports System.Web.UI
Imports System.Web.UI.WebControls
Imports System.ComponentModel

Namespace myControls
    <ParseChildren(True, "Items")> _
    Public Class ItemRotator
        Inherits CompositeControl
        Private _items As ArrayList = New ArrayList()

        <Browsable(False)> _
        Public ReadOnly Property Items() As ArrayList
            Get
                Return _items
            End Get
        End Property

        Protected Overrides Sub CreateChildControls()
            Dim rnd As Random = New Random()
            Dim index As Integer = rnd.Next(_items.Count)
            Dim item As Control = CType(_items(index), Control)
            Me.Controls.Add(item)
        End Sub
    End Class

    Public Class Item
        Inherits Control

    End Class
End Namespace
```

In Listing 31.26, the second value passed to the ParseChildren attribute is the name of a control property. The contents of the ItemRotator are parsed as items of the collection represented by the specified property.

Unlike the ContentRotator control, the controls contained in the ItemRotator control are not automatically parsed into child controls. After the CreateChildControls() method executes, the ItemRotator control contains only one child control (the randomly selected Item control).

The page in Listing 31.27 illustrates how you can use the ItemRotator control to randomly display page content.

LISTING 31.27   ShowItemRotator.aspx

```
<%@ Page Language="VB" Trace="true" %>
<%@ Register TagPrefix="custom" Namespace="myControls" %>
<!DOCTYPE html PUBLIC "-//W3C//DTD XHTML 1.0 Transitional//EN"
➥"http://www.w3.org/TR/xhtml1/DTD/xhtml1-transitional.dtd">
<html xmlns="http://www.w3.org/1999/xhtml" >
<head id="Head1" runat="server">
    <title>Show ItemRotator</title>
</head>
<body>
    <form id="form1" runat="server">
    <div>

    <custom:ItemRotator
        id="ItemRotator1"
        Runat="server">
        <custom:item ID="Item1" runat="server">
            First Item
        </custom:item>
        <custom:item ID="Item2" runat="server">
            Second Item
            <asp:Calendar
                id="Calendar1"
                Runat="server" />
        </custom:item>
        <custom:item ID="Item3" runat="server">
            Third Item
        </custom:item>
    </custom:ItemRotator>

    </div>
    </form>
</body>
</html>
```

There is no requirement that the contents of a control must be parsed as controls. When building a control that represents a collection of items, you can also represent the items as objects. For example, the ImageRotator control in Listing 31.28 contains ImageItem objects. The ImageItem class does not represent a control.

LISTING 31.28   ImageRotator.vb

```vb
Imports System
Imports System.Collections
Imports System.Web.UI
Imports System.Web.UI.WebControls
Imports System.ComponentModel


Namespace myControls

    <ParseChildren(True, "ImageItems")> _
    Public Class ImageRotator
        Inherits WebControl

        Private _imageItems As ArrayList = New ArrayList()

        Public ReadOnly Property ImageItems() As ArrayList
            Get
                Return _imageItems
            End Get
        End Property

        Protected Overrides Sub RenderContents(ByVal writer As HtmlTextWriter)
            Dim rnd As Random = New Random()
            Dim img As ImageItem = CType(_imageItems(rnd.Next(_imageItems.Count)),
➥ImageItem)
            writer.AddAttribute(HtmlTextWriterAttribute.Src, img.ImageUrl)
            writer.AddAttribute(HtmlTextWriterAttribute.Alt, img.AlternateText)
            writer.RenderBeginTag(HtmlTextWriterTag.Img)
            writer.RenderEndTag()
        End Sub
    End Class

    Public Class ImageItem
        Private _imageUrl As String
        Private _alternateText As String

        Public Property ImageUrl() As String
            Get
                Return _imageUrl
            End Get
            Set(ByVal Value As String)
                _imageUrl = value
            End Set
        End Property
```

LISTING 31.28   Continued

```
        Public Property AlternateText() As String
            Get
                Return _alternateText
            End Get
            Set(ByVal Value As String)
                _alternateText = value
            End Set
        End Property
    End Class
End Namespace
```

Notice that the ImageItem class is just a class. It does not derive from the base Control class. Because the ImageItem class does nothing more than represent a couple of properties, there is no reason to make it a full-blown control.

The page in Listing 31.29 illustrates how you can use the ImageRotator control to display different images randomly.

LISTING 31.29   ShowImageRotator.aspx

```
<%@ Page Language="VB" Trace="true" %>
<%@ Register TagPrefix="custom" Namespace="myControls" %>
<!DOCTYPE html PUBLIC "-//W3C//DTD XHTML 1.0 Transitional//EN"
➥"http://www.w3.org/TR/xhtml1/DTD/xhtml1-transitional.dtd">
<html xmlns="http://www.w3.org/1999/xhtml" >
<head id="Head1" runat="server">
    <title>Show ImageRotator</title>
</head>
<body>
    <form id="form1" runat="server">
    <div>

    <custom:ImageRotator
        id="ImageRotator1"
        Runat="server">
        <custom:ImageItem ImageUrl="Image1.gif" AlternateText="Image 1" />
        <custom:ImageItem ImageUrl="Image2.gif" AlternateText="Image 2" />
        <custom:ImageItem ImageUrl="Image3.gif" AlternateText="Image 3" />
    </custom:ImageRotator>

    </div>
    </form>
</body>
</html>
```

31

The page in Listing 31.29 has tracing enabled. If you look in the Control Tree section, you'll see that the ImageRotator control does not contain any child controls (see Figure 31.12).

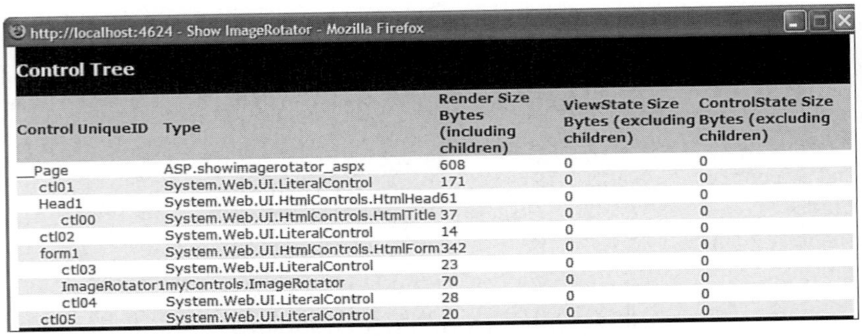

Control Tree				
		Render Size Bytes (including children)	ViewState Size Bytes (excluding children)	ControlState Size Bytes (excluding children)
Control UniqueID	Type			
__Page	ASP.showimagerotator_aspx	608	0	0
ctl01	System.Web.UI.LiteralControl	171	0	0
Head1	System.Web.UI.HtmlControls.HtmlHead	61	0	0
ctl00	System.Web.UI.HtmlControls.HtmlTitle	37	0	0
ctl02	System.Web.UI.LiteralControl	14	0	0
form1	System.Web.UI.HtmlControls.HtmlForm	342	0	0
ctl03	System.Web.UI.LiteralControl	23	0	0
ImageRotator1	myControls.ImageRotator	70	0	0
ctl04	System.Web.UI.LiteralControl	28	0	0
ctl05	System.Web.UI.LiteralControl	20	0	0

FIGURE 31.12   The ShowImageRotator.aspx page control tree.

Using the AddParsedSubObject() Method

When the ParseChildren attribute has the value false, the contents of a control are automatically added to the control's collection of child controls (represented by the Controls property). It is important to understand that all content contained in the control, even carriage returns and spaces, are added to the controls collection.

Any content contained in a control that does not represent a server-side control is parsed into a Literal control. In some cases, you might want to allow only a certain type of control to be added to the Controls collection.

The AddParsedSubObject() method is called as each control is added to the Controls collection. By overriding the AddParsedSubObject() method, you can block certain types of controls—such as Literal controls—from being added to the Controls collection.

For example, the ContentRotator control in Listing 31.20 overrides the base AddParsedSubObject() method and prevents anything that is not a Content control from being added to the ContentRotator Controls collection. If you removed the AddParsedSubObject() method from this control, then all of the carriage returns and spaces between the Content controls would be added to the Controls collection as Literal controls.

Using a ControlBuilder

The AddParsedSubObject() method enables you to specify which parsed controls get added to a Controls collection. Sometimes, you must take even more control over the parsing of a control.

When the ASP.NET Framework parses a page, the Framework uses a special type of class called a ControlBuilder class. You can modify the way in which the content of a control is parsed by associating a custom ControlBuilder with a control.

Here's a list of the most useful methods supported by the `ControlBuilder` class:

- `AllowWhiteSpaceLiterals()`—Enables you to trim white space from the contents of a control.

- `AppendLiteralString()`—Enables you trim all literal content from the contents of a control.

- `GetChildControlType()`—Enables you to specify how a particular tag gets parsed into a control.

The `GetChildControlType()` method is the most useful method. It enables you to map tags to controls. You can use the `GetChildControlType()` method to map any tag to any control.

For example, the file in Listing 31.30 contains a `ServerTabs` control that renders multiple tabs (see Figure 31.13). Each tab is represented by a `Tab` control.

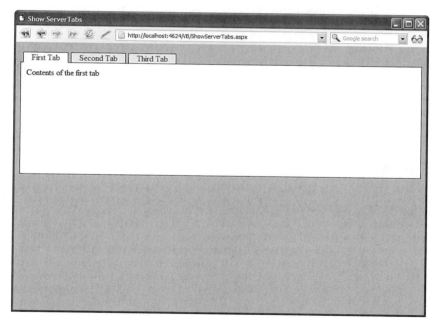

FIGURE 31.13   Using the `ServerTabs` control.

LISTING 31.30   `ServerTabs.vb`

```
Imports System
Imports System.Collections
Imports System.Web.UI
Imports System.Web.UI.WebControls

Namespace myControls
```

LISTING 31.30 Continued

```
    <ControlBuilder(GetType(ServerTabsBuilder))> _
    <ParseChildren(False)> _
    Public Class ServerTabs
        Inherits WebControl
        Implements IPostBackEventHandler

        Public Property SelectedTabIndex() As Integer
            Get
                If ViewState("SelectedTabIndex") Is Nothing Then
                    Return 0
                Else
                    Return CType(ViewState("SelectedTabIndex"), Integer)
                End If
            End Get
            Set(ByVal Value As Integer)
                ViewState("SelectedTabIndex") = Value
            End Set
        End Property

        Protected Overrides Sub RenderContents(ByVal writer As HtmlTextWriter)
            Dim i As Integer
            For i = 0 To Me.Controls.Count - 1 Step i + 1
                Dim tab As ServerTab = CType(Me.Controls(i), ServerTab)
                Dim eRef As String = _
➥Page.ClientScript.GetPostBackClientHyperlink(Me, i.ToString())

                If SelectedTabIndex = i Then
                    writer.AddAttribute(HtmlTextWriterAttribute.Class, _
➥"tab selectedTab")
                Else
                    writer.AddAttribute(HtmlTextWriterAttribute.Class, "tab")
                End If
                writer.RenderBeginTag(HtmlTextWriterTag.Div)
                writer.AddAttribute(HtmlTextWriterAttribute.Href, eRef)
                writer.RenderBeginTag(HtmlTextWriterTag.A)
                writer.Write(tab.Text)
                writer.RenderEndTag() ' A
                writer.RenderEndTag() ' Tab Div
            Next
            writer.Write("<br style='clear:both' />")

            writer.AddAttribute(HtmlTextWriterAttribute.Class, "tabContents")
            writer.RenderBeginTag(HtmlTextWriterTag.Div)
            Me.Controls(SelectedTabIndex).RenderControl(writer)
            writer.RenderEndTag() ' Tab Contents DIV
        End Sub
```

LISTING 31.30   Continued

```vbnet
        Protected Overrides Sub AddParsedSubObject(ByVal obj As Object)
            If TypeOf obj Is ServerTab Then
                MyBase.AddParsedSubObject(obj)
            End If
        End Sub

        Protected Overrides ReadOnly Property TagKey() As HtmlTextWriterTag
            Get
                Return HtmlTextWriterTag.Div
            End Get
        End Property

        Public Sub RaisePostBackEvent(ByVal eventArgument As String)
➥Implements IPostBackEventHandler.RaisePostBackEvent
            SelectedTabIndex = Int32.Parse(eventArgument)
        End Sub
    End Class

    Public Class ServerTabsBuilder
        Inherits ControlBuilder

        Public Overrides Function GetChildControlType(ByVal tagName As String,
➥ByVal attribs As IDictionary) As Type
            If String.Compare(tagName, "tab", True) = 0 Then
                Return GetType(ServerTab)
            Else
                Return Nothing
            End If
        End Function
    End Class

    Public Class ServerTab
        Inherits Control
        Private _Text As String

        Public Property Text() As String
            Get
                Return _Text
            End Get
            Set(ByVal Value As String)
                _Text = value
            End Set
        End Property
    End Class
End Namespace
```

Notice that the ServerTabs class is decorated with a ControlBuilder attribute. This attribute associates the ServerTabs control with a ControlBuilder class named ServerTabsBuilder.

The ServerTabsBuilder class overrides the base ControlBuilder GetChildControlType() method. The overridden method maps the <tab> tag to the Tab control. Because of this mapping, you do not need to use a prefix or use the runat="server" attribute when declaring a tab within the ServerTabs control.

The page in Listing 31.31 illustrates how you can use the ServerTabs control.

LISTING 31.31 ShowServerTabs.aspx

```
<%@ Page Language="VB" %>
<%@ Register TagPrefix="custom" Namespace="myControls" %>
<!DOCTYPE html PUBLIC "-//W3C//DTD XHTML 1.0 Transitional//EN"
➥"http://www.w3.org/TR/xhtml1/DTD/xhtml1-transitional.dtd">
<html xmlns="http://www.w3.org/1999/xhtml" >
<head id="Head1" runat="server">
    <style type="text/css">
        html
        {
            background-color:silver;
        }
        .tab
        {
            float:left;
            position:relative;
            top:1px;
            background-color:#eeeeee;
            border:solid 1px black;
            padding:0px 15px;
            margin-left:5px;
        }
        .tab a
        {
            text-decoration:none;
        }
        .selectedTab
        {
            background-color:white;
            border-bottom:solid 1px white;
        }
        .tabContents
        {
            border:solid 1px black;
            background-color:white;
            padding:10px;
```

LISTING 31.31   Continued

```
            height:200px;
        }
    </style>
    <title>Show ServerTabs</title>
</head>
<body>
    <form id="form1" runat="server">
    <div>

    <custom:ServerTabs
        ID="ServerTabs1"
        Runat="Server">
        <tab Text="First Tab">
          Contents of the first tab
        </tab>
        <tab Text="Second Tab">
          Contents of the second tab
        </tab>
        <tab Text="Third Tab">
          Contents of the third tab
        </tab>
    </custom:ServerTabs>

    </div>
    </form>
</body>
</html>
```

The `ControlBuilder` enables you to declare instances of the `Tab` control by using the `<tab>` tag instead of using a `<custom:Tab runat="server">` tab.

Creating a Better Designer Experience

Up to this point, we've ignored the Design view experience. In other words, we've ignored the question of how our custom controls appear in the Visual Web Developer or Visual Studio .NET Design view.

You can modify the appearance of your control in Design view in two ways. You can apply design-time attributes to the control, or you can associate a `ControlDesigner` with your control. We'll explore both methods in this section.

Applying Design-Time Attributes to a Control

Design-time attributes enable you to modify how control properties appear in Design view. Some attributes are applied to the control itself, whereas other attributes are applied to particular properties of a control.

Here is the list of the design-time attributes you can apply to a control:

- DefaultEvent—Enables you to specify the default event for a control. When you double-click a control in Visual Web Developer or Visual Studio .NET, an event handler is automatically created for the default event.

- DefaultProperty—Enables you to specify the default property for a control. When you open the Property window for a control, this property is highlighted by default.

- PersistChildren—Enables you to specify whether child controls or properties are persisted as control attributes or control contents.

- ToolboxData—Enables you to specify the tag added to a page when a control is dragged from the toolbox.

- ToolboxItem—Enables you to block a control from appearing in the Toolbox.

Here is the list of design-time attributes you can apply to a control property:

- Bindable—Enables you to indicate to display a Databindings dialog box for the property.

- Browsable—Enables you to block a property from appearing in the Properties window.

- Category—Enables you to specify the category associated with the property. The property appears under this category in the Properties window.

- DefaultValue—Enables you to specify a default value for the property. When you right-click a property in the Properties window, you can select Reset to the return the property to its default value.

- Description—Enables you to specify the description associated with the property. The description appears in the Properties window when the property is selected.

- DesignerSerializationVisibility—Enables you to specify how changes to a property are serialized. Possible values are Visible, Hidden, and Content.

- Editor—Enables you to specify a custom editor for editing the property in Design view.

- EditorBrowsable—Enables you to block a property from appearing in Intellisense.

- NotifyParentProperty—Enables you to specify that changes to a subproperty should be propagated to the parent property.

- PersistenceMode—Enables you to specify whether a property is persisted as a control attribute or control content. Possible values are Attribute, EncodedInnerDefaultProperty, InnerDefaultProperty, and InnerProperty.

- TypeConverter—Enables you to associate a custom type converter with a property. A type converter converts a property between a string representation and a type (or vice versa).

The Editor attribute enables you to associate a particular editor with a property. Certain types in the Framework have default editors. For example, a property which represents a System.Drawing.Color value is automatically associated with the ColorEditor. The ColorEditor displays a color picker (see Figure 31.14). To view the list of editors included in the .NET Framework, look up the UITypeEditor class in the .NET Framework SDK Documentation.

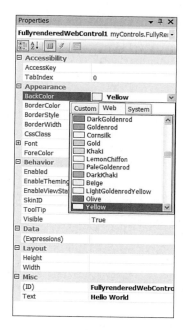

FIGURE 31.14   Using the ColorEditor to pick a color.

The MovieView control contained in Listing 31.32 illustrates how you can use several of these attributes. The control displays a single movie.

LISTING 31.32   MovieView.vb

```
Imports System
Imports System.Web.UI
Imports System.Web.UI.WebControls
Imports System.ComponentModel

Namespace myControls

    <DefaultProperty("Title")> _
    Public Class MovieView
        Inherits WebControl
```

LISTING 31.32   Continued

```vbnet
        Private _title As String = "Movie Title"
        Private _description As String = "Movie Description"

        <Category("Movie")> _
        <Description("Movie Title")> _
        Public Property Title() As String
            Get
                Return _title
            End Get
            Set(ByVal Value As String)
                _title = Value
            End Set
        End Property

        <Category("Movie")> _
        <Description("Movie Description")> _
        Public Property Description() As String
            Get
                Return _description
            End Get
            Set(ByVal Value As String)
                _description = Value
            End Set
        End Property


        Protected Overrides Sub RenderContents(ByVal writer As HtmlTextWriter)
            writer.RenderBeginTag(HtmlTextWriterTag.H1)
            writer.Write(_title)
            writer.RenderEndTag()

            writer.Write(_description)
        End Sub

        Protected Overrides ReadOnly Property TagKey() As HtmlTextWriterTag
            Get
                Return HtmlTextWriterTag.Div
            End Get
        End Property
    End Class
End Namespace
```

The page in Listing 31.33 contains the MovieView control. Open the page in Design view
to see the effect of the various design-time attributes. For example, notice that a category
and description are associated with both the Title and Description properties in the
Properties window (see Figure 31.15).

FIGURE 31.15   The `MovieView` control in Design view.

LISTING 31.33   `ShowMovieView.aspx`

```
<%@ Page Language="VB" %>
<%@ Register TagPrefix="custom" Namespace="myControls" %>
<!DOCTYPE html PUBLIC "-//W3C//DTD XHTML 1.0 Transitional//EN"
➥"http://www.w3.org/TR/xhtml1/DTD/xhtml1-transitional.dtd">
<html xmlns="http://www.w3.org/1999/xhtml" >
<head id="Head1" runat="server">
    <title>Show MovieView</title>
</head>
<body>
    <form id="form1" runat="server">
    <div>

    <custom:MovieView
        id="MovieView1"
        Runat="server" />

    </div>
    </form>
</body>
</html>
```

Creating Control Designers

You can modify the appearance of your custom controls in Design view by creating a
`ControlDesigner`. The ASP.NET 2.0 Framework enables you to implement a number of
fancy features when you implement a `ControlDesigner`. This section focuses on just two
of these advanced features.

First, you learn how to create a `ContainerControlDesigner`. A `ContainerControlDesigner` enables you to drag and drop other controls from the Toolbox onto your control in Design view.

You also learn how to add Smart Tags (also called Action Lists) to your control. When a control supports Smart Tags, a menu of common tasks pop up above the control in Design view.

Creating a Container ControlDesigner

If you associate a custom control with a `ContainerControlDesigner`, then you can add child controls to your control in Design view. For example, the file in Listing 31.34 contains a `GradientPanel` control. This control displays a gradient background behind its contents (see Figure 31.16).

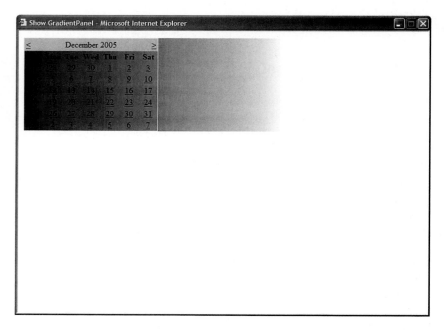

FIGURE 31.16   Displaying the `GradientPanel` control.

LISTING 31.34   `GradientPanel.vb`

```
Imports System
Imports System.Web.UI
Imports System.Web.UI.WebControls
Imports System.Web.UI.Design
Imports System.ComponentModel
Imports System.Drawing
```

LISTING 31.34   Continued

```
Namespace myControls
    <Designer(GetType(GradientPanelDesigner))> _
    <ParseChildren(False)> _
    Public Class GradientPanel
        Inherits WebControl

        Private _direction As GradientDirection = GradientDirection.Horizontal
        Private _startColor As Color = Color.DarkBlue
        Private _endColor As Color = Color.White

        Public Property Direction() As GradientDirection
            Get
                Return _direction
            End Get
            Set(ByVal Value As GradientDirection)
                _direction = Value
            End Set
        End Property

        Public Property StartColor() As Color
            Get
                Return _startColor
            End Get
            Set(ByVal Value As Color)
                _startColor = Value
            End Set
        End Property

        Public Property EndColor() As Color
            Get
                Return _endColor
            End Get
            Set(ByVal Value As Color)
                _endColor = Value
            End Set
        End Property


        Protected Overrides Sub AddAttributesToRender(ByVal writer
➥As HtmlTextWriter)
            writer.AddStyleAttribute(HtmlTextWriterStyle.Filter,
➥Me.GetFilterString())
            MyBase.AddAttributesToRender(writer)
        End Sub

        Public Function GetFilterString() As String
```

31

LISTING 31.34   Continued

```
                Return String.Format("progid:DXImageTransform.Microsoft.Gradient(
➥gradientType={0},startColorStr={1},endColorStr={2})", _
➥direction.ToString("d"), ColorTranslator.ToHtml(_startColor), _
➥ ColorTranslator.ToHtml(_endColor))
        End Function

        Public Sub New()
            Me.Width = Unit.Parse("500px")
        End Sub

        Protected Overrides ReadOnly Property TagKey() As HtmlTextWriterTag
            Get
                Return HtmlTextWriterTag.Div
            End Get
        End Property
    End Class

    Public Enum GradientDirection
        Vertical = 0
        Horizontal = 1
    End Enum

    Public Class GradientPanelDesigner
        Inherits ContainerControlDesigner

        Protected Overrides Sub AddDesignTimeCssAttributes(ByVal styleAttributes
➥As System.Collections.IDictionary)
            Dim gPanel As GradientPanel = CType(Me.Component, GradientPanel)
            styleAttributes.Add("filter", gPanel.GetFilterString())
            MyBase.AddDesignTimeCssAttributes(styleAttributes)
        End Sub
    End Class
End Namespace
```

The GradientPanel control uses an Internet Explorer filter to create the gradient background. The filter is applied in the AddAttributesToRender() method. You can set the StartColor, EndColor, and Direction properties to control the appearance of the gradient background.

Notice that the GradientPanel control is decorated with a ControlDesigner attribute. This attribute associates the GradientPanelDesigner class with the GradientPanel control.

The GradientPanelDesigner is also included in Listing 31.34. One method is overridden in the GradientPanelDesigner class. The AddDesignTimeCssAttributes() method is used to apply the gradient background in Design view.

The page in Listing 31.35 illustrates how you can declare the `GradientPanel` in a page. However, to understand the effect of the `ContainerControlDesigner`, you need to open the page in Design view in either Visual Web Developer or Visual Studio .NET.

LISTING 31.35   ShowGradientPanel.aspx

```
<%@ Page Language="VB" %>
<%@ Register TagPrefix="custom" Namespace="myControls" %>
<!DOCTYPE html PUBLIC "-//W3C//DTD XHTML 1.0 Transitional//EN"
➥"http://www.w3.org/TR/xhtml1/DTD/xhtml1-transitional.dtd">
<html xmlns="http://www.w3.org/1999/xhtml" >
<head id="Head1" runat="server">
    <title>Show GradientPanel</title>
</head>
<body>
    <form id="form1" runat="server">
    <div>

    <custom:GradientPanel
        id="GradientPanel1"
        Runat="server">
        <asp:Calendar
            ID="Calendar1"
            runat="server" />
    </custom:GradientPanel>

    </div>
    </form>
</body>
</html>
```

When you open the page in Listing 31.35 in Design view, you can drag other controls from the toolbox onto the `GradientPanel` control. For example, if you drag a `Calendar` control onto the `GradientPanel` control, the `Calendar` control is added automatically to the control collection of the `GradientPanel` (see Figure 31.17).

31

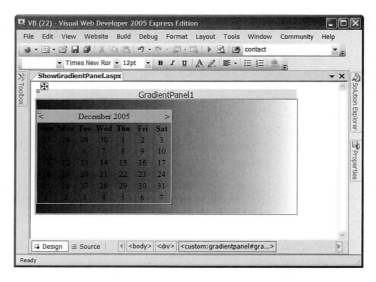

FIGURE 31.17   Editing the `GradientPanel` control in Design view.

Adding Smart Tasks

If you add a `GridView` control to a page when you are in Design view, you'll notice that a menu of common tasks appears above the `GridView`. For example, you can select a Smart Task to enable sorting or paging.

You can add your own Smart Tasks to a custom control by inheriting a new class from the base `DesignerActionList` class.

For example, the file in Listing 31.36 contains three classes. It contains a custom control, named the `SmartImage` control, which enables you to rotate and mirror images. It also contains a `ControlDesigner`. Finally, it contains a `DesignerActionList` class that contains two Smart Tasks.

LISTING 31.36   SmartImage.vb

```
Imports System
Imports System.Web.UI
Imports System.Web.UI.WebControls
Imports System.Web.UI.Design
Imports System.ComponentModel
Imports System.ComponentModel.Design

Namespace myControls

    <Designer(GetType(SmartImageDesigner))> _
    Public Class SmartImage
        Inherits WebControl
```

LISTING 31.36   Continued

```vb
Private _imageUrl As String
Private _alternateText As String
Private _rotation As Integer = 0
Private _mirror As Boolean = False

Public Property ImageUrl() As String
    Get
        Return _imageUrl
    End Get
    Set(ByVal Value As String)
        _imageUrl = Value
    End Set
End Property

Public Property AlternateText() As String
    Get
        Return _alternateText
    End Get
    Set(ByVal Value As String)
        _alternateText = Value
    End Set
End Property

Public Property Rotation() As Integer
    Get
        Return _rotation
    End Get
    Set(ByVal Value As Integer)
        _rotation = Value
    End Set
End Property

Public Property Mirror() As Boolean
    Get
        Return _mirror
    End Get
    Set(ByVal Value As Boolean)
        _mirror = Value
    End Set
End Property

Protected Overrides ReadOnly Property TagKey() As HtmlTextWriterTag
    Get
        Return HtmlTextWriterTag.Img
```

LISTING 31.36   Continued

```
                End Get
        End Property

        Private Function GetFilterString() As String
            Dim _mirrorValue As String = "0"
            If _mirror Then
                _mirrorValue = "1"
            End If
            Return String.Format("progid:DXImageTransform.Microsoft.BasicImage(
➥Rotation={0},Mirror={1})", _rotation, _mirrorValue)
        End Function


        Protected Overrides Sub AddAttributesToRender(ByVal writer
➥As HtmlTextWriter)
            writer.AddStyleAttribute(HtmlTextWriterStyle.Filter,
➥Me.GetFilterString())
            writer.AddAttribute(HtmlTextWriterAttribute.Src, _imageUrl)
            writer.AddAttribute(HtmlTextWriterAttribute.Alt, _alternateText)
            MyBase.AddAttributesToRender(writer)
        End Sub
    End Class

    Public Class SmartImageDesigner
        Inherits ControlDesigner
        Public Overrides ReadOnly Property ActionLists()
➥As DesignerActionListCollection
            Get
                Dim colActions As New DesignerActionListCollection()
                colActions.AddRange(MyBase.ActionLists)
                colActions.Add(New SmartImageActionList(Me))
                Return colActions
            End Get
        End Property
    End Class

    Public Class SmartImageActionList
        Inherits DesignerActionList

        Private items As DesignerActionItemCollection
        Private _parent As SmartImageDesigner

        Public Sub New(ByVal parent As SmartImageDesigner)
            MyBase.New(parent.Component)
            _parent = parent
        End Sub
```

LISTING 31.36   Continued

```
        Public Sub Rotate()

            Dim toCall As TransactedChangeCallback =
➥New TransactedChangeCallback(AddressOf DoRotate)
            ControlDesigner.InvokeTransactedChange(Me.Component, toCall,
➥"Rotate", "Rotate image 90 degrees")
        End Sub

        Public Sub Mirror()
            Dim toCall As TransactedChangeCallback =
➥New TransactedChangeCallback(AddressOf DoMirror)
            ControlDesigner.InvokeTransactedChange(Me.Component, toCall,
➥"Mirror", "Mirror Image")
        End Sub

        Public Overrides Function GetSortedActionItems()
➥As DesignerActionItemCollection
            If IsNothing(items) Then
                items = New DesignerActionItemCollection()
                items.Add(New DesignerActionMethodItem(Me, "Rotate",
➥"Rotate Image", True))
                items.Add(New DesignerActionMethodItem(Me, "Mirror",
➥"Mirror Image", True))
            End If
            Return items
        End Function

        Public Function DoRotate(ByVal arg As Object) As Boolean
            Dim img As SmartImage = CType(Me.Component, SmartImage)
            img.Rotation += 1
            If img.Rotation > 3 Then
                img.Rotation = 0
            End If
            _parent.UpdateDesignTimeHtml()
            Return True
        End Function

        Public Function DoMirror(ByVal arg As Object) As Boolean
            Dim img As SmartImage = CType(Me.Component, SmartImage)
            img.Mirror = Not img.Mirror
            _parent.UpdateDesignTimeHtml()
            Return True
        End Function
    End Class
End Namespace
```

31

The SmartImage control takes advantage of an Internet Explorer filter named the BasicImage filter. This filter enables you to manipulate images by rotating, mirroring, and changing the opacity of images. In Listing 31.36, the filter is applied in the AddAttributesToRender() method.

The SmartImage control is associated with a ControlDesigner named the SmartImageDesigner through the control's Designer attribute. The SmartImageDesigner class overrides the base class's ActionLists property to expose a custom DesignerActionList.

The DesignerActionList is the final class declared in Listing 31.36. This class contains four methods named Rotate(), DoRotate(), Mirror(), and DoMirror(). The GetSortedActionItems() method exposes the Rotate and Mirror actions.

When all is said and done, the custom ActionList enables you to display Rotate and Mirror Smart Tags for the SmartImage control in Design view. When you click the Rotate action in Design view, the SmartImage does in fact rotate (see Figure 31.18).

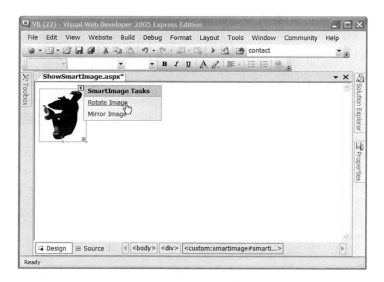

FIGURE 31.18   Adding Smart Tags to a control.

> **NOTE**
>
> You can view the SmartImage control by opening the ShowSmartImage.aspx page included on the CD that accompanies this book.

Summary

In this chapter, you learned how to build basic controls in the ASP.NET Framework. First, you learned how to create both fully rendered and composite controls. You also learned how to combine the features of fully rendered and composite controls by creating hybrid controls.

You also learned how to preserve the values of control properties in View State. You learned the difference between View State and Control State and how to use both features of the framework.

Next, you learned how to handle postback data and events. You saw how you can process form data submitted to the server. You also learned how you can raise a server-side event that is initiated by a postback.

This chapter examined the topic of building controls that represent a collection of items. You learned how to use the ParseChildren attribute to parse the inner content of a control in different ways. You also learned how to alter the parsing of a control's content by overriding the AddParsedSubObject() method and by creating custom ControlBuilders.

Finally, you saw two methods of modifying the appearance of a control in Design view. You learned how to apply design-time attributes to a control and its properties. You also learned how to associate a ControlDesigner with a custom control.

31

Integrating JavaScript in Custom Controls

Even though the ASP.NET Framework is a server-side programming framework, there is nothing to prevent you from taking advantage of JavaScript—a client-side programming language—in your custom controls. In fact, you can do many exciting things by integrating JavaScript into your custom controls.

If you want to create rich and interactive user interfaces then you have no choice but to use JavaScript. For example, by taking advantage of JavaScript, you can create controls that display floating windows, rich text boxes, and drag-and-drop interfaces. In other words, by taking advantage of JavaScript, you can create the same type of experience that users have come to expect from working with traditional desktop applications.

In this chapter, you learn how to integrate JavaScript into your custom controls. First, you learn how to take advantage of the methods and properties of the `ClientScriptManager` class. This class exposes the main application programming interface for working with client-side scripts. You also learn how to detect the features of different browsers by using the `HttpBrowserCapabilities` class.

Next, we get our hands dirty by building several controls that use client-side JavaScript. In the second part of this chapter, we build the following controls:

- `NewWindowLink`—This control renders a button that opens a new browser window. By setting properties of the control, you can configure the position and size of the new browser window.

- WebWindow—This control renders a virtual browser window by rendering a floating <div> tag. The WebWindow control enables you to display multiple windows in a single page.

- ClientTabs—This control enables you to divide the content displayed in a page into multiple tabs. Only the contents of a single tab are displayed at one time. When you switch tabs, the page is not posted back to the server.

In the final section of this chapter, we discuss my favorite topic in the universe: AJAX. By taking advantage of AJAX, a custom control can communicate with the web server without posting the page that contains the control back to the web server.

In the final section of this chapter, we build two AJAX controls:

- ServerTimeButton—This control renders a button. When you click the button, the current time is retrieved from the server and displayed in a browser alert dialog box.

- ComboBox—This control displays a drop-down list of matching records from a database as you type.

> **NOTE**
>
> One reason that many programmers avoid using JavaScript is the issue of browser compatibility. Client-side programming is a mess because different browsers implement JavaScript and the Browser Object Model in different ways. However, by taking advantage of feature detection, you can write JavaScript that works the same way across all modern browsers. All the controls discussed in this chapter are compatible with Internet Explorer 6, Firefox 1, and Opera 8.

Using the ClientScriptManager **Class**

The ClientScriptManager class contains the main application programming interface for working with JavaScript. You'll make heavy use of this class whenever you add JavaScript to your custom controls.

The ClientScriptManager class supports the following methods for adding JavaScript to a page:

- RegisterArrayDeclaration—Enables you to add a JavaScript array to a page.

- RegisterClientScriptBlock—Enables you to add a JavaScript script after the page's opening server-side <form> tag.

- RegisterClientScriptInclude—Enables you to add a JavaScript include after the page's opening server-side <form> tag.

- RegisterClientScriptResource—Enables you to add JavaScript in a page that has been compiled into an assembly.

- RegisterExpandoAttribute—Enables you to add script for adding an expando attribute to an element of the page.

- `RegisterHiddenField`—Enables you to add a hidden form field after the page's opening server-side `<form>` tag.

- `RegisterOnSubmitStatement`—Enables you to add JavaScript that executes immediately before a page is posted back to the server.

- `RegisterStartupScript`—Enables you to add a JavaScript script before the page's closing server-side `<form>` tag.

Notice that there are two methods for rendering a JavaScript script in the body of a page: `RegisterClientScriptBlock()` and `RegisterStartupScript()`. The only difference between these methods is the location where they render the JavaScript. The location of a JavaScript script in a page matters because you cannot refer to an HTML element in JavaScript unless the script is located after the element. If you use the `RegisterStartupScript()` method, then you know that all the HTML elements in the body of the server-side `<form>` tag have been created.

All the methods listed here were designed so that you can safely call them more than once. Because you might have multiple instances of the same control in the same page, you don't want to add duplicate instances of the same script to a page. For example, if you call the `RegisterClientScriptInclude()` method more than once, then only one JavaScript include is added to the page.

You can detect whether or not a script has already been registered in a page by using one of the following methods:

- `IsClientScriptBlockRegistered`—Returns true when a script has already been registered with the `RegisterClientScriptBlock()` method.

- `IsClientScriptIncludeRegistered`—Returns true when a JavaScript include has already been registered with the `RegisterClientScriptInclude()` method.

- `IsOnSubmitStatementRegistered`—Returns true when a script has already been registered with the `RegisterOnSubmitStatement()` method.

- `IsStartupScriptRegistered`—Returns true when a script has already been registered with the `RegisterStartupScript()` method.

Detecting Browser Capabilities

After you have entered the messy universe of JavaScript, you must handle the frustrating incompatibilities between different web browsers. For example, you don't want to call the `showModalDialog()` or `addEventListener()` method on a browser that doesn't support it. You can detect browser capabilities either on the client side or the server side.

On the client side, you can perform feature detection in your JavaScript scripts to check whether particular methods are supported by a browser. For example, Internet Explorer and Firefox use different methods for adding an event handler. Internet Explorer uses the `attachEvent()` method and Firefox uses the (more standards-compliant) `addEventListener()` method.

The following script correctly adds a load event handler in the case of both browsers:

```
if (window.addEventListener)
    window.addEventListener('load', doSomething, false);
else
    window.attachEvent('onload', doSomething);
```

When you request a page that contains this script with Internet Explorer, calling `window.addEventListener` returns a value equivalent to `false` and the `window.attachEvent()` method is used. When you request a page that contains this script with Firefox or Opera, on the other hand, the `window.addEventListener()` method is called.

On the server side, you can use the properties of the `HttpBrowserCapabilities` class to detect the features of the browser being used to request a page. This class has a huge number of properties (too many to list here). However, here are some of the more useful properties that you can detect:

- `ActiveXControls`—Returns `true` when a browser supports ActiveXControls.
- `AOL`—Returns `true` when a browser is an American Online browser.
- `Browser`—Returns the type of browser (for example, IE, Firefox, Opera).
- `ClrVersion`—Returns the latest version of the .NET Framework installed on the browser.
- `Cookies`—Returns `true` when a browser supports cookies.
- `EcmaScriptVersion`—Returns the version of JavaScript supported by the browser.
- `MajorVersion`—Returns the major version of the browser as an Integer.
- `MinorVersion`—Returns the minor version of the browser as a couble.
- `MinorVersionString`—Returns the minor version of the browser as a string.
- `MSDomVersion`—Returns the version of the Microsoft Document Object Model supported by the browser.
- `Platform`—Returns the platform of the client (for example, WinXP).
- `SupportsCallback`—Returns `true` when a browser supports AJAX.
- `SupportsCSS`—Returns `true` when a browser supports Cascading Style Sheets.
- `Version`—Returns the full version of the browser.
- `W3CDomVersion`—Returns the W3C Document Object Model version supported by the browser (for example, 1.0).

The `HttpBrowserCapabilities` object is exposed through the `Request` object. You use `Request.Browser` to get a reference to the `HttpBrowserCapabilities` object. For example, you can use the following code to execute a subroutine only when the requesting browser is Internet Explorer version 5.0 or greater:

```
If Request.Browser.Browser = "IE" And Request.Browser.MajorVersion >= 5 Then
    doSomething()
End If
```

Behind the scenes, the `HttpBrowserCapabilities` object uses the User-Agent header sent by a browser to determine the browser's capabilities. A database of browser capabilities is stored in a set of XML files located in the following folder:

```
\WINDOWS\Microsoft.NET\Framework\[version]\CONFIG\Browsers
```

The information reported back by these properties is only as accurate as the information stored in these XML files.

Building JavaScript Controls

In this section, you learn how to build three custom JavaScript controls. You start with a simple sample of a custom control that renders JavaScript. We build a `NewWindowLink` control that enables you to open a new browser window when you click a button.

Next, we build a `WebWindow` control that enables you to render a virtual browser window. This control enables you to simulate multiple windows in a single web form page.

Finally, we create a `ClientTabs` control. This control enables you to switch between different tabs of content on the client without a postback to the server.

Building a `NewWindowLink` Control

Being a good web developer is hard. To be a good web developer, you need to know HTML, Cascading Style Sheets, SQL, XML, and JavaScript. You also need to know about the different implementations of these technologies in the case of different browsers and different operating systems.

One of the main jobs of a framework, such as the ASP.NET Framework, is to shield you from all the underlying technologies on which the framework is built. If you integrate JavaScript into a custom control, then you can learn the JavaScript for five minutes and then never need to worry about it again.

For example, in this section, we build a `NewWindowLink` control that opens a new browser window (see Figure 32.1). The JavaScript required to open a new window is quite simple. However, the advantage of creating a control that opens a new window is that you don't need to remember the JavaScript in the future.

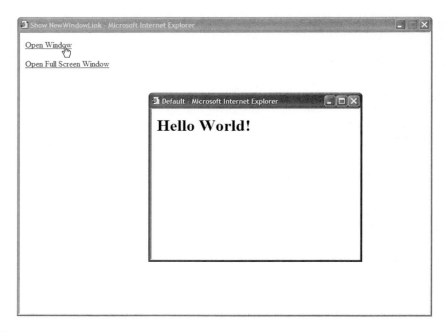

FIGURE 32.1   Opening a new browser window with the NewWindowLink control.

The code for the NewWindowLink control is contained in Listing 32.1.

LISTING 32.1   NewWindowLink.vb

```
Imports System
Imports System.Web
Imports System.Web.UI
Imports System.Web.UI.WebControls

Namespace myControls

    Public Class NewWindowLink
        Inherits WebControl
        Private _text As String = "Click Here!"
        Private _navigateUrl As String
        Private _target As String = "_blank"
        Private _windowWidth As Integer = 400
        Private _windowHeight As Integer = 300
        Private _windowLeft As Integer = 100
        Private _windowTop As Integer = 100
        Private _fullScreen As Boolean = False
        Private _resizable As Boolean = True

        Public Property Text() As String
```

LISTING 32.1   Continued

```
    Get
        Return _text
    End Get
    Set(ByVal Value As String)
        _text = value
    End Set
End Property

Public Property NavigateUrl() As String
    Get
        Return _navigateUrl
    End Get
    Set(ByVal Value As String)
        _navigateUrl = value
    End Set
End Property

Public Property Target() As String
    Get
        Return _target
    End Get
    Set(ByVal Value As String)
        _target = value
    End Set
End Property

Public Property WindowWidth() As Integer
    Get
        Return _windowWidth
    End Get
    Set(ByVal Value As Integer)
        _windowWidth = value
    End Set
End Property

Public Property WindowHeight() As Integer
    Get
        Return _windowHeight
    End Get
    Set(ByVal Value As Integer)
        _windowHeight = value
    End Set
End Property
```

32

LISTING 32.1   Continued

```
    Public Property WindowLeft() As Integer
        Get
            Return _windowLeft
        End Get
        Set(ByVal Value As Integer)
            _windowLeft = value
        End Set
    End Property

    Public Property WindowTop() As Integer
        Get
            Return _windowTop
        End Get
        Set(ByVal Value As Integer)
            _windowTop = value
        End Set
    End Property

    Public Property FullScreen() As Boolean
        Get
            Return _fullScreen
        End Get
        Set(ByVal Value As Boolean)
            _fullScreen = value
        End Set
    End Property

    Public Property Resizable() As Boolean
        Get
            Return _resizable
        End Get
        Set(ByVal Value As Boolean)
            _resizable = value
        End Set
    End Property

    Protected Overrides Sub AddAttributesToRender(ByVal writer As
➥HtmlTextWriter)
        Dim fullscreenValue As String = "no"
        If (_fullScreen) Then
            fullscreenValue = "yes"
        End If
        Dim resizableValue As String = "no"
        If (_resizable) Then
```

LISTING 32.1   Continued

```
                    resizableValue = "yes"
            End If
            Dim features As String =
➥ "width={0},height={1},left={2},top={3},fullscreen={4},
➥resizable={5},status=no,toolbar=no,menubar=no,location=no"
            Dim featuresValue As String =
➥String.Format(features, _windowWidth, _windowHeight, _windowLeft, _
➥windowTop, fullscreenValue, resizableValue)
            Dim script As String =
➥String.Format("window.open('{0}','{1}','{2}');return false;",
➥ Page.ResolveUrl(_navigateUrl), _target, featuresValue)
            writer.AddAttribute(HtmlTextWriterAttribute.Onclick, script)
            writer.AddAttribute(HtmlTextWriterAttribute.Href,
➥Page.ResolveUrl(_navigateUrl))
            MyBase.AddAttributesToRender(writer)
        End Sub


        Protected Overrides Sub RenderContents(ByVal writer As HtmlTextWriter)
            writer.Write(_text)
        End Sub


        Protected Overrides ReadOnly Property TagKey() As HtmlTextWriterTag
            Get
                Return HtmlTextWriterTag.A
            End Get
        End Property


    End Class
End Namespace
```

The majority of the code in Listing 32.1 is devoted to declaring a set of properties. The NewWindowLink control includes properties for the new window's position and size. It also includes properties you can set to open a window that is resizable or full screen.

The JavaScript for opening the window is contained in the AddAttributesToRender() method. This method adds a client-side OnClick handler to the link rendered by the control. When you click the link, the window.open() method is called on the client.

The page in Listing 32.2 illustrates how you can use the NewWindowLink control in an ASP.NET page. The page contains two instances of the NewWindowLink control. The first instance opens a normal window. The control opens the page specified by its NavigateUrl property in a new window.

The second instance of the NewWindowLink control opens a full-screen window. A full-screen window is supported only with Internet Explorer. (You get a normal new window when the control is used with other browsers such as Firefox.) After you open a full-screen window, you can close it by selecting Alt+F4.

LISTING 32.2   `ShowNewWindowLink.aspx`

```
<%@ Page Language="VB" %>
<%@ Register TagPrefix="custom" Namespace="myControls" %>
<!DOCTYPE html PUBLIC "-//W3C//DTD XHTML 1.0 Transitional//EN"
   "http://www.w3.org/TR/xhtml1/DTD/xhtml1-transitional.dtd">
<html xmlns="http://www.w3.org/1999/xhtml" >
<head id="Head1" runat="server">
    <title>Show NewWindowLink</title>
</head>
<body>
    <form id="form1" runat="server">
    <div>

    <custom:NewWindowLink
        id="NewWindowLink1"
        Text="Open Window"
        NavigateUrl="~/Default.aspx"
        Runat="server" />

    <br /><br />

    <custom:NewWindowLink
        id="NewWindowLink2"
        Text="Open Full Screen Window"
        NavigateUrl="~/Default.aspx"
        FullScreen="true"
        Runat="server" />

    </div>
    </form>
</body>
</html>
```

Building a `WebWindow` Control

There are several disadvantages that result from using separate browser windows in a web application. First, communicating information between multiple browser windows is difficult. When you update one window, you must reload the other windows to reflect the new information. Furthermore, new browser windows can be blocked by pop-up blockers.

A better alternative is to create virtual windows by creating floating <div> tags. Unlike true browser windows, you don't run into problems communicating information between virtual windows. Furthermore, a virtual window will never be blocked by a pop-up blocker.

By taking advantage of a little JavaScript, you can even drag and drop a virtual window. In other words, you can position a virtual window at different locations on the screen.

The code for the virtual window control, the WebWindow control, is contained in Listing 32.3.

LISTING 32.3   WebWindow.vb

```vb
Imports System
Imports System.Web.UI
Imports System.Web.UI.WebControls
Imports System.ComponentModel

Namespace myControls

    <ParseChildren(False)> _
    Public Class WebWindow
        Inherits WebControl
        Implements IPostBackEventHandler

        Private _windowTitleText As String = "Untitled"

        Public Event Closed As EventHandler

        Public Property WindowTitleText() As String
            Get
                Return _windowTitleText
            End Get
            Set(ByVal Value As String)
                _windowTitleText = value
            End Set
        End Property

        Protected Overrides Sub OnPreRender(ByVal e As EventArgs)
            If Not Page.ClientScript.IsClientScriptIncludeRegistered("WebWindow")
➥Then
                Page.ClientScript.RegisterClientScriptInclude("WebWindow",
➥Page.ResolveClientUrl("~/ClientScripts/WebWindow.js"))
            End If

            Dim startupScript As String =
➥String.Format("WebWindow.init('{0}');", Me.ClientID)
            Page.ClientScript.RegisterStartupScript(Me.GetType(), Me.ClientID,
➥startupScript, True)
        End Sub
```

LISTING 32.3   Continued

```
        Protected Overrides Sub RenderContents(ByVal writer As HtmlTextWriter)
            RenderTitleBar(writer)
            writer.AddAttribute(HtmlTextWriterAttribute.Class, "webWindowBody")
            writer.RenderBeginTag(HtmlTextWriterTag.Div)
            Me.RenderChildren(writer)
            writer.RenderEndTag()
        End Sub

        Private Sub RenderTitleBar(ByVal writer As HtmlTextWriter)
            writer.AddAttribute(HtmlTextWriterAttribute.Class, "webWindowTitleBar")
            writer.AddAttribute("onmousedown", "WebWindow.mouseDown(event)")
            writer.AddStyleAttribute(HtmlTextWriterStyle.TextAlign, "right")
            writer.RenderBeginTag(HtmlTextWriterTag.Div)

            writer.AddAttribute(HtmlTextWriterAttribute.Class,
➥"webWindowTitleText")
            writer.RenderBeginTag(HtmlTextWriterTag.Span)
            writer.Write(_windowTitleText)
            writer.RenderEndTag()

            RenderCloseButton(writer)

            writer.RenderEndTag()
        End Sub

        Private Sub RenderCloseButton(ByVal writer As HtmlTextWriter)
            Dim eventRef As String =
➥Page.ClientScript.GetPostBackEventReference(Me, String.Empty)
            writer.AddAttribute(HtmlTextWriterAttribute.Class, "webWindowClose")
            writer.AddAttribute(HtmlTextWriterAttribute.Onclick, eventRef)
            writer.RenderBeginTag(HtmlTextWriterTag.Span)
            writer.Write("X")
            writer.RenderEndTag()
        End Sub

        Protected Overrides Sub AddAttributesToRender(ByVal writer
➥As HtmlTextWriter)
            writer.AddStyleAttribute(HtmlTextWriterStyle.Position, "absolute")
            writer.AddAttribute(HtmlTextWriterAttribute.Class, "webWindow")
            MyBase.AddAttributesToRender(writer)
        End Sub

        Protected Overrides ReadOnly Property TagKey() As HtmlTextWriterTag
            Get
```

LISTING 32.3   Continued

```
                Return HtmlTextWriterTag.Div
            End Get
        End Property


        Public Sub RaisePostBackEvent(ByVal eventArgument As String)
➥Implements IPostBackEventHandler.RaisePostBackEvent
            RaiseEvent Closed(Me, EventArgs.Empty)
        End Sub
    End Class
End Namespace
```

The `RenderContents()` method in Listing 32.3 is responsible for rendering the virtual window. This method renders a title bar that contains a close button. It also renders a `<div>` tag that contains the window's contents.

All the magic happens in an external JavaScript file. A JavaScript `include` is rendered by the `WebWindow` control in its `OnPreRender()` method. The control assumes that a JavaScript file named `WebWindow.js` is located in a subfolder named ClientScripts.

The contents of the `WebWindow.js` file are contained in Listing 32.4.

LISTING 32.4   `ClientScripts\WebWindow.js`

```javascript
var WebWindow = new Object();

WebWindow.init = function(winId)
    {
        eval("place=" + this.getCookie(winId + "_place"));
        place = place || {left:20, top:20};

        var win = document.getElementById(winId);

        win.style.left = place.left;
        win.style.top = place.top;
    }


WebWindow.mouseDown = function(e)
    {
        var e = e || window.event;
        var src = e.target || e.srcElement;
        var win = src.offsetParent;

        var startWinX = win.offsetLeft;
        var startWinY = win.offsetTop;
        var startMouseX = e.clientX;
```

LISTING 32.4   Continued

```javascript
        var startMouseY = e.clientY;

        var move = function(e)
            {
                var e = e || window.event;
                win.style.left = (startWinX - (startMouseX - e.clientX)) + 'px';
                win.style.top = (startWinY - (startMouseY - e.clientY)) + 'px';

                if (document.all)
                {
                    e.cancelBubble = true;
                    e.returnValue = false;
                }
                if (e.preventDefault)
                {
                    e.preventDefault();
                }
            }

        var up = function(e)
            {
                document.onmousemove = null;
                document.onmouseup = null;
                WebWindow.setCookie(win.id + "_place", "{left:'" + win.style.left
+ "', top:'" + win.style.top + "'}");
            }

        document.onmousemove = move;
        document.onmouseup = up;
    }

WebWindow.setCookie = function(name, value)
{
    var expires = new Date();
    expires.setTime( expires.getTime() + 365 * 24 * 60 * 60 * 1000 );
    document.cookie = name + "=" + escape(value) +
";expires=" + expires.toGMTString();
        }

WebWindow.getCookie = function(name)
{
    var aCookie = document.cookie.split("; ");
    for (var i=0; i < aCookie.length; i++)
```

LISTING 32.4   Continued

```
    {
      var aCrumb = aCookie[i].split("=");
      if (name == aCrumb[0])
      return unescape(aCrumb[1]);
    }
    return null;
}
```

The JavaScript file in Listing 32.4 contains the methods that enable you to drag the WebWindow around the page. When you click your mouse on the WebWindow's title bar, the WebWindow.mouseDown() method executes and records your current mouse position. As you move your mouse, the move() method executes and updates the WebWindow's position on the screen by modifying the left and top style properties of the WebWindow's containing div element.

Whenever you move a WebWindow, its new position is recorded in a browser cookie. The next time that you open the page, the WebWindow appears in the same location.

> **WARNING**
>
> Be careful about where you declare the WebWindow control in a page. Do not declare the control inside of another <div> tag or you might encounter difficulties when you attempt to drag the control outside of its containing <div> tag. I've tested the WebWindow control with Internet Explorer 6.0, Firefox 1.0, and Opera 8.0.

The page in Listing 32.5 illustrates how you can use the WebWindow control in an ASP.NET page. When the page first opens, the WebWindow is not visible by default. When you click the Open Window link, the WebWindow is displayed (see Figure 32.2). Finally, when you click the WebWindow's Close button, the WebWindow1_Closed() event handler executes and the WebWindow is hidden.

LISTING 32.5   ShowWebWindow.aspx

```
<%@ Page Language="VB" %>
<%@ Register TagPrefix="custom" Namespace="myControls" %>
<!DOCTYPE html PUBLIC "-//W3C//DTD XHTML 1.0 Transitional//EN"
   "http://www.w3.org/TR/xhtml1/DTD/xhtml1-transitional.dtd">
<script runat="server">

    protected sub lnkOpenWindow_Click(sender As object, e As EventArgs)
        WebWindow1.Visible = true
    End Sub

    protected sub WebWindow1_Closed(sender As object, e As EventArgs)
        WebWindow1.Visible = false
```

LISTING 32.5   Continued

```
    End Sub
</script>
<html xmlns="http://www.w3.org/1999/xhtml" >
<head id="Head1" runat="server">
    <style type="text/css">
        .webWindow
        {
            width:400px;
            height:400px;
            border:Outset;
            background-color:white;
        }
        .webWindowBody
        {
            padding:10px;
        }
        .webWindowTitleBar
        {
            font:14px Verdana,Sans-Serif;
            padding-left:10px;
            background-color:Blue;
            color:white;
            cursor:move;
        }
        .webWindowTitleText
        {
            float:left;
        }
        .webWindowClose
        {
            background-color:Red;
            cursor:pointer;
        }
    </style>
    <title>Show WebWindow</title>
</head>
<body>
    <form id="form1" runat="server">

    <div>
    <asp:LinkButton
        id="lnkOpenWindow"
        Text="Open Window"
        OnClick="lnkOpenWindow_Click"
```

LISTING 32.5 Continued

```
         Runat="server" />
    </div>

    <custom:WebWindow
        id="WebWindow1"
        WindowTitleText="The WebWindow Title"
        Visible="false"
        OnClosed="WebWindow1_Closed"
        Runat="server">
        Here is some content
    </custom:WebWindow>

    </form>
</body>
</html>
```

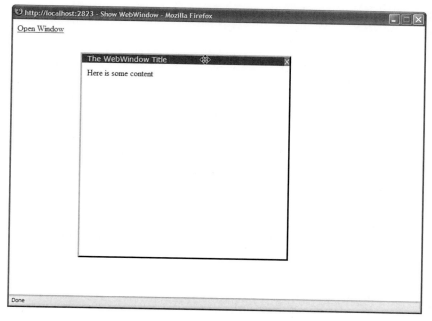

FIGURE 32.2 Displaying a virtual window with the `WebWindow` control.

Building a `ClientTabs` Control

In Chapter 4, "Using the Rich Controls," you learned how to use the `Menu` control with the `MultiView` control to display tabbed content in a page. The drawback of using these controls is that they require you to post the page containing the controls back to the server each and every time you click a tab.

In this section, you learn how to create a client-side tab control named the ClientTabs control (see Figure 32.3). This control renders the contents of all the tabs to the browser. However, it hides the contents of all the tabs except for the selected tab. When you select a new tab, JavaScript is executed on the browser to hide the contents of all the tabs except the newly selected tab.

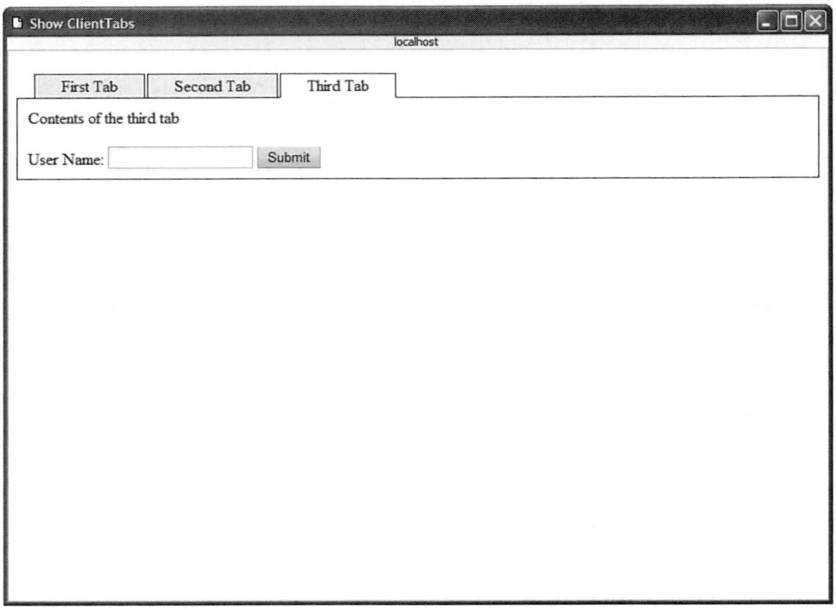

FIGURE 32.3   Displaying tabs with the ClientTabs control.

Unfortunately, the entire code for the ClientTabs control is too long to include in the body of this book. However, the complete source code (in both Visual Basic .NET and C#) is included on the CD that accompanies this book. Listing 32.6 contains a partial listing of the ClientTabs control.

LISTING 32.6   ClientTabs.vb (Partial Listing)

```
Namespace myControls
    <ParseChildren(False)> _
    Public Class ClientTabs
        Inherits WebControl
        Implements IPostBackDataHandler

        ''' <summary>
```

LISTING 32.6   Continued

```
''' Render tabs and tab content
''' </summary>
Protected Overrides Sub RenderContents(ByVal writer As HtmlTextWriter)
    RenderTabs(writer)
    RenderTabContent(writer)
End Sub


''' <summary>
''' Render the tab strip
''' </summary>
Private Sub RenderTabs(ByVal writer As HtmlTextWriter)
    writer.AddAttribute(HtmlTextWriterAttribute.Class, "tabs")
    writer.RenderBeginTag(HtmlTextWriterTag.Table)
    writer.RenderBeginTag(HtmlTextWriterTag.Tbody)
    writer.AddAttribute(HtmlTextWriterAttribute.Id, TabContainerID)
    writer.RenderBeginTag(HtmlTextWriterTag.Tr)

    Dim index As Integer
    For index = 0 To Controls.Count - 1 Step index + 1
        Dim currentTab As Tab = CType(Controls(index), Tab)
        Dim script As String = String.Format(
➥"ClientTabs.selectTab('{0}','{1}')", Me.ClientID, currentTab.ClientID)
        writer.AddAttribute(HtmlTextWriterAttribute.Onclick, script)
        If index = SelectedIndex Then
            writer.AddAttribute(HtmlTextWriterAttribute.Class,
➥"tab selectedTab")
        Else
            writer.AddAttribute(HtmlTextWriterAttribute.Class,
➥"tab unselectedTab")
        End If
        writer.AddAttribute(HtmlTextWriterAttribute.Id,
➥currentTab.ClientID + "_tab")
        writer.RenderBeginTag(HtmlTextWriterTag.Td)
        writer.Write(currentTab.Text)
        writer.RenderEndTag()
    Next

    writer.RenderEndTag()
    writer.RenderEndTag()
    writer.RenderEndTag()
End Sub


''' <summary>
''' Render the tab contents
```

LISTING 32.6   Continued

```
    ''' </summary>
    Private Sub RenderTabContent(ByVal writer As HtmlTextWriter)
        writer.AddAttribute(HtmlTextWriterAttribute.Id, TabContentContainerID)
        writer.AddAttribute(HtmlTextWriterAttribute.Class, "tabContent")
        writer.RenderBeginTag(HtmlTextWriterTag.Div)

        Dim index As Integer
        For index = 0 To Controls.Count - 1 Step index + 1
            Dim currentTab As Tab = CType(Controls(index), Tab)
            If index <> SelectedIndex Then
                currentTab.Style.Add("display", "none")
            End If

            currentTab.RenderControl(writer)
        Next
        writer.RenderEndTag()
    End Sub
End Class
End Namespace
```

Listing 32.6 contains the code for rendering the tabs. When the `ClientTab` control renders its contents, it iterates through its child controls in two passes. First, it renders the tab links. Next, it renders the body of each tab. Any tab that is not selected is hidden by the CSS `display:none` property.

One special feature of the `ClientTabs` control needs to be explained. Imagine that each of the tabs contains a separate form with a separate button. When you click the button and submit the form to the server, you want the same tab to be displayed again when the page is reloaded. In other words, to function properly, the `ClientTabs` control needs to retain state across postbacks.

The `ClientTabs` control registers a hidden form field in its `OnPreRender()` method. When you select a new tab, the ID of the selected tab is assigned to the hidden form field. When the page is posted back to the server, the value of the hidden form field is used to determine the currently selected tab. That way, when the `ClientTab` control renders its tabs again, the tab selected on the client remains selected when the control is rendered on the server.

The `ClientTabs` control uses a Cascading Style Sheet file to format the appearance of the tabs. This Cascading Style Sheet file is added to the page containing the ClientTabs control by the ClientTabs control's OnPreRender() method. The contents of the Cascading Style Sheet file are contained in Listing 32.7.

LISTING 32.7 ClientScripts\ClientTabs.css

```
.tab
{
    padding:2px 25px;
    border:solid 1px black;
    cursor:pointer;
}

.unselectedTab
{
    background-color:#eeeeee;
}

.selectedTab
{
    background-color:White;
    border-bottom:solid 1px white;
}

.tabs
{
    position:relative;
    top:3px;
    left:15px;
}


.tabContent
{
    border:Solid 1px black;
    background-color:White;
    padding:10px;
}
```

Finally, the ClientTabs control executes a client-side JavaScript function named ClientTabs.selectTab() when a user selects a new tab. The JavaScript library is added to the page in the ClientTabs control's OnPreRender() method. The ClientTabs control assumes that there is a JavaScript file named ClientTabs.js that is located in the ClientScripts folder. The contents of this JavaScript file are contained in Listing 32.8.

LISTING 32.8 ClientScripts\ClientTabs.js

```
var ClientTabs = new Object();

ClientTabs.selectTab = function(controlId, tabId)
    {
```

LISTING 32.8   Continued

```
        // Get previous value
        var hiddenField = document.getElementById(controlId + '_hidden');
        var prevTabId = hiddenField.value;

        // Hide previous tab
        document.getElementById(prevTabId + '_tab').className =
'tab unselectedTab';
        document.getElementById(prevTabId).style.display = 'none';

        // Show new tab
        document.getElementById(tabId).style.display = 'block';
        document.getElementById(tabId + '_tab').className = 'tab selectedTab';

        // Update hidden value
        hiddenField.value = tabId;
    }
```

The page in Listing 32.9 illustrates how you can use the ClientTabs control within an ASP.NET page. The page in Listing 32.9 contains a ClientTabs control that contains three Tab controls. The final Tab control includes a simple form with a Button control. Notice that after you submit the page to the server, the correct tab is selected when the tabs are rendered back to the client.

LISTING 32.9   ShowClientTabs.aspx

```
<%@ Page Language="VB" %>
<%@ Register TagPrefix="custom" Namespace="myControls" %>
<!DOCTYPE html PUBLIC "-//W3C//DTD XHTML 1.0 Transitional//EN"
   "http://www.w3.org/TR/xhtml1/DTD/xhtml1-transitional.dtd">
<html xmlns="http://www.w3.org/1999/xhtml" >
<head id="Head1" runat="server">
    <title>Show ClientTabs</title>
</head>
<body>
    <form id="form1" runat="server">
    <div>

    <custom:ClientTabs
        id="ClientTabs1"
        Runat="server">
        <custom:Tab ID="Tab1" Text="First Tab" runat="server">
            Contents of the first tab
        </custom:Tab>
        <custom:Tab ID="Tab2" Text="Second Tab" runat="server">
```

LISTING 32.9 Continued

```
            Contents of the second tab
        </custom:Tab>
        <custom:Tab ID="Tab3" Text="Third Tab" runat="server">
            Contents of the third tab
            <br /><br />
            <asp:Label
                id="lblUserName"
                Text="User Name:"
                AssociatedControlID="txtUserName"
                Runat="server" />
            <asp:TextBox
                id="txtUserName"
                Runat="server" />
            <asp:Button
                id="btnSubmit"
                Text="Submit"
                Runat="server" />
        </custom:Tab>
    </custom:ClientTabs>

    </div>
    </form>
</body>
</html>
```

32

Building AJAX Controls

AJAX (Asynchronous JavaScript and XML) is the future of the web. By taking advantage of AJAX, you can avoid performing a postback each and every time you perform an action in an ASP.NET page. A control that uses AJAX can communicate directly with a web server by performing a "sneaky postback."

Three of the standard ASP.NET controls use AJAX: the TreeView, GridView, and DetailsView controls. When you expand a node in a TreeView, the child nodes of the expanded node can be retrieved from the web server without a postback. When you sort or page rows in a GridView control, the rows can be retrieved from the server without a postback. Finally, when you page through records in a DetailsView control, you do not need to post the page back to the server.

> **NOTE**
>
> Microsoft has developed a new framework (code named Atlas) that enables you to build rich AJAX applications on top of the ASP.NET Framework. You can learn more about Atlas by visiting http://atlas.asp.net.

In this section, you learn how to take advantage of AJAX when building custom controls. We'll start simple. First, we create a `ServerTimeButton` control that retrieves the current time from the server and displays it in the browser without requiring a postback. Next, we'll create a more practical control. We re-create Google Suggest by creating an AJAX-enabled `ComboBox` control.

Implementing AJAX

To implement AJAX in a custom control, you must perform the following steps:

1. Render the JavaScript that initiates the AJAX call.

2. Create the methods on the server that reply to the AJAX call.

3. Create the JavaScript on the browser that displays the result from the server.

You initiate an AJAX call from the browser in order to execute methods on the server. The server returns a result that can be used on the client.

You create the JavaScript that initiates the AJAX call by calling the `Page.ClientScripts.GetCallbackEventReference()` method. This method returns a string that represents a JavaScript function call that looks like this:

```
WebForm_DoCallback('myControl',null,showResult,null,showError,false)
```

The `GetCallbackEventReference()` method is overloaded. Here are the parameters for one of the overloaded versions of this method:

- `control`—The control that initiates the AJAX call.

- `argument`—The argument that is sent to the web server in the AJAX call.

- `clientCallback`—The name of the JavaScript function that executes after a result is returned from the web server.

- `context`—The argument that is passed back to the `clientCallback()` and `clientErrorCallback()` methods after the AJAX call completes.

- `clientErrorCallback`—The name of the JavaScript function that executes when an error on the server results from an AJAX call.

- `useAsync`—When true, the AJAX call is performed asynchronously.

Next, you need to implement the methods on the server that respond to the AJAX call. To do this, you need to implement the `ICallbackEventHandler` interface.

> **NOTE**
>
> AJAX, in Microsoft terminology, is called *client callbacks*. The name AJAX was invented in a Blog post by Jesse James Garrett.

The ICallbackEventHandler interface has two methods that you must implement:

- RaiseCallbackEvent—This method is called first on the server when an AJAX call is performed.

- GetCallbackResult—This method returns the result of the AJAX call to the client.

Finally, you must implement a JavaScript function on the client that is called when the results are returned from the server.

Building a ServerTimeButton Control

We start by creating a really simple control that uses AJAX. The ServerTimeButton control retrieves the current time from the server and displays it in the web browser (see Figure 32.4). The ServerTimeButton control is contained in Listing 32.10.

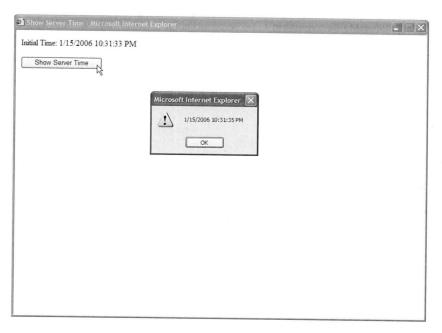

FIGURE 32.4   Displaying the server time with the ServerTimeButton control.

LISTING 32.10   ServerTimeButton.vb

```
Imports System
Imports System.Web.UI
Imports System.Web.UI.WebControls

Namespace myControls
    Public Class ServerTimeButton
```

LISTING 32.10   Continued

```
        Inherits WebControl
        Implements ICallbackEventHandler

        ''' <summary>
        ''' Add the onclick attribute that initiates the AJAX call
        ''' </summary>
        Protected Overrides Sub AddAttributesToRender(ByVal writer
➥As HtmlTextWriter)
            Dim eRef As String = Page.ClientScript.GetCallbackEventReference( _
                Me, _
                Nothing, _
                "showResult", _
                Nothing, _
                "showError", _
                False)

            writer.AddAttribute(HtmlTextWriterAttribute.Onclick, eRef)
            MyBase.AddAttributesToRender(writer)
        End Sub

        ''' <summary>
        ''' Add the Javascript file that process the AJAX call results
        ''' to the page
        ''' </summary>
        Protected Overrides Sub OnPreRender(ByVal e As EventArgs)
            Page.ClientScript.RegisterClientScriptInclude("serverTimeButton",
➥Page.ResolveClientUrl("~/ClientScripts/ServerTimeButton.js"))
        End Sub

        Protected Overrides Sub RenderContents(ByVal writer As HtmlTextWriter)
            writer.Write("Show Server Time")
        End Sub

        Protected Overrides ReadOnly Property TagKey() As HtmlTextWriterTag
            Get
                Return HtmlTextWriterTag.Button
            End Get
        End Property

        ''' <summary>
        ''' Called on server by AJAX
        ''' </summary>
        ''' <param name="eventArgument"></param>
        Public Sub RaiseCallbackEvent(ByVal eventArgument As String)
➥Implements ICallbackEventHandler.RaiseCallbackEvent
```

LISTING 32.10   Continued

```
        End Sub

        ''' <summary>
        ''' Returns result back to AJAX call
        ''' </summary>
        ''' <returns></returns>
        Public Function GetCallbackResult() As String
➥Implements ICallbackEventHandler.GetCallbackResult
            'throw new Exception("Server Exception");
            Return DateTime.Now.ToString()
        End Function
    End Class
End Namespace
```

The `ServerTimeButton` control renders an HTML button. Clicking the button initiates the AJAX call to the server. The script for initiating the AJAX call is generated in the `AddAttributesToRender()` method by a call to the `Page.ClientScript.GetCallbackEventReference()` method.

Notice that the `ServerTimeButton` control implements the `ICallbackEventHandler` interface. This interface includes two methods named `RaiseCallbackEvent` and `GetCallbackResult()`. In Listing 32.10, the `RaiseCallbackEvent()` does nothing. The `GetCallbackResult()` method returns the current time as a string.

Finally, the `ServerTimeButton` control uses a JavaScript file named `ServerTimeButton.js`. This file is registered in the control's `OnPreRender()` method. The contents of the `ServerTimeButton.js` file are contained in Listing 32.11.

LISTING 32.11   ClientScripts\ServerTimeButton.js

```
function showResult(result, context)
{
    alert( result );
}

function showError(error, context)
{
    alert( error );
}
```

The JavaScript file in Listing 32.11 includes two functions. The first function, named `showResult()`, displays the result of the AJAX call. This method simply displays the server time in a JavaScript alert box. The `showError()` function displays any error message returned by the server as a result of the AJAX call.

The page in Listing 32.12 uses the `ServerTimeButton` control.

LISTING 32.12   ShowServerTimeButton.aspx

```
<%@ Page Language="VB" %>
<%@ Register TagPrefix="custom" Namespace="myControls" %>
<!DOCTYPE html PUBLIC "-//W3C//DTD XHTML 1.0 Transitional//EN"
  "http://www.w3.org/TR/xhtml1/DTD/xhtml1-transitional.dtd">
<html xmlns="http://www.w3.org/1999/xhtml" >
<head id="Head1" runat="server">
    <title>Show Server Time</title>
</head>
<body>
    <form id="form1" runat="server">
    <div>

    Initial Time: <%= DateTime.Now.ToString() %>

    <br /><br />

    <custom:ServerTimeButton
        id="lnkServerTime"
        Runat="Server" />

    </div>
    </form>
</body>
</html>
```

If you open the page in Listing 32.12 and click the button, the time is retrieved from the server and displayed in the browser. At no time is the page posted back to the server. The server time is retrieved through an AJAX call.

Building an AJAX Combobox Control

The application that caused all the excitement over AJAX was Google Suggest (http://www.google.com/webhp?complete=1). Google Suggest is an enhanced version of Google Search. As you type a search phrase, Google Suggest automatically displays a list of matching entries in a drop-down list (see Figure 32.5).

The amazing thing about Google Suggest is that every time you enter a new letter into the search box, an AJAX call is performed to retrieve a list of matching results from the server. The fact that the AJAX calls can be performed in real time blew everyone's mind.

In this section, we create a `ComboBox` control that mimics the functionality of Google Suggest. Each time you enter a new letter into the combo box, a new AJAX call is performed against the web server to retrieve matching entries (see Figure 32.6).

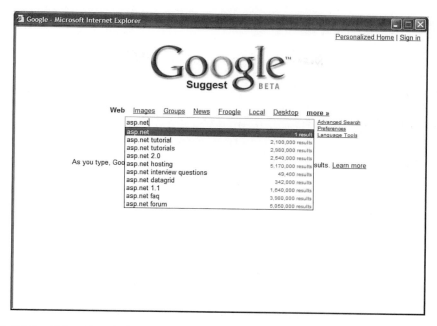

FIGURE 32.5   Using Google Suggest.

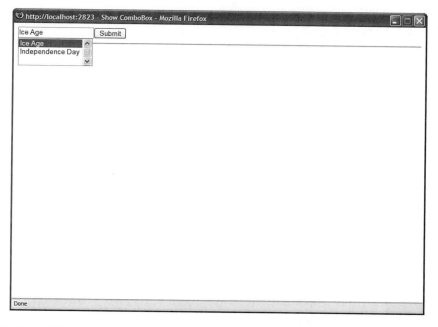

FIGURE 32.6   Displaying matching moves with the `ComboBox` control.

The ComboBox control is contained in Listing 32.13.

LISTING 32.13   ComboBox.vb

```vb
Imports System
Imports System.Collections.Generic
Imports System.Data
Imports System.Configuration
Imports System.Web
Imports System.Web.UI
Imports System.Web.UI.WebControls

Namespace myControls
    Public Class ComboBox
        Inherits CompositeControl
        Implements ICallbackEventHandler

        Private _comboTextBox As TextBox
        Private _dataKeyName As String = String.Empty
        Private _selectCommand As String = String.Empty
        Private _connectionString As String = String.Empty

        Private _clientArgument As String

        ''' <summary>
        ''' Name of the database field used for the lookup
        ''' </summary>
        Public Property DataKeyName() As String
            Get
                Return _dataKeyName
            End Get
            Set(ByVal Value As String)
                _dataKeyName = value
            End Set
        End Property

        ''' <summary>
        ''' SQL Select command issued against database
        ''' </summary>
        Public Property SelectCommand() As String
            Get
                Return _selectCommand
            End Get
            Set(ByVal Value As String)
                _selectCommand = value
            End Set
        End Property
```

LISTING 32.13 Continued

```
''' <summary>
''' Connection String for database
''' </summary>
Public Property ConnectionString() As String
    Get
        Return _connectionString
    End Get
    Set(ByVal Value As String)
        _connectionString = value
    End Set
End Property


Private ReadOnly Property ComboSelectId() As String
    Get
        Return Me.ClientID + "_select"
    End Get
End Property


Public Property Text() As String
    Get
        EnsureChildControls()
        Return _comboTextBox.Text
    End Get
    Set(ByVal Value As String)
        EnsureChildControls()
        _comboTextBox.Text = value
    End Set
End Property


Public Property Columns() As Integer
    Get
        EnsureChildControls()
        Return _comboTextBox.Columns
    End Get
    Set(ByVal Value As Integer)
        EnsureChildControls()
        _comboTextBox.Columns = value
    End Set
End Property


Protected Overrides Sub OnPreRender(ByVal e As EventArgs)
    ' Make sure all the properties are set
    If _dataKeyName = String.Empty Then
        Throw New Exception("DataKeyName cannot be empty")
    End If
```

32

LISTING 32.13   Continued

```
            If _connectionString = String.Empty Then
                Throw New Exception("ConnectionString cannot be empty")
            End If
            If _selectCommand = String.Empty Then
                Throw New Exception("SelectCommand cannot be empty")
            End If

            ' Register Include File
            If Not Page.ClientScript.IsClientScriptIncludeRegistered("ComboBox")
➥Then

                Page.ClientScript.RegisterClientScriptInclude("ComboBox", _
➥Page.ResolveUrl("~/ClientScripts/ComboBox.js"))
            End If
        End Sub

        Protected Overrides Sub CreateChildControls()
            ' Create the TextBox
            _comboTextBox = New TextBox()
            _comboTextBox.Attributes("autocomplete") = "off"
            Controls.Add(_comboTextBox)
        End Sub

        Protected Overrides Sub RenderContents(ByVal writer As HtmlTextWriter)
            ' Define the callback
        Dim callBackRef As String = Page.ClientScript.GetCallbackEventReference( _
                Me, _
                "this.value", _
                "comboBox_ClientCallback", _
                String.Format("'{0}'", ComboSelectId), _
                "comboBox_ErrorCallback", _
                True)

            ' Render the text box
            _comboTextBox.Attributes.Add("onkeyup", callBackRef)
            _comboTextBox.Attributes.Add("onblur", "comboBox_Blur(this)")
            _comboTextBox.RenderControl(writer)
            writer.WriteBreak()

            ' Render the drop-down
            writer.AddAttribute(HtmlTextWriterAttribute.Id, ComboSelectId)
            writer.AddStyleAttribute(HtmlTextWriterStyle.Display, "none")
            writer.AddStyleAttribute(HtmlTextWriterStyle.Position, "absolute")
            writer.RenderBeginTag(HtmlTextWriterTag.Select)
            writer.RenderEndTag()
        End Sub
```

LISTING 32.13   Continued

```
        Protected Overrides ReadOnly Property TagKey() As HtmlTextWriterTag
            Get
                Return HtmlTextWriterTag.Div
            End Get
        End Property

        Public Sub RaiseCallbackEvent(ByVal clientArgument As String)
➥Implements ICallbackEventHandler.RaiseCallbackEvent
            _clientArgument = clientArgument
        End Sub

        Public Function GetCallbackResult() As String
➥Implements ICallbackEventHandler.GetCallbackResult
            ' If no text, then return nothing
            If _clientArgument.Trim() = String.Empty Then
                Return "[]"
            End If

            ' Otherwise, get the matching rows
            Dim src As SqlDataSource = New SqlDataSource(_connectionString,
➥ _selectCommand)
            src.SelectParameters.Add(_dataKeyName, _clientArgument)
            Dim dvw As DataView
            Try
                dvw = CType(src.Select(DataSourceSelectArguments.Empty), DataView)
            Catch
                Return "[]"
            End Try

            ' Return matching rows in a JavaScript array
            Dim rows As New List(Of String)()
            Dim row As DataRowView
            For Each row In dvw
            rows.Add(String.Format("'{0}'", row(0).ToString().Replace("'", "\'")))
            Next

            Return "[" + String.Join(",", rows.ToArray()) + "]"
        End Function
    End Class
End Namespace
```

The control in Listing 32.13 renders a text box and a list box. As you type letters into the text box, a list of matching database records is displayed in the list box.

The ComboBox uses the JavaScript functions contained in Listing 32.14.

LISTING 32.14   ClientScripts\ComboBox.js

```javascript
// Display rows from database in the SELECT tag
function comboBox_ClientCallback(result, context)
{
    // convert rows into an array
    var rows;
    eval( 'rows=' + result );

    // Get the Select element
    var comboSelect = document.getElementById( context );

    // Add the options
    comboSelect.options.length = 0;
    for (var i=0;i<rows.length;i++)
    {
      var newOption = document.createElement("OPTION");
      newOption.text= rows[i];
      newOption.value= rows[i];
      if (document.all)
        comboSelect.add(newOption);
      else
        comboSelect.add(newOption, null);
    }

    // If results, show the SELECT, otherwise hide it
    if (comboSelect.options.length > 0)
    {
      comboSelect.size = comboSelect.options.length + 1;
      comboSelect.selectedIndex = 0;
      comboSelect.style.display='block';
    }
    else
      comboSelect.style.display='none';
}


// When leaving comboBox, get selected value from SELECT
function comboBox_Blur(src)
{
    var container = src.parentNode;
    var comboSelect = container.getElementsByTagName('select')[0];

    if ( comboSelect.style.display != 'none' && comboSelect.selectedIndex != -1)
        src.value = comboSelect.value;
```

LISTING 32.14   Continued

```
        comboSelect.style.display = 'none';
}


// If server error, just show it
function comboBox_ErrorCallback(result)
{
    alert( result );
}
```

The JavaScript library in Listing 32.14 contains three functions. The first function, comboBox_ClientCallback(), displays the results of a database lookup after each callback. This function updates the list of matching entries displayed by the list box.

The comboBox_Blur() function updates the TextBox with the item in the ListBox that matches the text entered into the TextBox. Finally, the comboBox_ErrorCallback() method displays any errors returned from the server.

The page in Listing 32.15 illustrates how you can use the ComboBox control. When you enter text into the combo box, a list of matching movie titles is displayed.

LISTING 32.15   ShowComboBox.aspx

```
<%@ Page Language="VB" %>
<%@ Register TagPrefix="custom" Namespace="myControls" %>
<!DOCTYPE html PUBLIC "-//W3C//DTD XHTML 1.0 Transitional//EN"
    "http://www.w3.org/TR/xhtml1/DTD/xhtml1-transitional.dtd">
<script runat="server">


    Protected Sub btnSubmit_Click(ByVal sender As Object, ByVal e As EventArgs)
        lblResult.Text = ComboBox1.Text
    End Sub
</script>


<html xmlns="http://www.w3.org/1999/xhtml" >
<head id="Head1" runat="server">
    <title>Show ComboBox</title>
</head>
<body>
    <form id="form1" runat="server">
    <div>


    <custom:ComboBox
        id="ComboBox1"
        ConnectionString='<%$ ConnectionStrings:Movies %>'
        DataKeyName="Title"
```

LISTING 32.15   Continued

```
        SelectCommand="SELECT Title FROM Movies
            WHERE Title LIKE @Title+'%'
            ORDER BY Title"
        Style="float:left"
        Runat="Server" />
    <asp:Button
        id="btnSubmit"
        Text="Submit"
        Runat="server" OnClick="btnSubmit_Click" />
    <hr />

    <asp:Label
        id="lblResult"
        Runat="server" />

    </div>
    </form>
</body>
</html>
```

In Listing 32.15, the ConnectionString, DataKeyName, and SelectCommand properties are set. The ConnectionString property represents a connection to a database. The DataKeyName property represents a primary key column from a database table. Finally, the SelectCommand uses a SQL SELECT command to retrieve a list of matching records. Notice that the SELECT command uses a LIKE operator to retrieve all records that begin with the text entered into the combo box.

Summary

In this chapter, you learned how to build custom controls that take advantage of client-side JavaScript. In the first section, you learned how to use the ClientScriptManager class to add JavaScript scripts to a page. You also learned how to detect browser capabilities with the HttpBrowserCapabilities object.

Next, we built three JavaScript controls. You learned how to create a NewWindowLink control that renders a button that opens a new browser window. We also created a virtual window control named the WebWindow control. Finally, we created a ClientTabs control that renders a client-side tab strip.

The final section of this chapter explored the exciting topic of AJAX. You learned how to initiate an AJAX call to the server and implement the ICallbackEventHandler interface. We also created a ComboBox that uses AJAX to retrieve matching database records from the web server with each key press.

CHAPTER **33**

Building Templated Databound Controls

T he ASP.NET Framework is a framework. If you don't like anything about the framework, you always have the option of extending it. In particular, if you discover that the standard databound controls in the framework don't do everything you need, you can create a custom databound control.

In this chapter, you learn how to create custom controls that work like the ASP.NET 2.0 GridView, DetailsView, and FormView controls. In the first part of this chapter, you learn how to create controls that support templates. You learn how to implement controls that support both standard templates and two-way databinding templates. You also learn how to supply a control with a default template.

The last part of this chapter is devoted to the topic of databound controls. You learn about the new base control classes included in the framework that were supplied to make it easier to create custom databound controls. We also create several custom databound controls. For example, at the end of this chapter, we create a custom FormView control that uses AJAX to insert and update database records from the client.

Creating Templated Controls

A template enables you to customize the layout of a control. Furthermore, a template can contain expressions that are not evaluated until runtime.

The ASP.NET 2.0 Framework supports two types of templates. First, you can create a one-way databinding template. You use a one-way databinding template to display data items. In a one-way databinding template, you use the Eval() expression to display the value of a data item.

Second, you have the option of creating a two-way databinding template. A two-way databinding template can be used not only to display data items, but to update data items. You can use the Bind() expression in a two-way databinding template to both display a data item and extract the value of a data item.

Typically, you use templates with a databound control. For example, the GridView, Repeater, DataList, FormView, and DetailsView controls all support an ItemTemplate that enables you to format the data items that these controls display. However, you can use a template even when you are not displaying a set of data items. For example, the Login control supports a LayoutTemplate that enables you to customize the appearance of the Login form.

This part of this chapter concentrates on creating non-databound controls that support templates. In the next part of this chapter, you learn how to use templates with databound controls.

Implementing the ITemplate Interface

You create a one-way databinding template by adding a property to a control that returns an object that implements the ITemplate interface. The ITemplate interface includes one method:

- InstantiateIn—Instantiates the contents of a template in a particular control.

You are not required to implement the InstantiateIn() method yourself. The ASP.NET Framework creates the method for you automatically. You call the InstantiateIn method in your control to add the contents of a template to your control.

For example, the control in Listing 33.1 represents an article. The Article control includes a template named ItemTemplate. The ItemTemplate is used to lay out the elements of the article: the title, author, and contents.

LISTING 33.1   Article.vb

```
Imports System
Imports System.Web
Imports System.Web.UI
Imports System.Web.UI.WebControls

Namespace myControls

    Public Class Article
        Inherits CompositeControl

        Private _title As String
        Private _author As String
        Private _contents As String

        Private _itemTemplate As ITemplate
```

LISTING 33.1 Continued

```
    Public Property Title() As String
        Get
            Return _title
        End Get
        Set(ByVal Value As String)
            _title = value
        End Set
    End Property

    Public Property Author() As String
        Get
            Return _author
        End Get
        Set(ByVal Value As String)
            _author = value
        End Set
    End Property

    Public Property Contents() As String
        Get
            Return _contents
        End Get
        Set(ByVal Value As String)
            _contents = value
        End Set
    End Property

    <TemplateContainer(GetType(Article))> _
    <PersistenceMode(PersistenceMode.InnerProperty)> _
    Public Property ItemTemplate() As ITemplate
        Get
            Return _itemTemplate
        End Get
        Set(ByVal Value As ITemplate)
            _itemTemplate = Value
        End Set
    End Property

    Protected Overrides Sub CreateChildControls()
        _itemTemplate.InstantiateIn(Me)
    End Sub
End Class

End Namespace
```

Notice that the Article control contains a property named ItemTemplate that returns an object that implements the ITemplate interface. Notice that this property is decorated with two attributes: a TemplateContainer and a PersistenceMode attribute.

The TemplateContainer attribute is used to specify the type of control that will contain the template. In the case of the Article control, the template will be contained in the Article control itself. Therefore, the Article control's type is passed to the TemplateContainer attribute.

The PersistenceMode attribute indicates how a property is persisted in an ASP.NET page. The possible values are Attribute, EncodedInnerDefaultProperty, InnerDefaultProperty, and InnerProperty. We want to declare the ItemTemplate like this:

```
<custom:Article
  runat="server">
  <ItemTemplate>
   ... template contents ...
  </ItemTemplate>
</custom:Article>
```

Because we want to declare the ItemTemplate inside the Article control, the PersistenceMode attribute needs to be set to the value InnerProperty.

The Article control overrides the base WebControl class's CreateChildControls() method. The ItemTemplate is added as a child control to the Article control. Any controls contained in the template become child controls of the current control.

The page in Listing 33.2 illustrates how you can use the Article control and its ItemTemplate.

LISTING 33.2   ShowArticle.aspx

```
<%@ Page Language="VB" %>
<%@ Register TagPrefix="custom" Namespace="myControls" %>
<!DOCTYPE html PUBLIC "-//W3C//DTD XHTML 1.0 Transitional//EN"
  "http://www.w3.org/TR/xhtml1/DTD/xhtml1-transitional.dtd">
<script runat="server">

    Sub Page_Load()
        Article1.Title = "Creating Templated Databound Controls"
        Article1.Author = "Stephen Walther"
        Article1.Contents = "Blah, blah, blah, blah..."
        Article1.DataBind()
    End Sub

</script>
<html xmlns="http://www.w3.org/1999/xhtml" >
<head id="Head1" runat="server">
    <title>Show Article</title>
</head>
```

LISTING 33.2 Continued

```
<body>
    <form id="form1" runat="server">
    <div>

    <custom:Article
        id="Article1"
        Runat="server">
        <ItemTemplate>

        <h1><%# Container.Title %></h1>
        <em>By <%# Container.Author %></em>
        <br /><br />
        <%# Container.Contents %>

        </ItemTemplate>
    </custom:Article>

    </div>
    </form>
</body>
</html>
```

When you open the page in Listing 33.2, the contents of the `ItemTemplate` are displayed (see Figure 33.1).

In the `Page_Load()` method, the `Title`, `Author`, and `Contents` properties of the article are set. Notice that these properties are used within databinding expressions within the `Article` control's `ItemTemplate`. For example, the value of the `Title` property is displayed with the following databinding expression:

```
<%# Container.Title %>
```

The `Container` keyword refers to the current *binding container*. In this case, the binding container is the `Article` control itself. Therefore, you can refer to any property of the `Article` control by using the `Container` keyword.

Notice that the `Article` control's `DataBind()` method is called at the end of the `Page_Load()` method. Don't forget to call this method when you include databinding expressions in a template. If you don't call this method, then the databinding expressions are never evaluated and displayed.

Creating a Default Template

The previous section discussed the `ITemplate` interface's `InstantiateIn()` method. Normally, you don't implement the `InstantiateIn()` method; you let the ASP.NET Framework do it for you. However, if you want to supply a control with a default template, then you need to implement this method.

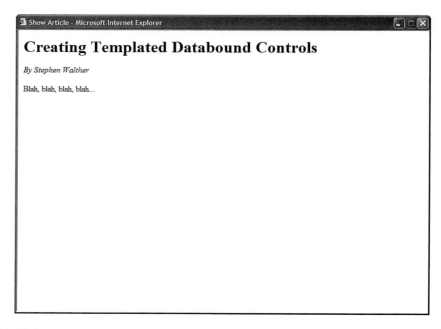

FIGURE 33.1   Using a template to display an article.

The modified Article control in Listing 33.3 includes a default template for the ItemTemplate. The default template is used when an ItemTemplate is not supplied.

LISTING 33.3   ArticleWithDefault.vb

```
Imports System
Imports System.Web
Imports System.Web.UI
Imports System.Web.UI.WebControls

Namespace myControls

    Public Class ArticleWithDefault
        Inherits CompositeControl

        Private _title As String
        Private _author As String
        Private _contents As String

        Private _itemTemplate As ITemplate

        Public Property Title() As String
            Get
                Return _title
```

LISTING 33.3   Continued

```
        End Get
        Set(ByVal Value As String)
            _title = value
        End Set
    End Property

    Public Property Author() As String
        Get
            Return _author
        End Get
        Set(ByVal Value As String)
            _author = value
        End Set
    End Property

    Public Property Contents() As String
        Get
            Return _contents
        End Get
        Set(ByVal Value As String)
            _contents = value
        End Set
    End Property

    <TemplateContainer(GetType(ArticleWithDefault))> _
    <PersistenceMode(PersistenceMode.InnerProperty)> _
    Public Property ItemTemplate() As ITemplate
        Get
            Return _itemTemplate
        End Get
        Set(ByVal Value As ITemplate)
            _itemTemplate = Value
        End Set
    End Property

    Protected Overrides Sub CreateChildControls()
        If _itemTemplate Is Nothing Then
            _itemTemplate = New ArticleDefaultTemplate()
        End If
        _itemTemplate.InstantiateIn(Me)
    End Sub
End Class

Public Class ArticleDefaultTemplate
    Implements ITemplate
```

LISTING 33.3   Continued

```vbnet
        Public Sub InstantiateIn(ByVal container As Control)
➡Implements ITemplate.InstantiateIn
            Dim lblTitle As New Label()
            AddHandler lblTitle.DataBinding, AddressOf lblTitle_DataBinding

            Dim lblAuthor As New Label()
            AddHandler lblAuthor.DataBinding, AddressOf lblAuthor_DataBinding

            Dim lblContents As New Label()
            AddHandler lblContents.DataBinding, AddressOf lblContents_DataBinding

            container.Controls.Add(lblTitle)
            container.Controls.Add(New LiteralControl("<br />"))
            container.Controls.Add(lblAuthor)
            container.Controls.Add(New LiteralControl("<br />"))
            container.Controls.Add(lblContents)
        End Sub

        Private Sub lblTitle_DataBinding(ByVal sender As Object,
➡ByVal e As EventArgs)
            Dim lblTitle As Label = CType(sender, Label)
            Dim container As ArticleWithDefault =
➡CType(lblTitle.NamingContainer, ArticleWithDefault)
            lblTitle.Text = container.Title
        End Sub

        Private Sub lblAuthor_DataBinding(ByVal sender As Object,
➡ByVal e As EventArgs)
            Dim lblAuthor As Label = CType(sender, Label)
            Dim container As ArticleWithDefault =
➡CType(lblAuthor.NamingContainer, ArticleWithDefault)
            lblAuthor.Text = container.Author
        End Sub

        Private Sub lblContents_DataBinding(ByVal sender As Object,
➡ByVal e As EventArgs)
            Dim lblContents As Label = CType(sender, Label)
            Dim container As ArticleWithDefault =
➡CType(lblContents.NamingContainer, ArticleWithDefault)
            lblContents.Text = container.Contents
        End Sub

    End Class

End Namespace
```

The control in Listing 33.3 is very similar to the control created in the previous section. However, notice that the CreateChildControls() method has been modified. The new version of the CreateChildControls() method tests whether there is an ItemTemplate. If there is no ItemTemplate, an instance of the ArticleDefaultTemplate class is created.

The ArticleDefaultTemplate class, which is also included in Listing 33.3, implements the ITemplate interface. In particular, the class implements the InstantiateIn() method. The instantiateIn() method creates all the controls that will appear in the template.

In Listing 33.3, three Label controls are created that correspond to the Title, Author, and Contents properties. Notice that the DataBinding event is handled for all three of these Label controls. When the DataBind() method is called, the DataBinding event is raised for each child control in the Article control. At that time, the values of the Title, Author, and Contents properties are assigned to the Text properties of the Label controls.

The page in Listing 33.4 illustrates how you can use the modified Article control.

LISTING 33.4   ShowArticleWithDefault.aspx

```
<%@ Page Language="VB" %>
<%@ Register TagPrefix="custom" Namespace="myControls" %>
<!DOCTYPE html PUBLIC "-//W3C//DTD XHTML 1.0 Transitional//EN"
    "http://www.w3.org/TR/xhtml1/DTD/xhtml1-transitional.dtd">
<script runat="server">

    Sub Page_Load()
        ArticleWithDefault1.Title = "Creating Templated Databound Controls"
        ArticleWithDefault1.Author = "Stephen Walther"
        ArticleWithDefault1.Contents = "Blah, blah, blah, blah..."
        ArticleWithDefault1.DataBind()
    End Sub

</script>
<html xmlns="http://www.w3.org/1999/xhtml" >
<head id="Head1" runat="server">
    <title>Show Article with Default Template</title>
</head>
<body>
    <form id="form1" runat="server">
    <div>

    <custom:ArticleWithDefault
        id="ArticleWithDefault1"
        Runat="server" />

    </div>
    </form>
</body>
</html>
```

33

The `ArticleWithDefault` control in Listing 33.4 does not include an `ItemTemplate`. When the page is displayed in a browser, the contents of the `ItemTemplate` are supplied by the `ArticleDefaultTemplate` class (see Figure 33.2).

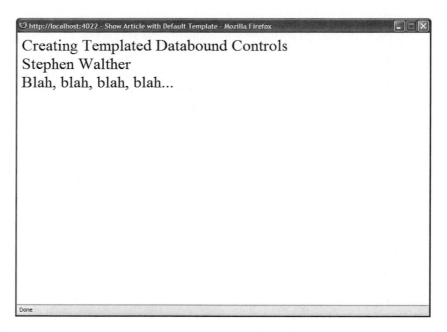

FIGURE 33.2   Displaying an article with a default template.

Supporting Simplified Databinding

The databinding expressions used in the previous two sections might seem a little odd. For example, we used the following databinding expression to refer to the `Title` property:

```
<%# Container.Title %>
```

When you use a databinding expression with one of the standard ASP.NET controls, such as the `GridView` control, you typically use a databinding expression that looks like this:

```
<%# Eval("Title") %>
```

Why the difference? The standard ASP.NET controls support a simplified databinding syntax. If you want to support this simplified syntax in your custom controls, then you must implement the `IDataItemContainer` interface.

The `IDataItemContainer` includes the following three properties, which you are required to implement:

- `DataItem`—Returns the value of the data item.

- `DataItemIndex`—Returns the index of the data item from its data source.

- `DisplayIndex`—Returns the index of the data item as it is displayed in a control.

Typically, you implement the `IDataItemContainer` when creating a databound control. For example, you wrap up each record retrieved from a database table in an object that implements the `IDataItemContainer` interface. That way, you can use a simplified data-binding expression to refer to the value of a particular database record column.

In this section, we create a non-databound control that supports the simplified databinding syntax. The control is named the `Product` control, and it is included in Listing 33.5.

LISTING 33.5   `Product.vb`

```vb
Imports System
Imports System.Web
Imports System.Web.UI
Imports System.Web.UI.WebControls

Namespace myControls

    Public Class Product
        Inherits CompositeControl

        Private _itemTemplate As ITemplate
        Private _item As ProductItem

        Public Property Name() As String
            Get
                EnsureChildControls()
                Return _item.Name
            End Get
            Set(ByVal Value As String)
                EnsureChildControls()
                _item.Name = Value
            End Set
        End Property

        Public Property Price() As Decimal
            Get
                EnsureChildControls()
                Return _item.Price
            End Get
            Set(ByVal Value As Decimal)
                EnsureChildControls()
                _item.Price = Value
            End Set
```

33

LISTING 33.5   Continued

```
        End Property

        <TemplateContainer(GetType(ProductItem))> _
        <PersistenceMode(PersistenceMode.InnerProperty)> _
        Public Property ItemTemplate() As ITemplate
            Get
                Return _itemTemplate
            End Get
            Set(ByVal Value As ITemplate)
                _itemTemplate = Value
            End Set
        End Property

        Protected Overrides Sub CreateChildControls()
            _item = New ProductItem()
            _itemTemplate.InstantiateIn(_item)
            Controls.Add(_item)
        End Sub
    End Class

    Public Class ProductItem
        Inherits WebControl
        Implements IDataItemContainer

        Private _name As String
        Private _price As Decimal

        Public Property Name() As String
            Get
                Return _name
            End Get
            Set(ByVal Value As String)
                _name = Value
            End Set
        End Property

        Public Property Price() As Decimal
            Get
                Return _price
            End Get
            Set(ByVal Value As Decimal)
                _price = Value
            End Set
        End Property
```

LISTING 33.5   Continued

```
        Public ReadOnly Property DataItem() As Object
➥Implements IDataItemContainer.DataItem
            Get
                Return Me
            End Get
        End Property


        Public ReadOnly Property DataItemIndex() As Integer
➥Implements IDataItemContainer.DataItemIndex
            Get
                Return 0
            End Get
        End Property


        Public ReadOnly Property DisplayIndex() As Integer
➥Implements IDataItemContainer.DisplayIndex
            Get
                Return 0
            End Get
        End Property
    End Class


End Namespace
```

The file in Listing 33.5 actually contains two classes: the `Product` and the `ProductItem` class. The `Product` control includes an `ItemTemplate` property. Notice that the `TemplateContainer` attribute that decorates this property associates the `ProductItem` class with the `ItemTemplate`.

In the `CreateChildControls()` method, the `ItemTemplate` is instantiated into the `ProductItem` class. The `ProductItem` class, in turn, is added to the controls collection of the `Product` class.

The `ProductItem` class implements the `IDataItemContainer` interface. Implementing the `DataItemIndex` and `DisplayIndex` properties is a little silly because there is only one data item. However, you are required to implement all the properties of an interface.

The page in Listing 33.6 illustrates how you can use the `Product` control with the simplified databinding syntax.

LISTING 33.6   ShowProduct.aspx

```
<%@ Page Language="VB" %>
<%@ Register TagPrefix="custom" Namespace="myControls" %>
<!DOCTYPE html PUBLIC "-//W3C//DTD XHTML 1.0 Transitional//EN"
  "http://www.w3.org/TR/xhtml1/DTD/xhtml1-transitional.dtd">
```

LISTING 33.6   Continued

```
<script runat="server">

    Sub Page_Load()
        Product1.Name = "Laptop Computer"
        Product1.Price = 1254.12
        Product1.DataBind()
    End Sub

</script>

<html xmlns="http://www.w3.org/1999/xhtml" >
<head id="Head1" runat="server">
    <title>Show Product</title>
</head>
<body>
    <form id="form1" runat="server">
    <div>

    <custom:Product
        id="Product1"
        Runat="Server">
        <ItemTemplate>
        Name: <%# Eval("Name") %>
        <br />
        Price: <%# Eval("Price", "{0:c}") %>
        </ItemTemplate>
    </custom:Product>

    </div>
    </form>
</body>
</html>
```

Notice that the Eval() method is used in the Product control's ItemTemplate. For example, the expression Eval("Name") is used to display the product name. If you prefer, you can still use the Container.Name syntax. However, the Eval() syntax is more familiar to ASP.NET developers.

Supporting Two-Way Databinding

Two-way databinding is a new feature of the ASP.NET 2.0 Framework. Two-way databinding enables you to extract values from a template. You can use a two-way databinding expression not only to display the value of a data item, but to update the value of a data item.

You create a template that supports two-way databinding expressions by creating a property that returns an object that implements the IBindableTemplate interface. This interface inherits from the ITemplate interface. It has the following two methods:

- InstantiateIn—Instantiates the contents of a template in a particular control.
- ExtractValues—Returns a collection of databinding expression values from a template.

For example, the ProductForm control in Listing 33.7 represents a form for editing an existing product. The control includes a property named EditItemTemplate that represents a two-way databinding template.

LISTING 33.7   ProductForm.vb

```vb
Imports System
Imports System.Web
Imports System.Web.UI
Imports System.Web.UI.WebControls
Imports System.ComponentModel
Imports System.Collections.Specialized

Namespace myControls

    Public Class ProductForm
        Inherits CompositeControl

        Public Event ProductUpdated As EventHandler

        Private _editItemTemplate As IBindableTemplate
        Private _item As ProductFormItem
        Private _results As IOrderedDictionary

        Public ReadOnly Property Results() As IOrderedDictionary
            Get
                Return _results
            End Get
        End Property

        Public Property Name() As String
            Get
                EnsureChildControls()
                Return _item.Name
            End Get
            Set(ByVal Value As String)
                EnsureChildControls()
                _item.Name = Value
            End Set
```

33

LISTING 33.7   Continued

```
        End Property

        Public Property Price() As Decimal
            Get
                EnsureChildControls()
                Return _item.Price
            End Get
            Set(ByVal Value As Decimal)
                EnsureChildControls()
                _item.Price = Value
            End Set
        End Property

        <TemplateContainer(GetType(ProductFormItem), BindingDirection.TwoWay)> _
        <PersistenceMode(PersistenceMode.InnerProperty)> _
        Public Property EditItemTemplate() As IBindableTemplate
            Get
                Return _editItemTemplate
            End Get
            Set(ByVal Value As IBindableTemplate)
                _editItemTemplate = Value
            End Set
        End Property

        Protected Overrides Sub CreateChildControls()
            _item = New ProductFormItem()
            _editItemTemplate.InstantiateIn(_item)
            Controls.Add(_item)
        End Sub

        Protected Overrides Function OnBubbleEvent(ByVal source As Object,
➥ByVal args As EventArgs) As Boolean
            _results = _editItemTemplate.ExtractValues(_item)
            RaiseEvent ProductUpdated(Me, EventArgs.Empty)
            Return True
        End Function
    End Class

    Public Class ProductFormItem
        Inherits WebControl
        Implements IDataItemContainer

        Private _name As String
        Private _price As Decimal

        Public Property Name() As String
```

LISTING 33.7   Continued

```
            Get
                 Return _name
            End Get
            Set(ByVal Value As String)
                 _name = Value
            End Set
        End Property

        Public Property Price() As Decimal
            Get
                 Return _price
            End Get
            Set(ByVal Value As Decimal)
                 _price = Value
            End Set
        End Property

        Public ReadOnly Property DataItem() As Object
➥Implements IDataItemContainer.DataItem
            Get
                 Return Me
            End Get
        End Property

        Public ReadOnly Property DataItemIndex() As Integer
➥Implements IDataItemContainer.DataItemIndex
            Get
                 Return 0
            End Get
        End Property

        Public ReadOnly Property DisplayIndex() As Integer
➥Implements IDataItemContainer.DisplayIndex
            Get
                 Return 0
            End Get
        End Property

    End Class
End Namespace
```

You should notice two special things about the `EditItemTemplate` property. First, notice that the property returns an object that implements the `IBindableTemplate` interface. Second, notice that the `TemplateContainer` attribute that decorates the property includes a `BindingDirection` parameter. You can assign one of two possible values to `BindingDirection`: OneWay and TwoWay.

The `ProductForm` includes an `OnBubbleEvent()` method. This method is called when a child control of the `ProductForm` control raises an event. For example, if someone clicks a `Button` control contained in the `EditItemTemplate`, the `OnBubbleEvent()` method is called.

In Listing 33.7, the `OnBubbleEvent()` method calls the `EditItemTemplate`'s `ExtractValues()` method. This method is supplied by the ASP.NET Framework because the `EditItemTemplate` is marked as a two-way databinding template.

The `ExtractValues()` method returns an `OrderedDictionary` collection that contains name/value pairs that correspond to each of the databinding expressions contained in the `EditItemTemplate`. The `ProductForm` control exposes this collection of values with its `Results` property. After the values are extracted, the control raises a `ProductUpdated` event.

The page in Listing 33.8 illustrates how you can use the `ProductForm` control to update the properties of a product.

LISTING 33.8   ShowProductForm.aspx

```
<%@ Page Language="VB" %>
<%@ Register TagPrefix="custom" Namespace="myControls" %>
<!DOCTYPE html PUBLIC "-//W3C//DTD XHTML 1.0 Transitional//EN"
    "http://www.w3.org/TR/xhtml1/DTD/xhtml1-transitional.dtd">

<script runat="server">

    sub Page_Load()
        If Not Page.IsPostBack Then
            ProductForm1.Name = "Laptop"
            ProductForm1.Price = 433.12
            ProductForm1.DataBind()
        End If
    End Sub

    Sub ProductForm1_ProductUpdated(ByVal sender As Object, ByVal e As EventArgs)
        lblName.Text = ProductForm1.Results("Name").ToString()
        lblPrice.Text = ProductForm1.Results("Price").ToString()
    End Sub
</script>

<html xmlns="http://www.w3.org/1999/xhtml" >
<head id="Head1" runat="server">
    <title>Show ProductForm</title>
</head>
<body>
    <form id="form1" runat="server">
```

LISTING 33.8   Continued

```
<div>

<custom:ProductForm
    id="ProductForm1"
    OnProductUpdated="ProductForm1_ProductUpdated"
    Runat="server">
    <EditItemTemplate>

    <asp:Label
        id="lblName"
        Text="Product Name:"
        AssociatedControlID="txtName"
        Runat="server" />
    <asp:TextBox
        id="txtName"
        Text='<%# Bind("Name") %>'
        Runat="server" />
    <br /><br />
    <asp:Label
        id="lblPrice"
        Text="Product Price:"
        AssociatedControlID="txtPrice"
        Runat="server" />
    <asp:TextBox
        id="txtPrice"
        Text='<%# Bind("Price") %>'
        Runat="server" />
    <br /><br />
    <asp:Button
        id="btnUpdate"
        Text="Update"
        Runat="server" />

    </EditItemTemplate>
</custom:ProductForm>

<hr />
New Product Name:
<asp:Label
    id="lblName"
    Runat="server" />

<br /><br />

New Product Price:
```

LISTING 33.8   Continued

```
    <asp:Label
        id="lblPrice"
        Runat="server" />

    </div>
    </form>
</body>
</html>
```

In the Page_Load() method in Listing 33.8, the ProductForm Name and Price properties are set. Next, the DataBind() is called in order to cause the ProductForm control to evaluate its databinding expressions.

Notice that the ProductForm control's EditItemTemplate includes Bind() expressions instead of Eval() expressions. You use Bind() expressions in a two-way databinding template.

The EditItemTemplate includes a Button control. When you click the Button control, the ProductForm control's OnBubbleEvent() method executes, the values are retrieved from the EditItemTemplate, and the ProductUpdated event is raised.

The page in Listing 33.8 handles the ProductUpdated event and displays the new values with two Label controls (see Figure 33.3).

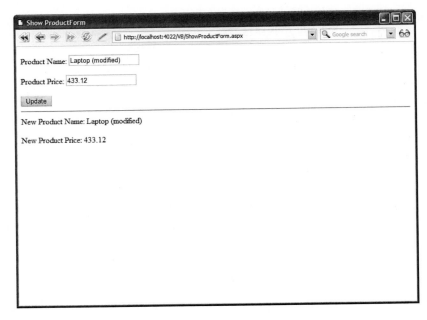

FIGURE 33.3   Using a two-way databinding template.

Creating Templated Databound Controls

In this section, you learn how to build templated databound controls. A databound control can be bound to a DataSource control such as the SqlDataSource or ObjectDataSource controls.

The ASP.NET 2.0 Framework provides you with a number of new base classes that you can use when creating a custom databound control. Creating a databound control using the previous version of the Framework was not a trivial matter (it took longer than a single afternoon). The ASP.NET 2.0 Framework, on the other hand, makes creating databound controls easy. (You can implement a custom databound control in less than 15 minutes.)

So, let's look at some tables and figures. Table 33.1 lists the base control classes for all the standard ASP.NET databound controls. Figure 33.4 displays the inheritance hierarchy of all the new databound controls in the ASP.NET 2.0 Framework. Typically, you'll inherit from one of the leaf nodes. You'll create a control that derives from the base CompositeDataBoundControl, HierarchicalDataBoundControl, or ListControl class.

This chapter concentrates on inheriting new controls from the base CompositeDataBoundControl class. This is the appropriate base class to use when you want to display one or more database records and use templates.

> **NOTE**
>
> You learned how to create controls that inherit from the base ListControl class in Chapter 10, "Using List Controls."

33

TABLE 33.1   Base Databound Control Classes

Control	Base Control
GridView, DetailsView, FormView	CompositeDataBoundControl
Menu, TreeView	HierarchicalDataBoundControl
DropDownList, ListBox, RadioButtonList, CheckBoxList, BulletedList	ListControl
DataList, DataGrid	BaseDataList
Repeater	Control

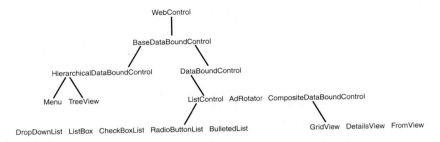

FIGURE 33.4   Databound control inheritance hierarchy.

Creating a `DivView` Control

Let's start simple. In this section, we create a custom databound control named the
`DivView` control. The `DivView` control displays a set of data items (database records) in
HTML <div> tags.

The `DivView` control inherits from the base `CompositeDataBoundControl` class and overrides a single method of the base class. The `DivView` control overrides the base class's
`CreateChildControls()` method.

The `DivView` control is contained in Listing 33.9.

LISTING 33.9   DivView.vb

```
Imports System
Imports System.Collections
Imports System.Web
Imports System.Web.UI
Imports System.Web.UI.WebControls

Namespace AspNetUnleashed
    Public Class DivView
        Inherits CompositeDataBoundControl

        Private _itemTemplate As ITemplate

        <TemplateContainer(GetType(DivViewItem))> _
        <PersistenceMode(PersistenceMode.InnerProperty)> _
        Public Property ItemTemplate() As ITemplate
            Get
                Return _itemTemplate
            End Get
            Set(ByVal Value As ITemplate)
                _itemTemplate = Value
            End Set
        End Property
```

LISTING 33.9 Continued

```vb
        Protected Overrides Function CreateChildControls(ByVal dataSource
➥As IEnumerable, ByVal dataBinding As Boolean) As Integer
            Dim counter As Integer = 0
            For Each dataItem As Object In dataSource
                Dim contentItem As New DivViewItem(dataItem, counter)
                _itemTemplate.InstantiateIn(contentItem)
                Controls.Add(contentItem)
                counter = counter + 1
            Next
            DataBind(False)
            Return counter
        End Function


        Protected Overrides ReadOnly Property TagKey() As HtmlTextWriterTag
            Get
                Return HtmlTextWriterTag.Div
            End Get
        End Property
    End Class


    Public Class DivViewItem
        Inherits WebControl
        Implements IDataItemContainer

        Private _dataItem As Object
        Private _index As Integer


        Public ReadOnly Property DataItem() As Object
➥Implements IDataItemContainer.DataItem
            Get
                Return _dataItem
            End Get
        End Property

        Public ReadOnly Property DataItemIndex() As Integer
➥Implements IDataItemContainer.DataItemIndex
            Get
                Return _index
            End Get
        End Property


        Public ReadOnly Property DisplayIndex() As Integer
➥Implements IDataItemContainer.DisplayIndex
```

LISTING 33.9   Continued

```
            Get
                Return _index
            End Get
        End Property

        Protected Overrides ReadOnly Property TagKey() As HtmlTextWriterTag
            Get
                Return HtmlTextWriterTag.Div
            End Get
        End Property

        Public Sub New(ByVal dataItem As Object, ByVal index As Integer)
            _dataItem = dataItem
            _index = index
        End Sub

    End Class
End Namespace
```

The `DivView` control supports an `ItemTemplate` that is used to format each of its data items. You are required to supply an `ItemTemplate` when you use the `DivView` control.

All the work happens in the `CreateChildControls()` method. Notice that this is not the same `CreateChildControls()` method that is included in the base `System.Web.UI.Control` class. The `DivView` control overrides the `CompositeDataBounControl`'s `CreateChildControls()` method.

The `CreateChildControls()` method accepts the following two parameters:

- `dataSource`—Represents all the data items from the data source.
- `dataBinding`—Represents whether or not the `CreateChildControls()` method is called when the data items are being retrieved from the data source.

The `CreateChildControls()` method is called every time that the `DivView` control renders its data items. When the control is first bound to a `DataSource` control, the `dataSource` parameter represents the data items retrieved from the `DataSource` control. After a postback, the `dataSource` parameter contains a collection of null values, but the correct number of null values.

After a postback, the contents of the data items can be retrieved from View State. As long as the correct number of child controls is created, the Framework can rebuild the contents of the databound control.

You can use the `dataBinding` parameter to determine whether the data items from the data source actually represent anything. Typically, the `dataBinding` parameter has the value `True` when the page first loads, and the value `False` after each postback.

Notice that the DataBind() method is called after the child controls are created. You must call the DataBind() method when a template includes databinding expressions. Otherwise, the databinding expressions are never evaluated.

The page in Listing 33.10 illustrates how you can bind the DivView control to a SqlDataSource control.

LISTING 33.10   ShowDivView.aspx

```
<%@ Page Language="VB" %>
<%@ Register TagPrefix="custom" Namespace="AspNetUnleashed" %>
<!DOCTYPE html PUBLIC "-//W3C//DTD XHTML 1.0 Transitional//EN"
    "http://www.w3.org/TR/xhtml1/DTD/xhtml1-transitional.dtd">
<html xmlns="http://www.w3.org/1999/xhtml" >
<head id="Head1" runat="server">
    <style type="text/css">
        .movies
        {
            width:500px;
        }
        .movies div
        {
            border:solid 1px black;
            padding:10px;
            margin:10px;
        }
    </style>
    <title>Show DivView</title>
</head>
<body>
    <form id="form1" runat="server">
    <div>

    <custom:DivView
        id="lstMovies"
        DataSourceID="srcMovies"
        CssClass="movies"
        Runat="Server">
        <ItemTemplate>
        <h1><%# Eval("Title") %></h1>
        Director: <%# Eval("Director") %>
        </ItemTemplate>
    </custom:DivView>


    <asp:SqlDataSource
```

LISTING 33.10   Continued

```
        id="srcMovies"
        ConnectionString="<%$ ConnectionStrings:Movies %>"
        SelectCommand="SELECT Title, Director FROM Movies"
        Runat="server" />

    <br />
    <asp:LinkButton
        id="lnkReload"
        Text="Reload"
        Runat="server" />


    </div>
    </form>
</body>
</html>
```

In Listing 33.10, the `SqlDataSource` control represents the Movies database table. The `DivView` control includes an `EditItemTemplate` that formats each of the columns from this database table (see Figure 33.5).

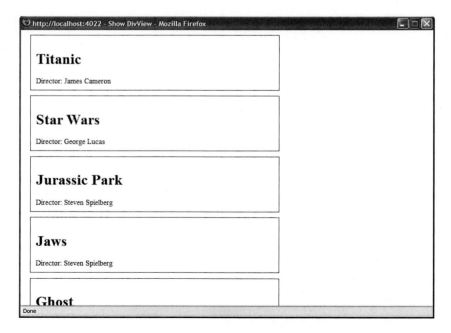

FIGURE 33.5   Displaying database records with the `DivView` control.

Creating an `AjaxDivView` Control

Two of the three ASP.NET controls that derive from the `CompositeDataBoundControl` class take advantage of AJAX. The `GridView` control supports AJAX when sorting and paging through database records. The `DetailsView` control supports AJAX when paging through database records.

There is a good reason for supporting AJAX when building databound controls. Using AJAX can significantly improve your application's performance. By taking advantage of AJAX, you can avoid re-creating an entire page each and every time you perform a database operation. AJAX enables you to transfer only the information you need back and forth between the web server and browser.

> **NOTE**
>
> Microsoft insists on using the term *Client Callbacks* to refer to AJAX. Because AJAX has become the standard name for this technology, I use AJAX instead of Client Callbacks in this book.

In this section, we add AJAX functionality to the `DivView` control. The modified `DivView` control, the `AjaxDivView` control, supports having its contents refreshed through an AJAX call.

The `AjaxDivView` control is contained in Listing 33.11.

LISTING 33.11   AjaxDivView.vb

```vb
Imports System
Imports System.Text
Imports System.IO
Imports System.Collections
Imports System.Web
Imports System.Web.UI
Imports System.Web.UI.WebControls

Namespace AspNetUnleashed
    Public Class AjaxDivView
        Inherits CompositeDataBoundControl
        Implements ICallbackEventHandler

        Private _itemTemplate As ITemplate

        ''' <summary>
        ''' The ItemTemplate is used to format each item
        ''' from the data source
        ''' </summary>
        <TemplateContainer(GetType(DivViewItem))> _
        <PersistenceMode(PersistenceMode.InnerProperty)> _
        Public Property ItemTemplate() As ITemplate
```

LISTING 33.11 Continued

```
            Get
                Return _itemTemplate
            End Get
            Set(ByVal Value As ITemplate)
                _itemTemplate = Value
            End Set
        End Property

        ''' <summary>
        ''' Register JavaScripts
        ''' </summary>
        Protected Overrides Sub OnPreRender(ByVal e As EventArgs)
            ' Register JavaScript library
            Page.ClientScript.RegisterClientScriptInclude("AjaxDivView",
➡Page.ResolveUrl("~/ClientScripts/AjaxDivView.js"))

            ' Register Refresh function
            Dim eRef As String = Page.ClientScript.GetCallbackEventReference(
➡Me, Nothing, "AjaxDivView_Result", "'" & Me.ClientID & "'",
➡"AjaxDivView_Error", False)
            Dim refreshFunc As String = "function AjaxDivView_Refresh() {" &
➡eRef & "}"
            Page.ClientScript.RegisterClientScriptBlock(Me.GetType(),
➡Me.UniqueID, refreshFunc, True)

            MyBase.OnPreRender(e)
        End Sub


        ''' <summary>
        ''' Iterate through the data items and instantiate each data
        ''' item in a template
        ''' </summary>
        Protected Overrides Function CreateChildControls(ByVal dataSource
➡As IEnumerable, ByVal dataBinding As Boolean) As Integer
            Dim counter As Integer = 0
            For Each dataItem As Object In dataSource
                Dim contentItem As New DivViewItem(dataItem, counter)
                _itemTemplate.InstantiateIn(contentItem)
                Controls.Add(contentItem)
                counter = counter + 1
            Next
            DataBind(False)
            Return counter
        End Function
```

LISTING 33.11 Continued

```vb
''' <summary>
''' Render this control's contents in a DIV tag
''' </summary>
Protected Overrides ReadOnly Property TagKey() As HtmlTextWriterTag
    Get
        Return HtmlTextWriterTag.Div
    End Get
End Property


''' <summary>
''' Whenever I get called through AJAX,
''' rebind my data
''' </summary>
Public Sub RaiseCallbackEvent(ByVal eventArgument As String)
➥Implements ICallbackEventHandler.RaiseCallbackEvent
    Me.DataBind()
End Sub


''' <summary>
''' Render my contents to a string
''' and send the result back to the client
''' </summary>
Public Function GetCallbackResult() As String
➥Implements ICallbackEventHandler.GetCallbackResult
    Dim builder As New StringBuilder()
    Dim sWriter As New StringWriter(builder)
    Dim hWriter As New HtmlTextWriter(sWriter)
    Me.RenderContents(hWriter)
    Return builder.ToString()
End Function

End Class



Public Class AjaxDivViewItem
    Inherits WebControl
    Implements IDataItemContainer

    Private _dataItem As Object
    Private _index As Integer


    Public ReadOnly Property DataItem() As Object
➥Implements IDataItemContainer.DataItem
```

33

LISTING 33.11   Continued

```
            Get
                  Return _dataItem
            End Get
      End Property

      Public ReadOnly Property DataItemIndex() As Integer
➥Implements IDataItemContainer.DataItemIndex
            Get
                  Return _index
            End Get
      End Property

      Public ReadOnly Property DisplayIndex() As Integer
➥Implements IDataItemContainer.DisplayIndex
            Get
                  Return _index
            End Get
      End Property

      Protected Overrides ReadOnly Property TagKey() As HtmlTextWriterTag
            Get
                  Return HtmlTextWriterTag.Div
            End Get
      End Property

      Public Sub New(ByVal dataItem As Object, ByVal index As Integer)
            _dataItem = dataItem
            _index = index
      End Sub

   End Class
End Namespace
```

The AjaxDivView control in Listing 33.11 is very similar to the DivView control created in the previous section, except for the fact that it implements the ICallbackEventHandler interface. This interface has two methods that you must implement: the RaiseCallbackEvent() and GetCallbackResult() methods.

The AjaxDivView control calls its DataBind() method in the RaiseCallbackEvent() method. When an AJAX call is made to this control, the control automatically refreshes its contents by rebinding to its data source.

The GetCallbackResult() returns a string that is sent to the browser as a result of an AJAX call. The AjaxDivView control renders its contents to a string and sends the string to the browser.

Notice that the `AjaxDivView` control registers two JavaScript scripts in its `OnPreRender()` method. First, the method registers an external JavaScript library named `AjaxDivView.js`. Second, it creates a JavaScipt function named `AjaxDivView_Refresh()` that refreshes the contents of the `AjaxDivView`.

The `AjaxDivView.js` file is contained in Listing 33.12.

LISTING 33.12   AjaxDivView.js

```
function AjaxDivView_Result(result, controlID)
{
    var control = document.getElementById(controlID);
    control.innerHTML = result;
}


function AjaxDivView_Error(error)
{
    alert( error );
}
```

The JavaScript file in Listing 33.12 includes two functions. The first function, named `AjaxDivView_Result()`, is called after `AjaxDivView` content is retrieved from the server. This function updates the `innerHTML` of the `AjaxDivView` control's containing `<div>` tag with the updated content.

The second function, the `AjaxDivView_Error()` function, is called only when there is an error on the server during an AJAX call. This function simply displays the error in a JavaScript alert box.

The page in Listing 33.13 illustrates how you can use the `AjaxDivView` control.

LISTING 33.13   ShowAjaxDivView.aspx

```
<%@ Page Language="VB" %>
<%@ Register TagPrefix="custom" Namespace="AspNetUnleashed" %>
<!DOCTYPE html PUBLIC "-//W3C//DTD XHTML 1.0 Transitional//EN"
    "http://www.w3.org/TR/xhtml1/DTD/xhtml1-transitional.dtd">
<html xmlns="http://www.w3.org/1999/xhtml" >
<head id="Head1" runat="server">
    <script type="text/javascript">

    window.onload = function()
    {
        window.setInterval("AjaxDivView_Refresh()", 5000);
    }
    </script>

    <style type="text/css">
```

33

LISTING 33.13   Continued

```
    h1
    {
        font-size:16px;
    }
    .ajaxDivView div
    {
        border:solid 1px black;
        padding:5px;
        margin:10px;
    }

    </style>
    <title>Show AjaxDivView</title>
</head>
<body language="javascript">
    <form id="form1" runat="server">
    <div>

    Page Time: <%= DateTime.Now.ToString() %>

    <br /><br />
    <button onclick="AjaxDivView_Refresh();return false;">Refresh</button>

    <br /><br />
    <custom:AjaxDivView
        id="AjaxDivView1"
        DataSourceID="srcMovies"
        CssClass="ajaxDivView"
        Runat="server">
        <ItemTemplate>

        <h1><%# Eval("Title") %></h1>
        <em>Director: <%# Eval("Director") %></em>

        </ItemTemplate>
    </custom:AjaxDivView>


    <asp:SqlDataSource
        id="srcMovies"
        ConnectionString="<%$ ConnectionStrings:Movies %>"
        SelectCommand="SELECT Id,Title,Director FROM Movies"
        Runat="server" />
```

LISTING 33.13   Continued

```
        </div>
    </form>
</body>
</html>
```

The page in Listing 33.13 displays the contents of the Movies database table. The AjaxDivView control is bound to a SqlDataSource control.

The page includes a little bit of JavaScript. The JavaScript causes the contents of the AjaxDivView to refresh automatically every five seconds. If you change one of the records in the Movies database table, then the contents of the AjaxDivView control automatically updates to reflect the change within five seconds (see Figure 33.6).

FIGURE 33.6   Displaying data with the AjaxDivView control.

The following JavaScript statement causes the AjaxDivView to update its contents every five seconds:

```
window.setInterval("AjaxDivView_Refresh()", 5000);
```

The AjaxDivView_Refresh() method initiates the AJAX call to refresh the AjaxDivView control's contents.

As an alternative to waiting the five seconds after a database update, if you are really impatient, you can click the button contained on the page. The button is a client-side button that calls the `AjaxDivView_Refresh()` method in its `onclick` handler.

Notice that the current time is displayed at the top of the page. This time never changes even when the contents of the `AjaxDivView` is updated. Only the `AjaxDivView` is refreshed, and not the rest of the page.

Creating an `AjaxFormView` Control

In this section, we create an `AjaxFormView` control. The `AjaxFormView` control works like the standard ASP.NET `FormView` control. However, the `AjaxFormView` control enables you to update and delete database records from the client by making AJAX calls back to the server.

Unfortunately, the code for the `AjaxFormView` control is too long to include in the pages of this book. The entire source code for the control is included on the CD that accompanies this book in both VB.NET and C# versions.

The `AjaxFormView` control has the following properties:

- `InsertItemTemplate`—Enables you to supply a template that is used when the control is in `Insert` mode.

- `EditItemTemplae`—Enables you to supply a template that is used when the control is in `Edit` mode.

- `DataKeyNames`—Enables you to specify one or more primary keys to use when updating a record.

- `DataKey`—Enables you to retrieve the value of the data key associated with the current record being edited.

- `DefaultMode`—Enables you to place the control in either `Edit` or `Insert` mode.

- `OnClientItemInserted`—Enables you to specify an optional script that executes when a new record is inserted.

- `OnClientItemUpdated`—Enables you to specify an optional script that executes when an existing record is updated.

The `AjaxFormView` control can be used to either insert or update a database record. You can set the control to either `Insert` or `Update` mode by setting the `DefaultMode` property.

> **WARNING**
>
> Make sure that you assign a value to the `AjaxFormView` control's `DataKeyNames` property when the control is set to `Edit` mode.

When you set the `AjaxFormView` control to `Insert` mode, the control renders an Insert button with its `RenderInsertButton()` method. This method creates a client-side button that initiates an AJAX call. The code for the `RenderInsertButton()` method is contained in Listing 33.14.

LISTING 33.14   `RenderInsertButton()`

```
''' <summary>
''' Render the Insert button with the AJAX onclick handler
''' </summary>
Private Sub RenderInsertButton(ByVal writer As HtmlTextWriter)
  Dim eRef As String = Page.ClientScript.GetCallbackEventReference(Me,
➥"'insert'", _onClientItemInserted, "'" & Me.ClientID & "'",
➥"AjaxFormView_Error", False)
  eRef = "__theFormPostData='';WebForm_InitCallback();" & eRef & ";return false"
  writer.AddAttribute(HtmlTextWriterAttribute.Onclick, eRef)
  writer.RenderBeginTag(HtmlTextWriterTag.Button)
  writer.Write("Insert")
  writer.RenderEndTag()
End Sub
```

The `RenderInsertButton()` method creates a button `onclick` handler that performs three actions. First, it sets the `__theFormPostData` variable to an empty string. Next, it calls the `WebForm_InitCallback()` method. These first two steps are required to pass the updated form field values back to the server in the AJAX call. By default, when an AJAX call is made back to the server, only the initial values of all the form fields are sent with the AJAX request.

Finally, the `onclick` handler actually makes the AJAX call. The necessary function call to initiate the AJAX request is retrieved with the help of the `Page.ClientScript.GetCallbackEventReference()` method.

When a user clicks the Insert button, an AJAX call is made back to the server and the control's `RaiseCallbackEvent()` method executes. When the Insert button is clicked, this method calls the `HandleInsert()` method. The code for the `HandleInsert()` method is contained in Listing 33.15.

LISTING 33.15   `HandleInsert()`

```
''' <summary>
''' Perform database insert by executing DataSource Insert method
''' </summary>
Private Sub HandleInsert()
  Dim values As IOrderedDictionary = _insertItemTemplate.ExtractValues(_item)
  Dim dataSource As DataSourceView = CType(Me.GetData(), DataSourceView)
  dataSource.Insert(values, AddressOf DataCallback)
End Sub
```

33

The HandleInsert() method gets the values of the databinding expressions from the InsertItemTemplate by calling the template's ExtractValues() method. This method is available because the InsertItemTemplate is marked as a template that supports two-way databinding.

The DataSource control to which the AjaxFormView control is bound has a DataSourceView associated with it. This DataSourceView is retrieved by a call to the GetData() method. The DataSourceView class includes Insert(), Update(), and Delete() methods you can call to modify the database data associated with the FormView. The HandleInsert() method in Listing 33.15 calls the Insert() method to insert a new database record.

The page in Listing 33.16 illustrates how you can use the AjaxFormView control. This page contains three controls: an AjaxFormView, AjaxDivView, and SqlDataSource control. The page enables you to add new records to the Movies database table (see Figure 33.7).

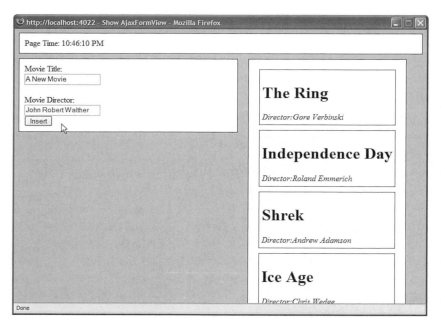

FIGURE 33.7 Inserting new records with the AjaxFormView control.

LISTING 33.16 ShowAjaxFormView.aspx

```
<%@ Page Language="VB" %>
<%@ Register TagPrefix="custom" Namespace="AspNetUnleashed" %>
<!DOCTYPE html PUBLIC "-//W3C//DTD XHTML 1.0 Transitional//EN"
  "http://www.w3.org/TR/xhtml1/DTD/xhtml1-transitional.dtd">
<html xmlns="http://www.w3.org/1999/xhtml" >
<head id="Head1" runat="server">
```

LISTING 33.16   Continued

```
<script type="text/javascript">

    function ItemInserted(error, controlID)
    {
        if (error == '')
        {
            var ajaxFormView = document.getElementById(controlID);
            var inputs = ajaxFormView.getElementsByTagName('input');
            for (var i=0;i < inputs.length;i++)
                inputs?.value = inputs?.defaultValue;

            window.setTimeout("AjaxDivView_Refresh()", 100);
        }
        else
            alert( 'Error: ' + error );
    }

</script>

<style type="text/css">
    html
    {
        background-color:silver;
    }

    .headerStrip
    {
        margin-bottom:10px;
        padding:10px;
        background-color:white;
        border:solid 1px black;
    }

    .frmMovie
    {
        background-color:white;
        width:400px;
        padding:10px;
        margin-right:20px;
        float:left;
        border:solid 1px black;
    }

    .listMovies
```

LISTING 33.16   Continued

```
            {
                background-color:white;
                float:left;
                padding:10px;
                border:solid 1px black;

            }

            .listMovies div
            {
                margin:10px;
                border:solid 1px black;
                padding:5px;
            }
    </style>

    <title>Show AjaxFormView</title>
</head>
<body>
    <form id="form1" runat="server">

    <div class="headerStrip">
    Page Time: <%= DateTime.Now.ToString("T") %>
    </div>

    <custom:AjaxFormView
        id="frmMovie"
        DataSourceID="srcMovies"
        DefaultMode="insert"
        OnClientItemInserted="ItemInserted"
        CssClass="frmMovie"
        Runat="server">
        <InsertItemTemplate>

        <asp:Label
            id="lblTitle"
            Text="Movie Title:"
            AssociatedControlID="txtTitle"
            Runat="server" />
        <br />
        <asp:TextBox
            id="txtTitle"
            Text='<%# Bind("Title") %>'
            Runat="server" />
```

LISTING 33.16   Continued

```
            <br /><br />
            <asp:Label
                id="Label1"
                Text="Movie Director:"
                AssociatedControlID="txtDirector"
                Runat="server" />
            <br />
            <asp:TextBox
                id="txtDirector"
                Text='<%# Bind("Director") %>'
                Runat="server" />

            </InsertItemTemplate>
        </custom:AjaxFormView>

        <custom:AjaxDivView
            id="listMovies"
            DataSourceID="srcMovies"
            CssClass="listMovies"
            Runat="server">
            <ItemTemplate>
            <h1><%# Eval("Title") %></h1>
            <em>Director:<%# Eval("Director") %></em>
            </ItemTemplate>
        </custom:AjaxDivView>

        <asp:SqlDataSource
            id="srcMovies"
            ConnectionString="<%$ ConnectionStrings:Movies %>"
            SelectCommand="SELECT Id,Title, Director
                FROM Movies ORDER BY Id DESC"
            InsertCommand="INSERT MOVIES (Title, Director)
                VALUES (@Title, @Director)"
            Runat="server" />

        </div>
        </form>
    </body>
    </html>
```

When you add new records to the Movies database table by clicking the AjaxFormView control's Insert button, the page is not posted back to the server. Instead, the new record is added to the database with an AJAX call.

The AjaxDivView displays the current contents of the Movies database table. The contents of the AjaxDivView control are refreshed automatically whenever a new record is added with the AjaxFormView control. The AjaxDivView control is refreshed by the AjaxFormView control's client-side ItemInserted() method.

The beautiful thing about both the AjaxFormView and AjaxDivView control is that both controls enable you to interact with the web server without posting the page that contains the controls back to the web server. This creates a user experience much closer to working with a desktop application. It also greatly improves the performance of your application because the entire page does not need to be re-created each and every time that you need to perform a database operation.

Summary

This chapter was devoted to the topic of building templated databound controls. In the first part, you learned how to support templates in your custom controls. You learned how to create templates that support both one-way and two-way databinding expressions. You also learned how to create a default template for a control.

The second half of this chapter focused on the topic of building databound controls. You learned how to create a simple DivView control that displays the records from a database table in a series of HTML <div> tags. Finally, you learned how to build two databinding controls that take advantage of AJAX. We created an AjaxDivView control that automatically refreshes its contents every five seconds. We also created a AjaxFormView control that enables you to insert and update database records directly from the client without a postback to the server.

PART X

Sample Application

IN THIS PART

Building an E-Commerce Application

The problem with most code samples in books is that they are way too simple. When building a full application, the world is often much more complex than the simple world that the book describes.

In this chapter, we build a complete ASP.NET application from start to finish. We build an entire online store with the ASP.NET Framework.

This chapter has several goals. The first is to discuss the issues that I encountered while building the application. Hard decisions had to be faced. Trade-offs were made.

Second, this book covers a lot of material. The ASP.NET 2.0 Framework includes an overwhelming number of new features (a fact which is both cool and scary). This chapter draws together many of the new ASP.NET 2.0 technologies discussed separately in previous chapters and shows you how you can apply these technologies in the context of a real-world application.

Finally, an important goal of this chapter is to provide you with a functioning application that you can use as a starting point for your projects. All the code for the e-commerce application is included on the CD that accompanies this book in both a Visual Basic .NET and C# version. If you need to build an e-commerce application, you can take advantage of this code to save yourself a significant amount of time.

Overview of the E-Commerce Application

In this chapter, we build the ASP.NET Beer Store. The e-commerce application is loaded with sample data that represents beer product information (see Figure 34.1).

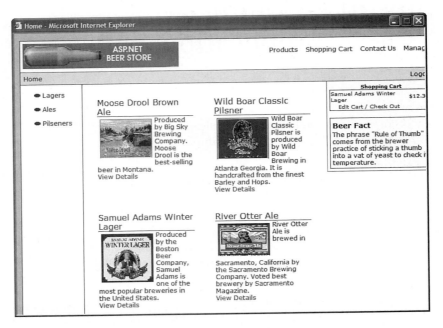

FIGURE 34.1   Home page of the ASP.NET Beer Store.

> **NOTE**
>
> The sample images used for the ASP.NET Beer Store were generously provided by Nathan Wiger and Corey Gray, the world-renowned experts on all excellent forms of beer. Visit their website at www.BeerLabels.com.

Before we get into the technical details of how the application works, I want to provide you with an overview of the different parts of the application. This application has two halves: The half that the world sees and the half that the store administrators see.

The public half of the ASP.NET Beer Store consists of the following ASP.NET pages:

- `Default.aspx`—The home page of the ASP.NET Beer Store. This page displays a list of featured products.

- `Products.aspx`—This page displays a list of products contained in a particular product category. If the category contains sub-categories, the sub-categories are also displayed.

- `ProductDetails.aspx`—This page displays details for a particular product. It also contains a link for adding a product to a shopping cart.

- `ShoppingCart.aspx`—This page displays a customer shopping cart. Customers can use this page to edit the items in their shopping carts.

- `CheckOut\Default.aspx`—This page enables customers to enter billing and shipping information and purchase the products in their shopping carts.

- `CheckOut\Confirmation.aspx`—This page displays an order confirmation number after a customer has placed an order.

- `ContactInfo.aspx`—This page displays contact information for the store.

- `Login.aspx`—This page enables an existing customer to log in or a new customer to register.

- `PasswordReminder.aspx`—This page enables customers to reset their passwords when they have forgotten their original passwords.

When you request the home page of the application, a list of featured products is displayed. Every page in the application also displays a list of product categories in a menu in the left column.

If you navigate to a product category, then you arrive at the `Products.aspx` page. This page displays a list of products contained in the category in a `DataList` control (see Figure 34.2). Next to each product description, a View Details link is rendered. If you click the View Details link, then you arrive at the `ProductDetails.aspx` page.

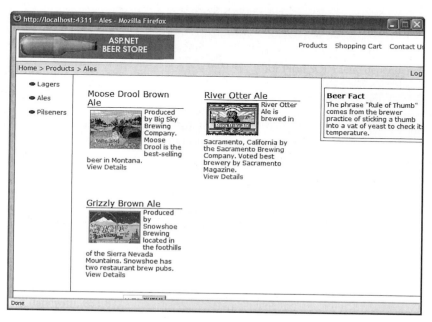

FIGURE 34.2   The `Products.aspx` page.

The ProductDetails.aspx page displays information on a particular product. You can click the Add to Cart link to add the product to your shopping cart.

You can view the contents of your shopping cart by clicking the Shopping Cart menu link that appears at the top of any page. The shopping cart is displayed by the ShoppingCart.aspx page. This page enables you to remove items from the shopping cart. It also includes a Check Out link (see Figure 34.3).

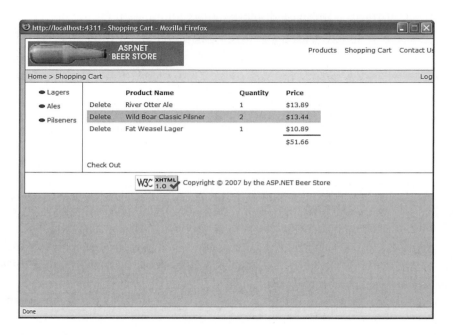

FIGURE 34.3   The ShoppingCart.aspx page.

If you click the Check Out link, and you are not authenticated, then you arrive at the Login.aspx page. This page enables existing customers to log in and new users to register. After you log in or register, you are redirected to the CheckOut\Default.aspx page (see Figure 34.4).

The CheckOut\Default.aspx page contains a form that enables a customer to enter credit card information, billing address, and shipping address. When the customer submits the form, the shopping cart associated with the customer is converted into a new product order.

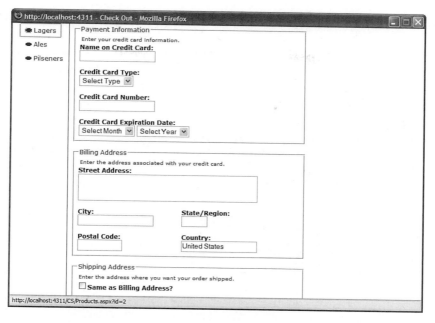

FIGURE 34.4   The check out page.

The private section of the application is no less important. A store manager uses this section to list new products and view customer orders. The private half of the ASP.NET Beer Store consists of the following pages:

- `Manage\Default.aspx`—Contains a list of links to other pages in the store management section.

- `Manage\Categories\Default.aspx`—This page enables store managers to create new product categories and edit existing product categories.

- `Manage\Products\Default.aspx`—This page enables store managers to list new products and edit existing products.

- `Manage\Orders\Default.aspx`—This page enables store managers to view customer product orders.

When the ASP.NET Beer Store first starts, an administrator role and user is created automatically. The role is named `StoreAdmins` and the user is named `Admin`. The Admin user has the password secret.

If you login with the Admin account, then an additional menu item labeled Manage appears at the top of every page. If you click the Manage link, then you are brought to the `Manage\Default.aspx` page. This page displays a menu of management options.

34

> **WARNING**
>
> Make sure that you modify the Admin password. Everyone who reads this book knows that the Admin password defaults to secret. You can modify the Admin password by opening the Web Site Administration Tool when the application is loaded in Visual Web Developer. Launch this tool by selecting the menu option Website, ASP.NET Configuration.

If you navigate to the `Manage\Categories\Default.aspx` page, then you can add, delete, and edit product categories. The hierarchy of current product categories is displayed in a `TreeView` control. Child categories of the selected category in the `TreeView` are displayed in a `GridView` control. If you click the Add Category link, a floating virtual window appears that enables you to add a new product category (see Figure 34.5).

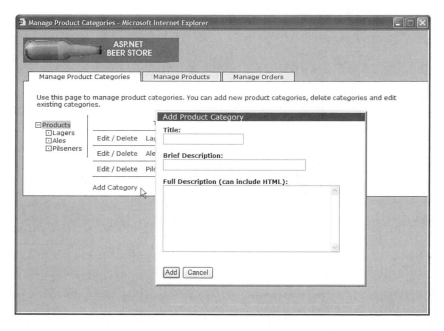

FIGURE 34.5   Adding a product category.

The `Manage\Products\Default.aspx` page enables you to add, delete, and edit products. The list of current products is displayed in a `GridView` control. If you click the Add New Product link, a new floating virtual window appears that contains a form for entering a new product (see Figure 34.6).

The `Manage\Orders\Default.aspx` page displays a list of product orders. This page doesn't display any product orders until a customer submits a shopping cart. You can click the Select link next to any order to view detailed order information, including the customer credit card information, billing address, and shipping address (see Figure 34.7).

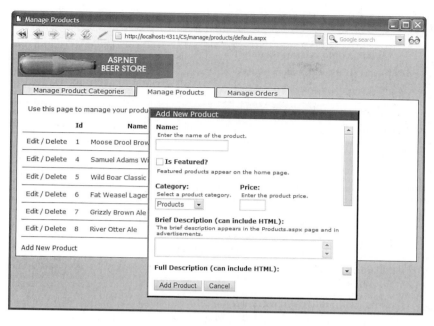

FIGURE 34.6 Adding a new product.

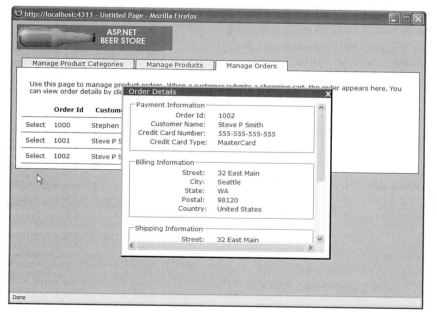

FIGURE 34.7 Viewing customer orders.

Using Master Pages, Themes, and User Controls

The ASP.NET Beer Store is designed with Master Pages, Themes, and User Controls. Master Pages and User Controls are used to share content across multiple pages. Themes are used to give the pages in the application a common style.

> **NOTE**
>
> Master Pages, Themes, and User Controls are covered in Part II of this book, "Designing ASP.NET Websites."

The application uses two Master Pages named `Store.master` and `Manage.master`. The `Store.master` Master Page contains the layout for the public section of the website. The `Manage.master` page contains the layout for the private section of the website.

The `Store.master` Master Page contains two of the standard ASP.NET Navigation controls: the `Menu` control and the `SiteMapPath` control. The `Menu` control is used to display the list of product categories. The `SiteMapPath` control is used to display the breadcrumb that appears near the top of every page.

The application takes advantage of two User Controls to create a standard layout for displaying products and product categories. The `Templates\ProductTemplate.ascx` User Control is used in both the Featured Products DataList and the Products DataList to display product information. The `Templates\CategoryTemplate.ascx` User Control is used in the Categories DataList to display product category information.

Building a Component Library

All the application logic for the e-commerce application was pushed out of the pages and into a separate component library. Placing as much of your application logic as possible into separate components makes it easier to reuse the same methods across multiple pages in your website.

The components are contained in the App_Code folder. The contents of this folder are dynamically compiled. You don't need to perform an explicit Build before using the components in the App_Code folder in your pages.

> **NOTE**
>
> Components are discussed in Part IV of this book, "Building Components."

The App_Code folder contains the following components:

- `Category`—Represents a product category. Contains methods for adding, deleting, and editing product categories.

- `Product`—Represents a product. Contains methods for adding, deleting, and editing products.

- `ShoppingCart`—Represents a shopping cart. Contains methods for adding and deleting shopping cart items.

- `Order`—Represents a product order. Contains methods for converting a shopping cart into a product order and retrieving orders.

Each component performs a dual role. Each component represents a particular type of object and it also represents methods for working with objects of that type. For example, the `Product` component represents a product. It includes all of the product properties such as the product `Name` and `Price` properties.

However, the `Product` component also contains all the methods for interacting with products. For example, it includes a method named `SelectByCategoryId()` that retrieves all the products contained in a particular category.

Creating a Custom Site Map Provider

One of the first issues that I encountered when building the e-commerce application was the problem of representing product categories.

On the one hand, I wanted to use all the standard Navigation controls. I wanted to use the `Menu`, `SiteMapPath`, and `TreeView` controls to display the product categories. For example, as you move from page to page in the website, I wanted the `SiteMapPath` control to display the current product category automatically so that a customer could navigate back up the category hierarchy. Because I wanted to use the product categories with the standard navigation controls, I needed to represent the categories in a Site Map.

> **NOTE**
>
> Navigation controls and Site Maps are discussed in Part V of this book, "Site Navigation."

On the other hand, I wanted to enable administrators of the application to be able to modify product categories easily through a form interface. I wanted an administrator to be able to add and edit categories through the form interface contained in the `Manage\Categories\Default.aspx` page.

Unfortunately, the default Site Map provider doesn't support both requirements. The default Site Map provider uses XML files to represents the navigational structure of a website. An administrator cannot easily update an XML file through a form interface. Therefore, I decided to write a custom Site Map provider.

Product categories are represented with the `CategorySiteMapProvider`. This class is contained in the App_Code folder. The `CategorySiteMapProvider` stores navigation information in a SQL database table. The `CategorySiteMapProvider` is configured to retrieve the categories from a database table named Categories.

The ASP.NET Beer Store actually uses both the standard `XmlSiteMapProvider` and the `CategorySiteMapProvider` to represent a Site Map. The root `Web.sitemap` file is contained in Listing 34.1.

LISTING 34.1   Web.sitemap

```xml
<?xml version="1.0" encoding="utf-8" ?>
<siteMap xmlns="http://schemas.microsoft.com/AspNet/SiteMap-File-1.0">
  <siteMapNode url="~/default.aspx" title="Home"  description="Home page">
    <siteMapNode provider="CategorySiteMapProvider" />
    <siteMapNode url="~/shoppingcart.aspx" title="Shopping Cart"
          description="View Shopping Cart" />
    <siteMapNode url="~/contactinfo.aspx" title="Contact Us"
          description="Contact us by phone or email" />
    <siteMapNode siteMapFile="~/manage/web.sitemap" />
  </siteMapNode>
</siteMap>
```

Notice that the second `siteMapNode` element in Listing 34.1 specifies a particular provider. This node retrieves all its subnodes from the `CategorySiteMapProvider`.

Notice, furthermore, that the last `siteMapNode` element uses the `siteMapFile` attribute. The Site Map for the management section of the website is contained in a separate XML Site Map file located at `\Manage\Web.sitemap`.

The ASP.NET Framework is smart enough to merge the `SiteMapNodes` from these different providers and locations seamlessly in the background. I was surprised with how little work I had to perform to combine the `SiteMapNodes` from the XML Site Map files and the SQL Server database table.

Creating a Shopping Cart

I also struggled with the issue of how to represent customer shopping carts. The obvious choice here is the ASP.NET Profile object. Using the Profile object offers several advantages.

> **NOTE**
>
> Browser cookies, `Session` state, and the `Profile` object are discussed in Chapter 22, "Maintaining Application State."

First, the `Profile` object is persistent. A customer can add items to a shopping cart during one visit and return many months later to complete a purchase.

Second, the `Profile` object is designed to handle both anonymous and authenticated users. Requiring a customer to register before adding items to a shopping cart does not create a good customer experience. An e-commerce application should make the process of adding an item to a shopping cart as easy as possible.

Finally, when you take advantage of the `Profile` object, you don't need to write any database logic to store shopping cart information. The Framework does all the hard work for you.

This all sounds good. Unfortunately, I encountered one issue with the `Profile` object that I could not overcome. I wanted to be able to perform database joins between the items in a shopping cart and other database tables such as the Products database table.

For example, when a customer views his shopping cart, the shopping cart should not display the price of a product when the customer added the item to their shopping cart. Instead, the shopping cart should display the current price of the product (imagine that a customer adds an item to the shopping cart while the item is on sale and returns many months later).

When you store items with the `Profile` object, all the items are stored as a blob. You can't perform database queries against the individual items contained in a `Profile`. In particular, you can perform database joins between items in a `Profile` and other database tables.

Therefore, I created a custom `ShoppingCart` component to represent customer shopping carts. The `ShoppingCart` component is in the App_Code folder.

The custom `ShoppingCart` component persists customer shopping carts. The component stores shopping carts in a database table named `ShoppingCarts`.

The custom `ShoppingCart` component handles both anonymous and authenticated users. It does it the same way that the `Profile` object does. Anonymous Identification is enabled in the web configuration file. When Anonymous Identification is enabled, a persistent cookie containing a unique identifier is added to each anonymous customer's browser. This unique identifier is used when an anonymous customer's shopping cart is stored and retrieved.

The `Global.asax` file includes a `Profile_OnMigrateAnonymous()` event handler. This event handler calls a method of the `ShoppingCart` class named `AuthenticateCart()` when an anonymous user logs in or registers. This method updates the ShoppingCarts database table by replacing the customer's anonymous identifier with the customer's authenticated username.

Finally, the custom `ShoppingCart` component caches customer shopping carts in `Sessions` state. A customer's shopping cart does not need to be retrieved from the database with each page request. Instead, the shopping cart is stored in the web server's memory while the customer browses the website. This is done to improve performance.

Protecting Credit Card Numbers

Storing credit card numbers in plain text in the database is an extremely bad idea. If a customer trusts you with a credit card number, you should do everything in your power to protect the information.

The best option is to never store credit card numbers at all. If you process a customer credit card number immediately after the customer submits it, then you can discard the credit card number when the transaction completes.

The e-commerce application stores credit card numbers in the Orders database table. Credit card numbers are not stored in plain text. Instead, they are encrypted before being added to the database.

The e-commerce application uses a component named `Secret` to encrypt and decrypt credit card numbers. The `Secret` component is located in the App_Code folder.

The `Secret` component uses the `RijndaelManaged` class from the `System.Security.Cryptography` namespace to encrypt and decrypt strings. The Rijndael algorithm is also known as the Advanced Encryption Standard (AES). It is the United States government encryption standard.

To use the `RijndaelManaged` class to encrypt a string, you must supply an encryption key and an initialization vector (IV). The encryption key must be kept secret. The IV, on the other hand, does not need to be kept secret. You need both the encryption key and IV to decrypt an encrypted string.

The `Secret` component loads the encryption key from the `machineKey` section of the web configuration file. The component reads the value of the `decryptionKey` attribute. The component uses the same key that is used by the ASP.NET Membership framework. The IV is generated from the first bytes of the encryption key.

If you change the value of the `decryptionKey` attribute in the web configuration file, then you can't retrieve any of the credit card numbers stored in the database. Credit card numbers are retrieved as a string of question marks.

Of course, all this encryption is meaningless if a hacker gets access to the Manage\Orders\Default.aspx page. This page displays order information, including the credit card number associated with an order. The page is password protected so that only members of the StoreAdmins role can access the page. However, if a hacker manages to bypass the ASP.NET Authentication framework, then all bets are off.

Handling Images

When you add a product with the Manage\Products\Default.aspx page, you can add an image for the product. The product image is stored in the Products database table.

> **NOTE**
>
> The FileUpload control in is covered in Chapter 4, "Using the Rich Controls."

The Manage\Products\Default.aspx page uses the standard ASP.NET FileUpload control to upload the image. The image is read from the FileUpload control and inserted into the database with the Product.InsertImage() method. To avoid clobbering the entire memory of your web server with a large image, this method adds the image to the database incrementally in 8040-byte chunks.

The product images are displayed by the Default.aspx, Products.aspx, and ProductDetails.aspx pages. All these pages use a Generic Handler named ProductImage.aspx to retrieve the image. This handler retrieves the image in 8040-byte chunks from the database and sends the image bytes to the browser.

> **NOTE**
>
> Generic Handlers are discussed in Chapter 25, "Working with the HTTP Runtime."

Retrieving Data with AJAX

No ASP.NET 2.0 application should be written without at least a little bit of AJAX (and a lot is great). The e-commerce application includes an AjaxRotator control that displays a random content item retrieved from the web server. The AjaxRotator updates its contents on the browser automatically every 15 seconds.

The AjaxRotator is included in the Store.master Master Page, so it is included on every public page in the website (see Figure 34.8). In the case of the ASP.NET Beer Store, the AjaxRotator is used to randomly display different beer facts (of questionable veracity).

The AjaxRotator retrieves its content items from an XML file named AjaxRotatorContent.config. This XML file contains a list of <item> elements, each of which represents a content item. The <item> elements can contain HTML content just as long as the content is XHTML-compliant.

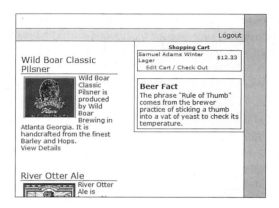

FIGURE 34.8   The AjaxRotator control displays beer facts.

Improving Performance Through Caching

The best way to improve the performance of an ASP.NET application is through caching. The e-commerce application takes extensive advantage of the new caching features of the ASP.NET 2.0 Framework.

The list of products, list of featured products, and list of categories are displayed with three user controls named ProductView.ascx, FeaturedProductView.ascx, and CategoryView.ascx. All three of these user controls include an <%@ OutputCache %> directive that includes a SqlDependency attribute.

All three user controls use a Polling SQL Cache dependency. The user controls cache data in memory until the data changes in the underlying database. For example, the list of featured products displayed on the home page (Default.aspx) is cached by the FeaturedProductView.ascx user control. The rendered output of this user control is cached in memory until the contents of the Products database table is changed.

The product information displayed by the ProductDetails.aspx page is also cached. However, in this case, the caching is performed at the level of the DataSource control rather than at the level of a User Control. The product information is retrieved from an ObjectDataSource control. The ObjectDataSource control is configured to use a Polling SQL Cache Dependency.

> **WARNING**
>
> The e-commerce application is configured to poll the database for changes every 15 seconds so data can be up to 15 seconds out of date. You can configure a shorter interval by modifying the `pollTime` attribute of the `<sqlCacheDependency>` element in the web configuration file.

Finally, the customer shopping carts are cached in `Session` state. When a shopping cart is first retrieved from the database for a customer, the shopping cart is added to `Session` state and remains there until the shopping cart is modified or the customer leaves the website.

Conforming to Standards

The e-commerce application is standards friendly. It was written to conform to the XHTML 1.0 Transitional standard. You'll notice that the footer includes an icon from the World Wide Web Consortium (W3C) that indicates that the website has successfully passed their XHTML 1.0 Transitional validator (see Figure 34.9).

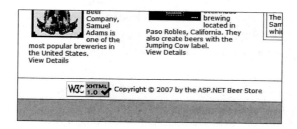

FIGURE 34.9   XHTML 1.0 Transitional W3C icon.

You can validate any page against the W3C validator by visiting http://validator.w3.org.

The e-commerce application does not use HTML tables for layout. All page layout is performed with Cascading Style Sheets. For example, the `Store.master` Master Page contains three `<div>` tags that represent the three page columns. The three columns are laid out from left to right with the following three CSS classes:

```
.leftColumn
{
    float:left;
    width:100px;
    padding:5px;
}


.middleColumn
```

```
{
    float:left;
    width:450px;
    border-left:solid 1px blue;
    padding:8px;
}

.rightColumn
{
    float:right;
    width:200px;
    border-left:solid 1px blue;
    border-bottom:solid 1px blue;
    padding:5px;
}
```

Furthermore, the e-commerce application was designed to be accessible to persons with disabilities. All images include an ALT attribute. All form elements are explicitly associated with a label. For example, the input field for a product name is created with the following Label and TextBox controls:

```
<asp:Label
  id="lblName"
  Text="Name:"
  AssociatedControlID="txtName"
  Runat="server" />

<asp:TextBox
  id="txtName"
  Text='<%# Bind("Name") %>'
  Runat="server" />
```

The AssociatedControlID property is used to explicitly associate the Label control with the TextBox control.

WEB STANDARDS NOTE

To learn more about how to make accessible ASP.NET 2.0 websites, see my article at the Microsoft MSDN website, "Building ASP.NET 2.0 Web Sites Using Web Standards."

Summary

The e-commerce application illustrates many of the new features of the ASP.NET 2.0 Framework. First, it illustrates how you can take advantage of Master Pages and Themes when designing your website. The e-commerce application takes advantage of both technologies to make it easy for you to change the appearance of the website.

The e-commerce application also takes advantage of the new Navigation controls and Site Map infrastructure included in the ASP.NET 2.0 Framework. The application uses `TreeView`, `Menu`, and `SiteMapPath` controls. These controls are bound to Site Map data retrieved from either the standard `XmlSiteMapProvider` or the custom `CategorySiteMapProvider`.

The e-commerce application also takes advantage of the new performance-enhancing features of the ASP.NET 2.0 Framework. The application uses Polling SQL Cache Dependencies to cache product and category data in memory just as long as the data does not change in the database.

Finally, the e-commerce application conforms to W3C standards such as XHTML and accessibility standards. The entire website validates as XHTML 1.0 Transitional.

34

Index

Symbols

A

C

ImageMap
 Click event, 113
 Focus() method, 112
 hot spots, 108
 navigation, 109
 postback, 110-112
 properties, 112
ImageRotator
 ImageRotator.vb file, 1731-1733
 ShowImageRotator.aspx page, 1733
ItemRotator
 ItemRotator.vb file, 1730
 ShowItemRotator.aspx page, 1731
Label, 61
 accessibility guidelines, 66
 displaying time with, 62-63
 form field labels, 65-66
 formatting, 63-65
 properties, 63
LayoutEditorPart, 1428, 1464-1468
LengthValidator
 LengthValidator.vb file, 171
 ShowLengthValidator.aspx page, 172-173
LinkButton, 88-91
 Click event, 91
 client scripts, 96-97
 Command event, 91, 103-106
 cross-page posts, 98-102
 displaying on pages, 88-89
 events, 91
 Focus() method, 91
 properties, 90
List controls
 appending list items, 448-450
 automatic postbacks, 450-451
 binding to data sources, 440-443
 BulletedList, 466-471
 CheckBoxList, 81, 464-466

 declaring list items, 437-439
 DropDownList, 455-457, 1292-1293
 EasyListBox, 457
 Items collection, 452-455
 ListBox, 460-464
 ListControl class, 437
 ListItem class, 437-439
 MultiSelectList, 471-481
 RadioButtonList, 457-459
 reordering list items, 452-455
 selected list items, determining, 443-448
Literal
 Mode property, 68-70
 modifying browser titles with, 67-68
Localize, 1318-1319
Login
 adding to Master Pages, 1029-1031
 custom authentication, 1034-1035
 hiding from authenticated users, 1029-1030
 Login.aspx page, 1024-1025
 properties, 1026-1028
 redirecting users, 1029
 templates, 1031-1034
LoginName, 1059-1060
LoginStatus, 1057-1059
LoginView
 roles, 1075-1077
 ShowLoginView.aspx sample page, 1073-1075
Menu, 886-887
 adding items to, 887-890
 binding to database data, 901-906
 binding to Site Maps, 894-897
 binding to SiteMapDataSource controls, 952-954
 binding to XML files, 898-901
 combining with MultiView control, 890-894

How can we make this index more useful? Email us at indexes@samspublishing.com

N

How can we make this index more useful? Email us at indexes@samspublishing.com

How can we make this index more useful? Email us at indexes@samspublishing.com

V

W

X